THE
ROYAL DESCENTS OF 900 IMMIGRANTS

Volume I
Acknowledgments, Introduction, and Descents from Kings or Sovereigns Who Died after 1200
[pp. i-cxcii, 1-734]

Edward III, King of England (1312–1377, reigned 1327–1377), a central figure of this work (see pages 107–93), from a rubbing of the Hastings Brass in Elsing Church, Norfolk, as published in Joseph Foster, *Some Feudal Coats of Arms* (James Parker and Co., Oxford and London, 1902), p. 78. Note that the king's tunic features his coat-of-arms, post 1340, as depicted also on the front cover.

THE
ROYAL DESCENTS
OF
900 IMMIGRANTS
to the American Colonies, Quebec,
or the United States

Who Were Themselves Notable
or Left Descendants
Notable in American History

Volume I

Gary Boyd Roberts

Computerized (from Manuscript) and Indexed
by Julie Helen Otto,
Who Also Undertook Research

Proofread by Margaret Foye Mill

Baltimore, 2018

For, among others, my four major contributors:

John C. Brandon
John Anderson Brayton
John Blythe Dobson
Douglas Richardson

Copyright © 2018
Gary Boyd Roberts
All Rights Reserved.
No part of this publication may be reproduced, in any form
or by any means, including electronic reproduction or
reproduction via the Internet, except by permission of the author.

Published by Genealogical Publishing Company
Baltimore, Maryland
2018

Library of Congress Preassigned Control Number 2018935565

ISBN, the two-volume set: 9780806320748
ISBN, Volume I: 9780806320755

Front cover: Shield of Edward III, King of England (died 1377), post 1340, with the arms of England (three lions) in the second and third quarters and those of France (fleurs-de-lis) in the first and fourth quarters, as drawn from the king's tomb at Westminster Abbey and published by C. S. Scott-Giles, *Looking at Heraldry* (rev. ed., Phoenix House, 1967), p. 7.

Table of Contents

Frontispiece	ii
Acknowledgments	v-xiv
Introduction (with ten appendices)	xv-cxcii
Appendix I: 255 Twentieth-Century Scholars (to 2018) and the Immigrants upon whose Royal Descents they have undertaken research	xlv
Appendix II: 925 Immigrants of Royal Descent: A Subject Index and Guide; 45 French-Canadian Immigrants of Royal Descent, both (1) France to Québec, and (2) Québec to the United States	lxxii
Appendix III: 610 Major Historical Figures Who Appear on the Charts; 30 Major Historical Figures Who Appear in the French-Canadian Section	cvi
Appendix IV: 84 Kings from Whom Descent is Outlined to the 970 Immigrants Herein	cxxxv
Appendix V	
Part 1: 140 Immigrants New to the 2004-2010 Editions	cxliii
Part 2: 75 Colonial Immigrants New to *RD900* With Notable American Descendants; Twelve Colonial Immigrants Notable in their own Right (or that of their Spouses) New to *RD900*; Six Colonial Immigrants of Speculative Royal Descent	cxlviii
Part 3: 161 Nineteenth- and Twentieth-Century Immigrants New to *RD900*	clii
Appendix VI: 227 (and Probably or Eventually Over 240) Royally Descended Immigrants Who Left 10 or More Notable Descendants	clx
Appendix VII: 198 Immigrants Whose Royal Descent is Much Altered since *RD500* or *RD600*	clxx
Appendix VIII: Immigrants with "Caveats", Some Aspect of Whose Royal Descent Merits Further Investigation	clxxix
Appendix IX: Speculative Descents (Immigrants for Whom a Line from Kings, not simply Gentry	

The Royal Descents of 600 Immigrants

Ancestry, has been Suggested but is Unproved or Seems Perhaps Problematic: A List [of 24] with Bibliography and Comments)	clxxxiii
10) Appendix X: 29 Immigrants Dropped from *RD600* or *RD900*, with Sources for Disproofs or Doubts	clxxxix
Immigrant Descendants of Late Medieval and Early Modern Kings (those dying after 1400, esp. Henry VII of England, James V and IV, and Robert III of Scotland)	1-268
Immigrant Descendants of 14th-Century Kings (those dying 1300-1400, esp. Edward III and I of England, Robert II and I of Scotland, and John II of France)	269-616
Immigrant Descendants of High Medieval Kings (those dying 1150-1300, esp. Henry III, John "Lackland" and Henry II of England, and William I "the Lion" and David I of Scotland)	617-803
Immigrant Descendants of Early Medieval Kings (those dying 900-1150, esp. Henry I and Ethelred II of England, and Henry I, Robert II and I, Hugh Capet, and Louis IV of France, plus one descent from Irish kings and one from Welsh princes)	804-887
Immigrants Whose Royal Descent or "Improved" Royal Descent was Received or Developed after Much of this Volume had been Indexed	888-915
Two Speculative Descents for Six Further Immigrants to New England	916-922
Presidential Addendum	923-927
Appendix: From Kings, via the American Colonies, to Recent Sovereigns: Lines from Royally Descended Immigrants to the Present British Royal Family, Princes of Monaco, and the late Queen Géraldine of the Albanians	929-935
French-Canadian Immigrants of Royal Descent, both France to Québec (or Acadia), and Québec to the United States	937-990
An Hispanic Royal Descent, Probably One of Hundreds	991-997
50 Remarkable Descents, Kinships, or Near-Kin of Near-Kin Connections Outlined on Charts Herein	999-1002
List of Abbreviated Sources	1003-1019
Index, with Introduction, and Postscript	1021-1611

Acknowledgments

This book cites hundreds of sources, and to their authors, especially the 255 twentieth-century scholars listed in the introduction that follows, I owe both this book and the enormous pleasure I have derived from tracing American notables of royal descent. Beyond its sources this book has two additional, mostly "silent," early sponsors—Ralph J. Crandall, from 1982 to 2005 Director of the New England Historic Genealogical Society in Boston and Michael Tepper, Managing Editor of Genealogical Publishing Company in Baltimore. Both have believed in me for forty years and acted accordingly. They are two of my best friends, each massively reinvigorated the institution he directed, and each is owed much by the genealogical community overall. Thus I am delighted that our partnership in producing 15 volumes of excerpts from *The New England Historical and Genealogical Register,* plus *American Ancestors and Cousins of The Princess of Wales* and several other books, continues with *The Royal Descents of 500, 600,* and now *900 Immigrants.* D. Brenton Simons, Ralph's successor, a sometime protégé, now the Society's President and CEO, has been another best friend, for over twenty-five years, nurturing in times of stress and promoter and protector of my career since the early 1990s. Brenton has more than doubled the Society's endowment, continued the massive expansion of NEHGS activities (especially the Newbury Street Press) and allowed me unprecedented access to NEHGS collections. Brenton also brought to my attention Henrietta Johnston, the "first woman painter in America," and the identification of one of her sitters, later an earl, as a nephew of her first husband.

A fourth partner in this endeavor, through 2010, was Alicia Crane Williams, editor 1985-1998 of *The* (then newly revived) *Mayflower Descendant,* who, as Williams Word Processing, formerly of 18 Martin's Cove Road, Hingham, Mass. 02043 (to whom I probably sent, and received, over 100 envelopes or packages of various drafts and parts of the book) read, keyboarded, indexed, and prepared camera-ready copy for both *RD500* and several editions of *RD600.* Alicia also typed or word-processed almost all of my genealogical articles through early 1989. Julie Helen Otto, former NEHGS librarian and editor of *NEXUS,*

The Royal Descents of 900 Immigrants

has computer-input all of my articles and lecture passouts since 1989, and beginning in Fall 2013, has prepared *RD900* for press, over many hours, nights, and questions about handwriting, discrepancies, "typos" or changed words. The volume in hand required much reformatting, massive fact-checking, and a new index, for all of which I am immensely grateful. Julie also reads Latin (and knows French and Spanish accent rules), undertook some research (see, for example, the charts for Ewen Somerled Cameron and Mrs. Margaret Stirling Forbes [Alexander], plus James Tytler's marriages and daughters), and is thus a fifth partner in this project. Only Alicia, Julie, Ralph, Mike, Brenton, Michael J. Wood of London (who indexed the 1966-77 American section of *The Mowbray Connection, TMC*), frequent presidential collaborator Christopher Challender Child, longtime colleague David Allen Lambert, a few other NEHGS staff members, William Birnie (Bill) Marsh (who prepared the French section of *TMC* for the NEHGS website) and a handful of "outside" genealogical scholars can readily read my handprinting, and without Alicia and the resources of Williams Word Processing, or without Julie and her (to me amazing) speed on computers, *RD500*, *RD600*, and *RD900*, and much of my scholarly life's work, would have come to fruition only with considerably more difficulty. Finally, among colleagues and friends who helped in the preparation of this work, I wish to thank Margaret Foye "Meg" Mill, who proofread the entire text and index, and identified various errors Julie and I had not noticed. Eileen Perkins, GPC Production Manager, and Joseph Garonzik, GPC Marketing Director, have, as always (since about 1983), been helpful and encouraging. They are among the best professionals in the field.

    I also wish to thank, profusely, the eight scholars who twice examined charts for *RD500* (1993), made various suggestions regarding additional immigrants or "better" lines, and detected numerous "gremlins" or typographical errors. These eight were (1) the late John Hutchinson Cook (see *NEXUS* 11 [1994]: 148), who suggested the line of biographer Ted Morgan (Sanche de Gramont), and whose magnificent gift to NEHGS of several thousand books on British and Continental genealogy I have used extensively; (2) the late H.M. West Winter, author of *The Descendants of Charlemagne (800-1400),* 10 vols., covering 16 generations, who added many diacritical marks and contributed both the line of George Mosle of N.Y., his maternal grandfather (Mosle's wife is an addition to this volume, the line taken largely from typescripts by West Winter at NEHGS), and a much improved royal descent for Peter

The Royal Descents of 900 Immigrants

Paul Rubens, the painter, and H.J. Stier of Maryland; (3) the late William Addams Reitwiesner of the Library of Congress (see *American Ancestors* 12 [2011], 1: 15), my colleague on *American Ancestors and Cousins of The Princess of Wales,* who contributed the line of (F.G.E.) Louis (W.) Viereck, had previously written on Louis Nicola, and extracted from Bartrum's *Welsh Genealogies* almost all of the Welsh lines herein (often unraveling the best or better descents for various Welsh immigrants, and considerably improving that section of the book); (4) the late Brice McAdoo Clagett, former NEHGS trustee, who allowed me to use all his research for "Seven Centuries: Ancestors for Twenty Generations of John Brice de Treville Clagett and Ann Calvert Brooke Clagett," unfortunately unpublished, including newly found material on John Cra(y)croft of Maryland and Gibbeses of South Carolina; (5) Douglas Richardson, prolific article writer, contributor to *Ancestral Roots, Magna Charta Sureties,* and *Plantagenet Ancestry of Seventeenth-Century Colonists,* and author of *Plantagenet Ancestry* (2004, 2011, the latter in 3 vols.), *Magna Carta Ancestry* (2005, 2011, the latter in 4 vols.), and *Royal Ancestry* (2013, 5 vols.), who added, among immigrants or other items, his identification of the mothers of Joan (Plantagenet), Princess of North Wales, and William Longespee, Earl of Salisbury, illegitimate children of, respectively, Kings John and Henry II of England; (6) Henry Bainbridge Hoff, editor of *The New England Historical and Genealogical Register* (*NEHGR*), former editor of *The New York Genealogical and Biographical Record,* Gignilliat, Nelson and Lloyd-Yale-Eaton scholar, who also brought to my attention the de Grasse and Rudyard descents; (7) Michael J. Wood, mentioned above, who undertook Henshaw and Ligon/Lygon research and contributed to the descent of Mrs. Thomasine Ward Thompson Buffum; and (8) the late David Faris, co-editor of later editions of *Ancestral Roots* and *Magna Charta Sureties* (responsible especially, in the seventh edition of the former, for the Holand-Swinnerton and Marmion notes at the end of lines 32 and 246A) and compiler before his death of two editions (1996 and 1999) of the just-mentioned *Plantagenet Ancestry of Seventeenth-Century Colonists.* Increase Nowell scholar Jerome E. Anderson, formerly of the NEHGS library staff, a contributing editor of *TAG* and consulting editor for *NEHGR,* also read the entire last draft and offered useful suggestions. The late Dudley, Winslow, Cotton, Bradbury and Errington scholar Marshall Kenneth Kirk, also formerly of the NEHGS

The Royal Descents of 900 Immigrants

library staff, carefully reviewed the introduction. Other readers of the first introduction were Michael Tepper and the late W.A. Reitwiesner.

For the 2004 edition of *RD600* the late Andrew B.W. MacEwen reviewed the Scottish charts in *RD500,* suggested elimination of some descents from Princess Annabella Stewart, Countess of Huntly, a daughter of James I of Scotland, and helped to develop the line for Magdalen Dalyell (Monteith). The late William Addams Reitwiesner reviewed all largely Continental (i.e. European) lines, traced the ancestry of Christoph(er), Baron de Graffenried and Mrs. Anne Coddington Fenner in considerable detail, and brought to my attention the line for Mrs. Kofi Annan (Bill also dictated by telephone the line of Sir John Gielgud, and led me to sources that would expand upon Leo van de Pas' published outline of the *RD* of Audrey Hepburn). The late Brice McAdoo Clagett, Henry Bainbridge Hoff, and John Anderson Brayton reviewed the pages for immigrants whose *RD*s they had developed or adjusted (since 1993, Cra[y]roft, the Dundas brothers, Eltonhead sisters, Neale, Mrs. Rivers, Henry Sewall of Md., Leighton Wilson, and the two Yonges for Brice; Mrs. Abigail Brewster Burr, Mrs. Lydia M. Latrobe Roosevelt, and Jan Otten van Tuyl for Henry; and Mrs. Ash[e], Branch, Calthorpe and Dobyns for John). Bill Marsh, my colleague on the French section of *The Mowbray Connection,* proofed the entire text and caught many "typos" and other errors. Correspondents whose research is incorporated herein, or who brought certain lines to my attention, include—in addition to the above eight, Jerome E. Anderson, Kirk, Tepper, MacEwen, Clagett, Brayton, and Marsh—Robert C. and Worth S. Anderson, Craig S. Ashley, Stewart Baldwin (who further reviewed Welsh Quaker *RD*s in the works of Thomas Allen Glenn), Robert Battle, the late Shirley Goodwin Bennett (sponsor of much research by Paul C. Reed), the late Miriam Elliott Bertelson, Ronny O. Bodine, Carl Boyer, 3rd (author of the *Ancestral Lines* series and other multi-ancestor works, and publisher of my *Notable Kin* and 1989 and 1995 *Ancestors of American Presidents* volumes), Kevin Bradford, John C. Brandon, Christos Christou, Jr., John A. Clark, the late John Insley Coddington, Robert Joseph Curfman, the late Francis James Dallett, David Curtis Dearborn of NEHGS, Sara B. Doherty, Marlene Eilers (Koenig), William Elliott, Thomas S. Erwin, Richard K. Evans (later author of *The Ancestry of Diana, Princess of Wales for Twelve Generations*), Todd A. Farmerie, the late Charles Fitch-Northen, Brandon Fradd, Thomas F. Gede, David L. Greene (former editor of *The American Genealogist, TAG*), Col. Charles M. Hansen (editor of *The*

The Royal Descents of 900 Immigrants

Genealogist [*TG*]), who confirmed or disproved several RDs for English Quaker immigrants), the late Ernest Flagg Henderson (III) (author of *Ancient, Medieval and More Recent Ancestors of Ernest Flagg Henderson IV and Roberta Campbell Henderson*, 4 vols., 2013), Douglas Hickling, Martin E. Hollick (who compiled *New Englanders in the 1600s*), the late Dorothy E. Hopkins, Anthony Glenn Hoskins, the late Jayne Simpson Huntington, Jack T. Hutchinson, the late David Humiston Kelley (the major ancient-world genealogist of his generation), Charles Kidd of *Debrett's Peerage*, Daniel MacGregor (author of "Brooke's Book" and "Close Ties"), Leslie Mahler, James Ross (Jay) Mellon (II) (author of *The Great Uprooting: Ancestors of the Mellon, Rüesch and Delafield Families*, 2008), the late Charles Mosley of *Burke's Peerage*, Albert H. Muth, the late General Herman Nickerson, Jr., Julie Helen Otto, Mrs. Gerald (Sarah) Polkinghorne, F.H. Pollard, John M. Plummer, Paul C. Reed, Douglas Richardson (see below), Dr. David A. Sandmire, the late Helen Jefferson Sanford, John L. Scherer, the late Walter Lee Sheppard, Jr. (editor of the *Ancestral Roots*, *AR*, and *Magna Charta Sureties*, *MCS*, series), D. Brenton Simons (see above), Bruce H. Sinkey, Scott C. Steward of NEHGS, Don Charles Stone (D.H. Kelley's successor as the major American genealogist of the "ancient world"), Patricia W. Strati, Henry Sutliff III, Davida E. Symonds, Nathaniel L. Taylor (current editor of *The American Genealogist*), Neil D. Thompson (former editor of *TG*), the late Sir Anthony Richard Wagner (Garter King of Arms and author of *English Genealogy* and *Pedigree and Progress*), and Wayne H.M. Wilcox. (I might not know of the deaths of some of the above.)

In 1996 and 1999 the late David Faris published, the first with GPC, the second with NEHGS, two editions of *Plantagenet Ancestry of Seventeenth-Century Colonists*, to both of which I contributed a few items and for the latter of which Douglas Richardson was almost a co-author. David's work, in effect, selected from *RD500*, *AR7* and *MCS4* most seventeenth-century English settlers (but only one group of Welsh, no Scots, no Continental Europeans, no eighteenth-, nineteenth-, or twentieth-century immigrants and few seventeenth-century governors unless they left American progeny) and covers almost all of their descents from Edward III, Edward I or Henry III of England, but no earlier or non-Plantagenet kings. Included, however, for the 155 or so immigrants so treated, and for each of their forebears in almost all of their descents from the above three kings, are pertinent dates, sometimes estimated, notes on Parliamentary or military service, royal allegiances,

The Royal Descents of 900 Immigrants

offices, titles and knighthood, residence or manorial holdings, university graduation or fellowship, etc. Some of my readers regret that I did not add such details to *RD500* and *RD600*, so I am especially glad that Faris, and later Richardson (see below), included them. Many outlines to baronial and gentry families, with full details, also comprise, in addition, three volumes by Carl Boyer 3rd – *Medieval English Ancestors of Robert Abell* (2001), covering roughly 1300-1650, *Medieval English Ancestors of Certain Americans* (also 2001), covering mostly 1000-1300, and *Medieval Welsh Ancestors of Certain Americans* (2004).

Douglas Richardson inherited all of David Faris's notes, manuscripts, and computer files, and reworked and massively expanded David's book. Doug's *Plantagenet Ancestry*, published in 2004 and 2011, covers many new Plantagenet descents, including lines from illegitimate children of Kings John and Henry II (plus those from Hamelin Plantagenet, Earl of Surrey, illegitimate half-brother of the latter), to approximately 205 immigrants. Sometime before his last illness, moreover, in June 2000, David Faris sent me a copy of *Magna Carta Ancestry (MCA)* as he and Douglas Richardson had outlined and developed the volume to that date. I combed this manuscript for new "best lines" (many developed by Doug) and Doug shared with me most of his new discoveries for the 2004 *Plantagenet Ancestry*. Doug's *Magna Carta Ancestry* appeared in 2005 and again in 2011, and allegedly covers every known descent for over 235 immigrants from the 17 sureties who left descendants past four generations. For specific additions of note to the 2004 and 2005 works, see *RD600* (2008, 2010 only), pp. 813-17, wherein I note and discuss *AR8*, *MCA5*, the Dudley, Marbury (Hutchinson and Scott) and Appleton works by Marston Watson, the fourth edition of *Adventurers of Purse and Person* (3 vols., by John Frederick Dorman), *The Ark and The Dove Adventurers* (by George E. and Donna Valley Russell) and Michel L. Call's *The Royal Ancestry Bible* (2005, 4 vols.). Thanks are also due to Kimball G. Everingham of Salt Lake City, editor of *Plantagenet Ancestry*, *Magna Carta Ancestry*, and *Royal Ancestry* (see the next paragraph), who moved David's files from Philadelphia to Utah and has greatly helped Doug with bibliography and computer matters as well.

In 2013 Douglas Richardson published *Royal Ancestry*, 5 vols., which amalgamates *PA* (2011) and *MCA* (2011) and adds 11 more immigrants (the total is now a few over 255) and is the first source I cite for each of these 255 in this volume (and for other immigrants whose

The Royal Descents of 900 Immigrants

best royal descent is through families Doug treats). In both the 2011 and the 2013 works Doug has added or amended many "High Medieval" lines, thus often "improving" or sometimes "downgrading" a "best royal descent." Doug has dropped, for lack of clinching proof, several immigrants I treat herein—Edward FitzRandolph, Anthony Savage, and Thomas Wingfield, plus the patrilineal descent for Thomas Dudley. The works of Faris and Richardson, each expanding its predecessor, are monumental, with thousands of citations and biographical facts that massively augment many of the charts, or parts of charts, in this book.

For *RD900* John C. Brandon, John A. Brayton and the late Andrew B.W. MacEwen, a few months before his death, reviewed the entire manuscript and brought various desired changes (and typos) to my attention (Mr. MacEwen for the Scottish sections especially). John C. Brandon has added over 60 new immigrants to this work or *RD600* (especially the 2006 and 2008 editions), easily the largest such contribution, including both colonial forefathers with large progenies (Mrs. Almy, Chambers, Chester, the Craighead and Mansfield siblings, Mrs. Frost, Izard, Mrs. Poole, Pordage, Spence and Traill of N.H. and Willing, sometimes with, or correcting, other scholars) and an almost equally large number of major twentieth-century figures (W.H. Auden, Borghese of Bomarzo, Helena Bonham Carter, the father of Olivia Wilde, Benedict Cumberbatch, Mrs. Negroponte, Lynn Redgrave [sister of Vanessa] and Natasha Richardson [Vanessa's daughter] and Frances "Fanny" Wright). John A. Brayton has contributed over 25 immigrants, many to the *RD600* editions of 2006 and 2008, mostly colonial; those with large progenies include the Batte brothers and Roger Mallory, Branch, Mrs. Burwell, Robert Drake, Hone, Mrs. Jones, Ludwell, Mrs. Meade, Stephens/Stevens Thompson and the much-married Frances Baldwin, once more with, or correcting, other scholars. Mr. Brandon finds more online clues to English origins than probably any genealogist now living. Mr. Brayton, especially in two series sponsored by the Order of First Families of North Carolina—*Registry of Ancestors* (2 vols., 2005-8) and *Ancestor Biographies* (2 vols., 2011-14), has become the major Southside Virginia, Albemarle and North Carolina genealogist of his generation (note also his 11-volume set of *Colonial Families of Surry and Isle of Wight Counties, Virginia, 1995-2011*—six volumes of wills and deeds and genealogies of Harris, Jennings, Pitt, Williams, and Bridger families). The late Andrew B.W. MacEwen, mentioned above, was long the major American, and perhaps world, authority on the genealogies of

The Royal Descents of 900 Immigrants

Scottish nobles, lairds, and clan chiefs, and contributed much—he is mentioned or cited in over 40 footnotes—to the ancestry of Henry Stewart, Lord Darnley, husband of Mary, Queen of Scots, outlined in Charles M. Hansen and Neil D. Thompson, *The Ancestry of Charles II, King of England* (2012, 2014).

Henry Bainbridge Hoff, also mentioned above and one of the major genealogical scholars of colonial and later New York, reviewed the lines of New York and New Jersey immigrants new to this volume, and brought various new lines to my attention, including (among late entries to this work) those for Mrs. Berg and Mrs. Tennent. John Blythe Dobson of Winnipeg, Manitoba, several years ago sent me outlines, some first seen on the websites of Daniel de Rauglaudre or the late Leo van de Pas, of "improved" Continental descents for various French and German immigrants in *RD600*, and then twice reviewed the entire Continental section of *RD900*. Dobson also contributed over two dozen immigrants to this edition, including Hinojosa and Cazenove from The Netherlands, Treasury Secretary Albert Gallatin, the von Trapp sibling singers, Russian novelist Vladimir Nabokov, British actor Daniel Craig, and five French-Canadian immigrants to the U.S., to be treated later. Anthony Glenn Hoskins of Santa Rosa, California, had earlier contributed descents for Thomas Brassey and John Umfreville and argued, often brilliantly, in the March 1997 issue of *Genealogists' Magazine*, that Mary Boleyn's son and daughter (for the latter see pp. 300-4) were children of King Henry VIII, not William Cary. To this volume Tony also contributed several Continental immigrants, including Mrs. Lester Armour (Alexandra, Princess Golitzin [Gallitzin]), "Peter Berlin" (Armin Hagen, Baron Hoyningen-Huene), (Prince) Alexi(s) Lubomirski, and Peter, Prince Golitzin (Gallitzin) and his wife (these last on p. 800-1). In addition, Tony was the first genealogist to suggest noble ancestry for Marcus Schenkenberg. My debt to various French Canadian scholars—especially Denis Beauregard, Roland-Yves Gagné, René Jetté, Diane Wolford Sheppard, Thomas Allaire, and John P. Hickey, Jr.—is acknowledged in the introductions to each part of the French Canadian (France to Québec and Québec to the U.S.) section at the end of this volume's main text.

Finally, I wish to acknowledge my own royally descended immigrant ancestors, Col. Thomas Ligon/Lygon of Virginia (first covered in *RD900* as a descendant of Edward III, via Henry, Cardinal Beaufort) and Act. Gov. Jeremiah Clarke of Rhode Island (traced

The Royal Descents of 900 Immigrants

matrilineally in *RA* to a granddaughter of Sancha de Ayala, below). My descent from Ligon inspired *The Mowbray Connection*, discussed in the introduction that follows. Learning in the late 1960s of my Jeremiah Clarke descent considerably reinforced my interest in Western royal genealogy generally. My two Ligon/Lygon (and four Mowbray) lines and my Jeremiah Clarke descent, largely but not quite fully outlined in Margaret Hardwick Miller, *Ligons and Their Kin of Graves County, Kentucky* (1978), *passim* (I appear on p. 117; the author, a cousin several times over, was matron of honor at the wedding of my parents), are derived through my maternal grandfather, George Wesley Boyd (1880-1952), farmer, oilman and sometime official of Navarro County, Texas, and three of his four grandparents. These lines may be outlined as follows, in the format used in my "Notable Kin" columns in *NEHGS NEXUS, New England Ancestors, American Ancestors*, and online (as "Royal Descents, Notable Kin, and Printed Sources" at www.americanancestors.org). Following my name and birth year are the names of my parents, a set of grandparents, great-grandparents, etc., backwards in time to the underlined immigrants of royal descent (RD), with semi-colons separating generations and commas separating couples of the same generation in my "Ahnentafel."

Gary Boyd Roberts, b. 1943; Jack Carl Roberts (1911-1990) & Mary Elizabeth Boyd (1912-2002); George Wesley Boyd (1880-1952) & Fannie Kate Root (1888-1964); Hugh Blair Boyd & Mary Elizabeth Bressie; John Boyd & Mary Stovall Puryear, Joseph Addison Bressie & Martha Ann Edens; William Puryear & Mary Ligon, John Bressie & Elizabeth Ligon, Ezekiel Edens & Mary Gammill; Joseph Ligon & Mary Church (parents of Mary and Elizabeth), James Edens & Fereby Averitt; Thomas Ligon & Ann ——, Benjamin Averitt & Amy Spooner; Matthew Ligon & Elizabeth Anderson, John Spooner & Hannah Stanton, Richard Ligon & Mary Worsham, Henry Stanton & Mary Hull; *Col. Thomas Ligon/Lygon* of Va. (*RD*, see pp. 295-99) & Mary Harris, John Stanton & Mary Clarke; *Jeremiah Clarke*, Acting Governor of R.I. (*RD*, see pp. 466-69) & Mrs. Frances Latham Dungan. Ligon's three descents from Thomas Mowbray, 1st Duke of Norfolk (d. 1399),

The Royal Descents of 900 Immigrants

centerpiece of *The Mowbray Connection*, are treated on p. 295; Clarke's from Sancha de Ayala (wife of Sir Walter Blount), is also treated herein, via a cross-reference to the chart for Ralph Izard on pp. 716-17. Sancha and Margaret Kerdeston (wife of John de Foix, 1st Earl of Kendal, treated herein on pp. 615-16) are usually the closest English commoner and often American links to Kings of Spain, Habsburgs, and many later European sovereigns.

Note: One of the speculative royal descents outlined at the end of the American charts herein, that for Mrs. Elizabeth Stoughton Scudder Chamberlain (pp. 920-22), was shared by my maternal grandmother, as follows:

Fannie Kate (Root) Boyd (1888-1964), above; Charles Mitchell Root & Mary Lucy Wade Peevey; Ephraim Hough Root & Caroline Pool; Judah Root & Sarah Hough; Ephraim Hough, Jr. & Eunice Andrews; Ephraim Hough & Hannah Royce, Andrew Andrews & Esther Royce; Robert Royce & Joanna Gaylord (parents of Hannah and Esther); Isaac Royce & Elizabeth Lathrop; Samuel Lathrop & Elizabeth Scudder; John *Scudder & Elizabeth Stoughton* of Mass. (possible *RD*), later married to Rev. Robert *Chamberlain*.

I might also call attention to the kinship between descendants of Mary (Worsham) Ligon above, and descendants of Pocahontas. John Bolling, the only American great-grandchild of the latter, married Mary Kennon, daughter of Richard Kennon and Elizabeth Worsham, Mary's sister. See my *Notable Kin, Volume Two* (1999), pp. 74-78.

Introduction

I

Royal descent is the "gateway" ancestry that links modern America to the ancient and feudal world. The pertinent Western genealogical evolution can be summarized as follows. Barbaric tribes invade and finally conquer the Roman Empire, and victors and vanquished—imperial or senatorial families, plus, later, possible descendants of Egyptian, Persian, Syrian, Parthian, Armenian, or Byzantine rulers—undoubtedly intermarry. During the "dark" and early "middle" ages, warrior chiefs of barbaric tribes become kings, feudalism begins, and territory and people begin to solidify into nations. Especially after 1200 or so, kings of England, Scotland, France, Aragón and Castile (later Spain), Denmark, and Sweden, plus Russian czars and finally Italian Renaissance princes, try to consolidate their possessions geographically and tame noble kinsmen into courtiers—processes still continuing as the New World is settled in the sixteenth and seventeenth centuries. From almost the beginning of each kingdom younger sons and non-reigning sons-in-laws of kings become noblemen, as do most kinsmen of conquerors. This nobility, which early assumes surnames, often rivals, in the aggregate, the power of its royal head (whom local peers often try to choose). The nobility's nemesis, often royal allies, consists in large part of its own younger sons and sons-in-law and their descendants, who form, or head, the European "gentry"—knights, manorial lords, gentlemen with coats-of-arms and "settled" estates, and finally baronets in England; lairds in Scotland; seigneurs in France; and counts, barons, lords or knights in Germany. In England, Scotland or Wales younger sons and sons-in-law of this gentry become leading merchants, lords mayor or aldermen; clergymen, Anglican bishops, or early Puritan leaders; university fellows, lawyers (via Inns of Court) or bureaucrats under Tudors and Stuarts; and professional soldiers (i.e., officers, sometimes under foreign kings). Younger sons and sons-in-law of these last groups – plus some gentlemen (especially among the "lesser gentry"), a few peers who often become governors, various Continental nobles (mostly later immigrants) and a handful of European "bourgeois,"

The Royal Descents of 900 Immigrants

mostly French Huguenots of mercantile and "robe" background—form the royally descended elite that settled the American colonies and is the subject of this book. The evolution that generates royal and "ancient" ancestry for millions of Americans—most, probably, with New England Yankee, Pennsylvania Quaker, or Tidewater planter forebears—is thus (1) *barbaric* chieftains solidifying into (2) *feudal kings*, whose own younger offspring become (3) *last-name national nobilities*, whose younger offspring form a (4) *landed gentry*, whose younger offspring in turn become (5) *merchants, ministers, intellectuals, bureaucrats and soldiers*. Offspring of these last, together with some members of (3) and (4) and many ambitious or discontented leaders of (5), help found the American colonies. Ministers, merchants and gentlemen go everywhere, but Puritans go to New England, Quakers (often Welsh) largely to Pennsylvania, Scots largely to mid-Atlantic states (some to Virginia), and Anglican "cavaliers" to Tidewater Maryland, Virginia, and South Carolina.

This volume outlines the "best" royal descents—from the most recent king—of 900 immigrants to the American colonies or the United States (but not English Canada, the Caribbean, Mexico, or Central or South America), from the seventeenth century to the present, who were notable themselves or left descendants notable in American history. My standard for notability is inclusion usually in *American National Biography (ANB)* or the *Dictionary of American Biography (DAB)*, but sometimes only *Who Was Who in America*, *Who's Who in America* or the *National Cyclopaedia of American Biography* (in a few cases even lesser compendia—usually biographical dictionaries of state legislatures or several states themselves but in a very few cases, Wikipedia entries). Included herein are all colonial governors for whom I could find royal descent, even if they returned to England or Scotland and left only British descendants, plus their wives if these wives were descended from a later king than their husbands or if the wives were very nearly related (to about second cousins, perhaps once or twice removed) to others of the 900. Included also were various town, settlement, or colony founders, officials other than governors, and British military officers of the French and Indian wars (but not the Revolution, at least past Lexington), and/or their wives, again if treated in *ANB* or the *DAB*; several clergymen or missionaries (and/or their wives) and engineers, if in *ANB* or the *DAB*; and a half-dozen or so European nobles—LaFayette and Noailles (brothers-in-law, plus their wives), Rochambeau, de Grasse, d'Estaing, Steuben and

The Royal Descents of 900 Immigrants

von Fersen—who played a significant role (on our side) in the American Revolution. Many of these last groups also returned to England, Scotland, or the Continent. Treated as immigrants too, even though they never came here, are Sir Ferdinando Gorges, founder and Lord Proprietor of Maine, and his four wives; Lady Juliana Fermor, wife of Pennsylvania proprietor Thomas Penn; and Cecil Calvert, 2nd Baron Baltimore, proprietor of Maryland, and his wife (Hon. Anne Arundell) and granddaughter-in-law (Lady Charlotte Lee), both baronesses Baltimore. Given this liberal counting of "immigrants," plus the probability, discussed below, that the royal descents of 5-10 percent or more of these immigrants may be disproved or (more often) significantly altered in the next decade or generation, I have extended their number to 925, and included 40 French Canadian immigrants. In future editions of this compendium, possibly assembled past my lifetime by other scholars, this final count may likewise vary.

These 900 immigrants fall into three categories. The first consists of the above-named colonial notables – governors and other officials, founders and proprietors, soldiers, clergymen and engineers – who often returned to their pre-American homes. The second consists of noted nineteenth- or twentieth-century figures, or their wives, parents or grandparents. Included herein are (1) Treasury Secretary Albert Gallatin, Irish patriot Thomas Addis Emmet, Texas pioneer Prince Carl of Solms-Braunfels, travelers Alexis de Tocqueville, Frances Trollope and Harriet Martineau (whose sister was an ancestor of the current Duchess of Cambridge), theosophist Madame Blavatsky and spouses of explorer Sir Henry Morton Stanley, *Monitor* builder John Ericsson and spiritualist Victoria Claflin Woodhull among nineteenth-century figures; (2) Christopher Isherwood, Jessica Mitford, Peter Lawford, Olivia de Havilland and Joan Fontaine (sisters), Sir John Gielgud, Audrey Hepburn, Lynn Redgrave and Natasha Richardson (aunt and niece), Ralph and Joseph Fiennes (brothers), Hugh Grant, Rupert Everett, Tilda Swinton, Helena Bonham Carter, Benedict Cumberbatch, Hermione Baddeley, Cary Elwes, Rachel Ward, Catherine Oxenberg, and Jack Huston, plus wives of Fritz Lang, David Niven, Raymond Massey, both Sir Ralph and Tony Richardson and Liam Neeson, and husbands of Hedy Lamarr, Adele Astaire, Beatrice Lillie, and Madonna, among California, Hollywood, Broadway or television writers and actors (sometimes also singers, dancers or comedians); (3) Robert Louis Stevenson, W.H. Auden, P.G. Wodehouse, Alec Waugh, Aldous Huxley and Noël

The Royal Descents of 900 Immigrants

Coward, plus the wives of Alfred North Whitehead and David Frost among British literary or intellectual figures some of whose career is associated with America; (4) journalists Arnaud de Borchgrave and Anthony West, biographer Ted Morgan, and wives of poets Ezra Pound and Robert Lowell (novelist Caroline Blackwood, earlier married to the painter Lucian Freud), of novelist Norman Mailer and of news commentator David R. Gergen; (5) Dag Hammarskjöld and wives of Averell Harriman and David K.E. Bruce among diplomats; (6) wives of James Cox Brady, Marshall Field III and Edgar Bronfman, among tycoons, plus a Guinness baronet of Maryland and the wife of a von Gontard scion of the Anheuser-Busch family of St. Louis; (7) rocket scientist Wernher von Braun and his wife, plus (sometime at U. of Calif. Berkeley) evolutionary biologist Richard Dawkins; (8) first and second husbands respectively of "society" figures Barbara Hutton and Lee Radziwill, plus two Hungarian counts who married Vanderbilt inheritors of "The Breakers" estate in Newport, R.I.; (9) the singing von Trapp siblings, record producer Peter Asher, Jeremy Clyde of "Chad and Jeremy", and the wife of soundtrack composer John Barry; (10) Kay Summersby, Eisenhower's friend; (11) Mother Alexandra (Ileana of Roumania) of the Orthodox Monastery of the Transfiguration in Ellwood City, Pennsylvania; (12) novelist Vladimir Nabokov; (13) adman David Ogilvy; (14) Sir Tim(othy) John Berners-Lee of the World Wide Web; (15) Dame Anna Wintour of *Vogue*; (16) husbands also of artist and patron Kay Linn Sage and writer Kay Boyle; (17) fathers of "Tammany" boss Richard Croker, cabinet officer Charles Joseph Bonaparte, Wyoming Senator Malcolm Wallop, and actresses Gloria Grahame and Olivia Wilde; (18) fathers-in-law of Lucien, 3rd Prince Murat, Czech president Tomas Garrigue Masaryk and novelist J.D. Salinger; (19) the mother of Sheraton Hotel founder Ernest Henderson; (20) both maternal grandparents of Mrs. Dean Acheson, wife of the Secretary of State; (21) the paternal grandmother of model and actress Brooke Shields; (22) a great-aunt of the late Diana, Princess of Wales; and (23) a daughter of Leo, Count Tolstoy, the novelist and seer. These colonial "notables in their own right" and nineteenth- and twentieth-century figures, their parents and grandparents I traced largely in the course of checking available printed sources for the known ancestry of all 15,000 figures in the *DAB*, a project I undertook at the Newberry Library in Chicago, 1966-74 (much multiplied by research, 1974-2017, at the New England Historic Genealogical Society in Boston, and elsewhere). Included herein

The Royal Descents of 900 Immigrants

are all my findings regarding the royal descents of traceable immigrant ancestors of these 15,000.

The remainder of these 900, only eleven less than 500, are very largely colonial immigrants who have left sizable, often huge, progenies. Almost 300 are ancestors of five or more figures in *ANB* or the *DAB* and over 225 are ancestors of at least ten. Probably over 100 are ancestors of five or more major figures in American history (the 500 or so who receive quarter-page or longer coverage in the *Concise DAB*). And over fifteen, including Governor Thomas Dudley, Samuel and Judith (Everard) Appleton, Rev. Peter Bulkeley, Mrs. Judith Knapp Hubbard, Percival Lowell, and Dr. Richard Palgrave of Massachusetts, Mrs. Audrey Barlow Almy and Mrs. Anne Marbury Hutchinson of Rhode Island, Mrs. Margaret Wyatt Allyn, Mrs. Anne Lloyd Yale Eaton, Mrs. Agnes Harris Spencer Edwards, Mrs. Alice Freeman Thompson Parke, and Thomas Trowbridge of Connecticut, Robert Livingston the elder of New York, and Henry Isham and William Randolph of Virginia – are ancestors of probably over 100 *ANB* or *DAB* notables. Immigrants with almost as many noted descendants as these last 15, perhaps 75 in the *DAB*, include Robert Abell, Griffith and Margaret (Fleming) Bowen, Mrs. Jane Allen Bulkeley (who died in England, first wife of Rev. Peter), Mrs. Mary Gye Maverick and Constant Southworth of Massachusetts; Leonard Chester, Mrs. Mabel Harlakenden Haynes (Eaton) and Governor William Leete of Connecticut; Mrs. Margaret Domville Hutton Banks of Maryland; and Mrs. Sarah Ludlow Carter, Henry and Alice (Eltonhead) Corbin, Theophilus Hone, Col. George Reade, Anthony Savage and Mrs. Mary Towneley Warner of Virginia (for comments or doubts about the descents of Southworth, Leete, and Savage see their respective charts).

Many of these 489 mostly colonial immigrants are treated in the six major modern compendia of such lines – (1) the 2013 *Royal Ancestry*, 5 vols., by Douglas Richardson, Doug's earlier *Plantagenet Ancestry* and *Magna Carta Ancestry*, my own *RD600*, and the 1996 and 1999 editions of *Plantagenet Ancestry of Seventeenth-Century Colonists*, much derived in turn from *RD500*; (2) the 2004 eighth edition of *Ancestral Roots of Certain American Colonists Who Came to America Before 1700* (formerly of *Sixty Colonists Who Came to New England Between 1623 and 1650*); (3) the 1999 fifth edition of *The Magna Charta Sureties, 1215*, by F.L. Weis, W.L. Sheppard, Jr., and William R. Beall (which included only one new immigrant, Gov. Thomas Greene of Md., from the 1991 fourth edition by Weis, Sheppard, and David Faris); (4) the often flawed

The Royal Descents of 900 Immigrants

(and weakly documented) five volumes of *Living Descendants of Blood Royal* (1959-73), by H.H. d'Angerville; (5) the three volumes of *Pedigrees of Some of the Emperor Charlemagne's Descendants* (1941, 1974, 1978), by M.D.A.R. von Redlich, A.L. Langston, J.O. Buck and T.F. Beard, also sometimes flawed, and without *any* references; and (6) *Lineage Book, Descendants of the Illegitimate Sons and Daughters of the Kings of Britain* (my copy covers 237 lines, some via immigrants whose RDs have been disproved, for members joining through 1987). Many of the New England immigrants herein were listed in my own royal descent bibliographies of such colonists in *The Connecticut Nutmegger* 10 (1977-78): 187-98, 400, and *The New England Historical and Genealogical Register* (*NEHGR*) 141 (1987): 92-109, plus *NEHGS NEXUS* 13 (1996): 124-30.[1] Still, well over 200 of these 489 have appeared in no such compendium or listing but have been culled from journal articles, genealogies, visitations, other printed sources or private research by good or widely known, reliable scholars (often correspondents) acknowledged on the charts. Archival or record sources are usually cited only when good printed sources do not cover the connection needing proof.

This book covers only immigrants notable in their own right or ancestors of notable Americans. Such limits include almost all royally descended colonial immigrants, for most Great Migration New Englanders who left children and grandchildren now have probably a million or more living descendants. Early New York or New Jersey settlers of royal descent (mostly English or Scots rather than Dutch), early Pennsylvanians of such descent (mostly Welsh or English Quakers, with some Scots) and Maryland, Virginia and South Carolina planters so descended (mostly English with some Scots; often Catholic in early Maryland, Anglican elsewhere) have thousands, often hundreds of thousands of such descendants. Thus every colonial immigrant who left issue that left issue in turn almost certainly has at least a few notable

---

[1] The sole immigrant in the 1987 article not covered herein is Mrs. Dorothy May Bradford (a *Mayflower* passenger who drowned off Cape Cod before the ship landed), first wife of Governor William Bradford (their one child d.s.p.). Dorothy's parentage has been disputed; Cordelia Bowes, her *alleged* mother, was descended from Hugh Lupus, Earl of Chester, d. 1101, [again] alleged kinsman of William the Conqueror). According to *TAG* 89 (2017): 81-94, 168-88 (Caleb Johnson, Sue Allan, and Simon Neal), however, Dorothy was instead the daughter of Henry and Katherine (____) May, son of John May and Thomasine Cross, daughter of John and Jacomine (____) Cross.

The Royal Descents of 900 Immigrants

descendants. The genealogical literature on the progeny of royally descended members of these colonial populations is also usually good enough that we can trace such descendants *from printed sources*. Finally, these 489 are a large enough group so that living Americans with 50 to 100 immigrant ancestors in New England (or Long Island), in Quaker (but not German or Scots-Irish) Pennsylvania, or in the Tidewater South (but often *not* the Piedmont, Shenandoah Valley, or mountainous "backcountry") can *expect* to find a royally descended forebear herein.

But many nineteenth- and twentieth-century immigrants have left only a few, a few dozen, a few hundred, or a few thousand descendants – not enough for at least one to be almost certainly notable, not enough for living Americans to expect to find any of a small group of such immigrants in their ancestry, and not yet enough to have generated a sizable body of published genealogy. Yet undoubtedly, because of their sheer quantity, many post-colonial immigrants have royal descents and my selection of them, discussed briefly above and despite much perusal of sources, is very partial. The late Joseph L. Druse, long of East Lansing, Michigan, combed various modern Burke's works, especially the *Peerage* and *Landed Gentry*, plus Arthur C. Addington's *Royal House of Stuart*, Ruvigny's *Plantagenet Roll of the Blood Royal*, and other sources, and found numerous nineteenth- or twentieth-century immigrants to America none of whose descendants yet seem to be covered in *ANB* or the *DAB*. Much similar combing could be undertaken in (1) the post-2000 volumes of the *Landed Gentry*, covering Scotland, Yorkshire, Wales and Cumbria; (2) F.A. Crisp's modern *Visitation of England and Wales* (and *Notes*) and *Visitation of Ireland* series; (3) *Genealogisches Handbuch des Adels*, *Europäische Stammtafeln*, the most recent *Almanach de Gotha* (2 vols., 2012-13), and Daniel A. Willis's books on the descendants of Maria Theresa, Louis XIII, and George I; (4) Jacques Arnold's volumes on descendants of late eighteenth- or nineteenth-century kings or sovereign princes; and (5) sources for the *Rolls of Arms Registered by The Committee on Heraldry of the New England Historic Genealogical Society, Parts 1-10* (2013, which added various immigrants from the 1976 *Burke's Irish Family Records*). I have checked most of these sets (the Arnold volumes page by page and the *Roll of Arms* entry by entry) for immigrants of royal descent *and notable progeny*. Many recent "gentry" immigrants from Great Britain, or royal, noble or royally descended immigrants from the Continent simply have not *yet* had notable progeny – they almost certainly eventually will. Some who may have had such

The Royal Descents of 900 Immigrants

descendants already, but are also not treated herein, are nineteenth-century Germans and Scandinavians, no doubt often of royal descent, sometimes studied by (1) the late Duderstadt scholar C. Frederick Kaufholz (see *National Genealogical Society Quarterly* 49 [1961]: 201-4, 63 [1975]: 268-71, and *The American Genealogist* 51 [1975]: 225-29, 59 [1983]: 150-56); (2) the late Norwegian-American scholar Gerhard Brandt Naeseth (see his *Naeseth-Fehn Family History* [1956] for midwestern kinsmen of Queen Sonja [Haraldsen] of Norway, p. 146, plus Erling Arnold Smedal, *The Smedal Family History and Genealogy* [1966] and *Supplement* [1973-77], and *Pedigrees of Some of the Emperor Charlemagne's Descendants*, vol. 3, pp. 240, 255-60); (3) the late W.L. Sheppard, Jr. (see *NEHGR* 111 [1957]: 99-103, reprinted in *English Origins of New England Families From NEHGR*, 1st ser. [1984], 3: 255-59); (4) R. Bruce Diebold (for Fritz Harbou, Mrs. Fritz Lang, and Claus von Bülow herein); (5) Thomas Frederick Gede (for V.E.H. von Finck, the Lewenhaupts, plus the California ancestors of Che Guevara); and others. I have, I think, combed the printed literature on *colonial immigrants* fairly thoroughly, and have looked at many sources for nineteenth- and twentieth-century immigrants of royal descent as well. Concerning non-noble mid-nineteenth-century Germans, Scandinavians, Dutch and others, however, I am ignorant of the record sources in Europe often necessary to trace their ancestry, and without the oral history or local documentation needed to know their progeny. The Continental nobility most frequently covered herein, perhaps surprisingly, is the Russian—immigrants largely from its Revolution who bear noble surnames (Troubetskoy, Golitzin [variously spelled], Obolensky, Tolstoy, etc.) and are treated, or whose spouses, children or grandchildren are covered, in *Who's Who in America* or *Who Was Who in America*. Often descended from near kinsmen of Czar Ivan I or the early Romanovs, these princes or counts are usually well covered in Nicolas Ikonnikov's *La Noblesse de Russie, Europäische Stammtafeln* (esp. vol. I, part 5 and vols. 23-25) and *Genealogisches Handbuch des Adels*. I shall consider French-Canadian lines following the main text of American charts.

II

Having discussed royal descent generally, the scope of this book, and the types of royally descended immigrants it covers, I now wish to say something about the history of this project, and of the massive

The Royal Descents of 900 Immigrants

scholarship it summarizes. In 1965-66, as a first-year graduate student at the University of Chicago (and after extensive earlier research at Yale and the New York Public Library), I began the almost encyclopedic genealogical study that has become my life's work – *The Mowbray Connection,* subtitled *An Analysis of the Genealogical Evolution of British, American, and Continental Nobilities, Gentries, and Upper Classes Since the End of the Middle Ages.* Twenty-three volumes – six of British charts, three of introductory text to the American section, ten of American charts, two of Continental charts, one of bibliography, and one (by Michael J. Wood of London) of index to the American charts compiled mostly before 1977 – are now at the New England Historic Genealogical Society (NEHGS) in Boston, the New York Public Library, and the Society of Genealogists in London. I wrote of *The Mowbray Connection* in *The Connecticut Nutmegger* 10 (1977-78): 3-12, 187-98, 393-400, *The Detroit Society for Genealogical Research Magazine* 41 (1977-78): 142, 42 (1978-79): 191, and *Genealogical Journal* 12 (1983-84): 70, 13 (1984-85): 66. As I suggested in these last, my aim was twofold. Since British and American genealogy are most frequently connected through the Tudor-Stuart gentry, and British and Continental genealogy through the common descent of most European nobilities from a common core of high medieval kings (mostly Plantagenets, Capets and Hohenstaufens), and since, as noted above, nobilities sire gentries from whom later intellectual and professional elites, twentieth-century "establishments" and even America's contemporary suburban middle class often derive – given these facts, I wanted to produce a single, stem study that by assimilating enough data would allow me to examine much of the genealogical history of the Western world. A secondary aim was to organize much of the best modern scholarship in our field, both Anglo-American and Continental. In so doing I hoped to examine further some of the suggestions in Sir Anthony Richard Wagner's *English Genealogy,* to develop hypotheses that genealogy could now offer demography, local, national, and world history, sociology and anthropology, and to document from *good* printed sources the sizable number of American immigrants of royal descent. In 1965, and to some extent still on the Internet, the magnificent ongoing literature on this last topic was marred by association with poor earlier compendia.

The focus of *The Mowbray Connection* is Thomas Mowbray, 1st Duke of Norfolk (d. 1399; his widow, Lady Elizabeth FitzAlan, who

The Royal Descents of 900 Immigrants

also left children by a later husband, Sir Robert Goushill, and survived until 1425), great-great-grandson of Edward I, King of England, d. 1307; heir to the English crown after the descendants of Edward III; a minor character in Shakespeare's *Richard II*; and ancestor of Lady Jane Grey, Queen Elizabeth I, and many Tudor-Stuart peers, including Dudleys and Howards. Mowbray is a forebear too of almost all major clans of the eighteenth-century Whig oligarchy (including the great ducal progeny of the 1st Earl Gower – see *NEHGS NEXUS* 14 [1997]: 70-73), most Prime ministers through Home (plus David Cameron), many nineteenth and twentieth-century intellectual figures (including Byron, Shelley, E.B. Browning, Tennyson, Swinburne, Jane Austen, Charles Reade, Lewis Carroll, Darwin, Bertrand Russell, Ralph Vaughan Williams, T.E. Lawrence and the Mitfords, Sitwells, and Trevelyans, plus, among genealogists, John and Sir J.B. Burke, J.H. Round, G.E. Cokayne and Vicary Gibbs) and most members of the last century's "British establishment." Mowbray and/or his above-named wife (also a great-great-grandchild of Edward I) were also ancestors, or siblings or first cousins of ancestors, of perhaps half of the 900 American immigrants treated herein. Mowbray's own American colonial progeny included the Ligon/Lygon-Gorges-Berkeley-Dudley-Dale and Delaware West-Pelham-Bellingham clusters of governors (pp. 295-304, as already noted), Saltonstalls and Dudleys (likely via Gov. Thomas, certainly by his second wife) of Massachusetts, Averys of Connecticut and among their descendants the Rockefellers of New York (via Mrs. Susanna Palmes Avery), Maryland's barons Baltimore (plus Bladens and Keys, these last via Mrs. Alicia Arnold Ross), and Randolphs and Carringtons of Virginia. Elizabeth FitzAlan's immigrant descendants, in addition, included Abells, Bulkeleys, Pynchons, (probably) Southworths, Tyngs, and Willards (these last via Mrs. Mary Launce Sherman) and Wellingtons (via Dr. Richard Palgrave) of Massachusetts; Mainwarings of Connecticut; Lloyds (via John Nelson) of Long Island; Abbotts, Fenwicks and Rudyards of New Jersey; Claypooles and Biddles (via Rebecca Owen) of Philadelphia; Darnalls, Gerards, Hattons, Neales, Sewalls and the Carrollton Carrolls of Maryland; Conways, Corbins, Wormeleys, Dades and probably Thorntons and Strothers (the last two via Anthony Savage) of Virginia; Alstons and Fenwicks of South Carolina; and J.E. Oglethorpe of Georgia. For Ligon/Lygon notable descendants, both British and American – a good sampling of the above larger progeny, I think – see *NEHGS NEXUS* 16

The Royal Descents of 900 Immigrants

(1999): 156-59, 200-2, and *New England Ancestors* 1 (2000), 1: 64-66, 2: 38-41, 3: 42-44.

Near kinsmen of Mowbray or his wife with many American descendants include (1) Mowbray's sisters Eleanor, wife of John de Welles, 5th Baron Welles (see pp. 310-13, 343-44, 389-91, 409, 415-16, 426, 462-65, 470-74, 486-88 [later "improved"], 526-27, 439-40, 545-46, 579-81, 609-10), Joan (Genet), wife of Sir Thomas Grey of Heton, Northumberland (pp. 310-13, 327-30, 519-21, 599), and Margaret, wife of Sir Reginald Lucy (pp. 425, 534-35); (2) Elizabeth's sisters, Alice FitzAlan, wife of John Cherleton, 4th Baron Cherleton of Powis and alleged (but sometimes thought not to be) mistress of Henry Beaufort, Cardinal Beaufort (see pp. 295-99, 337-38, 375-76, 382-83, 396-97, plus *Foundations* 1, #4 [July, 2004]: 246-68), and Joan FitzAlan, wife of William Beauchamp, Baron Abergavenny (pp. 500-2, 551-52, 588-89, 596-97) and mother of Richard Beauchamp, 1st Earl of Worcester, father by Isabel le Despencer of Elizabeth Beauchamp, first wife of Edward Neville, 1st Baron Abergavenny (see pp. 347-48, 357-58, 405-6, 417); (3) two double first cousins of Elizabeth FitzAlan – Mary Bohun, wife of the future Henry IV of England (see pp. 229-36) and Eleanor Bohun, wife of Thomas Plantagenet of Woodstock, 1st Duke of Gloucester (son of Edward III) (see pp. 331-32, 352-54, 392-95, 403-4, 420-22, 425, 428, 436-37); and (4) Elizabeth FitzAlan's aunt, another Alice FitzAlan, wife of Thomas Holand, 2nd Earl of Kent (half-brother of Richard II) and mother of Edmund Holand, 4th Earl of Kent (see pp. 377-78, 410-12, 423-24), of Eleanor Holand, wife secondly of Edward Cherleton, 5th Baron Cherleton of Powis (see pp. 515-16, 600), and of Margaret Holand, wife of John Beaufort, Marquess of Somerset and Dorset (see pp. 300-4, 345-46, 361-62, 399, 407-8, 418, 427, 431) and mother in turn of Queen Joan Beaufort (Stewart) of Scotland (see pp. 225, 239-42, 249, 261-62, 266, 271-72, 278-80, 283-86), plus (5) the progeny of James II, James IV and James V of Scotland, James I of England, etc.). I might also note that Margaret Kerdeston, wife of John de Foix, 1st Earl of Kendal, grandmother of Anne de Foix, Queen of Bohemia and Hungary, and most recent English ancestress of many European sovereigns (see Col. Charles M. Hansen and Neil D. Thompson, *The Ancestry of Charles II, King of England: A Medieval Heritage* [2012, 2014], pp. 58-63), appears on pp. 615-16; among her first cousins was Anne Morley, wife of John Hastings, *de jure* Baron Hastings (see pp. 317-18, 342-44, 349-50, 577).

The Royal Descents of 900 Immigrants

Furthermore, one-fourth of the ancestry of Mowbray and his wife – that derived through Edward I, both his queens (Eleanor of Castile and Margaret of France), his brother (Edmund Plantagenet, 1st Earl of Lancaster) and his brother's wife (Blanche of Artois) – was Continental and largely royal, sovereign, or comital. This quadrant of the Mowbray-FitzAlan ancestry was fairly widespread, I found, among several Continental nobilities, especially those of France, Spain, Rhineland Germany, and Austria. Among figures herein this quadrant, much or some of it, is shared by (among others) Steuben, LaFayette, Noailles, Rochambeau, de Grasse, von Fersen, Zinzendorf (and his granddaughter), de Graffenried, Madame Blavatsky, Alexandra, Countess Tolstoy (daughter of Leo), R.P. Garrigue and the Masaryks, Dag Hammarskjöld, Vladimir Nabokov, Audrey Hepburn, the von Trapp siblings, and G.P. Lannes de Montebello. Focused, then, on Mowbray, his wife and their near Continental cousins, my life's work outlines the best Mowbray-connected royal descent of over 500 major figures in European history, of 1000 British figures of note, and of roughly 25 percent of the almost 15,000 notable Americans who died before 1941 and are treated in the *DAB* and its first two supplements. When no major portion of the Mowbray-FitzAlan ancestry is shared by a royally descended figure the best "single strand" of royal descent is presented – often, for British or American figures, a line from King John, Henry II, Henry I or Ethelred II of England, William I (the Lion) or David I of Scotland, or Henry I, Robert II, Hugh Capet or Louis IV of France. Since my official retirement at the end of 2004 I have much expanded, redrawn and documented from printed sources over 2000 American charts (about half of the American section) and plan to expand the remaining American charts after this volume is published; Julie Helen Otto has subject-indexed these new charts by both immigrants and notable descendants.

The Royal Descents of 500 Immigrants (*RD500*), *The Royal Descents of 600 Immigrants* (*RD600*), and now their successor, *The Royal Descents of 900 Immigrants* (*RD900*) are, in effect, the first volume of *The Mowbray Connection* to be published. For this book, however, I undertook extensive research into immigrants not included in the 1966-77 or pre-2004 version of *The Mowbray Connection* – and deleted lines disproved since the late 1960s. For this book also I have tried to outline not the closest Mowbray connection of any immigrant, but the best (i.e. from the eldest child, sons preferred to daughters) descent from the most *recent* king. This last effort involved tracing various new descents from

The Royal Descents of 900 Immigrants

Edward III and later kings; various other more recent royal descents were called to my attention by correspondents and/or genealogical colleagues. All such "improved" lines will be welcome and will appear in any later editions or future addenda to this work.

III

As suggested above, this book rests upon, and is a distillation of, a massive quantity of scholarship – much of the best work of the Jacobus generation, and of contemporary American genealogists, plus many monographs in English journals; the great (New) *Complete Peerage, Scots Peerage* (by Sir J.B. Paul), and *Welsh Genealogies, 300-1400 AD* and *1400-1500* (by P.C. Bartrum); various Burke's works and earlier peerage compendia by Collins, Douglas, and Lodge; the sometimes erroneous but invaluable visitations, especially those published by the Harleian Society; the great seventeenth- through twentieth-century English county histories, Dugdale through the (New) *History of Northumberland* and the ongoing *Victoria County History* series; the also ongoing *History of Parliament*, especially the 1381-1421 and 1509-1629 volumes; and the various great Continental sets – Anselme, Courcelles, Saint Allais, *Dictionnaire de la Noblesse* and *Grand Armorial de France* for France, *Europäische Stammtafeln, Genealogisches Handbuch des Adels*, the *Almanach de Gotha* and *Deutsche Geschichte in Ahnentafeln* for Germany, Litta for Italy, Elgenstierna for Sweden, Ikonnikov for Russia, etc. I also readily acknowledge my great debt, in *RD500*, to the above-cited *Ancestral Roots* and *Magna Charta Sureties, 1215* volumes (the last two editions of both of which include various additions and changes I submitted to Messrs. Sheppard and Faris); and in *RD600* and *RD900*, to *Plantagenet Ancestry of Seventeenth Century Colonists* and the 2004/5, 2011 and 2013 *Plantagenet Ancestry, Magna Carta Ancestry* and *Royal Ancestry* by Douglas Richardson, all discussed in "Acknowledgments"; plus liberal use of *Living Descendants of Blood Royal, Pedigrees of Some of the Emperor Charlemagne's Descendants,* and the *Lineage Book, Descendants of the Illegitimate Sons and Daughters of the Kings of Britain*. I readily concede too that except for one of my own ancestors, Col Thomas Ligon (Lygon) of Virginia, I have undertaken or commissioned little work in English *record* sources – parish registers, wills, inquisitions post mortem, chancery or manorial data, etc., although several colleagues at NEHGS have found key items

The Royal Descents of 900 Immigrants

for me online. Instead I have – as exhaustively, I think, as time and my bibliographical knowledge allow – combed *printed* genealogical sources for royally descended immigrants who were notable themselves or left noted American progeny. I have undertaken this 50 years of research largely at the Newberry Library in Chicago and, most importantly, NEHGS in Boston, where I have been reference librarian or director of research, special projects or publications, and am now Senior Research Scholar, 1974-77 and 1981 to the present, emeritus since 2005. I have looked at most printed genealogies, examined most major periodicals issue-by-issue, used dozens of compendia (and I think exhausted the bad older compilations of Charles Henry Browning, John Sparhawk Wurts, and Frederick Adams Virkus, which, like the Mormon Family Group Sheet Archives in Salt Lake City and on microfilm, the Ancestral File and, alas, many Internet sources, may *sometimes* be used for clues but should never be cited), talked about their contributions to this subject with most living (and most recently deceased) authors named in Appendix I, and for virtually all British families or New England immigrants herein sought the *best* sources listed by George W. Marshall, J.B. Whitmore, Geoffrey B. Barrow or *Burke's Family Index* (1976) (England, Wales, and Ireland), Margaret Stuart (Scotland) or Clarence Almon Torrey and Martin Edward Hollick (New England).

    Most of the Continental sets I used for this book were well described by John Insley Coddington in "Royal and Noble Genealogy," *Genealogical Research: Methods and Sources*, Milton Rubincam, ed. (1st ed., 1960), pp. 299-319. The history of British genealogical literature was well covered by Sir A.R. Wagner in *English Genealogy* (3rd ed., 1983), pp. 351-407. I wrote on the Jacobus generation in *The Connecticut Nutmegger* 12 (1979-80): 372, on George Andrews Moriarty, Jr., W.G. Davis, and various other scholars of royal descents in my introductions to *English Origins of New England Families* (1st and 2nd series, 1984-85) and *Massachusetts and Maine Families in the Ancestry of Walter Goodwin Davis* (1996), all reprinted and updated in my 2004 and 2012 *The Best Genealogical Sources in Print* (chapters 5, 13, and 14), mentioned below, and on post-1960 scholarship concerning royally descended New Englanders in *NEHGR* 141 (1987): 92-109, 150 (1996): 461-64. To these discussions I think I can most usefully add simply (see Appendix I to this introduction) a list of 255 twentieth-century scholars (through 2017), many still living, and the immigrants on

The Royal Descents of 900 Immigrants

whom they have worked – sometimes establishing not the entire descent outlined in this book but nonetheless a significant part of it.

The list in Appendix I, which could be expanded even further, emphasizes *living* scholars, contributors to the major current American genealogical journals (*NEHGR, TAG, NYGBR, TG, NGSQ* and *TVG*, plus *Genealogists' Magazine* and *Foundations*, from England) or to the *Ancestral Roots* and *Magna Charta Sureties* series, and English, Welsh or Scottish genealogists with much interest in American families (Addington, Arnold, Bartrum, Coldham, Currer-Briggs, Evans, Gun, Hamilton, Kidd, Montague-Smith, Mosley, Ruvigny, Sanders, Tayler(s), Wagner, Walne, Whyte and Wood). A sizable number of scholars now work in this field, or at least trace gentry and noble connections of their own forebears. Numerous clues still remain to be pursued, including many discovered by a dozen or more "gleanings" abstractors – Henry FitzGilbert Waters (*Genealogical Gleanings in England*), Lothrop Withington (*Virginia Gleanings in England*), J. Henry Lea, J.R. Hutchinson and William Gilbert (*English Origins of American Colonists From NYGBR*), George Sherwood (*American Colonists in English Records*), Charles Edward Banks (*Topographical Dictionary of 2885 Emigrants to New England, 1620-1650*, with many mistakes), Donald Whyte (*A Dictionary of Scottish Emigrants to the U.S.A.*), David Dobson (various books on Scottish immigrants), Robert Barnes (*British Roots of Maryland Families*), William Armstrong Crozier (*Virginia Heraldica*) and the above Peter Wilson Coldham (note also the older *Aspinwall Notarial Records* and *Note-Book Kept by Thomas Lechford*, plus the various lists that compose appendices A-C of *English Origins of New England Families from NEHGR*, 1st ser., vol. 3). In addition, moreover, to a major flowering of scholars and a plethora of clues, the Great Migration Project of Robert Charles Anderson and NEHGS has produced two series to date (with complete coverage of all immigrants to New England 1620-35, using every known document and good printed sources, plus *Great Migration Directory*, which lists all immigrants 1636-40, with a bibliography for each), and the 400th anniversary in 2007 of the settlement of Virginia inspired much research on the Jamestown Colony (especially the fourth edition of *Adventurers of Purse and Person*). English source records at the county level are now being published in profusion (the complete Bedfordshire parish register series and the Elizabethan *Essex Wills* prepared by the late F.G. Emmison are particularly notable examples), parish registers continue to be copied,

The Royal Descents of 900 Immigrants

filmed, or published, *The Index Library* and other works list all PCC (and many local) wills and administrations through 1700, publication of Tudor inquisitions post mortem has begun, and the Mormon International Genealogical Index (IGI), now absorbed into FamilySearch (www.familysearch.org), contains almost 900 million birth, baptism or marriage entries (for probably almost 600 million events) from around the world, mostly from the early sixteenth to mid-nineteenth centuries. This last includes perhaps 30 percent of all English parish registers.

Thus many more English origins and royal descent discoveries are likely in the near future. Judging from my experience in trying to update *RD500* and *RD600* more or less continuously, and in following the periodical literature, I should estimate that the immediate origin or royal descent of as many as 20 percent (190) of these immigrants could be altered – and as "old" lines or immigrants are dropped, probably many more will be added – in the next decade. Between *RD500* and *RD900* (1993 and 2017, over two decades) various scholars and I added over 350 new immigrants (many, admittedly, from the nineteenth and twentieth centuries, but not counting the French Canadians), deleted 29, and made major changes in the *RDs* of 165 (see Appendices V-VII to this introduction). Thus this book, like its predecessors, will certainly expand to future editions, by myself or a successor. Many possible changes, or at least problems to explore, are in fact suggested on the charts herein. For I have both (1) noted near kinsmen of many (especially Welsh Quaker Pennsylvania) immigrants who also came here but for whom I can find no notable descendants, and (2) indicated any areas of doubt in the outlined royal descents. Such ancestry for almost all immigrants herein will stand, I think, but some lines may well be "improved" (i.e., superseded by another descent from a later king) or changed. On various charts I note that a thorough monograph on a certain family or person would be welcome. On others I note that a particular identification (as of an immigrant or an immigrant's parent) would benefit from further confirmation (and a few may, of course, be disproved). Some lines herein, including some I discovered, are "virtually proved" – seemingly validated by a series of reliable printed materials – but not yet the subject of a separate monograph that brings together printed and all record or documentary sources. A main purpose of this book is to generate and encourage articles on these "problem" families, persons, and identifications, and suggest detailed studies on

The Royal Descents of 900 Immigrants

immigrants whose "virtually proved" lines appear herein for perhaps the first time.

I shall conclude this section by referring readers to Appendix II to this introduction – a list, in page-number order, of 63 "immigrants with caveats," some aspect of whose royal descents, as noted on their charts, merits further study or could need further proof.

IV

Having completed my discussion of the genealogical scholarship that lies behind this work, with appendix listings that both evoke the contribution of my colleagues and suggest problems for further study, I now proceed to a further examination of the 489 royally descended colonial immigrants who left notable American progeny, even if only a single notable child or grandchild. Of my count of 489, 147 (30%) settled in New England (98, or 20%, in Massachusetts; 27, or 6%, in Connecticut; 11, or 2%, in Rhode Island; six, or 1%, in New Hampshire; and five, or 1%, in Maine); 171 (35%) in the Middle Atlantic states (29, or 6%, in New York; 16, or 3%, in New Jersey; 62, or 12%, in Pennsylvania; five, or 1%, in Delaware; and 47, or 10%, in Maryland); and 171 (35%) in the South (124, or 25%, in Virginia; 13, or 3%, in North Carolina; 27, or 4%, in South Carolina; six, or 1%, in Georgia; and one in Florida). One hundred and ninety-eight, the largest total, settled in the three major Tidewater colonies (Virginia, Maryland, and South Carolina). Of these 489, I believe 321, or 66%, were descendants of the above-discussed Thomas Mowbray, 1st Duke of Norfolk, and Elizabeth FitzAlan, his wife; of Elizabeth FitzAlan and her third husband, Sir Robert Goushill; of Mowbray's or his wife's sisters, her double first cousins or her aunt, also named above; or of various other cousins of Mowbray and his wife who bore over half their combined ancestry. These 321, of whom 90 settled in New England (62 in Massachusetts, twelve in Connecticut, nine in Rhode Island, four in New Hampshire, and three in Maine), 108 in the Middle Atlantic states (16 in New York, eleven in New Jersey, 34 in Pennsylvania, three in Delaware, 43 in Maryland, and one in the District of Columbia), and 123 in the South (87 in Virginia, eight in North Carolina, 22 in South Carolina, and six in Georgia), shared a sizable quantity of medieval baronial ancestry; sprang, in general, from the center, rather than the periphery, of the English, Scottish or Welsh gentry; and were usually descendants of Edward I (d. 1307), Edward III

The Royal Descents of 900 Immigrants

(d. 1377) or later English or Scottish kings. Over 65%, then, of these 489 – although often Puritans, Quakers, younger sons or cadets (sons or grandsons, etc., of younger sons), clergymen, merchants, or ambitious office holders – were usually descended from late medieval earls and often nearly related to peers and baronets (a few were such themselves). Descendants of Beauforts, St. Johns, Woodvilles, Nevilles, Sir Henry "Hotspur" Percy, Seymours, Wentworths, Boleyns, or Howards were often fifth (or closer) cousins of Tudor sovereigns, and the colonial descendants of these 321 were frequently fifth to seventh cousins of the ruling Whig families (the "ducal oligarchy") of post-Restoration and eighteenth-century Great Britain. The remaining 168 of these 489, descendants of earlier kings, often shared only a few "strands" of baronial ancestry and sometimes belonged to the middling or lesser gentry – families who owned only one or a few manors, were mostly non-knighted, did not produce many Tudor peers or perhaps even Stuart baronets, were perhaps "declining" by the time of the English civil war (1641-1660), and did not often figure in the ancestry of the Augustan ducal oligarchy. Note that three major Tidewater plantation colonies – Maryland, Virginia, and South Carolina – claimed 198 (41%) of the 489, but fully 152 (47%) of the 321.

As we consider smaller groups of royally descended immigrants with even more notable descendants, several trends become clear. New Englanders with royal ancestry left far more notable descendants than such immigrants to the Middle Atlantic states or the South, as one might expect from the prominence of New England in the nineteenth-century elites listed below. Since the New York Dutch community included very few royally-descended immigrants yet traced (Alexander de Hinojosa, Mrs. Sophia van Lodensteyn de Beauvois or Debevoise, Jan Otten van Tuyl, and A.H. de Huybert, with Théophile Cazenove only in the late eighteenth century, the last of whom lived largely in Philadelphia), the Middle Atlantic group herein is dominated by Pennsylvania Quakers, both English and Welsh. These last, however, and especially the Welsh, leave – relative to Puritan New Englanders, Tidewater planters, and New York Livingstons – comparatively few descendants, and the Welsh Quakers herein are mostly descendants of illegitimate children of either David, Prince of Wales, or William FitzRobert, 2nd Earl of Gloucester (themselves grandsons respectively, through other illegitimacies, of Kings John and Henry I of England). Virginia massively dominates the South, but if the three major Tidewater colonies – Maryland, Virginia, and South

The Royal Descents of 900 Immigrants

Carolina – are combined, such a region rivals only Massachusetts as a settlement area for immigrants with ten or more notable descendants. Virginia alone, however, rivals all of New England as a settlement area for such immigrants with considerable rather than meager baronial ancestry.

    Of the 227 royally descended immigrants who left ten or more notable descendants, 107 (47%) settled in New England (75, or 33%, in Massachusetts; 17, or 7%, in Connecticut; eight, or 3%, in Rhode Island; three, or 1%, in New Hampshire; and four, or 2%, in Maine); 54 (24%) in the Middle Atlantic states (15, or 7%, in New York; five, or 2%, in New Jersey; 18, or 8%, in Pennsylvania; one in Delaware; and 16, or 7%, in Maryland); 66 (29%) in the South (56, or 25%, in Virginia; four, or 2%, in North Carolina; four [1%] in South Carolina; and two [1%] in Georgia); and (rearranged) 76 (or 34%) in the three major Tidewater colonies. One hundred and twenty-eight (or 56%) of these 227 were descendants of Mowbray, his wife, their siblings or kinsmen sharing over half their ancestry. Of the 128, 55 settled in New England (37 in Massachusetts, seven in Connecticut, seven in Rhode Island, two in New Hampshire, and two in Maine), 27 in the Middle Atlantic states (seven in New York, two in New Jersey, seven in Pennsylvania, and eleven in Maryland), 46 in the South (39 in Virginia, two in North Carolina, three in South Carolina, and two in Georgia) and (rearranged) 53 in the three major Tidewater colonies. I might note that Mrs. Barbara Bennet Murray of North Carolina only died there; her also royally descended husband, James Murray, moved to Massachusetts, and their notable progeny is totally northern.

    These 227, the royally descended immigrants to the thirteen colonies who left ten or more notable descendants – only 25% of the 900 but ancestors of millions of Americans – are listed in Appendix III to this introduction, alphabetically, by colony.

V

    Almost as fascinating as the geographical distribution of the 489 royally descended immigrants who left notable progeny, and as the identification of those who left increasingly greater numbers of such descendants, are the numerous and complex kinships among these 900, and the connections forged in the colonies by intermarriage among their children, grandchildren, and great- or great-great-grandchildren. The

The Royal Descents of 900 Immigrants

charts that form the body of this book delineate 145 or more clusters of near kinsmen – siblings, uncles/aunts and nieces/nephews, first or second cousins, and for a few immigrants who returned to the "Old World," grandparents or great- or great-great-grandparents and grandchildren or great- or great-great-grandchildren. Over 380 of the 900 belonged to one of these 145 clusters. Four groups – the Ligon/Lygon (pp. 295-99), Delaware/de la Warr West (pp. 300-4), St. George-Tucker (pp. 462-65), and Evan Robert Lewis (pp. 650-52) progenies – included between eight and eleven immigrants. Clusters with five, six, or seven immigrants are Rutherford-Bennet-Murray (pp. 210-12), Wyatt (pp. 314-15), Blakiston-Mansfield (pp. 317-18), Oxenbridge-Coke-Blennerhasset-Emmet (pp. 324-26), Fenwick-Brent (pp. 331-32), Marbury (pp. 478-82), von Trapp (pp. 187-88), Hughes-Roberts (pp. 659-60), Towneley-Nowell-Whitaker (pp. 700-4), Bulkeley (pp. 746-48) and Lawrence (pp. 879-81, 883-84).

Furthermore, several dozen fourteenth- or fifteenth-century English, Welsh or Scottish peers, knights or gentlemen were ancestors of between 15 and 50 (or more) of these 900. In addition to the myriad Mowbray and FitzAlan descendants mentioned above, among the progeny herein of Edward III, King of England (d. 1377), I have charted over 40 immigrant descendants of Elizabeth Mortimer (d. ca. 1417/18) and Sir Henry "Hotspur" Percy and over 60 immigrant descendants (including the 26 covered on pp. 47-58, and the immigrant progeny charted on pp. 1-8, 11-18, and 24-46 could be added as well) of Joan Beaufort (d. 1440) and Ralph Neville, 1st Earl of Westmoreland. Once in the colonies, moreover, of the 489 royally descended immigrants who left notable progeny, and in only those lines that produced it, 70% or more had a child, grandchild, great-grandchild, or great-great-grandchild who married a child, grandchild, great-grandchild, or great-great-grandchild of another of the 489. The early progeny of most of these 70%, moreover, made two or more such connections, so even by the time of the American Revolution, major historical figures sometimes had three or more royally descended immigrant ancestors. Beginning with the late nineteenth century, some figures had ten or more such ancestors. The children of Confederate General Robert Edward Lee and Mary Anne Randolph Custis were descended from Henry and Alice (Eltonhead) Corbin (twice), William Randolph (twice), and Henry Isham (twice), Act. Gov. Edmund Jennings, Lawrence Towneley, Mrs. Mary Towneley Warner (Towneley's aunt), Mrs. Sarah Ludlow Carter (twice), Theophilus Hone, Mrs. Anne Lovelace Gorsuch, Col. William Bernard,

The Royal Descents of 900 Immigrants

Gov. Alexander Spotswood, Gov. Philip Ludwell, Cecil Calvert, 2nd Baron Baltimore, Hon. Anne Arundell Calvert, Baroness Baltimore, Jane Lowe Sewall Calvert, Baroness Baltimore, Lady Charlotte Lee Calvert, Baroness Baltimore, Thomas Gerard, Robert Peyton, and Col. Walter Aston, all of Virginia or Maryland. The children of President Franklin Delano Roosevelt and his cousin (Anna) Eleanor Roosevelt were descendants of Thomas Lawrence, Mrs. Margaret (Es)touteville Shepard, Mrs. Elizabeth Coytmore Tyng, John Nelson, Thomas Southworth, Dr. Richard Palgrave, Mrs. Anne Marbury Hutchinson, Mrs. Catherine Hamby Hutchinson, James Murray, Mrs. Barbara Bennet Murray of N.C., John Irvine of Ga., Col. Kenneth Baillie of Ga., Mrs. Diana Skipwith Dale of Va., Gabriel Ludlow, Robert Sinclair, and both Robert Livingstons, all except the designated southerners of Massachusetts, Rhode Island, or New York. The Lee offspring had 20 royally descended immigrant ancestors (or, in the case of the Baltimores, figures treated herein as immigrants); the Roosevelts, 17. Charted herein, I might add, are lines for the twin daughters of former President George Walker Bush and First Lady Laura Lane (Welch) Bush from 13 of these 489 immigrants – Dr. Richard Palgrave, Rev. Peter and Jane (Allen) Bulkeley, Mrs. Elizabeth Bullock Clement(s), Mrs. Catherine Hamby Hutchinson, and Mrs. Mary Gye Maverick of Mass., Mrs. Anne Marbury Hutchinson of Mass. and R.I., Col. Walter Aston and Mrs. Dorothy Beresford Brodnax of Va., Robert Livingston the elder of N.Y., Obadiah Bruen of Conn., George Elkington of N.J., and Christoph(er) von Graffenried, landgrave of N.C.

The colonial English, Scottish, Welsh and (small) Anglo-Irish contingent of these 900 compose, I wish to suggest, a significant section of the first British colonial gentry. Derived largely from the genealogical center, not the periphery, of their parent gentry, in numerous ways and complexly related when they arrived, often in clusters or following other kinsmen, the royally descended colonial immigrants and their immediate progeny intermarried here just as they would have in England, Scotland, Wales or Ireland. Consisting largely of colony or settlement founders, proprietors, acting or deputy governors, other appointed or elected officials, noted clergymen, large landowners, or wealthy merchants, this gentry also divides into four regional elites – the Puritans of New England; the Hudson Valley and Long Island manorial aristocracy (the least represented of these four elites among the 227 immigrants listed in Appendix III to this introduction, but including the Livingstons); the

The Royal Descents of 900 Immigrants

Philadelphia and Main Line Quakers; and the plantation aristocracy of Tidewater Virginia (plus Maryland and to a much lesser extent South Carolina). The first of these elites was clerical and political, later mercantile, and the third was America's first urban oligarchy. A mercantile section of the second elite developed colonial New York City, and the fourth, somewhat urbanized in Baltimore and Charleston, both owned and governed much of the South. From these four colonial elites and this first colonial British gentry are also genealogically derived the bulk of the nineteenth- and twentieth-century groups that dominate much of American history, i.e.:

1. The Salem-Boston mercantile "Brahmins" (Peabody-Endicott-Crowninshield-Higginson-Cabot-Lowell), dominant from 1800, or earlier, to 1830.
2. The intellectual aristocracy centered at Harvard (dominant 1830-60), which led the Unitarian, abolitionist, feminist, and other reform movements and produced the literary "flowering of New England"; and at Yale (dominant 1865-1900), which produced many business leaders (and "Wall Street") and developed social Darwinism and intercollegiate sports. The Harvard elite was often derived from #1, the Yale elite from locally notable families in Connecticut, the Connecticut Valley, and Connecticut-derived upstate New York or the Midwest.
3. The post-Civil War robber-baron industrial oligarchy.
4. The turn-of-the-century eastern inter-city "society" (Astors, Vanderbilts, and Whitneys), centered in New York City and Newport, to some extent a second-generation "gentrification" of #3 above.
5. The early twentieth-century "Social Register," a consolidation of #s 1-4.
6. The post-World War II suburban upper-middle-class, often corporation executives, descendants of nineteenth-century "pioneers" and largely associated with new provincial cities and the "Sunbelt" (Miami, Atlanta, Houston and Dallas, Phoenix, Denver, San Diego, and Los Angeles).
7. The current college-trained meritocracy, in part a second generation of #6, based on expanded civil rights, outreach to women, to African, Hispanic and Asian Americans, and to the poor; grade-school testing, SAT (Scholastic Aptitude Test) and GRE (Graduate Record

The Royal Descents of 900 Immigrants

Examination) scores, and remedial, second-language, and advanced placement programs; and/or the rapid advance of computer technology, the Internet, and social media (the Clintons and Obamas are examples of this meritocracy).

The first and second of these groups are derived almost solely from New England, a region that contributed heavily to the third, fourth, and fifth groups (and somewhat, as the colonial origin of many "pioneers," to the sixth group as well). For the royal descent of various major intellectual, literary and reform leaders, and of various tycoons see, in addition to *The Mowbray Connection*, my *Notable Kin, Volume One* (1998) and *Volume Two* (1999) plus, among post-1995 *NEXUS* or *New England Ancestors* articles, or my website column, "Royal Descents, Notable Kin, and Printed Sources" on www.americanancestors.com, items on Yale and Harvard presidents and the notable progeny of Lygons/Ligons, Gov. Thomas Dudley, Samuel and Judith (Everard) Appleton, Mrs. Alice Freeman Thompson Parke, the New York Livingstons, William Randolph and Henry Isham of Va., and Mrs. Anne Lloyd Yale Eaton.

Note: Since many eighteenth- through twentieth-century immigrants herein are British, I suggest that the five major hegemonous groups to which these latter belong are:

1. The "rising" gentry (the Tudors created few peers), often Puritan, that challenged royal power in the English Civil War; later Anglican Tories, usually associated with the "country," who supported the Revolution of 1688 but thereafter the sovereign, often bitter enemies of 2.
2. The mostly Whig "ducal oligarchy" of 1660-1832 (or 1685 to 1820), led by rich magnates who accumulated often vast estates, built "country house" palaces and governed England's "Augustan Age" almost by hereditary right.
3. The nineteenth-century British intellectual aristocracy (first defined by Noel Annan), associated with Cambridge and Oxford (but usually not the Oxford Movement), reform, the civil service and eventually Bloomsbury, often evangelical or Quaker and with some gentry ancestry (among families with at least one major historical figure, Arnold, Babington, Barclay, Darwin, Galton, Gurney, Lloyd, Stephen, Strachey, Trevelyan, Waugh, and Wilberforce).

The Royal Descents of 900 Immigrants

5. The twentieth-century British establishment, an amalgam of #s 1-4 (I date it from the 1857 marriage of the 3rd Marquess of Salisbury, later prime minister, to Darwin-Wedgwood cousin Georgiana Caroline Alderson), composed of families almost simultaneously associated with literary or intellectual pursuits, bureaucratic administration and business or property trusteeship. Examples include British Astors and Rothschilds (the latter now Strachey cousins), the Beaverbrook progeny, Mitford sisters, Redgrave-Richardson cluster of actors, Asquith-Bonham clan, and the Pakenham family of Lady Antonia Fraser, each covered or mentioned herein.

VI

Having completed my introduction to royal descent generally, to this book's scope and the types of royally descended immigrants it covers, to the history of this project and the scholarship on which it rests, and to the immigrants themselves, their geographical distribution, numbers of noted descendants, kinships to each other and participation in American history overall – having covered these major substantive topics, I now move to the more mundane subject of format. The body of this book consists of charts outlining, with numbered generations, the "best" royal descent – or sometimes two or more nearly equal descents – of the 900 immigrants discussed above and listed in the "immigrant subject index." The order of the charts is determined by the death year of the king who heads it, most recent first (the few exceptions are noted below). Except for birth and death years of immigrants notable in their own right and treated in *ANB* or the *DAB* (or sometimes *Who Was Who in America*, *Who's Who*, or, for a few immigrants, several biographical dictionaries of individual states), no other dates are used. Places are likewise omitted, except for Scottish lairds or gentlemen, but following each chart is a full list of sources documenting the descent. Over 150 of these sources are abbreviated (an abbreviations list immediately follows the text). Sources for the immigrant's immediate origin are listed first, and then those for each generation and family between immigrant and king, *in backward order from the immigrant.*

Clusters of very near kinsmen, and many immigrants sharing over seven or so generations of ancestors are treated together. Charts for such groups precede those for only one immigrant in the sequence under

The Royal Descents of 900 Immigrants

each king, and groups themselves are arranged by number of immigrants (charts treating six precede those treating five, which precede those treating four, etc.). Both groups and singles among each king's immigrant progeny are arranged geographically – New England colonists first, then Middle Atlantic settlers, and finally southerners, in the same order for colonies or states as the Appendix III list of 227 colonial immigrants who left 10 or more notable descendants. In the list of sources for groups of immigrants, the first immigrant on the chart is the first whose line is documented. The shared ancestry is usually referenced with the first immigrant, or soon thereafter, and for each additional immigrant, cited sources cover only his or her descent from the shared "stem," *sometimes in forward order* from the ancestry already documented. Groupings were organized for convenience of presentation only, are often changed from *RD500* or *RD600*, and will probably change even more in any future editions. For ease of presentation also I chose in some cases to treat immigrants who shared six or more outlined generations with other immigrants (but were not "very near" kinsmen) as "singles" and simply repeated the mutual lines.

    As regards "best" royal descents—those from the most recent king—within the progeny of the same king (especially that of Edward III or Edward I), elder sons were preferred to younger sons (Lionel of Antwerp to John of Gaunt, John of Gaunt to Edmund of Langley, and Edmund of Langley to Thomas of Woodstock), younger sons to daughters (Thomas of Brotherton or Edmund of Woodstock to their half-sisters Joan and Elizabeth), and the sons of daughters to the daughters of daughters (William de Bohun, 1st Earl of Northampton, to any of his female de Clare first cousins). Legitimate children were preferred to illegitimate children but illegitimate children of later kings were preferred to legitimate children of earlier kings. As it happens, however, all descents herein from Edward III, Edward I, and Henry III are through *legitimate* children, whereas all lines charted herein from Kings Edward IV, John "Lackland", Henry II, and Henry I of England, and James V, James IV, and William I "the Lion", Kings of Scotland, are from illegitimate children (of these kings or of John's son, Richard Plantagenet, King of the Romans).

    Three exceptions to the king-by-death-year order were suggested by close kinship to, but not descent from, later sovereigns. Descendants of Henry VII, King of England, via his daughter Mary Tudor are treated before descendants of James V, King of Scotland, as the immediate royal-heir kinsmen of Queen Elizabeth I (d. 1603). Descendants of

The Royal Descents of 900 Immigrants

James V of Scotland, all through illegitimate sons, follow as next-of-kin of Mary, Queen of Scots (d. 1587). Descendants of Edward IV, of his brother George Plantagenet, 1st Duke of Clarence, of their sister Anne Plantagenet and Sir Thomas St. Leger, and of their aunt Isabel Plantagenet and Henry Bourchier, Count of Eu and 1st Earl of Essex, precede those of James IV of Scotland as the closest royally descended kinsmen of Henry VIII (d. 1547). Two near connections of immigrants to late nineteenth- or twentieth-century kings or princes are also charted in the main body of this work – the line from LaFayette to Queen Paola and King Philippe of the Belgians and her children and the descent from Oglethorpe's sister to the kings of Italy. The line from Mrs. Alice Freeman Thompson Parke to Susan May Williams, wife of Jerome Napoleon Bonaparte, son of the King of Westphalia, and the kinship of Zinzendorf, de Schweinitzes and de Gersdorffs to Queen Victoria, are covered as well. An appendix (to the text, not this introduction) treats the descents of H.M. The Queen and the late Queen Elizabeth The Queen Mother from Richard and Anna (Cordray) Bernard, Mrs. Mary Towneley Warner and Col. George Reade, all of Virginia; of the late Diana, Princess of Wales, from Mrs. Alice Freeman Thompson Parke; of princes of Monaco (Louis II, Rainier III, and Albert II) from Rev. John Oxenbridge of Mass.; and of the late Queen Géraldine of the Albanians and her son and grandson from Thomas Trowbridge of Conn. Only two immigrants herein – Thomas O'Con(n)or of N.Y. and Thomas Lewis of Maine, the last two – are not descended from an English, Scots or Continental king, but from only a fifteenth-century king of Connaught and early Welsh rulers, respectively; Lewis's wife, however, was Mrs. Elizabeth Marshall Lewis of Maine, another of the 900 and a descendant of Edward I.

Following the charts for O'Con(n)or and Lewis are those for immigrants whose royal descents or "improved" royal descents were received or developed (or which I decided to include) after the index to the first half of this volume was completed; the d'Harnoncourt and Warren-Johnson-Dease-Mrs. Sheddon charts were improved and a Duncanson-Glen descent was traced for First Lady Jacqueline (Bouvier) Kennedy (Onassis). Next included are speculative descents—for the wife of John Carver, first governor of the Plymouth Colony and Isaac Robinson, her nephew, and for the Stoughton siblings of Massachusetts and Connecticut. Then, before the royal descendants, noted above, of RD American immigrants, and the two-part French-Canadian section to be

The Royal Descents of 900 Immigrants

introduced later, is a presidential addendum—covering royal descents of twenty-first century defeated candidates or contenders John Forbes Kerry, Howard (Brush) Dean (III), John Sidney McCain III, and (Willard) Mitt Romney; all but Romney were covered in the *RD600* of 2008 and 2010.

Whenever I mention doubts about any particular connection, and an alternate lesser descent is fully proved—or in many cases simply to cross-reference secondary descents that surprisingly link descendants of Edward III and (often illegitimate children of) earlier kings—I have noted that a spouse on one chart is a child, grandchild, etc., of a person or couple on a later chart. Sources for these secondary lines are included among the cited references for each chart. Many more secondary descents are outlined in *Royal Ancestry,* and the *Ancestral Roots* and *Magna Charta Sureties, 1215* series. About a few matters, too, I have been a bit arbitrary. *SETH* (see elsewhere in this volume) replaces the more standard *"q.v."* I sometimes use the article "de" for persons living after 1400 (who probably did not use it themselves) but omit it before a few surnames (Badlesmere, Baliol, Chaworth, Courtenay, Ferrers of Groby, Grey [of Codnor, Powis, Rotherfield, and Wilton], Hastings, Holand, Mortimer, Mowbray, Stafford and possibly others) whose pre-1400 family members probably used it. I also use "king of Scotland," not "king of Scots," and "baron" for Scottish lords, and refer to seventeenth-century immigrants with modern terms of address (Mrs. Anne Mauleverer Abbott, etc.) and modern titles (Hon. Anne Arundell Calvert, later Baroness Baltimore, Hon. Leonard Calvert, etc.). I do not use Scandinavian or Russian patrynomics or, usually, the female forms of Polish or Russian surnames. Catherine is *usually* spelled with a "C," and I consistently use Westmoreland instead of Westmorland. Other idiosyncracies may be noted by readers and changed, if deemed harmful, in any future editions.

I shall conclude this section on format with a referral to yet another list (Appendix IV) – of the 86 kings from whom descent to these 900 is outlined herein. The kings are listed in order, with death years and the pages on which immigrant progeny appear, and some notes on their near kinship to each other.

VII

The Royal Descents of 900 Immigrants both stands on its own as the most comprehensive compendium of such American lines to date and

The Royal Descents of 900 Immigrants

is topically the third of five books to date based in part on the American section of *The Mowbray Connection*. The first of these books, co-authored with the late William Addams Reitwiesner of the Library of Congress, was *American Ancestors and Cousins of The Princess of Wales* (GPC, 1984). It considered the British royal family as the genealogical centerpiece of the Anglo-American world and examined New England and mid-Atlantic connections of the late Diana, Princess of Wales, her granddaughter, Princess Charlotte (Elizabeth Diana, b. 2015), and Princes William (Arthur Philip Louis, b. 1982), Duke of Cambridge, George (Alexander Louis, b. 2013), and Harry (Henry Charles Albert David, b. 1984), plus the Virginia ancestors and cousins of the late Queen Elizabeth The Queen Mother – all key contemporary reinforcements of a "special kinship" centered on seventeenth-century immigration here but much strengthened since. (I later sponsored a posthumous work by W.A. Reitwiesner, *The Ancestry of Catherine Middleton* [2011], edited by Christopher Challender Child and Scott Campbell Steward, which covers the (royal) Fairfax-Martineau descent of H.R.H. The Duchess of Cambridge. Jane (Conyers) Hardy, a second "gateway ancestor" of royal descent, was found later and has since been twice treated in *American Ancestors*.)

My second book, *Ancestors of American Presidents* (Carl Boyer 3rd, publisher, 1989, 1995; NEHGS, 2009, 2012), considered the ancestry of our presidents through 2017 as a summary of much of the genealogical evolution of the United States. Twenty-three presidents (1789-2017) have been found to be of royal descent, or very likely so, as have the wives or "First Ladies" of eight others (John Adams, Tyler [Julia Gardiner, his second wife], Grant, Garfield, Wilson [both wives], Eisenhower, Kennedy, and Reagan). Note, however, that in addition to the 23, the very tentative line of James Buchanan, Sr., of Pennsylvania, father of the 15th president, appears only as a possibility on the chart for Lynn Redgrave and Natasha Richardson – more research on the Buchanans of Ramelton is required. The lines of these 23 presidents and of Mrs. John Adams, Mrs. W.H. Harrison, Mrs. Tyler, Mrs. Grant, Mrs. Garfield, both Mrs. Wilsons, Mrs. Truman (retained from *RD600*, although two "better" royal descents are outlined herein for her husband), Mrs. Eisenhower, Mrs. Kennedy, Mrs. Reagan, and both Barbara and Laura Bush from over 70 immigrants herein, some repeated from *AAP* 2009/2012. New to this volume are such lines for Mrs. Tyler, Mrs. Kennedy, Betty Ford, and Mrs. Carter, of whom Mrs. Tyler and Mrs. Kennedy were wives of presidents not of royal

The Royal Descents of 900 Immigrants

ancestry. Betty Ford, Mrs. Carter, and Barbara and Laura Bush are treated herein, even though their husbands were also of royal descent, in part because many living Americans still remember them.

Royal descents for "First Ladies" Jane Pierce, Edith and Eleanor Roosevelt, Helen Taft and Barbara Bush, plus Martha Jefferson and Alice Roosevelt, Theodore's first wife, all of whose husbands shared such ancestry, are also outlined in *Notable Kin, Volume One, AAP 2009, 2012,* and more recently, through Jacqueline Kennedy, plus Betty Ford and Nancy Reagan, in issues 3-13 (2006-16) of *Executive Papers*, edited by Alexander Bannerman. Much of the usefulness of *The Royal Descents of 900 Immigrants* to the genealogical public overall, and much of its centrality to American genealogical evolution, is suggested by noting that 31 of our 45 presidents, or their wives, have royal forebears. This compendium pinpoints the genealogical "connecting tissue" that links the modern U.S. and early medieval Europe. Having earlier examined the current British royal family and American presidents for their central roles I have now covered (herein) a major strand of Anglo-American kinship – easily the best documented and most nearly allied to the nobility of Continental Europe, and some think among the most intrinsically interesting as well.

My fourth and fifth books, published like the 1989 and 1995 presidential works, by Carl Boyer 3rd of Santa Clarita, California, were edited—but not condensed or merely selective—anthologies of my "Notable Kin" columns, 1985-1995, from *NEHGS NEXUS*. Begun in 1986, with some additions to the Princess of Wales volume that were first published in 1985, this column was my "genealogical voice" through 2000 (with various similar columns later, in *New England Ancestors* and *American Ancestors*) on many subjects. By the end of 1995 I and a few guest contributors—John Anderson Brayton, Richard E. Brenneman, David Curtis Dearborn, Julie Helen Otto, and Michael J. Wood had considered the ancestry of over 200 major figures in American history, plus a few Canadian, British, and Continental figures as well. These anthologies cover notable descendants of many of the immigrants herein, especially the 227 whose progeny includes at least ten subjects of biographies in *ANB,* the *DAB* or *Who's Who.*

My sixth book, *The Best Genealogical Sources in Print*, vol. 1, a set of updated bibliographical articles, introductions and reviews, published by NEHGS in early 2004, contains much further material on ancient and royal genealogy or immigrants of royal descent—see

The Royal Descents of 900 Immigrants

especially chapters 6, 7, 10, 13, 14, 21, 24, 28 and 29. This last volume was reprinted, with an introduction on "Genealogical Progress since 2004," in 2012. Together these six books offer not only a preview of many descents in *The Mowbray Connection* but also a distillation of much of my life's work to date. *In toto*, as already implied, my published and compiled work covers, I hope, many facets of the recorded genealogical evolution of the United States, Great Britain, and Continental Europe—in short, the Western world.

    Additions and corrections to this book are, of course, welcome and eagerly anticipated. Most—but undoubtedly not all—royal descents of colonial immigrants that have already appeared in printed sources, but are not included herein, have been seen and rejected. I shall be delighted to hear from scholars developing new or "better" lines from either printed or record sources (preferably both). In addition, however, to forwarding such lines to me (for much-appreciated inclusion in any future editions of, or supplements to, this compendium), I also wish to recommend monographic publication – both because I can then simply cite the book or article, and because the process of composing a monograph and passing some level of "peer review" often suggests new lines of inquiry or argument. The major American genealogical journals, especially the *Register, TAG,* and *The Genealogist*, plus, to a lesser extent, the *Record* and *Foundations*, are always pleased to publish well-documented, newly-proved royal descents. And I personally stand ready to assist (in person preferably, or via telephone) with finding printed corroboration.

Gary Boyd Roberts

The Royal Descents of 900 Immigrants

**Appendix I to the Introduction:
255 Twentieth-Century Scholars (to 2017)
and the immigrants upon whose royal descents
they have undertaken research
(those marked "deceased" were known
by the author personally
or via significant correspondence)**

1. Arthur Adams – George Elkington (superseded by Col. C.M. Hansen, below), Mrs. Margaret Halsnode Denne (with C.M. Hansen below), *MCS* and *LDBR* 1 (although his contribution to both of these last may have been slight)

2. Arthur Charles Addington (*The Royal House of Stuart*) – descendants herein, in legitimate lines, of James I, King of England – including, among well-known figures, Mother Alexandra; Catherine Oxenberg; Mrs. Avery Brundage; Mrs. E.F. Bronfman; Stanislaus Albert, Prince Radziwill (husband of Lee); Egon, Prince zu Fürstenberg (husband of Diane); Felix, Prince of Salm-Salm (husband of the Princess [Agnes Joy]) and husbands of Kay Boyle and Olivia Wilde

3. Mrs. Sarah Cantey Whitaker Allen – Whitakers (3)

4. Jerome E. Anderson – Increase Nowell (unpublished, partly used in *The Great Migration Begins*, with H. DeS. Bull below), Mrs. Audrey Divett Buller Parsons (with J.R. Mellon II below)

5. Robert Charles Anderson – Thomas Bradbury (rejection of FitzWilliam and Poyntz lines, with Marshall K. Kirk and J.B. Threlfall below), Lady Anne Bell Gorges, Mansfields (with John C. Brandon and Paul C. Reed below), Great Migration compendia

6. Worth S. Anderson – William Farrar (with Alvahn Holmes)

7. Jacques Arnold – *The Royal Houses of Europe* [since ca. 1750], 33 vols. to date (2006-), which largely supersede (except for full names), the works by Addington and Daniel Willis

8. Craig Stanley Ashley – Charles Barnes

The Royal Descents of 900 Immigrants

9. David A. Avant, Jr. – Lawrence Smith (with Mary B.T. McCurdy below)

10. Augustine H. Ayers – Joseph Bolles (with W.L. Sheppard, Jr. below) (deceased)

11. Stewart Baldwin – Mrs. Harriet Churchill Fawkener Pownall, review of various Welsh Quaker lines proposed by Thomas A. Glenn, with some disproofs (see Appendix VI)

12. Alexander Bannerman – Tucker sisters of N.C., *Executive Papers*, Duncanson-Glen descent of Mrs. Jacqueline L.B. Kennedy Onassis

13. Robert Barnes – Henry Jerningham, Mrs. Maria Johanna Somerset Lowther Smith, *BRMF* 1 & 2, and bibliography therein of Marylanders of royal descent (some speculative or unproved)

14. Joseph Gardner Bartlett – Peter Talbot (further research is requested)

15. Peter C. Bartrum (*Welsh Genealogies*) – Griffith and Margaret (Fleming) Bowen (with General Herman Nickerson, Jr., below); all Welsh lines herein through 1500 (as extracted by W.A. Reitwiesner and checked by me)

16. Robert Battle – Mrs. Margaret Mackenzie Avery, Andrew Myles Cockburn (father of Olivia Wilde, with John C. Brandon below), Cary Elwes, Mrs. Anne Derehaugh Stratton (with D.A. Sandmire and E.A. Stratton and H.W. "Hal" Bradley below) and (Sir) P.G. Wodehouse, plus various additions to websites of W.A. Reitwiesner, esp. an AT for Christoph(er), Baron von Graffenried

17. Timothy Field Beard – Robert Drake (with J.A. Brayton, Douglas Richardson, and Mrs. Henrietta Dawson Ayres Sheppard below), Mrs. Anne Lloyd Yale Eaton (with H.B. Hoff, below), T.L. Stuart-Menteth, Richard Wright, *PSECD* 2&3, plus corrections for Col. Walter Aston and Mrs. Muriel Gurdon Saltonstall, review of many hereditary society lineage papers covering royal descents (deceased)

The Royal Descents of 900 Immigrants

18. Joseph M. Beatty Jr. – Mrs. Christiana Clinton Beatty, Charles Clinton

19. Henry Lyman Parsons Beckwith, Jr. – comments on various immigrants in *A Roll of Arms Registered by The Committee on Heraldry of the New England Historic Genealogical Society, Parts 1-10 with Additions and Corrections and a History of the Committee on Heraldry* (2013)

20. Robert Behra – Mrs. Mary Mainwaring Gill and Oliver Mainwaring (with H.M. Buck, B. McA. Clagett, T.A. Farmerie and G.H. Goodman below)

21. Eversley M.G. Belfield – Henry Edward Bellew (6th Viscount Exmouth)

22. Col. John C. Bell – Joseph Bickley

23. Mrs. Shirley Goodwin Bennett – Robert Baillie (unpublished, with Paul C. Reed below), G.A. McKay, McLeans of Conn. (with T.F. Gede below), sponsor of Jernegan research by Neil D. Thompson below (with J.A. Brayton above) and Wentworth research by Paul C. Reed (with M.A. Guido, E.A. Stratton and N.L. Taylor below) (deceased)

24. Mrs. Miriam Elliott Bertelson – John Hughes (Hugh, Pugh) (deceased)

25. Harrison Black – Benjamin Harrison (deceased)

26. John Bennett Boddie II (*VHG, SVF, HSF*, not always reliable) – Col. Walter Aston (with Nathan W. Murphy and Paul C. Reed below), Lancelot Bathurst, two Battes and Roger Mallory (with J.A. Brayton and W.A. Reitwiesner below), William Boddie (and Mrs. Judith Everard Appleton, with W.G. Davis, Jr., Ernest Flagg and Leslie Mahler below), Thomas Boteler and Mrs. Elizabeth Boteler Claiborne, Act. Gov. Edmund Jennings, Richard Kempe (with David Faris below), Col. Thomas Ligon/ Lygon (per W.D. Ligon, corrected by G.B. Roberts, N.D. Thompson, and M.J. Wood, below), Col. George Reade (with Y.L. Wilson below), William Strother, Thomas Warren (with Noel Currer-Briggs below), three Washingtons (with G.S.H.L. Washington below)

27. Ronny O. Bodine – Thomas Owsley (co-author, with T.W. Spaulding below, of *The Ancestry of Dorothea Poyntz, Wife of Reverend John Owsley, Generations 1-12*)

28. Michael P. Bodman – Nathaniel Littleton, William Tazewell

29. Ross Boothe, Jr. – Mrs. Amy Wyllys Pynchon (with C.W. Faulkner below)

30. Richard LeBaron Bowen – Marburys (Mrs. Hutchinson, Mrs. Scott, Wentworth and Lawson, with M.B. Colket, Jr. and F.N. Craig below)

31. Carl Boyer, 3rd – Robert Abell (with Neil D. Thompson below), Percival Lowell (with Douglas Richardson below), Mrs. Grizel Campbell McNeill, Mrs. Jane Evans Dodge, *Medieval English Ancestors of Robert Abell* and *Medieval English Ancestors of Certain Americans* (both 2001), *Medieval Welsh Ancestors of Certain Americans* (2004), *Ancestral Lines* trilogy (2015-16)

32. Kevin Bradford – Thomas Rudyard, dep. gov. of East Jersey

33. Harold Wheeler ["Hal"] Bradley – Strattons (with Robert Battle, Dr. David A. Sandmire and E.A. Stratton below)

34. Homer Worthington Brainerd – Henry Isham, two Randolphs

35. John C. Brandon (over 60) – Mrs. Audrey Barlow Almy (with Leslie Mahler below), Jeffrey Amherst, 1st Baron Amherst, W.H. Auden, Mrs. Frances Ravenscroft Ball, Christopher Batt (with W.G. Davis, Jr. and Brandon Fradd below), Gov. Richard Bellingham, Lady Amelia Offley Bernard, Gov. Thomas Boone, Borghese of Bomarzo, John Bradstreet (in the French Canadian section), Mrs. Mary Woodcock Bridges, Helena Bonham Carter, Charles Chambers and Leonard Chester (both with Leslie Mahler below), John Clayton, James Clifton, Andrew Myles Cockburn (father of Olivia Wilde, with Robert Battle above and George Larson), Craighead siblings, Benedict and Sophie Irene (Hunter) Cumberbatch, Mrs. Helen Cuming Cuming, Mrs. Thomasine Clench Frost (with D.C. Stone below), Mrs. Elizabeth Wilson Glen, Culcheth Golightly, Mrs. Dorothea Scott Gotherson (Hogben) (with Bruce Despain below), (Lady) Elizabeth (Tate) Hardy, Sir Robert Hesilrige, 8th Bt., Mrs. Jane Whalley Hooke,

The Royal Descents of 900 Immigrants

Thomas Hussey (with Leslie Mahler below), Ralph Izard, Vernon H.P.S. Kennedy (with George Larson), Mrs. Anne Cheney Knollys (with Leslie Mahler below), Thomas Law, William James Linton, (Lady) Charlotte (Clayton) Lovelace, Mansfield siblings (with R.C. Anderson above and Paul C. Reed below), Mrs. Elizabeth Taylor (Tufton alias) Mason, Mellish sisters, Mrs. Diana Villiers Negroponte, Rev. Edward Norris (with Leslie Mahler), John Norton, Mrs. Deliverance Sheffield Peter(s), Rev. Thomas Peter(s), Mrs. Jane Greene Poole (with Douglas Richardson below), George Pordage, Redgrave-Richardson acting cluster (with Will Johnson below), Mrs. Elizabeth Hussey Scott (with Leslie Mahler below), Robert Sinclairs of N.H. and Pa., Keith Spence, George Symes (with Douglas Richardson), William Tatham, Richard Towneley, Robert Traill of N.H., Mrs. Penelope Spencer Treworgy (with Leslie Mahler), James Tytler, John Wallace, Charles Willing (with Don C. Stone, N.L. Taylor and David Topping below), Frances "Fanny" Wright; review of this entire volume.

36. James C. Brandow – George Carrington, Mrs. Elizabeth Hannah Carrington Willing

37. John Anderson Brayton (over 25) –Mrs. Mary Batt Ash(e) (Lillington), Mrs. Elizabeth Wood Barcroft, Henry and Thomas Batte and Roger Mallory (with J.B. Boddie II above and W.A. Reitwiesner below), Christopher Branch, Edward Buncomb, Mrs. Abigail Smith Burwell (with Clayton Torrence below), Christopher Calthorpe, Daniel Dobyns, Robert Drake (with T.F. Beard above and Douglas Richardson and Mrs. Henrietta D.A. Sheppard below), Richard Edgeworth, John Fisher, George Gale, Theophilus Hone (with Patricia Law Hatcher below), Thomas Jernegan (with Neil D. Thompson below), Mrs. Dorothy Walker Jones, Lightfoots (with Larry W. Cates below), Gov. Philip Ludwell, Mrs. Henrietta Constantia Worsam Meade, Gov. Seth Southill, Fortunatus Sydnor, Stephens/Stevens Thompson, Mrs. Frances Baldwin Townshend Jones Williams (with Jeffery A. Duvall below), and Edward Wyndham/Windham (plus disproof of John Hinton—see Appendix VI), review of the lines he developed. Several of these immigrants are treated in *AP&P*, 4th ed., by J.F. Dorman below.

The Royal Descents of 900 Immigrants

38. Richard E. Brenneman – Mrs. Catherine White Leggett Carver, Isaac Robinson (speculative)

39. Chester Horton Brent – Brents (4)

40. David T. Brown (with English researcher Karen Proudler) – Mrs. Elizabeth Pride Gibbs Sherwin

41. Howard M. Buck – Mrs. Mary Mainwaring Gill and Oliver Mainwaring (with Robert Behra above and B. McA. Clagett, T.A. Farmerie and G.H. Goodman below)

42. Henry DeSaussure Bull – Stephen Bull, Increase Nowell (with J.E. Anderson above)

43. Dr. Joseph Gaston Baillie Bulloch – Col. Kenneth Baillie, James Cuthbert, John Irvine

44. Adrian Benjamin Moreira Da Silva-Burke – Duncanson sisters (with Gordon Remington below), Stoughtons (speculative, with J.B. Dobson and Janet P.C. Wolfe below), further doubts about John Whitney

45. Larry W. Cates – Lightfoots (with J.A. Brayton above)

46. Harrison Dwight Cavanagh – Mrs. Anne Fielder Gantt Wight

47. Arnaud Chaffanjon – LaFayette, Noailles, and their wives

48. Christopher Challender Child – John Evans of Radnor, Pa. and John Morgan (with Christos Christou, Jr. immediately below and T.A. Farmerie below), Harriet Martineau and the Duchess of Cambridge (esp. their Fairfax ancestry, with W.A. Reitwiesner, S.C. Steward and M.J. Wood below), Norton Claypoole descendants, *The Nelson Family of Rowley, Massachusetts* (2014) (with J.H. Otto below), Wahlbergs in Mass.

49. Christos Christou, Jr. – John Evans of Radnor, Pa. and John Morgan (with C.C. Child immediately above and T.A. Farmerie below)

50. Brice McAdoo Clagett – Bulkeleys (6) (with J.G. Hunt, D.L. Jacobus, C.A. Torrey and H.J. Young below), Dr. Charles Carroll, Wiseman Clagett, John Cra(y)croft, two Dundases, Eltonhead sisters, Gibbeses of S.C. (3), Mrs. Mary Mainwaring Gill and Oliver Mainwaring (with Robert Behra and H.M. Buck

above, and T.A. Farmerie and G.H. Goodman below), James Neale, Lowes (3), Alexander Magruder (based on Dr. Charles G. Kurz, below), Mrs. Elizabeth Mallory Rivers, Anthony Savage (with N.D. Thompson, correcting W.D. Ligon, both below), Henry Sewall of Md., J.A.G., Vicomte de Sibour, Leighton Wilson, two Yonges (with Edward Yonge below, and Francis Yonge with Paul C. Reed below) (plus disproof of Act. Gov. Robert Brooke – see Appendix VI), "Seven Centuries: Twenty Generations of Ancestors of John Brice de Treville Clagett and Ann Calvert Brooke Clagett" (unpublished mss. frequently cited herein) (deceased)

51. John Insley Coddington – John Alstons (expanded or corrected by H.B. Hoff and D.L. Kent below), (Count) William Frederick Bentinck, Rev. John Davenport (with G.B. Roberts, below), two Eddoweses, John Fenwick of N.J. (with E.J. Sellers below), Edward FitzRandolph, Henry Gregory (with David Ebel below), Lady Christian Stuart Griffin, Rev. John Oxenbridge, Mrs. Elizabeth Coytmore Tyng (deceased)

52. Nicholas Dixie Coddington – Mrs. Anne Coddington Fenner

53. George Edward Cokayne and his nephew, Vicary Gibbs – *The Complete Peerage*, 1st ed. (Cokayne) and [New] *Complete Peerage*, 14 vols. (Gibbs) and *The Complete Baronetage* (Cokayne), 5 vols. (with the [New] *CP* reprinted in 6 vols. and *CB* in 1 vol.) (usually definitive coverage of all British peers and baronets herein, but without daughters or cadet lines)

54. Peter Wilson Coldham – Thomas Weston; *Complete Book of Emigrants* and *Emigrants in Bondage* series; *American Wills and Administrations in the Prerogative Court of Canterbury*; "Genealogical Gleanings in England" series in *NGSQ*

55. Meredith Bright Colket, Jr. – Marburys (4, with R. LeB. Bowen above and F.N. Craig below), Ludlows (3, with H.F. Seversmith below), Delaware West-Pelham cluster (with A.G. Hoskins below) (deceased)

56. Francis Northrop Craig – Gov. Thomas Dudley (with Brandon Fradd, D.H. Kelley, and M.K. Kirk below), Marburys (4, with R. LeB. Bowen and M.B. Colket, Jr. above), de Braose ancestry

The Royal Descents of 900 Immigrants

of Bressie, N. Browne, Davenport, and Hawes (with E.A. Stratton below) (for these last immigrants, with W.G. Davis, Jr. and G.B. Roberts for Bressie, D.L. Greene and D.L. Jacobus for Browne, J.I. Coddington and Roberts for Davenport, and J.W. Hawes and Roberts for Hawes) (deceased)

57. Leander Howard Crall – William Asfordby

58. G. Rodney Crowther – Lowes (3)

59. Robert Joseph Curfman – Thomas Dongan, 2nd Earl of Limerick (with T.T. Dongan below); Yales (3) (with P.G. Van der Poel below)

60. Noel Currer-Briggs – Thomas Warren (as reported in *PSECD* 3) (with J.B. Boddie II above)

61. Francis James Dallett – Countess Plater-Zyberk (deceased)

62. H. d'Angerville – *Living Descendants of Blood Royal*, 5 vols. (some descents disproved)

63. Edward J. Davies – Mrs. Harriet Churchill Fawkener Pownall

64. Walter Goodwin Davis, Jr. – two Appletons, two Batts, Thomas Bressie, two Lewises of Me., Mrs. Thomasine Ward Thompson Buffum (doubts) (two Appletons and Mrs. Lewis with Ernest Flagg below, Samuel Appleton with C.M. Hansen and J.J. Muskett below, Mrs. Appleton also with J.B. Boddie above and Leslie Mahler below, Christopher Batt with J.C. Brandon above and Brandon Fradd below, Bressie with G.B. Roberts below, Mrs. Buffum with M.J. Wood below); 16 multi-ancestor books covering each of his great-great-grandparents (consolidated by G.B. Roberts into *Massachusetts and Maine Families in the Ancestry of Walter Goodwin Davis*, 3 vols., 1996)

65. David Curtis Dearborn – James Taylor ("improved" by Douglas Richardson)

66. Rev. Henry Lyttelton Lyster Denny – Rev. William Narcissus Lyster

67. Bruce Despain – Mrs. Dorothea Scott Gotherson (Hogben) (with John C. Brandon above)

68. Katharine Dickson (Brown) – John Stockman (deceased)

The Royal Descents of 900 Immigrants

69. R. Bruce Diebold – Fritz Harbou, Claus von Bülow

70. John Blythe Dobson – Stoughtons (speculative, with A.B.M. Da Silva-Burke above and Janet P.C. Wolfe below), Sir T.J. Berners-Lee (with W.A. Reitwiesner and M.J. Wood below), Daniel (Wroughton) Craig and the improved Warren-Johnson-Dease-Mrs. Shedden descent; Continental descents improved (sometimes initially by Internet sources, including http://genealogics.org, compiled by Leo van de Pas) from *RD600*, including von Steuben; Lafayette and his de Noailles brother-in-law and Ted Morgan; Zinzendorf, his wife, de Gersdorff and the (de) (von) Schweinitz wives; the fifth (and last) wife of Sir Ferdinando Gorges; Carondelet; Mrs. Wernher von Braun; and Philippe Lannes de Montebello; plus, among new immigrants herein of Continental descent, Fernand Auberjonois, Mrs. Jeanne M. B. de M. Boal, Théophile Cazenove, Colloredo-Mansfeld, Baroness Irmgard (von Kiesenwetter) von Egloffstein, Albert Gallatin, Rene d'Harnoncourt (improved), Alexander de Hinojosa, William Johan Hoffman, Jan Samuel François van Hoogstraten, Baroness Caroline Eugénie von Lagerfelt, Vladimir Nabokov, two Ruspolis, the von Trapp siblings, and Prince Sergey Troubetskoy; review of this entire volume

71. Sara Doherty – Peter Worden

72. Thomas T. Dongan – Thomas Dongan, 2nd Earl of Limerick, and his kin (with R.J. Curfman above)

73. John Frederick Dorman (plus Virginia M. Meyer, Prentiss Price, Annie Lash Jester and Martha Woodruff Hiden - *AP&P*) – William Baugh, Col. William Bernard, Joseph Bickley, Christopher Branch, Mrs. Abigail Smith Burwell, Christopher Calthorpe, Calverts of Md., Mrs. Elizabeth Boteler Claiborne, John Clayton, Francis Dade, Gov. Edward Digges, William Farrar, John Fisher, Henry Fleete, Col. Gerard Fowke, Mrs. Anne Lovelace Gorsuch, Act. Gov. Edmund Jennings, Col. Thomas Ligon/Lygon, Lady Charlotte (Clayton) Lovelace, Nathaniel Littleton, Gov. Francis Lovelace, Henry Lowe, Col. George Reade, Mrs. Alicia Arnold Ross, St. Legers (Codd, Horsmanden and Mrs. Colepepper/Culpeper), Stracheys (3), Delaware Wests, Mrs. Frances Baldwin Townshend Jones Williams, John Woodliffe, Henry Woodhouse,

The Royal Descents of 900 Immigrants

Rev. Hawte Wyatt (all in *AP&P4*), many with other contributors listed herein

74. Hervé Douxchamps – Henri Joseph Stier
75. Jeffery A. Duvall – Mrs. Frances Baldwin Townshend Jones Williams (with John A. Brayton above)
76. David Ebel – Henry Gregory (with J.I. Coddington above)
77. Mrs. Marlene Eilers (Koenig) – Catherine Oxenberg, *Queen Victoria's Descendants*
78. William M. Ellicott – Mrs. Mary Fox Ellicott
79. William Elliott – Mrs. B.M.B.E. Burton, Mackintoshes/ McIntoshes (with G.B. Roberts below)
80. Lucy L. Erwin – William Clopton, Mrs. Thomasine Clopton Winthrop (with J.J. Muskett below)
81. Thomas S. Erwin – Mrs. Barbara Mitford Wyatt, Wentworth Day
82. Charles Frederick Holt Evans – John Bevan, two Robert Livingstons, Dep. Gov. Thomas and Mary (Jones) Lloyd (with I.H. Leet and Brad Verity below), Margaret of Teschen (with C.M. Hansen below, for Mrs. Margaret Tyndal Winthrop); *Complete Works of Charles Evans: Genealogy and Related Topics* (2003)
83. Richard K. Evans – Gov. Peter and Gov. Philip de Carteret (with W.P. Johnson below); Cecil-Vanderbilt *AT* and Queen Mother and 13th-18th generation Princess of Wales charts; *The Ancestry of Diana, Princess of Wales, for Twelve Generations*
84. Margaret Dickson Falley – George (Holmes) Pomeroy
85. David Faris – much editing of *AR6,7* and *MCS4*; *PASCC 1* and *2*; Edward Howell (with Douglas Richardson below), Thomas Booth, Kemps (with J.J. Muskett below), Christopher Isherwood (deceased)
86. Todd A. Farmerie – Mrs. Margaret Wyatt Allyn (with Ernest Flagg below), Mrs. Mary Butler Underwood, Oliver Mainwaring (with Robert Behra, H.M. Buck, and B. McA. Clagett above and

The Royal Descents of 900 Immigrants

G.H. Goodman below), John Evans of Radnor, Pa. and John Morgan (with C.C. Child and Christos Christou, Jr. above), Sancha de Ayala (1998 *Register* article with Nathaniel L. Taylor below, topic with Milton L. Rubincam below), co-owner of *soc.genealogy.medieval* (on which he leaves many postings, some formerly printed in *The Plantagenet Connection*)

87. Claude W. Faulkner – Thomas Gerard, Mrs. Amy Wyllys Pynchon (with Ross Boothe, Jr. above)

88. Charles Fitch-Northen – Thomas Trowbridge (with D.L. Jacobus below), Grenvilles of Devon and Cornwall (deceased)

89. Ernest Flagg – Samuel and Judith (Everard) Appleton and Mrs. Elizabeth Marshall Lewis (all with W.G. Davis, Jr. above), Mrs. Margaret Wyatt Allyn (with T.A. Farmerie above) (plus Samuel Appleton with C.M. Hansen and J.J. Muskett below and Judith [Everard] Appleton with J.B. Boddie above)

90. David M. Foley – various Scottish and other lines in *MCS3*,4, notably Home (41E), Spotswood (43A), Griffin (43B), Mercer (91B), Houstoun (92A), and probably Lunsford (88A), Coke (94A), Gorsuch (113A), and Dudley (149B)

91. Joseph Foster – *The Royal Lineage of Our Noble and Gentle Families*, 6 vols. (especially for Blennerhassett and Quaker Lloyd and Barclay descendants), *Dugdale's Visitations of Yorkshire, with Additions*, 3 vols., *PCF Yorkshire* and *PCF Lancashire*, *Foster's V of Yorkshire* (together almost all Yorkshire families herein); *Alumni Oxonienses*, 1500-1886, 8 vols.

92. Brandon Fradd – Christopher Batt (with John C. Brandon and W.G. Davis, Jr. above), Governor Thomas Dudley (with F.N. Craig above and D.H. Kelley and M.K. Kirk below), Percival Lowell (with Douglas Richardson below), and the (speculative) Winslows (with J.G. Hunt and Marshall K. Kirk below)

93. Thomas Frederick Gede – McLeans of Conn. (with Shirley G. Bennett above), V.E.H. von Finck, René d'Harnoncourt, Lewenhaupts, Francisco de Paula Eustaquio Lynch Zavaleta (behind Che Guevara) (with some New World research on this last by J.H. Otto)

The Royal Descents of 900 Immigrants

94. Paul McKee Gifford – two Falconers (with Charles R. Owens below), Rev. John Munro (with Douglas Hickling, G.H.S. King and R.W. Munro below)

95. Thomas Allen Glenn (*WFP* 1,2, *Merion*) – most Welsh immigrants to Pa. herein, as confirmed by Bartrum (Harrys, Hugh Jones, Robert Lloyd, William and John Edwards and John Evans of Merion and Radnor disproved; further research should be undertaken for John Roberts of Pencoyd, John Williams, Robert Jones and Mrs. Sidney Rees Roberts)

96. William Good – Mrs. Margaret Domville Hatton Banks (with Douglas Richardson below)

97. Glenn H. Goodman – Mrs. Mary Mainwaring Gill and Oliver Mainwaring (with Robert Behra, H.M. Buck, B. McA. Clagett and T.A. Farmerie above)

98. Raymond Gorges – Sir Ferdinando Gorges, his four wives and agnate kin

99. David L. Greene – Nathaniel Browne (with D.L. Jacobus below), Nathaniel Burrough (with J.J. Muskett, G.I. Nelson and G.E. Russell, below), Lawrences (5), Mrs. Alice Freeman Thompson Parke (with G.A. Moriarty, Jr., C.A. Torrey and H.J. Young below), editor of *TAG* (1984-2015)

100. Michael Anne Guido – William Wentworth and Christopher Lawson (with Paul C. Reed, E.A. Stratton and N.L. Taylor below)

101. W.J.T. Gun – John Henry and noted kin, Dryden-Swift-Walpole kin of Marbury sisters, from *Studies in Hereditary Ability*

102. George Hamilton (*A History of the House of Hamilton*) – two Alexander Hamiltons

103. Col. Charles M. Hansen – Mrs. Anne Mauleverer Abbott, Samuel Appleton (with W.G. Davis, Jr., and Ernest Flagg above and J.J. Muskett below), Matthew Clarkson, James and Norton Claypoole (with Milton Rubincam and W.L. Sheppard, Jr. below), Mrs. Margaret Halsnode Denne (with Arthur Adams above), George Elkington (with Arthur Adams above), William Rodney (with G.E. McCracken below) and two disproofs (see

The Royal Descents of 900 Immigrants

Appendix VI), Margaret of Teschen (with C.F.H. Evans above, for Mrs. Margaret Tyndal Winthrop), plus with N.D. Thompson, below, *The Ancestry of Charles II, King of England: A Medieval Heritage* (2012, 2013), editor of *TG* since vol. 11 (1997), and Margaret Kerdeston and Woodville studies

104. James L. Hansen – Rev. William Skepper/Skipper

105. Fairfax Harrison – Colepeppers/Culpepers (3)

106. Patricia Law Hatcher – Theophilus Hone (with J.A. Brayton above)

107. James William Hawes – Edmond Hawes (with G.B. Roberts and H.J. Young below)

108. Ernest Flagg Henderson III – Mrs. Berta von Bunsen Henderson, Rev. George Ross (with H.P. Read below), *Ancient, Medieval, and More Modern Ancestors of Ernest Flagg Henderson IV and Roberta Campbell Henderson*, 4 vols. (2013) (deceased)

109. John Goodwin Herndon – two Wingfields

110. Thomas Benjamin Hertzel – Thomas Prater/Prather

111. Douglas Hickling – Rev. John Munro (with P. McK. Gifford above and G.H.S. King and R.W. Munro below), Sherburnes and Christiana de Mowbray

112. Mrs. Napier Higgins – Bernards, especially Sir Francis, 1st Bt., and Amelia (Offley)

113. Philip Hoare – Noël (Pierce) Coward

114. Henry Bainbridge Hoff – Mrs. Josephine Alma (Danielsen) Berg, Mrs. Abigail Brewster Burr, Mrs. Anne Lloyd Yale Eaton (with T.F. Beard, above), Jean-François Gignilliat, Ephraim Golding, F.J.P., Count de Grasse, Nelsons (J. Alston of S.C., J. Nelson, Mrs. M.N. Teackle, Alston with J.I. Coddington above), Mrs. Lydia M. Latrobe Roosevelt, Mrs. Catherine Kennedy Tennent, Jan Otten van Tuyl, editor of *NEHGR* since 2001

115. William J. Hoffman – Mrs. Sophia van Lodensteyn de Beauvois or Debevoise, plus his own line on pp. 733-34

The Royal Descents of 900 Immigrants

116. Martin Edward Hollick – Thomas Bradbury (editor of *Register* article by M.K. Kirk), Mrs. Anne Skipwith Goforth Oxley, Mrs. Rose Stoughton Otis, *New Englanders in the 1600s*

117. Harry Hollingsworth – Mrs. Diana Skipwith Dale, Sir Grey Skipwith, 3rd Bt.

118. (Mrs.) Winifred Lovering Holman (Dodge) – Deighton sisters (3) (with W.D. Ligon and chart in *TG* 6 by N.D. Thompson below), Mrs. Sarah Woodward Henchman (with Leslie Mahler and Lothrop Withington below) (deceased)

119. Alvahn Holmes – William Farrar (with Worth S. Anderson above)

120. Dorothy E. Hopkins – William Goddard (with Paul C. Reed) (deceased)

121. Anthony Glenn Hoskins – twentieth-century noble German immigrants (esp. Peter Berlin), Marcus van Schenkenberg (with Leo van de Pas below), Thomas Brassey, John Umfreville/Humphreville, possible West-Pelham descent from Henry VIII and Mary Boleyn (with M.B. Colket, Jr., above)

122. Matthew Hovious – Mrs. Rebecca Ward Allen, Mrs. Mary Ward Cutting (Miller), and William Markham (with Leslie Mahler below)

123. Edgar Erskine Hume – George Home

124. John Griffiths Hunt – Bulkeleys (corrected by B. McA. Clagett, above, also with D.L. Jacobus, C.A. Torrey and H.J. Young below), plus Jane Allen (7), two Carletons (with G.A. Moriarty, Jr., and W.L. Sheppard, Jr., below), Mrs. Mary Gye Maverick, Robert Throckmorton (but note Paul C. Reed below), George Yate, Winslow speculations (with Brandon Fradd above and M.K. Kirk below)

125. Mrs. Jayne Simpson Huntington (with English researcher Maryan Egan-Baker of Salt Lake City) – Thomas Danvers (deceased)

126. Jack T. Hutchinson – Emmanuel Woolley (unpublished)

127. Donald Lines Jacobus – Nathaniel Browne (with D.L. Greene above), Obadiah Bruen, Bulkeleys (including Rev. Thomas

James, Jane Allen and Grace Chetwode) (8, with B. McA. Clagett and J.G. Hunt above and C.A. Torrey and H.J. Young below), Mrs. Mary Launce Sherman, Thomas Trowbridge (with Charles Fitch-Northen above), Mrs. Anne Rich Willis, first editor of *TAG*

128. Edward Miller Jefferys – Sir Herbert Jeffreys

129. Will Johnson –Redgrave-Richardson acting cluster (with J.C. Brandon above)

130. William Perry Johnson – Gov. Peter and Gov. Philip de Carteret (with R.K. Evans above)

131. Christopher Johnston – William Bladen, Blakistons (4), Christopher Lowndes, James Neale, Richard Tilghman (all articles in the *Maryland Historical Magazine*)

132. Edith Duncan Johnston – Sir Patrick Houston, 5th Bt.

133. Alfred Rudulph Justice – Act. Gov. Jeremiah Clarke

134. C. Frederick Kaufholz – Midwestern Kaufholz kin

135. David Humiston Kelley – various additions, including line 223 (Mrs. Olive Welby Farwell) to the *Ancestral Roots* series, Gov. Thomas Dudley (with F.N. Craig and Brandon Fradd above and M.K. Kirk below), Mrs. Dorothy May Bradford and John Whitcomb and William and John Munro/Monroe speculations (deceased)

136. David L. Kent – John Alston of N.C.

137. Charles Kidd – Reginald Michael Bloxam Hallward

138. Ann Robinson King – William Cumming

139. George Harrison Sanford King – Sir Marmaduke Beckwith, 3rd Bt., Rev. John Munro (with P. McK. Gifford and Douglas Hickling above and R.W. Munro below)

140. Kenneth W. Kirkpatrick (pseudonym for Marshall Kenneth Kirk) – Thomas Bradbury (with R.C. Anderson above and J.B. Threlfall above, with *Register* article edited by M.E. Hollick above), Gov. Thomas Dudley (with F.N. Craig, Brandon Fradd and D.H. Kelley above, plus speculations about five Winslows

The Royal Descents of 900 Immigrants

[with Brandon Fradd and J.G. Hunt above], Rev. John Cotton and Abraham Errington), *ATs* in Winslow article for Herbert Pelham and both his wives (deceased)

141. Dr. Charles G. Kurz – Alexander Magruder (per B. McA. Clagett above)

142. Christopher Carter Lee, K.M. – Mrs. Mathilde Denis de Lagarde Boal, Thomas Cornwallis/Cornwaleys, Thomas Duke, disproof of William Kennedy, William Mauduit descendants

143. Irene Haines Leet – Dep. Gov. Thomas and Mary (Jones) Lloyd (with C.F.H. Evans, above, and Brad Verity below)

144. Asselia Strobhar Lichliter – Essex Beville

145. William Daniel Ligon – Ligon/Lygon cluster (especially Col. Thomas Ligon/Lygon as also in J.B. Boddie above, both corrected by G.B. Roberts and M.J. Wood, and with N.D. Thompson below; Sir F. Gorges, with Raymond Gorges above; Berkeley; Foliot; H. Norwood; Deighton sisters (3), with W.L. Holman above and chart in *TG* 6 by N.D. Thompson below; and Savage, corrected by B. McA. Clagett, above, and N.D. Thompson, below), Henry Corbin

146. E.L. Lomax – Sir Thomas Lunsford

147. Charles M. Lord – James Veatch

148. Daniel MacGregor – Mrs. Vivian Rüesch Mellon (with J.R. Mellon II below), Mrs. Marina Torlonia Shields Slater

149. Doug McDonald – Rev. Robert Rose (with Christine Rose below)

150. Dr. George Harry McLaughlin – Guy Stuart Ritchie

151. Harry Macy, Jr. – Humphrey Underhill, Mrs. Mary Underhill Naylor Stites

152. Rev. A.A. Maddison – *Lincolnshire Pedigrees* (*HSPVS*, vols. 50-52, 55) (almost all Lincolnshire families herein)

153. Charles R. Maduell, Jr. – Carondelet

154. Leslie Mahler – Mrs. Rebecca Ward Allen, Mrs. Mary Ward Cutting (Miller) and William Markham (with Matthew Hovious above), Mrs. Audrey Barlow Almy (with John C. Brandon above),

The Royal Descents of 900 Immigrants

Mrs. Judith Everard Appleton (with J.B. Boddie, W.G. Davis, Jr., and Ernest Flagg above), Charles Chambers and Leonard Chester (both also with John C. Brandon), John Freake, Mrs. Sarah Woodward Henchman (with W.L. [Holman] Dodge above and Lothrop Withington below), Thomas Hussey and Mrs. Elizabeth Hussey Scott (both again with John C. Brandon), Mrs. Anne Cheney Knollys (once more with John C. Brandon), Samuel Levis and Joseph Need, Mrs. Elizabeth Bullock Clement(s), Mrs. Judith Knapp Hubbard, Rev. Edward Norris, Mrs. Penelope Spencer Treworgy (these last two also with Brandon), notes to me, sometimes via Christopher Challender Child, about other immigrants

155. George Englert McCracken – William Rodney (with C.M. Hansen above) (plus likely disproof of Dr. Thomas Wynne – see Appendix VI), *The Welcome Claimants*, second editor of *TAG* (deceased)

156. Mary Burton Derrickson McCurdy – Towneleys (L. Smith [with D.A. Avant, Jr., above], L. Towneley, and Mrs. M.T. Warner)

157. Andrew B.W. MacEwen – John William McEwen and Charles Russell McGregor (later Gregor), (Mrs.) Magdalen Dalyell (Monteith, later Dalyell) (with Donald Whyte below), review of all Scottish lines herein (deceased)

158. James Ross Mellon II – Mrs. Vivian Rüesch Mellon (wife) (with Daniel MacGregor above), Mrs. Audrey Divett Buller Parsons (behind Mrs. Henry C.S. Mellon) (with J.E. Anderson above), *The Great Uprooting: Ancestries of the Mellon, Rüesch and Delafield Families* (2008) (also for various European kinships)

159. Gerhard Meyer – Zinzendorf(s) and Schweinitz(es)

160. Elizabeth Mitchell – William Baugh

161. Patrick W. Montague-Smith – Mrs. Mary Wolseley Brooke, Mrs. Anne Wolseley Calvert, Mrs. Alicia Arnold Ross, Abneys

162. George Andrews Moriarty, Jr. – two Carletons (with J.G. Hunt above and W.L. Sheppard, Jr., below), Dr. Richard Palgrave, Rev. William Sargent (and Mrs. Alice Freeman Thompson Parke, with D.L. Greene above and C.A. Torrey and H.J. Young below),

The Royal Descents of 900 Immigrants

John Throckmorton (and George Yate) (possible John Throckmorton revision by Paul C. Reed is awaited), Mrs. Muriel Gurdon Saltonstall (with J.J. Muskett and M.J. Wood below), Namur-Rethel-Camville descent of Throckmortons

163. Charles Gordon Mosley – ed., *American Presidential Families* and 1999 and 2003 *Burke's Peerage* (see his "Introduction" to the 1999 ed. esp.) (deceased)

164. R.W. Munro – Rev. John Munro (with P. McK. Gifford, Douglas Hickling, and G.H.S. King above)

165. Nathan W. Murphy – Col. Walter Aston (with J.B. Boddie above and Paul C. Reed below), Mrs. Anne Fielder Gantt (Wight), Mrs. Margaret Domville Hatton Banks, and Mrs. Elizabeth Whetenhall Rozier

166. James Joseph Muskett – Winthrop and associated families, including Appleton (with W.G. Davis, Jr., Ernest Flagg, and C.M. Hansen above), Burrough[s] (with D.L. Greene above and G.I. Nelson and G.E. Russell below), Clopton (with L.L. Erwin above), Drury, Gurdon (with G.A. Moriarty, Jr., and M.J. Wood below), Mildmay and Tyndal (with C.F.H. Evans and C.M. Hansen above), from vol. 1 of *Suffolk Manorial Families*, plus Kempe from vol. 2 (with David Faris above)

167. Albert H. Muth – Mrs. Elizabeth Alsop Baldwin (Fowler) (with J.L. Scherer below)

168. Glade Ian Nelson – Nathaniel Burrough (with D.L. Greene and J.J. Muskett above, and G.E. Russell below), Ralph Hilton/Hylton

169. General Herman Nickerson, Jr. – Griffith and Margaret (Fleming) Bowen, with P.C. Bartrum, above, plus disproof of Henry and Walter Norton (see Appendix VI) (deceased)

170. J.B. Calvert Nicklin – Calverts (Barons Baltimore and wives, Hon. Leonard and Mrs. Anne Wolseley Calvert [also in *AP&P4* and *The Ark and The Dove Adventurers*]), Francis Dade, William Strother

171. Rev. V.F. O'Daniel – Cuthbert Fenwick

The Royal Descents of 900 Immigrants

172. Terri Bradshaw O'Neill – Gov. James Colleton and Mrs. Elizabeth Selwood Moore

173. Julie Helen Otto – Hermione Baddeley, Ewen S. Cameron, Richard Dawkins, Friedrich E.S.K. (Frederick W.), Baron von Egloffstein, Mrs. Margaret Stirling Forbes [Alexander] (with S.C. Steward below), Thomas Nelson (Sr.) (with C.C. Child above), Mrs. Hilda M.R.T. Otto and Mrs. Myrtle J.G. Ashmole, Richard Saltonstall (also with S.C. Steward below), Vernon H.P. Shaw Kennedy, James Tytler, Justin Bieber, F. de P.E. Lynch Zavaleta (behind Che Guevara) (this last with T.F. Gede above); Internet research on the immediate families or near ancestry of various nineteenth- and twentieth-century immigrants, and extensive preparation of this volume for press

174. Charles R. Owens – Alexander Falconer (with P. McK. Gifford above), Taronites and ancient ancestry of Irene of the East (wife of Philip of Swabia, German Emperor, with Don C. Stone below)

175. Gerald Paget – *The Lineage and Ancestry of H.R.H. Prince Charles, Prince of Wales*, 2 vols. (1977), filmed notebooks (at the Library of Congress and much used by W.A. Reitwiesner) on royal and noble families (deceased)

176. Sir James Balfour Paul – *The Scots Peerage* (all Scottish peers herein, plus many cadet lines)

177. Ann Naile Phelps – James Burd (with W.K. and A.C.Z. Rutherford below)

178. J. Hall Pleasants – Richard Curson

179. Mrs. Gerald (Sarah) Polkinghorne – Gov. William Leete of Conn. (with E.A. Stratton below for disproof of the Peyton descent) (deceased)

180. F.H. Pollard – George Mackay, Mrs. Sarah Blair Watkinson

181. Shawn H. Potter – Rev. Gregory Dexter, possible Buchanans

182. John M. Plummer – Mrs. Joan Price Cleeve

183. F.W. Pyne – John Pyne of S.C

184. M. Taylor Pyne – Thomas Pyne of N.Y.

The Royal Descents of 900 Immigrants

185. James A. Rasmussen – Edward Raynsford

186. Harmon Pumpelly Read – Rev. George Ross (with E.F. Henderson III above)

187. Franz V. Recum – Warren-Johnson-Shedden cluster (4)

188. Paul C. Reed – Col. Walter Aston (with J.B. Boddie and Nathan W. Murphy above), Robert Baillie (unpublished, with S.G. Bennett above), Mrs. Elizabeth Harleston Ball and John Harleston, John Baskerville, Mrs. Anna Cordray Bernard and two Ironmongers, Joseph Bickley, Leven Bufkin, James Cudworth (with Douglas Richardson below), William Goddard (with Dorothy E. Hopkins above), Mansfields (with R.C. Anderson and J.C. Brandon above), John and Robert Throckmorton (revisions to be published), William Wentworth and Christopher Lawson (with M.A. Guido above, and E.A. Stratton and N.L. Taylor below), John Woodliffe, Francis and Philip Yarnall, Francis Yonge (with B. McA. Clagett above), and Countess Ida (plus John Goode disproof – see Appendix VI)

189. William Addams Reitwiesner – Mrs. Kofi Annan, Sir John Gielgud, Sir T.J. Berners-Lee (with J.B. Dobson above and M.J. Wood below), Henry and Thomas Batte and Roger Mallory (with J.B. Boddie and J.A. Brayton above), Lady Charlotte Lee Calvert, Baroness Baltimore (in *MCS3,4,5*) (with Milton Rubincam below), Mrs. Anne Coddington Fenner, Christoph(er), Baron de Graffenried (with Robert Battle above), A.L. Gyllenhaal (with Stephen Robeson-Miller below), Louis Nicola, Louis Viereck, Harriet Martineau and The Duchess of Cambridge (with C.C. Child above and S.C. Steward and M.J. Wood below), extractions from *Bartrum 1,2* and general review of all Welsh and Continental lines in *RD600* (deceased)

190. Gordon Lewis Remington – Duncanson sisters (with A.B.M. Da Silva-Burke above)

191. Douglas Richardson – Mrs. Margaret Wyatt Allyn, Mrs. Margaret Domville Hatton Banks, John Baynard, Mrs. Dorothy Beresford Brodnax, Thomas Colepepper (Culpeper), Anthony Collamore, Mrs. Elizabeth Haynes Cooke, William Crymes, James Cudworth, Robert Drake, Mrs. Agnes Harris Spencer

The Royal Descents of 900 Immigrants

Edwards, George Elkington, Edward Howell, Mrs. Judith Knapp Hubbard, Lightfoots, Ligon/Lygon cluster (Beaufort descent), Percival Lowell, Simon Lynde, Richard More, Philip and Thomas Nelson, Mrs. Jane Greene Poole, Mrs. Rose Stoughton Otis, Richard Parker, Edward Raynsford, Mrs. Margaret Estouteville/Touteville Shepard, George Symes, James Taylor (for many of these immigrants, with one or more scholars listed herein), various additions to *AR6,7, MCS4*, and *PASCC 1 and 2*, plus *Plantagenet Ancestry* (3 vols.), *Magna Carta Ancestry* (4 vols.) and *Royal Ancestry* (5 vols.)

192. Hannah Benner Roach – Peter Penn-Gaskell

193. Clarence Vernon Roberts – Edward Foulke (with P.C. Bartrum and T.A. Glenn above), John Williams (with P.C. Bartrum above)

194. Gary Boyd Roberts – Thomas Bressie (with W.G. Davis, Jr. above), Rev. John Davenport (with J.I. Coddington, above), Edmond Hawes (with J.W. Hawes and H.J. Young below), Col. Thomas Ligon/Lygon (with M.J. Wood, below, in correcting W.D. Ligon and J.B. Boddie, and also with Neil D. Thompson below); Mackintoshes (McIntoshes, with William Elliott above), J.E. Oglethorpe, Robert Traill of N.H., Mrs. Stephen Breyer, Aldous Huxley and others in *NEXUS*; bibliographies in *The Connecticut Nutmegger* and *NEHGR*; various additions to *AR6,7, 8, MCS3,4, 5*, and *PASCC 1* and *2*; consolidation of the works by W.G. Davis, Jr., above; *The Mowbray Connection*; *RD500, RD600*, most nineteenth- and twentieth-century British and Continental figures new to *RD900*

195. Stephen Robeson-Miller – A.L. Gyllenhaal (with W.A. Reitwiesner above)

196. Christine Rose – Rev. Robert Rose (corrected by Doug McDonald above)

197. Mrs. Dunbar Rowland – William Dunbar

198. Milton Rubincam – John Barclay, Lady Charlotte Lee Calvert, Baroness Baltimore (with W.A. Reitwiesner above), James and Norton Claypoole (with C.M. Hansen above and W.L. Sheppard, Jr. below), Thomas Gordon, Sancha de Ayala and some of her

The Royal Descents of 900 Immigrants

American progeny (with T.A. Farmerie above and N.L. Taylor below), comments (sometimes superseded) on many lines in *NGSQ* book reviews (deceased)

199. Daniel Wood Rudgers – Dep. Gov. Thomas Rudyard

200. George Ely Russell – Nathaniel Burrough (with D.L. Greene, J.J. Muskett, and G.I. Nelson above), *The Ark and The Dove Adventurers*, editor of *NGSQ* (deceased)

201. William Kenneth and Anna Clay (Zimmerman) Rutherford – James Burd (with Anne N. Phelps above), Archibald Russell, Walter Rutherford

202. Marquis of Ruvigny and Raineval (*The Plantagenet Roll of the Blood Royal*) – most descendants herein, in legitimate lines, of Henry VII, King of England; George Plantagenet, Duke of Clarence; Anne St. Leger Manners, Baroness Ros; Walter Devereux, 1st Viscount Hereford; and Henry Percy, 4th Earl of Northumberland)

203. Charles Richard Sanders – Stracheys (3)

204. Dr. David A. Sandmire – Strattons (with Robert Battle and H.W. "Hal" Bradley above and E.A. Stratton below)

205. Helen Jefferson Sanford – two Mahons (deceased)

206. John L. Scherer – Mrs. Elizabeth Alsop Baldwin Fowler (with Albert H. Muth above), Archibald Dunlop, Andrew Elliott

207. Mrs. Elizabeth Wellborn Schieffelin – Col. Gerard Fowke

208. Detlev Schwennicke – editor of the *ES* volumes, new series, used for the first several, sometimes ten or more, generations of most Continental figures herein

209. Edwin Jaquett Sellers – John Fenwick of N.J. (with J.I. Coddington above), Thomas Fenwick, Mrs. Maria de Carpentier Jaquet

210. Herbert Furman Seversmith –Ludlows (3) (with M.B. Colket, Jr. above)

211. John Shakespeare – Mrs. Dorothy Shakespear Pound

212. Mrs. Henrietta Dawson Ayres Sheppard – Robert Drake (with J.A. Brayton, T.F. Beard, and Douglas Richardson above)

The Royal Descents of 900 Immigrants

213. Walter Lee Sheppard, Jr. – Joseph Bolles (with Augustine H. Ayers above), two Carletons (with G.A. Moriarty, Jr., and J.G. Hunt, above), James and Norton Claypoole (with C.M. Hansen and Milton Rubincam above), "Royal Bye-Blows" list in *NEHGR*, seven editions of *Ancestral Roots* and four of *Magna Charta Sureties, 1215*, 1952-1992 (more recent editions mostly with David Faris), *Feudal Genealogy*, founder of Descendants of the Illegitimate Sons and Daughters of the Kings of Britain (deceased)

214. D. Brenton Simons – Robert Dering, first husband of Mrs. Henrietta de Beaulieu Dering Johnston of S.C.

215. Bruce Harris Sinkey – John Ashby

216. Thomas W. Spaulding, Jr. – Thomas Owsley (co-author, with R.O. Bodine above, of *The Ancestry of Dorothea Poyntz, Wife of Reverend John Owsley, Generations, 1-12*)

217. G.D. Squibb – various post-1950 and esp. post-2000 editions of visitations of Wiltshire (and mostly late such for) Dorset, Nottinghamshire, Derbyshire, Hampshire, Somerset and Oxfordshire, much cited herein

218. Scott C. Steward – Mrs. Margaret Stirling Forbes [Alexander] (in a Vanderbilt *AT*) (with J.H. Otto above), Richard Saltonstall (also with J.H. Otto), Henry Wyche and Mrs. Anne Rich Willis, William Snelling, John Thorndike (husband of Elizabeth Stratton), Harriet Martineau and The Duchess of Cambridge (with C.C. Child and W.A. Reitwiesner above and M.J. Wood below)

219. Don Charles Stone – Mrs. Thomasine Clench Frost (with J.C. Brandon above), Mrs. Jane Vaughan Owen, Charles Willing (with J.C. Brandon above and N.L. Taylor and David Topping below), *Some Ancient and Medieval Descents of Edward I of England* (ongoing, 2000 version bound at NEHGS), Taronites and ancient ancestry of Irene of the East (wife of Philip of Swabia, German Emperor) (with C.R. Owens above), co-owner of *soc.genealogy.medieval*

220. Mrs. Patricia Wright Strati – Rudolph Pierre Garrigue

221. Eugene Aubrey Stratton – Strattons (with Robert Battle, H.W. "Hal" Bradley and D.A. Sandmire above), Gov. William

Leete (disproof of the Peyton descent) (with Mrs. Gerald Polkinghorne above), William Wentworth (with M.A. Guido and Paul C. Reed above and N.L. Taylor below), de Braose ancestry of Bressie, N. Browne, Davenport and Hawes (with F.N. Craig above, whom see for other scholars associated with these immigrants) (deceased)

222. Henry Sutliff III – Gov. John Seymour of Md.

223. Davida E. Symonds – Thomas Lechmere

224. Alistair and Henrietta Tayler (*The House of Forbes*) – John Forbes of Pa., Rev. John Forbes of Fla. and Forbes line of Hans Axel, Count von Fersen

225. Nathaniel Lane Taylor – Sancha de Ayala (1998 *Register* article with Todd A. Farmerie above, topic with Milton Rubincam above) and William Wentworth and Christopher Lawson (with M.A. Guido, P.C. Reed and E.A. Stratton above) among her descendants, James Blount (with K.S. Vanlandingham below), Charles Willing (with J.C. Brandon and D.C. Stone above and David Topping below), Mrs. Frances Walker Banister, editor of *TAG* since 2015

226. Neil D. Thompson – Robert Abell (with Carl Boyer, 3rd, above), Kenelm Cheseldine, Thomas Jernegan (with Shirley G. Bennett and J.A. Brayton above), Col. Thomas Ligon (with J.B. Boddie and W.D. Ligon above, corrected by G.B. Roberts above and M.J. Wood below), Anthony Savage (with B. McA. Clagett above, also correcting W.D. Ligon), much editing and additions to royal descent articles in *TG* (on Eve of Leinster, Llywelyn and Joan of Wales, 3 Nelsons, Mrs. A.F.T. Parke, Wolseleys and Mrs. A.A. Ross, de Braose ancestors of Bressie, Browne, Davenport and Hawes, the Deighton sisters [especially Mrs. Negus], George Elkington, William Wentworth, Bressie and Hawes, Thomas Trowbridge, H.J. Stier, two Harlestons, Lawrence siblings, unpublished Gibbes monograph by B. McA. Clagett, and Sir Thomas Greene [ancestors of the Marbury sisters]), plus, with C.M. Hansen, above, *The Ancestry of Charles II, King of England: A Medieval Heritage* (2012) and Margaret Kerdeston and Woodville studies) and disproofs of Daniel and Hugh Harry and John Underhill (see Appendix VI)

The Royal Descents of 900 Immigrants

227. Sydnor Thompson – Fortunatus Sydnor
228. John Brooks Threlfall – Thomas Bradbury (with R.C. Anderson and Marshall K. Kirk above)
229. David Topping – Charles Willing (with J.C. Brandon, D.C. Stone and N.L. Taylor above)
230. Clayton Torrence – Mrs. Abigail Smith Burwell (with J.A. Brayton above), Mrs. Anne Lovelace Gorsuch, Gov. Francis Lovelace
231. Clarence Almon Torrey – Rev. Thomas James (with B. McA. Clagett, J.G. Hunt and D.L. Jacobus above, and H.J. Young below), Mrs. Alice Freeman Thompson Parke (with D.L. Greene and G.A. Moriarty, Jr. above, and H.J. Young below), *New England Marriages Prior to 1700*
232. Robert Dennard Tucker – Tuckers and Booth-Tuckers
233. Leo van de Pas – Hugh Grant, Audrey Hepburn, Marcus Schenkenberg (with A.G. Hoskins above), *Genealogics* (website on royal and noble families), *Plantagenet Cousins* (deceased)
234. Peter G. Van der Poel – Gov. John Cranston (as noted in *MCS3,4,5*), Yales (3) (with R.J. Curfman above)
235. Kyle Samuel Vanlandingham – James Blount (with N.L. Taylor above)
236. Brad Verity – Mrs. Anne Talbot Darnall (with John Higgins), Mrs. Mary Jones Lloyd (with C.F.H. Evans and I.H. Leet above), medieval topics (Cardinal Henry Beaufort, Alice [de] Hales, Isabel de Beaumont, Bohun-Butler progeny)
237. Sir Anthony Richard Wagner – Mrs. Mabel Harlakenden Haynes (Eaton), Richard More, comments on others (especially Mrs. Anne Bainton Ball, Mark Catesby and Edward FitzRandolph, with doubts about Thomas Newberry) in *English Genealogy* or *Pedigree and Progress* (deceased)
238. Peter Walne – Christopher Branch, Col. John and Lawrence Washington (father) (with J.B. Boddie and Peter Walne above and G.S.H. Lee Washington immediately below)

The Royal Descents of 900 Immigrants

239. George Sydney Horace Lee Washington – three Washingtons (with J.B. Boddie and Peter Walne above) (and H.E. Pellew), with Calvert (and Stuart in America) speculations discarded

240. Henry FitzGilbert Waters – *Genealogical Gleanings in England*, 2 vols., the initial source for much research reported herein

241. Walter Kendall Watkins – Alexander Cochrane, Robert Gibbs

242. Frederick Lewis Weis – two Southworths, first several editions of *Ancestral Roots* and *Magna Charta Sureties, 1215*

243. Donald Whyte – (Mrs.) Magdalene Dalyell (Monteith, later Dalyell) (with Andrew B.W. MacEwen above), *A Dictionary of Scottish Emigrants to the U.S.A.*, 2 vols.

244. Wayne Howard Miller Wilcox – Mrs. Catherine Hamby Hutchinson

245. Kelsey Jackson Williams – William Stewart

246. David Geoffrey Williamson – Burke's, later Debrett's works of the 1970s and 1980s, esp. *Burke's Guide to the Royal Family*, *Royal Families of the World*, 2 vols. and the 1981 *Burke's Presidential Families of the U.S.A.*, 2nd edition (deceased)

247. Daniel Willis, formerly Brewer-Ward – *Descendants of Maria Theresa, Descendants of Louis XIII, Descendants of George I* (for various immigrants charted herein)

248. York Lowry Wilson – Thomas Chamberlayne, Mrs. Dorothy Chamberlayne Daniell, Col. George Reade (with J.B. Boddie II above)

249. Henry Mosle (H.M.) West Winter – George and Caroline D.D. Mosle; *The Descendants of Charlemagne* (covering 16 generations) (deceased)

250. Lothrop Withington – Mrs. Sarah Woodward Henchman and Mrs. Frances Woodward Oxenbridge (with W.L. [Holman] Dodge and Leslie Mahler above); *Virginia Gleanings in England*

251. Janet Paulette Chevalley Wolfe – Craigheads, Hartes of Ill., Stoughtons (speculative, with A.B.M. Da Silva-Burke and J.B. Dobson above), Mrs. Anne Revell Curtis (with her husband, Robert A. Wolfe)

The Royal Descents of 900 Immigrants

252. Michael Johnson Wood – Mrs. Thomasine Ward Thompson Buffum (with doubts by W.G. Davis, Jr. above), Joshua Henshaw, Col. Thomas Ligon/Lygon (with G.B. Roberts, correcting W.D. Ligon and J.B. Boddie, and with Neil D. Thompson, all four above), Mrs. Muriel Gurdon Saltonstall (with G.A. Moriarty, Jr., and J.J. Muskett above), Sir T.J. Berners-Lee (with J.B. Dobson and W.A. Reitwiesner above), Harriet Martineau and The Duchess of Cambridge (with C.C. Child, W.A. Reitwiesner and S.C. Steward above)

253. Edward Yonge – Francis and Robert Yonge (with B. McA. Clagett above and Francis also with Paul C. Reed above)

254. Gary E. Young – Francis and Philip Yarnall

255. Henry James Young – Edmond Hawes (with J.W. Hawes and G.B. Roberts above), Rev. Thomas James and the Bulkeleys (with B. McA. Clagett, J.G. Hunt, D.L. Jacobus and C.A. Torrey above), and Mrs. Alice Freeman Thompson Parke (with D.L. Greene, G.A. Moriarty, Jr., and C.A. Torrey above) (ancestor tables for Hawes, Rev. T. James, and Mrs. Parke)

Note: The specific works of these scholars, on each immigrant listed, are usually cited on the chart(s) outlining that immigrant's RD. Virginia scholars William Stanard Glover and Lyon Gardiner Tyler, editors between them of all three major Virginia genealogical journals of the early twentieth century, are omitted because most of their work, although widely used, has been superseded by later contributions from various of the above. John Horace Round is omitted because he wrote largely on the origins and medieval descents, usually patrilineal, of British noble families, not their colonial immigrant descendants.

Among useful websites, soc.genealogy.medieval, co-owned by Don Charles Stone and Todd A. Farmerie, and genealogics.com, that of the late Leo van de Pas, are mentioned above. Also of considerable use have been websites of (1) the late William Addams Reitwiesner above, printouts of the bulk of which have been bound in spring binders by J.H. Otto and G.B. Roberts; (2) Daniel de Rauglaudre (roglo.eu/roglo), on royal and noble families, sometimes used as a first source by J.B. Dobson to "improve" various Continental descents herein; and (3) George Larson, who sometimes collaborated with Reitwiesner and has worked with John C. Brandon.

The Royal Descents of 900 Immigrants

Appendix II:
925 Immigrants of Royal Descent:
A Subject Index and Guide
(Alphabetical by Title or Surname)

The following list of all non-French Canadian immigrants to the American colonies or the United States includes all such whose names appear in **bold** in the text. Also included are the dozen or so immigrants covered in the "Sources" sections following each chart. These latter, "lesser" immigrants were also (somewhat) notable in their own right, or parents or ancestors of figures notable in American history. Immigrants noted as having no NDTPS (notable descendants treated in printed sources), usually near kinsmen of immigrants treated in the text, are not listed below.

A

	Page
1. Abbott, Mrs. Anne Mauleverer, of N.J.	374
2. Abell, Robert, of Mass.	500
3. Abercromby, James, British commander at Ticonderoga	273
4. Alexandra, Mother (Ileana, Princess of Roumania, Archduchess of Austria, Princess of Tuscany, Mrs. S. V. Issarescu), of Pa.	2
5. Allen, Mrs. Rebecca Ward, of Mass.	655
6. Allyn, Mrs. Margaret Wyatt, of Conn.	672
7. Almy, Mrs. Audrey Barlow, of R.I.	763
8. Alston, John, of N.C.	826
9. Alston, John, of S.C.	356
10. Amherst of Holmesdale and Montreal, Jeffrey Amherst, 1st Baron of, governor of Va.	755
11. Annan, Mrs. Nina Maria (Nane) Lagergren Cronstedt, of N.Y.	60
12. Anson, Hon. William, of Texas	28
13. Appleton, Mrs. Judith Everard, of Mass.	882
14. Appleton, Samuel, of Mass.	813
15. Argall, Sir Samuel, governor of Va.	514
16. Armour, Princess Alexandra Romanoff, of Ill.	793-94
17. Asfordby, William, of N.Y.	343
18. Ashby, John, of S.C.	471

The Royal Descents of 900 Immigrants

19. Asher, Peter, sometime of Calif.	64
20. Ash(e) (Lillington), Mrs. Mary Batt, of S.C.	468
21. Mrs. Myrtle Jane Goodacre Ashmole, sometime of Conn.	323
22. Astaire, Adele (first husband, Lord Charles Arthur Francis Cavendish)	26
23. Aston, Col. Walter, of Va.	728
24. Atwater, Mrs. Anna Maria Drury, of N.Y.	371
25. Auberjonois, Princess Laure-Louise-Napoléone-Eugénie-Caroline Murat Frank, of N.Y.	83
26. Auberjonois, Fernand, of N.Y.	635
27. Auden, W.H. (Wystan Hugh), sometime of N.Y.	404
28. Avery, Mrs. Margaret Mackenzie, of S.C.	95

B

29. Bacon (Jarvis Mole), Mrs. Elizabeth Duke, of Va.	561
30. Bacon, Nathaniel, gov. of Va. (rebel)	494
31. Bacon, Nathaniel, act. gov. of Va.	878
32. Clinton-Baddeley (Tennant Willis), Mrs. Hermione Youlanda Ruby [Hermione Baddeley], sometime of Calif.	109
33. Bagration (-Mukhransky), Teymuraz, Prince (Prince of Georgia), of N.Y.	7
34. Baillie, Col. Kenneth, of Ga.	283
35. Baillie, Robert, of Ga.	152
36. Baldwin (Fowler), Mrs. Elizabeth Alsop, of Conn.	589
37. Ball, Mrs. Elizabeth Harleston, of S.C.	349
38. Ball, Mrs. Frances Ravenscroft, of Va.	518
39. Baltimore, Hon. Anne Arundell Calvert, Baroness (husband proprietor of Md.)	339
40. Baltimore, Cecil Calvert, 2nd Baron, proprietor of Md.	739
41. Baltimore, Lady Charlotte Lee Calvert (Crewe), Baroness (husband proprietor of Md.)	29
42. Baltimore, Jane Lowe Sewall Calvert, Baroness, of Md.	512
43. Baltimore, Mary Janssen Calvert, Baroness, of Md.	312
44. Ban(n)ister, Mrs. Frances Walker, of Mass.	399
45. Barclay, Mrs. Louisa Anna (or Louise Ann) Matilda Aufrere, of N.Y.	144

The Royal Descents of 900 Immigrants

46. Barcroft, Mrs. Elizabeth Wood, of Va.	772
47. Barham, Charles, of Va.	514
48. Baring-Gould, William Drake, of Minn.	136
49. Barnes, Charles, of N.Y.	359
50. Baskerville, John, of Va.	235
51. Bathurst, Lancelot, of Va.	883
52. Batt, Mrs. Anne Bainton, of Mass.	468
53. Batt, Christopher, of Mass.	678
54. Batte, Henry, of Va.	506
55. Batte, Thomas, of Va.	505
56. Bayfield, St. Clair [John St. Clair Roberts]	364
57. Baynard, John, of Md.	744
58. Beatty, Mrs. Christiana Clinton, of N.Y.	351
59. Beckwith, Sir Marmaduke, 3rd Bt., of Va.	127
60. Bellingham, Mrs. Elizabeth Backhouse, of Mass.	575
61. Bellingham, Mrs. Penelope Pelham, of Mass.	301
62. Bellingham, Richard, governor of Mass.	528
63. Bellomont, Catherine Nanfan Coote, Countess of (husband gov. of N.Y., Mass. and N.H.)	107
64. Bellomont, Richard Coote, 1st Earl of, governor of N.Y., Mass. and N.H.	462
65. Bentinck, (Count) Wilhelm Friedrich, of Missouri	54
66. Beresford, Mrs. Dorothy Mellish, of S.C.	311
67. Berg, Mrs. Josephine Alma Danielsen, of N.Y.	891
68. Berkeley, Sir William, governor of Va.	296
Berlin, Peter, *see* Hoyningen-Huene, Baron Armin Hoyer, of Calif.	
69. Bernard, Lady Amelia Offley, of Mass. (husband governor of N.J. and Mass.)	531
70. Bernard, Mrs. Anna Cordray, of Va.	739
71. Bernard, Sir Francis, 1st Bt., governor of N.J. and Mass.	495
72. Bernard, Richard, of Va.	495
73. Bernard, Col. William, of Va.	495
74. Berners-Lee, Sir Timothy John "Tim," of Mass.	520
75. Bevan, Mrs. Barbara Aubrey, of Pa.	338
76. Bevan, John, of Pa.	410
77. Beville, Essex, of Va.	420
78. Bickley, Joseph, of Va.	534
79. Birkin, Jane (Mrs. John Barry) (husband of N.Y.)	27

The Royal Descents of 900 Immigrants

80. Bladen, Mrs. Barbara Janssen, of Md.	312
81. Bladen, William, of Md.	327
82. Blakiston, George, of Md.	317
83. Blakiston, Nathaniel, governor of Md.	317
84. Blakiston, Nehemiah, of Md.	317
85. Blavatsky (Betanelly), Madame Helena Petrovna Hahn, of N.Y.	792
86. Blennerhasset, Harman, of Va.	325
87. Blennerhasset, Mrs. Margaret Agnew, of Va.	144, 325
88. Blount, James, of N.C.	530
89. Boal, Mrs. Jeanne-Marie-Bernarde de Menthon, sometime of Washington, D.C.	206
90. Boal, Mrs. Matilde Dolores Denis de Lagarde, of Pa.	443
91. Bobrinski, George Victor, of Ill.	14
92. Boddie, William, of Va.	882
93. Bohun, Edmund, of S.C.	353
94. Boissevain, Marie-Thérèse Zwetana, Countess von Hartenau, wife of Charles-Hercule Boissevain, sometime of N.Y. and Colo.	41
95. Bolles, Joseph, of Me.	471
96. Bonaparte, Jerome Napoleon, of Md.	858
97. Bonham Carter, Helena, sometime of N.Y. or Calif.	306
98. Boone, Thomas, governor of N.J. and S.C.	743
99. Booth, Thomas, of Va.	560
100. Booth-Tucker, Mrs. Emma Moss (husband Frederick St. George de Lautour Booth-Tucker)	464
101. Borchgrave d'Altena, Arnaud, Count, of N.Y.	112
102. Borghese, Francesco Maria Luigi Constanzo, 6th Duke of Bomarzo, sometime of N.J.	24
103. Boteler (Butler), Thomas, of Md.	754
104. Bourbon del Monte Santa Maria, Ranieri, Prince of San Faustino, husband of Kay Linn Sage, of Calif.	20
105. Botetourt, Norborne Berkeley, 1st Baron, gov. of Va.	345
106. Bowen, Griffith, of Mass.	811
107. Bowen, Mrs. Margaret Fleming, of Mass.	582
108. Bradbury, Thomas, of Mass.	579
109. Bradstreet, John, of N.Y.	949

The Royal Descents of 900 Immigrants

110. Brady, Lady Victoria May Pery, of N.Y.	116
111. Branch, Christopher, of Va.	822
112. le Brassieur, Mrs. Anne Mellish Splatt, of S.C.	311
113. Brassey, Thomas, of Pa.	817
114. von Braun, Maria Irmengard Emmy Luise Gisela von Quistorp, Baroness (wife and first cousin of Wernher), of Ala.	59
115. von Braun, Wernher Magnus Maximilian, Baron von, of Ala.	224
116. Brent, George, of Va.	332
117. Brent, Giles, of Va. and Md.	331
118. Brent, Margaret, of Md.	331
119. Brent, Mrs. Mary Brent, of Va.	332
120. Brereton, Rev. John, of Me.	760
121. Bressie, Thomas, of Conn.	670
122. Brett, Hon. Dorothy Eugénie, of N.M.	137
123. Breyer, Hon. Mrs. Joanna Freda Hare, of Mass.	81
124. Bridges, Mrs. Mary Woodcock, of Mass.	506
125. Brodnax, Mrs. Dorothy Beresford, of Va.	474
126. Bromfield, Edward, of Mass.	491
127. Bronfman, Lady Carolyn Elizabeth Ann Townshend Capellini, of N.Y.	9
128. Brooke, Mrs. Mary Wolseley, of Md.	676
129. Broughton, Thomas, of Mass.	750
130. Browne, Nathaniel, of Conn.	653
131. Bruce, Mrs. Evangeline Bell, of Va.	100
132. Bruce, (William) Nigel (Ernle), of Calif.	145
133. Bruen, Obadiah, of Conn.	688
134. Brundage, Mrs. Avery (later Mrs. Friedrich Karl Feldmann) (Marianne Charlotte Katharina Stefanie, Princess Reuss-Köstritz)	8
135. Buffum, Mrs. Thomasine Ward Thompson, of Mass.	761
136. Bufkin, Leven, of Va.	473
137. Bulkeley, Mrs. Grace Chetwode, of Mass.	574
138. Bulkeley, Mrs. Jane Allen (never immigrated, husband of Mass.)	702
139. Bulkeley, Rev. Peter, of Mass.	746
140. Bull, Stephen, of S.C.	369
141. Bullard, Mrs. Sarah Tucker Harris, of S.C.	463

The Royal Descents of 900 Immigrants

142. [Borberg, later] von Bülow, Claus Cecil, of R.I.   645
143. Buncombe, Edward, of N.C.   609
144. Burd, James, of Pa.   275
145. Burnet, William, governor of N.Y.   273
146. Burnham, Mrs. Mary Lawrence, of Mass.   881
147. Burr, Mrs. Abigail Brewster, of Conn.   539
148. Burrough(s), Nathaniel, of Mass. and Md.   484
149. Burton, Mrs. Beatrice Maud Boswell Eliott, of N.Y.   90
150. Burwell, Mrs. Abigail Smith, of Va.   878
151. Butler, Pierce, of S.C.   382

C

152. Cadwalader, Mrs. Jane John, of Pa.   651
153. Cadwalader, John, of Pa.   651
154. Cadwalader, Robert, of Pa.   694
155. Cahill, Mrs. Jeanne Maud Martineau Grewcock, of N.Y.   380
156. Calthorpe, Christopher, of Va.   606
157. Calvert, Mrs. Anne Wolseley, of Md.   676
158. Calvert, Hon. Leonard, governor of Md.   739
159. Cameron, Ewen Somerled, of Montana (husband of [Mrs.] Evelyn [Jephson Flower] Cameron)   85
160. Campbell, Lord William, governor of S.C.   93
161. Carleton, Edward, of Mass.   398
162. Carleton, Mrs. Ellen Newton, of Mass.   667
163. de Carondelet and de Noyelle, Francois Luis Hector, Vicomte de la Hestre and du Langue, Spanish governor of La. and W. Florida   438
164. Carrington, George, of Va.   557
165. Carroll, Dr. Charles, of Annapolis, Md.   602
166. Carter, Mrs. Sarah Ludlow, of Va.   503
167. de Carteret, Peter, governor of N.C.   868
168. de Carteret, Philip, governor of N.J.   868
 [Carver, Mrs. Catherine White Leggett, of Mass. (wife of first Plymouth Colony Governor John Carver)]   916
169. Cary, Hon. Mrs. Cynthia Burke Roche Burden, of R.I.   378
170. Catesby, Mark, traveler to Va., S.C., Ga., and Fla.   831
171. Cazenove, Théophile, sometime of Pa.   635

The Royal Descents of 900 Immigrants

172. Cecil, Hon. John Francis Amherst, sometime of N.C. 73-74
 [Chamberlain, Mrs. Elizabeth Stoughton Scudder,
    of Mass.] 921
173. Chamberlayne, Thomas, of Va. 133
174. Chambers, Charles, of Mass. 501
175. Chase, Mrs. Margaret Frances Towneley, of Md. 859
176. Chauncey, Rev. Charles, of Mass. 806
177. Chavchavadze, Princess Nina Romanoff (Grand
    Duchess of Russia), of Mass. 4
178. Cheseldine, Kenelm, atty. gen. of Md. 478
179. Chester, Leonard, of Conn. 757
180. Chichele, Lady Agatha Eltonhead Kellaway
    Wormeley, of Va. 498
181. Chichele, Sir Henry, deputy governor of Va. 491
182. Clagett, Wiseman, solicitor-general of N.H. 302
183. Claiborne, Mrs. Elizabeth Boteler, of Va. 754
184. Clarendon, Catherine O'Brien Hyde, Countess of
    (and Baroness Clifton) (husband
    governor of N.Y. and N.J.) 122
185. Clarendon, Edward Hyde, 3rd Earl of, governor
    of N.Y. and N.J. 122
186. Clarke, Mrs. Barbara Murray, of N.C. 21
187. Clarke, Jeremiah, acting governor of R.I. 468
188. Clarkson, Matthew, provincial secretary of N.Y. 750
189. Claypoole, James, of Pa. 554
190. Claypoole, Norton, of Del. 554
191. Clayton, John, of Va. 543
192. Cleeve, Mrs. Joan Price, of Me. 810
193. Clement(s), Mrs. Elizabeth Bullock, of Mass. 584
194. Clifton, Mrs. Anne Brent, of Md. 332
195. Clifton, James, of Md. 904
196. Clinton, Charles, of N.Y. 351
197. Clinton, Hon. George, governor of N.Y. 108
198. Clopton, William, of Va. 483
199. Clyde, (Michael) Jeremy (Thomas) Clyde (Jeremy
    of "Chad and Jeremy"), sometime of Calif. 74
200. Cochrane, Alexander, of Mass. 251
201. Cockburn, Andrew Myles, of N.Y. and Calif.
    (father of Olivia Wilde) 94

The Royal Descents of 900 Immigrants

202. Cocke, Mrs. Elizabeth Catesby, of Va.	831
203. Codd, St. Leger, of Va.	348
204. Coke, John, of Va.	325
205. Colepepper (Culpeper), Mrs. Katherine St. Leger, of Va.	347
206. Colepepper (Culpeper), Thomas, of Va.	839-40
207. Colepepper (Culpeper), Thomas Colepepper (Culpeper), 2nd Baron, governor of Va.	840
208. Collamore, Anthony, of Mass.	867
209. Colleton, James, governor of S.C.	742
210. Colloredo-Mansfeld, Franz Ferdinand Romanus, Count, of Mass.	198
211. Conway, Mrs. Martha Eltonhead, of Va.	497
212. Cooke, Mrs. Elizabeth Haynes, of Mass.	587
213. Copley, Mrs. Anne Boteler, of Md.	302
214. Copley, Lionel, governor of Md.	600
215. Copley, Thomas, of Md.	494
216. Corbin (Creek), Mrs. Alice Eltonhead Burnham, of Va.	498
217. Corbin, Henry, of Va.	697
218. Cornwallis (Cornwaleys), Thomas, of Md.	596
219. Cosby, Mrs. Grace Montagu (husband governor of N.Y. and N.J.)	115
220. Cosby, William, governor of N.Y. and N.J.	307
221. Cotton, Leonard, of N.H.	297
222. Coward, Noël (Pierce), sometime of N.Y.	242
223. Hamilton-Cox, Henry, of Pa.	167
224. Craig, Daniel (Wroughton), sometime of N.Y.	362
225. Craighead, Rev. Thomas, of Pa.	87
226. Cranston, John, governor of R.I.	241
227. Craven, Christopher, governor of S.C.	321
228. Cra(y)croft, John, of Md.	604
229. Croker, Eyre Coote, of N.Y.	480
230. Crowne, Mrs. Agnes Mackworth Watts (husband of Mass.)	319
231. Crymes, Dr. William, of Va.	426
232. Cudworth, James, of Mass.	580
233. Cumberbatch, Benedict, sometime of Calif.	101
234. Cumberbatch, Mrs. Sophie Irene Hunter, sometime of Calif.	179

The Royal Descents of 900 Immigrants

235. Cuming, Sir Alexander, 2nd Bt.	272
236. Cuming, Mrs. Helen Cuming, prob. of Mass.	272
237. Cumming, William, of Md.	281
238. Curson, Richard, of Md.	377
239. Curtis, Mrs. Alison E. McCarthy-Willis-Bund, of Calif. and R.I.	541
240. Curtis, Mrs. Anne Revell, of N.J.	757
241. Cuthbert, James, of S.C.	176
242. Cutting (Miller), Mrs. Mary Ward, of Mass.	655

D

243. D'Abo (Leonard), Olivia Jane, sometime of Calif.	135
244. Dade, Francis, of Va.	565
245. Dale, Mrs. Diana Skipwith, of Va.	470
246. Dale, Lady Elizabeth Throckmorton, of Va. (husband governor)	297
247. Dallas, Mrs. Arabella Maria Smith, of Pa.	666
248. Dalyell, (Mrs.) Magdalen (later Dalyell Monteith), of Va.	171
249. Dana, William Pulteney, of N.Y.	155
250. Daniell, Mrs. Dorothy Chamberlayne, of S.C.	133
251. Danvers, Thomas, of Pa.	629
252. Darnall, Mrs. Anne Talbot, of Md.	121
253. Davenport, Rev. John, of Conn.	654
254. Davie, Humphrey, of Mass.	308
255. Davison, Catherine, Countess Cheremetov (wife of Daniel Pomeroy Davison)	794
256. de Beauvois or Debevoise, Mrs. Sophia van Lodensteyn, of N.Y.	775
257. De Butts, Mrs. Marianne Welby, of Md.	115
258. Delaware (de la Warr), Cecily Shirley West, Baroness (husband governor of Va.)	491
259. Delaware (de la Warr), Thomas West, 3rd Baron, governor of Va.	300
260. Denne, Mrs. Margaret Halsnode, of N.J.	883
261. Denny, William, lt. gov. of Pa., governor of Del.	494
262. Dexter, Rev. Gregory, of R.I.	862
263. Digges, Edward, governor of Va.	347
264. Dixwell, John, of Conn., regicide	750

The Royal Descents of 900 Immigrants

265. Dobkin, Maria Immaculata Pia (Countess) von Habsburg, of N.Y.	6
266. Dobyns, Daniel, of Va.	467
267. Dodge, Mrs. Jane Evans, of N.Y.	690
268. Douglas, Robert Langton, of N.Y.	166
269. Drake, Robert, of Va.	419
270. Drexel, (Hon.) Mrs. Mildred Sophia Noreen Stonor, of R.I.	66
271. Dudley (Allyn), Mrs. Katherine Deighton Hackburne, of Mass.	297
272. Dudley, Thomas, governor of Mass.	370, 373
273. Duke, Thomas, of Va.	103
274. Dumaresq, Philip, of Mass.	527
275. Dunbar, William, of Miss.	266
276. Dundas, James, of Pa.	151
277. Dundas, Thomas, of Pa.	151
278. Dunlop, Archibald, of Conn.	218
279. Dunmore, Lady Charlotte Stewart Murray, Countess of (husband governor of N.Y. and Va.)	62
280. Dunmore, John Murray, 4th Earl of, gov. of N.Y. and Va.	62

E

281. Eaton, Mrs. Anne Lloyd Yale, of Conn. (second husband gov. of the New Haven Colony)	686
282. Eddowes, Ralph, of Pa.	367
283. Eddowes, Mrs. Sarah Kenrick, of Pa.	376
284. Eden, Sir Robert, 1st Bt., governor of Md.	100
285. Edgeworth, Richard, of N.C.	312
286. Edwards, Mrs. Agnes Harris Spencer, of Conn.	867
287. Egerton, Graham, of Washington, D.C.	150
288. von Egloffstein, Friedrich Wilhelm Ernst Sigismund Kamill, Baron, of N.Y.	641
289. von Egloffstein, Irmgard von Kiesenwetter, Baroness, of N.Y.	141
290. Elkington, George, of N.J.	768
291. Ellicott, Mrs. Mary Fox, of Pa.	595
292. Elliott, Andrew, of N.Y.	96

The Royal Descents of 900 Immigrants

293. Ellis, Mrs. Margaret Roberts, of Pa.	229
294. Ellis, Rowland, of Pa.	229
295. Elwes, (Ivan Simon) Cary, of Calif.	77
296. Emmet, Mrs. Mary Byrd Farley Tucker, of Va.	21
297. Emmet, Thomas Addis, of N.Y.	325
298. Ericsson, Mrs. Amelia Jane Byam, of N.Y.	302
299. Erskine, Robert, of N.J.	275
300. d'Estaing, Jean-Baptiste-Charles-Henri-Hector, Revolutionary commander	202
301. Evans, Cadwalader, of Pa.	651
302. Evans, Mrs. Ellen Morris, of Pa.	660
303. Evans, Mrs. Hannah Price Jones David, of Pa.	658
304. Evans, John, of Radnor, Pa.	555
305. Evans, Thomas, of Pa.	651
306. Everard, Sir Richard, 4th Bt., governor of N.C.	114
307. Everett, Rupert (Hector), of Calif.	34
308. Eyre, Sir Richard (Charles Hastings), sometime of N.Y.	383

F

309. Fagan, Nicholas FitzMaurice, of Pa.	545
310. Fairfax, Thomas Fairfax, 6th Baron, of Va.	129
311. Fairfax, William, of Va.	129
312. Falconer, Alexander, of Md.	256
313. Falconer, Patrick, of Conn. and N.J.	252
314. Farrar, William, of Va.	343
315. Farwell, Mrs. Olive Welby, of Mass.	519
316. Fauquier, Mrs. Catherine Dalston, of Va. (husband governor)	472
317. Fenner, Mrs. Anne Coddington, of N.J.	467
318. Fenwick, (Lady) Alice Apsley Boteler (second husband of Conn.)	662
319. Fenwick, Mrs. Catherine Haselrige (husband of Conn.)	331
320. Fenwick, Cuthbert, of Md.	599
321. Fenwick, Mrs. Elizabeth Covert (husband of N.J.)	691
322. Fenwick, George, of Conn.	328
323. Fenwick, Mrs. Jane Eltonhead Moryson, of Md.	498
324. Fenwick, John, of N.J.	366
325. Fenwick, John, of S.C.	366

The Royal Descents of 900 Immigrants

326. Fenwick, Thomas, of Del.	719
327. von Fersen, Hans Axel, Count, Revolutionary soldier	267
328. Field (Pleydell-Bouverie), Mrs. Audrey Evelyn James Coats, of N.Y.	68
329. Fiennes, Ralph (Nathaniel), of Calif.	158
330. Fiennes, Joseph (Alberic), of Calif.	158
331. Filmer, Henry, of Va.	514
332. von Finck, Victor Ernst Hermann, of Mo.	620
333. Fisher, John, of Va.	357
334. Fitzgerald, Desmond, of R.I. and Mass.	334
335. FitzRandolph, Edward, of Mass. and N.J.	725
336. Fleete, Henry, of Va.	314
337. Foliot, Rev. Edward, of Va.	296
338. Fontaine, Joan (Joan de Beauvoir de Havilland), of Calif.	463
339. Foot, Mrs. Philippa Ruth Bosanquet, of Calif.	335
340. Forbes, John, of Pa.	255
341. Forbes, Rev. John, of Fla.	790
342. Forbes (Alexander), Mrs. Margaret Stirling, of Va.	174
343. Foulke, Edward, of Pa.	658
344. Foulke, Mrs. Ellen Hughes, of Pa.	660
345. Foulke, Mrs. Gwen Evans, of Pa.	651
346. Fowke, Col. Gerard, of Va.	722
347. von and zu Franckenstein, Joseph, Baron, husband of Kay Boyle, sometime of N.Y. and Calif.	15
348. Frankland, Sir Charles Henry, 4th Bt. (husband of Lady Agnes Surriage Frankland of Mass.)	130
349. Fraser, Thomas, of S.C. and N.J.	82
350. Freake, John, of Mass.	493
351. Frost, Lady Corina Mary Gabriel Fitzalan-Howard, wife of David (Paradine) Frost, sometime of N.Y. and Calif.	72
352. Frost, Mrs. Thomasine Clench, of Mass.	680
353. zu Fürstenberg, Prince (Eduard) Egon (Peter Paul Giovanni), of N.Y.	20

G

354. Gagarin, Sergei, Prince, of N.Y.	793
355. Gage, Hon. Thomas, of Mass.	110

The Royal Descents of 900 Immigrants

356. Gale, George, of Va. and Md.	787
357. Galitzine, Nicolas, Prince, of Ill.	793
358. Gallatin, (Abraham Alphonse) Albert, of N.Y.	912
359. Gantt (Wight), Mrs. Anne Fielder/Feilder, of Md.	603
360. Garrigue, Rudolph Pierre, of N.Y.	635
361. Gerard, Thomas, of Md.	558
362. Gergen, Mrs. Anne Elizabeth Wilson, of Mass.	232
363. von (de) Gersdorff, Ernst Bruno, of Mass.	183
364. Gibbes, John, prob. of S.C.	779
365. Gibbes, Robert, governor of S.C.	779
366. Gibbes, Thomas, of S.C.	779
367. Gibbs, Robert, of Mass.	738
368. Giddings, Mrs. Jane Lawrence, of Mass.	888
369. Gielgud, Sir (Arthur) John, sometime of N.Y. and Calif.	803
370. Gignilliat, Jean François, of S.C.	873
371. Gill, Mrs. Mary Mainwaring, prob. of Md.	558
372. Glen, Mrs. Elizabeth Wilson, of S.C.	112
373. Glen, Mrs. Katherine Duncanson, of N.Y.	248
374. Goddard, William, of Mass.	526
375. Goforth (Oxley), Mrs. Anne Skipwith, of N.J.	409
376. Golding, Ephraim, of L.I., N.Y.	766
377. Golightly, Culcheth, of S.C.	366
378. Golitzin (Gallitzin), Prince Demetrius Augustine, of Md. and Pa.	798
379. Golitzin (Gallitzin), Maria Anna Charlotte Zita Elisabeth Regina Thérèse, Archduchess of Austria, of Ill.	800
380. Golitzin (Gallitzin), Prince Peter, of Ill.	800
381. von Gontard, Mrs. Susanne Schilling von Canstatt, of Mo.	57
382. Gordon, Thomas, of N.J.	250
383. Gorges, Lady Anne Bell (first wife of Sir Ferdinando)	838
384. Gorges, Lady Elizabeth Gorges (Courtenay) (Bligh) (fourth wife of Sir Ferdinando)	295
385. Gorges, Lady Elizabeth Gorges Smith (fifth wife of Sir Ferdinando)	307 457, 522
386. Gorges, Sir Ferdinando, founder and lord proprietor of Me.	295-96, 522

lxxxiv

The Royal Descents of 900 Immigrants

387. Gorges, Lady Mary Fulford Achims (second wife of Sir Ferdinando)	392
388. Gorsuch, Mrs. Anne Lovelace, of Md.	509
389. Gotherson (Hogben), Mrs. Dorothea Scott, of L.I., N.Y.	314
390. Graeme, Thomas, of Pa.	168
391. von Graffenried, Christoph(er), Baron, Landgrave of N.C.	832
392. de Gramont, Sanche Armand Gabriel (Ted Morgan), of N.Y.	49
393. Grant, Hugh (John Mungo), sometime of Calif.	66
394. de Grasse, François Joseph Paul, Count (also Marquis de Tilly), Revolutionary commander	616
395. Greene, Thomas, gov. of Md.	721
396. Gregor, Charles Russell (formerly McGregor), of N.Y.	146
397. Gregory, Henry, of Conn.	816
398. Griffin, Lady Christian Stuart, of Va.	155
399. Grove (Abernethy), Maria, Countess Cheremetoff (wife of Brandon Hambright Grove and Robert G. Abernethy), sometime of Washington, D.C.	7
400. Guest, Princess Caroline-Cécile-Alexandrine-Jeanne Murat, of Va.	83
401. Guest, Raymond Richard, of Va.	63
402. Guest, Winston Frederick Churchill, of N.Y.	63
403. Guillermo, Bernardo Frederico, of N.Y.	1
404. Guinness, Benjamin Seymour, sometime of N.Y.	481
405. Guinness, Mrs. Bridget Henrietta Frances Williams-Bulkeley, sometime of N.Y.	124
406. Guinness (Niarchos), Hon. Daphne Suzannah Diana Joan, of N.Y.	23
407. Guinness, Sir Kenelm Lee "Tim," 4th Bt., of Md.	308
408. Gwinnett, Button, president (governor) of Ga.	648
409. Gyllenhaal, Anders Leonard, of Ill.	662-63

H

410. Haig, Robert, of Ohio	285
411. Hallward, Reginald Michael Bloxam, of Calif.	362
412. Hamilton, Alexander, of Md.	270

The Royal Descents of 900 Immigrants

413. Hamilton, Alexander, of N.Y. 214
414. Hammarskjöld, Dag (Hjalmar Agne Carl) of N.Y. 51
415. Harbou, Fritz, of N.Y. 645
416. Hardy, Lady Elizabeth Tate, wife of Sir Charles
 Hardy, gov. of N.Y., admiral 346
417. Harleston, John, of S.C. 349
418. d'Harnoncourt, René, Count, of N.Y. 220, 895
419. Harriman, Hon. Pamela Beryl Digby Spencer-Churchill
 Hayward, of N.Y. and Washington, D.C. 67
420. Harrison, Benjamin, of Va. 496
421. Harte, Charles Edward, of Ohio 567
422. Hatton (Banks), Mrs. Margaret Domville, of Md. 560
423. Haugh, Mrs. Elizabeth Bulkeley Whittingham, of Mass. 747
424. Haugwitz-Hardenburg-Reventlow, Curt Henry
 Eberhard Erdmann George, Count, of N.Y. 44
425. de Havilland, Olivia (Mary), of Calif. 462
426. Hawes, Edmond, of Mass. 654
427. Haynes (Eaton), Mrs. Mabel Harlakenden, of Conn. 806-7
428. Henchman, Mrs. Sarah Woodward, of Mass. 647
429. Henckel von Donnersmarck, Christiane
 Asschenfeldt, Countess, of Calif. 37
430. Henckel von Donnersmarck, Count Florian
 (Maria Georg Christian), of Calif. 45
431. Henderson, Mrs. Berta von Bunsen, of Mass. 148
432. Heneage, Charles (second husband of Agnes
 Elizabeth Winona Leclerq Joy,
 Princess Salm-Salm, of Vt.) 30
433. Henry, John, of Va. 219
434. Henshaw, Joshua, of Mass. 397
435. Hepburn, Audrey, of Calif. (Mrs. Edda Kathleen
 van Heemstra Hepburn-Ruston Ferrer Dotti) 446
436. Herbert, Henry William ("Frank Forrester"), of N.Y. 76
437. Heron, Benjamin, of N.C. 732
438. Hesilrige, Sir Robert, 8th Bt., sometime of Mass. 901
439. Hess, Ludmilla Maria, Princess zu Schwarzenburg
 (wife of Carl Barton Hess), of N.Y. 11
440. Hilton (Hylton), Ralph, of N.Y. 106
441. de Hinojosa, Alexander, of N.Y. 447
442. Hoar (Usher), Mrs. Bridget Lisle, of Mass. 297

The Royal Descents of 900 Immigrants

443. Hoffman, Willem Johan (William J.), of N.Y.	734
444. Home, George, of Va.	90
445. Homes, Mrs. Catherine Craighead, of Mass.	87
446. Hone, Theophilus, of Va.	730
447. Hooke, Mrs. Jane Whalley, sometime of Mass. and Conn.	781
448. Hopkins, Mrs. Anne Yale, of Conn.	658
449. Horsmanden, Warham, of Va.	348
450. Houston, Sir Patrick, 5th Bt., of Ga.	156
451. Howard, Cecil DeBlaquiere, of N.Y.	109
452. Howard, George, of Washington, D.C.	127
453. Howard of Effingham, Francis Howard, 5th Baron, governor of Va.	605
454. Howard of Effingham, Lady Philadelphia Pelham, Baroness (husband governor of Va.)	350
455. Howard of Effingham, Lady Susan Felton (Harbord), Baroness (husband governor of Va.)	150 350
456. Howe, George Augustus, 3rd Viscount, French and Indian War commander	432
457. Howell, Edward, of L.I., N.Y.	643
458. Hoyningen-Huene, Armin Hoyer, Baron ("Peter Berlin"), of Calif.	850
459. Hubbard, Mrs. Judith Knapp, of Mass.	682
460. Hughes (Hugh, Pugh), John, of Pa.	659
461. Humphrey(s), Daniel, of Pa.	510
462. Hunter, Robert, governor of N.Y.	214
463. Hussey, Thomas, sometime of Md.	739
464. Huston, Allegra, of Taos, N.M.	9
465. Huston, Jack Alexander, sometime of Calif.	65
466. Hutchinson, Mrs. Anne Marbury, of R.I.	478
467. Hutchinson, Mrs. Catherine Hamby, of Mass.	715
468. Huxley, Aldous Leonard, of Calif.	436
469. Hyde, Edward, proprietary gov. of N.C.	427
470. Hyrne, Mrs. Elizabeth Massingberd, of S.C.	471

I

471. Ireland, John, of Md.	415
472. Ironmonger, Francis, of Va.	738
473. Ironmonger, William, of Va.	738

The Royal Descents of 900 Immigrants

474. Irvine, John, of Ga.	225
475. Isham, Henry, of Va.	710
476. (Bradshaw-) Isherwood, Christopher (William), of Calif.	549
477. Izard, Ralph, of S.C.	717

J

478. James, Rev. Thomas, of N.Y.	748
479. Jaquet, Mrs. Maria de Carpentier, of Del.	633
480. Jeffreys, Sir Herbert, governor of Va.	541
481. Jennings, Edmund, acting governor of Va.	607
482. Jernegan, Thomas, of Va.	489
483. Jerningham, Henry, of Md.	110
484. Johnson, Guy, of N.Y.	487, 488, 900
485. Johnson, Stanley Patrick, sometime of N.Y.	12
486. Johnson, Sir William, 1st Bt., of N.Y.	487, 900
487. Johnston, Charles, of N.Y.	111
488. Johnston, Mrs. Henrietta de Beaulieu Dering, of S.C. (first husband, Robert Dering)	430
489. Johnstone, Mrs. Euphan Scott, of N.J.	276
490. Jones, Mrs. Dorothy Walker, of Va.	706
491. Jones, Mrs. Jane Edward, of Pa.	651
492. Jones, John, of Mass.	340
493. Jones, Robert, of Pa.	809
494. Joplin(g), Ralph, of Va.	698
495. Josselyn, John, traveler to New England	852

K

496. Kaufholz, Friedrich George, of Ohio	450
497. Keith, Sir William, 4th Bt., governor of Pa. and Del.	223
498. Kemeys, William, of N.Y.	548
499. Kempe, Richard, secretary and acting governor of Va.	483-84
500. Kennedy, Archibald, of N.Y.	253
501. Kennedy, Vernon Hew Primrose Shaw, of Ill.	129
502. Kinloch, James, of S.C.	92
503. Knollys, Mrs. Anne Cheney, sometime of Mass.	667
504. Kravchenko, Anna, Princess Galitzine (wife of	

Sergei Kravchenko), of Mass. 799
505. Kyrle, Lady Mary Jephson, of S.C. 428
506. Kyrle, Sir Richard, governor of S.C. 466

L

507. La Fayette (Lafayette), Marie-Adrienne-Françoise de Noailles Motier, Marquise de 288
508. La Fayette (Lafayette), Marie-Joseph-Paul-Yves-Roch-Gilbert Motier, Marquis de, Revolutionary commander 201, 203
509. Lagerfelt, Caroline (Eugénie, Baroness von), of N.Y. 453
510. Lane, Sir Ralph, of Va. 368
511. Lang, Mrs. Thea von Harbou Klein-Rogge, wife of Fritz Lang, long of Calif. 645
512. Lannes de Montebello, Guy Philippe, of N.Y. 227
513. Law, Thomas, of Va. 363
514. Lawford, Peter (Sydney Ernest), of Calif. 564
515. Lawrence, John, of N.Y. 881
516. Lawrence, Thomas, of N.Y. 881
517. Lawrence, William, of N.Y. 881
518. Lawson, Christopher, of Mass. 708
519. Lechmere, Thomas, of Mass. 396
520. Lee, Charles, Revolutionary general 235
521. Leete, William, gov. of Conn. 854
522. Levis, Samuel, of Pa. 384
523. Lewenhaupt, Count Eric Emil Audley, of Calif. 893
524. Lewenhaupt, Countess Hedvig Margaretha, of Calif. 890
525. Lewis, Mrs. Elizabeth Marshall, of Me. 630
526. Lewis, Ellis, of Pa. 230
527. Lewis, Thomas, of Me. 886
528. Lightfoot, John, of Va. 329
529. Lightfoot, Philip, of Va. 329
530. Ligon (Lygon), Col. Thomas, of Va. 295
531. Lillie, Beatrice Gladys "Bea", of N.Y. (husband, Sir Robert Peel, 5th Bt.) 67
532. Limerick, Thomas Dongan, 2nd Earl of, gov. of N.Y. 486-87
533. Lindsay, Rev. David, of Va. 282
534. Lippe-Biesterfeld, (Ernst) Aschwin (Georg Carol Ignatz), Prince of, of N.Y. 47

The Royal Descents of 900 Immigrants

535. Littleton, Nathaniel, of Va.	233
536. Livingston, Robert, the elder, of N.Y.	243
537. Livingston, Robert, the younger, of N.Y.	244
538. Lloyd, Mrs. Mary Jones, of Pa.	233
539. Lloyd, Thomas, deputy governor of Pa.	231
540. Lobkowicz, Maximilian Erwin Maria Joseph Antonius von Padua Heinrich Thomas, Prince	19
541. Loder, John (William John Muir Lowe) (husband of Hedy Lamarr), sometime of Calif.	78
542. Logan, James, of Pa.	279
543. Loudoun, John Campbell, 4th Earl of, French and Indian War commander	143
544. Lourie, (Countess) Elisabeth Belevsky-Zhukovsky Perevostchikov, of N.Y.	5
545. Lovelace, Lady Charlotte Clayton Lovelace, Baroness, of N.Y.	543
546. Lovelace, Francis, governor of N.Y.	509
547. Lovelace, John Lovelace, 4th Baron, governor of N.Y.	781
548. Lovell, Mrs. Penelope Eleanore Elphinstone-Dalrymple Balston, of Mass.	128
549. Lowe, Henry, of Md.	512
550. Lowe, Nicholas, of Md.	512
551. Lowell, Lady Caroline Maureen Hamilton-Temple-Blackwood Freud Citkowitz, of N.Y.	31
552. Lowell, Percival, of Mass.	569
553. Lowndes, Charles, of S.C.	752
554. Lowndes, Christopher, of Md.	752-53
555. Lowndes, Mary Elizabeth, of Conn.	753
556. Lubomirski, Alexi(s) (Jean), Prince, of N.Y.	622
557. Ludlow, Gabriel, of N.Y.	504
558. Ludlow, Roger, of Mass. and Conn. (dep. gov. of Mass.)	503
559. Ludwell, Philip, of Va.	856
560. Lunsford, Sir Thomas, of Va.	551
561. Lynch Zavaleta, Francisco de Paula Eustaquio ("Frank E."), sometime of Calif.	996-97
562. Lynde, Simon, of Mass.	749
563. Lyster, Rev. William Narcissus, of Mich.	433

564. Lyttelton, William Henry Lyttelton, 1st Baron,
gov. of S.C. and Jamaica — 315

M

565. Mackay, George, of Washington, D.C. — 82
566. Mackintosh (McIntosh), Col. Henry, of Mass. and R.I. — 239
567. Mackintosh (McIntosh), John Mohr, of Ga. — 239
568. Mackintosh (McIntosh), Lachlan, of R.I. — 239
569. MacLean (McLean), Allan, of Conn. — 213
570. MacLean (McLean), John, of N.J. — 249
571. MacLean (McLean), Neil, of Conn. — 213
572. McLeod (MacLeod), Alexander, of N.Y. — 249
573. Magan, Percy Tilson, Jr., of Calif. — 120
574. Magruder (McGruder), Alexander, of Md. — 280
575. Mahon, George Charles, of Mich. — 364
576. Mahon, Mrs. Sarah L'Estrange, of Mich. — 434
577. Mailer (Cram), Lady Jeanne Louise Campbell,
of N.Y. and S.C. — 70
578. Mainwaring, Oliver, of Conn. — 400
579. Maitland, James William, of N.Y. — 161-62
580. Mallory, Roger, of Va. — 668
581. Markham, William, of Mass. — 656
582. Martin, Henry Austin, of Mass. — 144
583. Martineau, Harriet, traveler in the U.S. — 379
584. (Tufton alias) Mason, Mrs. Elizabeth Taylor, of N.H. — 537
585. Massey (Sebright), Mrs. Margery Hill Fremantle
(wife of Raymond Hart Massey), of Calif. — 341
586. Mather, Mrs. Margaret Wade Linton, of Conn. — 540
587. Mauduit, William, of Md. — 563
588. Maverick, Mrs. Mary Gye, of Mass. — 632
589. McAdam, John Loudon, sometime of N.Y. — 128
590. McEwen, John William, of Me. — 146
591. McKay, George Alexander, of Mass. — 217
592. McNeill, Mrs. Grizel Campbell, of N.C. — 263
593. Meade, Mrs. Henrietta Constantia Worsam, of Pa. — 385
594. Mellon, Mrs. Vivian Rüesch, of N.Y. — 190
595. Mellowes, Mrs. Martha Bulkeley, of Mass. — 747
596. Mercer, Hugh, of Va. — 276
597. Middleton, Mrs. Mary Helen Hering, of S.C. — 324

The Royal Descents of 900 Immigrants

598. Middleton, Lady Mary Mackenzie Clarke Drayton Ainslie, of S.C.   92
599. Miles, Mrs. Ada Elinor Harte, of Ill.   567
600. Miryazantz, Alexandra, Princess of Greece and Denmark, sometimes of N.Y. (wife of Nicholas Miryazantz)   3
601. Mitford (Romilly Treuhaft), Hon. Jessica Lucy, of Calif.   23
602. Monckton, Hon. Robert, governor of N.Y.   119
603. Montagu, Lord Charles Greville, governor of S.C.   135
604. Monteith, Thomas, of Va.   171, 258
605. Montgomery, Mrs. Isabel Burnett, of N.J.   250
606. Montgomery, William, of N.J.   269
607. Montrésor, Mrs. Frances Tucker, of N.Y.   464
608. Montrésor, Mrs. Henrietta Fielding (husband of N.Y.)   368
609. Moody, Lady Deborah Dunch, of N.Y.   738
610. Moore, Lady Catherine Maria Long, of N.Y.   346
611. Moore, Mrs. Katherine Selwood, of S.C.   742
612. Morawetz, Mrs. Cathleen Synge, of N.Y.   254
613. More, Richard, of Mass., *Mayflower* passenger   319
614. Morgan, Mrs. Anne Tucker, of S.C.   463
615. Morgan, John, of Pa.   555
616. Morton, Rev. Charles, of Mass.   836
617. Moryson, Francis, deputy and acting governor of Va.   517
618. Mosle, Mrs. Caroline Durnford Dunscombe, of N.Y.   626
619. Mosle, George, of N.Y.   440
620. Munro, Rev. John, of Va.   260
621. Murray, Mrs. Barbara Bennett, of N.C.   210
622. Murray, James, of N.C. and Mass.   210
623. Murray, John Boyles, of N.Y.   210

N

624. Nabokov, Vladimir, sometime of N.Y.   618
625. Neale, James, of Md.   875
626. Need, Joseph, of Pa.   384
627. Negroponte, Mrs. Diana Villiers, of Washington, D.C.   122
628. Negus, Mrs. Jane Deighton Lugg, of Mass.   297
629. Nelson, John, of Mass.   355
630. Nelson, Philip, of Mass.   126
631. Nelson, Thomas (Jr.), of Mass.   126

632. Nichols, Richard, governor of N.Y. 456
633. Nicola, Louis, of Pa. 736
634. Niven, Mrs. Primula Susan Rollo, of Calif. 70
635. de Noailles, Anne-Jeanne-Baptiste-Pauline-Adrienne-Louise-Catherine-Dominique de Noailles, Vicomtesse 288
636. de Noailles, Louis-Marie de Noailles, Vicomte, Revolutionary soldier 288
637. Norris, Rev. Edward, of Mass. 492
638. Norton, John, of Va. 467
639. Norwood, Henry, of Va. 296
640. Nott, Edward, governor of Va. 335
641. Nott, Mrs. Margaret Blakiston, of Va. 317
642. Nourse, James, of Pa. 123
643. Nowell, Increase, secretary of Mass. 701

O

644. Obolensky (-Neledinsky-Meletzky), Sergei, Prince, of N.Y. and Mich. 799-800
645. O'Con(n)or, Thomas, of N.Y. 885
646. Ogilvy, David Mackenzie, of N.Y. 97
647. Ogle, Samuel, governor of Md. (and his wife) 327-28
648. Oglethorpe, James Edward, of Ga. 613
649. Orr, John, of Va. 173
650. Osborne, Sir Danvers, 3rd Bt., gov. of N.Y. 346
651. Osborne, Lady Mary Montagu (husband gov. of N.Y.) 105
652. Otis, Mrs. Rose Stoughton, of N.H. 945
653. Otto, Mrs. Hilda Margaret Rose Thomas, of Calif. 321
654. Owen, Mrs. Jane Vaughan, of Pa. 229
655. Owen, Joshua, of N.J. 510
656. Owen, Mrs. Rebecca Owen, of Pa. 510
657. Owen, Robert, of Pa. (husband of Jane Vaughan) 770
658. Owen, Robert, of Pa. (husband of Rebecca Owen) 615
659. Owsley, Thomas, of Va. 423
660. Oxenberg, Catherine, of N.Y. 3
661. Oxenbridge, Mrs. Frances Woodward (husband of Mass.) 647
662. Oxenbridge, Rev. John, of Mass. 324

The Royal Descents of 900 Immigrants

P

663. von Pagenhardt, Maximilian Hugo, Baron, of Washington, D.C.	13
664. Palgrave, Dr. Richard, of Mass.	571
665. Palmes (Myles), Mrs. Anne Humphrey, of Mass.	301
666. Palmes, Edward, of Conn.	501
667. Parke, Mrs. Alice Freeman Thompson, of Mass. and prob. Conn.	858
668. Parsons, Mrs. Audrey Divett Buller, of R.I.	305
669. Pelham, Mrs. Elizabeth Bosvile Harlakenden, of Mass.	339
670. Pelham, Herbert, of Mass., first treasurer of Harvard College	301
671. Pelham, Mrs. Jemima Waldegrave (husband of Mass.)	661
672. Pellew, Henry Edward (6th Viscount Exmouth, a title never assumed), of N.Y. (and Washington, D.C.)	865
673. Penhallow, Samuel, of N.H.	836
674. Penn, Lady Juliana Fermor (husband proprietor of Pa.)	226
675. Penn-Gaskell, Peter, of Pa.	149
676. Percy, Hon. George, governor of Va.	418
677. Perkins, Mrs. Mary Frances Baker Wilbraham, of Mass.	120
678. Peter, Robert, of Md.	170
679. Peter(s), Mrs. Deliverance Sheffield, of Mass.	577
680. Peter(s), Rev. Hugh, of Mass.	665
681. Peter(s), Rev. Thomas, sometime of Conn.	665
682. Peyton, Robert, of Va.	360
683. Pierrefeu, Alain Dedons, Count de, of Mass.	185
684. Pitcairn, John, British commander at Lexington	215
685. Plater-Zyberk, Maria Malgarzata Paulina Wilhelmina Róza Leopoldyna Julia Wielopolska, Countess, of Pa.	11
686. de Polignac, Camille Armand Jules Marie, Prince, of the Confederacy	289
687. Pomeroy, George (Holmes), of Pa.	594
688. Poole, Mrs. Jane Greene, of Mass.	743
689. Poole, William, of Mass.	337
690. Popham, George, of Me.	337
691. Pordage, George, of Mass.	357

692. Pound, Mrs. Dorothy Shakespear, sometime
of Washington, D.C.   131
693. Pownall, Mrs. Harriet Churchill Fawkener, of Mass.   536
694. Prather, Thomas, of Va.   695
695. Pryce-Jones, Alan Payan, of R.I.   73
696. Pynchon, Mrs. Amy Wyllys, of Mass.   533
697. Pyne, John, of S.C.   744
698. Pyne, Thomas, of N.Y.   744

R

699. Radziwill, Stanislaus Albert, Prince, of N.Y.   16-17
700. Randolph, Henry, of Va.   387
701. Randolph, William, of Va.   387
702. Rantoul, Mrs. Matilda Charlotte Palgrave
Chetwynd-Talbot, of Mass.   137
703. Raynsford, Edward, of Mass.   625
704. Reade, Col. George, of Va.   310
705. Redgrave (Clark), (Mrs.) Lynn (Rachel),
sometime of Conn.   246
706. Richardson (Fox Neeson), Mrs. Natasha,
sometime of N.Y.   246
707. Richardson, Muriel Florence Forbes-Robertson,
Lady (wife of Sir Ralph Richardson),
sometime of N.Y. and Calif.   268
708. Ritchie, Guy Stuart, sometime of N.Y. or Calif.
(husband of Madonna [Louise Veronica]
Ciccone)   63
709. Rivers, Mrs. Elizabeth Mallory, of S.C.   847
710. Roberdeau, Daniel, of Pa.   244
711. Roberts, Mrs. Gainor Roberts, of (Pencoyd) Pa.   660
712. Roberts, Hugh, of Pa.   660
713. Roberts, Mrs. Jane Owen, of Pa.   651
714. Roberts, John, of (Pencoyd) Pa.   692
715. Roberts, Mrs. Sidney Rees, of Pa.   809
716. Robinson, Douglas, of N.Y.   163-64
[Robinson, Isaac, of Mass.]   917
717. de Rochambeau, Jean Baptiste Donatien de Vimeur,
Count, Revolutionary commander   455
718. Rodes, Charles, of Va.   343

The Royal Descents of 900 Immigrants

719. Rodney, William, of Del. and Pa. — 307
720. Romanoff, Andrew, Grand Duke of Russia, of Calif. — 5
721. Romanoff, Nikita, Grand Duke of Russia, of N.Y. — 5
722. Romanoff, Rostislav, Grand Duke of Russia, sometime of Ill. — 5
723. Romanovsky-Ilyinski, Paul, Prince [Paul R. Ilyinski], sometime of Fla. — 4
724. Roosevelt, Mrs. Lydia M. Latrobe, of N.Y. — 590
725. Rose, Rev. Robert, of Va. — 261
726. Ross, Mrs. Alicia Arnold, of Md. — 333
727. Ross, Rev. George, of Del. — 828
728. Roy (Vidmer), Mrs. Elizabeth Brooke, of Fla. — 137
729. Rozier, Mrs. Elizabeth Whetenhall, of Md. — 905
730. Rudyard, Thomas, deputy governor of East Jersey — 407
731. Russell, Archibald, of N.Y. — 165
732. Ruspoli, Bartolomeo, of Calif. — 21
733. Ruspoli, Tao, of Calif. — 21
734. Russell (Burgos Roubanis), Lady Sarah Cornelia Spencer-Churchill, sometime of Pa. and N.Y. — 27
735. Rutherford, Walter, of N.Y. — 211

S

736. St. George, George Baker Bligh, of N.Y. — 265
737. Salm-Salm, Prince Felix Constantin Nepomuk (first husband of Agnes Elizabeth Winona Leclerq Joy, Princess Salm-Salm, of Vt.) — 38
738. Saltonstall, Mrs. Muriel Gurdon, of Mass. — 353
739. Saltonstall, Richard, of Mass. — 374
740. Sanders, Mrs. Lillian May Caulfield, of Pa. — 308
741. Sandys, George, treasurer of Va. — 783
742. Sarg, Anthony Frederick "Tony," of N.Y. — 116
743. Sargent, Rev. William, of Mass. — 857
744. Savage, Anthony, of Va. — 532
745. Schenkenberg (van Mierop), Marcus (Lodewijk), sometime of Calif. — 908
746. de Schweinitz, Amalie Joanna Lydia von Tschirschky und Bögendorff, of Pa. — 183
747. von Schweinitz, Anna Dorothea Elizabeth (Baroness) von Watteville, of Pa. — 196

748. Scott, Mrs. Elizabeth Hussey, of Mass. 739
749. Scott, John, of N.Y. 211
750. Scott, Mrs. Katherine Marbury, of R.I. 478
751. Seton, Mrs. Margaret Seton, of N.Y. 222
752. Seton, William, of N.Y. 222
753. Sewall, Henry, secretary of Md. 819
754. Seymour, Mrs. Hester Newton, of Md. 413
755. Seymour, John, governor of Md. 598
756. Shedden, Mrs. Matilda Cecilia Dowdall, of N.J. 487, 900
757. Shepard, Mrs. Margaret Estouteville/Touteville, of Mass. 393
758. Sherman, Mrs. Mary Launce, of Mass. 395
759. Sherwin, Mrs. Elizabeth Pride Gibbs, of N.C. 103
760. Shields (Slater), Mrs. Marina Torlonia, of N.Y. 18
761. Shirley, William, governor of Mass. and the Bahamas 475
762. Shute, Samuel, governor of Mass. 684
763. de Sibour, Jean Antonin Gabriel, Vicomte, of Washington, D.C. 639
764. Sinclair, Robert, of N.Y. 88
765. Skepper/Skipper, Rev. William, of Mass. 342
766. Skinner, Mrs. Anne Storer Truman, of Md. 628
767. Skipwith, Sir Grey, 3rd Bt., of Va. 470
[Smead, Mrs. Judith Stoughton Denman, of Mass.] 921
768. Smith, Lawrence, of Va. 701
769. Smith, Mrs. Maria Jo(h)anna Somerset Lowther, of Md. 109
770. Snelling, John, of Mass. 573
771. Snelling, William, of Mass. 835
772. Solms-Braunfels, Prince (Frederick William) Charles (Louis George Alfred Alexander), known as Prince Carl, of Tex. 40-41
773. Southill (Sothild, Sothill, Sotehill, Sothel), Seth, gov. of N.C. 359
774. Southworth, Constant, of Mass. 524
775. Southworth, Thomas, of Mass. 524
776. Spence, Keith, of N.H. 86
777. Spencer, Nicholas, act. gov. of Va. 306
778. Spotswood, Alexander, gov. of Va. 278

The Royal Descents of 900 Immigrants

779. Stanley (Curtis), (Lady) Dorothy Tennant (husband,
    Sir Henry Morton Stanley, long in U.S.)   130
780. Stephens, Mrs. Mary Newdigate (husband
    governor of Ga.)   517
781. Steuben, Friedrich Wilhelm Ludolf Gerhard Augustin,
    Baron von, Revolutionary commander   181
782. Stevenson, Robert Louis, sometime of N.Y. and Calif.   270
783. Stewart, William, of N.C.   264
784. Drummond-Stewart, Sir William (George), 7th Bt.,
    sometime of Mo. and points west   897
785. Stier, Henri Joseph, Seigneur of Aertselaer, of Md.   804-5
786. Stites, Mrs. Mary Underhill Naylor, of N.Y.   875
787. Stock, Mrs. Jane Adams, of Idaho (under Thomas
    Owsley)   424
788. Stockman, John, of Mass.   476
789. Storer, Arthur, of Md.   628
    [Stoughton, Israel, of Mass.]   920-21
    [Stoughton, Thomas, of Mass.]   920
790. Strachey, John, of Va.   825
791. Strachey, William, first Secretary of the
    Virginia Colony   852
792. Strachey, William, of Va.   852
793. Strachwitz von Gross Zauche und Camminetz,
    Alexander Maria Hubertus Hyacinthus,
    Count, of Calif.   39
794. Stratton, Mrs. Anne Derehaugh, of Mass.   661-62
795. Stratton, John, of Mass.   661, 706
796. Strother, William, of Va.   421
797. Stuart-Menteth, Thomas Loughnan, of N.Y.   79
798. Summersby, Kay (Mrs. Kathleen Helen McCarthy-
    Morrogh Summersby Morgan), of N.Y.   546
799. Swain, Esaias Reinhold (originally Slettengren),
    of Mass.   53
800. Swinton (Byrne), (Mrs. Katherine Matilda) "Tilda,"
    of Calif.   177
801. Sydnor, Fortunatus, of Va.   490
802. Symes, George, of Va.   357
803. Szápáry, Anton Carl Sylvester, Count, sometime
    of Newport, R.I.   35

The Royal Descents of 900 Immigrants

804. Széchényi, Count Ladislaus (Laszló), of Newport, R.I.	209

T

805. Talbot, Mrs. Isabel Jenney (husband of N.J.)	489
806. Talbot, Rev. John, of N.J.	711
807. Talbot, Peter (George, Jr.), of Mass.	841
808. Taylor, Humphrey (John Fausett), of N.Y.	593
809. Taylor, James, of Mass.	670
810. Tazewell, William, of Va.	310
811. Teackle, Mrs. Margaret Nelson, of Va.	356
812. Teller, Mrs. Margaret Duncanson, of N.Y.	248
813. von Tempski, Mrs. Amy Dulcibella Wodehouse, of Hawaii	131
814. Tennent, Mrs. Catherine Kennedy, of Pa.	898
815. Thomas, Mrs. Anna Lloyd Braithwaite, of Md.	231
816. Thomas, Sir George, 1st Bt., governor of Pa. and Del.	714
817. Thompson, Stephens/Stevens, atty. gen. of Va.	322
818. Thornborough/Thornburgh, Edward, of Pa.	902
819. Thornborough/Thornburgh, Thomas, of Va.	909
820. Thorndike, Mrs. Elizabeth Stratton, of Mass.	661, 706
821. Throckmorton, John, of R.I.	508
822. Throckmorton, Robert, of Va.	720
823. Tilghman, Richard, of Md.	357
824. de Tocqueville, Alexis Henry de Clerel, traveler in the U.S.	294
825. Tolstoy, Alexandra, Countess, of N.Y.	794
826. Torrey, Mrs. Jane Haviland, of Mass.	351
827. Towneley, Lawrence, of Va.	701
828. Towneley, Richard, of N.J.	552
829. Traill, Robert, of N.H.	85
830. Traill, Robert, of Pa.	88
831. von Trapp, Agathe (Johanna Erwina Gobertina), of Vt. and Md.	187
832. von Trapp, Hedwig (Maria Adolphine Gobertina), of Vt.	187
833. von Trapp (Winter), Joanna Karolina, of N.Y.	187
834. von Trapp, Maria (Agathe) Franziska, of Vt.	187
835. von Trapp (Dupire), Martina, of Vt.	187

The Royal Descents of 900 Immigrants

836. von Trapp, Rupert (Georg), of Vt.	187
837. von Trapp, Werner, of Vt.	187
838. Treworgy, Mrs. Penelope Spencer, of Me., Mass., and Newfoundland	489
839. Trollope, Mrs. Frances Milton, traveler in the U.S.	320
840. Troubetskoy, Pierre, Prince, of Va.	194
841. Troubetskoy, Sergei, Prince, sometime of Va. (husband of [Dorothy Livingston] Ulrich, [Princess] Troubetskoy)	793
842. Troubetskoy, Vladimir, Prince, of Wisc.	195
843. Trowbridge, Thomas, of Conn.	870
844. Tryon, William, gov. of N.C. and N.Y.	134
845. Tucker, Henry, of Va.	463
846. Tucker, St. George, of Va.	464
847. Tyng, Mrs. Elizabeth Coytmore, of Mass.	375
848. Tytler, James, of Mass.	159

U

849. Uggla, Carl Magnus Helmfried, of N.Y.	458
850. Umfreville/Humphreville, John, of Conn.	843
851. Underhill, Humphrey, of N.Y.	875
852. Underwood, Mrs. Mary Butler, of Va.	674

V

853. Vane, Lady Frances Wray (husband gov. of Mass.)	115
854. Vane, Sir Henry, gov. of Mass.	315
855. van Hoogstraten, Jan Samuel François, of N.Y.	460
856. van Tuyl, Jan Otten, of N.Y.	776
857. Veatch, James, of Md.	241
858. Viereck, (Franz Georg Edwin) Louis (Withold), of N.Y.	16
859. Villiers, James Michael Hyde, briefly of N.Y.	125

W

860. Walker, Lady Margaret Gwendolen Mary Drummond, of Washington, D.C.	72
861. Wallace, John, of Pa.	152
862. Wallop, Hon. Oliver Malcolm, of Wyo.	77
863. Ward (Brown), Rachel (Claire), of Calif.	33

The Royal Descents of 900 Immigrants

864. Ward (Sheed), (Mrs.) Mary Josephine "Maisie," of N.Y.   71
865. Warner, Mrs. Mary Towneley, of Va.   700
866. Warren, Sir Peter, of N.Y.   487, 900
867. Warren, Thomas, of Va.   778
868. Washington, John, of Surry Co., Va.   515
869. Washington, John, of Westmoreland Co., Va.   515
870. Washington, Lawrence, of Va.   515
871. Watkinson, Mrs. Sarah Blair, of Conn.   150
872. Waugh, Alexander Robin "Alec," sometime of N.Y. and Fla.   402
873. Wedgwood, Josiah Ralph Patrick, of Seattle, Wash.   117
874. Wentworth, Thomas, of Va.   821
875. Wentworth, William, of N.H.   708
876. West, Anthony, of N.Y.   406
877. West, Hon. Francis, gov. of Va.   300
878. West, Hon. John, gov. of Va.   300
879. Weston, Thomas, of Mass.   723
880. Whalley, Edward, of Mass. and Conn., regicide   781
881. Whitaker, Rev. Alexander, of Va.   701
882. Whitaker, Jabez, of Va.   701
883. Whitaker, Mrs. Mary Bourchier, of Va.   354
884. Whitehead, Mrs. Evelyn Ada Maud Rice Willoughby-Wade, of Mass.   535
885. Whiting, Mrs. Elizabeth St. John, of Mass.   747
886. Wiggin, Frederick, of N.Y.   111
887. Williams, Mrs. Frances Baldwin Townshend Jones, of Va.   727
888. Williams, Mrs. Frances Deighton, of Mass.   297
889. Williams, John, of Pa.   693
890. Willing, Charles, of Pa.   411
891. Willing, Mrs. Elizabeth Hannah Carrington, of Pa.   557
892. Willis, Mrs. Anne Rich, of Va.   838
893. Wilson, Mrs. Elizabeth Mansfield, of Mass.   318
894. Wilson, Leighton, of Ga.   138
895. Wingfield, Edward Maria, of Va.   565
896. Wingfield, Thomas, of Va.   307
897. Winthrop, Mrs. Margaret Tyndal, of Mass.   713-14
898. Winthrop, Mrs. Thomasine Clopton (husband of Mass.)   483

The Royal Descents of 900 Immigrants

899. Wintour (Shaffer), Anna, Dame, of N.Y.	117
900. Wiseman, Mrs. Anna Capell, prob. of Md.	121
901. Wiseman, Robert, of Md.	484
902. Wodehouse, Ernest Hay, of Hawaii	131
903. Wodehouse, Sir Pelham Grenville (P.G.), sometime of N.Y.	335
904. Woodhouse, Henry, of Va.	846
905. Woodhull (Blood Martin), Mrs. Victoria Claflin, of N.Y. (third husband, John Biddulph Martin)	138
906. Woolley, Emmanuel, of R.I.	528
907. Worden, Peter, of Mass.	702
908. Wright (Phiquepal-Arusmont), Mrs. Frances "Fanny," of Tenn., Ohio, and N.Y.	390
909. Wright, Richard, of Va.	785
910. Wright, Robert, of S.C.	350
911. Wyatt, Mrs. Barbara Mitford, of Va.	425
912. Wyatt, Sir Francis, governor of Va.	314
913. Wyatt, Rev. Hawte, of Va.	314
914. Wyatt, Lady Margaret Sandys, of Va.	783
915. Wyche, Henry, of Va.	837
916. Wyndham/Windham, Edward, of Va.	385

Y

917. Yale, David, of Conn.	657
918. Yale, Thomas, of Conn.	657
919. Yarnall, Francis, of Pa.	553
920. Yarnall, Philip, of Pa.	553
921. Yate, George, of Md.	625
922. Yates, John, of Va.	361
923. Yonge, Francis, chief justice of S.C.	476
924. Yonge, Robert, of S.C.	311

Z

925. Zinzendorf and Pottendorf, Nicholas Ludwig, Count of, American resident 1741-43	237

The Royal Descents of 900 Immigrants

45 French-Canadian Immigrants of Royal Descent, both (i) France to Québec or Acadia, and (ii) Québec to the United States

(i) France to Québec or Acadia

1. Michel **d'Aigneaux d'Ouville** (p. 956)
2. Jean-Vincent **l'Abbadie**, Baron de Saint-Castin (p. 963)
3. Charles-Joseph **d'Ailleboust**, Seigneur des Musseaux (p. 940)
4. Anne (Couvent) **Amiot**, wife of Philippe Amiot and Jacques Maheu; *see also* Couvent (p. 945)
5. Marie-Louise-Élisabeth (Bazin) **Amiot**, wife of Jean-Baptiste Amiot and Gabriel-Elzéar Taschereau; *see also* Bazin (p. 951)
6. Élisabeth (**d'Amours**) Chartier, wife of Louis-Théandre Chartier, Sieur de Lotbinière; *see also* Chartier (p. 955)
7. Mathieu **d'Amours**, Sieur de Chauffours (p. 954)
8. Catherine (**Baillon**) Miville, wife of Jacques Miville; *see also* Miville (p. 950)
   Marie-Louise-Élisabeth (**Bazin**) Amiot, wife of Jean-Baptiste Amiot and Gabriel-Elzéar Taschereau; *see also* Amiot (p. 951)
9. Pierre **Bazin** (p. 950)
10. John **Bradstreet** (p. 953)
    Élisabeth (d'Amours) **Chartier**, wife of Louis-Théandre Chartier, Sieur de Lotbinière; *see also* d'Amours (p. 955)
11. Anne-Élisabeth (de Tarragon) **Couturier** dit la Bonté, wife of Gilles Couturier de la Bonté; *see also* de Tarragon (p. 948)
    Anne (**Couvent**) Amiot, wife of Philippe Amiot and Jacques Maheu (p. 945); *see also* Amiot
12. Marie (Martin) **Février**, wife of Christophe Février (p. 940); *see also* Martin (p. 940)
13. Louis-Joseph de **Gannes de Falaise** (p. 964)
14. Jacques **Guéret** dit Dumont (p. 946)
15. Nicolas **Leblond** (p. 957)
16. Toussaint **Ledran** [le Dran] (p. 945)
17. Louis-Joseph **Legouès**, Seigneur de Grais (p. 962)
18. Léon **Levrault**, Sieur de Langis (p. 941)
19. Jeanne (**Le Marchand**) Le Neuf, wife of Mathieu Le Neuf, Sieur du Hérisson (p. 959)

The Royal Descents of 900 Immigrants

Marie (**Martin**) Février, wife of Christophe Février; *see also* Février (p. 940)

20. Jeanne-Marie (Motin) (**de Menou**) Turgis de Saint-Étienne, wife of Charles de Menou, Seigneur d'Aulnay-Charnizay and of Charles-Amador Turgis de Saint-Étienne, both governors of Acadia; *see also* Motin and Turgis de Saint-Étienne (pp. 952, 953)

    Catherine (Baillon) **Miville**, wife of Jacques Miville; *see also* Baillon (p. 950)

    Jeanne-Marie (**Motin**) (de Menou) Turgis de Saint-Étienne; *see above and* Turgis de Saint-Étienne (pp. 952, 953)

    Jeanne (Le Marchand) **Le Neuf**, wife of Mathieu Le Neuf, Sieur du Hérisson (p. 959)

21. Pierre de **Saint-Ours**, Seigneur de Saint-Ours and Deschaillons (p. 965)

22. Julien-Charles **Sévigny** dit la Fleur (problematic) (p. 942)

    Anne-Élisabeth **de Tarragon**, wife of Gilles Couturier dit la Bonté; *see also* Couturier dit la Bonté (p. 948)

    Jeanne-Marie (Motin) (de Menou) **Turgis de Saint-Étienne**, wife of Charles de Menou, Seigneur d'Aulnay-Charnizay, and of Charles-Amador Turgis de Saint-Étienne, both governors of Acadia; *see also* de Menou and Motin (a royal descent has also been proposed for Charles-Amador Turgis de Saint-Étienne, but as noted on p. 953, I think further research may be required) (pp. 952, 953).

(ii) Québec to the United States

1. Louis J. **Bertrand** of Ill. (great-great-grandfather of Angelina Jolie) (p. 974)
2. Justin Drew **Bieber**, sometime of Calif. (p. 984)
3. Edward **Brisbois** of Mass. (great-grandfather of Donnie and Mark Wahlberg) (p. 976)
4. Godefroi **Brisson dit Tilly** of Mass. (ancestor of Chloë Sevigny) (p. 989)

5-6. François **Chrétien**, and his wife Mrs. Olivine **Laforme** Chrétien, both sometime of N.H. (grandparents of [Joseph-Jacques-] Jean Chrétien) (p. 970)

7. Jean-Baptiste **d'Amours de Louvières** of Louisiana (ancestor of Beyoncé [Giselle] Knowles) (p. 990)

The Royal Descents of 900 Immigrants

8. Eustache **Demers** (VI) of Mich. (great-great-grandfather of Madonna [Ciccone]) (p. 975)

   Céline-Marie-Claudette **Dion**, sometime of Nevada (fully treated herein but not added to this count since she lives in Nevada largely when performing in Las Vegas) (p. 977)
9. Narcisse ("Nelson") **Fortin**, of Mich. (great-grandfather of Madonna) (p. 988)
10. Nazaire ("Henry") **Fortin**, of Mich. (great-great-grandfather of Madonna) (p. 988)
11. Eric **Gagné** of Mass. (p. 982)
12. Ryan [Thomas] **Gosling** of Calif. (p. 979)
13. Joseph-Georges-André **Goulet** of Mass. (father of Robert Goulet) (p. 973)
14. Mrs. Marie (Bourassa) **Gravel** of Mass. (mother of U.S. Senator "Mike" Gravel (p. 972)
15. François-Xavier **Jean** of N.H. (great-grandfather of Jack Kerouac) (p. 971)
16. Léon-Alcide **Kerouac** of N.H. and Mass. (father of Jack Kerouac) (p. 971)
17. Mario **Lemieux** of Pa. (p. 981)
18. Mrs. Rose-Hermine (**Rose**) **Mercereau** of Mich. (great-great-grandmother of A.H. Vigneron, Archbishop of Detroit) (p. 983)
19. Alanis Nadine **Morrisette**, sometime of Calif. (p. 978)
20. Paul-Jean **Paquin**, sometime of Mass. (great-grandfather of Anna Paquin) (p. 980)
21. Joseph **Rose** of Mich. (great-great-grandfather of Archbishop A.H. Vigneron) (p. 983)
22. Jacques-Michel **Sarrazin** [Michael Sarrazin], sometime of Calif. (p. 987)
23. Joseph-Louis-Eugène **Theroux** of Mass. (grandfather and great-grandfather respectively of Paul Edward Theroux and Justin Paul Theroux) (p. 985)

When combined with the 925 immigrants in the preceding list, these 22 from France to Québec, and 23 from Québec to the U.S., total 970. Even if 70 descents herein—over 7 per cent of the 970—became problematic, the number in this book's title would still hold. The first chart in this section covers the descent from Anne (Couvent) Amiot to Prime Ministers Pierre Elliott Trudeau and his son Justin Pierre James Trudeau.

The Royal Descents of 900 Immigrants

Appendix III:
610 Major Historical Figures Who Appear on the Charts (sovereigns are included *only* if they appear at the center of the charts, or lower, not at the top)

1. Acheson, Dean Gooderham, pp. 364, 434
2. Adam, Robert, p. 219
3. Adams, Mrs. Abigail Smith, pp. 375, 393
4. Adams, John, Jr., pp. 375, 393
5. Adams, John Quincy, pp. 375, 393
6. Addington, Henry, 1st Viscount Sidmouth, P.M., p. 865
7. Agassi, Andre, p. 18
8. Alba, Fadrique Álvarez de Toledo, 3rd Duke of, p. 191
9. Albemarle, George Monck, 1st Duke of, pp. 103, 104
10. Albert II, King of the Belgians, pp. 142, 201, 204
11. Albert I (Honoré Charles Grimaldi), Sovereign Prince of Monaco, pp. 20, 933
12. Albert II (Alexandre Louis Pierre Grimaldi), Sovereign Prince of Monaco, p. 934
13. Albert, Prince of Saxe-Coburg-Gotha, Prince Consort of Great Britain, pp. 2, 45, 290
14. d'Albret, Jean, King of Navarre, p. 287, 293
15. Alexander I, King of Yugoslavia, p. 3
16. Alexander II, Czar of Russia, pp. 2, 3, 5, 799
17. Alexander III, Czar of Russia, p. 5
18. Alexander VI (Borgia), Pope, pp. 287, 293
19. Alexander Nevsky, Grand Prince of Kiev, p. 791
20. Alsop, Joseph Wright (V), p. 164
21. Alsop, Stewart (Johonnot Oliver), p. 164

The Royal Descents of 900 Immigrants

22. Annan, Kofi, p. 60
23. Anne, Queen of England (later Great Britain), pp. 300, 428, 539, 551, 588, 596
24. Anne (Elizabeth Alice Louise), Princess of Great Britain, the Princess Royal (formerly Mrs. Mark Anthony Peter Phillips, now Mrs. Timothy James Hamilton Laurence), p. 321
25. Armour, Philip Danforth, p. 794
26. Arnold, Matthew, p. 436
27. Arnold, Thomas, p. 436
28. Asher, Jane, p. 64
29. Asher, Peter, p. 64
30. Asquith, Herbert Henry, 1st Earl of Oxford and Asquith, p. 306
31. Astaire, Adele (Cavendish) (Douglas), Lady, p. 23, 26
32. Astaire, Fred, p. 26
33. Astor, John Jacob (IV), p. 799
34. Astor, Mrs. William (Backhouse, Jr.) (Mrs. Caroline Webster Schermerhorn Astor), pp. 44, 799
35. Astor, William Vincent, p. 66
36. Auberjonois, René (Murat), pp. 83, 635, 636
37. Auden, W.H. (Wystan Hugh), p. 404
38. Austen, Jane, p. 299
39. de Ayala, Sancha, Lady Blount (genealogical link), pp. 676, 709
40. Bacon, Francis, 1st Viscount St. Albans, pp. 684, 846
41. Bacon, Nathaniel, gov. of Va., rebel, p. 494
42. Bacon, Sir Nicholas, Lord Chancellor, pp. 684, 846, 877
43. Baliol, John, King of Scotland, p. 780
44. Baltimore, George Calvert, 1st Baron, p. 739
45. Barclay, Robert, Quaker apologist, pp. 148, 256

The Royal Descents of 900 Immigrants

46. Barry, John (Jonathan Barry Prendergast), pp. 27, 28
47. Beaverbrook, William Maxwell Aitken, 1st Baron, pp. 69, 371
48. Beckford, William (Jr.), p. 933
49. Belmont, August, p. 174
50. von Below, (Anton) George Hugo, p. 224
51. Berkeley, Sir William, gov. of Va., pp. 296, 347, 839
52. Berners-Lee, (Sir Timothy) "Tim" (John), p. 520
53. Berthier, Louis-Alexandre, Prince of Neuchâtel and Wagram, p. 83
54. Birkin, Jane, pp. 27, 28
55. Bischoffsheim, Maurice Jonathan, p. 227
56. Bland, Dorothy, Mrs. Jordan, mistress of William IV, King of Great Britain, p. 9
57. Blavatsky, Mrs. Helena Petrovna Hahn, later Betanelly (Madame), pp. 792, 795
58. Blennerhasset, Harmon (and his wife), pp. 144, 325

Blount, see also (de) Ayala

59. Blount, Elizabeth, mistress of Henry VIII, King of England, later Baroness Talboys and Countess of Lincoln, pp. 324, 405, 417, 462, 501, 503
60. Boleyn, Anne, Queen of England, pp. 300, 428, 539, 551, 588, 596
61. Boleyn, Mary, mistress of Henry VIII, King of England, pp. 300, 303
62. Bonaparte, Charles-Joseph, p. 858
63. Bonaparte, Jérôme, King of Westphalia, p. 858
64. Bonaparte, Joseph, King of Spain, p. 83
65. Bonham Carter, Helena, pp. 306, 309
66. Booth, William, founder of the Salvation Army, p. 464
67. de Borchgrave (d'Altena), Arnaud [Charles Paul Marie Philippe], Count, p. 112

The Royal Descents of 900 Immigrants

68. Borghese, Princess Marcella (Fazi), p. 24
69. Borgia, Cesare, Duc de Valentinois, pp. 287, 293
70. Borgia, Lucrezia, Duchess of Modena and Ferrara, pp. 287, 293
71. Bosanquet, Bernard, p. 335
72. Boswell, James, pp. 90, 150
73. Bowdoin, James, p. 923
74. Boyle, Kay, p. 15
75. Bradlee, Ben(jamin Crowninshield), p. 183
76. Bradstreet, Mrs. Anne Dudley, pp. 370, 371
77. Brahe, Tyge/Tycho, p. 646
78. von Braun, Wernher (Magnus Maximilian, Baron), pp. 59, 224
79. Brent, Margaret, pp. 331, 357, 429
80. Breyer, Stephen Gerald, p. 81
81. Brienne, John de, King of Jerusalem, Emperor of Constantinople, pp. 647, 909, 943
82. Bronfman, Edgar Miles, Jr., p. 9
83. Brooke, Sir Charles Vyner, H.H. the last Rajah of Sarawak, p. 137
84. Browne, Robert, the separatist, pp. 491, 730, 731
85. Browning, (Mrs.) Elizabeth Barrett, p. 355
86. Browning, Robert, p. 355
87. Bruce, David Kirkpatrick Este, pp. 100, 190
88. Brundage, Avery, p. 8
89. Brynner, Yul, p. 227
90. Buchanan, James, Jr., pp. 245, 247
91. Buckingham, George Villiers, 1st Duke of, pp. 430, 536
92. Bulkeley, Rev. Peter, pp. 574, 702, 746
93. von Bülow, Claus (Claus Cecil Borberg, later von Bülow), p. 645

The Royal Descents of 900 Immigrants

94. Burghley, William Cecil, 1st Baron, pp. 315, 345, 470, 554, 684
95. Burnet, Gilbert, Bishop of Salisbury, p. 273
96. Burroughs, Rev. George, witchcraft victim, p. 484
97. Busch, Adolphus, pp. 57, 136
98. Busch, August ("Gussie") Anheuser, Jr., p. 57
99. Bush, Mrs. Barbara Pierce, pp. 243, 474, 479, 572, 585, 688, 703, 716, 729, 747, 769
100. Bush, George Herbert Walker, 41st U.S. President, pp. 243, 474, 479, 572, 585, 688, 703, 716, 729, 747, 769
101. Bush, George Walker, 43rd U.S. President, pp. 243, 244, 474, 479, 572, 585, 688, 703, 716, 729, 747, 769, 833, 923
102. Bush, Mrs. Laura Lane Welch, pp. 243, 474, 479, 572, 585, 688, 703, 716, 729, 747, 769, 833, 834
103. Bute, James Stuart, 3rd Earl of, British Prime Minister, p. 299
104. Butler, Samuel, pp. 475, 476, 674
105. Byrd, William II, p. 348
106. Byron, George Gordon, later Noël, 6th Baron Byron, pp. 163, 298
107. Cambridge, H.R.H. The Duchess of (formerly Catherine Elizabeth Middleton) (for her husband, see under William), pp. 101, 380, 381, 931, 932
108. Campbell, Mrs. Patrick (Beatrice Stella Tanner), pp. 584, 648
109. Cameron, David William, British Prime Minister, p. 10
110. Carroll, Lewis (Charles Lutwidge Dodgson), p. 107
111. Carter, James Earl, Jr., 39th U.S. President, pp. 422, 696, 765, 773
112. Carter, Mrs. (Eleanor) Rosalyn Smith, pp. 422, 696
113. Carver, John, first governor of the Plymouth Colony, pp. 916, 917
114. Charles II, King of England, pp. 241, 430, 467
115. Charles VIII (Bonde), King of Sweden, pp. 457, 663, 664
116. Charles IX, King of France, p. 637

The Royal Descents of 900 Immigrants

117. Charles XIV John (Jean-Baptiste Bernadotte), King of Sweden, p. 83
118. Charles Albert, King of Sardinia, p. 614
119. Charles Philip Arthur George, Prince of Wales, pp. 380, 655, 832, 930, 932
120. Charlotte Elizabeth Diana of Cambridge, Princess of Great Britain, pp. 25, 380, 931, 932
121. Charlotte (Louise Juliette Grimaldi), Hereditary Princess of Monaco, Duchess of Valentinois, pp. 289, 933
122. Chauncey, Rev. Charles, second president of Harvard College, p. 806
123. Chesterfield, Philip Dormer Stanhope, 4th Earl of, p. 107
124. Christian, Fletcher, pp. 363, 365
125. Churchill, Arabella, mistress of James II, King of England, pp. 24, 536
126. (Spencer-) Churchill, Lord Randolph (Henry), pp. 63, 584, 648
127. (Spencer-) Churchill, Sir Winston (Leonard), pp. 63, 67, 585, 648, 755
128. Citkowitz, Israel, p. 31
129. Clarendon, Edward Hyde, 1st Earl of, pp. 626, 678, 780
130. Clary, Desirée (Desideria), Queen of Sweden, p. 83
131. Clary, (Marie-) Julie, Queen of Spain, p. 83
132. Cleeve, George, p. 810
133. Cleveland, (Stephen) Grover, 22nd and 24th U.S. President, pp. 335, 500
134. Clinton, DeWitt, p. 351
135. Clinton, Hon. George, gov. of N.Y., p. 108
136. Clinton, George, U.S. vice-president, p. 351
137. Clyde, (Michael) Jeremy (Thomas), of "Chad and Jeremy", p. 74

The Royal Descents of 900 Immigrants

138. Colbert, Jean-Baptiste, Marquis de Seignelay, p. 202
139. Coolidge, (John) Calvin (Jr.), 30th U.S. President, pp. 342, 526, 748, 758, 814, 882
140. Cornwall, H.R.H. The Duchess of (formerly Camilla [Rosemary Shand] Parker-Bowles), pp. 655, 656, 930
141. Cortés, Hernán, 1st Marquess of Valle de Oaxaca, conqueror of Mexico, p. 191
142. Coward, Noël (Pierce), pp. 240, 242
143. Croker, Richard Welstead, p. 480
144. Cromer, Evelyn Baring, 1st Earl of, p. 123
145. Cromwell, Oliver, Lord Protector, pp. 114, 130, 466, 476, 534, 554, 781
146. Cumberbatch, Benedict (Timothy Carlton), pp. 101, 179
147. Dallas, Alexander James, p. 666
148. Dallas, George Mifflin, p. 666
149. Dana, Francis, p. 155
150. Dana, Richard Henry, p. 155
151. Dana, Richard Henry, Jr., p. 155
152. Darwin, Charles Robert, pp. 116, 117
153. Davenport, Rev. John, pp. 654, 656
154. Davis, Jefferson, pp. 421, 533
155. Dawkins, (Clinton) Richard, pp. 108, 113
156. de Havilland (Goodrich Galante), (Mrs.) Olivia (Mary), p. 462
157. Dean, Howard (Brush) (III), pp. 161, 923, 924, 926
158. Dermot MacMurray (Diarmait MacMurrough), King of Leinster, pp. 837, 839, 847
159. Diana, Princess of Wales (formerly Lady Diana Frances Spencer), pp. 25, 32, 101, 306, 377, 380, 416, 417, 432, 482, 492, 543, 552, 576, 755, 858, 859, 930, 932

The Royal Descents of 900 Immigrants

160. Dixwell, John, regicide, p. 750
161. Donne, John, p. 426
162. Dryden, John, pp. 423, 478, 481, 482
163. Dudley, Edmund, pp. 321, 477, 691
164. Dudley, Thomas, gov. of Mass., pp. 297, 370, 372, 373, 924
165. Dufferin and Ava, Frederick Temple-Blackwood, 1st Marquess of, p. 32
166. Dugdale, Sir William, pp. 819, 820
167. Duke, Doris, p. 103
168. Duke, James Buchanan, p. 103
169. Duke, Washington, p. 103
170. Durocher, Leo, p. 424
171. Eaton, Theophilus, gov. of the New Haven Colony, pp. 252, 686
172. Eden, (Robert) Anthony, 1st Earl of Avon, pp. 585, 648
173. Edgeworth, Maria, p. 312
174. Edward VI, King of England, pp. 305, 705, 853
175. Edward VII, King of Great Britain, pp. 137, 655
176. Eisenhower, Dwight David, 34th U.S. President, pp. 546, 589
177. Eisenhower, Mrs. Mamie Geneva Doud, p. 589
178. Elizabeth I, Queen of England, pp. 134, 300, 345, 470, 539, 554, 588, 596, 684, 705
179. Elizabeth II, Queen of Great Britain, pp. 3, 41, 321, 930
180. Queen Elizabeth The Queen Mother of Great Britain (formerly Lady Elizabeth Angela Marguerite Bowes-Lyon), pp. 101, 121, 419, 451, 545, 930
181. Elliott, Maxine, p. 268
182. Emmet, Thomas Addis, p. 325
183. Ericsson, John, p. 302

The Royal Descents of 900 Immigrants

184. Esher, Reginald Baliol Brett, 2nd Viscount, p. 137
185. Essex, Robert Devereux, 2nd Earl of, pp. 134, 135, 136
186. d'Este, Hercules I, Duke of Modena and Ferrara, pp. 186, 189
187. Eugénie (Marie-Ignace-Augustine de Portocarrero y Kirkpatrick) (Bonaparte), Empress of the French, pp. 291, 292
188. Everett, Rupert (Hector), p. 34
189. Ferrer, Mel(chor Gastón), p. 446
190. von Fersen, Hans Axel, Count, pp. 240, 267
191. Field, Marshall (I), p. 68
192. Field, Marshall (III), p. 68
193. Fielding, Henry, p. 368
194. Fiennes, Ralph (Nathaniel), p. 158
195. FitzHerbert, Mrs. Maria (Mary Anna Smythe Weld FitzHerbert), first wife of George IV, King of Great Britain, p. 123
196. FitzWalter, Robert, leader of the Magna Charta barons, p. 880
197. Flagler, Henry Morrison, p. 306
198. Fleetwood, George, Swedish general and baron, pp. 662, 663
199. Fontaine, Joan (Mrs. Joan de Beauvoir de Havilland Aherne Dozier Young Wright), p. 463
200. Ford, Mrs. Elizabeth Ann (Betty) Bloomer Warren, pp. 631, 655, 867, 868, 887
201. Ford, Gerald Rudolph, Jr., 38th U.S. President, pp. 631, 655, 868, 877
202. Forster, Edward Morgan (E.M.), p. 107
203. Forster, William Edward, p. 436
204. Fox, Hon. Charles James, p. 31
205. Fox, Edward, p. 246
206. Francis II, King of France, p. 637

The Royal Descents of 900 Immigrants

207. Franklin, Benjamin, p. 87
208. Fraser (Pinter), Lady Antonia (Margaret Caroline Pakenham), pp. 73, 122
209. Frederick I, King of Prussia, pp. 56, 58, 432
210. Frederick I, the "Winter King" of Bohemia, p. 56
211. Freud, Lucian Michael, p. 31
212. Freud, Sigmund, p. 31
213. Frost, David (Paradine), p. 72
214. Fulton, Robert, p. 616
215. zu Fürstenberg, Maximilian Egon II, Prince, p. 20
216. von Fürstenberg, Diane (Halfin), p. 20
217. Gage, Hon. Thomas, p. 110
218. Gallatin, Abraham-Alphonse-Albert (Sec. of the Treasury), p. 912
219. Garfield, James Abram, 20th U.S. President, p. 480
220. Garfield, Mrs. Lucretia Rudolph, p. 480
221. de Gaveston, Piers, 1st Earl of Cornwall, p. 847
222. Genghis Khan, pp. 797, 800
223. George I, King of Great Britain, pp. 58, 432
224. George III, King of Great Britain, pp. 40, 615
225. George IV, King of Great Britain, p. 123
226. George VI, King of Great Britain, p. 930
227. George Alexander Louis, Prince of Cambridge and Great Britain, pp. 25, 380, 931, 932
228. Géraldine, Countess Apponyi de Nagy-Apponyi, Queen of the Albanians, pp. 929, 935
229. Gergen, David (Richmond), p. 232
230. Getty, John Paul, p. 645
231. Gielgud, Sir (Arthur) John, p. 803

The Royal Descents of 900 Immigrants

232. Giscard d'Estaing, Valéry, p. 185
233. Glendower, Owen, pp. 657, 813, 824
234. Godard, Jean-Luc, pp. 635, 636, 795
235. Goffe, William, regicide, pp. 585, 781
236. Gonzaga, Frederick II, Duke of Mantua, Marquess of Montferrat, pp. 186, 189
237. Gorges, Sir Ferdinando, pp. 295, 392, 457, 522, 838
238. Grace (Patricia Kelly), Princess of Monaco, p. 934
239. von Graffenried, Christoph(er), Baron, Landgrave of N.C., p. 832
240. Grafton, Augustus Henry FitzRoy, 3rd Duke of, British Prime Minister, p. 33
241. Grahame, Gloria (Mrs. Gloria Hallward Clements Ray Howard Ray), p. 362
242. Gramont, Antoine-Alfred-Agénor de Gramont, 10th Duc de, p. 49
243. Grant, Cary (Archibald Alexander Leach), p. 44
244. Grant, Hugh John (Mungo), pp. 66, 364
245. Grant, Mrs. Julia Boggs Dent, pp. 722, 921
246. Grant, Ulysses Simpson, 18th U.S. President, pp. 722, 921
247. Granville, John Carteret, 1st Earl, British Prime Minister, pp. 69, 226
248. de Grasse, François-Joseph-Paul, Count de Grasse, Marquis de Tilly, p. 616
249. Greene, (Henry) Graham, p. 549
250. Grenville, Hon. George, British Prime Minister, p. 77
251. Grey, Charles, 2nd Earl Grey, British Prime Minister, p. 72
252. Grey (Dudley), Lady Jane, pp. 69, 80, 477
253. Griffin, Cyrus, p. 155
254. Guevara, Ernesto "Che", pp. 991, 997
255. Guinness, Sir Benjamin Lee, 1st Bt., pp. 31, 308, 481

The Royal Descents of 900 Immigrants

256. Gustav VII Adolf, King of Sweden, p. 41
257. Gwinnett, Button, pp. 648, 649
258. Gwynn, Eleanor "Nell", p. 33
259. Gyllenhaal, Jacob Benjamin "Jake", p. 663
260. Gyllenhaal, Maggie (Ruth), p. 663
261. Hamilton, Alexander (of N.Y.), p. 214
262. Hammarskjöld, Dag (Hjalmar Agne Carl), p. 51
263. Hammarskjöld, (Knut) Hjalmar (Leonard), p. 51
264. Hampden, John, Parliamentary leader, pp. 300, 466
265. Harding, Warren Gamaliel, pp. 764, 859, 860
266. Hardwick, Elizabeth ("Bess of"), Countess of Shrewsbury, pp. 468, 512, 706
267. Harriman, (Hon. Mrs.) Pamela (Beryl Digby Spencer-Churchill Hayward), p. 67
268. Harriman, William Averell, p. 67
269. Harrison, Benjamin (V), signer, pp. 496, 503, 730, 878
270. Harrison, Benjamin, 23rd U.S. President, pp. 496, 503, 731, 867, 878
271. Harrison, William Henry, 9th U.S. President, pp. 496, 503, 731, 867, 878
272. Hayes, Mrs. Lucy Ware Webb ("Lemonade Lucy"), pp. 656, 702, 871
273. Hayes, Rutherford Birchard, 19th U.S. President, pp. 656, 702, 871
274. Hayward, Leland, p. 67
275. Henderson, Ernest Flagg, Jr., pp. 148, 149
276. Henry, Patrick, p. 219
277. Henry V, King of England, pp. 226, 603, 813, 824
278. Henry VIII, King of England, pp. 226, 603, 813, 824

The Royal Descents of 900 Immigrants

279. Henry II, King of France, pp. 202, 637, 735

280. Henry III, King of France, p. 637

281. Henry IV, King of France and Navarre, pp. 62, 192, 293, 615, 637, 638

282. Henry (Harry) Charles Albert David of Wales, Prince of Great Britain, pp. 25, 858, 931, 932

283. Hepburn, Audrey (Mrs. Edda Kathleen van Heemstra Hepburn-Ruston Ferrer Dotti), p. 446

284. Hervey, John, 1st Baron Hervey of Ickworth, pp. 117, 334

285. Hoar, Rev. Leonard, third president of Harvard College, p. 297

286. von Hoffmansthal, Hugo, pp. 799, 800

287. Home, Sir Alexander "Alec" Frederick, sometime 14th Earl of Home, British Prime Minister, p. 25

288. Hooker, Rev. Thomas, p. 757

289. Hooper, William, signer, p. 211

290. Hoover, Herbert Clark, 31st U.S. President, p. 371

291. Howard, Katherine, Queen of England, p. 468

292. Howe, George Augustus, 3rd Viscount Howe, p. 432

293. Howland, John, *Mayflower* passenger, pp. 654, 926, 982

294. Hume, David, p. 257

295. Huston, Angelica, p. 65

296. Huston, John, pp. 9, 65

297. Huston, Walter, p. 65

298. Hutchinson, Mrs. Anne Marbury, pp. 478, 480, 925, 926

299. Hutton, Barbara (Woolworth), pp. 44, 46, 63

300. Hutton, Edward Francis (E.F.), p. 44

301. Huxley, Aldous (Leonard), p. 436

302. Huxley, Sir Julian (Sorell), p. 436

The Royal Descents of 900 Immigrants

303. Hyde, Anne, Duchess of York (first wife of James II, King of England), pp. 22, 24, 122, 678, 679, 727, 780, 781, 782

304. Ibsen, Henrik, p. 645

305. (Bradshaw-)Isherwood, Christopher (William), p. 549

306. Ivan III, 1st Czar of Russia, p. 797

307. Ivan IV, the Terrible, Czar of Russia, p. 792

308. Jacques (Honoré Rainier Grimaldi), Prince of Monaco, Marquis des Baux, p. 934

309. James II, King of England, pp. 678, 727, 781

310. Jefferson, Thomas, 3rd U.S. President, pp. 387, 711, 823, 912

311. Jerome, Jennie (sometime Lady Randolph [Henry Spencer-] Churchill), pp. 63, 584, 585, 648

312. Jerome, Leonard Walter, pp. 548, 648

313. Johnson, Sir William, 1st Bt., p. 487, 900

314. Joplin, Janis Lyn, p. 698

315. Joséphine (Marie-Josèphe Tascher de la Pagerie de Beauharnais Bonaparte), Empress of the French, pp. 292, 442, 443, 444

316. Julius II (della Rovere), Pope, p. 192

317. Karl (Charles) I, Emperor of Austria, p. 800

318. Kemble (Butler), Mrs. Frances Anna "Fanny", p. 382

Kendal, see Kerdeston

319. Kennedy, Edward Moore (Sen.), pp. 26, 564, 914

320. Kennedy, John Fitzgerald, 35th U.S. President, pp. 26, 53, 564, 914, 915

321. Kennedy, Joseph Patrick, financier and diplomat, pp. 26, 564, 914

322. Kennedy, Robert Francis (Sen.), pp. 26, 564, 914

323. Keppel, (Hon. Mrs.) Alice (Edmonstone), p. 655

324. Kerdeston (de Foix), Margaret, Countess of Kendal (genealogical link), pp. 287, 289, 615, 616

The Royal Descents of 900 Immigrants

325. Kerry, John Forbes, p. 923
326. Key, Francis Scott, p. 333
327. Ladislaus V, King of Bohemia and Hungary, pp. 287, 615
328. de la Fayette (Lafayette), Marie-Joseph-Paul-Yves-Roch-Gilbert Motier, Marquis, pp. 201, 202, 203, 288
329. Lamarr, Hedy (Hedwig Eva Maria Kiesler), p. 98
330. Lang, Fritz, p. 645
331. Lannes de Montebello, Guy Philippe, p. 227
332. Lansdowne, William Petty, 1st Marquess of, British Prime Minister, p. 226
333. Latrobe, Benjamin Henry, p. 590
334. Lawford, Peter (Sydney Ernest), pp. 26, 564, 914
335. Lawrence, Thomas Edward (T. E.), "Lawrence of Arabia", pp. 101, 102
336. Lee, Robert E(dward) (Gen.), p. 29
337. Leicester, Robert Dudley, 1st Earl of, pp. 134, 477
338. Leka I and Leka II, styled Kings of the Albanians, p. 935
339. Leopold I, King of the Belgians, pp. 45, 182, 196, 237, 290
340. Leopold II, Holy Roman Emperor, p. 614
341. Leuchtenburg, Eugène (-Rose) de Beauharnais, 1st Duke of, pp. 442, 443
342. Lillie (Peel, Lady) Beatrice (Gladys) ("Bea"), p. 67
343. Liverpool, Robert Banks Jenkinson, 2nd Earl of, British Prime Minister, p. 34
344. Livingston, Robert the elder, of N.Y., pp. 243, 244
345. Lloyd, Thomas, dep. gov. of Pa., pp. 231, 232, 233
346. Logan, James, of Pa., colonial statesman, p. 279
347. Louis II (-Honoré-Charles-Antoine Grimaldi), Sovereign Prince of Monaco, p. 20

The Royal Descents of 900 Immigrants

348. Louis XIV, King of France, pp. 287, 288, 289

349. Louis-Philippe, King of the French, pp. 288, 290, 291, 294

350. Lovelace, Richard, poet, p. 509

351. Lowell, James Russell, p. 86

352. Lowell, Robert (Traill Spence IV), pp. 31, 86

353. Luce, Henry Robinson, Jr., p. 91

354. Ludlow, Roger (Dep. Gov.), pp. 503, 504

355. MacLean, John, Jr., tenth president of the College of New Jersey, later Princeton, p. 249

356. MacMillan, (Maurice) Harold, 1st Earl of Stockton, British Prime Minister, p. 26

357. Madison, Mrs. Dorothea "Dolly" Payne Todd, pp. 497, 532

358. Madison, James, Jr., pp. 497, 532

359. Madonna (Louise Veronica Ciccone Penn Ritchie), pp. 63, 380

360. Mailer, Norman, p. 70, 371

361. de Maintenon, Françoise-Charlotte-Amable d'Aubigné, Marquise (Madame), mistress and second wife of Louis XIV, King of France, p. 288

362. de Malesherbes, Chrétien-Guillaume de Lamoignon, Baron, p. 294

363. Malory, Sir Thomas, claimed to be the author of *Le Morte d'Arthur*, p. 847

364. Mann, Thomas, p. 404

365. Marlborough, John Churchill, 1st Duke of, pp. 24, 33, 70, 71, 536

366. Martineau, Harriet, p. 379

367. Marx, Karl, p. 147

368. Mary II, Queen of England, pp. 122, 615, 678, 679, 781

369. Masaryk, Jan Garrigue, p. 635

370. Masaryk, Tomas Jan (later Garrigue), p. 635

The Royal Descents of 900 Immigrants

371. Massey, Raymond (Hart), p. 341
372. Mathilde (-Marie-Christiane-Ghislaine) (d'Udekem d'Acoz), Queen of the Belgians, pp. 154, 155, 201, 203, 204
373. Mauriac, François, p. 795
374. Mazarin(i), Cardinal Jules (Giulio), p. 289
375. McAdam, John Loudon, p. 128
376. McGregor (or Campbell), Robert, "Rob Roy," p. 146
377. McNab, Sir Allan Napier, 1st Bt., p. 655
378. Meade, George Gordon (Gen.), p. 385
379. de'Medici, Catherine, Queen of France, p. 637
380. de'Medici, Cosimo I, Grand Duke of Tuscany, pp. 191, 192
381. de'Medici, Francesco Maria I, Grand Duke of Tuscany, p. 192
382. de'Medici, Marie, Queen of France, p. 192
383. Medina Sidonia, Alfonso Pérez de Guzmán y Sotomayor, 7th Duke of, admiral of the Spanish Armada, pp. 140, 142, 191
384. Mellon, Andrew William, p. 190
385. Mellon, Paul, p. 190
386. Mellon, Judge Thomas, p. 190
387. Merrill, Dina (Mrs. Nedenia Hutton Rumbrough Robertson), p. 44
388. Michael III, Czar of Russia, p. 792
389. Middleton, Henry, president of the Continental Congress, p. 92
390. (Freeman-) Mitford (Romilly Treuhaft), (Hon.) Jessica (Lucy), pp. 23, 26
391. (Freeman-) Mitford (Rodd), (Hon.) Nancy, p. 26
392. Monroe, James, 5th U.S. President, pp. 163, 260
393. de Montespan, Françoise-Athénaïs de Rochechouart, Marquise, mistress of Louis XIV, King of France, pp. 287, 289

The Royal Descents of 900 Immigrants

394. Montmorency, Anne, Duc de, p. 637
395. More, Richard, *Mayflower* passenger, p. 319, 322
396. Morgan, Ted (Sanche-Arnaud-Gabriel de Gramont), p. 49
397. Moseley, Sir Oswald Ernald, 6th Baronet, p. 23
398. Mountbatten, Louis Francis Albert Victor Nicholas, 1st Earl Mountbatten of Burma, p. 41
399. Murat, Joachim, 1st Prince Murat, King of Naples, p. 82
400. Napier, John, inventor of logarithms, p. 214
401. Napoléon I, Emperor of the French, pp. 11, 157, 292, 442, 858
402. Napoléon III, Emperor of the French, pp. 49, 291, 292
403. Neeson, Liam (John), p. 246
404. Nero, Franco, p. 246
405. Ney, Michel, Duke d'Elchingen and Prince of Moscow, p. 83
406. Niarchos, Stavros, p. 23
407. Niven, (James) David (Graham), p. 70
408. Nixon, Richard Milhous, 37th U.S. President, p. 764
409. de Noailles, Louis-Marie, Vicomte, pp. 200, 288
410. Northumberland, John Dudley, 1st Duke of, p. 477
411. Nottingham, Charles Howard, 1st Earl of, p. 605
412. Obama, Barack Hussein, Jr., 44th U.S. President, 498, 726, 923
413. O'Conor, Charles, p. 885
414. Ogilvy, David Mackenzie, p. 97
415. Oglethorpe, James Edward, pp. 613, 614
416. Olivares, Gaspar Felipe de Guzmán, Count-Duke of, minister of Philip IV, King of Spain, p. 191
417. Onassis, Aristotle Socrates, pp. 16, 915
418. Onassis, Mrs. Jacqueline Lee Bouvier Kennedy, pp. 16, 74, 914, 915

The Royal Descents of 900 Immigrants

419. Onorato II (Grimaldi), Prince of Monaco, p. 190
420. Orlov, Prince Gregori, p. 14
421. Orwell, George (Eric Arthur Blair), p. 122
422. Otto, (Karl Louis) Rudolf, p. 321
423. Oxford, Edward de Vere, 17th Earl of, p. 766
424. Paola (Ruffo di Calabria), Queen of the Belgians, p. 201, 204
425. Paul, Czar of Russia, p. 792
426. Paul III, Pope (Alessandro Farnese), pp. 186, 188, 189, 192
427. Peel, Sir Robert, 2nd Bt., pp. 66, 67
428. Pembroke, Richard "Strongbow" de Clare, 2nd Earl of, 837, 839, 847
429. Pembroke, William Marshall, 1st Earl of, pp. 837, 839, 845, 847
430. Penn, Sean, pp. 63, 975
431. Penn, William, pp. 149, 226
432. Pepys, Samuel, p. 480
433. Percy, Sir Henry "Hotspur" (Lord Henry Percy), pp. 305, 310, 317, 319, 327, 333, 342, 347, 349, 351, 355, 359, 361, 363, 374, 379, 384, 385, 389, 399, 401, 414, 418, 425, 431, 737, 901, 904, 905
434. Perry, Matthew Galbraith, p. 174
435. Perth, James Eric Drummond ("Sir Eric Drummond"), 16th Earl of, Secretary-General of the League of Nations, p. 72
436. Perry, Oliver Hazard (Cdre.), p. 174
437. Phelips, Sir Robert, p. 457
438. Philip II, King of Spain, pp. 18, 615
439. Philip, Prince of Greece and Denmark, Duke of Edinburgh, pp. 3, 41, 930
440. Philippe I, King of the Belgians, pp. 201, 204

The Royal Descents of 900 Immigrants

441. Phillips, Mark Anthony Peter, first husband of Anne Elizabeth Alice Louise, Princess of Great Britain, The Princess Royal, pp. 321, 322

442. Pickering, Timothy, Jr., p. 924

443. Pierce, Franklin, 14th U.S. President, pp. 582, 812

444. Pinter, Harold, pp. 73, 122

445. Pizarro, Francisco, the conqueror of Perú, p. 191

446. Platt, Oliver, p. 377

447. de Poitiers, Diane, Duchess de Valentinois, mistress of Henry II, King of France, pp. 202, 735

448. de Polignac, Auguste-Jules-Armand, Prince, minister of Charles X, King of France, p. 289

449. Poniatowski, Stanislaus II August, King of Poland, p. 154

450. Portland, Richard Weston, 1st Earl of, Lord Treasurer, p. 467

451. Portsmouth, Louise-Renée de Penancoët de Kéroualle, Duchess of, mistress of Charles II, King of England, pp. 25, 31, 226

452. Post (Close Hutton Davies May), Mrs. Marjorie Merriweather, p. 44

453. Pound, Ezra Loomis, p. 131

454. Pride, Sir Thomas, p. 103

455. Pynchon, William, p. 533

456. Rainier III (-Louis-Henry-Maxence-Bertrand Grimaldi), Sovereign Prince of Monaco, pp. 289, 290, 934

457. Randolph, William, Virginia planter, pp. 387, 711

458. Ray, Nicholas, p. 362

459. Read, George, signer, p. 828

460. Reagan, Mrs. Nancy Davis (Anne Francis Robbins), p. 673

461. Reagan, Ronald Wilson, p. 673

462. Redgrave, Lynn (Rachel Clark), p. 246

The Royal Descents of 900 Immigrants

463. Redgrave, Sir Michael Scudamore, p. 246
464. Redgrave, Vanessa (Richardson Nero), p. 246
465. Richard III, King of England, p. 118
466. Richardson, Sir Ralph (David), p. 268
467. Richardson, (Cecil Anthony) "Tony", p. 246
468. Rigg (Gueffen Stirling Silva), Diana (Dame), p. 23
469. Ripley, George, p. 155
470. Ritchie, Guy Stuart, pp. 63, 380, 975
471. Robertson, William (IV), historian, p. 219
472. Robinson, Rev. John, minister of the Pilgrims in Leyden, pp. 917, 918
473. de Rochambeau, Jean-Baptiste-Donatien de Vimeur, Count, pp. 267, 455
474. Rodney, Caesar, Jr., signer, p. 307
475. Romney, George Wilcken, pp. 924, 926
476. Romney, (Willard) Mitt, pp. 923, 924
477. Roosevelt, (Mrs. Anna) Eleanor (Roosevelt), pp. 211, 356, 376, 394, 479, 524, 571, 716, 881, 921
478. Roosevelt, Franklin Delano, 32nd U.S. President, pp. 49, 211, 356, 376, 394, 479, 524, 571, 716, 881, 921, 967
479. Roosevelt, Theodore, Jr., 26th U. S. President, pp. 164, 225, 283, 471, 858
480. Ross, George, Jr., signer, p. 828
481. Ross, Herbert David, pp. 16, 914
482. Rubens, Peter Paul, pp. 804, 805
483. Russell, Bertrand Arthur William, 3rd Earl Russell, pp. 22, 25
484. Russell, John, 1st Earl Russell, British Prime Minister, p. 25
485. Sackville-West, Victoria Mary "Vita" (Hon.), p. 299

The Royal Descents of 900 Immigrants

486. de Sade, Donatien-Alphonse-François de Sade, Count, known as the Marquis de Sade, p. 227

487. Sage, Kay Linn, p. 20

488. Salinger, Jerome David (J.D.), p. 166

489. Salisbury, Robert Cecil, 1st Earl of, p. 315

490. Saltonstall, Sir Richard, pp. 291, 353, 374, 837

491. Salm-Salm, Princess (Agnes Elizabeth Winona Leclerq Joy, later Heneage), pp. 30, 38

492. Saltykov, Sergei, Count, alleged father of Paul I, Czar of Russia, pp. 792, 796

493. Sarg, Anthony "Tony" Frederick, p. 116

494. Sarsgaard, (John) Peter, p. 663

495. Savoy, Prince Eugène of, p. 289

496. Schlesinger, Arthur Meier, Jr., p. 406

497. Schreiber, (Isaac) Liev, p. 129

498. Schwarzenegger, Arnold (Alois), pp. 26, 564, 914

499. Seymour, Jane, Queen of England, pp. 305, 705, 853

500. Shaftesbury, Anthony Ashley Cooper, 7th Earl of, p. 299

501. Shelley, (Mrs.) Mary Wollstonecraft Godwin, p. 474

502. Shelley, Percy Bysshe, p. 474

503. Shields, (Christa) Brooke (Camille), p. 18

504. Shirley, William, gov. of Mass., pp. 32, 475, 476

505. Shriver, Maria Owings (Mrs. Arnold Alois Schwarzenegger), pp. 26, 564, 914

506. Shriver, Sargent, p. 914

507. Sidney, Sir Philip, p. 477

508. Sitwell, (Sir Francis) Osbert Sacheverell, 5th Bt., Sir Sacheverell, 6th Bt., and Dame Edith (Louisa), p. 177

The Royal Descents of 900 Immigrants

509. Somerset, Edward Seymour, 1st Duke of, Lord Protector, pp. 305, 307

510. Sorel, Agnès, mistress of Charles VII, King of France, pp. 202, 208, 209

511. Spenser, Edmund, p. 478

512. Spotswood, Alexander, lieut. gov. of Va., p. 278

513. Stanislaus II (Augustus Poniatowski), King of Poland, p. 154

514. Stanley, Sir Henry Morton, p. 130

515. von Starhemberg, (Heinrich) Ernest Rüdiger, Count, p. 237

516. Stephen, Sir Leslie, p. 611

517. von Steuben, Friedrich Wilhelm Ludolf Gerhard Augustin, Baron, p. 181

518. Stevenson, Robert Louis, p. 270

519. Stoughton, Israel, pp. 916, 920

520. Stoughton, William, gov. of Mass., pp. 920, 921

521. Strachey, (Giles) Lytton, p. 825

522. Summersby (Morgan), (Mrs. Kathleen) "Kay" (Helen MacCarthy-Morrogh), p. 546

523. Surrey, Henry Howard, Earl of, poet, pp. 333, 431

524. Swift, Jonathan, p. 482

525. Swinton, Katherine Matilda "Tilda", p. 177

526. Synge, (Edmund) John Millington, p. 254

527. Taft, Alphonso, pp. 318, 881

528. Taft, William Howard, 27th U.S. President, pp. 291, 318, 881

529. Tait, Archibald Campbell, Archbishop of Canterbury, p. 177

530. Taney, Roger Brooke, p. 333

531. Taylor, Elizabeth (Rosemond) (Hilton Wilding Todd Fisher Burton Warner Fortensky), pp. 21, 190

The Royal Descents of 900 Immigrants

532. Taylor, Zachary, 12th U.S. President, pp. 421, 533
533. Tennyson, Alfred Tennyson, 1st Baron, p. 355
534. Terry, Dames Ellen and Kate, p. 803
535. Theroux, Paul Edward, p. 985
536. Thoreau, Henry David, p. 655
537. de Tocqueville, Hervé-Louis-François de Clerel, Count, p. 293
538. Tokhai, Khan of the Golden Horde, p. 797
539. Tolstoy, Count Leo, pp. 193, 794
540. Toynbee, Arnold, p. 299
541. von Trapp, siblings (Agathe, Hedwig, Joanna Karolina, Maria Franziska, Martina, Rupert, and Werner), p. 187
542. Trevelyan, George Macaulay, p. 436
543. Trollope, (Thomas) Anthony, p. 320
544. Trollope, Mrs. Frances (Milton), pp. 320, 322
545. Truman, Mrs. Elizabeth Virginia "Bess" Wallace, pp. 171, 259
546. Truman, Harry S, pp. 171, 259, 673
547. Tudor, Owen, pp. 226, 603, 813, 824
548. Tyler, John (IV), 10th U.S. President, p. 643
549. Vanderbilt (Belmont), (Mrs.) Alva (Erskine Smith), pp. 26, 174, 175
550. Vanderbilt, Cornelius II, pp. 35, 209
551. Vanderbilt, William Kissam, pp. 26, 174
552. Vane, Sir Henry (the younger), pp. 34, 115, 315
553. Vaughan Williams, Ralph, p. 117
554. Venn, John, and John Archibald, p. 611
555. Victor Emanuel II, King of Sardinia, first King of United Italy, p. 614
556. Victoria, Queen of Great Britain, pp. 2, 41, 45, 182, 19, 237, 290

The Royal Descents of 900 Immigrants

557. Villiers, Barbara, Duchess of Cleveland, mistress of Charles II, King of England, pp. 22, 29, 33, 34, 109

558. Wagner, Sir Anthony Richard, p. 25

559. Wallenberg, Raoul (Jr.), p. 60

560. Waller, Edmund, poet, p. 466

561. Walpole, Horace, 4th Earl of Orford, p. 482

562. Walpole, Robert, 1st Earl of Orford, p. 482

563. Ward, Mrs. (Thomas) Humphrey (Mary Augusta Arnold), p. 436

564. Ward, Rev. William George, p. 71

565. Warren, Sir Peter, pp. 487, 900

566. Warwick (and Salisbury), Richard Neville, 1st Earl of, the "Kingmaker", p. 419

567. Washington, George, 1st U.S. President, pp. 29, 310, 365, 515, 518, 611, 700, 787

568. Washington, Mrs. Martha Dandridge Custis, pp. 29, 170, 301, 310, 515, 700

569. Watts, Naomi, p. 129

570. Waugh, Alexander "Alec" Raban, p. 402

571. Waugh, Evelyn Arthur St. John, p. 401

572. Wedgwood, Josiah (and Francis and Clement Francis Wedgwood), master potter(s) of Etruria, pp. 116, 117

573. Wellesley, Richard Wellesley, 1st Marquess, pp. 340, 545

574. Wellington, Arthur Wellesley, 1st Duke of, pp. 74, 157, 341, 545

575. Wells, Herbert George (H.G.), p. 406

576. Wentworth, Paul, Parliamentary leader, p. 710

577. Wentworth, Peter, Parliamentary leader, p. 710

578. West, Dame Rebecca (Mrs. Cicely Isabel Fairfield Andrews), p. 406

579. Whalley, Edward, regicide, p. 781

The Royal Descents of 900 Immigrants

580. Whipple, William, Jr., signer, p. 85
581. Whitehead, Alfred North, p. 535
582. Whitgift, John, Archbishop of Canterbury, p. 579
583. Wiener de Croisset, Franz, p. 227
584. Wilde, Olivia (Olivia Jane Cockburn), pp. 21, 94
585. Wilding, Michael, p. 21
586. William I, Emperor of Germany, p. 41
587. William the Silent, Prince of Orange, 1st Stadholder of The Netherlands, pp. 62, 141, 181, 182, 184, 194, 196
588. William Arthur Philip Louis of Wales, Duke of Cambridge (for his wife see under Cambridge, and for his children see under George and Charlotte), Prince of Great Britain, pp. 25, 26, 380, 858, 931, 932
589. Wilson, Mrs. Edith Bolling Galt, pp. 278, 301, 387, 711, 823
590. Wilson, Mrs. Ellen Louise Axson, pp. 463, 465, 508, 673, 726
591. Wilson, (Thomas) Woodrow, pp. 278, 301, 387, 463, 465, 508, 673, 711, 726, 823
592. Winslow, Edward, gov. of Plymouth Colony, p. 479
593. Winthrop, John, gov. of Mass. Bay Colony, pp. 483, 501, 713, 714
594. Winthrop, Robert Charles, p. 923
595. Wintour (Shaffer), Anna (Dame), p. 117
596. Wister, Owen, pp. 382, 383
597. Witte, Count Sergei, pp. 792, 795
598. Wodehouse, Sir Pelham Grenville (P.G.), pp. 335, 336
599. Woodhull (Blood Martin), (Mrs.) Victoria (Claflin), p. 138
600. Woodville, Elizabeth, Queen of England, pp. 100, 103, 105, 106, 134, 208, 333, 339, 347, 370, 397, 412, 431, 902
601. Woolf, (Adeline) Virginia (Stephen), p. 611

The Royal Descents of 900 Immigrants

602. Woolworth, Frank Winfield, pp. 44, 63
603. Wortley Montagu, Lady Mary (Pierrepont), p. 64
604. Wrangel, Herman, p. 889
605. Wren, Sir Christopher, p. 350
606. Wright, Frances "Fanny" (Phiquepal-Arusmont), pp. 390, 391
607. Wyatt, Sir Francis, gov. of Va., pp. 314, 783
608. Yale, Elihu, p. 657
609. Zinzendorf and Pottendorf, Nicholas Ludwig, Count of, pp. 196, 237
610. Zog I, King of the Albanians, p. 935

The Royal Descents of 900 Immigrants

30 Major Historical Figures Who Appear in the French-Canadian Section at the End of This Volume

1. Jennifer [Joanna] Aniston, wife of #s16 and 22
2. Justin [Drew] Bieber
3. Shawn [Corey] Carter ("Jay Z") (w), husband of #12
4. [Joseph-Jacques-] Jean Chrétien
5. Madonna [Louise Veronica] Ciccone, wife of #s16 and 18
6. Céline [-Marie-Claudette] Dion
7. Eric Gagné
8. Robert [Gerard] Goulet
9. Ryan [Thomas] Gosling
10. Maurice Robert "Mike" Gravel
11. Jack Kerouac [Jean-Louis LeBris Kerouac]
12. Beyoncé [Giselle Knowles], wife of #3
13. Mario Lemieux

    Madonna, see Ciccone

14. Alanis [Nadine] Morrisette
15. Anna [Hélène] Paquin
16. Sean Penn (w), husband of #5
17. [William] Brad[ley] Pitt (w), husband of #s 1 and 27
18. Guy [Stuart] Ritchie (w), husband of #5
19. Michael [Jacques Michel André] Sarrazin
20. Chloë [Stevens] Sevigny
21. Justin Paul Theroux, husband of #1, nephew of #22
22. Paul [Edward] Theroux, uncle of #21
23. William Robert "Billy Bob" Thornton (w), husband of #27
24. Justin [Pierre James] Trudeau, son of #25

The Royal Descents of 900 Immigrants

25. Pierre [Elliott] Trudeau, father of #24
26. Allen Henry Vigneron, Archbishop of Detroit
27. Angelina Jolie [Voight], wife of #s 17 and 23, daughter of #28
28. Jon Voight (w), father of #27
29. Donald Edward "Donnie" Wahlberg, brother of #30
30. Mark [Robert Michael] Wahlberg, brother of #29

The Royal Descents of 900 Immigrants

Appendix IV to the Introduction: 84 Kings from whom Descent is Outlined to 970 Immigrants Herein

1. Juliana, Queen of The Netherlands, d. 2004 (p. 1)
2. Ferdinand I, King of Roumania, d. 1927 (p. 2)
3. George I, King of Greece, d. 1913 (pp. 3-4)
4. Alexander II, Czar of Russia, d. 1881 (p. 5), son of #6, grandson of #7
5. Ferdinand II, King of the Two Sicilies, d. 1859 (p. 6)
6. Nicholas I, Czar of Russia, d. 1855 (p. 7), grandson of #12, father of #4, son-in-law of #7, grandson-in-law of #11
7. Frederick William III, King of Prussia, d. 1840 (p. 8), son of #11, father-in-law of #6, grandfather of #4
8. William IV, King of Great Britain, d. 1837 (pp. 9-10)
9. Francis II, Holy Roman Emperor and Emperor of Austria, d. 1835 (p. 11), grandson of #13
10. Frederick I, King of Württemberg, d. 1816 (p. 12)
11. Frederick William II, King of Prussia, d. 1797 (p. 13), grandson of #14, father of #7, grandfather-in-law of #6
12. Catherine II, Empress of Russia, d. 1796 (p. 14), grandmother of #6
13. Francis I (of Lorraine), Holy Roman Emperor, d. 1765, husband of Maria Theresa, Empress of Austria, d. 1780 (p. 15) (grandparents of #9)
14. Frederick William I, King of Prussia, d. 1740 (pp. 16-17), grandfather of #11
15. Victor Amadeus II, King of Sardinia, d. 1730 (pp. 18-19)
16. Joseph I, Holy Roman Emperor, d. 1711 (p. 20-21), uncle of Maria Theresa, Empress of Austria, #13
17. James II, King of England (reigned 1685-1688), d. 1701 (pp. 22-24), grandson of #20, brother of #18

cxxxv

The Royal Descents of 900 Immigrants

18. Charles II, King of England, d. 1685 (pp. 22-23, 25-34), grandson of #20, brother of #17

    (all descents charted herein of 17 and 18 are through illegitimate children)

19. Christian IV, King of Denmark, d. 1648 (pp. 37), son of #22, grandson of #25, brother-in-law of #20

20. James I, King of England (and VI, King of Scotland, d. 1625) (pp. 38-39), grandson of #27, son-in-law of #22, brother-in-law of #19, grandfather of #17 and 18

21. Charles IX, King of Sweden, d. 1611 (pp. 40-46), half-brother of #23

22. Frederick II, King of Denmark, d. 1588 (pp. 47-50), son of #25, father of #19, father-in-law of #20

23. Eric XIV, King of Sweden, d. 1577 (pp. 51-53, 889-90), half-brother of #21

24. Ferdinand I, Holy Roman Emperor, d. 1564 (pp. 54-57, 891-92), grandson of #30, ancestor of Kings or Queens #1-18

25. Christian III, King of Denmark, d. 1559 (pp. 58-61, 893-94), father of #22, grandfather of #19, grandfather-in-law of #20

26. Henry VII, King of England, d. 1509 (pp. 62-81; pp. 62-68 also cover descendants of William the Silent, Prince of Orange, first Stadholder of The Netherlands, d. 1584, and pp. 69-78, 80-81 cover descendants of Edward Seymour, Baron Beauchamp, heir to the English throne in 1603 according to the will of Henry VIII), son-in-law of #28, father-in-law of #31, grandfather of #27

27. James V, King of Scotland, d. 1542 (pp. 82-99, 897), son of #31, grandson of #26, grandfather of #20

28. Edward IV, King of England, d. 1483 (pp. 100-6), father-in-law of #26, grandfather-in-law of #31

    (all descents charted herein of #27 and #28 are through illegitimate children)

29. George Plantagenet, 1st Duke of Clarence (pp. 107-18); Anne Plantagenet, wife of Sir Thomas St. Leger (pp. 119-33); and

cxxxvi

The Royal Descents of 900 Immigrants

Isabel Plantagenet, wife of Henry Bourchier, Count of Eu, 1st Earl of Essex (pp. 134-39) – brother, sister, and aunt of Kings Edward IV, #28 above, and Richard III, d. 1485

30. Ferdinand I, King of Aragón, first King of united Spain, d. 1516 (pp. 140-42), grandfather of #24

31. James IV, King of Scotland, d. 1513 (pp. 143-80), son-in-law of #26, father of #27 (all descents charted herein through illegitimate children)

32. John I, King of Denmark, d. 1513 (pp. 180-85), uncle of #25

33. Ferdinand I, King of Naples, d. 1494 (pp. 186-93) (pp. 189-93 includes Cortés of Mexico and de' Medici of Tuscany)

34. Casimir IV, King of Poland, d. 1492 (pp. 194-99, 196-97, via Reuss-Ebersdorf and Zinzendorf cousins of Leopold I, King of the Belgians, d. 1865, and Victoria, Queen of Great Britain, d. 1901), father of #84

35. Louis XI, King of France, d. 1483 (pp. 200-7), son of #36, grandson of #40

36. Charles VII, King of France, d. 1461 (pp. 202-4, 208-9), son of #40, father of #35

37. James II, King of Scotland, d. 1460 (pp. 210-19), son of #39, grandson of #43, grandfather of #31 (210-18 via his daughter, [Princess] Mary, wife of James Hamilton, 1st Baron Hamilton)

38. Albert II, Holy Roman Emperor, King of Hungary and Bohemia, d. 1439 (pp. 220-21)

39. James I, King of Scotland, d. 1437 (pp. 222-25, 898-99), son of #43, grandson of #44, father of #37

40. Charles VI, King of France, d. 1422 (pp. 226-28), grandson of #47, father of #36, grandfather of #35

41. Henry IV, King of England, d. 1413 (pp. 229-36), grandson of #46 (all through an illegitimate daughter of his son, Humphrey Plantagenet, Duke of Gloucester)

The Royal Descents of 900 Immigrants

42. Rupert III, Holy Roman Emperor, d. 1410 (pp. 237-38) (and pp. 287-91 via Zinzendorf cousins of Leopold I, King of the Belgians, d. 1865, and Victoria, Queen of Great Britain, d. 1901)

43. Robert III, King of Scotland, d. 1406 (pp. 239-68), son of #44, father of #39, grandfather of #37

44. Robert II, King of Scotland, d. 1390 (pp. 269-86), grandson of #50, father of #43, grandfather of #39

45. Charles II, King of Navarre, d. 1387 (pp. 287-94), son of #49, son-in-law of #47 (pp. 287-92, via Noailles cousins of Louis Philippe, King of the French, d. 1850, and the Empress Eugénie of the French, d. 1920, and pp. 287-91 also from Rupert III, Holy Roman Emperor, #42 above)

46. Edward III, King of England, d. 1377 (pp. 295-437, 900-6), pp. 300-4 through William Carey or perhaps Henry VIII, King of England, d. 1547, son of #26, grandson of #28, and Mary Boleyn, aunt of Queen Elizabeth I), grandson of #53, grandfather of #41

47. John II, King of France, d. 1364 (pp. 438-46), grandfather of #40

48. Louis IV, Holy Roman Emperor, d. 1347 (pp. 447-54, 907-8, 451-54 also from John III, King of Sweden, d. 1592, full brother of #21, half-brother of #23, who has no proved pre-Vasa royal ancestry)

49. Philip III, King of Navarre, d. 1343 (p. 455), father of #45

50. Robert I, King of Scotland, d. 1329 (p. 456), grandfather of #44

51. Haakon V, King of Norway, d. 1319 (pp. 457-58)

52. Charles II (of Anjou and France), King of Naples and Sicily, d. 1309 (pp. 459-61), nephew of the wives of #s57 and 58

53. Edward I, King of England, d. 1307 (pp. 462-616, 615-16 via John de Foix, 1st Earl of Kendal, and Margaret Kerdeston, grandparents of Anne de Foix, wife of Ladislaus V, King of Bohemia and Hungary, d. 1516), son of #57, grandson of #63, grandfather of #46

54. Adolf I of Nassau-Wiesbaden, Holy Roman Emperor, d. 1298 (pp. 617-18)

The Royal Descents of 900 Immigrants

55. Alfonso III, King of Portugal, d. 1279 (pp. 619-20)

56. Przemysl Ottokar II, King of Bohemia, d. 1278 (pp. 621-22) (also from Grand Princes of Moscow and Youri I, called King of Galicia), son of #59

57. Henry III, King of England, d. 1272 (pp. 623-33), son of #63, grandson of #66, father of #53

58. St. Louis IX, King of France, d. 1270 (pp. 634-39) (#57 and #58 were brothers-in-law, married to sisters), grandfather-in-law of #53

59. Wenceslaus I, King of Bohemia, d. 1253 (pp. 640-41), son-in-law of Philip of Swabia, King of the Romans, grandson-in-law of Frederick I Barbarossa, Holy Roman Emperor, #65, brother-in-law of #61, father of #56

60. Amadeus IV, Count of Savoy, ruler of Milan, d. 1253 (pp. 642-43), father-in-law of Manfred, King of Sicily, d. 1266

61. Waldemar II, King of Denmark, d. 1241 (pp. 644-46), brother-in-law of #59

62. Alfonso IX, King of Leon, d. 1230 (pp. 647-49, 909-10) (and John de Brienne, Emperor of Constantinople, d. 1237), grandfather-in-law of #53

63. John "Lackland," King of England, d. 1216 (pp. 650-99; pp. 653-56, 661-64, 672-75 via his son Richard Plantagenet, King of the Romans, and 650-52, 657-60, 686, 689-90, 692-94 via illegitimate children of David, Prince of North Wales, his grandson), son of #66, father of #57

64. William the Lion, King of Scotland, d. 1214 (pp. 700-32), all via illegitmate daughters (pp. 700-31 via Isabel of Scotland, wife of Robert de Ros, Magna Charta surety)

65. Frederick I Barbarossa, Holy Roman Emperor, d. 1190, and his son, Philip of Swabia, King of the Romans, d. 1208 (pp. 733-36), grandfather-in-law and son-in-law of #59

66. Henry II, King of England, d. 1189 (pp. 737-72), father of #63, grandfather of #57 (all via his illegitimate son, William Longespee, Earl of Salisbury)

The Royal Descents of 900 Immigrants

67. Louis VII, King of France, d. 1180 (pp. 774-77) (#66 and #67 both married the famed Eleanor of Aquitaine), son of #70

68. David I, King of Scotland, d. 1153 (pp. 778-90, pp. 778-90 via sisters of Robert I, King of Scotland, 780-82 via a sister of John Baliol, King of Scotland, d. 1313), grandfather of #64

69. Boleslaw III, King of Poland, d. 1138 (pp. 791-803, pp. 791-96 via a Romanov aunt of Michael III, Czar of Russia, d. 1645, and pp. 797-801 via a great-aunt of Ivan III, first Czar of Russia, d. 1505)

70. Louis VI, King of France, d. 1137 (pp. 804-5), grandson of #75, father of #67

71. Henry I, King of England, d. 1135 (pp. 806-27), son of #73, grandfather of #66 (all via one of two illegitimate sons, earls of Cornwall and Gloucester)

72. Donald III Bane, King of Scotland, d. 1099 (pp. 828-29)

73. William I, the Conqueror, King of England, d. 1087 (pp. 830-31, 911-13), father of #71, grandson-in-law of #77

74. Bela I, King of Hungary, d. 1063 (pp. 832-34)

75. Henry I, King of France, d. 1060 (pp. 835-48), son of #77, grandson of #79, grandfather of 70 (all via a granddaughter, Isabel of Vermandois, successively Countess of Leicester and Countess of Surrey in England)

76. Mieszko II Lambert, King of Poland, d. 1034 (pp. 849-50)

77. Robert II, King of France, d. 1031 (pp. 851-56), son of #79, father of #75, grandfather-in-law of #73

78. Ethelred II the Unready, King of England, d. 1016 (pp. 857-65, with Mrs. Jerome Napoleon Bonaparte, daughter-in-law of Jerome Bonaparte, King of Westphalia, on p. 858)

79. Hugh Capet, King of France, d. 996 (pp. 866-73), grandson of #81, father of #77, grandfather of #75

80. Louis IV, King of France, d. 954 (pp. 874-78)

81. Robert I, King of France, d. 923 (pp. 879-84), grandfather of #79 (all also from a sister of #73 and possibly #79 or #80)

The Royal Descents of 900 Immigrants

82. Turlough O'Conor Don, King of Connaught, d. 1406 (p. 885)

83. Angharad II, Queen of Powys (whose son Rhywallon, Prince of Powys, d. 1070) (pp. 886-87 – only Thomas Lewis of Maine, whose wife was descended from #53)

And, from "Immigrants...Received or Developed After Much of This Volume Had Been Indexed":

84. Sigismund I, King of Poland, d. 1548 (pp. 895-96), son of #34

The Royal Descents of 900 Immigrants

Appendix V to the Introduction, Part 1:
140 Immigrants New to the 2004-2010 Editions

1. Almy, Mrs. Audrey Barlow, of R.I.
2. Alston, John, of N.C.
3. Amherst of Holmesdale and Montreal, Jeffrey Amherst, 1st Baron of, governor of Va.
4. Annan, Mrs. Nina Maria (Nane) Lagergren Cronstedt, of N.Y.
5. Ashby, John, of S.C.
6. Ash(e) (Lillington), Mrs. Mary Batt, of S.C.
7. Baillie, Robert, of Ga.
8. Barcroft, Mrs. Elizabeth Wood, of Va.
9. Baring-Gould, William Drake, of Minn.
10. Barnes, Charles, of N.Y.
11. Baskerville, John, of Va.
12. Bellingham, Mrs. Elizabeth Backhouse, of Mass.
13. Blount, James, of N.C.
14. Boone, Thomas, gov. of N.J. and S.C.
15. Booth, Thomas, of Va.
16. Brassey, Thomas, of Pa.
17. Breyer, Hon. Mrs. Joanna Freda Hare, of Mass.
18. Bridges, Mrs. Mary Woodcock, of Mass.
19. Brodnax, Mrs. Dorothy Beresford, of Va.
20. Buncombe, Edward, of N.C.
21. Burr, Mrs. Abigail Brewster, of Conn.
22. Burton, Mrs. Beatrice Maud Boswell Eliott, of N.Y.
23. Burwell, Mrs. Abigail Smith, of Va.

The Royal Descents of 900 Immigrants

24. Calthorpe, Christopher, of Va.
25. Cary, Hon. Mrs. Cynthia Burke Roche Burden, of R.I.
26. Cheseldine, Kenelm, atty gen. of Md.
27. Cleeve, Mrs. Joan Price, of Me.
28. Clement(s), Mrs. Elizabeth Bullock, of Mass.
29. Cooke, Mrs. Elizabeth Haynes, of Mass.
30. Cotton, Leonard, of N.H.
31. Coward, Noël (Pierce), sometime of N.Y.
32. Hamilton-Cox, Henry, of Pa.
33. Dalyell, (Mrs.) Magdalen (Dalyell Monteith, later), of Va.
34. Danvers, Thomas, of Pa.
35. Dobkin, Maria Immaculata Pia, (Countess) von Habsburg, of N.Y.
36. Dobyns, Daniel, of Va.
37. Dodge, Mrs. Jane Evans, of N.Y.
38. Dunlop, Archibald, of Conn.
39. Edgeworth, Richard, of N.C.
40. Elwes, (Ivan Simon) Cary of Calif.
41. Evans, John, of Radnor, Pa.
42. Everett, Rupert (Hector), of Calif.
43. Falconer, Alexander, of Md.
44. Falconer, Patrick, of Conn. and N.J.
45. Fenner, Mrs. Anne Coddington, of N.C.
46. Fiennes, Ralph (Nathaniel), of Calif.
47. Fiennes, Joseph (Alberic), of Calif.
48. Gage, Hon. Thomas, of Mass.
49. Gale, George, of Va. and Md.

The Royal Descents of 900 Immigrants

50. Golding, Ephraim, of L.I., N.Y.
51. Gotherson (Hogben), Mrs. Dorothea Scott, of L.I., N.Y.
52. von Graffenried, Christoph(er), Baron, Landgrave of N.C.
53. Grant, Hugh (John Mungo), sometime of Calif.
54. Greene, Thomas, gov. of Md.
55. Gyllenhaal, Anders Leonard, of Ill.
56. Harbou, Fritz, of N.Y.
57. Hardy, Lady Elizabeth Tate, wife of Sir Charles Hardy, gov. of N.Y., admiral
58. Harrison, Benjamin, of Va.
59. Haugwitz-Hardenburg-Reventlow, Curt Henry Eberhard Erdmann George, Count, of N.Y.
60. Henchman, Mrs. Sarah Woodward, of Mass.
61. Hepburn, Audrey, of Calif. (Mrs. Edda Kathleen van Heemstra Hepburn-Ruston Ferrer Dotti)
62. Hubbard, Mrs. Judith Knapp, of Mass.
63. Hughes (Hugh, Pugh), John, of Pa.
64. Huxley, Aldous Leonard, of Calif.
65. Hyde, Edward, proprietary gov. of N.C.
66. Jernegan, Thomas, of Va.
67. Jerningham, Henry, of Md.
68. Johnston, Mrs. Henrietta de Beaulieu Dering, of S.C. (first husband, Robert Dering)
69. Jones, Mrs. Dorothy Walker, of Va.
70. Kennedy, William, of N.C.
71. Kyrle, Lady Mary Jephson, of S.C.
72. Kyrle, Sir Richard, governor of S.C.
73. Law, Thomas, of Va.

The Royal Descents of 900 Immigrants

74. Lechmere, Thomas, of Mass.
75. Levis, Samuel, of Pa.
76. Lillie, Beatrice Gladys, "Bea," of N.Y. (husband, Sir Robert Peel, 5th Bt.)
77. Lovell, Mrs. Penelope Eleanor Elphinstone-Dalrymple Balston, of Mass.
78. Lowell, Percival, of Mass.
79. Ludwell, Gov. Philip, of N.C. and S.C. (descendants in Va.)
80. Lunsford, Lady Katherine Neville, of Va.
81. Mackay, George, of Washington, D.C.
82. Maitland, James William, of N.Y.
83. McEwen, John William, of Me.
84. McKay, George Alexander, of Mass.
85. Meade, Mrs. Henrietta Constantia Worsam, of Pa.
86. Mellon, Mrs. Vivian Rüesch, of N.Y.
87. Moore, Mrs. Katherine Selwood, of S.C.
88. Nelson, Philip, of Mass.
89. Nelson, Thomas (Jr.), of Mass.
90. Niven, Mrs. Primula Susan Rollo, of Calif.
91. Norwood, Henry, of Va.
92. Nowell, Increase, secretary of Mass.
93. Ogilvy, David Mackenzie, of N.Y.
94. Otis, Mrs. Rose Stoughton, of N.H.
95. Oxenbridge, Mrs. Frances Woodward (husband of Mass.)
96. Parsons, Mrs. Audrey Divett Buller, of R.I.
97. Peter, Robert, of Md.
98. Peter(s), Mrs. Deliverance Sheffield, of Mass.

The Royal Descents of 900 Immigrants

99. Plater-Zyberk, Maria Malgarzata Paulina Wilhelmina Róza Leopoldyna Julia Wielopolska, Countess, of Pa.

100. Poole, Mrs. Jane Greene, of Mass.

101. Radziwill, Stanislaus Albert, Prince, of N.Y.

102. Ritchie, Guy Stuart, sometime of N.Y. or Calif. (husband of Madonna [Louise Veronica] Ciccone)

103. Rivers, Mrs. Elizabeth Mallory, of S.C.

104. Roosevelt, Mrs. Lydia M. Latrobe, of N.Y.

105. Sewall, Henry, secretary of Md.

106. Seymour, Mrs. Hester Newton, of Md.

107. Seymour, John, governor of Md.

108. Shepard, Mrs. Margaret Estouteville/Touteville, of Mass.

109. Skepper/Skipper, Rev. William, of Mass.

110. Skinner, Mrs. Anne Storer Truman, of Md.

111. Smith, Mrs. Maria Jo(h)anna Somerset Lowther, of Md.

112. Snelling, William, of Mass.

113. Southill (Sothild, Sothill, Sotehill, Sothel), Seth, gov. of N.C.

114. Stevenson, Robert Louis, sometime of N.Y. and Calif.

115. Stites, Mrs. Mary Underhill Naylor, of N.Y.

116. Storer, Arthur, of Md.

117. Stratton, Mrs. Anne Derehaugh, of Mass.

118. Summersby, Kay (Mrs. Kathleen Helen McCarthy-Morrogh Summersby Morgan), of N.Y.

119. Sydnor, Fortunatus, of Va.

120. Taylor, James, of Mass.

121. Thompson, Stephens/Stevens, atty. gen. of Va.

122. Tucker, Henry, of Va.

123. Umfreville/Humphreville, John, of Conn.

124. Underhill, Humphrey, of N.Y.
125. van Tuyl, Jan Otten, of N.Y.
126. Ward (Sheed), (Mrs.) Mary Josephine "Maisie," of N.Y.
127. Wedgwood, Josiah Ralph Patrick, of Seattle, Wash.
128. West, Anthony, of N.Y.
129. Whitehead, Mrs. Evelyn Ada Maud Rice Willoughby-Wade, of Mass.
130. Williams, Mrs. Frances Baldwin Townshend Jones, of Va.
131. Willing, Charles, of Pa.
132. Wilson, Mrs. Elizabeth Mansfield, of Mass.
133. Wilson, Leighton, of Ga.
134. Wodehouse, Sir Pelham Grenville (P.G.), sometime of N.Y.
135. Woolley, Emmanuel, of R.I.
136. Worden, Peter, of Mass.
137. Wyatt, Mrs. Barbara Mitford, of Va.
138. Wyndham/Windham, Edward, of Va.
139. Yonge, Francis, chief justice of S.C.
140. Yonge, Robert, of S.C.

The Royal Descents of 900 Immigrants

Appendix V, Part 2:
75 Colonial Immigrants New to *RD900* with Notable American Descendants

1. Mrs. Rebecca Ward Allen of Mass.
2. Mrs. Margaret Mackenzie Avery of S.C.
3. Mrs. Frances Ravenscroft Ball of Va.
4. Mary Janssen Calvert, Baroness Baltimore, of Md.
5. Mrs. Frances Walker Ban(n)ister of Mass.
6. William Baugh of Va.
7. Mrs. Dorothy Mellish Beresford of S.C.
8. Mrs. Barbara Janssen Bladen of Md.
9. John Bradstreet of N.Y.
10. Mrs. Anne Mellish Splatt le Brassieur of S.C.
11. Levin Bufkin of Va.
12. Mrs. Sarah Tucker Harris Bullard of S.C.
13. Charles Chambers of Mass.
14. Leonard Chester of Conn.
15. Norton Claypoole of Del.

16-17. James and Anne (Brent) Clifton of Md.

18. Rev. Thomas Craighead of Pa.
19. Dr. William Crymes of Va.
20. Mrs. Helen Cuming Cuming of Mass.
21. William Cumming of Md.
22. Mrs. Anne Revell Curtis of N.J.
23. Mrs. Mary Ward Cutting (Miller) of Mass.
24. Mrs. Anne Talbot Darnall of Md.
25. Rev. Gregory Dexter of R.I.
26. Thomas Duke of Va.

The Royal Descents of 900 Immigrants

27. Thomas Fraser of S.C. and N.J.
28. John Freake of Mass.
29. Mrs. Thomasine Clench Frost of Mass.
30. Mrs. Anne Fielder Gantt (Wight) of Md.
31. Mrs. Katherine Duncanson Glen of N.Y.
32. Mrs. Anne Skipwith Goforth (Oxley) of N.J.
33. Culcheth Golightly of S.C.
34. Dr. Thomas Graeme of Pa.
35. Henry Gregory of Conn.
36. Mrs. Margaret Domville Hatton (Banks) of Md.
37. Sir Robert Hesilrige, 8th Bt., sometime of Mass.
38. Mrs. Catherine Craighead Homes of Mass.
39. Theophilus Hone of Va.
40. Edward Howell of L.I., N.Y.
41. Thomas Hussey of Md.
42. John Ireland of Md.
43. Ralph Izard of S.C.
44. Ralph Joslin(g) of Va.
45. John Lightfoot of Va.
46. Philip Lightfoot of Va.
47. Mrs. Mary Jones Lloyd of Pa.
48. Mrs. Grizel Campbell McNeill of N.C.
49. William Markham of Mass.
50. William Mauduit of Md.
51. Thomas Monteith of Va.
52. Mrs. Anna Tucker Morgan of S.C.
53. Joseph Need of Pa.
54. John Norton of Va.

The Royal Descents of 900 Immigrants

55. George Pordage of Mass.
56. Thomas Prater/Prather of Va.
57. Mrs. Elizabeth Whetenhall Rozier of Md.
58. Mrs. Elizabeth Hussey Scott of Mass.
59. Mrs. Elizabeth Pride Gibbs Sherwin of N.C.
60. Keith Spence of N.H.
61. William Stewart of N.C.
62. George Symes of Va.
63. William Tazewell of Va.
64. Mrs. Margaret Duncanson Teller of N.Y.
65. Mrs. Catherine Kennedy Tennent of Pa.
66. Edward Thornborough/Thornburgh of Pa.
67. Thomas Thornborough/Thornburgh of Va.
68. Robert Traill of Pa.
69. Mrs. Penelope Spencer Treworgy of Maine, Mass., and Newfoundland
70. John Wallace of Pa.
71. Thomas Wentworth of Va.
72. Robert Wiseman of Md.
73. Mrs. Anne Capell Wiseman, prob. of Md.
74. Francis Yarnall of Pa.
75. Philip Yarnall of Pa.

Colonial Immigrants Notable in Their Own Right (or that of their spouses) New to *RD900*

1. Mrs. Elizabeth Duke Bacon (Jarvis Mole), of Va.
2. Nathaniel Bacon, Act. Gov. of Va. (not the husband of 1. above)
3. Mrs. Barbara Janssen Bladen of Md. (British descendants only)
4. John Clayton of Va.

The Royal Descents of 900 Immigrants

5. Thomas Cornwaleys (Cornwallis) of Md.
6. Mrs. Elizabeth Wilson Glen of S.C.
7. Mrs. Anne Cheney Knollys, sometime of Mass.
8. Lady Charlotte Clayton Lovelace, Baroness Lovelace, of N.Y.
9. Mrs. Elizabeth Taylor (Tufton alias) Mason of N.H.
10. Mrs. Katherine Selwood Moore of S.C.
11. Rev. Edward Norris of Mass.
12. Rev. Thomas Peter(s), sometime of Conn.
13. William Tatham of Washington, D.C.

Colonial Immigrants of Speculative Royal Descent

1. Mrs. Catherine White Leggett Carver of Mass. (wife of first Plymouth Colony Governor John Carver) (no issue)
2. Mrs. Elizabeth Stoughton Scudder Chamberlain of Mass.
3. Isaac Robinson of Mass.
4. Mrs. Judith Stoughton Denman Smead of Mass.
5. Israel Stoughton of Mass.
6. Thomas Stoughton of Mass.

Of the first 75 of the above, those with large progenies (so most likely to be in the ancestry of possibly millions of Americans) are Mrs. Allen, Chambers, Chester, Mrs. Cutting, Mrs. Darnall, Dexter, Mrs. Gantt, Mrs. Katherine D. Glen, Mrs. Goforth, Gregory, Mrs. Hatton, Mrs. Homes, Hone, Howell, Izard, John Lightfoot, Mrs. Lloyd, Markham, Prat(h)er, Mrs. Teller, and the Yarnalls (twenty-two in all).

The Royal Descents of 900 Immigrants

Appendix V, Part 3:
160 Nineteenth- and Twentieth-Century Immigrants New to *RD900*

1. Hon. William **Anson** of Texas
2. Princess Alexandra Galitzine Romanoff **Armour** of Ill.
3. Peter **Asher**, sometime of Calif.
4. Mrs. Myrtle Jane Goodacre **Ashmole**, sometime of Conn.
5. Adele **Astaire** (first husband – Lord Charles Arthur Cavendish), sometime of N.Y. and Arizona
6. Mrs. Anna Maria Drury **Atwater** of N.Y.
7. Fernand **Auberjonois** of N.Y.
8. Princess Laure-Louise-Napoléone-Eugénie-Caroline Murat **Frank Auberjonois** of N.Y.
9. W.H. (Wystan Hugh) **Auden**, sometime of N.Y.
10. Mrs. Hermione Youlanda Ruby Clinton-**Baddeley** (Tennant Willis) [Hermione Baddeley], sometime of Calif.
11. Prince Teymuraz **Bagration** (-Mukransky), Prince of Georgia, of N.Y.
12. St. Clair **Bayfield** (John St. Clair Roberts) of N.Y.
13. (Count) William Frederick **Bentinck** of Missouri
14. Mrs. Josephine Alma Danielsen **Berg** of N.Y.

Peter **Berlin**, *see* Hoyningen-Huene, Baron Armin Hagen, of Calif.

15. Sir Timothy John "Tim" **Berners-Lee** of Mass.
16. Jane **Birkin**, wife of John **Barry** of N.Y.
17. Mrs. Jeanne-Marie-Bernarde de Menthon **Boal**, sometime of Washington, D.C.
18. Mrs. Mathilde Denis de Lagarde **Boal** of Pa.
19. George Vladimir [Gregori, Count] **Bobrinskoy** of Ill.
20. Marie-Thérèse-Vera-Zwetana, Countess von Hartenau, wife of Charles Hercules **Boissevain**, sometime of N.Y. and Colo.

The Royal Descents of 900 Immigrants

21. Helena **Bonham Carter**, sometime of N.Y. or Calif.
22. Francesco Marco Luigi Costanzo **Borghese**, 6th Duke of Bomarzo, sometime of N.Y.
23. Ranieri **Bourbon del Monte Santa Maria**, Prince of San Faustino, husband of Kay Linn Sage, of Calif.
24. (William) Nigel (Ernle) **Bruce** of Calif.
25. Claus [Cecil Borberg, later] **von Bülow** of R.I.
26. Mrs. Jeanne Maud Martineau Grewcock **Cahill** of N.Y.
27. Ewen Somerled **Cameron** of Montana (husband of [Mrs.] Evelyn [Jephson Flower] Cameron)
28. Théophile **Cazenove**, sometime of Pa.
29. Hon. John Francis Amherst **Cecil**, sometime of N.C.
30. Princess Nina Romanoff **Chavchadze** (Grand Duchess of Russia) of Mass.
31. (Michael) Jeremy (Thomas) **Clyde** (Jeremy of "Chad and Jeremy"), sometime of Calif.
32. Andrew Myles **Cockburn** of N.Y. and Calif. (father of Olivia Wilde)
33. Franz Ferdinand Romanus, Count **Colloredo-Mansfeld** of Mass.
34. Daniel (Wroughton) **Craig**, sometime of N.Y.
35. Benedict **Cumberbatch**, sometime of Calif.
36. Mrs. Sophie Irene Hunter **Cumberbatch**, sometime of Calif.
37. Mrs. Alison E. MacCarthy-Willis-Bund **Curtis** of Calif. and R.I.
38. Mrs. Olivia Jane **D'Abo** Leonard, sometime of Calif.
39. William Pulteney **Dana**, of N.Y.
40. Catherine, Countess Cheremetov, wife of Daniel Pomeroy **Davison** of N.Y.
41. (Hon.) Mrs. Mildred Sophia Noreen Stonor **Drexel** of R.I.

The Royal Descents of 900 Immigrants

42. Friedrich Ernst Sigismond Kamill (Frederick W.), Baron **von Egloffstein**, of N.Y.

43. Irmgarde (von Kiesenwetter), Baroness **von Egloffstein**, of N.Y.

44. Andrew **Elliott** of N.Y.

45. Jean-Baptiste-Charles-Henri-Hector **d'Estaing**, Revolutionary commander

46. Sir Richard (Charles Hastings) **Eyre**, sometime of N.Y.

47. Nicholas FitzMaurice **Fagan** of Pa.

48. Victor Ernst Hermann **von Finck** of Mo.

49. Mrs. Philippa Ruth Bosanquet **Foot** of Calif.

50. Joseph Baron **von and zu Franckenstein**, husband of Kay Boyle, sometime of N.Y. and Calif.

51. Lady Carina Mary Gabriel FitzAlan-Howard, wife of David (Paradine) **Frost**, sometime of N.Y. and Calif.

52. Sergei, Prince **Gagarin**, of N.Y.

53. Nicholas, Prince **Galitzine**, of Ill.

54. (Abraham Alphonse) Albert **Gallatin** of N.Y.

55. Mrs. Anne Elizabeth Wilson **Gergen** of Mass.

56. Sir (Arthur) John **Gielgud**, sometime of N.Y. and Calif.

57. Prince Demetrius Augustine **Golitzin (Gallitzine)** of Md. and Pa.

58. Maria Anna (C.Z.E.R.T.), Archduchess of Austria, Princess **Golitzin (Gallitzine)** of Ill.

59. Prince Peter **Golitzin (Gallitzine)** of Ill.

60. Mrs. Susanna Schilling von Canstatt **von Gontard** of Mo.

61. Charles Russell McGregor, later **Gregor**, of N.Y.

62. Maria, Countess Cheremetoff, wife of Brandon Hambright **Grove** (and Robert G. Abernethy), sometime of Washington, D.C.

63. Princess Caroline-Cécile-Alexandrine-Jeanne Murat **Guest** of Va.

64. Bernardo Frederico **Guillermo** of N.Y.

The Royal Descents of 900 Immigrants

65. Benjamin Seymour **Guinness**, sometime of N.Y.
66. Mrs. Bridget Henrietta Frances Williams-Bulkeley **Guinness** of N.Y.
67. Hon. Daphne Suzannah Diana Joan **Guinness** Niarchos
68. Sir Kenelm Ernest Lee "Tim" **Guinness**, 4th Bt., of Md.
69. Robert **Haig** of Ohio
70. René (Count) **d'Harnoncourt** of N.Y.
71. Charles Edward **Harte** of Ohio
72. Christiane Asschenfeldt, Countess **Henckel von Donnersmarck** of Calif.
73. Florian (Maria Georg Christian), Count **Henckel von Donnersmarck**, of Calif.
74. Ludmilla Maria, Princess zu Schwarzenburg, wife of Carl Barton **Hess**, of N.Y.
75. Alexander **de Hinojosa** of N.Y.
76. William Johan (William J.) **Hoffman** of N.Y.
77. Cecil DeBlaquiere **Howard** of N.Y.
78. George **Howard** of Washington, D.C.
79. Armin Hagen, Baron **Hoyningen-Huene** ("Peter Berlin") of Calif.
80. Allegra **Huston** of Taos, N.M.
81. Jack Alexander **Huston**, sometime of Calif.
82. Stanley (Patrick) **Johnson**, sometime of N.Y.
83. Charles **Johnston** of N.Y.
84. Friedrich George **Kaufholz** of Ohio
85. Vernon Hew Primrose Shaw **Kennedy** of Ill.
86. Anna, Princess Galitzine, wife of Sergei **Kravchenko** of Mass.
87. Caroline (Eugénie, Baroness von) **Lagerfelt** of N.Y.

The Royal Descents of 900 Immigrants

88. Lang, Mrs. Thea von Harbou Klein-Rogge, wife of Fritz **Lang**, long of Calif.
89. Count Eric Emil Audley **von Lewenhaupt**, of Calif.
90. Countess Hedvig Margaretha **von Lewenhaupt**, of Calif.
91. (Ernst) Aschwin (Georg Carol Heinrich Ignatz), Prince of **Lippe-Biesterfeld**, of N.Y.
92. Maximilian Erwin (Maria Joseph Antonius von Padua Heinrich Thomas), Prince **Lobkowicz**, sometime of Mass.
93. William John Muir Lowe, known as John **Loder**, husband of Hedy Lamarr, sometime of Calif.
94. (Countess) Elizabeth Belevsky-Zhukovsky Perevostchikov **Lourie** of N.Y.
95. Mary Elizabeth **Lowndes** of Conn.
96. Alexi(s), Prince **Lubomirsky** of N.Y.
97. Francisco de Paula Eustaquio (Frank E.) **Lynch Zavaleta**, sometime of Calif.
98. Percy Tilson **Magan**, Jr. of Calif.
99. Henry Austin **Martin** of Mass.
100. Harriet **Martineau**, traveler in the U.S.
101. Mrs. Margery Hilda Fremantle Massey Sebright, wife of Raymond Hart **Massey** of Calif.
102. Mrs. Margaret Wade Linton **Mather** of Conn.
103. John Loudon **McAdam**, sometime of N.Y.
104. Mrs. Ada Harte **Miles** of Ill.
105. Alexandra, Princess of Greece and Denmark, sometime of N.Y., wife of Nicolas **Miryazantz**
106. Mrs. Cathleen Synge **Morawetz** of N.Y.
107. Mrs. Caroline Durnford Dunscomb **Mosle** of N.Y.
108. Vladimir **Nabokov**, sometime of N.Y.

The Royal Descents of 900 Immigrants

109. Mrs. Diana Mary Villiers **Negroponte** of Washington, D.C.
110. Sergei, Prince **Obolensky** (-Neledinsky-Meletzky) of N.Y. and Mich.
111. Thomas **O'Con(n)or** of N.Y.
112. Maximilian Hugo, Baron **von Pagenhardt**, of Washington, D.C.
113. Camille-Armand-Jules-Marie, Prince **de Polignac**, of the Confederacy
114. Mrs. Dorothy Shakespear **Pound**, sometime of Washington, D.C.
115. Alan Payan **Pryce-Jones**, of Newport, R.I.
116. Mrs. Matilda Charlotte Palgrave Chetwynd-Talbot **Rantoul** of Mass.
117. (Mrs.) Lynn (Rachel) **Redgrave** (Clark), sometime of Conn.
118. Mrs. Natasha **Richardson** (Fox Neeson), sometime of N.Y.
119. Muriel (Elsa Florence) Forbes-Robertson Richardson, wife of Sir Ralph (David) **Richardson**, sometime of N.Y. and Calif.
120. Andrew **Romanoff**, Grand Duke of Russia, of Calif.
121. Nikita **Romanoff**, Grand Duke of Russia, of N.Y.
122. Rostislav **Romanoff**, Grand Duke of Russia, sometime of Ill.
123. Paul, Prince **Romanovsky-Ilyinski** (Paul R. Ilyinski), sometime of Fla.
124. Bartolomeo **Ruspoli** of Calif.
125. Tao **Ruspoli** of Calif.
126. Lady Sarah Cornelia Spencer-Churchill **Russell** (Burgos Roubanis), sometime of Pa. and N.Y.
127. Mrs. Lilian May Caulfield **Sanders** of Pa.
128. Anthony Frederick "Tony" **Sarg** of N.Y.
129. Marcus (Lodewijk) **Schenkenberg** (**van Mierop**), sometime of Calif.

The Royal Descents of 900 Immigrants

130. Sir William (George) **Douglas-Stewart**, 7th Bt., sometime of Mo. and points west

131. Mrs. Jane Adams **Stock** of Idaho (under Thomas Owsley)

132. Alexander Maria Hubertus Hyacinthus, Count **Strachwitz von Gross Zauche und Camminetz**, of Calif.

133. Esais Reinhold Slettengren, later **Swain**, of Mass.

134. (Mrs. Katherine Matilda) "Tilda" **Swinton** (Byrne) of Calif.

135. Anton Carl Sylvester, Count **Szápáry**, sometime of Newport, R.I.

136. Ladislaus (László), Count **Széchényi**, sometime of Newport, R.I.

137. Humphrey (John Fausit) **Taylor** of N.Y.

138. Mrs. Amy Dulcibella Wodehouse **von Tempski** of Hawaii

139. Alexis Henry de Clerel **de Tocqueville**, traveler in the U.S.

140. Alexandra, Countess **Tolstoy**, of N.Y.

141. Agathe (Johanna Erwina Gobertina) **von Trapp** of Vt. and Md.

142. Hedwig (Maria Adolphine Gobertina) **von Trapp** of Vt.

143. Johanna Karolina/Joanna Carolina **von Trapp** Winter of N.Y.

144. Maria (Agathe) Franziska Gobertina **von Trapp** of Vt.

145. Martina **von Trapp** Dupire of Vt.

146. Rupert (Georg) **von Trapp** of Vt.

147. Werner **von Trapp** of Vt.

148. Mrs. Frances Milton **Trollope**, traveler in the U.S.

149. Pierre, Prince **Troubetskoy** of Va.

150. Sergei, Prince **Troubetskoy**, sometime of Va.

151. Vladimir, Prince **Troubetskoy**, of Wisc.

152. James **Tytler**, of Mass.

153. Carl Magnus Helmfrid **Uggla** of N.Y.

The Royal Descents of 900 Immigrants

154. Jan Samuel François **van Hoogstraten**, of N.Y.
155. James Michael Hyde **Villiers**, briefly of N.Y.
156. Alexander Raban "Alec" **Waugh**, sometime of N.Y. and Fla.
157. Frederick **Wiggin** of N.Y.
158. (Dame) Anna **Wintour** Shaffer of N.Y.
159. Ernest Hay **Wodehouse** of Hawaii
160. Mrs. Frances ("Fanny") **Wright** (Phiquepal-Arusmont) of Tenn., Ohio and N.Y.

The Royal Descents of 900 Immigrants

Appendix VI to the Introduction: 227 (and Probably or Eventually Over 240) Royally Descended Immigrants Who Left 10 or More Notable Descendants

Massachusetts

    1. Robert Abell

    2. Mrs. Rebecca Ward Allen

    3-4. Samuel and Judith (Everard) Appleton

    5-6. Christopher and Anne (Bainton) Batt

    7-8. Griffith and Margaret (Fleming) Bowen

    9. Thomas Bradbury

    10. Edward Bromfield

    11. Mrs. Thomasine Ward Thompson Buffum

12-14. Rev. Peter, Jane (Allen) and Grace (Chetwode) Bulkeley

    15. Mrs. Mary Lawrence Burnham

    16. Nathaniel Burroughs

17-18. Edward and Ellen (Newton) Carleton

    19. Charles Chambers

    20. Rev. Charles Chauncey

    21. Mrs. Elizabeth Bullock Clement(s)

    22. James Cudworth

    23. Mrs. Mary Ward Cutting (Miller)

24-25. Gov. Thomas and Katherine (Deighton Hackburne, later Allyn) Dudley

    26. Mrs. Olive Welby Farwell

    27. Robert Gibbs

    28. Mrs. Jane Lawrence Giddings

    29. William Goddard

The Royal Descents of 900 Immigrants

30. Mrs. Elizabeth Bulkeley Whittingham Haugh
31. Edmond Hawes
32. Mrs. Sarah Woodward Henchman
33. Joshua Henshaw
34. Mrs. Catherine Craighead Homes
35. Mrs. Judith Knapp Hubbard
36. Mrs. Catherine Hamby Hutchinson
37. Percival Lowell
38. Simon Lynde
39. William Markham
40. Mrs. Mary Gye Maverick
41. Mrs. Martha Bulkeley Mellowes
42. James Murray (husband of #212)
43. Mrs. Jane Deighton Lugg Negus
44. John Nelson of Boston
45. Philip Nelson of Rowley
46. Increase Nowell

47-48. Rev. John and Frances (Woodward) Oxenbridge
   49. Dr. Richard Palgrave
   50. Mrs. Anne Humphrey Palmes (Myles)

51-52. Herbert and Jemima (Waldegrave) Pelham
53-54. William and Jane (Greene) Poole
   55. Mrs. Amy Wyllys Pynchon
   56. Edward Raynsford

57-58. Richard and Muriel (Gurdon) Saltonstall
   59. Rev. William Sargent
   60. Mrs. Margaret (Es)Touteville Shepard

The Royal Descents of 900 Immigrants

- 61. Mrs. Mary Launce Sherman
- 62. Gov. William Shirley (some of whose notable progeny is British)
- 63. Rev. William Skepper/Skipper
- 64-65. Constant and Thomas Southworth
- 66. Mrs. Anne Derehaugh Stratton
- 67. Peter Talbot
- 68. James Taylor
- 69. Mrs. Elizabeth Stratton Thorndike
- 70. Mrs. Jane Haviland Torrey
- 71. Mrs. Elizabeth St. John Whiting
- 72. Mrs. Frances Deighton Williams
- 73. Mrs. Elizabeth Mansfield Wilson
- 74. Mrs. Margaret Tyndal Winthrop (some of whose notable progeny is British)
- 75. Peter Worden

plus Maine (part of Massachusetts until 1820)
- 76. Joseph Bolles
- 77. Mrs. Joan Price Cleeve
- 78-79. Thomas and Elizabeth (Marshall) Lewis

Connecticut
- 80. Mrs. Margaret Wyatt Allyn
- 81. Mrs. Elizabeth Alsop Baldwin (Fowler)
- 82. Thomas Bressie
- 83. Obadiah Bruen

The Royal Descents of 900 Immigrants

84. Leonard Chester
85. Rev. John Davenport
86. Mrs. Anne Lloyd Yale Eaton
87. Mrs. Agnes Harris Spencer Edwards
88. Henry Gregory
89. Mrs. Mabel Harlakenden Haynes (Eaton)
90. Gov. William Leete
91. Dep. Gov. (of Mass.) Roger Ludlow
92. Oliver Mainwaring
93. Mrs. Alice Freeman Thompson Parke
94. Thomas Trowbridge
95. John Umfreville
96. Thomas Yale

Rhode Island
97. Mrs. Audrey Barlow Almy
98. Act. Gov. Jeremiah Clarke
99. Gov. John Cranston
100. Mrs. Anne Marbury Hutchinson
101-102. Henry and Lachlan Mackintosh/McIntosh
103. Mrs. Katherine Marbury Scott
104. John Throckmorton

New Hampshire
105. Keith Spence
106. Robert Traill
107. William Wentworth

The Royal Descents of 900 Immigrants

New York
- 108. Matthew Clarkson
- 109. Thomas Addis Emmet
- 110. Mrs. Katherine Duncanson Glen
- 111. Alexander Hamilton
- 112. Edward Howell
- 113. Rev. Thomas James
- 114. John Lawrence
- 115. Thomas Lawrence
- 116. William Lawrence
- 117. Robert Livingston the elder
- 118. Robert Livingston the younger
- 119. Gabriel Ludlow
- 120. Walter Rutherford
- 121. Robert Sinclair
- 122. Mrs. Sarah (Brewster?) Smith

New Jersey
- 123. George Elkington
- 124. Edward FitzRandolph
- 125. Mrs. Euphan Scott Johnstone
- 126-27. William and Isabel (Burnett) Montgomery

Pennsylvania
- 128. John Cadwalader
- 129. James Claypoole

The Royal Descents of 900 Immigrants

130. Mrs. Arabella Smith Dallas (who immigrated in 1783)
131. Mrs. Mary Fox Ellicott
132. Robert Jones
133-34. Dep. Gov. Thomas and Mary (Jones) Lloyd
135. James Logan
136. Mrs. Henrietta Constantia Worsam Meade
137-38. Robert and Rebecca (Owen) Owen
139-40. Hugh and Jane (Owen) Roberts
141-42. John and Gainor (Roberts) Roberts
143. Mrs. Sidney Rees Roberts (daughter-in-law of 120-21)
   (some of the notable progeny of 135-37 is British)
144. Charles Willing

Delaware
145. Rev. George Ross

Maryland
146. Hon. Anne Arundell Calvert, Baroness Baltimore
147. Cecil Calvert, 2nd Baron Baltimore (husband of #138)
148. Lady Charlotte Lee Calvert (Crewe), Baroness Baltimore
149. Jane Lowe Sewall Calvert, Baroness Baltimore
   (some of the notable progeny of #s 139-42 is British)
150. William Bladen
151. Thomas Boteler (Butler)
152. Mrs. Anne Talbot Darnall
153. Thomas Gerard
154. Mrs. Mary Mainwaring Gill

The Royal Descents of 900 Immigrants

155. Mrs. Anne Lovelace Gorsuch
156. Mrs. Margaret Domville Hatton (Banks)
157. Alexander Magruder
158. James Neale
159. Mrs. Alicia Arnold Ross
160. Henry Sewall, Secretary of Md. (first husband of #143)
161. Richard Tilghman

Virginia

162. Col. Walter Aston
163. Lancelot Bathurst
164-65. Henry and Thomas Batte
166-67. Richard and Anna (Cordray) Bernard
168. Col. William Bernard
169. Christopher Branch
170. Mrs. Abigail Smith Burwell
171. George Carrington
172. Mrs. Sarah Ludlow Carter
173. Lady Agatha Eltonhead Kellaway Wormeley Chichele
174. Mrs. Elizabeth Boteler Claiborne
175. William Clopton
176. Mrs. Elizabeth Catesby Cocke (Holloway)
177. Mrs. Martha Eltonhead Conway
178-79. Henry and Alice (Eltonhead Burnham, later Creek) Corbin
180. Francis Dade
181. Mrs. Diana Skipwith Dale
182. Gov. Edward Digges

The Royal Descents of 900 Immigrants

183. Robert Drake
184. William Fairfax
185. Henry Filmer
186. Rev. Edward Foliot
187. Mrs. Margaret Stirling Forbes (Alexander)
188. Col. Gerard Fowke
189. Benjamin Harrison
190. John Henry
191. Theophilus Hone
192. Warham Horsmanden
193. William Ironmonger
194. Henry Isham
195. Act. Gov. Edmund Jennings
196. Mrs. Dorothy Walker Jones
197. Col. Thomas Ligon/Lygon
198. Philip Ludwell (gov. of N.C. and S.C., descendants in Va.)
199. Roger Mallory
200. Rev. John Munro
201. Robert Peyton
202. William Randolph
203. Col. George Reade
204. Anthony Savage
205. Sir Grey Skipwith, 3rd Bt.
206. Lawrence Smith
207. Gov. Alexander Spotswood
208. William Strother
209. Lawrence Towneley

The Royal Descents of 900 Immigrants

    210. Stephens/Stevens Thompson

    211. St. George Tucker

    212. Mrs. Mary Towneley Warner

    213. John Washington of Surry Co.

    214. John Washington of Westmoreland Co.

    215. Gov. Hon. John West

    216. Mrs. Frances Baldwin Jones Williams

    217. Mrs. Anne Rich Willis

North Carolina

    218. John Alston

    219. James Blount

    220. Sir Richard Everard, 4th Bt.

    221. Mrs. Barbara Bennet Murray (wife of #39)

South Carolina

    222. John Alston

    223. Stephen Bull

    224. Gov. Robert Gibbes

    225. Ralph Izard

Georgia

    226. Col. Kenneth Baillie

    227. John Irvine

Three other immigrants—Mrs. Margaret Duncanson Teller of N.Y., Mrs. Anne Fielder Gantt of Md., and Thomas Prater/Prather of Va., very

The Royal Descents of 900 Immigrants

probably left over 10 notable descendants. A fourth such immigrant, with progeny in both New England and French Canada, is Mrs. Rose Stoughton Otis of N.H. I look forward to finding more notable descendants for each of these RD immigrants.

Immigrants herein for whom I have found 7-9 notable descendants, and hope to find more, include Thomas Evans of Pa., Francis Yarnall of Pa., Daniel Humphreys of Pa., William Rodney of Del. and Pa., Gov. Leonard Calvert of Md., George Brent of Va., Rev. David Lindsay of Va., Thomas Warren of Va., Mrs. Barbara Murray Clarke of N.C., Mrs. Mary Batt Ashe (Lillington) of S.C., Pierce Butler of S.C., Charles Lowndes of S.C., and Rev. John Forbes of Fla. (with the four immigrants named in the preceding paragraph, a total of 17).

The Royal Descents of 900 Immigrants

Appendix VII to the Introduction:
198 Immigrants Whose Royal Descent is Much Altered Since *RD500* or *RD600*

Those listed below, in the order of the charts herein, usually descend from an earlier or later king or have alternate "equal" descents or new alternate lines (although in a few cases, but perhaps not all that are improved, the altered information is only a spouse or much better source[s]). Improved descents for Continental figures are sometimes from the websites of Daniel de Rauglaudre or the late Leo van de Pas, as reported to me by John Blythe Dobson of Winnipeg, Manitoba, Canada, and then confirmed by Mr. Dobson and myself from reliable printed sources.

1. (F.W.) Charles (L.G.A.A.), Prince of Solms-Braunfels, of Texas
2. Sanche-Armand-Gabriel de Gramont, known as Ted Morgan, of N.Y.
3. Maria (I.E.L.G., Baroness) von Quistorp von Braun, of Ala.
4. Robert Traill of N.H.
5. Robert Sinclair of N.Y.
6. James Dundas of Pa.
7. Thomas Dundas of Pa.
8. Douglas Robinson of N.Y.
9. Mrs. Amalia (J.L.) von Tschirschky und Bögendorf de Schweinitz of Pa.
10. Ernst Bruno von (de) Gersdorff of Mass.
11. Mrs. Vivian Rüesch Mellon of N.Y.
12. Anne (D.E., Baroness) von Watteville von Schweinitz of Pa.
13. Louis Marie de Noailles, Vicomte Noailles, Revolutionary War leader
14. M.J.P.Y.R. Gilbert Motier, Marquis de la Fayette (Lafayette), Revolutionary War general
15. Neil MacLean (McLean) of Conn.

The Royal Descents of 900 Immigrants

16. Allan MacLean (McLean) of Conn.
17. (Guy) Philippe Lannes de Montebello of N.Y.
18. Mrs. Jane Vaughan Owen of Pa.
19. Thomas Lloyd, dep. gov. of Pa.
20. Mrs. Anna Lloyd Braithwaite of Md.
21. Mrs. Mary Jones Lloyd of Pa.
22. Nicholas Ludwig, Count of Zinzendorf and Pottendorf, American resident 1741-43
23. Col. Henry Mackintosh (McIntosh) of Mass. and R.I.
24. Lachlan Mackintosh (McIntosh) of R.I.
25. John Mohr Mackintosh (McIntosh) of R.I.
26. John Cranston, gov. of R.I.
27. James Veatch of Md.
28. Noël (Pierce) Coward, sometime of N.Y.
29. Robert Livingston the elder of N.Y.
30. Robert Livingston the younger of N.Y.
31. Daniel Roberdeau of Pa.
32. John MacLean of N.J.
33. Alexander MacLeod of N.Y.
34. Thomas Gordon, chief justice of N.J.
35. Mrs. Isabel Burnett Montgomery of N.J.
36. Alexander Falconer of Md.
37. Rev. John Munro of Va.
38. Rev. Robert Rose of Va.
39. William Burnet, gov. of N.Y.
40. James Abercromby (of Ticonderoga)
41. Alexander Spotswood, (lt.) gov. of Va.

The Royal Descents of 900 Immigrants

42. James Logan of Pa.
43. Col. Kenneth Baillie of Ga.
44. Marie-Adrienne-Françoise de Noailles Motier, Marquise de La Fayette (Lafayette)
45. Anne-Jeanne-Baptiste (P.A.L.C.D.) de Noailles, Vicomtesse de Noailles
46. Col. Thomas Ligon/Lygon of Va.
47. Sir Ferdinando Gorges, lord proprietor of Me.
48. Sir William Berkeley, gov. of Va.
49. Rev. Edward Foliot of Va.
50. Henry Norwood, treasurer of Va.
51. Mrs. Katherine Deighton Hackburne Dudley Allyn of Mass.
52. Mrs. Frances Deighton Williams of Mass.
53. Mrs. Jane Deighton Lugg Negus of Mass.
54. Mrs. Bridget Lisle Hoar (Usher) of Mass.
55. Leonard Cotton of N.H.

(#s 46-55 descend from Edward I via Mowbray, as noted in *RD600*, but there only the designation "probably" was used for the descent from Edward III via Cardinal Beaufort)

56. Richard More of Mass.
57. Rev. John Oxenbridge of Mass.
58. William Poole of Mass.
59. William Farrar of Va.
60. William Asfordby of N.Y.
61. Robert Peyton of Va.
62. George Charles Mahon of Mich.
63. Mrs. Henrietta Fielding Montrésor of N.Y.
64. Thomas Dudley, gov. of Mass.

The Royal Descents of 900 Immigrants

65. Pierce Butler of S.C.
66. Oliver Mainwaring of Conn.
67. Thomas Rudyard, dep. gov. of East Jersey
68. Charles Willing of Pa.
69. Robert Drake of Va.
70. Thomas Owsley of Va.
71. François (L.H.) de Carondelet and de Noyelle, Vicomte de la Hestre et du Langue, Spanish gov. of La. and W. Fla.
72. Lady Elizabeth Gorges Smith Gorges (fourth wife of Sir Ferdinando Gorges)
73. John Ashby of S.C.
74. Mrs. Anne Marbury Hutchinson of R.I.
75. Mrs. Katherine Marbury Scott of R.I.
76. Eyre Coote Croker of N.Y.
77. Thomas Dongan, 2nd Earl of Limerick, gov. of N.Y.
78. Sir Peter Warren of N.Y.
79. Sir William Johnson, 1st Bt., of N.Y.
80. Guy Johnson of N.Y.
81. Mrs. Matilda Cecilia Dowdall Sheddon of N.J.

(the lineage of #s 77-81 is improved on p. 900—from a descent from Edward I to one from Edward III)

82. Col. William Bernard of Va.
83. Richard Bernard of Va.
84. Sir Francis Bernard, 1st Bt., gov. of N.J. and Mass.
85. Mrs. Martha Eltonhead Conway of Va.
86. Mrs. Alice Eltonhead Burnham Corbin (Creek) of Va.
87. Mrs. Jane Eltonhead Moryson Fenwick of Md.
88. (Lady) Agatha Eltonhead Kellaway Wormeley (Chichele) of Va.

The Royal Descents of 900 Immigrants

89. Edward Palmes of Conn.
90. Gabriel Ludlow of N.Y.
91. Thomas Batte of Va.
92. Henry Batte of Va.
93. John Throckmorton of R.I.
94. Joshua Owen of Pa.
95. Mrs. Rebecca Owen Owen of Pa.
96. Daniel Humphreys of Pa.
97. Lady Jane Lowe Sewall Calvert, Baroness Baltimore, of Md.
98. Nicholas Lowe of Md.
99. Henry Lowe of Md.
100. Mrs. Olive Welby Farwell of Mass.
101. Constant Southworth of Mass.
102. Thomas Southworth of Mass.
103. William Goddard of Mass.
104. Philip Dumaresq of Mass.
105. Richard Bellingham, gov. of Mass.
106. James Blount of (Va. and) N.C.
107. Lady Amelia Offley Bernard of Mass.
108. Joseph Bickley of Va.
109. William Kemeys of N.Y.
110. Christopher (W. Bradshaw-) Isherwood of Calif.
111. Richard Towneley of N.J.
112. John Evans of (Radnor) Pa.
113. John Morgan of Pa.
114. Peter (Sydney Ernest [Aylen, later]) Lawford of Calif.
115. Thomas Bradbury of Mass.

The Royal Descents of 900 Immigrants

116. James Cudworth of Mass.
117. Mrs. Margaret Fleming Bowen of Mass.
118. Mrs. Elizabeth Bullock Clement[s] of Mass.
119. Mrs. Elizabeth Alsop Baldwin (Fowler) of Conn.
120. George Holmes Pomeroy of Pa.
121. Cuthbert Fenwick of Md.
122. John Cra(y)croft of Md.
123. Mrs. Rose Stoughton Otis of N.H. (and her French-Canadian children and grandchildren)
124. Edward Raynsford of Mass.
125. George Yate of Md.
126. Mrs. Mary Gye Maverick of Mass.
127. Nathaniel Browne of Conn.
128. Rev. John Davenport of Conn.
129. Edmond Hawes of Mass.
130. Mrs. Arabella Maria Smith Dallas of Pa.
131. Thomas Bressie of Conn.
132. Mrs. Margaret Wyatt Allyn of Conn.
133. Mrs. Mary Butler Underwood of Va.
134. Mrs. Anne Wolseley Calvert of Md.
135. Mrs. Mary Wolseley Brooke of Md.
136. Christopher Batt of Mass. (and his granddaughter, Mrs. Mary Batt Ash[e] Lillington of S.C.)
137. Mrs. Judith Knapp Hubbard of Mass. (initially improved in *RD600*, p. 848)
138. Obadiah Bruen of Conn.
139. Mrs. Elizabeth Covert Fenwick of N.J.
140. Henry Corbin of Va.

The Royal Descents of 900 Immigrants

141. John Stratton of Mass.
142. Mrs. Elizabeth Stratton Thorndike of Mass.
143. Mrs. Dorothy Walker Jones of Va.
144. William Wentworth of N.H.
145. Christopher Lawson of Mass.
146. Mrs. Margaret Tyndal Winthrop of Mass.
147. Sir George Thomas, 1st Bt., gov. of Pa. and Del.
148. Mrs. Catherine Hamby Hutchinson of Mass.
149. Thomas Greene, gov. of Md.
150. Col. Gerard Fowke of Va.
151. Thomas Weston of Mass.
152. Edward FitzRandolph of Mass. and N.J.
153. Col. Walter Aston of Va.
154. Benjamin Heron of N.C.
155. Mrs. Anna Cordray Bernard of Va.
156. Francis Ironmonger of Va.
157. William Ironmonger of Va.
158. Lady Deborah Dunch Moody of L.I., N.Y.
159. Robert Gibbs of Mass.
160. Cecil Calvert, 2nd Baron Baltimore, proprietor of Md.
161. Hon. Leonard Calvert, gov. of Md.
162. Rev. Peter Bulkeley of Mass.
163. Mrs. Elizabeth Bulkeley Whittingham Haugh of Mass.
164. Mrs. Martha Bulkeley Mellowes of Mass.
165. Mrs. Elizabeth St. John Whiting of Mass.
166. Rev. Thomas James of L.I., N.Y.
167. Simon Lynde of Mass.

The Royal Descents of 900 Immigrants

168. Matthew Clarkson of N.Y.
169. John Dixwell, regicide, of Conn.
170. Thomas Broughton of Mass.
171. Thomas Boteler of Md.
172. Mrs. Elizabeth Boteler Claiborne of Va.
173. Jeffrey Amherst, 1st Baron Amherst of Holmesdale and Montréal
174. Mrs. Thomasine Ward Thompson Buffum of Mass.
175. George Elkington of N.J.
176. Robert Owen of Pa.
177. Edward Whalley, regicide, of Mass. and Conn.
178. John Lovelace, 4th Baron Lovelace, gov. of N.Y.
179. George Sandys, treasurer of Va.
180. Mrs. Margaret Sandys Wyatt, of Va.
181. Madame (Helena Petrovna Hahn) Blavatsky (Betanelly) of N.Y. (1873-78)
182. Demetrius Augustine, Prince Golitzin (Gallitzin) of Md. and Pa.
183. Rev. Charles Chauncey of Mass.
184. Mrs. Mabel Harlakenden Haynes (Eaton) of Mass.
185. Christopher Branch of Va.
186. Thomas Colepepper (Culpeper) of Va.
187. Thomas Colepepper (Culpeper), 2nd Baron Colepepper (Culpeper), gov. of Va.
188. George Talbot, Jr., known as Peter Talbot, of Mass.
189. Henry Woodhouse of Va.
190. John Josselyn, traveler to N.E., naturalist
191. William Strachey, first Secretary of the Virginia Company (and his grandson, another William Strachey of Va.)

The Royal Descents of 900 Immigrants

192. William Leete of Conn., gov. of Conn.
193. Rev. William Sargent of Mass.
194. Mrs. Alice Freeman Thompson Parke of Mass. and (prob.) Conn.
195. Mrs. Margaret Frances Towneley Chase of Md.
196. Philip de Carteret, gov. of N.J.
197. Peter de Carteret, gov. of N.C.
198. James Neale of Md.

The Royal Descents of 900 Immigrants

Appendix VIII:
"Immigrants with Caveats," Some Aspect of Whose Royal Descent Merits Further Investigation

1. Mrs. Dorothy Chamberlayne Daniell of S.C. (p. 133)
2. Robert Langton Douglas of N.Y. (p. 166)
3. John Cranston, gov. of R.I. (p. 241)
4-5. Hugh Mercer of Va. and Mrs. Euphan Scott Johnstone of N.J. (p. 276)
6. Col. Kenneth Baillie of Ga. (p. 283)
7. Thomas Wingfield of Va. (dropped from *RA*) (p. 307)
8. Mrs. Margaret Nelson Teackle of Va. (p. 356)
9. Joshua Henshaw of Mass. (p. 397)
10. William Strother of Va. (p. 421)
11. Fortunatus Sydnor of Va. (p. 490)
12. John Washington of Surry Co., Va. (p. 515)
13-14. Constant and Thomas Southworth of Mass. (p. 524)
15. Anthony Savage of Va. (p. 532)
16. Mrs. Elizabeth Taylor (Tufton alias) Mason of N.H. (p. 537)
17-18. George Carrington of Va. and Mrs. Elizabeth Hannah Carrington Willing of Pa. (p. 557)
19. John Snelling of Mass. (p. 573)
20. Mrs. Deliverance Sheffield Peters of Mass. (p. 577)
21. Mrs. Elizabeth Bullock Clements of Mass. (p. 584)
22. Mrs. Mary Fox Ellicott of Pa. (p. 595)
22. Cuthbert Fenwick of Md. (p. 599)
23. John Cra(y)croft of Md. (p. 604)
24-26. Mrs. Rebecca Ward Allen, Mrs. Mary Ward Cutting (Miller), and William Markham, all of Mass. (pp. 654-56)

The Royal Descents of 900 Immigrants

27. Mrs. Mary Butler Underwood of Va. (p. 674)

28. Mrs. Thomasine Clench Frost of Mass. (p. 680)

29. John Roberts of (Pencoyd, Lower Merion), Pa. (p. 692)

30. John Williams of Pa. (p. 693)

31. Thomas Prater/Prather of Va. (p. 695)

32. Lawrence Smith of Va. (p. 701)

33. Robert Throckmorton of Va. (p. 720)

34. Thomas Weston of Mass. (p. 723)

35. Theophilus Hone of Va. (p. 730)

36. Benjamin Heron of N.C. (p. 732)

37. Mrs. Thomasine Ward Thompson Buffum of Mass. (p. 761)

38. Jan Otten Van Tuyl of N.Y. (p. 776)

39. John Gibbes of Goose Creek, S.C. (p. 779)

40-41. Robert Jones and Mrs. Sidney Rees Roberts of Pa. (p. 809)

42. Henry Gregory of Conn. (p. 815)

43. Christopher Branch of Va. (p. 822)

44-45. Mark Catesby, traveler to the South, and Mrs. Elizabeth Catesby Cocke of Va. (p. 831)

46. Peter Talbot of Mass. (p. 841)

47. John Umfreville/Humphreville of Conn. (p. 843)

48. Henry Woodhouse of Va. (p. 846)

49. John Josselyn, traveler to New England, naturalist (p. 850)

50-51. William Strachey, first Secretary of the Virginia Colony, and his grandson, another William Strachey of Va. (p. 850)

52. William Leete, gov. of Conn. (p. 852)

53. Rev. Gregory Dexter of R.I. (p. 862)

54. Anthony Collamore of Mass. (p. 867)

The Royal Descents of 900 Immigrants

55. James Neale of Md. (p. 874)

56. Humphrey Underhill of N.Y. (p. 875)

57. Mrs. Mary Underhill Naylor Stites of N.Y. (p. 875)

58. Nathaniel Bacon, act. gov. of Va. (p. 878)

59. Mrs. Abigail Smith Burwell (p. 878)

Note: #s 55 through 59 are included because Douglas Richardson, and perhaps other scholars, doubt that Millicent of Rethel married (1) Robert Marmion and (2) Richard de Camville, and was the mother of William de Camville (= Auberée de Marmion) and Robert Marmion (= ——), as shown on pp. 874 and 877. I cite vol. 6, pp. 472-73, of the manuscript notes of George Andrews Moriarty, Jr., and *TAG* 20 (1943-44): 255-56.

60. William Boddie of Va. (p. 882)

The Royal Descents of 900 Immigrants

Among immigrants whose royal descent herein I believe is correct but for whom some information is missing, or for whom an alternate line is the only certain RD, are the following, with a brief description of the unknown item:

1. Thomas Fraser of S.C. and N.J. (placement of mother among Frasers; RD of father correct) (p. 82)
2. Thomas Dudley, gov. of Mass. (origin of father; RD of mother fully proved) (p. 370)
3. Mrs. Barbara Mitford Wyatt of Va. (maternity uncertain) (p. 425)

4-5. Thomas and Henry Batte of Va. (the Perry descent, questioned by J.A. Brayton; the Mallory descent is proved) (pp. 505-6)

6. John Throckmorton of R.I. (a possible alternate line to an agnate cousin, also of royal descent, has been suggested, but not published, by Paul C. Reed) (p. 508)

7-8. Joshua Owen of N.J. and Mrs. Rebecca Owen Owen of Pa. (maternity uncertain) (p. 510)

9. Mrs. Abigail Brewster Burr of Conn. (first name of mother) (p. 539)
10. Mrs. Mary Mainwaring Gill of Md. (whether she immigrated, or died in England) (p. 558)
11. Mrs. Mary Gye Maverick of Mass. (Echingham descent through father; mother's descent correct) (p. 632)
12. Roger Mallory of Va. (maternity uncertain) (p. 668)
13. Edward FitzRandolph of Mass. and N.J. (St. Quintin descent; Douglas Richardson also questions the Bigod connection) (p. 725)
14. Mrs. Frances Baldwin Townshend Jones Williams of Va. (parentage; paternal grandparentage is certain) (p. 727)
15. Mrs. Audrey Barlow Almy of R.I. (identification of mother) (p. 763)

16-17. Edward Thornborough/Thornburgh of Pa. and Thomas Thornborough/Thornburg of Va. (placement among other Thornboroughs by Charles C. Thornburgh III, whose work was hastily assembled)

The Royal Descents of 900 Immigrants

**Appendix IX to the Introduction:
Speculative Descents (Immigrants for Whom a Line
from Kings, not simply Gentry Ancestry,
has been Suggested but is Either Unproved
or Seems Perhaps Problematic:
A List and Bibliography with Comments)**

1-5. Five Winslow brothers of Mass. (Edward, governor of the Plymouth Colony and *Mayflower* passenger; Gilbert, *Mayflower* passenger, died unmarried; John, husband of *Mayflower* passenger Mary Chilton; Josiah; and Kenelm) – Brandon Fradd, *The Winslow Families of Worcestershire, 1400-1700* (2008), which massively amplifies *NEHGR* 154 (2000): 78-108 (the late M.K. Kirk) with English documents but rejects a Greville descent and suggests instead (pp. 29-35) that the immigrants' grandfather, Kenelm Winslow, possibly married a granddaughter, or was himself a grandson, of Kenelm Buck and Ellen Neville, daughter (by his second wife, Lettice Harcourt) of Thomas Neville, son of Sir Henry Neville and Joan Bourchier, SETH.

6-7. Rev. Henry Whitfield of Conn. and Richard Waters of Mass., 2nd cousins – John Brooks Threlfall, *The Ancestry of Reverend Henry Whitfield (1590-1657) and His Wife Dorothy Sheafe (159?-1669) of Guilford, Connecticut* (1989, 1995), *NEHGR* 103 (1949): 102-7, reprinted in *EO1*: 3: 82-87, and *GGE*: 1323 (and chart preceding)–54 (Waters). Could Hugh John, a witness of the 1491 probate of Sir William Brandon (SETH, husband of Elizabeth Wingfield), be the husband of Sir William's daughter, Margaret Brandon the younger, and the Hugh Manning (son of John), great-great-grandfather of the two immigrants? The 1619 visitation of Kent gives the wife of Hugh Manning as a paternal aunt of Charles Brandon, 1st Duke of Suffolk, husband of Princess Mary Tudor, SETH. See note following this appendix.

8-9. William Munro (Monroe) of Lexington, Mass., and John Munro (Monroe) of Bristol, R.I. – *TAG* 45 (1969): 65-78 (D.H. Kelley), which outlines possible, perhaps likely, patrilineal descents from the Munros of Foulis and ancient kings of Ireland. See also Joan S. Guilford, *The Monroe Book* (1993), pp. 3-480 and, for an almost certain agnate kinsman, p. 260 herein.

The Royal Descents of 900 Immigrants

10-11. John Washburn of Mass. and William Washburn of L.I. – see the endnote on the chart of Mrs. Mary Woodcock Bridges of Mass. (p. 507 of this volume, plus *AR7*, line 91, dropped from *AR8*); the parentage of John Washburn of Bengeworth, Worcestershire, great-grandfather of the immigrants, is unproved.

12. Capt. Myles Standish of Mass., *Mayflower* passenger and soldier – G.V.C. Young, *Pilgrim Myles Standish, First Manx-American* (1984), and Lawrence Hill, *Gentlemen of Courage—Forward* (1987), esp. charts at end, a descent Jeremy D. Bangs considers only *possible*; see *The Mayflower Quarterly* 72 (2006): 133-59. If the Young and Hill hypotheses are correct, however, Myles Standish would be a son of John Standish (and Christian Lace), son of John Standish (and Mallie Moore), son of Huan Standish (first on the Isle of Man, and ——), son of Robert Standish (and Margaret Croft), son of Gilbert Standish (and ——), son of Hugh Standish (first of Ormskirk, and ——), son of Sir Alexander Standish and Constance Gerard, SETH.

13. Rev. John Cotton of Mass. – *New Hampshire Genealogical Record* 16 (1999): 145-70 (J.A. Brayton and the late M.K. Kirk). The authors suggest that the Cotton pedigree compiled by Horatio Gates Somerby, although "clinched" by two forged documents, may be largely correct, with a *possible* patrilineal descent from Walter Cotton and Joan Rede, SETH, and "better" RDs through either Katherine Sampson or Katherine Hungerford, wives of Nicholas Leventhorpe, and daughters respectively of George Sampson (and —), SETH, and Robert Hungerford, 2nd Baron Hungerford, and Margaret Botreaux, SETH. See also *NEHGR* 150 (1996): 91-93. Constance Leventhorpe, daughter of Nicholas and one of the above Katherines, married Clement Cotton, grandson of the above Walter and Joan, and was possibly a great-grandmother of the immigrant minister.

[Note: The conjectural descent for Thomas Newberry of Mass., prepared by Joseph Gardner Bartlett in *Newberry Genealogy* (1914), but doubted by Sir Anthony Richard Wagner in *English Genealogy*, 3rd ed. (1983), p. 66, was disproved by Clifford L. Stott of Salt Lake City, whose as yet unpublished work on this line was brought to my attention by Douglas Richardson. A "Newberry

Summary" by Don Charles Stone contains, with comments, postings on soc.genealogy.medieval by Paul C. Reed (1999), Richardson (2011), and Robert Forrest (2011). I should now like further evidence for Bartlett's identification of George Talbot (Jr.) as Peter Talbot of Mass.]

14. John Whitney of Mass. – *TAG* 81 (2006): 249-62 (Robert Leigh Ward and Tim Doyle), which suggests that the immigrant's almost certain father, Thomas Whitney of Westminster (m. Mary Bray), was a son of Robert Whitney of Castleton (m. Elizabeth ferch Morgan ap William), son by an unknown wife of an elder Robert Whitney of Castleton, son of Robert Whitney of Whitney (and his second wife Elizabeth Vaughan), for whom see *RA* 1: 354-55, son of Eustace Whitney and Joan Trussell, daughter of Sir William Trussell and Margery Ludlow, SETH. Doubts about the parentage of Thomas Whitney of Westminster, however, were raised by Adrian Benjamin Moreira Da Silva-Burke in *TAG* 86 (2012-13): 209-12, 88 (2016): 312-13. Research on John Whitney's likely ancestry is updated by the above R.L. Ward (cohost with Tim Doyle) on the Whitney Research Group website at http://whitneygen.org.

15. John Whitcomb of Mass. – *AR7,* lines 158A, 158, 148 (incorporating Boulogne/Bolonia research by David H. Kelley); *The Pedigree Register* 2 (1910-1913): 52-57; and Norman K. Whitcomb, *The Whitcomb Family History* (2008), esp. chapter 3. This last suggests that the immigrant John Whitcomb (m. 1623 Frances Cogan) was the son of Thomas Whetcombe (and Joanna Pope), son of Jesper/Jasper Whitcombe (and ——), son of William Witdecombe of Martock, Somerset (and Elizabeth ——), whose patrilineal descent is charted in *Ped. Reg.* 2: 52-53. Agnate descent from First Crusade leader Godfrey of Boulogne is almost certain.

16. Abraham Errington of Mass. *NEHGR* 132 (1978): 44-50 (Kerry William Bate) plus further unpublished Cresswell-Lumley research by the late M.K. Kirk, who thought that the mother of Catherine Cresswell, daughter of Robert Cresswell of Cresswell and wife of Roger Errington, was indeed Elizabeth Lumley, daughter of Thomas Lumley and Margaret Plantagenet,

SETH, the latter an illegitimate daughter of Edward IV, King of England, and Elizabeth (Wayte) Lucy.

17. Mrs. Phebe Leete Parkhurst of Mass. (wife of George), daughter of Robert Leete (and Alice Grundy), son of John Leete and Ellen Burgoyne. The parentage of both of these last is unknown – J.B. Threlfall, *Fifty Great Migration Colonists to New England and Their Origins* (1990), pp. 261-64, 267-79. Undoubtedly a kinswoman of Gov. William Leete of Conn., ARD, SETH, via both Leetes and Burgoynes, Phebe may also share the Staverton-Dabridgecourt descent outlined herein.

18. George Wyllys, gov. of Conn. – *NEHGR* 141 (1987): 98 and sources cited therein, esp. *NEHGR* 22 (1868): 186, 31 (1879): 350 (reprinted in *EO2*: 3: 800, 808), *LDBR* 4: 112-14, plus my suggestion that the line includes only one pair of Richard and Thomas Willises/Wyllyses. Full documentation of the Willis-Jeames-Keverell-Napton-Beauchamp descent, or some *RD* alternative, is still required.

19. James Buchanan of Pa., father of the 15th President, as noted on pp. 245-47 herein. More research in Ramelton (Rathmelton), Donegal, is required. As also noted on pp. 245, Shawn H. Potter of Woodbridge, Va., has assembled considerable circumstantial evidence that William Buchanan, second son of George Buchanan and Elizabeth Mayne, was the father by Janet —— of likely brothers Robert, Walter, William, Andrew, George and John Buchanan, all also immigrants to Pa.

20. Mrs. Mary Drake Chetham Heath of Md. – *LDBR* 3: 721-22. I can find no pertinent printed Stansby, Hiett or Bromwich pedigrees.

21. Humphrey Warren of Md. – H.W. Newman, *Charles County Gentry* (1940), pp. 278-89; see also *BRMF1*, pp. 452-57. This line was brought to my attention by Neil D. Thompson of Salt Lake City.

22. Thomas Gascoigne or Gaskins of Va. – J.F. Dorman states in *AP&P* 4: 2: 54 that Thomas Gascoigne/Gaskin was apparently the "Thomas son of Henry Gascoigne" baptized 16 May 1609 at Aberford, Yorkshire. Given the lack of a clinching statement of kinship in a will or property inheritance, and the middling status

of the Virginia Gaskins family, I am skeptical enough to want more evidence. The English Thomas was the son (by a second wife, Mrs. Anna Hobbes Mompeson, married in 1589) of Henry Gascoigne, son of Francis Gascoigne of Mickleforth, Yorkshire, by Elizabeth Singleton, daughter of William Singleton and Elizabeth Cornwallis, daughter of William Cornwallis and Elizabeth Stanford, SETH. See *PCF Yorkshire* (Gascoigne pedigree) and *RA* 2: 375-76 (Cornwallis, Tyrrell). For Singleton see Harl. 1560, 1820, Additional 19149 and Rawlinson Mss. 393, all at the British Library.

23. Evan Ragland of Va. – Charles J. Ragland, Jr., *The Raglands: The History of the British-American Family* (1978). The English and American Evan Raglands are not, I believe, proved identical by documentary sources; Ragland was brought to my attention by John A. Brayton of Memphis, Tenn.

24. Thomas Willoughby of Va. – In "Searching for Thomas Willoughby," *Virginia Genealogical Society Newsletter* 39, #3 (June 2013): 1-6, Raymond Gill of Brooklyn, N.Y. presents the strong circumstantial (and traditional) evidence, not yet proved but not contradicted by anything yet found, that the immigrant was a son of Thomas and Clemence (Willoughby) Willoughby, second cousins, of Bore Place, Kent, grandson of Sir Thomas Willoughby, sheriff of Kent, and Catherine Hart, and of Kenelm Willoughby of Rickmansworth, Hertfordshire, and Catherine Goldwell, and great-grandson of Robert Willoughby of Bore Place (and Dorothy Willoughby of Wollaston, Nottinghamshire) and of Christopher Willoughby and Margery Totteshurst. Robert and Christopher were brothers, sons of Sir Thomas Willoughby, chief justice of the Common Pleas (and Bridget Read), son of Sir Christopher Willoughby, *de jure* 10th Baron Willoughby d'Eresby, and Margaret Jenney, SETH. See also Frederick Arthur Crisp, *Visitation of England and Wales, Notes*, vol. 9 (1911) (to the immigrant's father and to Christopher Willoughby and Margery Totteshurst), and the will of Kenelm Willoughby, the immigrant's maternal grandfather (who mentions his late daughter Clemence, late son-in-law Thomas, and grandson Thomas Willoughby, the last a principal heir), dated 31 Oct. 1618,

The Royal Descents of 900 Immigrants

signed 22 May 1620 and proved 24 June 1620 (PCC PROB 11/135, Soame Quire, folio 463v-465).

Note 1: Some readers may think the RDs outlined in the text for "Immigrants with Caveats" are somewhat speculative also. I hope especially for further monographs on Mrs. Thomasine Ward Thompson Buffum, Anthony Collamore, the Southworth brothers and Peter Talbot of Mass.; Henry Gregory and Gov. William Leete of Conn.; Gov. John Cranston of R.I.; Cuthbert Fenwick of Md.; Anthony Savage, Lawrence Smith, William Strother, Mrs. Margaret Nelson Teackle and John Washington (Surry Co.) of Va.; and Col. Kenneth Baillie of Ga.

Note: A recent discussion on soc.genealogy.medieval, among Don Charles Stone, John Higgins, Nathan W. Murphy (who cites an email from Matthew Tompkins) and Douglas Richardson, shows that (1) another Hugh John lived in Bulcamp and Halesworth, Suffolk, much closer to Sir William Brandon's estate at Wangford, Suffolk, than Hugh Manning in St. Mary's Cray, Kent, and this Hugh John (or another of a closer place also) is more likely the witness to Sir William's will; and (2) the IPM of Henry Brandon, 2nd Duke of Suffolk, son of Princess Mary, mentioned the then representatives of the duke's five Brandon great-aunts, Sir William's daughters Anne, Margaret, Elizabeth, Eleanor and Catherine, but none from the second Margaret and no Manning. A more distant kinship between Hugh Manning's wife, who could also have been illegitimate, remains possible and other Manning forebears treated by Waters and Threlfall should be investigated.

The Royal Descents of 900 Immigrants

Appendix X to the Introduction:
29 Immigrants Dropped from *RD600* or This Edition, with Sources for the Disproofs or Doubts

1. Brooke, Robert, acting gov. of Md. –correspondence with the late Brice McAdoo Clagett, plus his Elmeden bibliographical note in his manuscript *Seven Centuries: Ancestors for Twenty Generations of John Brice de Treville Clagett and Ann Calvert Brooke Clagett*. Elizabeth de Umfreville (ca. 1392-1424), wife of Sir William de Elmeden could not be the grandmother of Thomas Foster, fl. 1414-27, husband of Elizabeth Etherstone.

2-3. Bye, Thomas, and his wife, Mrs. Margaret Davis Bye of Pa. – I, too, especially after eliminating the alleged Kirkbride and Dalston descents of Joseph Kirkbride, 16 below, have concluded that as regards English origins at least, the work of Arthur Edward Bye is unreliable and should not be used or cited.

4. Calvert alias Lazenby alias Butler, Charles, of Md. – The late W.A. Reitwiesner brought to my attention two later articles by George Sydney Horace Lee Washington – in *Notes and Queries* 198, #12 (Dec. 1953): 527-29 and 210, #2 (Feb. 1965): 43-47 – in which Charles Calvert (d. 1733) is said still to be the son of "Countess Henrietta" (alleged to be Henrietta FitzJames, illegitimate daughter of James II, King of England, and Arabella Churchill) but by either of two possible lovers, not her (later) second husband, Piers Butler, 3rd Viscount Galmoye. In the first of these articles the mother of Benedict "Swingate" Calvert, illegitimate son of Charles Calvert, 5th Baron Baltimore, colonial governor of Md., is guessed to be "Mary Granville, Mrs. Delany"; in the second article she is not identified. Given such changes of opinion, plus the consensus of various contemporary genealogists that G.S.H.L. Washington sometimes published during one of his unfortunate "mad" or delusional periods, Charles Calvert, said to be alias Lazenby alias Butler, should be deleted from this volume until some *record* evidence is found of his origins.

The Royal Descents of 900 Immigrants

5-6. Cope, Oliver, of Pa. and Fisher, Mrs. Margery Maude, of Del. – *TAG* 70 (1995): 156-71, 72 (1997): 244-56 (Charles M. Hansen), 81 (2006): 314-15 (Leslie Mahler).

7-8. Corwin, Matthew of L.I., N.Y., and Curwen, George of Mass. – Recent research by J.C.B. Sharp, sponsored by Barbara Fricke, has found Curwens in Kimcote and Walton, Leicestershire (about six miles from Sibbertoft), a 1401 Coventry, Warwickshire, record of a Curwayn "otherwise called Sybertoft" and a family of "Corwenne" in Coventry by 1280. "Corwin" is also an occupational surname derived from "cordwainer" [shoemaker] and a John Curwayn of Coventry is called a "corvisor" in 1395. The immigrant Curwen/Corwin brothers from Sibbertoft, Northamptonshire were thus probably *not* descended from the Curwens of Workington, Cumberland.

9-11. Edwards, William (ap Edward, or Bedward) and John (ap Edward), brothers, of Pa., and their nephew, John Evans of Merion and Radnor, Pa. – *TAG* 82 (2007): 17-31 (Stewart Baldwin).

12. Goode, John, of Va. – conversations with Paul C. Reed, who states that he has disproved Goode's parentage, about which I was also doubtful.

13. Hinton, John, of N.C. – conversations with John Anderson Brayton, who tells me that Hinton's origin is unknown; once again I too had been doubtful, or at least desired more proof.

14-15. Harry, Daniel and Hugh, brothers, of Pa. – *TAG* 69 (1994): 95-97 (Neil D. Thompson).

16. Jones, Hugh, of Pa., alleged but disproved kinsman of #9-11 above – *TAG* 80 (2005): 117-20 (Stewart Baldwin).

17. Kennedy, William of N.C. – The Bible record at the N.C. State Archives indeed contains the entry shown to me by the late Miriam Elliott Bertelson, as transcribed in *RD500* and *RD600*. As strongly suspected by Christopher Carter Lee, who obtained a copy of the record, the entry is clearly in a later hand and is certainly false. Mr. Lee also found a copyrighted online article by Iain Kennedy that fully covers the career of William Kennedy (brother of the governor of N.Y.), who became a merchant in Edinburgh, never immigrated to the American colonies, married

The Royal Descents of 900 Immigrants

Helen Smith, and left immediate descendants who remained in Scotland.

18. Kirkbride, Joseph of Pa. – Correspondent Roger Clayton reports that Bernard Kirkbride (ca. 1639/30 [36 in 1665]-1677) and Jane Featherstonehaugh died childless and the immigrant's father, Matthew Kirkbride, a Quaker (and formerly said to be son of this couple) was born ca. 1636, possibly son of a previous Bernard Kirkbride. The immigrant's mother, according to *LDBR* 3: 210-13, was Magdalen, daughter of Sir John Dalston of Dalston. In the major monograph on this Dalston family, in *TCWAAS*, new ser., 10 (1910): 231-68, an earlier Elizabeth Kirkbride married a John Dalston, but no contemporary Sir John had a daughter Magdalen (Sir John Dalstons of Dalston were born in 1523 and 1556, and Sir John, 1st Bt., in 1639). A younger son John, b. 1610 to Sir George Dalston and Catherine Tamworth, is untraced ["about whom I know nothing"], This last John might merit further investigation, but was certainly *not* Sir John Dalston of Dalston.

19. Lloyd, Robert, of Pa. – *TAG* 71 (1996): 77-84 (Stewart Baldwin).

20. Lovecraft, Mrs. Mary Fulford, of N.Y. – *NEXUS* 13 (1996): 129-30 (Ken Faig Jr. to H.L.P. Beckwith)

21-23. Norton, Henry, of Me., and Walter, of Mass., nephew and uncle – *NEHGR* 150 (1996): 327-28 (the late Lt. Gen. Herman Nickerson, Jr.)

24. Tilghman, Christopher, of Va. – Elizabeth M. Tillman, *Getting to the Roots of the Family Tree: The Story of A Saxon Family*, 3 vols. (1997), vols. 2 and 3, esp. the chart at end of vol. 3, opposite p. 1139.

25. Underhill, John, of N.Y. – Carl J. Underhill, ed., *Underhill Genealogy, Vol. VII* (2002), Foreword, "Captain John Underhill's English Lineage," citing research by Neil D. Thompson sponsored by Ludlow Elliman.

26-27. Waller, Col. John, and Herndon, Mrs. Mary (Waller?), probable siblings – Douglas Richardson has found, from the 10 April 1707 PCC will of Anne (Keate) Waller, that her son John was Mr. John Waller of London, merchant, not "John Waller, gent." of

The Royal Descents of 900 Immigrants

Newport Pagnell, Buckinghamshire, d. 1723, husband of Mary Pomfrett and father of Col. John and Mary. Waller, however, was a major gentry family in Buckinghamshire; some kinship to the poet Edmund Waller seems almost certain, and an alternate royal descent may be likely. Further research is eagerly awaited.

28. Witter, Thomas, of N.Y. – R.D. Tucker, *The Descendants of William Tucker of Throwleigh, Devon* (1991), pp. 52-53, 157-59, 381-82, 384.

29. Wynne, Dr. Thomas, of Pa. – *WC*, pp. 566-67, wherein G.E. McCracken pronounces the identification of Dr. Thomas Wynne of Philadelphia, barber-surgeon and Quaker pamphleteer, with Thomas (bp. Bonfari, Flintshire 20 July 1627), son of Thomas ap John Wyn, as "not yet proved." Flintshire archivist Elizabeth L. Pettit found that the latter was buried at Bonfari 7 October 1633, information kindly relayed to me by Mrs. Becky Thill of Richardson, Texas. The identification is not disproved, but note that on p. 570, McCracken states "when he wrote the *Reply,* [Dr. Thomas] Wynne was living near the place where he was born and where he says his father died before he was eleven" [not seven, or a few months after his sixth birthday]. I might also note that none of the names of siblings of Thomas Wynne, bp. 1627 (Anne, Harrie, Edward, Peter and [a base brother] John), are repeated among the names of children of Dr. Thomas Wynne of Philadelphia (Mary, Tabitha, Rebecca, Sidney, Hannah and Jonathan).

THE
ROYAL DESCENTS OF 900 IMMIGRANTS

Volume I

Acknowledgments, Introduction, and Descents from Kings or Sovereigns Who Died after 1200
[pp. i-cxcii, 1-734]

The Royal Descents of 900 Immigrants

1. Juliana, Queen of The Netherlands, 1948-1980, d. 2004 = Bernhard (Leopold Friedrich Eberhard Julius Kurt Karl Gottfried Peter), Prince of Lippe-Biesterfeld, Prince of The Netherlands, SETH

2. Maria Cristina of The Netherlands = Jorge Perez Guillermo

3. **Bernardo Frederico Guillermo** (b. 1977) of N.Y., furniture designer = Eva Prinz-Valdes.

Sources: Jacques Arnold, *The Royal Houses of Europe: The Benelux Monarchies: The Netherlands, Belgium, Luxembourg* (2006), chart A7DQ (two pages) and *The Hohenzollern Dynasty of Prussia: The Descendants of King Friedrich Wilhelm I, Volume 2* (2011), chart 8FE (two pages) (Bernardo's marriage and daughter Isabel Christina), *BRFW* 1: 226 (Lippe-Biesterfeld).

The Royal Descents of 900 Immigrants

1. Ferdinand I, King of Roumania, d. 1927 = Marie of Edinburgh, daughter of Alfred of Great Britain, Duke of Edinburgh (and Marie of Russia, daughter of Alexander II, Czar of Russia and Marie of Hesse), son of Albert, Prince of Saxe-Coburg and Gotha and Victoria, Queen of Great Britain (SETH for both of these last)

2. **Ileana of Roumania** (1909-1991), Mother Abbess (known as **Mother Alexandra**) of the Monastery of the Transfiguration, Ellwood City, Pa. = (1) Anton Maria Franz Leopold Blanka Karl Joseph Ignaz Raphael Michael Margareta Nicetas, Archduke of Austria, Prince of Tuscany; (2) Stefan Virgil Issarescu. Her eldest son, Stefan, Archduke of Austria and Prince of Tuscany, was an American citizen as Stefan Habsburg-Lothringen of Farmington, Mich., and married Mary Jerrine Soper; their five children were born in Boston, Mass., and Detroit, Mich.

Sources: Marlene A. Eilers, *Queen Victoria's Descendants*, 2nd ed. (1997), pp. 68-73, 146, 148-50; *BRFW* 1: 457-58, 344-45 and Jacques Arnold, *The Royal Houses of Europe: The Balkan and Italian Monarchies* (2007), charts B3 (two pages), J4K (two pages).

The Royal Descents of 900 Immigrants

1. George I, King of Greece, d. 1913 = Olga of Russia (parents of Andrew, Prince of Greece and Denmark, who married Alice of Battenberg, SETH, and was the father of Philip of Greece and Denmark, Duke of Edinburgh, consort of Elizabeth II, Queen of Great Britain, SETH)

2. Nicholas, Prince of Greece and Denmark = Helen of Russia

3. Olga of Greece = Paul (Karadjordjevic), Prince Regent of Yugoslavia, first cousin of Alexander I, King of Yugoslavia

4. Elizabeth (Karadjordjevic) of Yugoslavia = (1) Howard Oxenberg of N.Y.; (2) Neil Roxburgh Balfour; (3) Manuel Ulloa Elias

5. (By 1) **Catherine Oxenberg** (b. 1961) of N.Y., actress = (1) Robert J. Evans (b. 1930, born Robert J. Shapera), movie producer (annulled after 12 days); (2) Casper Robert Van Dien (b. 1968), actor. Her two Van Dien children were born in Los Angeles.

2. Christopher, Prince of Greece and Denmark (brother of Nicholas) = Françoise Isabella of Guise (Orléans/France)

3. Michael, Prince of Greece and Denmark = Marina Karella

4. **Alexandra, Princess of Greece and Denmark**, sometime of N.Y. = Nicolas **Mirzayantz** (b. 1963), cosmetics executive (see *WWA*, 2012, p. 3084, with no spouse named). Their eldest child was born in New York City.

Sources: *BRFW* 1: 325-27, 474-75, 543-44, *Almanach de Gotha*, 188th ed., vol. 1 (2012), pp. 162-64, 339-41, 374-76 (Greece, Russia, Yugoslavia), *RIIS* 2: 392-94, Jacques Arnold, *The Royal Houses of Europe: The Balkan and Italian Monarchies* (2007), charts D3C, A2D, A1, A2G, and Oxenberg notes of Marlene A. Eilers Koenig.

Note: Alexandra of Greece and Denmark, sister of Nicholas and Christopher, married Paul, Grand Duke of Russia (son of Alexander II, Czar of Russia, and Marie of Hesse). Their son, Dimitri, Grand Duke of Russia, married (Anna) Audrey Emery of Cincinnati, and was the father

The Royal Descents of 900 Immigrants

of Paul, Prince Romanovsky-Ilyinski (1928-2004), sometime Paul R. Ilyinski, of Fla., councilman and mayor of Palm Beach, photographer, who married (1) Mary Evelyn Prince and (2) Angela Philippa Kaufman. In 2012 the four children (all born in Palm Beach) of Prince Romanovsky-Ilyinski lived in Litchfield, Conn., and Cincinnati and Dayton, Ohio.

In addition, Marie of Greece and Denmark, a sister of Nicholas, Christopher, Andrew, and Alexandra, married George, Grand Duke of Russia, and left an elder daughter Nina, Grand Duchess of Russia, who married Prince Paul Chavchavadze of Georgia and immigrated to Massachusetts. Their son, Prince David Chavchavadze, long worked for the U.S. Central Intelligence Agency and authored several books on history and politics. This last married Helen Husted, Judith Clippinger and Eugenie de Smitt; three of his four children and five of his six grandchildren were born in either Washington, D.C. or New York City.

The Royal Descents of 900 Immigrants

1. Alexander II, Czar of Russia, d. 1881 = (1) Marie of Hesse; (2) Catherine, Princess Dolguruki, created Princess Yourievsky

2. (by 1) Alexei, Grand Duke of Russia, who allegedly married morganatically Alexandra Zhukovsky, daughter of Vassili Zhukovsky, the Russian poet

3. Alexis, Count Belevsky-Zhukovsky (also Belewsky-Joukovsky and Bjelewskji-Jukowskij in Ferrand and Schwennicke, respectively) = Maria, Princess Troubetskoy

4. **Elisabeth, Countess Belevsky-Zhukovsky** of N.Y. = (1) Peter Ghika-Perevostchikov; (2) Arthur Vincent **Lourie**, 1892-1966, musical composer and writer.

Sources: *WWWA*, vol. 4, *1961-1968* (1968), p. 587 (A.V. Lourie), *ES2*: 2: 152 and *ES2*: 3: 3: 418 plus, for more detail, Jacques Ferrand, *Les Familles Comitales de l'Ancien Empire de Russie*, 2nd ed., vol. 1 (1997), pp. 17-19. For the figures below see *BRFW1*, pp. 469-74.

Alexander III, Czar of Russia, d. 1894, son of Alexander II and Marie above, married Marie Sophie Frederikke Dagmar (Maria Feodorovna) of Denmark and left (in addition to Nicholas II, last Czar of Russia) an eldest daughter, Xenia, Grand Duchess of Russia, who married Alexander, Grand Duke of Russia, a cousin (son, by Cäcilie Auguste of Baden, of Michael, Grand Duke of Russia, son of Nicholas I, Czar of Russia, and Charlotte Louise of Prussia, SETH). Of the sons of Xenia and Alexander, [1] Andrew, Grand Duke of Russia, married Elizabeth Ruffo and was the father of Andrew, Grand Duke of Russia, known as *Andrew Romanoff*, b. 1923, of Calif., an artist, who married (1) Helen Dourneff, (2) Mrs. Kathleen Norris Roberts, and (3) Mrs. Inez von Bachelin Storer, known as Inez Storer, b. 1933, also an artist; [2] Nikita, Grand Duke of Russia, who married Maria, Countess Vorontzov-Dachkov, and was the father of Nikita, Grand Duke of Russia, known as *Nikita Romanoff* (1923-2007) of N.Y., co-author of *Ivan the Terrible* (1975), who married Janet Anne Schoenwald; and [3] Rostislav, Grand Duke of Russia, sometime of Ill., who married (1) Alexandra, Princess Galitzine, SETH (later Mrs. Lester Armour), (2) Mrs. Alice Eilken Baker, and (3) Mrs. Hedwig Maria Gertrud Eva van Chappuis Gage, and was the father by Alexandra of Rostislav, Grand Duke of Russia, known as *Rostislav Romanoff* (1938-1999), vice president and head of international banking at Northern Trust Co., Chicago, who married Stephena Verdel Cook.

The Royal Descents of 900 Immigrants

1. Ferdinand II, King of the Two Sicilies, d. 1859 = (1) Maria Cristina of Sardinia; (2) Maria Theresa of Austria

2. (by 2) Maria Immaculata of the Two Sicilies = Karl Salvator, Archduke of Austria, Prince of Tuscany

3. Leopold Salvator, Archduke of Austria, Prince of Tuscany = Blanca of Spain (parents of Anton, Archduke of Austria, Prince of Tuscany, and husband of Ileana of Roumania, known as Mother Alexandra, of the Monastery of the Transfiguration, Ellwood City, Pa., ARD, SETH)

4. Karl (Pius Maria Adelgonde Blanka Leopold Ignaz Raphael Michael Salvator Kyrill Angelus Barbara), Archduke of Austria, Prince of Tuscany, Carlist pretender to the Spanish throne = Christa Satzger de Bálványos

5. **Maria Immaculata Pia, Countess von Habsburg**, of N.Y. = John Howard **Dobkin**, b. 1942, art museum administrator (of the Cooper-Hewitt Museum, the National Academy of Design, and Historic Hudson Valley). Their three children were born in Washington, D.C., and New York City.

Sources: *Who's Who in America*, recent editions (J.H. Dobkin); Daniel Willis, *The Descendants of Louis XIII* (1999), pp. 633, 625, 308, 300 and Jacques Arnold, *The Royal Houses of Europe: The Balkan and Italian Monarchies* (2007), charts J4M, J3F, J2C, I3B (two pages).

The Royal Descents of 900 Immigrants

1. Nicholas I, Czar of Russia, d. 1855 = Charlotte Louise of Prussia

2. Constantine, Grand Duke of Russia = Alexandra of Saxe-Altenburg

3. Constantine, Grand Duke of Russia = Elizabeth of Saxe-Altenburg, a cousin

4. Tatiana, Grand Duchess of Russia, of the Orthodox Convent of the Mount of Olives = Constantine, Prince Bagration-Mukhransky, a prince of Georgia

5. **Teymuraz** (Prince) **Bagration**(-Mukhransky, a prince of Georgia) (1912-1992) of N.Y., senior executive of the Tolstoy Foundation, author = (1) Ekaterina Ratchitch; (2) Irina, Countess Czernichew-Besobrasow.

2. Maria, Grand Duchess of Russia (sister of the elder Constantine) = (2) Grigori, Count Stroganov

3. Elena, Countess Stroganov = Vladimir, Count Cheremeteff

4. Sergei, Count Cheremeteff = Alexandra, Countess Cheremeteff, a cousin

5. Nikita, Count Cheremeteff = Catherine Vandoro

6. **Maria, Countess Cheremeteff**, sometime of Washington, D.C. = (1) Brandon Hambright **Grove**, Jr. (b. 1929), U.S. diplomat; (2) Robert G. **Abernethy**. Her four children by Grove were either born or married in Washington, D.C.; a daughter by Abernethy was born in New Haven, Conn.

Sources: Jacques Arnold, *The Royal Houses of Europe: Great Britain and Ireland*, vol. 5, *The Descendants of George I, the Stuart-Hanover Connection* (2009), charts 6H, 7H, 8R, and *The Hohenzollern Dynasty*, vol. 1, charts 7BV (second husband), 6AU (two pages), 5AM (two pages); *WWA*, 2012, p. 1753 (Grove); *BRFW* 1: 469-70 (and 2: 64) (Russia, Georgia) and *WWWA* 13, 1998-2000 (2000): 13 (Bagration).

The Royal Descents of 900 Immigrants

1. Frederick William III, King of Prussia, d. 1840 = (1) Louise of Mecklenburg-Strelitz; (2) Augusta von Harrach, Princess of Liegnitz, Countess of Hohenzollern

2. (by 1) Albert, Prince of Prussia = Marianne of The Netherlands, daughter of William I, King of The Netherlands (and Wilhelmine of Prussia, sister of King Frederick William III), son of William V of Orange, Stadholder of The Netherlands (and Wilhelmine of Prussia, sister of Frederick William II, King of Prussia, and aunt of Frederick William III), son of William IV of Orange, Stadholder of The Netherlands, and Anna of Great Britain, daughter of George II, King of Great Britain, d. 1760, and Caroline of Brandenburg-Anspach

3. Alexandrine of Prussia = William, Duke of Mecklenburg (uncle of Henry, Duke of Mecklenburg, husband of Wilhelmina, Queen of the Netherlands, and son of Paul Frederick, Grand Duke of Mecklenburg-Schwerin, and Alexandrine of Prussia, daughter of Frederick William III, King of Prussia, and Louise of Mecklenburg-Strelitz, above

4. Charlotte of Mecklenburg-Schwerin = Henry XVIII, Prince Reuss-Köstritz, son of Henry II, Prince Reuss-Köstritz (and Clotilde, Countess of Castell-Castell), son of Henry LV, Count Reuss-Köstritz and Maria Justina, Baroness von Watteville, daughter of Johann Michael, Baron von Watteville and Henrietta Benigna Justina, Countess of Zinzendorf and Pottendorf, sometime of Pa., etc., ARD, SETH

5. Henry XXXVII, Prince Reuss-Köstritz = Anna Christa Stefanie Clemm von Hohenberg

6. **Marianne Charlotte Katharina Stefanie, Princess Reuss-Köstritz** = (1) Avery **Brundage** (1887-1975), president of the U.S. Olympic Association, 1929-53, and of the International Olympic Committee, 1952-72; (2) Friedrich Karl **Feldmann**.

Sources: *BRFW* 1: 256 and *passim*; *RHS* 2: 240-41 and *passim*; *Almanach de Gotha*, 188th ed., vol. 1 (2012), p. 332; *The Hohenzollern Dynasty*, vol. 1, charts 8AH, 7AE, 5AY, 4L; and Gerhard Meyer, *Nikolas Ludwig, Reichsgraf von Zinzendorf, Eine Genealogische Studie mit Ahnen-und Nachfahrenliste* (1966), pp. 228-29, 256-57.

The Royal Descents of 900 Immigrants

1. William IV, King of Great Britain, d. 1837 = Adelaide of Saxe-Meiningen

2. (illegitimate by Dorothy Bland, the actress Mrs. Jordan) Elizabeth FitzClarence = William George Hay, 18th Earl of Erroll

3. Agnes Georgiana Elizabeth Hay = James Duff, 5th Earl of Fife. A son, Alexander William George Duff, 1st Duke of Fife, married H.R.H. Princess Louise Victoria Alexandra Dagmar of Great Britain, daughter of King Edward VII. Descendants of the only grandchild of the latter couple, James George Alexander Bannerman Carnegie, 3rd Duke of Fife, are heirs to the British throne after descendants (now numerous) of King George V.

4. Anne Elizabeth Clementina Duff = John Villiers Stuart Townshend, 5th Marquess Townshend

5. John James Dudley Stuart Townshend, 6th Marquess Townshend = Gladys Ethel Gwendolen Eugenie Sutherst

6. George John Patrick Dominic Townshend, 7th Marquess Townshend = Elizabeth Pamela Audrey Luby

7. **Lady Carolyn Elizabeth Ann Townshend** of N.Y. = (1) Antonio **Capellini**; (2) (=Dec. 1973, annulled Dec. 1974) Edgar Miles **Bronfman** (1929-2013), chairman and chief executive officer of Seagram Co., Ltd., distillers.

4. Agnes Cecil Emmeline Duff (sister of Anne Elizabeth Clementina) = Sir Alfred Cooper

5. (Alfred) Duff Cooper, 1st Viscount Norwich
   = Diana Olivia Winifred Maud Manners, society leader as Lady Diana Cooper

6. John Julius Cooper, 2nd Viscount Norwich, historian
   = (1) Anne Frances May Clifford; (2) Hon. Mary Makins

7. (illegitimate by ballerina Enrica "Ricki" Soma, fourth wife of John Huston, the film director and actor, SETH, who raised Allegra) **Allegra Huston**, b. 1964, now of (Taos), New Mexico, writer, author of *Love Child: A Memoir of Family Lost and Found* (2009), partner of Cisco Guevara.

The Royal Descents of 900 Immigrants

Sources: *BP* (Townshend, Fife, Erroll, Munster, Norwich); Jacques Arnold, *The Royal Houses of Europe: Great Britain and Northern Ireland*, vol. 3, *The Descendants of King George III, Including the FitzClarence Family (but Excluding the Descendants of Queen Victoria)* (2008), charts A1, A2C, A3H, A4O, A4Q, A5W, A5BB, A6BG. Sybil Mary Cooper, third daughter of Sir Alfred and Agnes C.E. Duff, married Richard Vaughan Hart-Davis; their son, Sir Rupert Charles Hart-Davis, was an actor and publisher whose first wife was the actress Dame Peggy Ashcroft. Stephanie Agnes Cooper, eldest daughter of Sir Alfred and Agnes C.E. Duff, married (1) Arthur Francis Levita. Their daughter, Edith Agnes Levita, married (1) Ewen Donald Cameron and left a son, Ian Donald Cameron, who married Mary Fleur Mount and is the father of British Prime Minister David William Cameron, who married Samantha Gwendoline Sheffield (see charts A5Z and A5BA).

The Royal Descents of 900 Immigrants

1. Francis II, Holy Roman Emperor and Emperor of Austria, d. 1835 = (1) Elizabeth of Württemberg; (2) Maria Theresa of the Two Sicilies; (3) Maria Ludovika of Austria-Este; (4) Caroline Augusta of Bavaria

2. (by 2) Marie Louise of Austria = (1) Napoleon I, Emperor of the French, d. 1821; (2) Adam Adalbert, Count von Neipperg; (3) Charles René, Count Bombelles

3. (by 2) William Albert, 1st Prince of Montenuovo = Juliana, Countess Batthyány Német-Ujvár

4. Albertine Leopoldine Wilhelmine Julia Maria, Princess of Montenuovo = Zygmunt, Count Wielopolski, Marquis Gonzaga-Myszkowski

5. **Maria Malgorzata Paulina Wilhelmina Róza Leopoldyna Julia Wielopolska** of Philadelphia = Józafat, Count **Plater-Zyberk**. Their son, Józafat, Count Plater-Zyberk, married Maria Meysztowicz, and was the father of architectural educator Elizabeth (Elzbieta) Maria Plater-Zyberk, b. 1950, wife of Andres M. Duany.

4. Alfred, 2nd Prince of Montenuovo (brother of Albertine) = Franziska, Countess Kinsky von Wchinitz und Tettau

5. Franziska, Princess of Montenuovo = Leopold Willibald, Prince of Lobkowicz

6. Amelia Franziska, Princess of Lobkowicz = Franz Friedrich, Prince of Schwarzenberg

7. **Ludmilla Maria, Princess of Schwarzenberg**, of N.Y. = Carl Barton **Hess** (1912-2011), private equity firm executive. They left no children.

Sources: *The Habsburg Dynasty*, charts 3A (2 pages), 4A, 5B, 6AA, 7AB, 8AF (to Elizabeth [Elzbieta] Maria, Countess Plater-Zyberk, but without naming a husband), 6AB, 7AE (two pages) (to Mrs. Hess); *WWA* 1996, p. 3308 (Plater-Zyberk), and *WWWA*, vol. 22, *2010-2011* (2011), p. 95 (Hess). The Plater-Zyberk descent was brought to my attention by the late Francis James Dallett, archivist of the University of Pennsylvania.

The Royal Descents of 900 Immigrants

1. Frederick I, King of Württemberg, d. 1816 = (1) Augusta of Brunswick, daughter of Charles II William Ferdinand, Duke of Brunswick and Augusta of Great Britain, daughter of Frederick Louis, Prince of Wales (and Augusta of Saxe-Gotha), son of George II, King of Great Britain, d. 1760, and Caroline of Brandenburg-Anspach; (2) Charlotte of Great Britain

2. (by 1) Paul, Prince of Württemberg = Charlotte of Saxe-Hildburghausen

3. (illegitimately by Friederike Margarethe Porth) Karoline Adelheid Pauline von Rothenburg = Karl, Baron von Pfeffel

4. Hubert, Baron von Pfeffel = Helene von Rivière

5. Marie Luise, Baroness von Pfeffel = Stanley Fred Williams

6. Irene Williams = Osman Ali Wilfred Kemal, alias Wilfred Johnson, son of Ali Kemal Bey, Interior Minister of Turkey, and Winifred Brun

7. **Stanley (Patrick) Johnson**, b. 1940, writer and environmentalist, sometime of N.Y. = Charlotte Fawcett. Their son, (Alexander) Boris (de Pfeffel) Johnson, b. 1964, a former M.P., editor of the *Spectator*, mayor of London, and British Foreign Secretary, was born in New York City and retains joint U.S. and U.K citizenship; Boris = (1) Allegra G. A. Mostyn-Owen; (2) Marina Claire Wheeler.

Sources: Wikipedia entries for Prince Paul of Württemberg, Stanley Johnson and Boris Johnson, the first of which cites http://www.augsburger-allgemeine.de/bayern/London/OB-entdeckt-beruehmte-vermandtschaft-id 4054426.html (*ES* 2: 1: 2 does not cover the illegitimate children of Paul, Prince of Württemberg; *GH des A* does not include an article on von Pfeffel; and some middle names above are taken from other Internet sources); *ES* 2, charts for Württemberg, Brunswick-Wolfenbüttel and Great Britain. This descent was also featured on the British Broadcasting Company (BBC) program "Who Do You Think You Are"; see vademecumgenealogy.blogspot.com/2012/02/london.html.

The Royal Descents of 900 Immigrants

1. Frederick William II, King of Prussia, d. 1797 = (1) Elizabeth Christina of Brunswick-Wolfenbüttel; (2) Frederica of Hesse-Darmstadt

2. (by 2) Augusta of Prussia = William II, Elector of Hesse

3. Frederick William, Elector of Hesse = (morganatic) Gertrude Falkenstein, Princess von Hanau and zu Horowitz, Countess von Schaumburg

4. Augusta Marie Gertrude, Princess von Hanau and zu Horowitz, Countess von Schaumburg = Ferdinand Maximilian, Prince of Isenburg-Budingen

5. Gertrude Philippina Alexandra Marie Augustine Louise, Princess of Isenburg-Büdingen = Robert, Baron von Pagenhardt

6. **Maximilian Hugo, Baron von Pagenhardt** (1884-1943) of Washington, D.C., naval architect and construction engineer = Marie Dupuy Adams.

Sources: Daniel A. Willis, *The Descendants of King George I of Great Britain* (2002), pp. 275-76, 290-91. Note also *BRFW* 1: 204-7, 136-37 (Hesse, Prussia), *ES* 2: 17: 68 (Isenburg-Büdingen-Wachtersbach), *WWWA*, vol. 2, *1943-1950* (1950), p. 549 (M.H. [Baron] von Pagenhardt). Maximilian (Ferdinand) Robert, Baron von Pagenhardt, policy sciences educator and diplomat, son of Maximilian Hugo and Marie, who married Hope Allen, Sylvia Hommel and Heidi Schweiger, is treated in *WWWA*, vol. 13, *1998-2000* (2000), p. 289.

The Royal Descents of 900 Immigrants

1. Catherine II (of Anhalt-Zerbst), Empress of Russia, d. 1796 (= Peter III, Czar of Russia)

2. (illegitimate by Gregory, Count [later Prince] Orlov) Alexis, Count Bobrinski = Anna Dorothea, Baroness Ungern-Sternberg

3. Paul, Count Bobrinski = Julia Junosha-Belinslava (Junòsza-Biélinska)

4. Alexis, Count Bobrinski = Alexandra Pizarjewa

5. Vladimir, Count Bobrinski = Maria Nikonowa

6. **Gregori, Count Bobrinski**, known as **George Vladimir Bobrinskoy** (1901-1985) of Ill., professor of Sanskrit, department chairman (South Asian studies, linguistics), University of Chicago = Theodora Platt. Their three children were born in Chicago.

Sources: *WWWA*, vol. 9, 1985-1989 (1989), p. 39 (G.V. Bobrinskoy) and *ES* 2: 3: 3: 415-16 (Bobrinski). Note also Jacques Ferrand, *Les Familles Comitales de l'Ancien Empire de Russie*, 2nd ed., vol. 1 (1997), pp. 22, 31-33, and David Geoffrey Williamson, *The Counts Bobrinskoy: A Genealogy* (1962). This line is the only illegitimate descent herein from a reigning queen.

The Royal Descents of 900 Immigrants

1. Francis I (of Lorraine), Holy Roman Emperor, d. 1765 = Maria Theresa, Empress of Austria, d. 1780
2. Ferdinand, Archduke of Austria, Duke of Modena = Maria Beatrice (d'Este) of Modena
3. Maria Leopoldina of Modena, Archduchess of Austria = Louis Joseph, Count von Arco-Zinneberg
4. Maximilian Joseph, Count von Arco-Zinneberg = Leopoldina, Countess von Waldburg-Zeil
5. Helena, Countess von Arco-Zinneberg = Heinrich, Baron von and zu Franckenstein
6. Konrad, Baron von and zu Franckenstein = Anna Maria, Countess Esterhazy de Galantha
7. **Joseph, Baron von and zu Franckenstein**, sometime of N.Y. and Calif. = **Kay Boyle** (1902-92), poet, novelist and short-story writer, formerly wife of Laurence Vail. This last was formerly married to art collector and patron Marguerite "Peggy" Guggenheim, who herself later married Surrealist painter Max Ernst. The two children of Baron Joseph and Kay (Boyle) von and zu Franckenstein were born in New York City.

Sources: *The Habsburg Dynasty*, charts 6BS (two pages), 5W, 4J (two pages), 3F, 2B, 1 (two pages) and *ANB* (Kay Boyle, Peggy Guggenheim and Max Ernst).

The Royal Descents of 900 Immigrants

1. Frederick William I, King of Prussia, d. 1740 = Sophie Dorothea of Great Britain
2. Ferdinand, Prince of Prussia =   3. Louise of Brandenburg-Schwedt, his niece, daughter of Frederick William, Margrave of Brandenburg-Schwedt and 2. Sophie of Prussia, elder sister of Ferdinand and daughter of Frederick William I, King of Prussia, and Sophie Dorothea of Great Britain, above
3,4. August, Prince of Prussia, d. unm.
4,5. (illegitimate by Auguste Arend, enobled as "von Prillwitz") (Friedrich Wilhelm August) Ludwig von Prillwitz = Georgine Marie Elizabeth Eugenie, Countess von Moltke
5,6. (illegitimate by Edwina Viereck, actress) (**Franz Georg Edwin) Louis (Withold) Viereck** of N.Y. = Laura Viereck, a first cousin (parents of George Sylvester Viereck, 1884-1962, writer and pro-German propagandist, who married Margaret Edith Hein).

3,4. (Frederica Dorothea) Louise (Philippine) of Prussia (sister of August) = Anthony Henry, Prince Radziwill, Polish statesman
4,5. (Frederick William Louis Maria Ferdinand Henry August) Boguslav, Prince Radziwill = Leontine, Countess von Clary and Aldringen
5,6. Ferdinand (Frederick William Alexander), Prince Radziwill, chairman of the Polish Party in the German Reichstag = Pelagia, Princess Sapieha
6,7. Janusz (Francis Xavier Joseph Labre Bonislaus Maria), Prince Radziwill, Polish political leader = Anna, Princess Lubomirska
7,8. **Stanislaus Albert, Prince Radziwill**, sometime of N.Y. = (1) Rose de Monléon; (2) Grace Kolin; (3) Mrs. Caroline Lee Bouvier Canfield, known as Lee Radziwill, b. 1933, socialite, SETH, later wife of film and broadway producer/director Herbert David Ross, sister of First Lady Mrs. Jacqueline Lee Bouvier Kennedy Onassis, wife of 35th U.S. President John Fitzgerald Kennedy and Greek shipping magnate Aristotle Socrates Onassis, society and fashion leader, editor, SETH. The only son

The Royal Descents of 900 Immigrants

of Stanislaus and Lee was noted television producer Anthony (Stanislaus Albert, Prince) Radziwill, 1959-1999, who married Caroli Di Falco, the television actress known as Carole Radziwill.

Sources: *DAB* (G.S. Viereck), G.S. Viereck, *My Flesh and Blood: A Lyric Autobiography with Indiscreet Annotations* (1931), pp. 236-38; *Gothaisches Genealogisches Taschenbuch der Briefadeligen Häuser* (1915), pp. 739-40 (von Prillwitz); *ES,* charts for Prillwitz (2: 1: 142B), Prussia and Brandenburg-Schwedt.; *RHS* 2:209, 216, 286, 309-10, 317, 319-20 and *GHdesA*, vol. 42, *Fürstliche Häuser*, vol. 8 (1968), pp. 417, 423-27 (Radziwill). The Viereck line was brought to my attention by the late William Addams Reitwiesner of Washington, D.C.

The Royal Descents of 900 Immigrants

1. Victor Amadeus II, King of Sardinia, d. 1732 = (1) Anne Marie of Orleans; (2) Anna Teresa Canali, Marchesa di Spigno

2. (illegitimate by Jeanne Baptiste d'Albret) Victoria Francesca of Savoy, Madamigella di Susa = Victor Amadeus I of Savoy, Prince of Carignan, a cousin, son of Emanuel Philibert of Savoy, Prince of Carignan (and Angelina Caterina d'Este of Modena), son of Thomas, Prince of Carignan (and Marie of Bourbon-Soissons), son of Charles Emanuel I, Duke of Savoy, and Catherine of Spain, daughter of Philip II, King of Spain, d. 1598, and Elizabeth of France

3. Louis Victor of Savoy, Prince of Carignan = Christine Henrietta of Hesse-Rheinfels-Rotenburg

4. Leopolda of Savoy-Carignan (great-aunt of Charles Albert, King of Sardinia, and great-great aunt of this latter's son, Victor Emanuel II, King of Italy) = Giovanni Andrea, Prince Doria-Pamfili-Landi, 2nd Prince of Torriglia

5. Luigi Doria-Pamfili-Landi, Prince of Valmontore, 3rd Prince of Torriglia = Teresa Orsini of Gravina

6. Leopoldina Doria-Pamfili-Landi = Sigismundo, Prince Chigi-Albani, 6th Prince of Farnese

7. Teresa Chigi-Albani = Giulio Torlonia, 2nd Duke of Poli and Guadagnolo

8. Marino Torlonia, 4th Prince of Civitella-Cesi = Mary Elsie Moore of N.Y.

9. **Marina Torlonia** of N.Y. = (1) Francis Xavier **Shields**; (2) Edward W. **Slater**. Marina's son, Francis Alexander Shields, married firstly Teri Schmon and is the father of (Christa) Brooke (Camille) Shields (b. 1965), model, actress, and former wife of tennis champion Andre Agassi.

4. Gabriella of Savoy-Carignan (sister of Leopolda) = Ferdinand Philip Joseph, Prince of Lobkowicz

5. Franz Joseph Maximilian, Prince of Lobkowicz = Marie Caroline, Princess von Schwarzenberg

The Royal Descents of 900 Immigrants

6. Ferdinand Joseph, Prince of Lobkowicz = Marie of Liechtenstein
7. Moritz (Aloyse Joseph Marcellin), Prince of Lobkowicz = Marie Anna of Oettingen-Wallerstein
8. Ferdinand (Zdenko Maria), Prince of Lobkowicz = Maria Anna Bertha, Countess von Neipperg
9. **Maximilian Erwin (Maria Joseph Antonius von Padua Heinrich Thomas), Prince of Lobkowicz** (1888-1967), Czech ambassador to the U.K., later of Dover, Mass. = Gillian Margaret Hope Somerville. Their three sons, ten grandchildren, and ten great-grandchildren all live in the U.S.

Sources: Daniel MacGregor, *Brooke's Book: Ancestry of Brooke Shields* (privately distributed, 1988); *BRFW* 1:360, 362-63 (generations 1-4), Christoph Weber, *Kardinäle und Prälaten in den Letzten Jahrzehnten des Kirchenstaates* (1978), tafel 34 (Doria-Pamphili) and tafel 3 (Albani/Chigi), *GHdesA*, *Fürstliche Häuser*, Band IV (1956), pp. 530, 532, and newspaper accounts (*N.Y. Times*, etc.) of the marriage of Marina Torlonia and Francis Xavier Shields; *ES* 1: 3: 26 and *Almanach de Gotha*, 188th ed., vol. 1 (2012), pp. 585-88 (Lobkowicz).

The Royal Descents of 900 Immigrants

1. Joseph I, Holy Roman Emperor, d. 1711 = Wilhelmine Amalie of Brunswick-Lüneburg

2. Maria Josepha of Austria = Frederick Augustus II, Elector of Saxony, (elected) King of Poland, d. 1763

3. Francis Xavier of Saxony = Clara Spinucci, Countess von der Lausitz

4. Maria Christina Sabina of Saxony, Countess von der Lausitz = Camillo (VIII) Massimiliano Massimo, Prince of Arsoli

5. Camillo Vittorio Emanuele Massimo, Prince of Arsoli = Giacinta della Porta-Rodiani

6. Maria Francesca Massimo = Ranieri Bourbon del Monte Santa Maria, Prince of San Faustino

7. Carlo Bourbon del Monte Santa Maria, Prince of San Faustino = Jane Allen Campbell of Montclair, N.J.

8. **Ranieri Bourbon del Monte Santa Maria, Prince of San Faustino**, of Calif. = (1) Kay [Katherine] Linn **Sage** (1898-1963), surrealist painter and poet, patron of the Museum of Modern Art, who later married surrealist painter Yves Tanguy; (2) Lydia Bodrero; (3) Mrs. Géneviève B. Lyman Casey.

8. Virginia Bourbon del Monte Santa Maria = Edoardo Agnelli

9. Clara Jeanne Agnelli (sister of Giovanni Agnelli, industrialist, head of Fiat) = Tassilo (Egon Maria Karl Georg Leo), Prince zu Fürstenberg, son of (Karl) Emil (Anton Maximilian Leo Wratislaw), Prince zu Furstenberg, and Maria Matilda Georgina, Countess Festetics von Tolna, daughter of Tassilo, Prince Festetics von Tolna and Lady Mary Victoria Douglas-Hamilton, SETH (who = [1] Albert I [Honoré Charles Grimaldi], sovereign Prince of Monaco); nephew of Maximilian Egon II, Prince zu Fürstenberg, "Beer Baron," adviser and friend of William II, German Emperor; and half-nephew of Louis II, Sovereign Prince of Monaco

10. **(Eduard) Egon (Peter Paul Giovanni), Prince zu Fürstenberg** (1946-2004) of N.Y., fashion designer = (1) Diane Halfin, known as Diane von Fürstenberg (b. 1946), fashion designer; (2) Lynn Marshall.

The Royal Descents of 900 Immigrants

5. Barbara Massimo (sister of Camillo Vittorio Emanuele, Prince of Arsoli) = Giovanni Ruspoli, Prince of Cerveteri

6. Francesco Maria Ruspoli, Prince of Cerveteri = Egle Franchese

7. Alessandro Ruspoli, Prince of Cerveteri = Marianita Montefeltro della Rovere

8. Francesco Maria Quinto Ruspoli, Prince of Cerveteri = Claudia Matarazzo

9. Alessandro Ruspoli, Prince of Cerveteri, illegitimate by Debra Berger

10. **Tao Ruspoli** (b. 1975) of Calif., filmmaker, photographer and musician = Olivia Wilde (born Olivia Jane Cockburn) (b. 1984), actress, ARD, SETH.

10. **Bartolomeo Ruspoli** of Calif. = Aileen Getty (b. 1957), AIDS activist, granddaughter of oil tycoon John Paul Getty and former wife of Christopher Edward Wilding, son of Michael Wilding, actor, and Elizabeth (Rosemond) Taylor (Hilton Wilding Todd Fisher Burton Warner Fortensky), the actress.

Sources: *RHS* 2:8-9, 13, 62, 65, 66, 71-72, 75, and Jacques Arnold, *The Royal Houses of Europe: The Stuart Dynasty of Great Britain*, vol. 1 (2010), charts 5I, 6I, 7R, 8BG, 9BZ, 10FA, 11KB, 12PE, 13JY, 13JZ, 9CA, 10FB, 11KF (the entire Bourbon del Monte Santa Maria/Agnelli descent and the Ruspoli line to generation 9 in both sources); Stephen Robeson Miller, *Kay Sage: The Biographical Chronology and Four Surrealist One-Act Plays* (2011), *passim*, plus *NAW Modern Period*, pp. 618-19 (Kay Sage); *WWA*, various editions (Egon and Diane von Fürstenberg), *Almanach de Gotha*, 188th ed., vol. 1 (2012), pp. 515-17 (von Fürstenberg), *GH des A*, vol. 8, *Fürstliche Häuser*, vol. 3 (1955), pp. 334-35 (Festetics von Tolna), *BP* (Hamilton) and *BRFW*, vol. 1, p. 406 (Monaco); Wikipedia or Internet Movie Database entries for "Dado" Ruspoli, Debra Berger, Tao Ruspoli, Olivia Wilde, and Aileen Getty. The Ruspoli line was brought to my attention by John Blythe Dobson of Winnipeg, Manitoba, Canada. In generation 9, Prince "Dado" Ruspoli and Debra Berger were a minor actor and actress.

The Royal Descents of 900 Immigrants

1. Charles II, King of England, d. 1685 = Catherine of Braganza

2. (illegitimate by Barbara Villiers, Duchess of Cleveland) Charlotte Fitzroy = Edward Henry Lee, 1st Earl of Lichfield

3. George Henry Lee, 2nd Earl of Lichfield = Frances Hales

4. Charlotte Lee = Henry Dillon, 11th Viscount Dillon

5. Charles Dillon-Lee, 12th Viscount Dillon =

1. James II, King of England, reigned 1685-88, d. 1701 = (1) Anne Hyde; (2) Mary of Modena

2. (illegitimate by Catherine Sidley, Countess of Dorchester) Catherine Darnley = James Annesley, 3rd Earl of Anglesey

3. Catherine Annesley = William Phipps

4. Constantine Phipps, 1st Baron Mulgrave = Lepell Hervey

5. Henrietta Maria Phipps

6. Henry Augustus Dillon-Lee, 13th Viscount Dillon = Henrietta Browne

7. Henrietta Maria Dillon-Lee = Edward John Stanley, 2nd Baron Stanley of Alderley. Their daughter, Katherine Louisa Stanley, married John Russell, Viscount Amberley (son of John Russell, 1st Earl Russell, British Prime Minister, SETH, and Frances Anna Maria Elliot) and was the mother of Bertrand Arthur William Russell, 3rd Earl Russell, mathematician and peace advocate.

8. Henrietta Blanche Stanley = David Graham Drummond Ogilvy, 7th Earl of Airlie

9. Clementina Gertrude Helen Ogilvy = Algernon Bertram Freeman-Mitford, 1st Baron Redesdale

10. David Bertram Ogilvy Freeman-Mitford, 2nd Baron Redesdale = Sydney Bowles. Their other daughters included the writer (Hon.) Nancy (Freeman-) Mitford, wife of Hon. Peter Murray Rennell Rodd; Fascist sympathizer and martyr (Hon.) Unity Valkyrie (Freeman-) Mitford; and (Hon.) Deborah Vivian

The Royal Descents of 900 Immigrants

(Freeman-) Mitford, Duchess of Devonshire, SETH (see under Adele Astaire).

11. **Hon. Jessica Lucy Freeman-Mitford**, known as **Jessica Mitford** (1917-1996) of Calif., writer = (1) Esmond Marcus David **Romilly**; (2) Robert Edward **Treuhaft**.

11. Hon. Diana Freeman-Mitford = (1) Bryan Walter Guinness, 2nd Baron Moyne, son of Walter Edward Guinness, 1st Baron Moyne (and Evelyn Hilda Stuart Erskine), son of Edward Cecil Guinness, 1st Earl of Iveagh, and Adelaide Maria Guinness, SETH; (2) Sir Oswald Ernald Mosley, 6th Bt., leader of British Fascists

12. (by 1) Jonathan Bryan Guinness, 3rd Baron Moyne = Suzanne Lisney

13. **Hon. Daphne Suzannah Diana Joan Guinness** (b. 1967) of N.Y., fashion designer, art collector, and model = Spyros (Stavros) **Niarchos**, son of Greek shipping magnate Stavros Niarchos and Eugenia Livanos. A son is Nicolas Stavros Niarchos (b. 1989), writer for *The New Yorker*.

Sources: *CP* (Lichfield, Dillon, Anglesey, Mulgrave, Stanley of Alderley, Airlie, Redesdale, Russell); *BP* (Redesdale, Moyne, Iveagh, Guinness Bt.); *ANB, Supplement* (2002): 416-18 (Jessica Mitford), and Wikipedia entries for Daphne Guinness and Spyros and Stavros Niarchos. Lepell Hervey above was a daughter of John Hervey, 1st Baron Hervey, the man of letters, and Mary Lepell, SETH.

Note: Frances Dillon, a sister of the 12th Viscount Dillon, married (Sir) William Jerningham, 6th Bt., 1st Baron Stafford; their son, George William Jerningham, 2nd Baron Stafford, married Frances Henrietta Sulyarde; their daughter, Charlotte Georgiana Jerningham, married Thomas Fraser, 12th Baron Lovat; their son, Simon Fraser, 13th Baron Lovat, married Alice Mary Blundell; their daughter, Margaret Mary Fraser, married Archibald Stirling (-Maxwell); their son, William Joseph Stirling, married Susan Rachel Bligh; and their son, Archibald Hugh Stirling, married (1) Charmian Rachel Montagu-Douglas-Scott; (2) Dame Diana Rigg, b. 1938, part of whose television career was American, former wife of Israeli painter Menachem Gueffen; and (3) Sharon Helene Silver. See *BP* or *CP* (Dillon, Stafford, Lovat and, for Stirling, Heron-Maxwell, baronets).

The Royal Descents of 900 Immigrants

1. James II, King of England, 1685-88, d. 1701 = (1) Anne Hyde; (2) Mary of Modena

2. (illegitimate by Arabella Churchill, sister of John Churchill, 1st Duke of Marlborough, the victor at Blenheim, SETH) James FitzJames, 1st Duke of Berwick = Anne Bulkeley

3. Charles FitzJames, 2nd Duke of FitzJames = Victoire-Louise-Josèphe Gouyon

4. Jacques-Charles FitzJames, 3rd Duke of FitzJames = Marie-Claudine-Silvie de Thiard

5. Edouard FitzJames, 4th Duke of FitzJames = Elisabeth Alexandrine le Vassor

6. Jacques-Marie-Emanuel FitzJames, 5th Duke of FitzJames = Marguerite de Marmier

7. Arabella FitzJames = Scipione Borghese (of maternal Salviati descent), Duca Salviati

8. Francesca Salviati = Francesco Borghese, 3rd Duke of Bomarzo, a cousin

9. Marco Borghese, 4th Duke of Bomarzo = Isabel-Fanny-Louise Porgès

10. Paolo Borghese, 5th Duke of Bomarzo = (1) Anna dei Conti Scheibler; (2) (Mrs.) Marcella Fazi (Mauritzi), founder of "Princess Marcella Borghese" cosmetics (carried by Revlon)

11. (by 2) **Francesco Marco Luigi Costanzo Borghese, 6th Duke of Bomarzo**, b. 1938, sometime of N.J., former head of his mother's cosmetics company = Amanda Leigh. A son is Prince Lorenzo Borghese, businessman, animal advocate and television personality.

Sources: *Almanach de Gotha*, 188th ed., vol. 2 (2013), pp. 147-48 (Borghese of Bomarzo) and Wikipedia entry for Lorenzo Borghese; *GH des A*, vol. 19, *Fürstliche Häuser*, vol. 5 (1959), pp. 389-90 (Borghese), vol. 3, *Fürstliche Häuser*, vol. 2 (1943), p. 455 (Salviati); *ES* 2: 3: 2: 368b, 387-88 (Berwick, FitzJames). This line was developed and brought to my attention by John C. Brandon of Columbia, S.C.

The Royal Descents of 900 Immigrants

1. Charles II, King of England, d. 1685 = Catherine of Braganza
2. (illegitimate by Louise Renée de Penancoët de Kéroualle, Duchess of Portsmouth) Charles Lennox, 1st Duke of Richmond and Lennox = Anne Brudenell
3. Anne Lennox = William Anne Keppel, 2nd Earl of Albemarle
4. Elizabeth Keppel = Francis Russell, Marquess of Tavistock, son of John Russell, 4th Duke of Bedford, and Gertrude Leveson-Gower, SETH
5. John Russell, 6th Duke of Bedford = Georgiana Gordon, daughter of Alexander Gordon, 4th Duke of Gordon and Jane Maxwell, SETH. By a second wife, Georgiana Elizabeth Byng, the 6th Duke was also the father of Prime Minister John Russell, 1st Earl Russell, SETH, and a great-grandfather of Bertrand Arthur William Russell, 3rd Earl Russell, the philosopher and mathematician, also SETH.
6. Louisa Jane Russell = James Hamilton, 1st Duke of Abercorn. See *NEHGS NEXUS* 14 (1997): 70-73 for their noted British descendants—including the late Diana, Princess of Wales, the Duke of Cambridge, Princes Harry and George, and Princess Charlotte; Sarah (Margaret Ferguson), Duchess of York and Princesses Beatrice and Eugenie; Princess Alice, Duchess of Gloucester, Richard, 2nd Duke of Gloucester, and the latter's children and grandchildren; Prime Minister Alexander Frederick (Sir "Alec") Douglas-Home, 14th Earl of Home; and Gillian Mary Millicent Graham, wife of Garter King of Arms Sir Anthony Richard Wagner.
7. Maud Evelyn Hamilton = Henry Charles Keith Petty-Fitzmaurice, 5th Marquess of Lansdowne
8. Evelyn Petty-Fitzmaurice = Victor Christian William Cavendish, 9th Duke of Devonshire, son of Lord Edward Cavendish and Emma Lascelles, his first cousin, grandson of William Cavendish, 7th Duke of Devonshire and Blanche Georgiana Howard and of Hon. William Saunders Sebright Lascelles and Caroline Georgiana Howard, and great-grandson twice over of George Howard, 6th Earl of Carlisle, and Georgiana Dorothy Cavendish, SETH. The 9th Duke and Evelyn Petty-Fitzmaurice

The Royal Descents of 900 Immigrants

were also parents of Lady Dorothy Evelyn Cavendish, wife of Prime Minister (Maurice) Harold Macmillan, 1st Earl of Stockton.

8. Lord Charles Arthur Francis Cavendish = **Adele Astaire**, born Marie Austerlit (1898-1981), sometime of N.Y. and Arizona, musical theatre dancer, longtime partner of her brother, the dancer Fred Astaire. She = (2) Kingman Douglass. Two of Lord Charles A.F. Cavendish's nephews, sons of Edward William Spencer Cavendish, 10th Duke of Devonshire and Lady Mary Alice Gascoyne-Cecil, were (1) William John Robert Cavendish, Marquess of Hartington, who married Kathleen Kennedy, daughter of Joseph Patrick Kennedy, the financier and diplomat; sister of John Fitzgerald Kennedy, 35th U.S. President, SETH, of Robert Francis Kennedy, U.S. Senator and Attorney-General, of Edward Moore Kennedy, U.S. Senator, of Mrs. Jean Ann Kennedy Smith, diplomat, of (Mrs.) (Robert) Sargent Shriver, Jr. (Eunice Mary Kennedy), wife of the Democratic vice-presidential nominee in 1972, and of Mrs. Peter (Sydney Ernest [Aylen, later]) Lawford, wife of the actor, SETH; and aunt of Congressmen Joseph Patrick Kennedy (III) and Patrick Joseph Kennedy, and of Maria (Owings) Shriver, television newscaster and wife of Arnold (Alois) Schwarzenegger, bodybuilder, actor, and governor of California; and great-aunt of Congressman Joseph Patrick Kennedy (IV); and Andrew Robert Buxton Cavendish, 11th Duke of Devonshire, who married Hon. Deborah Vivien Freeman-Mitford, sister of the writers (Hon.) Jessica (Lucy Freeman-) Mitford (Romilly Treuhaft), and (Hon.) Nancy (Freeman-) Mitford (Rodd) (all three sisters SETH)

7. Albertha Frances Anne Hamilton (sister of Maud Evelyn) = George Charles Spencer-Churchill, 8th Duke of Marlborough, son of John Winston Spencer-Churchill, 7th Duke of Marlborough, and Frances Anne Emily Vane-Stewart, SETH

8. Charles Richard John Spencer-Churchill, 9th Duke of Marlborough = Consuelo Vanderbilt, memoirist, daughter of railroad tycoon William Kissam Vanderbilt and society leader and suffragette Mrs. Alva Erskine Smith Vanderbilt Belmont, SETH

The Royal Descents of 900 Immigrants

9. John Robert Edward Spencer-Churchill, 10th Duke of Marlborough = Alexandra Mary Cadogan

10. **Lady Sarah Consuelo Spencer-Churchill**, sometime of Pa. and N.J. = (1) Edwin Fairman **Russell** (1914-2001), American newspaper and magazine publisher (of the *Patriot Evening News* of Harrisburg, Pa., and *Vogue*), president of Metro Suburbia, Inc., Newhouse Newspapers (his first wife; his second was Cynthia Cary, former wife of Charles Penrose Van Pelt and daughter of Guy Fairfax Cary and Hon. Mrs. Cynthia Burke Roche Burden, SETH); (2) Guy **Burgos**; (3) Theodorus **Roubanis**.

6. Lord Charles James Fox Russell (brother of the Duchess of Abercorn) = Isabella Clarissa Davies, daughter of William Griffith Davies and Elizabeth Seymour, daughter of Lord Robert Seymour (and Anne Delmé), son of Francis Seymour, 1st Marquess of Hertford, and Isabella Fitzroy, daughter of Charles Fitzroy, 2nd Duke of Grafton, and Henrietta Somerset, SETH

7. Henry Charles Russell = Lelia Louisa Millicent Willoughby, daughter of Henry Willoughby, 8th Baron Middleton, and Julia Louisa Bosville, daughter of Alexander William Robert Macdonald and later Bosville, de jure 12th Bt. (and Matilda Eliza Moffat), son of Godfrey Bosville Macdonald, 3rd Baron Macdonald, and Louisa Maria LaCoast, long said to be an illegitimate daughter (by Lady Almeria Carpenter) of H.R.H. Prince William Henry of Great Britain, Duke of Gloucester, son (by Augusta of Saxe-Gotha) of Frederick Louis, Prince of Wales, son of George II, King of Great Britain (d. 1760), and Caroline of Brandenburg-Anspach

8. Olive Isobel Russell = Henry Laurence Birkin

9. David Leslie Birkin = Judy Mary Gamble, the actress Judy Campbell. Their son is Andrew (Timothy) Birkin, screenwriter, director, and sometime actor.

10. **Jane** (Mallory) **Birkin** (b. 1946), singer and actress = **John Barry** (Jonathan Barry Prendergast) (1933-2011), soundtrack

composer (the James Bond series [especially *Goldfinger*], *Midnight Cowboy*, *The Lion in Winter*, *Dances with Wolves*, *Born Free*, *Out of Africa*, etc.), of N.Y. post 1980 (after his divorce from Jane Birkin). Jane was later the partner of Serge Gainsbourg, singer and songwriter, and of Jacques Doillon, director.

Sources: *ANB* (Adele Astaire) and *WWA*, 1994, p. 2979 (E.F. Russell), *BP* and *CP* (Devonshire, Lansdowne, Abercorn, Bedford, Albemarle, Richmond, Gordon, Harewood, Carlisle, Marlborough, Hertford, Grafton, Middleton, Macdonald, and Gloucester [and *CP* 8: 340, note b, and Averil Stewart, *A Family Tapestry* (1961), pp. 5-7, 21, 23, 36, 76 for Louisa Maria LaCoast]) and *BP* only for Birkin, baronets; *Diana 12G*, endpapers and pp. 16-17, 23, 35, 53, 82, 127-28, 104-7, 342, 344, 347, 353, 364, 379 (#s 40-41, 82-83, 164-67, 328-31, 662-63, 1324-25) (generations 1-6, with biographies of #s 41, 1324 [=1096] and 1325). The alleged line from George II to Jane Birkin was brought to my attention by John C. Brandon of Columbia, S.C. Harriet Georgiana Louisa Hamilton, another daughter of the 1st Duke of Abercorn and Louisa Jane Russell, married Thomas George Anson, 2nd Earl of Lichfield. Their youngest son, Hon. William Anson (1872-1926), became a rancher in Texas, selected horses for the American Army during World War I, and married Louisa Goddard Van Wagenen of N.Y. A daughter and grandson of these last remained in Texas. See *BP* (Lichfield) and *NCAB* 28 (1940): 243-44.

One might note, in addition, that of the seven daughters of the 1st Duke of Abercorn and his wife—daughter of the 6th Duke of Bedford by a daughter of the 4th Duke of Gordon—wives of the 8th Duke of Marlborough, the 5th Marquess of Lansdowne, and the 2nd Earl of Lichfield, appear above. The remaining four daughters, Beatrice Frances, Louisa Jane (grandmother of Princess Alice, Duchess of Gloucester, above), Katherine Elizabeth, and Georgiana Susan, married respectively George Frederick D'Arcy Lampton, 2nd Earl of Durham; William Henry Montagu Douglas Scott, 6th Duke of Buccleuch; William Henry Edgcumbe, 4th Earl of Mount Edgcumbe; and Edward Turnor, 5th Earl of Winterton (in total for these daughters, two dukes, one marquess, and four earls).

The Royal Descents of 900 Immigrants

1. Charles II, King of England, d. 1685 = Catherine of Braganza
2. (illegitimate by Barbara Villiers, Duchess of Cleveland) Charlotte Fitzroy = Edward Henry Lee, 1st Earl of Lichfield
3. **Lady Charlotte Lee** = (1) Benedict Leonard **Calvert**, 4th Baron Baltimore, proprietor of Maryland, ARD, SETH; (2) Christopher **Crewe**.
4. (by 1) Charles Calvert, 5th Baron Baltimore, colonial governor of Md. = Mary Janssen of Md., SETH.
5. Hon. Caroline Calvert = Sir Robert **Eden**, 1st Bt. of Maryland (1741-1784), colonial governor of Md., ARD, SETH.
5. (illegitimate by ——) Benedict "Swingate" Calvert (of Md.) = Elizabeth Calvert, daughter of Charles Calvert, colonial governor of Md., and Rebecca Gerard, daughter of John Gerard (and Elizabeth ——), son of Thomas Gerard of Md., ARD, SETH, and Susannah Snow. Among the children of Benedict and Elizabeth, Eleanor Calvert married firstly John Parke Custis, step-son of George Washington, 1st U.S. President, SETH, and son of Daniel Parke Custis and Martha Dandridge. George Washington Parke Custis, son of John and Eleanor, married Mary Lee FitzHugh and was the father of Mary Anne Randolph Custis, wife of Confederate commander Robert E(dward) Lee.

Sources: *MCS5,* line 17C and *GVFVM* 2:621-27; *MG* 1:140-41, 159-61; *CB* and *BP* (Eden of Maryland, later also of West Auckland, baronets); E.W. Beitzell, *The Cheseldine Family: Historical* (1949), pp. 8, 10.

The Royal Descents of 900 Immigrants

1. Charles II, King of England, d. 1685 = Catherine of Braganza
2. (illegitimate by Mary Davies) Mary Tudor = Edward Radcliffe, 2nd Earl of Derwentwater
3. James Radcliffe, 3rd Earl of Derwentwater = Anna Maria Webb
4. Anna Maria Barbara Radcliffe = Robert James Petre, 8th Baron Petre
5. Catherine Petre = George Fieschi Heneage
6. George Robert Heneage = Frances Anne Ainslie
7. George Fieschi Heneage = Frances Tasburgh
8. **Charles Heneage = Agnes Elizabeth Winona Leclerq Joy** of Vt., known as **Princess (Agnes Elizabeth Winona Leclerq Joy of) Salm-Salm** (1840-1912), adventuress who attempted the rescue of Emperor Maximilian of Mexico (Heneage was her second husband; she = (1) Felix Constantin Alexander Johann Nepomuk, Prince of Salm-Salm, ARD, SETH).

Sources: *BP* (Heneage) and *CP* (Heneage, Petre, Derwentwater); *Clarence*, pp. 384-85 (where Charles Heneage is unfortunately omitted), 425; *BLG*, 8th ed. (1894), p. 935 and *DAB* (A.E.W.L. Joy, Princess Salm-Salm).

The Royal Descents of 900 Immigrants

1. Charles II, King of England, d. 1685 = Catherine of Braganza
2. (illegitimate by Louise Renée de Penancoët de Kéroualle, Duchess of Portsmouth) Charles Lennox, 1st Duke of Richmond and Lennox = Anne Brudenell
3. Charles Lennox, 2nd Duke of Richmond and Lennox = Sarah Cadogan. Their daughter, Georgiana Caroline Lennox, married Henry Fox, 1st Baron Holland, politician, and was the mother of (Hon.) Charles James Fox, the Whig leader, orator and statesman.
4. Lord George Henry Lennox = Louisa Kerr
5. Charles Lennox, 4th Duke of Richmond and Lennox = Charlotte Gordon, daughter of Alexander Gordon, 4th Duke of Gordon and Jane Maxwell, SETH
6. Lord Arthur Lennox = Adelaide Constance Campbell
7. Constance Charlotte Elisa Lennox = Sir George Russell, 4th Bt.
8. Marie Clotilde Russell = Hon. Arthur Ernest Guinness, son of Edward Cecil Guinness, 1st Earl of Iveagh (and Adelaide Maria Guinness, a cousin), son of Sir Benjamin Lee Guinness, 1st Bt., the brewer and "richest man in Ireland," SETH, and Elizabeth Guinness, also a cousin
9. Maureen Constance Guinness = Basil Sheridan Hamilton-Temple-Blackwood, 4th Marquess of Dufferin and Ava
10. **Lady Caroline Maureen Hamilton-Temple-Blackwood**, known as Caroline Blackwood (1931-1996), sometime of N.Y., writer = (1) Lucian Michael **Freud** (1922-2011), painter, grandson of Sigmund Freud, the founder of psychoanalysis; (2) Israel **Citkowitz** (1909-1974), composer; (3) Robert (Traill Spence) **Lowell** (IV) (1917-1977), the American poet.

Sources: *CP* (Dufferin and Ava, Richmond, Holland, Gordon, Aberdeen, Atholl), and *BP* (Dufferin and Ava, Iveagh, Russell of Swallowfield, baronets, Richmond, Ilchester, Gordon, Aberdeen, Atholl, and Guinness). See also *BRB*, tables I, LXXXII, CIV, CVIII, CIX, pp. 1, 48, 64-67, 467. The 4th Duke of Richmond and Lennox and Lady Charlotte Gordon, generation 5 above, are ancestors 92-93 in *Diana 12G*, p. 26. *CP* also covers the descent of the 4th Marquess of Dufferin and Ava, via his

The Royal Descents of 900 Immigrants

grandfather, Frederick Temple-Blackwood, 1st Marquess of Dufferin and Ava, Governor-General of Canada and Viceroy of India, from William Shirley, colonial governor of Massachusetts and of the Bahamas, SETH.

The Royal Descents of 900 Immigrants

1. Charles II, King of England, d. 1685 = Catherine of Braganza

2. (illegitimate by Barbara Villiers, Duchess of Cleveland) Henry Fitzroy, 1st Duke of Grafton = Isabella Bennet

3. Charles Fitzroy, 2nd Duke of Grafton = Henrietta Somerset

4. Lord Augustus Fitzroy = Elizabeth Cosby, daughter of William Cosby, colonial governor of N.Y. and N.J., ARD, SETH, and Grace Montagu, ARD, SETH

5. Augustus Henry Fitzroy, 3rd Duke of Grafton, British Prime Minister = Elizabeth Wrottesley, daughter of Sir Richard Wrottesley, 7th Bt., and Mary Leveson-Gower, daughter of John Leveson-Gower, 1st Earl Gower, and Evelyn Pierrepont, SETH

6. Lord Henry Fitzroy = Caroline Pigot

7. Henry Fitzroy = 6. Jane Elizabeth Beauclerk, daughter of 5. Charles George Beauclerk (and Emily Charlotte Ogilvie), son of 4. Topham Beauclerk (and Diana Spencer, daughter of Charles Spencer, 3rd Duke of Marlborough, and Elizabeth Trevor, SETH), son of 3. Lord Sidney Beauclerk (and Mary Norris), son (by Diana de Vere) of Charles Beauclerk, 1st Duke of St. Albans, illegitimate son (by actress Eleanor "Nell" Gwynn) of King Charles II above

8. Blanche Adeliza Fitzroy = Robert Francis St. Clair-Erskine, 4th Earl of Rosslyn

9. Millicent Fanny St. Clair-Erskine = Cromartie Leveson-Gower, 4th Duke of Sutherland, son of George Granville William Leveson-Gower, 3rd Duke of Sutherland (and Anne Hay-Mackenzie), son of George Granville Sutherland-Leveson-Gower, 2nd Duke of Sutherland, and Harriet Elizabeth Georgiana Howard, SETH

10. Rosemary Millicent Leveson-Gower = William Humble Eric Ward, 3rd Earl of Dudley

11. Hon. Peter Alistair Ward = Claire Leonora Baring

12. **Rachel (Claire) Ward** (b. 1957) of Calif., actress, later of Australia = Bryan Brown (b. 1947), actor.

Sources: *BP* (Dudley, Sutherland, Rosslyn, Grafton, St. Albans, Marlborough).

The Royal Descents of 900 Immigrants

1. Charles II, King of England, d. 1685 = Catherine of Braganza
2. (illegitimate by Barbara Villiers, Duchess of Cleveland) Charles Fitzroy, 2nd Duke of Cleveland, 1st Duke of Southampton = Anne Pulteney
3. Grace Fitzroy = Henry Vane, 1st Earl of Darlington, son of Gilbert Vane, 2nd Baron Barnard (and Mary Randyll), son of Christopher Vane, 1st Baron Barnard (and Elizabeth Holles), son of Sir Henry Vane, Puritan statesman and colonial governor of Massachusetts, and Frances Wray, both ARD, SETH
4. Anne Vane = Charles Hope-Vere
5. Charles Hope = Susan Anne Sawyer
6. Frederick Hope = Eliza Cockburn
7. Charles Hope = Leonora Louisa Isabella Orde
8. Gwendoline Katherine Leonora Hope = Donald Charles Hugh MacLean
9. Sir Hector Charles Donald MacLean = Opre Vyvyan
10. Sara MacLean = Anthony Michael Everett
11. **Rupert (Hector) Everett**, b. 1959, sometime of Calif., actor, unm.

Sources: *BP* 1999, p. 2902 (Everett, Vyvyan), 1967, pp. 2895-96 (Vice-Adm. Sir Hector Charles Donald MacLean); *BP* (Linlithgow, Barnard) and *CP* (Darlington, Cleveland); *Clarence*, tables LXXIII, pp. 62, 584, 304 (Hope, Vane).

The Royal Descents of 900 Immigrants

1. Christian IV, King of Denmark, d. 1648 (brother of Anne of Denmark, Queen of James I, King of England) = (1) Anna Katharina of Brandenburg; (2) Christine Munk

2. (by 2) Leonora Christina, Countess of Schleswig-Holstein = Corfitz, Count von Ulfeld

3. Leo, Count von Ulfeld = Anna Maria, Countess von Zinzendorf

4. Corfitz Anton, Count von Ulfeld = Maria Elisabeth, Princess of Lobkowicz, daughter of Philip Hyacinth, Prince of Lobkowicz (and Anna Maria, Countess von Althann), son of Ferdinand August, Prince of Lobkowicz (and Claudia of Nassau-Hadamar), son of Wenceslaus Eusebius, Prince of Lobkowicz and Augusta Sophie of Sulzbach, daughter of Augustus, Count Palatine of Sulzbach and Hedwig of Holstein-Gottorp, daughter of John Adolf, Duke of Holstein-Gottorp and Augusta of Denmark, SETH, sister of the above Christian IV, King of Denmark.

5. Anna Elisabeth Maria, Countess von Ulfeld = George Christian Anton Michael Joseph Paternus Franz de Paula, Count of Waldstein-Wartenburg

6. Maria Elisabeth Joanna Baptista, Countess of Waldstein-Wartenburg = August, Count Keglevich von Buzin

7. Augusta, Countess Keglevich von Buzin = Anton, Count Szápáry

8. Geza, Count Szápáry = Maria, Countess Gvöry von Radvány

9. Paul Anton Ladislaus Agoston Maria, Count Szápáry = Maria, Countess Przezdziecka

10. **Anton Carl Sylvester, Count Szápáry** (1905-1972), Red Cross official and sportsman, imprisoned at Mauthausen concentration camp for nine months, 1944-45 = Sylvia, Countess Széchényi, daughter of Ladíslaus (László), Count Széchényi, Hungarian diplomat, ARD, SETH, and Gladys Moore Vanderbilt. Countess Szápáry (1918-1998) was the last Vanderbilt family member to live at The Breakers (built by Gladys's parents, Cornelius Vanderbilt II and Alice Claypoole Gwynne) in Newport, R.I., and a patron of the Newport Preservation Society.

The Royal Descents of 900 Immigrants

Sources: *New York Times* obituary of Anthony, Count Szápáry, issue of 26 December 1972 and *GH des A*, vol. 23, *Gräfliche Häuser B*, vol. 2 (1960), pp. 411-13 (Szápáry), 419-20 (Széchényi); *ES* 2: 5: 183 (Waldstein-Wartenburg), 2: 25: 64-65 (Ulfeld), 1: 3: 26 (Lobkowicz); *ES* 1: 1 or *ES* 2: 1 (Sulzbach, Holstein-Gottorp) and *ES* 1: 2 or *ES* 2: 2 (Denmark).

The Royal Descents of 900 Immigrants

1. Christian IV, King of Denmark, d. 1648 = (1) Anna Katharina of Brandenburg; (2) Christine Munk
2. (by 2) Sofie Elisabeth, Countess of Schleswig-Holstein = Christian, Count von Pentz
3. Armgaard Agnes, Countess von Pentz = Hartwig Diedrich von Bülow
4. Sibilla Sophie Hedwig von Bülow = Barthold Diedrich von Bülow
5. Clara Eleonore von Bülow = August Friedrich von Bernstorff
6. Andreas Hans August von Bernstorff = Eleonore Katharina von Bülow
7. Auguste Friederike von Bernstorff = Friedrich Studemund
8. Luise Studemund = Emanuel Sigismund von Schreiber
9. Sigismund von Schreiber = Anna Charlotte Elisabeth Beinroth
10. George Adolf Carl von Schreiber = Adelaide Frohne
11. Edith-Marie Lehmann-von Schreiber = Friedrich Gustav Kuno Asschenfeldt
12. Dr. Herbert Christian Asschenfeldt = Siga Rosenberger
13. **Christiane Asschenfeldt** of Calif. = Florian (Maria Georg Christian), Count **Henckel von Donnersmarck**, film director (*The Lives of Others*, *The Tourist*), ARD, SETH.

Sources: This descent from *Genealogics* was developed by José Verheecke. For generations 1-2 and 4-7 see *ES* 2: 1: 3: 297a and *ES* 2: 22: 35 respectively (no husbands for the four daughters of Andreas Hans August and Eleonore Katharina, however, are given). For generations 10-12 see *Deutsches Geschlechterbuch* 142 (1966): 14-15. For older sections of the von Pentz and von Bülow pedigrees see (per *GH des A*, vol. 22, *Adelige Häuser* A, vol. 4 [1960], pp. 510, 91), *Adel. Taschenbuch* A 1906 (Pentz) and A 1911, 1942 (von Bülow), not at NEHGS.

The Royal Descents of 900 Immigrants

1. James I, King of England (and VI, King of Scotland), d. 1625 = Anne of Denmark

2. Elizabeth of England = Frederick V of the Palatinate, Elector Palatine of the Rhine, (elected) King of Bohemia, d. 1632

3. Edward of the Palatinate = Anna Gonzaga of Nevers and Mantua

4. Louise Marie of the Palatinate = Charles Theodore, Prince of Salm-Neufville

5. Louis Otto, Prince of Salm-Neufville = Albertine Johannette of Nassau-Hadamar

6. Dorothea Francisca of Salm-Neufville = Nicholas Leopold, Prince of Salm-Salm

6. Christina of Salm-Neufville = Joseph, Landgrave of Hesse-Rheinfels-Rotenburg

7. Maximilian Friedrich, Prince of Salm-Salm, Duke of Hoogstraeten = 7. Marie Louise of Hesse-Rheinfels-Rotenburg

8. Constantin, Prince of Salm-Salm = (1) Victoria Felicitas of Löwenstein-Wertheim-Rochefort; (2) Maria Walpurga of Sternberg-Mandersheid

9. (by 1) Florentin, Prince of Salm-Salm = Flaminia di Rossi

10. Felix Constantin Alexander Johann Nepomuk, Prince of **Salm-Salm** = **Agnes Elizabeth Winona Leclerq Joy** of Vt., known as Princess (Agnes Elizabeth Winona Leclerq Joy of) Salm-Salm (1840-1912), adventuress who attempted the rescue of Emperor Maximilian of Mexico (Salm-Salm was her first husband; she = [2] Charles Heneage, ARD, SETH).

9. (by 2) Eleanore Wilhelmine Louise of Salm-Salm = Alfred, Prince (and 10th Duke) of Croy

10. Berthe Rosine Ferdinande of Croy = Ignaz, Baron von Landsburg-Velen

The Royal Descents of 900 Immigrants

11. Emma, Baroness von Landsberg-Velen = Hermann Franz Arthur, Count Strachwitz von Gross-Zauche und Kamminetz

12. **Alexander Maria Hubertus Hyacinthus, Count Strachwitz von Gross-Zauche und Kamminetz** of California = Friederike Frances Adelheid von Bredow. A son is Christian Alexander Maria, Count Strachwitz von Gross-Zauche und Kamminetz, known as Chris Strachwitz, b. 1931, founder of **Arhoolie Records** and patron of jazz, rhythm and blues, folk and Mexican music.

Sources: Wikipedia entry for Chris Strachwitz, Jr., *GH des A*, vol. 47 (*Fürstliche Häuser A*, vol. 6, 1970), p. 435, *RHS* 1: 3, 7, 151-53, 162-63, 174, 176, and Jacques Arnold, *The Royal Houses of Europe: The Stuart Dynasty of Great Britain, Volume 3A* (*The Lines Descended from*) *Ludwig Otto, 5th Prince of Salm* (2010), charts 5C, 6C, 7I, 8Q, 9AV (to Agnes, Princess Salm-Salm), 9AW, 10CD, 11EC (both to Christian Alexander Maria).

The Royal Descents of 900 Immigrants

1. Charles IX, King of Sweden, d. 1611, son of Gustavus I (Vasa), King of Sweden, and Margaretta Leijonhufvud, for whom no medieval royal descent can be traced = (1) Anna Maria of Simmern

2. Catherine of Sweden = John Casimir, Count Palatine of Zweibrücken-Kleeberg, son of John I, Count Palatine of Zweibrücken and Magdalena of Cleves, SETH, daughter of William III, Duke of Cleves, Juliers, and Berg, and Maria of Austria, daughter of Ferdinand I, Holy Roman Emperor, d. 1564, and Anne of Bohemia, SETH

3. Christine Magdalen of Zweibrücken-Kleeberg = Frederick VI, Margrave of Baden-Durlach

4. Joanna of Baden-Durlach = John Frederick, Margrave of Brandenburg-Anspach

5. Dorothea Frederica of Brandenburg-Anspach = John Reinhold III, Count of Hanau-Lichtenberg

6. Charlotte Christine of Hanau-Lichtenberg = Louis VIII, Landgrave of Hesse-Darmstadt

7. George William, Landgrave of Hesse-Darmstadt = Louise of Leiningen-Hildesheim

8. Frederica of Hesse-Darmstadt = Charles II, Grand Duke of Mecklenburg-Strelitz, brother of (Sophie) Charlotte of Mecklenburg-Strelitz, wife of George III, King of Great Britain. Frederica and Charles II were the parents of Louise of Mecklenburg-Strelitz, wife of Frederick William III, King of Prussia, SETH.

9. Frederica of Mecklenburg-Strelitz = (2) Frederick, Prince of Solms-Braunfels; (3) Ernest Augustus, King of Hanover

10. **(Frederick William) Charles (Louis George Alfred Alexander), Prince of Solms-Braunfels**, known as **Prince Carl of Solms-Braunfels** (1812-1875), founder of New Braunfels and German colonization in Texas, where he resided 1 July 1844-15 May 1845; = (Marie Josephine) Sophie, Princess of Löwenstein-Wertheim-Rosenberg. Note that Prince Carl was

The Royal Descents of 900 Immigrants

a first cousin of William I, German Emperor, and a second cousin of Victoria, Queen of Great Britain.

7. Louis IX, Landgrave of Hesse-Darmstadt (brother of George William) = Caroline Henrietta Christine, Countess Palatine of Zweibrücken-Birkenfeld

8. Louis I, Grand Duke of Hesse = Louise Henriette of Hesse-Darmstadt

8. Amelia of Hesse-Darmstadt = Charles Louis, Prince of Baden

9. Louis II, Grand Duke of Hesse = 9. Wilhelmine of Baden

10. Alexander, Prince of Hesse = Julia, Countess von Haucke. Their son, Louis, Prince of Battenberg, 1st Marquess of Milford Haven, married Victoria of Hesse, granddaughter of Queen Victoria, and was the father of (1) Louis Francis Albert Victor Nicholas Mountbatten, 1st Earl Mountbatten of Burma, First Lord of the Admiralty, Supreme Allied Commander in Southeast Asia during World War II and last Viceroy of India, (2) Lady Louise Mountbatten, second wife of Gustav VI Adolf, King of Sweden, and (3) Alice of Battenberg, wife of Andrew, Prince of Greece and Denmark, SETH, and mother of Philip, sometime Prince of Greece and Denmark, Duke of Edinburgh, husband of Elizabeth II, Queen of Great Britain, SETH.

11. Alexander, Prince of Battenberg, Prince of Bulgaria, Count von Hartenau = Johanna Maria Loisinger

12. **(Marie-Thérèse-Vera-) Zwetana, Countess von Hartenau**, sometime of N.Y. and Colorado, = Charles-Hercule **Boissevain**, physician and educator. They left no children.

Sources: C.W. and E.H. Geue, *A New Land Beckoned. German Immigration to Texas, 1844-1847* (rev ed., 1972), p. 20 esp., plus any *Almanach de Gotha*, 1812-75, for Prince Carl himself; *ES*, charts for Solms-Braunfels, Mecklenburg-Strelitz, Hesse-Darmstadt, Hanau-Lichtenberg, Brandenburg-Anspach, Baden-Durlach, Zweibrücken-Kleeberg, Sweden, Cleves, Austria, Hesse, Baden and Battenberg; *BRFW* 1: 58 (generations 10-12), Jacques Arnold, *The Royal Houses of Europe: The German Dynasty of Hesse* (2012), charts A1, A2, A3B, A4D and *WWWA*, vol. 2,

The Royal Descents of 900 Immigrants

1943-1950 (1950), p. 69 (C.H. Boissevain). See also *Prince Charles*, vol. 2, pp. 1-3 and #s D 5-6, E 9-10, F 17-20, G 33-36 (p. 5), H 65-66 (p. 7), I 131-32 (pp. 11-12), J 263-64 (p. 19), K 527-28 (p. 31), K 285-86 (p. 30), L 571-72 (p. 47), K 215-16 (p. 29), L 429-32 (p. 45), M 859-60 (p. 69), M 279-80 (p. 66), N 559-60 (p. 100).

The Royal Descents of 900 Immigrants

1. Charles IX, King of Sweden, d. 1611, son of Gustav I (Vasa), King of Sweden, and Margaretta Leijonhufvud, for whom no medieval royal descent can be traced = (1) Anna Maria of Simmern

2. Catherine of Sweden = John Casimir, Count Palatine of Zweibrücken-Kleeberg, son of John I, Count Palatine of Zweibrücken and Magdalena of Cleves, SETH, daughter of William III, Duke of Cleves, Juliers, and Berg, and Maria of Austria, daughter of Ferdinand I, Holy Roman Emperor, d. 1564, and Anne of Bohemia, SETH

3. Christine Magdalen of Zweibrücken-Kleeberg = Frederick VI, Margrave of Baden-Durlach

4. Frederick VII, Margrave of Baden-Durlach = Augusta Marie of Holstein-Gottorp

5. Catherine of Baden-Durlach = John Frederick, Count of Leiningen-Hartenburg

6. Anna Marie Louise of Leiningen-Hartenburg = Frederick Ferdinand, Count zu Pappenheim

7. Frederick William, Count zu Pappenheim = Frederica Joanna, Baroness von Seckendorff

8. Charles Frederick Theodore, Count zu Pappenheim = Lucie, Countess von Hardenburg-Reventlow

9. Adelaide, Countess zu Pappenheim =

4. Charles Gustav, Margrave of Baden-Durlach = Anna Sophia of Brunswick-Wolfenbüttel

5. Christine Juliane of Baden-Durlach = John William, Duke of Saxe-Eisenach

6. Caroline Christine of Saxe-Eisenach = Charles I, Landgrave of Hesse-Philippsthal

7. Charlotte Amelia Caroline of Hesse-Philippsthal = Anthony Ulric, Duke of Saxe-Meiningen

8. Amelia Augusta of Saxe-Meiningen = Charles Erdmann, Prince of Carolath-Beuthen

9. Henry, Prince of Carolath-Beuthen

The Royal Descents of 900 Immigrants

10. Lucie, Princess of Carolath-Beuthen = Curt Ulrich Henry, Count Haugwitz-Hardenburg-Reventlow

11. George Erdmann Charles Ferdinand, Count Haugwitz-Hardenburg-Reventlow = Gabrielle Schneider

12. **Curt Henry Eberhard Erdmann George, Count Haugwitz-Hardenburg-Reventlow,** sometime of N.Y. = (1) Barbara Woolworth Hutton (1912-1979), American heiress, socialite and philanthropist, daughter of Franklyn Laws Hutton (brother of Edward Francis Hutton, founder of E.F. Hutton & Co., brokers, father by social leader and General Foods, Inc., founder Marjorie Merriweather Post of Mrs. Nedenia Hutton Rumbrough Robertson, known as Dina Merrill, actress and wife of Cliff[ord Parker] Robertson [III], actor) and Edna Woolworth, daughter (by Jennie Creighton) of Woolworth Department Store founder Frank Winfield Woolworth (Reventlow was Barbara Hutton's second husband; her third was Archibald Alec Leach, known as Cary Grant, actor, and her fifth was playboy Porfirio Rubirosa); (2) Margaret Astor Drayton, daughter of William Backhouse Astor Drayton (and Helen Fargo Squiers), son of James Coleman Drayton and Charlotte Augusta Astor, daughter of financier William (Backhouse) Astor (Jr.) and society leader Caroline Webster Schermerhorn. Lance George William Detlev, Count Haugwitz-Hardenburg-Reventlow, only child of Curt and Barbara, married (1) Jill Oppenheim, known as Jill St. John, actress, and (2) Cheryl Holdridge.

3. Eleanor Catherine of Zweibrücken-Kleeberg (sister of Christine Magdalen) = Frederick, Landgrave of Hesse-Eschewege

4. Christine of Hesse-Eschewege = Ferdinand Albert I, Duke of Brunswick-Bevern

5. Ferdinand Albert II, Duke of Brunswick-Wolfenbüttel = Antoinette Amalia of Brunswick-Wolfenbüttel, niece of the Anna Sophia of Brunswick-Wolfenbüttel who married Charles Gustav, Margrave of Baden-Durlach, see generation 4 above

6. Sophia Antoinette of Brunswick-Wolfenbüttel = Ernest Frederick II, Duke of Saxe-Coburg-Saalfeld

The Royal Descents of 900 Immigrants

7. Francis, Duke of Saxe-Coburg-Saalfeld = Augusta Caroline Sophia of Reuss-Ebersdorf, SETH. Among their children were Leopold I, King of the Belgians; Victoria of Saxe-Coburg-Saalfeld, who married secondly Edward, Prince of Great Britain and Duke of Kent, and was the mother of Victoria, Queen of Great Britain, SETH; and Ernest I, Duke of Saxe-Coburg-Gotha, who married firstly Louise Dorothea of Saxe-Gotha, and was the father of Albert, Prince of Saxe-Coburg-Gotha, Prince Consort of Great Britain, SETH, the husband of Queen Victoria. Descendants of Francis and Augusta include kings or sovereigns of Austria, Belgium, Bulgaria, Denmark, Germany, Great Britain, Greece, Italy, Luxembourg, Norway, Portugal, Roumania, Saxony, Spain and Sweden (and wives of sovereigns of Mexico, Russia and Yugoslavia).

8. Sophie Frederica of Saxe-Coburg-Saalfeld = Emanuel, 1st Count von Mensdorff-Pouilly

9. Alfonso Frederick, Count von Mensdorff-Pouilly = Theresia Rosa, Countess von Dietrichstein-Proskau-Leslie

10. Sophie, Countess Mensdorff-Pouilly = Friedrich Karl, Count Kinsky von Wchinitz und Tettau

11. Wilhelmina, Countess Kinsky von Wchinitz und Tettau = Edwin Hugo, Count Henckel von Donnersmarck

12. Friedrich Carl, Count Henckel von Donnersmarck = Annalise von Zitzewitz

13. Leo Ferdinand, Count Henckel von Donnersmarck = Anna Maria von Berg

14. **Florian (Maria Georg Christian), Count Henckel von Donnersmarck**, b. 1973, film director (*The Lives of Others*, *The Tourist*) = Christiane Asschenfeldt, ARD, SETH.

Sources: *GH des A*, vol. 94, *Gräfliche Häuser*, vol. 12 (1988): 278-79 (Haugwitz-Hardenburg-Reventlow), vol. 14, *Fürstliche Häuser*, vol. 4 (1950): 42 (Kinsky von Wchinitz und Tettau), 543-45, 549 (Saxe-Coburg-Saalfeld to Kinsky), *ANB* (B.W. and E.F. Hutton, F.W. Woolworth) and Howland Davis and Arthur Kelly, *A Livingston Genealogical Register* (1995), charts F37 and H77; *ES* 2: 4:61 for Pappenheim, *ES* 1: 4:94b for

The Royal Descents of 900 Immigrants

Hardenburg-Reventlow, 4:92 for Carolath-Beuthen, 4:22 for Leiningen-Hartenburg 9: 69 for Henckel von Donnersmarck (and *ES* 2: 3: 24 for Mensdorff-Pouilly) and tables for Saxe-Meiningen, Hesse-Philippsthal, Saxe-Eisenach, Baden-Durlach, Zweibrücken-Kleeberg, Sweden, Cleves, Austria, Saxe-Coburg-Saalfeld, Brunswick-Wolfenbüttel, Brunswick-Bevern, Hesse-Eschewege, Belgium, Great Britain, and Saxe-Coburg-Gotha; Wikipedia entry for Florian, Count Henckel von Donnersmarck and Jacques Arnold, *The Royal Houses of Europe: Saxe-Coburg-Gotha* (2006), charts 1, 2A, 3A, 4A, 5AC, 6AF. Francis, Duke of Saxe-Coburg-Saalfeld and Augusta Caroline Sophia of Reuss-Ebersdorf are #s G 57-58, p. 5, Anthony Ulric, Duke of Saxe-Meiningen, and Charlotte Amelia Caroline of Hesse-Philippsthal are #s I 235-36, p. 13, and Frederick VII, Margrave of Baden-Durlach and Augusta Marie of Holstein-Gottorp #s J 143-44, p. 18, in *Prince Charles*. I first noticed princely ancestry for this second husband of Barbara Hutton in examining D.L. Jacobus's manuscript on the descendants of Ferdinand of Aragón and Isabella of Castile (then at the Connecticut Historical Society in Hartford, now at NEHGS). I was told of royal descent for Henckel von Donnersmarck by the late Leo van de Pas.

The Royal Descents of 900 Immigrants

1. Frederick II, King of Denmark, d. 1588 = Sophie of Mecklenburg-Güstrow (parents of Anne of Denmark, wife of James I, King of England)

2. Augusta of Denmark = John Adolf, Duke of Holstein-Gottorp

3. Frederick III, Duke of Holstein-Gottorp = Marie Elizabeth of Saxony, daughter of John George I, Elector of Saxony, and Magdalen Sybilla of Prussia, daughter of Albert Frederick, Duke of Prussia, and Marie Eleanor of Cleves, SETH

4. Magdalen Sybil of Holstein-Gottorp = Gustav Adolf, Duke of Mecklenburg-Güstrow

5. Christine of Mecklenburg-Güstrow = Louis Christian I, Count of Stolberg-Gedern

6. Frederick Carl, Prince of Stolberg-Gedern = Louise of Nassau-Saarbrücken

7. Caroline, Princess of Stolberg-Gedern = Christian Albert Louis, Prince of Hohenlohe-Langenburg

8. Charles Louis, Prince of Hohenlohe-Langenburg = Amalie Henriette Charlotte of Solms-Baruth, SETH

9. Frederica Christine Emilie, Princess of Hohenlohe-Langenburg = Frederick Louis Henry, Count of Castell-Castell

10. Adelaide Clotilde Augusta of Castell-Castell = Julius Peter Hermann August, Count of Lippe-Biesterfeld

11. Ernest Casimir Frederick Charles Eberhard, Count of Lippe-Biesterfeld = Caroline Frederica, Countess von Wartensleben

12. Bernhard Casimir Frederick Gustav Henry Wilhelm Edward, Prince of Lippe = Armgard Cunigunde Alharda Agnes Oda von Cramm. Their elder son was Bernhard (Leopold Friedrich Eberhard Julius Kurt Karl Gottfried Peter), Prince of Lippe-Biesterfeld, created Prince of The Netherlands, married Juliana, Queen of The Netherlands, SETH.

13. **(Ernst) Aschwin (Georg Carol Heinrich Ignatz), Prince of Lippe-Biesterfeld** (1914-1988) of N.Y., authority on Chinese painting and Indian sculpture, at the Metropolitan Museum of Art, 1949-73 = Simone-Louise Arnoux.

The Royal Descents of 900 Immigrants

Sources: *BRFW* 1: 225-26 (Lippe-Biesterfeld), *GH des A*, vol. 33 (*Fürstliche Häuser*, vol. 7, 1964), pp. 547-49, 552, 557 (an AT of the children of Queen Juliana and Prince Bernhard of The Netherlands) (generations 6-12) and *ES*, charts for Stolberg-Gedern (2: 17: 101-2), Mecklenburg-Güstrow, Holstein-Gottorp, Denmark, Saxony, Prussia (dukes of), and Austria.

The Royal Descents of 900 Immigrants

1. Frederick II, King of Denmark, d. 1588 = Sophie of Mecklenburg-Güstrow (parents of Anne of Denmark, wife of James I, King of England)

2. Augusta of Denmark = John Adolf, Duke of Holstein-Gottorp

3. Hedwig of Holstein-Gottorp = Augustus, Count Palatine of Sulzbach

4. Augusta Sophie of Sulzbach = Wenceslaus Eusebius, Prince of Lobkowicz

5. Ferdinand August, Prince of Lobkowicz = Maria Anna of Baden-Baden

6. Maria Ludovica of Lobkowicz = Anselm Franz, Prince of Thurn und Taxis

7. Maria Augusta of Thurn und Taxis = Charles Alexander, Duke of Württemberg-Stuttgart

8. Frederick Eugene, Duke of Württemberg = Dorothea of Brandenburg-Schwedt

9. (illegitimate by Anne Eleanora Franchi) Eleanor von Württemberg, Baroness von Franquement = (Jean-François-Louis-Marie) Albert-Gaspard Grimaud, Count d'Orsay

10. Anna-Quintana-Albertine-Ida-Grimaud, Comtesse d'Orsay = Antoine-Héraclius-Geneviève-Agénor de Gramont, 9th Duc de Gramont, son of Antoine-Louis-Marie de Gramont, 8th Duc de Gramont, and Louise-Gabrielle-Aglaë de Polignac, daughter of Jules-François-Armand de Polignac, 1st Duc de Polignac, and Gabrielle-Yolande-Claude-Martine de Polastron, SETH.

11. Antoine-Alfred-Agénor de Gramont, 10th Duc de Gramont, foreign minister of Napoleon III = Emma Mary Mackinnon

12. Antoine-Alfred-Agénor de Gramont, 11th Duc de Gramont = Maria Ruspoli

13. Count Gabriel-Antoine-Armand de Gramont = Marie Negroponte

14. **Sanche-Armand-Gabriel de Gramont** (b. 1932), known as **Ted Morgan** (pseudonym), of N.Y., historian, biographer of Churchill, FDR, Somerset Maugham, and William S. Burroughs = (1) Margaret Kinnicutt; (2) Nancy Ryan.

The Royal Descents of 900 Immigrants

Sources: Ted Morgan, *On Becoming American* (1978), plus *GF*: 93-95, *GH des A, Fürstliche Häuser*, vol. 3 (1955), pp. 353-56, *Anselme*, vol. 9, part 2, pp. 233-4 (Gramont), part 1, pp. 854-55 (Polignac), vol. 4, pp. 582-83 (Gramont), and Jean, Duc de Polignac, *La Maison de Polignac: Étude d'une Évolution Sociale de la Noblesse* (1975), *passim*; *ES* 2: 3: 267a (illegitimate Württemberg), 2: 10: 74-75 (Gramont); *Paget* G 19 (p. 4), H 38 (p. 7), I 76 (p. 11), J 151 (p. 18), K 302 (p. 30), L 604 (p. 44), M 411 (p. 67) (generations 1-8). This "improved" descent was brought to my attention by John Blythe Dobson of Winnipeg, Manitoba, Canada.

The Royal Descents of 900 Immigrants

1. Eric XIV, King of Sweden, d. 1577, son of Gustav I (Vasa), King of Sweden and Katherine of Saxe-Lauenburg, see below = Katherine Månsdotter

2. (illegitimate by Agda Persdotter) Constantia Eriksdotter = Henrik Frankelin

3. Maria Catharina Frankelin = Anders Koskull

4. Erik Koskull = Anna Maria Gyllensvärd

5. Anders, Baron Koskull = Anna Catharina Stromberg

6. Eleonora, Baroness Koskull = Claes Didrik Breitholtz

7. Catharina Mariana Breitholtz = Carl Gustaf Hammarskjöld

8. Carl Ake Hammarskjöld = Charlotta Eleonora Rääf i Smaland

9. Knut Vilhelm Hammarskjöld = Maria Louisa Cecilia Vilhelmina Cöster

10. (Knut) Hjalmar (Leonard) Hammarskjöld, prime minister of Sweden (1914-17), diplomat = Agnes Maria Caroline Almquist

11. **Dag (Hjalmar Agne Carl) Hammarskjöld** (1905-1961), Swedish economist and statesman, second Secretary-General of the United Nations (and resident of New York City), 1953-61, d. unm.

Sources: *Elgenstierna*, vol. 3, pp. 470-73, vol. 1, p. 606, vol. 4, pp. 241-44, vol. 2, p. 817 (Hammarskjöld, Breitholtz, Koskull, Frankelin); *ES* (Sweden, Denmark, Saxe-Lauenburg, Brandenburg, Bavaria, Saxony, etc.).

1. Louis IV (of Bavaria), Holy Roman Emperor, d. 1347 = (1) Beatrix of Glogau; (2) Margaret of Holland

2. (by 1) Stephen III, Duke of Bavaria-Landshut = Elizabeth of Sicily and Aragón, daughter of Frederick II, King of Sicily, d. 1336 (and Eleanor of Sicily and Anjou), son of Peter II, King of Aragón, d. 1285, and Constance of Sicily

3. Frederick, Duke of Bavaria-Landshut = Magdalena Visconti of Milan

The Royal Descents of 900 Immigrants

4. Elizabeth of Bavaria-Landshut = Frederick I, Elector of Brandenburg, also a great-grandchild of Louis IV, HRE, above, and patrilineal ancestor of kings of Prussia

5. Frederick II, Elector of Brandenburg = Katherine of Saxony, daughter of Frederick I, Elector of Saxony, and Katherine of Brunswick-Lüneburg, SETH

6. Dorothea of Brandenburg = John V, Duke of Saxe-Lauenburg

7. Magnus II, Duke of Saxe-Lauenburg = Katherine of Brunswick-Wolfenbüttel, also a descendant of Louis IV, HRE, above. Their daughter, Dorothea of Saxe-Lauenburg, married Christian III, King of Denmark (also a great-grandson of Frederick I, Elector of Brandenburg and Elizabeth of Bavaria-Landshut above). Their son, Frederick II, King of Denmark, SETH, married Sophie of Mecklenburg-Güstrow and was the father of both Christian IV, King of Denmark, SETH, and Anne of Denmark, wife of James I, King of England, also SETH.

8. Katherine of Saxe-Lauenburg = Gustav I (Vasa), King of Sweden, for whom no descent from a previous king is now generally accepted

The Royal Descents of 900 Immigrants

1. Eric XIV, King of Sweden, d. 1577, son of Gustav I (Vasa), King of Sweden, and Katherine of Saxe-Lauenburg (see preceding chart) = Katherine Månsdotter

2. (illegitimate by Agda Persdotter) Virginia Eriksdotter = Håken Hand

3. Catherina Hand = Johann Rytter

4. Virginia Rytter = Göran Stierna

5. Christina Stierna = Bengt Hierta

6. Catharina Hierta = Hans Silfverswård

7. Bengt Silfverswård = Margareta Maria Klingspor

8. Eva Sofia Silfverswård = Per Bråkenhielm

9. Christina Margaretha Bråkenhielm = Christian Slettengren

10. Per Gustav Slettengren = Caroline Wilhelmina Fogelberg

11. **Esaias Reinhold Slettengren**, who changed his name to **Swain**, of Mass. = Betsy Miller Chase. Their daughter, Susan Wilhelmina Swain, married Frederick Wilson Borden and was the mother of Alice Louisa Borden, wife of Raymond Carl Lawson. Nancy Custer Lawson, a daughter of these last, married Richard King Donahue, b. 1927, advisor to President John Fitzgerald Kennedy, president of the Massachusetts Bar Association, and business executive (with Nike).

Sources: Slettengren research of Kurt Anthony Lawson, U.S.N., son of Anthony Borden Lawson and Susan Ritchie and nephew of Mrs. Donahue, and *WWA* (2001), p. 1350 (R.K. Donahue); *Svenska Släktkalendern 1915-16*, pt. 2, pp. 697, 699 and *1919*, pt. 3, pp. 743-45 (Slettengren); *Elgenstierna*, vol. 1, p. 649, vol. 7, pp. 252, 255, vol. 3, pp. 582-83, vol. 7, p. 611, vol. 6, p. 242, vol. 3, pp. 481-82 (Bråkenhielm, Silfverswård, Hierta, Stierna, Rytter [Reuter], Hand). Mr. Lawson also wishes to credit and thank Nils W. Olsson, who first identified the immigrant's original surname as Slettengren.

The Royal Descents of 900 Immigrants

1. Ferdinand I, Holy Roman Emperor, d. 1564 = Anne of Bohemia, SETH

2. Maria of Austria = William III, Duke of Cleves, Juliers and Berg

3. Marie Eleanor of Cleves = Albert Frederick, Duke of Prussia

4. Sophie of Prussia = William, Duke of Courland

4. Anna of Prussia = John Sigismund, Elector of Brandenburg

5. George William, Elector of Brandenburg = Elizabeth Charlotte of the Palatinate

5. James, Duke of Courland = 6. Louise Charlotte of Brandenburg

6, 7. Louise Elizabeth of Courland = Frederick II, Landgrave of Hesse-Homburg

7, 8. Wilhelmina Marie of Hesse-Homburg = Anthony II, Count von Aldenburg

8, 9. Charlotte Sophie von Aldenburg = William, 1st Count Bentinck, son of British Minister Hans William Bentinck, 1st Earl of Portland, and Jane Martha Temple

9, 10. Christian Frederick Anthony, Count Bentinck = Mary Catherine van Tuyll van Serooskerken

10, 11. William Gustavus Frederick, 2nd Count Bentinck = Sarah Margaret Gerdes

11, 12. **William Frederick** (Wilhelm Friedrich) (**Count**) **Bentinck**, of Missouri = Wilhelmina Sara Gerdes, a cousin. Their daughter, (Wilhelmine) Auguste (Friederike) Bentinck, married James Smith, and left a son, William Frederick Bentinck-Smith, who married Marion Jordan. William Bentinck-Smith, a son of these last and husband of Phebe Keyes, was a noted Harvard University official and editor.

Sources: *WWWA*, vol. 11, 1993-1996 (1996), p. 22 (William Bentinck-Smith), Bentinck notes by John Insley Coddington in his mss. collection

The Royal Descents of 900 Immigrants

at NEHGS, *ES* 2: 28: 123 (Bentinck) and *BP* (Portland); *ES* charts for Hesse-Homburg, Courland, Prussia, Austria and Brandenburg. Frederick II, Landgrave of Hesse-Homburg and Louise Elizabeth of Courland at generation 6, 7 above are ancestors J 433-34 in *Prince Charles*.

The Royal Descents of 900 Immigrants

1. Ferdinand I, Holy Roman Emperor, d. 1564 = Anne of Bohemia, SETH

2. Maria of Austria = William III, Duke of Cleves, Juliers and Berg

3. Magdalene of Cleves = John I, Count Palatine of Zweibrücken

3. Marie Eleanor of Cleves = Albert Frederick, Duke of Prussia

4. John II, Count Palatine of Zweibrücken = Louisa Juliane of Pfalz, sister of Frederick I, "Winter King" of Bohemia

4. Sophie of Prussia = William, Duke of Courland

5. Frederick, Count Palatine of Zweibrücken = Anna Juliane of Nassau-Saarbrücken

5. James, Duke of Courland = Louise Charlotte of Brandenburg, SETH, see previous chart

6. Elizabeth of Zweibrücken = Victor Amadeus, Prince of Anhalt-Bernberg

6. Frederick Casimir, Duke of Courland = Sophia Amalia of Nassau-Siegen

7. Charles Frederick, Prince of Anhalt-Bernberg = Sophie Albertine of Solms-Sonnenwalde

7. Marie Dorothea of Courland = Albert Frederick of Brandenburg-Schwedt, brother of Frederick I, King of Prussia

8. Charlotte of Anhalt-Bernberg = Augustus I, Prince of Schwarzburg-Sondershausen

8. Victor Frederick, Prince of Anhalt-Bernberg

= 8. Albertine of Brandenburg-Schwedt

9. Augustus II, Prince of Schwarzburg-Sondershausen = 9. Christiane of Anhalt-Bernberg

10. Augusta, Princess of Schwarzburg-Sondershausen = George, Prince of Waldeck-Pyrmont

11. Frederick Louis, Prince of Waldeck-Pyrmont = Ursula Polle ("unequal marriage"), Countess of Waldeck

The Royal Descents of 900 Immigrants

12. Frederick, Count of Waldeck = Cornelia, Countess Bethlen von Bethlen

13. Augusta, Countess of Waldeck = Karl Wilhelm Friedrich, Baron Schilling von Canstatt

14. Victor Georg Wilhelm Friedrich Ödön Arpad, Baron Schilling von Canstatt = Lilli Kann

15. **Susanna, Baroness Schilling von Canstatt**, of Mo. = **Adalbert von Gontard**, 1900-1976, business executive with Anheuser-Busch, grandson of Adolphus Busch, founder of the company, and first cousin of August Anheuser "Gussie" Busch, the brewer's major later executive.

Sources: *GH des A, Freiherrl. Häuser* A, vol. 1 (1952), pp. 350-51 (Schilling von Canstatt), *ES* 2: 1: 3: 330, 333 F (Waldeck) and charts for Schwarzburg-Sondershausen, Anhalt-Bernberg, Zweibrücken, Cleves, Austria, Prussia, Courland, Brandenburg, and Brandenburg-Schwedt.

The Royal Descents of 900 Immigrants

1. Christian III, King of Denmark, d. 1559 = Dorothea of Saxe-Lauenburg

2. Dorothea of Denmark = William, Duke of Brunswick-Lüneburg

3. George, Duke of Brunswick-Kalenberg = Anna Eleanor of Hesse-Darmstadt

4. Ernest Augustus, Elector of Hanover (father by Sophie of the Palatinate of George I, King of Great Britain and Sophie Charlotte of Hanover, wife of Frederick I, King of Prussia); by Klara Elisabeth von Meysenburg, wife of Franz Ernst, Count von Platen and Hallermund. Ernest Augustus is now thought to be the father of

5. Sophia Charlotte, Countess von Platen and Hallermund, Countess of Leinster and Darlington = Johann Adolf, Baron von Kielmansegge

6. Georg Ludwig, Count von Kielmansegge = Melusina Agnes, Baroness von Spörcken

7. Friedrich, Count von Kielmansegge = Charlotte Wilhelmine Hedwig, Baroness von Spörcken

8. Friedrich Otto Gotthardt, Count von Kielmansegge = Friederike Charlotte Sabine Wilhelmine von dem Bussche-Lohe

9. Louise Charlotte Sophia Friederike, Countess von Kielmansegge = Carl Wilhelm Georg, Count zu Innhausen und Knyphausen

10. Hyma Friederike Georgine Elisabeth Pauline Johanna Magdalena, Countess zu Innhausen und Knyphausen = Philipp Friedrich Ernst, Baron von Dörnberg

11. Luise Marie Emilie Pauline, Baroness von Dörnberg = Eugene Georg Nikolaus von Falkenhayn

12. Thesa Elisabeth Klementine Franzische von Falkenhayn = Alexander August Gustav Henrik Achim Albrecht von Quistorp, son of Wernher Theodor August Friedrich Wilhelm von Quistorp and Marie Eleonore Dorothea von Below, ARD, SETH

13. **Maria Irmengard Emmy Luise Gisela von Quistorp** of Ala.
= Wernher Magnus Maximilian, Freiherr (Baron) **von Braun** (1912) of Huntsville, Ala., the rocket scientist, ARD, SETH.

Sources: *GH des A*, vol. 21, *Freiherrliche Häuser A*, vol. 3 (1959), pp. 519-28 (an ancestor table of the rocket scientist's children), #s 3, 7, 15, 31, 63, 126 (gens. 7-13), *Gothaisches Genealogisches Taschenbuch der Gräflichen Häuser auf das Jahr 1868*, pp. 414-15, 417 (Kielmansegge, gens. 5-9), *Neue Deutsche Biographie*, vol. 11 (1977), pp. 579-80 and German sources cited therein, and *Diana 12G*, pp. 84, 131-32, 193, 290, 365, 380, 405, 444 (generations 1-5). This "improved" descent was brought to my attention by John Blythe Dobson of Winnipeg, Manitoba.

The Royal Descents of 900 Immigrants

1. Christian III, King of Denmark, d. 1559 = Dorothea of Saxe-Lauenburg
2. Dorothea of Denmark = William, Duke of Brunswick-Lüneburg
3. Dorothea of Brunswick-Lüneburg = Charles I, Count Palatine of Zweibrücken-Birkenfeld
4. Sophie of Zweibrücken-Birkenfeld = Kraft, Count of Hohenlohe-Neuenstein
5. Charlotte Susanna Maria of Hohenlohe-Neuenstein = Ludvig Wierich, Count Lewenhaupt
6. Carl Julius, Count Lewenhaupt = Christina Gustaviana, Baroness Horn, a descendant of John III, King of Sweden, son of Gustav I Vasa, King of Sweden
7. Mauritz Casimir, Count Lewenhaupt = (1) Ulrika Charlotta, Countess Lewenhaupt, SETH
8. Adolf Fredrik, Count Lewenhaupt = Hedvig Amalia, Countess Lewenhaupt, also a cousin
9. Hedvig Sophie Charlotta Amalia, Countess Lewenhaupt = Georg Alexander Dardel
10. Fritz Ludvig Dardel = Augusta Charlotta Silfverschiöld
11. Fritz August Dardel = Sofia Matilda Norlin
12. Fredrik Elias August Dardel = Maria Sofia Wising, mother by her first husband, Raoul Wallenberg, of Raoul Wallenberg (Jr.), 1912-1947?, Swedish diplomat and businessman known for saving thousands of Hungarian Jews from Nazi extermination
13. Nina Viveka Maria Dardel = Gunnar Karl Andreas Lagergren
14. **Nina Maria (Nane) Lagergren**, sometime of N.Y. = (1) Claes **Cronstedt**; (2) Kofi Atta **Annan**, b. 1938, seventh Secretary General of the United Nations (1997-2006).

Sources: *The International Who's Who 2005* (2004), pp. 58, 1017 (K.A. Annan and G.K.A. Lagergren); *Sveriges Ridderskap och Adels Kalender 1963*, pp. 188-89 (Dardel); *Elgenstierna*, vols. 2, pp. 168-69 (Dardel), 4, pp. 610-14 (Lewenhaupt); *ES*, charts for Hohenlohe-Neuenstein (2: 17: 6),

The Royal Descents of 900 Immigrants

Zweibrücken-Birkenfeld, Brunswick-Lüneburg and Denmark. This line was brought to my attention by the late William Addams Reitwiesner.

The Royal Descents of 900 Immigrants

1. Henry VII, King of England, d. 1509 = Elizabeth Plantagenet
2. Princess Mary Tudor = Charles Brandon, 1st Duke of Suffolk
3. Eleanor Brandon = Henry Clifford, 2nd Earl of Cumberland, SETH
4. Margaret Clifford = Henry Stanley, 4th Earl of Derby, SETH
5. William Stanley, 6th Earl of Derby = Elizabeth de Vere
6. James Stanley, 7th Earl of Derby = Charlotte de la Trémouille, daughter of Claude de la Trémouille, Duc de Thouars, SETH, and Charlotte of Nassau-Dillenburg, daughter of William the Silent, Prince of Orange, 1st Stadholder of the Netherlands (d. 1584), and Charlotte of Bourbon-Montpensier, a second cousin once removed of Henry IV, King of France
7. Amelia Ann Sophia Stanley = John Murray, 1st Marquess of Atholl

8. Charles Murray, 1st Earl of Dunmore = Catherine Watts

8. William Murray, 2nd Baron Nairne = Margaret Nairne

9. William Murray, 3rd Earl of Dunmore = 9. Catherine Murray
10. **John Murray, 4th Earl of Dunmore** (1730-1809), colonial governor of N.Y. and Va. = Lady Charlotte Stewart, see below.

9. Anne Murray (sister of the 3rd Earl of Dunmore) = John Cochrane, 4th Earl of Dundonald
10. Catherine Cochrane = Alexander Stewart, 6th Earl of Galloway
11. **Lady Charlotte Stewart** = John **Murray**, 4th Earl of Dunmore (1730-1809), colonial governor of N.Y. and Va., see above.

11. John Stewart, 7th Earl of Galloway = Anne Dashwood
12. Susan Stewart = George Spencer-Churchill, 5th Duke of Marlborough, son of George Spencer, 4th Duke of Marlborough (son by Elizabeth Trevor of Charles Spencer, 3rd Duke of Marlborough, son of noted statesman Robert Spencer, 3rd Earl of Sunderland, and Anne Churchill, SETH) and Caroline Russell, daughter of John Russell, 4th Duke of Bedford, and Gertrude Leveson-Gower, daughter of John Leveson-Gower, 1st Earl Gower, and Evelyn Pierrepont, see below

The Royal Descents of 900 Immigrants

13. George Spencer-Churchill, 6th Duke of Marlborough = Jane Frances Clinton Stewart, his first cousin, daughter of George Stewart, 8th Earl of Galloway (and Jane Paget), son of the 7th Earl of Galloway and Anne Dashwood, above

14. John Winston Spencer-Churchill, 7th Duke of Marlborough = Frances Anne Emily Vane-Stewart. Their son, Lord Randolph (Henry Spencer-) Churchill, chancellor of the exchequer in 1886, married Jennie Jerome, social leader, SETH, and was the father of Sir Winston (Leonard Spencer-) Churchill, the British statesman and historian, also SETH.

15. Cornelia Henrietta Maria Spencer-Churchill = Ivor Bertie Guest, 1st Baron Wimborne

16. Hon. Frederick Edward Guest = Amy Phipps of Pittsburgh

17. **Winston Frederick Churchill Guest** (1906-1982) of N.Y., sportsman = (1) Helena Woolworth McCann, granddaughter of department store magnate Frank Winfield Woolworth and first cousin of Barbara Hutton, SETH; (2) Lucy Douglas Cochrane.

17. **Raymond Richard Guest** (1907-1992) of Va., U.S. diplomat = (1) Elizabeth Sturgis Polk; (2) Mrs. Ellen Tuck French Astor, formerly wife of John Jacob Astor VI; (3) Princess Caroline-Cécile-Alexandrine-Jeanne Murat, SETH.

12. Charlotte Stewart (sister of the 8th Earl of Galloway and Susan, Duchess of Marlborough) = Sir Edward Crofton, 3rd Bt.

13. Frederica Crofton = Hubert McLaughlin

14. Edward McLaughlin = Anne Bromilow

15. Vivian Guy Ouseley McLaughlin = Edith Jane Martineau

16. Doris Margaretta McLaughlin = Stewart John Ritchie

17. John Vivian Ritchie = Amber Mary Parkinson

18. **Guy Stuart Ritchie**, b. 1968, filmmaker, sometime of N.Y. or Calif. = (1) (div.) Madonna (Louise Veronica) Ciccone, b. 1958, SETH, rock star and actress, formerly wife of Sean Penn, actor; (2) Jacqui Ainsley.

The Royal Descents of 900 Immigrants

11. Susannah Stewart (sister of the Countess of Dunmore and the 7th Earl of Galloway) = Granville Leveson-Gower, 1st Marquess of Stafford (second wife), son of John Leveson-Gower, 1st Earl Gower, and Evelyn Pierrepont (for whose notable progeny see *NEHGS NEXUS* 14 [1997]: 70-73), sister of the famed letter-writer and traveler Lady Mary (Pierrepont) Wortley-Montagu and daughter of Evelyn Pierrepont, 1st Duke of Kingston-upon-Hull and Mary Feilding, daughter of William Feilding, 3rd Earl of Denbigh, 2nd Earl of Desmond, and Mary King, daughter of Sir Robert King and Frances Folliott (Folliot), SETH

12. Georgiana Augusta Leveson-Gower = William Eliot, 2nd Earl of St. Germans

13. Edward Granville Eliot, 3rd Earl of Saint Germans = Jemima Cornwallis, daughter of Charles Cornwallis, 2nd Marquess Cornwallis, and Louisa Gordon, daughter of Alexander Gordon, 4th Duke of Gordon and Jane Maxwell, below

14. Charles George Cornwallis Eliot = Constance Rhiannon Guest, sister of the 1st Baron Wimborne above

15. Edward Granville Eliot = Clare Louisa Phelips

16. Margaret Augusta Eliot = Richard Alan John Asher. Their daughter Jane Asher, b. 1946, actress, novelist and wife of illustrator Gerald Scarfe, was sometime the girlfriend, fiancée and "muse" of (Sir James) Paul McCartney of "The Beatles."

17. **Peter Asher**, b. 1944, sometime of Calif., child actor, musician (Peter of Peter and Gordon [Waller], who released 20 albums), Apple Records and Sony executive, promoter/manager for James Taylor, Linda Ronstadt and Bonnie Raitt; = (1) Elizabeth Duster; (2) Wendy Worth. Peter Asher's daughter by Wendy is Victoria (Jane) Asher, "keytarist" for the American punk band Cobra Starship.

12. Charlotte Sophia Leveson-Gower (sister of the Countess of Saint Germans) = Henry Charles Somerset, 6th Duke of Beaufort

13. Isabella Frances Anne Somerset = Thomas Henry Kingscote

The Royal Descents of 900 Immigrants

14. Sir Robert Nigel Fitzharding Kingscote = Emily Mary Curzon, daughter of Richard William Penn Curzon, 1st Earl Howe, and Harriet Georgiana Brudenell, daughter of Robert Brudenell, 6th Earl of Cardigan (and Penelope Anne Cooke), son of Hon. Robert Brudenell (and Anne Bishop), daughter of George Brudenell, 3rd Earl of Cardigan, and Elizabeth Bruce, SETH

15. Winifred Agnes Kingscote = George Henry Hugh Cholmondeley, 4th Marquess of Cholmondeley

16. George Horatio Charles Cholmondeley, 5th Marquess of Cholmondeley = Betty Cecile Sassoon, daughter of Sir Richard Sassoon, 2nd Bt., and Betty Caroline de Rothschild of the French branch of the banking family

17. George Hugh Cholmondeley, 6th Marquess of Cholmondeley = Lavina Margaret Leslie

18. Lady Margaret Lavina Cholmondeley = Walter Anthony Huston, screenwriter, son of John Huston, the film director and actor, and Enrica "Ricki" Soma, and brother of Anjelica Huston the actress. John Huston was the son of actor Walter Huston and Rhea Gore.

19. **Jack Alexander Huston**, b. 1982, sometime of Calif., also an actor, unm., partner of actress Shannan Click.

9. Margaret Murray (sister of Catherine Murray, Countess of Dunmore) = William Drummond, 4th Viscount Strathallan

10. Robert Drummond = Winifred Thompson

11. Henry Roger Drummond = Susannah Wells

12. Catherine Elizabeth Drummond = George Randolph

13. Cyril Randolph = Frances Selina Hervey

14. Felton George Randolph = Emily Margaret Nepean

15. Margaret Isobel Randolph = John Cassilis Maclean

16. Fynvola Susan Maclean = James Murray Grant

The Royal Descents of 900 Immigrants

17. **Hugh (John Mungo) Grant**, b. 1960, sometime of Calif., actor, unm.

11. Charlotte Theresa Drummond (sister of Henry Roger Drummond) = Peregrine Edward Towneley
12. Frances Towneley = Thomas Stonor, 3rd Baron Camoys
13. Francis Stonor = Elise Peel, daughter of Sir Robert Peel, 2nd Bt., British Prime Minister, and Julia Floyd, see below
14. Francis Robert Stonor, 4th Baron Camoys = Jessica (Jessie) Philippa Carew
15. Ralph Francis Julian Stonor, 5th Baron Camoys = Mildred Sherman
16. **(Hon. Mildred Sophia) Noreen Stonor** (the Hon. Mrs. Drexel), b. 1922, of Newport, R.I., social leader = John R. **Drexel** (III). Their son, John Nicholas Drexel, married (1) Pamela Braga; (2) (Mary) Jacqueline Astor, daughter of John Jacob Astor VI and Gertrude Gartsch and niece of (William) Vincent Astor, the real estate magnate, philanthropist, and head of the American Astor family.

8. John Murray, 1st Duke of Atholl (brother of the 1st Earl of Dunmore and Lord Nairne) = Catherine Hamilton

9. John Murray, 3rd Duke of Atholl = Jean Frederick	9. Lord George Murray = Emilia Murray
10. Charlotte Murray, = Baroness Strange, Lady of the Isle of Man	10. John Murray, 4th Duke of Atholl

11. Lord George Murray = Anne Charlotte Grant
12. Caroline Leonora Murray = Henry Stephen Fox-Strangways, 3rd Earl of Ilchester
13. Theresa Anne Maria Fox-Strangways = Edward St. Vincent Digby, 9th Baron Digby

The Royal Descents of 900 Immigrants

14. Edward Henry Trafalgar Digby, 10th Baron Digby = Emily Beryl Sissy Hood

15. Edward Kenelm Digby, 11th Baron Digby = Constance Pamela Alice Bruce

16. **Hon. Pamela Beryl Digby, known as Mrs. Pamela Beryl Digby Spencer-Churchill Hayward Harriman** (1920-1996), diplomat, of N.Y. and Washington, D.C. = (1) Randolph Frederick Edward Spencer-Churchill (1911-1968), British M.P., author, biographer of his father, Sir Winston Leonard Spencer-Churchill, the statesman, SETH, who married Clementine Ogilvie Hozier; (2) Leland Hayward (1902-1971), theatrical producer; (3) (William) Averell Harriman (1891-1986), governor of N.Y., U.S. Secretary of Commerce, diplomat.

9. Susan Murray (sister of the 3rd Duke of Atholl and Lord George Murray) = William Gordon, 2nd Earl of Aberdeen

10. Catherine Gordon = Cosmo George Gordon, 3rd Duke of Gordon

11. Alexander Gordon, 4th Duke of Gordon = Jane Maxwell

12. Susan Gordon = William Montagu, 5th Duke of Manchester

13. Susan Montagu = George Hay, 8th Marquess of Tweeddale

14. Emily Hay = Sir Robert Peel, 3rd Bt., son of Sir Robert Peel, 2nd Bt., British Prime Minister, and Julia Floyd, see above

15. Sir Robert Peel, 4th Bt. = Mercedes de Graffenried

16. Sir Robert **Peel**, 5th Bt. = **Beatrice Gladys "Bea" Lillie** (1894-1989) of N.Y., comic actress.

8. Amelia Murray (sister of the 1st Duke of Atholl, the 1st Earl of Dunmore, and Lord Nairne) = Hugh Fraser, 9th Baron Lovat

9. Catherine Fraser = Sir William Murray, 3rd Bt.

10. Catherine Murray = Sir Thomas Moncreiffe, 3rd Bt.

11. Sir William Moncreiffe, 4th Bt. = Clara Guthrie

12. Sir Thomas Moncreiffe, 5th Bt. = Elizabeth Ramsay

The Royal Descents of 900 Immigrants

13. Sir David Moncreiffe, 6th Bt. = Helen Mackay
14. Sir Thomas Moncreiffe, 7th Bt. = Louisa Hay
15. Helen Moncreiffe = Sir Charles John Forbes, 4th Bt.
16. Evelyn Elizabeth Forbes = William Dodge James
17. **Audrey Evelyn James**, sometime of N.Y. = (1) Muir Dudley Coats; (2) Marshall **Field** III (1893-1956), Chicago newspaper publisher and grandson of department store magnate Marshall Field I; (3) Peter **Pleydell-Bouverie**.

Sources: *BRB*, tables I, XIV, LXXXII, CIV, CXIII-CXV, CXXIII, pp. 1, 48, 64-65, 69-71, 75 (Dunmore and his wife); CXV, CXVIII, pp. 71-72, 498-99, *BP* (Wimborne, Marlborough), *BRFW* 1: 121, 123-24 and *GF*: 185-86 (Guest brothers); CXV, CXX, CXI, CX, pp. 71-72, *Essex*, pp. 495-96, http://www.harrymclaughlin.com/Descent_From_Edward_II.pdf, downloaded 10 April 2007 (and earlier), chart by Dr. George Harry McLaughlin of Syracuse and Toronto universities, outlining the entire McLaughlin-Ritchie descent, *BLG* 1952, pp. 1648-49 and Andrew Morton, *Madonna* (2001), pp. 303-14); CXV, CXX, CXI, CIX, pp. 71, 73, 67, 66, 516, 479-80, *BP* (St. Germans, Kingston, Denbigh, King), and Wikipedia entries for several Ashers (esp. Richard, Margaret and Jane); CXX (Somerset, Kingscote), XIV, XV, XXI (Bruce, Cardigan, Howe), pp. 73, 13, 14, 16, 522, 171, 174, *BLG*, 18th ed., vol. 3 (1972), p. 377 (Kingscote), *BP* (Beaufort, Cholmondeley, Howe, Cardigan, Sassoon) and Wikipedia entry for Jack Alexander Huston; CXXIV, CXXV, pp. 75-76, *BP* (Perth, Nairne), *BLG*, 18th ed., vol. 3 (1972), p. 746 (Randolph, to Mrs. Grant), (British) *Who's Who*, 2006, p. 888 (Hugh J.M. Grant, naming parents); CXXV, pp. 76, 537 and *BP* (Camoys, O'Hagan [Towneley], Perth) (Mrs. Drexel); CIV, CV, pp. 64-66, 453-54 and *BP* (Digby) (Mrs. Harriman); CIV, CVII, CIX, CX, pp. 64-68, 473, 475, and *BP* (Peel, Tweeddale, Manchester, Gordon, Aberdeen) (Beatrice Lillie); CIV, CXXVII, CXXXI, CXXXII, pp. 64, 77, 79, 555-56, *BP* (Moncreiffe and Forbes of Newe, baronets) and *BLG* (James of West Dean Park) (Mrs. Field). The Hugh Grant line was traced by the late Leo van de Pas of Erindale, Australia.

Elizabeth de Vere at generation 5 was a daughter of Edward de Vere, 17th Earl of Oxford (son of John de Vere, 16th Earl of Oxford and Margery Golding, SETH) and Anna Cecil, daughter of William Cecil, 1st Baron Burghley, minister of Elizabeth I, and Mildred Cooke, SETH. See *GM* 11 (1951-54): 406-7 (part of an AT of Lady Amelia Ann Sophia Stanley).

The Royal Descents of 900 Immigrants

1. Henry VII, King of England, d. 1509 = Elizabeth Plantagenet
2. Princess Mary Tudor = Charles Brandon, 1st Duke of Suffolk
3. Frances Brandon = Henry Grey, 1st Duke of Suffolk
4. Katherine Grey (sister of Lady Jane Grey, aspirant to the English crown) = Edward Seymour, 1st Earl of Hertford
5. Edward Seymour, Baron Beauchamp (whose progeny were heirs to the English throne after the descendants of James I) = Honora Rogers
6. William Seymour, 2nd Duke of Somerset = Frances Devereux
7. Mary Seymour = Heneage Finch, 3rd Earl of Winchilsea
8. Frances Finch = Thomas Thynne, 1st Viscount Weymouth
9. Frances Thynne = Sir Robert Worsley, 4th Bt.
10. Frances Worsley = John Carteret, 1st Earl Granville, British Prime Minister
11. Georgiana Caroline Carteret = Hon. John Spencer
12. John Spencer, 1st Earl Spencer = Margaret Georgiana Poyntz
13. Georgiana Spencer = William Cavendish, 5th Duke of Devonshire
14. Georgiana Dorothy Cavendish = George Howard, 6th Earl of Carlisle, see below
15. Harriet Elizabeth Georgiana Howard = George Granville Sutherland-Leveson-Gower, 2nd Duke of Sutherland, see below
16. Elizabeth Georgiana Sutherland-Leveson-Gower = George Douglas Campbell, 8th Duke of Argyll
17. Lord Walter Campbell = Olivia Rowlandson Milns
18. Douglas Walter Campbell = Aimee Marie Suzanne Lawrence
19. Ian Douglas Campbell, 11th Duke of Argyll = Janet Gladys Aitken, daughter of William Maxwell Aitken, 1st Baron Beaverbrook, the British and Canadian financier, newspaper publisher, public official, and member of Churchill's war cabinet, and Gladys Henderson Drury, SETH

The Royal Descents of 900 Immigrants

20. **Lady Jeanne Louise Campbell** of N.Y. and S.C. = (1) Norman Mailer (1923-2007), the American novelist (his third wife); (2) John Sergeant **Cram**.

11. Louisa Carteret (sister of Mrs. Spencer) = Thomas Thynne, 2nd Viscount Weymouth, great-nephew of the above 1st Viscount
12. Thomas Thynne, 1st Marquess of Bath = Elizabeth Cavendish-Bentinck
13. Thomas Thynne, 2nd Marquess of Bath = Isabella Elizabeth Byng, see below.
14. Elizabeth Thynne = John Frederick Campbell, 1st Earl Cawdor, see below
15. Georgiana Isabella Campbell = John Balfour
16. Georgiana Elizabeth Balfour = Arthur Wills Blundell Trumbull Sandys Roden Hill, 5th Marquess of Downshire
17. Arthur Wills John Wellington Trumbull Blundell Hill, 6th Marquess of Downshire = Katherine Mary Hare
18. Kathleen Nina Hill = William Hereward Charles Rollo
19. **Primula Susan Rollo**, sometime of Calif. = (James) David (Graham) **Niven** (1910-1983), actor, recipient of an Academy Award for *Separate Tables*.

3. Eleanor Brandon (sister of Frances) = Henry Clifford, 2nd Earl of Cumberland, see below
4. Margaret Clifford = Henry Stanley, 4th Earl of Derby, see below
5. Ferdinando Stanley, 5th Earl of Derby = Alice Spencer
6. Frances Stanley = John Egerton, 1st Earl of Bridgwater
7. John Egerton, 2nd Earl of Bridgwater = Elizabeth Cavendish
8. John Egerton, 3rd Earl of Bridgwater = Jane Powlett
9. Scroope Egerton, 1st Duke of Bridgwater = (1) Elizabeth Churchill, daughter of John Churchill, 1st Duke of Marlborough, SETH, English commander during the War of the Spanish

The Royal Descents of 900 Immigrants

Succession and hero of the Battle of Blenheim, and Sarah Jennings, the favorite of Queen Anne; (2) Rachel Russell

10. (by 2) Louisa Egerton = Granville Leveson-Gower, 1st Marquess of Stafford (first wife), SETH

11. Margaret Caroline Leveson-Gower = Frederick Howard, 5th Earl of Carlisle

12. George Howard, 6th Earl of Carlisle = Georgiana Dorothy Cavendish, see above

12. Caroline Howard (sister of the 6th Earl of Carlisle) = John Campbell, 1st Baron Cawdor

13. John Frederick Campbell, 1st Earl Cawdor = Elizabeth Thynne, see above

11. George Granville Leveson-Gower, 1st Duke of Sutherland (brother of the Countess of Carlisle) = Elizabeth Gordon, Countess of Sutherland

12. George Granville Sutherland-Leveson-Gower, 2nd Duke of Sutherland = Harriet Elizabeth Georgiana Howard, his cousin, see above

12. Charlotte Sophia Sutherland-Leveson-Gower (sister of the 2nd Duke of Sutherland) = Henry Charles Fitzalan-Howard, 13th Duke of Norfolk

13. Henry Granville Fitzalan-Howard, 14th Duke of Norfolk = Augusta Mary Minna Catherine Lyons

14. Victoria Alexandrina Fitzalan Howard = James Robert Hope-Scott

15. Josephine Mary Hope = Wilfrid Philip Ward, Catholic apologist and biographer of his father, Oxford Movement leader William George Ward, and of Cardinal John Henry Newman

16. **Mary Josephine "Maisie" Ward**, 1889-1975, sometime of N.Y., Catholic writer and social activist, founder of Sheed and Ward Publishing House = Francis Joseph Sheed.

The Royal Descents of 900 Immigrants

13. Edward George Fitzalan-Howard, 1st Baron Howard of Glossop (brother of the 14th Duke of Norfolk) = Augusta Talbot

14. Francis Edward Fitzalan-Howard, 2nd Baron Howard of Glossop = Clara Louise Greenwood

15. Bernard Edward Fitzalan-Howard, 3rd Baron Howard of Glossop = Mona Josephine Stapleton, Baroness Beaumont

16. Miles Francis Fitzalan-Howard, 17th Duke of Norfolk = Anne Mary Teresa Constable-Maxwell

17. **Lady Carina Mary Gabriel Fitzalan-Howard = David (Paradine) Frost** (1939-2013), television commentator and personality, much of whose career was American.

14. Angela Mary Charlotte Fitzalan-Howard (sister of the 2nd Baron Howard of Glossop) = Marmaduke Francis Constable-Maxwell, 11th Baron Herries

15. Angela Mary Constable-Maxwell = James Eric Drummond, 16th Earl of Perth, known earlier as Sir Eric Drummond, Secretary-General of the League of Nations

16. **Lady Margaret Gwendolen Mary Drummond** of Washington, D.C. = John **Walker** (3rd) (1906-1995), director of the National Gallery of Art, 1956-1969.

10. (by 1) Anne Egerton (half-sister of Louisa) = William Villiers, 3rd Earl of Jersey

11. George Bussy Villiers, 4th Earl of Jersey = Frances Twysden

12. Harriet Villiers = Richard Bagot, Bishop of Bath and Wells

13. Sidney Leveson Lane Bagot = William Henry Dawnay, 8th Viscount Downe

14. Hon. Lewis Payan Dawnay = Victoria Grey, granddaughter of Charles Grey, 2nd Earl Grey, British Prime Minister

15. Marion Vere Dawnay = Henry Morris Pryce-Jones

The Royal Descents of 900 Immigrants

16. **Alan (Payan) Pryce-Jones** (1908-2000) of R.I., author, editor and literary critic = (1) Thérèse Carmen May (Poppy), Baroness Fould-Springer; (2) Mary Jean Thorne.

7. Elizabeth Egerton (sister of the 2nd Earl of Bridgwater) = David Cecil, 3rd Earl of Exeter
8. John Cecil, 4th Earl of Exeter = Frances Manners
9. John Cecil, 5th Earl of Exeter = Anne Cavendish
10. Elizabeth Cecil = Charles Boyle, 4th Earl of Orrery
11. John Boyle, 5th Earl of Cork and Orrery = Margaret Hamilton
12. Lucy Boyle = George Byng, 4th Viscount Torrington
13. Isabella Elizabeth Byng = Thomas Thynne, 2nd Marquess of Bath, see above

10. John Cecil, 6th Earl of Exeter (brother of Elizabeth) = Elizabeth Brownlow
11. Brownlow Cecil, 8th Earl of Exeter = Hannah Sophia Chambers
12. Hon. Thomas Chambers Cecil = Charlotte Garnier
13. Henry Cecil, 1st Marquess of Exeter = Sarah Hoggins
14. Brownlow Cecil, 2nd Marquess of Exeter = Isabella Poyntz
15. William Alleyne Cecil, 3rd Marquess of Exeter = Georgina Sophia Pakenham, whose brother, William Lygon Pakenham, 4th Earl of Longford, was the patrilineal great-great-grandfather of Lady Antonia (Pakenham) Fraser (Pinter), SETH, the biographer and wife of playwright Harold Pinter
16. Lord William Cecil = Mary Rothes Margaret Tyssen Amherst, Baroness Amherst of Hackney
17. **Hon. John Francis Amherst Cecil** of the British Diplomatic Service, sometime of N.C. = Cornelia Stuyvesant Vanderbilt, daughter of forestry pioneer and philanthropist George Washington Vanderbilt, builder of Biltmore, and Edith

The Royal Descents of 900 Immigrants

Stuyvesant Dresser. The forest lands surrounding Biltmore were inherited by George Henry Vanderbilt Cecil (who married Nancy Owen), elder son of Hon. John and Cornelia, and Biltmore, the largest house in America and a major tourist attraction, was inherited by younger son William Amherst Vanderbilt Cecil (who married Mary Lee Ryan, a first cousin of First Lady Mrs. Jacqueline Lee Bouvier Kennedy Onassis and Princess [Caroline] Lee [Bouvier Canfield] Radziwill [Ross], both SETH).

14. Sophia Cecil (sister of the 2nd Marquess of Exeter) = Hon. Henry Manvers Pierrepont

15. Augusta Sophia Anne Pierrepont = Lord Charles Wellesley, son of Arthur Wellesley, 1st Duke of Wellington, Field Marshal and victor at Waterloo, SETH, and Catherine Pakenham

16. Arthur Charles Wellesley, 4th Duke of Wellington = Kathleen Emily Bulkeley Williams-Bulkeley

17. Gerald Wellesley, 7th Duke of Wellington = Dorothy Violet Ashton

18. Lady Elizabeth Wellesley = Thomas Clyde

19. (**Michael**) **Jeremy** (**Thomas**) **Clyde**, b. 1941, sometime of Calif. (as was his mother), singer, actor, "Jeremy" of the rock group "Chad and Jeremy," much of whose success was in the U.S. = Vanessa Field.

Sources: *BRB*, tables I, XIV, XXIV, XXXII, XXXVII, XXXVIII, LXXXII, LXXXIII, LXXXV, XCVII, pp. 1, 13, 18, 22, 24-25, 48-50, 59, 230, 371, 276, 368, 370-72, 414-15 and *BP* (Argyll) (Lady J.L.C.M. Cram); tables XXXVI, XCVII, pp. 24, 59, 214, 216-17 and *BP* (Rollo, Downshire, Cawdor) (Mrs. Niven); pp. 371-72 and *BP* (Norfolk, Howard of Glossop, Herries, Perth) (Lady C.M.G.F.-H. Frost, Lady M.G.M.D. Walker); *BP* (Linlithgow), *BLG* 1952, p. 2630 (Ward) and *ANB*, vol. 22, pp. 644-45 (Maisie Ward); pp. 368-70, *Oxford DNB*, vol. 30, pp. 434-35 and *BP* (Pryce-Jones, Downe, Bagot, Jersey) (A.P. Pryce-Jones); *BP* (Exeter, Amherst and Wellington), *NEXUS* 13 (1996): 20-21, 76-77, 79-82 (Vanderbilt Cecil), and L.G. Pine, *The New Extinct Peerage, 1884-1971* (1973), p. 190 (Manvers) (Jeremy Clyde). The 1st Earl Spencer and Margaret Georgiana Poyntz, the first generation 12 above, are #s 64-65 in

The Royal Descents of 900 Immigrants

Diana 12G, p. 21. For the Bernard/Haselwood, Lygon/Foliot and Wyche/ Saltonstall ancestry of Granville Leveson-Gower, 1st Marquess of Stafford, and the major British descendants of his parents—John Leveson-Gower, 1st Earl Gower, and Evelyn Pierrepont—see *NEXUS* 13 (1996): 208, 210, 14 (1997): 70-73, 16 (1999): 156-59. An extensive AT (to no. 2047) for G.H.V. Cecil and W.A.V. Cecil has been compiled by Richard K. Evans.

Lady Miriam Howard, a sister of the 17th Duke of Norfolk (at generation 16 above) married Theodore (Bernard Peregrine) Hubbard; their daughter, Vanessa Mary Teresa Hubbard, married John Austen Anstruther-Gough-Calthorpe and is the mother of British actress Gabriella Zanna Vanessa Anstruther-Gough-Calthorpe, known as Gabriella Wilde, whose husband is musician Alan Pownall. See *BP* (Norfolk, Lindsey and Abington, and Anstruther-Gough-Calthorpe, baronets).

The above Frances Devereux at generation 6, p. 69, was a daughter of Robert Devereux, 2nd Earl of Essex, the favorite of Elizabeth I and leader of "Essex's Rebellion," and Frances Walsingham, SETH. Hon. John Spencer at generation 11, p. 69, was the son of noted statesman Robert Spencer, 3rd Earl of Sunderland, and Anne Churchill, daughter, like Elizabeth Churchill at generation 9 on p. 70, of John Churchill, 1st Duke of Marlborough, SETH, English commander during the War of the Spanish Succession and hero of the Battle of Blenheim, and Sarah Jennings. Lady Georgiana (Spencer) Cavendish, Duchess of Devonshire, a famed society leader and political hostess, has been the subject of a well-received biography and film. George Douglas Campbell, 8th Duke of Argyll, and Elizabeth Georgiana Sutherland-Leveson-Gower were parents of of John Douglas Sutherland Campbell, 9th Duke of Argyll, governor-general of Canada and husband of H.R.H. Princess Louise (Caroline Alberta), daughter of Queen Victoria. Henry Clifford, 2nd Earl of Cumberland at generation 3, p. 70, was a son of Henry Clifford, 1st Earl of Cumberland, and Margaret Percy, SETH. Henry Stanley, 4th Earl of Derby at generation 4, p. 70, was a son of Edward Stanley, 3rd Earl of Derby and Dorothy Howard, SETH. And Rachel Russell at generation 9, p. 71, was a sister of John Russell, 4th Duke of Bedford, who married Gertrude Leveson-Gower, SETH. See *Essex* and *BP* or *CP* (Essex, Spencer, Sunderland, Marlborough, Devonshire, Argyll, Cumberland, Derby, and Bedford) plus sections of *Diana 12G* and *Prince Charles*.

The Royal Descents of 900 Immigrants

1. Henry VII, King of England, d. 1509 = Elizabeth Plantagenet
2. Princess Mary Tudor = Charles Brandon, 1st Duke of Suffolk
3. Frances Brandon = Henry Grey, 1st Duke of Suffolk
4. Katherine Grey (sister of Lady Jane Grey, aspirant to the English crown) = Edward Seymour, 1st Earl of Hertford
5. Edward Seymour, Baron Beauchamp (whose progeny were heirs to the English throne after the descendants of James I) = Honora Rogers
6. Francis Seymour, 1st Baron Seymour of Trowbridge = Frances Prynne
7. Charles Seymour, 2nd Baron Seymour of Trowbridge = Elizabeth Alington
8. Charles Seymour, 6th Duke of Somerset = Elizabeth Percy
9. Catherine Seymour = Sir William Wyndham, 3rd Bt.
10. Charles Wyndham, 1st Earl of Egremont = Alicia Maria Carpenter
11. Elizabeth Alicia Maria Wyndham = Henry Herbert, 1st Earl of Carnarvon
12. Hon. William Herbert = Letitia Dorothea Allen
13. **Henry William Herbert** (1807-1858) of N.Y., field sports writer under the pseudonym "Frank Forrester" = (1) Sarah Barker; (2) Adela R. Budlong.

12. Henry George Herbert, 2nd Earl of Carnarvon (brother of Hon. William Herbert) = Elizabeth Acland
13. Henry John George Herbert, 3rd Earl of Carnarvon = Henrietta Anna Howard
14. Eveline Alicia Juliana Herbert = Isaac Newton Wallop, 5th Earl of Portsmouth, see below
15. Oliver Henry Wallop, 8th Earl of Portsmouth = Marguerite Walker

The Royal Descents of 900 Immigrants

16. Hon. **Oliver Malcolm Wallop** of Wyo. = Jean Moore. They were the parents of Malcolm Wallop, b. 1933, U.S. Senator from Wyoming, who married (1) Josephine Vail Stebbins; (2) Judith Warren; (3) Mrs. French Addison Gamble Goodwin; (4) Isabel Thompson.

12. Frances Herbert (sister of Hon. William Herbert and the 2nd Earl of Carnarvon) = Thomas Reynolds Moreton, 1st Earl of Ducie
13. Mary Elizabeth Kitty Moreton = William Basil Percy Feilding, 7th Earl of Denbigh
14. Rudolph William Basil Feilding, 8th Earl of Denbigh = Mary Berkeley
15. Winefride Mary Elizabeth Feilding = Gervase Henry Elwes
16. Simon Edmund Vincent Paul Elwes = Gloria Ellinor Rodd
17. (Bebe Evelyn) Dominick Elwes = Tessa Georgina Kennedy
18. **(Ivan Simon) Cary Elwes** (b. 1962) of Calif., actor, unm.

10. Elizabeth Wyndham (sister of the 1st Earl of Egremont) = Hon. George Grenville, Prime Minister, Chancellor of the Exchequer. A daughter, Catherine Grenville, married Richard Aldworth Neville, 2nd Baron Braybrooke. Their daughter, Mary Neville, married Sir Stephen Richard Glynne, 8th Bt., and was the mother of Catherine Glynne, wife of William Ewart Gladstone, the British Prime Minister and statesman.
11. Hester Grenville = Hugh Fortescue, 1st Earl Fortescue
12. Catherine Fortescue = Newton Fellowes Wallop, 4th Earl of Portsmouth
13. Isaac Newton Wallop, 5th Earl of Portsmouth = Eveline Alicia Juliana Herbert, see above

Sources: *BRB*, tables I, XIV, L, LI, LIII, LVI, pp. 1, 13, 31-34, 265, 269-70, *BP* (Carnarvon), and *BLG*, 18th ed., vol. 1 (1965), p. 236 (H.W. Herbert and Cary Elwes); and tables L, LI, LIII, LV, pp. 31-34, 264, 284 and *BP* (Portsmouth). See also V.J. Watney, *The Wallop Family and Their*

The Royal Descents of 900 Immigrants

Ancestry, 4 vols. (1928), *passim*. The descent of Cary Elwes was brought to my attention by Robert Battle of Tacoma, Washington.

Note: George O'Brien Wyndham, 2nd Earl of Egremont, son of Charles Wyndham, 1st Earl of Egremont, and Alicia Maria Carpenter above, married Elizabeth Ilive/Iliffe, but before marriage had by her an illegitimate son, George Wyndham, 1st Baron Leconfield, who married Mary Fanny Blunt. A second son of these last, Hon. Percy Scawen Wyndham, married Madeline Caroline Frances Eden Campbell, and was the father of Pamela Adelaide Genevieve Wyndham, who married Edward Priaulx Tennant, 1st Baron Glenconner. Hon. David Francis Tennant, a son of these last, married (1) Hermione Youlanda Ruby Clinton-Baddeley, the actress Hermione Baddeley (1906-86), sometime of Calif., SETH; (2) Virginia Penelope Parsons; and (3) Shelagh Ann Rainey. See *BP* and *CP* (Egremont, Leconfield, Glenconner).

The Royal Descents of 900 Immigrants

1. Henry VII, King of England, d. 1509 = Elizabeth Plantagenet
2. Princess Mary Tudor = Charles Brandon, 1st Duke of Suffolk
3. Eleanor Brandon = Henry Clifford, 2nd Earl of Cumberland, SETH
4. Margaret Clifford = Henry Stanley, 4th Earl of Derby, SETH
5. Ferdinando Stanley, 5th Earl of Derby = Alice Spencer
6. Elizabeth Stanley = Henry Hastings, 5th Earl of Huntingdon, son of Francis Hastings, Lord Hastings, and Sarah Harrington, SETH
7. Ferdinando Hastings, 6th Earl of Huntingdon = Lucy Davies
8. Theophilus Hastings, 7th Earl of Huntingdon = Frances Leveson Fowler
9. Catherine Maria Hastings = Granville Wheeler
10. Catherine Maria Wheeler = James Stuart-Menteth
11. Sir Charles Granville Stuart-Menteth, 1st Bt. = Ludivina Loughnan
12. **Thomas Loughnan Stuart-Menteth** of Canandaigua, N.Y. = Isabella Maria Tobin.

Sources: *BRB*, tables I, LXXXII, CII, CIII, pp. 1, 48, 63, 441, *Clarence*, tables I-IV, pp. 1-3, 77 and *BP* (Stuart-Menteth, baronets, Huntingdon, Derby, Cumberland). Note also *PSECD* 2:268-75, which includes the line to genealogist Timothy Field Beard (1930-2015), husband of Annette Knowles Huddleston and son of Stuart-Menteth Beard (and Natalie Sudler Turner), son of Maximillian Beard (and Gertrude Field Finley), son of Cornelius Collins Beard and Philadelphia Stuart-Menteth, daughter of Thomas and Isabella Maria above.

The Royal Descents of 900 Immigrants

1. Henry VII, King of England, d. 1509 = Elizabeth Plantagenet
2. Princess Mary Tudor = Charles Brandon, 1st Duke of Suffolk
3. Frances Brandon = Henry Grey, 1st Duke of Suffolk
4. Katherine Grey (sister of Lady Jane Grey, aspirant to the English crown) = Edward Seymour, 1st Earl of Hertford
5. Edward Seymour, Baron Beauchamp (whose progeny were heirs to the English throne after the descendants of James I) = Honora Rogers
6. William Seymour, 2nd Duke of Somerset = Frances Devereux
7. Henry Seymour, Baron Beauchamp = Mary Capell
8. Elizabeth Seymour, heiress to the English throne after the descendants of James I = Thomas Bruce, 3rd Earl of Elgin, 2nd Earl of Ailesbury
9. Elizabeth Bruce = George Brudenell, 3rd Earl of Cardigan
10. Thomas Brudenell-Bruce, 1st Earl of Ailesbury = Susanna Hoare
11. Charles Brudenell-Bruce, 1st Marquess of Ailesbury = Henrietta Maria Hill
12. Ernest Augustus Charles Brudenell-Bruce, 3rd Marquess of Ailesbury = Louisa Elizabeth Horsley-Beresford
13. Ernestine Mary Brudenell-Bruce = William Hare, 3rd Earl of Listowel
14. Richard Granville Hare, 4th Earl of Listowel = Freda Johnstone
15. John Hugh Hare, 1st Viscount Blakenham = Beryl Nancy Pearson, daughter of Weetman Harold Miller Pearson, 2nd Viscount Cowdray and Agnes Beryl Spencer-Churchill, daughter (by Augusta Warburton) of Lord Edward Spencer-Churchill, son of George Spencer-Churchill, 6th Duke of Marlborough, SETH, and his second wife and first cousin, Jane Frances Clinton Stewart, daughter (by Katharine Charteris-Wemyss) of Hon. Edward Richard Stewart, son of John Stewart, 7th Earl of Galloway, and Anne Dashwood, SETH

16. **Hon. Joanna Freda Hare** of Mass. = Stephen Gerald **Breyer**, b. 1938, appellate judge, educator, Supreme Court Justice since 1994.

Sources: *NEXUS* 11 (1994): 94-95 and sources listed therein, esp. *BP*, *CP* and *BRB*: 1, 13-14, 17, 48, 64, 69-72, 178-79, 506, 510. See *NK* 2: 217-22 for the royal descendants (including kings of Roumania, Yugoslavia and the Belgians) of Thomas Bruce, 3rd Earl of Elgin, 2nd Earl of Ailesbury, whose first wife was Elizabeth Seymour, 8 above, by his second wife, Charlotte Jacqueline D'Argenteau, *suo jure* Countess of Esneux and Baroness of Melsbroeck.

The Royal Descents of 900 Immigrants

1. James V, King of Scotland, d. 1542 = (1) Madeleine of France; (2) Mary of Guise

2. (illegitimate by Eupheme Elphinstone) Robert Stewart, 1st Earl of Orkney = Janet Kennedy, daughter of Gilbert Kennedy, 3rd Earl of Cassillis, and Margaret Kennedy, SETH

3. Elizabeth Stewart = Sir James Sinclair of Murchil

4. Agnes Sinclair = John Mackay of Dirlot and Strathy, son of Hugh (Huistern Dhu) Mackay of Farr and Jean Gordon, daughter of Alexander Gordon, 12th Earl of Sutherland, and Jean Gordon, SETH

5. Hugh Mackay of Strathy = Jane Mackay of Reay

6. John Mackay of Strathy = Elizabeth Sinclair of Brims

7. Hugh Mackay of Strathy = Barbara Murray of Pennyland

8. James Mackay, sometime of Ga. = Ann —— (poss. Mrs. Ann Stephens)

9. (probably illegitimate by Henrietta Sinclair of Olrig) John Mackay = Sarah More

10. Sinclair Mackay = Margaret Henderson

11. **George Mackay** (b. 1809) of Washington, D.C. = Ann Crerar.

5. Jean Mackay (sister of Hugh) = William Mackay of Bighouse

6. Angus Mackay of Bighouse = Jane Sinclair of Ulbster

7. Anne Mackay = Alexander Fraser of Errogie

8. Angus Fraser of Errogie = Jean Fraser, said to be a full or half-sister (or full or half-niece) of Simon Fraser, British army officer who died at Saratoga

9. **Thomas Fraser** of S.C. and N.J. = Anne Laughton Smith.

10. Caroline Georgina Fraser = Lucien-Charles-Joseph-Napoléon, 3rd Prince Murat, son of Joachim Murat, 1st Prince Murat, King of Naples, and (Marie-Annonciade-) Caroline Bonaparte, sister of Napoléon I, Emperor of the French

The Royal Descents of 900 Immigrants

11. Joachim-Joseph-Napoléon, 4th Prince Murat = Malcy-Louise-Caroline-Frédérique Berthier, daughter of Napoléon Berthier, Prince and Duke de Wagram (son of Napoleonic Marshal Louis-Alexandre Berthier, Prince of Neuchâtel and Wagram and Marie Françoise Lhutilier de la Serre) and Zénaïde Clary, niece of (Marie) Julie [Clary], Queen of Spain, wife of Joseph Bonaparte, King of Spain, and Desirée [Clary], Queen of Sweden, wife of Jean-Baptiste Bernadotte, King of Sweden as Charles XIV (John)

12. Joachim-Napoléon, 5th Prince Murat = (Marie-) Cécile (-Michèle) Ney, great-granddaughter of Napoleonic Marshal Michel Ney, Duke d'Elchingen and Prince of Moscow

13. Prince Alexandre-Michel-Eugène-Joachim-Napoléon Murat = Yvonne-Noele-Marie Gillois

14. **Princess Caroline-Cécile-Alexandrine-Jeanne Murat** of Va. = Raymond Richard **Guest** (1907-1992), U.S. diplomat, SETH.

11. Prince Louis-Napoléon Murat (brother of Joachim-Joseph-Napoléon, 4th Prince Murat) = Eudoxia Somov

12. Prince Michel-Anne-Charles-Joachim-Napoléon Murat = Helen McDonald Stallo

13. **Princess Laure-Louise-Napoléone-Eugénie-Caroline Murat** of N.Y. = (1) Jean-Paul **Frank**; (2) **Fernand Auberjonois** (1910-2004), of N.Y. (a naturalized U.S. citizen), journalist, foreign correspondent, and writer, SETH. Her son by (2) is actor René (Murat) Auberjonois, who married Judith Helen Mahalyi.

Sources: research of F.H. Pollard, great-grandson of George and Ann (Crerar) Mackay (esp. in the baptismal register of the English Chapel in Perth and OPRs [Old Parish Registers] of Thurso), *The Scottish Genealogist* 41 (1994). 15-19, 21, Angus Mackay, *The Book of Mackay* (1906), pp. 305-6, 310-12, *SP* 2: 340 (Sinclair of Caithness) and *CP* or *SP* (Orkney, Cassilis) (courtesy of F.H. Pollard; note that James Mackay of Ga. left both descendants there and the above, probably illegitimate, son in Scotland); Duncan Warrand, *Some Fraser Pedigrees* (1934), p. 111, *TAG* 64 (1989): 171-78 (Fraser, Murat, by J.I. Coddington), *BRFW* 1, pp. 120-24 (Murat), *ES* 1: 4: 149, 150a and b (Murat, Ney and Berthier) and Jacques Arnold, *The*

The Royal Descents of 900 Immigrants

Royal Blood of Europe: The Bonaparte Dynasty of France (2008), Murat section, charts 3G, 4T, 4W, 5AY, 5BD, 6BC.

The parentage of Janet Kennedy, wife of Robert Stewart, 1st Earl of Orkney, is given above but not on several following charts since she is first included in this volume on this chart.

The Royal Descents of 900 Immigrants

1. James V, King of Scotland, d. 1542 = (1) Madeleine of France; (2) Mary of Guise

2. (illegitimate by Eupheme Elphinstone) = Robert Stewart, 1st Earl of Orkney = Janet Kennedy

3. (illegitimate by Janet Robertson of Struan) James Stewart of Graemsay = Helen Menteith

4. Margaret Stewart = Francis Moodie of Breckness

5. Barbara Moodie = Patrick Balfour of Pharay

6. George Balfour of Pharay = Marjorie Baikie

7. Barbara Balfour = William Traill of Westness

8. William Traill of Kirkwall = Isabell Fea

9. **Robert Traill** of N.H. = Mary Whipple, sister of William Whipple, Jr., signer of the Declaration of Independence. Several kinsmen of Robert Traill may also have immigrated to New England. An uncle, John Traill (son of William and Barbara and husband of Mary Gale), was of Boston, Mass., but left no NDTPS.

10. William Traill (returned to Scotland) = Mary Colebrook

11. George William Traill, C.S. [Civil Service] India

12. (illegitimate by ____) Mary Colebrooke Traill = Allan Gordon Cameron

13. **Ewen Somerled Cameron** of Montana = (1) Julia Wheelock; (2) Evelyn Jephson Flower (1868-1928), known as Evelyn Cameron, Montana photographer.

4. Harry Stewart of Graemsay (brother of Margaret) = Sibella Primrose

5. Barbara Stewart = John Graham of Breckness

6. Mary Graham = George Traill of Holland, uncle of the half-blood of both William Traill of Westness above, and the George Traill of Quendall who married Anna Baikie, SETH

7. Mary Traill = William Blaw

85

The Royal Descents of 900 Immigrants

8. Janet Blaw = James Spence

9. **Keith Spence** of N.H. = Mary Traill, daughter of Robert Traill of N.H., above, and Mary Whipple. Among their children Harriet Brackett Spence married Charles Lowell, a descendant of Percival Lowell, Charles Chambers, and Mrs. Elizabeth Bullock Clement(s), all of Mass., and was the mother of James Russell Lowell, the poet and diplomat. Later Spence-Traill descendants include the poet Robert (Traill Spence) Lowell (IV), presidential advisor McGeorge Bundy, and philanthropist and social leader (Mrs. Roberta) Brooke (Roswell Kuser Marshall) Astor.

Sources: *NEXUS* 6 (1989): 205-6 and *NK1*: 11, 14, 178-83, 185-87, *NK2*: 18-20, 210 (entire line of J.R. Lowell, Robert Lowell, Bundy and Brooke Astor), William Traill of Woodwick, *A Genealogical Account of the Traills of Orkney* (1883), pp. 25-26, 63-64, 73-76 esp., *The New Hampshire Genealogical Record* 4 (1907): 1-6 (Traill, Spence) (Robert Traill), Hew Scott, ed., *Fasti Ecclesiae Scoticanae*, vol. 7 (1948), p. 277 (William Blaw), William Brown, *Or and Sable: A Book of the Graemes and Grahams* (1903), pp. 513-17, H.L. Norton Smith, *A Collection of Armorials of the County of Orkney* (1902), pp. 13-14, 138 esp. (Stewart of Graemsay, Moodie, Balfour) and *SP* and *CP* (Orkney); Cecil H.C. Howard, *Genealogy of the Cutts Family in America* (1892), pp. 53, 106 (incomplete), 215-16, 360-61, 433-34, Alexander Mackenzie, *History of the Camerons* (1884), pp. 407-8, and Donna M. Lucey, *Photographic Montana, 1894-1928, The Life and Work of Evelyn Cameron* (2001), *passim*, esp. p. 10. The long 1847 will of G.W. Traill (1848 Traill, George William) [reference SC 70/4/5 Edinburgh Sheriff Court Wills, accessed 7 Nov. 2012 at www.scotlandspeople.gov.uk] mentions "my natural children Mary and Charles"). Mary's birth record, as Mary Traill born in Almorh, India 4 January 1834, daughter of George William Traill, commissioner of Kumaon, and a "native unmarried woman" is recorded in N/1/38f.193, India Office records (Bengal Presidency) at the British Library; see http://indiafamily.bl.uk/UI/FullDisplay.aspx?RecordId=014-000273372. Julie Helen Otto traced the career and family of G.W. Traill. *Fasti* and Graeme-Grahame references were brought to my attention by John C. Brandon of Columbia, S.C.

The Royal Descents of 900 Immigrants

1. James V, King of Scotland, d. 1542 = (1) Madeleine of France; (2) Mary of Guise

2. (illegitimate by Eupheme Elphinstone) Robert Stewart, 1st Earl of Orkney = Janet Kennedy

3. (illegitimate by ———) Christian Stewart = John Mowat of Hugoland, Shetland

4. Jean Mowat = David Heart/Hart of Rusland

5. John Heart/Hart = Agnes Baxter

6. Agnes Heart/Hart = Robert Craighead (Craghead), Presbyterian minister

7. **Rev. Thomas Craighead (Craghead)** (c. 1670-1739) of Pa., Presbyterian clergyman = Margaret Wallace.

7. **Catherine Craighead** of Mass. = Rev. William **Ho(l)mes** (correctly **Homes**) (1663-1746), Presbyterian minister. Their son, Robert Homes, married Mary Franklin, sister of Benjamin Franklin, the statesman and scientist.

Sources: *Dictionary of Irish Biography* (2009), vol. 2, pp. 947-50 (Rev. Robert, Rev. Thomas [the immigrant] and the latter's son, Alexander Craghead [not Craighead], with some errors), vol. 4, pp. 763-64 (Rev. William and Robert Ho[l]mes), plus *Oxford DNB* for Rev. Robert (both notices of Rev. Robert name his wife and father-in-law); Rev. Hew Scott, *Fasti Ecclesiae Scoticanae...Ministers in the Parish Churches of Scotland*, new ed., vol. 4 (1923), p. 155 (John Heart/Hart, noting his 1637 matriculation, 1643 ordination, 1644 marriage to Agnes Baxter, and daughter Agnes); John Anderson, ed., *Calendar of the Laing Charters, A.D. 854-1851* (1899), pp. 529-30 ("David Heart of Russland, William and Mr. John Heart his sons" witness a 1638 charter) and SC 11/5/1644/1 at the Orkney Archives ("Dauid Heart.. William Heart his eldest sone and of Mr John Heart Minister his second sone" mentioned in the 1644 marriage settlement of Margaret Heart, David's daughter); Francis J. Grant, *The County Families of the Zetland Islands* (1893), pp. 180-81 (Mowat) and *SP* (Stewart, Earls of Orkney, for Christian Stewart). Extensive Heart/Hart research by Janet (Paulette Chevalley) Wolfe, John C. Brandon and others, has been posted online. Among cited documents is the Dunino, Fife 17 Dec. 1648 baptism of "Agnes, daughter of Mr. Jhon Hart minister and Agnes Backstare".

The Royal Descents of 900 Immigrants

1. James V, King of Scotland, d. 1542 = (1) Madeleine of France; (2) Mary of Guise

2. (illegitimate by Helen Stewart, SETH, later wife of John Gordon, 11th Earl of Sutherland, SETH) Lord Adam Stewart = Janet Ruthven

3. Mary Stewart = John Sinclair of Toab

4. William Sinclair = Joanna Gordon of Cairston

5. James Sinclair of Kirkwall = Anna Sinclair

6. **Robert Sinclair** of N.Y. = Maria Duyckinck.

3. Barbara Stewart (sister of Mary) = Henry Halcro of that Ilk

4. Hugh Halcro of that Ilk = Esther Thomson

5. Hugh Halcro of that Ilk = Jean Stewart, daughter of Henry Stewart (and Margaret Urie), son of James Stewart, 1st Earl of Arran, and Elizabeth Stewart, daughter of John Stewart, 4th Earl of Atholl and Margaret Fleming, SETH

6. Sibella Halcro = James Baikie

7. Anna Baikie = George Traill of Quendall

7. Barbara Baikie = Alexander Grant

8. Thomas Traill = 8. Sibella Grant. Among their children, Isabella Traill immigrated to Mass., married William Tate and left children but no NDTPS, and Thomas Traill, probably sometime of Mass., later settled in Grenada and left issue by Azubah, a Creole of Barbados.

9. **Robert Traill** of Pa. = Elizabeth Grotz.

Sources: *NYGBR* 50 (1919): 46-47 (Robert Sinclair), as corrected by *RA* 1: 674-75, 681-82 (generations 1-3) and among sources cited therein esp. Alfred W. Johnston, Amy Johnston and Jón Stefánsson, *Orkney and Shetland Records*, vol. 1, Part 1 (1907), pp. 196-99 ("instrument of resignation and sasine, Magnus Sinclair in Skaill in favour of John Sinclair, his eldest son, and Mary Stewart his spouse, of Tohoip and Brabester," dated 17 May 1580, which calls this Mary Stewart "brother dochter to ane nobil and potent Lord Robert Stewartt, fewar [*sic*, feuar] of Orkney"), a copy of which was kindly sent to me by John C. Brandon of Columbia, S.C.; *NEHGR* 164 (2010): 145-52, corrected in 165 (2011): 297 and among sources cited therein esp. James W. Moore, *Rev. John Moore of Newtown, Long Island, and Some of His Descendants* (1903), p. 338 (Robert Traill), William Traill of Woodwick, *A Genealogical Account of the Traills of Orkney* (1883), pp. 23-25, 61-66, 73-74, E.E. Scott, *The Erskine-Halcro Genealogy* (1895), pp. 14-15, 18-21 and Peter D. Anderson, *Robert Stewart, Earl of Orkney, Lord of Shetland, 1533-1593* (1982), pp. 80, 104, 131-32, 156-58. The above George Traill of Quendall was a brother of William Traill of Westness who married Barbara Balfour, SETH, and nephew of the half-blood of the George Traill of Holland who married Mary Graham, SETH.

The Royal Descents of 900 Immigrants

1. James V, King of Scotland, d. 1542 = (1) Madeleine of France; (2) Mary of Guise
2. (illegitimate by Elizabeth Carmichael) John Stewart, prior of Coldingham = Jean Hepburn, sister of James Hepburn, 4th Earl of Bothwell, third husband of Mary, Queen of Scots
3. Francis Stewart, 1st Earl of Bothwell = Margaret Douglas, daughter of David Douglas, 7th Earl of Angus, and Margaret Hamilton, SETH
4. John Stewart of Coldingham = Margaret Home
5. Margaret Stewart = Sir John Home of Renton
6. Sir Patrick Home, 1st Bt. = Jean Dalmahoy
7. Margaret Home = Sir George Home, 3rd Bt.
8. **George Home** of Va. = Elizabeth Proctor.

4. Elizabeth Stewart (sister of John) = Hon. James Cranston
5. Isabella Cranston = Sir Gilbert Eliott, 1st Bt.
6. Sir William Eliott, 2nd Bt. = Margaret Murray
7. Sir Gilbert Eliott, 3rd Bt. = Eleanor Elliot, a cousin
8. Sir John Eliott, 4th Bt. = Mary Andrews
9. Sir Francis Eliott, 5th Bt. = Euphan Dickson
10. Sir William Eliott, 6th Bt. = Mary Russell
11. Sir William Francis Eliott, 7th Bt. = Theresa Boswell, daughter of Sir Alexander Boswell, 1st Bt. (and Griselle/Graca Cumming), son of James Boswell of Auchinleck, SETH, the man of letters and biographer of Samuel Johnson, and Margaret Montgomerie
12. Alexander Boswell Eliott = Catherine Craigie
13. Sir Arthur Augustus Boswell Eliott, 9th Bt. = Lilia Burbank
14. **Beatrice Maud Boswell Eliott** of N.Y. = Frank Vincent **Burton**, Jr. Their daughter, Leila Eliott Burton, b. 1925, travel author = (1) Arthur Twining Hadley II; (2) Yvor Hyatt Smitter; (3) William C. Musham; (4) Henry Robinson Luce III, b. 1925,

vice-president of Time, Inc., and publisher of *Fortune* and *Time*, son of Henry Robinson Luce, Jr., founder of Time, Inc., and Lila Hotz.

Sources: *MCS5*, lines 41E and 92B, *CB* (Home of Lumsden and Home of Wedderburn, baronets), *SP* and *CP* (Bothwell, Angus), The Dowager Lady Eliott of Stobs and Sir Arthur Eliott, 11th Baronet of Stobs, *The Elliots: The Story of a Border Clan* (1974), pp. 77-95, 102-12, 116-19, *BP* (Eliott of Stobs), *SP* (Cranstoun), and *BLG* (Boswell); *Who's Who of American Women* (L.E.B. Hadley) and *WWA* (H.R. Luce III) (courtesy of William Elliott). See also *BLG* (Home-Robertson of Wedderburn and Paxton) and E.E. Hume, *A Colonial Scottish Jacobite Family: The Establishment in Virginia of a Branch of the Humes of Wedderburn* (1931) and *Memorial to George Hume, Esquire, Crown Surveyor of Virginia and Washington's Teacher of Surveying* (1939, originally published in *TM* and reprinted in *GVFT* 2:263-377).

The Royal Descents of 900 Immigrants

1. James V, King of Scotland, d. 1542 = (1) Madeleine of France; (2) Mary of Guise

2. (illegitimate by Eupheme Elphinstone) Robert Stewart, 1st Earl of Orkney = Janet Kennedy

3. Jean Stewart = Patrick Leslie, 1st Baron Lindores

4. David Leslie, 1st Baron Newark, parliamentary general in the English Civil War = Joan Yorke

5. Mary Leslie = Sir Francis Kinloch, 2nd Bt.

6. **James Kinloch** of S.C. = (1) Mrs. Susannah —— Strode; (2) Marie Esther Page.

4. Elizabeth Leslie (sister of the 1st Baron Newark) = Sir James Sinclair, 1st Bt.

5. Anne Sinclair = George Mackenzie, 1st Earl of Cromarty

6. John Mackenzie, 2nd Earl of Cromarty = Mary Murray

7. George Mackenzie, 3rd Earl of Cromarty = Isabel Gordon

8. **Lady Mary Mackenzie** of S.C. = (1) Robert **Clarke**; (2) Thomas **Drayton**; (3) John **Ainslie**; (4) Henry **Middleton** (1717-1784), planter, South Carolina legislator, president of the Continental Congress. Lady Anne Mackenzie, a sister of Lady Mary, also immigrated to S.C. and married (1) Edmund Atkins, president of His Majesty's Council for S.C. and first Superintendent of Indian Affairs for the Southern District of the American Colonies; (2) John Murray, asst. and act. sec. of the Province of S.C. Both of Lady Anne's husbands, however, are omitted from the *DAB, ANB* and *NCAB*.

Sources: *CP* or *SP* (Orkney, Lindores, Newark, Cassilis), *CB* and *BP* (Kinloch of Gilmerton, baronets) and *SCG* 3:58-59 (James Kinloch); *CB* (Sinclair of Mey, baronets), *CP* or *SP* (Cromarty/ie) and *NGSQ* 52 (1964): 25 (Lady M.M.C.D.A. Middleton).

The Royal Descents of 900 Immigrants

1. James V, King of Scotland, d. 1542 = (1) Madeleine of France; (2) Mary of Guise
2. (illegitimate by Margaret Erskine) James Stewart, 1st Earl of Moray, Regent of Scotland = Agnes Keith, daughter of William Keith, 3rd Earl Marischal, and Margaret Keith, SETH
3. Elizabeth Stewart = James Stewart, 2nd Earl of Moray, a cousin
4. James Stewart, 3rd Earl of Moray = Anne Gordon, daughter of George Gordon, 1st Marquess of Huntly and Henrietta Stewart, SETH
5. James Stewart, 4th Earl of Moray = Margaret Home
6. Mary Stewart = Archibald Campbell, 9th Earl of Argyll
7. Hon. John Campbell = Elizabeth Elphinstone
8. John Campbell, 4th Duke of Argyll = Mary Bellenden
9. **Lord William Campbell** (d. 1778), colonial governor of S.C. = Sarah Izard, daughter of Ralph Izard (and Mary Blake), son of Walter Izard (and Mary Turgis), son of Ralph Izard of S.C., SETH and Mrs. Mary ____ Smith Middleton.

6. Henrietta Stewart (sister of Mary) = Sir Hugh Campbell of Cawdor
7. Jean Campbell = John Urquhart of Meldrum
8. William Urquhart of Meldrum = Mary Forbes of Monymusk
9. Jean Urquhart = John Urquhart of Craigston
10. Mary Urquhart = Robert Arbuthnot of Haddo

11. Sir William Arbuthnot, 1st Bt. = Anne Alves	11. George Arbuthnot = Eliza Fraser
12. John Alves Arbuthnot =	12. Mary Arbuthnot

13. George Arbuthnot = Caroline Emma Nepean Aitchison
14. John Bernard Arbuthnot = Olive Blake
15. Patricia Evangeline Anne Arbuthnot
    = (Francis) Claud Cockburn, Communist journalist, author of *Beat the Devil*

16. **Andrew Myles Cockburn** (b. 1947), journalist, documentarian, of N.Y. and Calif. = Leslie Corkill Redlich. Their daughter is Olivia Jane Cockburn, b. 1984, known as Olivia Wilde, actress and former wife of Tao Ruspoli, b. 1975, of Calif., filmmaker, photographer and musician, SETH.

Sources: *SP, CP* and *BP* (Argyll, Moray) and *South Carolina Genealogies*, vol. 2 (1983), pp. 417-20, 438-42, 445-47 (Izard); *BLG* 1906, pp. 1711-12 (Urquhart of Meldrum and Byth, Pollard-Urquhart of Craigston and Castle Pollard), *BP* 2003, vol. 1, p. 120 (Arbuthnot of Edinburgh, baronets, to Olivia Wilde, where her birth year is given as 1983), *BLG* 1939, pp. 42-43 (Arbuthnot of Elderslie) and Wikipedia entry for Olivia Wilde (and several Cockburns). The Olivia Wilde descent was developed by George Larson and Robert Battle, who prepared an AT for 8+ generations, and brought to my attention by John C. Brandon of Columbia, S.C.

The Royal Descents of 900 Immigrants

1. James V, King of Scotland, d. 1542 = (1) Madeleine of France, (2) Mary of Guise

2. (illegitimate by Margaret Erskine) James Stewart, 1st Earl of Moray, Regent of Scotland = Agnes Keith, daughter of William Keith, 3rd Earl Marischal, and Margaret Keith, SETH

3. Elizabeth Stewart = James Stewart, 2nd Earl of Moray, a cousin

4. Grizel Stewart = Sir Robert Innes, 1st Bt.

5. Sir Robert Innes, 2nd Bt. = Jean Ross

6. Jean Innes = Alexander Rose of Clava

7. Elizabeth Rose = Alexander Mackenzie of Davochmaluag

8. **Margaret Mackenzie** of S.C. = Joseph **Avery** (ca. 1685-1744), surveyor of Georgia.

TAG 84 (2010): 52-64 (Robert Battle) and sources cited therein. Mr. Battle has now concluded, however, that Mrs. Elizabeth Avery Spencer, wife of William Spencer and ancestor of various English notables, was a daughter of Joseph Avery's unknown first wife, not Margaret Mackenzie.

The Royal Descents of 900 Immigrants

1. James V, King of Scotland, d. 1542 = (1) Madeleine of France; (2) Mary of Guise

2. (illegitimate by Elizabeth Carmichael) John Stewart, prior of Coldingham = Jean Hepburn

3. Francis Stewart, 1st Earl of Bothwell = Margaret Douglas, daughter of David Douglas, 7th Earl of Angus, and Margaret Hamilton, SETH

4. Jean Stewart = Robert Eliot of Redhaugh

5. Margaret Eliot = James Eliot of Larriston

6. Janet Eliot = William Scott of Milsington (parents of Walter)

7. Walter Scott of Girnwood = Jean Scott (of Oakwood)

8. Janet Scott = Robert Eliot (of Whitthaugh)

9. Walter Eliot (of Hermitage) = Helen Crozier

10. Janet or Jean Eliot = Henry Eliot (of Dinfee, of the family of Lodgewill)

11. William Eliot, d. unm. (but mentioned an illegitimate son Andrew in his will)

12. (illegitimate by Betty Beattie) **Andrew Elliott** of N.Y. = Margaret Schuman (ancestors of John L. Scherer of Rexford, N.Y.).

Sources: *American Ancestors* 11 (2010), 2: 28-29; research of John L. Scherer of Rexford, N.Y., confirmed in part by George Tancred, *Annals of a Border Club* (1899), pp. 153-57, 167 (Eliots of Redhaugh and Larriston).

The Royal Descents of 900 Immigrants

1. James V, King of Scotland, d. 1542 = (1) Madeleine of France; (2) Mary of Guise

2. (illegitimate by Margaret Erskine) James Stewart, 1st Earl of Moray, Regent of Scotland = Agnes Keith, daughter of William Keith, 3rd Earl Marischal, and Margaret Keith, SETH

3. Elizabeth Stewart = James Stewart, 2nd Earl of Moray, a cousin

4. James Stewart, 3rd Earl of Moray = Anne Gordon, daughter of George Gordon, 1st Marquess of Huntly, and Henrietta Stewart, SETH

5. Mary Stewart = James Grant of Freuchie

6. Lodovick Grant of Freuchie and Grant = Janet Brodie

7. Janet Grant = Sir Roderick Mackenzie, 2nd Bt. (of Scatwell)

8. Janet Mackenzie = Sir Alexander Mackenzie, 2nd Bt. (of Gairloch)

9. Sir Alexander Mackenzie, 3rd Bt. = Margaret Mackenzie of Redcastle

10. Sir Hector Mackenzie, 4th Bt. = Christian Henderson

11. John Mackenzie of Eileanach = Mary Jane Inglis

12. Kythé Caroline Mackenzie = Francis Mackenzie Ogilvy

13. Francis John Longley Ogilvy = Dorothy Fairfield, daughter of Arthur Fairfield (and Sophie Blew-Jones), son of Charles George Fairfield and Arabella Rowan, SETH

14. **David Mackenzie Ogilvy** (1911-1999) of N.Y., advertising executive = (1) Melinda Street; (2) Anne Cabot; (3) Herta Lans.

Sources: David Ogilvy, *An Autobiography* (1997), pp. 1-3, 5-7, 16-19, 59, *Who's Who in America*, 1996, pp. 3119-20 and *Oxford DNB* (D.M. Ogilvy and Sir H.D. Rolleston, 1st Bt.); *BP* 1940 (Lady Henry Davy Rolleston [Eila Ogilvy], his paternal aunt), *BP* 1999 (Mackenzie of Gairloch, baronets, under Inglis of Glencorse, baronets; Mackenzie of Scatwell, baronets; Strathspey [Grant of Grant and Freuchie]; Moray).

The Royal Descents of 900 Immigrants

1. James V, King of Scotland, d. 1542 = (1) Madeleine of France; (2) Mary of Guise

2. (illegitimate by Eupheme Elphinstone) Robert Stewart, 1st Earl of Orkney = Janet Kennedy

3. Mary Stewart = Patrick Gray, 6th Baron Gray

4. Jean Gray = John Wemyss, 1st Earl of Wemyss

5. David Wemyss, 2nd Earl of Wemyss = (1) Anna Balfour; (3) Elizabeth Sinclair

6. (by 3) Margaret Wemyss, Countess of Wemyss = James Wemyss, 1st Baron Brantisland

6. (by 1) Jean Wemyss = George Gordon, 15th Earl of Sutherland

7. John Gordon, 16th Earl of Sutherland = Helen Cochrane

7. David Wemyss, 4th Earl of Wemyss = (1) Anne Douglas (3) Elizabeth Sinclair

8. William Gordon, later Sutherland, Lord Strathnaver = Katherine Morison

8. (by 1) James Wemyss, 5th Earl of Wemyss = Janet Charteris

8. (by 3) Elizabeth Wemyss

9. William Sutherland, 17th Earl of Sutherland

9. Hon. James Wemyss = 9, 10. Elizabeth Sutherland

10, 11. James Wemyss = Caroline Charlotte Binfield

11, 12. Elizabeth Huntly Wemyss = Sir William Muir, Islamicist and administrator in India

12, 13. Caroline Charlotte Muir = William Henry Lowe

13, 14. William Henry Muir Lowe = Frances Bruster de Salvo

14, 15. **William John Muir Lowe**, the actor **John Loder**, sometime of Calif. = (1) Sophie Künzig; (2) Micheline Cheirel; (3) Hedy Lamarr (1914-2000), the film star and inventor (born Hedwig Eva Maria Kiesler); (4) Evelyn Auffemordt; (5) Alba Julia Lagomarsino.

The Royal Descents of 900 Immigrants

Sources: *GM* 27 (2001-3): 322-26; *BLG*, various editions (Muir) and *CP*, *BP*, and *SP* (Wemyss, Sutherland, Gray, Orkney). The above Patrick Gray, 6th Baron Gray, was a son of Patrick Gray, 5th Baron Gray (and Barbara Ruthven), son of Patrick Gray, 4th Baron Gray and Marion Ogilvy, SETH.

The Royal Descents of 900 Immigrants

1. Edward IV, King of England, d. 1483 = Elizabeth Woodville
2. (illegitimate by Elizabeth [Wayte] Lucy) Margaret (not Elizabeth) Plantagenet = Thomas Lumley
3. Roger Lumley = Isabel Radcliffe
4. Agnes Lumley = John Lambton
5. Robert Lambton = Frances Eure, daughter of Sir Ralph Eure and Margery Bowes, SETH
6. John Lambton = Katherine Kirby
7. John Lambton = Margaret Hall
8. Margaret Lambton = Sir Robert Eden, 1st Bt.
9. Sir John Eden, 2nd Bt. = Catherine Shafto, daughter of Mark Shafto (and Margaret Ingleby), son of Sir Robert Shafto and Catherine Widdrington, daughter of Sir Thomas Widdrington, Speaker of the House of Commons and Frances Fairfax, SETH.
10. Sir Robert Eden, 3rd Bt. = Mary Davison. Their daughter Mary Eden married John Moore, Archbishop of Canterbury.
11. **Sir Robert Eden, 1st Bt**. of Maryland (1741-1784), colonial governor of Md. = Hon. Caroline Calvert, ARD, SETH.

6. Ralph Lambton (brother of John) = Eleanor Tempest
7. William Lambton = Catherine Widdrington
8. Sir Thomas Lambton = Margaret Freville
9. Freville Lambton = Thomasine Milwood
10. Thomas Lambton = Dorothy Bewicke
11. Dorothy Lambton = Robert Surtees
12. Jane Surtees = Crosier Surtees, a cousin
13. Robert Surtees = Elizabeth Cookson
14. Charles Freville Surtees = Bertha Chauncey
15. Sir Herbert Conyers Surtees = Madeleine Augusta Crabbe
16. Bertha Etelka Surtees = Edward Bell
17. **Evangeline Bell** of Va. = David Kirkpatrick Este **Bruce** (1898-1977), diplomat, whose first wife was Mrs. Ailsa Nora Mellon Bruce, philanthropist and art patron.

The Royal Descents of 900 Immigrants

6. Jane Lambton (sister of John and Ralph) = Sir William Blakiston (they are ancestors also of Catherine Elizabeth "Kate" Middleton, now H.R.H. The Duchess of Cambridge; see *American Ancestors* 12 [2011], 4: 34-35, 14 [2013], 4: 52-55, also for Lawrence of Arabia)
7. Sir Ralph Blakiston, 1st Bt. = Margaret Fenwick
8. Sir Francis Blakiston, 3rd Bt. = Anne Bowes
9. Elizabeth Blakiston = Sir William Bowes. Their son, George Bowes, married Mary Gilbert and was the father of Mary Eleanor Bowes, wife of John Bowes-Lyon, 9th Earl of Strathmore, and mother (a third son) of Thomas Bowes-Lyon, 11th Earl of Strathmore, who married Mary Elizabeth Louisa Rodney Carpenter. Thomas Bowes-Lyon, Lord Glamis, their son, married Charlotte Grinstead and was the father (a second son) of Claude Bowes-Lyon, 13th Earl of Strathmore, who married Frances Dora Smith, SETH. A granddaughter of these last was H.M. the late Queen Elizabeth The Queen Mother.
10. Anne Bowes = Edward Chaloner
11. William Chaloner = Mary Finney. They are ancestors #654-55 of the late Diana, Princess of Wales.
12. William Chaloner = Emma Harvey
13. Caroline Chaloner = Abraham Perry Cumberbatch
14. Robert William Cumberbatch = Louisa Hanson
15. Henry Alfred Cumberbatch = Helene Gertrude Rees
16. Henry Carlton Cumberbatch = Pauline Ellen Laing Congdon
17. Timothy Carlton (Cumberbatch), actor = Wanda Ventham
18. **Benedict Timothy Carlton Cumberbatch**, b. 1976, sometime of Calif., film actor = Sophie Irene Hunter, b. 1978, also sometime of Calif., theater director, ARD, SETH.

Sources: *RA* 5: 460-62, 468-69 (Edward IV and Elizabeth [Wayte] Lucy) plus conversations with Douglas Richardson about Margaret (not Elizabeth) Plantagenet and Isabel Radcliffe; *Surtees* 2: 163 (Lumley), 174-75, 3: 36 (Lambton), 3: 295 (Shafto); *CB* and *BP* (Eden of Auckland, Eden of Md., baronets, Auckland, Brougham, Vansittart [*BP* 1956], Chapman of Gillua Castle, baronets [*BP* 1921], and Strathmore);

The Royal Descents of 900 Immigrants

Oxford DNB (Moore, T.E. Lawrence, and Brougham), *NHN* 12: 496 (Eure); *BLG* (Surtees of Redworth and Surtees of Mainsforth Hall) and various Harvard class books for the class of 1904 (Edward Bell); Internet biographies of Benedict and H.C. Cumberbatch and Timothy Carlton, *Times* marriage notice of H.C. Cumberbatch and Pauline E.L. Congdon (= 26 April 1934), *Who Was Who, 1916-1920* [British] (1929), p. 252 (H.A. Cumberbatch), SAR application of Robert Cecil Cumberbatch (brother of H.C.), #85245 (national; state #6277, Mass.); George W. Marshall, *Collections for a Genealogical Account of the Family of Comberbach* (1866), chart on pp. 38-39, *DVY*, vol. 2, pp. 233-35 (Chaloner), *Diana 12G*, pp. 79, 125, 183, 275, 364, 378, 402, 438 (Chaloner, Bowes, and Blakiston, generations 8-11 of the Blakiston-Chaloner line), and *Prince Charles*, #s A 1-2, B 3-4, C 7-8, D 13-14, E 25-26, F 49-50, G 97-98, H 195-96, I 389-90, J 779-80, K 1557-58, L 3113-14, M 6227-28, N 12453-54, O 24907-8, P 49813-14, Q 99627-28 (entire line to H.M. the late Queen Elizabeth The Queen Mother) and *Surtees* 2: 255 (Blakiston), 4, part I, pp. 108-9 (Bowes and Bowes-Lyon). William Eden, 1st Baron Auckland, diplomat and younger brother of the colonial governor of Md., married Eleanor Elliott and was the father of Caroline Eden, wife of Arthur Vansittart and mother of Louisa Vansittart, wife of William Chapman. A son of these last, Sir Thomas Robert Tighe Chapman, 7th Bt., who assumed the surname Lawrence, was the father illegitimately, by Sarah Junner, of Thomas Edward (T.E.) Lawrence, "Lawrence of Arabia," the soldier, Arabist and author of *Seven Pillars of Wisdom*. Thomas Eden, another son of Sir Robert and Mary, married Marianna Jones and was the father of Mary Anne Eden, wife secondly of Henry Peter Brougham, 1st Baron Brougham and Vaux, the politician, reformer and abolitionist. See *American Ancestors* 14 (2013): 4: 55.

The Royal Descents of 900 Immigrants

1. Edward IV, King of England, d. 1483 = Elizabeth Woodville
2. (illegitimate by Elizabeth [Wayte] Lucy) Arthur Plantagenet, 1st Viscount Lisle = Elizabeth Grey, *suo jure* Baroness Lisle
3. Frances Plantagenet = (1) John Basset; (2) Thomas Monck
4. (by 1) Sir Arthur Basset = Eleanor Chichester
5. Margaret Basset = Richard Duke
6. **Thomas Duke** of Va. = Mary (Hampton?). Thomas Duke was the patrilineal ancestor of Washington and James Buchanan Duke (and Doris Duke, the latter's daughter).

4. (by 2) Anthony Monck = Mary Arscott
5. Sir Thomas Monck = Elizabeth Smythe (parents of George Monck, 1st Duke of Albemarle, the Cromwellian general who facilitated the Restoration of Charles II)
6. Thomas Monck = Mary Gould
7. Elizabeth Monck = Sir Thomas Pride, the regicide and parliamentary army officer associated with "Pride's Purge"
8. **Elizabeth Pride** (of N.C.) = (1) John **Gibbs** (fl. 1682-95), governor of N.C. ("Albemarle"); (2) William **Sherwin** (d. post 1709), engraver. Anne Gibbs, daughter of Elizabeth and John, married Nathaniel Rice (d. 1753), governor of N.C.

Sources: Duke of Virginia research by Christopher Carter Lee, *MGH*, 4th ser., vol. 3 (1910), p. 30 (where the immigrant Thomas Duke is confused with an uncle of the same name, who d. 1652), *VD*, p. 47 (Basset) and *RA* 5: 460-62, 469-70 (generations 1-3); *BRB*, Table LXXXII, p. 48, note 4, which cites a pedigree showing Elizabeth Pride as a sister of Thomas Pride and wife of John Gibbs and William Sherwin; *Oxford DNB* (2004), 50: 344-45 (William Sherwin), and William S. Powell, ed., *Dictionary of North Carolina Biography*, vol. 2 (1986), pp. 294-96 (John Gibbs), both with likely errors or omissions; 4 July 1687 will of Christopher Monck, 2nd Duke of Albemarle, which mentions "cousins Mrs. Elizabeth Gibbs and Thomas Pride" (British Record Association collection, ref. ZDDX31/17/9); *Journal of the House of Lords*, vol. 19, 1709-1714

(1802), pp. 38-39 (lawsuit against William Sherwin, Anne Gibbs [under age 21], Martin Bladen and Mary his wife, etc.); Romney Sedgwick, ed., *The History of Parliament: The House of Commons, 1715-1754*, vol. 1 (1970), pp. 465-66 (Martin Bladen, brother of William Bladen, colonial publisher and attorney-general of Md., SETH, and husband of Mary Gibbs, Anne's sister); *Register Book for St. Clement Danes* [London], *This Book Rebound 1862* (24 August 1726 marriage of Nathaniel Rice and Anne Gibbs); William L. Saunders, ed., *Colonial Records of North Carolina, Vol. III—1728 to 1734* (1886, repr. 1993), pp. 139-40 (1731 letter from Gov. George Burrington referring to "Mr. Rice Secretary of this Province Col[l]: Bladen's Brother in Law"); *VD*, pp. 569-70 (Monck) and *CP* (Lisle, Albemarle). The above and various other sources, especially concerning the above-cited lawsuit (which claimed that Thomas Pride, brother of Mrs. Elizabeth Pride Gibbs Sherwin, was the true heir-at-law of the 1st Duke of Albemarle) have been collected by Bladen researcher Karen Proudler and Rice descendant David T. Brown, the latter of Franklin, Tenn. Mr. Brown kindly sent me the results of their research and copies of relevant documents. A John Monck, cacique in 1682 (nominated by the 2nd Duke of Albemarle) left a 1684 will in South Carolina but I can trace no NDTPS. See *Records in the British Public Record Office Relating to South Carolina, 1663-1684* (1928), pp. 13, 209 (where Mr. John Monck is called of Knightsleere)-210 (where he is Mr. John Monck of Kings Cleere, "drapper"), 237, and C.T. Moore and A.A. Simmons, *Abstracts of the Wills of the State of South Carolina, 1670-1740* (Volume 1) (1960), p. 5. Note also Ted R. Jamison, Jr., *George Monck and the Restoration: Victory without Bloodshed* (1975), p. 151 (chart, with errors).

The Royal Descents of 900 Immigrants

1. Edward IV, King of England, d. 1483 = Elizabeth Woodville
2. (illegitimate by Elizabeth [Wayte] Lucy) Margaret (not Elizabeth) Plantagenet = Thomas Lumley
3. Richard Lumley, 5th Baron Lumley = Anne Conyers
4. Hon. Anthony Lumley = —— Gray
5. Roger Lumley = Anne Kurtwich
6. Richard Lumley, 1st Viscount Lumley = Frances Shelley
7. Hon. John Lumley = Mary Compton
8. Richard Lumley, 1st Earl of Scarbrough = Frances Jones
9. Mary Lumley = George Montagu, 1st Earl of Halifax, son of Edward Montagu and Elizabeth Pelham, SETH
10. **Lady Mary Montagu** = Sir Danvers **Osborne**, 3rd Bt., colonial governor of N.Y., ARD, SETH.

Sources: *CB* (Osborne of Chicksands, baronets); *CP* (Halifax, Scarbrough, Lumley); *Surtees* 2: 163-64 (Lumley); *RA* 5: 460-62, 468-69 (Edward IV and Elizabeth [Wayte] Lucy), plus conversations with Douglas Richardson about Margaret (not Elizabeth) (Plantagenet) Lumley.

The Royal Descents of 900 Immigrants

1. Edward IV, King of England, d. 1483 = Elizabeth Woodville
2. (illegitimate by Elizabeth [Wayte] Lucy) Margaret (not Elizabeth) Plantagenet = Thomas Lumley
3. Sibyl Lumley = Sir William Hilton
4. William Hilton = Margaret Metcalfe
5. Sir William Hilton = Anne Yorke
6. Henry Hilton = —— Brandling
7. Henry Hilton = Elizabeth Kitchen
8. Robert Hilton = Isabel Selby
9. Henry Hilton = Sarah Clarke
10. John Hilton = Mrs. Hannah —— Moore
11. **Ralph Hilton** (Hylton) of N.Y. = Mehitabel Lawrence.

Sources: *TAG* 50 (1974): 81-86 and sources cited therein; *RA* 5: 460-62, 468-69 (Edward IV and Elizabeth [Wayte] Lucy), plus conversations with Douglas Richardson about Margaret (not Elizabeth) (Plantagenet) Lumley.

The Royal Descents of 900 Immigrants

1. Edward III, King of England, d. 1377 = Philippa of Hainault
2. Lionel of Antwerp, Duke of Clarence = Elizabeth de Burgh
3. Philippa Plantagenet = Edmund Mortimer, 3rd Earl of March
4. Roger Mortimer, 4th Earl of March = Eleanor Holand, daughter of Thomas Holand, 1st Earl of Kent, and Joan Plantagenet, "The Fair Maid of Kent," SETH
5. Anne Mortimer = Richard Plantagenet, Earl of Cambridge, son of Edmund of Langley, 1st Duke of York (and Isabel of Castile), son of Edward III, King of England, and Philippa of Hainault, above
6. Richard Plantagenet, 3rd Duke of York = Cecily Neville, daughter of Ralph Neville, 1st Earl of Westmoreland, and Joan Beaufort, SETH
7. George Plantagenet, 1st Duke of Clarence, brother of Kings Edward IV (d. 1483) and Richard III (d. 1485) = Isabel Neville
8. Margaret Plantagenet, Countess of Salisbury = Sir Richard Pole
9. Henry Pole, 1st Baron Montagu = Joan Neville
10. Katherine Pole = Francis Hastings, 2nd Earl of Huntingdon
11. George Hastings, 4th Earl of Huntingdon = Dorothy Port
12. Francis Hastings, Lord Hastings = Sarah Harington. A daughter, Katherine Hastings, married Philip Stanhope, 1st Earl of Chesterfield, and was a great-great-grandmother of Philip Dormer Stanhope, 4th Earl of Chesterfield, the man of letters and literary patron. Sarah Stanhope, a daughter of Katherine and the 1st Earl, married Sir Richard Houghton, 3rd Bt. For the descent from this last couple to Charles Lutwidge Dodgson (Lewis Carroll), author of *Alice in Wonderland*, and Edward Morgan (E.M.) Forster, the novelist, see *NEHGS NEXUS* 15 (1995): 205-7.
13. Sir George Hastings = Seymour Prynne
14. Catherine Hastings = Bridges Nanfan
15. **Catherine Nanfan** = Richard **Coote**, 1st Earl of Bellomont (1636-1701), colonial governor of N.Y., Mass. and N.H., ARD, SETH.

11. Katherine Hastings (sister of the 4th Earl of Huntingdon) = Henry Clinton, 2nd Earl of Lincoln. Their son, Thomas Clinton,

The Royal Descents of 900 Immigrants

3rd Earl of Lincoln, married Elizabeth Knevet and left two daughters who immigrated to Mass.—Lady Susan Clinton, who left issue but no NDTPS, third wife of John Humphrey, dep. gov. of Mass., widower of Elizabeth Pelham, SETH; and Lady Arbella Clinton, who died childless, for whom the Winthrop fleet flagship *Arbella* was named, wife of Isaac Johnson.

12. Sir Edward Clinton = Mary Deighton
13. Francis Clinton = Priscilla Hill
14. Francis Clinton, 6th Earl of Lincoln = Susan Penniston
15. **Hon. George Clinton** (c. 1686-1761), colonial governor of N.Y. = Anne Carle.
16. Sir Henry Clinton = Harriet Carter
17. Augusta Clinton = Henry Dawkins
18. Clinton George Augustus Dawkins = Marianne Jane Robarts
19. Francis Henry Dawkins = Alice Clara Tufnell
20. Clinton George Evelyn Dawkins = Frances Enid Smythies
21. Clinton John Dawkins = Jean Mary Vyvyan Ladner
22. (Clinton) Richard Dawkins, b. 1941, British evolutionary biologist and atheist, of the University of California at Berkeley, 1967-69, a participant in the anti-Vietnamese war movement and the 1968 presidential campaign (for the Democratic nomination of U.S. Senator Eugene Joseph McCarthy), author of *The Selfish Gene* and *The Blind Watchman*, = (1) Marion Ellina Stamp; (2) Eve Barham; (3) Hon. Sarah Ward, the British television actress Lalla Ward.

17. (almost certain illegitimate children by Mrs. Mary [O'Callaghan] Baddeley include) Frederick Henry Clinton-Baddeley (half-brother of Augusta) = Susan le Mesurier
18. Henry Salkeld Clinton-Baddeley = Constance Louisa Dyer
19. William Herman Clinton-Baddeley = Louise Rosalie Bourdin. Another daughter was English actress (Madeleine) Angela Baddeley, best known to American audiences as the cook Mrs. Bridges on the BBC series *Upstairs, Downstairs*.

The Royal Descents of 900 Immigrants

20. **Hermione Youlanda Ruby Clinton-Baddeley**, 1906-86, known as **Hermione Baddeley**, sometime of Calif. = (1) Hon. David Francis Tennant, SETH; (2) Maj. J. H. "Dozey" Willis.

11. Elizabeth Hastings (sister of the 4th Earl of Huntingdon and the Countess of Lincoln) = Edward Somerset, 4th Earl of Worcester
12. Henry Somerset, 1st Marquess of Worcester = Anne Russell
13. Lord John Somerset = Mary Arundell, daughter of Thomas Arundell, 1st Baron Arundell of Wardour and Anne Philipson, SETH
14. Charles Somerset = Catherine Baskerville
15. **Maria Jo(h)anna Somerset** of Md. = (1) John **Lowther**; (2) Richard **Smith**.

13. Elizabeth Somerset (sister of Lord John Somerset) = Thomas Browne, 3rd Viscount Montagu, son of Anthony Maria Browne, 2nd Viscount Montagu, and Jane Sackville, SETH
14. Elizabeth Browne = Christopher Roper, 5th Baron Teynham
15. Henry Roper, 6th Baron Teynham = Anne Lennard, Baroness Dacre, daughter of Thomas Lennard, 1st Earl of Sussex and Anne Palmer, daughter of Barbara Villiers, Duchess of Cleveland, possibly by Roger Palmer, 1st Earl of Castlemaine, or by Charles II, King of England, SETH, or by Philip Stanhope, 1st Earl of Chesterfield
16. Henry Richard Roper = Mary Tenison
17. William Roper = Elizabeth Fish
18. Eliza Roper = Peter Boyle de Blaquiere
19. Louisa Emily de Blaquiere = Arthur Augustus Farmer
20. Alice Augusta Farmer = George Henry Howard
21. **Cecil de Blaquiere Howard** (1888-1956) of N.Y., sculptor = Cecile Coupet.

The Royal Descents of 900 Immigrants

12. Anne Somerset (sister of the 1st Marquess of Worcester) = Sir Edward Winter

13. Anne Winter = Benedict Hall

14. Henry Benedict Hall = Frances Fortescue, daughter of Sir John Fortescue, 2nd Bt. (and Margaret Arundell, daughter of Thomas Arundell, 1st Baron Arundell of Wardour, and Anne Philipson, his second wife, SETH), son of Sir John Fortescue (and Frances Stanley), son of Sir Francis Fortescue and Grace Manners, daughter of Sir John Manners and Dorothy Vernon, SETH

15. Benedict Hall = Jane ——

16. Benedicta Maria Theresa Hall = Thomas Gage, 1st Viscount Gage

17. Hon. **Thomas Gage** (c. 1720-1787), last royal governor of Mass., commander-in-chief of British forces in North America, 1763-72 = Margaret Kemble of N.J.

14. Mary Hall (sister of Henry Benedict Hall) = Sir Henry Jerningham, 2nd Bt.

15. Sir Francis Jerningham, 3rd Bt. = Anne Blount

16. Henry Jerningham = Mary L'Espine

17. **Henry Jerningham** of Md.= Catherine ——.

12. Blanche Somerset (sister of the 1st Marquess of Worcester and Lady Anne [Somerset] Winter) = Thomas Arundell, 2nd Baron Arundell of Wardour, son of Thomas Arundell, 1st Baron Arundell of Wardour above, by Mary Wriothesley, his first wife)

13. Henry Arundell, 3rd Baron Arundell of Wardour = Cecily Compton

14. Thomas Arundell, 4th Baron Arundell of Wardour = Margaret Spencer

15. Henry Arundell, 5th Baron Arundell of Wardour = Elizabeth Panton

16. Elizabeth Arundell = James Touchet, 6th Earl of Castlehaven

17. Mary Touchet = Philip Thicknesse

The Royal Descents of 900 Immigrants

18. George Thicknesse-Touchet, 19th Baron Audley = Elizabeth Delaval
19. Elizabeth Susanna Thicknesse-Touchet = John Cossins
20. Sarah Beresford Cossins = Sir John Hay, 7th Bt.
21. Georgiana Barbara Hay = William Johnston
22. **Charles Johnston** (1867-1931) of N.Y., author, translator of Hindu and Russian writers = Vera Jelihorvaky.

11. Sir Edward Hastings (brother of the 4th Earl of Huntingdon, the Countess of Lincoln and the Countess of Worcester) = Barbara Devereux, daughter of Sir William Devereux and Jane Scudamore, SETH
12. Sir Henry Hastings = Mabel Faunt
13. Henry Hastings = Jane Goodhall
14. Walter Hastings = Hannah Cradock
15. Jane Hastings = Edward Holme
16. William Holme = Elizabeth Chetham
17. John Holme = Elizabeth Bowker
18. Catherine Holme = Timothy Wiggin (parents of Augustus Wiggin of N.Y., who married Ann E. Loder but left no NDTPS. Another son, William Wiggin, married Frances Emma Rice and was the father of Augustus Holme Wiggin of Minn., who married Hannah Hansen but also left no NDTPS).
19. **Frederick Wiggin** of N.Y. = Elizabeth Sumner Gerard (parents of Frederick Holme Wiggin, 1853-1910, surgeon, who married Abigail Fiske Merriam and Christina Ferguson).

11. Frances Hastings (sister of the 4th Earl of Huntingdon, the Countess of Lincoln, the Countess of Worcester, and Sir Edward Hastings) = Henry Compton, 1st Baron Compton
12. William Compton, 1st Earl of Northampton = Elizabeth Spencer
13. Spencer Compton, 2nd Earl of Northampton = Mary Beaumont

The Royal Descents of 900 Immigrants

14. James Compton, 3rd Earl of Northampton = Mary Noel

15. George Compton, 4th Earl of Northampton = Jane Fox

16. James Compton, 5th Earl of Northampton = Elizabeth Shirley, Baroness Ferrers of Chartley

17. Charlotte Compton, Baroness Ferrers of Chartley = George Townshend, 1st Marquess Townshend

18. Lord John Townshend = Georgiana Anne Poyntz

19. Lord George Osborne Townshend (brother of John Townshend, 4th Marquess Townshend) = Jessie Victoria MacKellar

20. Charles Thornton Townshend = Louise Graham

21. Sir Charles Vere Ferrers Townshend, British World War I commander = Alice Cahen d'Anvers

22. Audrey Dorothy Louise Townshend = Baudouin, Count Borchgrave d'Altena

23. **Arnaud Charles Paul Marie Philippe, Count Borchgrave d'Altena**, known as Arnaud de Borchgrave (b. 1926) of N.Y., editor and correspondent (associated with *Newsweek* magazine) = (1) Dorothy Solon; (2) Eileen Ritschel; (3) Alexandra D. Villard.

15. Spencer Compton, 1st Earl of Wilmington, Speaker of the House of Commons (brother of the 4th Earl of Northampton), d. unm. but was "by general repute" the father by Jane Towneley, wife of William Wilson (and later of Anthony Trumble) of Elizabeth Wilson below. Jane Towneley was the daughter of Nicholas Towneley (and Jane Gildredge), son of Nicholas Towneley and Joan White, SETH; William Wilson was the son of Sir William Wilson, 2nd Bt., and Ricarda Peacock.

16. (likely illegitimate) **Elizabeth Wilson** of S.C. = James **Glen** (1701-77), governor of S.C.

Sources: *Clarence*, tables I, II, V, pp. 1-2, 5 (Lady Bellomont); II, XVII, XVIII, pp. 2, 13-14 (Clinton, plus *GM* 3: 462-68 and *GMB* 2: 1104-5), 177-78 (to F.H. Dawkins, plus *BLG* 1952, p. 629 [to C.J. Dawkins] and Richard Dawkins, *An Appetite for Wonder: The Making of a Scientist*

The Royal Descents of 900 Immigrants

[2013], initial chart, pp. 3-25); Hermione Baddeley, *The Unsinkable Hermione Baddeley* (1984), *passim*, and various English wills, esp. those of Frederick Henry Clinton-Baddeley (1879) and Gen. Sir Henry Clinton (1796, PCC, mentioning Mrs. Mary [O'Callaghan], widow of Thomas Baddeley, and her son John, plus Henry, William, Harriet, Elizabeth, and Frederick Baddeley, the last five almost certainly Clinton's illegitimate children by Mary, born after Thomas Baddeley's 1782 death), *BLG* 1952, p. 84 (Baddeley, covering Thomas, John, and the latter's two elder sons, Paul Frederick Henry and William Clinton Baddeley, who carry first and/or middle names shared by the later Clinton-Baddeleys); II, XXXV, pp. 2, 28 (plus *Maryland Genealogical Society Bulletin* 37 [1996]: 299-303, *BRMF1*, pp. 402-5, and *BRMF2*, pp. 202-5 for Mrs. M.J.S.L. Smith); XXXV, XLV, XLVI, pp. 1-2, 28, 36-37, 409-10 (to C. de B. Howard) and *WWWA*, vol. 3, *1951-1960* (1960), p. 420; XXXV, pp. 2, 28, *Transactions of the Bristol and Gloucestershire Archaeological Society* 7 (1882-83): 244, 248, 265-66 (Hall, Gage), W.P.W. Phillimore, *Visitations of Worcester, 1569* (*HSPVS*, vol. 27, 1888), p. 149 (Winter), plus *Parliament, 1558-1603*, vol. 3, pp. 673-75 (Sir Edward Winter/Wynter), and *CB* (Fortescue of Selden) (Gov. Thomas Gage); *BRMF* 1, pp. 269-70, *BP* or *CP* (Jerningham, baronets, and Stafford, barons); XXXV, LVI, pp. 28, 45, 470-71 (to Charles Johnston) and *WWWA*, vol. 1, *1899-1942* (1943), pp. 642-63; II, XV, pp. 2, 11, 169 and *Essex* (*The Clarence Volume Supplement*, Chart II), pp. 508-9, 529, 531-32 (to Frederick Wiggin) and *WWWA*, vol. 1, *1899-1942* (1943), p. 1343; II, XX, pp. 2, 16-17, 195, *BP* (Townshend) and *WWA* (Arnaud de Borchgrave); *CP* (Wilmington), *BP* (Maryon-Wilson), *ANB* (James Glen), Historical Manuscripts Commission, *Manuscripts of the Earls of Egmont: Diary of the First Earl of Egmont, Vol. III, 1739-1747* (1923), p. 49 and three letters (dated 1725-27) relating to failed marriage negotiations for Elizabeth Wilson, listed among its acquisitions in *East Sussex Record Office: Report to the County Archivist, April 2009 to March 2010*, pp. 11-12, plus F.A. Hill, *The Mystery Solved: Facts Relating to the "Lawrence-Townley" "Chase-Townley" Marriages and Estate Question* (1888), Townley chart C in back. The Wilson letters and the Towneley descent were first brought to my attention by John C. Brandon of Columbia, S.C. Likely gentry ancestry for (Clinton) Richard Dawkins and Hermione (Y.R. Clinton-) Baddeley was first suggested to me by Julie Helen Otto. Among spouses of the above immigrants, Hon. Sarah (Lalla) Ward and Hon. D.F. Tennant were also of royal descent, but never settled in the U.S.

The Royal Descents of 900 Immigrants

1. Edward III, King of England, d. 1377 = Philippa of Hainault
2. Lionel of Antwerp, Duke of Clarence = Elizabeth de Burgh
3. Philippa Plantagenet = Edmund Mortimer, 3rd Earl of March
4. Roger Mortimer, 4th Earl of March = Eleanor Holand
5. Anne Mortimer = Richard Plantagenet, Earl of Cambridge, son of Edmund of Langley, 1st Duke of York (and Isabel of Castile), son of Edward III, King of England, and Philippa of Hainault, above
6. Richard Plantagenet, 3rd Duke of York = Cecily Neville, daughter of Ralph Neville, 1st Earl of Westmoreland, and Joan Beaufort, SETH
7. George Plantagenet, 1st Duke of Clarence, brother of Kings Edward IV (d. 1483) and Richard III (d. 1485) = Isabel Neville
8. Margaret Plantagenet, Countess of Salisbury = Sir Richard Pole
9. Henry Pole, 1st Baron Montagu = Joan Neville
10. Winifred Pole = Sir Thomas Barrington
11. Sir Francis Barrington, 1st Bt. = Joan Cromwell, aunt of Oliver Cromwell, the Lord Protector
12. Joan Barrington = Sir Richard Everard, 1st Bt.
13. Sir Richard Everard, 2nd Bt. = Elizabeth Gibbs
14. Sir Hugh Everard, 3rd Bt. = Mary Brown
15. **Sir Richard Everard**, 4th Bt., colonial governor of N.C. = Susan Kidder.

9. Ursula Pole (sister of the 1st Baron Montagu) = Henry Stafford, Baron Stafford
10. Dorothy Stafford = Sir William Stafford
11. Elizabeth Stafford = Sir William Drury
12. Frances Drury = (1) Sir Nicholas Clifford; (2) Sir William Wray
13. (by 1) Frances Clifford = Sir Edward Ayscough

The Royal Descents of 900 Immigrants

14. Anne Ayscough = Edward King
15. Edward King = Bridget Neville
16. Neville King = Mary Middlemore
17. Anne King = Richard Welby
18. **Marianne Welby** of Md. = Samuel **De Butts**.

13. (by 2) Frances Wray = Sir Anthony Irby
14. Elizabeth Irby = George Montagu
15. Edward Montagu = Elizabeth Pelham
16. **Grace Montagu** = William **Cosby** (c. 1690-1735/6), colonial governor of N.Y. and N.J., ARD, SETH.

13. (by 2) Sir Christopher Wray (brother of Frances) = Albinia Cecil
14. **Frances Wray** = Sir Henry **Vane** (1613-1662), Puritan statesman, colonial governor of Mass., ARD, SETH.

14. Sir Drury Wray, 6th Bt. (brother of Frances) = Anne Casey
15. Diana Wray = William Twigge, Archdeacon of Limerick
16. Jane Twigge = Stackpole Pery
17. William Cecil Pery, 1st Baron Glentworth = Jane Walcot
18. Edmund Henry Pery, 1st Earl of Limerick = Mary Alice Ormsby
19. Henry Hartstonge Pery, Viscount Glentworth = Annabella Edwards
20. William Henry Tennison Pery, 2nd Earl of Limerick = Susannah Sheaffe
21. William Hale John Charles Pery, 3rd Earl of Limerick =
20. Emilie Caroline Pery = Henry Gray
21. Caroline Maria Gray

115

The Royal Descents of 900 Immigrants

22. William Henry Edmond de Vere Sheaffe Pery, 4th Earl of Limerick = May Imelda Josephine Irwin

23. **Lady Victoria May Pery** of N.Y. = James Cox **Brady** (1882-1927), businessman, founder of Maxwell Motor Co., later absorbed into Chrysler Corp.

14. Cecil Wray (brother of Frances and Sir Drury) = Susanna Cressy

15. William Wray = Isabella Ullithorne

16. Sir John Wray, 6th Bt. = Frances Fairfax Norcliffe

17. Isabella Wray = John Dalton

18. Thomas Norcliffe Dalton, later Norcliffe = Anne Wilson

19. Mary Norcliffe Dalton = Charles Best

20. Mary Ellen Best = Johann Philip Anton Sarg

21. Francis Charles Anthony Sarg = Mary Elizabeth Parker

22. **Anthony Frederick "Tony" Sarg** (1880-1942), of N.Y., illustrator (for the *Saturday Evening Post, Collier's*, etc.), author of children's books, puppeteer (who designed the large animal balloons long used in Macy's Thanksgiving Day Parades) = Bertha Eleanor McGowan.

14. Theodosia Wray (sister of Frances, Sir Drury, and Cecil) = Rowland Laugharne

15. Anne Laugharne = David Allen

16. John Allen = Joan Bartlett

17. John Bartlett Allen = Elizabeth Hensleigh

18. Elizabeth Allen = Josiah Wedgwood, master potter of Etruria, M.P., brother of Susanna Wedgwood, wife of Robert Waring Darwin (see *NK*1: 45-51) and mother of naturalist Charles Robert Darwin

19. Francis Wedgwood, master potter of Etruria (brother of [1] Emma Wedgwood, wife of her first cousin Charles Robert

The Royal Descents of 900 Immigrants

Darwin, the naturalist; and [2] Josiah Wedgwood, husband of another first cousin, Caroline Sarah Darwin [sister of the naturalist] and father of Margaret Susan Wedgwood, Mrs. Arthur Charles Vaughan Williams, mother of composer Ralph Vaughan Williams) = Frances Mosley

20. Clement Francis Wedgwood, master potter of Etruria = Emily Catherine Rendel
21. Josiah Clement Wedgwood, 1st Baron Wedgwood, M.P., Labor Party official = Ethel Kate Bowen
22. Josiah Wedgwood = Dorothy Mary Winser
23. **Josiah Ralph Patrick Wedgwood**, b. 1924, of Seattle, Wash., pediatrician, educator = Virginia Lloyd Hunt.

14. Albinia Wray (sister of Frances, Sir Drury, Cecil, and Theodosia) = Richard Betenson
15. Theodosia Betenson = Thomas Farringdon
16. Albinia Farringdon = Robert Bertie, 1st Duke of Ancaster
17. Lord Vere Bertie = Anne Casey
18. Albinia Bertie = George Hobart, 3rd Earl of Buckinghamshire
19. George Vere Hobart = Jane Cataneo
20. Albinia Jane Hobart-Hampden = Sir Augustus John Foster, 1st Bt., son of John Thomas Foster and Lady Elizabeth Hervey, known as Lady Elizabeth Foster, the scandalous second wife of William Cavendish, 5th Duke of Devonshire and later a patron of the arts in Rome, daughter of Frederick Augustus Hervey, 4th Earl of Bristol (and Elizabeth Davers), son of John Hervey, 1st Baron Hervey of Ickworth, man of letters, and Mary Lepell, SETH).
21. Sir Cavendish Hervey Foster, 3rd Bt. = Isabella Todd
22. John Frederick Foster = Caroline Emily Marsh
23. Alice Jane Blanche Foster = Fitzgerald Wintour
24. Charles Vere Wintour, British newspaper editor (*Evening Standard*, *Daily Express*) = Eleanor "Nonie" Trego Baker
25. **(Dame) Anna Wintour**, b. 1949, of N.Y., editor of the British and American *Vogue* = David Shaffer.

The Royal Descents of 900 Immigrants

Sources: *Clarence*, tables II, LVII, LXIII, pp. 2, 46, 53 and *CB* (Everard of Much Waltham, baronets); LXVII, LXVIII, LXX, LXXV, pp. 56-57, 59, 64, *TG* 12 (1998): 158-67 (De Butts), Rev. A.R. Maddison, ed., *Lincolnshire Pedigrees* (*HSPVS*, vols., 50-52, 55), vol. 1 (1902), pp. 65-66 (Ayscough), vol. 2 (1903), p. 566 (King), *BLG* (Reeve-King of Ashby de la Launde), and *GVFWM* 1: 586 (Mrs. De Butts); LXX, LXXVI, pp. 59, 65 (G.M. Cosby); LXX, LXXIII, pp. 59, 62 (Lady Vane); LXX, LXXI, pp. 59-60, 558-60 and *BP* (Limerick) (Lady V.M.P. Brady); LXX, LXXII, pp. 59, 61, 574-75 (entire line to A.F. Sarg) and *DAB*; *Essex*, pp. 508-9, 512 (*The Clarence Volume Supplement*, II, VII), 580-82, 137, *BP* 1999, pp. 2960-62 (Wedgwood), and *Who's Who in America* (Dr. J.R.P. Wedgwood); LXX, LXXIV, pp. 59, 63, 591-93 (to Alice J.B. Foster) (and *BP* for Ancaster, Buckinghamshire, Devonshire, Bristol, and Foster, baronets), (British) *Who Was Who, 1941-50* (1952), p. 1253 (Fitzgerald Wintour), (British) *Who's Who, 1981-82*, pp. 2830-31 (C.V. Wintour) and *WWA* (Anna Wintour), plus Jerry Oppenheimer, *Front Row: What Lies Beneath the Chic Exterior of Vogue's Editor-in-Chief* (2005), pp. 1-11, esp. 1, 4. See also *RA* 4: 661-64 (Somerset, for Maria Jo[h]anna).

The Isabel and Joan Neville at generations 7 and 9 above were daughters respectively of Richard Neville, "the Kingmaker," Earl of Warwick and Salisbury, and Anne Beauchamp, SETH; and George Neville, 2nd Baron Abergavenny, and Margaret Fenne, SETH. Anne Neville, sister of Isabel, was the wife and Queen of Richard III, King of England, SETH.

The Royal Descents of 900 Immigrants

1. Edward III, King of England, d. 1377 = Philippa of Hainault
2. Lionel of Antwerp, Duke of Clarence = Elizabeth de Burgh
3. Philippa Plantagenet = Edmund Mortimer, 3rd Earl of March
4. Roger Mortimer, 4th Earl of March = Eleanor Holand
5. Anne Mortimer = Richard Plantagenet, Earl of Cambridge, son of Edmund of Langley, 1st Duke of York (and Isabel of Castile), son of Edward III, King of England, and Philippa of Hainault, above
6. Richard Plantagenet, 3rd Duke of York = Cecily Neville, daughter of Ralph Neville, 1st Earl of Westmoreland and Joan Beaufort, SETH
7. Anne Plantagenet, sister of Kings Edward IV (d. 1483) and Richard III (d. 1485) = Sir Thomas St. Leger
8. Anne St. Leger = George Manners, Baron Ros, son of Sir Robert Manners and Eleanor de Ros, SETH
9. Thomas Manners, 1st Earl of Rutland = Eleanor Paston
10. Sir John Manners = Dorothy Vernon
11. Sir George Manners = Grace Pierpont
12. John Manners, 8th Earl of Rutland = Frances Montagu
13. John Manners, 1st Duke of Rutland = Catherine Noel
14. John Manners, 2nd Duke of Rutland = Catherine Russell
15. Elizabeth Manners = John Monckton, 1st Viscount Galway
16. **Hon. Robert Monckton** (1726-1782), colonial governor of N.Y., British commander in America during the French and Indian wars, d. unm.

15. John Manners, 3rd Duke of Rutland (brother of Viscountess Galway) = Bridget Sutton

16. John Manners, Marquess of Granby = Frances Seymour

16. Lord George Manners-Sutton = Diana Chaplin

The Royal Descents of 900 Immigrants

17. (illegitimate by ——) = 17. John Manners-Sutton
    Anne Manners
18. Mary Georgiana Manners-Sutton = Robert Nassau Sutton
19. Mary Isabella Sutton = Sir George Baker, 3rd Bt.
20. Sir George Barrington Baker Wilbraham, 5th Bt. = Katherine Frances Wilbraham
21. Sir Philip Wilbraham Baker Wilbraham, 6th Bt. = Joyce Christabel Kennaway
22. **Mary Frances Baker Wilbraham** of Mass. = Elliot **Perkins** (1901-1985), educator, master of Lowell House at Harvard.

13. Grace Manners (sister of the 1st Duke of Rutland) = Patrick Chaworth, 3rd Viscount Chaworth
14. Juliana Chaworth = Chambré Brabazon, 5th Earl of Meath
15. Mary Brabazon = William Tisdall
16. Mary Tisdall = William Lyster, son of John Lyster and Elizabeth Coddington, SETH
17. Elizabeth Lyster = James Saurin, Bishop of Dromore
18. Emily Saurin = Edward Richards
19. Anne Catherine Richards = Percy Tilson Magan
20. **Percy Tilson Magan, Jr.** (1867-1947) of Calif., physician and medical college president = (1) Ida May Bauer; (2) Lillian Eshelman.

11. Grace Manners (sister of Sir George) = Sir Francis Fortescue
12. Mary Fortescue = John Talbot, 10th Earl of Shrewsbury
13. Hon. Gilbert Talbot = Jane Flatsbury
14. Anne Talbot = Edward Talbot, possibly a cousin

The Royal Descents of 900 Immigrants

15. **Anne Talbot** of Md. = Henry **Darnall**. Their son, Henry Darnall, married Rachel Brooke and was the father of Mary Darnall, wife of Charles Carroll (III) of Carrollton, signer of the Declaration of Independence, Revolutionary leader and U.S. senator, SETH.

10. Katherine Manners (sister of Sir John) = Sir Henry Capell
11. Sir Gamaliel Capell = Jane Browne
12. **Anne Capell**, probably of Md. = Robert **Wiseman** of Md., SETH.

11. Sir Arthur Capell (brother of Sir Gamaliel) = Margaret Grey
12. Sir Henry Capell = Theodosia Montagu
13. Arthur Capell, 1st Baron Capell = Elizabeth Morrison
14. Arthur Capell, 1st Earl of Essex = Elizabeth Percy
15. Algernon Capell, 2nd Earl of Essex = Mary Bentinck
16. William Capell, 3rd Earl of Essex = Jane Hyde
17. Charlotte Capell = Thomas Villiers, 1st Earl of Clarendon
18. Hon. George Villiers = Theresa Parker, daughter of John Parker, 1st Baron Barrington, and Theresa Robinson, daughter of Thomas Robinson, 1st Baron Grantham, and Frances Worsley, daughter of Thomas Worsley and Mary Frankland, daughter of Sir Thomas Frankland, 2nd Bt., and Elizabeth Russell, SETH, see following chart, also a descendant of George Manners, Baron Ros, and Anne St. Leger
19. George William Villiers, 4th Earl of Clarendon = Catherine Grimston
20. Sir Francis Hyde Villiers = Virginia Katharine Smith, daughter of Eric Carrington Smith (and Mary Maberly), son of Oswald Smith and Henrietta Mildred Hodgson, SETH, great-grandparents of the late H.M. Queen Elizabeth The Queen Mother
21. Algernon Hyde Villiers = Beatrix Elinor Paul

The Royal Descents of 900 Immigrants

22. Charles English Hyde Villiers = Countess Marie José De La Barre d'Erquelinnes

23. **Diana Mary Villiers** of Washington, D.C. = John Dimitri **Negroponte**, b. 1939, diplomat, U.S. ambassador to the United Nations, director of the Office of Intelligence.

14. Theodosia Capell (sister of the 1st Earl of Essex) = Henry Hyde, 2nd Earl of Clarendon, brother of Anne Hyde, wife of James II, King of England, and uncle of Queens Mary II and Anne

15. **Edward Hyde**, 3rd **Earl of Clarendon** (1661-1723), colonial governor of N.Y. and N.J. = Catherine O'Brien, Baroness Clifton, see below.

10. Elizabeth Manners (sister of Sir John and Katherine) = Sir John Savage

11. Margaret Savage = William Brereton, 1st Baron Brereton

12. Mary Brereton = Henry O'Brien, 4th Earl of Thomond

13. Anne O'Brien = Henry O'Brien, 6th Earl of Thomond, a cousin

14. Henry O'Brien, Lord Ibrackan = Catherine Stuart, Baroness Clifton

15. **Catherine O'Brien, Baroness Clifton** = Edward **Hyde**, 3rd Earl of Clarendon (1661-1723), colonial governor of N.Y. and N.J., see above.

10. Frances Manners (sister of Sir John, Katherine, and Elizabeth) = Henry Neville, 4th Baron Abergavenny, son of George Neville, 3rd Baron Abergavenny and Mary Stafford, SETH

11. Mary Neville, Baroness le Despencer = Sir Thomas Fane

12. Francis Fane, 1st Earl of Westmoreland = Mary Mildmay. Among their descendants, via Thomas Fane, 8th Earl of Westmoreland, are Eric Arthur Blair, who wrote under the name George Orwell, and biographer Lady Antonia (Margaret Caroline Pakenham) Fraser, whose second husband is the playwright Harold Pinter. See *NEHGS NEXUS* 16 (1999): 72-73.

The Royal Descents of 900 Immigrants

13. Elizabeth Fane = William Cope
14. Elizabeth Cope = Thomas Geers
15. Elizabeth Geers = William Gregory
16. Elizabeth Gregory = John Nourse
17. **James Nourse** of Pa. = Sarah Fouace.

10. Anne Manners (sister of Sir John, Katherine, Elizabeth, and Frances) = Henry Neville, 5th Earl of Westmoreland
11. Charles Neville, 6th Earl of Westmoreland = Jane Howard, daughter of Henry Howard, Earl of Surrey, the poet, and Frances Vere, SETH
12. Anne Neville = David Ingleby
13. Mary Ingleby = Sir Peter Middleton
14. William Middleton = Catherine Constable
15. Peter Middleton = Elizabeth Langdale
16. Elizabeth Middleton = Sir Carnaby Haggerston, 3rd Bt., son of William Haggerston and Anne Constable, daughter of Sir Philip Constable, 3rd Bt. (and Margaret Radcliffe), son of Sir Marmaduke Constable, 2nd Bt. (and Anne Sherborne), son of Sir Philip Constable, 1st Bt. (and Anne Roper), son of Sir Marmaduke Constable (and Frances Metham), son of Sir Philip Constable (and Margaret Tyrwhit), son of Sir Marmaduke Constable (and Jane Conyers), SETH, next chart, also a Manners-St. Leger descendant
17. Sir Thomas Haggerston, 4th Bt. = Mary Silvertop
18. Sir Carnaby Haggerston, 5th Bt. = Frances Smythe, sister of Mrs. Mary Anne Smythe Weld FitzHerbert (Mrs. Maria FitzHerbert), unacknowledged first wife of George Augustus Frederick, Prince of Wales, later George IV, King of Great Britain. For these sisters' Lygon descent see *NEHGS NEXUS* 16 (1999): 200-1.
19. Mary Haggerston = Sir Thomas Stanley (-Massey-Stanley), 9th Bt. A son, Sir Rowland [Stanley] Errington, 11st Bt., married Julia MacDonald and was the father of Ethel [Stanley] Errington, first wife of Evelyn Baring, 1st Earl of Cromer, the British Imperial commander and Egyptian administrator.

The Royal Descents of 900 Immigrants

20. Maria Frances Stanley (-Massey-Stanley) = Sir Richard Williams-Bulkeley, 10th Bt.
21. Sir Richard Lewis Mostyn Williams-Bulkeley, 11th Bt. = Margaret Elizabeth Williams
22. **Bridget Henrietta Frances Williams-Bulkeley**, sometime of N.Y. = Benjamin Seymour **Guinness**, also sometime of N.Y., SETH. Bridget's and Benjamin's daughter, Tanis Eva Bulkeley Guinness, married (1) Hon. William Drogo Sturgis Montagu; (2) Howard **Dietz**, 1896-1983, American lyricist ("That's Entertainment"), the MGM publicist who designed its lion logo; (3) (Charles Edward) Harold John **Phillips**.

Sources: Sources: *Exeter*, tables I, II, VII, pp. 1-2, 9 and *BP* (Galway, Rutland) (Monckton); table VII, pp. 9, 159-62 and *BP* (Baker Wilbraham, baronets, for Mrs. Perkins); table X, pp. 12, 208, *BIFR*, pp. 1104 (Tisdall), 770 (Magan), *BLGI* 1912, pp. 426-27 (Lyster), 590 (Richards), *BLG* 1939, p. 1996 (Saurin), Rev. H.L.L. Denny, *Memorials of an Ancient House: A History of the Family of Lister or Lyster* (1913), pp. 61-63, 70-72 and *NCAB* 36 (1950): 202-3 (P.T. Magan); tables II, VII, XV, XVI, pp. 2, 9, 17-18 (to Anne Talbot, wife of —— Talbot) and Talbot-Darnall research by Brad Verity, aided by John Higgins; tables II, XXVII, pp. 2, 30, Walter C. Metcalfe, ed., *Visitations of Essex, 1552, 1558, 1590, 1612, 1634* (*HSPVS*, vol. 13, 1878), pp. 171, 370, 130 (Capell, Wiseman), and G.E. and D.V. Russell, *The Ark and The Dove Adventurers* (2005), pp. 199-200 and sources cited therein (Mrs. Wiseman); tables II, XXVII, XXXV, XLII, pp. 2, 30-31, 39, 65, 379-80, 638, 642-43, *BP* (Clarendon) and *WWA 2012* (2011), p. 3224 (to Mrs. Negroponte) and *CP* (Clarendon) (Clarendon and his wife); tables II, XXIV, pp. 2, 27, *MGH*, 3rd ser., 4 (1902): 219-20 (Cope), *Duncumb* 4: 30 (Geers), 3: 233 (Gregory) and Maria Catharine Nourse Lyle, *James Nourse and His Descendants* (1897), pp. 2-23 (Nourse); tables II, XXII, XLVII, pp. 2, 25, 52, 333-34, 529 (to Mrs. Guinness), *BP* 2003 (Guinness, baronets), and *ANB* (Howard Dietz). I first noticed the gentry origin of P.T. Magan while perusing Henry L.P. Beckwith, ed., *A Roll of Arms* [of] *the Committee on Heraldry of the New England Historic Genealogical Society* (2013), at p. 268.

For Mrs. Anne Talbot Darnall Mr. Verity cites, among other documents, a 1735 indenture (recorded in the land records of Prince

The Royal Descents of 900 Immigrants

George's County, Maryland) between Henry Darnall (Jr.), son of Henry and Anne, and George Talbot, "Earl of Shrewsbury" (whose elder brother, Gilbert Talbot, 13th Earl of Shrewsbury, was a Jesuit priest) and John Talbot of Longford (son of Thomas Talbot of Longford [and Anne Yate], son of John Talbot, 10th Earl of Shrewsbury by a second wife, Frances Arundel, see *Collins*, 3: 36-38), which mentions the £500 marriage portion of Anne [Talbot Darnall]; a 1719 petition by George Talbot ("Earl of Shrewsbury") to alienate some of the lands of the late Charles Talbot, 1st Duke of Shrewsbury (George's first cousin) to provide marriage portions for George's nieces Anne and Mary, daughters of Anne (Talbot) Talbot; and a 1715 census of English Catholic non-jurors, which includes Edward Talbot of "Bowling Green," Albrighton, Shropshire, and his daughters Anne and Mary. "Royal Descents of Anne Talbot Darnall and Mary Talbot Salvin," a soc.gen.medieval thread first posted 17 Oct. 2012 by Brad Verity (royaldescent@hotmail.com), with further posts by John Higgins (jhigginsgen@yahoo.com) and Will Johnson (wjhonson@aol.com), appears on soc.gen.medieval (http://archiver.rootsweb.ancestry.com/read/GEN-MEDIEVAL/2012-10/1350516036, and was brought to my attention by John C. Brandon of Columbia, S.C.

Eric Hyde Villiers, the elder son of Sir Francis Hyde Villiers and Virginia Katharine Smith at generation 20 on p. 121 (and a great-uncle of Mrs. Diana Mary Villiers Negroponte) married Joan Ankaret Talbot; their second son was James (Michael Hyde) Villiers, 1933-1998, an English actor (who = [1] Patricia Donovan and [2] Lucinda Claire Nex), various of whose movies (*The Entertainer*, *Repulsion*, *The Nanny*, *The Ruling Class*, *Joseph Andrews*, *For Your Eyes Only*, etc.) were widely distributed and well received in the U.S. (see *BP* and *Oxford DNB*).

The Royal Descents of 900 Immigrants

1. Edward III, King of England, d. 1377 = Philippa of Hainault
2. Lionel of Antwerp, Duke of Clarence = Elizabeth de Burgh
3. Philippa Plantagenet = Edmund Mortimer, 3rd Earl of March
4. Roger Mortimer, 4th Earl of March = Eleanor Holand
5. Anne Mortimer = Richard Plantagenet, Earl of Cambridge, son of Edmund of Langley, 1st Duke of York (and Isabel of Castile), son of Edward III, King of England, and Philippa of Hainault, above
6. Richard Plantagenet, 3rd Duke of York = Cecily Neville, daughter of Ralph Neville, 1st Earl of Westmoreland and Joan Beaufort, SETH
7. Anne Plantagenet, sister of Kings Edward IV (d. 1483) and Richard III (d. 1485) = Sir Thomas St. Leger
8. Anne St. Leger = George Manners, Baron Ros
9. Katherine Manners = Sir Robert Constable
10. Sir Marmaduke Constable = Jane Conyers
11. Katherine Constable = Sir Robert Stapleton
12. Philip Stapleton = Dorothy Hill
13. Dorothy Stapleton (d. 1637 in England) = Thomas Nelson of Rowley, Mass.
14. **Philip Nelson** of Mass. = (1) Sarah Jewett; (2) Elizabeth Lowell, daughter of John Lowell (and Elizabeth Goodale), son of Percival Lowell, ARD, SETH, and Rebecca ——.
14. **Thomas Nelson, Jr**. of Mass. = (1) Anne Lambert; (2) Mrs. Mary Lunt; (3) Mrs. Philippa Andrews Felt Platts.

12. Jane Stapleton (sister of Philip) = Christopher Wyvill
13. Sir Marmaduke Wyvill, 2nd Bt. = Isabel Gascoigne. Their son, Sir Christopher Wyvill, 3rd Bt., married Ursula Darcy and was the father of Sir William Wyvill, 4th Bt., who himself married Anne Brooke and left a second son, Darcy Wyvill, father (by wife Jane Hessell) of William Wyvill of Md. This last married

The Royal Descents of 900 Immigrants

Elinor Boyd and left agnate progeny entitled to the baronetcy but no NDTPS.

14. Mary Wyvill = Arthur Beckwith
15. Sir Roger Beckwith, 1ˢᵗ Bt. = Elizabeth Jennings, daughter of Sir Edmund Jennings and Margaret Barkham, and sister of Act. Gov. Edmund Jennings of Va., ARD, SETH
16. **Sir Marmaduke Beckwith, 3ʳᵈ Bt.**, of Va. = Mrs. Elizabeth Brockenbrough Dickenson.

14. Grace Wyvill (sister of Mary) = George Witham
15. John Witham = Elizabeth Standish
16. William Witham = Anne Lawson
17. Henry Witham = Catherine Meaburne
18. Anne Witham = Philip Howard of Corby Castle
19. Henry Howard = Catherine Mary Neave
20. Sir Henry Francis Howard = Marie Ernestine von der Schulenberg
21. Sir Henry Howard = Cecilia Dowdall Riggs, daughter of George Washington Riggs, banker and Washington, D.C. civic leader and Janet Madeleine Cecilia Shedden, SETH
22. **George Howard** of Washington, D.C. = Mrs. Mary Allen Clagett Perrin. Their son, Henry Howard, married Natalie Bayard Merrill and was the father of Natalie Bayard Howard, wife of (1) Peter Alan Gordon and (2) William Thompson Baker, Jr., b. 1944, lawyer and Yale College classmate of the author.

10. Barbara Constable (sister of Sir Marmaduke) = Sir William Babthorpe
11. Margaret Babthorpe = Sir Henry Cholmley
12. Sir Richard Cholmley = Susanna Legard
13. Margaret Cholmley = Sir William Strickland, 1ˢᵗ Bt.

The Royal Descents of 900 Immigrants

14. Margaret Strickland = Sir John Cochrane
15. William Cochrane = Mary Bruce
16. Thomas Cochrane, 8th Earl of Dundonald = Jane Stuart
17. Elizabeth Cochrane = Patrick Heron
18. Mary Heron = Sir John Shaw Heron-Maxwell, 4th Bt.
19. Helenora Catherine Heron-Maxwell = Hew Drummond Elphinstone-Dalrymple
20. Sir Robert Graeme Elphinstone-Dalrymple, 5th Bt. = Flora Loudoun MacLeod
21. Sir Francis Napier Elphinstone-Dalrymple, 7th Bt. = Edith Ethel LeBreton
22. **Penelope Eleanor Elphinstone-Dalrymple** of Mass. = (1) James Peter Henry **Balston**; (2) Russell Alexander **Lovell**, Jr., b. 1918, historian and archivist of Sandwich, Mass.

15. John Cochrane (brother of William) = Hannah deWitt/Worth
16. Susannah Cochrane = James McAdam
17. **John Loudon McAdam** (1756-1836), sometime of N.Y., merchant, road builder, surveyor and administrator = (1) Gloriana Margaret Nicoll of N.Y.; (2) Anne Charlotte Delancey.

17. Wilhelmina Hannah McAdam (sister of John Loudon McAdam) = John Shaw
18. Sir James Shaw Kennedy = Mary Primrose Kennedy, daughter of David Kennedy of Kirkmichael and Henrietta Whiteford, daughter of Sir John Whiteford, 3rd Bt. (and Anne Cartwright), son of Sir John Whiteford, 2nd Bt. (and Alice Muir), son of Sir Adam Whiteford, 1st Bt., and Margaret Cathcart, daughter of Alan Cathcart, 7th Baron Cathcart (and Elizabeth Dalrymple), son of Alan Cathcart, 6th Baron Cathcart and Marion Boswell, daughter of David Boswell of Auchinleck (a great-great-grandson of James IV, King of Scotland, d. 1513, and Agnes Stewart, Countess of Boswell) and Isabel Wallace, SETH

The Royal Descents of 900 Immigrants

19. John Shaw Kennedy = Eleanor Green Wilkinson

20. **Vernon Hew Primrose Shaw Kennedy** of Ill. = Grace Dunlop Cummings. Their daughter, Ruth Melville Shaw Kennedy, married Albert Prime, Jr., and left a daughter, Pamela Dutton Prime, who married Tell Carroll Schreiber. T.C. Schreiber, Jr., stage actor and director, son of these last, married Heather Milgram and is the father of actor (Isaac) Liev Schreiber, husband of actress Naomi Watts (see 18 July 1890, Traverse City, Mich. birth record of Ruth Shaw Kennedy, 1911 Yale College classbooks [for William Albert Prime, Jr.], *Brooklyn Daily Eagle* of 15 Nov. 1936, p. 6B, column 1, which identifies Mrs. Tell C. Schreiber as Pamela Prime, and identifies her parents), plus Internet sources, including Wikipedia, for Tell C., Jr., and (Isaac) Liev Schreiber.

12. Mary Cholmley (sister of Sir Richard) = Hon. Henry Fairfax

13. Henry Fairfax, 4th Baron Fairfax = Frances Barwick

14. Thomas Fairfax, 5th Baron Fairfax = Catherine Colepepper (Culpeper), daughter of Thomas Colepepper (Culpeper), 2nd Baron Colepepper (Culpeper), colonial governor of Va., ARD, SETH, and Margaret van Hesse

15. **Thomas Fairfax, 6th Baron Fairfax** (1692-1781) of Va., proprietor of the Northern Neck of Virginia, d. unm.

14. Hon. Henry Fairfax (brother of the 5th Baron Fairfax) = Anne Harrison

15. **William Fairfax** of Va., governor of the Bahamas, president of the Colonial Council of Va. = (1) Sarah Walker; (2) Mrs. Deborah Clarke Gedney.

12. Barbara Cholmley (sister of Sir Richard and Mary) = Thomas Belasyse, 1st Viscount Fauconberg

13. Hon. Henry Belasyse = Grace Barton

14. Arabella Belasyse = Sir William Frankland, 1st Bt.

The Royal Descents of 900 Immigrants

15. Sir Thomas Frankland, 2nd Bt. = Elizabeth Russell, granddaughter of Oliver Cromwell, the Lord Protector
16. Henry Frankland, Governor of Bengal = Mary Cross
17. Sir Charles Henry Frankland, 4th Bt., British consular officer = **Agnes Surriage, known as Lady Agnes Surriage Frankland** (1726-1783), Boston, Mass., social leader.

17. Sir Thomas Frankland, 5th Bt., admiral (brother of Sir C.H.) = Sarah Rhett of S.C.
18. Charlotte Frankland = Robert Nicholas
19. Harriet Nicholas = Henry Theodosius Browne Collier, admiral
20. Gertrude Barbara Rich Collier = Charles Tennant
21. **Dorothy Tennant** = (1) Sir Henry Morton **Stanley** (1841-1904), the journalist and African explorer, long an American resident; (2) Henry **Curtis**.

13. Barbara Belasyse (sister of Hon. Henry) = Sir Henry Slingsby, 1st Bt.
14. Barbara Slingsby = Sir John Talbot
15. Anne Talbot = Sir John Ivory

16. John Ivory Talbot = Mary Mansel
16. Barbara Ivory = Henry Davenport
17. Martha Talbot = 17. William Davenport

18. Mary Davenport = John Shakespear
19. Henry Davenport Shakespear = Louisa Caroline Tobin Muirson
20. Alexander Shakespear = Catherine Mary Tayler
21. Henry Hope Shakespear = Olivia Tucker, daughter of Henry Tod(d) Tucker (and Maria Johnson), son of John Coulston Price Tucker (and Anne Mulcaster), son of Henry Tucker III and Frances Bruere, SETH

22. **Dorothy Shakespear**, sometime of Washington, D.C. = Ezra Loomis **Pound** (1885-1972), the poet

10. Everilda Constable (sister of Sir Marmaduke and Barbara) = Thomas Crathorne
11. Katherine Crathorne = Ralph Creyke
12. Ralph Creyke = Margaret Thornborough
13. Katherine Creyke = James Boyd, 9th Baron Boyd
14. William Boyd, 1st Earl of Kilmarnock = Jean Cuninghame
15. William Boyd, 2nd Earl of Kilmarnock = Lettice Boyd
16. William Boyd, 3rd Earl of Kilmarnock = Euphemia Ross
17. William Boyd, 4th Earl of Kilmarnock = Agnes Livingston
18. James Boyd, later Hay, 15th Earl of Erroll = Isabel Carr
19. William Hay, 17th Earl of Erroll = Jane Bell
20. Dulcibella Jane Hay = Charles Nourse Wodehouse, son of Philip Wodehouse and Apollonia Nourse, SETH
21. James Hay Wodehouse = Annette Fanny Massey
22. **Ernest Hay Wodehouse** (1869-1957) of Hawaii, business executive = Mary Augusta Ward.
22. **Amy Dulcibella Wodehouse** of Hawaii = Louis **von Tempski**. Their daughter, Armine von Tempski (who married Alfred L. Ball), was a noted writer on Hawaii.

Sources: *Exeter*, tables II, XLVII, XLIX, LII, pp. 2, 52, 54, 56, 549-550, 554, *NEHGR* 148 (1994):130-40 and sources cited therein (Nelsons, by Douglas Richardson) and Christopher Challender Child [and Julie Helen Otto], *The Nelson Family of Rowley, Massachusetts* (2014), pp. 59-64, 445-563, 593-603 and endpapers; *BRMF1*: 479-82 (Wyvill), *CB* (Beckwith of Aldborough, Wyvill of Constable Burton), *LDBR* 2:532-33 and G.H.S. King, *Marriages of Richmond County, Virginia, 1668-1853* (1964), pp. 13-14 (Beckwith); tables LII and pp. 558-59 (Howard), *BP*

The Royal Descents of 900 Immigrants

(Norfolk), *WWA* (W.T. Baker) and Franz V. Recum, *The Families of Warren and Johnson of Warrenstown, County Meath* (1950, for Shedden and Riggs); tables XLVII, LIV, LVIII, LIX, pp. 52, 58, 63, 64, 627, 629 and *BP* (Elphinstone-Dalrymple, baronets); table LIX, pp. 64, 631, James Paterson, *History of the Counties of Ayr and Wigton*, vol. 2, *Carrick* (1864), pp. 145-47 (McAdam), 281 (Kennedy, Shaw) and John and J.B. Burke, *The Royal Families of England, Scotland, and Wales, with Their Descendants*, vol. 1 (1851), pedigree 73 (Cholmley to J.L. McAdam); *Oxford DNB* (McAdam, Sir James Shaw Kennedy), A.O. Cummings, *Cummings Genealogy: Isaac Cummings, 1601-1677, of Ipswich in 1638 and Some of His Descendants* (1904), p. 400, *TG*, 1st ser., 4 (1880): 141-44 and *CB* (Whiteford), *SP* and *CP* (Cathcart); table LXIII, p. 68, and *CP* and *BP* (Fairfax) (two Fairfaxes); tables LVIII, LX, pp. 63, 65, *CB* and *BP* (Frankland, baronets) and *DAB* (Lady A.S. Frankland); table LX, pp. 65, 635-36, *SCG* 4:3-4, 9 (Rhett, Frankland, Nicholas, Collier), *MGH*, new ser., 3 (1878-80): 129 (Collier, Tennant) and *BLG* (Coombe Tennant of Cadoxton) (Lady H.M. Stanley); tables LX, LXII, pp. 65, 67, 651, 654-55 (to Henry D. Shakespear), Lt. Col. John Shakespear, *John Shakespear of Shadwell and His Descendants, 1619-1931* (1931), pp. 80, 139-43, 259-60, 373, 381 and chart at end (to Mrs. Pound) and Robert Dennard Tucker, *Descendants of William Tucker of Throwleigh, Devon* (1991), pp. 196-98, 246-47; tables XLVII, LXVI, pp. 52, 71, 680, 682-83 (to E.H. and Amy D. Wodehouse, with the husband of the latter given as Louis von Tunpsky), *BP* (Kimberley) and *WWWA*, vol. 7, *1977-1981* (1981), p. 622 (E.H. Wodehouse), vol. 2, *1943-1950* (1950), p. 549 (Armine von Tempski). Several nieces, nephews, great-nephews or great-nieces lived or now live in the U.S.; see *BP* (Kimberley). The descent of V.H.P. Shaw Kennedy was developed by George Larson and brought to my attention by John C. Brandon. Some American Shaw Kennedy, Prime and Schreiber research was undertaken by Julie Helen Otto.

Pages 445-463 of the above-cited Nelson genealogy contains an AT for Philip Stapleton at 12 above for 13 generations, with descent from many other couples in this work, especially Sir William Mallory and Jane Norton (AT #s 10-11) and Sir Robert Greystock and Elizabeth Grey (AT #s 62-63).

The Royal Descents of 900 Immigrants

1. Edward III, King of England, d. 1377 = Philippa of Hainault
2. Lionel of Antwerp, Duke of Clarence = Elizabeth de Burgh
3. Philippa Plantagenet = Edmund Mortimer, 3rd Earl of March
4. Roger Mortimer, 4th Earl of March = Eleanor Holand
5. Anne Mortimer = Richard Plantagenet, Earl of Cambridge, son of Edmund of Langley, 1st Duke of York (and Isabel of Castile), son of Edward III, King of England, and Philippa of Hainault, above
6. Richard Plantagenet, 3rd Duke of York = Cecily Neville, daughter of Ralph Neville, 1st Earl of Westmoreland and Joan Beaufort, SETH
7. Anne Plantagenet, sister of Kings Edward IV (d. 1483) and Richard III (d. 1485) = Sir Thomas St. Leger
8. Anne St. Leger = George Manners, Baron Ros
9. Margaret Manners = Sir Henry Strangways
10. Sir Giles Strangways = Joan Wadham
11. John Strangways = Dorothy Thynne
12. Grace Strangways = Edmund Chamberlayne
13. Edmund Chamberlayne = Eleanor Colles
14. **Thomas Chamberlayne** of Va. = (1) Mary Wood; (2) Elizabeth Stratton.
14. **Dorothy Chamberlayne** of S.C. = Robert **Daniell**, colonial governor of S.C.

Sources: *Exeter*, tables II, LXIX, pp. 2, 74, J.P. Rylands, ed., *Visitation of Dorset, 1623* (*HSPVS*, vol. 25, 1885), pp. 86-87 (Strangways), T.F. Fenwick and W.C. Metcalfe, eds., *Visitation of the County of Gloucester, 1682-1683* (1884), pp. 37-38 (where, however, Dorothy Chamberlayne is said to have married "Edward Ridley, Steward to the Duke of Somerset"), and *Wilson*, pp. 4-5, 8-25 (esp. chart opp. p. 20) (Chamberlayne and Mrs. Daniell).

The Royal Descents of 900 Immigrants

1. Edward III, King of England, d. 1377 = Philippa of Hainault
2. Lionel of Antwerp, Duke of Clarence = Elizabeth de Burgh
3. Philippa Plantagenet = Edmund Mortimer, 3rd Earl of March
4. Roger Mortimer, 4th Earl of March = Eleanor Holand
5. Anne Mortimer = Richard Plantagenet, Earl of Cambridge, son of Edmund of Langley, 1st Duke of York (and Isabel of Castile), son of Edward III, King of England, and Philippa of Hainault, above
6. Isabel Plantagenet = Henry Bourchier, Count of Eu, 1st Earl of Essex, son of William Bourchier, Count of Eu, and Anne Plantagenet, SETH
7. William Bourchier, Viscount Bourchier = Anne Woodville, sister of Elizabeth Woodville, Queen of Edward IV
8. Cecily Bourchier = John Devereux, 2nd Baron Ferrers of Chartley
9. Walter Devereux, 1st Viscount Hereford = (1) Mary Grey; (2) Margaret Garneys
10. (by 1) Sir Richard Devereux = Dorothy Hastings
11. Walter Devereux, 1st Earl of Essex = Lettice Knollys, former wife of Robert Dudley, 1st Earl of Leicester, early favorite of Elizabeth I and daughter of Sir Francis Knollys and Catherine Cary, SETH
12. Robert Devereux, 2nd Earl of Essex, favorite of Elizabeth I, leader of "Essex's Rebellion" = Frances Walsingham
13. Dorothy Devereux = Sir Henry Shirley, 2nd Bt.
14. Sir Robert Shirley, 4th Bt. = Catherine Okeover
15. Robert Shirley, 1st Earl Ferrers = Selina Finch
16. Mary Shirley = Charles Tryon
17. **William Tryon** (1729-1788), colonial governor of N.C. and N.Y. = Margaret Wake.

The Royal Descents of 900 Immigrants

16. George Shirley (brother of Mary) = Mary Sturt
17. Evelyn Shirley = Phyllis Byam Wollaston
18. Emily Harriet Shirley = Edward Harbord, 2nd Baron Suffield
19. Ralph Harbord = Elizabeth Pole Schenley
20. Edward Ralph Harbord = Anne Elizabeth Riley-Smith
21. Dorothy Primrose Harbord = Edward d'Abo
22. Michael David (Mike) d'Abo, musician, sometime with the rock band Manfred Mann = Margaret Evelyn Lyndon
23. **Olivia (Jane) d'Abo**, b. 1969, sometime of Calif., actress, singer and songwriter = Patrick Raymond Leonard, American musician.

12. Penelope Devereux (sister of the 2nd Earl of Essex) = Robert Rich, 1st Earl of Warwick
13. Robert Rich, 2nd Earl of Warwick = Frances Hatton
14. Anne Rich = Edward Montagu, 2nd Earl of Manchester
15. Robert Montagu, 3rd Earl of Manchester = Anne Yelverton
16. Charles Montagu, 1st Duke of Manchester = Doddington Greville
17. Robert Montagu, 3rd Duke of Manchester = Harriet Dunch
18. **Lord Charles Greville Montagu**, colonial governor of S.C. = Elizabeth Bulmer.

13. Henry Rich, 1st Earl of Holland (brother of the 2nd Earl of Warwick) = Isabel Cope
14. Frances Rich = William Paget, 6th Baron Paget
15. Frances Paget = Rowland Hunt
16. Thomas Hunt = Jane Ward
17. Thomas Hunt = Sarah Witts

The Royal Descents of 900 Immigrants

18. Sarah Hunt = Joseph Sabine

19. Diana Amelia Sabine = William Baring-Gould

20. Sabine Baring-Gould, antiquarian = Grace Taylor. Their son, Edward Sabine Baring-Gould, also immigrated to Minnesota, married Marian Darragh Linton and left issue but no NDTPS.

21. **William Drake Baring-Gould** of Minneapolis, Minnesota = Harriet R. Stuart. Their son, Sherlock Holmes authority William Stuart Baring-Gould, married Ceil Moody and was the father of Judith A. Baring-Gould, wife of Adolphus Busch Orthwein, Jr., now of Atlanta, sportsman and developer, sometime college roommate of the author (at Yale, 1962-63), great-nephew of August Anheuser "Gussie" Busch, longtime head of Anheuser-Busch, and great-great-grandson of Adolphus Busch, the brewery's founder.

12. Dorothy Devereux (sister of the 2nd Earl of Essex and the Countess of Warwick) = Sir Thomas Perrott, son of Sir John Perrott (and Anne Cheyney), now known not to be an illegitimate son of Henry VIII, King of England, d. 1547, by Mary Berkeley, wife of Sir Thomas Perrott, Sir John's father (see p. 233 herein and *Oxford DNB* 43: 810, 815)

13. Penelope Perrott = Sir William Lower

14. Dorothy Lower = Sir Maurice Drummond

15. Henrietta Maria Drummond = Robert Middlemore

16. Mary Middlemore = Sir John Gage, 4th Bt.

17. Mary Gage = Sir John Shelley, 3rd Bt.

18. Richard Shelley = Mary Fleetwood

19. Frances Shelley = James Best

20. George Best = Caroline Scott

21. Dorothy Best = Joseph George Brett

22. William Baliol Brett, 1st Viscount Esher = Eugénie Mayer

The Royal Descents of 900 Immigrants

23. Reginald Baliol Brett, 2nd Viscount Esher, army reformer and diplomat, friend of Edward VII, King of Great Britain = Eleanor Frances Weston Van de Weyer

24. **Hon. Dorothy Eugénie Brett** (1883-1977) of Taos, N.M., artist, patroness, friend of the novelist D.H. Lawrence, d. unm.

24. Hon. Sylvia Leonora Brett, known as H.H. The Ranee of Sarawak = H.H. Sir Charles Vyner Brooke, last Rajah of Sarawak

25. **Elizabeth Brooke** of Fla. = (1) Harry **Roy** (1904-1971), bandleader; (2) Richard **Vidmer**.

11. Elizabeth Devereux (sister of the 1st Earl of Essex) = Sir John Vernon

12. Elizabeth Vernon = Henry Wriothesley, 3rd Earl of Southampton

13. Penelope Wriothesley = William Spencer, 2nd Baron Spencer

14. Alice Spencer = Henry Moore, 1st Earl of Drogheda

15. Henry Moore, 3rd Earl of Drogheda = Mary Cole

16. Elizabeth Moore = George Rochfort

17. Thomasina Rochfort = Gustavus Lambart

18. Charles Lambart = Frances Dutton

19. Frances Thomasine Lambart = Charles Talbot, 2nd Earl Talbot

20. Gerard Chetwynd-Talbot = Margaret Mackay

21. Charles Alexander Price Chetwynd-Talbot = Maud Fleming

22. **Matilda Charlotte Palgrave Chetwynd-Talbot** of Mass. = Augustus Neal **Rantoul** (1865-1934), architect.

10. (by 1) Sir William Devereux (brother of Sir Richard) = Jane Scudamore

11. Margaret Devereux = Sir Edward Littleton

12. Margaret Littleton = Richard Skinner

13. Margaret Skinner = Thomas Joliffe

The Royal Descents of 900 Immigrants

14. Benjamin Joliffe = Mary Joliffe, a cousin
15. Anne Joliffe = Robert Biddulph
16. Michael Biddulph = Penelope Dandridge
17. John Biddulph = Augusta Roberts
18. Mary Anne Biddulph = Robert Martin
19. John Biddulph Martin = **Mrs. Victoria Claflin Woodhull Blood, known as Mrs. Victoria Claflin Woodhull** (1838-1927) of N.Y., spiritualist, suffragette, American presidential candidate of the Equal Rights Party in 1892 [she = (1) Canning Woodhull and (2) James H. Blood].

10. (by 2) Sir Edward Devereux, 1st Bt. (half-brother of Sir Richard and Sir William) = Catherine Arden
11. Anne Devereux = Robert Leighton
12. Edward Leighton = Abigail Stephens
13. Robert Leighton = Gertrude Baldwin
14. Abigail Leighton = Basil Wood
15. Basil Wood = Elizabeth Richards. A son, Leighton Wood, was the father (possibly by Elizabeth ——) of Leighton Wood, auditor and solicitor-general of Va., who married and left issue but no NDTPS.
16. Basil Wood = Sarah Bond
17. Mary Wood = Joseph Wilson
18. **Leighton Wilson** of Ga. = (1) Anne Adams; (2) Sarah Adams.

Sources: *Essex*, tables I-III, pp. 1-4, *DNB* and *DAB* (William Tryon); tables II, III, pp. 2-4, 43, 45, 48 (to E.R. Harboard), *BP* (Suffield), *BLG*, 18th ed., vol. 1 (1965), p. 182 (d'Abo) and Wikipedia entries for Mike and Olivia d'Abo; tables II, VIII, pp. 2, 9, 103 and *BP* (Manchester, for Lord C.G. Montagu); tables VIII, IX, pp. 9-11, 124, 126-27, *BLG* 18th ed., vol. 3 (1972), pp. 387-88, 1958 Minnesota death record (#020676) of Mrs. Harriet Stuart Baring-Gould, plus Hennepin County, Minnesota, census data, 1870-1930 (under Thomas or Estelle Stewart/Stuart, Platt B.

The Royal Descents of 900 Immigrants

Walker, and William D. Baring-Gould), *N.Y. Times* obituary (12 Aug. 1967, 25:5) of W.S. Baring-Gould, plus recent social registers (A.B. Orthwein); table II, p. 2, *DNB* (Sir John Perrott and Sir Robert Naunton), *VC,* p. 300 (Lower, Drummond), W.P.W. Phillimore and W.F. Carter, *Some Account of the Family of Middlemore of Warwickshire and Worcestershire* (1901), pp. 68-69, *BP* (Gage, Shelley [baronets] and Esher), *BLG*, 18th ed., vol. 3 (1972), pp. 120-21 (Brooke of Sarawak), *BLG* 1937, pp. 149-50 (Best, now Best-Davison of Park House) and *RLNGF* 1:74 (Shelley, Best) (Hon. D.E. Brett, Mrs. Roy); tables II, XI, XV, pp. 2, 13, 17, 217, 220-22 (to Mrs. Rantoul), *WWWA*, vol. 4, *1961-1968* (1968), p. 777 and *BP* (Shrewsbury); tables II, XVII, XXVIII, pp. 2, 19, 30, 342, 345, and *BLG* 1937, p. 1541 (Martin late of Ledbury) (J.B. Martin); tables XXIX, XXXI, pp. 31, 33, 376-77 and *TG* 16 (2002): 68-70 (1st Viscount Hereford via Leighton Wilson to Brice McAdoo Clagett) and sources cited therein.

The Royal Descents of 900 Immigrants

1. Ferdinand I, King of Aragón, first King of united Spain, d. 1516 = (1) Isabella I, Queen of Castile, first Queen of united Spain; (2) Germaine (Germana) de Foix

2. (illegitimate by Aldonza Ruíz de Alemany) Alonzo de Aragón, Archbishop of Zaragoza

3. (illegitimate by Ana de Gurrea) Ana de Aragón = Juan Alonzo Pérez de Guzmán, 6th Duke of Medina-Sidonia (a son, Juan Carlos de Guzmán, Count of Niebla, married Eleanor de Zuñiga y Sotomayor and was the father of Alfonso Pérez de Guzmán y Sotomayor, 7th Duke of Medina-Sidonia, the admiral who led the Spanish Armada, see below, and married Ana de Silva y Mendoza)

4. Ana de Guzmán y Aragón = Íñigo Fernández de Velasco, 4th Duke of Frias

5. Juan Fernández de Velasco, 5th Duke of Frias = (1) María Girón de Guzmán; (2) Juana Fernández de Córdova y Aragón. By (1) he was the father of Ana de Velasco y Girón, wife of Teodosio (Theodore) II, Duke of Braganza, and mother of John IV, King of Portugal. This last married Luisa Francisca de Guzmán, daughter of Juan Manuel Domingo de Guzmán y Silva, 8th Duke of Medina-Sidonia (and Juana de Sándoval y Rojas), son of the above 7th Duke of Medina-Sidonia and Ana de Silva y Mendoza.

6. (by 2) Bernardino Fernández de Velasco, 6th Duke of Frias = Isabel de Guzmán

7. Íñigo Melchior Fernández de Velasco, 8th Duke of Frias = María Teresa de Benavides

8. (illegitimate by María de la Torre) Francisco de Velasco = ——

9. (illegitimate by ——) María Francisca de Velasco = Isidro Casado de Acevedo y del Mazo, 1st Marquess of Monteleón, son of Pedro Casado de Acevedo y Rosales and María Teresa Martínez del Mazo y Velásquez, daughter of Juan Bautista Martínez del Mazo and Francisca Velásquez, daughter of Diego Rodríguez de Silva y Velásquez, the Spanish painter (of the court of Philip IV, King of Spain) and Juana Pacheco de Miranda

10. Antonio Casado de Acevedo y Velasco, 3rd Marquess de Monteleón = Margareta Huguetan, Countess of Gyldensteen

The Royal Descents of 900 Immigrants

11. Enriqueta (Henrietta) Juana Francisca Susanna de Casado y Huguetan = Henry VI, Count Reuss-Köstritz. Their daughter, Friederike Luise Sophie, Countess Reuss-Köstritz, married John Christian II, Count of Solms-Baruth; their daughter, Amalie Henriette Charlotte, Countess of Solms-Baruth, married Charles Louis, Prince of Hohenlohe-Langenburg, SETH. This last couple are ancestors of the current Kings of Spain, Sweden, The Netherlands, and the Belgians, plus the Grand Duke of Luxembourg and Sovereign Prince of Liechtenstein.

12. Henry XLVIII, Count Reuss-Köstritz = Christiane Henriette Antonie of Schönberg-Wechselburg, see below

13. (Ernestine) Adelaide, Countess Reuss-Köstritz = Ernst Philip von Kiesenwetter

14. **Irmgard von Kiesenwetter** of N.Y. = **Friedrich Ernst Sigismund Kamill von Egloffstein**, known as **Frederick W. Egloffstein** (1824-1885), explorer, mapmaker and engraver (esp. of the Gunnison or "Grand River," now in Colorado, engravings long thought, erroneously, to be of the Grand Canyon), of various U.S. cities, lastly New York, 1846-78, SETH. A son was sometime of Davenport, Iowa, where his own two sons were born.

Since the above line (developed and brought to my attention by John Blythe Dobson of Winnipeg, Manitoba, Canada, after Egloffstein was himself brought to my attention by Julie Helen Otto) passes through four illegitimacies I outline below Irmgard von Kiesenwetter's descent from Christian, Count of Waldeck-Wildungen and Elizabeth of Nassau-Siegen. Christian was a descendant of John I, King of Denmark, d. 1513, and Margaret of Saxony, as shown on the following chart for Friedrich W.L.G.A., Baron von Steuben, and Elizabeth of Nassau was a great-niece of William the Silent, first Stadholder of The Netherlands, as also shown on the von Steuben chart.

6. (from John I, King of Denmark, d. 1513) Christian, Count of Waldeck-Wildungen = Elizabeth of Nassau-Siegen

7. Maria Magdalena of Waldeck-Wildungen = Simon VII, Count of Lippe-Detmold

The Royal Descents of 900 Immigrants

8. Sophie Elizabeth of Lippe-Detmold = George William, Count of Leiningen-Westerburg-Schaumburg

9. Sophia Magdalena of Leiningen-Westerburg = Otto Louis, Count of Schönburg-Hartenstein

9. Joanna Elizabeth of Leiningen-Westerburg = George Hermann Reinhard von Runkel, Count of Wied

10. George Albert, Count of Schönburg-Hartenstein = 10. Sophie Sabine of Wied

11. Joanna Sophie Elizabeth of Schönburg-Harteinstein = Francis Henry, Count of Schönburg-Wechselburg

12. Charles Henry, Count of Schönburg-Wechselburg = Christiane Wilhelmine, Countess von Einsiedel

13. Christiane Henriette Antonie of Schönburg-Wechselburg = Henry XLVIII, Count Reuss-Köstritz, see above

Sources: *GH des A*, vol. 30 (*Freiherrliche Häuser, A*, vol. 5 [1963], pp. 62-63 (Egloffstein) and *ES* 2: 1: 3: 364 (Reuss-Köstritz), 2: 4: 154 (Schönburg-Wechselburg), 2: 4: 147 (Schönburg-Hardenstein), 2: 29: 77 (Wied), 2: 29: 73 (Leiningen-Westerburg), plus charts for Lippe, Waldeck and Nassau-Siegen); *NEHGS NEXUS* 14 (1997): 204-6 and sources cited therein (descent from Velásquez); Leo Lindemans, *Voorouderstafel van het Belgisch Koningshuis/Tableau d'Ascendance de la Maison Royale Belge/Ahnentafel des Belgischen Königshauses* (1998), #s 182-83, 766-67, 1532-33, 3064-67, 6130-35, 12262-65, 704-5, 1408-11, 2818-19, 5636-37, 11274-11275, 2820-21, 5640-41, 12280-81 (descent from Velásquez, kinship to Medina-Sidonia of the Armada and Kings of Portugal, and generations 2-11); Alonzo López de Haro, *Nobiliario Genealógico de los Reyes y Títulos de España* (1622), pp. 188-91 (Velasco, generations 4-6 and both wives of the 5th Duke of Frias); Johann Lanz, *Die 64 Ahnen der Katharina von Braganza, Königin von England*, in *Charles Evans*, pp. 94-114 (generations 1-5, Medina-Sidonia and John IV, King of Portugal, and his wife). Otto Louis and Sophia Magdalena at generation 9 of the second descent are ancestors K 879-80 in *Prince Charles* and as suggested above, and Henry VI and Enriqueta at generation 11 in the first descent are ancestors #382-83 of Kings Baudouin and Albert II of the Belgians.

The Royal Descents of 900 Immigrants

1. James IV, King of Scotland, d. 1513 = Margaret Tudor of England

2. (illegitimate by Margaret Drummond) Margaret Stewart = Sir John Drummond of Innerpeffry

2. (illegitimate by Agnes Stewart, Countess of Bothwell) Joan Stewart = Malcolm Fleming, 3rd Baron Fleming

3. Agnes Drummond = Hugh Montgomery, 3rd Earl of Eglinton

3. Agnes Fleming = William Livingston, 6th Baron Livingston

4. Margaret Montgomery = Robert Seton, 1st Earl of Winton

4. Alexander Livingston, 1st Earl of Linlithgow = Eleanor Hay, see note below

5. Alexander Montgomery, = 6th Earl of Eglinton (heir of his maternal grandfather)

5. Anne Livingston

6. Hugh Montgomery, 7th Earl of Eglinton = Mary Leslie

7. Margaret Montgomery = James Campbell, 2nd Earl of Loudoun

8. Hugh Campbell, 3rd Earl of Loudoun = Margaret Dalrymple

9. **John Campbell, 4th Earl of Loudoun** (1705-1782), British commander in America during the French and Indian War, d. unm.

7. Alexander Montgomery, 8th Earl of Eglinton (brother of the Countess of Loudoun) = Elizabeth Crichton, daughter of William Crichton, 2nd Earl of Dumphries (and Elizabeth Swift), son of William Crichton, 1st Earl of Dumphries (and Elizabeth Seton), son of William Crichton (and Catherine Carmichael), son of William Crichton, 5th Baron Crichton and Elizabeth Fleming, daughter of Malcolm Fleming, 3rd Baron Fleming and Joan Stewart, above.

8. Alexander Montgomery, 9th Earl of Eglinton = Margaret Cochrane

9. Euphemia Montgomery = George Lockhart of Carnwath

The Royal Descents of 900 Immigrants

10. George Lockhart of Carnwath = Fergusia Wishart

11. Sir James Lockhart-Wishart (1st Count of Lockhart in the Holy Roman Empire) = Annabella Crawford

12. Mariana Matilda Lockhart-Wishart = Anthony Aufrere

11. **Louisa Anna (or Louise Ann) Matilda Aufrere** of N.Y. = George **Barclay**. Matilda Antonia Barclay, their daughter, married Francis Robert Rives and was the mother of George Lockhart Rives, lawyer, historian, public official and trustee and board chairman or president of Columbia College/University and the New York Public Library, who married Caroline Maria King and Mrs. Sara Whiting Belmont.

8. Mary Montgomery (sister of the 9th Earl of Eglinton) = Sir James Agnew, 4th Bt.

9. James Agnew of Howlish = Elizabeth Wilkinson

10. James Agnew of Howlish = Elizabeth Saunders

11. Robert Agnew = Catherine Blennerhasset, daughter of Conway Blennerhasset and Elizabeth Lacy, ARD, SETH

12. **Margaret Agnew** of Va. = her uncle, Harman **Blennerhasset** (1765-1831) of Va., ARD, SETH, adventurer and "Western Empire" associate of Aaron Burr.

12. Elizabeth Agnew (sister of Margaret) = Austin Martin

13. Henry James Martin = Mary McLean

14. **Henry Austin Martin** (1824-1884) of Mass., surgeon = Frances Coffin Crosby.

9. Sir Andrew Agnew, 5th Bt. (brother of James of Howlish) = Eleanor Agnew, a cousin

10. Mary Agnew = Sir Michael Bruce, 6th Bt.

11. Sir William Bruce, 7th Bt. = Anne Colquhoun Fairlie

12. William Cunningham Bruce = Jane Catherine Clark

13. Sir William Cunningham Bruce, 9th Bt. = Charlotte Isabella O'Grady
14. Sir William Waller Bruce, 10th Bt. = Angelica Mary Selby
15. **(William) Nigel (Ernle) Bruce** (1895-1953), of Calif., actor (Dr. Watson in Sherlock Holmes films, also in first full Technicolor and first 3-D movies) = Violet Pauline Shelton, British actress as Violet Campbell.

Sources: *SP* and *CP* (Loudoun, Eglinton, Winton, Linlithgow, Livingston, Fleming, Hay, Lennox, Dumphries, Crichton) (4th Earl of Loudoun); *MP*, table XI, pp. 12, 185, *BP* 1898, pp. 914-15, and *NEXUS* 8 (1991): 150 (Mrs. Barclay); *DAB* (H.A. Martin) and Joseph Foster, *The Royal Lineage of Our Noble and Gentle Families, Together with Their Paternal Ancestry*, vol. 4 (1887), pp. 586-89, 593a-94 (Neville-Throckmorton-Lynne-Blennerhasset-Agnew-Martin descents), and *Oxford DNB* (Nigel Bruce), *BP*, 107th ed. (2003), pp. 47, 547-48, 550-51 and *CB* (Agnew of Lucknow, Bruce of Stenhouse), *BP* or *CP* (Eglinton, Dumfries, Crichton). Mary Agnew, a sister of Margaret and Elizabeth, married Edward Stafford; their son, Bulkeley Buckingham Stafford, married Anne Tyler and was the father of Sir Edward William Stafford, Prime Minister of New Zealand. Eleanor Hay, at generation 4, was a daughter of Andrew Hay, 8th Earl of Erroll, and Jean Hay, and a granddaughter of George Hay, 7th Earl of Erroll and Margaret Robertson, SETH, and of William Hay, 6th Earl of Erroll (brother of the 7th Earl) and Helen Stewart, daughter of John Stewart, 3rd Earl of Lennox and Anne Stewart, also SETH. Thus Eleanor Hay had legitimate descents from daughters of both James II and James I, Kings of Scotland. The parentage of Nigel Bruce was brought to my attention by Julie Helen Otto.

The Royal Descents of 900 Immigrants

1. James IV, King of Scotland, d. 1513 = Margaret Tudor of England
2. (illegitimate by Agnes Stewart, Countess of Bothwell) Joan Stewart = Malcolm Fleming, 3rd Baron Fleming
3. Margaret Fleming = John Stewart, 4th Earl of Atholl
4. Jean Stewart = Sir Duncan Campbell, 1st Bt.
5. Sir Robert Campbell, 3rd Bt. = Isabel Mackintosh, daughter of Lachlan Mackintosh of Mackintosh and Agnes Mackenzie of Kintail, SETH.
6. Jean Campbell = Archibald Campbell of Glenlyon
7. Margaret Campbell = Donald Glas McGregor of Glengyle
8. Robert McGregor or Campbell, the celebrated highland freebooter "Rob Roy," of Inversnaid = Mary McGregor of Comermore
9. James (took surname) Drummond of Innervonchell = Annabella McNicoll
10. John (resumed surname) McGregor of P.E.I. = Margaret McGregor
11. James McGregor = Jane Brown
12. **Charles Russell McGregor**, later **Gregor**, of N.Y. = Hester Ann Gregory. Their son, Elmer Russell Gregor (1878-1954), who married Ida M. Frame, was a noted author of Indian stories and pioneer of the outdoor camping movement that led to the Boy Scouts of America.

11. Margaret McGregor (sister of James), illegitimately by Benjamin McEwen
12. Benjamin McEwen, Jr. = Mary Ann Robinson
11. **John William McEwen** of Me. = Matilda Sarah Robinson, a cousin. Their son, Benjamin Beecher McEwen, married Mary Emma Coles, also a cousin, and left a son, Maynard Leslie MacEwen, who married Aimee Maxine Barnes and was the

father of Andrew Brian Wendover MacEwen (1939-2015), noted Scottish genealogist, late of Stockton Springs, Me.

6. Isabella Campbell (sister of Jean) = Sir James Campbell of Ardkinglass
7. Robert Campbell of Orchard = Jean Campbell of Ardentinny
8. John Campbell of Orchard = Anne Campbell of Kinochtree
9. Anne Campbell of Orchard = George Wishart
10. Jane Wishart of Pittarow = Christian Heinrich Philip, Baron von Westphalen
11. Johann Ludwig, Baron von Westphalen = Caroline Heubel
12. Johanna (Jenny) Bertha Julie von Westphalen = Karl Marx (1818-1883), founder of socialism, author of "A Communist Manifesto"

Sources: Research by the late Andrew B.W. MacEwen in Maine and P.E.I. esp., *WWWA*, vol. 3, *1951-1960* (1960), p. 346 (E.R. Gregor), plus, among printed Scottish sources, A.G.M. MacGregor, *History of the Clan Gregor,* vol. 2 (1901), pp. 256-58, 273-81, 335-38, *The Scottish Antiquary* 7 (1892-93): 43, 88, 93, 94 (McGregor, Campbell of Glenlyon), Duncan Campbell, *The Lairds of Glenlyon* (1886), and *SP*, *CB* or *CP* (Breadalbane [and Campbell of Glenorchy, baronets], Atholl, Fleming [under Wigtown in *SP*]). See also W.H. Murray, *Rob Roy MacGregor, His Life and Times* (1982), pp. xiv, 1-26, 264-68, 279 esp., and Donald Whyte, *A Dictionary of Scottish Emigrants to Canada Before Confederation* (1886), pp. 231-32, entries for John McGregor (1745-16 Feb. 1832), and his wife, Margaret McGregor (1760-1844). For Mrs. Marx see *NK1*: 45-47, 52-54, and sources cited therein, esp. G. Harvey Johnston, *The Heraldry of the Campbells*, vol. 2 (1921), pp. 55-56 (Glenurchy), 13 (Ardkinglass), 21 (Orchard), *Transactions of the Royal Historical Society*, 1st ser., 4 (1876): 352 esp. (in "Memoir of George Wishart, the Scottish Martyr," by Rev. Charles Rogers), *GM* 19 (1997-99): 237-41 (Wishart to Mrs. Marx) and *GH des A, Adeligen Häuser B*, vol. 12 (1977): 489-91 (Westphalen).

The Royal Descents of 900 Immigrants

1. James IV, King of Scotland, d. 1513 = Margaret Tudor of England

2. (illegitimate by Margaret Drummond) Margaret Stewart = John Gordon, Lord Gordon

3. Alexander Gordon, Bishop of the Isles and of Galloway

4. (illegitimate by Barbara Logie) John Gordon = Geneviève Petau

5. Louisa (Lucy) Gordon = Sir Robert Gordon, 1st Bt., son of Alexander Gordon, 12th Earl of Sutherland (and Jean Gordon, daughter of George Gordon, 4th Earl of Huntly, and Elizabeth Keith, SETH), son of John Gordon, 11th Earl of Sutherland and Helen Stewart, daughter of John Stewart, 3rd Earl of Lennox (and Elizabeth Stewart), son of Matthew Stewart, 2nd Earl of Lennox and Elizabeth Hamilton, daughter of James Hamilton, 1st Baron Hamilton, and Princess Mary Stewart, daughter of James II, King of Scotland, d. 1460, and Mary of Guelders

6. Katherine Gordon = David Barclay of Urie (parents of John Barclay of N.J., who = Katherine [Rescarrick?] but left no NDTPS)

7. Robert Barclay, Quaker apologist and nominal governor of East N.J. (East Jersey) = Christian Mollison.

8. David Barclay = Priscilla Freame

9. John Barclay = Susanna Willet

10. Robert Barclay = Ann Ford

11. Elizabeth Lucy Barclay = Henry Birkbeck

12. Emma Birkbeck = Georg Friedrich von Bunsen

13. **Berta von Bunsen** of Mass. = Ernest Flagg **Henderson**. Among their children was Ernest Flagg Henderson, Jr. (1897-1967), founder of the Sheraton hotel chain, who married Mary Gill Caldwell Stephens and Faryl Finn.

8. Jean Barclay (sister of David) = Alexander Forbes of Aquorthies and London

The Royal Descents of 900 Immigrants

9. Christian Forbes = William Penn (III), son of William Penn, Jr. (and Mary Jones), son of William Penn, the founder of Pennsylvania, and Gulielma Maria Springett
10. Christiana Gulielma Penn = Peter Gaskell
12. **Peter Penn-Gaskell** of Pa. = Elizabeth Edwards.

Sources: Ernest Flagg Henderson III, *Ancient, Medieval, and More Recent Ancestors of Ernest Flagg Henderson IV and Roberta Campbell Henderson*, 4 vols. (2013), which charts the full known ancestry of Mrs. Berta von Bunsen Henderson for many generations, based in part, for the above descent, on *MP*, pp. 470-71; *BLG*, Birkbeck of Westacre, Barclay of Leyden, and Barclay of Bury Hill (formerly of Mathers and Urie); *AR8*, line 252 (John Barclay of N.J.); *SP* and *CP* (Sutherland, Lennox, and Hamilton — under Arran); *GPFPGM* 2: 574-75, 579-83 and R. Burnham Moffatt, *The Barclays of New York* (1904), pp. 74-77, 222-23 (for Peter Penn-Gaskell). E.F. Henderson III was a son of E.F. Henderson, Jr. and Mary Gill Caldwell Stephens above.

The Royal Descents of 900 Immigrants

1. James IV, King of Scotland, d. 1513 = Margaret Tudor of England
2. (illegitimate by Agnes Stewart, Countess of Bothwell) Joan Stewart = Malcolm Fleming, 3rd Baron Fleming
3. Joan Fleming = David Crawford of Kerse
4. Marion Crawford = James Boswell of Auchinleck
5. David Boswell of Auchinleck = Isabel Wallace
6. Margaret Boswell = David Blair of Adamton
7. Margaret Blair = William Blair of Giffordland
8. David Blair of Giffordland = Mrs. Sarah —— Lawson
9. **Sarah Blair** of Conn. = Samuel **Watkinson**.

5. James Boswell (younger brother of David of Auchinleck) = Margaret Cunningham
6. David Boswell of Auchinleck = Anne Hamilton
7. James Boswell of Auchinleck = Elizabeth Bruce (their son, Alexander Boswell, senator of the College of Justice as Lord Auchinleck, married Euphemia Erskine and was the father of James Boswell of Auchinleck, SETH, the man of letters, traveler, and biographer of Samuel Johnson)
8. John Boswell, president of the Royal College of Physicians (Edinburgh) = Anne Cramond
9. Robert Boswell of St. Boswells = Sibella Sandeman
10. Sibella Boswell = William Egerton
11. Philip Henry Egerton = Mary Marjoribanks
12. **Graham Egerton** of Washington, D.C. = Julia Easley (their son, William Graham Egerton, married Rebecca Crenshaw White and was the father of John Walden Egerton, b. 1935, author of *The Americanization of Dixie*, etc., who married Ann Elizabeth Bleidt).

Sources: *TAG* 47 (1971): 65-69, 48 (1972):79-80 (Mrs. Watkinson); *BLG*, 18th ed., vol. 3 (1972): 80 (Boswell of Auchinleck), *BP* (Grey Egerton, baronets), and *Who's Who in America* (J.W. Egerton) (for Graham Egerton).

The Royal Descents of 900 Immigrants

1. James IV, King of Scotland, d. 1513 = Margaret Tudor of England
2. (illegitimate by Agnes Stewart, Countess of Bothwell) Joan Stewart = Malcolm Fleming, 3rd Baron Fleming
3. Margaret Fleming = Robert Graham
4. John Graham, 3rd Earl of Montrose = Jean Drummond, daughter of David Drummond, 2nd Baron Drummond, and Lilias Ruthven, SETH
5. John Graham, 4th Earl of Montrose = Margaret Ruthven, daughter of William Ruthven, 1st Earl of Gowrie, and Dorothea Stewart, daughter of Henry Stewart, 1st Baron Methven, and Janet Stewart, daughter of John Stewart, 2nd Earl of Atholl and Janet Kennedy, SETH
6. Lilias Graham = Sir John Colquhoun, 1st Bt.
7. Sir John Colquhoun, 2nd Bt. = Margaret Baillie
8. Lilias Colquhoun = Sir John Stirling of Keir
9. Lilias Stirling = John Murray of Polmais
10. Anne Murray = John Dundas of Manour
11. **James Dundas** of Pa. = Elizabeth Moore.
11. **Thomas Dundas** of Pa. = ——, sister of Mrs. Hannah Russell.

Sources: *CRLA* 8 (1941), pp. 143-44 (Dundas), Francis de Sales Dundas, *Dundas, Hesselius* (1938), pp. 15-16, 35-45, and *Douglas*, pp. 179-80 (Dundas); Andrew Ross and Francis J. Grant, eds., *Alexander Nisbet's Heraldic Plates* (1892), pp. 53-54 (with 1705 and 1681 dates for the births of Anne Murray and Lilias Stirling); William Fraser, *The Stirlings of Keir* (1858), pp. 66-68 and A.M. Sterling, *The Sterling Genealogy*, 2 vols. (1909), pp. 74-76; *BP*, 106th ed. (1999), p. 630 (Colquhoun, baronets), *SP* and *CP* (Montrose, Fleming – in *SP* under Wigtown, Drummond, Gowrie, Methven and Atholl). The Murray-Stirling-Colquhoun-Graham-Fleming descent was first developed and brought to my attention by Brice McAdoo Clagett of Friendship, Maryland.

The Royal Descents of 900 Immigrants

1. James IV, King of Scotland, d. 1513 = Margaret Tudor of England

2. (illegitimate by Agnes Stewart, Countess of Bothwell) Joan Stewart = Malcolm Fleming, 3rd Baron Fleming

3. John Fleming, 5th Baron Fleming, = Elizabeth Ross

3. Margaret Fleming = Robert Graham

4. John Graham, 3rd Earl of Montrose = Jean Drummond

4. John Fleming, 1st Earl of Wigtown = 5. Lilias Graham

5, 6. Malcolm Fleming of Gilmerton = Helen Bruce, daughter of Alexander Bruce of Cultmalundie and Jean Oliphant, daughter of Lawrence Oliphant, 4th Baron Oliphant and Margaret Hay, daughter of George Hay, 7th Earl of Erroll (and Margaret Robertson), SETH, a descendant of James I, King of Scotland, d. 1437, and Joan Beaufort.

6, 7. Jean Fleming = Adam Murray of Cardon

7, 8. William Murray of Cardon = Christian Veitch

8, 9. Christian Murray = John Wallace

9. 10. **John Wallace** of Pa. = Mary Maddox.

7, 8. Helen Murray (sister of William) = Alexander Bertram of Nisbet

8, 9. William Bertram of Nisbet = Cecilia Kennedy

9, 10. Euphemia Bertram = George Baillie of Hardington

10, 11. **Robert Baillie** of Ga. = Mary Ann Mackintosh, daughter of John Mohr Mackintosh of Ga., ARD, SETH, and Marjory Fraser.

Sources: William White Bronson, *The Inscriptions in St. Peter's Church Yard: Philadelphia* (1879), p. 24 (the immigrant John Wallace, naming his parents and maternal grandfather), Sir Bernard Burke, *Royal Descents and Pedigrees of Founders' Kin* (1864), #SVI (submitted by

The Royal Descents of 900 Immigrants

John William Wallace, the immigrant's great-grandson), *Heraldic Journal* 3 (1867): 184-86 and Rev. Charles Rogers, *The Book of Wallace* (1889), vol. 1, pp. 212-16 (Wallace); J.W. Buchan and Rev. Henry Paton, *A History of Peebleshire*, vol. 3 (1927), chart between pp. 16 and 17, p. 301 (Murray of Cardon), William Drummond, *The Genealogy of the Most Noble and Ancient House of Drummond* (1831), p. 173 (Helen Bruce), M.E. Cumming Bruce, *Family Records of the Bruces and the Cumyns* (1870), p. 337, *SP* (Wigtown, Montrose, Oliphant, Erroll); research of Paul C. Reed and Shirley Goodwin Bennett, based in part on Robert G(ranberry) Baillie, "Lives of the Baillies," mss. at the Georgia Historical Society (No. 42, item 1); American Loyalist Claims (PRO originals and Family History Library microfilms) AO 13/38-4-10 (FHL #366,734), AO 12/99/306 (FHL #1,401,491), AO 12/101/94-5 and AO 13/38; *BLG*, 11th ed. (1906), p. 118 (Bertram); Walter H. McIntosh, *McIntosh-Mackintosh: American and Canadian Lineage,* vol. 7 (1988), p. 45. The Wallace descent was noted and brought to my attention by John C. Brandon of Columbia, S.C.

The Royal Descents of 900 Immigrants

1. James IV, King of Scotland, d. 1513 = Margaret Tudor of England

2. (illegitimate by Margaret Boyd) Catherine Stewart = James Douglas, 3rd Earl of Morton

2. (illegitimate by Margaret Drummond) Margaret Stewart = John Gordon, Lord Gordon

3. Margaret Douglas = James Hamilton, 2nd Earl of Arran, Duke of Châtellerault, regent of Scotland, son of James Hamilton, 1st Earl of Arran (and Janet Beaton), son of James Hamilton, 1st Baron Hamilton, and Princess Mary Stewart, daughter of James II, King of Scotland, d. 1460, and Mary of Guelders

3. George Gordon, 4th Earl of Huntly = Elizabeth Keith

4. Anne Hamilton =

4. George Gordon, 5th Earl of Huntly

5. George Gordon, 1st Marquess of Huntly = Henrietta Stewart, daughter of Esmé Stewart, 1st Duke of Lennox, Scottish political leader, and Catherine de Balsac, SETH.

6. George Gordon, 2nd Marquess of Huntly = Anne Campbell, daughter of Archibald Campbell, 7th Earl of Argyll, and Agnes Douglas, granddaughter of Colin Campbell, 6th Earl of Argyll and Annabel or Agnes Keith and great-granddaughter of Archibald Campbell, 4th Earl of Argyll, and Margaret Graham, SETH, and of William Keith, 3rd Earl Marischal, and Margaret Keith, SETH. Their daughter Lady Catherine Gordon married John Andrew, Count Morstyn, poet and Great Treasurer of Poland. For the Polish, Russian, Austrian, French and Belgian descendants of this last couple, matrilineal great-grandparents of Stanislaus II August Poniatowski, King of Poland (1732-98, King 1764-95), ancestor of the sovereign princes of Liechtenstein since 1938, the current

The Royal Descents of 900 Immigrants

Queen Mathilde (d'Udekem d'Acoz) of the Belgians, SETH, and her children, various princes or counts Poniatowski, Czartoryski, Lubomirski, Sapieha, Potocki and Zamoyski, see *NEHGS NEXUS* 14 (1997): 157-59, 16 (1999): 202.

7. Charles Gordon, 1st Earl of Aboyne = Elizabeth Lyon
8. Charles Gordon, 2nd Earl of Aboyne = Elizabeth Lyon, a cousin
9. Helen Gordon = George Kinnaird
10. Charles Kinnaird, 6th Baron Kinnaird = Barbara Johnstone
11. Helen Kinnaird = Edmund Dana, brother of the diplomat Francis Dana, uncle of Richard Henry Dana, man of letters, and great-uncle of both Richard Henry Dana, Jr., author of *Two Years Before the Mast*, and Sophia Willard Dana, wife of George Ripley, Transcendentalist leader of Brook Farm
12. **William Pulteney Dana**, sometime of N.Y. = (1) Anne Fitzhugh of Md.; (2) Charlotte Elizabeth Bayley. His daughter (by Anne), Anne Frisbie Dana, married Daniel Holker Fitzhugh, a cousin. Among the notable descendants of these last, via FitzHugh, Ayrault, Colt and Shattuck, is John Shattuck (born Howard Francis Shattuck III), government official, diplomat, foundation executive (of the JFK Library Foundation in Boston), educator (president of the Central European University in Budapest), and author of *Freedom on Fire*, 1965 Yale classmate (and likewise in History, the Arts and Letters humanities honors major) of this work's author. See Malcolm Storer, *Annals of the Storer Family* (1927), p. 82 (Ayrault) and B.M. Larson, *Shattuck Memorials, No. II* (1977), pp. 559, 649.

6. Mary Gordon (sister of the 2nd Marquess of Huntly) = William Douglas, 1st Marquess of Douglas
7. Lucy Douglas = Robert Maxwell, 4th Earl of Nithsdale
8. Mary Maxwell = Charles Stuart, 4th Earl of Traquair
9. John Stuart, 6th Earl of Traquair = Christian Anstruther
10. **Lady Christian Stuart** of Va. = Cyrus **Griffin** (1748-1810), jurist, last president of the Continental Congress.

The Royal Descents of 900 Immigrants

4. Claud Hamilton, 1st Baron Paisley (brother of the Countess of Huntly) = Margaret Seton

5. Margaret Hamilton = William Douglas, 1st Marquess of Douglas, who = (2) Mary Gordon, above

6. Jean Douglas = John Hamilton, 1st Baron Bargeny

7. Anne Hamilton = Sir Patrick Houston, 1st Bt.

8. Patrick Houston = Isabel Johnstone

9. **Sir Patrick Houston, 5th Bt.**, president of the colonial council of Ga. = Priscilla Dunbar.

Sources: E.E. Dana, *The Dana Family in America* (1956), pp. 499-503; and *NGSQ* 52 (1964): 25-36 (Lady Griffin, generations 4-10); *SP* and *CP* (Kinnaird, Aboyne, Huntly, Morton, Arran, Douglas, Nithsdale, Traquair, Lennox, Housto[u]n [baronets], Bargeny, Douglas, and Paisley); *MCS5*, line 92A and Edith Duncan Johnston, *The Houstouns of Georgia* (1950). The Morstyn-Poniatowski article in *NEHGS NEXUS* includes an ancestor table for the 2nd Marquess of Huntly and his wife for six generations, with most lines extended in *Prince Charles* and *Charles II*.

The Royal Descents of 900 Immigrants

1. James IV, King of Scotland, d. 1513 = Margaret Tudor of England

2. (illegitimate by Margaret Boyd) Catherine Stewart = James Douglas, 3rd Earl of Morton

2. (illegitimate by Margaret Drummond) Margaret Stewart = Sir John Drummond of Innerpeffry

3. Margaret Douglas = James Hamilton, 2nd Earl of Arran, Duke of Châtellerault, regent of Scotland, son of James Hamilton, 1st Earl of Arran (and Janet Beaton), son of James Hamilton, 1st Baron Hamilton, and Princess Mary Stewart, daughter of James II, King of Scotland, d. 1460, and Mary of Guelders

3. Isabel Drummond = Sir Matthew Campbell of Loudoun

4. Claud Hamilton, 1st Baron Paisley = Margaret Seton

4. Margaret Campbell = Thomas Boyd, 6th Baron Boyd

5. James Hamilton 1st Earl of Abercorn =

5. Marion Boyd

6. Sir George Hamilton, 1st Bt. = Mary Butler

7. James Hamilton = Elizabeth Colepepper

8. James Hamilton, 6th Earl of Abercorn = Elizabeth Reading

9. Mary Hamilton = Henry Colley, great-uncle of Arthur Wellesley, 1st Duke of Wellington, victor over Napoleon I at Waterloo

10. Mary Colley = Arthur Pomeroy, 1st Viscount Harberton

11. John Pomeroy, 4th Viscount Harberton = Esther Spencer

12. George Francis Pomeroy Colley = Frances Trench

The Royal Descents of 900 Immigrants

13. Henry FitzGeorge Colley = Elizabeth Isabella Wingfield
14. Gertrude Theodosia Colley = Alberic Arthur Twisleton-Wykeham-Fiennes
15. Sir Maurice Alberic Twisleton-Wykeham-Fiennes = Sylvia Joan Finlay
16. Mark Fiennes = Jennifer Anne Mary Alleyne Lash
17. **Ralph (Nathaniel) Fiennes**, b. 1962, certainly sometime of Calif., actor, Academy Award nominee for *Schindler's List* (Best Supporting Actor) and *The English Patient* (Best Actor) = Alex(andra) Elizabeth Kingston.
17. **Joseph (Alberic) Fiennes**, b. 1970, certainly sometime of Calif., actor (in *Shakespeare in Love*), married María Dolores Diéguez. A sister, Martha Maria Fiennes, b. 1964, is a film director; a third brother, Magnus Hubert Fiennes, b. 1965, is a composer; and a second sister, Sophia Victoria Fiennes, b. 1967, is a photographer.

Sources: *BP* (Saye and Sele, Harberton, Wellington, Abercorn), *CP* or *SP* (Abercorn, Paisley, Arran, Morton, Boyd [under Kilmarnock in *SP*], Loudoun).

The Royal Descents of 900 Immigrants

1. James IV, King of Scotland, d. 1513 = Margaret Tudor of England

2. (illegitimate by Margaret Drummond) Margaret Stewart = Sir John Drummond of Innerpeffry

2. (illegitimate by Agnes Stewart, Countess of Bothwell) Joan Stewart = Malcolm Fleming, 3rd Baron Fleming

3. Margaret Drummond = Robert Elphinstone, 3rd Baron Elphinstone

3. Agnes Fleming = William Livingston, 6th Baron Livingston

4. Alexander Elphinstone, 4th Baron Elphinstone = 4. Jean Livingston,

5. Jean Elphinstone = Arthur Forbes, 10th Baron Forbes

6. Elizabeth (or Elspeth) Forbes = James Skene of Skene

7. John Skene of Skene = Jean Burnett, daughter of Alexander Burnett of Leys (and Jean Arbuthnot), son of Sir Thomas Burnett, 1st Bt., and Margaret Douglas, SETH

8. Barbara Skene = John Tytler

9. George Tytler = Janet Robertson

10. **James Tytler** (1745-1804), of Mass., British balloonist, editor of the *Encyclopaedia Britannica*, 2nd edition, radical journalist; = (1) Elizabeth Rattray (div. 1788); (2) (bigamously) —— Cairns (d. by 1782); (3) (also bigamously, 7 Dec. 1782) Jean Aikenhead. Twin daughters by the last, Eleanor Tytler (d. Peabody, Mass. 11 Jan. 1880 aged 92:6, dau. of James, maternity uncertain) and Margaret Tytler (d. Boston 26 Oct. 1861 aged 74:3:13, dau. of James and Jane), married, at Salem, Mass., William Rue or Rhue and Daniel Anderson, respectively; both sisters left American descendants.

Sources: *Oxford DNB* (James Tytler) and *MGH*, 5th ser., vol. 2 (1916-17), p. 250 (Tytler); W.F. Skene, *Memorials of the Family of Skene of Skene* (1887), pp. 35-39 and *Burnett of Leys*, pp. 41-72 (esp. 61); *SP*, *CP*, or *BP* (Elphinstone, Livingston or Linlithgow, Fleming or Wigtown), *Mass. VRs, Deaths* [Peabody], 1880, 319: 274 (Eleanor Rhue), 1861, 149: 149

The Royal Descents of 900 Immigrants

(Margaret Anderson); *Salem, Mass. VRs* 4: 410 (marriages), 2: 38, 6: 182, 200 (Rhue/Rue/"Ruee" births, deaths), and 1: 38, 5: 46 (Anderson births, deaths); Scottish OPR Marriages 685/01 0490 0280 Edinburgh (Tytler-Rattray) and OPR Marriages 685/02 0170 0119 St. Cuthbert's [Edinburgh] (Tytler-Aikenhead). This line was developed and brought to my attention by John C. Brandon of Columbia, S.C.; Tytler's Scottish marriages to Elizabeth Rattray and Jean Aikenhead, and the Salem VRs, were found by Julie Helen Otto.

William Livingston, 6th Baron Livingston, first listed in this volume at generation 3 above and on several following charts, was a son of Alexander Livingston, 5th Baron Livingston, and Agnes Douglas, daughter of John Douglas, 2nd Earl of Morton (grandson of James I, King of Scotland, d. 1437, and Joan Beaufort) and Janet Crichton, SETH. This descent is noted here but not subsequently (or on p. 145) because the 6th Baron Livingston first appears on this chart as the first link for an immigrant descended from a *legitimate* child of an earlier Scottish king.

The Royal Descents of 900 Immigrants

1. James IV, King of Scotland, d. 1513 = Margaret Tudor of England

2. (illegitimate by Agnes Stewart, Countess of Bothwell) Joan Stewart = Malcolm Fleming, 3rd Baron Fleming

3. Agnes Fleming = William Livingston, 6th Baron Livingston

4. Alexander Livingston, 1st Earl of Linlithgow = Eleanor Hay

5. Alexander Livingston, 2nd Earl of Linlithgow = = 6. Elizabeth Gordon, daughter of 5. George Gordon, 1st Marquess of Huntly, and Henrietta Stewart, SETH

6, 7. George Livingston, 3rd Earl of Linlithgow = Elizabeth Maule

7, 8. Alexander Livingston, 3rd Earl of Callendar   =

3. Margaret Fleming = Robert Graham

4. John Graham, 3rd Earl of Montrose = Jean Drummond

5. John Graham, 4th Earl of Montrose = Margaret Ruthven

6. James Graham, 1st Marquess of Montrose, Royalist general = Magdalen Carnegie

7. James Graham, 2nd Marquess of Montrose = Isabel Douglas

8. Anne Graham

8, 9. Mary Livingston = James Graham of Airth

9, 10. Elizabeth Graham = William Macdowall of Garthland

10, 11. James Macdowall = Margaret Jamieson

11, 12. Isabella Graham Macdowall = Thomas Maitland of Dundrennan

12, 13. **James William Maitland** of N.Y. = Agnes Jane O'Reilly. Their son Thomas A. Maitland married Helen Abbie Van Voorhis; their son James William Maitland married Sylvia Wigglesworth; their daughter Andrea Belden Maitland married Howard Brush Dean, Jr., and was the mother of Howard (Brush) Dean (III), b. 1948,

The Royal Descents of 900 Immigrants

governor of Vermont and presidential candidate in 2004, who married Judith Steinberg.

Sources: *MGH* 2 (1876): 213 (Maitland), *BLG*, 18th ed., vol. 3 (1972), p. 578 (Macdowall of Garthland), and 1937, p. 939 (Graham of Airth), plus James P. Maher, *Index to Marriages and Deaths in the New York Herald*, vol. 2, *1856-1863* (1991), pp. 71, 492 (marriage and death notices for the immigrant J.W. Maitland); *SP* and *CP* (Callendar, Livingston, Linlithgow, Fleming [Wigton], Huntly, and Montrose). For sources from Maitland to Howard B. Dean (III), see *RD600*, p. 574.

The Royal Descents of 900 Immigrants

1. James IV, King of Scotland, d. 1513 = Margaret Tudor of England

2. (illegitimate by Margaret Drummond) Margaret Stewart = Sir John Drummond of Innerpeffry

2. (illegitimate by Agnes Stewart, Countess of Bothwell) Joan Stewart = Malcolm Fleming, 3rd Baron Fleming

3. Margaret Drummond = Robert Elphinstone, 3rd Baron Elphinstone

3. Agnes Fleming = William Livingston, 6th Baron Livingston

3. John Fleming, 5th Baron Fleming = Elizabeth Ross

4. Alexander Elphinstone 4th Baron Elphinstone =

4. Jean Livingston

4. Jean Fleming = William Bruce of Airth

5. Margaret Elphinstone = 5. Sir John Bruce of Airth

6. Christian Bruce = John Innes of Edingight

7. John Innes of Edingight = Elizabeth Gordon

8. John Innes of Edingight = Helen Strachen

8. Anne Innes = Patrick Duff of Craigston

9. John Innes of Edingight = 9. Jean Duff
(siblings of John and Jean, Alexander Innes of Rosieburn and Margaret Duff, married respectively Katherine Abercromby and Alexander Gordon of Gight. Two of their children, Katherine Innes and George Gordon of Gight, married each other and were parents of Catherine Gordon of Gight, Mrs. John Byron, mother of George Gordon Byron, later Noel, 6th Baron Byron, the poet)

10. John Innes of Edingight = Elizabeth Grant

11. Elizabeth Innes = George Robinson of Gask

12. William Rose Robinson of Clermiston = Mary Douglas

13. **Douglas Robinson** of N.Y. = Fanny Monroe, great-niece of James Monroe, 5th U.S. President. Their son, Douglas

The Royal Descents of 900 Immigrants

Robinson, Jr., married Corinne Roosevelt, sister of Theodore Roosevelt, Jr., 26th U.S. President, SETH, and was the father of Corinne Douglas Robinson, wife of Joseph Wright Alsop (IV) and mother of political columnists Joseph (Wright) Alsop (V) (1910-1989) and Stewart (Johonnot Oliver) Alsop (1914-1974).

Sources: *BLG* 1952, pp. 2171-72 (Robertson of Orchardton); *BP* (Innes of Balvenie, baronets); M.E. Cuming Bruce, *Family Records of the Bruces and the Cumyns* (1870), pp. 322-23, *SP* and *CP* (Fleming [under Wigtown in *SP*], Elphinstone and Livingston [under Linlithgow in *SP*]); *Gordon*, vol. 1 (1903), Gordon of Gight section, pp. 117-46.

The Royal Descents of 900 Immigrants

1. James IV, King of Scotland, d. 1513 = Margaret Tudor of England

2. (illegitimate by Margaret Drummond) Margaret Stewart = Sir John Drummond of Innerpeffry

2. (illegitimate by Agnes Stewart, Countess of Bothwell) Joan Stewart = Malcolm Fleming, 3rd Baron Fleming

3. Margaret Drummond = Robert Elphinstone, 3rd Baron Elphinstone

3. Agnes Fleming = William Livingston, 6th Baron Livingston

4. Alexander Elphinstone = 4th Baron Elphinstone

4. Jean Livingston

5. Helen Elphinstone = Sir William Cockburn, 1st Bt.

6. Sir William Cockburn, 2nd Bt. = Margaret Acheson

7. Sir Alexander Cockburn, 4th Bt. = Marion Sinclair, daughter of John Sinclair of Stevenson and Isabel Boyd, daughter of Robert Boyd, 7th Baron Boyd, and Christian Hamilton, SETH

8. Helen Cockburn = Sir Robert Steuart, 1st Bt.

9. Helen Steuart = Sir Gilbert Elliot, 2nd Bt.

10. Eleanor Elliot = John Rutherford of Edgerston (and N.Y.), SETH

11. Jane Rutherford = William Oliver of Dinlabrye

12. Eleanor Oliver = James Russell

13. **Archibald Russell** of N.Y. = Helen Rutherford Watts, daughter of John Watts and Anne Rutherford, daughter of John Rutherford (and Magdalen Morris), son of Walter Rutherford of N.Y., ARD, SETH (brother of John Rutherford of Edgerston and N.Y., above) and Catherine Alexander. Archibald Douglas Russell, son of Archibald and Helen, married Robertina Rivington Pyne (daughter by Albertina Shelton Taylor of Percy Rivington Pyne, son of Thomas Pyne of N.Y., ARD, SETH, and Anna Rivington), and was the father of Constance Rivington Russell, who married (1) John Gilbert Winant, diplomat and governor of N.H., and (2) Marion Eppley, physical chemist and widower of Ethelberta Pyne Russell, sister of Constance.

The Royal Descents of 900 Immigrants

Sources: Livingston Rutherfurd, *Family Records and Events* [Rutherfurd family] (1894), chapters 2-3 (pp. 85-256), esp. 255-56; *DNB* (James Russell, 1754-1836); *Rutherford*, vol. 1, pp. 70-71, 73-74, 98-99, and 2nd rev. ed., vol. 2, p. 802, 815; Hon. George F.S. Elliot, *The Border Elliots and The Family of Minto* (1897), pp. 308-24; *CB* (Steuart of Allanbank); Thomas H. Cockburn-Hood, *The House of Cockburn of That Ilk and the Cadets Thereof* (1888), pp. 83-95; *SP* and *CP* (Boyd, under Kilmarnock in *SP*; Elphinstone; and Livingston, under Linlithgow in *SP*).

Following the above chart, an immigrant was inadvertently omitted, viz.:

1. James IV, King of Scotland, d. 1513 = Margaret Tudor of England
2. (illegitimate by Agnes Stewart, Countess of Bothwell) Joan Stewart = Malcolm Fleming, 3rd Baron Fleming
3. John Fleming, 5th Baron Fleming = Elizabeth Ross
4. Mary Fleming = Sir James Douglas
5. William Douglas, 1st Earl of Queensberry = Isabel Ker
6. Sir Archibald Douglas of Dornock = Eleanor Davis
7. James Douglas of Jamaica = ——
8. Thomas Douglas of Jamaica = —— Watson
9. Samuel Douglas of Jamaica = —— James
10. Samuel Douglas of Jamaica = Isabella Moncreiffe
11. Robert Douglas = ——
12. Samuel Douglas = ——
13. Robert Douglas = Annie Johnson
14. **Robert Langton Douglas**, sometime of N.Y. = (1) Margaret Jane Cannon (parents of William Sholto Douglas, 1st Baron Douglas of Kirtleside, British Air Marshal); (2) Mary Henchman; (3) Jean Stewart (parents of Claire Alison Douglas, wife of Jerome David [J.D.] Salinger [1919-2010], the American novelist, author of *Catcher in the Rye*).

Sources: *BP* (Douglas of Kirtleside), *SP* (Queensberry, Fleming—under Wigtown). Further documentation of generations 7-12 would be desirable.

The Royal Descents of 900 Immigrants

1. James IV, King of Scotland, d. 1513 = Margaret Tudor of England
2. (illegitimate by Margaret Boyd) Catherine Stewart = James Douglas, 3rd Earl of Morton
3. Margaret Douglas = James Hamilton, 2nd Earl of Arran, Duke of Châtellerault, regent of Scotland, son of James Hamilton, 1st Earl of Arran (and Janet Beaton), son of James Hamilton, 1st Baron Hamilton, and Princess Mary Stewart, daughter of James II, King of Scotland, d. 1460, and Mary of Guelders
4. Claud Hamilton, 1st Baron Paisley = Margaret Seton
5. Sir Frederick Hamilton = Sidney Vaughan
6. Gustavus Hamilton, 1st Viscount Boyne = Elizabeth Brooke
7. Joshua Hamilton = Mary Cox
8. **Henry Hamilton-Cox** (c. 1769-c. 1821), sometime of Pa., farmer, poet, and religionist = Letitia Eleanor Hutcheson.

Sources: *DAB* (as H.H. Cox), *BP* (Boyne, as Henry Hamilton-Cox; Abercorn), *CP* (Boyne, Paisley, Arran, Hamilton and Morton).

The Royal Descents of 900 Immigrants

1. James IV, King of Scotland, d. 1513 = Margaret Tudor of England

2. (illegitimate by Margaret Boyd) Catherine Stewart = James Douglas, 3rd Earl of Morton

2. (illegitimate by Margaret Drummond) Margaret Stewart = Sir John Drummond of Innerpeffry

3. Margaret Douglas = James Hamilton, 2nd Earl of Arran, Duke of Châtellerault, Regent of Scotland, son of James Hamilton, 1st Earl of Arran (and Janet Beaton), son of James Hamilton, 1st Baron Hamilton, and Princess Mary Stewart, daughter of James II, King of Scotland, d. 1460, and Mary of Guelders

3. Jean Drummond = Sir James Chisholm of Cromlix

4. Jean Chisholm = James Drummond, 1st Baron Maderty

4. John Hamilton, 1st Marquess of Hamilton = Margaret Lyon

5. (illegitimate by——) Sir John Hamilton of Lettrick = Jean Campbell

6. Catherine Hamilton =

5. Sir James Drummond of Machany

6, 7. Sir James Drummond of Machany = Anne Hay of Keillor

7, 8. Anne Drummond = Thomas Graeme of Balgowan

8, 9. **Dr. Thomas Graeme** of Pa. = Anne Diggs. Their daughter was Mrs. Elizabeth Graeme Ferguson, 1737-1801, poet, translator, journal and letter writer, who married Henry Hugh Ferguson.

Sources: Charles P. Keith, *The Provincial Councillors of Pennsylvania* (1883, repr. 1997), pp. 158-64 (Graeme), citing a pedigree in the appendix to the 1880 *Life of Lord Lynedoch* by Capt. Delavoye; Louisa G. Graeme,

The Royal Descents of 900 Immigrants

Or and Sable: A Book of the Graemes and Grahams (1903), pp. 580-82; *SP*, *CP* or *BP* (Perth, Strathallan, Maderty, Hamilton, and Morton), *RA* 1: 242-43, 668-74 (Drummond of Innerpeffry [under Barclay], Scotland).

The Royal Descents of 900 Immigrants

1. James IV, King of Scotland, d. 1513 = Margaret Tudor of England

2. (illegitimate by Agnes Stewart, Countess of Bothwell) Joan Stewart = Malcolm Fleming, 3rd Baron Fleming

3. Margaret Fleming = Robert Graham

4. John Graham, 3rd Earl of Montrose = Jean Drummond, daughter of David Drummond, 2nd Baron Drummond, and Lilias Ruthven, SETH

5. John Graham, 4th Earl of Montrose = Margaret Ruthven, daughter of William Ruthven, 1st Earl of Gowrie, and Dorothea Stewart, daughter of Henry Stewart, 1st Baron Methven, and Janet Stewart, daughter of John Stewart, 2nd Earl of Atholl and Janet Kennedy, SETH

6. Lilias Graham = Sir John Colquhoun, 1st Bt.

7. Lilias Colquhoun = John Napier of Kilmahew

8. Katherine Napier = Robert Campbell of Woodside

9. Lilias Campbell = James Dunlop of Garnkirk, son of James Dunlop of Garnkirk and Elizabeth Roberton, SETH

10. Jean Dunlop = Thomas Peter. Their sons John Peter (m. Elizabeth Cocke) and Walter Peter (m. Katherine Cocke and Sarah Norfleet) also settled in Va. or Md. and left descendants but I have found no NDTPS.

11. **Robert Peter** of Md., first mayor of Georgetown, D.C. = Elizabeth Scott. Their eldest son, Thomas Peter, married Martha Parke Custis, a granddaughter of First Lady Martha Dandridge Custis Washington. America Pinckney Peter, daughter of Thomas and Martha, married George Williams and was the mother of Katherine Alicia Williams, wife of naval officer John Henry Upshur.

Sources: A. McC. Dunlop, *A Genealogical Study of the Dunlop and Peter Families* (1956), esp. charts 1b, 10, 20, 28 (undocumented), *BRMF1*:173-74, 353 (Dunlop, Peter), *BP* 1898, p. 335 (Colquhoun, with the correct parentage for Lilias, wife of John Napier of Kilmahew), *CP* and *SP* (Montrose, Fleming – in *SP* under Wigtown, Drummond, Gowrie, Methven, and Atholl). Detailed documentation for generations 8-11 would be welcome.

The Royal Descents of 900 Immigrants

1. James IV, King of Scotland, d. 1513 = Margaret Tudor of England
2. (illegitimately by Margaret Drummond) Margaret Stewart = Sir John Drummond of Innerpeffry
3. Elizabeth Drummond = Malcolm Drummond of Bourland
4. David Drummond of Bourland = Helen Menteith of Maner
5. Agnes Drummond = James Menteith of Auldcathie
6. James Menteith of Auldcathie = Margaret Sandilands
7. James **Menteith** or **Monteith**, later Dalyell, of Auldcathie = Magdalen Dalyell of Va., SETH (their eldest son, Sir James Monteith, later Dalyell, 3rd Bt., is an ancestor of [Sir] Thomas "Tam" Dalyell [11th Bt.], Labor M.P. and author).
8. **Thomas Monteith** of Va. = Phillis Gallop.
9. Magdalen Monteith = Anderson Doniphan
10. Elizabeth Doniphan = Richard Shipp
11. Emma Grant Shipp = William Truman, Jr.
12. Anderson Shipp Truman = Mary Jane Holmes
13. John Anderson Truman = Martha Ellen Young
14. Harry S Truman (1884-1972), 33rd U.S. President = Elizabeth Virginia "Bess" Wallace

Sources: *Family History: The Journal of the Institute of Heraldic and Genealogical Studies* 20 (#168, July 2001), pp. 350-53, 358-59 (Donald Whyte on the Menteiths of Auldcathie, generations 5-8 above); Sir James Dalyell of Binns, (9th) Bt., and James Beveridge, eds., *The Binns Papers (Publications of the Scottish Record Society*, vol. 70, 1938), pp. 119 (#578, which abstracts a letter of 17 Nov. 1734 from Thomas Menteith of Rappahannock Co., Va., to his brother Sir James Dalyell, 3rd Bt.), 112 (#545, item 42, the marriage contract between James Monteith and Magdalen Dalyell), 65, 92 (#s 338 and 446, which cover Margaret Sandilands and Christian Mylne, the latter of whom was said in the 1681 Drummond genealogy below and elsewhere to be the wife of the second James Menteith at generation 6 above); Hon. William Drummond, later

The Royal Descents of 900 Immigrants

1st Viscount Strathallan, *The Genealogy of the Most Noble and Ancient House of Drummond* (1889, compiled 1681), p. 49 (Bourland, generations 2-7), 148-51 (Innerpeffry), and Henry Drummond, *History of Our Noble British Families*, vol. 2 (1846), Drummond section, pp. 34-35 (Bourland), 12-13 (Innerpeffry).

The Royal Descents of 900 Immigrants

1. James IV, King of Scotland, d. 1513 = Margaret Tudor of England

2. (illegitimate by Margaret Drummond) Margaret Stewart = Sir John Drummond of Innerpeffry

3. Agnes Drummond = Hugh Montgomery, 3rd Earl of Eglinton, son of Hugh Montgomery, 2nd Earl of Eglinton, and Mariot Seton, daughter of George Seton, 3rd Baron Seton, and Janet Hepburn, daughter of Patrick Hepburn, 1st Earl of Bothwell, and Janet Douglas, daughter of James Douglas, 1st Earl of Morton and Princess Joan Stewart, "the dumb lady," daughter of James I, King of Scotland, d. 1437, and Joan Beaufort

4. Agnes Montgomery = Robert Semphill, 4th Baron Semphill, son of Hon. Robert Semphill (and Barbara Preston), son of Robert Semphil, 3rd Baron Semphill and Isabel Hamilton, SETH

5. Barbara Semphill = Sir Colin Lamont of Ineryne

6. Anne Lamont = William Crauford of Auchenames

7. Barbara Crauford = Alexander Orr

8. Alexander Orr of Hazelside = Agnes Dalrymple

9. **John Orr** of Va. = Susannah Monroe Grayson.

Sources: *GVFT* 2:783-86 and H.B. McCall, *Some Old Families: A Contribution to the Genealogical History of Scotland* (1890), pp. 145-53 (Orr, Crauford); *SP* and *CP* (Semphill, Eglinton, Seton, Bothwell, Morton).

The Royal Descents of 900 Immigrants

1. James IV, King of Scotland, d. 1513 = Margaret Tudor of England
2. (illegitimate by Margaret Drummond) Margaret Stewart = Sir John Drummond of Innerpeffry
3. Isabel Drummond = Sir Matthew Campbell of Loudoun
4. Margaret Campbell = Thomas Boyd, 6th Baron Boyd
5. Hon. Robert Boyd = Jean Ker
6. Robert Boyd, 7th Baron Boyd = Christian Hamilton
7. Marion Boyd = Sir James Dundas of Arniston
8. Christian Dundas = Sir Charles Erskine, 1st Bt., son of Sir Charles Erskine (and Mary Hope), SETH, a descendant of James II, King of Scotland, d. 1460, and Mary of Gueldres
9. Mary Erskine = Sir William Stirling, 2nd Bt.
10. Christian Stirling = John Stirling of Herbertshire
11. George Stirling of Herbertshire = ——
12. (perhaps or probably illegitimate) **Margaret Stirling** of Va. = (1) David **Forbes**; (2) —— **Alexander**. Her daughter by Forbes, Delia Stirling Forbes, married Scottish native George Smith and was the mother of Murray Forbes Smith, father by Phoebe Ann Desha of society leader and suffragette Alva Erskine Smith, wife of railroad tycoon William Kissam Vanderbilt and congressman Oliver Hazard Perry Belmont, the latter a son of financier August Belmont and grandson and great-nephew respectively of naval officers Matthew Galbraith Perry and Oliver Hazard Perry.

Sources: OPR Marriages 685/01 0500 0416 (Edinburgh) (marriage on 17 April 1774 of "David Forbes Surgeon in Lady Yester's Kirk parish and Margaret Stirling in Old Kirk parish Daughter of the deceased George Stirling of Herbertshire") (found by Julie Helen Otto); A.M. Sterling, *The Sterling Genealogy* (1909), 1:120, 178, 2: 1209 and *NEXUS* 13 (1996): 76-78, 81-82; *CB* (Stirling of Ardoch, Erskine of Alva); *Douglas*, p. 180 (Dundas of Arniston); *SP* and *CP* (Boyd — under Kilmarnock in *SP*; Loudoun). I cannot find David Forbes (the immigrant's first husband), or his alleged (by A.M. Sterling) parents, "Sir William Forbes of Pitsligo and his wife Jean Erskine" in *Forbes*. William Fraser, *The*

The Royal Descents of 900 Immigrants

Stirlings of Keir (1858), p. 173 (not p. 177, as per *NEXUS* 13: 78, 82) states that George Stirling of Herbertshire died childless (so Margaret was probably illegitimate). He was succeeded by his sister Jean Stirling, wife of Sir William Stirling of Glorat, 3rd Bt., and James Erskine, a lord of session, styled Lord Alva. For this last, in part, Mrs. Vanderbilt was undoubtedly named.

The Royal Descents of 900 Immigrants

1. James IV, King of Scotland, d. 1513 = Margaret Tudor of England

2. (illegitimate by Margaret Drummond) Margaret Stewart = John Gordon, Lord Gordon, son of Alexander Gordon, 3rd Earl of Huntly (and Janet Stewart), son of George Gordon, 2nd Earl of Huntly (son of Alexander Gordon, 1st Earl of Huntly, SETH, and Elizabeth Crichton) and (prob.) Princess Annabella Stewart, daughter of James I, King of Scotland, d. 1437, and Joan Beaufort

3. George Gordon, 4th Earl of Huntly = Elizabeth Keith

4. Elizabeth Gordon = John Stewart, 4th Earl of Atholl

5. Elizabeth Stewart = Hugh Fraser, 5th Baron Lovat

6. Simon Fraser, 6th Baron Lovat = Jean Stewart

7. Sir James Fraser of Brae = Beatrix Wemyss

8. Magdalen Fraser = George Cuthbert of Castle Hill

9. John Cuthbert of Castle Hill = Jean Hay

10. **James Cuthbert** of S.C. = (1) Mrs. Patience Stobo Hamilton; (2) Mrs. Mary Hazzard Wigg.

Sources: J.G.B. Bulloch, *The Cuthberts, Barons of Castle Hill, and Their Descendants in South Carolina and Georgia* (1908), pp. 8-14, 35-37; *SP* and *CP* (Lovat, Atholl, Huntly).

The Royal Descents of 900 Immigrants

1. James IV, King of Scotland, d. 1513 = Margaret Tudor of England

2. (illegitimate by Agnes Stewart, Countess of Bothwell) Joan Stewart = Malcolm Fleming, 3rd Baron Fleming

3. James Fleming, 4th Baron Fleming = Barbara Hamilton, daughter of James Hamilton, 2nd Earl of Arran, Duke of Châtellerault, Regent of Scotland, and Margaret Douglas, SETH

4. Jean Fleming = John Maitland, 1st Baron Thirlestane

5. John Maitland, 1st Earl of Lauderdale = Isabel Seton

6. John Maitland, 1st Duke of Lauderdale = Anne Home

7. Mary Maitland = John Hay, 2nd Marquess of Tweeddale

8. Lord William Hay = Margaret Hay

9. Jean Hay = Archibald Murray of Murrayfield

10. Susan Mary Murray = Sir Hay Campbell, 1st Bt.

11. Susan Campbell = Crawford Tait of Harviestown (parents of Archibald Campbell Tait, Archbishop of Canterbury)

12. Susan Murray Tait = Sir George Sitwell, 2nd Bt. (parents of Sir Sitwell Reresby Sitwell, 3rd Bt., father by Louisa Lucy Hely-Hutchinson of Sir George Reresby Sitwell, 4th Bt., father by Lady Ida Emily Augusta Denison, of the literary Sitwell siblings—(Sir Francis) Osbert Sacheverell Sitwell (5th Bt.), (Sir) Sacheverell Sitwell (6th Bt.), and Dame Edith (Louisa) Sitwell.

13. Georgiana Caroline Sitwell = Archibald Campbell Swinton, also a descendant of illegitimate daughters of James IV, King of Scotland

14. George Sitwell Campbell Swinton = Elizabeth Ebsworth

15. Alan Henry Campbell Swinton = Mariora Beatrice Evelyn Rochfort Hankey

16. Sir John Swinton = Judith Balfour Killen

17. **Katherine Matilda Swinton**, the actress **Tilda Swinton**, b. 1960, sometime of Calif. = John **Byrne**, artist and playwright.

The Royal Descents of 900 Immigrants

Sources: *BLG* (Swinton of that Ilk or of Kimmerghame) and *Oxford DNB* (A.C. Tait, Sitwells), *BP* or *CP* (Sitwell, Bt., Campbell of Succoth, Bt., Murray of Blackbarony, Bt., Lauderdale, Thirlestane, Fleming, Arran).

The Royal Descents of 900 Immigrants

1. James IV, King of Scotland, d. 1513 = Margaret Tudor of England
2. (illegitimate by Margaret Boyd) Catherine Stewart = James Douglas, 3rd Earl of Morton
3. Margaret Douglas = James Hamilton, 2nd Earl of Arran, Duke of Châtellerault, regent of Scotland, son of James Hamilton, 1st Earl of Arran (and Janet Beaton), son of James Hamilton, 1st Baron Hamilton, and Princess Mary Stewart, daughter of James II, King of Scotland, d. 1460, and Mary of Guelders
4. Claud Hamilton, 1st Baron Paisley = Margaret Seton
5. Sir Claud Hamilton of Shawfield = Janet Hamilton of Leckprevick
6. Sir William Hamilton of Manor Elieston = Beatrix Campbell
7. Claud Hamilton of Montalony and Fahy = Isabella Wingfield
8. William Hamilton of Beltrim = Mary ——
8. Claud Hamilton of Strabane = Isabella ——
9. Claud Hamilton of Beltrim =
9. Letitia Hamilton
10. Letitia Hamilton = Hon. Arthur Cole (-Hamilton)
11. Claud William Cole-Hamilton = Nicola Sophia Chaloner
12. Arthur Willoughby Cole-Hamilton = Emilia Katherine Beresford
13. Letitia Grace Cole-Hamilton = Hon. Sir Henry George Louis Crichton
14. Emily Florence Crichton = John Edward Bernard Seely, 1st Baron Mottistone
15. Irene Florence Seely = Mason Hogarth Scott
16. Jane Emily Scott = Sir (James) Michael Gow
17. Anna Katherine Gow = Charles Hunter
18. **Sophie Irene Hunter**, b. 1978, sometime of Calif., theater director = Benedict (Timothy Carlton) **Cumberbatch**, b. 1976, also sometime of Calif., film actor, ARD, SETH.

The Royal Descents of 900 Immigrants

Sources: Wikipedia and other notices of the Cumberbatch-Hunter marriage; *BP* (Scott of Beauclerc, baronets, Mottistone, Erne [for Crichton], Enniskillen [for Cole-Hamilton]), *Hamilton*, pp. 14-18, 31-34, 1002-5, 918-21, 1034, *CP* (Paisley, Arran, Morton) and *SP* (Abercorn, Arran, Morton).

The Royal Descents of 900 Immigrants

1. John I, King of Denmark, d. 1513 = Christine of Saxony
2. Elizabeth of Denmark = Joachim I, Elector of Brandenburg
3. Margaret of Brandenburg = John II, Prince of Anhalt-Zerbst
4. Maria of Anhalt-Zerbst = Albert V, Count of Barby-Mühlingen
5. Maria of Barby-Mühlingen = (1) Josias, Count of Waldeck
6. Christian, Count of Waldeck-Wildungen = Elizabeth of Nassau-Siegen, daughter of John II, Count of Nassau-Siegen (and Magdalena of Waldeck), son of John I, Count of Nassau-Dillenburg (and Elizabeth of Leuchtenberg), brother of William the Silent, Prince of Orange, d. 1584, first Stadholder of The Netherlands
7. Louise Sybil of Waldeck-Wildungen = Gerhard Ludwig, Baron von Effern
8. Charlotte Dorothea, Countess von Effern = Augustin von Steuben
9. Wilhelm Augustin von Steuben = Maria Justina Dorothea von Jagow
10. **Friedrich Wilhelm Ludolf Gerhard Augustin, Baron von Steuben** (1730-1794), Prussian soldier, American Revolutionary commander, d. unm.

Sources: *DGA*, vol. 1 (1939), pp. 259, 264-65; *ES*, tables for Denmark, Brandenburg, Anhalt-Zerbst, Barby-Mühlingen (*ES* 2: 12: 138), Waldeck, Nassau-Siegen, and Nassau-Dillenburg.

The Royal Descents of 900 Immigrants

1. John I, King of Denmark, d. 1513 = Christine of Saxony
2. Elizabeth of Denmark = Joachim I, Elector of Brandenburg
3. Margaret of Brandenburg = John II, Prince of Anhalt-Zerbst
4. Maria of Anhalt-Zerbst = Albert V, Count of Barby-Mühlingen
5. Maria of Barby-Mühlingen = (2) George III, Count of Erbach
6. Dorothea of Erbach = Louis Eberhard, Count of Hohenlohe-Waldenburg-Pfedelbach
7. Sophie Juliana of Hohenlohe-Waldenburg-Pfedelbach = Wolfgang George, Count of Castell-Remlingen
8. Wolfgang Dietrich, Count of Castell-Remlingen = Dorothea Renata, Countess of Zinzendorf and Pottendorf, daughter of Maximilian Erasmus, Count of Zinzendorf and Pottendorf, and Anna Amelia of Dietrichstein-Hollenburg, SETH.
9. Sophia Theodora of Castell-Remlingen = Henry XXIX, Count Reuss-Ebersdorf, son of Henry X, Count Reuss-Ebersdorf (and Erdmuthe Benigna of Solms-Laubach), son of Henry X, Count Reuss-Lobenstein (and Marie Sybil of Reuss-Obergreitz), son of Henry II, Count Reuss-Gera, and Magdalena of Schwarzburg-Rudolstadt, daughter of Albert VII, Count of Schwarzburg-Rudolstadt and Juliana of Nassau-Dillenburg, sister of William the Silent, Prince of Orange, d. 1584, 1st Stadholder of The Netherlands. Henry XXIX and Sophie Theodora were the parents of Henry XXIV, Count Reuss-Ebersdorf, who married Caroline Ernestine of Erbach-Schönberg and left a daughter, Augusta Caroline of Reuss-Ebersdorf, who married Francis, Duke of Saxe-Coburg-Saalfeld and was both the mother of Leopold I, King of the Belgians, and the maternal grandmother of Victoria, Queen of Great Britain.
10. Joanna Dorothea, Countess Reuss-Ebersdorf = Christoph Friedrich Levin von Trotta genannt Treyden
11. Frederica Theodora Elizabeth von Trotta genannt Treyden = Friedrich Ludwig von Tschirschky und Bögendorff
12. Franz Ludwig von Tschirschky und Bögendorff = Wilhelmine Maximiliane Luise Marina von Schönberg

The Royal Descents of 900 Immigrants

13. **Amalie Joanna Lydia von Tschirschky und Bögendorff** of Pa. = Edmund Alexander **de Schweinitz** (1825-1887), Moravian Bishop and historian, SETH.

12. Augusta Theodora von Tschirschky und Bögendorff (sister of Franz Ludwig) = Heinrich August von Gersdorff

13. **Ernst Bruno von (de) Gersdorff of Mass.** = Caroline Choate. Their son, Carl August de Gersdorff, married Helen Suzette Crowninshield and left a daughter, Josephine de Gersdorff, wife of Frederick Josiah Bradlee, Jr., and mother of Benjamin Crowninshield ("Ben") Bradlee (1921-2014), managing or executive editor of *The Washington Post*, 1965-92.

Sources: *ES*, tables for Denmark, Brandenburg, Anhalt-Zerbst, Barby-Mühlingen (2: 12: 38), Erbach (2: 5: 3), Hohenlohe-Waldenburg-Pfedelbach (2: 17: 15), Castell-Remlingen (2: 16: 125), Schwarzburg-Rudolstadt, Nassau-Dillenburg, Reuss-Gera, Reuss-Lobenstein, Reuss-Ebersdorf, Saxe-Coburg-Saalfeld, Belgium, and Great Britain; Dr. Walter von Boetticher, *Geschichte des Oberlausitzischen Adels und Seiner Güter, 1635-1815*, vol. 2 (1913), pp. 1004-5 (Trotta genannt Treyden); *Gothaisches Genealogisches Taschenbuch der Uradeligen Häuser, 1913*, pp. 726-28 (von Tschirschky und Bögendorff), *1923*, p. 263 (von Gersdorff) and *GH des A*, vol. 15, *Adelige Häuser A*, vol. 3 (1957), p. 218 (E.B. von [de] Gersdorff); Gerhard Meyer, *Nikolas Ludwig von Zinzendorf, Eine Genealogische Studie mit Ahnen und Nachfahrenliste* (1966), *DAB* (E.A. de Schweinitz) and *NK1*: 68-70, 72-75, 77-78 (generations 9-13 to both immigrants). See also *Prince Charles*, vol. 2 (1977), I 229-30 (p. 13), J 457-60 (p. 21), K 917-20 (p. 33), also K 111-12 (p. 28), L 223-24 (p. 44), M 447-48 (p. 67), also K 1465-66 (p. 36), L 2931-32 (p. 54), M 5863-64 (p. 81), also M 965-66 (p. 69), N 1931-32 (p. 104), also M 5763-64 (p. 80), N (11527-28) (p. 112) (John I and Christina), K 913-14 (p. 33), L 1825-26 (p. 50), M 3651-52 (p. 75), also L 497-98 (p. 75, Albert VII and Juliana), etc., and *NK1*: 68-70, 72-75, 77-78. This "improved" descent was brought to my attention by John Blythe Dobson of Winnipeg, Manitoba, Canada.

The Royal Descents of 900 Immigrants

1. John I, King of Denmark, d. 1513 = Christine of Saxony
2. Elizabeth of Denmark = Joachim I, Elector of Brandenburg
3. Margaret of Brandenburg = John II, Prince of Anhalt-Zerbst
4. Joachim Ernest, Prince of Anhalt-Zerbst = Agnes of Barby
5. Sybil of Anhalt-Zerbst = Frederick, Duke of Württemberg-Mömpelgard
6. Louis Frederick, Duke of Württemberg-Mömpelgard = Anna Eleanor of Nassau-Weilberg, daughter of John Casimir, Count of Nassau-Weilberg (and Elizabeth of Hesse-Darmstadt), son of Albert, Count of Nassau-Weilberg and Anna of Nassau-Dillenburg, sister of William the Silent, Prince of Orange, d. 1564, 1st Stadholder of the Netherlands
7. George, Duke of Württemberg-Mömpelgard = Anne de Coligny
8. Leopold Eberhard, Duke of Württemberg-Mömpelgard, d. 1723 = (1) Anna Sabina von Hedwiger, Countess von Sponeck; (2) Henrietta Hedwige Curie, Baroness von l'Esperance
9. (by 2) Karl Leopold, Baron von l'Esperance and Sandersleben, Count of Coligny = 9. (by 1) Leopoldine Eberhardine, Countess von Sponeck
(This extraordinary marriage, and that of one of his sisters to one of her brothers, was of a half-brother and a half-sister.)
10. Anna Elizabeth de Sandersleben, Countess of Coligny = Thomas de Pillot, seigneur de Chenecey, Marquis de Coligny
11. Charles-Ignace de Pillot, Marquis de Coligny = Marie-Anne-Claude de Bernard de Sassenay
12. (Charles-Francois-) Emmanuel (-Edwige) de Pillot, Marquis de Coligny = Charlotte-Victorine-Clémentine-Angélique de Messey-Beaupré
13. (Marie-Simone-) Léopoldine de Pillot = (Louis-Joseph-) Léonce Dedons, Marquis de Pierrefeu
14. (Louis-Dolorès-Emmanuel-) Alphonse Dedons, Count de Pierrefeu = (Aline-) Anne de Quérangal

The Royal Descents of 900 Immigrants

15 **Alain Dedons, Count de Pierrefeu** of Mass. = Elsa Tudor. Their daughters Dolores and Katharine Dedons de Pierrefeu married respectively Arthur Noyes Daniels and Horace Durham Gilbert, New Hampshire businessmen treated in *Who's Who in America*.

Sources: Henri, Baron de Woelmont de Brumagne, *Notices Généalogiques,* 6th ser. (1930), pp. 470-73 (Dedons de Pierrefeu); *GAdeF*, vol. 5, p. 288 (Pillot); Michel Huberty, etc., eds., *L'Allemagne Dynastique,* vol. 2, *Anhalt-Lippe-Wurtemberg* (1979), pp. 567-93, 605-9 (children of generation 8, with a chart showing the descent of Anne-Aymone Sauvage de Brantes, wife of French president Valéry Giscard d'Estaing, from the extraordinary marriage of half-siblings at generation 9 via counts and princes of Lucinge and Faucigny-Lucinge); *ES* 2: 3: 2: 268 for the illegitimate agnate progeny of Leopold Eberhard, Duke of Württemberg-Mömpelgard and charts for Württemberg, Nassau, Anhalt, Brandenburg, and Denmark. See also Leo van de Pas, *Ancestors* [of Frédéric, Sophie, and May Giscard d'Estaing, grandchildren of the French president and Anne-Aymone Sauvage de Brantes] (ca. 2000).

The Royal Descents of 900 Immigrants

1. Ferdinand I, King of Naples, d. 1494, illegitimate son (by Giraldona Carlino) of Alfonso V, King of Aragón, Sicily and Naples, d. 1458 (and a first cousin of the younger Ferdinand I, first King of united Spain) = (1) Isabella of Clermont; (2) Joanna of Aragón

2. (by 1) Eleanor of Naples = Hercules I, Duke of Modena and Ferrara, Renaissance patron

3. Isabella of Este, Renaissance patroness = Francis II Gonzaga, Marquess of Mantua

4. Frederick II Gonzaga, Duke of Mantua, Marquess of Montferrat, Renaissance patron = Margaret Palaeologina of Montferrat, a descendant, via counts of Savoy and dukes of Berry, of John II, King of France, d. 1364

5. Isabella Gonzaga = Ferdinando Francesco II d'Avalos, Prince of Francavilla and Montesarchio

6. Alfonso II Felice d'Avalos, Prince of Francavilla and Montesarchio = Lavinia Feltrina della Rovere of Urbino, daughter of Guidobaldo II della Rovere, Duke of Urbino (and Vittoria Farnese, granddaughter of Pope Paul III [Alessandro Farnese]), son of Francesco Maria I della Rovere, Duke of Urbino, and Eleanor Gonzaga, daughter of Francis II Gonzaga, Marquess of Mantua, and Isabella of Este, Renaissance patroness, generation 3 above

7. Caterina d'Avalos = Camillo Gonzaga, Count of Novellara

8. Lavinia Teresa Gonzaga = Wratislaus I, Prince zu Fürstenberg

9. Katharina Eleanora, Princess zu Fürstenberg = Francis William, Count of Hohenems

10. Maria Franziska, Countess of Hohenems = (Johann) Ferdinand Franz Leopold, Count of Enkevoirth

11. Maria Antonia Cäcilia, Countess Enkevoirth = Johann Joseph von Rottal, Reichsgraf von Rottal

12. Maria Franziska Emanuela von Rottal = (Franz) Anton, Reichsgraf Breunner-Enkevoirth

The Royal Descents of 900 Immigrants

13. Karl Borromäus Ignaz Josef, Count Breunner-Enkevoirth = Maria Josepha Franziska Anna Judith Walpurga Magdalena, Countess von Khevenhüller zu Frankenburg

14. Josef Ludwig Nepomuk Franz de Paula Kajetan Xavier, Count Breunner-Enkevoirth = Maria Anna Josefa Franziska Walpurgis, Countess von Pergen

15. August Ferdinand Paul Ludwig, Count Breunner-Enkevoirth = Maria Teresia, Countess Esterházy de Galántha, a descendant via Limburg-Stirum, Limburg-Bronckhorst, Hohstein-Schaumberg, Brunswick-Lüneburg-Celle, Mecklenburg-Schwerin, Brandenburg, Saxony, and Austria, of Albert II, Holy Roman Emperor, King of Hungary and Bohemia, d. 1439, and Elizabeth of Bohemia

16. August Johann Evangelist Karl Borromäus Josef, Count Breunner-Enkevoirth = Maria Agatha Franzisca Ludovica Stephanie, Countess Széchényi

17. Agathe Johanna Maria Gobertina, Countess Breunner-Enkevoirth = John Whitehead, son of Robert Whitehead, inventor of the torpedo

18. Agatha Whitehead = Georg(e) (Johannes, Ritter, not Baron) von Trapp (1880-1947) of Vermont, who with second wife, Maria Augusta Kutschera, and the seven children below, formed the noted Trapp Family Singers, inspiration for the Broadway musical and film *The Sound of Music*

19. **Agathe (Johanna Erwina Gobertina) von Trapp** of Vt. and Md., d. unm.

19. **Hedwig (Maria Adolpine Gobertina) von Trapp** of Vt., d. unm.

19. **Johanna Karolina von Trapp** of N.Y. = Ernst Florian **Winter**.

19. **Maria (Agatha) Franziska (Gobertina) von Trapp** of Vt., d. unm.

19. **Martina von Trapp** of Vt. = Jean **Dupire**.

19. **Dr. Rupert Georg von Trapp** of Vt. = (1) Henriette Lajoie; (2) Janice Tyre.

19. **Werner von Trapp** of Vt. = Erika Klambauer.

The Royal Descents of 900 Immigrants

Sources: Wikipedia entries for George, Rupert, Agathe, Maria Franziska, Werner, Hedwig, Johanna (Karolina), and Martina von Trapp, and Robert Whitehead, the last of which misidentifies the parents of Agathe (Whitehead) von Trapp; Martin Gschwandtner, *Auguste Caroline Lammer (1885-1937)* (2015), esp. p. 130 (Whitehead chart-Auguste Caroline married Frank Whitehead, brother of Agatha [Whitehead] von Trapp); *Gothaisches Genealogisches Taschenbuch der Gräflichen Häuser, 1893*, p. 162 (Breunner-Enkevoirth, generations 15-16); *GH des A*, vol. 133 (*Fürstliche Häuser*, vol. 7, 1966), pp. 569, 571, 576 (generations 13-16, in a Schönburg-Hartenstein ahnentafel), Prof. Dr. Ernst Heinrich Kneschke, *Neues Allgemeines Deutsches Adels-Lexikon*, vol. 2 (1860), pp. 66-68 (Breunner-Enkevoirth, generations 12-15); Franz Xavier Schweickhardt, *Darstellung des Erzherzogthums Oesterreich unter der Ens, Viertel unterm Manhartsberg*, vol. 2 (1834), pp. 163-64 (Rottal, Enkevoirth); *ES* 2: 12: 145 (Hohenems), 2: 5: 15 (Fürstenberg); Jacobus Wilhelmus Imhof, *Corpus Historiæ Genealogicæ Italiæ et Hispaniæ* (1702), pp. 148-49 (d'Avalos) and James Ross Mellon, *The Great Uprooting: Ancestors of the Mellon, Rüesch and Delafield Families* (2008), chart XXIII, sheets II and III, chart XVIII, sheet II (generations 1-6) and chart XXXVII, sheet I (Farnese, to Pope Paul III). This descent was developed and brought to my attention by John Blythe Dobson of Winnipeg, Manitoba, Canada. Various of the von Trapp siblings had later careers.

The Royal Descents of 900 Immigrants

1. Ferdinand I, King of Naples, d. 1494, illegitimate son (by Giraldona Carlino) of Alfonso V, King of Aragón, Sicily and Naples, d. 1458 (and a first cousin of the younger Ferdinand I, first King of united Spain) = (1) Isabella of Clermont; (2) Joanna of Aragón

2. (by 1) Eleanor of Naples = Hercules I, Duke of Modena and Ferrara, Renaissance patron

3. Isabella of Este, Renaissance patroness = Francis II Gonzaga, Marquess of Mantua

4. Frederick II Gonzaga, Duke of Mantua, Marquess of Montferrat, Renaissance patron = Margaret Palaeologina of Montferrat, a descendant, via counts of Savoy and dukes of Berry, of John II, King of France, d. 1364

5. Isabella Gonzaga = Ferdinando Francesco d'Avalos, Prince of Francavilla and Montesarchio

6. Alfonso II Felice d'Avalos, Prince of Francavilla and Montesarchio = Lavinia Feltrina della Rovere of Urbino, daughter of Guidobaldo II della Rovere, Duke of Urbino (and Vittoria Farnese, granddaughter of Pope Paul III [Alessandro Farnese]), son of Francesco Maria I della Rovere, Duke of Urbino, and Eleanor Gonzaga, daughter of Francis II Gonzaga, Marquess of Mantua, and Isabella of Este, Renaissance patroness, generation 3 above

7. Isabella d'Avalos, Princess of Francavilla = Íñigo d'Avalos, Prince of Francavilla

8. Francesca d'Avalos = Marino II Caracciolo, Prince of Avellino

9. Francesco Marino Caracciolo, Prince of Avellino = Geronima Pignatelli, see below

10. Giovanna Caracciolo = Nicolo d'Avalos, Prince of Montesarchio and Troia

11. Ippolita d'Avalos = Francesco Ruffo, Duke of Bagnara, Prince of Motta San Giovanni

12. Carlo Ruffo, Prince of Sant'Antimo = Anna Giuseppa Cavaniglia, see below

13. Cecilia Ruffo = Andrea Colonna, Prince of Stigliano

The Royal Descents of 900 Immigrants

14. Clelia Colonna = Francesco Maria Correale, Count of Terranova

15. Matilda Correale = Giovanni Antonio Maresca Donnorso, Count of Tronco, son of Nicola Maresca Donnorso, 3rd Duke of Serracapriola, prime minister of the Kingdom of Naples, and Maria Margherita di Sangro, a descendant, via dukes of Sangro and Andria, princes of Francavilla, and marquesses of Baux, of Onorato II Grimaldi, Prince of Monaco, d. 1662, himself a descendant, via Landi, Cordova, and señores/senhores de Salvatierra (and two illegitimacies) of Edward I, King of Portugal, d. 1438

16. Margherita Maresca Donnorso Correale = Arturo, Count de la Feld

17. Giuseppe Uberto, Count de la Feld = Angela Bianchi

18. Maria Luisa, Countess de la Feld = Hans Rüesch

19. **Vivian Rüesch** of N.Y. = James Ross **Mellon** II, b. 1942, African hunter, author and editor, scion of the Gulf Oil family, a great-great-grandson of Judge Thomas Mellon, founder of the Mellon Bank, great-great-nephew of the latter's son, Andrew William Mellon, financier, Secretary of the Treasury, diplomat and founder of the National Gallery of Art, and first cousin twice removed of the latter's children: Paul Mellon and Ailsa (Nora) Mellon, both art patrons and philanthropists (Paul of the National Gallery and Yale Center for British Art). Ailsa was the first wife of diplomat David Kirkpatrick Este Bruce, SETH. A second cousin once removed of J.R. Mellon II is Paul Mellon's daughter, Catherine Conover Mellon, wife of (1) John William Warner, Jr., Secretary of the Navy and U.S. senator (who later married Elizabeth [Rosemond] Taylor [Hilton Wilding Todd Fisher Burton Warner Fortensky]) and (2) Ashley Carrithers. J.R. "Jay" Mellon's most recent book is *The Judge: A Life of Thomas Mellon, Founder of a Fortune* (2012).

1. Henry II, King of Castile, d. 1379 = Joanna of Peñafiel

2. (illegitimate by Beatríz Ponce de León y Xérica, daughter of Pedro Ponce de León, II. Señor de Marchena, and Beatríz de Xérica, SETH) Fadrique of Castile, Duke of Benavente = Leonor Sánchez

The Royal Descents of 900 Immigrants

of Castile, illegitimate daughter (by ———) of Sancho of Castile, Count of Albuquerque, brother of the above Henry II

3. Leonor of Castile = Pedro Manrique de Lara y Mendoza, lord of Amusco and Treviño

4. Leonor Manrique = Álvaro de Zuñiga, Duke of Plasencia, Arévalo and Béjar, d. 1488. By a second wife, his niece Leonor Pimentel, he was the father of Isabel de Zuñiga y Pimentel, wife of Fadrique Álvarez de Toledo, 2nd Duke of Alba and mother of Pedro Álvarez de Toledo, Marquess of Villafranca del Bierzo. This last married María Osorio Pimentel, Marquesa of Villafranca del Bierzo, and was the father of Leonor Álvarez de Toledo, wife of Cosimo I de' Medici, Grand Duke of Tuscany, see below. García Álvarez de Toledo, Marquess of Coria, eldest son of the 2nd Duke of Alba and Isabel de Zuñiga y Pimentel, married Beatríz Pimentel y Pacheco and was the father of Fernando Álvarez de Toledo, 3rd Duke of Alba, infamous governor of the Spanish Netherlands.

5. Pedro de Zuñiga y Manrique, Count of Bañares = Teresa de Guzmán. A daughter, Leonor de Zuñiga y Guzmán, married Juan Alonso de Guzmán y Ribera, 3rd Duke of Medina Sidonia, and was a great-grandmother of both Alfonso Pérez de Guzmán y Sotomayor, 7th Duke of Medina-Sidonia, the admiral of the Spanish Armada, and Gaspar Philip de Guzmán, known as the Count-Duke of Olivares, the Spanish statesman and chief minister of Philip IV, King of Spain.

6. Juana Manrique de Zuñiga = Carlos de Arellano, Count of Aguilar

7. Juana de Zuñiga y Arellano = Hernán Cortés, 1st Marquess del Valle de Oaxaca, conqueror of Mexico, and a first cousin once removed of Francisco Pizarro, conqueror of Perú

8. Martín Cortés (de Monroy), 2nd Marquess del Valle de Oaxaca = Ana de Arellano, a first cousin, daughter of Pedro Ramírez de Arellano (brother of 6. Juana above) and Ana Ramírez de Arellano

9. Juana Cortés y Arellano = Pedro de Mendoza Carrillo de Albornoz, Count of Priego

The Royal Descents of 900 Immigrants

10. Juana Estefanía Cortés, Marquesa del Valle de Oaxaca, who assumed the surname Cortés = Diego Tagliavia d'Aragona, Duke of Terranova

11. Giovanna Tagliavia d'Aragona, Duchess of Terranova = Ettore Pignatelli, Prince of Nola, etc.

12. Geronima Pignatelli = Francesco Marino Caracciolo, Prince of Avellino, see above

The major de' Medici line is:

1. Cosimo I de' Medici, Grand Duke of Tuscany, d. 1574 = Leonor Álvarez de Toledo, see above. Their son, Francesco Maria de' Medici, Grand Duke of Tuscany, married Joanna, Archduchess of Austria (daughter of Ferdinand I, Holy Roman Emperor, and Anne of Bohemia, SETH), and was the father of Marie de' Medici, Queen of Henry IV, King of France.

2. Isabella de' Medici = Paolo Giordano Orsini, Duke of Bracciano, great-grandson of Pope Julius II (della Rovere) and Pope Paul III (Farnese)

3. Eleanora Orsini = Alessandro Sforza, Duke of Segni

4. Paolo II Sforza, Marquess of Procena = Olympia Cesi

5. Francesco Sforza, Duke of Onano = Dorotea di Tocco

6. Eleanora Sforza = Carlo Onero Cavaniglia, Duke of San Giovanni

7. Troiano Cavaniglia, Marquess of San Marco = Cecilia de Ponte Carafa Tovar

8. Anna Giuseppa Cavaniglia = Carlo Ruffo, Prince of Sant' Antimo, see above

Sources: James Ross Mellon II, *The Great Uprooting: Ancestries of the Mellon, Rüesch and Delafield Families* (2008), esp. chart XXIII, sheets II and III and chart XVIII, sheets II and III (with the Cortés descent on chart XXXIX-B, sheets I and II [and note chart XIV, sheets II-IV], the de' Medici on chart XII, sheets I and II, the Grimaldis on chart XXXVI, sheets II and III, 5 Renaissance popes [of the Cibò, Borgia, della Rovere,

The Royal Descents of 900 Immigrants

Farnese, and Boncompagni families] on chart XXXVII, sheets I and II, and a kinship via Trubetskoy to Leo, Count Tolstoy on chart XLVI, sheet IV). This remarkable work is based in part, among other printed sources, on *Libro d'Oro della Nobilità Italiana,* vol. 6 (1923-25), pp. 744-45 (de la Feld); *G H des A, Fürstliche Häuser,* Band VI (1961), pp. 477-79 (Maresca Donnorso), Band V (1959), pp. 440 (Colonna), 555-56 (Ruffo), Band XV (1997), pp. 540-41, 543, 547-51 (d'Avalos), Band IV (1956), p. 382 (Caracciolo); Conte Pompeo Litta and Lucino Basdonna, *Famiglie Celebri Italiane,* vol. 3 (1833), Colonna section, Table 15 esp. (for Clelia Colonna) and 2nd ser., vol. 1 (1902), Caracciolo section, Table 5 esp. (for Giovanna Caracciolo); Daniel MacGregor, *Brooke's Book: Ancestry of Brooke Shields* (privately distributed, 1988), #s 747-48, p. 14 (generation 10 above), #s 1495-96, p. 21 (and #s 755-56, p. 14) (generation 9), #s 1509-10, p. 21 (generation 8), #s 3019-20, p. 32 (generation 7), #s 6039-40, p. 49 (and #s 2347-48, p. 25) (generation 6), #s 4693-94, p. 38 (generation 5), #s 9387-88, p. 59 (generation 4), #s 18773-74, p. 88 (and #s 11559-60, p. 71) (generation 3), #s 23119-20, p. 106 (and #s11553-54, p. 70) (generation 2) and #s 23107-8, p. 106 (generation 1, all for the descent from Ferdinand, first King of Naples), plus, for the Cortés descent, #s 1511-12, p. 21, #s 3023-24, p. 32, #s 6047-48, p. 49, #s 12095-96, p. 76, and #s 24189-90, p. 114, plus *ES* 2: 3: 3: 544 and 2: 2: 64 (Castile). See also *Who's Who in the World,* 16th ed. (1999), p. 1391 (Hans Rüesch) and *ES*1: 2: 129-30 (Gonzaga of Mantua), 124 (Este of Modena and Ferrara), 48 (Castile, Aragón and Naples). For the Alva, Medina-Sidonia and Olivares connections see the Manrique (12) Zuñiga (5, 6), (Álvarez) de Toledo (8, 10) and Guzmán (8, 12) charts in Christoph Weber, *Genealogien zur Papstgeschichte* (*Päpste und Papsttum,* vol. 29 in 6 vols.), vols. 5-6 (2002) and *TG* 28 (2014): 124-25, plus *Charles II,* pp. 3-6, 9-10, 17-18, 31, 54.

The Royal Descents of 900 Immigrants

1. Casimir IV, King of Poland, d. 1492 = Elizabeth of Austria

2. Sophie of Poland = Frederick, Margrave of Brandenburg-Anspach

3. Barbara of Brandenburg-Anspach = George, Landgrave of Leuchtenberg

4. Elizabeth of Leuchtenberg = John I, Count of Nassau-Dillenburg, brother of William the Silent, Prince of Orange, d. 1584, first Stadholder of The Netherlands

5. George, Count of Nassau-Dillenburg = Amalia of Sayn-Wittgenstein

6. Margaret of Nassau-Dillenburg = Otto, Count of Lippe-Brake

7. Casimir, Count of Lippe-Brake = Anna Amelia of Sayn-Wittgenstein-Homburg

8. Sophia Hedwig of Lippe-Brake = Ludwig Franz, Count of Sayn-Wittgenstein-Berleburg

9. Ludwig Franz, Count of Sayn-Wittgenstein-Berleburg = Helena Amelia of Solms-Baruth, see below

10, 11. Christian Ludwig Casimir, Count of Sayn-Wittgenstein-Berleburg = Amelia Louisa Finck von Finckelstein

11, 12. (Ludwig Adolf) Peter, Prince of Sayn-Wittgenstein, Marshal of Russia = Antonia Snarska

12, 13. Amelia of Sayn-Wittgenstein = Pierre (Peter), Prince Troubetskoy

13, 14. Pierre (Peter), Prince Troubetskoy = Varvara, Princess Troubetskoy. He was the father by Ada Winans/Wynans, later his second wife, of both Paul (Paolo, Prince) Troubetskoy (1866-1938), who lived in the U.S. 1914-20 and married Elin Sundström and Muriel Marie Beddam, and of

14, 15. **Pierre (Prince) Troubetskoy** (1864-1936) of Va., portrait painter = Mrs. Amélie Louise Rives Chanler, known as Amélie Rives, author of *The Quick or the Dead?*

13, 14. Nicolas, Prince Troubetskoy, brother of the second Pierre/Peter = Sophia Lopuchin

14, 15. Sergei, Prince Troubetskoy = Praskovia, Princess Obolensky

15, 16. Vladimir, Prince Troubetskoy = Elisabeth, Princess Galitzine

16, 17. Sergei, Prince Troubetskoy = Nina Gugajew

17, 18. **Vladimir, Prince Troubetskoy**, b. 1957, of Wisc., polymer chemist = Olga Merzelikin.

3. Elizabeth of Brandenburg-Anspach = Ernest, Margrave of Baden-Durlach

4. Anna of Baden-Durlach = Charles I, Count of Hohenzollern

5. Joachim, Count of Hohenzollern = Agnes, Countess of Honstein

6. John George, Count of Hohenzollern = Eleanor von Promnitz

7. Anna Ursula of Hohenzollern = Johann Bernard II von Maltzan, Baron of Wartenberg and Penzlin

8. Barbara Helena, Baroness von Maltzan = Elias Andreas, Count Henckel von Dommersmarck

9. Helena Constantia, Countess Henckel von Dommersmarck = John Christian I, Count of Solms-Baruth

10. Helena Amelia of Solms-Baruth = Ludwig Franz, Count of Sayn-Wittgenstein-Berleberg, also a descendant of Casimir IV and Elizabeth of Austria, see above

Sources: *WWA 2009* (2008), p. 5044; *ES* 2: 24: 158, 160 (Trubetskoy), 2: 4: 123, 127 (Sayn-Wittgenstein-Berleburg), 1: 3: 336, 338 (Lippe-Brake), 2: 17: 58 (Solms-Baruth), 2: 9: 68 (Henckel von Donnersmarck), 2: 20: 27 (von Maltzan), 2: 1: 147 (Hohenzollern), and *ES*, tables for Poland, Brandenburg-Anspach, Leuchtenberg, Nassau-Dillenburg and Baden-Durlach. See also *ANB* (under Amélie Rives) and J.R. Childs, *Reliques of the Rives (Ryves)* (1929), p. 585, and W.D. Taylor, *Amélie Rives (Princess Troubetskoy)* (1973).

The Royal Descents of 900 Immigrants

1. Casimir IV, King of Poland, d. 1492 = Elizabeth of Austria
2. Sophie of Poland = Frederick, Margrave of Brandenburg-Anspach
3. Sophie of Brandenburg-Anspach = Frederick II, Duke of Liegnitz
4. Frederick III, Duke of Liegnitz = Catherine of Mecklenburg-Schwerin
5. Helena of Liegnitz = Sigismund VI, Herr von Kurzbach
6. Sophia von Kurzbach = Heinrich Anselm, Herr von Promnitz
7. Sigismund Siegfried, Count von Promnitz = Catherine Elizabeth of Schönburg-Lichtenstein
8. Benigna von Promnitz = John Frederick, Count of Solms-Laubach
9. Erdmuthe Benigna of Solms-Laubach = Henry X, Count Reuss-Ebersdorf, son of Henry X, Count Reuss-Lobenstein (and Marie Sybil of Reuss-Obergreitz), son of Henry II, Count Reuss-Gera, and Magdalena of Schwarzburg-Rudolstadt, daughter of Albert VII, Count of Schwarzburg-Rudolstadt and Juliana of Nassau-Dillenburg, sister of William the Silent, Prince of Orange, d. 1584, 1st Stadholder of The Netherlands. Henry X and Erdmuthe Benigna were great-great-grandparents of Leopold I, King of the Belgians, and great-great-great-grandparents of Victoria, Queen of Great Britain.
10. Erdmuthe Dorothea, Countess Reuss-Ebersdorf = Nicholas Ludwig, Count of Zinzendorf and Pottendorf (1700-1760), religious reformer, founder of the Moravian brotherhood, American resident Dec. 1741-Jan. 1743, ARD, SETH.
11. Henrietta Benigna Justina, Countess of Zinzendorf and Pottendorf (accompanied her father to America) = Johann Michael, Baron von Watteville
12. **Anna Dorothea Elizabeth, Baroness von Watteville**, of Pa. = Hans Christian Alexander **von Schweinitz**.

The Royal Descents of 900 Immigrants

13. Lewis David von Schweinitz (1780-1834), Moravian clergyman, botanist, pioneer mycologist = Louise Amalia Ledoux

14. Edmund Alexander de Schweinitz (1825-1887), Moravian Bishop and historian = (1) 17. Amalie Joanna Lydia von Tschirschky und Bögendorff of Pa., ARD, SETH; (2) Isabel Allen Bogge.

Sources: *ES,* tables for Poland, Brandenburg-Anspach, Liegnitz, Kurzbach (1: 4: 89b), Promnitz (2: 19: 161) and Solms-Schwarzburg-Rudolstadt, Nassau-Dillenburg, Reuss-Gera, Reuss-Lobenstein, and Reuss-Ebersdorf; *DAB* (N.L. von Zinzendorf and L.D. and E.A. von [de] Schweinitz); Gerhard Meyer, *Nikolas Ludwig von Zinzendorf, Eine Genealogische Studie mit Ahnen und Nachfahrenliste* (1966). See also *Prince Charles*, vol. 2 (1977), J 457-58 (p. 21), K 877-78 (p. 33), L 1755-56 (p. 50), M 3509-10 (p. 74), N 7019-20 (p. 110), O 14039-40 [not 10437] (p. 110), P 28076-77, also N 1341-42 (pp. 237-38, 102), O 2683-84, also M 5765-66 (pp. 148, 80), N 11531-32 (p. 112, Casimir IV and Elizabeth), K 913-14 (p. 33), L 1825-26 (p. 50), M 3651-52, also L 497-98 (pp. 75, 46, Albert VII and Juliana), etc., *NK1*:68-70, 72-75, 77-78, and J.H. Martin, *Historical Sketch of Bethlehem in Pennsylvania, with Some Account of the Moravian Church*, 2nd ed. (1873), pp. 10-11. This "improved" descent was brought to my attention by John Blythe Dobson of Winnipeg, Manitoba, Canada.

The Royal Descents of 900 Immigrants

1. Casimir IV, King of Poland, d. 1492 = Elizabeth of Austria
2. Sophie of Poland = Frederick, Margrave of Brandenburg-Anspach
3. Elizabeth of Brandenburg-Anspach = Ernest, Margrave of Baden-Durlach
4. Anna of Baden-Durlach = Charles I, Count of Hohenzollern
5. Marie Jacoba of Hohenzollern = Leonhard V, Count of Harrach
6. Carl, Count of Harrach = Maria Elisabeth von Schrattenbach
7. Leonhard VII Karl, Count of Harrach = Maria Franziska, Princess von Eggenberg
8. Maria Anna Elisabeth, Countess von Harrach = Franz Maximilian, Count of Mansfeld-Vorterort
9. Carl Franz, Count of Mansfeld-Vorterort = Maria Eleanore of Mansfeld-Vorderort, a first cousin
10. Heinrich Franz, Count of Mansfeld-Vorterort = Anna, Countess Czernin
11. Maria Isabella, Countess of Mansfeld-Vorterort = Franz Gundaccar, Prince of Colloredo-Mansfeld
12. Ferdinand, Count of Colloredo-Mansfeld = Margareta von Ziegler
13. Joseph, Prince of Colloredo-Mansfeld = Theresia von Lebzeltern
14. Franz de Paula Ferdinand Gundaccar, Count of Colloredo-Mansfeld = Maria, Baroness Lexa von Aehrenthal, a descendant of Gustav I Vasa, King of Sweden, d. 1560) and Margareth Leijonhufvud (SETH, neither of whom has proved royal medieval ancestry) via Counts of Östfriesland, Princes of Liechtenstein, and von Aehrenthal
15. Ferdinand Johannes Hieronymus Maria, Count of Colloredo-Mansfeld = Eleanor (Nora) Iselin of N.Y.
16. **Franz Ferdinand Romanus, Count of Colloredo-Mansfeld** of Mass. = Mabel Bayard Bradley. Their son, Ferdinand Peter Ernst, Count Colloredo-Mansfeld, b. 1939, is a founding

The Royal Descents of 900 Immigrants

partner and CEO of Cabot, Cabot & Forbes (real estate) in Boston, and married Suzanna Lawrence.

Sources: *WWA 2006* (2005), p. 909, *Almanach de Gotha* 2012, pp. 477-79 and *ES* 1: 3: 37 (Colloredo-Mansfeld), *ES* 2: 19: 87 (Mansfeld-Vorderort), *ES* 2: 5: 30-31 (Harrach), Hohenzollern (2: 1: 147), and tables for Baden-Durlach, Brandenburg-Anspach and Poland). The descent from Gustav I Vasa, King of Sweden, was developed and brought to my attention by John Blythe Dobson of Winnipeg, Manitoba, Canada.

The Royal Descents of 900 Immigrants

1. Louis XI, King of France, d. 1483 = (1) Margaret of Scotland; (2) Charlotte of Savoy

2. (illegitimate by Marguerite de Sassenage) Jeanne of Valois = Louis de Bourbon, Count of Roussillon, see next chart

3. Anne de Bourbon = Jean II, Baron d'Arpajon

4. Jacques d'Arpajon, Vicomte d'Hauterive = Charlotte de Castelpers

5. Charles, Baron d'Arpajon = Françoise de Montal

6. Jean V, Baron d'Arpajon = Jacquette de Castelnau-Clermont-Lodeve

7. Louis, Duc d'Arpajon = Gloriande de Lauzières

8. Jean Louis d'Arpajon, Marquis de Severac = Charlotte de Vernou de la Rivière-Bonneuil

9. Louis, Marquis d'Arpajon = Anne-Charlotte le Bas de Montargis

10. Anne Claudine Louise d'Arpajon = Philippe de Noailles, Duc de Mouchy, SETH

11. **Louis-Marie de Noailles, Vicomte de Noailles** (1756-1804), leader in the American and French revolutions and in the American émigré community of the 1790s (fought at the battles of Savannah and Yorktown, resided in Philadelphia from 1793 to 1800) = Anne-Jeanne-Baptiste-Adrienne-Louise-Catherine Dominique de Noailles, SETH.

5. Jeanne d'Arpajon (sister of Charles) = Guyon de Belvezer, Baron de Jalavoux and d'Oradour, Seigner de Joncheres

6. Anne de Belvezer = Antoine de Douhet de Marlat, Seigneur de Védrine

7. Françoise de Douhet de Marlat = François de Pons, Seigneur de la Grange de Bart (du Bou[s]chet)

8. Marie de Pons = Charles Motier de Champetières, Baron de Vissac

The Royal Descents of 900 Immigrants

9. Édouard Motier de la Fayette, Baron de Vissac = Marie-Catharine de Chavaniac

10. Michel-Louis-Christophe-Roch-Gilbert Motier, Marquis de La Fayette = Marie-Louise-Julie de la Rivière, see below

11. **Marie-Joseph-Paul-Yves-Roch-Gilbert Motier, Marquis de La Fayette (Lafayette)** (1757-1834), the American Revolutionary general and French statesman = Marie-Adrienne-Françoise de Noailles, ARD, SETH.

12. Anastasie-Louise-Pauline Motier = Just-Charles-César de Fay, Count de la Tour-Maubourg

13. Adrienne-Jenny-Florimonde de Fay = Charles-Joseph-Maurice Hector, Count Perrone de San Martino

14. Louise Perrone di San Martino = Félix-Henri-Victor-Gaspard-Édouard-Alexandre, Count Rignon

15. Maria Cristina Giovanna Luigia Rignon = Augusto Filippo Stanislas Gazelli di Rossana

16. Luisa Albertina Cristina Giovanna Gazelli di Rossana = Fulco Antonio Francesco Benjamino, 1st Prince Ruffo di Calabria

17. Paola Margherita Giuseppina Consiglia Ruffo di Calabria (Queen Paola of the Belgians) = Albert II, King of the Belgians (1993-2013, abdicated), b. 1934

18. Philippe I, King of the Belgians (since 2013), b. 1960 = Mathilde-Marie-Christiane-Ghislaine d'Udekem d'Acoz (Queen Mathilde of the Belgians)

18. Astrid-Josephine-Charlotte-Fabrizia-Elisabeth-Paola-Maria, Princess of the Belgians, b. 1962 = Lorenz Otto Carl Amadeus Thadeus Maria Pius Andreas Marcus d'Aviano, Archduke of Austria, grandson of Karl (Charles) I, Emperor of Austria

18. Laurent-Benoit-Baudouin-Marie, Prince of the Belgians, b. 1963 = Claire Coombs

4. Charlotte d'Arpajon (sister of Jacques) = Gabriel, Vicomte d'Estaing

The Royal Descents of 900 Immigrants

5. François, Vicomte d'Estaing = Catherine de Chabannes

6. Jean III, Vicomte d'Estaing = Gilberte de la Rochefoucauld

7. Jacques d'Estaing, Baron de Plauzet = Catherine du Bourg

8. Jean d'Estaing, Baron de Saillans = Claude de Combourcier

9. Gaspard d'Estaing, Comte de Saillans = Philiberte de la Tour de Saint-Vidal

10. Charles-François d'Estaing, Marquis de Saillans = Marie-Henriette de Colbert, great-niece of Jean-Baptiste Colbert, Marquis of Seignelay, financial minister of Louis XIV

11. **Jean-Baptiste-Charles-Henri-Hector, Comte d'Estaing** (1729-1794), French general and admiral in the early years of the American and French Revolutions, also active in the Caribbean = Marie-Sophie Rousselet de Châteaurenault.

Given the interest in a descent from Agnès Sorel and Diane de Poitiers, Duchess of Valentinois, a second line is offered below.

1. Charles VII, King of France, d. 1461 = Marie of Anjou

2. (illegitimate by Agnès Sorel) Charlotte de Valois = Jacques de Brezé, Count de Maulévrier

3. Louis de Brezé, Count de Maulévrier = Diane de Poitiers, Duchess de Valentinois, mistress of Henry II, King of France

4. Françoise de Brezé = Robert de la Marck, Duc de Bouillon

5. Diane de la Marck = Henri de Clermont, Count de Tonnerre

6. Charles-Henri de Clermont, Count de Clermont et de Tonnerre = Catherine-Marie d'Escoubleau de Sourdis

7. Isabeau de Clermont = Jacques de Beauvau, Seigneur du Rivau

8. Françoise de Beauvau = Jacques de Voyer, Vicomte de Paulmy

9. Jean-Armand de Voyer, Marquis de Paulmy = Radegonde de Mauroy

The Royal Descents of 900 Immigrants

10. Marie-Françoise-Céleste de Voyer = Charles-Yves-Jacques de La Rivière, Marquis de Paulmy, Count de La Rivière

11. Charles-Yves-Thibault de La Rivière, Marquis de La Rivière = Julie-Célestine Barberin de Reignac

12. Julie-Louise-Céleste de La Rivière = Joseph-Yves-Thibault-Hyacinthe de La Rivière, Marquis de La Rivière

13. Marie Louise Julie de La Rivière = Michel Louis Christophe Roch Gilbert Motier, Marquis de La Fayette, see above

14. **Marie-Joseph-Paul-Yves-Roch-Gilbert Motier, Marquis de La Fayette (Lafayette)** (1757-1834), the American revolutionary general and French statesman = Marie-Adrienne-Francoise de Noailles, ARD, SETH.

Sources: For the line from Louis XI, see *ES* 2: 3: 2: 305, 328 (Bourbon bastard), *ES* 2: 3: 4: 808-9 and *Anselme*, vol. 5, pp. 895-900 (d'Arpajon, with Anselme naming the husband of Jeanne d'Arpajon, generation 5 above), Leo Lindemans, *Voorouderstafel van het Belgisch Koninghuis/ Tableau d'Ascendance de la Maison Royale Belge/Ahnentafel des Belgischen Königshauses*, vol. 2, Ruffo di Calabria (1999), #s 1-3, 6-7, 14-15, 30-31, 62-63, 126-27, 252-53, 504-5, 1008-9, 2018-19, 4038-39 (generations 7-18, with different from the above [and I infer erroneous] parents for Françoise de Douhet de Marlat) and Arnaud Chaffanjon, *La Fayette et sa Descendance* (1976), pp. 38-41, 99-101, 113-20, 131-34, 139-40, 143-44, 155-56, 160-61 (generations 7-18); Jacques Dupont, *Cahiers de St. Louis*, #21 (1982), pp. 1733-35 (generations 6-10, with the parents for Françoise de Douhet de Marlat given as the above "Antoine [de Douhet], Seigneur de Marlat and Anne de Belvezer" [cited by Lindemans, in the above, who also cites Count Albert de Remacle, *Dictionnaire Généalogique des Familles d'Auvergne*, 3 vols. (1995-96), 1: 453, 2: 25, 275 and 3: 131]), *Saint Allais*, vol. 8, pp. 236-37 (Belvezer); *ANB* and *D de la N*, vol. 7, pp. 466-67, 469-72 (d'Estaing), vol. 6, pp. 20-25, 32-35 (Colbert). This "improved" line from King Louis XI of France was brought to my attention by John Blythe Dobson of Winnipeg, Manitoba, Canada.

For the descent from Charles VII see Chaffanjon above, pp. 73-75 (generations 4-14); *Anselme*, vol. 7, pp. 168-69 (de la Marck), vol. 8, pp. 271-72 (Brezé). For Mathilde d'Udekem d'Acoz see *NEXUS* 16 (1999):

The Royal Descents of 900 Immigrants

202. Each of the children of Albert II, King of the Belgians, and Queen Paola now have children themselves; those to date of King Philippe and Queen Mathilde are Princess Élisabeth, b. 2001, Prince Gabriel Baudouin, b. 2003, Prince Emmanuel Leopold, b. 2005, and Princess Éleanore, b. 2008 (see *Almanach de Gotha*, 188th ed. [2012, in English], pp. 101-3).

The Royal Descents of 900 Immigrants

1. Louis XI, King of France, d. 1483 = (1) Margaret of Scotland; (2) Charlotte of Savoy

2. (illegitimate by Marguerite de Sassenage) Jeanne de Valois = Louis de Bourbon, Count of Roussillon, illegitimate son, by Jeanne de Burman, of Charles I, Duke of Bourbon, son of John I, Duke of Bourbon, and Marie of Berry, daughter of John I, Duke of Berry (and Jeanne of Armagnac), son of John II, King of France, d. 1364, and Bona of Bohemia, SETH

3. Suzanne de Bourbon = Jean de Chabannes, Count of Dammartin

4. Antoinette de Chabannes = René d'Anjou, 2nd Baron de Mézières, son of Louis d'Anjou, 1st Baron de Mézières (and Anne de la Trémouille), illegitimate son of Charles of Anjou, Duke of Maine (and ——), son of Charles, Count of Maine (and Cobella Ruffo, Countess of Montalto), son of Louis II, King of Naples, Sicily, Jerusalem and Aragón, d. 1384, and Marie of Châtillon-Blois

5. Françoise d'Anjou = (2) Jean III, Seigneur de Rambures, Count of Dammartin and Guines

6. Jean IV, Seigneur de Rambures = Claude de Bourbon, granddaughter of an illegitimate son of of John II, Count of Vendôme

7. Charles I, Seigneur de Rambures = 8. Renée de Boulainvilliers, daughter of 7. Antoine de Boulainvilliers, Count of Courtenay (and Jeanne-Catherine de Vieuxpont), son of 6. Philippe de Boulainvilliers, Count of Courtenay (and Jeanne de Briçon), son of Philippe de Boulainvilliers, Count of Fauquemberghe (her first husband) and Françoise d'Anjou, #5 above

8, 9. Charlotte de Rambures = François de La Roche, 1st Marquis de Fontenilles

9, 10. Renée-Charlotte de La Roche = (Catherine) Jean-Emmanuel de Timbrune de Valence, Marquis de Valence

10, 11. Eméric-Emmanuel de Timbrune de Valence, Marquis de Valence = Marie-Anne du Breulh

The Royal Descents of 900 Immigrants

11, 12. Vincent-Sylvestre de Timbrune de Valence, Marquis de Ferrières = Marie-Louise de Losse

12, 13. (Jean-Baptiste) Cyrus (Marie-Adélaïde) de Timbrune, Count de Valence = Edmée-Nicole-Pulchérie Brûlart

13, 14. Louise-Philippine-Séraphine-Félicité de Timbrune = (Antoine) Philippe-Fiacre-Ghislain de Vischer, Baron de Celles

14, 15. Pulchérie-Félicité-Cyrette de Vischer = Henri-Louis-Espérance de Laërce (des Acres), Count de L'Aigle

15, 16. (Marie Louise) Geneviève-Ghislaine des Acres = (Bernard-Auguste) René, Count de Menthon

16, 17. Bernard-Auguste-Marie-Ghislaine, Count de Menthon = Marie-Thérèse-Anne-Luglienne de La Bourdonnaye

17, 18. **Jeanne-Marie-Bernarde de Menthon**, sometime of Washington, D.C. = Pierre de Lagarde **Boal** (1895-1966), U.S. diplomat, SETH, and was the mother of Margaret Mathilde Boal, wife of (Francis Preston) Blair Lee (III) (1916-1985), Secretary of State, lt. gov., and act. gov. of Maryland.

Sources: *WWWA*, vol. 4, *1961-1968* (1968), p. 97 (P. de L. Boal) and *WWA* (F.P. Blair Lee III) plus undoubtedly much research in French Archives by the Boal Mansion Museum in Boalsburg, Pa., which has traced the French ancestry of Mrs. Lee over many years. Independently, John Blythe Dobson of Winnipeg, Manitoba, Canada, has found and sent to me copies of various printed materials, including the death notice of Jeanne Marie (Bernard de Menthon) Boal in *The Washington Post* of 24 Sept. 1984 and *Rex Annuaire Généalogique de la Noblesse de France*, 6th ed. (1914, at NEHGS), p. 890 (Menthon); death notice of Pulchérie-Félicité-Ghislaine (de Vischer de Celles), Comtesse de l'Aigle, which names her parents and daughters) in *Le Bulletin Heraldique* 7 (1888), columns 119-20 and L. de Magny et al., *Nobiliaire Universal de France*, vol. 17 (1885, also at NEHGS), p. 8 (de l'Aigle); Henri, Baron de Woëlmont de Brumagne, *Notices Généalogiques*, 9th series, vol. 3 (1925), pp. 796-801 (Timbrune); *Courcelles*, vol. 1, pp. 10-11 (de La Roche-Fontenilles); *Anselme*, vol. 8, pp. 67-69 (Rambures); *ES* 2: 3: 2: 305, 314, 328, 337 (illegitimate lines

The Royal Descents of 900 Immigrants

from Kings of France and their agnate kinsmen) and *ES* 2: 2: 26 (Anjou to Louis II of Naples, etc.); *De Favigny-Renansart* (anonymous pamphlet, 1851), pp. 11-12 (Boulainvilliers). See also *Revue de l'Agenais et des Anciennes Provinces du Sud-Ouest* 26 (1899): 333-41 (generations 9/10-13/14) and W.J. d'Ablaing, Baron van Giesenburg, *De Ridderschappen in het Konigrijk der Nederlanden* (1875), p. 190 (Vischer).

The Royal Descents of 900 Immigrants

1. Charles VII, King of France, d. 1461 = Marie of Anjou

2. (illegitimate by Agnès Sorel) Marie-Marguerite of Valois = Olivier de Coëtivy, seigneur de Taillebourg

3. Gillette de Coëtivy = Jacques d'Estouteville, Seigneur de Beyne, Baron d'Ivry

4. Charlotte d'Estouteville = Charles of Luxembourg, Count of Brienne, great-nephew of Jacqueline of Luxembourg, wife secondly of Richard Woodville, 1st Earl Rivers, and mother of Elizabeth Woodville, SETH, Queen of Edward IV, King of England

5. Françoise of Luxembourg = Bernhard III, Margrave of Baden-Baden

6. Christopher II, Margrave of Baden-Rodemachern = Cecily of Sweden, daughter of Gustav I (Vasa), King of Sweden, d. 1560, and Margaretta Leijonhujvud, SETH, for neither of whom, however, is a descent from earlier kings now generally accepted.

7. Edward [Fortunatus], Margrave of Baden-Baden = Maria von Eychen

8. Hermann [Fortunatus], Margrave of Baden-Rodemachern = Antoinette Elisabeth von Criechingen

9. Maria Sidonia of Baden-Rodemachern = Philip, Count of Hohenzollern-Hechingen

10. Hermann Friedrich, Count of Hohenzollern-Hechingen = Maria Josepha (Josephine) Theresia of Oettingen-Spielberg

11. Maria Josepha of Hohenzollern-Hechingen = Francis Wenceslaus, Prince von Clary and Aldringen

12. Maria Josepha, Countess von Clary and Aldringen = Caspar Benedikt Anthon Johann Nepomuk, Baron von Ledebur zu Wicheln

13. Maria Josepha, Baroness von Ledebur zu Wicheln = Heinrich (Wilhelm) Gundaccar (Vincenz Ferrerius Franz Xavier Anton von Padua Joseph Alois Felix), Count von Wurmbrand-Stuppach

The Royal Descents of 900 Immigrants

14. Francizka de Paula, Countess von Wurmbrand-Stuppach = Ludwig Maria Alois, Count Széchényi (von Sárvár Felsővidek)

15. Emmerich (Irme), Count Széchényi = Alexandra, Countess Sztáray-Szirmay

16. **Ladislaus (Lásyló), Count Széchényi** (1899-1938), Hungarian diplomat, sometime of Newport, R.I. = Gladys Moore Vanderbilt, daughter of Cornelius Vanderbilt II, financier, railroad president and philanthropist, and Alice Claypoole Gwynne. Their youngest daughter Sylvia, Countess Széchényi, married Anton Carl Sylvester, Count Szápáry, ARD, SETH.

Sources: *GH des A, Gräfliche Häuser* B, vol. 2 (1960), pp. 417-20 and *Gothaisches Genealogisches Taschenbuch des Gräfliche Häuser* B, vol. 114 (1941), pp. 489-91 (Széchényi), *GH des A, Fürstliche Häuser*, vol. 4 (1956), p. 335, and *Almanach de Gotha, 1844*, pp. 252-53 (Wurmbrand-Stuppach); *Allgemeines Genealogisches und Staats-Handbuch* (1811), pp. 909-10 (Wurmbrand-Stuppach), 641-42 (Ledebur-Wicheln), 262-63 (Clary und Aldringen), 119-20 (Hohenzollern-Hechingen) and *ES*, charts for Hohenzollern-Hechingen, Baden-Baden and Sweden); *Anselme* 3: 726-30 (Luxembourg), 8: 99 (d'Estouteville). For Ledebur-Wicheln see also *Gothaisches Genealogisches Taschenbuch der Uradeligen Häuser, 1914*, p. 487, Luxembourg and d'Estouteville pedigrees appear on *ES* 2: 1: 2: 231-32 and *ES* 2: 13: 108 respectively and Edward, Margrave of Baden-Baden and Maria von Eychen, generation 7 above, are L 605-6, p. 47, in *Prince Charles*, and Charles VII of France and Agnes Sorel appear under Q 19344, p. 355.

The Royal Descents of 900 Immigrants

1. James II, King of Scotland, d. 1460 = Mary of Guelders
2. Mary Stewart = James Hamilton, 1st Baron Hamilton
3. James Hamilton, 1st Earl of Arran = (1) Elizabeth Home; (2) Janet Beaton
4. (illegitimate by ――) Sir John Hamilton of Samuelston = Janet Home
5. Margaret Hamilton = David Douglas, 7th Earl of Angus
6. Margaret Douglas = Sir Walter Scott of Buccleuch

7. Mary Scott = William Eliot of Larriston	7. Walter Scott, 1st Baron Scott of Buccleuch = Margaret Kerr
8. Jean Eliot = Thomas Rutherford of Edgerston	8. Walter Scott, 1st Earl of Buccleuch = Mary Hay
9. Robert Rutherford of Edgerston = Marion Riddell	9. (illegitimate by ――) Francis Scott of Mangerton = ――
10. John Rutherford of Edgerston = Barbara Abernethy	10. Elizabeth Scott = Sir John Scott, 1st Bt.
11. Barbara Rutherford = Archibald Bennet of Chesters	11. Margaret Scott of Ancrum = John Murray of Bowhill
12. Andrew Bennet of Chesters = Dorothy Collingwood	12. Anne Bennet = 12. John Murray of Unthank

13. **Barbara Bennet** of N.C. = 13. **James Murray** of N.C. and Mass.
14. Elizabeth Murray = Edward Hutchinson Robbins
15. Anne Jean Robbins = Joseph Lyman (III)

The Royal Descents of 900 Immigrants

16. Catherine Robbins Lyman = Warren Delano, Jr.
17. Sara Delano = James Roosevelt
18. Franklin Delano Roosevelt (1882-1945), 32nd U.S. President = (Anna) Eleanor Roosevelt

11. **John Scott** of N.Y. (brother of Mrs. Murray) = Magdalen Vincent. Their son John Scott (Jr.) married Marion Morin and was the father of John Morin Scott, lawyer, New York legislator and revolutionary leader, who married Helena Rutgers.

13. **Barbara Murray** of N.C. (sister of James Murray of N.C. and Mass.) = Thomas **Clarke**. A daughter, Anne Clarke, married William Hooper, lawyer and signer of the Declaration of Independence from North Carolina.

13. John Murray (brother of James and Barbara) = Mary Boyles
14. **John Boyles Murray** of N.Y. = Martha McClenachan.

11. Thomas Rutherford of Edgerston (brother of Barbara) = Susanna Riddell
12. Sir John Rutherford of Edgerston = Elizabeth Cairncross
13. **Walter Rutherford** of N.Y. = Catherine Alexander.
13. John Rutherford of Edgerston (and N.Y.) = Eleanor Elliot, ARD, SETH (John's family returned to Scotland but a great-grandson, Archibald Russell, SETH, also immigrated to N.Y. and married Helen Rutherford Watts, a great-granddaughter of John's brother Walter).

Sources: *DAB* (John Morin Scott), M.S.B. Chance & M.A.E. Smith, *Scott Family Letters* (1930), p. 318 esp. and N.M. Tiffany, *Letters of James Murray, Loyalist* (1901), pp. 292-94 esp.; *MGH*, 4th ser., vol. 2 (1906-7):166-68 (Scotts, Murrays, and Bennets); T.H. Cockburn-Hood, *The Rutherfords of That Ilk & Their Cadets* (1884), chart at end esp., Livingston Rutherfurd, *Family Records and Events* [Rutherfurd family] (1894), chapters 2-3 (pp. 85-256) and chart at end esp., and *Rutherford*, vol. 1, pp. 27, 31, 37-38, 47, 57, 70-71, 73-74 and rev. ed., vol. 1, pp. 76,

The Royal Descents of 900 Immigrants

79-81, 83, 85-86, 89-90, 93, 103; *Douglas*, p. 217 (Scott of Ancrum); *SP*, articles on the Scotts of Buccleuch, Douglases of Angus, and Hamiltons of Arran.

The Royal Descents of 900 Immigrants

1. James II, King of Scotland, d. 1460 = Mary of Guelders
2. Mary Stewart = James Hamilton, 1st Baron Hamilton
3. James Hamilton, 1st Earl of Arran = Janet Beaton
4. Jean Hamilton = Alexander Cunyngham, 5th Earl of Glencairn
5. William Cunyngham, 6th Earl of Glencairn = Janet Gordon
6. Margaret Cunyngham = Sir Lachlan MacLean of Duart, son of Hector MacLean of Duart and Janet Campbell, SETH
7. Lachlan Maclean of Torloisk = Marian MacDonald of Clanranald
8. Mary MacLean = John Garbh MacLean of Drimnin
9. Catherine MacLean = Hugh (Ewen) MacLean of Balliphetrish
10. Catherine MacLean = Allan MacLean of Grisiboll, son of Neil MacLean of Drimnacross and Florence MacDonald of Morrer, SETH
11. **Neil MacLean (McLean)** of Conn. = Mrs. Hannah Stillman Caldwell.
11. **Allan MacLean (McLean)** of Conn. = (1) Susanna Beauchamp; (2) Mary Loomis. John MacLean, a brother of the immigrants Neil and Allan, married Anne MacLean of Kilmore in Mull and was the father of John MacLean, a merchant of Norfolk, Va., said to have married there and left a daughter, but for whom I can find no NDTPS.

Sources: J.P. MacLean, *A History of the Clan MacLean* (1889), pp. 295-96 (Drimnacross and Grisiboll), 302 (Drimnin), 312 (Torloisk), 90-137 (Duart) and *The Scottish Genealogist* 36 (1989): 94-95 (MacLean of Balliphetrish); *SP* and *CP* (Glencairn, Arran, Hamilton). See also John J. McLean, *A Brief History of the Ancestry and Posterity of Doctor Neil McLean of Hartford, Conn., U.S.A.* (1900), and Mary McLean Hardy, *A Brief History of the Ancestry and Posterity of Allan MacLean, 1715-1786, Vernon, Colony of Connecticut, New England, U.S.A.* (1905). These immigrants were first brought to my attention by Thomas Frederick Gede of Davis, California, and part of the line was suggested as well by Shirley Goodwin Bennett.

The Royal Descents of 900 Immigrants

1. James II, King of Scotland, d. 1460 = Mary of Guelders
2. Mary Stewart = James Hamilton, 1st Baron Hamilton
3. James Hamilton, 1st Earl of Arran = Janet Beaton
4. Jean Hamilton = Alexander Cunyngham, 5th Earl of Glencairn
5. William Cunyngham, 6th Earl of Glencairn = Janet Gordon
6. Elizabeth Cunyngham = (1) James Crawford of Crosbie; (2) Alexander Cunyngham of Craigends
7. (by 1) Jane Crawford = Patrick Crawford of Auchenames
8. Elizabeth Crawford = Robert Hunter of Hunterston
9. James Hunter = Margaret Spalding
10. **Robert Hunter** (d. 1734), colonial governor of N.Y. and N.J., lt. gov. of Va., governor of Jamaica, soldier, dramatist = Elizabeth Orby.

7. (by 2) William Cunyngham of Craigends = Elizabeth Stewart
8. William Cunyngham of Craigends = Elizabeth Napier, daughter of John Napier, the mathematician and inventor of logarithms, and Ann Chisolm
9. Alexander Cunyngham of Craigends = Janet Cunyngham
10. Rebecca Cunyngham = John Hamilton of Grange
11. Alexander Hamilton of Grange = Elizabeth Pollok
12. James Hamilton of Nevis, B.W.I.
13. (illegitimate by Mrs. Rachel Faucette Levine) **Alexander Hamilton** (1755 or 1757-1804) of N.Y., the statesman, first U.S. Secretary of the Treasury = Elizabeth Schuyler.

Sources: *BLG*, 18th ed., vol. 3 (1972), p. 473 (Hunter of Hunterston) and *BLG* 1939, p. 505 (Craufurd of Auchenames); *SP* and *CP* (Glencairn, Arran, Hamilton); *Hamilton*, pp. 1069-70, 221; Roberdeau Buchanan, *Genealogy of the Roberdeau Family* (1876), p. 20 (Cunyngham of Craigends), *BP* and *SP* (Napier).

The Royal Descents of 900 Immigrants

1. James II, King of Scotland, d. 1460 = Mary of Guelders
2. Mary Stewart = James Hamilton, 1st Baron Hamilton
3. Elizabeth Hamilton = Matthew Stewart, 2nd Earl of Lennox
4. John Stewart, 3rd Earl of Lennox = Anne Stewart
5. John Stewart, lord of Aubigny = Anne de la Queuille
6. Esmé Stewart, 1st Duke of Lennox, Scottish political leader = Catherine de Balsac
7. Mary Stewart = John Erskine, 2nd Earl of Mar
8. Sir Charles Erskine = Mary Hope
9. Mary Erskine = William Hamilton of Wishaw
10. Katherine Hamilton = David Pitcairn
11. **John Pitcairn** (1722-1775), British commander at the Battle of Lexington in April 1775 = Elizabeth Dalrymple.

Sources: *DAB*; Constance Pitcairn, *The History of the Fife Pitcairns* (1905), pp. 409-53 (esp. 419); *SP*, *BP* and *CP* (Belhaven, Rosslyn, Mar, Lennox, Hamilton — under Arran in *SP*).

The Royal Descents of 900 Immigrants

1. James II, King of Scotland, d. 1460 = Mary of Guelders
2. Mary Stewart = James Hamilton, 1st Baron Hamilton
3. James Hamilton, 1st Earl of Arran = Janet Beaton
4. Jean Hamilton = Alexander Cunyngham, 5th Earl of Glencairn
5. William Cunyngham, 6th Earl of Glencairn = Janet Gordon
6. Margaret Cunyngham = Sir Lachlan MacLean of Duart

7. Beathag MacLean = Hector Maclaine of Lochbuie	7. Hector MacLean of Duart = Isabella Acheson
8. Lachlan Maclaine of Lochbuie = 9. Margaret MacLean, daughter of 8. Hector MacLean of Torloisk (and Janet MacLean), son of 7. Lachlan MacLean of Torloisk (and Marian Campbell), son of Sir Lachlan MacLean of Duart and Margaret Cunyngham, 6. above	8. Sir John MacLean, 1st Bt. (and 1st Adlad Macklier in Sweden) = Anna Gubbertz
9. Hector Maclaine of Lochbuie = Margaret Campbell of Lochnell	9. David, Baron MacLean (Friherre in Sweden) = Eleanora Elisabet, Countess von Ascheberg
10. Mary Maclaine = Lachlan MacLean of Kingairloch	10. Anna Isabella, Baroness MacLean = Andrew Fraser of Torosay
11. Hugh MacLean of Kingairloch = Elizabeth McLachlan of McLachlan	11. John Fraser of Inverlochy and Pictou, N.S. (1783) = (Mary Stewart?)
12. Hector MacLean of Kingairloch, of Pictou, N.S. 1803-4 =	12. Elizabeth Fraser

13. Elizabeth McLachlan MacLean = George McKay (Mackay)

The Royal Descents of 900 Immigrants

14. **George Alexander McKay** of Mass. = Christina McMillan. Their daughter, Elizabeth Florence McKay, married Osborne Maguire and left a daughter, Edna Beatrix Maguire, wife of Harold Goodwin and mother of Shirley Elizabeth Goodwin, former NEHGS trustee and wife of Exxon director and U.S. Treasury Under-Secretary Jack Franklin Bennett (1924-2010).

Sources: Research of Shirley Goodwin Bennett and Paul C. Reed based in part on the N.S. baptismal record and Mass. VRs for G.A. McKay; *BLG* 18th ed., vol. 3 (1972), pp. 590 (MacLean of Kingairloch, to Mrs. McKay), 583 (Maclaine of Lochbuie); J.P. MacLean, *A History of the Clan MacLean* (1889), pp. 91-159, 240-42, 261-63, 312-13; *The Scottish Genealogist* 16 (1969): 29-30 (Fraser), James N.M. MacLean, *The MacLeans of Sweden* (1971), pp. 24-29, 32-38, and *Elgenstierna*, vol. 5, pp. 139-40, 142-43 (MacLean, Makeleer); *SP* and *CP* (Glencairn, Arran, Hamilton).

The Royal Descents of 900 Immigrants

1. James II, King of Scotland, d. 1460 = Mary of Guelders
2. Mary Stewart = James Hamilton, 1st Baron Hamilton

3. Elizabeth Hamilton = Matthew Stewart, 2nd Earl of Lennox
3. James Hamilton, 1st Earl of Arran = Janet Beaton

4. Margaret Stewart = John Fleming, 2nd Baron Fleming
4. Jean Hamilton = Alexander Cunyngham, 5th Earl of Glencairn

5. Margaret Fleming = Patrick Murray of Philiphaugh
5. William Cunyngham, 6th Earl of Glencairn = Janet Gordon

6. Katherine Murray = John Somerville of Cambusnethan
6. Elizabeth Cunyngham = Alexander Cunyngham of Craigends

7. Jean Somerville = James Dunlop of Dunlop
7. William Cunyngham of Craigends = Elizabeth Stewart

8. James Dunlop of Garnkirk = Bessie ——
8. Jean Cunyngham = James Roberton of Bedlay

9. James Dunlop of Garnkirk = 9. Elizabeth Roberton

10. **Archibald Dunlop** of Conn. = Mary Beach.

Sources: *NEHGR* 152 (1998): 186-96, 154 (2000): 321-24, both by John L. Scherer, much aided on the 1998 article by Andrew B.W. MacEwen of Stockton Springs, Maine, plus the 5 April 1654 marriage contract between James Dunlop, 2nd of Garnkirk, and Elizabeth Roberton (Dunlop of Garnkirk Papers, Mitchell Library, Glasgow) and Alexander Nesbit, *A System of Heraldry*, new ed. (1816), appendix 2, p. 147 (Roberton).

The Royal Descents of 900 Immigrants

1. Robert II, King of Scotland, d. 1390 = (1) Elizabeth Mure
2. Marjorie Stewart = John Dunbar, 1st Earl of Moray
3. Thomas Dunbar, 2nd Earl of Moray = Margaret (Seton?)
4. Janet Dunbar = James Crichton, 2nd Baron Crichton
5. William Crichton, 3rd Baron Crichton = Marion Livingston
6. Sir James Crichton (*not* an illegitimate son of Princess Margaret Stewart, daughter of James II, King of Scotland, and Mary of Guelders) = Catherine Borthwick
7. Margaret Crichton = John Robertson of Muirton, son of Alexander Robertson of Struan and Elizabeth Stewart, daughter of John Stewart, 1st Earl of Atholl, and Eleanor Sinclair, SETH, and granddaughter of Dowager Queen Joan Beaufort of Scotland
8. David Robertson of Muirton = —— Innes
9. William Robertson of Muirton = Isabel Petrie
10. William Robertson of Gledney = Margaret Mitchell (parents of William [= Eleanor Pitcairn] and Mary Robertson [= William Adam], and grandparents of historian William Robertson [IV], [author of *The History of America*, who married Mary Nesbit, a cousin], and classical architect Robert Adam, who d. unm.).
11. Jean Robertson = Alexander Henry
12. **John Henry** of Va. = Mrs. Sarah Winston Syme (parents of Patrick Henry, 1736-1799, orator and revolutionary statesman, who married Sarah Shelton and Dorothea Spotswood Dandridge).

Sources: *ANB* (William Robertson IV, who never visited America, and Patrick Henry), W.T.J. Gun, *Studies in Hereditary Ability* (1928), pp. 170-81 and Mary Selden Kennedy, *Seldens of Virginia and Allied Families*, vol. 2 (1911), pp. 387-92; *BLG* 1937, p. 2452 (Robertson, under Williamson of Lawers) and Rev. Hew Scott, *Fasti Ecclesiae Scoticanea* (1914 ed.), vol. 1, p. 40, #1736 (for the forename of Margaret *Mitchell*), this latter noted by John A. Clark of Cambridge, Mass.; *Oxford DNB* (William Robertson, Robert Adam); *SP* and *CP* (Crichton, Frendrault, Moray).

    This chart is *out of order*, and should follow that for Rev. David Lindsay of Va. It is retained here to emphasize the deleted descent from James II, King of Scotland, erroneously given in *BLG* 1937, as above.

The Royal Descents of 900 Immigrants

1. Albert II, Holy Roman Emperor, King of Hungary and Bohemia, d. 1439 = Elizabeth of Bohemia

2. Anna of Austria = William, Duke of Saxony and Landgrave of Thuringia

3. Margaret of Saxony = John Cicero, Elector of Brandenburg

4. Ursula of Brandenburg = Henry V, Duke of Mecklenburg-Schwerin

5. Sophia of Mecklenburg-Schwerin = Ernest, Duke of Brunswick-Lüneburg-Celle

6. Margaret of Brunswick-Lüneburg-Celle = John, Count of Mansfeld-Hinterort

7. Maria of Mansfeld-Hinterort = Philip V, Count of Mansfeld-Vorderort

8. Susanna Polyxena Catharina, Countess Mansfeld-Vorderort = Mathias Ernest, Count Berchtold

9. Franz Karl, Count Berchtold = Esther Elisabeth Prazmová de Bilkova

10. Franz Anthony, Count Berchtold = Marie Esther Elisabeth von Sinzendorf

11. Prosper Anthony, Count Berchtold = Marie Teresa Eleanora Petrvaldská de Petrvaldu

12. Leopold, Count Berchtold = Marie Johanna von Magnis

13. Sigismund Andreas Corsinus, Count Berchtold = Ludmilla Maria Theresa Wratislavová, Countess Mitrowicz and Schönfeld

14. Ludmilla Gizella Theresa, Countess Berchtold = Hubert Heinrich, Count de la Fontaine and d'Harnoncourt-Unverzagt

15. Hubert Karl Sigismund Joseph Franz, Count de la Fontaine and d'Harnoncourt-Unverzagt = Josepha Juliane, Countess Mittrowsky von Mitrowicz (see pp. 895-96)

16. **René Vladimir Hubert Maria, Count de la Fontaine and d'Harnoncourt-Unverzagt**, known as **René d'Harnoncourt**

The Royal Descents of 900 Immigrants

(1901-68), director of the Museum of Modern Art in New York City, authority on Native American art = Sara Carr. Their daughter, Anne Julie d'Harnoncourt (1943-2008), wife of Joseph Rishel, was director and CEO of the Philadelphia Museum of Art, 1982-2008.

This line, noted from online sources by Thomas Frederick Gede, SETH, is confirmed by *ES* 2, charts for Hapsburgs (Holy Roman Emperors), Saxony, Brandenburg-Schwerin and Brunswick-Lüneburg and *ES* 1: 3: 44 (Mansfeld-Hinterort), 42 (Mansfeld-Vorderort); *Gothaisches Genealogisches Taschenbuch der Gräflichen Häuser, 1827* (Berchtold) or Duchlau Berchtold, *Haus Berchtold mit Wappenabbildung* (1893) (neither at NEHGS); *G H des A*, vol. 23, *Gräfliche Häuser B*, vol. 2 (1960), pp. 117, 119 (de la Fontaine and d'Harnoncourt-Unverzagt).

An "improved" line from Sigismund I, King of Poland, d. 1548, brought to my attention by John Blythe Dobson of Winnipeg, Manitoba, appears on pp. 895-96 herein.

The Royal Descents of 900 Immigrants

1. James I, King of Scotland, d. 1437 = Joan Beaufort, daughter of John Beaufort, Marquess of Somerset and Dorset, and Margaret Holand, SETH
2. Joan Stewart ("the dumb lady," both deaf and mute) = James Douglas, 1st Earl of Morton
3. Janet Douglas = Patrick Hepburn, 1st Earl of Bothwell
4. Janet Hepburn = George Seton, 3rd Baron Seton
5. George Seton, 4th Baron Seton = Elizabeth Hay
6. John Seton of Cariston = Isabel Balfour
7. George Seton of Cariston = Margaret Ayton
8. George Seton of Cariston = Cecilia Kynnynmond
9. Isabella Seton = Sir George Seton of Parbroath
10. Robert Seton = ——
11. James Seton = Margaret Newton
12. John Seton = Elizabeth Seton of Belsies
13. **William Seton** of N.Y. = (1) Rebecca Curson, daughter of Richard Curson of Md., ARD, SETH, and Elizabeth Becker (their son, William Magee Seton, married Elizabeth Ann Bayley, known as Mother (later Saint) [Elizabeth Ann Bayley] Seton, foundress of the American Sisters of Charity); (2) Anna Maria Curson.
13. **Margaret Seton** of N.Y. = Andrew **Seton** (of Barnes, almost certainly a kinsman). Mary Seton, their daughter, married John de Ponthieu Wilkes and was the mother of Charles Wilkes, naval officer and explorer, who married Jane Jeffrey Renwick and Mrs. Mary H. Lynch Bolton.

Sources: Monsignor Robert Seton, *An Old Family or the Setons of Scotland and America* (1899), pp. 176-78, 197-98, 239-73, 312-13 esp.; *SP* and *CP* (Seton [under Winton in *SP*], Bothwell, Morton).

The Royal Descents of 900 Immigrants

1. James I, King of Scotland, d. 1437 = Joan Beaufort
2. Joan Stewart, "the dumb lady" = James Douglas, 1st Earl of Morton
2. Annabella Stewart = George Gordon, 2nd Earl of Huntly
3. John Douglas, 2nd Earl of Morton = Janet Crichton
3. Isabel Gordon = William Hay, 3rd Earl of Erroll
4. Elizabeth Douglas = Robert, Lord Keith
4. Thomas Hay = Margaret Logie
5. William Keith, 3rd Earl Marischal = Margaret Keith, a cousin
5. George Hay, 7th Earl of Erroll = Margaret Robertson
6. William, Lord Keith =
6. Elizabeth Hay
7. Margaret Keith = Sir William Keith of Ludquhairn
8. Sir William Keith, 1st Bt. = ——
9. Sir Alexander Keith, 2nd Bt. = Margaret Bannerman
10. Sir William Keith, 3rd Bt. = Jean Smith
11. **Sir William Keith, 4th Bt.** (1680-1749), colonial governor of Pa. and Del. = Anne Newbury.

7. George Keith, 4th Earl Marischal (brother of Lady William Keith) = Margaret Ogilvy
8. Sir James Keith of Benholm = Margaret Lindsay
9. Elizabeth Keith = Sir Archibald Primrose, 1st Bt.
10. Margaret Primrose = Sir John Foulis, 1st Bt.
11. Elizabeth Foulis = Alexander Gibson of Durie
12. Archibald Gibson, Baron von Gibson in Prussia = Renata Clark
13. Helen Gibson = Otto Ernst, Count von Keyserlingk
14. Otto Alexander Heinrich Dietrich, Count von Keyserlingk = Emilie Alexandrine, Countess von Dönhoff

The Royal Descents of 900 Immigrants

15. Friederike Caroline Alexandrine Emma, Countess von Keyserlingk = Gustav Friedrich Eugen von Below (their son, Friedrich Karl Bogislav von Below, married Maria Karoline Elizabeth von der Goltz and was the father of [Anton] Georg Hugo von Below, German historian)

16. Karl Emil Gustav von Below = Eleonore Melitta Behrend

17. Marie Eleonore Dorothea von Below = Wernher Theodor August Friedrich Wilhelm von Quistorp

18. Emmy Melitta Cécile von Quistorp = Magnus Alexander Maximilian, Freiherr (Baron) von Braun

19. **Wernher Magnus Maximilian, Freiherr (Baron) von Braun** (1912-1977) of Huntsville, Ala., the rocket scientist = 19. Maria Irmengard Emmy Luise Gisela von Quistorp of Ala., ARD, SETH, his first cousin, daughter of 18. Alexander August Gustav Henrik Achim Albrecht von Quistorp (son of generation 17 above) and Theda Elisabeth Klementine Franziska von Falkenhayn, SETH.

Sources: *DAB*, *GPFPM* 472-80, *CB* (Keith of Ludquhairn); *SP* and *CP* (Marischal, Morton, Erroll, Huntly) (Sir William Keith, 4th Bt.); *GHdesA,* vol. 21, *Freiherrliche Häuser A*, vol. 3 (1959), pp. 519-28, and *Ahnentafeln Berühmter Deutscher*, vol. 4 (1938), for Georg von Below, esp. tafeln 1 and 7, pp. 284, 288 (von Braun).

The Royal Descents of 900 Immigrants

1. James I, King of Scotland, d. 1437 = Joan Beaufort
2. Joan Stewart, "the dumb lady" = James Douglas, 1st Earl of Morton
3. Janet Douglas = Patrick Hepburn, 1st Earl of Bothwell
4. Janet Hepburn = George Seton, 3rd Baron Seton
5. George Seton, 4th Baron Seton = Elizabeth Hay
6. Beatrix Seton = Sir George Ogilvy of Dunlugas
7. Janet Ogilvy = William Forbes of Tolquhon
8. Thomas Forbes of Waterton = Jean Ramsay
9. Grizel Forbes = John Douglas of Inchmarlo
10. John Douglas of Tilquhillie = Agnes Horn
11. Euphemia Douglas = Charles Irvine of Over Boddam
12. **John Irvine** of Ga. = Ann Elizabeth Baillie.
13. Anne Irvine = James Bulloch
14. James Stephens Bulloch = Martha Stewart
15. Martha Bulloch = Theodore Roosevelt
16. Theodore Roosevelt, Jr. (1858-1919), 26th U.S. President = (1) Alice Hathaway Lee; (2) Edith Kermit Carow

Sources: *MCS5*, line 93; *BSIC*, pp. 85-87; *TSA* 8 (1893-94): 40-42; *Forbes*, pp. 396-97, 416; *SP*, articles on Ogilvys (of Dunlugas, later Lords Banff), Setons (Lords Seton, later Earls of Winton), Hepburns (Earls of Bothwell) and Douglases (Earls of Morton).

The Royal Descents of 900 Immigrants

1. Charles VI, King of France, d. 1422 = Isabella of Bavaria (parents of Catherine of France, wife of Henry V, King of England, and of Owen Tudor, and paternal grandmother of Henry VII, King of England)

2. Joanna of France = John VI, Duke of Brittany, son of John V, Duke of Brittany and Joanna of Navarre, SETH

3. Isabel of Brittany = Guy XIV, Count of Laval

4. Louise de Laval = Jean III de Brosse, Count of Penthièvre

5. Isabel de Brosse = Jean IV, Sire de Rieux and de Rochefort, Count of Harcourt

6. Jean de Rieux, Seigneur de Châteauneuf = Béatrix de Jonchères

7. René de Rieux, Seigneur de Sourdéac = Susanne de Sainte-Melaine

8. Marie de Rieux = Sébastien de Ploëuc, Marquis de Timeur

9. Marie de Ploëuc = Guillaume de Penancoët, Seigneur de Kéroualle

10. Henriette-Mauricette de Penancoët de Kéroualle (sister of Louise-Renée de Penancoët de Kéroualle, Duchess of Portsmouth and mistress of Charles II, King of England, SETH) = Philip Herbert, 7th Earl of Pembroke

11. Charlotte Herbert = John Jeffreys, 2nd Baron Jeffreys

12. Henrietta Louisa Jeffreys = Thomas Fermor, 1st Earl of Pomfret. Their daughter, Sophia Fermor, married John Carteret, 1st Earl Granville, British prime minister, and was the mother of Sophia Carteret, wife of William Petty, 1st Marquess of Lansdowne, 2nd Earl of Shelburne, also a British prime minister.

13. **Lady Juliana Fermor** = Thomas **Penn** (1702-1775), proprietor of Pa., son of William Penn, the founder of Pennsylvania, and Hannah Callowhill.

9. Mauricette de Ploëuc (sister of Marie) = Donatien de Maillé, Marquis de Kerman

10. Henri de Maillé, Marquis de Kerman = Marie-Anne du Puy

The Royal Descents of 900 Immigrants

11. Donatien de Maillé, Marquis de Kerman = Marie-Louise Binet de Marcognet

12. Marie-Eléonore de Maillé = Jean-Baptiste-Francois-Joseph, Count de Sade

13. Donatien-Alphonso-François, Count de Sade, known as the Marquis de Sade, 1740-1814, erotic writer, from whose name the word "sadism" is derived = Renée-Pélagie Cordier de Launay de Montreuil

14. Donatien-Claude-Armand, Count de Sade = (Louise-Gabrielle-) Laure de Sade, a cousin

15. (Marie-Antoine-) Auguste, Count de Sade = Charlotte-Germaine de Maussion

16. Laure-Marie-Charlotte de Sade, friend of Marcel Proust, on whom is based the Duchesse de Guermantes in *Remembrance of Things Past* = Adhéaume-Marie-Mériadec de Chevigné

17. Marie-Thérèse-Anne-Josèphe-Germaine de Chevigné = (1) Maurice-Jonathan Bischoffsheim, Paris banker (by whom she was the mother of Marie-Laure (Henriette Anne) Bischoffsheim, wife of (Arthur Anne Marie) Charles, Vicomte de Noailles, and patroness of the arts (Dali, Cocteau, Buñuel, and other Surrealist artists, writers and filmmakers); (2) Franz Wiener de Croisset, French playwright and opera librettist. Her son by the latter, Philippe Wiener de Croisset, was the second husband of Jacqueline Thion de la Chaume, sometime fashion editor of the French *Vogue* and later the third wife of actor Yul Brynner.

18. Germaine Wiener de Croisset = André-Roger Lannes de Montebello, son of George-Ernest-Casimir Lannes de Montebello (and Emilie d'Aviles), son of René Lannes de Montebello and Marie, Princess Lubomirska, daughter of Casimir, Prince Lubomirski and Zénaïde Holynska, SETH

19. **(Guy) Philippe Lannes de Montebello** (b. 1936) of N.Y., museum curator, head of the Metropolitan Museum (of Art) of New York = Edith Bradford Myles.

The Royal Descents of 900 Immigrants

Sources: *DAB* (Thomas Penn) and *GPFPGM* 2: 566-70; *CP* (Pomfret, Grenville, Lansdowne, Jeffreys, Pembroke, Portsmouth); *D de la N*, vol. 15, pp. 628-29 (Penancoët de Kéroualle), 954 (Ploëuc); *Anselme*, vol. 6, pp. 767-68, 771-73 (Rieux), vol. 5, pp. 574-75 (Brosse); *ES2*: 14: 145 (Laval) and for Brittany and France; *ES2*: 10: 60 (Maillé), *D de la N*, vol. 18, pp. 34-35 (de Sade), and Maurice Lever (trans. by Arthur Goldhammer), *Sade: A Biography* (1993), pp. 13-16, 30-35, 99-102 esp.; Laurence Benaïm, *Marie Laure de Noailles: La Vicomtesse du Bizarre* (2001), chart before Chapter 1 and Chapters 1 and 3 esp. (generations 13-17) and note also Princess Marthe Bibesco, *Proust's Oriane, A Diptych* (1952), on Laure Marie Charlotte de Sade, Comtesse de Chevigné); *GF*, pp. 171-73, *GH des A, Fürstliche Häuser*, vol. 5 (1959), p. 508 (Lannes de Montebello) and *Almanach de Gotha* 1855, pp. 182-83 (Lubomirski); Yul "Rock" Brynner II, *Empire and Odyssey: The Brynners in Far East Russia and Beyond* (2006), esp. p. 129. This "improved" descent was brought to my attention by John Blythe Dobson of Winnipeg, Manitoba, Canada.

The Royal Descents of 900 Immigrants

1. Henry IV, King of England, d. 1413 = (1) Mary Bohun; (2) Joanna of Navarre
2. (by 1) Humphrey Plantagenet, Duke of Gloucester = (1) Jacqueline of Bavaria; (2) Eleanor Cobham
3. (illegitimate) Antigone Plantagenet = Henry Grey, 2nd Earl of Tankerville
4. Elizabeth Grey = Sir Roger Kynaston
5. Mary Kynaston = Hywel ap Jenkin
6. Humphrey ap Hywel = Anne Herbert
7. Jane ferch Humphrey ap Hywel = Gruffudd Nannau ap Hywel
8. Hugh ap Gruffudd (Hugh Nannau) = Anne ferch Rhys Vaughan
9. Gruffudd Nannau = Elen ferch John Wynne
10. Catherine Nannau = Robert Vaughan, antiquary, son of Hywel Vaughan ap Gruffudd ap Hywel, and Margaret Owen, daughter of Edward Owen (and Elen Llwyd ferch Robert ap Morgan), son of Lewis Owen and Margaret Puleston, SETH
11. **Jane Vaughan** of Pa. = Robert **Owen** of Pa., ARD, SETH, her second cousin once removed.

8. John ap Gruffudd (John Nannau) (brother of Hugh) = Elsbeth ferch Dafydd Llwyd
9. Lewys ap John Gruffudd = Elen ferch Hywel ap Gruffudd

10. Rees Lewys ap John Gruffudd = Catrin ferch Elisha ap Dafydd
11. Ellis ap Rees (alias Ellis Price) = Anne Humphrey, ARD, SETH
12. **Rowland Ellis** of Pa. = (1) Margaret ferch Ellis Morris.

10. Owain ap Lewys = Mary ferch Tudur Vaughn
11. Robert ab Owain = Margaret ferch John ap Lewys
12. = (2) **Margaret Roberts** of Pa. (no children by Rowland)

12. Lewis ap Robert (brother of Mrs. Margaret Roberts Ellis of Pa.) = Mary ——

13. **Ellis Lewis** of Pa. = (1) Elizabeth Newlin; (2) Mrs. Mary Beakbaine Baldwin.

Sources: *RA* 2: 492-93; 3: 589-92 (generations 3-12 for Rowland Ellis and Margaret Roberts); *PACF*, pp. 200-1 (generations 7-11 for Mrs. Jane Vaughan Owen, brought to my attention by Don Charles Stone of Colorado Springs, Colo.; *Merion*, pp. 216-29, 235-37 (R. Ellis and E. Lewis); *WFP1*, p. 116, footnote 1 and chart between pp. 116-17; *Bartrum* 2, pp. 131, 1428, 148 (generations 4-7).

Note: Ellis Lewys, a third son of Lewys ap John Gruffudd and Elen ferch Hywel ap Gruffudd, married Elen ferch Gruffudd ap Hywel and left a daughter, Elen Ellis, who married Thomas ap Robert. Their son, Robert ap Thomas, by Catrin ——, his wife, left a son, Thomas Roberts, bp. 19 April 1691 at Mallwyn, Merionethshire, suggested in *CVR*, pp. 224-33 as the immigrant Thomas Roberts of Milford, Pa. (= Alice ——).

The Royal Descents of 900 Immigrants

1. Henry IV, King of England, d. 1413 = (1) Mary Bohun; (2) Joanna of Navarre
2. (by 1) Humphrey Plantagenet, Duke of Gloucester = (1) Jacqueline of Bavaria; (2) Eleanor Cobham
3. (illegitimate) Antigone Plantagenet = Henry Grey, 2nd Earl of Tankerville
4. Elizabeth Grey = Sir Roger Kynaston
5. Humphrey Kynaston = Elsbeth ferch Maredudd ap Hywel
6. Margaret Kynaston = John ab Ieuan ab Owain
7. Humphrey Wynn = Mawd ferch Oliver ap Thomas Pryce
8. Catrin Wynn = John Lloyd
9. Charles Lloyd = Elizabeth Stanley
10. **Thomas Lloyd** (1640-1694), dep. gov. of Pa., physician, colonial statesman = (1) Mary Jones of Pa., ARD, SETH; (2) Mrs. Patience Gardiner Story.

10. Charles Lloyd (brother of Dep. Gov. Thomas) = Elizabeth Lort
11. Sampson Lloyd = Mary Crowley
12. Sampson Lloyd = Rachel Champion
13. Charles Lloyd = Mary Farmer
14. Anna Lloyd = Isaac Braithwaite
15. Joseph Bevan Braithwaite = Martha Gillett
16. **Anna Lloyd Braithwaite** of Md. – Richard Henry **Thomas** (1854-1904), physician, Quaker minister, author.

15. Charles Lloyd Braithwaite (brother of Joseph Bevan Braithwaite) = Susanna Wilson
16. Anna Mary Braithwaite = Thomas Crewdson Wilson, a cousin
17. Charles Braithwaite Wilson = Ellen Blanch Hargrove

The Royal Descents of 900 Immigrants

18. Henry Braithwaite Wilson = Margarethe Agnes "Grete" Bodden
19. **Anne Elizabeth Wilson** of Mass. = David Richmond **Gergen** (b. 1942), presidential advisor and historian.

Sources: *RA* 3: 589-93 and *Merion*, pp. 340-42 (Lloyd), and Charles F.H. Evans and Irene Haines Leet, *Thomas Lloyd, Dolobran to Pennsylvania* (1982) (including an ancestor table of Dep. Gov. Thomas Lloyd for 8 generations); *Bartrum 2,* pp. 131, 21 (generations 4-7); David Curtis Dearborn, *Ancestors of David Richmond Gergen and Anne Elizabeth Wilson* (2013, presented to its subjects by NEHGS at its April 2013 annual meeting), pp. 229, 231-32, 237, 239, 241, 243, 245-46, 250, 255, 260, 263, 267, 271, 273, 275, 277, 279, 281, 321-25; Sandys B. Foster, *The Pedigree of Wilson of High Wray and Kendal and the Families Connected with Them* (1890), pp. 100-1, 103-4, 189-91, 197-98 (Catrin/Catherine Wynn to Gov. Thomas Lloyd, Mrs. Thomas, and Charles Braithwaite Wilson above), which takes much of its text from *RLNGF* 2, *passim*; "Oma and Opa: Their Lives" (privately printed for the Braithwaite and Wilson families).

In *RD500* and *RD600* I added to the Lloyd-Braithwaite and G.C. Mahon charts a descent from Sir John Perrot, a sometime alleged illegitimate son of Henry VIII, King of England, by Mary Berkeley. The *Oxford DNB* 43: 810 (and 815 for sources) dismisses this allegation and cites R.K. Turvey, "Sir John Perrot, Henry VIII's Bastard? The Destruction of a Myth," in *Transactions of the Honourable Society of Cymmrodorion* (1992), pp. 79-94.

The Royal Descents of 900 Immigrants

1. Henry IV, King of England, d. 1413 = (1) Mary Bohun; (2) Joanna of Navarre

2. (by 1) Humphrey Plantagenet, Duke of Gloucester = (1) Jacqueline of Bavaria; (2) Eleanor Cobham

3. (illegitimate) Antigone Plantagenet = Henry Grey, 2nd Earl of Tankerville

4. Elizabeth Grey = Sir Roger Kynaston

5. Jane Kynaston = Roger Thornes, son of Thomas Thornes and Mary Corbet, daughter of Sir Roger Corbet and Elizabeth Hopton, SETH

6. John Thornes = Elizabeth Astley

7. Richard Thornes = Margaret —— or Joan ferch Evan Lloyd Fychan

8. Alice Thornes = John Lyttelton (Littleton)

9. Sir Edward Lyttelton (Littleton) = Mary Walter

10. **Nathaniel Littleton** of Va. = Mrs. Anne South(e)y Harmar.

10. Mary Littleton = Gilbert Jones, son of Gilbert Jones (and Joan Moore), son of Humphrey Jones and Gainor Penrhyn, daughter of William Penrhyn and Alice Salway, daughter of Richard Salway and Anne Vaughan, daughter of Roger Vaughan and Eleanor Cornewall, daughter of Sir Thomas Cornewall and Anne Corbet, daughter of Sir Richard Corbet and Elizabeth Devereux, SETH

11. **Mary Jones** of Pa. = Thomas **Lloyd** (1640-1694), dep. gov. of Pa., physician, colonial statesman, ARD, SETH.

Sources: *RD 3*: 586-92 (generations 3-10), and sources cited therein, esp. *Transactions of the Shropshire Archaeological and National History Society*, 4th ser., vol. 3 (1913), pp. 302-32 (Littleton), which notes the marriage of Mary Littleton and "Gilbert Jones, barrister at law, son of Gilbert Jones of Welshpool," A.T. Butler, ed., *Visitation of Worcestershire, 1634* (*HSPVS*, vol. 90, 1938), p. 64, and George Grazebrook and J.P. Rylands, *Visitation of Shropshire, 1623*, vol. 2 (*HSPVS*, vol. 29, 1889), pp. 458-60 (Thornes), 295 (Kynaston), vol. 1

The Royal Descents of 900 Immigrants

(*HSPVS,* vol. 28, 1889), pp. 135-36 (Corbet, Hopton); Littleton-Jones research by Brad Verity, posted on soc.gen.medieval and brought to my attention by John C. Brandon of Columbia, S.C.; Charles F.H. Evans and Irene Haines Leet, *Thomas Lloyd, Dolobran to Pennsylvania* (1982), pp. 4, 14 (Jones), Rev. W.V. Lloyd, *The Sheriffs of Montgomeryshire* (1876), pp. 294, 153 (Penrhyn, Salway), *Bartrum 2*, p. 457 (Vaughan) and *Cornewall*, pp. 189, 203-8. See also *NEHGR* 41 (1887): 364-68, *AP&P* 4: 3: 217-19, and *Foundations* 6 (2014): 53-68 (Michael P. Bodman, who cites Matthew M. Wise, *The Littleton Heritage: Some American Descendants of Col. Nathaniel Littleton [1605-1684] of Nansemond Co., Virginia and His Royal Ancestors* [1997]).

The Royal Descents of 900 Immigrants

1. Henry IV, King of England, d. 1413 = Mary Bohun
2. Humphrey Plantagenet, Duke of Gloucester = (1) Jacqueline of Bavaria; (2) Eleanor Cobham
3. (illegitimate) Antigone Plantagenet = Henry Grey, 2nd Earl of Tankerville
4. Elizabeth Grey = Sir Roger Kynaston
5. Margaret Kynaston = Richard Hanmer
6. Ermin Hanmer = Sir Edward Puleston
7. Margaret Puleston = William Hope
8. John Hope = Maud Ravenscroft
9. George Hope = Elizabeth Knight
10. Magdalen Hope = John Baskerville
11. **John Baskerville** of Md. = Mary Barber.

6. Sir Thomas Hanmer (brother of Ermin) = Jane Brereton
7. Sir Thomas Hanmer = Catherine Salter
8. John Hanmer = Jane Salusbury
9. Sir Thomas Hanmer = Catherine Mostyn
10. Sir John Hanmer, 1st Bt. = Dorothy Trevor
11. Sir Thomas Hanmer, 2nd Bt. = Susan Hervey
12. William Hanmer = Peregrine North
13. Susan Hanmer = Sir Henry Bunbury, 3rd Bt.
14. Isabella Bunbury = John Lee
15. **Charles Lee** (1731-1782), soldier of fortune, U.S. revolutionary general, d. unm.

Sources: P.H. Baskerville, *Genealogy of the Baskerville Family* (1912), pp. 10, 40-45, and *Additional Baskerville Genealogy* (1917), pp. 87-88; *VGE*, pp. 416-17 and Lewys Dwnn and Sir S.R. Meyrick, *Heraldic*

The Royal Descents of 900 Immigrants

Visitations of Wales, vol. 2 (1846), pp. 316 (Hope), 310 (Puleston); *Bartrum 2*, pp. 1458, 949, 131 (Puleston, Hanmer, Kynaston), *DAB* and *Oxford DNB* (Charles Lee); *Ormerod*, vol. 1, pp. 630-31 (Lee), vol. 2, pp. 395-96 (Bunbury); *CB* and *BP* (Bunbury of Stanney and Hanmer of Hanmer, baronets). Note also Calvert Hanmer, *The Hanmers of Marton and Montford, Salop* (1916), pp. 41-44 and chart at end entitled "Extract from the Pedigree of the Hanmers of Hanmer, showing their connection with the families of Bunbury and Lee." The Baskerville descent was developed by Paul C. Reed and anticipated in *TG* 10 (1989, published 1994) and *TVG* 49 (2005): 257-58. From printed sources doubtlessly used by Mr. Reed some time ago, I have, I believe, reconstructed the correct line. Mr. Reed's monograph on this descent is eagerly awaited.

The Royal Descents of 900 Immigrants

1. Rupert III, Holy Roman Emperor, d. 1410 = Elizabeth of Nürnberg

2. Otto of Bavaria, Count Palatine of Mosbach = Joanna of Bavaria-Landshut

3. Amalia of Bavaria = Philip I, Count of Rieneck

4. Dorothea of Rieneck = Frederick IV, Landgrave of Leuchtenberg

5. Amalia of Leuchtenberg = Leonard II von Frauenberg, Count of Haag

6. Maximiliana von Frauenberg = Charles I, Count of Ortenberg

7. Anna Maria of Ortenburg = Hartman II of Liechtenstein-Feldsberg

8. Judith of Liechtenstein-Feldsberg = Johann Joachim, Baron von Zinzendorf and Pottendorf. Their daughter, Anna, Baroness von Zinzendorf and Pottendorf, married Conrad, Count von Starhemberg, and was the mother of [Heinrich] Ernst Rüdiger, Count von Starhemberg, defender of Vienna against the Turks in 1683.

9. Otto Henry, Baron von Zinzendorf and Pottendorf = Anna Apollonia von Zelking

10. Maximilian Erasmus, Count of Zinzendorf and Pottendorf = Anna Amelia of Dietrichstein-Hollenburg

11. George Louis, Count of Zinzendorf and Pottendorf (brother of Dorothea Renata, Countess of Zinzendorf and Pottendorf, wife of Wolfgang Dietrich, Count of Castell-Remlingen, a great-great-grandmother of Leopold I, King of the Belgians, and a great-great-great-grandmother of Victoria, Queen of Great Britain) = Carlotta Justina von Gersdorff

12. **Nicholas Ludwig, Count of Zinzendorf and Pottendorf** (1700-1760), religious reformer, founder of the Moravian brotherhood, American resident Dec. 1741-Jan. 1743 = (1) Erdmuthe Dorothea, Countess Reuss-Ebersdorf, ARD, SETH; (2) Anne Nitschmann.

The Royal Descents of 900 Immigrants

Sources: Meyer per the preceding chart for Erdmuthe Dorothea, *et al.*; *ES*, tables for Bavaria, Rienick (2: 18: 59), Leuchtenberg (2: 16: 97), Frauenburg zum Haag (2: 16: 60), Ortenburg (2: 5: 80), and Liechteinstein-Feldsberg (2: 3: 1: 33); *DGA*, vol. 1 (1939), p. 117 (Starhemberg). Generations 2-10 of this line are followed in *Prince Charles*, #s K919-920, L1837-1838, M3673-3674, N7347-7348, O14695-14696, P 29391-92, Q 58783-84 (P6825-26), Q 13651-52). See also Adelaide L. Fries, ed., *Records of the Moravians in North Carolina, Volume I, 1752-1771* (1922), p. 228, *Volume II, 1752-1775* (1925), pp. 543-46. This "improved" descent was brought to my attention by John Blythe Dobson of Winnipeg, Manitoba, Canada.

The Royal Descents of 900 Immigrants

1. Robert III, King of Scotland, d. 1406 = Annabella Drummond
2. Mary Stewart = Sir James Kennedy of Dunure
3. Gilbert Kennedy, 1st Baron Kennedy = Katherine Maxwell
4. John Kennedy, 2nd Baron Kennedy = Elizabeth Montgomery
5. Janet Kennedy = Sir Alexander Gordon of Lochinvar
6. Janet Gordon = Lachlan Mackintosh of Mackintosh
7. William Mackintosh of Mackintosh = Margaret Ogilvie of Deskford
8. Lachlan Mackintosh of Mackintosh = Agnes Mackenzie, daughter of Sir Kenneth Mackenzie of Kintail and Elizabeth Stewart, SETH
9. William Mackintosh of Borlum = Elizabeth Innes
10. Lachlan Mackintosh of Borlum = Helen Gordon
11. **Col. Henry Mackintosh (McIntosh)** of Mass. and R.I. = Elizabeth Byfield.
12. Elizabeth Mackintosh (McIntosh) = Lachlan Mackintosh (McIntosh) of Mass., her cousin, see below.

11. William Mackintosh of Borlum (brother of Col. Henry of Mass.) = Mary Baillie, sister of the Alexander Baillie of Dunain who married Jean Mackenzie, SETH
12. William Mackintosh of Borlum = Mary Reade
13. **Lachlan Mackintosh (McIntosh)** of R.I. = Elizabeth Mackintosh (McIntosh), his cousin, see above.

12. Lachlan Mackintosh of Knocknagel (brother of the younger William) = Mary Lockhart
13. **John Mohr Mackintosh (McIntosh)** of Ga. = Marjory Fraser.

Sources: Walter H. McIntosh, *A Genealogical Record of Families in New England Bearing the Name McIntosh* (1981), p. 40, and *McIntosh, Mackintosh Families of Scotland and America* (1982), pp. 26, 49-51;

The Royal Descents of 900 Immigrants

Alexander M. Mackintosh, *The Mackintoshes and Clan Chattan* (1903), pp. 106-92, 377-83; *SP&CP* (Kenmure [Gordon] and Cassillis [Kennedy]). See also *BLG,* 18th ed., vol. 1 (1965), pp. 479-80 (generations 6-9) and *NK 1*:45-46, 52-54 (notable descendants of and kinship to Mrs. Karl Marx). Part of this line was brought to my attention by William Elliott.

Note that most immigrant descendants charted herein of Robert III, King of Scotland—all except John MacLean, Alexander McLeod, Rev. Robert Rose, Mrs. Grizel Campbell McNeill, and William Stewart—are through his youngest daughter Mary Stewart, Princess of Scotland, by four of her five husbands: George Douglas, 1st Earl of Angus; Sir James Kennedy of Dunure; Sir William Graham of Kincardine; and Sir William Edmonstone of Culloden. And among Princess Mary's immigrant descendants charted herein, all except the three Mackintosh/McIntosh kinsmen above, the two Robert Livingstons, Daniel Roberdeau, the Redgrave/Richardson cluster, Archibald Kennedy, and Rev. John Munro were through the Earl of Angus. Among Princess Mary's immigrant descendants charted herein by George Douglas, 1st Earl of Angus, all except Gov. John Cranston, James Veitch, Noël Coward, John Forbes of Fort Duquesne, William Dunbar and Hans Axel, Count von Fersen, were through Princess Mary's eldest son William Douglas, 2nd Earl of Angus. Princess Mary's immigrant descendants charted herein by Sir James Kennedy of Dunure were all through their son Gilbert Kennedy, 1st Baron Kennedy.

The Royal Descents of 900 Immigrants

1. Robert III, King of Scotland, d. 1406 = Annabella Drummond
2. Mary Stewart = George Douglas, 1st Earl of Angus
3. Mary Douglas = Sir David Hay of Yester
4. John Hay, 1st Baron Hay of Yester = Elizabeth Cunningham
5. John Hay, 2nd Baron Hay of Yester = Elizabeth Crichton
6. Christian Hay = William Stewart of Traquair, son of James Stewart of Traquair (and Catherine Rutherford), illegitimate son (by Margaret Murray) of James Stewart, 1st Earl of Buchan, SETH, husband of Margaret Ogilvy and son of Sir James Stewart, "The Black Knight of Lorne," and Joan Beaufort, Queen Dowager of Scotland)
7. James Stewart of Traquair = Katherine Kerr
8. Sir Robert Stewart of Schillinglaw = Alice Cockburn
9. Christian Stewart = John Cranston of Bold
10. James Cranston, a chaplain to King Charles I = ——
11. **John Cranston** (c. 1626-1680), physician, colonial governor of R.I. = Mary Clarke, daughter of Jeremiah Clarke, acting governor of R.I., ARD, SETH, and Mrs. Frances Latham Dungan.

8. Janet Stewart (sister of Sir Robert) = John Veatch of Dawyck
9. Malcolm Veatch of Muirdeen = ——
10. **James Veatch** of Md. = Mary Gakerlin.

9. Alexander Veitch (brother of Malcolm) of Manor = Margaret Scott
10. William Veitch of Redpath = ——
11. Robert Veitch of Bromley = ——
12. John Veitch of Selkirk = Barbara Ainslie
13. Henry Veitch = Margaret Harrison

The Royal Descents of 900 Immigrants

14. Henry Gordon Veitch = Mary Kathleen Synch
15. Violet Agnes Veitch = Arthur Sabin Coward
16. **Noël (Pierce) Coward** (1899-1973), sometime of N.Y., playwright, songwriter and performer, d. unm.

Sources: *MCS5*, lines 41, 91 and *AR8*, line 1 (Cranston); *TAG* 53 (1977):152-53 and William Robert Veitch, *In Search of Yesterday* (Veatch/Veitch family), c. 1969; Philip Hoare, *Noel Coward, A Biography* (1995), pp. xiv-xv (Veitch chart), 1-11, *BLG* 1906, p. 1721 and J.W. Buchan and Rev. Henry Paton, *A History of Peeblesshire*, vol. 3 (1927), pp. 439-40 (Veitch). I reported Andrew B.W. MacEwen's doubts about the immediate ancestry of Gov. John Cranston in *NEXUS* 11 (1994): 41 and *NK2*: 193-94.

The Royal Descents of 900 Immigrants

1. Robert III, King of Scotland, d. 1406 = Annabella Drummond
2. Mary Stewart = Sir James Kennedy of Dunure
3. Gilbert Kennedy, 1st Baron Kennedy = Katherine Maxwell
4. Catherine Kennedy = Alexander Montgomery (parents of Hugh Montgomery, 1st Earl of Eglinton)
5. Euphemia Montgomery = Sir Robert Bruce of Airth
6. Janet Bruce = William Livingston of Kilsyth, son of William Livingston of Kilsyth and Elizabeth Graham, daughter of Patrick Graham, 1st Baron Graham, and Christian Erskine, daughter of Robert Erskine, 1st Baron Erskine, and Elizabeth Lindsay, SETH
7. Alexander Livingston of Over and Nether Inches = Barbara Forrester
8. Barbara Livingston = Alexander Livingston, minister of Monyabroch
9. William Livingston, minister of Monyabroch = Agnes Livingston
10. John Livingston, minister of Ancrum = Janet Fleming
11. **Robert Livingston the elder** (1654-1728) of N.Y., first lord of Livingston Manor, landowner, merchant, public official = Mrs. Alida Schuyler Van Rensselaer.
12. Gilbert Livingston = Cornelia Beekman
13. James Livingston = Judith Newcomb
14. Gilbert James Livingston = Susanna Lewis
15. Judith Livingston = Samuel Herrick Butler
16. Courtland Philip Livingston Butler = Elizabeth Slade Pierce
17. Mary Elizabeth Butler = Robert Emmet Sheldon
18. Flora Sheldon = Samuel Prescott Bush
19. Prescott Sheldon Bush, U.S. Senator = Dorothy Walker
20. George Herbert Walker Bush (b. 1924), 41st U.S. President = Barbara Pierce
21. George Walker Bush (b. 1946), 43rd U.S. President = Laura Lane Welch

The Royal Descents of 900 Immigrants

11. James Livingston (brother of Robert the elder) = ——

12. **Robert Livingston the younger** of N.Y. = Margareta Schuyler.

7. Elizabeth Livingston (sister of Alexander) = Gabriel Cunyngham of Craigends

8. James Cunyngham of Achenyeard = Margaret Fleming

9. William Cunyngham of Edinburgh, Clerk of the Signet = Rebecca Muirhead

10. Richard Cunyngham of Glengarnock = Elizabeth Heriot

11. Robert Cunyngham of St. Christopher, B.W.I. = Judith Elizabeth de Bonneson

12. Mary Cunyngham = Isaac Roberdeau

13. **Daniel Roberdeau** (c. 1727-1795) of Pa., merchant, revolutionary patriot = (1) Mary Bostwick; (2) Jane Milligan.

Sources: *MCS5*, lines 42, 42B, 43 and sources cited therein, esp. Florence Van Rensselaer, *The Livingston Family in America and Its Scottish Origins* (1949), pp. 5-7, 45-46, 49-50, 52, 81, 301 and E.B. Livingston, *The Livingstons of Callendar and Their Principal Cadets* (1920), pp. 446-49, 212-17 (the Robert Livingstons); Bruce research of John P. Ravilious, largely concerning lands in Baldorane, which passed from "Robert Levingstone" (1524, 1545) (presented to soc.gen.medieval on 19 Jan. 2004 as part of "Crusaders in the Ancestry of President George W. Bush"). Ravilious cites William Bruce Armstrong, *The Bruces of Airth and their Cadets* [1892], pp. xiv, xxxv and *SP* 5: 187); *SP* and *CP* (Kilsyth, Montgomery or Eglinton, Kennedy or Cassillis, Graham or Montrose, Erskine or Mar); *LDBR* 1:227-28 and Roberdeau Buchanan, *Genealogy of the Roberdeau Family* (1876), chart opposite p. 9 (which contains some errors) and pp. 19, 21-102.

The Royal Descents of 900 Immigrants

1. Robert III, King of Scotland, d. 1406 = Annabella Drummond
2. Mary Stewart = Sir William Edmonstone of Culloden
3. Sir William Edmonstone = Matilda Stewart
4. Sir Archibald Edmonstone = Janet Shaw
5. Margaret Edmonstone = George Buchanan of that Ilk
6. Janet Buchanan = Thomas Buchanan of Carbeth
7. John Buchanan of Gartincaber = —— ——
8. George Buchanan of Gartincaber = Elizabeth Leckie
9. John Buchanan of Blairlusk = —— ——
10. George Buchanan of Blairlusk = Elizabeth Mayne. Their fourth son, Thomas Buchanan of Ramelton, Donegal, is said to be the grandfather (the intervening generation is unknown) of John Buchanan of The Cairn, Ramelton, who married Jane Russell and was the father of James Buchanan of Ramelton and later Pa. This last married Elizabeth Spear and was the father of 15th U.S. President James Buchanan (1791-1868), who died unmarried. And Shawn H. Potter of Woodbridge, Va., has assembled considerable evidence that William Buchanan, second son of George and Elizabeth, married Janet —— and was the father of brothers Robert, Walter, William, Andrew, George and John Buchanan, all also of Pa., from whom I have not yet tried to find notable descendants.
11. John Buchanan, eldest son = Catherine Black
12. John Buchanan of Donaghanie, Tyrone = Jane Nixon
13. John Buchanan of Omagh, Tyrone – Sarah Sproule. Their son, James Buchanan, sometime British Consul in N.Y., later moved to Montreal, and by his wife Elizabeth Clarke left descendants in Canada and Ireland (including Robert Stewart Buchanan of N.Y., who married Elizabeth Curzon but left no children, and Canadian civil servant Alexander Carlisle Buchanan, treated in the *Dictionary of Canadian Biography*, vol. 9, *1861-1870* [1976], pp. 97-98).
14. Jane Buchanan = James Robinson

The Royal Descents of 900 Immigrants

15. Sarah Jane Robinson = James Jay

16. Julia Madeleine Jay = Frederick Robertson Kempson

17. Eric William Edward Kempson = Beatrice Hamilton Ashwell

18. Rachel Kempson (1910-2003), British actress = Sir Michael Scudamore Redgrave (1908-1983), British actor, of Shakespeare especially. Their son was British actor and political activist Corin (William) Redgrave, who married Deirdre Hamilton-Hill and Kika Markham.

19. Vanessa Redgrave, b. 1937, sometime of N.Y. (when acting on Broadway) or Calif. (for films), British actress (among films, *A Man for All Seasons*, *Blow-Up*, *Camelot*, *Isadora*, *The Charge of the Light Brigade*, *The Seagull*, *Mary, Queen of Scots*, *Murder on the Orient Express*, *Julia*, *The Bostonians*, *Howard's End*, *Crime and Punishment*, *Mission Impossible*, *Atonement*) = (1) (Cecil Antonio) **"Tony" Richardson** (1928-91), stage and film producer or director, of Calif. post 1974 (among films, *Look Back in Anger*, *The Entertainer*, *Sanctuary*, *A Taste of Honey*, *The Loneliness of the Long Distance Runner*, *Tom Jones*, *The Loved One*, *Charge of the Light Brigade*, *Hamlet*, *A Delicate Balance*, *Joseph Andrews*, *Antony and Cleopatra*, *Phantom of the Opera*); (2) **Franco Nero** (Francesco Sparanero), b. 1941, actor (among many films, *Camelot*, *Querelle*, and *Django Unchained*).

20. **Natasha Richardson** (1963-2009), sometime of N.Y., stage, film and television actress (among films, *Past Midnight* and *Wild Child*) = (1) Robert (Michael John) **Fox**, b. 1953, stage and film producer, brother of actors James Fox and Edward Fox; (2) **Liam** (John) **Neeson**, b. 1952, also sometime of N.Y., Irish actor (among films, *Schindler's List*, *Rob Roy*, *Les Misérables*, *Star Wars I* and *II*, *Gangs of New York*, *Kinsey*, *The Simpsons*, *The Chronicles of Narnia*, *Clash of the Titans*).

19. **Lynn (Rachel) Redgrave** (1943-2010), sometime of Conn. (a naturalized U.S. citizen), actress (among films, *Tom Jones*, *Georgy Girl*, *The Happy Hooker*, *Gods and Monsters*, *Kinsey*), memoirist and playwright = (Ivan) John Clark, b. 1932, British actor.

The Royal Descents of 900 Immigrants

Younger members of this acting clan include Joely Richardson (b. 1965), television and film actress ("The Tudors" and "Nip/Tuck", *The Affair of the Necklace, Wallis and Edward, The Girl with the Dragon Tattoo*), formerly married to producer Timothy Bevan; screenwriter and director Carlo Gabriel (Redgrave) Nero, b. 1969; Jemma (Rebecca) Redgrave (b. 1965, daughter of Corin Redgrave and Deirdre Hamilton-Hill), also a television and film actress (Eve Granger in "Cold Blood," *Howard's End, Lassie*); singer-songwriter Puma (formerly Kelly) Clark, b. 1970, and author and photographer Annabel Lucy Clark (b. 1981).

Sources: Wikipedia entries for the various Redgraves and their spouses; *Oxford DNB* entries for Sir Michael Redgrave and Rachel Kempson, and Rachel Kempson, Lady Redgrave, *A Family and Its Fortunes* (1986), pp. 1-2 (where Rachel names her parents and all four grandparents); *WWWA* entries for Tony and Natasha Richardson and Lynn Redgrave, *WWA* entries for Vanessa Redgrave and Liam Neeson; *Kelly's Handbook to the Titled, Landed and Official Classes for 1918*, p. 889 (F.R. Kempson, giving his wife as J. Madeleine, daughter of the late Jas. Jay of Litley Court, Herefordshire, J.P.) and Edward Walford, *The County Families of the United Kingdom*, 6th ed. (1871), p. 544 (James Jay, esq., of Litley Court, Herefordshire, "magistrate for the city of Hereford," which names his wife and father-in-law); A.W. Patrick Buchanan, *The Buchanan Book: The Life of Alexander Buchanan, Q.C., of Montreal, Followed by an Account of the Family of Buchanan* (1911), pp. 253, 189-250 (189-91 esp.) (covering the progeny of James Buchanan of N.Y. and Montreal); John Guthrie Smith, *Strathendrick and Its Inhabitants from Early Times* (1896), pp. 346-47, 350-51 (copied in *NGSQ* 24 [1936]: 85-87, 25 [1937]: 14-15, 67) and *The Parish of Strathbane* (1886), pp. 104-10; Sir Archibald Edmonstone, *Genealogical Account of the Family of Edmonstone of Duntreath* (1875); and correspondence from the late Andrew B. W. MacEwen of Stockton Springs, Maine. The presidential Buchanan descent, with an unidentified generation, requires further research. The Buchanan-Robinson-Jay-Kempson descent was developed by California genealogist Will Johnson (wjhonson@aol.com) and John C. Brandon of Columbia, S.C., the latter of whom brought it to my attention.

The Royal Descents of 900 Immigrants

1. Robert III, King of Scotland, d. 1406 = Annabella Drummond
2. Mary Stewart = George Douglas, 1st Earl of Angus
3. William Douglas, 2nd Earl of Angus = Margaret Hay
4. Helen Douglas = William Graham, 2nd Baron Graham
5. Agnes Graham = Sir Walter Forrester of Torwood and Garden
6. Sir James Forrester = Elizabeth Erskine, daughter of Robert Erskine, 4th Baron Erskine, and Isabel Campbell, SETH
7. Margaret Forrester = Henry Livingston of Falkirk
8. Henry Livingston, minister of St. Ninian's = Agnes Gray
9. Helen Livingston = James Duncanson, minister of Alloa. Daughter Janet/Jannette married (1) Jan Aerdes (corruption of an unknown Scottish surname; nothing is known about the later history of their marriage, or whether they had children); (2) Thomas Powell; (3) Robert Orchard (David M. Riker, comp., *Genealogical and Biographical Directory to Persons in New Netherland*, vol. 3 [1999], page for Robert Orchard, lists no children for Robert, and vol. 5, 2004 *Supplement* (2004), p. 230, lists no children for Thomas Powell by any of three wives). A probable daughter of James and Helen, Ann/Annette Duncanson, was the first wife of the above Thomas Powell. A possible daughter of James and Helen, Maria Duncanson, married (1) Jan MacFasse, also a Scot, and (2) possibly Pieter Loockermans.
10. **Marg(a)ret Duncanson** of N.Y. = William **Teller (Taillier).**
10. **Katherine/Catalin Duncanson** of N.Y. = Sander [Alexander] Leendertsz. **Glen.**

Sources: *NYGBR* 128 (1997): 1-10 (Duncanson, by Gordon Remington); *TG* 27 (2013): 28-50 (Duncanson, Livingston), 162-81 (Forrester, and the above royal descent, by Adrian Benjamin Burke) and sources cited in each (*TG* 28 [2014]: 58-89 covers Gray, and 28: 91, 201 cover additions and corrections). For the descent from Mrs. Glen above to First Lady Jacqueline Lee (Bouvier) (Kennedy) Onassis, see the section at the end of the main text herein, covering royal descents submitted or traced after much of this book was indexed.

The Royal Descents of 900 Immigrants

1. Robert III, King of Scotland, d. 1406 = Annabella Drummond
2. Margaret Stewart = Archibald Douglas, 4th Earl of Douglas
3. Archibald Douglas, 5th Earl of Douglas = Eupheme Grant
4. Margaret Douglas = (his first wife) John Stewart, 1st Earl of Atholl, son of Sir James Stewart, "The Black Knight of Lorne" and Joan Beaufort, Dowager Queen of Scotland
5. Janet Stewart = Alexander Gordon, 3rd Earl of Huntly
6. Jean Gordon = Colin Campbell, 3rd Earl of Argyll
7. Archibald Campbell, 4th Earl of Argyll = Margaret Graham
8. Janet Campbell = Hector MacLean of Duart, chief of the Clan MacLean
9. Marion MacLean = Hector Roy MacLean of Coll, a cousin
10. Lachlan MacLean of Coll = Florence MacLeod of MacLeod
11. Neil MacLean of Drimnacross = Florence MacDonald of Morrer
12. Florence MacLean = Charles MacLean of Borreray
13. Archibald MacLean = Susanna Campbell of Scamadall
14. John MacLean = Anne Long or Lang
15. **John MacLean** (1771-1814) of N.J., chemist, educator = Phebe Bainbridge. Their son, another John MacLean (1800-1886), was tenth president of the College of New Jersey, later Princeton University, who died unmarried.

14. Margaret MacLean (sister of John) = Neil McLeod (MacLeod)
15. **Alexander McLeod** (MacLcod) (1774-1833) of N.Y., Reformed Presbyterian clergyman, author and editor = Maria Anne Agnew.

Sources: *DAB* (John MacLean and Alexander McLeod); J.P. MacLean, *A History of the Clan MacLean* (1889), pp. 90-91, 285-87, 295-96, 273-74 (Duart, Coll, Drimnacross, Borreray); *SP* and *CP* (Argyll, Huntly, Atholl, Douglas).

The Royal Descents of 900 Immigrants

1. Robert III, King of Scotland, d. 1406 = Annabella Drummond
2. Mary Stewart = George Douglas, 1st Earl of Angus
3. William Douglas, 2nd Earl of Angus = Margaret Hay
4. George Douglas, 4th Earl of Angus = Isabel Sibbald
5. Archibald Douglas, 5th Earl of Angus = Elizabeth Boyd
6. Sir William Douglas of Glenbervie = Elizabeth Auchinleck
7. Sir Archibald Douglas of Glenbervie = Agnes Keith
8. William Douglas, 9th Earl of Angus = Giles (Egidia in Latin) Graham
9. Sir Robert Douglas of Glenbervie = Elizabeth Auchinleck
10. Margaret Douglas = Sir Thomas Burnet, 1st Bt., son of Alexander Burnet of Leys, and Katherine Gordon, SETH
11. Catherine Burnet = Robert Gordon of Pitlurg
12. **Thomas Gordon,** chief justice of N.J. = (1) Helen Riddell; (2) Janet Mudie.

9. Margaret Douglas (sister of Sir Robert) = William Forbes of Monymusk
10. Sir William Forbes, 1st Bt. = Elizabeth Wishart
11. Robert Forbes of Barnes = ——
12. Jean Forbes = Alexander Forbes of Ballogie
13. —— Forbes = Robert Burnett of N.J.
14. **Isabel Burnett** of N.J. = William **Montgomery** of N.J., ARD, SETH.

Sources: *AR8,* line 256 (Thomas Gordon, generations 10-12), and NGSQ 763 (1983): 8 (Helen Riddell); *Burnett of Leys,* pp. 32-72, *CB* and *BP* (Burnet of Leys and Douglas of Glenbervie, baronets); *SP* and *CP* (Angus); *Montgomery,* pp. 79-83 and *Forbes,* pp. 301-2, 410.

The Royal Descents of 900 Immigrants

1. Robert III, King of Scotland, d. 1406 = Annabella Drummond
2. Mary Stewart = George Douglas, 1st Earl of Angus
3. William Douglas, 2nd Earl of Angus = Margaret Hay
4. George Douglas, 4th Earl of Angus = Isabel Sibbald
5. Archibald Douglas, 5th Earl of Angus = Elizabeth Boyd
6. Sir William Douglas of Glenbervie = Elizabeth Auchinleck
7. Sir Archibald Douglas of Glenbervie = Elizabeth Irvine
8. John Douglas (half-brother of William Douglas, 9th Earl of Angus) = ——
9. John Douglas of Leith = ——
10. Rev. William Douglas of Aboyne = ——
11. Rev. William Douglas of Midmar = ——
12. Robert Douglas of Blackmiln = Barbara Farquharson
13. Francis Douglas of Aberdeen and Paisley = Elizabeth Ochterloney
14. Bethiah Douglas = Hugh Cochrane of Glanderston
15. John Cochrane of Glanderston = Isabella Ramsay
16. **Alexander Cochrane** of Mass. = Margaret Rae.

Sources: Walter Kendall Watkins, *The Cochranes of Renfrewshire, Scotland: The Ancestry of Alexander Cochrane of Billerica and Malden, Mass., U.S.A.* (1904) and Cochrane tabular pedigree compiled by same (TP COC 735 at NEHGS), which contains some errors; *NEHGR* 56 (1902):192 (reprinted in *EO* 2:2:802) and *SP* and *CP* (Angus).

The Royal Descents of 900 Immigrants

1. Robert III, King of Scotland, d. 1406 = Annabella Drummond
2. Mary Stewart = George Douglas, 1st Earl of Angus
3. William Douglas, 2nd Earl of Angus = Margaret Hay
4. George Douglas, 4th Earl of Angus = Isabel Sibbald
5. Archibald Douglas, 5th Earl of Angus = Elizabeth Boyd
6. Sir William Douglas of Glenbervie = Elizabeth Auchinleck
7. Sir Archibald Douglas of Glenbervie = Agnes Keith
8. Elizabeth Douglas = Alexander Falconer of Halkerton, son of David Falconer of Halkerton (and Mariot Dunbar), son of George Falconer of Halkerton and Elizabeth Erskine, SETH
9. Archibald Falconer of Coltfield = Jean Dunbar
10. John Falconer of Tulloch and Phesdo = Agnes Spens
11. **Patrick Falconer** of Conn. and N.J. = Hannah Jones, daughter of Dep. Gov. William Jones and Hannah Eaton, daughter of Theophilus Eaton, colonial statesman and merchant, governor of the New Haven Colony, and Mrs. Anne Lloyd Yale of Conn., ARD, SETH.

Sources: Paul McKee Gifford, *Falconer of Halkerton: A Genealogy of a Scottish Family and its Branches in England, the United States, and Jamaica, including those spelled "Falconar" and "Faulkner"* (1997), pp. 5-9, 35-38, 427, 429, 431-32, 435-36, 439-41, 501; *SP* and *CP* (Angus).

The Royal Descents of 900 Immigrants

1. Robert III, King of Scotland, d. 1406 = Annabella Drummond
2. Mary Stewart = Sir James Kennedy of Dunure
3. Gilbert Kennedy, 1st Baron Kennedy = Katherine Maxwell
4. John Kennedy, 2nd Baron Kennedy = Elizabeth Montgomery
5. David Kennedy, 1st Earl of Cassillis = Agnes Borthwick
6. Gilbert Kennedy, 2nd Earl of Cassillis = Isabel Campbell
7. Gilbert Kennedy, 3rd Earl of Cassillis = Margaret Kennedy
8. Sir Thomas Kennedy of Culzean = Elizabeth Makgill
9. Sir Alexander Kennedy of Culzean = Agnes Kennedy
10. Alexander Kennedy of Craigoch and Kilhenzie = Anna Crawford
11. **Archibald Kennedy** (c. 1685-1763) of N.Y., British colonial official (collector of customs and provincial councillor) = (1) —— Mussam (by whom he was the father of Archibald Kennedy, 11th Earl of Cassillis); (2) Mrs. Mary Walter Schuyler.

Sources: *BP* (Ailsa), *SP* and *CP* (Cassillis).

The Royal Descents of 900 Immigrants

1. Robert III, King of Scotland, d. 1406 = Annabella Drummond
2. Mary Stewart = George Douglas, 1st Earl of Angus
3. William Douglas, 2nd Earl of Angus = Margaret Hay
4. Helen Douglas = William Graham, 2nd Baron Graham
5. Christian Graham = Sir James Haldane of Gleneagles
6. Sir John Haldane of Gleneagles = Marjorie Lawson
7. Sir James Haldane of Gleneagles = Margaret Erskine
8. John Haldane of Gleneagles = Elizabeth Lundin
9. Joseph Haldane of Myreton = Euphemia Shaw
10. James Haldane of Myreton = ――
11. John Haldane of Myreton = Janet Higgins
12. Jean Haldane = Robert Trail(l)
13. Robert Trail(l) = Mary Dow
14. Anthony Trail(l) = Agnes Gayer
15. Robert Trail(l) = Anne Hayes
16. Kathleen Trail(l) = John Hatch Synge. Their fifth son was (Edmund) John Millington Synge, the playwright and poet, who died unmarried.
17. Edward Synge = Ellen Frances Price
18. John Lighton Synge, Irish mathematician = Elizabeth Eleanor Mabel Allen
19. **Cathleen Synge**, known as Mrs. Cathleen Synge **Morawetz**, b. 1923, of N.Y., mathematician = Herbert Morawetz, polymer chemist.

Sources: *BIFR* (Synge, Trail[l]); *BLG* (and 2003 *BP*) (Haldane) and General Sir Aylmer L. Haldane, *The Haldanes of Gleneagles* (1929), esp. pp. 45-48; *SP* and *CB* (Montrose [for Graham], Angus).

The Royal Descents of 900 Immigrants

1. Robert III, King of Scotland, d. 1406 = Annabella Drummond
2. Mary Stewart = George Douglas, 1st Earl of Angus
3. Elizabeth Douglas = Alexander Forbes, 1st Baron Forbes
4. James Forbes, 2nd Baron Forbes = Giles (Egidia in Latin) Keith
5. Duncan Forbes of Corsindae = Christian Mercer
5. Margaret Forbes = Malcolm Forbes of Tolquhon
6. William Forbes of Corsindae = Margaret Lumsden
6. William Forbes of Tolquhon = —— Leith
7. James Forbes of Corsindae = Janet Gordon
7. Alexander Forbes of Tolquhon = Alison Anderson
8. William Forbes of Tolquhon = Elizabeth Gordon
8. John Forbes of Bandley = Elizabeth Keith
8. William Forbes of Corsindae = 9. Janet Forbes of Tolquhon
9,10. James Forbes of Corsindae = Katherine Mortimer
10,11. Janet Forbes = 9. Duncan Forbes of Culloden (Their daughter, Elizabeth Forbes, married William Baillie of Dunain and was the mother of the Alexander Baillie of Dunain, who married Jean Mackenzie, and of the Mary Baillie who married William Mackintosh of Borlum, both SETH.)
10-12. John Forbes of Culloden = Anna Dunbar
11-13. John Forbes of Pittencrieff = Elizabeth Graham
12-14. **John Forbes** (c.1710-1759) of Pa., British army officer, hero of Fort Duquesne = ——.

Sources: *Oxford DNB*, supp.; *Forbes*, pp. 406-7 (Pittencrieff), 403 (Culloden), 394-95 (Tolquhon), 294-97 (Corsindae), 25-42 (1st and 2nd barons Forbes); *SP* and *CP* (Forbes, Angus).

255

The Royal Descents of 900 Immigrants

1. Robert III, King of Scotland, d. 1406 = Annabella Drummond
2. Margaret Stewart = Archibald Douglas, 4th Earl of Douglas
3. Archibald Douglas, 5th Earl of Douglas = Eupheme Grant
4. Margaret Douglas = (his first wife) John Stewart, 1st Earl of Atholl, son of Sir James Stewart, "The Black Knight of Lorne" and Joan Beaufort, Queen Dowager of Scotland
5. Elizabeth Stewart = Andrew Gray, 2nd Baron Gray, son of Patrick Gray and Annabel Forbes, daughter of Alexander Forbes, 1st Baron Forbes, and Elizabeth Douglas, SETH
6. Gilbert Gray = Giles (Egidia in Latin) Mercer
7. Patrick Gray, 4th Baron Gray = Marion Ogilvy, daughter of James Ogilvy, 4th Baron Ogilvy of Airlie (and Helen Sinclair), son of James Ogilvy, 3rd Baron Ogilvy of Airlie (and Isabel Lindsay), son of John Ogilvy, 2nd Baron Ogilvy of Airlie and Jean Graham, daughter of William Graham, 2nd Baron Graham, and Helen Douglas, SETH.
8. Isabel Gray = Alexander Falconer of Halkerton, son of Alexander Falconer (and Elizabeth Douglas, daughter of Sir Archibald Douglas of Glenbervie and Agnes Keith, SETH), son of David Falconer of Halkerton (and Mariot Dunbar), son of George Falconer of Halkerton and Elizabeth Erskine, SETH.
9. Sir Alexander Falconer of Halkerton = Agnes Carnegie
10. Sir John Falconer, Master of the Mint of Scotland = Sybilla Ogilvy
11. David Falconer = Margaret Mollison, sister of Christian Mollison, wife of Robert Barclay, Quaker apologist and nominal governor of East N.J., SETH. Their sons John and Gilbert Falconer, who married Anna Quare and Hannah Hardiman respectively, immigrated to Md., and left issue but no NDTPS. A daughter, Jane Falconer, also immigrated to Md., and married Simon Wilmer but almost certainly left no children.
12. **Alexander Falconer** of Md. = Susanna Duvall.

The Royal Descents of 900 Immigrants

Sources: Paul McKee Gifford, *Falconer of Halkerton: A Genealogy of a Scottish Family and Its Branches in England, the United States, and Jamaica, including those spelled "Falconar" and "Faulkner"* (1997), pp. 5-12, 36-39, 69-72, 79, 83-98, 119-20, 125-27, 135; *SP* or *CP* (Gray, Atholl, Douglas, Forbes, Ogilvy of Airlie, Graham [Montrose], Angus). Paul Gifford and Charles R. Owens have investigated the ancestry of Sybilla Ogilvy (daughter of John Ogilvy of Powrie, a Catholic spy, and Elizabeth Scrymgeour) but the late Andrew B.W. MacEwen showed that John Ogilvy of Powrie was a son of Gilbert Ogilvy of that Ilk by Janet Beaton, not Sybilla Drummond. The cross-referenced Douglas-Forbes and Douglas-Graham-Ogilvy lines at generations 3 and 7 above, and the Erskine-Halkerton and Douglas-Falconer lines at generation 8, all trace to Robert III. In particular Elizabeth Douglas, Lady Forbes, was a daughter of George Douglas, 1st Earl of Angus, and Princess Mary Stewart, daughter of Robert III and Annabella Drummond above. Helen Douglas, Lady Graham, was a niece of Lady Forbes and daughter of William Douglas, 2nd Earl of Angus, and Margaret Hay. This last couple were great-great-grandparents of Sir Archibald Douglas of Glenbervie at generation 8.

Sir David Falconer of Glenfarquhar, another son of Sir Alexander Falconer and Agnes Carnegie, married firstly Margaret Hepburn and was the father of Sir David Falconer of Newton, who married secondly Mary Norvell. Catherine Falconer, a daughter of these last, married Joseph Hume and was the mother of David Hume, the philosopher, who died unmarried. See the above-cited Falconer of Halkerton genealogy, pp. 53-54, 56, 59-61 (Falconer) and the *Oxford DNB* articles on Sir David Falconer of Newton and David Hume.

The Royal Descents of 900 Immigrants

1. Robert III, King of Scotland, d. 1406 = Annabella Drummond
2. Mary Stewart = George Douglas, 1st Earl of Angus
3. William Douglas, 2nd Earl of Angus = Margaret Hay
4. Helen Douglas = William Graham, 2nd Baron Graham
5. Agnes Graham = Sir Walter Forrester of Torwood and Garden
5. William Graham, 1st Earl of Montrose = Annabella Drummond
6. Margaret Forrester = Sir John Stirling of Keir
6. Jean Graham illegitimately by James Chisholm, Bishop of Dunblane
6. Elizabeth Graham = Walter Drummond, a cousin
7. Sir James Stirling of Keir = (said to be) Jean Chisholm
7. David Drummond, 2nd Baron Drummond = Lilias Ruthven
8. Sir Archibald Stirling of Keir = 8. Mary Drummond
9. Jean Stirling = Sir William Drummond of Riccarton, a cousin
10. William Drummond of Riccarton = Magdalen Dalyell
11. Katherine Drummond = Sir Thomas Dalyell, 1st Bt., a cousin
12. **Magdalen Dalyell** of Va. = James **Menteith** or **Monteith** of Auldcathie, later Dalyell, SETH (their eldest son, Sir James Monteith, later Dalyell, 3rd Bt., is an ancestor of [Sir] Thomas [Tam] Dalyell [11th Bt.], Labor M.P. and author).
13. **Thomas Monteith** of Va. = Phillis Gallop.
14. Magdalen Monteith = Anderson Doniphan
15. Elizabeth Doniphan = Richard Shipp
16. Emma Grant Shipp = William Truman, Jr.
17. Anderson Shipp Truman = Mary Jane Holmes
18. John Anderson Truman = Martha Ellen Young

The Royal Descents of 900 Immigrants

19. Harry S Truman (1884-1972), 33rd U.S. President = Elizabeth Virginia "Bess" Wallace

Sources: *Family History* 20 (#168, July 2001): 350-53 (Donald Whyte on the Menteiths/Monteiths); correspondence with Mrs. Tam Dalyell of The Binns and the late Andrew B.W. MacEwen, *GVFT* 3:615, 622, G.H.S. King, *Marriages of Richmond County, Virginia, 1668-1853* (1964), p. 136 and *BP* and *CB* (Dalyell, baronets); Sir James Dalyell of Binns, (9th) Bt. and James Beveridge, eds., *The Binns Papers* (*Publications of the Scottish Record Society*, vol. 70, 1938), pp. 119 (#578, which abstracts a letter of 17 Nov. 1734 from Thomas Monteith of Rappahannock Co., Va., to his brother, Sir James Dalyell, 3rd Bt.), 112 (#545, 42, marriage contract between James Monteith and Magdalen Dalyell), 76-77 (#s 385-86), 66 (#342), 56 (#285), 47 (#258), 41 (#232), 26 (#124 and notes 2 and 3, marriage contracts of William Drummond and Magdalen Dalyell and of Sir William Drummond and Jean Stirling); A.M. Sterling, *The Sterling Genealogy,* vol. 1 (1909), pp. 53-70; J.C. Gibson, *Lands and Lairds of Larbert and Duniplace Parishes* (1908), pp. 137-38 and chart following p. 156 (Forrester); *SP* and *CP* (Drummond, Montrose, Graham, Angus). The line was first brought to my attention by Mrs. Dalyell and further developed by the late Andrew B.W. MacEwen.

The Royal Descents of 900 Immigrants

1. Robert III, King of Scotland, d. 1406 = Annabella Drummond
2. Mary Stewart = Sir William Graham of Kincardine
3. Sir Robert Graham of Fintry = (1) Janet Lovell, (2) Matilda ——
4. (probably by 1) Marjory (or Elizabeth) Graham = John Erskine of Dun
5. John Erskine of Dun = Katherine Monypenny
6. Elizabeth Erskine = George Falconer of Halkerton
7. Jean Falconer = Sir Alexander Dunbar of Cumnock
8. Margaret Dunbar = Robert Munro, 14th Baron of Foulis
9. George Munro of Katewell = ——
10. George Munro of Katewell = Euphemia Munro of Pittonachy
11. David Munro of Katewell = Agnes Munro of Durness
12. **Rev. John Munro** of Va. = Christian Blair (their daughter, Mary Munro, married John Blair, her first cousin, colonial governor of Va. and president of its council). Rev. John's brother, Rev. Andrew Munro of Isle of Wight Co., Va., married Mrs. Sarah Smith Pitt and left issue but probably no NDTPS. Rev. Andrew was not, however, the Andrew Munroe/Munro of St. Mary's Co., Md., and Westmoreland Co., Va., patrilineal great-great-grandfather of U.S. President James Monroe.

Sources: *Clan Munro Magazine*, no. 6 (1959-60):14-18, R.W. Munro, ed., *The Munro Tree: A Genealogy and Chronology of the Munros of Foulis and Other Families of the Clan, a Manuscript Compiled in 1734 Edited with Introduction and Notes* (1978), pp. 15, 17 and notes Q, Q45-48, and Alexander Mackenzie, *History of the Munros of Foulis* (1898), pp. 40-43, 173 (which corrects p. 42 as to the mother of Margaret Dunbar), 480-81; Paul McKee Gifford, *Falconer of Halkerton* (1997), pp. 5-6, 36-37; Violet Jacob, *The Lairds of Dun* (1931), pp. 32-47 (Erskine); J.G. Smith, *Strathendrick and its Inhabitants from Early Times* (1896), pp. 154-56 (Graham of Fintry); *SP* (Kintore and Montrose for Falconer and Graham). The first seven generations of this line were developed and brought to my attention by Douglas Hickling of Piedmont, California.

The Royal Descents of 900 Immigrants

1. Robert III, King of Scotland, d. 1406 = Annabella Drummond
2. Mary Stewart = George Douglas, 1st Earl of Angus
3. Elizabeth Douglas = Alexander Forbes, 1st Baron Forbes
4. James Forbes, 2nd Baron Forbes = Giles (Egidia in Latin) Keith
5. William Forbes, 3rd Baron Forbes = Christian Gordon
6. John Forbes, 6th Baron Forbes = (1) Catherine Stewart, daughter of John Stewart, 1st Earl of Atholl (and Eleanor Sinclair, per Andrew B.W. MacEwen), son of Sir James Stewart, "the Black Knight of Lorne," and Joan Beaufort, Dowager Queen of Scotland, SETH; (2) Christian Lundin, SETH
7. (by 1) Elizabeth Forbes = James Grant of Freuchie
8. John Grant of Freuchie = Margaret Stewart, daughter of John Stewart, 3rd Earl of Atholl (and Grizel Rattray), son of John Stewart, 2nd Earl of Atholl and Janet Campbell, SETH
9. Grizel Grant = Patrick Grant of Ballindalloch
10. Patrick Grant of Ballindalloch = Helen Ogilvy
11. John Grant of Ballindalloch = Elizabeth Innes
12. Patrick Grant of Whytree = ——
13. Margaret Grant = John Rose of Lochiehills
14. **Rev. Robert Rose** of Va. = (1) Mary Tarent; (2) Anne Fitzhugh. John Rose (= Anne Cuming), Rev. Charles Rose (= Catharine Brooke), and Alexander Rose (prob. = Nelly Grant), brothers of Rev. Robert, also immigrated to Va., but left no NDTPS.

Sources: Christine Rose, *Ancestors and Descendants of the Brothers Rev. Robert Rose and Rev. Charles Rose of Colonial Virginia and Wester Alves, Morayshire, Scotland* (1985), pp. 13-14, 17-38, 243-46, 267-68, 273-76, which supersedes W.G. Stanard, *A Chart of the Ancestors and Descendants of Rev. Robert Rose* (1895, with various errors) and *BLG* 1952, p. 2199 (Rose). A Rose-Grant posting by Professor Doug McDonald on soc.genealogy.medieval cites, in addition to *SP* (Seafield, for Grants of Freuchie), *SP* and *CP* (Forbes, Atholl) and William Fraser, *The Chiefs*

The Royal Descents of 900 Immigrants

of Grant, vol. 1 (1883), pp. 520-21 (Grant of Ballindalloch, but without Patrick Grant of Whytree), Inquisitions General #8035, 11 Nov. 1698, where Margaret Grant is called "*heres Patricii Grant in Whytree, patris*"; Banff Sasines 1600-1780 (LDS film #896591, where a Patrick Grant in 1662 is said to be a brother of John Grant, feuar of Ballindalloch, and Patrick Grant of Whytree appears on sasines of 1694 and 1697); and the 1780 Matriculation of Arms in Scotland of William Rose of Montcoffer (son of John Rose, sometime of Va., and Anne Cum[m]ing), arms that include Rose of Kilvarock, Grant of Ballindalloch, and Gordon of Huntly. Professor McDonald's doubts about a Falconer descent for the Rose brothers of Va. are noted in *RD600* (2008, 2010), p. 845.

The Royal Descents of 900 Immigrants

1. Robert III, King of Scotland, d. 1406 = Annabella Drummond
2. (illegitimate by ——) Sir John Stewart of Ardgowan, Blackhall and Auchingoun = ——
3. Margaret Stewart = Duncan Campbell, 1st Baron Campbell
4. Duncan Campbell of Kilmichael = Anna, daughter of Iain [John], son of Alan M'Cowle
5. Dugald Campbell of Auchinbreck and Kilmichael = Agnes Lamont of that Ilk
6. Archibald Campbell of Auchinbreck and Kilmichael = Margaret Campbell of Ardkinglas, a cousin
7. Donald Campbell of Kilmory = Grizel (or Elizabeth) Stewart of Kildon[n]an
8. Patrick Campbell of Stuck = Helen Woddrop
9. John Campbell of Fernoch = Florence Lamont of Silvercraigs
10. Archibald Campbell of Auchindarroch = Jean MacLachlan
11. **Grizel Campbell** of N.C. = Neill [Dubh "Black Neill"] **McNeill**.

Sources: Carl Boyer 3rd, *Ancestral Lines from Maine to North Carolina: 182 Families...with Medieval and Royal Ancestries of Percival[1] Lowell and* [Grizel Campbell, wife of] *Neill Dubh[1] McNeill* (2015), pp. 331-32 (McNeill), 52-56 (Campbell), 433-34, and sources cited therein, esp. G. Harvey Johnston, *Heraldry of the Campbells* (1920, repr. 1977), pp. 18, 87, 90, 92 (generations 3-10 but omitting 5); *BLG*, 19th ed., vol. 1, *The Kingdom of Scotland* (2001), pp. 165-66 (generations 3-6) and *BP* (Campbell of Auchinbreck). The wife of generation 4 was supplied by the late Andrew B.W. MacEwen of Stockton Springs, Maine; see "Genealogies of the Family of Auchinbreck," in J.R.N. MacPhail, ed., *Highland Papers*, vol. 4 (*Publications of the Scottish History Society*), 3rd ser., vol. 22 (1934, repr. 1995), pp. 63-65, 68, 71-72, 77-78.

The Royal Descents of 900 Immigrants

1. Robert III, King of Scotland, d. 1406 = Annabella Drummond
2. (illegitimate by ——) Sir John Stewart of Ardgowan, Blackhall and Auchingoun = ——
3. Margaret Stewart = Duncan Campbell, 1st Baron Campbell
4. Sir Colin Campbell of Glenorchy = Margaret Stirling
5. Mariot Campbell = William Stewart of Baldoran, son of James Stewart of Baldoran (and Annabel Buchanan), illegitimate son (by —— MacDonald) of Sir James Stewart of Baldoran, son (by Isabel, Countess of Lennox) of Murdoch Stewart, 2nd Duke of Albany, son of Robert Stewart, 1st Duke of Albany, and Margaret Graham, Countess of Menteith, SETH
6. Walter Stewart of Baldoran = Euphemia Reddich
7. James Stewart of Baldoran = —— Stewart of Glenbuckie
8. Alexander Stewart of Ardvorlich = Margaret Drummond of Drummonderinoch
9. Janet Stewart = Duncan Stewart of Glenogle
10. Alexander Stewart = ——
11. Catherine Stewart = Alexander Stewart of Ledcreish. Their son Patrick Stewart also immigrated to N.C., married (1) —— and (2) Elizabeth Menzie and left a sizeable progeny but no NDTPS (yet found).
12. **William Stewart** of N.C. = (1) —— Colvin; (2) Mrs. Janet McDougal Williamson. A son by Janet was Duncan Stewart, Tennessee legislator and lt. governor of Mississippi, who married Penelope Jones and was the father of Catherine Stewart, wife of Hugh Cage, Mississippi congressman and judge.

Sources: *TAG* 80 (2005): 11-22 and sources cited therein (Kelsey Jackson Williams), plus *BLG*, 19th ed., vol. 1, *The Kingdom of Scotland* (2001), pp. 1264-65 (Stewart of Ardvorlich), *SP*, *CP* and *BP* (Breadalbane, for Campbell, Royal House of Scotland and Moray, for Stewart). Note the patrilineal descent from Robert II, King of Scotland, to 9. Janet Stewart of Ardvorlich, and the three Stewart-Stewart intermarriages. For Duncan

The Royal Descents of 900 Immigrants

Stewart and Mrs. Cage see *Biographical and Historical Memoirs of Mississippi*, vol. 2 (1891), pp. 833-36 and for this family generally, *Stewart Clan Magazine* C (1933-38): 189 (Duncan), 34 (1956-57): 177-79, 181-92, 194-96, 35 (1957-58): 240.

The Royal Descents of 900 Immigrants

1. Robert III, King of Scotland, d. 1406 = Annabella Drummond
2. Mary Stewart = George Douglas, 1st Earl of Angus
3. Elizabeth Douglas = Alexander Forbes, 1st Baron Forbes
4. James Forbes, 2nd Baron Forbes = Giles (Egidia in Latin) Keith
5. William Forbes, 3rd Baron Forbes = Christian Gordon
6. John Forbes, 6th Baron Forbes = (2) Christian Lundin
7. Elizabeth Forbes = Alexander Dunbar of Conzie and Kilbuyack
8. William Dunbar of Hempriggs = Margaret Anderson
9. John Dunbar of Hempriggs = ——
10. James Dunbar of Newton = ——
11. Archibald Dunbar of Newton and Thunderton = Elizabeth Hacket
12. Robert Dunbar of Newton and Thunderton = Margaret Mackenzie, daughter of Colin Mackenzie of Pluscardine (and Margaret Heatley), son of Thomas Mackenzie of Pluscardine (and Jean Grant, daughter of John Grant of Freuchie and Lillias Murray, for whom see *NEXUS* 16 [1999]:31), son of Kenneth Mackenzie, 1st Baron Mackenzie of Kintail (and Isabel Ogilvie), son of Colin Mackenzie of Kintail, SETH, and Barbara Grant, daughter of John Grant of Freuchie and Margaret Stewart, daughter of John Stewart, 3rd Earl of Atholl (and Grizel Rattray), son of John Stewart, 2nd Earl of Atholl, SETH, and Janet Campbell.
13. (Sir) Archibald Dunbar of Newton and Thunderton (*de jure* 4th Bt. of Northfield) = Anne Bayne
14. **William Dunbar** (1749-1810) of Natchez, Mississippi, planter and scientist = Dinah Clark.

Sources: Mrs. Dunbar Rowland, *The Life, Letters and Papers of William Dunbar* (1930), pp. 14-15 esp.; *BP* and *CB* (Dunbar of Northfield [or Hempriggs]); *SP* and *CP* (Forbes, Angus); *SP* (Seaforth, for Mackenzie; Seafield, for Grant; and Atholl). The Mackenzie and Grant descents were brought to my attention by the late Andrew B.W. MacEwen of Stockton Springs, Maine.

The Royal Descents of 900 Immigrants

1. Robert III, King of Scotland, d. 1406 = Annabella Drummond
2. Mary Stewart = George Douglas, 1st Earl of Angus
3. Elizabeth Douglas = Alexander Forbes, 1st Baron Forbes
4. James Forbes, 2nd Baron Forbes = Giles (Egidia in Latin) Keith
5. Duncan Forbes of Corsindae = Christian Mercer
6. James (Jacob) Forbes of Sweden = Helen Lundie
7. Mattias (Matthew) Forbes = Margareta Penters
8. Ernald Forbes = Carin Björnram
9. Arvid (Forbes), Baron Forbus = Margareta Boije
10. Sofia Juliana, Baroness Forbus = Axel Julius, Count de la Gardie, son of Jacob, Count de la Gardie (and Ebba, Countess Brahe), SETH, son of Pontus, Baron de la Gardie, by Sophia Gyllenhielm, illegitimate daughter (by Catherine Hannuntytär) of John III, King of Sweden, d. 1592, son of Gustav Vasa, King of Sweden, and Margrieta Leijonhufvud, SETH, neither of whom have proved royal medieval ancestry.
11. Magnus Julius, Count de la Gardie = Hedwig Catharina, Countess Lillie
12. Hedwig Catharina, Countess de la Gardie = Frederick Axel, Count von Fersen
13. **Hans Axel, Count von Fersen** (1755-1810), Swedish soldier, aide-de-camp to Rochambeau during the American Revolution, favorite and benefactor of Marie Antoinette, Queen of France, d. unm.

Sources: *DAB* and *ES*, vol. 8, tables 153-154 (de la Gardie); *Elgenstierna*, vol. 2, pp. 686 (von Fersen), 227-28 (de la Gardie), 787-88, 792-93 (Forbes, Forbus); *SP* (Forbes, Angus). See also *Forbes*, pp. 469-71.

The Royal Descents of 900 Immigrants

1. Robert III, King of Scotland, d. 1406 = Annabella Drummond
2. Mary Stewart = George Douglas, 1st Earl of Angus
3. Elizabeth Douglas = Alexander Forbes, 1st Baron Forbes
4. James Forbes, 2nd Baron Forbes = Giles (Egidia in Latin) Keith
5. Duncan Forbes of Corsindae = Christian Mercer
6. William Forbes of Corsindae = Margaret Lumsden
7. James Forbes of Corsindae = Janet Gordon
8. William Forbes of Tolquhon = Elizabeth Gordon
9. John Forbes of Pitnacardell = —— Hay of Burnthill
10. William Forbes of Tombeg = ——
11. John Forbes of Tombeg = Anna Lunan
12. James Forbes of Inverurie = Jean Forbes in Mills of Drum
13. Alexander Forbes = Mary Bairnsfather
14. Margaret Forbes = John Robertson
15. John Forbes-Robertson, art critic and journalist = Frances Cox (parents of the actor Sir Johnston Forbes-Robertson, who married [Mary] Gertrude Elliott, sister of Maxine Elliott, both actresses, all three of whom performed in the U.S.)
16. Norman Forbes-Robertson, actor = Louise Wilson
17. Frank Forbes-Robertson, actor-manager = (1) Honoria (Helen) McDermott, actress; (2) Sydney Thornton, actress
18. (by 1) Muriel Elsa Florence Forbes-Robertson, actress, stage name Muriel Forbes = **Sir Ralph (David) Richardson** (1902-1983), stage and movie actor, sometime of N.Y. or Calif. Films include *Richard III*, *A Long Day's Journey into Night*, *Doctor Zhivago*, *A Doll's House*, and *Time Bandits*.

Sources: *Forbes*, pp. 394-95, 409, 411-13, J.M. Bulloch, *The Picturesque Ancestry of Sir Johnston Forbes-Robertson* (1926) and *Who's Who in the Theatre*, 1936 ed., p. 1608. Note also *Oxford DNB* for Sir Johnston Forbes-Robertson and Sir Ralph (David) Richardson, and their wives.

The Royal Descents of 900 Immigrants

1. Robert II, King of Scotland, d. 1390 = (1) Elizabeth Mure
2. Robert Stewart, 1st Duke of Albany = Margaret Graham, Countess of Menteith

3. Marjory Stewart = Duncan Campbell, 1st Baron Campbell	3. Joan Stewart = Robert Stewart, 1st Baron Lorne
4. Hon. Archibald Campbell = Elizabeth Somerville	4. John Stewart, 2nd Baron Lorne = Fingula of the Isles
5. Colin Campbell, 1st Earl of Argyll =	5. Isabel Stewart

6. Helen Campbell = Hugh Montgomery, 1st Earl of Eglinton
7. Sir Neil Montgomery of Lainshaw = Margaret Mure
8. Sir Neil Montgomery of Lainshaw = Jean Lyle
9. Sir Neil Montgomery of Lainshaw = Elizabeth Cunyngham
10. William Montgomery of Brigend = Jean Montgomery
11. John Montgomery of Brigend = Elizabeth Baxter
12. Hugh Montgomery of Brigend = Katharine Scott
13. **William Montgomery** of N.J. = Isabel Burnett, daughter of Robert Burnett and Mrs. —— Forbes Burnett of N.J., ARD, SETH.

7. Margaret Montgomery = William Semphill, 2nd Baron Semphill
8. Robert Semphill, 3rd Baron Semphill = Isabel Hamilton
9. Margaret Semphill = David Hamilton of Broomhill
10. Katherine Hamilton = James Hamilton of Torrence
11. Robert Hamilton of Torrence = Beatrix Hamilton
12. Janet Hamilton = John Hamilton of Airdrie
13. Gavin Hamilton of Airdrie = Jane Montgomery

14. William Hamilton, professor of divinity and principal, University of Edinburgh = Mary Robertson

15. **Alexander Hamilton** (1712-1756) of Md., physician and social historian = Margaret Dulany.

14. Sir Robert Hamilton, 3rd Bt., of Airdrie (brother of William) = Elizabeth Cochrane

15. Louisa Hamilton = James Balfour of Pilrig

16. James Balfour of Pilrig, professor of moral philosophy, University of Edinburgh = Cecilia Elphinstone

16. Louisa Balfour = Robert Whytt (Whyte) of Bennochie, professor of medicine, University of Edinburgh

17. John Balfour of Pilrig   =   17. Jean Whytt

18. Lewis Balfour = Henrietta Scott Smith

19. Margaret Isabella Balfour = Thomas Stevenson, lighthouse engineer

20. **Robert Louis Stevenson**, 1850-1894, sometimes of N.Y. and Calif., novelist, author and traveler = Mrs. Frances Matilda (Fanny) Van de Grift Osborne.

Sources: *Montgomery*, pp. 55-58, 62-68, 71-83; *SP* and *CP* (Semphill, Eglinton, Argyll, Campbell, Lorne, Albany); *Hamilton*, pp. 704-9, 853-56, 187 and *BP* (Stirling-Hamilton of Preston, baronets); *BLG* 1906, p. 1149 (Balfour), 1846, pp. 857-58 (Whyte), *Oxford DNB* (James Balfour, Robert Whytt, Thomas and R.L. Stevenson) and *ANB*, vol. 20, pp. 731-33. See also the Lorne-Fingula of the Isles marriage source cited under Alexander Magruder (McGruder) of Md., herein.

The Genealogical Magazine of New Jersey 89 (2014): 3-20, 73-81, proposes another immigrant descendant of Helen Campbell and Hugh Montgomery, 1st Earl of Eglinton. He is John Campbell of Freehold, N.J., whose wife is unknown and for whom I can readily find no notable descendants. The immigrant was the son of William Campbell of Middlewellwood (and ——), son of Hugh Campbell of Middlewellwood (and Rachel Farquhar), son of Thomas Campbell of Middlewellwood and

The Royal Descents of 900 Immigrants

Margaret Campbell, daughter probably of George Campbell of Cesnock (and Agnes Shaw), son of John Campbell of Cesnock (and Janet Campbell of Loudoun), son of George Campbell of Glasnock and Cesnock and Janet Montgomery, daughter of the above Hugh Montgomery, 1st Earl of Eglinton, and Helen Campbell, at generation 6.

The Royal Descents of 900 Immigrants

1. Robert II, King of Scotland, d. 1390 = (1) Elizabeth Mure
2. Robert Stewart, 1st Duke of Albany = Margaret Graham, Countess of Menteith
3. Margaret Stewart = Sir John Swinton of that Ilk
4. Sir John Swinton of that Ilk = Marjory Dunbar
5. Sir John Swinton of that Ilk = ——
6. Sir John Swinton of that Ilk = Katherine Lauder
7. John Swinton of that Ilk = Marion Home
8. John Swinton of that Ilk = Katherine Lauder, a cousin
9. Robert Swinton of that Ilk = Jean Hepburn
10. Sir Alexander Swinton of that Ilk = Margaret Home
11. Sir Alexander Swinton of Mersington = Alison Skene
12. Elizabeth Swinton = Sir Alexander Cuming, 1st Bt.
13. **Sir Alexander Cuming, 2nd Bt.** (c. 1690-1775), English agent who persuaded the Creek and Cherokee Indians to accept British sovereignty in 1730, treated in the *DAB* = Amy Whitehall.
13. **Helen Cuming** of Mass. = Robert **Cuming**. Their son, Dr. John Cuming of Concord, Mass., who married Abigail Wesson, was an early benefactor of the Harvard Medical School. Isabella Cuming, daughter of Helen and Robert, married James Nevin, sometime a N.H. state councilor, and left English gentry descendants.

Sources: *CB* (Cuming of Culter); A.C. Swinton, *The Swintons of that Ilk and Their Cadets* (1883), pp. 10-64 and *BLG*, 18th ed., vol. 3 (1972), p. 878 (Swinton); *SP* and *CP* (Albany); *The Pedigree Register* 1 (1907-10), pp. 105-6 (a matrilineal line from Elizabeth [Swinton] Cuming) and Lemuel Shattuck, *A History of the Town of Concord, Middlesex County, Massachusetts* (1835), pp. 253-54 (Dr. John Cuming). Helen (Cuming) Cuming was brought to my attention by John C. Brandon of Columbia, S.C.

The Royal Descents of 900 Immigrants

1. Robert II, King of Scotland, d. 1390 = (1) Elizabeth Mure
2. Robert Stewart, 1ˢᵗ Duke of Albany = Margaret Graham, Countess of Menteith
3. —— Stewart (daughter, possibly Mary) = William Abernethy of Saltoun
4. Sir William Abernethy = Margaret Borthwick
5. Laurence Abernethy, 1ˢᵗ Baron Saltoun of Abernethy = Margaret ——
6. James Abernethy, 3ʳᵈ Baron Saltoun of Abernethy = ——
7. Alexander Abernethy, 4ᵗʰ Baron Saltoun of Abernethy = —— Stewart, daughter of James Stewart, 1ˢᵗ Earl of Buchan (and Margaret Ogilvy), son of Sir James Stewart, the "Black Knight of Lorne" and Joan Beaufort, Dowager Queen of Scotland
8. Beatrix Abernethy = Alexander Forbes of Pitsligo
9. Marion Forbes = Alexander Gordon of Lesmoir
10. Katherine Gordon = Alexander Burnet of Leys
11. Robert Burnet = Rachel Johnston
12. Gilbert Burnet, Bishop of Salisbury, the historian = Mary Scott
13. **William Burnet** (1688-1729), colonial governor of N.Y., N.J., Mass. and N.H. = (1) Maria Stanhope; (2) Anna Maria Van Horne.

10. Sir James Gordon, 1ˢᵗ Bt. (brother of Katherine) = Rebecca Keith
11. Sir James Gordon of Lesmoir = Helen Urquhart
12. Katherine Gordon = John Abercromby of Glassaugh
13. Alexander Abercromby of Glassaugh = Katherine Dunbar
14. Alexander Abercromby of Glassaugh = Helen Meldrum
15. **James Abercromby** (1706-1781), British commander in America during the French and Indian War, the loser at Ticonderoga = Mary Duff.

The Royal Descents of 900 Immigrants

Sources: *DAB* (William Burnet), *Burnett of Leys*, pp. 32-40, 130-42, *Gordon*, vol. 2, Lesmoir section, pp. 37-61, *Forbes*, p. 346, and *SP* and *CP* (Forbes of Pitsligo, Saltoun, Buchan, Albany) (Burnet); *DAB* (James Abercromby) and Cavendish D. Abercromby, *The Family of Abercromby* (1927), pp. 61, 87-89 and chart opposite p. 86.

The Royal Descents of 900 Immigrants

1. Robert II, King of Scotland, d. 1390 = (2) Euphemia of Ross
2. Katherine (also called Jean or Elizabeth) Stewart = David Lindsay, 1st Earl of Crawford
3. Elizabeth Lindsay = Robert Erskine, 1st Baron Erskine
4. Thomas Erskine, 2nd Baron Erskine = Janet Douglas
5. Alexander Erskine, 3rd Baron Erskine = Christian Crichton
6. Robert Erskine, 4th Baron Erskine = Isabel Campbell
7. James Erskine of Little Sauchie and Balgownie = Christian Stirling
8. Alexander Erskine of Shielfield = Elizabeth Haliburton
9. Ralph Erskine of Shielfield = (1) Isabella Cairncross; (2) Janet Wilson
10. (probably by 2) Henry Erskine of Chirnside = Margaret Halcro
11. Ralph Erskine of Dunfermline = Margaret Simpson
12. **Robert Erskine** (1735-1780) of N.J., geographer and hydraulic engineer = Elizabeth ――――.

10. (by 1) John Erskine of Shielfield = Margaret Haliburton
11. James Erskine of Shielfield = Elizabeth Carre
12. ―――― Erskine (daughter) = Patrick Haliburton of Muirhouselaw
13. George Haliburton, Lord Provost of Edinburgh = Jean Clark
14. Jean Haliburton = Edward Burd of Ormiston
15. **James Burd** of Pa. = Sarah Shippen.

Sources: *DAB* (Robert Erskine) and *Oxford DNB* (Henry and Ralph Erskine); Ebenezer Erskine Scott, *The Erskine-Halcro Genealogy*, 2nd ed. (1895), charts I and V, part 2, and p. 51 (R. Erskine); *PSFCD* 3:85-87 (undocumented), W.K. and A.C. (Zimmerman) Rutherford, *Genealogical History of the Halliburton Family*, rev. ed., vol. 1 (1983), pp. 12, 21, 23, 41-42, plus materials on the Erskines of Shielfield and Chirnside submitted to the Order of the Crown of Charlemagne by Ann Naile Phelps (according to Timothy Field Beard) (James Burd); *SP* and *CP* (Erskine or Mar, Crawford).

The Royal Descents of 900 Immigrants

1. Robert II, King of Scotland, d. 1390 = (2) Euphemia of Ross
2. Katherine (also called Jean or Elizabeth) Stewart = David Lindsay, 1st Earl of Crawford
3. Elizabeth Lindsay = Robert Erskine, 1st Baron Erskine
4. Thomas Erskine, 2nd Baron Erskine = Janet Douglas
5. Alexander Erskine, 3rd Baron Erskine = Christian Crichton
6. Christian Erskine = David Stewart of Rosyth
7. Christian Stewart = John Bethune of Balfour
8. John Bethune of Balfour = Agnes Anstruther
9. Margaret Bethune = John Row
10. John Row = Grizel Ferguson
11. John Row = Elspeth Gillespie
12. Lilias Row = John Mercer (the three John Rows and John Mercer, plus William Mercer below, were all ministers)
13. Thomas Mercer of Todlaw = Isabel Smith
14. William Mercer = Anne Munro
15. **Hugh Mercer** (1726-1777) of Va., physician and revolutionary officer = Isabel Gordon.

10. Catherine Row (sister of the second John) = William Rigg
11. William Rigg of Aithernie = Sarah Inglis
12. Thomas Rigg of Aithernie = Bethia Carstairs
13. Margaret Rigg = George Scott of Pitlochie, writer on America
14. **Euphan Scott** of N.J. = John **Johnstone**.

Sources: *MCS5*, line 91B (generations 14-22) and sources cited therein, esp. J.T. Clark, ed., *Genealogical Collections Concerning Families in Scotland Made by Walter Macfarlane, 1750-1751*, vol. 1 (1900), pp. 11-12, 21 (Bethune of Balfour) (for Hugh Mercer); *TSA* 5 (1891): 5 (Stewart of Rosyth); *SP* (Mar) and *CP* (Erskine, Crawford); *NYGBR* 33 (1902):

The Royal Descents of 900 Immigrants

246-47, *Oxford DNB* (George Scott or Scot, d. 1685) and Rev. Walter Wood, *The East Neuk of Fife, Its History and Antiquities*, 2nd ed. (1887), pp. 40-41 (Rigg) (for Mrs. Johnstone). Macfarlane (and Wood, p. 375) state that Christian Stewart, wife of John Bethune of Balfour, was a daughter of the laird of Rosyth. Chronology and naming patterns (the three Christians) make the above descent almost certain; a full monograph centered on Christian Stewart, however, would be welcome.

The Royal Descents of 900 Immigrants

1. Robert II, King of Scotland, d. 1390 = (2) Euphemia of Ross
2. Giles (Egidia in Latin) Stewart = Sir William Douglas of Nithsdale
3. Giles (Egidia in Latin) Douglas = Henry Sinclair, 2nd Earl of Orkney
4. William Sinclair, 3rd Earl of Orkney, 1st Earl of Caithness = Marjory Sutherland
5. Eleanor Sinclair = (his second wife) John Stewart, 1st Earl of Atholl, son of Sir James Stewart, "The Black Knight of Lorne," and Joan Beaufort, Dowager Queen of Scotland
6. Jean Stewart = James Arbuthnott of Arbuthnott
7. Isabel Arbuthnott = Robert Maule of Panmure
8. William Maule = Bethia Guthrie
9. Eleanor Maule = Alexander Morrison of Prestongrange
10. Bethia Morrison = Sir Robert Spotswood of Dunipage, son of John Spotswood, Archbishop of St. Andrews, and Rachel Lindsay, daughter of David Lindsay, Bishop of Ross, and Janet Ramsay, SETH
11. Robert Spotswood = Catherine ——
12. **Alexander Spotswood** (1676-1740), colonial (lt.) governor of Va. = Anne Butler Brayne.
13. Dorothea Spotswood = Nathaniel West Dandridge
14. Martha Dandridge = Archibald Payne
15. Catherine Payne = Archibald Bolling
16. Archibald Bolling, Jr. = Anne E. Wigginton
17. William Holcombe Bolling = Sallie Spiers White
18. Edith Bolling = (1) Norman Galt; (2) (Thomas) Woodrow Wilson (1856-1924), 28th U.S. President

9. Isabel Maule (sister of Eleanor) = James Dundas of Doddington

The Royal Descents of 900 Immigrants

10. Bethia Dundas = James Hume

11. Isabel Hume = Patrick Logan

12. **James Logan** (1674-1751) of Pa., colonial statesman, jurist, Indian trader and scholar = (1) Sarah Read; (2) Amy Child.

Sources: *RA* 5: 1-5, 41-44, 1: 615-17, 640-41 (entire line) and sources cited therein, especially *CP* and *SP* (Spotswood); *MCS5*, line 111B and C.P. Keith, *The Provincial Councillors of Pennsylvania* (1883, reprint 1997), pp. 1-14 (Logan), *Drummond*, vol. 2 (Dundas and Hume pedigrees), and *SP* (Maule, earls of Panmure).

The Royal Descents of 900 Immigrants

1. Robert II, King of Scotland, d. 1390 = (1) Elizabeth Mure

2. Robert Stewart, 1st Duke of Albany = Margaret Graham, Countess of Menteith

3. Marjory Stewart = Duncan Campbell, 1st Baron Campbell

3. Joan Stewart = Robert Stewart, 1st Baron Lorne, brother of Sir James Stewart, the "Black Knight of Lorne," second husband of Joan Beaufort, Dowager Queen of Scotland, SETH

4. Hon. Archibald Campbell = Elizabeth Somerville

4. John Stewart, 2nd Baron Lorne = Fingula of the Isles

5. Colin Campbell, 1st Earl of Argyll = 5. Isabel Stewart

6. Archibald Campbell, 2nd Earl of Argyll = Elizabeth Stewart

7. Donald Campbell, Abbot of Coupar Angus

8. (illegitimate, allegedly by Margaret ——) Nicholas Campbell, Dean of Lismore Cathedral = Katherine Drummond

9. Margaret Campbell (of Keithick) = Alexander McGruder

10. **Alexander Magruder (McGruder)** of Md. = (1) Sarah ——; (2) Elizabeth ——.

Sources: *PSECD* 3:202-4 (undocumented); *Yearbook of the American Clan Gregor Society* 52(1978):55-65, 53(1979):53-71 ("The Ancestral History of Margaret Campbell of Keithick" and "The McGruder Lineage in Scotland to Magruder Family in America," both by Dr. Charles G. Kurz, based on research of Thomas Garland Magruder, Jr.), kindly brought to my attention by Brice McAdoo Clagett of Friendship, Md.; *SP* and *CP* (Argyll, Campbell, Lorn [Innermeath in *SP*], and Albany [Stewart]). For the marriage of John Stewart, 2nd Baron Lorne, to Fingula of the Isles, see Jean and R.W. Munro, *Acts of the Lords of the Isles, 1336-1493* (1986), pp. 244, 301, brought to my attention by Douglas Hickling of Piedmont, Calif.

The Royal Descents of 900 Immigrants

1. Robert II, King of Scotland, d. 1390 = (1) Elizabeth Mure

2. Marjorie of Scotland = John Dunbar, 1st Earl of Moray, son of Sir Patrick Dunbar and Isabel Randolph, SETH

3. Euphemia Dunbar = Sir Alexander Comyn of Altyre

4. Sir Thomas Comyn of Altyre = Margaret Gordon of Haddo

5. Jean Comyn (illegitimately with but sometimes alleged to have married) Alexander Gordon, 1st Earl of Huntly

6. Margaret Gordon = Hugh Rose of Kilvarock

7. John Rose of Bellivat = Marjorie Dunbar of Conzie and Kilbuick

8. John Rose of Bellivat = Janet Urquhart of Burdsymonds

9. Jean Rose (more likely a daughter of 8 than of 7) = William Cumming of Presley

10. William Cumming of Presley = Margaret Leslie of Aikenway

11. David Cumming = Anna Tulloch

12. **William Cumming** of Md. = Elizabeth Coursey. A son was N.C. legislator and Continental Congressman William Cumming, Jr., who died unmarried.

Sources: Research of Miss Ann Robinson King of Birmingham, Ala., based on a deposition by the immigrant in Chancery Court records, Anne Arundel Co., Md., Liber #4, fol. 235, dated 29 Sept. 1718; PRs of Forres, co. Moray, Scotland; the 6 Nov. 1714 will of Alexander Cumming, brother of David, in County Moray Testaments, vol. 2; General Register of Sasines, Book 108, p. 435ff. (6 March 1716) and instrument of sasine 21 Feb. 1639, RS 28/4/196, 197 and RS 28/4/195, 196; M.E. Cumming Bruce, *Family Records of the Bruces and the Cumyns* (1870), pp. 456-57, 657; C. Innes, ed., *A Genealogical Deduction of the Family of Rose of Kilvarock* (1848, repr. 1981), pp. 54-55, 523; and *SP* and *CP* (Huntly, Moray). For William Cumming, Jr., see William S. Powell, ed., *Dictionary of North Carolina Biography*, vol. 1 (1979), p. 473. The late Andrew B. W. MacEwen wrote that he had developed a line from Robert II to Alexander Gordon, 1st Earl of Huntly, in "Some Notes on the Keith and Gordon Pedigrees," in Lindsay L. Brook, ed., *Studies in Genealogy and Family History in Tribute to Charles Evans on the Occasion of his Eightieth Birthday* (1989), pp. 153-189.

The Royal Descents of 900 Immigrants

1. Robert II, King of Scotland, d. 1390 = (2) Euphemia of Ross
2. Katherine (also called Jean or Elizabeth) Stewart = David Lindsay, 1st Earl of Crawford
3. Alexander Lindsay, 2nd Earl of Crawford = Marjory ———
4. David Lindsay, 3rd Earl of Crawford = Marjory Ogilvy
5. Sir Walter Lindsay of Beaufort and Edzell = Isabel Livingston
6. Sir David Lindsay of Beaufort and Edzell = Katherine Fotheringham
7. Sir Walter Lindsay of Beaufort and Edzell = ——— Erskine
8. Alexander Lindsay of Haltoun (younger brother of the 9th Earl of Crawford) = ——— Barclay
9. David Lindsay, Bishop of Ross = Janet Ramsay
10. Sir Jerome Lindsay of Annatland and the Mount = Margaret Colville
11. **Rev. David Lindsay** of Va. = (1) ———; (2) Susanna ———

Sources: *MCS5*, line 43 and Margaret Isabella Lindsay, *The Lindsays of America* (1889), charts opp. 8 and 22 esp.

The Royal Descents of 900 Immigrants

1. Robert II, King of Scotland, d. 1390 = (1) Elizabeth Mure
2. Robert Stewart, 1st Duke of Albany = Margaret Graham, Countess of Menteith
3. Marjory Stewart = Duncan Campbell, 1st Baron Campbell
3. Joan Stewart = Robert Stewart, 1st Baron Lorne
4. Hon. Archibald Campbell = Elizabeth Somerville
4. John Stewart, 2nd Baron Lorne = Fingula of the Isles
5. Colin Campbell, 1st Earl of Argyll = 5. Isabel Stewart
6. Archibald Campbell, 2nd Earl of Argyll = Elizabeth Stewart
7. Janet Campbell = John Stewart, 2nd Earl of Atholl, son of John Stewart, 1st Earl of Atholl (and Eleanor Sinclair), son of Sir James Stewart, "The Black Knight of Lorne," and Joan Beaufort, Dowager Queen of Scotland
8. Elizabeth Stewart = Sir Kenneth Mackenzie of Kintail
9. Colin Mackenzie of Kintail = Barbara Grant
10. (illegitimate by Mary Mackenzie) Alexander Mackenzie of Coul = Christian Munro
11. Sir Kenneth Mackenzie, 1st Bt. = Jean Chisholm
12. Jean Mackenzie = Alexander Baillie of Dunain
13. John Baillie "of Balrobert" (almost certainly son or son-in-law[the husband of Jean Baillie] of the above)
14. **Col. Kenneth Baillie** of Ga. = Elizabeth Mackay.
15. Anne Elizabeth Baillie = John Irvine of Ga., ARD, SETH
16. Anne Irvine = James Bulloch
17. James Stephens Bulloch = Martha Stewart
18. Martha Bulloch = Theodore Roosevelt
19. Theodore Roosevelt, Jr. (1858-1919), 26th U.S. President = (1) Alice Hathaway Lee; (2) Edith Kermit Carow.

The Royal Descents of 900 Immigrants

Sources: *Baillie*, pp. 3-6, 12-25, 40-46; *CB*, vol. 4, p. 296 (Mackenzie of Coul); *SP*, articles on Mackenzies (of Kintail, later Earls of Seaforth) and Stewarts (Earls of Atholl); *SP* and *CP* (Argyll, Campbell, Lorne, Albany) and the Lorne-Fingula of the Isles marriage source cited elsewhere herein. Documentary proof of the identity of John Baillie "of Balrobert" would be welcome.

The Royal Descents of 900 Immigrants

1. Robert II, King of Scotland, d. 1390 = (2) Euphemia of Ross
2. Katherine (also called Jean or Elizabeth) Stewart = David Lindsay, 1st Earl of Crawford
3. Elizabeth Lindsay = Robert Erskine, 1st Baron Erskine
4. Thomas Erskine, 2nd Baron Erskine = Janet Douglas
5. Alexander Erskine, 3rd Baron Erskine = Christian Crichton
6. Robert Erskine, 4th Baron Erskine = Isabel Campbell
7. Catherine Erskine = Alexander Elphinstone, 2nd Baron Elphinstone
8. Marjorie Elphinstone = Sir Robert Drummond of Carnock
9. Patrick Drummond of Carnock = Margaret Scott
10. Agnes Drummond = John Abercromby of Abbots-Kerse
11. Elspeth Abercromby = Robert Haig of St. Ninians, son of James Haig of Bemersyde (and Elizabeth McDougall), son of Robert Haig of Bemersyde (and Margaret Kerr), son of Andrew Haig of Bemersyde (by which of three wives is uncertain), son of Robert Haig of Bemersyde (and Barbara Spotswood), son of William Haig of Bemersyde and Isabel Home, daughter of Mungo Home and Elizabeth Stewart, illegitimate daughter (by Margaret Murray) of James Stewart, 1st Earl of Buchan, SETH
12. John Haig of Orchard Farm = Isabel Ramsey
13. George Haig of Newbigging = Janet Anderson
14. James Haig of Alloa = Mary Mackenzie
15. John Haig of the Garthlands = Margaret Stein
16. John Haig of Bonnington = Christina Jameson
17. James Haig = Marie de St. Paule
18. **Robert Haig** of Columbus, Ohio = Hattie Leamon. Their son, James Haig, married firstly Mary Caroline Murray and was the father of Robert Murray Haig, political economist, who married Gertrude Marguerite Hoppin.

The Royal Descents of 900 Immigrants

Sources: *BLG*, 18th ed., vol. 2 (1969), pp. 265-66, 268-69 (Haig), *The Scottish Antiquary* 10 (1896), pp. 68, 99-100 (Abercromby, Drummond), *SP* and *CP* (Elphinstone, Erskine or Mar, Crawford, Home, and Buchan).

The Royal Descents of 900 Immigrants

1. Charles II, King of Navarre, d. 1387 = Joanna of France, daughter of John II, King of France, and Bona of Bohemia

2. Joanna of Navarre = John V, Duke of Brittany (Joanna married secondly Henry IV, King of England)

3. Margaret of Brittany = Alain IX, Vicomte de Rohan

4. Catherine de Rohan = Jean d'Albret, Vicomte de Tartas

5. Alain d'Albret, Count of Gavre = Françoise de Châtillon-Blois (their children included Jean d'Albret, King of Navarre, and Charlotte d'Albret, wife of Cesare Borgia, Duc de Valentinois, tyrant of Italy, son of Pope Alexander VI and brother of Lucretia Borgia, Duchess of Modena and Ferrara)

6. Isabelle d'Albret = Gaston II de Foix, Count of Benauges, son of John de Foix, 1st Earl of Kendal, and Margaret Kerdeston, SETH. Gaston II de Foix, Count of Benauges married firstly Catherine de Foix, a cousin, and left a daughter, Anne de Foix, who married Ladislaus V, King of Bohemia and Hungary. Their daughter, Anne of Bohemia, married Ferdinand I, Holy Roman Emperor, and is an ancestress of many later European kings.

7. Louise de Foix = François de Melun, Baron d'Antoing

8. Hugh de Melun, Prince d'Épinoy = Yolande de Barbançon

9. Pierre de Melun, Prince d'Épinoy = Hippolite de Montmorency

10. Anne de Melun = Alexander de Bournonville, Duc de Bournonville, SETH, p. 291 below

11. Ambrose-François de Bournonville, Duc de Bournonville = Lucrèce-Françoise de la Vieuville

12. Marie-Françoise de Bournonville = Anne-Jules de Noailles, Duc de Noailles. Their daughter, Marie-Victoire-Sophie de Noailles, married secondly Louis-Alexandre de Bourbon, Count of Toulouse, legitimized son of Louis XIV, King of France, and Françoise-Athénaïs de Rochechouart, Marquise de Montespan. Louis-Jean-Marie de Bourbon, Duke of Penthièvre, son of Louis-Alexandre and Marie-Victoire-Sophie, married Maria Theresa Felicitas d'Este of Modena and was the father of Louise-Marie-Adélaïde of Bourbon-Penthièvre, wife of Louis-Philippe-Joseph

The Royal Descents of 900 Immigrants

"Égalité," Duke of Orléans, supporter and victim of the French Revolution, and mother of Louis-Philippe, King of the French (1773-1850), a refugee in the U.S. 1796-1800, who married Maria Amelia (Theresa) of the Two Sicilies. Descendants of these last include Kings of the Belgians, Spain and Bulgaria, Grand Dukes of Luxembourg, Princes Napoléon, and the wives of Crown Prince Rudolf of Austria, Maximilian, Emperor of Mexico, and the last King (later prime minister) of Roumania.

13. Adrien-Maurice de Noailles, Duc de Noailles, French soldier and statesman = Françoise-Charlotte-Amable d'Aubigné (niece of Françoise d'Aubigné, Marquise [known as Madame] de Maintenon, mistress and second wife of Louis XIV, King of France)

14. Louis de Noailles, Duc de Noailles = Catherine-Françoise-Charlotte de Cossé

15. Jean-Louis-François-Paul de Noailles, Duc de Noailles = Henriette-Anne-Louise d'Aguessau

16. **Marie-Adrienne-Françoise de Noailles** = Marie-Joseph-Paul-Yves-Roch-Gilbert **Motier, Marquis de La Fayette (Lafayette)** (1757-1834), the American revolutionary general and French statesman, ARD, SETH.

16. **Anne-Jeanne-Baptiste-Pauline-Adrienne-Louise-Catherine-Dominique de Noailles** = Louis-Marie **de Noailles,** Vicomte de Noailles (1756-1804), leader in the American and French revolutions and in the American emigré community of the 1790s, his wife's first cousin once removed, see below.

14. Philippe de Noailles, Duc de Mouchy (brother of Louis de Noailles, Duc de Noailles) = Anne-Claudine-Louise d'Arpajon, SETH

15. **Louis-Marie de Noailles, Vicomte de Noailles** (1756-1804), leader in the American and French revolutions and in the American emigré community of the 1790s (fought at the battles of Savannah and Yorktown, resided in Philadelphia from 1793 to 1800) = Anne-Jeanne-Baptiste-Pauline-Adrienne-Louise-Catherine-Dominique de Noailles, see above.

13. Anne-Louise de Noailles (sister of Adrien-Maurice) = Jacques-Hippolyte Mancini-Mazarini, Marquis de Mancini, a first cousin of Eugène, Prince of Savoy, Austrian commander in the War of the Spanish Succession, and great-nephew of both Cardinal Jules (Giulio) Mazarin(i), minister of Louis XIII, King of France, and Francoise-Athénaïs de Rochechouart, Marquise de Montespan, see above, mistress of Louis XIV, King of France

14. Diane-Adélaide-Zéphirine Mancini-Mazarini = Louis-Melchior-Armand de Polignac, Marquis de Chalencon

15. Jules-François-Armand de Polignac, 1st Duc de Polignac = Gabrielle-Yolande-Claude-Martine de Polastron. Their son, Camille-Henri-Melchior, Count de Polignac, married Marie-Charlotte-Calixte-Alphonsine le Vassor de la Touche, and was the father of Charles-Marie-Thomas, Count de Polignac, who married Caroline-Josephine le Normand de Mora. A son of these last, Maxence-Melchior-Édouard-Marie-Louis, Count de Polignac, married Suzanne-Marie-Anne-Stéphanie-Françoise de la Torre y Mier and was the father of Pierre (-Marie-Xavier-Raphael-Antoine-Melchior), Count de Polignac, who married Charlotte (-Louise-Juliette Grimaldi), Hereditary Princess of Monaco, and Duchess of Valentinois, SETH, and was the father of Rainer III (Louis-Henry-Maxence-Bertrand), Sovereign Prince of Monaco, SETH.

16. Auguste-Jules-Armand Marie, Prince of Polignac, minister of Charles X, King of France = (1) Barbara Campbell; (2) Mary Charlotte Parkyns

17. (by 2) **Camille-Armand-Jules-Marie, Prince de Polignac** (1832-1913), sometime Confederate general, 1861-65; = (1) Marie Adolfine Langenberger; (2) Margaret Elizabeth Knight.

Sources: Arnaud Chaffanjon, *La Fayette et sa Descendance* (1976), pp. 58-64, and *Anselme* (and Potier de Courcy), vol. 9, part 2, pp. 242-44 (Noailles), vol. 5, pp. 837-39 (Bournonville), 231-32 (Melun), vol. 3, pp. 383-84 (Foix), vol. 6, pp. 213-15 (Albret), vol. 4, pp. 55-56 (Rohan); *ES*, tables for Navarre, Brittany, Rohan, Albret, Foix, Melun, Noailles, France (illegitimate progeny of Louis XIV) and Orléans. See also *Charles II*, pp. 10, 18-19, 34, 58-63, 106-7, 170, 272-73, 396-98, on Margaret Kerdeston and

The Royal Descents of 900 Immigrants

her immediate ancestry and royal progeny. For Camille A.J.M., Prince de Polignac and Rainier III, Sovereign Prince of Monaco, see also *ES* 2: 9: 91-92, 95, *ES* 2: 2: 203, *BRFW* 1: 408-9 and E.S. Branda, ed., *The Handbook of Texas: A Supplement*, vol. 3 (1976), p. 742 (reprinted in Ron Tyler, Douglas E. Barnett and Roy R. Barkley, *The New Handbook of Texas*, 6 vols. [1996], https://tshaonline.org/handbook/online/articles/fpo07); Jean, Duc de Polignac, *La Maison de Polignac: Étude d'Une Évolution Sociale de la Noblesse* (1975), *passim*, Anselme, vol. 9, part 1, pp. 854-55 (Polignac), vol. 5, pp. 463-64 (Mancini). For descendants of Louis-Philippe, King of the French, the only great-grandchild of Marie-Victoire-Sophie de Noailles to leave issue, see Jacques Arnold, *The Royal Houses of Europe: The Bourbon Dynasty of France: The Descendants of King Louis XIII* (2008), section A. Among these descendants, in addition to the sovereigns listed above, was Elizabeth (Bianca Maria Constance), Princess Czartoryski, sometime of Washington, D.C. and New York City (where two of her three children were born), wife of Stefan Adam, Count Zamoyski, and mother of Polish historian and writer Adam Stefan, Count Zamoyski, b. New York 1949, who was educated and has lived largely in England, and married noted painter Emma Sargeant. Princess Elizabeth was the daughter of Adam Louis, Prince Czartoryski (and Maria Louisa, Countess Krasinski), son of Wladyslaw, Prince Czartoryski, and Marguerite-Adélaïde (Marie) of Orléans, daughter of Louis-Charles (-Philippe-Raphael) of Orléans, Duke of Nemours (and Victoire [-Françoise-Antoinette-Julienne-Louise] of Saxe-Coburg-Gotha, sister of Fernando (Ferdinand) II, King of Portugal, niece of Leopold I, King of the Belgians and first cousin of both Queen Victoria and Prince Albert), son of Louis-Philippe and Maria Amelia Theresa of the Two Sicilies. See Arnold, above, charts A1, A2D, A3H, A4P, and *RHS*, pp. 43, 48, 51, plus Wikipedia entries for S.A. and A.J., Counts Zamoyski. I first noted this Zamoyski line while perusing Ian Fettes and Leo van de Pas, *Plantagenet Cousins* (2007), where it appears on p. 334.

The above descent from Charles II, King of Navarre, d. 1387, is preferred to that below, from a later king, because the line above treats the nearest immigrant kinsmen herein of Anne of Bohemia, wife of Ferdinand I, Holy Roman Emperor, d. 1564. The line below is not only from a more recent king than Charles II of Navarre; it also includes the executed Netherlandish and Belgian hero Lamoral, Count of Egmont and Prince of Gavre.

The Royal Descents of 900 Immigrants

1. Rupert III, Holy Roman Emperor, d. 1410 = Elizabeth of Nürnberg

2. Margaret of Pfalz = Charles I, Duke of Lorraine

3. Catherine of Lorraine = James I, Margrave of Baden

4. Charles I, Margrave of Baden = Catherine of Austria, sister of Frederick III, Holy Roman Emperor

5. Catherine of Baden = George II, Count of Werdenberg

6. Magdalen of Werdenberg = John I, Count of Egmont

7. John II, Count of Egmont = Françoise of Luxembourg, Countess of Gavre

8. Lamoral, Count of Egmont, Prince of Gavre, Belgian martyr in the revolt of The Netherlands against Spain = 7. Sabina of Simmern, daughter of John II, Count Palatine of Simmern and 6. Beatrix of Baden, daughter of 5. Christopher I, Margrave of Baden (and Ottilie of Katzenelnbogen), son of Charles I, Margrave of Baden and Catherine of Austria, #4 above. For Ottilie of Katzenelnbogen see *The Genealogist* 28 (2014): 130-32.

8, 9. Marie Christine of Egmont = Oudard de Bournonville, Count of Hennin-Lietard

9, 10. Alexander de Bournonville, Duc de Bournonville = Anne de Melun, SETH, see above, p. 287

Sources: *ES* 2: 18: 32 (Egmont), 2: 12: 51 (Werdenberg) and charts for Pfalz and Simmern (Counts Palatine), Lorraine, and Baden. This descent was noticed and brought to my attention by John Blythe Dobson of Winnipeg, Manitoba, Canada.

The following remarkable descent links (1) the kings listed on p. 615; (2) Louis-Philippe, King of the French, his royal descendants noted above, and his Noailles kinsmen, including Lafayette's wife, Mancini-Mazarins, Gramonts, Polignacs, and the royal family of Monaco; and (3) via de Foix, Kerdeston and de la Pole, various American immigrants, including wives of Herbert Pelham (Elizabeth Bosvile) and Richard Saltonstall, plus an RD ancestor of President Taft—to the Empress Eugénie, wife of Napoléon III (Bonaparte), Emperor of the French.

The Royal Descents of 900 Immigrants

9. Anne-Marie de Melun (sister of Pierre de Melun, Prince d'Épinoy, p. 287) = Lamoral, 1st Prince of Ligne

10. Yolande of Ligne = Charles Alexander, Duke of Croy

11. Marie-Claire of Croy = (2) Philip Francis, Duke of Croy-Havre

12. Ferdinand Joseph Francis, Duke of Croy-Havre = Marie Josephine Barbara de Hallwin

13. Jean Baptiste Francois Joseph, Duke of Croy-Havre = Marie Anna Césarine Lante della Rovere

14. Marie Anna Charlotte Josephine of Croy = Joachim Antoine Ximeniz de Palafox, 6th Marquis of Arriza

15. Philip Antoine José de Palafox y Croy-Havre = María Francisca de Sales de Portocarrero de Guzmán, Countess of Montijo

16. Cipriano de Palafox y Portocarrero, Count of Montijo = María Manuela Kirkpatrick of Closeburn, a first cousin of Ferdinand-Marie de Lesseps, French diplomat and promoter of the Suez Canal

17. Eugenia (Maria [Ignace Augustine] de Portocarrero de Guzmán y Kirkpatrick, the Empress Eugénie of the French (1826-1920) = Napoleon III (Louis Napoleon Bonaparte), Emperor of the French (1808-1873), nephew of Napoleon I (Bonaparte), Emperor of the French, and grandson of the Empress Josephine (Marie-Josèphe-Rose de Tascher de la Pagerie), SETH, whose first husband was Alexandre-Marie, Vicomte de Beauharnais. See *Anselme*, vol. 9, pt. 1, pp. 804-5 (Portocarrero), Joël Aubailly, *Les Ancêtres de Napoléon III* (1998), pp. 61-63, 65 (generations 13-17) and *ES* 2: 18: 107, 110, 115 (Croy), 97 (Ligne), 2: 7: 56 (Melun).

The Royal Descents of 900 Immigrants

1. Charles II, King of Navarre, d. 1387 = Joanna of France, daughter of John II, King of France, d. 1364, and Bona of Bohemia

2. Joanna of Navarre = John V, Duke of Brittany (Joanna married secondly Henry IV, King of England)

3. Margaret of Brittany = Alain IX, Vicomte de Rohan

4. Catherine de Rohan = Jean d'Albret, Vicomte de Tartas

5. Alain d'Albret, Count of Gavre = Françoise de Châtillon-Blois. They were parents of Jean d'Albret, King of Navarre, and great-grandparents of Henry IV, King of France.

6. Charlotte d'Albret = Cesare Borgia, Duc de Valentinois, tyrant of Italy, son of Pope Alexander VI and brother of Lucretia Borgia, Duchess of Ferrara and Modena

7. Louisa, Princess Borgia = Philip of Bourbon, Baron de Busset, son of Peter of Bourbon, Baron de Busset (and Marguerite de Tourzel), illegitimate son of Louis of Bourbon, Bishop of Liège, son of Charles I, Duke of Bourbon, and Agnes of Burgundy, SETH

8. Claude of Bourbon, Count of Busset = Marguerite de la Rochefoucauld

9. Cesare of Bourbon, Count of Busset = Louise de Montmorillon

10. Anne of Bourbon = Antoine de Pracomtal, Baron de Soussey

11. Louise de Pracomtal = François Damas, Count de Cruz

12. Antoine-Louis Damas, Count de Cruz = Marie-Anne Coutier

13. Étienne Damas, Count de Cruz = Marguerite-Étiennette d'Achey

14. Louis-Alexander Damas, Count de Cruz = Marie-Louise de Menou

15. Catherine-Antoinette Damas = Bernard-Bonaventure de Clerel, Count de Tocqueville

16. Hervé-Louis-François de Clerel, Count de Tocqueville = Louise-Madeleine le Peltier, daughter of Louis V le Peltier, Marquis de Rosambo, and Marie-Thérèse de Lamoignon,

daughter (by Françoise-Thérèse Grimod) of Chrétien-Guillaume (Christian William) de Lamoignon, Baron de Malesherbes, French minister (under Louis XVI), and of royal descent via le Potier, Baillet, d'Aunoy and Montmorency

17. **Alexis-Henry de Clerel de Tocqueville**, known as **Alexis de Tocqueville** (1805-1852), sometime traveler in the U.S., 1831-32, French minister of foreign affairs under Louis Philippe, author of *Democracy in America* = Mary Mottley.

Sources: Henri Jougla de Morenas, *Grand Armorial de France*, vol. 2 (1938), p. 460 (Clerel de Tocqueville), vol. 5 (1948), p. 239 (le Pelletier); *Courcelles*, vol. 1 (1822), pp. 32-34 (Damas); *ES* 2: 3: 2: 332 (Bourbon-Busset), 2: 9: 11 (Borgia), 2: 2: 14B (d'Albret), 2: 3: 1: 72 (Bourbon), *Charles II*, pp. 28, 48, 87, 51. 91, 83-84, 139-40, 230 (generations 1-5); *D de la N*, vol. 15, p. 593 (le Pelletier), 11, pp. 383-88 (Lamoignon), 16, pp. 230-32 (Potier), 2, pp. 196-97 (Baillet) and *ES* 1: 3: 117 (III), 113 (Montmorency).

The Royal Descents of 900 Immigrants

1. Edward III, King of England, d. 1377 = Philippa of Hainault
2. John of Gaunt, Duke of Lancaster = Catherine Roët
3. Henry Beaufort, Cardinal Beaufort
4. (illegitimate, allegedly, but probably not, by Alice FitzAlan, who = John Cherleton, 4th Baron Cherleton of Powis) Jane Beaufort = Sir Edward Stradling
5. Katherine (or Joan) Stradling = Morris Dennis
6. Sir Walter Dennis = Agnes Danvers
7. Sir William Dennis = Anne Berkeley, daughter of Maurice Berkeley and Isabel Mead, SETH (and granddaughter of James Berkeley, 6th Baron Berkeley, and Isabel Mowbray, also SETH)
8. Eleanor Dennis = William Lygon, son of Sir Richard Lygon and Margaret Grevile, SETH (and grandson of Richard Lygon and Anne Beauchamp, also SETH)
9. Thomas Lygon = 8. Frances Dennis, see below

9, 10. Thomas Lygon = Elizabeth Pratt

10, 11. **Col. Thomas Ligon (Lygon)** of Va. = Mary Harris.

   6. John Dennis (brother of Sir William) = Fortune Norton

   7. Hugh Dennis, nephew of Sir William Dennis, above = Katherine Trye, daughter of Edward Trye (and Sybil Monington, daughter of Thomas Monington and Elizabeth Milborne, daughter of Simon Milborne and Jane Baskerville, SETH), son of William Trye (and Anne Baynham), son of William Trye and Isabel Berkeley, daughter of James Berkeley, 6th Baron Berkeley, and Isabel Mowbray, SETH

   8. Frances Dennis = Thomas Lygon, see above

   9. Cecily Lygon (sister of the first Thomas Lygon) = Edward Gorges, SETH

  10. **Sir Ferdinando Gorges** (c. 1565-1647), founder and lord proprietor of Maine, = (1) Anne Bell; (2) Mrs. Mary Fulford Achims; (3) Mrs. Elizabeth ____ Coffin; (4) Mrs. Elizabeth

The Royal Descents of 900 Immigrants

(Gorges) (Courtenay) Bligh; (5) Lady Elizabeth (Gorges) Smith (all except the third wife ARD, SETH). Deputies of Gorges in Maine included his son (by Anne Bell), Robert Gorges, gov.-general of New England 1623-24 (d. unm.) and his nephew, William Gorges, gov. of New Somersetshire, Maine, 1636-37 (also d. unm.), son of Sir Edward Gorges and Dorothy Speke.

9. Margaret Lygon (sister of Thomas and Cecily) = Sir Henry Berkeley
10. Sir Maurice Berkeley = Elizabeth Killigrew
11. **Sir William Berkeley** (1608-1677), colonial governor of Va. = Mrs. Frances Colepepper (Culpeper) Stephens (1634-c.1695), Virginia political figure, daughter of Thomas and Katherine (St. Leger) Colepepper (Culpeper), both of Va. and ARD, SETH. Sir William's brother, John Berkeley, 1st Baron Berkeley of Stratton, is an ancestor of George Gordon Byron, 6th Baron Byron, the poet; see NEHGS *NEXUS* 15 (1998): 116-17.

9. Katherine Lygon (sister of Thomas, Cecily, and Margaret) = Thomas Foliot, son of John Foliot and Elizabeth Moore, daughter of John Moore and Eleanor Milborne, daughter of Simon Milborne and Jane Baskerville, SETH
10. Sir John Foliot = Elizabeth Aylmer
11. **Rev. Edward Foliot** of Va. = ———.

9. Elizabeth Lygon (sister of Thomas, Cecily, Margaret, and Katherine) = William Norwood
10. Henry Norwood = Elizabeth Rodney. Their son Charles Norwood was clerk of the Virginia Assembly 1654-56 but returned to England and left no NDTPS.
11. **Henry Norwood** (1614-1689), treasurer of Va., lt. gov. of Tangier, royalist soldier, M.P., d. unm.

8. Isabel Dennis (sister of Eleanor) = Sir John Berkeley
9. Elizabeth Berkeley = Henry Lygon (brother of William above)

The Royal Descents of 900 Immigrants

10. Elizabeth Lygon = Edward Bassett
11. Jane Bassett = John Deighton
12. **Katherine Deighton** of Mass. = (1) Samuel **Hackburne**; (2) Thomas **Dudley** (1576-1653), colonial governor of Mass., ARD, SETH; (3) Rev. John **Allyn**.
12. **Frances Deighton** of Mass. = Richard **Williams**.
12. **Jane Deighton** of Mass. = (1) John **Lugg**; (2) Jonathan **Negus**.

9. Sir Richard Berkeley (brother of Elizabeth) = (1) Elizabeth Reade; (2) Elizabeth Jermy
10. (by 2) Elizabeth Berkeley = Sir Thomas Throckmorton
11. **Elizabeth Throckmorton** of Va. = Sir Thomas **Dale** (d. 1619), colonial governor of Va.

10. Mary Berkeley (sister of Elizabeth [Lady Throckmorton]) = Sir John Hungerford
11. Bridget Hungerford = Sir William Lisle
12. John Lisle, regicide = Alice Beckenshaw
13. **Bridget Lisle** of Mass. = (1) Leonard **Hoar** (c. 1630-1675), third president of Harvard College; (2) Hezekiah **Usher**.
14. Bridget Hoar = Thomas Cotton, London rector
15. **Leonard Cotton** of N.H. and Mass. = Hannah Freese.

Sources: *RA* 3: 576-81 (Ligon/Lygon, Berkeley, Norwood), 3: 5-7 (Foliot, Moore), 2: 433-35 (Dennis), 5: 193 (Trye), 4: 86-88 (Milborne), 5: 52-56 (Stradling, Beaufort, which accepts the Beaufort-Stradling-Dennis descent), 1: 337-41 (Berkeley), 4: 187-92 (Mowbray), 4: 256-66 (Norfolk), 5: 193-94 (Trye), 2: 410-12 (Deighton, Basset); *MCS5*, lines 66 (Ligon), 68 (Norwoods), 69 (Sir Wm. Berkeley), 70 (Foliot), 29 (Gorges), 28, 28B (Deighton sisters) and *AR8*, lines 16 (generations 1-5), 209 (Gorges), 84, 187 (Deightons); *TVG* 22 (1978): 253-55, 23 (1979): 80, 38 (1994): 48-51 (Ligon); *TG* 6 (1985): 195-97, 216-18 (Deightons);

The Royal Descents of 900 Immigrants

Ligon, passim, esp. pp. 196-97, 211-12 (Trye), 177-80 (Gorges), 219-20, 222, 229-34 (Sir William Berkeley), 45-46, 101-3 (Foliot, Norwoods), 861-62 (Deightons), 214-15 (Sir Richard Berkeley); *Gorges,* pp. 119-40, 163-67, 172-73 and chart at end esp.; *ANB* 16: 531-33 and *Parliament, 1660-1690,* vol. 3, pp. 163-64 (Henry Norwood); *DAB* (Sir Thomas Dale) and *Lives of the Berkeleys,* vol. 2, pp. 178, 180-81 (Lady Dale); *Oxford DNB* (Leonard Hoar, John and Alice Lisle), W.H. Rylands, ed., *Visitations of Hampshire, 1530, 1575, and 1622-34* (*HSPVS,* vol. 64, 1913), pp. 52-53 (Lisle[y]), and Sir John MacLean and W.C. Heane, *Visitation of Gloucester, 1623* (*HSPVS,* vol. 21, 1885), p. 89 (Hungerford) (for Mrs. Hoar), pp. 49-51 (Dennis). See also *Ligon,* vols. 2-3, *passim, NEXUS* 16 (1999): 156-59, 200-2, *AP&P4*: 2: 265-69, 271-96 (and for my own colonial Ligon descent, 2: 265-66, 268-69, 275, 292, esp.), *M&G,* p. 435 (Stradling) and *Parliament, 1386-1421,* vol. 2, pp. 771-72 (Sir Gilbert Denys/Dennis, father of Morris). Douglas Richardson, the late Marshall K. Kirk, Anthony G. Hoskins and I all think the legitimacy of Katherine (Stradling) Dennis is virtually certain, given the association of Cardinal Beaufort, Sir Gilbert Dennis, and Sir Edward Stradling. The lack of contemporary evidence and another Dennis-Stradling connection via Russell, however, are noted by Brad Verity in *Foundations* 1, #4 (July 2004), pp. 254, note 11, and 256 (chart).

For Leonard Cotton of N.H. and Mass., see *NEHGR* 53 (1899): 298-99, *GGE*: 90-93 (Cotton), *FMG,* vol. 1, pp. 122-23 (Cotton); R.L. Nickipor, *Vital Records from the Town Records of Hampton Falls, New Hampshire, Through 1899* (1976), p. 9, and *Vital Records of Newbury, Massachusetts, to the End of the Year 1849,* vol. 1 (1911), p. 129 (births or baptisms of children of Leonard Cotton and Hannah ——); *York* [Maine] *Deeds,* Book XVIII (1910), p. 48 (fo. 16) (identification of Hannah Freese). Note also Robert J. Hunter, "Dublin to Boston, 1719," *Éire-Ireland: A Journal of Irish Studies* 6 (2) (Summer 1971): 18-24 (a 1719 letter written by Leonard Cotton, referring to his then-living grandmother in Boston). The last two items were brought to my attention by John C. Brandon of Columbia, S.C.

For notable British and American Ligon/Lygon descendants see *NEHGS NEXUS,* vols. 14-16 (1997-99) and *New England Ancestors,* vol. 1 (2000)—articles so titled plus separate coverage of the Leveson-Gower progeny and George Gordon Byron, 6th Baron Byron, the poet. In addition, Catherine Berkeley, daughter of Sir Richard Berkeley and Elizabeth Reade at generation 9 above, married firstly Rowland Leigh. Their son, Sir William Leigh, married Elizabeth Whorwood and was the father of William Leigh, husband of Joanna Pury and father of Theophilus Leigh, husband of Mary Brydges (sister of James Brydges, 1st Duke of Chandos) and father of Thomas Leigh, Fellow of All Souls College, Oxford, husband of Jane Walker and father of Cassandra Leigh, wife of Hampshire rector George Austen and mother of Jane Austen, the novelist. See G.H. Tucker, *A Goodly Heritage: A History of Jane Austen's Family* (1983), *passim*, esp. pp. 57-65, 216-18 (Leigh). For the major notable descendant I have found to date for Leonard Cotton of N.H. and Mass.—investor and philanthropist Warren Edward Buffett—see *Mayflower Descendant* 65 (2017): 73-83, esp. p. 77, note 34 (G.B. Roberts and J.H. Otto).

Lygon descendants through (1) Henry Folliott, 1st Baron Folliott (Foliot) (p. 308), and (2) Lady Evelyn Pierrepont (wife of John Leveson-Gower, 1st Earl Gower, p. 64) appear on pp. 25-28, 33, 62-63, 63-64, 69-73, 648. Other Lygon and Leveson-Gower descendants treated herein, but through only other lines, include the literary Sitwell siblings and biographer Lady Antonia (Margaret Caroline Pakenham) Fraser, wife of playwright Harold Pinter. Figures treated herein whose spouses were Lygon and Leveson-Gower descendants include William Petty, 1st Marquess of Lansdowne, 2nd Earl of Shelburne, British Prime Minister (his second wife, Lady Louise FitzPatrick, daughter of John FitzPatrick, 1st Earl of Upper Ossory, and Lady Evelyn Leveson-Gower, daughter of the 1st Earl Gower and Lady Evelyn) and Louis Francis Albert Victor Nicholas, 1st Earl Mountbatten of Burma (Hon. Dame Edwina Cynthia Annette Ashley). Lygon and Leveson-Gower descendants covered in *NEHGS NEXUS* 14 (1997): 70-73 but not in this volume include the philanthropist Anthony Ashley Cooper, 7th Earl of Shaftesbury (great-grandfather of Lady Mountbatten and son of Cropley Ashley Cooper, 6th Earl of Shaftesbury, and Lady Anne Spencer, daughter of George Spencer, 4th Duke of Marlborough, and Lady Caroline Russell, SETH), novelist (Hon. Victoria Mary) "Vita" Sackville-West (Nicholson) and Rosalind Murray, wife of historian Arnold (Joseph) Toynbee. Lastly, Lady Mary Wortley-Montagu, daughter of Edward Wortley-Montagu and the famed Lady Mary (Pierrepont) Wortley-Montagu, SETH, sister of Lady Evelyn, married John Stuart, 3rd Earl of Bute, British Prime Minister and favorite of King George III.

The Royal Descents of 900 Immigrants

1. Edward III, King of England, d. 1377 = Philippa of Hainault
2. John of Gaunt, Duke of Lancaster = Catherine Roët
3. John Beaufort, Marquess of Somerset and Dorset = Margaret Holand
4. Edmund Beaufort, 1st Duke of Somerset = Eleanor Beauchamp
5. Eleanor Beaufort = Sir Robert Spencer
6. Margaret Spencer = Thomas Cary
7. William Cary = Mary Boleyn, sister of Anne Boleyn, second Queen of Henry VIII, d. 1547, and aunt of Elizabeth I, Queen of England (Mary Boleyn was the mistress of Henry VIII at the time, ca. 1524, of Catherine's birth, and Catherine and her brother Henry Cary, 1st Baron Hunsdon, are thought by Anthony G. Hoskins to be children of the king). Mary and Queen Anne Boleyn were children of Thomas Boleyn, 1st Earl of Wiltshire (and Earl of Ormonde) and Elizabeth Howard, and grandchildren of Sir William Boleyn and Margaret Butler, SETH, and Thomas Howard, 2nd Duke of Norfolk, SETH, and his first wife, Elizabeth Tilney, SETH, widow of Sir Humphrey Bourchier.
8. Catherine Cary = Sir Francis Knollys. A second Sir Francis Knollys, one of their sons, married Lettice Barrett and was the father of Lettice Knollys, wife secondly of Parliamentary leader John Hampden, SETH.
9. Anne Knollys = Thomas West, 2nd Baron Delaware (de la Warr)
10. **Thomas West, 3rd Baron Delaware** (de la Warr) (1577-1618), colonial governor of Va. = Cecily Shirley, ARD, SETH.
10. **Hon. Francis West** (1586-1634), colonial governor of Va. = (1) Mrs. Margaret Blayney; (2) Lady Temperance Flowerdew Yeardley, widow of Sir George Yeardley, colonial governor of Va.; (3) Jane Davye.
10. **Hon. John West**, colonial governor of Va. = Anne ——.
11. John West, Jr. = Unity Croshaw
12. Nathaniel West = Martha Woodward

The Royal Descents of 900 Immigrants

13. Unity West = William Dandridge, uncle of First Lady Mrs. Martha Dandridge Custis Washington

14. Nathaniel West Dandridge = Dorothea Spotswood

15. Martha Dandridge = Archibald Payne

16. Catherine Payne = Archibald Bolling

17. Archibald Bolling, Jr. = Anne E. Wigginton

18. William Holcombe Bolling = Sallie Spiers White

19. Edith Bolling = (1) Norman Galt; (2) (Thomas) Woodrow Wilson (1856-1924), 28th U.S. President

10. Hon. Elizabeth West (sister of the 3rd Baron Delaware, Hon. Francis and Hon. John) = Herbert Pelham (who = [1] Catherine Thatcher)

11. Elizabeth Pelham = John Humphrey, dep. gov. of Mass. (who = [3] Lady Susan Clinton, SETH). Two older children of Elizabeth and John, John Humphrey, Jr., and another Elizabeth, also apparently immigrated to Mass. but their later history is unknown. Elizabeth probably married Adam Ot(t)ley of Lynn.

12. **Anne Humphrey** of Mass. = (1) William **Palmes**, likely son of a Stephen Palmes of Ireland (and ——), son of Sir Francis Palmes and Mary Hadnall, SETH; (2) Rev. John **Myles** (c. 1621-1683), Baptist minister.

10. Hon. Penelope West (sister of the 3rd Baron Delaware, Hon. Francis, Hon. John, and Hon. Elizabeth) = Herbert Pelham (Jr., son of Herbert Pelham and Catherine Thatcher). Two of their younger sons, William (d.s.p.) and John Pelham, also immigrated to Mass. but left no NDTPS.

11. **Herbert Pelham** of Mass., first treasurer of Harvard College = (1) Jemima Waldegrave; (2) Mrs. Elizabeth Bosvile Harlakenden of Mass. Both of his wives were ARD, SETH.

11. **Penelope Pelham** of Mass. = Richard **Bellingham** (c. 1592-1672), colonial governor of Mass., ARD, SETH. Note: Hon. Nathaniel West, another son of Thomas West, 2nd Baron

The Royal Descents of 900 Immigrants

Delaware (de la Warr) and Anne Knollys, also immigrated to Va., and = Frances Greville, but his only known child returned to England and left no NDTPS.

9. Catherine Knollys (sister of Anne) = Sir Philip Boteler
10. Sir John Boteler = Anne Spencer
11. Sir Philip Boteler = Elizabeth Langham
12. **Anne Boteler** of Md. = Lionel **Copley** (d. 1693), colonial governor of Md., ARD, SETH.

9. Sir Thomas Knollys (brother of Anne and Catherine) = Ottilia de Merode
10. Lettice Knollys = Sir Rowland Rugeley
11. Mary Rugeley = John Wiseman
12. Elizabeth Wiseman = Richard Clagett
13. Wiseman Clagett = Martha Clifton
14. **Wiseman Clagett** (1721-1784) of N.H., lawyer, King's Attorney for and Solicitor-General of N.H. = Lettice Mitchell.

9. Richard Knollys (brother of Anne, Catherine and Sir Thomas) = Jane Heigham
10. Francis Knollys = Alice Beecher
11. Dorothy Knollys = William Byam
12. Edward Byam = Lydia Thomas
13. William Byam = Anne Gunthorpe
14. William Byam = Mary Burgh
15. Edward Samuel Byam = Eleanor Prior
16. (illegitimate by Mrs. Jane Davis Browning) **Amelia Jane Byam** of N.Y. = John **Ericsson** (1803-1889), engineer, builder of the *Monitor* (for the U.S.) in 1861.

The Royal Descents of 900 Immigrants

Sources: *RA* 5: 352-58 (West, Pelham, Palmes), 2: 102-10 (Cary, Spencer), 4: 645-57 (Somerset); *AR8*, lines 1, 228, 229, *MCS5*, lines 4, 80; *GM* 25:9 (March 1997), 345-52 (Anthony G. Hoskins); *AP&P4*: 3: 486-89 (West), *TAG* 16 (1939-40): 129-32, 201-5, 18 (1941-42): 137-46, 210-18, 19 (1942-43): 197-202 (Pelham, Humphrey) and sources cited therein, esp. *CP* (generations 1-5, 8-9); *DAB* (Lionel Copley), *Clutterbuck*, vol. 2, p. 477 (Boteler), and *CP* VII, 239 (Gerald FitzGerald, Lord Gerald). See also *NEHGR* 154 (2000): 87-88 (ancestor table of Herbert Pelham of Mass.). For John Humphrey, Jr., and Adam Ot(t)ley, see O.A. Roberts, *History of...The Ancient and Honorable Artillery Company of Massachusetts, 1637-1888*, vol., 1, *1637-1738* (1895), pp. 116-17, *Records and Files of the Quarterly Courts of Essex County, Massachusetts*, vol. 2, *1656-1662* (1912), pp. 394-95, and *GM* 3, pp. 462-68 (John Humphrey), with thanks to Rixford A. Beals of Somerset, N.J., and John C. Brandon of Columbia, S.C.

For **Wiseman Clagett**: *DAB* (Clagett); research by Brice McAdoo Clagett, largely sent to the author, which cites, among other sources, *NGSQ* 62 (1974): 207, L.B. McQuiston, *The McQuiston, McCuiston, and McQuesten Families, 1620-1937* (1937), pp. 138-39, *Morant*, vol. 2, p. 559 (Clagett, Wiseman), W.C. Metcalfe, ed., *Visitations of Essex 1552, 1558, 1570, 1612 and 1634*, vol. 1 (*HSPVS*, vol. 13, 1878), p. 528 (Wiseman); *MGH*, new ser., 3 (1878-80): 201-2 (Rugeley, Knollys), *DNB* (Sir Francis and Thomas Knollys), and the lengthy inscription of the sepulchral monument of Mary (Rugeley) Wiseman in the Wimbish, Essex, parish church.

For **Mrs. Ericsson**: Ruth White, *Yankee From Sweden: The Dream and the Reality in the Days of John Ericsson* (1960), pp. 40-41 and research by Daniel Browning of Sydney, Australia, great-great-great-grandson of a half-brother of Mrs. Ericsson; V.L. Oliver, *History of the Island of Antigua*, vol. 1 (1894), pp. 97-99 (Byam, Knollys); *DAB* (Sir Francis and Richard Knollys) and J.B. Burke, *The Royal Families of England, Scotland, and Wales, with Their Descendants, Sovereigns, and Subjects*, vol. 1 (1851), pedigree CXCVI (an unreliable work, seemingly good in this instance). Some printed sources confuse the brothers Robert and Richard Knollys, sons of Sir Francis. If Catherine Cary was indeed the daughter of Mary Boleyn by Henry VIII, King of England, d. 1547, then that famed monarch is an ancestor of all American (and any other) descendants of the following immigrants who left colonial progeny:

The Royal Descents of 900 Immigrants

1. Hon. John West, gov. of Va.
2. Mrs. Anne Palmes Laing of N.Y.
3. Mrs. Susanna Palmes Avery of Conn. Mrs. Laing and Mrs. Avery were children of Mrs. Anne Humphrey Palmes Myles.
4. Herbert Pelham of Mass.
5. Wiseman Clagett of N.H.

Descendants of the first four of the above, for six or more generations, are the subject of Marston Watson, *Americans of Royal and Noble Ancestry, Volume Four: Pelham-Avery-West: Descendants for Nine Generations of Thomas West, 2nd Baron de la Warr: The Possible American Progeny of King Henry VIII* (2017). Thomas West, 2nd Baron Delaware (de la Warr) was the son of William West, 10th Baron Delaware (de la Warr) (first of this title with the surname West) and Elizabeth Strange, SETH.

The Royal Descents of 900 Immigrants

1. Edward III, King of England, d. 1377 = Philippa of Hainault
2. Lionel of Antwerp, Duke of Clarence = Elizabeth de Burgh
3. Philippa Plantagenet = Edmund Mortimer, 3rd Earl of March
4. Elizabeth Mortimer = Sir Henry "Hotspur" Percy
5. Elizabeth Percy = John Clifford, 7th Baron Clifford
6. Mary Clifford = Sir Philip Wentworth, see below
7. Sir Henry Wentworth = Anne Saye, see below
8. Margery Wentworth = Sir John Seymour (parents of Jane Seymour, third Queen of Henry VIII, King of England, and maternal grandparents of Edward VI, King of England, d. 1553)
9. Edward Seymour, 1st Duke of Somerset, Lord Protector = (1) Catherine Filliol (2) Anne Stanhope
10. (by 1) Sir (Lord) Edward Seymour = Margaret Walsh
11. Sir Edward Seymour, 1st Bt. = Elizabeth Champernowne
12. Sir Edward Seymour, 2nd Bt. = Dorothy Killigrew
13. Mary Seymour = Sir Jonathan Trelawny, 2nd Bt.
14. Sir Jonathan Trelawny, 3rd Bt., Bishop of Winchester = Rebecca Hele
15. Rebecca Trelawny = John Francis Buller
16. James Buller = Elizabeth Gould   16. John Buller = Elizabeth Caroline Hunter
17. James Buller = Husey Gould
18. William Buller   =   17. Caroline Buller
18, 19. Charles George Buller = Frances Boucher
19, 20. Frank Buller = Jean Brien
20, 21. **Audrey Divett Buller** of R.I. = Lloyd Halman **Parsons** (1893-1969), artist. Their daughter, Audrey Jane Penelope Parsons, married Henry Flagler Harris, son of John Andrews Harris (III) and Elizabeth Lamont Flagler, daughter of Harry Harkness

The Royal Descents of 900 Immigrants

Flagler (and Anne Louise Lamont), son of Florida developer Henry Morrison Flagler and Mary Harkness. Elizabeth Harkness Harris, daughter of A.J.P. Parsons and H.F. Harris, married Gulf Oil scion Henry Coxe Stokes Mellon.

12. Mary Seymour (sister of Sir Edward Seymour, 2nd Bt.) = Sir George Farwell
13. George Farwell = Anne Browne
14. Anne Farwell = George Wroughton
15. James Wroughton = Anne Eyre (ancestors #698-99 and 700-1 of Diana, Princess of Wales)
16. Henrietta Wroughton = James Norman
17. George Norman = Charlotte Beadon
18. George Warde Norman = Sibella Stone
19. Sibella Charlotte Norman = Henry Bonham Carter
20. Sir Maurice Bonham Carter = Helen Violet Asquith, Baroness Asquith of Yarnbury, Liberal Party official, daughter of Herbert Henry Asquith, 1st Earl of Oxford and Asquith, British Prime Minister, and Helen Kelsall Melland
21. Raymond Henry Bonham Carter = Elena Propper de Callejon
22. **Helena Bonham Carter**, b. 1966, actress, sometime of N.Y. or Calif., unm., but has two children with film director Timothy William (Tim) Burton.

10. (by 2) Anne Seymour (sister of Sir Edward) = Sir Edward Unton
11. Cecilia Unton = John Wentworth
12. Anne Wentworth = Sir Edmund Gostwick, 2nd Bt.
13. Mary Gostwick = Nicholas Spencer
14. **Nicholas Spencer**, acting colonial governor of Va., president of its council = Frances Mottrom.

The Royal Descents of 900 Immigrants

10. Mary Seymour (sister of Anne) = Francis Cosby
11. Alexander Cosby = Dorcas Sidney
12. Richard Cosby = Elizabeth Pigott
13. Francis Cosby = Anne Loftus
14. Alexander Cosby = Elizabeth L'Estrange
15. **William Cosby** (c. 1690-1735/6), colonial governor of N.Y. and N.J. = Grace Montagu, ARD, SETH.

9. Sir Henry Seymour (brother of the 1st Duke of Somerset) = Barbara Morgan
10. Jane Seymour = Sir John Rodney, son of George Rodney and Elizabeth Kirton, SETH
11. William Rodney = Alice Caesar. Their son, John Rodney, immigrated to Antigua and Philadelphia, married Mrs. Frances Mall Richardson and Anne ——, but left progeny only in Antigua.
12. William Rodney, sometime of New York City = Rachel ——
13. **William Rodney** of Del. and Pa. = (1) Mary Hollyman; (2) Sarah Jones. Caesar Rodney, a son by Sarah, married Elizabeth Crawford and was the father of Caesar Rodney, Jr., Revolutionary statesman and signer of the Declaration of Independence, who died unm.

9. Elizabeth Seymour (sister of the 1st Duke of Somerset and of Sir Henry) = Gregory Cromwell, 1st Baron Cromwell
10. Henry Cromwell, 2nd Baron Cromwell = Mary Paulet
11. Edward Cromwell, 3rd Baron Cromwell = Frances Rugge
12. Frances Cromwell = Sir John Wingfield
13. John Wingfield = Mary Owen
14. **Thomas Wingfield** of Va. = (1) Mary ——; (2) Mary ——.

12. Anne Cromwell (sister of Frances) = Sir Edward Wingfield
13. Lewis Wingfield = Sidney Gore

The Royal Descents of 900 Immigrants

14. Edward Wingfield = Eleanor Gore, a cousin
15. Isabella Wingfield = Sir Henry King, 3rd Bt., a cousin, son of Sir Robert King, 1st Bt. (and Frances Gore), son of Sir Robert King and Frances Folliott (Foliot), daughter of Henry Folliot (Foliot), 1st Baron Folliot (Foliot) (and Anne Strode), son of Thomas Foliot and Katherine Lygon, SETH
16. Isabella King = Thomas St. Lawrence, 1st Earl of Howth
17. William St. Lawrence, 2nd Earl of Howth = Margaret Burke
18. Thomas St. Lawrence, 3rd Earl of Howth = Henrietta Elizabeth Digby Barfoot
19. Henrietta Eliza St. Lawrence = Benjamin Lee Guinness, son of Sir Benjamin Lee Guinness, 1st Bt., the brewer and onetime "richest man in Ireland," SETH, and Elizabeth Guinness, a cousin
20. Kenelm Edward Lee "Bill" Guinness = Josephine Strangman
21. **Sir Kenelm Ernest Lee "Tim" Guinness, 4th Bt.** (1928-2011), of Md., engineer, World Bank official = Mrs. Jane Nevin Dickson.

16. Frances King (sister of Isabella) = Hans Wadman Wood
17. Margaret Wood = Charles Caulfield
18. Hans Caulfield = Anne Rothe
19. Hans Caulfield = Mary Anne Ellis
20. Hans James Caulfield = Jenny Brasher
21. **Lilian May Caulfield** of Pa. = Henry Nevill **Sanders**, 1869-1943, educator (professor at McGill and Bryn Mawr).

10. Frances Cromwell (sister of the 2nd Baron Cromwell) = Richard Strode
11. Sir William Strode = Mary Southcott
12. Juliana Strode = Sir John Davie, 1st Bt.
13. **Humphrey Davie** of Mass. = (1) Mary White; (2) Mrs. Sarah Gibbon Richards.

The Royal Descents of 900 Immigrants

Sources: Canadian and U.S. Buller research by James Ross Mellon (II) and Jerome E. Anderson, plus *BLG*, 18th ed., vol. 1 (1965), pp. 95-96 (Buller), *BP* and *CB* (Salusbury-Trelawny, baronets, and Somerset, dukes of); *RA* 4: 618-22 (Seymour, Rodney), 4: 216-20 (Wentworth), 2: 246 (Clifford), 4: 355-57 (Percy), 4: 174-75 (Mortimer), *BP* (Oxford and Asquith), *BLG*, 18th ed., vol. 1 (1965), p. 469 (Bonham Carter), 531-32 (Norman), PCC will, proved 1746, of James Wroughton of Wilcot, Wiltshire, which mentions a younger daughter Henrietta, and PCC will, proved 1779, of George Wroughton, son of James and Anne, which mentions his beloved brother James Norman, *Diana 12G*, pp. 86, 133-34, 196, 296, 365-66, 407, 447 (generations 12-15) and *VD*, pp. 702-3 (Seymour); *VM* 2 (1894-95): 32-34 (Spencer), *EB* and *CB* (Gostwick), W.H. Rylands, ed., *Four Visitations of Berkshire 1532, 1566, 1623 and 1665-6*, vol. 2 (*HSPVS*, vol. 57, 1908), p. 222 (Unton) and *BP* and *CP* (Somerset); *BLGI*, 1958, p. 181 (Cosby of Stradbally) and W.G. Duke, *Henry Duke, Councilor, His Descendants and Connections* (1949), pp. 294-99 (Cosby, Seymour); *MCS5*, line 38, *WC*, pp. 447-55, *TAG* 64 (1989): 97-111 (Rodney) and *Collins*, vol. 1, pp. 149-50 (Seymour); *MCS5*, line 21, *GVFVM5*: 822-26, 840-41 (Wingfield, dropped, however, from *RA*) and *EP* and *CP* (Cromwell); *BP*, *CP* or *EP* (Guinness, Bt., Howth [also in L.G. Pine, *The New Extinct Peerage* (1971), p. 152], Kingston, Powerscourt, Folliott [Foliot], Charlemont), *Ligon*, vol. 1, p. 101 (Foliot), and *WWWA*, vol. 22, *2010-2011* (2011), p. 85 (Sir K.E.L. Guinness), vol. 5, *1969-1973* (1973), p. 632 (H.N. Sanders); *RA* 2: 404-6 (Davie, Strode), *TAG* 23 (1946-47): 206-10 and *CB* (Davie), *VD*, pp. 270 (Davie), 718-19 (Strode) and F.A. Crisp, ed., *Visitation of England and Wales, Notes*, vol. 12 (1917), pp. 121, 127 (Strode, Cromwell). The line for Helena Bonham Carter was posted on soc.genealogy.medieval, then further developed and brought to my attention by John C. Brandon of Columbia, S.C.

Sir Philip Wentworth at generation 6 above, and Anne Saye at generation 7 above, were children respectively of Sir Roger Wentworth and Margery Despencer, SETH, and Sir John Saye and Elizabeth Cheyne, SETH. The parentage of Sir Philip and Anne is given here and not subsequently because in this volume both first appear on this chart.

The Royal Descents of 900 Immigrants

1. Edward III, King of England, d. 1377 = Philippa of Hainault
2. Lionel of Antwerp, Duke of Clarence = Elizabeth de Burgh
3. Philippa Plantagenet = Edmund Mortimer, 3rd Earl of March
4. Elizabeth Mortimer = Sir Henry "Hotspur" Percy
5. Henry Percy, 2nd Earl of Northumberland = Eleanor Neville
6. Henry Percy, 3rd Earl of Northumberland = Eleanor Poynings
7. Margaret Percy = Sir William Gascoigne, son of Sir William Gascoigne and Jane Neville, SETH
8. Elizabeth Gascoigne = Sir George Talboys, son of Sir Robert Talboys and Elizabeth Heron, SETH
9. Anne Talboys = Sir Edward Dymoke
10. Frances Dymoke = Sir Thomas Windebank
11. Mildred Windebank = Robert Reade
12. **Col. George Reade** of Va. = Elizabeth Martiau.
13. Mildred Reade = Augustine Warner Jr.
14. Mildred Warner = Lawrence Washington
15. Augustine Washington = Mary Ball
16. George Washington (1731/2-1799), 1st U.S. President = Mrs. Martha Dandridge Custis

11. Anne Windebank (sister of Mildred) = Henry Reade, a brother of Robert Reade above
12. Francis Reade (a double first cousin of Col. George Reade of Va.) = Frances Shelley
13. Frances Reade = John Kingsmill, son of William Kingsmill (and Margaret Pistor), son of Thomas Kingsmill (and Anne Warcop), son of Sir John Kingsmill and Constance Goring, SETH
14. Anne Kingsmill = James Tazewell
15. **William Tazewell** of Va. = Sophia Harmanson, daughter of Henry Harmanson and Gertrude Littleton, daughter of Southey

The Royal Descents of 900 Immigrants

Littleton (and Elizabeth Bowman), son of Nathaniel Littleton of Va., ARD, SETH, and Mrs. Anne South(e)y Harmar.

9. Elizabeth Talboys (sister of Anne) = Sir Christopher Willoughby
10. Anne Willoughby = Edward Hall, son of Francis Hall and Elizabeth Wingfield, SETH
11. Anne Hall = George Mackworth
11. Henry Hall = (1) Jane Neale (2) Margaret Elmes
12. Sir Thomas Mackworth, 1st Bt. = 12. (by 1) Elizabeth Hall
13. Sir Henry Mackworth, 2nd Bt. = 13. Mary Hopton, daughter of 12. Robert Hopton (and Jane Kemeys), son of Sir Arthur Hopton and 11. Rachel Hall, daughter of Edward Hall and Anne Willoughby, 10. above
14. Margaret Mackworth = (as his 2nd w.) Philip Yonge
15. Mackworth Yonge = Margaret Bourne
16. **Robert Yonge**, of S.C. by 1723 = (1) Mrs. Hannah Eve, (2) Mrs. Elizabeth Elliott Butler D'Arques.

12. (by 2) Alice Hall (half-sister of Elizabeth) = Robert Metham, son of Charles Metham and Anne Dymoke, daughter of Sir Robert Dymoke (and Bridget Fiennes), son of Sir Edward Dymoke and Anne Talboys, above
13. Anne Metham = Reason Mellish
14. Edward Mellish = Bridget Eldridge
15. **Dorothy Mellish** of S.C. = Richard **Beresford**, d. 1722, S.C. legislator. A son, Richard Beresford, who married Mrs. Sarah Blakeway Logan, was also a S.C. legislator.
15. **Anne Mellish** of S.C. = (1) Richard **Splatt**; (2) Francis **le Brassieur**. Mary Splatt, daughter of Anne and Richard, married (1) William Cripps; (2) Alexander Gillon, S.C. merchant, naval officer and financial agent. Anne le Brassieur, daughter of Anne

and Francis, married Joseph Pinckney and S.C. legislator Jacob Motte.

12. Frances Hopton (sister of Robert) = Rice Jones
13. Rachel Jones = Anthony Hungerford
14. Catherine Hungerford = Sir Robert Henley
15. Willamsa Henley = Sir Theodore Janssen, 1st Bt.
16. **Mary Janssen** of Md. = Charles **Calvert**, 5th Baron Baltimore, colonial governor of Md., ARD, SETH (parents of Hon. Caroline Calvert, wife of Sir Robert Eden, 1st Bt., colonial governor of Md., ARD, SETH).
16. **Barbara Janssen** of Md. = Thomas Bladen (1698-1780), colonial governor of Md., son of William Bladen, colonial publisher and attorney-general of Md., ARD, SETH, and Anne Van Swearingen.

14. Sir Edward Hungerford (brother of Catherine) = (3) Jane Digby
15. Edward Digby Gerard Hungerford = Elizabeth Baker
16. Mary Hungerford = Paul Elers
17. Anna Maria Elers = Richard Lovell Edgeworth (their daughter was the novelist Maria Edgeworth)
18. **Richard Edgeworth** of N.C. = Elizabeth ——.

Sources: *RA* 4: 466-68 (Reade, Windebank, Dymoke), 5: 114 (Talboys), 3: 79-80 (Gascoigne), 4: 355-60 (Percy), *MCS5,* lines 86, 108, *AR8,* lines 3, 19, 5 and *Wilson,* pp. 253-335 (Reade); *AAP* 2009, 2012, pp. 1-4, 224-25, 623 (Washington AT, bibliography and chart); *Foundations* 5 (2013): 65-76 (Michael P. Bodman) and sources cited therein (Tazewell), plus G.D. Squibb, ed., *Visitation of Hampshire and the Isle of Wight, 1686* (*HSPVS*, new ser., vol. 10, 1991), pp. 35-36 (Kingsmill) and W.H. Turner, ed., *Visitation of Oxford, 1566, 1574, 1634* (*HSPVS*, vol. 5, 1871), p. 163 (Warcop); research of Brice McAdoo Clagett based in part on *BDSCHR*, vol. 2, pp. 740-41 (Robert Yonge), C.A. Langley, *South Carolina Deed*

The Royal Descents of 900 Immigrants

Abstracts, 1719-1772, vol. 1 (1983), p. 207 (Francis to Robert Yonge), Egmond, Shropshire parish registers and Edward Yonge, *The Yonges of Caynton, Egmond, Shropshire* (1969), pp. 98-99, 107-9, 225-29 (where Robert Yonge the immigrant is said erroneously to have probably died young), *Blore*, p. 128 and *CB,* vol. 1, p. 122 (Mackworth), *Lincolnshire Pedigrees*, pp. 441-43 (Hall), 670-71 (Metham), 946-47 (Talboys), 1205-7 (Dymoke) and *Collins,* vol. 6, p. 610 (Willoughby); *MGH*, 3rd ser., 3 (1900): 11-12 (Hopton); *FMG,* vol. 3, pp. 975-76 and G.D. Squibb, ed., *Visitation of Nottinghamshire, 1662-64* (*HSPVS*, new ser., vol. 5, 1986), p. 77 (both for Mellish), W.B. Edgar and N. Louise Bailey, eds., *Biographical Directory of the South Carolina House of Representatives*, vol. 2 (1977), pp. 77-79 (Richard Beresford Sr. and Jr.), 478-80 (Jacob Motte) and vol. 3 (1981), pp. 268-72 and *DAB* (Alexander Gillon); *Visitations of Oxford, 1566, 1574, 1634*, as above, p. 292 (Jones), Sir R.C. Hoare, 2nd Bt., *Hungerfordiana, or Memoirs of the Family of Hungerford* (1823), pp. 31-32 (with errors), 67, and G.W. Marshall, ed., *Le Neve's Pedigrees of the Knights* (HSPVS, vol. 8, 1873), pp. 34 (Hungerford), 171 (Henley); *CB*, vol. 5, pp. 26-27 and *EB* (Janssen), CP (Baltimore), and *MG* 1: 44-45 (Bladen); James C. Pigg, *Descendants of Richard Edgeworth* (2001), pp. i-ii, part 1, pp. 1-5, part 2, pp. 1-2, and H.J. and H.E. Butler, *The Black Book of Edgeworthstown and Other Edgeworth Memories, 1585-1817* (1927), chart at end and *passim*, esp. pp. 125-32 (and 127-29, 152), BTs of Blackbourton, Oxfordshire, 1678-1853 (FHL #95215, item 3) (1748, 1749, 1766, 1773, 1775 and 1781 burials of Edward [D.G.] Hungerford, Edward Hungerford Elers [son of Paul], Elizabeth [Baker] Hungerford, Anna Maria [Elers] Edgeworth, Mary [Hungerford] Elers and Paul Elers respectively and the 1743 birth of Anne Marie Elers, daughter of Paul), and *Parliament, 1660-1690*, vol. 2, pp. 613-14 (Sir Edward Hungerford). The Mellish descent was developed by John C. Brandon of Columbia, S.C., and the Edgeworth descent was developed and contributed by John Anderson Brayton of Memphis, Tenn. Barbara Bladen, younger daughter of Thomas and Barbara, married Hon. Henry St. John, M.P., but left no issue. Harriot Bladen, elder daughter of Thomas and Barbara, married William Anne Capell, 4th Earl of Essex and left, as did Lady Caroline Calvert Eden, a large British progeny.

    The parentage of Sir William Gascoigne and Sir George Talboys is given on p. 310 but not later, because the above is their first mention in this book.

The Royal Descents of 900 Immigrants

1. Edward III, King of England, d. 1377 = Philippa of Hainault
2. John of Gaunt, Duke of Lancaster = Catherine Roët
3. Joan Beaufort = Ralph Neville, 1st Earl of Westmoreland, son of John Neville, 3rd Baron Neville, and Maud Percy, SETH
4. Edward Neville, 1st Baron Abergavenny = Catherine Howard, daughter of Sir Robert Howard and Margaret Mowbray, SETH
5. Margaret Neville = John Brooke, 7th Baron Cobham
6. Thomas Brooke, 8th Baron Cobham = Dorothy Heydon
7. Elizabeth Brooke = Sir Thomas Wyatt, poet
8. Sir Thomas Wyatt, conspirator = Jane Hawte, daughter of Sir William Hawte and Mary Guilford, SETH
9. George Wyatt = Jane Finch
10. **Sir Francis Wyatt** (1588-1644), colonial governor of Va. = Margaret Sandys of Va., ARD, SETH.
10. **Rev. Hawte Wyatt** of Va. = (1) Barbara Mitford of Va., ARD, SETH; (2) Elizabeth ——; (3) Anne Cox.

9. Jane Wyatt (sister of George) = Charles Scott, son of Sir Reginald Scott and Mary Tuke, SETH
10. Deborah Scott = William Fleete
11. **Henry Fleete** (c. 1602-1661) of Va., merchant, Indian interpreter = Mrs. Sarah —— Burden. His brothers Reginald, Edward and John also immigrated to Md. and served in its assembly but left no NDTPS.

10. Thomas Scott (brother of Deborah) = Mary Knatchbull
11. Thomas Scott = Judith Thomson
12. **Dorothea Scott** (1628/9-post 1680), late in life of L.I., N.Y., Quaker preacher and writer = (1) Maj. Daniel **Gotherson**; (2) Joseph **Hogben**.

9. Anne Wyatt (sister of George and Jane) = Roger Twisden

The Royal Descents of 900 Immigrants

10. Margaret Twisden = Henry Vane
11. Sir Henry Vane, English Secretary of State = Frances Darcy
12. **Sir Henry Vane** (1613-1662), Puritan statesman, colonial governor of Mass. = Frances Wray, ARD, SETH.
12. Margaret Vane = Sir Thomas Pelham, 2nd Bt.
13. **Philadelphia Pelham** = Francis **Howard**, 5th Baron Howard of Effingham, colonial governor of Va., ARD, SETH.

7. George Brooke, 9th Baron Cobham (brother of Elizabeth) = Anne Bray
8. William Brooke, 10th Baron Cobham = Frances Newton. Their daughter, Elizabeth Brooke, married Robert Cecil, 1st Earl of Salisbury and Lord Treasurer, SETH, son of William Cecil, 1st Baron Burghley, SETH, minister of Elizabeth I, and Mildred Cooke, SETH.
9. Margaret Brooke = Sir Thomas Sondes
10. Frances Sondes = Sir John Leveson
11. Christian Leveson = Sir Peter Temple, 2nd Bt.
12. Sir Richard Temple, 3rd Bt. = Mary Knapp
13. Christian Temple = Sir Thomas Lyttelton, 4th Bt.
14. **William Henry Lyttelton, 1st Baron Lyttelton** (1724-1808), colonial governor of S.C. and Jamaica, diplomat = (1) Mary Macartney; (2) Caroline Bristow.

Sources: *RA* 5: 409-13 (Wyatt, Brooke), 1: 320-22 (Neville), 4: 598-601 (Scott, Fleete, Hogben); *Oxford DNB* (Sir Francis and both Sir Thomas Wyatts, both Sir Henry Vanes), J. Cave-Browne, *The History of Boxley Parish, Including an Account of the Wiat Family* (1892), chart opp. p. 133 esp., *MCS5*, line 72, *AP&P* 4: 3: 850-51 (Wyatt), 1: 970-72 (Fleete), and *VGE*, pp. 623-33 (Wyatt), 567-68 (Fleete); *Berry's Kent*, p. 310 (Twisden); *CB* (Pelham, Temple and Lyttelton, baronets); *CP* or *BP* (Howard of Effingham or Effingham, Chichester [Pelham], Barnard [Vane], Lyttelton, viscounts and barons Cobham, Abergavenny). The correct placement of Dorothea Scott in this pedigree resulted from research exchanged online by Bruce Despain, "Susan" (dicentraexima@yahoo.com), and John C. Brandon, especially the 24 June 1650 marriage at Saint Bartholomew the Less, London, of Daniel Gotherson and Dorathie Scott (in the IGI); the 30 Jan. 1628/9 baptism at St. Alphege, Kent, of Dorothea Scott (and the 1627 and 1635/6 deaths of her brothers Charles and Thomas); the 5 Oct. 1626 marriage in Lenham, Kent, of Thomas Scott (aged 15 in 1619, according to the 1619 visitation of Kent) and Judith Thomson; the 1611 baptism and 1614 burial of Doryte Scott, daughter of the elder Thomas above; Ecclesiastical Cause Papers (DCb/J/J/58/169, date 11 Feb. 1635) of the Diocese of Canterbury (on The National Archives [UK] website, www.nationalarchives.gov.uk), noting a contention between Mary [Knatchbull] Scott and her daughters (Ann Paramor, Catherine Scott and Mary Bragg) and grandchildren Thomas and Dorothy Scott, children of Thomas Scott, Junior, Mary's son, deceased; 1653 Chancery suits between John Bragg and Mary his wife and Daniel Gotherson, Dorothy his wife, and another, and between Mary Paramour and Daniel Gotherson and Dorothy his wife (Lists and Indexes, *Index of Chancery Proceedings, Bridges' Division, 1613-1714*, vol. 39, p. 164, Bundle 379, No. 10 and vol. 44, p. 327, Bundle 403, No. 225); plus Robert Hovenden, ed., *The Visitation of Kent, 1619-21* (*HSPVS*, vol. 42, 1898), p. 128 (Scott). G.D. Scull, *Dorothea Scott Otherwise Gotherson and Hogben* (1883) and the *Oxford DNB* (2004), 23: 24 both omit the generation of Dorothea's parents and mistake her for her aunt, who died aged 3.

  The parentage of Ralph Neville, 1st Earl of Westmoreland, is noted above but not on subsequent charts because he first appears here with his wife and her royal descent, not merely as a cross-reference.

The Royal Descents of 900 Immigrants

1. Edward III, King of England, d. 1377 = Philippa of Hainault
2. Lionel of Antwerp, Duke of Clarence = Elizabeth de Burgh
3. Philippa Plantagenet = Edmund Mortimer, 3rd Earl of March
4. Elizabeth Mortimer = Sir Henry "Hotspur" Percy
5. Elizabeth Percy = John Clifford, 7th Baron Clifford
6. Thomas Clifford, 8th Baron Clifford = Joan Dacre
7. John Clifford, 9th Baron Clifford = Margaret Bromflete
8. Henry Clifford, 10th Baron Clifford = Anne St. John
9. Elizabeth Clifford = Sir Ralph Bowes
10. Sir George Bowes = Muriel Eure, daughter of William Eure, 1st Baron Eure (and Elizabeth Willoughby), son of Sir Ralph Eure and Muriel Hastings, daughter of Sir Hugh Hastings (and Anne Gascoigne), son of John Hastings, *de jure* Baron Hastings, and Anne Morley, SETH
11. Elizabeth Bowes = John Blakiston
12. Marmaduke Blakiston = Margaret James
13. **George Blakiston** of Md. = Barbara Lawson.
13. John Blakiston, regicide = Susan Chambers
14. **Nehemiah Blakiston** of Md. = Elizabeth Gerard, daughter of Thomas Gerard of Md., ARD, SETH, and Susannah Snow. Elizabeth m. (2) Ralph Rymer, (3) Joshua Guibert.
14. John Blakiston = Phebe Johnston
15. **Nathaniel Blakiston**, colonial governor of Md. = ——.
15. **Margaret Blakiston** of Va. = Edward **Nott**, colonial governor of Va., ARD, SETH.

10. Margery Bowes (sister of Sir George) = Sir Ralph Eure, brother of Muriel above and son of William Eure, 1st Baron Eure and Elizabeth Willoughby above
11. Anne Eure = Lancelot Mansfield

The Royal Descents of 900 Immigrants

12. John Mansfield, M.P. = Elizabeth ——. Their daughter Anne Mansfield also immigrated to Mass., married (1) wealthy Boston merchant Robert Keayne and (2) Samuel Cole, and left issue (through great-grandchildren) but no NDTPS.

13. **John Mansfield** of Mass. = Mrs. Mary Shard Gove.

13. **Elizabeth Mansfield** of Mass. = Rev. John **Wilson** (c. 1591-1667), Boston minister and writer.

14. John Wilson, Jr. = Sarah Hooker

15. Susanna Wilson = Grindall Rawson

16. Edmund Rawson = Elizabeth Hayward

17. Abner Rawson = Mary Allen

18. Rhoda Rawson = Aaron Taft

19. Peter Rawson Taft = Sylvia Howard

20. Alphonso Taft, diplomat, U.S. Secretary of War and Attorney General = Louisa Maria Torrey

21. William Howard Taft (1857-1930) 27th U.S. President = Helen Herron

Sources: *RA* 1: 382-83 (Blakiston), 1: 494-95 (Bowes), 2: 246-49 (Clifford), 4: 355-59 (Percy), 2: 527-29 (Eure), 2: 499-500 (Hastings), 2: 372-74 (Dacre); *MG* 1: 48-55 (Blakiston); *Surtees*, vol. 4, pp. 107-8 (Bowes), *CP* (Eure, Hastings), *NHN*, vol. 12, p. 496 (Eure) and *Foster's V of Yorkshire*, p. 373 (Hastings); *NEHGR* 155 (2001): 3-35 (Mansfield), based partly on sources cited in *NEHGR* 153 (1999): 353-54, plus Robert H. Rodgers, ed., *Middlesex County Records of Probate and Administration, October 1649-December 1660* (1999), pp. 235-40, *Parliament, 1558-1603*, vol. 3, p. 13 (John Mansfield, M.P., generation 12 above), and *Connecticut Historical Society Bulletin* 7 (1940-41): 10-12, which discusses the Lancelot Mansfield coat of arms.

Joan Dacre at generation 6 above was the daughter of Thomas Dacre, 6th Baron Dacre of Gilsland and Philippa Neville, daughter of Ralph Neville, 1st Earl of Westmoreland and Margaret Stafford, SETH. And Anne St. John at generation 8 was a daughter of Sir John St. John and Alice Bradshaw, SETH. Joan's and Anne's parentage is given here but not subsequently because in this volume they first appear on this chart.

The Royal Descents of 900 Immigrants

1. Edward III, King of England, d. 1377 = Philippa of Hainault
2. Lionel of Antwerp, Duke of Clarence = Elizabeth de Burgh
3. Philippa Plantagenet = Edmund Mortimer, 3rd Earl of March
4. Elizabeth Mortimer = Sir Henry "Hotspur" Percy
5. Elizabeth Percy = John Clifford, 7th Baron Clifford
6. Thomas Clifford, 8th Baron Clifford = Joan Dacre
7. Matilda Clifford = Sir Edmund Sutton (or/alias Dudley), SETH, who = (1) Joyce Tiptoft, SETH
8. Dorothy Sutton = Richard Wrottesley
9. Walter Wrottesley = Isabella Harcourt
10. Eleanor Wrottesley = Richard Lee, son of Sir Thomas Lee and Jane Corbet, daughter of Sir Robert Corbet and Elizabeth Vernon, SETH
11. Dorothy Lee = Thomas Mackworth
12. Richard Mackworth = Dorothy Cranage
13. **Agnes Mackworth** = (1) Richard **Watts**; (2) William **Crowne** (ca. 1617-1683) of Mass., adventurer and land speculator.

9. Joan Wrottesley (sister of Walter) = Richard Cresset, son of Thomas Cresset and Jane Corbet, daughter of Sir Roger Corbet and Elizabeth Hopton, SETH
10. Margaret Cresset = Thomas More
11. Jasper More = Elizabeth Smalley
12. Katherine More = Samuel More, a cousin; by Jacob Blakeway she was the mother of
13. **Richard More** (1614-1693/4-96) of Mass., a passenger on the *Mayflower* = (1) Christian Hunter, (2) (almost certainly) Elizabeth Woolnaugh (a bigamous union), (3) Mrs. Jane —— Crumpton. Ellen More (b. 1612), Jasper More (b. 1613) and undoubtedly Mary More (b. 1616), siblings of Richard More,

were also passengers on the *Mayflower* but died before reaching adulthood.

12. Joan More (sister of Katherine) = John Gresley, son of Sir Thomas Gresley and Katherine Walsingham, daughter of Sir Thomas Walsingham and Dorothy Guilford, SETH
13. Henry Gresley = Mary Allye
14. Charles Gresley = Joan ——
15. Francis Gresley = Cecilia Leeson
16. Mary Gresley = William Milton
17. **Frances Milton**, known as Frances **Trollope** (1779-1863), in U.S. (Tennessee and Ohio) 1827-31, later of England and Italy, travel writer and novelist, author of the (critical) *Domestic Manners of the Americans*, = Thomas Anthony Trollope. The novelist Anthony Trollope (who married Rose Heseltine and Louisa Ellen Harris) was their son.

9. Eleanor Wrottesley (sister of Walter and Joan) = Sir Henry Long
10. Margery Long = Robert Hungerford, see note below
11. Walter Hungerford = Frances Cocke, see note below
12. Anne Hungerford = William Gostlett
13. Charles Gostlett = Marie, widow of —— Short
14. Benjamin Gostlett = Elizabeth Chetwynd, see note below
15. Helena Gostlett = John Harington
16. Henry Harington = Mary Backwell
17. Henry Harington = Martha Musgrove
18. Susanna Isabella Harington = Josiah Thomas, Archdeacon of Bath. Their daughter, Jane Anne Thomas, married Edward Musgrave Harington (her first cousin, son of Henry Harington and Esther Lens, and grandson of 17 above) and was the mother

The Royal Descents of 900 Immigrants

of Edward Templer Harington, father (by Ada Drew) of Ada Constance Helen Harington, wife of John Gerhard Tiarks. Their son, John Gerhard Edward Tiarks, married Evelyn Florence Cripps and left a daughter, Anne Patricia Tiarks, wife of Peter William Garside Phillips and mother of Mark Anthony Peter Phillips, first husband of H.R.H. Princess Anne (Elizabeth Alice Louise) of Great Britain, The Princess Royal, daughter of H.M. Queen Elizabeth II.

19. George Hudleston Thomas = Mary Anne Broadhurst
20. Edgar Hastings Thomas = Christian Jean Wallace
21. **Hilda Margaret Rose Thomas** of Calif. = (Theodor) Ernst (Heinrich) **Otto**, brother of (Karl Louis) Rudolf Otto, German theologian and philosopher of religion. Gerhard Gottfried (Gerald Godfrey) Otto, son of Ernst and Hilda, married Jean Blackman and was the father of genealogist Julie Helen Otto (b. 1954), my collaborator on this work, co-editor of the NEHGS *NEXUS*, 1989-96, who drew the charts in *Ancestors of American Presidents*, contributed to *Notable Kin, Volume One* and various works published by NEHGS, and indexed NEHGS journals *post* 1989.

8. Thomas Dudley (brother of Dorothy Sutton) = Grace Threlkeld
9. Richard Dudley = Dorothy Sanford
10. Edmund Dudley = Catherine Hutton
11. Mary Dudley = Thomas Ferrand
12. Eleanor Ferrand = Thomas Heber
13. Martha Heber = George Clapham
14. Sir Christopher Clapham = Margaret Oldfield
15. Margaret Clapham = Sir William Craven
16. **Christopher Craven**, colonial gov. of S.C. = Elizabeth Staples.

9. Winifred Dudley (sister of Richard) = Anthony Blencowe
10. Richard Blencowe = Apollonia Tolson

The Royal Descents of 900 Immigrants

11. Sir Henry Blencowe = Grace Sandford
12. John Blencowe = Anne Mallison
13. Elizabeth Blencowe = Henry Thompson
14. Sir William Thompson = Mary Stephens/Stevens
15. **Stephens/Stevens Thompson** (1674-ca. 1713/4), attorney-general of Va. = Dorothea Tanton.

Sources: *RA* 3: 686-88 (Mackworth, Lee, Wrottesley, Sutton), 5: 104-5 (Sutton), 2: 246-47 (Clifford), 3: 210-11 (Harcourt), 4: 146-48 (More, Cressett); *MCS5*, lines 39, 36, 161, *AR8*, lines 198, 5 and sources cited therein, plus *NEHGR* 108 (1954): 176-77 (reprinted in *EO* 1: 3: 774-75) and George Wrottesley, *History of the Family of Wrottesley of Wrottesley, co. Stafford* (1903), pp. 244-57, 266-75, 400 (Mrs. Mackworth); *NEHGR* 114 (1960): 163-68, 124 (1970): 85-87 (reprinted in *EO2*: 2: 763-71 and *Genealogies of Mayflower Families From The New England Historical and Genealogical Register*, 3 vols. [1986], 2: 743-51), R.M. Sherman, R.S. Wakefield and Lydia Dow Finlay, *Mayflower Families Through Five Generations,* vol. 15 (1997), pp. 151-55 and David Lindsay, *Mayflower Bastard: A Stranger Among the Pilgrims* (2002) (Richard More), George Grazebrook and J.P. Rylands, eds., *Visitation of Shropshire, 1623, Part II* (*HSPVS*, vol. 29, 1889), pp. 365-66 (Mo[o]re) 319 (Lee), *Part I* (*HSPVS*, vol. 28, 1889), pp. 157 (Cresset[t]), 135-36 (Corbet), 255-56 (Hopton); *The Gresleys of Drakelowe*, pp. 71-72, 135-36, 138-39, 226, 272, 293 (Gresley, Milton, More, Walsingham), and *Oxford DNB*, article on Frances Trollope; research of Julie Helen Otto, Rev. Francis J. Poynton, *Memoranda, Historical and Genealogical, Relating to the Parish of Kelston in the County of Somerset,* part IV (1885), pp. 53-56, 1-4, 110 (Benjamin Gostlett to Edgar Hastings Thomas), F.W. Todd, *Humphrey Hooke of Bristol and His Family and Descendants in England and America During the Seventeenth Century* (1938), charts opposite pp. 10 and 141, and T.F. Fenwick and Walter C. Metcalfe, eds., *Visitation of the County of Gloucester, 1682-83* (1884), pp. 73-74 (Gostlett), G.D. Squibb, ed., *Wiltshire Visitation Pedigrees, 1623* (*HSPVS*, vol. 105-6, 1954), pp. 92, 94 (Hungerford), 117 (Long), *RA* 3: 158-60 (Grey, Ferrers), plus *GM* 17 (1972-74): 407-19 (Edward III to Mark Phillips) (for Mrs. Otto); *TCWAAS* 9 (1888): 318 (and chart opp.) 23 (Dudley), *DVY* 3: 96 (Ferrand), 2: 475-76, 378 (Clapham, Heber) and *BP* (Craven); P.C. Copeland and R.K.

The Royal Descents of 900 Immigrants

MacMaster, *The Five George Masons: Patriots and Planters of Virginia and Maryland* (1975), pp. 54-56, John and J.A. Venn, *Alumni Cantabrigienses, Part 1: From the Earliest Times to 1751*, vol. 4 (1927), pp. 227-28 (Stephen[s] Thompson and his brother, another Sir William), M.S. Kennedy, *Seldens of Virginia and Allied Families*, vol. 2 (1911), pp. 329-31 (Thompson/Thomson), 1675, 1693/4 and 1706 wills of Henry (PCY), Sir William (PCC, Bond 87-130) and Mary (Stephens, PCC) Thompson, J.W. Blencowe, *The Blencowe Families: The Descendants of the Blencowe Families of Cumbria and Northamptonshire* (2001, used with caution by J.A. Brayton), *BLG*, 1863, p. 115 (Blencowe of Thoby Priory), *Parliament, 1558-1603*, vol. 2, pp. 63-64 (Thomas Dudley, brother of Richard and Winifred) and Sir Richard St. George, *Visitations of Cumberland, 1615* (*HSPVS*, vol. 7, 1872), p. 36 (Dudley). The Stephens/Stevens descent was developed and contributed by John Anderson Brayton of Memphis, Tenn.

Christian Jeannette Paton Thomas, daughter of Edgar Hastings Thomas and Christian Jean Wallace at generation 20 above, married Cunliffe McNeile Parsons. Their daughter, Nancy Jacqueline Parsons, married Hugh John Mackenzie Goodacre; Myrtle Jane Goodacre (b. 1934, daughter of these last), often her husband's collaborator, married (Nelson) Philip Ashmole (b. 1934), zoologist (esp. on island birds), conservationist, and assistant or associate professor at Yale, 1966-1972. See Wikipedia for Philip Ashmole, *BLG* 1952, p. 1003 (Goodacre), and research by J.H. Otto and John Duncan Goodacre (Mrs. Ashmole's brother).

Isabella Harcourt at generation 9 above was a daughter of John Harcourt (and Margaret Bracy), son of Sir Thomas Harcourt and Jane Francys, SETH. Among ancestors of J.H. Otto, Mrs Ashmole, and Peter and Zara Phillips (grandchildren of H.M. Queen Elizabeth II), Robert Hungerford at generation 10 above was the son of Robert Hungerford (and Mary Yorke), son of Sir Edward Hungerford and Anne Grey, sister of Sir John Grey, first husband of Elizabeth Woodville, later Queen of England (wife of King Edward IV), SETH. Frances Cocke at generation 11 was a daughter of John Cocke and Anne Goodere, daughter of Thomas Goodere and Jane Hawte, SETH. And Elizabeth Chetwynd at generation 14 was a daughter of Edward Chetwynd (and Helena Harington), son of John Chetwynd (and Margerie Middlemore), son of Thomas Chetwynd and Jane Salter, SETH. See Hungerford, Grey, and Ferrers sources cited above; *Parliament 1509-1558*, vol. 1, pp. 662-64, *Clutterbuck*, vol. 2, p. 55 (both for Cocke), and *Mary Isaac*, pp. 175-79 (Goodere, Hawte); and H.E. Chetwynd-Stapylton, *The Chetwynds of Ingestre* (1872), pp. 140-60.

The Royal Descents of 900 Immigrants

1. Edward III, King of England, d. 1377 = Philippa of Hainault
2. John of Gaunt, Duke of Lancaster = Catherine Roët
3. Joan Beaufort = Ralph Neville, 1st Earl of Westmoreland
4. Richard Neville, 1st Earl of Salisbury = Alice Montagu
5. Alice Neville = Henry FitzHugh, 5th Baron FitzHugh
6. Elizabeth FitzHugh = Nicholas Vaux, 1st Baron Vaux of Harrowden

4. Edward Neville, 1st Baron Abergavenny = Elizabeth Beauchamp
5. George Neville, 2nd Baron Abergavenny = Margaret Fenne
6. Sir Edward Neville = Eleanor Windsor, daughter of Andrews Windsor, 1st Baron Windsor, and Elizabeth Blount, SETH

7. Katherine Vaux = Sir George Throckmorton
8. Clement Throckmorton =
7. Katherine Neville

8,9. Katherine Throckmorton = Thomas Harby

9,10. Katherine Harby = Daniel Oxenbridge

10,11. **Rev. John Oxenbridge** (1608/9-1674) of Mass., Puritan clergyman = (1) Jane Butler; (2) Frances Woodward, ARD, SETH; (3) Mary Hackshaw; (4) Mrs. Susanna Parris Abbott (his daughter by 2, Theodora Oxenbridge, married Rev. Peter Thacher of Milton, Mass., noted theologian and Congregational clergyman).

10,11. (by 1) Elizabeth Oxenbridge = Caleb Cockcroft

11,12. Elizabeth Cockcroft = Nathaniel Hering

12,13. Oliver Hering = Elizabeth Hughes

13,14. Oliver Hering = Anna Maria Morris

14,15. Julines Hering = Mary Inglis

15,16. **Mary Helen Hering** of S.C. = Henry **Middleton** (1770-1846), governor of S.C., congressman, diplomat.

The Royal Descents of 900 Immigrants

9,10. Emma Harby (sister of Katherine) = Robert Charlton

10,11. Catherine Charlton = Richard Coke

11,12. Richard Coke = Elizabeth Robie

12,13. **John Coke** of Va. = Sarah Hoge.

8,9. Martha Throckmorton (sister of Katherine) = George Lynne

9,10. George Lynne = Isabel Forrest

10,11. Martha Lynne = John Blennerhasset

11,12. Robert Blennerhasset = Avice Conway

12,13. John Blennerhasset = Elizabeth Cross

13,14. Conway Blennerhasset = Elizabeth Harman

14,15. Conway Blennerhasset = Elizabeth Lacy

15,16. **Harman Blennerhasset** (1765-1831) of Va., adventurer, "western empire" associate of Aaron Burr = 16,17. **Margaret Agnew** of Va., his niece, daughter of Robert Agnew and 15,16. Catherine Blennerhasset.

12,13. Catherine Blennerhasset (sister of John) = Richard McLaughlin

13,14. Avice McLaughlin = John Mason

14,15. James Mason = Catherine Power

15,16. Elizabeth Mason = Robert Emmet

16,17. **Thomas Addis Emmet** (1764-1827) of N.Y., lawyer, Irish patriot − Jane Patten.

17,18. John Patten Emmet = Mary Byrd Farley Tucker of Va., ARD, SETH.

Sources: *RA* 4: 295-300 (Oxenbridge, Harby, Throckmorton, Vaux, Lucy), 1: 320-23, 4: 233-37 (Neville), 2: 633-34 (FitzHugh), 4: 124-26 (Montagu); *Oxford DNB* (Rev. John Oxenbridge), *NEHGR* 140 (1986): 111-12 (Parris, brought to my attention by Henry Bainbridge Hoff in *NEXUS* 14 [1997]: 192, 196), *AR8*, lines 201 and 78, *TAG* 31 (1955): 60, and

The Royal Descents of 900 Immigrants

NEHGR 108 (1954): 178 (reprinted in *EO* 1: 3: 776), plus *Throckmorton*, pp. 105-6, 165-66, *EP, BP* or *CP* (Vaux of Harrowden, FitzHugh, Salisbury, Abergavenny); J.A. Inglis, *The Family of Inglis of Auchindenny and Redhall* (1914), pp. 72-77, John Britton, *Graphical and Literary Illustrations of Fonthill Abbey, Wiltshire, with Heraldical and Genealogical Notices of the Beckford Family* (1823), pp. 64-65 (table VII — Hering), *Oxford DNB* (Oliver St. John, d. 1673, second husband of Elizabeth [Oxenbridge] Cockcroft) (for Mrs. Middleton); *MCS5*, line 94A and *BLG*, 18th ed., vol. 1, 1965, pp. 147-48 (Coke); *BIFR*, pp. 136-37, 140 (Blennerhasset), Rev. H.I. Longden, ed., *Visitation of Northamptonshire, 1681* (*HSPVS*, vol. 87, 1935), pp. 127-28 (Lynne); Thomas Addis Emmet II, *A Memoir of John Patten Emmet* (1898) (Emmet pedigree) and *Memoir of Thomas Addis and Robert Emmet*, 2 vols. (1915) (vol. 1, p. 175 and vol. 2, pp. 360-61 for Mason esp.). The above Sir George Throckmorton was a son of Sir Robert Throckmorton and Catherine Marrow, SETH. The above Nicholas Vaux, 1st Baron Vaux of Harrowden, was a son of Sir William Vaux (and Katherine Peniston), son of Sir William Vaux and Maud Lucy, daughter of Sir Walter Lucy and Eleanor l'Archdekne, SETH. See also G.A. Moriarty's extensive Vaux of Harrowden monograph in *MGH*, 5th ser., 5 (1923-1925): 277-301, 342-62, esp. 342.

The Royal Descents of 900 Immigrants

1. Edward III, King of England, d. 1377 = Philippa of Hainault
2. Lionel of Antwerp, Duke of Clarence = Elizabeth de Burgh
3. Philippa Plantagenet = Edmund Mortimer, 3rd Earl of March
4. Elizabeth Mortimer = Sir Henry "Hotspur" Percy
5. Henry Percy, 2nd Earl of Northumberland = Eleanor Neville
6. Henry Percy, 3rd Earl of Northumberland = Eleanor Poynings
7. Margaret Percy = Sir William Gascoigne
8. Agnes Gascoigne = Sir Thomas Fairfax
9. Sir Nicholas Fairfax = Jane Palmes, SETH
10. Mary Fairfax = Sir Henry Curwen
11. Mabel Curwen = 12. Sir William Fairfax, see below
12,13. Sir Philip Fairfax = Frances Sheffield, daughter of Edmund Sheffield, 1st Earl of Mulgrave, and Ursula Tyrwhitt, daughter of Sir Robert Tyrwhitt (and Elizabeth Oxenbridge), son of Sir William Tyrwhitt (son of Sir Robert Tyrwhitt and Maud Talboys, SETH) and Isabel Girlington (widow of Christopher Kelke), SETH, who shares the de la Pole-Stafford ancestry of the Habsburgs.
13,14. Sir William Fairfax, Parliamentary general in the English Civil War = Frances Chaloner
14,15. Isabella Fairfax = Nathaniel Bladen. A daughter, Elizabeth Bladen, married secondly Edward Hawke and was the mother of Edward Hawke, 1st Baron Hawke, the British admiral, who married Catherine Brooke.
15,16. **William Bladen** (1673-1718), colonial publisher, attorney-general of Md. = Anne Van Swearingen.
16,17. Anne Bladen = Benjamin Tasker, president of the council (and act. gov.) of Md.
17,18. Anne Tasker = 16,17. Samuel Ogle (c. 1702-1752), colonial governor of Md., see below.

The Royal Descents of 900 Immigrants

8. Margaret Gascoigne (sister of Agnes) = Ralph Ogle, 3rd Baron Ogle

9. Dorothy Ogle = Sir Thomas Forster

10. Eleanor Forster = George Craster

11. Edmund Craster = Alice Mitford

12. Isabel Craster = Luke Ogle, a cousin

13. Nicholas Ogle = ——

14. Luke Ogle = Katherine Graham

15. Samuel Ogle = 16. Ursula Markham, see below

16,17. **Samuel Ogle** (c. 1702-1752), colonial governor of Md. = 17,18. Anne Tasker, see above.

10. Thomas Forster (brother of Eleanor) = Florence Wharton

11. Thomas Forster = Isabel Brewster

12. Phyllis Forster = John Forster, a cousin

13. Dorothy Forster = George Fenwick. Their daughter, Elizabeth Fenwick, also immigrated to Conn., married John Cullick and Richard Ely, but left no NDTPS.

14. **George Fenwick** (1603-1656/7), colonist, a founder of Saybrook, Conn. = (1) Alice Apsley, ARD, SETH; (2) Catherine Haselrige, ARD, SETH.

5. Elizabeth Percy (sister of the 2nd Earl of Northumberland) = John Clifford, 7th Baron Clifford

6. Thomas Clifford, 8th Baron Clifford = Joan Dacre

7. John Clifford, 9th Baron Clifford = Margaret Bromflete

8. Elizabeth Clifford = Sir Robert Aske

9. John Aske = Eleanor Ryther

10. Robert Aske = (1) Eleanor Markenfield; (2) Anne Sutton

11. (by 2) Elizabeth Aske = Gabriel Fairfax

The Royal Descents of 900 Immigrants

12. Sir William Fairfax = 11. Mabel Curwen, see above

11. (by 1) Robert Aske (half-brother of Elizabeth) = Elizabeth Dawney
12. Helen Aske = Thomas Fairfax, 1st Baron Fairfax
13. Ferdinando Fairfax, 2nd Baron Fairfax, Parliamentary general in the English Civil War = Mary Sheffield, sister of Frances above, who also shares the de la Pole-Stafford ancestry of the Habsburgs
14. Frances Fairfax = Sir Thomas Widdrington, Speaker of the House of Commons
15. Mary Widdrington = Sir Robert Markham, 3rd Bt.
16. Ursula Markham = 15. Samuel Ogle, see above

11. (illegitimate by ——) Robert Aske (half-brother of Elizabeth and Robert) = Elizabeth Lacy
12. Jane Aske = Richard Lightfoot
13. John Lightfoot = Elizabeth Phillips
14. **John Lightfoot** of Va. = Elizabeth Tailer/Taylor.
15. **Philip Lightfoot** of Va. = Alice Corbin, daughter of Henry Corbin of Va., ARD, SETH, and Mrs. Alice Eltonhead Burnham, ARD, SETH.

Sources: *RA* 1: 378-80 (Bladen, Fairfax), 2: 544-45 (Fairfax, Curwen), 3:78-80 (Gascoyne), 4: 355-60 (Percy), 2: 246-48 (Clifford), 1: 168-71 (Aske, Lightfoot), 2: 280-81 (Sheffield), 5: 225-27 (Tyrwhitt), 4: 638-39 (Girlington, Hildyard, Hastings); *MG* 1:43-47 (Bladen) and *Oxford DNB* (Hawke), *PCF Yorkshire* (Fairfax and Gascoigne pedigrees), William Jackson, *Papers and Pedigrees Mainly Relating to Cumberland and Westmorland,* vol. 1 (1892), chart at end (Curwen) and *BP* and *CP* (Northumberland, March) (for William Bladen); Sir H.A. Ogle, 7th Bt., *Ogle and Bothal, or a History of the Baronies of Ogle, Bothal and Hepple, and of the Families of Ogle and Bertram* (1902), *passim* (and chart between pp. 220 and 221), *NF* 2:148-49, 154-55, 197, 199-299, 203-5 (Ogle), 259-60, 264 (Craster), 131 (Widdrington) and *NHN*, vol. 1

(1893), pp. 228, 276 (Forster), vol. 7 (1904), p. 473 (Fenwick) (for Samuel Ogle and George Fenwick); *Oxford DNB* (Sir William and the 2nd Baron Fairfax, Sir Thomas Widdrington) and *CB* (Markham of Sedgebrooke, baronets), *Foster's V of Yorkshire*, pp. 118-19 (Aske) and *Collins*, vol. 6, pp. 516-18 (Clifford). For Mrs. Elizabeth Fenwick Cullick Ely, see J. Hammond Trumbull, ed., *The Public Records of the Colony of Connecticut,* vol. 1, *1636-1665* (1850), pp. 573-76, 585-86 and M.S. Beach, Rev. William Ely and G.B. Vanderpoel, *The Ely Ancestry* (1902), pp. 32-35. Lightfoot research was undertaken by Larry W. Cates, plus Paul C. Reed, Belinda Myrick-Bennett, Jerry E. Jones and Joyce L. Grissom, who used T.C. Wales and C.P. Hartley, eds., *Visitation of London Begun in 1687, Part I* (*HSPVS*, new ser., vol. 16 (2004), pp. 324-26 (Lightfoot), *GVFWM* 3: 239-40 (Jones, Lightfoot, Aske and Fairfax), and two Lightfoot items, both with errors, in *GVFVM* 4: 225-27, 230, and *GVFWM* 3: 409-17, 420-24. Sir Henry Curwen and Mary Fairfax at generation 10 above are ancestors also of William Wordsworth, the poet; see NEHGS *NEXUS* 15 (1998): 116-17.

The Royal Descents of 900 Immigrants

1. Edward III, King of England, d. 1377 = Philippa of Hainault
2. John of Gaunt, Duke of Lancaster = Catherine Roet
2. Thomas of Woodstock, 1st Duke of Gloucester = Eleanor Bohun
3. Joan Beaufort = Ralph Neville, 1st Earl of Westmoreland
3. Anne Plantagenet = William Bourchier, Count of Eu
4. George Neville, 1st Baron Latymer = Elizabeth Beauchamp
4. John Bourchier, Baron Berners = Margery Berners
5. Sir Henry Neville =
5. Joan Bourchier
6. Richard Neville, 2nd Baron Latymer = Anne Stafford, daughter of Humphrey Stafford and Katherine Fray, SETH
7. Margaret Neville = Edward Willoughby
8. Elizabeth Willoughby = Sir Fulke Grevile
9. Robert Grevile = Blanche Whitney
10. Fulke Grevile = Mary Copley
11. Dorothy Grevile = Sir Arthur Haselrige, 2nd Bt., Puritan leader
12. **Catherine Haselrige** = George **Fenwick** (1603-1656/7), colonist, a founder of Saybrook, Connecticut, ARD, SETH.

9. Katherine Grevile (sister of Robert) = Giles Reed
10. Elizabeth Reed = Richard Brent (parents also of Fulke and Mary Brent of Md., who died childless and unmarried respectively)
11. **Margaret Brent** (1600-1670/1) of Md., feminist, d. unm.
11. **Giles Brent** of Va. and Md., dep. gov. of Md. = (1) Kittamaquund, an Indian; (2) Mrs. Frances Whitgreaves Harrison.
11. George Brent = Mariana Peyton (parents also of Henry Brent of Md., who married Mrs. Anne Calvert Brooke but had no surviving issue, and Robert Brent of Va., who married Anne Baugh but left no NDTPS)

The Royal Descents of 900 Immigrants

12. **George Brent** of Va. = (1) Elizabeth Greene; (2) Mrs. Mary Sewall Chandler, daughter of Henry Sewall, secretary of Md., and Lady Jane Lowe Sewall Calvert, Baroness Baltimore, of Md., ARD, SETH.

12. **Mary Brent** of Va. = (1) Giles **Brent** Jr., her first cousin, son of Giles Brent, dep. gov. of Md., and Kittamaquund; (2) Francis Hammersley.

12. **Anne Brent** of Md. = James **Clifton** of Md., ARD, SETH.

Sources: *RA* 1: 519-21 (Brent); 3: 122-23 (Read, Greville), 1: 578-80 (Willoughby), 3: 538-41 (Neville), 1: 479-85 (Bourchier); *Oxford DNB* (George Fenwick, Sir Arthur Haselrige [Hesilrige], 2nd Bt.), *CB* (Hasilrigg), *BP* (Warwick) or *Collins*, vol. 4, pp. 337-43 (Grevile), *CP* (Willoughby de Broke, Latymer, Berners, Eu, etc.); *DAB* (Margaret Brent), *LDBR* 5: 492-95, 666-73, and Chester Horton Brent, *The Descendants of Colonel Giles Brent, Capt. George Brent, and Robert Brent, Gent., Immigrants to Maryland and Virginia* (1946), pp. 42-89. See also *NEHGR* 154 (2000): 88-89, 92-93 (ancestor tables of the parents of Mrs. Fenwick), 95-106 (Grevile). Edward Willoughby at generation 7 above was the son of Richard Willoughby, 2nd Baron Willoughby de Broke, and Elizabeth Beauchamp, daughter of Richard Beauchamp, 2nd Baron Beauchamp of Powyck and Elizabeth Stafford, SETH.

The immigrant James Clifton was brought to my attention by John C. Brandon of Columbia, S.C. Clifton's marriage to Anne Brent is covered in the above Brent genealogy, pp. 43, 80, 105-7, and descendants in *GVFVM* 2: 87-92 and *Genealogies of Kentucky Families From the Register of the Kentucky Genealogical Society*, vol. 1 (1981), pp. 643-48. Since the descents for Clifton and his wife were traced after charts of the immigrant descendants of King Edward III, d. 1377, had been indexed, Mrs. Clifton is included on this chart largely because she was a sister of two of the immigrants above. Royal descents developed too late for inclusion in the main text (see pp. 888-915) are largely those, unlike that for Mrs. Clifton above, that treat immigrants not very nearly related to other immigrants in this work. In its correct order this chart would follow that for Mrs. Agnes Mackworth Watts Crowne, Richard More of the *Mayflower*, the writer Mrs. Frances Milton Trollope, Mrs. Hilda Margaret Rose (Thomas) Otto, Christopher Craven, governor of S.C., and Stephens/Stevens Thompson, attorney-general of Va.

The Royal Descents of 900 Immigrants

1. Edward III, King of England, d. 1377 = Philippa of Hainault
2. Lionel of Antwerp, Duke of Clarence = Elizabeth de Burgh
3. Philippa Plantagenet = Edmund Mortimer, 3rd Earl of March
4. Elizabeth Mortimer = Sir Henry "Hotspur" Percy
5. Henry Percy, 2nd Earl of Northumberland = Eleanor Neville
6. Henry Percy, 3rd Earl of Northumberland = Eleanor Poynings
7. Henry Percy, 4th Earl of Northumberland = Maud Herbert
8. Eleanor Percy = Edward Stafford, 3rd Duke of Buckingham, son of Henry Stafford, 2nd Duke of Buckingham, and Catherine Woodville, sister of Elizabeth Woodville, Queen of Edward IV
9. Elizabeth Stafford = Thomas Howard, 3rd Duke of Norfolk, son of Thomas Howard, 2nd Duke of Norfolk, and Elizabeth Tilney, SETH
10. Henry Howard, Earl of Surrey, the poet = Frances Vere
11. Catherine Howard = Henry Berkeley, Baron Berkeley
12. Mary Berkeley = Sir John Zouche
13. Sir John Zouche = Isabel Lowe, sister of Vincent Lowe, husband of Anne Cavendish, SETH
14. Elizabeth Zouche = Devereux Wolseley, son of Sir Thomas Wolseley and Ellen Broughton, SETH
15. Anne Wolseley = Thomas Knipe
16. Anne Knipe = Michael Arnold
17. **Alicia Arnold** of Md. = John **Ross**. Their daughter, Anne Arnold Ross, married Francis Key and was the mother of John Ross Key, father by Anne Phoebe Penn Dagworthy of Francis Scott Key (1779-1843), author of "The Star Spangled Banner," who married Mary Tayloe Lloyd, and of Anne Phoebe Charlton Key, wife of Roger Brooke Taney (1777-1864), second U.S. chief justice, attorney general and secretary of the Treasury.

The Royal Descents of 900 Immigrants

11. Thomas Howard, 4th Duke of Norfolk (brother of Lady Berkeley) = Margaret Audley

12. Thomas Howard, 1st Earl of Suffolk = Catherine Knevet

13. Theophilus Howard, 2nd Earl of Suffolk = Elizabeth Home

14. James Howard, 3rd Earl of Suffolk = Barbara Villiers

15. Elizabeth Howard = Sir Thomas Felton, 4th Bt.

16. Elizabeth Felton = John Hervey, 1st Earl of Bristol

17. John Hervey, 1st Baron Hervey of Ickworth, man of letters = Mary Lepell. Their son, Frederick Augustus Hervey, 4th Earl of Bristol, married Elizabeth Davers and was the father of Louisa Theodosia Hervey, wife of Robert Banks Jenkinson, 2nd Earl of Liverpool, British prime minister.

18. Mary Hervey = George Fitzgerald

19. Charles Lionel Fitzgerald = Dorothea Butler

20. Edward Thomas Fitzgerald = Emma Green

21. Lionel Charles Henry William Fitzgerald = Sarah Caroline Brown

22. **Desmond Fitzgerald** (1846-1926) of R.I. and Mass., hydraulic engineer = Elizabeth Parker Clark Salisbury.

13. Catherine Howard (sister of the 2nd Earl of Suffolk) = William Cecil, 2nd Earl of Salisbury

14. Hon. Algernon Cecil = Dorothy Neville

15. Diana Cecil = John Turnor

16. Edmund Turnor = Elizabeth Ferne

17. Edmund Turnor = Mary Disney

18. Elizabeth Frances Turnor = Samuel Smith

19. Sophia Smith = William Dickinson

20. Caroline Dickinson = William Bence-Jones

The Royal Descents of 900 Immigrants

21. Philippa Frances Bence-Jones = Sir Frederick Albert Bosanquet, a second cousin of Bernard Bosanquet, the Idealist philosopher
22. William Sidney Bence Bosanquet = Esther Cleveland, daughter of (Stephen) Grover Cleveland, 22nd and 24th U.S. President, and Frances Folsom
23. **Philippa Ruth Bosanquet**, known as **Philippa Foot** (1920-2010), ethicist (moral philosopher) = M(ichael) R(ichard) D(aniel) Foot, historian

12. Lord William Howard (brother of the 1st Earl of Suffolk) = Elizabeth Dacre
13. Margaret Howard = Sir Thomas Cotton, 2nd Bt.
14. Lucy Cotton = Sir Philip Wodehouse, 3rd Bt.
15. Sir Thomas Wodehouse = Anne Armine
16. Sir John Wodehouse, 4th Bt. = Mary Fermor
17. Sir Armine Wodehouse, 5th Bt. = Letitia Bacon
18. Philip Wodehouse = Apollonia Nourse
19. Philip Wodehouse = Lydia Lea
20. Henry Ernest Wodehouse = Eleanor Deane
21. (Sir) **Pelham Grenville (P.G.) Wodehouse** (1881-1975), sometime of N.Y., a U.S. citizen *post* 1955, comic writer and lyricist, author of *The Inimitable Jeeves*, etc. = Mrs. Ethel Newton Rowley.

10. Thomas Howard, 1st Viscount Howard of Bindon (brother of the Earl of Surrey) = Gertrude Lyte
11. Charles Lyte-Howard = Rebecca Webb
12. Catherine Howard = Sir Thomas Thynne
13. Anne Thynne = Sir Thomas Nott
14. **Edward Nott**, colonial governor of Va. = Margaret Blakiston of Va., ARD, SETH.

The Royal Descents of 900 Immigrants

Sources: *AP&P* 4: 3: 873-76 (Ross, Arnold, Knipe, Wolseley, Zouche), *MP*, tables I-II, XXI, pp. 1-2, 22, 434, *Lives of the Berkeleys*, vol. 2, pp. 402-3 esp. and *NGSQ* 51 (1963): 36-37 esp. (Lowe) (for Mrs. Ross); *MP*, tables I-II, XXI, pp. 1-2, 22-23, 336-37, *CP* (Liverpool), and Desmond Fitzgerald, *Family Notes* (1911), pp. 6-8, 31, 71-136 esp. (for Fitzgerald); *MP*, tables XXI, XXII, pp. 22, 24, 392-93, 395 (to William S.B. Bosanquet), *BIFR*, p. 640 (Bence-Jones), *BLG*, 18th ed., vol. 1 (1965), pp. 77-79 (Bosanquet) and Hugh Brogan and Charles Mosley, *American Presidential Families* (1993), pp. 518-19 (Cleveland to Mrs. Foot); *MP*, table I-II, XXI, XXIII, pp. 1-2, 22, 25, 404, 406-7, and *BP* (Kimberley) (P.G. Wodehouse); *MG*1: 50, *VGE*, pp. 171-72, *Oxford DNB* (Sir Thomas Nott), *CP* (Howard of Bindon — vol. 6, p. 584, note [c] esp.) and *MP*, tables I-II, XXI, XXIV, pp. 1-2, 22, 26, 440 (for Nott). See also *RA* 3: 338-39 (Howard), 5: 19-24 (Stafford), 4: 355-62 (Percy) and *AR*8, line 81C. The descent of P.G. Wodehouse was brought to my attention by Robert Battle of Tacoma, Wash.

    The above Henry Berkeley, Baron Berkeley, at generation 11 above was the son of Thomas Berkeley, Baron Berkeley (and Anne Savage, daughter of Sir John Savage and Anne Bostock, SETH), son of Thomas Berkeley, Baron Berkeley, and Eleanor Constable, SETH. William Cecil, 2nd Earl of Salisbury, at generation 13 was a son of Robert Cecil, 1st Earl of Salisbury and Lord Treasurer, and Elizabeth Brooke, SETH. See *CP* (Berkeley, Salisbury).

The Royal Descents of 900 Immigrants

1. Edward III, King of England, d. 1377 = Philippa of Hainault
2. John of Gaunt, Duke of Lancaster = Catherine Roët
3. Henry Beaufort, Cardinal Beaufort
4. (illegitimate allegedly, but probably not, by Alice FitzAlan, who = John Cherleton, 4th Baron Cherleton of Powis) Jane Beaufort = Sir Edward Stradling
5. Sir Henry Stradling = Elizabeth Herbert, daughter of Sir William ap Thomas and Gwladys Gam, SETH
6. Thomas Stradling = Janet Mathew
7. Sir Edward Stradling = Elizabeth Arundel
8. Jane Stradling = Alexander Popham
9. Edward Popham = Jane Norton
10. **George Popham** (d. 1608), Maine colonist, = ——.

9. Sir John Popham (brother of Edward) = Amy Adams
10. Jane Popham = Thomas Horner
11. Amy Horner = John Symes
12. Thomas Symes = Amy Bridges
13. George Symes = Dorothy Everard
14. **George Symes** (descendants mostly use Sims) of Va. = ——. John, Matthew and Edward Symes, also early in Virginia, could be either sons or kinsmen of George.

9. Catherine Popham (sister of Edward and Sir John) = Sir William Pole
10. Sir William Pole, antiquary = Mary Periham (their daughter, Elizabeth Poole, also immigrated to Mass. and helped to found Taunton, but died unmarried).
11. **William Poole** of Mass. = Jane Greene of Mass., ARD, SETH.

8. (illegitimate by Felice Gwyn ferch John ap Llwyd Kemeys) Elizabeth Stradling (half-sister of Jane) = Edmund Morgan, son of Thomas Morgan and Elizabeth Vaughan, daughter of Sir Roger Vaughan and Joan Whitney, SETH

9. Mary Morgan = John Thomas

10. William Thomas = Joan Lewis

11. Thomas Thomas = Dorothy Carew

12. Elizabeth Thomas = William Aubrey, son of William Aubrey and Jane Mathew, daughter of Humphrey Mathew (and Mary Lewis), son of Miles Mathew (and Katherine Mathew), son of William Mathew and Alice Raglan, daughter of Sir John Raglan and Anne Dennis, daughter of Sir William Dennis and Anne Berkeley, SETH.

13. **Barbara Aubrey** of Pa. = John **Bevan** of Pa., ARD, SETH.

Sources: *RA* 5: 52-61 (Poole, Popham, Stradling), 1: 197-99 (Aubrey, Mathew, Dennis), 5: 149-50 (Thomas, Morgan); *DAB* (George Popham), *BLG* 1952 (Buller-Leyborne-Popham of Huntstrete) and F.T. Colby, *Visitation of Somerset, 1623* (*HSPVS*, vol. 11, 1876), p. 87 (Popham); Jane Morris, *Adam Symes and His Descendants* (1938), esp. pp. 5-16, 367-76, *MGH*, new series 4 (1884): 162 (Horner) and *RA* 5: 58, note 6 (Symes); *MCS5*, line 27, and sources cited therein, esp. *TAG* 31 (1955): 171-72, 32 (1956): 9-12 and *M&G*, pp. 435-36 (Stradling) (for William Poole); *Keeler-Wood*, pp. 415-19 (partly corrected or confirmed by *M&G*, pp. 435-36, 241, 311, 317, 31-32, 347 and *Bartrum 2*, p. 1623, which gives no mother for Elizabeth Stradling, wife of Edmund Morgan) and S.W. Pennypacker, *The Descent of Samuel Whitaker Pennypacker... From the Ancient Counts of Holland* (1898), pp. 10-16 (Mrs. Bevan). Douglas Richardson's footnote about the George Symes descent was brought to my attention by John C. Brandon of Columbia, S.C.

The Royal Descents of 900 Immigrants

1. Edward III, King of England, d. 1377 = Philippa of Hainault
2. John of Gaunt, Duke of Lancaster = Catherine Roët
3. Joan Beaufort = Ralph Neville, 1st Earl of Westmoreland
4. Richard Neville, 1st Earl of Salisbury = Alice Montagu
5. Catherine Neville = William Bonville, Baron Harington and Bonville
6. Cecily Bonville, Baroness Harington and Bonville = Thomas Grey, 1st Marquess of Dorset, son of Sir John Grey and Elizabeth Woodville, later Queen of Edward IV, King of England
7. Thomas Grey, 2nd Marquess of Dorset = Margaret Wotton
8. Lord John Grey = Mary Browne, daughter of Sir Anthony Browne and Alice Gage, see next page
9. Elizabeth Grey = Sir Edward Grevile, son of Sir Fulke Grevile and Elizabeth Willoughby, SETH
10. Margaret Grevile = Godfrey Bosvile
11. **Elizabeth Bosvile** of Mass. = (1) Roger **Harlakenden**; (2) Herbert **Pelham** of Mass., first treasurer of Harvard College, ARD, SETH.

  8. Anne Grey (sister of Lord John) = Sir Henry Willoughby
  9. Margaret Willoughby = Sir Matthew Arundell, son of Sir Thomas Arundell (and Margaret Howard, SETH, sister of Queen Katherine Howard), son of Sir John Arundell and Elizabeth Grey, daughter of generation 8 above
10. Thomas Arundell, 1st Baron Arundell of Wardour = Anne Philipson
11. **Hon. Anne Arundell** = Cecil **Calvert**, 2nd Baron Baltimore (1605-1675), proprietor of Md., ARD, SETH.
12. Charles Calvert, 3rd Baron Baltimore (1637-1715), colonial governor of Md. = (1) Mary Darnall, probably a near relative of the Henry Darnall who married Anne Talbot of Md., ARD, SETH; (2) Mrs. Jane Lowe Sewall of Md., ARD, SETH; (3) Mrs. Mary Banks Thorpe; (4) Margaret Charleton

The Royal Descents of 900 Immigrants

13. (by 2) Benedict Leonard Calvert, 4th Baron Baltimore, proprietor of Md. = Lady Charlotte Lee, ARD, SETH.

7. Dorothy Grey (sister of the 2nd Marquess of Dorset) = William Blount, 4th Baron Mountjoy
8. Dorothy Blount = John Bluet
9. Richard Bluet = Mary Chichester
10. Arthur Bluet = Joan Lancaster
11. John Bluet = Elizabeth Portman
12. Anne Bluet = Cadwallader Jones
13. Cadwallader Jones = Elizabeth Creswick
14. William Jones = Martha Smith
15. **John Jones** of Mass. = Hannah Francis.

7. Elizabeth Grey (sister of the 2nd Marquess of Dorset and Dorothy, Baroness Mountjoy) = Gerald FitzGerald, 9th Earl of Kildare, son of Gerald FitzGerald, 8th Earl of Kildare, and Alison Eustace, SETH
8. Gerald FitzGerald, 11th Earl of Kildare = Mabel Browne, daughter of Sir Anthony Browne (and Alice Gage), son of Sir Anthony Browne and Lucy Neville, SETH
9. Mary FitzGerald = Christopher Nugent, 3rd Baron Delvin
10. Mabel Nugent = Murrough O'Brien, 4th Baron Inchiquin
11. Dermod O'Brien, 5th Baron Inchiquin = Ellen FitzGerald
12. Mary O'Brien = Michael Boyle, Archbishop of Armagh
13. Eleanor Boyle = William Hill
14. Michael Hill = Anne Trevor. Their son, Arthur Hill, 1st Baron Dungannon, married Anne Stafford and was the father of Anne Hill, wife of Garret Wesley, 1st Earl of Mornington and mother of Richard Wellesley, 1st Marquess Wellesley, Foreign Secretary, Governor-General of India and colonial statesman,

The Royal Descents of 900 Immigrants

and Arthur Wellesley, 1st Duke of Wellington, field marshal and victor of Waterloo, both SETH

15. Anne Hill = St. John Brodrick

16. Anne Brodrick = James Jefferyes

17. James St. John Jefferyes = Arabella Fitzgibbon

18. Albinia Frances Jefferyes = Stephen Francis William Fremantle

19. John Fremantle = Agnes Lyon

20. Delvin David Fremantle = Emma Isaacs

21. Leila Hope Fremantle = Sir Sidney Robert Fremantle, a cousin

22. Margery Hilda Fremantle = (1) **Raymond (Hart) Massey** (1896-1983) of Calif., actor, a naturalized U.S. citizen; (2) Sir Giles Edward Sebright, 13th Bt.

Sources: *RA* 1: 443-44 (Bosvile), 3: 123-24 (Grevile), 3: 161-70 (Grey), 1: 436 (Bonville), 4: 124-26 (Neville), 2: 168-70 (Arundell), 2: 64-65 (Calvert), 3:42-43 (Willoughby); *NEHGR* 154 (2000): 90-91 (a five-generation ancestor table), *MCS5*, line 95 and sources cited therein (esp. *PCF Yorkshire* — Bosvile pedigree), *Collins*, vol. 4, p. 342 and *BP* (Grevile, later earls of Warwick, and Greys, earls of Stamford) and *CP* (Dorset, Bonville, Salisbury, Westmoreland) (for Mrs. Pelham); *MG* 1: 138-40, *MCS5*, line 63, and Joseph Jackson Howard and H. Seymour Hughes, *Genealogical Collections Illustrating the History of Roman Catholic Families of England, Based on the Lawson Manuscript*, part III (Arundell) (1887?), pp. 226, 229, 233-34 (for Lady A.A. Calvert, Baroness Baltimore); *NEHGR* 113 (1959): 216-21 (reprinted in *EO* 2: 2: 570-75), *VD*, pp. 93-94 (Bluet), 102 (Blount, Grey) and *CP* (Mountjoy) (John Jones); *ANB* and *Oxford DNB* (R.H. Massey); *BP* (Cottesloe [Fremantle], Colthurst [Jefferyes], Midleton [Brodrick], Downshire [Hill], Wellington, Cork [Boyle], Inchiquin, Westmeath [Nugent], Leinster [FitzGerald of Kildare]). For generations 4-14 of Mrs. Massey's (Lady Sebright's) descent see also *Prince Charles* I 469-70 (p. 15), J 937-38 (p. 25), K 1875-76 (p. 40), L 3751-52 (p. 61), M 7501-2 (p. 92), N 15003-4 (p. 131), O 3007-8 (p. 191), P 60013-16 (p. 279), Q 120027-28 (p. 467), O 28837-38 (p. 179), P 57549-50 (p. 262), P57673-74 (p. 264), Q 115097-100 (p. 435), Q 5328 (p. 321).

The Royal Descents of 900 Immigrants

1. Edward III, King of England, d. 1377 = Philippa of Hainault
2. Lionel of Antwerp, Duke of Clarence = Elizabeth de Burgh
3. Philippa Plantagenet = Edmund Mortimer, 3rd Earl of March
4. Elizabeth Mortimer = Sir Henry "Hotspur" Percy
5. Elizabeth Percy = John Clifford, 7th Baron Clifford
6. Mary Clifford = Sir Philip Wentworth
7. Elizabeth Wentworth = Sir Martin at See
8. Joan/Jane at See = Sir Piers Hildyard, son of Sir Robert Hildyard and Elizabeth Hastings, daughter of John Hastings, *de jure* Baron Hastings, and Anne Morley, SETH
9. Isabel Hildyard = Ralph Legard
10. Joan Legard = Richard Skepper
11. Edward Skepper = Mary Robinson
12. **Rev. William Skepper/Skipper** of Boston, Mass., where he died 1640-50 = (1) Jane ——; (2) Sarah Fisher.
13. (by 2) Sarah Skepper/Skipper = Walter Fairfield
14. William Fairfield = Esther Gott
15. Abigail Fairfield = John Parkman
16. Esther Parkman = Adam Brown
17. Adam Brown, Jr. = Priscilla Putnam
18. Israel Putnam Brown = Sally Briggs
19. Sally Brown = Israel C. Brewer
20. Sarah Almeda Brewer = Calvin Galusha Coolidge
21. John Calvin Coolidge = Victoria Josephine Moor
22. (John) Calvin Coolidge (Jr.), 1872-1933, 30th U.S. President = Grace Anna Goodhue

9. Katherine Hildyard (sister of Isabel) = William Holme

The Royal Descents of 900 Immigrants

10. John Holme = Anne Aislaby
11. Catherine Holme = Marmaduke Constable
12. Frances Constable = Sir John Rodes
13. Sir Francis Rodes, 1st Bt. = Elizabeth Lascelles
14. John Rodes = Elizabeth Jason
15. **Charles Rodes** of Va. = Frances ———.

8. Elizabeth at See (sister of Joan/Jane) = Roger Kelke
9. Christopher Kelke = Isabel Girlington, daughter of William Girlington and Katherine Hildyard, daughter of Sir Robert Hildyard and Elizabeth Hastings, daughter of John Hastings, *de jure* Baron Hastings, and Anne Morley, SETH
10. William Kelke = Thomasine Skerne
11. Cecily Kelke = John Farrar, son of William Farrar and Margaret Lacy, daughter of Hugh Lacy (and Agnes Savile), son of Gerard Lacy and Alice Symmes, daughter of William Symmes and Margaret Bosvile, daughter of Thomas Bosvile and Isabel Hastings, sister of Elizabeth (Hastings) Hildyard above
12. **William Farrar** of Va. = Mrs. Cecily ——— Jordan.

10. Christopher Kelke (brother of William) = Jane St. Paul
11. Christopher Kelke = Elizabeth Carr
12. Anne Kelke = Roger Leming
13. Anne Leming = William Wolley
14. Alice Wolley = John Asfordby, son of William Asfordby and Eleanor Newcomen, daughter of John Newcomen and Mary Skipwith, daughter of John Skipwith (and Eleanor Kingston), son of Sir William Skipwith and Alice Dymoke, SETH
15. **William Asfordby** of N.Y. = Martha Burton.

The Royal Descents of 900 Immigrants

Sources: *RA* 4: 638-40 (Skepper, Legard, Hildyard) (and 2: 499 [Hastings], 4: 156-57 [Morley], and 2: 416-20 [de la Pole, Kerdeston]), 2: 546-57 (Farrar, Kelke), 3: 410-12 (Wolley, Leming, Kelke), 4: 218-19 (at See, Wentworth), 2: 246 (Clifford), 4: 355-57 (Percy), 4: 174-76 (Mortimer), 1: 158-59 (Asfordby, Newcomen, Skipwith), 4: 642 (Skipwith), 4: 342-43 (Lacy); *TAG* 20 (1942-43): 77-85, 69 (1994):129-39 and sources cited in both (Skepper/Skipper royal descents); *PSECD* 3: 241-43 (undocumented), *GVFVM*5: 188-90 and *FMG*, vol. 2, pp. 585-86 (Rodes), *DVY*, vol. 2, pp. 118-19 (Holme), vol. 3, pp. 47-48 (Constable); Alvahn Holmes, *The Farrar's Island Family and its English Ancestry*, vol. 1 (1972, repr. 1977), chapters 1-3 and Farrar and Kelke charts at end, and *Papers, Reports, etc., Read Before the Halifax Antiquarian Society 1922*, pp. 129-32, *1924*, pp. 159-61 (Lacy, Symmes, Bosvile); *PCF Yorkshire* (Bosvile and Hildyard pedigrees); *Foster's V of Yorkshire*, pp. 330-31 (Lacy), 372-73 (Hastings) (the Hastings-Bosvile-Symmes-Lacy-Farrar descent was developed and brought to my attention by Worth S. Anderson of Arlington, Va.); Frank Allaben, *The Ancestry of Leander Howard Crall* (1908), pp. 92-93 (Asfordby), 161-62 (Wolley), 153-54 (Newcomen), 191-92 (Skipwith), 203-6 and *Lincolnshire Pedigrees*, pp. 595 (Leming), 556-57 (Kelke), 404-5 (Girlington). Marmaduke Constable at generation 11 was the son of Marmaduke Constable (and Elizabeth Stokes), son of Sir William Constable and Joan Fulthorpe, SETH.

As editing of this work's index was ending, news arrived of the engagement of Prince Henry (Harry) Charles Albert David of Wales and American actress (Rachel) Meghan Markle, a descendant of Rev. William Skepper/Skipper as follows: (Rachel) Meghan Markle; Thomas Wayne Markle & Doria Loyce Ragland; Gordon Arnold Markle & Doris May Sanders; Frederick George Sanders & Gertrude May Merrill; George David Merrill & Mary Bird; Jacob Lee Merrill & Mary Smith; John Smith, Jr. & Mary Mudgett; John Smith & Martha Drake; Abraham Drake & Martha Eaton; Nathaniel Drake & Jane Lunt; Henry Lunt, Jr. & Jane Browne; Abraham Browne & Jane Skipper; *Rev. William Skepper/Skipper* of Mass. & ──. See a Markle AT (through Smith/Mudgett, confirmed for the author from record sources by Alex Bannerman of Charleston, W. Va.), on www.famechain.com; Mildred D. Mudgett, *Thomas Mudgett of Salisbury, Massachusetts and His Descendants* (1961), p. 69 (Merrill, Smith), Alice Smith Thompson, *The Drake Family of New Hampshire* (1962), pp. 43-44 (which mistakenly calls the wife of Henry Lunt, Jr., Jane Skipper), 55, 79-80, and Lunt, Browne, and Skepper/Skipper sources as per p. 925.

The Royal Descents of 900 Immigrants

1. Edward III, King of England, d. 1377 = Philippa of Hainault
2. John of Gaunt, Duke of Lancaster = Catherine Roët
3. John Beaufort, Marquess of Somerset and Dorset = Margaret Holand, daughter of Thomas Holand, 2nd Earl of Kent, and Alice FitzAlan, SETH
4. Edmund Beaufort, 1st Duke of Somerset = Eleanor Beauchamp
5. Henry Beaufort, 2nd Duke of Somerset, d. unm.
6. (illegitimate by Joan Hill) Charles Somerset, 1st Earl of Worcester = Elizabeth Herbert
7. Henry Somerset, 2nd Earl of Worcester = Elizabeth Browne, daughter of Sir Anthony Browne (son of Sir Thomas Browne and Eleanor Arundel, SETH) and Lucy Neville, daughter of John Neville, 1st Marquess of Montagu (and Isabel Ingoldsthorpe), son of Richard Neville, 1st Earl of Salisbury and Alice Montagu, SETH
8. Lucy Somerset = John Neville, 4th Baron Latymer
9. Dorothy Neville = Thomas Cecil, 1st Earl of Exeter, son of William Cecil, 1st Baron Burghley, minister of Elizabeth I
10. Dorothy Cecil = Sir Giles Alington
11. Susan Alington = Sir Robert Crane, 1st Bt.
12. Elizabeth Crane = Sir Edmund Bacon, 4th Bt.
13. Frances Bacon = Walter Norborne
14. Elizabeth Norborne = John Symmes Berkeley
15. **Norborne Berkeley, 1st Baron Botetourt** (c. 1718-1770), colonial governor of Va., d. unm.

11. Katherine Alington (sister of Susan) = Zouche Tate
12. William Tate = Mary Stedman
13. Bartholomew Tate = Mary Noel
14. Bartholomew Tate = Arundel Stratford

The Royal Descents of 900 Immigrants

15. **Elizabeth Tate** = Sir Charles **Hardy** (the younger) (c. 1716-1780), colonial governor of N.Y., admiral.

14. Mary Tate (sister of the younger Bartholomew) = Samuel Long

15. **Catherine Maria Long** of N.Y. = (1) Sir Henry **Moore**, 1st Bt. (1713-1769), colonial governor of N.Y.; (2) Richard Vincent.

9. Elizabeth Neville (sister of Dorothy) = Sir John Danvers

10. Dorothy Danvers = Sir Peter Osborne

11. Sir John Osborne, 1st Bt. = Eleanor Danvers, a cousin

12. Sir John Osborne, 2nd Bt. = Elizabeth Strode

13. John Osborn(e) = Sarah Byng

14. **Sir Danvers Osborne, 3rd Bt.**, colonial governor of N.Y. = Lady Mary Montagu, ARD, SETH.

Sources: *DAB*, *EP* and *CP* (Botetourt), *CB* (Bacon of Redgrave, Crane of Chilton), *BP* and *CP* (Exeter, Latymer, Worcester [under Beaufort in *BP*], Somerset and Pembroke, plus the *CP* entry for Edward Devereux, 8th Viscount Hereford, first husband of Elizabeth Norborne) (for Botetourt); *Oxford DNB* (Sir Charles Hardy the younger) and *Nichols*, vol. 2, pt. 2, p. 888 (Tate), a connection brought to my attention by John C. Brandon of Columbia, S.C.; Robert Mowbray Howard, *Records and Letters of the Family of the Longs of Longville, Jamaica, and Hampton Lodge, Surrey*, vol. 1 (1925), pp. 113, 120, 185 esp. (for Lady Moore); *BP* and *CB* (Osborn[e] of Chicksands Priory, baronets), and F.N. McNamara, *Memorials of the Danvers Family* (1895), chart opposite p. 103 and pp. 284-86 (for Osborne). For the first eight generations see also *RA* 4: 645-61 (Somerset), 3: 279-81 (Herbert).

The above Elizabeth Herbert at generation 6 was a daughter of William Herbert, 2nd Earl of Pembroke, Earl of Huntingdon (son of William Herbert, 1st Earl of Pembroke of the first creation, and Anne Devereux, SETH) and Mary Woodville, sister of Elizabeth Woodville, the wife and queen of King Edward IV.

The Royal Descents of 900 Immigrants

1. Edward III, King of England, d. 1377 = Philippa of Hainault
2. Lionel of Antwerp, Duke of Clarence = Elizabeth de Burgh
3. Philippa Plantagenet = Edmund Mortimer, 3rd Earl of March
4. Elizabeth Mortimer = Sir Henry "Hotspur" Percy
5. Henry Percy, 2nd Earl of Northumberland = Eleanor Neville
6. Henry Percy, 3rd Earl of Northumberland = Eleanor Poynings
7. Henry Percy, 4th Earl of Northumberland = Maud Herbert
8. Eleanor Percy = Edward Stafford, 3rd Duke of Buckingham, son of Henry Stafford, 2nd Duke of Buckingham, and Catherine Woodville, sister of Elizabeth Woodville, Queen of Edward IV
9. Mary Stafford = George Neville, 3rd Baron Abergavenny (their progeny shares the entire known ancestry of Elizabeth Plantagenet of York, Queen of Henry VII), son of George Neville, 2nd Baron Abergavenny and Margaret Fenne, SETH
10. Ursula Neville = Sir Warham St. Leger
11. Anne St. Leger = Thomas Digges, mathematician
12. Sir Dudley Digges, diplomat, judge = Mary Kempe, daughter of Sir Thomas Kempe and Dorothy Thompson, SETH
13. **Edward Digges**, colonial governor of Va. = Elizabeth Page.

11. Sir Anthony St. Leger (brother of Anne) = Mary Scott
12. Sir Warham St. Leger = Mary Heyward
13. **Katherine St. Leger** of Va. = Thomas **Colepepper (Culpeper)** of Va., ARD, SETH. Their daughter, Frances Colepepper (Culpeper) (1634-c.1695), Virginia political figure, married (1) Samuel Stephens, colonial gov. of N.C.; (2) Sir William Berkeley (1608-1677), colonial gov. of Va., ARD, SETH; and (3) Philip Ludwell (d. 1717), planter, Virginia councillor, colonial gov. of N.C. and S.C., ARD, SETH. Their son, John Colepepper (Culpeper), was Surveyor General of S.C., later lived in Albemarle Co., N.C., and married Judith ——, Mrs. Margaret Bird, and Sarah Mayo.

13. Ursula St. Leger = Daniel Horsmanden

14. **Warham Horsmanden** of Va. = Susanna Beeching. Their daughter, Mary Horsmanden, married (1) Samuel Filmer; (2) William Byrd I (1652-1704), Virginia planter, Indian trader, merchant and councilor, and was the mother of diarist and colonial official William Byrd II, who married Lucy Parke and Maria Taylor. Rev. Daniel Horsmanden, son of Warham and Susanna, married Mrs. Susanna Woolston Bowyer and was the father of Daniel Horsmanden, Jr. (1694-1778), last chief justice of the province of New York, who married Mrs. Mary Reade Vesey and Anne Jevon.

13. Mary St. Leger = William Codd

14. **St. Leger Codd** of Va. = (1) Mrs. Anne Mottrom Wright Fox; (2) Mrs. Anne Bennett Bland; (3) Mrs. Anne Hynson Randall Wickes.

Sources: *RA* 3: 105-6 (Digges), 4: 537-39 (St. Leger, Horsmanden, Codd), 2: 370-72 (Culpeper, Berkeley), 1: 323-25 (Neville), 5: 22-24 (Stafford), 4: 355-62 (Percy), *MCS5*, lines 48, 47, 44, 36, 161, *AR8*, lines 3, 19, 5, *AP&P*, 4: 3: 103-9 (St. Leger), *Oxford DNB* (Berkeley, Ludwell, Byrd, Horsmanden), *DNB* (Sir Warham St. Leger) and sources cited in all, especially *CP* (for generations 1-9). The entire ancestry of Elizabeth Plantagenet of York, Queen of Henry VII, is covered in Ernest Flagg Henderson III, *Ancient, Medieval, and More Recent Ancestors of Ernest Flagg Henderson IV and Roberta Flagg Henderson*, 4 vols. (2013). For Digges, Horsmanden, Byrd, and Codd see also *AP&P* 4: 1: 821-24 (Digges), 4: 3: 103-11 (St. Leger).

The Royal Descents of 900 Immigrants

1. Edward III, King of England, d. 1377 = Philippa of Hainault
2. Lionel Plantagenet, Duke of Clarence = Elizabeth de Burgh
3. Philippa Plantagenet = Edmund Mortimer, 3rd Earl of March
4. Elizabeth Mortimer = Sir Henry "Hotspur" Percy
5. Elizabeth Percy = John Clifford, 7th Baron Clifford
6. Mary Clifford = Sir Philip Wentworth
7. Sir Henry Wentworth = Anne Saye
8. Sir Richard Wentworth = Anne Tyrrell, daughter of Sir James Tyrrell and Anne Arundell, SETH, the latter of whom shared the de la Pole-Stafford ancestry of the Habsburgs.
9. Thomas Wentworth, 1st Baron Wentworth = Margaret Fortescue. Their daughter, Anne Wentworth, married John Poley and left a daughter, Mirabel Poley, who married William Brewster and herself left a son, William Brewster, who married Catherine Offley and was the father of Thomas (alias Seckford) Brewster of Va., who married Mrs. Elizabeth —— Watkins but left no NDTPS.
10. Philip Wentworth = Elizabeth Corbett
11. Jane Wentworth = John Harleston (their daughter, Affra Harleston, married John Comin[g] and immigrated to S.C., but left no children)
12. John Harleston = Elizabeth ——
13. **John Harleston** of S.C. = Elizabeth Willis.
13. **Elizabeth Harleston** of S.C. = Elias **Ball**.

9. Dorothy Wentworth (sister of the 1st Baron Wentworth) = Sir Lionel Tollemache
10. Lionel Tollemache = Susan Jermyn
11. Sir Lionel Tollemache, 1st Bt. = Elizabeth Cromwell, daughter of Henry Cromwell, 2nd Baron Cromwell, and Mary Paulet, see below

The Royal Descents of 900 Immigrants

12. Sir Lionel Tollemache, 2nd Bt. = Elizabeth Stanhope

13. Susan Tollemache = Sir Henry Felton, 2nd Bt.

14. **Susan Felton** = (1) Philip Harbord; (2) Francis **Howard**, 5th Baron Howard of Effingham, colonial governor of Va., ARD, SETH.

10. Mary Tollemache (sister of Lionel) = John Jermyn

11. Thomas Jermyn = Sarah Stephens

12. Jane Jermyn = Thomas Wright

13. Jermyn Wright = Anne Blatchford

14. Sir Robert Wright = Susan Wren, a first cousin of Sir Christopher Wren, the architect

15. **Robert Wright**, chief justice of S.C. = Mrs. Isabella Wright Pitts, possibly a cousin (parents of Sir James Wright, 1st Bt., colonial governor of Ga. = Sarah Maidman).

Sources: *RA* 3: 331-32 (Harleston), 4: 218-21 (Wentworth), 2: 246 (Clifford), 4: 355-57 (Percy), 4: 174-76 (Mortimer); *TG* 9 (1988): 163-225, esp. 179-88, 190-91, 211-21, and sources cited therein (Harlestons, plus Brewster); *CP* (Effingham), *CB* (Felton, Tollemache), Walter C. Metcalfe, ed., *Visitations of Suffolk, 1561, 1577, and 1612* (1882), p. 71 (Talmache or Tollemache), and *Wentworth*, vol. 1, pp. 38-42; *DNB* (Sir James Wright, 1st Bt., and Sir Robert Wright), *MCS5*, line 37, *SMF* 2: 256 (Wright, Jermyn).

The Royal Descents of 900 Immigrants

1. Edward III, King of England, d. 1377 = Philippa of Hainault
2. Lionel of Antwerp, Duke of Clarence = Elizabeth de Burgh
3. Philippa Plantagenet = Edmund Mortimer, 3rd Earl of March
4. Elizabeth Mortimer = Sir Henry "Hotspur" Percy
5. Henry Percy, 2nd Earl of Northumberland = Eleanor Neville
6. Catherine Percy = Edmund Grey, 1st Earl of Kent
7. Anne Grey = John Grey, 8th Baron Grey of Wilton
8. Tacy Grey = John Guise
9. William Guise = Mary Rotsy
10. John Guise = Joan Pauncefoot
11. Elizabeth Guise = Robert Haviland
12. **Jane Haviland** (of Mass.) = William **Torrey**.

7. George Grey, 2nd Earl of Kent (brother of Lady Anne) = Catherine Herbert
8. Anne Grey = John Hussey, 1st Baron Hussey
9. Bridget Hussey = Sir Richard Morrison
10. Elizabeth Morrison = Henry Clinton, 2nd Earl of Lincoln
11. Sir Henry Clinton alias Fynes = Elizabeth Hickman
12. William Clinton = Elizabeth Kennedy
13. James Clinton = Elizabeth Smith
14. **Charles Clinton** of N.Y. = Elizabeth Denniston. Their sons included U.S. Vice-President George Clinton (1739-1812), also governor of N.Y., and General James Clinton (1733-1812), noted revolutionary soldier and father by Mary DeWitt of Republican statesman DeWitt Clinton (1769-1828), U.S. senator, governor of N.Y., and promoter of the Erie Canal.
14. **Christiana Clinton** of N.Y. = John **Beatty**.

The Royal Descents of 900 Immigrants

Sources: *RA* 3: 268-69 (Haviland, Guise), 5: 375-77 (Grey of Wilton), 3: 131-34 (Grey of Kent), 4: 355-59 (Percy), 2: 533-38 (Holand), 3: 279-80 (Herbert), 5: 250-51 (Devereux), *AR8*, lines 197, 207, 19, 5 and *NEHGR* 108 (1954): 177-78, 110 (1956): 232, reprinted in *EO* 1: 3: 775-77 (Mrs. Torrey); *NYGBR* 51 (1920): 360-62, 66 (1935): 330-35, *EP* and *CP* (Lincoln, Hussey, Kent) (Clinton and Mrs. Beatty).

Edward Grey, 1st Earl of Kent, at generation 6 above was a son of Sir John Grey and Constance Holand, daughter of John Holand, 1st Duke of Exeter, and Elizabeth Plantagenet, SETH. Catherine Herbert at generation 7 was a daughter of William Herbert, 1st Earl of Pembroke of the first creation, SETH (son of Sir William ap Thomas and Gwladys Gam, SETH) and Anne Devereux, daughter of Sir Walter Devereux (and Elizabeth Merbury), son of Walter Devereux and Elizabeth Bromwich, SETH.

The Royal Descents of 900 Immigrants

1. Edward III, King of England, d. 1377 = Philippa of Hainault
2. Thomas of Woodstock, 1ˢᵗ Duke of Gloucester = Eleanor Bohun
3. Anne Plantagenet = William Bourchier, Count of Eu
4. John Bourchier, Baron Berners = Margery Berners
5. Sir Humphrey Bourchier = Elizabeth Tilney, who married secondly Thomas Howard, 2ⁿᵈ Duke of Norfolk, SETH
6. John Bourchier, Baron Berners = Catherine Howard, daughter of John Howard, 1ˢᵗ Duke of Norfolk, SETH and Margaret Chedworth, a second wife
7. Joan Bourchier = Sir Edmund Knevet
8. John Knevet = Agnes Harcourt, daughter of Sir John Harcourt and Margaret Barantyne, daughter of William Barantyne (and Mary Reade), son of John Barantyne and Mary Stonor, daughter of Thomas Stonor and Joan de la Pole, illegitimate daughter (possibly by Malyne de Cay) of William de la Pole, 1ˢᵗ Duke of Suffolk, son of Habsburg ancestors Michael de la Pole, 2ⁿᵈ Earl of Suffolk, and Katherine Stafford, SETH.
9. Abigail Knevet = Sir Martin Sedley
10. Muriel Sedley = Brampton Gurdon
11. **Muriel Gurdon** of Mass. = Richard **Saltonstall** (c. 1610-1694) of Mass., colonial official, ARD, SETH.

8. Elizabeth Knevet (sister of John) = Francis Bohun
9. Nicholas Bohun = Audrey Coke
10. Edmund Bohun = Dorothy Baxter
11. Baxter Bohun = Margaret Lawrence
12. **Edmund Bohun**, chief justice of S.C. = Mary Brampton.

7. (illegitimate by Elizabeth Bacon) Sir James Bourchier (half-brother of Lady Knevet) = Mary Banister

8. Sir Ralph Bourchier = Elizabeth Hall, daughter of Francis Hall (and Ursula Sherington), son of Francis Hall and Elizabeth Wingfield, SETH

9. Sir John Bourchier = Elizabeth Verney

10. **Mary Bourchier** of Va. = Jabez **Whitaker** of Va., ARD, SETH.

Sources: *RA* 3: 180-83 (Gurdon, Sedley, Knevet); 1: 479-92 (Bourchier, Whitaker), 3: 334-36 (Howard), 5: 388-89 (Harcourt), 4: 407-8 (Barantyne), 2: 416-31 (Stonor, de la Pole), *AR8*, line 4, *MCS5*, line 18, *SMF* 1: 286-88 and *Foundations* 6 (2014): 96-97 (Gurdon), *Blomefield*, vol. 1, pp. 378-79 (Knevet), and *PSECD* 2, pp. xcviii-cxix (Mrs. Saltonstall); S. Wilton Rix, ed., *The Diary and Autobiography of Edmund Bohun, Esq., with an Introductory Memoir, Notes and Illustrations* (1853), pp. vii (and pedigree opposite)-xxxii; *MCS5*, line 73, Sarah C.W. Cantey, *Our Children's Ancestry* [Whitaker family] (1935), pp. 59 (and chart opposite)-64, and *Lincolnshire Pedigrees*, p. 441 (Hall) (for Mrs. Whitaker). Edmund Bohun is also treated in Richard B. McConnell, *Ancestral Peregrinations, Part One: A Series of Genealogical Charts Dealing with Some Phases of the Bohun Ancestry and with That of a Few of the Maternal Lines Involved* (Houston, Texas: Charles Greene Fleetwood, 1979), examined at the Fondren Library at Rice University, whose copy is said to be #323 of 500.

The Royal Descents of 900 Immigrants

1. Edward III, King of England, d. 1377 = Philippa of Hainault
2. Lionel of Antwerp, Duke of Clarence = Elizabeth de Burgh
3. Philippa Plantagenet = Edmund Mortimer, 3rd Earl of March
4. Elizabeth Mortimer = Sir Henry "Hotspur" Percy
5. Henry Percy, 2nd Earl of Northumberland = Eleanor Neville
6. Anne Percy = Sir Thomas Hungerford
7. Mary Hungerford = Edward Hastings, 2nd Baron Hastings
8. Anne Hastings = Thomas Stanley, 2nd Earl of Derby, son of George Stanley, Baron Strange, and Joan Strange, SETH. Edward Stanley, 3rd Earl of Derby, son of Anne Hastings and the 2nd Earl, married Dorothy Howard, SETH (daughter of Thomas Howard, 2nd Duke of Norfolk, and Agnes Tilney, SETH) and was the father of Elizabeth Stanley, wife of Henry Parker, 2nd Baron Morley. For descents from this last couple to poets (Mrs.) Elizabeth Barrett Browning, wife of Robert Browning, and Alfred Tennyson, 1st Baron Tennyson, see *NEHGS NEXUS* 15 (1998): 161-62.
9. Margaret Stanley = Robert Radcliffe, 1st Earl of Sussex
10. Jane Radcliffe = Anthony Browne, 1st Viscount Montagu, SETH
11. Hon. Anthony Browne = Mary Dormer
12. Dorothy Browne = Edmund Lee
13. Dorothy Lee = Sir John Temple
14. Mary Temple = Robert Nelson
15. **John Nelson** (c. 1654-1734) of Mass., merchant, proponent of French expulsion from North America, and public official = Elizabeth Tailer.
16. Rebecca Nelson = Henry Lloyd
17. Margaret Lloyd = William Henry Smith
18. Rebecca Smith = John Aspinwall
19. John Aspinwall, Jr. = Susan Howland

20. Mary Rebecca Aspinwall = Isaac Roosevelt
21. James Roosevelt = Sara Delano
22. Franklin Delano Roosevelt (1882-1945), 32nd U.S. President = (Anna) Eleanor Roosevelt

15. **Margaret Nelson** (sister of John Nelson of Mass.) said to be of Va. and to have = Rev. Thomas **Teackle**.

14. Dorothy Temple (sister of Mary) = John Alston
15. William Alston = Thomasine Brooke
16. **John Alston** of S.C. = Mrs. Elizabeth Turgis Harris.

Sources: *RA* 5: 134-40 (Nelson, Teackle, Alston, Temple, Lee, Browne), 2: 43-44 (Radcliffe), 5: 32 (Stanley), 3: 370-71 (Hastings), 3: 363-64 (Hungerford), 4: 355-7 (Percy); *TG* 2 (1981): 123-28, and sources cited therein, especially the works of Temple Prime and John Alexander Temple; John A. Upshur, *Upshur Family in Virginia* (1955), pp. 24-25 (Mrs. Teackle); *Lineage Book, Descendants of the Illegitimate Sons and Daughters of the Kings of Britain,* #212 (John Alston of S.C.), and sources cited therein. Sir Thomas Temple, 1st Bt., brother of Mary, was governor of Nova Scotia, lived briefly in Boston, and died unmarried; his two wills are transcribed in Temple Prime, *Some Account of the Temple Family*, 2nd ed. (1894), pp. 61-65. John Nelson, the above nephew, was Sir Thomas's principal heir.

The Royal Descents of 900 Immigrants

1. Edward III, King of England, d. 1377 = Philippa of Hainault
2. John of Gaunt, Duke of Lancaster = Catherine Roët
3. Joan Beaufort = Ralph Neville, 1st Earl of Westmoreland
4. Edward Neville, 1st Baron Abergavenny = Elizabeth Beauchamp, daughter of Richard Beauchamp, 1st Earl of Worcester, and Isabel le Despenser, SETH
5. George Neville, 2nd Baron Abergavenny = Margaret Fenne
6. Elizabeth Neville = Thomas Berkeley
7. Alice Berkeley = George Whetenhall, son of William Whetenhall and Anne Cromer, SETH
8. Thomas Whetenhall = Dorothy Vane
9. Susanna Whetenhall = William Tilghman
10. Oswald Tilghman = Elizabeth Packnam
11. **Richard Tilghman** of Md. = Mary Foxley.

10. Dorothy Tilghman (sister of Oswald) = Thomas St. Nicholas, son of Vincent St. Nicholas and Marion Brockhull, SETH, widow of Thomas Harfleet
11. Dorothy St. Nicholas = Edward Pordage
12. Joshua Pordage = Anne Mellish
13. **George Pordage** of Mass. = Elizabeth Lynde, daughter of Simon Lynde of Mass., ARD, SETH, and Hannah Newgate.

7. Anne Berkeley (sister of Alice) = John Brent
8. Margaret Brent = John Dering
9. Richard Dering = Margaret Twisden
10. Benetta Dering = John Fisher, whose sister Thomasine Fisher married John Epes and was the mother of William, Francis and Peter Epes, all of Va.
11. **John Fisher** of Va. = Elizabeth ―――.

The Royal Descents of 900 Immigrants

Sources: *MG* 2: 444-48 (Richard Tilghman) and sources cited therein, S.F. Tillman, *Spes Alit Agricolam* [Tilghman Family] (1962), pp. 1-2, W. Bruce Bannerman, *Visitations of Kent, 1530-1, 1574 and 1592*, vol. 2 (*HSPVS*, vol. 75, 1924), p. 116 (Whetenhall), *RA* 2: 594 (Berkeley), 1: 320-23 (Neville); *GGE*, pp. 891-92 (wills of Joshua Pordage, naming his "son George of Boston in New England" and of Jerman Major, husband of Deborah St. Nicholas, great-aunt of George Pordage; Major mentions his partner Joshua Pordage and brothers-in-law Thomas and John St. Nicholas), 1110 (will of Rebecca Angell [sister of Anne Mellish above], who mentions "fifty pounds owing me by my brother Joshua Pordage to his son my cousin George Pordage," and brother Henry Mellish); *TG*, new ser., vol. 29 (1913): 36 (Mellish) and *Nichols*, vol. 4, pt. 1, pp. 269-70 (St. Nicholas); *TVG* 38 (1994): 284-89 (John Fisher, by John Anderson Brayton), *AP&P* 4: 1: 954-55, 854-56 (Fisher, Epes), *RA* 2: 594-96 (Berkeley to Fisher), 2: 351-53 (Whetenhall to Fisher). The Pordage descent was developed by John C. Brandon of Columbia, S.C., and first mentioned to me by Leslie Mahler. Margaret Twisden at generation 9 above was the daughter of William Twisden and Elizabeth Roydon, daughter of Thomas Roydon and Elizabeth Whetenhall, SETH.

Note: *LDBR* 5: 847-48 cites research of Francis G. Leeson on Christopher Tilghman of Selling, Kent and Va., husband supposedly of Ruth Devonshire (S.F. Tillman, above, p. 72) and son of Christopher Tilghman (and ——), son of Christopher Tilghman and Anna Sanders, said to be a daughter of John Sanders and Anna Whetenhall, daughter of George Whetenhall and Alice Berkeley above. But the Whetenhall pedigree cited above states that this Anna/Anne Whetenhall married John Code of London, merchant, and Robert Hovenden, ed., *Visitation of Kent, 1619-1621* (*HSPVS*, vol. 42, 1898), pp. 77-78 and *Berry's Kent*, p. 159, give the parents of Anna (Sanders) Tilghman as Edward Sanders (son of Amyas Sanders and —— Austen and grandson of John Sanders) and Anne Prendreth, daughter of Milo Prendreth and Elizabeth Lowin. Elizabeth M. Tillman, *Getting to the Roots of the Family Tree: The Story of a Saxon Family,* 3 vols. (1997), vols. 2 and 3, esp. the chart at the end of vol. 3, opposite p. 1139, considers the immigrant Christopher Tilghman a probable nephew, not grandson, of the Christopher Tilghman who married Anna Sanders.

The Royal Descents of 900 Immigrants

1. Edward III, King of England, d. 1377 = Philippa of Hainault
2. Lionel of Antwerp, Duke of Clarence = Elizabeth de Burgh
3. Philippa Plantagenet = Edmund Mortimer, 3rd Earl of March
4. Elizabeth Mortimer = Sir Henry "Hotspur" Percy
5. Elizabeth Percy = John Clifford, 7th Baron Clifford
6. Thomas Clifford, 8th Baron Clifford = Joan Dacre
7. Elizabeth Clifford = Sir William Plumpton
8. Elizabeth Plumpton = John Sotehill
9. Robert Sotehill = Elizabeth Middleton
10. Henry Southill = Agnes Paver
11. Arthur Southill = Susan Whitfield
12. William Southill = Dorothy ——
13. William Southill = Elizabeth Skelton
14. **Seth Southill** (Soothill, Sothill, Sotehill, Sothel[l], governor of N.C. = (1) —— Foster; (2) Mrs. Anna Willix Riscoe Blount, widow of Robert Riscoe and James Blount of N.C., colonial official and leader in Culpeper's Rebellion, ARD, SETH.

9. Henry Sotehill (brother of Robert) = Joan Empson
10. Elizabeth Sotehill = Sir William Drury, son of Sir Robert Drury and Anne Calthorpe, SETH
11. Robert Drury = Audrey Rich
12. Dorothy Drury = Edward Barnes
13. William Barnes = Thomasine Shepherd
14. **Charles Barnes** of L.I., N.Y. = Mary Hand.

11. Bridget Drury (sister of Robert) = Henry Yelverton
12. Sir William Yelverton, 1st Bt. = Dionysia Stubbs
13. Sir William Yelverton, 2nd Bt. = Ursula Richardson

The Royal Descents of 900 Immigrants

14. Elizabeth Yelverton = Thomas Peyton

15. **Robert Peyton** of Va. = Mary ──.

Sources: Unpublished Sotehill/Southill research by John Anderson Brayton based in part on G.D. Lumb, ed., *The Registers of the Parish Church of Leeds from 1612 to 1639* (Publications of the Thoresby Society, vol. 3, 1895), pp. 199, 254, 373 (birth of Seth, marriage and burial of the younger William), and J.W. Walker, *Yorkshire Pedigrees, G-S* (*HSPVS*, vol. 95, 1943), p. 345 (Soothill; see also William S. Powell, ed., *Dictionary of North Carolina Biography*, vol. 5 [1994], pp. 399-401); *NEHGR* 157 (2004): 321-31 (Craig Stanley Ashley), based in part on *LG 1939* (later *Burke's American Families with British Ancestry*), pp. 2548-49, *NEHGR* 123 (1969): 86-88, A.W. Hughes Clarke and Arthur Campling, eds., *The Visitation of Norfolk, 1664, Volume I, A-L* (*HSPVS*, vol. 85, 1933), p. 3 (for Charles Barnes and his parentage); parish registers of Soham, Cambridgeshire (12 May 1581 baptism of William, son of Edward and Dorothy Barnes, 19 Feb. 1598 or 1599 death of Dorothy Barnes) and Hawstead, Suffolk (25 Aug. 1577 marriage of Edward Barnes and Dorothy Drury), plus W.M. Palmer, *Monumental Inscriptions and Coats of Arms from Cambridgeshire* (1932), pp. 152-53, plate xxvii and key (MIs of Edward and Dorothy Barnes); *SMF1*: 354 and Arthur Campling, *The History of the Family of Drury* (1937), pp. 47-51 esp.; *RA* 4: 372 (Peyton), 5: 444-45 (Yelverton), 2: 472-74 (Drury), 4: 392-93 (Sot[e]hill, Plumpton), 2: 246-47 (Clifford), 4: 355-59 (Percy); *Chester of Chicheley*, vol. 1, pp. 238-43 (Peyton) and Rev. G.H. Dashwood, ed., *Visitation of Norfolk, 1563*, vol. 1 (1878), pp. 267-68 (Yelverton); *PCF Yorkshire* (Plumpton pedigree); *Collins*, vol. 6, pp. 516-17 (Clifford); *CP* (Clifford, Northumberland, March). See also J.A. Brayton, as above, *Order of First Families of North Carolina: Ancestor Biographies*, vol. 1 (2011), pp. 160-61 (Robert Peyton). The *Oxford DNB* says mistakenly that the parentage of Gov. Seth "Sothel" is unknown.

The Royal Descents of 900 Immigrants

1. Edward III, King of England, d. 1377 = Philippa of Hainault
2. Lionel of Antwerp, Duke of Clarence = Elizabeth de Burgh
3. Philippa Plantagenet = Edmund Mortimer, 3rd Earl of March
4. Elizabeth Mortimer = Sir Henry "Hotspur" Percy
5. Henry Percy, 2nd Earl of Northumberland = Eleanor Neville
6. Henry Percy, 3rd Earl of Northumberland = Eleanor Poynings
7. Henry Percy, 4th Earl of Northumberland = Maud Herbert
8. Henry Algernon Percy, 5th Earl of Northumberland = Catherine Spencer
9. Margaret Percy = Henry Clifford, 1st Earl of Cumberland, son of Henry Clifford, 10th Baron Clifford, and Anne St. John, SETH
10. Henry Clifford, 2nd Earl of Cumberland (who = [1] Eleanor Brandon, SETH, granddaughter of Henry VII) = Anne Dacre (his second wife)
11. Frances Clifford = Philip Wharton, 3rd Baron Wharton
12. Frances Wharton = Sir Richard Musgrave, 1st Bt.
13. Sir Philip Musgrave, 2nd Bt. = Juliana Hutton
14. Sir Christopher Musgrave, 4th Bt. = Mary Cogan
15. Philip Musgrave = Mary Legge
16. Sir Christopher Musgrave, 5th Bt. = Julia Chardin
17. Anne Musgrave = Henry Aglionby
18. Mary Aglionby = John Orfeur Yates
19. **John Yates** of Va. = Julia Lovell.

17. Dorothy Musgrave (sister of Anne) = William Wroughton
18. George Wroughton = Diana Elizabeth Denton
19. John Chardin Wroughton = Georgina Grace Chamier
20. Grace Matilda Wroughton = Charles Mayvore Smith
21. Rosa(linde) Zeiman Smith = Howard Edward Jones

The Royal Descents of 900 Immigrants

22. Rosalinde Maud Jones = William John Gartland Craig
23. Timothy John Wroughton Craig = Carol Mary Williams
24. **Daniel (Wroughton) Craig**, b. 1968, actor (in three James Bond films especially), sometime of N.Y.; = (1) Fiona Loudon, actress; (2) Rachel Weisz, actress (who holds both British and U.S. citizenship).

11. Francis Clifford, 4th Earl of Cumberland (brother of Lady Wharton) = Grisold Hughes
12. Frances Clifford = Sir Gervase Clifton, 1st Bt.
13. Sir Clifford Clifton = Frances Finch
14. Catherine Clifton = Sir John Parsons, 2nd Bt.
15. Sir William Parsons, 3rd Bt. = Frances Dutton
16. Grace Parsons = Thomas Lambarde
17. Mary Lambarde = John Hallward
18. John Hallward = Emily Jane Leslie
19. Charles Berners Hallward = Elizabeth Anne Morgan
20. Reginald Francis Hallward = Adelaide Caroline Bloxam
21. **Reginald Michael Bloxam Hallward** of Calif. = Jeannie McDougall, actress under the name Jean Grahame (parents of the actress Gloria Grahame, 1925-1981, born Gloria Hallward, wife of Stanley Clements, film director Nicholas Ray, 1911-1978, Cy Howard, and Anthony Ray [her step-son]).

Sources: *MP*, tables I-II, VIII, X, XII, pp. 1-2, 9, 11, 13, 207 (for Yates), 210, 212-13 (to Rosalinde Zeiman Smith); *Discover Your Ancestors*, no. 4 (Laura Berry on the Chamier-Wroughton-Smith-Jones-Craig ancestry of Daniel Craig, an article noticed by the late Leo van de Pas), and Daniel Craig's entry in Wikipedia; *MP*, tables I-II, VIII, IX, pp. 1-2, 9-10, 137 and Charles Kidd, *Debrett Goes to Hollywood* (1986), pp. 124-28 (for R.M.B. Hallward). See also *RA* 4: 355-62 (Percy). The royal descent of Daniel Craig was posted on soc.gen.medieval by Jim Baker and brought to my attention by John Blythe Dobson of Winnipeg, Manitoba, Canada.

The Royal Descents of 900 Immigrants

1. Edward III, King of England, d. 1377 = Philippa of Hainault
2. Lionel of Antwerp, Duke of Clarence = Elizabeth de Burgh
3. Philippa Plantagenet = Edmund Mortimer, 3rd Earl of March
4. Elizabeth Mortimer = Sir Henry "Hotspur" Percy
5. Elizabeth Percy = John Clifford, 7th Baron Clifford
6. Thomas Clifford, 8th Baron Clifford = Joan Dacre
7. John Clifford, 9th Baron Clifford = Margaret Bromflete
8. Henry Clifford, 10th Baron Clifford = Florence Pudsey
9. Dorothy Clifford = Sir Hugh Lowther
10. Sir Richard Lowther = Frances Middleton
11. Sir Christopher Lowther = Eleanor Musgrave
12. Sir John Lowther = Eleanor Fleming
13. Agnes Lowther = Roger Kirkby
14. William Kirkby = Joanna Furness
15. Eleanor Kirkby = Humphrey Senhouse
16. Bridget Senhouse = John Christian. Their son, Charles Christian, married Anne Dixon and was the father of Fletcher Christian, leader of the mutiny on the *Bounty*.
17. Mary Christian = Edmund Law, Bishop of Carlisle
18. **Thomas Law** (1759-1834), East India Company official, promoter of an American National currency, of Washington, D.C. = Elizabeth Parke Custis, daughter of John Parke Custis and Eleanor Calvert, ARD, SETH.
18. Edward Law, 1st Baron Ellenborough, Lord Chief Justice of the King's Bench and cabinet minister = Anne Towry
19. Edward Law, 1st Earl of Ellenborough, Governor-General of India = (1) Octavia Catherine Stewart; (2) Jane Elizabeth Digby
20. (illegitimate by ——) Ida Catherine Villiers Law = George Blakemore Bayfield John Roberts

The Royal Descents of 900 Immigrants

21. **John St. Clair Roberts**, known as **St. Clair Bayfield**, 1875-1967, actor, a founder of Actors' Equity, and longtime common-law husband of music patron (and notorious operatic soprano) (Mrs.) (Narcissa) Florence Foster Jenkins (1868-1944), subject of the film *Florence Foster Jenkins* (2016; Bayfield was played by actor Hugh John Mungo Grant, ARD, SETH) = Kathleen Weatherley.

13. Sir John Lowther, 1st Bt. (brother of Agnes) = Mary Fletcher

14. Eleanor Lowther = Sir Christopher Wandesford, 1st Bt.

15. Frances Wandesford = Robert Maude

16. Anthony Maude = Alice Hartstonge

17. Anne Maude = Jerome Ryves, Dean of St. Patrick's

18. Alice Ryves = Thomas Le Hunte

19. Anne Le Hunte = Abraham Symes

20. Anne Symes = Henry Mahon

21. **George Charles Mahon** of Mich. = Sarah L'Estrange of Mich., ARD, SETH.

Sources: *Oxford DNB* (Thomas Law—not in *DAB* or *ANB*), and *BP* (Ellenborough), *Oxford DNB* for the 1st Earl of Ellenborough, Susan Law, *Through the Keyhole: Sex, Scandal, and the Secret Life of the Country House* (2015), *passim*, 8 June 1869 marriage license of George B.B.J. Roberts and Ida C.V. Law, and Wikipedia entries for the Earl of Ellenborough, St. Clair Bayfield, and Mrs. Jenkins; *BLG*, 18th ed., vol. 2 (1969), pp. 98-99 (Christian) and 11th ed. (1906), p. 1502 (Senhouse); John Corry, *History of Lancashire*, vol. 1 (1825), pp. 412-21, esp. 418-19 (Kirkby); Hugh Owen, *The Lowther Family* (1990), charts on pp. 9, 60, 65, 167-68 esp.; George C. Mahon, "Family History of Mahon of Castlegar, County of Galway, Ireland" (typescript, 1889) and further notes and data gathered by his granddaughter, Mrs. Dean Gooderham Acheson (Alice Caroline Stanley, wife of the U.S. Secretary of State and daughter of Louis Crandall Stanley and Jane Caroline Mahon) and by his great-granddaughter, the late Helen Jefferson Sanford, former trustee of

NEHGS; *BP* (Mahon of Castlegar, baronets; Hawarden [for Maudes], Lonsdale [for Lowthers]), and John O'Hart, *Irish Pedigrees*, 5th ed., vol. 1 (1892, reprint 1976), pp. 578-79 (Mahon); *CP* (Clifford, Northumberland, March), and *CB* (Wandesford of Kirklington, Lowther of Lowther); *Collins*, vol. 6, pp. 516-21 (Clifford) and *Lodge*, vol. 7, pp. 277-78 (Maude, Ryves); *BLG* 4th ed. (1863), p. 856 (Le Hunte). See also *RA* 2: 246-49 (Clifford), 4: 355-57 (Percy). The Thomas Law descent was brought to my attention by John C. Brandon of Columbia, S.C., and the St. Clair Bayfield descent by Julie Helen Otto. Generations 16-18 of the Thomas Law line demonstrate a surprising lateral connection—a step-granddaughter of George Washington married to a first cousin of *Bounty* mutineer Fletcher Christian.

The Royal Descents of 900 Immigrants

1. Edward III, King of England, d. 1377 = Philippa of Hainault
2. John of Gaunt, Duke of Lancaster = Catherine Roët
3. Joan Beaufort = Sir Robert Ferrers
4. Elizabeth Ferrers = John de Greystock, 4th Baron Greystock
5. Ralph de Greystock, 5th Baron Greystock = Elizabeth FitzHugh
6. Margery de Greystock = Sir Thomas Grey
7. Sir Ralph Grey = Elizabeth ——
8. Mary Grey = John Fenwick, son of Ralph Fenwick and Margery Mitford, SETH
9. Ralph Fenwick = Barbara Ogle
10. Richard Fenwick = Margaret Mills
11. William Fenwick = Elizabeth Gargrave
12. **John Fenwick** (1618-1683), colonist, founder of Salem, N.J. = (1) Elizabeth Covert, ARD, SETH; (2) Mary Marten, sister of the younger Sir Henry Marten, regicide.
12. Edward Fenwick = Sarah Neville
13. Robert Fenwick = Anne Culcheth. Another son, Robert Fenwick, also immigrated to S.C., was a colony assemblyman, and married Sarah Patey, but died without issue.
14. **John Fenwick** of S.C. = Elizabeth Gibbes, daughter of Robert Gibbes, gov. of S.C., ARD, SETH, and —— Davis.

14. Dorothy Fenwick (sister of John of S.C.) = Robert Golightly
15. **Culcheth Golightly** of S.C. = Mrs. Mary Butler Elliott.

12. Priscilla Fenwick (sister of John of N.J. and of Edward) = Roland Nevet
13. Elizabeth Nevet = Roger Eddowes
14. Ralph Eddowes = Eleanor Carter

The Royal Descents of 900 Immigrants

15. John Eddowes = Catherine Moulson
16. **Ralph Eddowes** of Pa. = Sarah Kenrick of Pa., ARD, SETH.

Sources: *RA* 2: 558-59 (two John Fenwicks and Mrs. Nevet), 3: 111-12 (Grey, Gray); 3: 138-40 (Greystock), 5: 340-41 (Ferrers); *DAB* (John Fenwick of N.J.), *MCS5,* line 65, and *SCG* 2: 188-91 (John Fenwick of S.C., who named nephew Culcheth Golightly in his 1745/6 will); *TCWAAS* 81 (1981): 38 (D. Fenwick and R. Golightly), PRs of St. Nicholas, Newcastle-upon-Tyne (7 Nov. 1706 baptism of Culcheth Golightly) and W.B. Edgar and N. Louise Bailey, *Biographical Directory of the South Carolina House of Representatives*, vol. 2 (1977), pp. 244-45 (John and Robert Fenwick), 286-87 (Culcheth Golightly), John Hodgson, *A History of Northumberland*, Part II, vol. 2 (1832), p. 113 (Fenwick), *NHN,* vol. 12, chart opp. p. 328 (Grey), J.W. Clay, *The Extinct and Dormant Peerages of the Northern Counties of England* (1913), pp. 97-98 (Greystock) and *AR8,* lines 62, 2, 1; *FMG,* vol. 1, pp. 109-13 (Eddowes) and unpublished research by John Insley Coddington (whose manuscript collection is now at NEHGS) showing that his ancestor, Elizabeth Nevet, wife of Roger Eddowes, was a daughter of Rev. Roland Nevet, d. 1675, rector of Stanton-on-Hine Heath and Oswestry, Shropshire, and Priscilla Fenwick, sister of John Fenwick of N.J. (for Ralph Eddowes).

Culcheth Golightly of S.C. was kindly brought to our attention by John C. Brandon of Columbia, S.C., but after charts of the immigrant descendants of King Edward III, d. 1377, had been indexed. Golightly is included on this chart largely because he was a nephew, not a more distant relative, of another immigrant of royal descent (his uncle, John Fenwick of S.C.). Immigrants treated in the section near this book's end, covering those "Whose Royal Descents or Improved Royal Descents were Received or Developed after Completion of this Volume's Index" (pp. 889-915) are not very nearly related to immigrants treated in the main body of this text. In its correct order, this chart would follow that for John Harleston and Mrs. Elizabeth Harleston Ball, both of S.C., Lady Susan Felton Harbord Howard (wife secondly of Francis Howard, 5th Baron Howard of Effingham, colonial governor of Va.), and Robert Wright, Chief Justice of S.C.

The Royal Descents of 900 Immigrants

1. Edward III, King of England, d. 1377 = Philippa of Hainault
2. John of Gaunt, Duke of Lancaster = Catherine Roët
3. Joan Beaufort = Ralph Neville, 1st Earl of Westmoreland
4. Richard Neville, 1st Earl of Salisbury = Alice Montagu
5. Alice Neville = Henry FitzHugh, 5th Baron FitzHugh
6. Elizabeth FitzHugh = Sir William Parr
7. William Parr, 1st Baron Parr = Mary Salisbury
8. Maud Parr = Sir Ralph Lane
9. **Sir Ralph Lane** (c. 1530-1603), Virginia colonist (commander of the Roanoke Island settlement 1585-86), d. unm.

9. Dorothy Lane (sister of Sir Ralph) = Sir William Feilding
10. Basil Feilding = Elizabeth Aston, daughter of Sir Walter Aston (and Elizabeth Leveson), son of Sir Edward Aston and Joan Bowles, SETH
11. William Feilding, 1st Earl of Denbigh = Susan Villiers
12. George Feilding, 1st Earl of Desmond = Bridget Stanhope
13. John Fielding = Bridget Cokayne
14. Edmund Fielding = Sarah Gould
15. Henry Fielding, the novelist = Charlotte Craddock
16. **Henrietta Fielding** = James Gabriel **Montrésor** (1702-1776), British military engineer who served in the American colonies from 1754 to 1760 (father by Mary Haswell, his first wife, of John Montrésor, also a British military engineer who served in the American colonies, who married Frances Tucker of N.Y., ARD, SETH).

8. Elizabeth Parr (sister of Maud) = Sir Nicholas Woodhull
9. Anne Woodhull = Richard Burnaby
10. Thomas Burnaby = Elizabeth Sapcotts

The Royal Descents of 900 Immigrants

11. Susan Burnaby = Stephen Agard, son of Ambrose Agard (and ——), son of Stephen Agard and Elizabeth Raynsford, SETH

12. Katherine Agard = Josias Bull, son of William Bull and Sarah Nowell, daughter of Laurence Nowell, Dean of Lichfield, and Mary ——, SETH

13. **Stephen Bull** of S.C. = ——. A brother, Burnaby Bull, also came to S.C., married, and left issue but no NDTPS. Their sister Mary Bull, wife of Jeremiah Webb, John Limbrey, and John Quinten, immigrated to S.C. after the death of her second husband, but also left no NDTPS.

Sources: *Oxford DNB* (Sir Ralph Lane and J.G. Montrésor), *RA* 4: 306-9 (Bull, Burney, Woodhull, Parr), 2: 632-34 (Fitz Hugh), 4: 124-26 (Neville), *BP* (Denbigh), *TAG* 52 (1976):15-17 (Parr, Woodhull) and *Stephen Bull* pp. 2-11, 92-94 esp.; W.C. Metcalfe, ed., *Visitations of Northamptonshire, 1564 and 1618-19* (1887), pp. 165 (Agard), 172 (Burnaby), and *Lincolnshire Pedigrees*, p. 853 (Sapcotts).

Henry FitzHugh, 5th Baron FitzHugh at generation 5 above and his sister Elizabeth FitzHugh (wife of Ralph de Greystock, 5th Baron Greystock) at generation 5 on the immediately preceding chart (p. 366) were both children of William FitzHugh, 4th Baron FitzHugh, and Margery Willoughby, SETH.

The Royal Descents of 900 Immigrants

1. Edward III, King of England, d. 1377 = Philippa of Hainault
2. John of Gaunt, Duke of Lancaster = Catherine Roët
3. Joan Beaufort = Ralph Neville, 1st Earl of Westmoreland
4. Richard Neville, 1st Earl of Salisbury = Alice Montagu
5. Catherine Neville = William Bonville, Baron Harington and Bonville
6. Cecily Bonville, Baroness Harington and Bonville = Thomas Grey, 1st Marquess of Dorset, son of Sir John Grey and Elizabeth Woodville, later Queen of Edward IV, King of England
7. Cecily Grey = John Sutton alias Dudley, 3rd Baron Dudley, son of Edward Sutton alias Dudley, 2nd Baron Dudley, and Cecily Willoughby, daughter of Sir William Willoughby and Joan Strangeways, daughter of Sir Thomas Strangeways and Catherine Neville, daughter of 3 above.
8. Henry Dudley = —— Ashton
9. Roger Dudley (parentage likely but not fully proved) = Susanna Thorne, see below
10. **Thomas Dudley** (1576-1653), colonial governor of Mass. = (1) Dorothy Yorke; (2) Mrs. Katherine Deighton Hackburne, ARD, SETH.
11. (by 1) Anne Dudley, known as Mrs. Anne Bradstreet, poet = Simon Bradstreet, Governor of Mass.
12. Dudley Bradstreet = Anne Wood
13. Margaret Bradstreet = Job Tyler
14. Hannah Tyler = John Spofford (IV)
15. Phoebe Spofford = John Grout, Jr.
16. Phoebe Grout = Jacob Winn (III)
17. Endymia Winn = Thomas Sherwood
18. Lucinda Sherwood = John Minthorn
19. Theodore Minthorn = Mary Wasley

The Royal Descents of 900 Immigrants

20. Hulda Randall Minthorn = Jesse Clark Hoover
21. Herbert Clark Hoover (1874-1964), 31st U.S. President = Lou Henry

16. Patience Dudley (sister of Anne) = Daniel Denison
17. Elizabeth Denison = John Rogers, sixth President of Harvard College
18. Daniel Rogers = Sarah Appleton, daughter of John Appleton, SETH (and Priscilla Glover), son of Samuel and Judith (Everard) Appleton, both ARD, SETH
19. Priscilla Rogers = Nathaniel Leonard
20. Sarah Leonard = Joseph LeBaron
21. Sarah LeBaron = William Hazen, Loyalist, New Brunswick official and businessman
22. Frances Amelia Hazen = Charles Vallancy Drury. Their son, Ward Chipman Drury, was the father (by Charlotte Augusta Hayne) of Charles William Drury, British army officer, father (by Mary Louise Henderson) of Gladys Henderson Drury, wife of William Maxwell Aitken, 1st Baron Beaverbrook, the British and Canadian financier and newspaper publisher, public official and member of Churchill's war cabinet. Janet Gladys Aitken, daughter of these last, married Ian Douglas Campbell, 11th Duke of Argyll, SETH, and was the mother of Lady Jeanne Louise Campbell Mailer Cram, SETH, third wife of American novelist Norman Mailer.
23. LeBaron Drury = Elizabeth Sophia Poyntz
24. **Anna Maria Drury** of N.Y. = Henry Green **Atwater**. Their daughter, Margaret Atwater, married Frederick Augustus Preston and was the mother of Frederick Willard Preston, noted surgeon and medical writer, who married Gertrude Eldred Bradford and Barbara Gay Hess.

Sources: *PIA*: 279-81 (Dudley), *RA* 5: 106-7 (Sutton alias Dudley), 3: 161-64 (Grey), 1: 436 (Bonville), 4: 124-26 (Neville), 5: 364-66 (Willoughby),

The Royal Descents of 900 Immigrants

4: 192-95 (Strangeways), 4: 233-37 (Neville); research of David Humiston Kelley and Marshall Kenneth Kirk, as reported in "The Filiation of Capt. Roger Dudley: A Terse Summary of Points Made in Marshall K. Kirk's Talk, 20 Nov. 1993"; *CP* (Dudley, Dorset, Bonville, Harington, Salisbury, Westmoreland, Berkeley [for Joan Strangeways, wife of Sir William Willoughby and William Berkeley, 1st Marquess of Berkeley]); *AR8*, lines 2, 207, 78, *MCS5*, lines 161, 45, 94. For Mrs. Atwater, see *WWWA*, vol. 12, *1996-1998* (1998), p. 199 (F.W. Preston), C.H. Attwater, *Atwater History and Genealogy*, vol. 5 (1956), pp. 195, 237, *BLG*, 18th ed., vol. 2 (1969), pp. 165-66 (Drury) and *BP* (Beaverbrook, Argyll); T.E. Hazen, *The Hazen Family in America* (1947), pp. 93-94, 185-86 and Watson, *Thomas Dudley* (2004), pp. 1-3, 7-8, 23-24, 74-75, 246-47 (to Sarah Leonard) and *Samuel Appleton* (2007), pp. 1-2, 4-5, 15-16, 51-52, 203-4 (to Mrs. Hazen). As the parentage of Roger Dudley remains unproved (Brandon Fradd plans a monograph; Douglas Richardson has dropped the Roger Dudley descent from his 2011 and 2013 compendia), the best royal descent of Gov. Thomas Dudley through his mother, Susanna Thorne, is outlined below.

1. John "Lackland," King of England, d. 1216 = (2) Isabel of Angoulême
2. (illegitimate by —— de Warenne) Richard FitzRoy = Rohese of Dover
3. Lorette de Dover = Sir William Marmion
4. John Marmion, 1st Baron Marmion = Isabel ——
5. John Marmion, 2nd Baron Marmion = Maud Furnival
6. Avice Marmion = John Grey, 1st Baron Grey of Rotherfield
7. Maud Grey = Sir Thomas Harcourt
8. Sir Thomas Harcourt = Jane Franceys
9. Sir Richard Harcourt = Edith St. Clair
10. Alice Harcourt = William Bessiles
11. Elizabeth Bessiles = Richard Fettiplace

12. Anne Fettiplace = Edward Purefoy, for whose descent from Amy de Gaveston, via Morton, Malory, and Driby see *RA* 2: 474-76, 4: 453-54.

13. Mary Purefoy = Thomas Thorne

14. Susanna Thorne = Roger Dudley, see above

15. **Thomas Dudley** (1576-1653), colonial governor of Mass. = (1) Dorothy Yorke; (2) Mrs. Katherine Deighton Hackburne, ARD, SETH.

Sources: *RA* 2: 476-77 (Dudley, Thorne, Purefoy), 1: 353-54 (Bessiles), 5: 386-87 (Harcourt), 3: 206-11 (Harcourt), 1: 460 (Grey), 4:274-76 (Grey), 4: 31-33 (Marmion), 1: 184-85 (Dover), *AR8*, lines 50, 30, 219, 218, and sources cited therein.

Sir Thomas Harcourt at generation 7 above was a son of Sir William Harcourt (and Joan Grey), son of Sir John Harcourt and Ellen la Zouche, SETH.

The Royal Descents of 900 Immigrants

1. Edward III, King of England, d. 1377 = Philippa of Hainault
2. Lionel of Antwerp, Duke of Clarence = Elizabeth de Burgh
3. Philippa Plantagenet = Edmund Mortimer, 3rd Earl of March
4. Elizabeth Mortimer = Sir Henry "Hotspur" Percy
5. Henry Percy, 2nd Earl of Northumberland = Eleanor Neville
6. Henry Percy, 3rd Earl of Northumberland = Eleanor Poynings
7. Margaret Percy = Sir William Gascoigne
8. Dorothy Gascoigne = Sir Ninian Markenfield
9. Alice Markenfield = Robert Mauleverer
10. Dorothy Mauleverer = John Kaye
11. Robert Kaye = Anne Flower
12. Grace Kaye = Sir Richard Saltonstall, a founder of the Massachusetts Bay Colony. Five further children – sons Robert, Samuel and Henry, and daughters Rosamond and Grace – also immigrated to Mass. with their father, but either died unmarried or returned with Sir Richard to England.
13. **Richard Saltonstall** (c. 1610-1694) of Mass., colonial official = Muriel Gurdon of Mass., ARD, SETH.

10. Sir Edmund Mauleverer (brother of Dorothy) = Mary Danby
11. William Mauleverer = Eleanor Aldeborough
12. James Mauleverer = Beatrice Hutton
13. Edmund Mauleverer = Anne Pearson
14. **Anne Mauleverer** of N.J. = John **Abbott**.

Sources: *RA* 4: 550-52 (Saltonstall), 4: 62-65 (Mauleverer, to Mrs. Abbott, Markenfield), 3: 79-80 (Gascoigne), 4: 355-60 (Percy); *AR8*, lines 3, 19, 5, Scott C. Steward, *The Descendants of Dr. Nathaniel Saltonstall of Haverhill, Massachusetts* (2013), pp. 23-49, *Saltonstall*, pp. 7-8, 12-13, first chart opp. p. 84 (Kaye), *PCF Yorkshire* (Mauleverer and Gascoigne pedigrees), C.B. Norcliffe, ed., *Visitation of Yorkshire, 1563-64* (*HSPVS*, vol. 16, 1881), p. 197 (Markenfield) and *MP*, charts I-II, XXX, pp. 1-2, 33; *TAG* 69 (1994): 160-64 (Col. Charles M. Hansen), *Yorkshire Archaeological Journal* 16 (1902): 196-203 (Mauleverer) and sources cited therein (Mrs. Abbott).

The Royal Descents of 900 Immigrants

1. Edward III, King of England, d. 1377 = Philippa of Hainault
2. John of Gaunt, Duke of Lancaster = Catherine Roët
3. Henry Beaufort, Cardinal Beaufort
4. (illegitimate allegedly, but probably not, by Alice FitzAlan, who = John Cherleton, 4th Baron Cherleton of Powis) Jane Beaufort = Sir Edward Stradling
5. Sir Henry Stradling = Elizabeth Herbert
6. Thomas Stradling = Janet Mathew
7. Jane Stradling = Sir William Griffith
8. Dorothy Griffith = William Williams
9. Jane Williams = William Coytmore
10. Rowland Coytmore = Mrs. Katherine Myles Gray of Mass. Their son, Thomas Coytmore, also immigrated to Mass. and married Martha Rainsborough, but left no surviving descendants.
11. **Elizabeth Coytmore** of Mass. = William **Tyng**.
12. Anna Tyng = Thomas Shepard, Jr.
13. Anna Shepard = Daniel Quincy
14. John Quincy = Elizabeth Norton
15. Elizabeth Quincy = William Smith, Jr.
16. Abigail Smith = John Adams, Jr. (1735-1826), 2nd U.S. President
17. John Quincy Adams (1767-1848), 6th U.S. President = Louisa Catherine Johnson

13. Thomas Shepard (III) (brother of Anna) = Mary Anderson
14. Anna Shepard = Henry Smith
15. William Henry Smith = Margaret Lloyd
16. Rebecca Smith = John Aspinwall

The Royal Descents of 900 Immigrants

17. John Aspinwall, Jr. = Susan Howland
18. Mary Rebecca Aspinwall = Isaac Roosevelt
19. James Roosevelt = Sara Delano
20. Franklin Delano Roosevelt (1882-1945), 32nd U.S. President = (Anna) Eleanor Roosevelt

10. Alice Coytmore (sister of Rowland) = Hugh Wynne
11. William Wynne = ──
12. Sarah Wynne = Archibald Hamilton
13. Sarah Hamilton = John Kenrick
14. John Kenrick = Mary Quarrell
15. **Sarah Kenrick** of Pa. = Ralph **Eddowes** of Pa., ARD, SETH. John Kenrick, brother of Mrs. Eddowes and an American resident for about three years, married Sarah Savage and left two sons, Samuel Savage Kenrick and Edward Kenrick, who settled in Hillsdale, Mich., but probably left no NDTPS.

Sources: *RA* 2: 345-47 (Tyng, Coytmore, Williams, Griffith), 5: 52-57 (Stradling, Beaufort); *AR8*, lines 199, 199A, 234; *MCS5*, lines 103, 104; *TAG* 32 (1956): 9-23 (reprinted in *JIC* 136-49, entire line), 24 (1948): 219-22.

The Royal Descents of 900 Immigrants

1. Edward III, King of England, d. 1377 = Philippa of Hainault
2. Edmund of Langley, 1st Duke of York = Isabel of Castile
3. Constance Plantagenet = Thomas le Despencer, 1st Earl of Gloucester
4. (illegitimate by Edmund Holand, 4th Earl of Kent) Eleanor Holand = James Touchet, 2nd Baron Audley
5. Margaret Touchet (or Audley) = (1) Sir Roger Vaughan; (2) Richard Grey, Baron Grey of Powis, son of Henry Grey, 2nd Earl of Tankerville, and Antigone Plantagenet, SETH
6. Elizabeth Vaughan or Grey (but see note below) = Sir John Ludlow
7. Anne Ludlow = Thomas Vernon, son of Sir Henry Vernon and Anne Talbot, SETH
8. Eleanor Vernon = Francis Curzon
9. George Curzon = ──
10. Francis Curzon = Isabel Symonds
11. Samuel Curzon = Elizabeth Stevens
12. Samuel Curson = Susanna ──
13. Samuel Curson = Rebecca Clark
14. **Richard Curson** of Md. = Elizabeth Becker.

9. John Curzon (brother of George) = Millicent Sacheverell
10. Eleanor Curzon = Richard Boothby
11. Richard Boothby = Grisel Halford
12. Thomas Boothby = Susanna ──
13. Benjamin Boothby = ── ──
14. William Boothby = Martha Hobson
15. William Boothby = Anne Brownell
16. James Brownell Boothby = Charlotte Cunningham

17. Elizabeth Caroline Boothby = Edmund Burke Roche, 1ˢᵗ Baron Fermoy

18. James Boothby Burke Roche, 3ʳᵈ Baron Fermoy = Frances Eleanor (Ellen) Work, SETH. Their son, Edmund Maurice Burke Roche, 4ᵗʰ Baron Fermoy, born in England but raised in the U.S., returned to England in 1920, married Ruth Sylvia Gill, and was the maternal grandfather of the late Diana, Princess of Wales, SETH.

19. **Hon. Cynthia Burke Roche** of Newport, R.I. = (1) Arthur Scott **Burden**, (2) Guy Fairfax **Cary**. Her daughter by (1), Eileen Burden, married (1) Walter Maynard and (2) Thomas Robins, Jr., and left a daughter by (1), Sheila Maynard, who married Nicholas Platt, diplomat, and is the mother of actor Oliver Platt.

Sources: J. Hall Pleasants, *The Curzon Family of New York and Baltimore* (1919), pp. 11-41 and chart opp. pp. 51 esp.; *Diana 12G*, pp. 9, 13, 18-19, 27, 39, 58, 92, 144, 214, 328, 285, 339-40, 342, 349, 356, 368, 413-14 (generations 8-18 in line of Mrs. Cary); *Collins*, vol. 7, pp. 401-3 (Vernon); *CP* (Grey of Powis, Audley and Kent, esp. vol. 6, appendix C, pp. 697-701); *AACPW*, pp. 92-95, and *BP* (Fermoy, Boothby, Scarsdale). See also *TAG* 74 (1999): 105-11, 189-92 and *RA* 5: 197-99 (Touchet), 3: 436-37 (Holand).

Although the matter is not covered in *RA*, Douglas Richardson reports that the identity of Elizabeth, wife of Sir John Ludlow, has been resolved; she was a Grey, daughter of Richard Grey, Baron Grey of Powis and Margaret Touchet or Audley (a Grey-Ludlow monograph is eagerly awaited) and so a great-great-granddaughter of Henry IV, King of England, and Mary Bohun. If this solution is correct, then this chart should follow that for Dep. Gov. Thomas Lloyd, Mrs. Anne Lloyd Braithwaite Thomas, and Mrs. Anne Elizabeth Wilson Gergen.

The Royal Descents of 900 Immigrants

1. Edward III, King of England, d. 1377 = Philippa of Hainault
2. Lionel of Antwerp, Duke of Clarence = Elizabeth de Burgh
3. Philippa Plantagenet = Edmund Mortimer, 3rd Earl of March
4. Elizabeth Mortimer = Sir Henry "Hotspur" Percy
5. Henry Percy, 2nd Earl of Northumberland = Eleanor Neville
6. Henry Percy, 3rd Earl of Northumberland = Eleanor Poynings
7. Margaret Percy = Sir William Gascoigne
8. Agnes Gascoigne = Sir Thomas Fairfax
9. William Fairfax = ——
10. John Fairfax = Mary Birch
11. Benjamin Fairfax = Sarah Galliard
12. Benjamin Fairfax = Bridget Springer
13. Sarah Fairfax = John Meadows (see *Oxford DNB*)
14. Philip Meadows = Margaret Hall
15. Sarah Meadows = David Martineau
16. Thomas Martineau = Elizabeth Rankin
17. **Harriet Martineau** (1802-1876), sometime traveler in the U.S., author of *Society in America*, 3 vols. (1837) and *Retrospect of Western Travel*, 2 vols. (1838), d. unm.
17. Elizabeth Martineau = Thomas Michael Greenhow
18. Frances Elizabeth Greenhow, known as Frances Lupton, advocate for women's education (see *Oxford DNB*) = Francis Lupton
19. Francis Martineau Lupton = Harriet Albina Davis
20. Olive Christiana Lupton = Richard Noel Middleton
21. Peter Francis Middleton = Valerie Glassborow
22. Michael Francis Middleton = Carole Elizabeth Goldsmith

The Royal Descents of 900 Immigrants

23. Catherine Elizabeth "Kate" Middleton, now H.R.H. The Duchess of Cambridge, b. 1982 = 2011 H.R.H. Prince William Arthur Philip Louis of Great Britain, Duke of Cambridge, b. 1982, son of H.R.H. Prince Charles Philip Arthur George of Great Britain, Prince of Wales, and Lady Diana Frances Spencer, later Diana, Princess of Wales, both SETH. A son, Prince George Alexander Louis of Cambridge, was b. 2013; a daughter, Princess Charlotte Elizabeth Diana of Cambridge, was b. 2015.

16. Peter Finch Martineau (brother of Thomas) = Catherine Marsh

17. Edward Martineau = Eleanor Rogers

18. William Martineau = Margaretta Sarah Mason

19. Edith Jane Martineau = Vivian Guy Ouseley McLaughlin, SETH (great-grandparents of filmmaker Guy Stuart Ritchie, husband of rock star and actress Madonna [Louise Victoria Ciccone], SETH)

16. John Martineau (brother of Thomas and Peter Finch Martineau) = Marriot Margaret Bunny

17. Philip Martineau = Elizabeth Frances Batty

18. Hubert Martineau = Elizabeth Mary Alston

19. Sir Philip Hubert Martineau = Alice Margaret Vaughan Williams

20. Hubert Melville Martineau = Mrs. Maud Morris Schwab of Chicago

21. **Jeanne Maud Martineau** of N.Y. = (1) Derek **Grewcock**; (2) John Thomas **Cahill** (1903-1966), lawyer.

W.A. Reitwiesner, C.C. Child and S.C. Steward, *The Ancestry of Catherine Middleton* (2011), esp. pp. 3, 5, 7, 9, 11, 15-16, 22-23, 31-33, 38, 45, 49-50, 54, 58-59, 61, 63, 116-17, 121, 124, 127-28, 131-32, 134, 136-40, which cites Edgar Taylor, *The Suffolk Bartholomeans* (1840), *passim* (Meadows, Fairfax), *FMG*, vol. 3, pp. 1130 (Meadows), 1107-8

(Martineau), *BLG*, 18th ed., vol. 3 (1972), pp. 618-21 (Martineau), F.M. Lupton, *Descendants of Charles Hobbs, 1596-1700* (1914), p. 165 (F.M. and O.C. Lupton) and C.A. Lupton, *The Lupton Family in Leeds* (1965), pp. 44, 64-66, 72-74, 84-88, 92-97 and chart at end (to M.F. Middleton). See also *PCF Yorkshire* (Fairfax pedigree, to Benjamin Fairfax, husband of Bridget Springer), *WWWA*, vol. 4, *1961-1968* (1968), p. 146 (J.T. Cahill), and Claudia Joseph, *Kate: Kate Middleton, Princess in Waiting* (2009), esp. chapters 7, 8, 10-12, pp. 68-84, 105-29 (Lupton, Middleton), 270-71 (chart). For the "ejected minister" near kin of Sarah (Fairfax) Meadows, see *Oxford DNB*, under John Meadows (1622-1697), John Fairfax (1623/4-1700) and Nathaniel Fairfax (1637-1690), the last also a noted physician, author, and antiquary. For the middle part of the Fairfax pedigree see *GM* 30 (2010-12): 407-11, 31 (2013-15): 156 (Anthony Adolph). For a second royal descent of The Duchess of Cambridge, via Conyers of Horden, Durham, baronets (and Blakiston, Bowes, Eure, Lambton and Lumley, all SETH) see *American Ancestors* 12 (2011), 4: 35-36.

The Royal Descents of 900 Immigrants

1. Edward III, King of England, d. 1377 = Philippa of Hainault
2. John of Gaunt, Duke of Lancaster = Catherine Roët
3. Henry Beaufort, Cardinal Beaufort
4. (illegitimate, allegedly, but probably not, by Alice FitzAlan, who = John Cherleton, 4th Baron Cherleton of Powis) Jane Beaufort = Sir Edward Stradling
5. Sir Henry Stradling = Elizabeth Herbert
6. Thomas Stradling = Janet Mathew
7. Jane Stradling = Sir William Griffith
8. Edward Griffith = Jane Puleston
9. Eleanor Griffith = Sir Nicholas Bagenall
10. Anne Bagenall = Sir Dudley Loftus
11. Nicholas Loftus = Margaret Chetham
12. Sir Nicholas Loftus = Eleanor Butler, daughter of Sir Edmund Butler, 2nd Bt. (and Juliana Hyde), son of Sir Thomas Butler, 1st Bt. (and Anne Colclough), illegitimate (by ——) son of Sir Edmund Butler (= Eleanor Eustace), son of James Butler, 9th Earl of Ormonde (and Joan FitzGerald), son of Piers Butler, 8th Earl of Ormonde and Margaret FitzGerald, SETH
13. Eleanor Loftus = James Butler, son of Sir Thomas Butler, 3rd Bt. (and Jane Boyle), son of Sir Edmund Butler, 2nd Bt., and Juliana Hyde, above
14. Sir Richard Butler, 5th Bt. = Henrietta Percy
15. **Pierce Butler** (1744-1822) of S.C., planter, legislator, one of the first two U.S. senators from S.C. = Mary Middleton, daughter of Thomas Middleton and Mary Bull, daughter of John Bull (and Mary Branford), son of Stephen Bull of S.C., ARD, SETH, and ——). Sarah Butler, daughter of Pierce Butler of S.C. and Mary Middleton, married James Mease and left a son, Pierce Butler (Mease, used mother's surname), who married Frances Anne (Fanny) Kemble, the actress. Sarah Butler, a daughter of these last, married Owen Jones Wister and was the mother of Owen Wister (1860-1938), "cowboy" novelist, author of *The*

The Royal Descents of 900 Immigrants

Virginian (see *NK2*: 197, 200), who married Mary Channing Wister, a cousin.

11. Sir Adam Loftus (brother of Nicholas) = Jane Vaughan
12. Sarah Loftus = Sir Thomas Dancer, 1st Bt.
13. Sir Loftus Dancer, 3rd Bt. = Catherine Amyrold
14. Sir Thomas Dancer, 4th Bt. = Anchoretta Rogers
15. Charity Dancer = Samuel Eyre
16. Anchoretta Eyre = Richard Eyre, a cousin
17. John Eyre = Jane Purefoy
18. Richard Eyre = Eleanor Baldwin
19. Philip Homan Eyre = Lucy Catherine Louisa Clarke
20. Hastings Elles John Eyre = Joan White
21. Richard Galfridus Hastings Giles Eyre = Minna Mary Jessica Royds
22. **Sir Richard (Charles Hastings) Eyre**, b. 1943, sometime of N.Y., British television and film director/producer, who also directed on Broadway and at the Metropolitan Opera in New York City = Susan Elizabeth Birtwistle, British television and film director/producer.

Sources: *DAB* (Pierce Butler), *SCG3*: 155 (Middleton, Butler), *BP* and *CB* (Butler of Cloughgrenan), *Lodge*, vol. 7, pp. 265-66 (Loftus), *BP* and *CP* (Ely, for Loftus; Ormonde); *BP* 2003, p. 1367 (Sir Richard Eyre), *BLG*, 18th ed., vol. 1 (1965), p. 614 (Royds), *BLGI* 1912, p. 212 (Eyre), *CB* (Dancer), *BIFR*, p. 45 (Bagenall), *PACF*, pp. 56-57, *RA* 5: 52-57 (Stradling, Beaufort), 2: 345-46 (Griffith, which, however, omits the above Edward Griffith at generation 8).

The Royal Descents of 900 Immigrants

1. Edward III, King of England, d. 1377 = Philippa of Hainault
2. Lionel of Antwerp, Duke of Clarence = Elizabeth de Burgh
3. Philippa Plantagenet = Edmund Mortimer, 3rd Earl of March
4. Elizabeth Mortimer = Sir Henry "Hotspur" Percy
5. Elizabeth Percy = John Clifford, 7th Baron Clifford
6. Thomas Clifford, 8th Baron Clifford = Joan Dacre
7. John Clifford, 9th Baron Clifford = Margaret Bromflete
8. Henry Clifford, 10th Baron Clifford = Anne St. John
9. Anne Clifford = Ralph Melford
10. Thomas Melford = Dionise ——
11. Mary Melford = Humphrey Need
12. Humphrey Need = Dorothy ——.
13. Nathaniel Need = Anne ——. Their daughter, Mary Need of Pa., married Edmund Cartledge and left issue but no NDTPS.
14. **Joseph Need** of Pa. = Rebecca ——.

13. Mary Need (sister of Nathaniel) = Christopher Levis. Their daughters Sarah and Hannah Levis also immigrated to Pa. and married respectively Thomas Bradshaw and Michael Blunston. Hannah apparently died without issue; Sarah left issue but no NDTPS.
14. **Samuel Levis** of Pa. = Elizabeth Claytor.

Sources: *RA* 4: 204-6 (Need, Levis, Melford), 2: 246-49 (Clifford), 4: 355-57 (Percy) and *TG* 13 (1999): 30-36 (Leslie Mahler); J. Smith Futhey and Gilbert Cope, *History of Chester County, Pennsylvania, with Genealogical and Biographical Sketches* (1881), p. 628, and Jacob Martin and Gilbert Cope, eds., *Abstracts of Wills of Chester County, Pennsylvania, vol. 1, 1714-1758* (1900), pp. 68 (Bradshaw), 133 (Levis), 146-47 (Blunston), 198 (Need), 452 (Cartledge).

The Royal Descents of 900 Immigrants

1. Edward III, King of England, d. 1377 = Philippa of Hainault
2. Lionel Plantagenet, Duke of Clarence = Elizabeth de Burgh
3. Philippa Plantagenet = Edmund Mortimer, 3rd Earl of March
4. Elizabeth Mortimer = Sir Henry "Hotspur" Percy
5. Elizabeth Percy = John Clifford, 7th Baron Clifford
6. Mary Clifford = Sir Philip Wentworth
7. Sir Henry Wentworth = Anne Saye
8. Elizabeth Wentworth = (1) Roger Darcy
9. Elizabeth Darcy = Humphrey Colles
10. John Colles = Anne Thynne
11. Elizabeth Colles = Humphrey Walrond
12. Humphrey Walrond, governor of Bermuda = Grace Seaman
13. Grace Walrond = Constant Sylvester
14. Mary Sylvester = Richard Worsam
15. Richard Worsam = Catherine Tomlinson
16. **Henrietta Constantia Worsam** of Pa. = George **Meade** (1741-1808), merchant, Revolutionary patriot. A son, Richard Worsam Meade, merchant, married Margaret Coats Butler and was the father of Union general George Gordon Meade, the victor at Gettysburg, who married Margaretta Sergeant.

8. Elizabeth Wentworth = (2) Sir Thomas Wyndham, SETH, whose first wife was Eleanor Scrope
9. Sir Thomas Wyndham = —— Colles, sister of Humphrey Colles, husband of Elizabeth Darcy, above
10. Sir Henry Wyndham = Bridget Mannock
11. Sir Thomas Wyndham = Susan Clere
12. **Edward Wyndham/Windham** of Va. = ——.

The Royal Descents of 900 Immigrants

Sources: *GPFPM*: 881-82 (Meade), Joanne McCree Sanders, *Barbados Records, Wills and Administrations, Volume III, 1701-1725* (1981), p. 381 (will of the elder Richard Worsam), Barbados record book 6/16, p. 255 (1705 will of Sir Henry Pickering, 2nd Bt., whose second wife was Grace Sylvester and who named his nephew "Richard Warsam" and the latter's three sisters, Constantia Richilinda, Henrietta Maria and Maria Richard), PRs of St. Martin in the Fields, Westminster (1745 marriage of the younger Richard Worsam), and Warfield, Berkshire (FHL #88472, item 1, 1745/6 baptism of Henrietta Constantia Worsam); *GGE*, pp. 17-18 (1671 will of Constant Sylvester, which mentions daughter Mary, wife Grace, and wife's brother Henry Walrond; *VD*, p. 770 (Walrond), *Oxford DNB* (Humphrey Walrond, governor of Bermuda); F.W. Weaver, *Visitations of Somerset, 1531, 1575, 1591* (1885), p. 17 (Colles), *Parliament, 1558-1603*, vol. 1, pp. 631-32 (John Colles), and *Parliament, 1509-1558*, vol. 1, p. 673 (Humphrey Colles); *SP* (Darcy of Chiche) and *RA* 4: 218-20 (Wentworth), 2: 246 (Clifford), 4: 355-57 (Percy), 4: 174-75 (Mortimer); Hon. H.A. Wyndham, *A Family History: The Wyndhams of Norfolk and Somerset* (vol. 1, *1410-1688* [1939]), *The Wyndhams of Somerset, Sussex and Wiltshire* (vol. 2, *1688-1837* [1950]), *passim*, esp. first chart at end of vol. 1 and fourth chart at end of vol. 2, 1: 40 and 2: 216-17, corrected by *Pedigrees, Norfolk County, England*, vol. 7, p. 90, so cited by Colles sources cited above. These two descents were developed and contributed by John Anderson Brayton of Memphis, Tenn.

The Royal Descents of 900 Immigrants

1. Edward III, King of England, d. 1377 = Philippa of Hainault
2. John of Gaunt, Duke of Lancaster = Catherine Roët
3. Joan Beaufort = Ralph Neville, 1st Earl of Westmoreland
4. Edward Neville, 1st Baron Abergavenny = Catherine Howard
5. Catherine Neville = Robert Tanfield
6. William Tanfield = Isabel Stavely
7. Francis Tanfield = Bridget Cave, SETH
8. Anne Tanfield = Clement Vincent
9. Elizabeth Vincent = Richard Lane
10. Dorothy Lane = William Randolph
11. **Henry Randolph** of Va. = (1) Elizabeth ――; (2) Judith Soane.
11. Richard Randolph = Elizabeth Ryland
12. **William Randolph** (c. 1651-1711) of Va., planter, merchant and colonial official = Mary Isham, daughter of Henry Isham of Va., ARD, SETH, and Mrs. Katherine Banks Royall.
13. Isham Randolph = Jane Rogers
14. Jane Randolph = Peter Jefferson
15. Thomas Jefferson (1743-1826), 3rd U.S. President = Mrs. Martha Wayles Skelton

15. Mary Jefferson (sister of Thomas) = John Bolling (III), a great-great-great-grandson of Pocahontas and John Rolfe
16. Archibald Bolling = Catherine Payne
17. Archibald Bolling, Jr. = Anne E. Wigginton
18. William Holcombe Bolling = Sallie Spiers White
19. Edith Bolling = (1) Norman Galt; (2) (Thomas) Woodrow Wilson (1856-1924), 28th U.S. President

Sources: *RA* 4:457-58 (plus 451-57 for the Vincent descent from Amy de Gaveston), 5: 129-31 (Tanfield), 1: 320-22 (Neville), *MCS5*, lines 71, 47,

45, and sources cited therein; Wassell Randolph, *Pedigree of the Descendants of Henry Randolph I (1623-1673) of Henrico County, Virginia* (1957), pp. 2-7. See also *DAB* (William Randolph), *Isham*, pp. 81-89 (Randolph), *Nichols*, vol. 4, part 2, p. 870 (Vincent), and *Baker*, vol. 2, p. 276 (Tanfield).

The Royal Descents of 900 Immigrants

1. Edward III, King of England, d. 1377 = Philippa of Hainault
2. Lionel of Antwerp, Duke of Clarence = Elizabeth de Burgh
3. Philippa Plantagenet = Edmund Mortimer, 3rd Earl of March
4. Elizabeth Mortimer = Sir Henry "Hotspur" Percy
5. Henry Percy, 2nd Earl of Northumberland = Eleanor Neville
6. Henry Percy, 3rd Earl of Northumberland = Eleanor Poynings

7. Henry Percy, 4th Earl of Northumberland = Maud Herbert
7. Margaret Percy = Sir William Gascoigne

8. Henry Algernon Percy 5th Earl of Northumberland = Catherine Spencer
8. Elizabeth Gascoigne = Sir George Talboys

9. Sir Thomas Percy = Eleanor Harbottle
9. Anne Talboys = Sir Edward Dymoke

10. Mary Percy = Sir Francis Slingsby
10. Margaret Dymoke = William Eure, 2nd Baron Eure, son of Sir Ralph Eure and Margery Bowes, SETH

11. Sir Henry Slingsby = Elizabeth Vavasour
11. Anne Eure = Sir John Mallory
11. Martha Eure = Sir William Airmine

12. Eleanor Slingsby = Sir Arthur Ingram
12. William Mallory = Alice Bellingham
12. Sir William Airmine, 1st Bt. = Elizabeth Hicks

13. Sir John Mallory = Mary Moseley
13. Elizabeth Airmine = Sir Thomas Style, 2nd Bt.

13. Arthur Ingram
14. Jane Mallory
14. Susan Style = Thomas Dalison, son of Maximilian Dalison and Frances Stanley, SETH

389

The Royal Descents of 900 Immigrants

14,15. Arthur Ingram = Elizabeth Barns

15. Thomas Dalison = Jane Etherington

15,16. Isabella Ingram = George Cary (brother of Lucius Charles Cary, 6th Viscount Falkland)

16,17. Elizabeth Cary (2) = **Jeffery** = (1) 16. Jane Dalison
Amherst, 1st Baron Amherst of Holmesdale and Montreal (1716/17-1797), Commander-in-Chief of British forces in North America, Governor of Virginia (1759-68), ARD, SETH.

12. Frances Slingsby (sister of Eleanor) = Bryan Stapleton

13. Sir Henry Stapleton, 1st Bt. = Elizabeth Darcy

14. Grace Stapleton = Thomas Robinson

15. William Robinson = Anne Walters (parents of Richard Robinson, 1st Baron Rokeby, Church of Ireland Archbishop of Armagh)

16. Grace Robinson = William Freind, Dean of Canterbury

17. Elizabeth Freind = Duncan Campbell

18. Camilla Elizabeth Campbell = James Wright, Jr.

19. **Frances "Fanny" Wright** (1795-1852) of Tenn., Ohio, and N.Y., social reformer (abolition, women's rights, education) and utopian = Guillaume Sylvan Phiquepal d'Arusmont.

Sources: *CP* (Amherst); *BLG* 1952, p. 596 (Dalison), *Kimber*, vol. 1, p. 269 (Style); *Lincolnshire Pedigrees*, pp. 40-41 (Airmine), 1205 (Dymoke), and *NHN*, vol. 12 (1926), pp. 496-97 and *CP* (Eure); *BP* (Falkland), *PCF Yorkshire* (Ingram pedigree), and Sheila V. Mallory

The Royal Descents of 900 Immigrants

Smith, *A History of the Mallory Family* (1985), pp. 143-44 esp.; *MCS* 5, lines 86, 108, *AR8*, lines 3, 19, 5 and *RA* 4: 466 (Dymoke), 5: 114 (Talboys), 3: 79-80 (Gascoigne), 4: 355-62 (Percy); *MP*, charts I, II, IV, VII, XXX, XXXII, pp. 1-2, 5, 8, 33, 35, 103, 109, 120-21 (Ingram, Slingsby, Percy, Mortimer, Plantagenet, Gascoigne, Talboys, Stapleton, Robinson, Freind), Celia Morris Eckhardt, *Fanny Wright: Rebel in America* (1984), *passim*, esp. pp. 4-7 (with some genealogical errors), *Gentleman's Magazine* 68 (1798): 259 (obituary of Mrs. Camilla Eliza Campbell Wright, mistakenly called a great-granddaughter, not great-niece, of the Archbishop) and Henry John Todd, *Some Account of the Deans of Canterbury* (1793), pp. 220-24, which identifies the husband of William Freind's daughter Elizabeth as Captain Duncan Campbell of the Chatham Division of Marines ["now Lt. Colonel"]; *Oxford DNB* for Richard Robinson, 1st Baron Rokeby, and William Freind. The line for "Fanny" Wright was developed and brought to my attention by John C. Brandon of Columbia, S.C.

The Royal Descents of 900 Immigrants

1. Edward III, King of England, d. 1377 = Philippa of Hainault
2. Thomas of Woodstock, 1st Duke of Gloucester = Eleanor Bohun
3. Anne Plantagenet = William Bourchier, Count of Eu
4. William Bourchier, Baron Fitzwarin = Thomasine Hankford, half-sister of the Anne Hankford who married Thomas Butler, 7th Earl of Ormonde, SETH
5. Fulk Bourchier, Baron Fitzwarin = Elizabeth Dinham
6. John Bourchier, 1st Earl of Bath = Cecily Daubeney
7. Dorothy Bourchier = Sir John Fulford
8. Sir John Fulford = Anne Dennis
9. Thomas Fulford = Ursula Bamfield
10. **Mary Fulford** = (1) Thomas **Achims**; (2) Sir Ferdinando **Gorges** (c. 1565-1647), founder and lord proprietor of Maine, ARD, SETH.

Sources: *Ligon*, vol. 1, pp. 178-80 (Gorges), *TG* 14 (2000): 9-19 (Achims), *VD*, pp. 379-80, 106-7 (Fulford, Bourchier) and *CP* (Bath, Fitzwarin, Eu). See also *RA* 2: 666-68, 1: 479-84 (Bourchier), 3: 198-99 (Hankford).

The Royal Descents of 900 Immigrants

1. Edward III, King of England, d. 1377 = Philippa of Hainault

2. John of Gaunt, Duke of Lancaster = Catherine Roët

2. Thomas of Woodstock, 1st Duke of Gloucester = Eleanor Bohun

3. Joan Beaufort = Ralph Neville, 1st Earl of Westmoreland

3. Anne Plantagenet = Edmund Stafford, 6th Earl of Stafford (later wife of William Bourchier, Count of Eu)

4. Anne Neville = 4. Humphrey Stafford, 1st Duke of Buckingham

5. Joan Stafford = Sir William Knevet

6. Charles Knevet = Anne Lacy

7. Elizabeth Knevet = Richard FitzWilliam, son of Sir William FitzWilliam and Anne Hawes, ARD, SETH

8. Margaret FitzWilliam = Bryan Robertson

9. Anne Robertson = Charles Estouteville/Touteville

10. **Margaret Estouteville/Touteville** of Mass. = Thomas **Shepard** (1605-1649), Puritan divine.

11. Thomas Shepard, Jr. = Anna Tyng

12. Anna Shepard = Daniel Quincy

13. John Quincy = Elizabeth Norton

14. Elizabeth Quincy = William Smith, Jr.

15. Abigail Smith = John Adams, Jr. (1735-1826), 2nd U.S. President

16. John Quincy Adams (1767-1848), 6th U.S. President = Louisa Catherine Johnson

12. Thomas Shepard (III) (brother of Anna) = Mary Anderson

13. Anna Shepard = Henry Smith

393

The Royal Descents of 900 Immigrants

14. William Henry Smith = Margaret Lloyd
15. Rebecca Smith = John Aspinwall
16. John Aspinwall, Jr. = Susan Howland
17. Mary Rebecca Aspinwall = Isaac Roosevelt
18. James Roosevelt = Sara Delano
19. Franklin Delano Roosevelt (1882-1945), 32nd U.S. President = (Anna) Eleanor Roosevelt

Sources: *RA* 2: 678-84 (Estouteville, Touteville, Robertson, FitzWilliam), 3: 176-79 (Knevet), 5: 13-17 (Stafford), 1: 479-84 (Bourchier, Gloucester), 4: 233-37 (Neville), 3: 491-500 (Worcester). This descent, developed by Douglas Richardson, is based in part on G.F. Shepard and D.L. Jacobus, *The Shepard Families of New England*, vol. 3 (1973), pp. 293-95 and *NEHGR* 100 (1946): 73; *Foster's V of Yorkshire*, p. 516, *Yorkshire Genealogist* 1 (1888): 92-94, and *DVY*, vol. 3, p. 143 (Estouteville, Stouteville); 1597 PCC will of John Robertson of London, brother of Anne, which mentions his "aunte Hall" and cousin Jane Gannock (Rachel FitzWilliam, daughter of Richard and Elizabeth [Knevet/Knyvett] FitzWilliam and wife of Richard Huddleston, —— Hall, John Reppes, and Richard Cure, and her daughter, Jane Huddleston, wife of William Gannock—see *Lincolnshire Pedigrees*, pp. 519-20 [Huddleston], 383 [Gannock]; *Lodge*, vol. 2, pp. 169-70 [FitzWilliam]; and *Blackmansbury* 9 [1972]: 4-7 [Knevet/Knyvett]).

The Royal Descents of 900 Immigrants

1. Edward III, King of England, d. 1377 = Philippa of Hainault
2. John of Gaunt, Duke of Lancaster = Catherine Roët
3. Joan Beaufort = Sir Robert Ferrers
4. Elizabeth Ferrers = John de Greystock, 4th Baron Greystock
5. Joan de Greystock = John Darcy
6. Richard Darcy = Eleanor Scrope
7. Sir William Darcy = Eupheme Langton
8. Thomas Darcy, 1st Baron Darcy of Darcy = Dowsabel Tempest
9. Sir Arthur Darcy = Mary Carew, daughter of Sir Nicholas Carew and Elizabeth Bryan, SETH
10. Sir Edward Darcy = Elizabeth Astley, daughter of Thomas Astley and Mary Denny, SETH
11. Isabella Darcy = John Launce
12. **Mary Launce** of Mass. = Rev. John **Sherman** (1613-1685), Puritan theologian and mathematician.

Sources: *RA* 3: 541-48 (Launce, Darcy), 3: 138-39 (Greystock), 5: 340-41 (Ferrers), *AR8*, lines 13, 62, 2 and sources cited therein, esp. *TAG* 21 (1944-45): 169-77.

The Royal Descents of 900 Immigrants

1. Edward III, King of England, d. 1377 = Philippa of Hainault
2. John of Gaunt, Duke of Lancaster = Catherine Roët
3. John Beaufort, Marquess of Somerset and Dorset = Margaret Holand
4. Edmund Beaufort, 1st Duke of Somerset = Eleanor Beauchamp
5. Henry Beaufort, 2nd Duke of Somerset, d. unm.
6. (illegitimate by Joan Hill) Charles Somerset, 1st Earl of Worcester = Elizabeth Herbert
7. Elizabeth Somerset = Sir John Savage, son of Sir John Savage (and Anne Bostock), son of Sir John Savage (and Dorothy Vermon), son of Sir John Savage and Catherine Stanley, SETH
8. Margaret Savage = Sir Richard Bulkeley, son of Sir Richard Bulkeley and Catherine Griffith, daughter of Sir William Griffith and Jane Stradling, SETH
9. Sir Richard Bulkeley = Mary Burgh
10. Katherine Bulkeley = Sir Edwin Sandys, son of Sir Samuel Sandys and Mercy Colepepper/Culpeper, SETH
11. Penelope Sandys = Nicholas Lechmere
12. Edmund Lechmere = Lucy Hungerford
13. **Thomas Lechmere** (1683-1765) of Mass., royal official = Anne Winthrop, daughter of Waitstill Winthrop (and Mary Browne), brother of Mrs. Lucy Winthrop Palmes, SETH.

Sources: E.P. Shirley, *Hanley and the House of Lechmere* (1883), pp. 20, 24, 44-45, 47, plus *AA* 4 (2003), 4: 54-55 (Lechmere-Cook Bible records, including the deaths of Thomas Lechmere and his wife); *PFC Yorkshire* (Sandys pedigree); *Lodge*, vol. 5, pp. 19, 24-26 (Bulkeley); *Ormerod*, vol. 1, p. 715 and *RA* 4: 557-58 (Savage); *Collins*, vol. 1, pp. 222-27 (Beaufort and Somerset); *PACF*, pp. 42 (Bulkeley), 185 (Griffith). See also *RA* 4: 645-60 (Somerset). This line was first brought to my attention by Davida Symonds of Agoura Hills, California.

The Royal Descents of 900 Immigrants

1. Edward III, King of England, d. 1377 = Philippa of Hainault
2. John of Gaunt, Duke of Lancaster = Catherine Roët
3. Joan Beaufort = Ralph Neville, 1st Earl of Westmoreland
4. Richard Neville, 1st Earl of Salisbury = Alice Montagu
5. Eleanor Neville = Thomas Stanley, 1st Earl of Derby, son of Thomas Stanley, 1st Baron Stanley, and Joan Goushill, SETH
6. George Stanley, Baron Strange = Joan Strange, daughter of John Strange, 8th Baron Strange of Knokyn and Jacquetta Woodville, sister of Elizabeth Woodville, Queen of Edward IV, King of England
7. Sir James Stanley = Anne Hart
8. Henry Stanley = Margaret Stanley
9. Margaret Stanley (possibly illegitimate) = Richard Houghton
10. Evan Houghton = Ellen Parker
11. Katherine Houghton = William Henshaw
12. **Joshua Henshaw** of Mass. = Elizabeth Sumner.

Sources: *NEHGR* 22 (1868): 105-115 (115 esp.), reprinted in *EO* 2: 2: 329-39, *Chetham Society Publications* 51 (1860): 95-97 (1598 will of Henry Stanley of Bickerstrath, which does not mention a daughter Margaret, wife of Richard Houghton), 82 (1871): 111 (a Stanley of Bickerstrath pedigree, again with no mention of Margaret, wife of Richard Houghton), *BP* (Derby-Crosshall, Aughton and Bickerstrath cadet line) and *CP* (Derby, Strange, Salisbury, Westmoreland). The 1701 pedigree reproduced in *NEHGR* 22 (1868): 115 cites a marriage settlement between Richard Houghton and "Margaret, daughter of Henry Stanley of Bickerstagh" dated 8 Oct. 1585 and as reported in 1980 by Michael J. Wood to W. Charles Barnard. Richard Houghton and his wife enfeoffed Edward, James and William Stanley (sons of Henry, of whom William was illegitimate) with lands in Great Carleton, etc. (William Farrer and John Brownbill, eds., *The Victoria History of the County of Lancaster*, vol. 3 [1907, rep. 1966], p. 278, note 8 and vol. 7 [1913, rep. 1966], p. 230, note 29). Very likely Margaret Stanley, wife of Richard Houghton, was also illegitimate, despite her forename. A definitive monograph on this descent would be welcome. See also *RA* 5: 28-31 (Stanley), 4: 124-26 (Neville).

The Royal Descents of 900 Immigrants

1. Edward III, King of England, d. 1377 = Philippa of Hainault
2. John of Gaunt, Duke of Lancaster = Catherine Roët
3. Joan Beaufort = Sir Robert Ferrers
4. Mary Ferrers = Sir Ralph Neville, her step-brother
5. John Neville = Elizabeth Newmarch
6. Jane Neville = Sir William Gascoigne
7. Margaret Gascoigne = Sir Christopher Warde, son of Sir Roger Warde and Joan Tunstall, daughter of Sir Thomas Tunstall and Eleanor FitzHugh, SETH
8. Anne Warde = Ralph Neville, a cousin
9. Katherine Neville = Sir Walter Strickland
10. Walter Strickland = (1) Agnes (Hamerton?); (2) Alice Tempest
11. (prob. by 1) Ellen Strickland = John Carleton
12. Walter Carleton = Jane Gibbon
13. **Edward Carleton** of Mass. = Ellen Newton of Mass., ARD, SETH.

Sources: *RA* 2: 111-14 (Carleton, Strickland), 5: 153-54 (Neville), 5: 218-20 (Warde, Tunstall), 3: 77-79 (Gascoigne, Neville), 5: 340-41 (Ferrers), *AR8*, line 2 and sources cited therein, esp. Walter Lee Sheppard, Jr., "The Ancestry of Edward Carleton and Ellen Newton, his Wife" (microfilm, 1978), which incorporates much data from *Moriarty*, plus much research also by John G. Hunt.

The Royal Descents of 900 Immigrants

1. Edward III, King of England, d. 1377 = Philippa of Hainault
2. Lionel of Antwerp, Duke of Clarence = Elizabeth de Burgh
3. Philippa Plantagenet = Edmund Mortimer, 3rd Earl of March
4. Elizabeth Mortimer = Sir Henry "Hotspur" Percy
5. Henry Percy, 2nd Earl of Northumberland = Eleanor Neville
6. Henry Percy, 3rd Earl of Northumberland = Eleanor Poynings
7. Margaret Percy = Sir William Gascoigne
8. Elizabeth Gascoigne = Sir George Talboys
9. Anne Talboys = Sir Edward Dymoke
10. Margaret Dymoke = William Eure, 2nd Baron Eure, son of Sir Ralph Eure and Margery Bowes, SETH
11. Sir Francis Eure = Elizabeth Lennard
12. Frances Eure = John Harborne
13. John Harborne = Anne Radcliffe
14. Katherine Harborne = Edward Walker
15. **Frances Walker** of Mass. = Thomas **Ban(n)ister**.

Sources: *NEHGR* 165 (2011): 96-98, 215-22 (Nathaniel Lane Taylor and Michael Andrews-Reading) and sources cited therein. See also *RA* 4: 466 (Dymoke), 5: 114 (Talboys), 3: 79-80 (Gascoigne), 4: 355-60 (Percy), 4: 174-76 (Mortimer), 2: 529 (Eure).

The Royal Descents of 900 Immigrants

1. Edward III, King of England, d. 1377 = Philippa of Hainault
2. John of Gaunt, Duke of Lancaster = Blanche Plantagenet of Lancaster
3. Elizabeth Plantagenet = John Holand, 1st Duke of Exeter, son of Thomas Holand, 1st Earl of Kent and Joan Plantagenet, "the Fair Maid of Kent", SETH
4. John Holand, 2nd Duke of Exeter = (1) Anne Stafford; (2) Beatrice of Portugal; (3) Anne Montagu
5. (illegitimate by ——) Robert Holand, "Bastard of Exeter" = Margaret ——
6. Jane Holand = John Kendall
7. Walter Kendall = Jane Rous
8. Lawrence Kendall = Katherine Munday
9. Mary Kendall = Richard Moyle
10. Loveday Moyle = Henry Ashe
11. Prudence Ashe = Oliver Mainwaring, son of Oliver Mainwaring and Margaret Torbock, SETH. Their son Richard was perhaps the Richard Mainwaring of L.I., = Mary ——, and left issue.
12. **Oliver Mainwaring** of Conn. = Hannah Raymond.

Sources: *RA* 4: 25-28 (Mainwaring), 3: 416-18 (Ashe, Moyle, Kendall), 2: 533-42 (Exeter, Holand), *TAG* 76 (2001): 46-49 and sources listed in both, plus the Oliver Mainwaring materials assembled and brought to my attention by Robert Behra of Salt Lake City (listed under Mrs. Mary Mainwaring Gill, prob. of Md., SETH) and an unpublished monograph by Glenn H. Goodman, "The Ancestry of Oliver Mainwaring of New London, Ct., Compiled from Published Sources," n.d.).

The Royal Descents of 900 Immigrants

1. Edward III, King of England, d. 1377 = Philippa of Hainault
2. Lionel of Antwerp, Duke of Clarence = Elizabeth de Burgh
3. Philippa Plantagenet = Edmund Mortimer, 3rd Earl of March
4. Elizabeth Mortimer = Sir Henry "Hotspur" Percy
5. Henry Percy, 2nd Earl of Northumberland = Eleanor Neville
6. Henry Percy, 3rd Earl of Northumberland = Eleanor Poynings
7. Henry Percy, 4th Earl of Northumberland = Maud Herbert
8. Henry Algernon Percy, 5th Earl of Northumberland = Catherine Spencer
9. Margaret Percy = Henry Clifford, 1st Earl of Cumberland
10. Catherine Clifford = John Scrope, 8th Baron Scrope of Bolton
11. Margaret Scrope = Sir John Constable
12. Sir Henry Constable = Margaret Dormer
13. Catherine Constable = Thomas Fairfax, 1st Viscount Fairfax, son of Sir William Fairfax (and Jane Stapleton), son of Sir Nicholas Fairfax and Jane Palmes, SETH
14. Dorothy Fairfax = Sir Thomas Norcliffe
15. Antonia Norcliffe = John Hatfield
16. Dorothy Hatfield = William Woodhouse
17. John Woodhouse = Hannah Dell
18. Susanna Woodhouse = William Morgan
19. John Morgan − Anne Gosse
20. Anne Gosse Morgan = Alexander Waugh
21. Arthur Waugh, publisher and writer = Catherine Charlotte Raban. Their younger son was Evelyn (Arthur St. John) Waugh, the comic novelist and author of *Brideshead Revisited* (who married two first cousins, Evelyn Florence Margaret Winifred Gardner and Laura Letitia Gwendolyn Evelyn Herbert).

The Royal Descents of 900 Immigrants

22. **Alexander Raban "Alec" Waugh** (1898-1981), sometime of N.Y. and Florida, novelist, author of *The Loom of Youth* and *Island in the Sun*, = (1) Barbara Annis Jacobs; (2) Joan Chirnside; (3) Mrs. Virginia (Eggertsen) Sorensen (1912-1991), American novelist and children's writer.

Sources: *Oxford DNB* (Arthur, "Alec" and Evelyn Waugh), *WWWA*, vol. 10, *1989-1993* (1993), p. 340 (Virginia Sorensen, Mrs. Alec Waugh); *BLG* 1952, pp. 2663-64 (Waugh), *GM* 12 (1955-58): 329-32, 334-35 (Waugh, Morgan), *FMG*, vol. 1, pp. 26-27, 32 (Woodhouse, Hatfield) and *MP*, Tables II, VIII, XIII, XIV, XVII, pp. 2, 9, 14, 15, 18 (generations 1-16). Note also *PCF Yorkshire* (Fairfax pedigree).

John Scrope, 8th Baron Scrope of Bolton at generation 10 above, was a son of Henry Scrope, 7th Baron Scrope of Bolton (and Mabel Dacre), son of Henry Scrope, 6th Baron Scrope of Bolton, and Elizabeth Percy, daughter of Henry Percy, 3rd Earl of Northumberland, and Eleanor Poynings at generation 6 above. Sir John Constable at generation 11 was a son of Sir John Constable and Joan Neville, daughter of Ralph Neville and Joan Warde, SETH. And Margaret Dormer at generation 12 above was a sister of the Mary Dormer who married Hon. Anthony Browne, SETH. See *CP* (Scrope, Northumberland), *Foster's V of Yorkshire*, pp. 57-58 (Constable) and W. Harry Rylands, ed., *Visitations of Buckinghamshire, 1566, 1634* (*HSPVS*, vol. 58, 1909), p. 41 (Dormer).

The Royal Descents of 900 Immigrants

1. Edward III, King of England, d. 1377 = Philippa of Hainault
2. John of Gaunt, Duke of Lancaster = Catherine Roët
3. Joan Beaufort = Ralph Neville, 1st Earl of Westmoreland
4. Anne Neville = Humphrey Stafford, 1st Duke of Buckingham, son of Edmund Stafford, 6th Earl of Stafford and Anne Plantagenet, SETH, later married to William Bourchier, Count of Eu
5. Anne Stafford = Sir Thomas Cobham, *de jure* 5th Baron Cobham
6. Anne Cobham, *de jure* Baroness Cobham = Edmund Burgh, 2nd Baron Burgh
7. Thomas Burgh, 3rd Baron Burgh = Agnes Tyrwhit, daughter of Sir William Tyrwhit and Anne Constable, SETH
8. William Burgh, 4th Baron Burgh = Catherine Clinton
9. Thomas Burgh, 5th Baron Burgh = Frances Vaughan
10. Catherine Burgh = Thomas Knevet, son of Sir Thomas Knevet (and Elizabeth Bacon), son of Sir Thomas Knevet (and Muriel Parry), son of John Knevet and Agnes Harcourt, SETH
11. Elizabeth Knevet = Sir John Rous, 1st Bt., son of Sir John Rous and Elizabeth Yelverton, daughter of Sir Christopher Yelverton and Margaret Catesby, daughter of Thomas Catesby and Isabel Tresham, daughter of Sir Thomas Tresham and Anne Parr, daughter of William Parr, 1st Baron Parr, and Mary Salisbury, SETH
12. Sir John Rous, 2nd Bt. = Anne Wood
13. Sir Robert Rous, 4th Bt. = Lydia Smith
14. Sir John Rous, 5th Bt. = Judith Bedingfield
15. Louisa Judith Rous = John Brereton Birch
16. Henry William Rous Birch = Lydia [daughter of Daniel] Mildred
17. Selina Acton Birch = Richard Henry Bicknell
18. Constance Rosalie Bicknell = George Augustus Auden

The Royal Descents of 900 Immigrants

19. **Wystan Hugh (W.H.) Auden** (1907-1973), sometime of N.Y. (and a U.S. citizen), the poet and man of letters = Erika Julia Hedwig Gründgens Mann, daughter of Thomas Mann, the German novelist.

Sources: *BLG*, 18th ed., vol. 1 (1965), p. 27 and F.A. Crisp, ed., *Visitation of England and Wales*, vol. 13 (1905), p. 174 and vol. 14 (1906), p. ii (additions and corrections) (Auden, Bicknell); Joseph Foster, *Alumni Oxonienses, 1715-1886* (1887), vol. 1, p. 111 and *Proceedings of the Suffolk Institute of Archaeology*, vol. 8, pt. 1 (1894), p. 50 (H.W.R. Birch); *Collins*, vol. 8, pp. 478-80 and *BP* (Stradbroke) (Rous); G.W. Marshall, ed., *Le Neve's Pedigrees of the Knights* (*HSPVS*, vol. 8, 1873), p. 22 (Knevet/ Knyvett) and *BP* (Berners) (Knyvett); *CP* (Burgh, Cobham, Buckingham, Stafford). For the Parr line see Walter Rye, ed., *Visitation of Norfolk, 1563, 1589 and 1613* (*HSPVS*, vol. 32, 1891), p. 329 (second daughter Elizabeth of Sir Christopher Yelverton, no marriage for her listed), W.C. Metcalfe, ed., *Visitations of Northamptonshire, 1564, 1618-19* (1887), p. 174 (Catesby), Mary E. Finch, *The Wealth of Five Northamptonshire Families, 1540-1640* (*Publications of the Northamptonshire Record Society*, vol. 19, 1956), Tresham chart at end; and *RA* 4: 307 (Parr), plus *Oxford DNB* for Sir Christopher Yelverton, there said to have eight daughters, and Sir Thomas Tresham. This line was developed and brought to my attention by John C. Brandon of Columbia, S.C.

The Royal Descents of 900 Immigrants

1. Edward III, King of England, d. 1377 = Philippa of Hainault
2. John of Gaunt, Duke of Lancaster = Catherine Roët
3. Joan Beaufort = Ralph Neville, 1st Earl of Westmoreland
4. Edward Neville, 1st Baron Abergavenny = Elizabeth Beauchamp, daughter of Richard Beauchamp, 1st Earl of Worcester and Isabel le Despencer, SETH
5. George Neville, 2nd Baron Abergavenny = Margaret Fenne
6. Sir Edward Neville = Eleanor Windsor, daughter of Andrews Windsor, 1st Baron Windsor, and Elizabeth Blount, SETH
7. Edward Neville, 5th Baron Abergavenny = Katharine Brome
8. Edward Neville, 6th Baron Abergavenny = Rachel Lennard
9. Henry Neville, 7th Baron Abergavenny = Mary Sackville
10. Cecily Neville = FitzWilliam Coningsby
11. Humphrey Coningsby = Lettice Loftus
12. Thomas Coningsby, 1st Earl of Coningsby = Barbara Gorges
13. Letitia Coningsby = Edward Denny
14. Sir Thomas Denny = Agnes Blennerhasset, daughter of John Blennerhasset (and Jane Denny, sister of Edward), son of John Blennerhasset (and Margaret Crosbie), son of John Blennerhasset (and Elizabeth Denny, great-aunt of Edward and Jane), son of John Blennerhasset and Martha Lynne, SETH
15. Jane Denny = Sir Barry Denny, 1st Bt., son of Barry Denny (and Jane O'Connor) son of Edward Denny and Letitia Coningsby above
16. Letitia Denny = William Rowan, son of George Rowan (and Mary Gorham) son of George Rowan (and —— Chute), son of George Rowan and Mary Blennerhasset, daughter of Thomas Blennerhasset and Ruth Blennerhasset, daughter of John Blennerhasset and Elizabeth Denny above
17. Arabella Rowan = Charles George Fairfield
18. Charles Fairfield = Isabella Campbell Mackenzie

19. Cicely Isabel Fairfield, known as (Dame) Rebecca West, 1892-1983, novelist, reporter, and literary critic = Henry Maxwell Andrews; illegitimately by H.G. (Herbert George) Wells, 1866-1946, utopian and science fiction/futurist writer and historian, she was the mother of

20. **Anthony West** (1914-1987), of Conn., novelist and writer for the *New Yorker* = (1) Katharine Church, (2) Lily Dulany Emmet (sister of Alexandra Temple Emmet, second wife of historian and presidential adviser Arthur Meier Schlesinger, Jr.).

Sources: *ANB* 23: 62-63 (Anthony West) and *Oxford DNB* (H.G. Wells and Rebecca West), Bonnie Kime Scott, ed., *Selected Letters of Rebecca West* (2000), pp. xxxii-iii (Fairfield-Mackenzie chart, based largely on Rebecca West and Faith Evans, *Family Memories: An Autobiographical Journey,* 1987, Victoria Glendinning, *Rebecca West: A Life,* 1987, and Carl Rollyson, *Rebecca West: A Life* [same title], 1996); A.E. Casey, *O'Kief, Coshe Mang, Slieve Lougher and Upper Blackwater in Ireland: Historical and Genealogical Items Relating to North Cork and East Kerry,* vol. 5 (1962), pp. 395, 489 (Rowan, photocopies of Mary Agnes Hickson, *Selections From Old Kerry Records* [1st ser.], 1872, p. 333, and 2nd ser. 1874, pp. 320-21) and vol. 6 (1963), pp. 141, 2140 (1833 marriage of "Charles George Fairfield, Esq. to Arabella Rowan, only dau. of late William Rowan, Esq.," from B.M. and D.B. O'Connell, "All Births, Marriages, and Deaths Reported in *Kerry Evening Post,* 1828-1864"), 2298; *BP* (Denny of Castle Moyne, baronets) and M.C.D. Dixon and E.C.D. Vann, *Denny Genealogy,* vol. 1 (1944), pp. 60-61, 63-66; *CP, EP* (confused) and *Collins,* vol. 9, pp. 411-12 (Coningsby); *BP* 2003, pp. 16-20 (Abergavenny); *BIFR,* pp. 136-37, 140-41 (Blennerhasset).

The Barbara Gorges at generation 12 was a daughter of Ferdinando Gorges (undoubtedly a namesake of the Maine proprietor) (and Meliana Hilliard), son of Henry Gorges and Barbara Baynard, SETH, for whom see the notes on p. 522 and *Gorges,* pp. 180-82, 200-3.

The Royal Descents of 900 Immigrants

1. Edward III, King of England, d. 1377 = Philippa of Hainault
2. John of Gaunt, Duke of Lancaster = Catherine Roët
3. John Beaufort, Marquess of Somerset and Dorset = Margaret Holand
4. Edmund Beaufort, 1st Duke of Somerset = Eleanor Beauchamp
5. Anne Beaufort = Sir William Paston
6. Anne Paston = Sir Gilbert Talbot, son of Sir Gilbert Talbot and Elizabeth Greystock, daughter of Ralph de Greystock, 5th Baron Greystock and Elizabeth Fitz Hugh, SETH.
7. Elizabeth Talbot = John Lyttelton
8. Roger Littleton = Elizabeth Stanley, daughter of John Stanley (and Cecily Freebody), son of George Stanley and Eleanor Sutton, SETH
9. Bridget Littleton = Henry James
10. Anne James = Thomas Rudyard
11. Anthony Rudyard = Anne Newton, daughter of William Newton (and Margery Wright), son of William Newton (and Margaret Mere), son of William Newton (and Parnell Davenport), son of William Newton and Katherine Mainwaring, daughter of Sir John Mainwaring and Katherine Hondford, daughter of John Hondford and Margaret Savage, daughter of Sir John Savage and Catherine Stanley, SETH
12. **Thomas Rudyard**, deputy governor of East Jersey = Alice Boscawen.

Sources: *RA* 4: 504-9 (Rudyard, James, Littleton, Talbot, Paston, Beaufort), 4: 645-57 (Beaufort); 4: 284 (Mainwaring), 5: 182 (Honford), 4: 557-58 (Savage), *NYGBR* 121 (1990): 193-97 and John Sleigh, *A History of the Ancient Parish of Leek in Staffordshire,* 2nd ed. (1883), pp. 125, 129 (Rudyard); James research by Kevin Bradford plus A.T. Butler, ed., *Visitation of Worcestershire, 1634* (*HSPVS,* vol. 90, 1938), p. 62 (Lyttelton, Littleton); *Cornewall,* pp. 218-19 (generations 1-7); *Earwaker,* vol. 1, pp. 127-28 (Newton), 251 (Hondford), *Ormerod,* vol. 1, pp. 482 (Mainwaring), 713 (Savage); *AR8,* lines 1, 57, plus *TG* 5 (1984): 164-65,

The Royal Descents of 900 Immigrants

171. Henry Bainbridge Hoff reports that further research undertaken since publication of the 1990 Rudyard article confirms the above identification of the immigrant's mother, and the "improved" Edward III descent above was first developed and brought to my attention by the above-named Kevin Bradford of Paducah, Ky.

The Royal Descents of 900 Immigrants

1. Edward III, King of England, d. 1377 = Philippa of Hainault
2. Thomas of Woodstock, 1st Duke of Gloucester = Eleanor Bohun
3. Anne Plantagenet = William Bourchier, Count of Eu
4. William Bourchier, Baron Fitzwarin = Thomasine Hankford
5. Fulk Bourchier, Baron Fitzwarin = Elizabeth Dinham
6. Elizabeth Bourchier = Sir Richard Page
7. Elizabeth Page = Sir William Skipwith, half-brother of the John Skipwith who married Eleanor Kingston, SETH, and of the Henry Skipwith who married Jane Hall, SETH
8. Sir Richard Skipwith = Mary Chamberlain
9. William Skipwith = 9. Anne Portington, daughter of Thomas Portington (and 8. Elizabeth Skipwith, daughter of Sir William Skipwith and 7. Elizabeth Page, above), son of John Portington (and Anne Langton), son of Henry Portington and Maud Tyrwhit, daughter of Sir Robert Tyrwhit and Maud Talboys, SETH)
10. Willoughby Skipwith = Honora Saunders
11. **Anne Skipwith** of N.J. = (1) William **Goforth**; (2) William **Oxley**.

Sources: *RA* 2: 666-71, 1: 479-84 (entire line of Mrs. Oxley), 5: 225-26 (Tyrwhit, Portington), 4: 642-43 (Skipwith) and among sources cited therein (with additional pages), George Tuttle Goforth, *The Goforth Genealogy: A History of the Descendants of George Goforth of Knedlington, England*, 3rd ed. (1981), pp. 1-4, and *Lincolnshire Notes and Queries* 8 (1905): 188-89 (Skipwith, Goforth); *Lincolnshire Pedigrees*, pp. 889-90, 895-96 (Skipwith, to Willoughby and Honora, but without their daughters), 794-95 (Portington), 1019 (Tyrwhit); *Oxford DNB* (2004), 42: 330 (Sir Richard Page, covering generations 5-7). This descent was first developed and brought to my attention by Martin Edward Hollick of West Roxbury, Mass.

The Royal Descents of 900 Immigrants

1. Edward III, King of England, d. 1377 = Philippa of Hainault
2. Edmund of Langley, 1st Duke of York = Isabel of Castile
3. Constance Plantagenet = Thomas le Despencer, 1st Earl of Gloucester
4. (illegitimate by Edmund Holand, 4th Earl of Kent) Eleanor Holand = James Touchet, 2nd Baron Audley
5. Constance Touchet (or Audley) = Robert Whitney (who later married Elizabeth Vaughan, SETH)
6. Joan Whitney = Sir Roger Vaughan
7. Watkyn Vaughan = Joan ferch Ieuan ap Gwilym Fychan
8. Sir William Vaughan = Catrin ferch Jenkin ap Havard
9. Catrin Vaughan = David Evans
10. Mary Evans = Thomas Basset
11. Catrin Basset = Richard ab Ieuan
12. Jane Richards = Ieuan ap John
13. **John Bevan** of Pa. = Barbara Aubrey of Pa., ARD, SETH.

Sources: *RA* 1: 355-57 (Bevan, Richards, Basset, Evans, Vaughan, Whitney), 5: 197-99 (Touchet or Audley), 3: 436-37 (Holand), *TAG* 59 (1983): 1-2, *Merion*, pp. 168-69, corrected by *M&G*, p. 241, and *Whitney*, pp. 114-15 and chart opposite p. 216. See also *Keeler-Wood*, pp. 403-5, 413 (ignore 412, which repeats the error in *Merion*, p. 168-69, that the mother of Watkyn Vaughan was Eleanor Somerset. She was instead Joan Whitney, as above).

The Royal Descents of 900 Immigrants

1. Edward III, King of England, d. 1377 = Philippa of Hainault
2. Edmund of Langley, 1st Duke of York = Isabel of Castile
3. Constance Plantagenet = Thomas le Despencer, 1st Earl of Gloucester
4. (illegitimate by Edmund Holand, 4th Earl of Kent) Eleanor Holand = James Touchet, 2nd Baron Audley
5. Margaret Touchet (or Audley) = (1) Sir Roger Vaughan; (2) Richard Grey, Baron Grey of Powis, son of Henry Grey, 2nd Earl of Tankerville, and Antigone Plantagenet, SETH
6. Elizabeth Vaughan or Grey (but see note below) = Sir John Ludlow
7. Anne Ludlow = Thomas Vernon
8. Elizabeth Vernon = John Steventon
9. Anne Steventon = George Barker, for whom see *RD600*, p. 865
10. Margaret Barker = Richard Griffith
11. Dorothy Griffith = John Mayne
12. Blanche Mayne = Charles Harrison
13. Anne Harrison = Thomas Willing
14. **Charles Willing** of Pa. = Anne Shippen.

Sources: Craig W. Horle, *Lawmaking and Legislatures in Pennsylvania: A Biographical Dictionary, Volume Three, 1757-1775* (2005), pp. 1427-28, 1453 (Thomas Willing, son of Charles and Anne, which mentions Dorothy Mayne); Thomas Balch, *Letters and Papers Relating Chiefly to the Provincial History of Pennsylvania* (1855), pp. c-cii, and C.P. Keith, *The Provincial Councillors of Pennsylvania* (1883, repr. 1997), pp. (89)-(90) (and note children Thomas, Dorothy and Margaret and grandchildren Thomas Mayne Willing and Dorothy Byrd) (Charles Willing); John Fetherston, ed., *Visitation of Warwick*[shire], *1619* (*HSPVS*, vol. 12, 1877), p. 331 and W.H. Rylands, ed., *Visitation of Warwick*[shire], *1682-83* (*HSPVS*, vol. 62, 1911), pp. 122-23 (Mayne, and note Dorothy and Margaret, sisters of Blanche); W.H. Turner, ed.,

The Royal Descents of 900 Immigrants

Visitations of Oxfordshire, 1566, 1574, 1634 (*HSPVS*, vol. 5, 1871), p. 294 (Dorothy b. ca. 1615, no marriage given, sister and niece of Johns, daughter of Richard and Margaret [Barker] Griffith and sister of Elizabeth Griffith, ca. 1607-1683); George Grazebrook and J.P. Rylands, eds., *Visitation of Shropshire, 1623* (*HSPVS*, vol. 28, 1889), p. 29 (Barker). Generations 9-14 were brought to my attention and partly developed on *soc.genealogy.medieval* by John C. Brandon of Columbia, S.C. Generations 7-9, proposed by David Topping of Wales, depend on the 1583 PROB 11/65 will of Elizabeth Steventon, who appoints George Barker, her son-in-law, as an executor, makes bequests to nephews Henry (Esq.) and Francis Vernon, and as a second executor names Francis Newport. This last was the son of Thomas Newport and Anna Corbet, daughter of Sir Robert Corbet and Elizabeth Vernon, aunt of the Thomas Vernon above. For further confirmation of generations 12-13 see also R. Winder Johnson, *The Ancestry of Rosalie Morris Johnson* (1905), p. 241, where three of Charles Willing's four sisters are given as Dorothy, Blanche, and Anne, names which follow the immediate matrilineal descent, and F.F. Starr, ed., *English Goodwin Family Papers*, vol. 1 (1921), p. 300, where the 5 Oct. 1692 will of "Margaret Goodwin, now wife of Stephen Goodwin of Horley, Oxon," proved 25 Nov. 1700, mentions "sister Blanch Harrison, use of £100 for life, then to her two children John and Anna Harrison." Also mentioned were sister Dorothy Mayne, brother James Mayne, cousin "Symon Maine," and "sister[s] Blanche, Dorothy and Ann." These last two sources were brought to my attention by John C. Brandon and Don Charles Stone. Nathaniel L. Taylor, moreover, has developed other royal descents, via Anthony Woodville, 2nd Earl Rivers (brother of Elizabeth Woodville, Queen of Edward IV), Poyntz, Wykes and Lowle, to Ava Lowle, wife of Joseph and mother of Thomas Willing above. For generations 1-7 see *Collins*, vol. 7, p. 401 (Vernon), *CP* (Grey of Powis, Audley and Kent, esp. vol. 6, appendix C, pp. 697-701) and *RA* 5: 197-99 (Touchet), 3: 436-47 (Holand), 5: 445-49 (York). Note also the 13-generation matrilineal descent of Charles Willing of Pa. from Isabel of Castile, Duchess of York.

For comments on a possible solution to the Elizabeth Vaughan or Grey issue, and then a descent from Henry IV, King of England, and Mary Bohun, see p. 378 herein. If Elizabeth is indeed the daughter of Baron Grey of Powis, then this chart should instead follow that for John Baskerville of Md. and U.S. Revolutionary general Charles Lee.

The Royal Descents of 900 Immigrants

1. Edward III, King of England, d. 1377 = Philippa of Hainault
2. John of Gaunt, Duke of Lancaster = Catherine Roët
3. Joan Beaufort = Sir Robert Ferrers
4. Mary Ferrers = Sir Ralph Neville, her step-brother
5. John Neville = Elizabeth Newmarch
6. Jane Neville = Sir William Gascoigne
7. Agnes Gascoigne = Sir Robert Plumpton, half-brother of the Sir William Plumpton who married Elizabeth Clifford, SETH
8. Agnes Plumpton = German Pole
9. Elizabeth Pole = Anthony Eyre, son of Edward Eyre and Elizabeth Reresby, SETH
10. Gervase Eyre = Mary Neville
11. Anthony Eyre = Anne Markham
12. Sir Gervase Eyre = Elizabeth Babington
13. Mary Eyre = Sir John Newton, 2nd Bt.
14. **Hester Newton** of Md. = John **Seymour** (1649-1709), colonial governor of Md., ARD, SETH.

Sources: Rev. Henry Thomas Ellacombe, *The History of the Parish of Bitton in the County of Gloucester* (1881), p. 89 (Seymour), *MGH,* new ser., vol. 1 (1874), p. 169 (Newton); *FMG,* vol. 2, pp. 555-58 (Eyre); *BLG,* 8th ed. (1894), p. 1625 (Pole, under Chandos-Pole); *Foster's V of Yorkshire*, pp. 387 (Plumpton), 384-85 (Gascoigne); *AR8,* line 2 and *RA* 4: 391-92 (Plumpton), 3: 77-79 (Gascoigne, Neville), 5: 340-41 (Ferrers).

The Royal Descents of 900 Immigrants

1. Edward III, King of England, d. 1377 = Philippa of Hainault
2. Lionel of Antwerp, Duke of Clarence = Elizabeth de Burgh
3. Philippa Plantagenet = Edmund Mortimer, 3rd Earl of March
4. Elizabeth Mortimer = Sir Henry "Hotspur" Percy
5. Henry Percy, 2nd Earl of Northumberland = Eleanor Neville

6. Henry Percy, 3rd Earl of Northumberland = Eleanor Poynings

6. Catherine Percy = Edmund Grey, 1st Earl of Kent

7. Margaret Percy = Sir William Gascoigne

7. George Grey, 2nd Earl of Kent = Catherine Herbert

7. Elizabeth Grey = Sir Robert Greystock

8. Elizabeth Gascoigne = Sir George Talboys

8. Anne Grey = John Hussey, 1st Baron Hussey

8. Elizabeth Greystock = Thomas Dacre, 3rd Baron Dacre of Gilsland

9. Anne Talboys = Sir Edward Dymoke

9. Elizabeth Hussey = Sir Robert Throckmorton

9. William Dacre, 4th Baron Dacre of Gilsland = Elizabeth Talbot

10. Margaret Dymoke = William Eure, 2nd Baron Eure, son of Sir Ralph Eure and Margery Bowes, SETH

10. Muriel Throckmorton = Sir Thomas Tresham

10. Margaret Dacre = Anthony Browne, 1st Viscount Montagu

11. Catherine Tresham = Sir John Webb

11. Elizabeth Browne = Robert Dormer, 1st Baron Dormer

11. Ralph Eure, 3rd Baron Eure = Mary Dawney

12. Mary Dormer = Sir John Caryll

12. William Eure, 4th Baron Eure = Lucy Noel

12. Sir John Webb, 1st Bt. = 13. Mary Caryll

13. Elizabeth Eure = Sir Francis Ireland

14. William Ireland
 = Barbara Eure,
   a cousin

15. William Ireland = 13, 14. Mariana Webb

14, 15, 16. John Ireland = Isabel Jessop

15, 16, 17. **John Ireland** of Md. = Sarah ——.

Sources: Research of Ferdinand Henry Onnen III of Washington, D.C., aided by English researcher Susan Moore, derived in part from (1) references to Mr. Ireland in the Carroll correspondence edited by Ronald Hoffman, Sally D. Mason and Eleanor S. Darcy as *Dear Papa, Dear Charley*, 3 vols. (2001); (2) the 1712 marriage record of John Ireland and Isabel Jessop; (3) several 17th- or 18th-century wills (in 1735, of John Ireland of Crofton, Yorkshire, which mentions brother Ralph, sons John [the eldest], and James, and daughters Mary, Elizabeth and Mariana; in 1705, of Francis Ireland, which mentions "Sir John Webb my late uncle" and brother Charles; in 1712, of Mary Ireland of the city of York, which mentions brothers Charles, Ralph and John and servant Isabel Jessup [who married Mary's brother John that same year]; in 1724, of Ralph Ireland, to brother John and the latter's son John and daughters Mary, Elizabeth, Marina and Winifred); and in 1681, of Sir John Webb, 1st Bt., which mentions his daughter Marina, wife of William Ireland; and (4) Chancery record C11/1389/28, showing that William Ireland and Mariana Webb were parents of Ralph, John, Charles [and Francis], Winifred and Mary Webb. Other sources include J.W. Walker, *Yorkshire Pedigrees, G-S* (*HSPVS*, vol. 95, 1943), p. 249 (Ireland); Sir Richard Colt Hoare, 2nd Bt., *The Modern History of South Wiltshire*, vol. 3, pt. 5, *The Hundred of Cawden* (1835): 20 and *CB* (Webb); *Horsham*, pp. 48-49 (Caryll); *CP* (Eure, Northumberland, Kent, Hussey, Greystock, Dacre of Gilsland, Montague, Dormer); *RA* 4: 466 (Dymoke), 5: 114 (Talboys), 3: 79-80 (Gascoigne), 4: 355-59 (Percy), 4: 174-76 (Mortimer); *Oxford DNB* (Sir Thomas Tresham, 1543-1605), *Parliament 1509-1558*, vol. 3, pp. 460-61 (Robert Throckmorton) and *BP* (through 1975) (Throckmorton; unfortunately *Throckmorton*, pp. 116, 121-23, does not list Catherine [Tresham] Webb among the children of Sir Thomas Tresham and Muriel Throckmorton, but see Mary Anne Everett Green, ed., *Calendar of State Papers, Domestic Series, of the Reign of James I, 1623-1625* [1859], p. 108—

The Royal Descents of 900 Immigrants

"Lady Webb, sister to Sir Lewis Tresham"). Sir John Webb, 1st Bt., and Mary Caryll are ancestors 2216-17 of the late Diana, Princess of Wales (see *Diana*, pp. 165, 393). Margery Bowes, wife of Sir Ralph Eure above, was also a Percy-Mortimer descendant; Sir Robert Throckmorton, husband of Elizabeth Hussey, was a son of Sir George Throckmorton and Katherine Vaux, SETH; and Lucy Noel, wife of William Eure, 4th Baron Eure, was a daughter of Sir Andrew Noel and Mabel Harington, daughter of Sir James Harington and Lucy Sidney, SETH.

The Royal Descents of 900 Immigrants

1. Edward III, King of England, d. 1377 = Philippa of Hainault
2. John of Gaunt, Duke of Lancaster = Catherine Roët
3. Joan Beaufort = Ralph Neville, 1st Earl of Westmoreland
4. Edward Neville, 1st Baron Abergavenny = Elizabeth Beauchamp, daughter of Richard Beauchamp, 1st Earl of Worcester (and Isabel le Despencer, daughter of Thomas le Despencer, 1st Earl of Gloucester, and Constance Plantagenet, SETH), son of William Beauchamp, Baron Abergavenny, and Joan FitzAlan, SETH
5. George Neville, 2nd Baron Abergavenny = Margaret Fenne
6. Sir Edward Neville = Eleanor Windsor, daughter of Andrews Windsor, 1st Baron Windsor, and Elizabeth Blount, SETH
7. Sir Henry Neville = Elizabeth Gresham
8. Sir Henry Neville = Anne Killigrew
9. Sir Henry Neville = Elizabeth Smythe
10. **Katherine Neville** of Va. = Sir Thomas **Lunsford** (c. 1610-c.1653) of Va., royalist army officer, ARD, SETH.

Sources: *BP* 1999, 2003 (Abergavenny), E.L. Lomax, *Genealogy of the Virginia Family of Lomax* (1913), pp 57-63 and *RA* 1: 320-23 (Neville, to the first Sir Henry), 4: 233-37 (Neville), 3: 491-500 (Lancaster) (3: 676-77, under Lunsford, names only Katherine's parents). Sir Thomas Lunsford and Katherine Neville were ancestors #s 1054-55 of the late Diana (Frances Spencer), Princess of Wales; see *Diana 12G*, pp. 100, 156, 232, 371, 391, 422 (generations 8-10).

The Royal Descents of 900 Immigrants

1. Edward III, King of England, d. 1377 = Philippa of Hainault
2. Lionel of Antwerp, Duke of Clarence = Elizabeth de Burgh
3. Philippa Plantagenet = Edmund Mortimer, 3rd Earl of March
4. Elizabeth Mortimer = Sir Henry "Hotspur" Percy
5. Henry Percy, 2nd Earl of Northumberland = Eleanor Neville, daughter of Ralph Neville, 1st Earl of Westmoreland, and Joan Beaufort, SETH
6. Henry Percy, 3rd Earl of Northumberland = Eleanor Poynings
7. Henry Percy, 4th Earl of Northumberland = Maud Herbert, daughter of William Herbert, 1st Earl of Pembroke of the first creation, SETH, and Anne Devereux, daughter of Sir Walter Devereux (and Elizabeth Merbury), son of Walter Devereux and Elizabeth Bromwich, SETH
8. Henry Algernon Percy, 5th Earl of Northumberland = Catherine Spencer, daughter of Sir Robert Spencer and Eleanor Beaufort, SETH
9. Sir Thomas Percy = Eleanor Harbottle, daughter of Sir Guischard Harbottle (and Joan Willoughby), son of Sir Ralph Harbottle (and Margaret ——), son of Bertram Harbottle and Joan Lumley, SETH
10. Henry Percy, 8th Earl of Northumberland = Katherine Neville, daughter of John Neville, 4th Baron Latymer and Lucy Somerset, SETH
11. **Hon. George Percy** (1580-1632), colonial governor of Va., d. unm.

Sources: *Oxford DNB* (Hon. George Percy), *CP* (Northumberland, Pembroke), and *MP*, tables I-III, pp. 1-4, *NHN*, vol. 9 (1909), p. 266 (Harbottle). *RA* 4: 355-62, 4: 174-76, 1: 80-85, 87-88 covers generations 1-8. The parentage of Eleanor Neville and Catherine Spencer is given above, but not on other charts, because Hon. George Percy, colonial governor of Va., was their first (and only agnate) immigrant descendant.

The Royal Descents of 900 Immigrants

1. Edward III, King of England, d. 1377 = Philippa of Hainault
2. John of Gaunt, Duke of Lancaster = Catherine Roët
3. Joan Beaufort = Ralph Neville, 1st Earl of Westmoreland
4. Richard Neville, 1st Earl of Salisbury = Alice Montagu
5. Richard Neville, "the Kingmaker," Earl of Warwick and Salisbury = Anne Beauchamp
6. (illegitimate by ——) Alice Neville = Christopher Conyers
7. Agnes Conyers = Geoffrey Lee, son of Richard Lee and Joyce Worsley, daughter of Sir Otewell Worsley and Rose Trevor, SETH
8. Richard Lee = Elizabeth Crispe
9. Mary Lee = Henry Drake
10. **Robert Drake** of Va. = Joan Gawton.

Sources: *RA* 2: 465-67 (Drake, Lee, Conyers), 4: 124-29 (Neville), 4: 233-37 (Neville), 3: 491-500 (Lancaster); *PSECD* 3: 122-23, *LDBR* 5, p. 381, and W.B. Bannerman, ed, *Visitations of Surrey, 1530, 1572, and 1623* (*HSPVS*, vol. 43, 1899), p. 102 (Drake) plus Robert Hovenden, *Visitation of Kent, 1619-1621* (*HSPVS*, vol. 42), p. 56 (Lee); *Parliament 1509-1558*, vol. 2, pp. 506-7 (Geoffrey Lee, brother of Edward Lee, Archbishop of York) and *Mary Isaac*, pp. 331-35, 340-42 (Lee, Worsley); F.W. Weaver, ed., *Visitations of Somerset, 1531, 1575* (1885), p. 14 (Conyers, under Carlisle). See also, for Drake, Mrs. Henrietta Dawson Ayres Sheppard, *Ayres-Dawson and Allied Families*, vol. 1 (1961), pp. 149-85. Elizabeth Drake, a sister of Robert of Virginia, married James Morley, a clerk in Chancery, and was an ancestor of H.M. the late Queen Elizabeth The Queen Mother; see *TG* 1 (1980): 115.

The Royal Descents of 900 Immigrants

1. Edward III, King of England, d. 1377 = Philippa of Hainault
2. Thomas of Woodstock, 1st Duke of Gloucester = Eleanor Bohun
3. Anne Plantagenet = William Bourchier, Count of Eu
4. John Bourchier, Baron Berners = Margery Berners
5. Sir Humphrey Bourchier = Elizabeth Tilney
6. Margaret Bourchier = Sir Thomas Bryan
7. Elizabeth Bryan = Sir Nicholas Carew, son of Sir Richard Carew and Malyn Oxenbridge, SETH
8. Isabel Carew = Nicholas Saunders
9. Mary Saunders = Robert Beville
10. John Beville = Mary Clement
11. **Essex Beville** of Va. = Mrs. Amy —— Butler.

Sources: *RA* 1: 359-62 (Deville, Saunders, Carew), 1: 479-88 (Bryan, Bourchier); Asselia Strobhar Lichliter, *700 Years of the Beville Family: The Lives and Times of 18 Generations of the Beville Family of Huntingdonshire, England* (1976), *passim*, esp. pp. 343-44, 399; Sir Henry Ellis, ed., *Visitation of Huntingdon*[shire, 1613] (Camden Society Publications, No. 43, 1849), p. 9 (Beville); W. Bruce Bannerman, ed., *Visitations of Surrey*, 1530, 1572, and 1623 (*HSPVS*, vol. 43, 1899), pp. 69 (Saunders), 17, 214 (Carew); *Oxford DNB* (Sir Francis Bryan and Sir Nicholas Carew); S.C.W. Allen, *Our Children's Ancestry* [Whitaker family] (1935), pp. 59 (and chart opposite)-60 (Bourchier) and *AR8*, line 4.

The Royal Descents of 900 Immigrants

1. Edward III, King of England, d. 1377 = Philippa of Hainault
2. John of Gaunt, Duke of Lancaster = Catherine Roët
2. Thomas of Woodstock, 1st Duke of Gloucester = Eleanor Bohun
3. Joan Beaufort = Ralph Neville, 1st Earl of Westmoreland
3. Anne Plantagenet = William Bourchier, Count of Eu
4. George Neville, 1st Baron Latymer = Elizabeth Beauchamp
4. John Bourchier, Baron Berners = Margery Berners
5. Sir Henry Neville = 5. Joan Bourchier
6. Richard Neville, 2nd Baron Latymer = Anne Stafford
7. Dorothy Neville = Sir John Dawney
8. Anne Dawney = Sir George Conyers
9. Sir John Conyers = Agnes Bowes
10. Eleanor Conyers = Lancelot Strother
11. William Strother = Elizabeth ——
12. **William Strother**, allegedly the immigrant to Va. = Dorothy —
13. William Strother, Jr. = Margaret Thornton
14. Francis Strother = Susannah Dabney
15. William Strother = Sarah Bayly
16. Sarah Dabney Strother = Richard Taylor
17. Zachary Taylor (1784-1850), 12th U.S. President = Margaret Mackall Smith. A daughter, Sarah Knox Taylor, was the first wife of Jefferson Davis, later President of the Confederacy (Confederate States of America).

13. Robert Strother (brother of William, Jr.) = Elizabeth Berry
14. Elizabeth Strother = Robert Kay
15. (probably) James Kay = Grace Elgin

The Royal Descents of 900 Immigrants

16. James Kay, Jr. = Elizabeth Ann Clinkscales
17. Mary Kay = John Pratt
18. James E. Pratt = Sophronia C. Cowan
19. Nina Pratt = William Archibald Carter
20. James Earl Carter = Bessie Lillian Gordy
21. James Earl Carter, Jr., b. 1924, 39th U.S. President = (Eleanor) Rosalynn Smith

Sources: *Lineage Book, Descendants of the Illegitimate Sons and Daughters of the Kings of Britain*, no. 76, which cites pp. 25-26 of a Strother manuscript I cannot locate; *CP*, Latymer article, *AR8*, line 2, and *RA* 3: 538-41 (Neville), 1: 479-85 (Bourchier). The above-given parentage and grandparentage of the immigrant William Strother first appeared, perhaps, in George Norbury Mackenzie's *Colonial Families of the United States of America*, vol. 5 (1915, rep. 1966), pp. 492-93.

The Royal Descents of 900 Immigrants

1. Edward III, King of England, d. 1377 = Philippa of Hainault
2. Edmund of Langley, 1st Duke of York = Isabel of Castile
3. Constance Plantagenet = Thomas le Despencer, 1st Earl of Gloucester
4. (illegitimate by Edmund Holand, 4th Earl of Kent) Eleanor Holand = James Touchet, 2nd Baron Audley
5. Sir Humphrey Audley = Elizabeth Courtenay, SETH
6. Elizabeth Audley = John Sydenham
7. Sir John Sydenham = Ursula Bridges
8. John Sydenham = Mary Poyntz, daughter of Sir Nicholas Poyntz (and Anne Verney), son of Sir Nicholas Poyntz and Joan Berkeley, SETH.
9. Anne Sydenham = John Poyntz
10. Newdigate Poyntz = Sarah Foxley, daughter of Francis Foxley and Mary Dryden, daughter of John Dryden and Elizabeth Cope, SETH
11. Dorothea Poyntz = John Owsley
12. **Thomas Owsley** of Va. = Anne ——.

Sources: *RA* 4: 294-95 (Owsley, Poyntz), 5: 108 (esp. note 8)-9 (Sydenham), 5: 197-99 (Touchet/Audley), 3: 436-37 (Holand), 3: 15-16 (Foxley); Harry Bryan Owsley, *Genealogical Facts of the Owsley Family in England and America* (1890), chapters 2-6; *BLG*, 18th ed., vol. 1 (1965), pp. 580-82 and Sir John Maclean, *Historical and Genealogical Memoir of the Family of Poyntz* (1886), pp. 95-96 esp.; *Diana 12G*, pp. 68, 99, 154, 358, 371, 390, 420-21 (generations 9-10); G.F. Sydenham, *The History of the Sydenham Family* (1928), pp. 117-36; *MGH*, 2nd Series, 3 (1890): 326-27, 349 (Sydenham, Audley); Ronny O. Bodine and Thomas W. Spalding, Jr., *The Ancestry of Dorothea Poyntz, Wife of Reverend John Owsley, Generations 1-14*, 3rd ed. (1999), *passim*.

Note: Poyntz Owsley, a brother of Thomas Owsley of Va., married Mary David (Davis) and left a daughter, Elizabeth Poyntz, who married firstly

The Royal Descents of 900 Immigrants

a Watts and secondly a Spriggs (H.B. Owsley above, pp. 51, 150). Mormon records, which may be correct, and a copy of which was sent to me by Stephen Ralph Boswell of Los Angeles, identify Elizabeth's first husband as Thomas Watts (= 18 July 1721 at Langton, Leicestershire). Their daughter Elizabeth Watts (d. 5 December 1787 in St. Margaret's, Leicestershire), married John Adams and left a son, Robert Adams, who married in Kibworth Beauchamp, Leicestershire, 6 Sept. 1779 Sarah Foxton and himself left a son, Poyntz Adams (1789-1870). This last married in Stoke Albany, Northamptonshire, 10 March 1822 Mary Staines and left a daughter, **Jane Adams** (1823-1865) of South Africa and later Idaho, wife of John **Stock**. Their daughter, Jane Susanne Stock, married Charles Coulson Rich II (d. 8 June 1890, Vernal, Utah) and herself left a daughter, Ada May Rich, wife of Clarence Irwin Johnson and mother of Laraine Johnson, 1920-2007, the movie and television actress Laraine Day, who married (1) James Ray Hendricks, (2) Leo Durocher, 1905-1991, baseball player and/or manager (for the Yankees, Reds, Cardinals, Dodgers, Giants, Cubs and Astros) and, (3) Michel Mark Grilikhes, movie producer.

The Royal Descents of 900 Immigrants

1. Edward III, King of England, d. 1377 = Philippa of Hainault
2. Lionel of Antwerp, Duke of Clarence = Elizabeth de Burgh
3. Philippa Plantagenet = Edmund Mortimer, 3rd Earl of March
4. Elizabeth Mortimer = Sir Henry "Hotspur" Percy
5. Henry Percy, 2nd Earl of Northumberland = Eleanor Neville
6. Sir Ralph Percy = Eleanor Acton
7. Sir Henry Percy = Constance ——
8. Margery Percy = Sir Henry Widdrington, son of Sir Ralph Widdrington (and Felicia Claxton), son of Sir Gerard Widdrington (and Elizabeth Boynton), son of Roger Widdrington and Alice Grey, daughter of Sir Thomas Grey (and Alice Neville, daughter of Ralph Neville, 1st Earl of Westmoreland, and Margaret Stafford, SETH), son of Sir Thomas Grey and Joan Mowbray, SETH
9. Mary Widdrington = John Mitford
10. John Mitford = Barbara Lawson
11. Philip Mitford = Alice (Abrahall?)
12. (maternity uncertain) **Barbara Mitford** of Va. = Rev. Hawte **Wyatt** of Va., ARD, SETH.

Sources: Research of Thomas S. Erwin of Raleigh, N.C., based in part on parish registers of St. Swithun's (Barbara Mitford, daughter of Philip, was bp. there 2 April 1594) and St. Helen's, Worcester, naming patterns among Philip Mitford's children (who included John and Barbara for his parents and Henry and Margery for siblings), *NHN,* vol. 9 (1909), p. 65 (Mitford), vol. 14 (1935), chart between pp. 328-29 (Neville), *NF* 2:103-4 (Widdrington), 15-16 (Percy), *CP* (Northumberland, March, Clarence) and *RA* 4: 355-59 (Percy), 4: 174-76 (Mortimer).

The Royal Descents of 900 Immigrants

1. Edward III, King of England, d. 1377 = Philippa of Hainault
2. John of Gaunt, Duke of Lancaster = Catherine Roët
3. Joan Beaufort = Ralph Neville, 1st Earl of Westmoreland
4. Richard Neville, 1st Earl of Salisbury = Alice Montagu
5. John Neville, 1st Marquess of Montagu = Isabel Ingoldsthorpe
6. Isabel Neville = William Huddleston
7. Sir John Huddleston = Elizabeth Sutton, daughter of Edward Sutton alias Dudley, 2nd Baron Dudley, and Cecily Willoughby, SETH
8. Sir John Huddleston = Bridget Cotton
9. Alice Huddleston = Sir Thomas Lovell
10. Charles Lovell = Elizabeth le Gros, daughter of Sir Thomas le Gros and Elizabeth Cornwallis, SETH
11. Alice Lovell = Sir George Crymes, 1st Bt., son of Sir Thomas Crymes and Margaret More (sister of Anne More, wife of John Donne, the poet), daughter of Sir George More and Anne Poynings, daughter of Sir Adrian Poynings and Mary West, daughter of Sir Owen West (and Mary Guilford, daughter of George Guildford and Elizabeth Mortimer, SETH), son of Thomas West, 8th Baron Delaware (de la Warr) and Eleanor Copley, SETH
12. Sir Thomas Crymes, 2nd Bt. = Mary Bond
13. **Dr. William Crymes** of Va. = (1) ——; (2) Christiana ——.

Sources: *RA* 2: 359-62 (Crymes, More, Poynings, West), 2: 480-82 (Lovell), 3: 394-400 (Huddleston, Neville), 4: 124-26, 233-37 (Neville), 3: 171-72 (Guilford), 5: 434 (le Gros), 5: 105-7 (Sutton); *Collectanea Topographica et Genealogica* 3 (1836): 155-57 (Crymes, therein Grymes, which mentions son William, "living in Virginia having issue a daughter") and *CB* 3: 15-16 (Crymes, Crimes, Grymes, Grimes); *Blomefield*, vol. 1, pp. 323, 328 (Lovell); *BLG* 1952, p. 1306 (Huddleston); *EP* and *CP* (Montagu, Salisbury).

The Royal Descents of 900 Immigrants

1. Edward III, King of England, d. 1377 = Philippa of Hainault
2. John of Gaunt, Duke of Lancaster = Catherine Roët
3. John Beaufort, Marquess of Somerset and Dorset = Margaret Holand
4. Edmund Beaufort, 1st Duke of Somerset = Eleanor Beauchamp
5. Margaret Beaufort = Sir Richard Dayrell
6. Margaret Dayrell = James Touchet, 7th Baron Audley
7. John Touchet, 8th Baron Audley = Mary Griffin
8. George Touchet, 9th Baron Audley = Elizabeth Tuke
9. Henry Touchet, 10th Baron Audley = Elizabeth Sneyd
10. Anne Touchet = Thomas Brooke
11. Sir Richard Brooke = Katherine Neville, daughter of Sir Henry Neville and Anne Killigrew, SETH
12. Anne Brooke = Edward Hyde
13. Robert Hyde = Phillis Sneyd
14. **Edward Hyde,** proprietary governor of N.C. = Katherine Rigby. Their daughter, Anne Hyde, married George Clarke, lt. gov. of N.Y.

Sources: *Ormerod* 3: 811 (Hyde), *Kimber,* vol. 2, p. 278 (Brooke), *Collins*, vol. 6, pp. 552-54 (Touchet) and *CP* (Audley, Somerset) and *BP* 1999, p. 17-18 (Neville, under Abergavenny). See also *RA* 5: 199-200 (Touchet), 5: 17-19 (Darrell/Dayrell), 4: 645-57 (Somerset).

The Royal Descents of 900 Immigrants

1. Edward III, King of England, d. 1377 = Philippa of Hainault
2. Thomas of Woodstock, 1st Duke of Gloucester = Eleanor Bohun
3. Anne Plantagenet = William Bourchier, Count of Eu
4. John Bourchier, Baron Berners = Margery Berners
5. Sir Humphrey Bourchier = Elizabeth Tilney
6. Anne Bourchier = Thomas Fiennes, 8th Baron Dacre
7. Mary Fiennes = Henry Norris (Norreys), executed for alleged adultery with Queen Anne Boleyn, son of Richard Norris (Norreys) (and ____), son of Sir William Norris (Norreys) and Joan de Vere, SETH.
8. Henry Norris, 1st Baron Norris (Norreys) of Rycote = Margaret Williams
9. Sir Thomas Norris (Norreys) = Bridget Kingsmill, daughter of Sir William Kingsmill and Bridget Raleigh, SETH
10. Elizabeth Norris (Norreys) = Sir John Jephson
11. **Mary Jephson** of S.C. = Sir Richard **Kyrle** (d. 1684), colonial governor of S.C., ARD, SETH.

Sources: *The Augustan, Book Five: An Omnibus Publication* (1974), "The Colonial Genealogist" section, pp. 709-10, which cites *Journal of the Cork Historical and Archaeological Society,* 1895, p. 523, and 1906, p. 4, and *South Carolina Archives, Records of the Secretary of the Province, 1675-1695,* pp. 214-15; W.H. Rylands, ed., *Visitations of Hampshire, 1530, 1575, 1622 and 1634* (*HSPVS*, vol. 64, 1913), p. 149 and *BIFR,* pp. 633-34 (Jephson); *Oxford DNB* (Henry Norris; Henry Norris, 1st Baron Norris and Sir Thomas Norris) and *BLGI,* 1912, p. 370 (Kingsmill); *Parliament, 1509-1558,* vol. 3, p. 19 (Henry Norris, 1st Baron Norris of Rycote); *CP* (Dacre, Berners, Eu and Gloucester) and *RA* 1: 479-86 (Bourchier).

The Royal Descents of 900 Immigrants

1. Edward III, King of England, d. 1377 = Philippa of Hainault
2. John of Gaunt, Duke of Lancaster = Catherine Roët
3. Joan Beaufort = (1) Sir Robert Ferrers, (2) Ralph Neville, 1st Earl of Westmoreland

4. Elizabeth Ferrers = John de Greystock, 4th Baron Greystock

4. Edward Neville, 1st Baron Abergavenny = Elizabeth Beauchamp, daughter of Richard Beauchamp, 1st Earl of Worcester, and Isabel le Despencer, SETH

5. Joan de Greystock = John Darcy

5. George Neville, 2nd Baron Abergavenny = Margaret Fenne

6. Joan Darcy = John Beaumont

6. Elizabeth Neville = Thomas Berkeley

7. George Beaumont = Joan Pauncefoot

7. Lora Berkeley = John Ashburnham

7. Anne Berkeley = John Brent

8. William Beaumont = Mary Basset

8. John Ashburnham = Isabel Sackville, daughter of John Sackville and Margaret Boleyn, SETH

8. Margaret Brent = John Dering

9. Richard Beaumont = Colette Clarke

9. John Ashburnham = Mary Fane

9. Richard Dering = Margaret Twisden

10. Nicholas Beaumont = Anne Saunders

10. Sir Anthony Dering = Frances Bell

11. Sir Thomas Beaumont = Catherine Farnham

The Royal Descents of 900 Immigrants

12. Elizabeth Beaumont Baroness of Chamond = 10. Sir John Ashburnham

11,13. Anne Ashburnham = 11. Sir Edward Dering

12,14. Sir Edward Dering, 2nd Bt. = Mary Harvey

13,15. **Robert Dering** = Henrietta de Beaulieu, known as **Henrietta Johnston**, 1674-1729, artist ("first woman painter in America"), of S.C. She married (2) Rev. Gideon Johnston.

Sources: Research by D. Brenton Simons for John Herdeg, based in part on *ANB* 12:152-53 (note esp. the identification of an early sitter, John Percival, later 1st Earl of Egmont, as her husband's nephew); Rev. Francis Haslewood, *Genealogical Memoranda Relating to the Family of Dering of Surrenden Dering, Kent* (1876), *passim* and *Archaeologia Cantiana* 10 (1876): 327-28 (and chart opposite), 331 (Dering); *RA* 2: 594-95 (Dering, Brent, Berkeley), 1: 320-23 (Neville), 3: 541-42 (Darcy), 3: 138-39 (Greystock), 5: 340-41 (Ferrers); *BP* 1924, pp. 148-49 (Ashburnham), *Lives of the Berkeleys,* vol. 1, p. 354, and *Collins*, vol. 2, pp. 104-6 (Sackville); *BP* 2003, pp. 311-12 (Beaumont), *CP* (Cramond), and J.W. Clay, *The Extinct and Dormant Peerages of the Northern Counties of England* (1913), p. 42 (Darcy). Anthony Beaumont, son of William Beaumont and Mary Basset (generation 8 above) married Anne Armstrong and was the father of Mary Beaumont, Countess of Buckingham, wife of Sir George Villiers and mother of George Villiers, 1st Duke of Buckingham, the favorite of Kings James I and Charles I. For the extraordinary Villiers progeny see Paul Bloomfield, *Uncommon People* (1955), pp. 26ff.

The Royal Descents of 900 Immigrants

1. Edward III, King of England, d. 1377 = Philippa of Hainault
2. Lionel of Antwerp, Duke of Clarence = Elizabeth de Burgh
3. Philippa Plantagenet = Edmund Mortimer, 3rd Earl of March
4. Elizabeth Mortimer = Sir Henry "Hotspur" Percy
5. Henry Percy, 2nd Earl of Northumberland = Eleanor Neville
6. Henry Percy, 3rd Earl of Northumberland = Eleanor Poynings
7. Henry Percy, 4th Earl of Northumberland = Maud Herbert

8. Henry Algernon Percy, 5th Earl of Northumberland = Catherine Spencer

9. Margaret Percy = Henry Clifford, 1st Earl of Cumberland, son of Henry Clifford, 10th Baron Clifford, and Anne St. John, SETH

8. Eleanor Percy = Edward Stafford, 3rd Duke of Buckingham, son of Henry Stafford, 2nd Duke of Buckingham, and Catherine Woodville, sister of Elizabeth Woodville, Queen of Edward IV

9. Elizabeth Stafford = Thomas Howard, 3rd Duke of Norfolk, SETH

10. Catherine Clifford = John Scrope, 8th Baron Scrope of Bolton, SETH

10. Henry Howard, Earl of Surrey, the poet = Frances Vere, SETH

11. Henry Scrope, 9th Baron Scrope of Bolton = 11. Margaret Howard

12. Thomas Scrope, 10th Baron Scrope of Bolton = Philadelphia Carey
13. Emanuel Scrope, 1st Earl of Sunderland = Elizabeth Manners
14. (illegitimate by Martha Jeanes) Annabella Scrope = John Grubham Howe
15. Scrope Howe, 1st Viscount Howe = Juliana Alington, daughter of William Alington, 2nd Baron Alington (and Juliana Noel), son of William Alington, 1st Baron Alington, and Elizabeth

Tollemache, daughter of Sir Lionel Tollemache, 2nd Bt., and Elizabeth Stanhope, SETH

16. Emanuel Scrope Howe, 2nd Viscount Howe = 6. Sophie Charlotte Marie von Kielmansegge, see below

7,17. **George Augustus Howe, 3rd Viscount Howe** (c. 1724-1758), British commander in America during the French & Indian wars, d. unm.

1. Christian III, King of Denmark, d. 1559 = Dorothea of Saxe-Lauenburg

2. Dorothea of Denmark = William, Duke of Brunswick-Lüneburg

3. George, Duke of Brunswick-Kalenberg = Anna Eleanor of Hesse-Darmstadt

4. Ernest Augustus, Elector of Hanover (father by Sophie of the Palatinate of George I, King of Great Britain and Sophie Charlotte of Hanover, wife of Frederick I, King of Prussia); by Klara Elisabeth von Meysenburg, wife of Franz Ernst, Count von Platen and Hallermund, Ernest Augustus is now thought to be the father of

5. Sophia Charlotte, Countess von Platen and Hallermund, Countess of Leinster and Darlington = Johann Adolf, Baron von Kielmansegge

6. Sophie Charlotte Marie von Kielmansegge = 16. Emanuel Scrope Howe, 2nd Viscount Howe, see above

Sources: *MP*, tables I-II, VIII, XIII, XXI, pp. 1-2, 9, 14, 22; *EP*, *BP* or *CP* (Howe, Sunderland, Scrope, Alington, etc.); Ragnhild Hatton, *George I, Elector and King* (1978), *passim*, esp. pp. 23-24, 157, 340-41, 412 (Howe, Kielmansegge, Hanover); *ES*, charts for Denmark, Brunswick-Lüneburg (Hanover) and Platen-Hallermund. See also *RA* 4: 355-62 (Percy). Generation 16 above are #s 340-41 in the ancestry of the late Diana, Princess of Wales; see *Diana 12G*, pp. 54, 83-84, 131-32, 192-93, 289-90, 354, 365, 380, 405, 444 (generations 12-16, 1-6).

The Royal Descents of 900 Immigrants

1. Edward III, King of England, d. 1377 = Philippa of Hainault
2. John of Gaunt, Duke of Lancaster = Catherine Roët
3. Joan Beaufort = Ralph Neville, 1st Earl of Westmoreland
4. Richard Neville, 1st Earl of Salisbury = Alice Montagu
5. Eleanor Neville = Thomas Stanley, 1st Earl of Derby
6. George Stanley, Baron Strange = Joan Strange, daughter of John Strange, 8th Baron Strange of Knokyn and Jacquetta Woodville, sister of Elizabeth Woodville, Queen of Edward IV, King of England
7. Margaret Stanley = Sir John Osbaldeston
8. Edward Osbaldeston = Maud Halsall
9. Geoffrey Osbaldeston, Chief Justice of Connaught = Lucy Warren
10. Deborah Osbaldeston = Walter Lyster
11. Anthony Lyster = Christiana Killkeny
12. Thomas Lyster = —— O'Kelly
13. John Lyster = Elizabeth Coddington
14. John Lyster = Jane Ducasse
15. William John Lyster = Martha Hatton
16. **Rev. William Narcissus Lyster** of Mich. = Ellen Emily Cooper (parents of Henry Francis LeHunte Lyster, 1837-1894, noted physician), who married Winifred Lee Brent. W.N.'s brother, Armstrong Lyster, who married Anne Isabella Isdell, also immigrated to the U.S. but left no NDTPS.

Sources: Rev. H.L.L. Denny, *Memorials of an Ancient House: A History of The Family of Lister or Lyster* (1913), pp. 19-22 (and chart opposite), 32-33, 61, 94-100. See also *BLGI*, 1912, pp. 426-27 (Lyster), *CP* (Derby, Salisbury, Westmoreland), and *RA* 5: 28-31 (Stanley), 4: 124-26 (Neville).

The Royal Descents of 900 Immigrants

1. Edward III, King of England, d. 1377 = Philippa of Hainault
2. John of Gaunt, Duke of Lancaster = Catherine Roët
3. Joan Beaufort = Ralph Neville, 1st Earl of Westmoreland
4. Richard Neville, 1st Earl of Salisbury = Alice Montagu
5. Alice Neville = Henry FitzHugh, 5th Baron FitzHugh
6. Elizabeth FitzHugh = Nicholas Vaux, 1st Baron Vaux of Harrowden
7. Anne Vaux = Sir Thomas Le Strange
8. Richard Le Strange = Anne Astley
9. Thomas Le Strange = Elizabeth ——
10. Hamon Le Strange = Dorothy Moore
11. Thomas Le Strange = ——
12. Henry Le Strange = Elizabeth Sandes
13. Thomas L'Estrange = Frances Atkinson

14. George L'Estrange = Anne Crosbie	14. Henry L'Estrange = Elizabeth Malone
15. William L'Estrange = Anne Atkinson, a cousin	15. Henry Peisley L'Estrange = Mary Carleton
16. Edmund L'Estrange =	16. Henrietta Maria L'Estrange

17. William L'Estrange = Caroline Stewart Atkinson, a cousin
18. **Sarah L'Estrange** of Mich. = George Charles **Mahon** of Mich., ARD, SETH. Their daughter, Jane Caroline Mahon, married Louis Crandall Stanley and was the mother of Alice Caroline Stanley, wife of Dean Gooderham Acheson (1893-1971), U.S. Secretary of State.

Sources: George C. Mahon, "Family History of L'Estrange of Kilcummin, King's County, Ireland" (typescript, 1885, owned by G.C. and Sarah's great-granddaughter, the late Helen Jefferson Sanford, former trustee of NEHGS), pp. 14-22 esp.; *BIFR*, pp. 722-25 (L'Estrange), 39-41 (Atkinson); *BLG*, 18th ed., vol. 3 (1972), p. 533 (Le Strange of

The Royal Descents of 900 Immigrants

Hunstanton); Godfrey Anstruther, *Vaux of Harrowden, A Recusant Family* (1953), pp. 7-8; *AR8*, lines 201, 78, 2. See also *RA* 4: 296-97 (Vaux), 2: 632-34 (Fitz Hugh), 4: 124-26 (Neville).

The Royal Descents of 900 Immigrants

1. Edward III, King of England, d. 1377 = Philippa of Hainault
2. Thomas of Woodstock, 1st Duke of Gloucester = Eleanor Bohun
3. Anne Plantagenet = William Bourchier, Count of Eu
4. William Bourchier, Baron Fitzwarin = Thomasine Hankford
5. Fulk Bourchier, Baron Fitzwarin = Elizabeth Dinham
6. John Bourchier, 1st Earl of Bath = Cecily Daubeney
7. Elizabeth Bourchier = Edward Chichester
8. Sir John Chichester = Gertrude Courtenay
9. Elizabeth Chichester = Hugh Fortescue
10. John Fortescue = Mary Speccot
11. Hugh Fortescue = Mary Rolle
12. Elizabeth Fortescue = Sir George Chudleigh, 2nd Bt.
13. Dorothy Chudleigh = Charles Ford
14. Elizabeth Ford = John Vinicombe
15. Elizabeth Vinicombe = John Penrose
16. John Penrose = Jane Trevenen
17. Mary Penrose = Thomas Arnold, headmaster of Rugby (parents of poet and literary critic Matthew Arnold and of Jane Arnold, wife of M.P., cabinet minister and educator reformer William Edward Forster)
18. Thomas Arnold = Julia Sorell (parents of Mary Augusta Arnold, Mrs. [Thomas] Humphrey Ward, novelist and mother of author Janet Penrose Ward, wife of social historian George Macaulay Trevelyan)
19. Julia Frances Arnold = Leonard Huxley (parents of zoologist Sir Julian [Sorell] Huxley)
20. **Aldous (Leonard) Huxley** (1894-1963), of Calif. post 1937, novelist and writer, author of *Brave New World* = (1) Maria Nys; (2) Laura Archera.

The Royal Descents of 900 Immigrants

Sources: *NEXUS* 16 (1999): 72-73 and sources cited therein, esp. *BLG,* 18th ed., vol. 1 (1965), pp. 405-6 (Huxley), *The Genealogical Magazine* 5 (1901-2): 24, 55-61, 116-18, 162-64, 176-77 ("Royal Descent of the Arnolds of Rugby" by Lionel Cresswell, covering the entire line but esp. generations 12-19), *VD*, pp. 190, 354, 173, 106-7 (Chudleigh, Fortescue, Chichester, Bourchier, corrected by Cresswell, however, as to the parentage of Dorothy [Chudleigh] Ford), and *CP* (Bath, Fitzwarin, Eu and Gloucester), *RA* 2: 666-68, 1: 479-84 cover generations 1-6.

The Royal Descents of 900 Immigrants

1. John II, King of France, d. 1364 = Bona of Bohemia

2. Philip II, Duke of Burgundy = Margaret of Flanders

3. John, Duke of Burgundy = Margaret of Bavaria

4. Philip III, Duke of Burgundy = (1) Michelle of France, (2) Bona of Artois, (3) Isabella of Portugal. By (3) Philip was father of Charles the Bold, Duke of Burgundy, father by Isabelle of Bourbon of Mary of Burgundy, wife of Maximilian I, Holy Roman Emperor, through whom the Habsburgs inherited the "Spanish" Netherlands.

5. (illegitimate by Jeanne de Presles) Anthony de Bourgogne, Count de la Roche, Heer van Beveren = Marie de la Viéville

6. (illegitimate by Marie de Braem) Antoine de Bourgogne, Seigneur de Capelle = Claude Andries

7. Anne de Bourgogne = Nicolas Triest, Seigneur de l'Auwerghem

8. Jacqueline Triest = Jean de Coudenhove, Seigneur de Gendtbrugghe

9. Nicolas de Coudenhove, Seigneur de Coudenhove = Charlotte de Baudrenghien

10. Jeanne de Coudenhove = Jean-Baptiste de Lannoy, Seigneur de Hautpont

11. Jeanne-Louise, Countess de Lannoy = Antoine de Carondelet, Baron de Noyelle, Vicomte de la Hestre, for whose French royal descent see *RD600*, pp. 383-84

12. Alexandre de Carondelet, Baron de Noyelle, Vicomte de la Hestre = Marie-Bonne de Bacquehem

18. Jean-Louis de Carondelet, Baron de Noyelle, Vicomte de la Hestre and du Langue = Marie-Angélique-Bernard de Rasoir

19. **François-Louis-Hector de Carondelet, Baron de Noyelle, Vicomte de la Hestre and du Langue** (c. 1748-1807), Spanish governor of Louisiana and West Florida = María Castaños Aragorri Uriarte y Olivide.

Sources: *New Orleans Genesis* 16 (1977): 123-36; *ES* 2: 3: 2: 320, 322, 323 (illegitimate agnate Burgundy descendants), 2: 28: 68 (Lannoy);

The Royal Descents of 900 Immigrants

___ Dumont (Official de la Chambre des Comptes à Bruxelles), *Fragmens Généalogiques*, vol. 3 (1862), pp. 112-13 and Baron J.S.F.J.L. de Berckenrode, *Nobiliaire des Pays-Bas et du Comté de Bourgogne*, vol. 2 (1865), p. 535 (Coudenhove); *Annuaire de la Noblesse de Belgique*, vol. 12 (1858), pp. 236-37 and Leo Lindemans, *Voorouderstafel van het Belgisch Koninghuis/Tableau d'Ascendance de la Maison Royale Belge/Ahnentafel des Belgischen Königshaus* [d'Udekem d'Acoz], vol. 3 (1998), #s 4748-49, 9498-99 (Triest). This "improved descent" was brought to my attention by John Blythe Dobson of Winnipeg, Manitoba, Canada.

The Royal Descents of 900 Immigrants

1. John II, King of France, d. 1364 = Bona of Bohemia
2. John I, Duke of Berry = Jeanne of Armagnac
3. Marie of Berry = John I, Duke of Bourbon
4. Charles I, Duke of Bourbon = Agnes of Burgundy
5. (illegitimate by Jeanne de Souldet), Sidoine alias Edmée de Bourbon = René du Bus, Seigneur de Tizon
6. Renée du Bus = Claude d'Anlezy, Seigneur de Menetou-Couture
7. Robert d'Anlezy, Seigneur de Menetou-Couture = Charlotte de Chastellux
8. Francoise d'Anlezy alias de Menetou = François de Celle, Seigneur du Puy
9. Gabrielle de Celle = Gilbert de Besse, Seigneur de la Richardie
10. Marguerite de Besse = Jérôme de Laizer, Seigneur de Siougeat
11. Louise de Laizer = Jean-Baptiste de Saignes, Seigneur de Grizols
12. Louise de Saignes = François des Rosiers, Seigneur de Moncelet
13. Charles-Annet des Rosiers, Seigneur de Moncelet = Anne de Bonnet de la Chabanne
14. Jean-Charles de Moncelet alias Moslé = Catharine Elisabeth Koehler
15. Alexander Samuel Mosle = Dorothea Catharina Rendorff
16. Georg Rudolf Mosle = Charlotte Amalie Schultze
17. **George Mosle** of N.Y. = Caroline Durnford Dunscomb of N.Y., ARD, SETH. Their daughter, Marie Caroline Mosle, married Keyes Winter, President Justice of the New York Municipal Court, and was the mother of (1) Henry Mosle (H.M.) West Winter (1915-2000, who married Elizabeth Tatham Dick), Pepsi-Cola executive, economic consultant, and author of *The Descendants of Charlemagne* (800-1400), 10 vols. (1987-91), covering sixteen generations; and (2) Susan Winter, who married Murray Salisbury Stedman, Jr. (1917-2006), political scientist and educator.

The Royal Descents of 900 Immigrants

Sources: H.M. West Winter (who compiled and contributed this line), "Genealogy of Hawtayne and West of Banbury (Oxon.) and London" (1965-70, typescript at NEHGS), pp. 144-45, "Magill and Dunscomb of Middletown, Conn., Chicago and New York" (1980, also a typescript at NEHGS), pp. 38-42, and "Durnford Family Records in Hampshire, Wiltshire, Dorset, Somerset and Canada" (1981, another typescript at NEHGS), pp. 31-33 (generations 13-17); A.G. Mosle, *Die Familie Mosle* (1912), pp. 1-11, and Otto Lasius, *Aus dem literarischen Nachlasse von Johann Ludwig Mosle, Grossherzoglich-Oldenburgischem General-major* (1879), vol. 1, pp. 1-2 (de Moncelet alias Moslé); Dr. de Ribier, *Preuves de noblesse des pages auvergnats admis dans les écuries du roi,* vol. 1 (1909), pp. 229, 231 (de Saignes and des Rosiers); *D de la N* (Laizer); Comte Jean de Remacle, *Généalogies des familles nobles de la Basse-Auvergne* (mms. at Family History Library in Salt Lake City, microfilm 661,782, no date or pagination) (de Besse) and *Dictionnaire des fiefs de la Basse-Auvergne,* in *Mémoires de l'Académie des Sciences Belles-Lettres and Arts de Clermont-Ferrand,* vol. 42/1 (1941), col. 642 (de Celle); Hugues A. Desgranges, *Nobiliaire de Berry,* vol. 1 (1965), p. 222 (du Bus and d'Anlezy); *ES*, tables for France, Berry, and Bourbon, and illegitimate children of the Bourbon house.

The Royal Descents of 900 Immigrants

1. John II, King of France, d. 1364 = Bona of Bohemia
2. Philip II, Duke of Burgundy = Margaret of Flanders
3. Marie of Burgundy = Amadeus VIII, Duke of Savoy
4. Louis I, Duke of Savoy = Anne de Lusignan, Princess of Cyprus, daughter of John I, titular King of Cyprus, Jerusalem, and Armenia, d. 1432, and Charlotte of Bourbon-Vendôme
5. Philip I, Duke of Savoy = (1) Margaret of Bourbon; (2) Claudia de Brosse
6. (illegitimate by Libera Portoneria) René de Savoie, Count de Villars-en Bresse = Anna Lascaris
7. Honorat II de Savoie, Count of Tenbe and Sommerive = Jeanne-Françoise de Foix
8. (illegitimate by ——) Jeanne de Villars = Nicolas de Thiene, Seigneur de Razay
9. Edmé de Thiene, Seigneur de Razay = Bonne de Burgat
10. Henry de Thiene, Seigneur de Razay = Jacqueline de Carnazet
11. Agathe de Thiene = Henri I du Plessis, Seigneur de Savonnières
12. Edmée-Henriette-Madeleine du Plessis = Gaspard de Tascher, Seigneur de la Pagerie
13. Gaspard-Joseph de Tascher, Seigneur de la Pagerie = Marie Françoise Boureau (Bourreau) de la Chevalerie
14. Joseph-Gaspard de Tascher, Seigneur de la Pagerie = Rose-Claire des Vergers de Sannois, a descendant, via Longvilliers, Choiseul, Sully, Chauvigny, and Counts of Vendôme, of Arthur II, Duke of Brittany (and Yolande of Dreux), son of John II, Duke of Brittany and Beatrix (Plantagenet) of England, SETH
15. Marie-Josèphe-Rose *dite* Joséphine de Tascher de la Pagerie, known as the Empress Josephine (1763-1814) = (1) Alexandre Marie, Vicomte de Beauharnais; (2) Napoléon I (Bonaparte), Emperor of the French (1769-1821)
16. (by 1) Eugène (Rose) de Beauharnais, 1st Duke of Leuchtenberg, Viceroy of Italy = Augusta Amalia Ludovica Georgia of Bavaria

17. (said to be illegitimate by Louise-Jeanne-Arnolde-Nicolasse-Marie Denis de Kerendern de Trobriand, whose much older husband was Barthélémy, Comte Dervieu du Villars; her child, certainly illegitimate, was given the surname of Minister of Police Pierre Denis-Lagarde) Louis-Pierre-Marie-Auguste Denis de Lagarde = Marie-Victoire-Desirée d'Haussy

18. Ludovic-Eugène Denis de Lagarde = Matilde-Ignacia de la Caridad Montalvo y Rodríguez

19. **Mathilde Dolores Denis de Lagarde** of Pa. = Theodore Davis **Boal**. Their son, Pierre de Lagarde Boal (1895-1966), was a diplomat of note, married Jeanne-Marie-Bernarde de Menthon, ARD, SETH, and was the father of Margaret Mathilde Boal, wife of (Francis Preston) Blair Lee (III) (1916-85), secretary of state, lt. gov. and act. gov. of Maryland.

Sources: *WWWA*, vol. 4, *1961-1968* (1968), p. 97 (P. de L. Boal), *WWA* (Blair Lee III) and *NYGBR* 127 (1996): 166; research in French archives by the Boal Mansion Museum in Boalsburg, Pa. That Eugène de Beauharnais was a lover of Louise-Jeanne-Arnolde-Nicolasse-Marie (known as Fanny) Denis de Kerendern de Trobriand is noted in Marie Arana, *Bolívar: American Liberator* (2013), pp. 53-55, 67, 476-78; Marie Caroline Post, *The Life and Mémoirs of Comte Régis de Trobriand, Major-General in the Army of the United States* (1910), pp. 27-30 covers Louise (Fanny), stating that "she pursued the gay life of the Imperial Court and became one of its most brilliant ornaments." The alleged descent from the 1st Duke of Leuchtenberg to Boal and Lee was brought to my attention by Christopher Carter Lee, an agnate kinsman of (Francis Preston) Blair Lee (III). The paternity of Louis P.M.A. Denis de Lagarde is generally accepted but documentary evidence, if any exists, would be welcome. Louise (Fanny)'s parents were François-Marie Denis de Kerendern, Baron de Trobriand, and Anna María Teresa Massa de Leunda y Aristiguieta (Post, as above, pp. 4-6).

For the ancestry of the Empress Josephine, see Joël Aubailly, *Les Ancêtres de Napoléon III* (1998), #s 6-7, 14-15, 28-29, 56-59, 114-15, 230-31, 460-61, 920-21, 1842 and p. 56 (entire line) and Leo Lindemans, *Voorouderstafel van het Belgisch Konighaus* [title also given in French and German], vol. 1 (1998), #s 50, 100-1, 202-3, 404-5, 808-9, 1618-19, 3238-39, 6476-77, 12952-53 (generations 8-16), each with bibliographies (Lindemans to books *and pages*); *ES* 2: 3: 3: 423b (generations 6-8) and *ES*

The Royal Descents of 900 Immigrants

2: 2: 192, 194-95 (Savoy), 2: 3: 3: 566 (Lusignan of Cyprus). For the Empress Josephine, note also *Bulletin Généalogique d'Information* 4 (1963): 37-40 and *Héraldique et Généalogie* 3 (1971): 60-65.

The Empress Joséphine is an ancestor of kings (and a reigning queen) of Sweden, Norway, Denmark and the Belgians, plus the Grand Duke of Luxembourg. For descendants of the legitimate children of the 1st Duke of Leuchtenberg see Jacques Arnold, *The Royal Houses of Europe: The Bonaparte Dynasty of France* (2008), pt. 2.

The Royal Descents of 900 Immigrants

1. John II, King of France, d. 1364 = Bona of Bohemia
2. Philip III, Duke of Burgundy = Margaret of Flanders
3. John, Duke of Burgundy = Margaret of Bavaria
4. Philip III, Duke of Burgundy = (1) Michelle of France, (2) Bona of Artois, (3) Isabella of Portugal. By (3), Philip was the father of Charles the Bold, Duke of Burgundy, father by Isabelle of Bourbon, of Mary of Burgundy, wife of Maximilian I, Holy Roman Emperor, through whom the Habsburgs inherited the "Spanish" Netherlands.
5. (illegitimate by Jeanne de Presles) Anthony de Bourgogne, Count de la Roche, Heer van Beveren = Marie de la Viéville
6. Jeanne de Bourgogne = Jasper van Culemborg, Heer van Werth
7. Magdalena van Culemborg = Guillaume de Noyelles
8. Elisabeth de Noyelles = Dirk van Bronckhorst-Batenburg, Heer van Anholt
9. Elisabeth van Bronckhorst-Batenburg = Johan (III) van Raesfeld, Heer van Ostendorf
10. Elisabeth van Raesfeld = Johan (II) van Pallandt, Heer van Voorst
11. Adolf Werner I van Pallandt, Heer van Bovenholt and Griethuysen = Ida Margaretha van Bottlenberg genaamd von Schirp
12. Adolf Werner (II) van Pallandt, Heer van Zuthem and Egede = Agnes Amalia van Pallandt
13. August Leopold van Pallandt, Heer van Eerde, Beerse, and Oosterveen = Anna Elisabeth van Haersolte
14. Adolph Werner, Baron van Pallandt = Anna Elisabeth Schimmelpenninck van der Oye
15. Guisbert Jan Anne Adolph, Baron van Pallandt = Cornelia Martina van der Goes
16. Henrietta Philippina Jacoba, Baroness van Pallandt = Frans Julius Johan, Baron van Heemstra

445

17. William Hendrik Johan, Baron van Heemstra = Wilhelmina Cornelia de Beaufort

18. Arnoud Jan Anne Aleid, Baron van Heemstra = Elbrig Willemine Henriette, Baroness van Asbeck

19. Ella, Baroness van Heemstra = (3) Joseph Victor Anthony Hepburn-Ruston

20. **Edda Kathleen van Heemstra Hepburn-Ruston,** born Audrey Kathleen Ruston, known as **Audrey Hepburn** (1929), actress, five-time Academy Award nominee (and winner for *Roman Holiday*), sometime of Calif. = (1) Melchor Gastón (Mel) Ferrer, actor; (2) Andrea Dotti.

Sources: *ANB* 10: 628-69 (Audrey Hepburn), which lists the several biographies, plus Sean Hepburn Ferrer, *Audrey Hepburn, An Elegant Spirit: A Son Remembers* (2003), pp. xiv-xvi esp.; *Nederland's Adelsboek,* 1956, pp. 61, 65-67 (van Heemstra), 1949, pp. 340-41, 362-63, 366-67 (van Pallandt); *ES* 2: 8: 85 (Raesfeld), 2: 18: 43-44 (Bronckhorst-Batenburg, Culemborg), 2: 3: 2: 322 (Burgundy-Beveren), and tables for Burgundy and France. This descent was developed, and Miss Hepburn's ancestry traced in considerable detail, by Leo van de Pas of Erindale, Australia. With advice from the late William Addams Reitwiesner I was readily able to trace this descent from the outline of it (contributed by Mr. van de Pas) in *The Plantagenet Connection* 9 (2001): 328-29.

The Royal Descents of 900 Immigrants

1. Louis IV (of Bavaria), Holy Roman Emperor, d. 1347 = (1) Beatrix of Glogau; (2) Margaret of Holland

2. (by 2) William, Count of Holland = Matilda Plantagenet of Lancaster

3. (illegitimate by Catharina Gerrit Busendochter) Elisabeth van Beieren = Brustijn van Herwijnen, Heer van Stavenisse

4. Adelise van Herwijnen = Otto, Heer van Haeften

5. Walraven, Heer van Haeften = Hendrika van Varick

6. Elisabeth van Haeften = Willem van Aeswijn

7. Henrica van Aeswijn = Seyno, Heer van Dorth

8. Dirck, Heer van Dorth = Joanna van Rossem

9. Seyno, Heer van Dorth = Maria Dorothea Droste zu Senden

10. Josina van Dorth = Alexander Tengnagell, Heer van Oploo

11. Maria Tengnagell = Abraham de Hinojosa

12. **Alexander de Hinojosa** (ca. 1629-1672), sometime of N.Y., "the last Dutch Director on the Delaware," also in Brazil = Margaret de Haes.

Sources: *TAG* 79 (2004): 260-63 (Henry Bainbridge Hoff) and *NYGBR* 73 (1942): 246-50 (William J. Hoffman) and sources cited in both, plus Otto Schutte, "De Hinojosa" in *Virtus: Bulletin van de Werkgroep Adelsgeschiedenis* 9 (2012), 1-2: 12-26; *Nederlands Adelsboek* 45 (1952): 322 (van Tengnagell, generations 9-10), 39 (1941): 256-57 (van Dorth, generation 7), 35 (1937): 117 (van Haeften, generations 4-5) and *ES* 2: 1: 1: 104, 91 (generations 1-2); and among articles not at NEHGS, *Gelre* 27 (1924): 115, 3 (1900): 81-116 and *Die Navorscher* 92 (1950-51): 33-44 (van Tengnagell and van Dorth), *Aqua Vitae: Genealogisch Tijdschrift NGV Afdeling Betuwe* 12 (1) (2009): 21-28 (Walraven van Haeften) and *Gens Nostra* 45 (1990): 380-87 (first six generations), plus J.A. de Chalmont, *Biographisch Woordenboek der Nederlanden*, 8 vols. (1798-1800, all published), 1: 358 (Willem van Aeswyn). This line was developed and brought to my attention by John Blythe Dobson of Winnipeg, Manitoba, Canada, who also used Ian Fettes and the late Leo

The Royal Descents of 900 Immigrants

van de Pas, *Plantagenet Cousins* (2007), pp. 18-20 (generations 1-5, for male model and actor Marcus [van] Schenkenberg, also a descendant of Walraven and Henrika above) and van de Pas's *Genealogics* website (which, for Marcus van Schenkenberg, cites at least two sources not at NEHGS or available to Mr. Dobson).

The Royal Descents of 900 Immigrants

1. Louis IV (of Bavaria), Holy Roman Emperor, d. 1347 = (1) Beatrix of Glogau; (2) Margaret of Holland

2. (by 1) Matilda of Bavaria = Frederick II, Margrave of Meissen, Landgrave of Thuringia

3. Frederick III, Margrave of Meissen = Katherine of Henneberg, daughter of Henry VI, Count of Henneberg, and Judith of Brandenburg, daughter of Herman V, Margrave of Brandenburg, and Anna of Austria, daughter of Albert I (Habsburg), Holy Roman Emperor, d. 1308 (and Elizabeth of Tirol), son of Rudolf I (Habsburg), Holy Roman Emperor, d. 1291, and Gertrude of Hohenberg

4. Frederick I, Elector of Saxony = Katherine of Brunswick-Lüneburg

5. Anna of Saxony = Louis I, Landgrave of Hesse

6. Louis II, Landgrave of Hesse = Matilda of Württemberg

7. (illegitimate by ——) Margaretha von Hessen = Heinrich Furster

8. —— Furster = Hermann von Medehem (Medem)

9. Anna von Medehem (Medem) = Marcus Stockeleff

10. Ilsabe Stockeleff = Barthold von Sothen

11. David von Sothen = —— von Sothen, a cousin

12. David von Sothen = Catharina Hartung

13. Anna Margaretha von Sothen = Sebastian Knoche (several descendants, or likely such, with the surname Wancke also immigrated to Cleveland)

14. Christine Elizabeth Knoche = Georg Valentin Kuehle

15. Johann Heinrich Kuehle = Anna Dorothea Eleonore Christine Gerlach (two grandsons named Kuehle also immigrated to Cleveland)

16. Anna Justina Kuehle = Ernst Philipp Wilhelm Kaufholz (a daughter and a likely son also immigrated to Cleveland, and a second daughter is said to have died in New Orleans).

17. **Friedrich Georg Kaufholz** of Cleveland, Ohio = Catharina Elisabeth Bauer. Their son, Frederick Gottlieb Kaufholz, married Elizabeth Trautman, and had Charles Frederick Kaufholz, who married Grace Maud Worst and had (Charles) Frederick Kaufholz (Jr.) (1915-2002), German-American genealogist (especially of Duderstadt, Hanover), trustee of NEHGS and donor of much of its German collection, who married Mary Roth.

Sources: *NGSQ* 49 (1961): 201-4 (generations 6-17), *TAG* 31 (1955): 177-78, *New England Ancestors* 3 (2002), 2: 6 and *TG* 16 (2002): 256 (the latter three are an ancestor table, to Johann Heinrich Kuehle, and obituaries of C. Frederick Kaufholz); *Deutsche Familienarchiv* 14 (1960): 294-95, 268, 297, 330, 250 (ancestor table of Louis II, Landgrave of Hesse) (generations 1-6), plus *ES* for Hesse, Saxony, Meissen, Bavaria, Henneberg, Brandenburg, and Austria (Habsburg).

The Royal Descents of 900 Immigrants

1. Louis IV (of Bavaria), Holy Roman Emperor, d. 1347 = (1) Beatrix of Glogau; (2) Margaret of Holland

2. (by 1) Matilda of Bavaria = Frederick II, Margrave of Meissen, Landgrave of Thuringia

3. Frederick III, Margrave of Meissen = Katherine of Henneberg, daughter of Henry VI, Count of Henneberg, and Judith of Brandenburg, daughter of Herman V, Margrave of Brandenburg, and Anna of Austria, daughter of Albert I (Habsburg), Holy Roman Emperor, d. 1308 (and Elizabeth of Tirol), son of Rudolf I (Habsburg), Holy Roman Emperor, d. 1291, and Gertrude of Hohenberg

4. Frederick I, Elector of Saxony = Katherine of Brunswick-Lüneburg

5. Frederick II, Elector of Saxony = Margaret of Austria, also a descendant of Albert I (Habsburg), Holy Roman Emperor, above

6. Ernest, Elector of Saxony = 6. Elizabeth of Bavaria, daughter of 5. Albert III, Duke of Bavaria-Munich (and Anna of Brunswick-Grubenhagen), son of 4. Ernest, Duke of Bavaria-Munich (and Elizabeth Visconti), son of 3. John, Duke of Bavaria-Munich (and Katharina of Gorz), son of 2. Stephen II, Duke of Bavaria-Landshut (son of Louis IV, Holy Roman Emperor, and Beatrix of Glogau, above) and Elizabeth of Sicily, daughter of Frederick II, King of Sicily, and Prince of Aragón, d. 1336, and Eleanor of Sicily and Anjou. Anna of Brunswick-Grubenhagen was a daughter of Eric, Duke of Brunswick-Grubenhagen and Elizabeth of Brunswick-Göttingen, daughter of Otto II, Duke of Brunswick-Göttingen and Margaret of Juliers, daughter of William III, Duke of Juliers and Catherine of Bavaria, daughter of Albert I, Duke of Bavaria and Count of Holland (and Margaret of Brieg), son of Louis IV, Holy Roman Emperor, above, and Margaret of Holland.

7. Margaret of Saxony = Henry, Duke of Brunswick-Lüneburg

8. Otto I, Duke of Brunswick-Lüneburg = Meta of Campe

The Royal Descents of 900 Immigrants

9. Otto II, Duke of Brunswick-Lüneburg = Margaret of Schwarzburg-Leutenberg

10. Elizabeth of Brunswick-Lüneburg = Eric Brahe, Count of Visingsborg

11. Beata Margareta, Countess Brahe = Gustaf Stenbock, Baron of Kronobäck and Öresten

12. Eric Stenbock, Count of Bogesund = Katharina von Schwerin

13. Magdalena, Countess Stenbock = Bengt, Count Oxenstierna, for whom Scandinavian royal descents are as follows:

1. Haakon V, King of Norway, d. 1319 = (1) Isabel de Joigny; (2) Eufemia of Rügen

2. (illegitimate by ——) Agnes (Agnes Haakonsdotter) of Norway = Havtore Jonson, knight

3. Jon Havtoreson, Lord of Borregaard and Huseby = ——

4. Ulv Jonson, Lord of Ervalla, Faanoe, Vreta, Saeby and Huseby = ——

5. Katarina Ulfsdotter = Tord Bonde, Lord of Bordsjoe

6. Marta Tordsdotter = Bengt Königsmark, Lord of Briby

7. Karin Königsmark = Johan Gädda, Lord of Faallnes

8. Kristina Gädda = Arvid Trolle, Lord of Bergkvara and Bo

9. Erik Trolle, Lord of Faanoe and Lagnoe = Karin Gyllenstierna

10. Beata Trolle = Gabriel, Baron Oxenstierna. A son, Gustav, Baron Oxenstierna, married Barbro Bielke (daughter of Axel Bielke and Elsa Posse, daughter of Axel Posse, Lord of Saatenes and Tun, and Elsa Nilsdotter, see below) and was the father of Axel (Gustafson), Count Oxenstierna, Swedish statesman and chancellor.

11. Bengt, Baron Oxenstierna = Sigrid Tre Rosor

12. Gabriel, Count Oxenstierna = Anna Banér. A daughter, Anna, Countess Oxenstierna, married Christopher Delphicus, Burggraf

The Royal Descents of 900 Immigrants

von Dohna-Carminden; among their descendants was Christian IX, King of Denmark, and among the grandsons of this last, in addition to Kings of Denmark, Norway, and Greece, were George V, King of Great Britain, and Nicholas II, last Czar of Russia.

13. Bengt, Count Oxenstierna = 12, 13. Magdalena, Countess Stenbock

14. Eva Magdalena, Countess Oxenstierna = Magnus, Count Stenbock, a cousin, son of Gustav Otto, Count Stenbock (a son of Gustaf Stenbock, Baron of Kronobäck and Öresten, and Beata Margareta, Countess Brahe, above) and Christina Katarina, Countess de la Gardie (sister of Axel Julius, Count de la Gardie, husband of Sofia Juliana, Baroness Forbus, SETH), daughter of Jacob, Count de la Gardie (and Ebba, Countess Brahe), son of Pontus, Baron de la Gardie, by Sophia Gyllenhielm, illegitimate daughter (by Catherine Hansdotter) of **John III, King of Sweden**, d. 1592, son of Gustav Vasa, King of Sweden, and Margareta Leijonhufvud, SETH; neither of the latter has proved royal medieval ancestry.

15. Ulrika Magdalena, Countess Stenbock = Karl Hans Wachtmeister, 2nd Count of Skunkberg

16. Magdalena Sophia, Countess Wachtmeister = Axel Gustaf, Baron Wachtmeister, a cousin

17. Hedwig Eleonora, Baroness Wachtmeister = Melker, Count Falkenberg

18. Magdalena Sophia, Countess Falkenberg = Israel, Baron Lagerfelt

19. Gustav Adolf, Baron Lagerfelt = Kristina Beata Wilhelmina, Baroness Funck

20. Adolf Israel Gustav, Baron Lagerfelt = Ebba Frederica Regina Grill

21. Gustav Adolf, Baron Lagerfelt = Gertrude Ida Eugenia, Baroness von Essen

22. Israel Karl Gustav Eugène, Baron Lagerfelt, diplomat = Mary Charmian Sara Champion de Crespigny

23. **Caroline (Eugénie, Baroness) Lagerfelt**, b. 1947, of N.Y., actress (most recently on television), unm.

The Royal Descents of 900 Immigrants

Sources: Wikipedia entry for Caroline Lagerfelt; *Elgenstierna*, vol. 4, pp. 453, 453-56 (Lagerfelt), 2, p. 642 (Falkenberg), 8, pp. 608, 614 (Wachtmeister), 7, pp. 572-77 (Stenbock), 1, p. 556 (Brahe), 5, pp. 591-93, 599-600, 604-5 (Oxenstierna), 8, pp. 371-72 (Trolle), 2, pp. 224-26 (de la Gardie); *ES* 2: 8: 151 (Brahe), 153-56 (de la Gardie, Oxenstierna), 158-60 (Stenbock), plus tables for Brunswick-Lüneburg, Saxony, Meissen, Bavaria, Henneberg, Brandenburg, Austria, Brunswick-Grubenhagen, Brunswick-Göttingen, and Juliers, and *Foundations* 2 (2006-9): 260-62 (line from Haakon V, King of Norway). Note also that Henry, Duke of Brunswick-Lüneburg and Margaret of Saxony at generation 7 are M 833-34 in *Prince Charles*, and the descent of Gabriel, Count Oxenstierna, from Bengt Königsmark, Lord of Briby, and Marte Tordsdotter (Bonde) (generations 6-12) is covered in *Prince Charles*, K 22-23, L 45-46, M 89-90, N 179-890, O 357-58, P 715-16, Q 1431-32. This descent was first developed and brought to my attention by John Blythe Dobson of Winnipeg, Manitoba, Canada.

The Royal Descents of 900 Immigrants

1. Philip III, King of Navarre, d. 1343 = Joanna of France, daughter of Louis X, King of France, d. 1316, and Margaret of Burgundy
2. Joanna of Navarre = Jean I, Vicomte de Rohan
3. Charles de Rohan, Seigneur de Guémené = Catherine de Guesclin
4. Louis I de Rohan, Seigneur de Guémené = Marie de Montauban
5. Pierre de Rohan, Seigneur de Gié = Françoise de Penhoët
6. Charles de Rohan, Seigneur de Gié = Jeanne de Saint-Severin
7. François de Rohan, Seigneur de Gié = Catherine de Silly

    (5. Pierre de Rohan was also Count de Marle, 6. Charles de Rohan was also Vicomte de Fronsac, and 7. François de Rohan was also Baron de Château-du-Loir)

8. Françoise (called Diane) de Rohan = François de Maillé de la Tour-Landry, Baron de la Tour-Landry, Count de Châteauroux
9. Madeleine de Maillé de la Tour-Landry = François de Menon, Seigneur de Turbilly
10. Urbain de Menon, Seigneur de Turbilly, Count de Brestau = Marie de Chahannai
11. Elizabeth de Menon = René IV de Vimeur, Seigneur de Rochambeau
12. Joseph-Charles I de Vimeur, Seigneur de Rochambeau = Marie-Madeleine Brachet
13. Joseph-Charles II de Vimeur, Marquis de Rochambeau = Marie-Claire-Thérèse Bégon
14. **Jean-Baptiste-Donatien de Vimeur, Count de Rochambeau** (1725-1807), commander of the French expeditionary army in America during the last three years of the American Revolution, treated in the *DAB* = Jeanne-Thérèse Tellez d'Acosta.

Sources: *Armorial General, ou Registres de la Noblesse de France*, vol. 2, pt. 2 (1742), pp. 13-18 (Vimeur de Rochambeau, Menon, Maillé) and *ES* 2: 10: 54 (Maillé), 2: 10: 14-16, 23 (Rohan) and charts for Navarre and France. See also *D de la N* (Vimeur de Rochambeau and Maillé) and *Anselme* (Rohan and Navarre).

The Royal Descents of 900 Immigrants

1. Robert I, King of Scotland, d. 1329 = (2) Elizabeth de Burgh
2. Matilda Bruce = Thomas Isaac or Ysac
3. Joanna Isaac or Ysac = John de Ergadia [of Argyll] of Lorne
4. Isabel de Ergadia [of Argyll] = Sir John Stewart of Innermeath and Lorne
5. Jean Stewart = Sir David Bruce of Clackmannan
6. John Bruce of Clackmannan = Elizabeth Stewart
7. Sir David Bruce of Clackmannan = Mariot Herries
8. Sir David Bruce of Clackmannan = Janet Blackadder
9. Sir Edward Bruce of Blairhall = Alison Reid
10. Sir George Bruce of Carnock = Margaret Primrose
11. Margaret Bruce = Francis Nichols (Nicolls)
12. **Richard Nichols** (Nicolls) (c. 1624-1672), first English colonial governor of N.Y., d. unm.

Sources: *Oxford DNB*; *Drummond*, vol. 1 (Bruce) and *BP* (Bruce, earls of Elgin); *BP* (recent editions, Moray — for Stewart of Lorne); *CP* (Lorn), *MCS5*, line 42, and *RA* 5: 39-41 (Stewart of Lorne [de Ergadia]), 1: 605-10 (Scotland). See also *TAG* 68 (1993): 113-14 (on the governor, his parents and [alleged] siblings) and William F. Skene, ed., *Gesta Annalia* (Edinburgh, 1871), in *Historians of Scotland*, vol. 1, section CLXIX, pp. 369-370 (Isaac or Ysac, Argyll).

The Royal Descents of 900 Immigrants

1. Haakon V, King of Norway, d. 1319 = (1) Isabel de Joigny; (2) Eufemia of Rügen

2. (illegitimate by ——) Agnes (Agnes Haakonsdotter) of Norway = Havtore Jonson, knight

3. Jon Havtoreson, Lord of Borregaard and Huseby = ——

4. Ulv Jonson, Lord of Ervalla, Faanoe, Vreta, Saeby and Huseby = ——

5. Peder Ulfsson, Lord of Ervalla and Huseby = ——

6. Ulf Pedersson, knight, Lord of Ervalla = ——

7. Elin Ulfsdotter of Ervalla = Henrik Erlandsson, Lord of Fyllingarum

8. Ulf Henriksson, Lord of Fyllingarum = Agneta Lillie

9. Helena Bååt (Snakenborg) = Sir Thomas Gorges, ARD, SETH. Their daughter Bridget Gorges married Sir Robert Phelips, the Parliamentary leader.

10. **Elizabeth Gorges** = (1) Sir Hugh **Smith**; (2) Sir Ferdinando **Gorges** (ca. 1565-1647), founder and Lord Proprietor of Maine (his fifth wife), ARD, SETH.

9. Karin Snakenborg (sister of Helena Bååt [Snakenborg]) = Filip Bonde, Lord of Bordsjoe and Seckestad, a kinsman of Charles VIII (Bonde), King of Sweden

10. Mårta Bonde = Lindorm Ribbing, Lord of Boxholm

11. Maria Ribbing = Carl Mörner, Baron Mörner

12. Christina Maria Mörner = Johan Ribbing

13. Bengt, Baron Ribbing = Ulrika Eleanora, Countess Piper

14. Ture, Baron Ribbing = Hedvig Juliana, Baroness Roos

15. Juliana, Baroness Ribbing = Carl Fredrik Uggla

16. Carl Fredrik Uggla = Maria Elisabet Brockman

17. Pontus Helmfrid Uggla = Malvina Sofia Ulrika Berggren

18. **Carl Magnus Helmfrid Uggla** of N.Y. = Annie Bass. Their son, Arnold Helmfrid Uggla, married Helen Jane Ryder and was the father of John Carl Uggla, who married Elizabeth Armistead Cooley and was the father of Dan(iel Cooley) Uggla, b. 1980, professional baseball player for the Florida Marlins, 2006-10, and the Atlanta Braves, 2011-14, San Francisco Giants, 2014, and Washington Nationals, 2014-15, who married (1) Tara Sims; (2) Janette Repsch.

Sources: *Foundations* 2: 4 (July 2007): 260-70 (Lady Gorges, and generations 1-10); *ES* 2: 2: 111 (Norway, which includes Agnes Haakonsdotter and Havtore Jonson); *Elgenstierna*, vol. 1, p. 517 (Bonde), vol. 6, pp. 291, 296, 312-13 (Ribbing), vol. 5, pp. 369-70 (Mörner af Tuna) and vol. 8, pp. 461-62 (Uggla, to the 1914 birth of A.H. Uggla); Social Security Death Index for Arnold Uggla (1914-96) and Helen Jane Ryder Uggla (1919-93), and Commonwealth of Virginia marriage record 71016970 (John Carl Uggla, son of Arnold H. Uggla and Helen Jane Ryder, and Elizabeth Armistead Cooley, daughter of Hollis Welbourn Cooley and Carey Shands) and the Wikipedia entry for Dan Uggla. The Uggla descent was developed and placed online by the late William Addams Reitwiesner.

The Royal Descents of 900 Immigrants

1. Charles II (of Anjou and France), King of Naples and Sicily, d. 1309 = Marie of Hungary, daughter of Stephen V, King of Hungary, d. 1272, and Elizabeth of the Kumans

2. Margaret of Anjou = Charles, Count of Valois, son of Philip III, King of France, d. 1285, and Isabella of Aragón

3. Jeanne of Valois (sister of Philip VI, King of France, d. 1350) = William III, Count of Holland and Hainault (parents of Philippa of Hainault, wife of Edward III, King of England), son of John II, Count of Hainault, and Philippa of Luxembourg, SETH

4. Joanna of Hainault = William V, Duke of Juliers

5. William VI, Duke of Juliers = Maria of Guelders

6. Joanna of Juliers = John V, Lord of Arkel

7. Maria of Arkel, heiress of Guelders = John II, Lord of Egmont. They were grandparents of Mary of Guelders, wife of James II, King of Scotland.

8. William, Count of Egmont = Walpurga of Mörs and Saarwerden, daughter of Frederick IV, Count of Mörs and Saarwerden, and Engelberta of Mark and Cleves, daughter of Adolf of Cleves, Count of Mark, and Margaret of Juliers, daughter of Gerhard VI of Juliers, Count of Berg (and Margaret of Ravensberg), son of William V, Duke of Juliers, and Joanna of Hainault, generation 4 above. John I, Count of Egmont, son of William and Walpurga, married Magdalena of Werdenberg, SETH, and was the father of John II, Count of Egmont, who married Françoise of Luxembourg, Countess of Gavre, and was the father of Lamoral, Count of Egmont, Prince of Gavre, also SETH, the Belgian leader and martyr in the revolt of The Netherlands against Spain.

9. Frederick of Egmont, Count of Buren = (1) Aleid von Culemburg; (2) Walpurga of Manderscheid

10. (illegitimate by Catharina von Kessel) Catharina van Egmond = Lodewijk van Praet, Heer van Moerkerke

11. Françoise/Francina van Praet = Wessel van den Boetzelaer, lord of Langerak and Asperen

The Royal Descents of 900 Immigrants

12. Rutger van den Boetzelaer, lord of Langerak, Merwede, Asperen and Carnisse = Agnes de Bailleul

13. Wessel van den Boetzelaer, lord of Asperen and Merwede = Amélie van Marnix

14. Philip Jacob van den Boetzelaer, lord of Asperen = Anne van der Noot

15. Anna Florentina van den Boetzelaer = Lodewijk van Marlot, Heer van Bavey

16. Anna Maria van Marlot = Gijsbert Johan van Hardenbroek, Heer van Groenewoude and Hinderstein

17. Anna Charlotte van Hardenbroek = Arnold Hendrik Feith

18. Gijsbert Jan Feith = Anna van Scherpenberg

19. Ursula Matha Feith = Jacob Pieter van Braam

20. Jacob Andreas van Braam = Ambrosina Wilhelmina van Rijck

21. Geertruida Helena van Braam = Hendrik Stephanus van Son

22. Hendrik Jan Abraham van Son = Wilhelmina Vincentia Maria Baud

23. Louise Dorothea Adrienne van Son = Jan Samuel François van Hoogstraten

24. François van Hoogstraten = Alida Hendrika Maria Wigman

25. **Jan Samuel François van Hoogstraten**, 1922-2011, of N.Y., official of Church World Service (with the U.N. High Commissioner for Refugees), the Tolstoy Foundation, and the International Human Assistance Program = Eleanor Colson Curtis. Sons David Jan van Hoogstraten, b. 1954, and Nicholas Frans van Hoogstraten, b. 1956 are respectively at British Petroleum Wind Energy, North America, and a television news producer in Los Angeles. This latter is also the author of *Lost Broadway Theaters*).

Sources: Internet coverage of J.S.F. van Hoogstraten and his sons; R.F. Vulsma, ed., *Van Aken naar Heden: Gezamenlijke uitgave van de Karel de*

The Royal Descents of 900 Immigrants

Grote-Nummers van "Gens Nostra" 1968, 1990 en 1991 (1994), pp. 352-55 (generations 16-25); *Nederlands Adelsboek* 40 (1942): 295 (van Hardenbroek), 38 (1940): 333 (van Boetzelaer); *Gens Nostra* 23 (1968): 376, 383 (generations 14-16), Simon van Leeuwen, *Batavia Illustrata*, vol. 2 (1685), pp. 1008-9 (Moerkerke); A.W.E. Dek, *Genealogie der Heren en Graven van Egmond* (1958), *passim* and *ES* 2: 18: 30-32 (Egmond) and charts for Guelders, Arkel (2: 5: 68), Juliers, Hainault/Holland, France, Naples, Saarwerden (2: 7: 168), and Mark and Cleve (2: 18: 17). Note also *Charles II*, pp. 121, 197, 305-6 (generations 5-7). This line was developed and brought to my attention by John Blythe Dobson of Winnipeg, Manitoba, Canada.

The Royal Descents of 900 Immigrants

1. Edward I, King of England, d. 1307 = Margaret of France
2. Thomas of Brotherton, Earl of Norfolk = Alice de Hales
3. Margaret Plantagenet, Duchess of Norfolk = John de Segrave, 4th Baron Segrave
4. Elizabeth de Segrave = John Mowbray, 4th Baron Mowbray
5. Eleanor Mowbray = John de Welles, 5th Baron Welles, son of John de Welles, 4th Baron Welles, and Maud de Ros, SETH
6. Eudo de Welles = Maud de Greystock
7. Lionel de Welles, 6th Baron Welles = Joan Waterton
8. Eleanor de Welles = Thomas Hoo, 1st Baron Hoo
9. Eleanor Hoo = James Carew
10. Sir Richard Carew = Malyn Oxenbridge
11. Margaret Carew = John St. John
12. Nicholas St. John = Elizabeth Blount
13. Elizabeth St. John = Sir Richard St. George
14. Sir George St. George = Catherine Gifford
15. Mary St. George = Richard Coote, 1st Baron Coote of Coloony
16. **Richard Coote, 1st Earl of Bellomont** (1636-1701), colonial gov. of N.Y., Mass. and N.H. = Catherine Nanfan, ARD, SETH.
16. Letitia Coote = Robert Molesworth, 1st Viscount Molesworth
17. Hon. William Molesworth = Anne Adair
18. Richard Molesworth = Catherine Cobb
19. John Molesworth = Louise Tomkyns
20. Margaret Letitia Molesworth = Charles Richard de Havilland
21. Walter Augustus de Havilland = Lilian Augusta Ruse
22. **Olivia (Mary) de Havilland** (b. 1916) of Calif., actress, recipient of the Academy Award in 1946 and 1949 = (1) Marcus Aurelius Goodrich; (2) Pierre Paul Galante.

The Royal Descents of 900 Immigrants

22. **Joan de Beauvoir de Havilland**, known as **Joan Fontaine** (1917-2013) of Calif., actress, recipient of the Academy Award in 1941 = (1) Brian de Lacey Aherne (1902-1986), actor; (2) William Dozier; (3) Collier Young; (4) Alfred Wright, Jr.

14. Sir Henry St. George (brother of Sir George) = Mary Dayrell
15. Frances St. George = George Tucker of Bermuda
16. **Henry Tucker** of Va. = Elizabeth Bridger.

16. William Tucker (brother of Henry of Va.) = Ann Stone
17. Benjamin S(tone) Tucker = Love (Gibbs?). Another daughter, Mary Tucker, wife of John Ballentine, also migrated to S.C. but left no NDTPS.
18. **Anna Tucker** of S.C. = Nathaniel **Morgan**.
19. Sarah Morgan = Job Palmer
20. Sarah Anne Palmer = Samuel Edward Axson
21. Isaac Stockton Keith Axson = Rebecca Longstreet FitzRandolph
22. Samuel Edward Axson = Margaret Jane Hoyt
23. Ellen Louise Axson = (Thomas) Woodrow Wilson (1856-1924), 28th U.S. President

18. **Sarah Tucker** of S.C. = (1) William **Harris**; (2) Edward **Bullard**.

16. St. George Tucker (brother of Henry and William of Va.) = Jane Hubbard. A son, John Tucker, immigrated to S.C., married Elizabeth —— and left issue but no NDTPS. Sons George and Mansfield may have immigrated to S.C. and Va. respectively.
17. Henry Tucker = Frances Tudor
18. Henry Tucker (Jr.) = Anne Butterfield

The Royal Descents of 900 Immigrants

19. **St. George Tucker** (1752-1827) of Va., revolutionary soldier, Virginia jurist, professor of law at William and Mary = (1) Frances Bland; (2) Lelia Skipwith.

19. Henry Tucker (III) = Frances Bruere. A son was British Rear Admiral Thomas Tudor Tucker.

20. Henry St. George Tucker = Jane Boswell. A daughter was children's writer Charlotte Maria Tucker.

21. William Thornhill Tucker = Wilhelmina Douglas de Lautour

22. **Frederick St. George de Lautour (Tucker, later) Booth-Tucker,** Salvation Army officer = (1) Louise Mary Bode; (2) Emma Moss Booth, known as Mrs. Emma Moss Booth-Tucker (1860-1903), Salvation Army officer, American resident from 1896 to 1903, daughter of William Booth, founder of the Salvation Army (and Catherine Mumford); (3) Mary Reid.

19. Frances Tucker (sister of Henry III and St. George) = Henry Tucker, a cousin

20. John Henry Tucker = Eliza Jane Tucker, a cousin

21. **Mary Byrd Farley Tucker** of Va. = John Patten **Emmet**, SETH.

18. Thomas Tucker (brother of Henry, Jr.) = Mary Nichols

19. **Frances Tucker** of N.Y. = John **Montrésor** (1736-1799), British military engineer who served in the American colonies from 1754 to 1778, son of James Gabriel Montrésor, also a noted British military engineer who served in the American colonies, SETH, by Mary Haswell, his first wife

14. Richard St. George (brother of Sir George and Sir Henry) = Anne Pinnock

15. Henry St. George = Anne Hatfield

16. George St. George = Elizabeth Bligh

17. Sir Richard St. George, 1st Bt. = Sarah Persse

The Royal Descents of 900 Immigrants

18. Sir Richard Bligh St. George, 2nd Bt. = Bridget Blakeney
19. Robert St. George = Sophia Madelina Olivia Mahon, daughter of James Mahon, Dean of Dromore (and Frances Catherine Ker), son of Ross Mahon and (Lady) Anne Browne, for whom see *RD600*, p. 243, but ignore the claimed royal parentage for Sir John Perrott
20. Howard Bligh St. George = Florence Evelyn Baker of N.Y.
21. **George Baker Bligh St. George** of N.Y. = Katherine Delano Price Collier, known as Mrs. Katherine D.P.C. St. George (1896-1983), congresswoman from N.Y.

Sources: *CP* (Bellomont, Coote of Coloony, Hoo, Welles), *EP* and *BP* (St. George, in *BP* to G.B.B. St. George, plus *BLGI* 1912, p. 452 for Mahon), *BP* (Bolingbroke), *Manning and Bray*, vol. 2, chart opp. p. 532 (Carew), and *RA* 1: 358-60 (Carew), 3: 308-11 (Hoo), 5: 331-38 (Welles), 4: 187-88 (Mowbray), 4: 256-66 (Norfolk); *BP* (Molesworth) and *BLG*, 18th ed., vol. 1 (1965), pp. 196-97 (de Havilland and Fontaine); Robert Dennard Tucker, *Descendants of William Tucker of Throwleigh, Devon* (1991), chapters 2-5, esp. pp. 50-53, 55-56, 139-40, 167-69, 177, 181, 184-85, 187, 191-227, 231-37, 249-51, 253-78, Caroline T. Moore, ed., *Abstracts of the Wills of the State of South Carolina, 1760-1784* (1969), pp. 45 (John Ballentine, wife Mary), 84 (Edward Bullard, wife Sarah and her son, Tucker Harris), and Brent H. Holcomb, *South Carolina Marriages, 1688-1799* (1980), pp. 112 (William Harris and Sarah Tucker), 31 (Edward Bullard and Sarah Harris, widow) (for Mrs. Morgan and Mrs. Bullard), and *Executive Papers* 8 (2011), pp. 14-15, 25, 70, 9 (2012), pp. 36-37 (Mrs. [Thomas] Woodrow Wilson to Margaret [Carew] St. John); Thomas Addis Emmet II, *A Memoir of John Patten Emmet* (1898), Tucker pedigrees esp. (for Henry and St. George Tucker, Booth-Tucker, Mrs. Emmet and Mrs. Montrésor). See also *NEXUS* 16 (1999): 116-19 (for the Molesworth descent of H.R.H. The Countess of Wessex, formerly Sophie Helen Rhys-Jones).

The parentage of John de Welles, 5th Baron Welles, is given above but not subsequently because in this volume he first appears on this chart.

The Royal Descents of 900 Immigrants

1. Edward I, King of England, d. 1307 = Eleanor of Castile
2. Joan Plantagenet = Gilbert de Clare, 3rd Earl of Gloucester, 7th Earl of Hertford
3. Elizabeth de Clare = Sir Theobald de Verdun
4. Isabel de Verdun = Henry Ferrers, 2nd Baron Ferrers of Groby
5. William Ferrers, 3rd Baron Ferrers of Groby = Margaret Ufford
6. Henry Ferrers, 4th Baron Ferrers of Groby = Joan Poynings
7. William Ferrers, 5th Baron Ferrers of Groby = Philippa Clifford
8. Sir Thomas Ferrers = Elizabeth Freville, daughter of Sir Baldwin Freville and Maud le Scrope, SETH
9. Sir Henry Ferrers = Margaret Heckstall (who married firstly William Whetenhall, and was also the mother of another William Whetenhall who married Anne Cromer, SETH, and was the father of Rose Whetenhall below)
10. Sir Edward Ferrers = Constance Brome, daughter of Nicholas Brome, SETH (who married [2] Katherine Lampeck) and Elizabeth Arundel
11. Elizabeth Ferrers = John Hampden
12. Griffith Hampden = Anne Cave, see below (parents also of William Hampden, who married Elizabeth Cromwell, aunt of Oliver Cromwell, the Lord Protector, and was the father of Parliamentary leader John Hampden, who = [2] Lettice Knollys, SETH)
13. Anne Hampden = Robert Waller (parents also of poet and M.P. Edmund Waller)
14. Anne Waller = James Kyrle
15. **Sir Richard Kyrle,** colonial governor of S.C. = (1) ———; (2) Mary Jephson of S.C., ARD, SETH.

14. Ursula Waller (sister of Anne) = Daniel Dobyns
15. Edmund Dobyns = ———

16. **Daniel Dobyns** of Va. = (1) Elizabeth Dudding; (2) Mrs. Elizabeth Godson (?) Smith; (3) Elizabeth Billington.

14. Robert Thomas Waller (brother of Anne and Ursula) = ———, a niece of John Bramhall, Archbishop of Armagh
15. John Waller = Hannah Coddington
16. Robert Waller = Anne Hughes
17. Hannah Waller = Dixie Coddington
18. **Anne Coddington** of N.C. = Richard **Fenner** (d. c. 1766), lawyer.

13. Dorothy Hampden (sister of Anne) = Robert Hatley
14. John Hatley = Anne Porter
15. Henry Hatley = Hester/Esther Whitaker
16. Jane Hatley = Daniel Norton
17. **John Norton** of Va. = Courtenay Walker.

10. Elizabeth Ferrers (sister of Sir Edward) = James Clerke
11. George Clerke = Elizabeth Wilsford, daughter of Thomas Wilsford (whose first wife was the above Rose Whetenhall, SETH) and Elizabeth Colepepper (Culpeper), sister of the William Colepepper (Culpeper) who married Cecily Barrett, SETH. Bridget Wilsford, a full sister of Elizabeth, married Leonard Digges and was the mother of Thomas Digges, husband of Anne St. Leger, SETH.
12. James Clerke = Mary Saxby
13. William Clerke = Mary Weston, sister of Richard Weston, 1st Earl of Portland, Lord Treasurer under Charles I, and daughter of Sir Jerome Weston and Mary Cave, sister of the Anne Cave who married Griffith Hampden above, and daughter of Anthony Cave and Elizabeth Lovett, SETH.

The Royal Descents of 900 Immigrants

14. **Jeremiah Clarke**, acting governor of R.I. = Mrs. Frances Latham Dungan. Their daughter, Mary Clarke, married (1) John Cranston (c. 1626-1680), physician, colonial governor of R.I., ARD, SETH; (2) Philip Jones; (3) John Stanton.

   8. Elizabeth Ferrers (sister of Sir Thomas) = Sir William Colepepper (Culpeper), a kinsman of Sir John Colepepper (Culpeper) above

   9. Richard Colepepper (Culpeper) = Isabel Worsley

   10. Joyce Colepepper (Culpeper) = (1) Ralph Leigh; (2) Lord Edmund Howard, SETH

   11. (by 1) Isabel Leigh (half-sister of Katherine Howard, fifth Queen of Henry VIII) = Sir Edward Baynton

   12. Henry Baynton/Bainton = Anne Cavendish, daughter (by Margaret Bostock, a first wife) of Sir William Cavendish, husband of Elizabeth Hardwick, the well-known "Bess of Hardwick," later Countess of Shrewsbury, adventuress, SETH

   13. Ferdinando Bainton = Joan Weare alias Browne

   14. **Anne Bainton** of Mass. = Christopher **Batt** of Mass., ARD, SETH.

   15. Samuel Batt (returned to England, rector of Coulston, Wiltshire) = Mary ——

   16. **Mary Batt** of S.C. = (1) John **Ash(e)** (parents of John Baptista Ashe, colonial official of N.C.); (2) Rev. William **Livingston.**

Sources: *The Augustan, Book Five: An Omnibus Publication* (1974), "The Colonial Genealogist" section, pp. 709-10, which cites *Journal of the Cork Historical and Archaeological Society,* 1895, p. 523 and 1906, p. 4, and *South Carolina Archives, Records of the Secretary of the Province, 1675-1695*, pp. 214-15, Duncumb, vol. 3, p. 185 (Kyrle) and *BIFR*, pp. 1174-75 (Waller), 252 (Coddington), Charles Croslegh, *Descent and Alliances of Croslegh or Crossle or Crossley of Scaitcliffe and Coddington of Oldbridge and Evans of Eyton Hall* (1904), p. 286 (Coddington) and William S. Powell, ed., *Dictionary of North Carolina Biography,* vol. 2 (1986), p. 186 (Richard Fenner); *TVG* 46 (2002): 163-

66 (Dobyns, by John Anderson Brayton), Kenneth W. Dobyns and Margaret S. Thorpe, *Daniel Dobyns of Colonial Virginia: His English Ancestry and American Descendants* (1969), pp. 9, 12-18, 21-26 esp.; *William and Mary Quarterly*, 3rd ser., 19 (1962): 383-84, 400-7 (Norton, Hatley), *MGH*, 5th ser., 9 (1935-37): 91-92 (Hatley, Hampden), *Chester of Chicheley*, vol. 1, pp. 73-110, and *Lipscomb*, vol. 2, pp. 234-36, 259 (Cave, Waller, Hampden), and Rev. Henry Norris, *Baddesley Clinton, Its Manor, Church, and Hall, with Some Account of the Family of Ferrers from the Norman Conquest to the Present Day* (1897), pp. 112-17 esp. and *CP* (Ferrers of Groby); *RA* 2: 212-15 (Clarke, Ferrers), 3: 153-58 (Ferrers), 5: 245-48 (Verdun), 2: 195-206 (Clare), 3: 39 (Freville), 2: 351-52 (Whetenhall), 3: 271 (Brome), 1: 260-62 (Wilsford, Colepepper), 2: 369 (Colepepper), 3: 104-5 (Digges), 3: 637-38 (Cave), 5: 44-46 (Colepepper/ Culpeper, Leigh), 1: 275-76 (Baynton), 1: 267-68 (Batt), *AR8*, lines 11 and 8 (Clarke), 248 (Mrs. Batt); *NEHGR* 74 (1920): 68-76, 130-40, reprinted in *EO* 1: 1: 570-88, and *Jeremy Clarke*, pp. 10-54 (34-35 esp.) (for Jeremiah Clarke); *Davis* 1: 81-86, 89-135 (129 esp.), and *Mary Isaac*, pp. 343-54 (for Mrs. Batt); C.T. Moore and A.A. Simmons, *Abstracts of the Wills of the State of South Carolina, 1670-1740,* vol. 1 (1960), pp. 23-24 (will of John Ash, mentioning his wife and father-in-law), plus N.C. research by John Anderson Brayton, who brought Mrs. Mary Batt Ash(e) to my attention. The descent of Mrs. Fenner was developed by Nicholas Dixie Coddington and the late W.A. Reitwiesner (who brought it to my attention). The descent of John Norton was developed, posted on the Internet, and brought to my attention by John C. Brandon of Columbia, S.C.

Philippa Clifford at generation 7 above was a sister of Thomas Clifford, 6th Baron Clifford, who married Elizabeth de Ros and was the father of John Clifford, 7th Baron Clifford, who married Elizabeth Percy, SETH; see *RA* 2: 244-46. And the Elizabeth Colepepper (Culpeper) Wilsford and William Colepepper (Culpeper) at generation 11, p. 467, were children of Walter Colepepper (Culpeper) (and Anne Aucher), son of Sir John Colepepper (Culpeper) and Agnes Gainsford, SETH. Anne Aucher was a daughter of Henry Aucher and Elizabeth Guilford, whose brother Sir Richard Guilford married Anne Pympe and was the father of Sir Edward Guilford (m. Eleanor West), George Guilford (m. Elizabeth Mortimer), and Frideswide Guilford (m. Sir Matthew Browne), all SETH. See *Sussex Archaeological Collections* 47 (1904): 58-63 and charts between pp. 56 and 57, and 72 and 73, and *Mary Isaac*, pp. 78-96.

The Royal Descents of 900 Immigrants

1. Edward I, King of England, d. 1307 = Margaret of France
2. Thomas of Brotherton, Earl of Norfolk = Alice de Hales
3. Margaret Plantagenet, Duchess of Norfolk = John de Segrave, 4th Baron Segrave
4. Elizabeth de Segrave = John Mowbray, 4th Baron Mowbray
5. Eleanor Mowbray = John de Welles, 5th Baron Welles
6. Eudo de Welles = Maud de Greystock
7. Lionel de Welles, 6th Baron Welles = Joan Waterton
8. Margaret de Welles = Sir Thomas Dymoke
9. Sir Lionel Dymoke = Joanna Griffith
10. Alice Dymoke = Sir William Skipwith
11. Henry Skipwith = Jane Hall, daughter of Francis Hall (and Ursula Sherington), son of Francis Hall and Elizabeth Wingfield, SETH
12. Sir William Skipwith = Margaret Cave, daughter of Roger Cave and Margaret Cecil, sister of William Cecil, 1st Baron Burghley, minister of Elizabeth I
13. Sir Henry Skipwith, 1st Bt. = Amy Kempe, daughter of Sir Thomas Kempe and Dorothy Thompson, SETH
14. **Sir Grey Skipwith, 3rd Bt.**, of Va. = Elizabeth ——.
14. **Diana Skipwith** of Va. = Edward **Dale**.
15. Katherine Dale (whose maternity has been disputed; see *TAG* 75 [2000]: 27-29 [*con*] and *The Plantagenet Connection* 9 [2001]: 117-20 [Douglas Richardson and Michael Anne Guido] [*pro*]; Katherine is included on *RA* 4: 644) = Thomas Carter
16. Thomas Carter, Jr. = Arabella Williamson
17. Daniel Carter = Elizabeth Pannill
18. Thomas Carter, probably (but DNA evidence may disprove) the Thomas Carter of Liberty Co., Ga. = Mary ——
19. Anne Carter = Joseph Oswald, Jr.
20. Susannah Oswald = General Daniel Stewart

The Royal Descents of 900 Immigrants

21. Martha Stewart = James Stephens Bulloch
22. Martha Bulloch = Theodore Roosevelt
23. Theodore Roosevelt, Jr. (1858-1919), 26th U.S. President = (1) Alice Hathaway Lee; (2) Edith Kermit Carow

11. Dorothy Skipwith (sister of Henry) = Andrew Gedney
12. Mary Gedney = George Ashby
13. George Ashby = Elizabeth Bennet
14. John Ashby = Elizabeth Thorowgood
15. **John Ashby** of S.C. (assemblyman 1698-1702) = Constantia Broughton.

11. Mary Skipwith (sister of Henry and Dorothy) = 13. George FitzWilliam, son of 12. John FitzWilliam (and Margaret Wygersley), son of 11. Thomas FitzWilliam (and Joan Gunby), son of 10. John FitzWilliam (and Joan Britt), son of Thomas FitzWilliam and 9. Margaret Dymoke, daughter of Sir Thomas Dymoke and 8. Margaret de Welles, above
12, 14. Frances FitzWilliam = Thomas Massingberd
13, 15. Thomas Massingberd = Frances Halton
14, 16. Sir Dra(y)ner Massingberd = Anne Mildmay
15, 17. **Elizabeth Massingberd** of S.C. = Edward **Hyrne**.

10. Anne Dymoke (sister of Alice) = John Goodrick
11. Lionel Goodrick = Winifred Sapcott
12. Anne Goodrick = Benjamin Bolles
13. Thomas Bolles = (1) Elizabeth Perkins; (2) Mary Witham, Baronetess of Nova Scotia
14. (by 1) **Joseph Bolles** of Me. = Mary (Howell?).
14. (by 2) Anne Bolles = Sir William Dalston, 1st Bt.

15. Sir John Dalston, 2nd Bt. = Margaret Ramsden
16. Sir Charles Dalston, 3rd Bt. = Susan Blake
17. **Catherine Dalston** of Va. = Francis **Fauquier** (c. 1704-1768), colonial (lt.) governor of Va.

Sources: *RA* 4: 642-44 (Skipwith), 1: 428 and 4: 464-65 (Dymoke), 5: 331-36 (Welles), 4: 187-88 (Mowbray), 4: 256-66 (Norfolk), 1: 428-30 (Bolles, Goodrick); *MCS5*, lines 84-85, 82, 63, *TAG* 75 (2000): 27-29, 79 (2004): 155-56, *BP* and *CB* (Skipwith of Prestwould, baronets), J.L. Miller, *The Descendants of Capt. Thomas Carter of "Barford," Lancaster County, Virginia* (1912), pp. 12-35, and J.B. Price and Harry Hollingsworth, *The Price, Blakemore, Hamblen, Skipwith and Allied Lines* (1992), pp. 15-43 (Skipwith and Mrs. Dale); *Lincolnshire Pedigrees*, pp. 889-90 (Skipwith), 441 (Hall), 1204 (Dymoke), 396 (Gedney), 46, 357-58 (FitzWilliam), 657-58, 660 (Massingberd), 416 (Goodrick); *BDSCHR* 2, pp. 41-42 (John Ashby "Jr."), H.A.M. Smith, *The Baronies of South Carolina* (1931), pp. 149-56, and *Nichols*, vol. 3, part 1, p. 298 (Ashby); *SCG* 2: 397-401 (Mrs. Hyrne); *AR8*, line 202, George E. Williams, *A Genealogy of the Descendants of Joseph Bolles of Wells, Maine,* vol. 1 (1970), pp. 1-10, 14-21, *CB* (Dalston of Dalston, Bolles of Osberton), W.H. Bowles, *Records of the Bowles Family* (1918), pp. 158-59, C.A. Goodricke, *History of the Goodricke Family* (1885), pp. 4-5, *DAB* (Francis Fauquier), *TCWAAS*, new ser. 10 (1910): 221-27 (Dalston), and J.W. Walker, ed., *Yorkshire Pedigrees, G-S* (*HSPVS*, vol. 95, 1943), pp. 254, 256-57 (Witham, Bolles, Dalston) (for Bolles and Mrs. Fauquier). Much material on the ancestry of Joseph Bolles was also collected by the late Augustine H. Ayers. The John Ashby line was brought to my attention by Bruce Harris Sinkey.

    The above Sir William Skipwith at generation 10 was by his first wife, Elizabeth Tyrwhit, the father of Sir William Skipwith, husband of Elizabeth Page, SETH.

The Royal Descents of 900 Immigrants

1. Edward I, King of England, d. 1307 = Margaret of France
2. Thomas of Brotherton, Earl of Norfolk = Alice de Hales
3. Margaret Plantagenet, Duchess of Norfolk = John de Segrave, 4th Baron Segrave
4. Elizabeth de Segrave = John Mowbray, 4th Baron Mowbray

5. Thomas Mowbray, 1st Duke of Norfolk = = Elizabeth FitzAlan
6. Margaret Mowbray = Sir Robert Howard
7. John Howard, 1st Duke of Norfolk = Katherine Moleyns
8. Isabel Howard = Robert Mortimer
9. Elizabeth Mortimer = George Guilford

5. Eleanor Mowbray = John de Welles, 5th Baron Welles
6. Eudo de Welles = Maud de Greystock
7. Lionel de Welles, 6th Baron Welles = Joan Waterton
8. Eleanor de Welles = Thomas Hoo, 1st Baron Hoo
9. Anne Hoo = Sir Roger Copley
10. Eleanor Copley = Thomas West, 8th Baron Delaware (de la Warr)

10. Sir John Guilford = 11. Barbara West
11, 12. Anne Guilford = Levin Bufkin
12, 13. Henry Bufkin = Sarah Flood
13, 14. Levin Bufkin (in Md. 1650-51, returned to England) = (1) Anne Walthall; (2) Anne Garrett
14, 15. (by 1) **Levin Bufkin** (1634-*ante* 1699) of Va., captive of Barbary pirates, 1678-80, who wrote (at least a letter) on his captivity, and whose "Barbary captivity narrative" has been a subject of several articles by historians = Mary Newby. They left issue but no NDTPS.

The Royal Descents of 900 Immigrants

11, 12. Elizabeth Guilford (sister of Anne) = William Cromer, son of James (and Anne Wotton) Cromer, son of Sir William (and Alice Hawte) Cromer, son of Sir James Cromer and Catherine Cantilupe (Cantelow), SETH. Barbara Cromer, daughter of Elizabeth and William, married Henry Shelley. Their son, Richard Shelley, married Joan Fuste and was the father of John Shelley, husband of Bridget Eversfield and father of Timothy Shelley, husband of Catherine Michell and father of another John Shelley, husband of Helen Bysshe and father of another Timothy Shelley, husband of Joanna Plum(b) of New Jersey, and father of Sir Bysshe Shelley, 1st Bt., father by Mary Catherine Michell (a cousin) of Sir Timothy Shelley, 2nd Bt., husband of Elizabeth Pilford and father of Percy Bysshe Shelley, the poet, who married secondly the Gothic novelist Mary Wollstonecraft Godwin.

12, 13. Dorothy Cromer = William Seyliard

13, 14. Elizabeth Seyliard = Cornelius Beresford

14, 15. **Dorothy Beresford** of Va. = John **Brodnax**.

15, 16. Robert Brodnax, London goldsmith = Anne ──

16, 17. William Brodnax, who returned to Va. (as did his brother John Brodnax, husband of Mary Skerme, who left five children but no NDTPS) = Mrs. Rebecca Champion Travis

17, 18. Edward Brodnax = Mary Brown

18, 19. Anne Brodnax = Robert Munford/Montfort

19, 20. Clarissa Montfort = John Shellman, Jr.

20, 21. Susan Shellman = Samuel Howard Fay

21, 22. Harriet Eleanor Fay = James Smith Bush

22, 23. Samuel Prescott Bush = Flora Sheldon

23, 24. Prescott Sheldon Bush, U.S. Senator = Dorothy Walker

24, 25. George Herbert Walker Bush (b. 1924), 41st U.S. President = Barbara Pierce, SETH

25, 26. George Walker Bush (b. 1946), 43rd U.S. President = Laura Lane Welch, SETH

The Royal Descents of 900 Immigrants

11,12. Dorothy Guilford (sister of Anne and Elizabeth) = Sir Thomas Walsingham

12,13. Barbara Walsingham = Anthony Shirley, brother of the Sir Thomas Shirley who married Anne Kempe, SETH

13,14. Thomas Shirley = Jane Essex

14,15. Thomas Shirley = Elizabeth Stapley

15,16. William Shirley = Anne Oglander

16,17. William Shirley = Elizabeth Godman

17,18. **William Shirley** (1694-1771), colonial governor of Mass. and the Bahamas = Frances Barker. A daughter, Elizabeth Shirley, married Massachusetts Loyalist Eliakim Hutchinson, and was the mother of Elizabeth Hutchinson, wife of Anglican clergyman East Apthorpe. Harriet Apthorpe, a daughter of these last, married Samuel Butler, Bishop of Lichfield and Coventry, and headmaster of Shrewsbury School; their son, Thomas Butler, married Fanny Worsley and was the father of Samuel Butler, the British novelist and printer, author of *The Way of All Flesh*, who died unmarried.

11. Sir George West (brother of Lady Guilford) = Elizabeth Morton

12. William West, 10th Baron Delaware (de la Warr) = Elizabeth Strange

13. Jane West = Sir Thomas Wenman

14. Richard Wenman, 1st Viscount Wenman = Agnes Fermor

15. Mary Wenman = Sir Martin Lister

16. Agnes Lister – Sir William Hartopp

17. Dorothy Hartopp = William Yonge, son of Philip Yonge (who married secondly Margaret Mackworth, SETH) and his first wife, Anne Archer

18. **Francis Yonge**, chief justice of S.C. = (1) Mrs. Elizabeth —— Fletcher; (2) Lydia ——.

The Royal Descents of 900 Immigrants

12. Sir Thomas West (brother of William, 10th Baron) = Elizabeth Huttoft

13. Elizabeth West = Sir John Leigh, son of John Leigh (and Margery Saunders), son of Ralph Leigh (and Margaret Ireland), son of Ralph Leigh and Joyce Colepepper (Culpeper), SETH

14. Thomas Leigh = Mary Fleming, daughter of Sir Thomas Fleming and Dorothy Cromwell, aunt of Oliver Cromwell, the Lord Protector

15. Anne Leigh = Joseph Stockman

16. **John Stockman** of Mass. = Mrs. Sarah Pike Bradbury.

Sources: *TAG* 84 (2010): 29-45, 133-43 (Paul C. Reed) and sources cited therein (Bufkin); *RA* 1: 562-66 (Brodnax, Beresford, Seyliard, Cromer), 3: 171-72 (Guilford, Mortimer), 3: 333-36 (Howard), 4: 187-92 (Mowbray), 4: 256-66 (Norfolk), 5: 348-53 (West), 3: 308-12 (Copley, Hoo), 5: 331-38 (Welles), 5: 44-49 (Stockman, Leigh); W.B. Bannerman, ed., *Visitations of Kent, 1530-1, 1574, and 1596,* vol. 1 (*HSPVS*, vol. 74, 1923), pp. 43-44 (Cromer), 77 (Guilford), *Parliament, 1558-1603,* vol. 1, pp. 678-79 (William Cromer), *Parliament, 1509-1558,* vol. 2, pp. 265-66 (Sir John Guil[d]ford), *MGH,* new ser. 3: 421-25 (Shelley), *CP* (de la Warr, Hoo, Welles, Norfolk) and *Horsham,* pp. 70-71 (Copley); *Lewes,* pp. 258-59, 261-65 (Shirley of Wiston and Preston), the 14 July 1664 marriage record of William Shirley and Anne Oglander in the St. Benet Fink, London, parish register, mss. notes by William Shirley biographer John A. Schutz on the governor's American and British descendants, E. Alfred Jones, *The Loyalists of Massachusetts* (1930), p. 169 (Hutchinson, Apthorp) and *Oxford DNB* for both Samuel Butlers, and *Manning and Bray,* vol. 2, p. 540 (Walsingham) (for Gov. Shirley); research of Brice McAdoo Clagett, based in part on *TG* 10 (1989, published 1994): 55 (Yonge, by Paul C. Reed), C.A. Langley, *South Carolina Deed Abstracts, 1719-1772,* vol. 1 (1983), p. 207 (F. to R. Yonge), Kenneth Coleman and C.S. Gurr, eds., *Dictionary of Georgia Biography,* vol. 2 (1983), pp. 1102-3 (Henry Yonge, son of Francis) (which cites P.K. Yonge, "The Yonge Family in America," tss. at the Univ. of Florida, Gainesville) and Edward Yonge, *The Yonges of Caynton, Edgmond, Shropshire* (1969), pp. 98-99, 109-12, 133-45, viii-x; *Nichols,* vol. 2, part 1, p. 267 (Hartopp), *PCF Yorkshire,* vol. 1, Lister pedigree, *The Herald and Genealogist* 2 (1865): 521-23, and *CP* (Wenman,

The Royal Descents of 900 Immigrants

Delaware/de la Warr); Katharine Dickson, *The Stockman Story: The English Ancestry of Mr. John Stockman of Salisbury, Massachusetts* (1992), esp. pp. 126-28 and sources cited therein, including W.H. Rylands, ed., *Visitations of Hampshire, 1530, 1575, and 1622-34* (*HSPVS*, vol. 64, 1913), pp. 158 (Leigh), 59 (West) (or *Berry's Hants,* pp. 294 [Leigh], 200 [West]). See also, for Stockman, Harry L.P. Beckwith, ed., *A Roll of Arms Registered by the Committee on Heraldry of the NEHGS, Parts 1-10* (2013), p. 8, *NEHGR* 125 (1971): 263. For the Howard-Mortimer-Guilford descent see also the IPMs of Robert Mortimer (1486) and his widow Isabel (1507). For Mrs. Brodnax, a line developed by Douglas Richardson, see also (Percival) "Boyd's Marriage Index" (at the Society of Genealogists in London, the New York Public Library, and the Family History Library in Salt Lake City), for the 1629 marriage in Chartham, Kent, of John Brodnax and Dorothy Beresford; Joseph Jackson Howard and Robert Hovenden, eds., *Some Pedigrees from the Visitation of Kent, 1663-68* (1887), esp. pp. 29, 63, 89 (1611 will of Dorothy [Cromer] [Seyliard] Beresford, Seyliard pedigree, and 1639 will of William Syliard, which mentions "my niece Dorothy Brodnox, wife of Mr. John Brodnox"); and Robert Hovenden, ed., *Visitation of Kent, 1619-1621* (*HSPVS*, vol. 42, 1898), p. 172 (Beresford). For Brodnaxes in Virginia, see *GVFVM1*: 435-38, *GVFWM1*: 455-67, esp. 460, 463, and Mildred S. Ezell, *Brodnax: The Beginning* (1995) and *Brodnax: The Beginning, Addendum* (2000).

Note: The above George Guilford, husband of Elizabeth Mortimer, and his sister Frideswide (Guilford) Browne, SETH, were siblings of Sir Edward Guilford, husband of Eleanor West—daughter by another, unrelated Elizabeth Mortimer, of Thomas West, 8th Baron Delaware, who later married Eleanor Copley, SETH. The three siblings were children of Sir Richard Guilford and Anne Pympe, SETH. Jane Guilford, daughter of Sir Edward and Eleanor, married John Dudley, 1st Duke of Northumberland (son of Edmund Dudley, SETH, minister of Henry VII, and Elizabeth Grey), Tudor courtier and instigator of the plot to crown his and Jane Guilford's daughter-in-law, Lady Jane Grey, wife of Lord Guilford Dudley. Siblings of Lord Guilford Dudley included early Elizabethan favorite Robert Dudley, 1st Earl of Leicester (who married Lettice Knollys, SETH) and Mary Dudley, wife of Sir Henry Sidney (son of Sir William Sidney and Anne Pagenham, SETH) and mother of Sir Philip Sidney, the poet. See, in addition to Guilford and West sources cited above, *RA* 2: 340-43 (Dudley, under Covert), and *CP* and *EP* (de la Warr, Northumberland, Leicester).

The Royal Descents of 900 Immigrants

1. Edward I, King of England, d. 1307 = Eleanor of Castile
2. Elizabeth Plantagenet = Humphrey de Bohun, 4th Earl of Hereford and Essex
3. Eleanor de Bohun = James Butler, 1st Earl of Ormonde
4. Petronilla Butler = Gilbert Talbot, 3rd Baron Talbot
5. Richard Talbot, 4th Baron Talbot = Ankaret le Strange
6. Mary Talbot = Sir Thomas Greene
7. Sir Thomas Greene = Philippa Ferrers, daughter of Robert de Ferrers, 5th Baron Ferrers of Chartley, and Margaret Despencer, SETH
8. Elizabeth Greene = William Raleigh
9. Sir Edward Raleigh = Margaret Verney
10. Edward Raleigh = Anne Chamberlayne
11. Bridget Raleigh = Sir John Cope. Their daughter Joan Cope married Stephen Boyle and was the mother of Elizabeth Boyle, wife of the poet Edmund Spenser, author of *The Faerie Queene.*
12. Elizabeth Cope = John Dryden
13. Stephen Dryden = Ellen Neale, daughter of John Neale and Grace Butler, SETH
14. Grace Dryden = Kenelm Cheseldine/Cheseldyne
15. **Kenelm Cheseldine**, atty. gen. of Md. = (1) Bridget Faulkner; (2) Mary Gerard, daughter of Thomas Gerard of Md., ARD, SETH, and Susannah Snow.

13. Bridget Dryden (sister of Stephen) = Francis Marbury, brother of Katherine Marbury, wife of Christopher Wentworth, SETH
14. **Katherine Marbury** of R.I. = Richard **Scott**.
14. **Anne Marbury**, known as **Mrs. Anne Hutchinson** (1591-1643), the religious reformer, heretic and founder of R.I. = William **Hutchinson**.

The Royal Descents of 900 Immigrants

15. Edward Hutchinson = Catherine Hamby of Mass., ARD, SETH
16. Elisha Hutchinson = (1) Hannah Hawkins; (2) Elizabeth Clarke
17. (by 2) Edward Hutchinson = Lydia Foster
18. Elizabeth Hutchinson = Nathaniel Robbins
19. Edward Hutchinson Robbins = Elizabeth Murray
20. Anne Jean Robbins = Joseph Lyman (III)
21. Catherine Robbins Lyman = Warren Delano, Jr.
22. Sara Delano = James Roosevelt
23. Franklin Delano Roosevelt (1882-1945), 32nd U.S. President (Anna) Eleanor Roosevelt

17. (by 1) Hannah Hutchinson = John Ruck
18. Hannah Ruck = Theophilus Lillie
19. John Lillie = Abigail Breck
20. Anna Lillie = Samuel Howard
21. Harriet Howard = Samuel Prescott Phillips Fay
22. Samuel Howard Fay = Susan Shellman
23. Harriet Eleanor Fay = James Smith Bush
24. Samuel Prescott Bush = Flora Sheldon
25. Prescott Sheldon Bush, U.S. Senator = Dorothy Walker
26. George Herbert Walker Bush (b. 1924), 41st U.S. President = Barbara Pierce, SETH
27. George Walker Bush (b. 1946), 43rd U.S. President = Laura Lane Welch, SETH

16. Elizabeth Hutchinson (sister of Elisha) = Edward Winslow
17. Anne Winslow = John Taylor
18. Elizabeth Taylor = Nathaniel Greene, Jr.

The Royal Descents of 900 Immigrants

19. John Greene = Azubah Ward

20. Lucretia Greene = 19. Elijah Mason, son of 18. Peleg Sanford Mason (and Mary Stanton), son of John Mason and 17. Anne Sanford, daughter of 16. Peleg Sanford, governor of R.I. (and Mary Coddington), son of John Sanford, acting governor of R.I., and 15. Bridget Hutchinson, daughter of William Hutchinson and 14. Anne Marbury, the famed Mrs. Anne Hutchinson, above

20, 21. Arabella Mason = Zebulon Rudolph

21, 22. Lucretia Rudolph = James Abram Garfield (1831-1881), 20th U.S. President

11. George Raleigh (brother of Bridget) = ——, widow of Sir Thomas Fitzgerald

12. Bridget Raleigh = Sir William Kingsmill, son of Sir John Kingsmill and Constance Goring, SETH

13. Sir Francis Kingsmill = —— Clifford (their daughter Dorothea Kingsmill married Alexander Marchant, Sieur de St. Michel and was the mother of Elizabeth Marchant, wife of the diarist Samuel Pepys)

14. William Kingsmill = Dorothy St. Leger

15. Levina Kingsmill = Matthew Pennefather

16. Kingsmill Pennefather = Elizabeth Bolton

17. Richard Pennefather = Charity Graham

18. Mary Pennefather = John Croker

19. Henry Croker = Harriet Dillon

20. **Eyre Coote Croker** of N.Y. = Frances Welstead (parents of Tammany Hall "boss" Richard Welstead Croker, 1841-1922, who married Elizabeth Frazier and Beula Benton Edmondson).

15. Mary Kingsmill (sister of Levina) = Ulysses Burgh, Bishop of Armagh

16. Dorothea Burgh = Thomas Smyth, Bishop of Limerick. A son was Arthur Smyth, Archbishop of Dublin.

17. John Smyth, Chancellor of the Diocese of Connor = ──

18. Susanna Smyth = Benjamin Lee

19. Anne Lee = Arthur Guinness. A son was Sir Benjamin Lee Guinness, 1ˢᵗ Bt., the brewer and "richest man in Ireland," who married Elizabeth Guinness, a cousin.

20. Susanna Guinness = John Darley

21. Elizabeth Jane Darley = Richard Seymour Guinness, also a cousin

22. **Benjamin Seymour Guinness**, sometime of N.Y. = Bridget Henrietta Frances Williams-Bulkeley, also sometime of N.Y., SETH. Bridget's and Benjamin's daughter, Tanis Eva Bulkeley Guinness, married (1) Hon. William Drogo Sturgis Montagu; (2) Howard **Dietz**, 1896-1983, American lyricist ("That's Entertainment"), the MGM publicist who designed its film logo; (3) (Charles Edward) Harold John Phillips.

Sources: *RA* 2: 144-48 (Cheseldine, Dryden, Marbury, Raleigh), 3: 112-14 (Greene), 5: 118-22 (Talbot), 2: 47-48 (Butler), 1: 420-24 (Bohun), plus Neale research by Neil D. Thompson, commissioned by John Steele Gordon and confirmed by *MG2*: 248-49; Edwin W. Beitzell, *The Cheseldine Family, Historical* (1949), pp. 8-10, 20-23, addenda pages 3-6 and *Baker*, vol. 2, p. 6 (Dryden); *AR8*, lines 14, 13, 7, and *Marbury*; *NEHGR* 123 (1969): 180-81 (reprinted in *EO* 2: 2: 483-84) and *TG* 13 (1999): 24-29 (Greene); *BIFR*, pp. 295-96 (Croker), 1033 (Smyth), 338-39 (de Burgh), *BLGI* 1899, p. 414 (Smyth of Mount Henry), *BLGI* 1958, pp. 568-70 (Pennefather), 1912, p. 370 (Kingsmill), *BP* 2003, pp. 1695-96, 1700 (Guinness) plus John Fetherston, ed., *Visitations of Warwickshire, 1619* (*HSPVS*, vol. 12, 1877), p. 77 and *NEHGR* 145 (1991): 15-21 (Raleigh).

Of the other sons of Elizabeth Cope and John Dryden (first generation 12 above), (1) Sir Erasmus Dryden, 1ˢᵗ Bt., married Frances Wilkes and was the father of another Erasmus Dryden, who married Mary Pickering (daughter of Henry Pickering [and Isabel Smith], son of John Pickering and Lucy Kaye, SETH) and was the father of John

The Royal Descents of 900 Immigrants

Dryden, the poet; and (2) Nicholas Dryden, who married Mary Emyley and was the father of Elizabeth Dryden, wife of Thomas Swift. Jonathan Swift, a son of these last, married Mary Erick and was the father of Jonathan Swift (Jr.), Dean of St. Patrick's and author of *Gulliver's Travels*, who died unmarried. In addition, Elizabeth Dryden, daughter of Sir Erasmus Dryden (1st Bt.) and Frances, married Sir Richard Phillips, 2nd Bt., and was the mother of Sir Erasmus Phillips, 3rd Bt., who married Katherine Darcy. Elizabeth Phillips, a daughter of these last, married John Shorter, and was the mother of Charlotte Shorter, wife of Robert Walpole, 1st Earl of Orford, "the first British Prime Minister," and mother of Horace Walpole, 4th Earl of Orford, the man of letters, who also died unmarried. For these Dryden descents see *NK* 2, pp. 216-19, 221-22, 193 (which also covers the Dryden and two Shorter descents of the late Diana, Princess of Wales) and W.T.J. Gun, *Studies in Hereditary Ability* (1928), pp. 122-27. For Pickering see Walter C. Metcalfe, ed., *Visitations of Northamptonshire, 1564, 1618-19* (1887), pp. 126-27. John Dryden's wife was Elizabeth Howard, daughter of Thomas Howard, 1st Earl of Berkshire (son of Thomas Howard, 1st Earl of Suffolk, and Catherine Knevet, SETH) and Elizabeth Cecil, daughter of William Cecil, 2nd Earl of Exeter (son of Thomas Cecil, 1st Earl of Exeter, and Dorothy Neville, SETH) and Elizabeth Drury, daughter of Sir William Drury and Elizabeth Stafford, SETH.

The Royal Descents of 900 Immigrants

1. Edward I, King of England, d. 1307 = Eleanor of Castile
2. Joan Plantagenet = Gilbert de Clare, 3rd Earl of Gloucester, 7th Earl of Hertford
3. Elizabeth de Clare = Roger Damory, 1st Baron Damory
4. Elizabeth Damory = John Bardolf, 3rd Baron Bardolf
5. William Bardolf, 4th Baron Bardolf = Agnes Poynings
6. Cecily Bardolf = Sir Brian Stapleton
7. Sir Miles Stapleton = Catherine de la Pole
8. Elizabeth Stapleton = Sir William Calthorpe
9. Anne Calthorpe = Sir Robert Drury, Speaker of the House of Commons
10. Anne Drury = George Waldegrave, son of Sir William Waldegrave and Margery Wentworth, SETH
11. Edward Waldegrave = Joan Acworth
12. Margery Waldegrave = William Clopton
13. **Thomasine Clopton** = John **Winthrop** (1587/8-1649), the colonial statesman, founder and governor of the Massachusetts Bay Colony (his second wife; Winthrop married thirdly Margaret Tyndal/Tindal of Mass., ARD, SETH).

13. Walter Clopton = Margaret Maidstone
14. William Clopton = Elizabeth Sutcliffe
15. **William Clopton** of Va. = Mrs. Anne Booth Dennett.

11. Sir William Waldegrave (brother of Edward) = Juliana Raynsford
12. Dorothy Waldegrave = Arthur Harris
13. Dorothy Harris = Robert Kempe
14. **Richard Kempe**, secretary and acting governor of Va. = Elizabeth Wormeley (who married secondly Sir Thomas Lunsford of Va., royalist army officer, ARD, SETH, and thirdly Robert Smith), niece of Ralph Wormeley, second husband of

The Royal Descents of 900 Immigrants

(Lady) Agatha Eltonhead (Kellaway) Wormeley (Chichele) of Va., ARD, SETH. Of Richard Kempe's brothers Edward Kempe, and possibly John Kempe, also came to Virginia; the secretary mentioned a nephew Edmund Kempe, presumably a son of Edmund Kempe and Bridget ——, in his will, and Matthew Kempe of Gloucester Co., Va., son evidently of Sir Robert Kempe, 1st Bt., and Jane Browne, was apparently a nephew as well.

12. Margery Waldegrave (sister of Dorothy) = John Wiseman
13. Thomas Wiseman = Alice Miles
14. **Robert Wiseman** of Md. = Anne Capell, probably of Md., SETH.

11. Phyllis Waldegrave (sister of Edward and Sir William) = Thomas Higham
12. Bridget Higham = Thomas Burrough
13. George Burrough = Frances Sparrow
14. **Nathaniel Burrough** of Mass. and Md., who returned to England = Rebecca Style.
15. Rev. George Burroughs of Mass., executed for witchcraft at Salem, 19 Aug. 1692 = (1) Hannah Fisher; (2) Mrs. Sarah Ruck Hathorne; (3) Mary ——

Sources: *RA* 2: 266-68 (Clopton), 5: 295-97 (Waldegrave), 2: 472-73 (Drury), 5: 35-38 (Calthorpe, Stapleton), 1: 253-60 (Bardolf), 2: 19-22 (Damory), 2: 195-206 (Clare), 3: 412-14 (Kempe), 2: 44-45 (Burrough); *MCS5*, lines 5 (Mrs. Winthrop and Clopton), 74, 75 (Burroughs, Kempe), 49, 40; *AR8*, lines 200 (Burroughs), 257, 11; *William Clopton*, esp. pp. 12-18, 49-50, 57-58, 71-73, 75-78 (generations 5-15, Bardolf-Clopton); *Kempe*, section II, pp. 32-36, *HSF*, vol. 10 (1966), pp. 164-69, 11 (1967), pp. 156-58; *SMF* 1: 354, 144, 26, 311 esp. (Drury, Clopton, Winthrop, Burrough), *SMF* 2: 237 (Kempe); Walter C. Metcalfe, ed., *Visitations of Essex, 1552, 1558, 1590, 1612, 1634* (*HSPVS*, vol. 13, 1878), pp. 120-21 (Waldegrave), 129-30 (Wiseman) and G.E. and D.V. Russell, *The Ark and*

The Royal Descents of 900 Immigrants

The Dove Adventurers (2005), pp. 199-200, and sources cited therein (Wiseman); *TAG* 48 (1972): 140-46, 56 (1980): 43-45, 60 (1984): 140-42, 76 (2001): 17-19 (for Nathaniel Burrough and Rev. George Burroughs).

The Royal Descents of 900 Immigrants

1. Edward I, King of England, d. 1307 = Margaret of France
2. Thomas of Brotherton, Earl of Norfolk = Alice de Hales
3. Margaret Plantagenet, Duchess of Norfolk = John de Segrave, 4th Baron Segrave
4. Elizabeth de Segrave = John Mowbray, 4th Baron Mowbray
5. Eleanor Mowbray = John de Welles, 5th Baron Welles
6. Eudo de Welles = Maud de Greystock
7. Sir William de Welles, Lord Deputy of Ireland = Anne Barnewall

8. Elizabeth de Welles = Christopher Plunkett, 2nd Baron Killeen
9. Genet Plunkett = Nicholas St. Lawrence, 16th Baron Howth
10. Alison St. Lawrence = (1) John Netterville (2) Patrick White
11. (by 2) Margaret White = Walter Foster
12. Margaret Foster = John Dongan
13. Sir Walter Dongan, 1st Bt. = Jane Rochfort
14. Sir John Dongan, 2nd Bt. =

8. Eleanor de Welles = Walter Chevers
9. Margaret Chevers = Bartholomew Aylmer
10. Anne Aylmer = Sir Thomas Luttrell
11. (by 1) Lucas Netterville
11. Margaret Luttrell
12. Margaret Netterville = John Netterville, a cousin
13. Alison Netterville = Sir William Talbot, 1st Bt.
14. Mary Talbot

15. **Thomas Dongan, 2nd Earl of Limerick** (1634-1715), colonial governor of N.Y., soldier = Mary Cooke. Three great-nephews of the earl/governor – John, Thomas and Walter Dongan, sons of John Dongan (and ——, possibly Margaret Browne) and grandsons of Michael Dongan (and —— Talbot, probably a

cousin) – also immigrated to N.Y. John and Thomas Dongan apparently died without issue. Walter Dongan married Ruth Floyd and Sarah Towneley and left descendants but no NDTPS.

10. Sir Gerald Aylmer, Lord Chief Justice of Ireland (brother of Anne) = Alison Fitzgerald

11. Bartholomew Aylmer = Ellen Warren

12. Christopher Aylmer = ──

13. Gerald Aylmer = ──

14. Sir Christopher Aylmer, 1st Bt. = Margaret Plunkett, SETH, for whom a descent from King Edward III has recently been traced and appears in "Immigrants Whose Royal Descents or Improved Royal Descents Were Received or Developed after Completion of the First Half of this Volume's Index," at the end of this book.

15. Catherine Aylmer = Michael Warren

16. **Sir Peter Warren** (1703-1752) of N.Y., naval officer in the American colonies, 1730-47 = Susannah De Lancey.

16. Anne Warren = Christopher Johnson. Their daughter, Anne Johnson, married Richard Dease and was the mother of Loyalist John Dease of N.Y., Detroit, and Montréal, also an official of the Indian Department, who married Anne French and was the father of Peter Warren Dease, Canadian Arctic explorer, who married Élisabeth Chouinard.

17. **Sir William Johnson, 1st Bt.** (1715-1774) of N.Y., Mohawk Valley pioneer and superintendent of Indian affairs in the American colonies = Catherine Weissenburg. A daughter, Anne Johnson, married Loyalist Christian Daniel Claus of Philadelphia, Albany, Montréal, and Québec, and was the mother of later Indian Department official, soldier and officeholder William Claus (who married Catherine Jordan).

18. Mary Johnson = 18. Guy Johnson (c. 1740-1788) of N.Y., northern superintendent of Indian affairs, 1774-82, loyalist, her first cousin, see below

17. John Johnson (brother of Sir William, 1ˢᵗ Bt.) = Catherine Nangle. Their son, Charles Robert Johnson, also immigrated to N.Y., = (1) ——; (2) Anne —— and left issue, but no NDTPS.

18. **Guy Johnson** (c. 1740-1788) of N.Y., northern superintendent of Indian affairs, 1774-82 = 18. Mary Johnson, his first cousin, above

18. Anne Johnson = Walter Dowdall

19. **Matilda Cecilia Dowdall** of N.J. = Thomas **Shedden**. Their daughter, Janet Madeleine Cecilia Shedden, married George Washington Riggs, banker and Washington, D.C. civic leader.

Sources: *CP* (Limerick, Howth, Killeen), *CB* (Dongan of Castletown and Talbot of Carton), *Lodge*, vol. 4, pp. 204-7 (Netterville), vol. 3, pp. 189-91 (St. Lawrence), 408-9 (Luttrell), vol. 7, pp. 44-45 (Aylmer), *BIFR*, p. 228 (Chevers), *Forebears* 15, #2 (Spring 1972): 103-6, and *The Colonial Genealogist* 8, #4 (1977): 200-12 (for Thomas Dongan, 2ⁿᵈ Earl of Limerick, but see *TG* 4 [1983]: 187-202, 10 [1989, published 1998]: 167-94 for disproof of the RD of William Dungan of St. Martin-in-the-Fields, first husband of Mrs. Frances [Latham] [Dungan] [Clarke] Vaughan of R.I. [who married (2) Act. Gov. Jeremiah Clarke of R.I., ARD, SETH] and father of Thomas Dungan of Pa., Barbara [Dungan] Barker of R.I., and Frances [Dungan] Holden of R.I.); *Oxford DNB* (Guy and Sir Wm. Johnson, Sir Peter Warren, and Sir Wm. de Welles under Lionel de Welles, 6ᵗʰ Baron Welles), *CB* (Johnson/Johnston of N.Y., Aylmer of Balrath) and Franz V. Recum, *The Families of Warren and Johnson of Warrenstown, County Meath* (1950) (for all four immigrants). See also *CP* 12, part I, p. 9 (forename of Anne Barnewall), *RA* 5: 331-32 (Welles), 4: 187-88 (Mowbray), 4: 256-66 (Norfolk), and Thomas P. Dungan, *John Dongan of Dublin: An Elizabethan Gentleman and His Family* (1996), esp. pp. 103-13, 125-28, 141-63, 183-88 (John of the title was the husband of Margaret Foster), *Richard Dungan, Master Plasterer of London in Shakespeare's Time* (2003), esp. pp. 113, 116, and *The Dungan Source Book* (2010), *passim*.

The Dease and Claus connections were brought to my attention by John Blythe Dobson. Sir Peter Warren, Sir William, 1ˢᵗ Bt., Sir John, 2ⁿᵈ Bt., and Guy Johnson, John and Peter Warren Dease, and Christian Daniel and William Claus all appear (vols. 4-6, 9) in the *Dictionary of Canadian Biography*, and Warren, Guy, and Sir Wm. in both the *DAB* and *ANB*. Note also the long, detailed will of Sir William Johnson in Milton W. Hamilton, ed., *The Papers of Sir William Johnson*, vol. 12 (1957), pp. 1062-76.

The Royal Descents of 900 Immigrants

1. Edward I, King of England, d. 1307 = Eleanor of Castile
2. Joan Plantagenet = Gilbert de Clare, 3rd Earl of Gloucester, 7th Earl of Hertford
3. Elizabeth de Clare = Roger Damory, 1st Baron Damory
4. Elizabeth Damory = John Bardolf, 3rd Baron Bardolf
5. William Bardolf, 4th Baron Bardolf = Agnes Poynings
6. Cecily Bardolf = Sir Brian Stapleton
7. Sir Miles Stapleton = Catherine de la Pole
8. Elizabeth Stapleton = Sir William Calthorpe
9. Anne Calthorpe = Sir Robert Drury, Speaker of the House of Commons
10. Bridget Drury = Sir John Jernegan
11. George Jernegan = Ela Spelman
12. Thomas Jernegan = Elizabeth Thompson
13. Thomas Jernegan = Elinor —— (Wentworth?)
14. **Thomas Jernegan** of Va. = —— ——.

13. Penelope Jernegan (sister of the second Thomas) = Thomas Spencer. Their son, John Spencer, also immigrated to Me. and later to Jamaica, but d. unm.
14. **Penelope Spencer** of Me. and Mass. = John **Treworgy(e)** (c. 1618-post 1660), merchant, colonizer, governor of Newfoundland.

12. Ela Jernegan (sister of the first Thomas) = Arthur Jenney
13. Francis Jenney = Anne Reade
14. Sir Arthur Jenney = Helen Stonard
15. **Isabel Jenney** = John **Talbot** (c. 1645-1727) of N.J., Anglican missionary clergyman, ARD, SETH.

11. Sir John Jernegan (brother of George) = Anne Tassell

12. Bridget Jernegan = William Sydnor

13. Paul Sydnor = Hester Catelyn/Catlin

14. William Sydnor = Joan Acton

15. (almost certainly) **Fortunatus Sydnor** of Va. = Mrs. Joanna Lawson Sockwell.

Sources: *TVG* 48 (2004): 163-68 (Thomas Jernegan by Neil D. Thompson, commissioned by Shirley Goodwin Bennett), 50 (2006): 73-74 (John Anderson Brayton), *TAG* 84 (2010): 46-49 (Mrs. Treworgy and Spencer, by John C. Brandon and Leslie Mahler) (Jernegan, Spencer) and sources cited in all three, plus George W. Brown, ed., *Dictionary of Canadian Biography, Volume I, 1000 to 1750* (1966), pp. 652-53 (John Treworgie); A.W.H. Clarke and Arthur Campling, eds., *Visitation of Norfolk, 1664*, vol. 1 (*HSPVS*, vol. 85, 1933), p. 109 (Jenney); Joan Corder, ed., *Visitation of Suffolk, 1561, Part II* (*HSPVS*, new ser., vol. 3, 1984), pp. 299-300 (Jenney), 335-36 (Jernegan); Sydnor Thompson, Jr., *The Sydnor Family Saga: The English Forebears and American Descendants of Fortunatus Sydnor (ca. 1640-ca. 1682), the Immigrant* (2000), pp. 11-16, 18-21 (generations 12-15 of the Sydnor descent, plus wills of Sir John Jernegan (193 Adams, Consistory Court of Norwich) and William Sydnor (PCC, 15 Cope); *SMF* 1:354 (Drury); *AR8*, line 257. See also *RA* 2: 472-73 (Drury), 5: 35-38 (Calthorpe, Stapleton), 1: 253-60 (Bardolf), 2: 19-22 (Damory), 2: 195-206 (Clare).

The Royal Descents of 900 Immigrants

1. Edward I, King of England, d. 1307 = Eleanor of Castile
2. Joan Plantagenet = Gilbert de Clare, 3rd Earl of Gloucester, 7th Earl of Hertford
3. Eleanor de Clare = Hugh le Despencer, 1st Baron Despencer
4. Sir Edward le Despencer = Anne Ferrers
5. Edward le Despencer, 3rd Baron Despencer = Elizabeth Burghersh
6. Elizabeth le Despencer = John FitzAlan, 2nd Baron Arundel
7. Sir Thomas Arundel = Joan Moyns
8. Eleanor Arundel = Sir Thomas Browne
9. Robert Browne = Anne ——
10. Eleanor Browne = Sir William Kempe
11. Sir Thomas Kempe = (1) Catherine Cheney; (2) Amy Moyle
12. (by 1) Anne Kempe = Sir Thomas Shirley
13. **Cecily Shirley** = Thomas **West**, 3rd Baron Delaware (de la Warr) (1577-1618), colonial governor of Va., ARD, SETH.

12. (by 2) Sir Thomas Kempe (half brother of Lady Shirley) = Dorothy Thompson
13. Dorothy Kempe = Sir Thomas Chichele
14. **Sir Henry Chichele**, colonial deputy-governor of Va. = Mrs. Agatha Eltonhead Kellaway Wormeley of Va., ARD, SETH.

11. Edward Kempe (brother of Sir Thomas) = Elizabeth Wilmot
12. Thomas Kempe = Mary Oglander
13. Frances Kempe = Henry Bromfield
14. **Edward Bromfield** of Mass. = (1) Elizabeth Brading; (2) Mary Danforth.

9. Sir George Browne = (brother of Robert) = Elizabeth Paston

10. Sir Matthew Browne = Frideswide Guilford, sister of the Sir Edward and George Guilford who married respectively Eleanor West and Elizabeth Mortimer, both SETH.

11. Catherine Browne = John Poyntz

12. Matthew Poyntz = Winifred Wilde

13. Silvester Poyntz (daughter) = Edward Norris

14. **Rev. Edward Norris** (1583-1659) of Mass., Congregational clergyman = Eleanor ——.

Sources: *RA* 4: 279-81 (Kempe, to Lady Shirley and Lady Chichele), 1: 568-70 (Bromfield), 4: 293-94 (Poyntz, to Matthew), 1: 580-83 (Browne, Arundel), 1: 151-52 (FitzAlan), 2: 443-47 (Despenser), *CP* (de la Warr), *Shirleiana*, pp. 235, 256-58 esp.; *Kempe*, section I, pp. 24-31, 34-38, charts opp. pp. 14 and 20, and section IV, p. 32 and chart opp. p. 20, *CP* (Arundel, Despencer, Gloucester), and *AR8*, lines 8, 74; *VGE*, pp. 421-23 (for Sir Henry Chichele); *NEHGR* 25 (1871): 182-85, 329-35, reprinted in *EO* 2: 1: 316-26, E.E. Salisbury, *Family Memorials* (1885), Bromfield pedigree post p. 610 (for Edward Bromfield); *TAG* 84 (2010): 200-11 and sources cited therein (for Rev. Edward Norris, by John C. Brandon and Leslie Mahler), plus *Mary Isaac*, pp. 85-94.

Note: In perusing the charts by Richard K. Evans on thirteenth- through eighteenth-generation ancestors of the late Diana, Princess of Wales, I noted that Sir Thomas Chichele, husband of Dorothy Kempe above, was a son of Thomas Chichele and Anne Bourne, daughter of John Bourne and Dorothy Lygon, daughter of Richard Lygon and Anne Beauchamp, ARD, SETH. See *Parliament, 1509-1558*, vol. 1, pp. 466-68 (John Bourne), *Parliament, 1558-1603*, vol. 1, p. 602 (Sir Thomas Chicheley, husband of Dorothy Kempe), and Benjamin Buckler, *Stemmata Chicheleana* (1765), pp. 5, 13 (8.7, 21.8, and 21.9).

The Royal Descents of 900 Immigrants

1. Edward I, King of England, d. 1307 = Margaret of France
2. Thomas of Brotherton, Earl of Norfolk = Alice de Hales
3. Margaret Plantagenet, Duchess of Norfolk = John de Segrave, 4th Baron Segrave
4. Elizabeth de Segrave = John Mowbray, 4th Baron Mowbray
5. Thomas Mowbray, 1st Duke of Norfolk = Elizabeth FitzAlan
6. Margaret Mowbray = Sir Robert Howard
7. John Howard, 1st Duke of Norfolk = Katherine Moleyns
8. Margaret Howard = Sir John Wyndham
9. Sir Thomas Wyndham = Eleanor Scrope
10. Sir John Wyndham = Elizabeth Sydenham
11. Margaret Wyndham = John Francis
12. Elizabeth Francis = Christopher Anketill
13. Margaret Anketill = John Doddington
14. Mary Doddington = Thomas Freake
15. **John Freake** of Mass. = Elizabeth Clarke.

10. Margaret Wyndham (sister of Sir John) = Sir Andrew Luttrell, son of Sir Hugh Luttrell and Margaret Hill, SETH
11. Sir John Luttrell = Mary Ryce
12. Catherine Luttrell = Sir Thomas Copley
13. William Copley = Magdalen Prideaux
14. **Thomas Copley** (1595-c. 1652) of Md., Jesuit missionary, d. unm.

11. Margaret Luttrell (sister of Sir John) = Peter Edgcumbe
12. Margaret Edgcumbe = Sir Edward Denny
13. Henry Denny = Mary Fitch
14. Peter Denny = Anne Hill

15. Hill Denny = Abigail Berners

16. **William Denny**, lt. gov. of Pa., gov. of Del. = Mary Hill.

10. Mary Wyndham (sister of Sir John and Margaret) = Erasmus Paston

11. Frances Paston = Thomas le Gros

12. Sir Thomas le Gros = Elizabeth Cornwallis, daughter of Sir Charles Cornwallis and Anne Fincham, SETH

13. Anne le Gros = Nathaniel Bacon

14. Thomas Bacon = Elizabeth Brooke

15. **Nathaniel Bacon** (1647-1676), colonial governor of Va., leader of Bacon's Rebellion = Elizabeth Duke, ARD, SETH.

Sources: *TAG* 86 (2012-13): 257-66 (Leslie Mahler) and sources cited therein (entire line for John Freake); *Oxford DNB* (Copley and Bacon); *Horsham*, pp. 71-72 (Copley of Roughey and Gatton), *VD*, pp. 537, 539 (Luttrell), Walter Rye, ed., *Visitation of Norfolk, 1563, 1589 and 1613* (*HSPVS*, vol. 32, 1891), pp. 324 (Wyndham), 217 (Paston), 186 (le Gros), *BP* and *CP* (Norfolk) and *AR8*, lines 16, 22 (for Thomas Copley); *PMHB* 44 (1920): 97-121, *MGH*, 4th ser., 5 (1914): 367-71, *BP* (Denny of Castle Moyne, baronets), and M.C.D. Dixon and E.C.D. Vann, *Denny Genealogy*, vol. 1 (1944), pp. 47-55, 64, 68 (all for Denny), plus *VC*, p. 142 (Edgcombe); W.H. Rylands, ed., *Visitation of Suffolk, 1664-8* (*HSPVS*, vol. 61, 1910), p. 39 (Bacon), A.W. Hughes Clarke and Arthur Campling, eds., *Visitation of Norfolk, 1664* (*HSPVS*, vol. 85, 1933), p. 120 (le Gros) and G.W. Marshall, *Visitations of Nottingham, 1569, 1614* (*HSPVS*, vol. 4, 1871), p. 162 (Cornwallis). See also *Dunster*, vol. 1, pp. 134-65, H.A. Wyndham, *A Family History: The Wyndhams of Norfolk and Somerset* (vol. 1, *1440-1688* [1939]), pp. 22-46, and *RA* 5: 432-33 (Wyndham), 3: 333-36 (Howard), 4: 256-66 (Norfolk), 5: 168-69 (Scrope).

The above Eleanor Scrope at generation 9 above was the daughter of Richard Scrope (and Eleanor Washburne), son of Henry Scrope, 4th Baron Scrope of Bolton, and Elizabeth Scrope, SETH.

The Royal Descents of 900 Immigrants

1. Edward I, King of England, d. 1307 = Eleanor of Castile
2. Joan Plantagenet = Gilbert de Clare, 3rd Earl of Gloucester, 7th Earl of Hertford
3. Margaret de Clare = Hugh de Audley, 1st Earl of Gloucester
4. Margaret de Audley = Ralph Stafford, 1st Earl of Stafford
5. Hugh Stafford, 2nd Earl of Stafford = Philippa Beauchamp
6. Margaret Stafford = Ralph Neville, 1st Earl of Westmoreland
7. Margaret Neville = Richard Scrope, 3rd Baron Scrope of Bolton
8. Henry Scrope, 4th Baron Scrope of Bolton = Elizabeth Scrope
9. Margaret Scrope = John Bernard
10. John Bernard = Margaret Daundelyn
11. John Bernard = Cecily Muscote
12. Francis Bernard = Alice Haselwood
13. Francis Bernard = Mary Woolhouse
14. **Col. William Bernard** of Va. = Mrs. Lucy Higginson Burwell.

13. Richard Bernard (brother of Francis) = Elizabeth Woolhouse (sister of Mary)
14. **Richard Bernard** of Va. = (1) Dorothy Alwey; (2) Anna Cordray of Va., ARD, SETH.

13. Thomas Bernard (brother of Francis and Richard) = Sarah ——
14. Francis Bernard = Sarah ——
15. Francis Bernard = Margery Winslowe
16. **Sir Francis Bernard, 1st Bt.** (1712-1779), barrister, colonial governor of N.J. and Mass. = Amelia Offley of Mass., ARD, SETH.

13. Elizabeth Bernard (sister of Francis, Richard and Thomas) = Thomas Harrison (one of their older sons, Thomas, Richard, Jonathan, Joseph or William, *might* be the father of Joseph and/or Richard Harrison of Md.)

14. **Benjamin Harrison**, almost certainly of Va. = Mary ——.

15. Benjamin Harrison, Jr. = Hannah ——

16. Benjamin Harrison (III) = Elizabeth Burwell

17. Benjamin Harrison (IV) = Anne Carter

18. Benjamin Harrison (V), signer of the Declaration of Independence = Elizabeth Bassett

19. William Henry Harrison (1773-1841), 9th U.S. President = Anna Tuthill Symmes

20. John Scott Harrison = Elizabeth Ramsey Irwin

21. Benjamin Harrison (1833-1901), 23rd U.S. President = (1) Caroline Lavinia Scott; (2) Mrs. Mary Scott Lord Dimmick

Sources: *RA* 1: 344-46 (Bernard), 5: 167-68 (Scrope), 4: 233-37 (Neville), 5: 9-13 (Stafford), 5: 79-81 (Audley); *MCS5*, line 46 and sources cited therein, esp. *MGH*, 5th ser., 7 (1929-31): 304-6 (Richard) and *Bernards of Abington*, vol. 1, chapters 1-2, 5, 8-9; *AR8*, lines 8-10 and *CP* (Scrope of Bolton, Westmoreland, Stafford, Gloucester, Hertford); *GVFVM3*: 936-47, Walter C. Metcalfe, *The Visitations of Northamptonshire Made in 1564 and 1618-19* (1887), pp. 98 (Harrison), 3 (Bernard), and Harrison Black, *The Ancestry and Descendants of Learner Blackman Harrison, 1815-1902, Entrepreneur and Bank President, of Cincinnati, Ohio* (2006), pp. 19-23. See also *NK1*: 1-8 and *AAP* (2009, 2012), pp. 22-25, 27, 231-32, 320-21.

Note: I have long known of the alleged descent for Benjamin Harrison of Va. and mentioned it as a possibility in my 1995 *Ancestors of American Presidents*, pp. 17-18, 145. A rereading of Francis Burton Harrison's article in *GVFVM* 3: 936-47 and the family's inclusion in Harrison Black's 2006 Harrison work cited above convince me of the probability of this line.

The Royal Descents of 900 Immigrants

1. Edward I, King of England, d. 1307 = Eleanor of Castile
2. Elizabeth Plantagenet = Humphrey de Bohun, 4th Earl of Hereford and Essex
3. William de Bohun, 1st Earl of Northampton = Elizabeth Badlesmere
4. Elizabeth de Bohun = Richard FitzAlan, 10th Earl of Arundel
5. Elizabeth FitzAlan = Sir Robert Goushill
6. Joan Goushill = Thomas Stanley, 1st Baron Stanley
7. Catherine Stanley = Sir John Savage, son of Sir John Savage and Eleanor Brereton, SETH
8. Dulcia/Dulce Savage = Sir Henry Bold
9. Maud Bold = Thomas Gerard
10. Jennet Gerard = Richard Eltonhead
11. William Eltonhead = Anne Bowers
12. Richard Eltonhead = Anne Sutton, daughter of Edward Sutton and Anne Stanley, daughter of Peter Stanley (and Cecily Tarleton), son of Sir William Stanley (and Anne Harington), son of Sir William Stanley (and Alice Grosvenor), son of William Stanley (and Alice Houghton), son of William Stanley and Mary Savage, daughter of Sir John Savage and Maud Swinnerton, SETH
13. **Martha Eltonhead** of Va. = Edwin **Conway**.
14. Edwin Conway, Jr. = Elizabeth Thornton
15. Francis Conway = Rebecca Catlett
16. Eleanor Rose Conway = James Madison
17. James Madison, Jr. (1750/1-1836), 4th U.S. President = Mrs. Dorothea "Dolly" Payne Todd

14. Eltonhead Conway (sister of Edwin, Jr.) = Henry Thacker
15. Martha Thacker = Thomas Hickman, Jr.
16. Edwin Hickman = Eleanor Elliott (or Ellis)

The Royal Descents of 900 Immigrants

17. James Hickman = Hannah Lewis
18. Susannah Hickman = James Browning
19. Anne Browning = Robert Overall
20. George Washington Overall = Louisiana Duvall
21. Susan Catherine Overall = Christopher Columbus Clark
22. Gabriella Clark = Harry Ellington Armour
23. Ruth Lucille Armour = Ralph Waldo Emerson Dunham
24. Stanley Armour Dunham = Madelyn Lee Payne
25. Stanley Ann Dunham = Barack Hussein Obama
26. Barack Hussein Obama, Jr., b. 1961, 44th U.S. President = Michelle LaVaughn Robinson

13. **Alice Eltonhead** of Va. = (1) Rowland **Burnham**; (2) Henry **Corbin** of Va., ARD, SETH; (3) Henry **Creek**.
13. **Jane Eltonhead** of Md. = (1) Robert **Moryson**; (2) Cuthbert **Fenwick** of Md., probably ARD, SETH.
13. **Agatha Eltonhead** of Va. = (1) William **Kellaway**; (2) Ralph **Wormeley**; (3) Sir Henry **Chichele**, colonial (deputy) governor of Va., ARD, SETH. Eleanor Eltonhead, a fourth sister, also immigrated to Va. and married (1) William Brocas; (2) John Carter (who later married Sarah Ludlow of Va., ARD, SETH); Katherine Eltonhead, a fifth sister, married "Thomas Mease of Burras, Ireland," thought by H.E. Hayden to be probably Thomas Mears, later of Va.; and William Eltonhead of Md. (d. 1655, m. Jane ——), was thought by Hayden to be a brother of these five sisters, although omitted (because dead and childless?) from the 1664 visitation of Lancashire. Neither Eleanor, Katherine, nor William left NDTPS.

Sources: *HVG*, pp. 227-30 (Eltonhead); *Baines* 2, vol. 4, pp. 375-76 (Gerard), vol. 5, p. 25 (Bold); William Farrer and John Brownbill, eds., *The Victoria History of the County of Lancaster*, vol. 3 (1907), p. 405, note 12; Savage bibliographical note on the placement of Dulcia Savage, based largely on chronology, in Brice McAdoo Clagett, *Seven Centuries:*

The Royal Descents of 900 Immigrants

Ancestors for Twenty Generations of John Brice de Treville Clagett and Ann Calvert Brooke Clagett, mss. sent to various scholars during Brice's lifetime; *RA* 2: 500-5 (Eltonhead, Sutton, Stanley of Hooton), 4: 556-68 (Savage, not including Dulcia), 5: 27-28 (Stanley), 2: 610-18 (FitzAlan, Goushill), 1: 420-26 (Bohun); Lancashire Parish Register Society, vol. 85 (*The Parish Register of Huyton, 1578-1727* (1948), p. 8 [1590 baptism of Anne Sutton]), vol. 13 (*The Register of the Parish Church of Ormskirk, 1557-1626* [1902], pp. 6, 263, 184 [baptism and marriage of Anne Stanley, burial of Peter Stanley]); P.E. Stanley, *The House of Stanley* (1998), pp. 68-70, 88, 93-94, 99 and *Ormerod* 2: 416 (Stanley); *AR8*, lines 57, 20, 15. See also Corbin, Cuthbert Fenwick, and Chichele sources cited elsewhere.

    The parentage of the younger Sir John Savage at generation 7 is given above, but not subsequently, since he first appears on this chart.

The Royal Descents of 900 Immigrants

1. Edward I, King of England, d. 1307 = Eleanor of Castile
2. Elizabeth Plantagenet = Humphrey de Bohun, 4th Earl of Hereford and Essex
3. William de Bohun, 1st Earl of Northampton = Elizabeth Badlesmere
4. Elizabeth de Bohun = Richard FitzAlan, 10th Earl of Arundel
5. Joan FitzAlan = William Beauchamp, Baron Abergavenny
6. Joan Beauchamp = James Butler, 4th Earl of Ormonde, son of James Butler, 3rd Earl of Ormonde, and Anne de Welles, SETH
7. Elizabeth Butler = John Talbot, 2nd Earl of Shrewsbury
8. Anne Talbot = Sir Henry Vernon
9. Elizabeth Vernon = Sir Robert Corbet, son of Sir Richard Corbet and Elizabeth Devereux, SETH
10. Dorothy Corbet = Sir Richard Mainwaring
11. Sir Arthur Mainwaring = Margaret Mainwaring, a cousin, daughter of Sir Randall Mainwaring (and Elizabeth Brereton), son of Sir John Mainwaring and Katherine Hondford, SETH
12. Mary Mainwaring = Richard Cotton
13. Frances Cotton = George Abell
14. **Robert Abell** of Mass. = Joanna ——.
15. Caleb Abell = Margaret Post
16. Experience Abell = John Hyde
17. James Hyde = Sarah Marshall
18. Abiah Hyde = Aaron Cleveland (IV)
19. William Cleveland = Margaret Falley
20. Richard Falley Cleveland = Anne Neal
21. (Stephen) Grover Cleveland (1837-1908), 22nd and 24th U.S. President = Frances Folsom

10. Sir Roger Corbet (brother of Dorothy) = Anne Windsor, daughter of Andrews Windsor, 1st Baron Windsor, and Elizabeth Blount, SETH

11. Margaret Corbet = Sir Francis Palmes, son of Bryan Palmes (and Isabel Linley), brother of the Jane Palmes who married Sir Nicholas Fairfax, SETH

12. Sir Francis Palmes = Mary Hadnall

13. Andrew Palmes = Elizabeth Harrison

14. **Edward Palmes** of Conn. = (1) Lucy Winthrop, daughter of John Winthrop, Jr., colonial governor of Conn. (and Elizabeth Reade), son of John Winthrop, the colonial statesman, SETH, and Mary Forth, his first wife; (2) Mrs. Sarah Farmer Davis.

14. Elizabeth Palmes = Robert Chambers

15. **Charles Chambers** of Mass. = Rebecca Patefield.

Sources: Carl Boyer 3rd, *Medieval English Ancestors of Robert Abell* (2001), *RA* 1: 106-7 (Abell, Cotton), 4: 1-2 (Mainwaring of Ightfield), 2: 294-95 (Corbet), 5: 283-84 (Vernon), 5: 125-26 (Talbot), 2: 49-52 (Butler), 1: 317-19 (Beauchamp), 2: 610-16 (FitzAlan), 1: 420-24 (Bohun), 4: 284 (Mainwaring of Over Rover); H.A. and L.P. Abell, *The Abell Family in America* (1940), pp. 41-46, *AR8*, lines 56A, 7, 120, 15, and *TG* 5 (1984): 131-39, 150-51, 154-56, 158-71, 9 (1988): 89 (R. Abell); *NEHGR* 11 (1857): 28, 28 (1874): 90 (reprinted in *EO* 2:2:964), 65 (1911): 379, *PCF Yorkshire* (Palmes pedigree), *Foster's V of Yorkshire,* pp. 91-92, and *Nichols*, vol. 2, p. 295 (E. Palmes); A.E.B. Corbet, *The Family of Corbet,* vol. 2 (1920), chart at end, *Roger Ludlow*, pp. 2193-2209 (Windsor), *TAG* 84 (2010): 124-31 (John C. Brandon and Leslie Mahler) and sources cited therein. Edward Palmes Shurick Sr., "The Palmes Family of England and America, Book No. 1," 1943, mss. at NEHGS, pp. 5-10, places William Palmes (b. ca. 1625), first husband of Anne Humphrey, SETH, as a son of Stephen Palmes (and ——) of Ireland, brother of the above Edward Palmes of Conn., and Mrs. Chambers, which is chronologically impossible. Their brother Bryan Palmes said that their sibling Stephen died at sea unmarried. John C. Brandon has found evidence of Stephen Palmes in Ireland in 1617.

The Royal Descents of 900 Immigrants

This last Stephen is more likely the father of William and probably the Stephen of an older generation, son of Sir Francis Palmes and Mary Hadnall, and named in Mary's monumental inscription. A further monograph is merited.

The parents of James Butler, 4th Earl of Ormonde, are given above since in this volume he first appears on this chart.

The Royal Descents of 900 Immigrants

1. Edward I, King of England, d. 1307 = Eleanor of Castile
2. Elizabeth Plantagenet = Humphrey de Bohun, 4th Earl of Hereford and Essex
3. Margaret de Bohun = Hugh Courtenay, 2nd Earl of Devon
4. Elizabeth Courtenay = Sir Andrew Luttrell
5. Sir Hugh Luttrell = Catherine Beaumont
6. Elizabeth Luttrell = John Stratton
7. Elizabeth Stratton = John Andrews
8. Elizabeth Andrews = Thomas Windsor
9. Andrews Windsor, 1st Baron Windsor = Elizabeth Blount
10. Edith Windsor = George Ludlow
11. Thomas Ludlow = Jane Pyle
12. Gabriel Ludlow = Phyllis ——. Three of their sons, Thomas, Francis and John Ludlow, also immigrated to Virginia, but left no NDTPS.
13. **Sarah Ludlow** of Va. = John **Carter.**
14. Robert "King" Carter = Elizabeth Landon
15. Anne Carter = Benjamin Harrison (IV)
16. Benjamin Harrison (V), Signer of the Declaration of Independence = Elizabeth Bassett
17. William Henry Harrison (1773-1841), 9th U.S. President = Anna Tuthill Symmes
18. John Scott Harrison = Elizabeth Ramsey Irwin
19. Benjamin Harrison (1833-1901), 23rd U.S. President = (1) Caroline Lavinia Scott; (2) Mrs. Mary Scott Lord Dimmick

12. **Roger Ludlow** (1590-1666, brother of Gabriel), of Mass. and Conn., dep. gov. of Mass., author of the Fundamental Orders of Connecticut = Mary Cogan (almost certainly the parents of Sarah, second wife of Rev. Nathaniel Brewster of Brookhaven,

L.I.). George Ludlow, a brother of Roger and Gabriel, also immigrated to Massachusetts, and later settled in Virginia, but apparently left no descendants.

12. Thomas Ludlow (brother of Gabriel and Roger) = Jane Bennett
13. Gabriel Ludlow = Martha Cary
14. **Gabriel Ludlow** of N.Y. = Sarah Hanmer.

Sources: *RA* 3: 662-68 (Ludlow, Windsor, Andrews, Stratton), 3: 644-45 (Luttrell), 2: 326-31 (Courtenay), 1: 420-24 (Bohun); *AR8*, lines 12, 6 and *MCS5*, line 88; *Roger Ludlow*. In his 1668 will John Carey of Castle Cary, Somerset, mentions his daughter Martha Ludlow (F.A. Crisp, *Abstracts of Somersetshire Wills*, etc., 3rd series [1889], p. 93), as brought to my attention by John C. Brandon of Columbia, S.C.

The Royal Descents of 900 Immigrants

1. Edward I, King of England, d. 1307 = Eleanor of Castile
2. Joan Plantagenet = Gilbert de Clare, 3rd Earl of Gloucester, 7th Earl of Hertford
3. Margaret de Clare = Hugh de Audley, 1st Earl of Gloucester
3. Eleanor de Clare = Hugh le Despencer, 1st Baron Despencer
4. Margaret de Audley = Ralph Stafford, 1st Earl of Stafford
4. Sir Edward Despencer = Anne Ferrers
5. Elizabeth Stafford = John de Ferrers, 4th Baron Ferrers of Chartley
5. Edward Despencer, 3rd Baron Despencer = Elizabeth Burghersh
6. Robert de Ferrers, 5th Baron Ferrers of Chartley = 6. Margaret Despencer
7. Sir Edmund Ferrers = Ellen Roche
8. Sir William Ferrers = Elizabeth Belknap
9. Anne Ferrers = Walter Devereux, 1st Baron Ferrers of Chartley (of the second creation)
10. Sybil Devereux = Sir James Baskerville
11. Sybil Baskerville = Watkin Vaughan (of Hergest)
12. James Vaughan (of Hergest) = Elizabeth Croft
13. Isabel Vaughan = George Parry
14. Roger Parry = Mary Crosley
15. Elizabeth Parry = Robert Batte
16. John Batte = Martha Mallory, daughter of Thomas Mallory, Dean of Chester, and Elizabeth Vaughan, SETH
17. **Thomas Batte** of Va. = (1) Mary ——; (2) Mrs. Amy —— Butler.

17. **Henry Batte** of Va. = Mary Lounds. William Batte, a brother of Thomas and Henry, also came to Va., married Mrs. Susan Aston Major (dau. of Col. Walter Aston of Va., ARD, SETH, and Hannah Jordan), and Elizabeth Horton, but also returned to England and left no NDTPS.

  8. Margaret Ferrers (sister of Sir William) = John Beauchamp, 1st Baron Beauchamp of Powyck

  9. Richard Beauchamp, 2nd Baron Beauchamp of Powyck = Elizabeth Stafford, daughter of Sir Humphrey Stafford and Eleanor Aylesbury, SETH

10. Margaret Beauchamp = William Reade

11. Richard Reade = Jane Rudhall, daughter of William Rudhall and Anne Milborne, SETH

12. Anne Reade = Anthony Washburn, son of John Washburn (and Margaret Tracy), son of Robert Washburn (and Eleanor Steple/ Stapylles), son of John Washburn and Joan Mitton, daughter of William Mitton (and Margaret Corbet), son of Sir Richard Mitton and Margaret Peshall, daughter of Sir Adam Peshall and Joyce de Botetourte, SETH (who married [1] Sir Baldwin Freville).

13. Robert Washburn = Mary Heriott

14. Alice Washburn = William Woodcock

15. **Mary Woodcock** of Mass. = Robert **Bridges**, d. 1656, Lynn iron manufacturer and magistrate.

Sources: *TVG* 42 (1998): 217-33, 44 (2000): 304-5, 46 (2002): 83-90 (Batte, Mallory) (both by John A. Brayton); M.P. Siddons, ed., *Visitation of Herefordshire, 1634* (*HSPVS*, new ser., vol. 15, 2002), pp. 57-58 (Parry), *M&G*, p. 238 (which erroneously gives the father of Sybil Baskerville as Sir John) (Vaughan of Hergest) and *Bartrum* 2, pp. 484 (Parry), 457 (Vaughan of Hergest), 56 (Baskerville); *RA* 2: 570-77 (Ferrers), 5: 9-11 (Stafford), 5: 79-81 (Audley), 2: 443-53 (Despencer), 2: 195-205 (Clare), 4: 419-21 (Beauchamp), 1: 399-400 (Reade), 5: 393-94 (Rudhall), 4: 88-89 (Mitton), 1: 448-64 (Peshall, Botetourte, FitzThomas, FitzOtho,

Beauchamp); *DAB* 3, pp. 34-35 (Robert Bridges); G.F. Dow, ed., *Records and Files of the Quarterly Courts of Essex County, Massachusetts, Volume I, 1636-1656* (1911), pp. 382-86 (Woodcock, Washburn); James Davenport, *The Washbourne Family of Little Washbourne and Wichenford, in the County of Worcester* (1907), pp. 30-35, 65-83, which omits Mary (Woodcock) Bridges, however. The Batte sources are correctly cited and outlined but Mr. Brayton reports that he has found no documentary evidence for the Parry pedigree as given in the 1634 Visitation of Herefordshire. The descent of Mrs. Bridges was developed and brought to my attention by John C. Brandon of Columbia, S.C.

Note: Joan Mitton and John Washburn of Wichenford, Worcestershire, for whom see the cross-reference at generation 12 above (and SETH for the Botetourte descent from Henry II, King of England), were said in the above-cited *The Washbourne Family of Little Washbourne and Wichenford*, pp. 30-58, and E.A.B. Barvard, *Some Notes on the Evesham Branch of the Washbourne Family* (1914), pp. 42-54, to be very probably (1907) or only possibly (1914) the parents of John Washburn of Bengeworth, near Little Washbourne, although Washburnes had lived in Bengeworth, Evesham, or nearby, for at least two centuries. By Emma ____ this John Washburne (I) of Bengeworth was the father of John Washburne (II), who married secondly Joan Whitehead, perhaps a kinswoman of Daniel Whitehead of Hempstead and Oyster Bay, L.I. John Washburn (III), burgess of Bengeworth, son of John (II) and Joan, married Mrs. Martha Timbrell Stevens and was the father of John Washburn (IV), b. 1597, who married Margery Moore and immigrated to (Duxbury) Mass. William Washburn, b. 1601, a younger brother of John (IV), is said in Ada C. Haight, *The Richard Washburn Family Genealogy* (1937), pp. 3-9, and Mabel T.R. Washburne, *Washburn Family Foundations in Normandy, England and America* (1953), pp. 50-58, 83-103, to be the immigrant to Hempstead, L.I. (married Joan ____), an identification that is probably correct. Further proof of the parentage of John Washburn (I) of Bengeworth is certainly required; see also *TAG* 36 (1960): 62-64 (John G. Hunt), *AR7*, line 91, Eugene Aubrey Stratton, *Plymouth Colony: Its History and People, 1620-1691* (1996), pp. 368-69, and Robert Charles Anderson, *The Pilgrim Migration: Immigrants to Plymouth Colony, 1620-1633* (2004), pp. 480-83.

The Royal Descents of 900 Immigrants

1. Edward I, King of England, d. 1307 = Eleanor of Castile
2. Joan Plantagenet = Gilbert de Clare, 3rd Earl of Gloucester, 7th Earl of Hertford
3. Eleanor de Clare = Hugh le Despencer, 1st Baron Despencer
4. Isabel le Despencer = Richard FitzAlan, 9th Earl of Arundel
5. Sir Edmund FitzAlan = Sybil Montagu
6. Philippa FitzAlan = Sir Richard Sergeaux
7. Philippa Sergeaux = Sir Robert Pashley
8. Anne Pashley = Edward Tyrrell
9. Philippa Tyrrell = Thomas Cornwallis
10. William Cornwallis = Elizabeth Stanford
11. Sir John Cornwallis = Mary Sulyard
12. Elizabeth Cornwallis = John Blennerhasset
13. Elizabeth Blennerhasset = Lionel Throckmorton, son of John Throckmorton (and Jane Baynard), son of Sir Thomas Throckmorton and Margaret Olney, SETH
14. Bassingborne Throckmorton = Mary Hill
15. **John Throckmorton** of R.I. = Rebecca Farrand.
16. John Throckmorton, Jr. = Alice Stout
17. Patience Throckmorton = Hugh Coward
18. John Coward = Alice Britton
19. Deliverance Coward = James FitzRandolph
20. Isaac FitzRandolph = Eleanor Hunter
21. Rebecca Longstreet FitzRandolph = Isaac Stockton Keith Axson
22. Samuel Edward Axson = Margaret Jane Hoyt
23. Ellen Louise Axson = (Thomas) Woodrow Wilson (1856-1924), 28th U.S. President

11. Affra Cornwallis (sister of Sir John) = Sir Anthony Aucher

12. Edward Aucher = Mabel Wroth, daughter of Sir Thomas Wroth and Mary Rich, SETH

13. Elizabeth Aucher = Sir William Lovelace

14. Sir William Lovelace = Anne Barne, daughter of Sir William Barne and Anne Sandys, daughter of Edwin Sandys, Archbishop of York, and Cecily Wilsford, SETH. Another son of Sir William and Anne was the Cavalier poet Richard Lovelace, who died unm.

15. **Francis Lovelace** (c. 1621-1675), colonial governor of N.Y., d. unm.

15. **Anne Lovelace** of Va. (progeny in Md.) = Rev. John **Gorsuch**. Thomas and Dudley Lovelace, brothers of Francis and Mrs. Gorsuch, also immigrated to N.Y. Both had wives named Mary, but neither brother left NDTPS.

Sources: *RA* 5: 154-55 (Throckmorton, Blennerhasset), 2: 375-7 (Cornwallis, Tyrrell), 4: 309-10 (Pashley), 1: 119-22 (Sergeaux, FitzAlan [Arundel]), 2: 606-9 (FitzAlan), 2: 443-47 (Despencer), 2: 195-206 (Clare), 3: 632-34 (Lovelace, Aucher), 1: 260-62 (Barne, Sandys, Wilsford); *AR8*, line 208, *NEHGR* 98 (1944): 67-72, 111-23, 271-79, 117 (1963): 234 (Throckmorton, Blennerhasset), 110 (1956): 122-27 (Cornwallis), 109 (1955): 17-31, 236 (Tyrrell) (reprinted in *EO* 2: 3: 478-98, *EO* 1: 2: 765-73, 3: 240-45, 204-19), plus *Moriarty* and *TAG* 77 (2002): 110, 229-34 (Farrand); *MCS5*, lines 117, 113B, 113A, 134, 34; *AP&P* 4: 2: 472-74 (Lovelace), *NYGBR* 51 (1920): 175-94 (Francis Lovelace and his brothers) and *WV*, end packet, "A Chart of the Ancestry of Anne Lovelace, Wife of The Reverend John Gorsuch." Paul C. Reed is collecting material to suggest that another John Throckmorton, also of royal descent and an agnate kinsman of the Throckmorton above, was the immigrant of R.I.; an article on this subject is eagerly anticipated.

The Royal Descents of 900 Immigrants

1. Edward I, King of England, d. 1307 = Eleanor of Castile
2. Elizabeth Plantagenet = Humphrey de Bohun, 4th Earl of Hereford and Essex
3. William de Bohun, 1st Earl of Northampton = Elizabeth Badlesmere
4. Elizabeth de Bohun = Richard FitzAlan, 10th Earl of Arundel
5. Elizabeth FitzAlan = Sir Robert Goushill
6. Joan Goushill = Thomas Stanley, 1st Baron Stanley
7. Margaret Stanley = (1) Sir William Troutbeck; (2) Sir John Boteler
8. (by 1) Joan Troutbeck = Sir William Griffith
9. Sir William Griffith (whose first wife was Jane Stradling, SETH) = Jane Puleston
10. Sybil Griffith = Owen ap Hugh
11. Jane Owen = Hugh Gwyn
12. Sybil Gwyn = John Powell
13. Elizabeth Powell = Humphrey ap Hugh
14. Owen Humphrey = (1) Margaret Vaughan; (2) Elizabeth Thomas
15. (maternity uncertain) **Joshua Owen** of N.J. = Martha Shinn.
15. (maternity uncertain) **Rebecca Owen** (sometimes called Rebecca Humphrey[s]) of Pa. = Robert **Owen** of Pa., ARD, SETH (John Owen and Elizabeth Owen, wife of John Roberts, a brother and sister of Joshua and Rebecca, also came to Pa. John Owen seems to have died unmarried. Mrs. Elizabeth Owen Roberts left no NDTPS).

14. Samuel Humphrey (brother of Owen) = Elizabeth Rees
15. **Daniel Humphrey(s)** of Pa. = Hannah Wynne. All of Daniel's siblings also came to Pa. — Lydia Humphrey, wife of Ellis Ellis; Joseph Humphrey = Elizabeth Medford; Benjamin Humphrey = Mary Llewelyn; Rebecca Humphrey = Edward

The Royal Descents of 900 Immigrants

Rees; Anne Humphrey = Edward Roberts; Goditha Humphrey; and Elizabeth Humphrey = Thomas Abel. To date I have found NDTPS only for Daniel.

14. Anne Humphrey = Ellis ap Rees (alias Ellis Price), ARD, SETH (parents of Rowland Ellis of Pa.) (John Humphrey, a brother of Owen, Samuel and Anne also came to Pa. = Jane Humphrey, and d.s.p.)

Sources: *RA* 4: 285-87 (generations 10-15), 2: 345-46 (Griffith), 5: 190-92 (Troutbeck), 5: 27-28 (Stanley), 2: 610-18 (FitzAlan), *WFP* 1, pedigree IV, pp. 44-47, and chart facing p. 44 (which includes the since-corrected Touchet-Whitney-Puleston descent), plus *Merion*, pp. 241-51. See also *PACF*, pp. 185, 58, 273 (Griffith, Owen, Gwyn [later Wynn]).

The Royal Descents of 900 Immigrants

1. Edward I, King of England, d. 1307 = Eleanor of Castile
2. Elizabeth Plantagenet = Humphrey de Bohun, 4th Earl of Hereford and Essex
3. Eleanor de Bohun = James Butler, 1st Earl of Ormonde
4. Petronilla Butler = Gilbert Talbot, 3rd Baron Talbot
5. Richard Talbot, 4th Baron Talbot = Ankaret le Strange
6. Mary Talbot = Sir Thomas Greene
7. Sir Thomas Greene (widower of Philippa Ferrers) = Marina Bellers
8. Anne Greene = Sir Thomas Pinchbeck, son of Richard Pinchbeck and Margaret Talboys, SETH
9. Elizabeth Pinchbeck = John Hardwick
10. John Hardwick = Elizabeth Leke
11. Elizabeth Hardwick, the well-known "Bess of Hardwick," Countess of Shrewsbury, adventuress, = Sir William Cavendish (second of four husbands)
12. Henry Cavendish = Grace Talbot
13. (illegitimate by ——) Anne Cavendish = Vincent Lowe
14. **Jane Lowe** of Md. = (1) Henry **Sewall**, secretary of Md., SETH; (2) Charles **Calvert**, 3rd Baron Baltimore (1637-1715), colonial governor of Md., ARD, SETH.
14. John Lowe = Catherine Pilkington
15. **Nicholas Lowe** of Md. = Mrs. Elizabeth Roe Combes
15. **Henry Lowe** of Md. = Mrs. Susannah Maria Bennett Darnall, daughter of Richard Bennett, Jr. and Henrietta Maria Neale, daughter of James Neale of Md., ARD, SETH, and Anna Maria Gill. (Note: Nicholas and Vincent Lowe, younger brothers of Lady Baltimore, also came to Md., and Vincent married Elizabeth Foster. Neither brother, however, left NDTPS.)

Sources: *RA* 3: 642-43 (Lowe), 4: 376-80 (Cavendish, Hardwick, Pinchbeck), 3: 112-14 (Greene), 5: 118-21 (Talbot), 2: 47-48 (Butler),

The Royal Descents of 900 Immigrants

1: 420-24 (Bohun); *NGSQ* 51 (1963): 32-43 (Lowe) and *The Reliquary* 22 (1881-82): 242 (Hardwick); *Lincolnshire Notes and Queries* 1 (1888-89): 173-77 and Pinchbeck bibliographical note by Brice McAdoo Clagett in *Seven Centuries: Ancestors for Twenty Generations of John Brice de Treville Clagett and Ann Calvert Brooke Clagett* (mss. sent to various scholars in Brice's lifetime), which notes mention in the 1492 (proved 1495/6, PCC 29 Vox) will of Richard Pinchbeck, of a granddaughter Elizabeth, "daughter of his deceased son Thomas and his surviving wife Ann"; *TG* 13 (1999): 24-29 (Greene); *AR8*, lines 14, 13, 7.

The Royal Descents of 900 Immigrants

1. Edward I, King of England, d. 1307 = Eleanor of Castile
2. Joan Plantagenet = Gilbert de Clare, 3rd Earl of Gloucester, 7th Earl of Hertford
3. Eleanor de Clare = Hugh le Despencer, 1st Baron Despencer
4. Isabel le Despencer = Richard FitzAlan, 9th Earl of Arundel
5. Sir Edmund FitzAlan = Sybil Montagu
6. Philippa FitzAlan = Sir Richard Sergeaux
7. Philippa Sergeaux = Sir Robert Pashley
8. Sir John Pashley = Elizabeth Woodville, sister of Richard Woodville, 1st Earl Rivers, SETH, and aunt of Elizabeth Woodville, Queen of Edward IV, King of England
9. Sir John Pashley = Lowys Gower
10. Elizabeth Pashley = Reginald Pympe
11. Anne Pympe = Sir John Scott
12. Sir Reginald Scott = Mary Tuke
13. Mary Scott = Richard Argall
14. **Sir Samuel Argall** (c. 1572-1626), colonial governor of Va., d. unm.
14. Elizabeth Argall = Sir Edward Filmer (parents of Sir Robert Filmer, political writer, author of *Patriarcha*)
15. **Henry Filmer** of Va. = Elizabeth ——.
15. Katherine Filmer = Robert Barham
16. **Charles Barham** of Va. = Elizabeth Ridley.

Sources: *RA* 2: 583-84 (Barham, Filmer, Argall), 4: 596-98 (Scott), 4: 309-11 (Pashley), 1: 119-22 (Sergeaux, FitzAlan), 2: 606-10 (FitzAlan), 2: 443-48 (Despencer), 2: 195-206 (Clare); *MCS5*, line 134, *AR8*, lines 8, 28, *DAB* (Argall), and *LDBR* 1:66-67 (Filmer), 435-36 (Barham) and sources cited therein; *VGE*, pp. 199-200, 346-47, 394-96, 583, 664-66; *GVFVM* 4: 528-32 (Barham); *Scot of Scots Hall*, pp. 170-71, 185, 254 esp.

The Royal Descents of 900 Immigrants

1. Edward I, King of England, d. 1307 = Margaret of France
2. Edmund of Woodstock, 1st Earl of Kent = Margaret Wake
3. Joan Plantagenet, "The Fair Maid of Kent" = Thomas Holand, 1st Earl of Kent
4. Thomas Holand, 2nd Earl of Kent = Alice FitzAlan
5. Eleanor Holand = Edward Cherleton, 5th Baron Cherleton of Powis, brother of John Cherleton, 4th Baron Cherleton of Powis, who married Alice FitzAlan (niece of the Alice above), SETH
6. Joyce Cherleton = John Tiptoft (Tibetot), 1st Baron Tiptoft
7. Joyce Tiptoft = Sir Edmund Sutton (or alias Dudley, who = [2] Matilda Clifford, SETH), son of John Sutton, 1st Baron Dudley, and Elizabeth Berkeley, SETH
8. John Sutton = Anne Clarell
9. Margaret Sutton = John Butler
10. William Butler = Margaret Greeke
11. Margaret Butler = Lawrence Washington, SETH
12. Lawrence Washington = Amphyllis Twigden. Their daughter, Martha Washington, also immigrated to Va. and married Samuel Hayward, but died without issue.
13. **Lawrence Washington** of Va. (second son) = (1) Mary Jones; (2) Mrs. Joyce Jones Hoskins Fleming.
13. **Col. John Washington** of Westmoreland County, Va. = (1) Anne Pope; (2) Mrs. Anne Gerard Broadhurst Brett; (3) Mrs. Frances Gerard Speake Peyton Appleton (2 and 3, who d.s.p., were daughters of Thomas Gerard of Md., ARD, SETH, and Susannah Snow).
14. (by 1) Lawrence Washington = Mildred Warner
15. Augustine Washington = Mary Ball
16. George Washington (1731/2-1799), 1st U.S. President = Mrs. Martha Dandridge Custis

12. Richard Washington (brother of Lawrence) = Frances Browne

13. **John Washington**, probably the immigrant to Surry Co., Va. = Mrs. Mary Flood Blunt Ford.

Sources: *RA* 5: 321-23 (Washington, Butler, Sutton), 5: 103-5 (Sutton), 3: 390-93 (Tiptoft), 2: 141-43 (Cherleton), 3: 419-36 (Holand, Kent), 2: 606-16 (FitzAlan); *MCS5*, lines 30, 30A, 94, 90, 114 (plus *AR8*, lines 47, 155); *BLG* (1939), whose American section was reprinted in 1971 as *Prominent Families in America with British Ancestry*, pp. 2959-63; *HSF* 4: 149-55 (Washington of Surry Co.) and *VHG*, pp. 301-4 (Flood); *TAG* 53 (1977): 15. Note also *AAP* (2009, 2012), pp. 1-3, 224-25, 306 (Washington AT, bibliography and chart) and Charles Mosley, ed., *American Presidential Families* (1993), pp. 49-53, 57.

The Royal Descents of 900 Immigrants

1. Edward I, King of England, d. 1307 = Eleanor of Castile
2. Elizabeth Plantagenet = Humphrey de Bohun, 4th Earl of Hereford and Essex
3. William de Bohun, 1st Earl of Northampton = Elizabeth Badlesmere
4. Elizabeth de Bohun = Richard FitzAlan, 10th Earl of Arundel
5. Elizabeth FitzAlan = Sir Robert Goushill
6. Elizabeth Goushill = Sir Robert Wingfield
7. Elizabeth Wingfield = Sir William Brandon
8. Anne Brandon = Nicholas Sidney
9. Sir William Sidney = Anne Pagenham
10. Lucy Sidney = Sir James Harington
11. Sir Henry Harington = Ruth Pilkington
12. Elizabeth Harington = Sir Richard Moryson
13. **Francis Moryson**, deputy and acting colonial governor of Va. = ——. (Richard [= Winifred ——] and Robert Moryson, brothers of Dep. and Acting Gov. Francis Moryson, also immigrated to Va. but left no NDTPS).

11. Frances Harington (sister of Henry) = Sir William Leigh
12. Sir Francis Leigh = Mary Egerton, see below
13. Juliana Leigh = Sir Richard Newdigate, 1st Bt.
14. Sir Richard Newdigate, 2nd Bt. = Mary Bagot
15. **Mary Newdigate** = William **Stephens**, colonial governor of Ga.

6. Joan Goushill (sister of Lady Wingfield) = Thomas Stanley, 1st Baron Stanley
7. Sir John Stanley = Elizabeth Weever
8. Anne Stanley = Ralph Ravenscroft

517

The Royal Descents of 900 Immigrants

9. George Ravenscroft = Eleanor ferch Richard ap Howell
10. Thomas Ravenscroft = Katherine Grosvenor
11. Elizabeth Ravenscroft = Thomas Egerton, 1st Viscount Brackley, Lord Chancellor
12. Mary Egerton = Sir Francis Leigh, see above

9. John Ravenscroft (brother of George) = Margaret Dod
10. Arthur Ravenscroft = Elizabeth ——
11. Martyn Ravenscroft = ——
12. Samuel Ravenscroft = Anne Goodfellow
13. William Ravenscroft = Margaret Greenstreet
14. **Frances Ravenscroft** of Va. = Joseph **Ball**, half-brother of Mary Ball, second wife of Augustine Washington, SETH, and mother of George Washington, 1st U.S. President.

Sources: *VM* 2 (1894-95): 383-85, *VGE*, pp. 320-21 (Moryson), *Oxford DNB* (Sir Richard Moryson, under Fynes Moryson; Sir Henry Sidney), *BP* (Harington, baronets) and G.J. Armitage, ed., *Visitation of Rutland, 1618-19* (*HSPVS*, vol. 3, 1870), pp. 38-39 (Harington), *NEHGR* 103 (1949): 102-7, 287-95 (reprinted in *EO* 1: 3: 82-96) (Brandon, Wingfield) and *AR8*, lines 15 (for Dep. and Act. Gov. Francis Moryson); *ANB* and *Oxford DNB* (William Stephens), *EB* and *CB* (Newdigate of Arbury), *CP* (Chichester [Leigh] and Brackley [Egerton]) and *EP*, p. 187 (Egerton), *MGH*, 5th ser., 1 (1916): 212-17, 223, 260-61, 266-67 (Ravenscroft, for both Mrs. Stephens and Mrs. Ball), *PCF Lancashire* (Stanley pedigree) and *AR8*, lines 20, 15 (for Mrs. Stephens); and HVG, pp. 56-59, 76-79 (for Mrs. Ball). See also *RA* 1: 506-7 (Brandon), 5: 381-82 (Wingfield), 2: 610-18 (Goushill, FitzAlan), 1: 420-26 (Bohun), 4: 25 (Stanley), 5: 27-28 (Stanley). The descent of Mrs. Ball was brought to my attention by John C. Brandon of Columbia, S.C.

The Royal Descents of 900 Immigrants

1. Edward I, King of England, d. 1307 = Margaret of France
2. Thomas of Brotherton, Earl of Norfolk = Alice de Hales
3. Margaret Plantagenet, Duchess of Norfolk = John de Segrave, 4th Baron Segrave
4. Elizabeth de Segrave = John Mowbray, 4th Baron Mowbray
5. Joan Mowbray = Sir Thomas Grey
6. Maud Grey = Sir Robert Ogle
7. Anne Ogle = Sir William Heron
8. Elizabeth Heron = Sir John Heron, a cousin
9. Elizabeth Heron = Sir Robert Talboys
10. Maud Talboys = Sir Robert Tyrwhit, SETH
11. Katherine Tyrwhit = Sir Richard Thimbleby, see note below
12. Elizabeth Thimbleby = Thomas Welby
13. Richard Welby = Frances Bulkeley, daughter of Edward Bulkeley and Olive Irby, SETH
14. **Olive Welby** of Mass. = Henry **Farwell.**

Sources: *RA* 5: 328-30 (Welby, Thimbleby), 5: 225-26 (Tyrwhit), 5: 113-14 (Talboys), 3: 281-83 (Heron, Ogle), 3: 106-9 (Gray/Grey), 4: 187-88 (Mowbray), 4: 255-56 (Norfolk), *AR8*, lines 223, 16, and sources cited therein.

15. Joseph Farwell – Hannah Learned
16. Henry Farwell = Susannah Richardson
17. Jonathan Farwell = Susannah Blanchard
18. Rachel Farwell = Nehemiah Lovewell
19. Catherine Lovewell = John Taplin, Jr.
20. Henry Taplin (Vt. to Ontario) = Melinda Huntley

The Royal Descents of 900 Immigrants

21. Lucinda Taplin = Charles Lane
22. Adelaide Lane = John S. Gray
23. Helen Lane Campbell Gray (Manitoba to Birmingham, England) = Cecil Burford Berners-Lee
24. Conway Berners-Lee = Mary Lee Woods
25. **Sir Timothy John "Tim" Berners-Lee**, b. 1955, sometime of Mass. since 1974, inventor of the World Wide Web (1991), unm.

Sources: Research in English and Canadian censuses, civil registrations, etc., by W.A. Reitwiesner, John Blythe Dobson and Michael J. Wood (reported on http://wargs.com/other/bernerslee.html, an AT by Reitwiesner), plus birth announcements (9 June 1955, p. 1A and 26 Sept. 1921, p. 1A) for T.J. and Conway Berners-Lee, obituaries for C.B. Berners-Lee (3 March 1931, p. 1C), Helen L.C. Gray Berners-Lee (12 June 1968, p. 20A), marriage (1 Sept. 1920, p. 1C) of Cecil and Helen, all in *The Times* [London] of those dates and pages; *NCAB* 16 (1937): 420-21 (Mortimer Mason Taplin, grandson of Henry and Melinda) and Frederic P. Wells, *History of Newbury, Vermont* (1902), p. 706 (Taplin); John D. Farwell, Jane A. Abbott and Lillian M. Wilson, *The Farwell Family* (1929, henceforth *Farwell*), pp. 25-37, 41-44, 52-55, 85-86, 136 (to Mrs. Taplin).

16. Hannah Farwell (sister of the second Henry) = Samuel Woods
17. Alice Woods = Peter Joslin
18. Esther Joslin = William Richardson
19. Samuel Richardson = Lucy Merrick, daughter of John Merrick (IV) (and Keziah Stratton), son of John Merrick (III) (and Abigail Harrington), son of John Merrick, Jr. and Elizabeth Trowbridge, SETH, daughter of James Trowbridge (and Margaret Atherton), son of Thomas Trowbridge and Elizabeth Marshall, SETH
20. Peter Richardson = Mehitable Spencer Prentiss
21. William Everett Richardson = Vesta Hodsdon
22. William Blaney Richardson, b. Boston, Mass., later of Matagalpa, Nicaragua, naturalist = Rosaura Ojeda Medero of Mexico. Their daughter Lucia Richardson Ojeda married

The Royal Descents of 900 Immigrants

Francisco Navarro Lugo, Vice-President of Nicaragua, 1937-1938 (under Anastasio Somoza García) and was the mother of (1) Ernest "Tito" Navarro Richardson, Nicaraguan Minister of Labor (under Anastasio Somoza Debayle), who married Perla Amador Pineda; and (2) Lucia Navarro Richardson, who married Francisco Fiallos Gil and was the mother in turn of Francisco Fiallos Navarro, Nicaraguan diplomat (Ambassador to the U.S.) and Attorney General, defeated candidate for President of Nicaragua in 2006. This last married Salvadora Somoza Urcuyo, daughter of Luís Somoza Debayle, granddaughter of Anastasio Somoza García, and niece of Anastasio Somoza Debayle, all presidents of Nicaragua (1937-47, 1950-56, 1956-63, 1967-72, 1974-79).

23. **William Blaney/Blaine Richardson, Jr.** of Mexico, sometime of Calif., banker = María Luisa López-Collada (of Mexico).
24. William Blaine "Bill" Richardson, Jr. (b. Calif. 1947), congressman, diplomat (U.S. Ambassador to the United Nations [1997-1998]), U.S. Secretary of Energy (1998-2001), Governor of New Mexico (2003-2011) = Barbara Flavin

Sources: AT by the late William Addams Reitwiesner (on http://wargs.com/political/richardson.html), confirmed by *WWA*, SSDI 091-26-0177 (William B. Richardson, Jr.) and 1868 Mass. birth record of W.B. Richardson, Sr.), J.A. Vinton, *The Richardson Memorial* (1876), pp. 572-74, 618, 679-80 (to W.E. Richardson); Edith S. Wessler, *The Jocelyn-Joslin-Joslyn-Josselyn Family* (1961), p. 104 and *Farwell*, pp. 25-37, 41-44, 49-50, 71; G.B., *Genealogy of the Merrick-Mirick-Myrick Family of Massachusetts, 1636-1902* (1902), pp. 101-3, 105, and F.B. Trowbridge, *The Trowbridge Genealogy* (1908), pp. 48, 503-6. The Nicaraguan research was undertaken by Eddy Kühl, whom I thank profusely, and brought to my attention by Christopher Challender Child of NEHGS.

Sir Richard Thimbleby at generation 11 was a son of John Thimbleby (and Margaret Boys), son of Richard Thimbleby and Elizabeth Hilton, SETH.

The Royal Descents of 900 Immigrants

1. Edward I, King of England, d. 1307 = Margaret of France
2. Thomas of Brotherton, Earl of Norfolk = Alice de Hales
3. Margaret Plantagenet, Duchess of Norfolk = John de Segrave, 4th Baron Segrave
4. Elizabeth de Segrave = John Mowbray, 4th Baron Mowbray
5. Thomas Mowbray, 1st Duke of Norfolk = Elizabeth FitzAlan
6. Margaret Mowbray = Sir Robert Howard
7. John Howard, 1st Duke of Norfolk = Katherine Moleyns
8. Anne Howard = Sir Edmund Gorges
9. Sir Edward Gorges = Mary Poyntz
10. Edward Gorges = Anne Walsh   10. Sir William Gorges = Winifred Butshead   10. Sir Thomas Gorges = Helen Bååt (Snakenborg), SETH
11. Edward Gorges = Cecily Lygon, SETH   11. Tristram Gorges = Elizabeth Cole
12. Sir Ferdinando Gorges (c. 1565-1647) founder and lord proprietor of Maine = (1) Anne Bell, ARD, SETH; (2) Mrs. Mary Fulford Achims, ARD, SETH; (3) Mrs. Elizabeth ―― Coffin   12. (4) **Elizabeth Gorges** (1) Edward Courtenay (2) William Bligh   11. (5) **Elizabeth Gorges** = (1) Sir Hugh Smith

Sources: *Gorges*, esp. pp. 43-51, 86-109, 114-15, 119-39, 178-99 and chart at end, and *Ligon*, pp. 172-80; *BP* and *CP* (Norfolk), *AR8*, lines 16, 22, and *RA* 3: 578. A third agent of Sir Ferdinando in Maine was his cousin Thomas Gorges, dep. gov. of Maine 1640-43 (= [1] Mary Sanford and [2] Mrs. Rose Alexander Mallock), son of Henry Gorges (and Barbara Baynard), son of Robert Gorges (and Anne Webb), son of Sir William Gorges (and ――), son of Sir Edmund Gorges and Anne

The Royal Descents of 900 Immigrants

Howard, above. Alexander Gorges, a son of Dep. Gov. Thomas and Rose, immigrated to Virginia and married Mrs. Mary —— Vaulx but left no NDTPS. This chart is considered as treating two immigrants (the two wives, both named Elizabeth Gorges) because Sir Ferdinando Gorges has been treated earlier, among the Lygon/Ligon kinsmen descended from Edward III.

The Royal Descents of 900 Immigrants

1. Edward I, King of England, d. 1307 = Eleanor of Castile
2. Elizabeth Plantagenet = Humphrey de Bohun, 4th Earl of Hereford and Essex
3. William de Bohun, 1st Earl of Northampton = Elizabeth Badlesmere
4. Elizabeth de Bohun = Richard FitzAlan, 10th Earl of Arundel
5. Elizabeth FitzAlan = Sir Robert Goushill
6. Joan Goushill = Thomas Stanley, 1st Baron Stanley
7. Margaret Stanley = (1) Sir William Troutbeck; (2) Sir John Boteler
8. (by 2) Sir Thomas Boteler = Margaret Delves
9. Margery Boteler = Sir Thomas Southworth
10. Sir John Southworth = Mary Ashton
11. Thomas Southworth = Rosamond Lister
12. Edward Southworth, probably the Leyden Pilgrim = Alice Carpenter of Mass., who later married William Bradford, *Mayflower* passenger and governor of the Plymouth Colony
13. **Constant Southworth** of Mass. = Elizabeth Collier.
13. **Thomas Southworth** of Mass. = Elizabeth Reynor.
14. Elizabeth Southworth = Joseph Howland
15. Nathaniel Howland = Martha Cole
16. Nathaniel Howland, Jr. = Abigail Burt
17. Joseph Howland = Lydia Bill
18. Susan Howland = John Aspinwall, Jr.
19. Mary Rebecca Aspinwall = Isaac Roosevelt
20. James Roosevelt = Sara Delano
21. Franklin Delano Roosevelt (1882-1945), 32nd U.S. President = (Anna) Eleanor Roosevelt

The Royal Descents of 900 Immigrants

Sources: *AR8*, lines 9, 46, 20, 15, and sources cited therein. See also *RA* 1: 446-48 (Boteler, to Margery), 5: 27-28 (Stanley), 2: 610-18 (Goushill, FitzAlan), 1: 420-26 (Bohun).

  An alternative Nottinghamshire origin for Edward Southworth was first suggested by Robert L. French in *The Mayflower Quarterly* 58 (1992): 10-15. In a 2017 online monograph by Sue Allan, "In Search of Separatist Edward Southworth of Leiden," the author strongly argues against the above origin for Edward of Leyden (his father, Thomas Southworth of Salmesbury, Lancashire, was seemingly the family's first Protestant; Thomas's father, Sir John Southworth, and two of Thomas's brothers, John and Christopher, were sometime ardent Catholics variously imprisoned). Ms. Allan argues instead, and gathers considerable circumstantial evidence favoring her argument, that Edward Southworth of Leyden was born at Clarborough, Nottinghamshire, 12 April 1585; an elder brother, Thomas Southworth, thought to be the man of that name also in Leyden, was born at Clarborough 28 July 1583. These latter brothers were sons of Richard Southworth of Clarborough (and Immyn Aston, married there in 1579), son of Richard Southworth of Clarborough and Welham and Emma Levesey of Keeton, all in Nottinghamshire, of whom the latter couple appear in G.W. Marshall, *Visitation of Nottingham, 1569 and 1614* (*HSPVS*, vol. 4, 1871), p. 114, and share a coat of arms somewhat similar to that of the Southworths of Salmesbury. Ms. Allan especially notes that Robert Bradford, a cousin of Gov. William, married Elizabeth Southworth, sister of the proposed Edward and Thomas of Clarborough.

  Note that the surname of the mother of the newly-alleged Leyden Southworths of Clarborough, if Ashton rather than Aston (a common error), is that of the paternal grandmother of the formerly alleged Leyden Pilgrim, Edward Southworth of Salmesbury above. Further Ashton and Levesey research is eagerly awaited, as is more information on earlier Southworths of Clarborough, and clinching proof (or disproof) of one of these Edward Southworths as the Leyden Pilgrim and father of Constant and Thomas of Mass.

The Royal Descents of 900 Immigrants

1. Edward I, King of England, d. 1307 = Margaret of France
2. Thomas of Brotherton, Earl of Norfolk = Alice de Hales
3. Margaret Plantagenet, Duchess of Norfolk = John de Segrave, 4th Baron Segrave
4. Elizabeth de Segrave = John Mowbray, 4th Baron Mowbray
5. Eleanor Mowbray = John de Welles, 5th Baron Welles
6. Eleanor de Welles = Sir Hugh Poynings
7. Constance Poynings = Sir John Paulet
8. John Paulet = Eleanor Ros
9. Sir John Paulet = Alice Paulet, a cousin
10. Eleanor Paulet = Sir William Gifford
11. John Gifford = Joan Bruges/Brydges
12. Anne Gifford = Thomas Goddard
13. Richard Goddard = Elizabeth Walrond
14. Edward Goddard = Priscilla D'Oyley
15. **William Goddard** of Mass. = Elizabeth Miles.
16. Josiah Goddard = Rachel Davis
17. Rachel Goddard = Obadiah Coolidge, Jr.
18. Josiah Coolidge = Mary Jones
19. John Coolidge = Hannah Priest
20. Calvin Coolidge = Sarah Thompson
21. Calvin Galusha Coolidge = Sarah Almeda Brewer
22. John Calvin Coolidge = Victoria Josephine Moor
23. (John) Calvin Coolidge (Jr.) (1872-1933), 30th U.S. President = Grace Anna Goodhue

10. Sir George Paulet (brother of Eleanor) = Barbara Hamden
11. Sir Hamden Paulet = Margaret More

12. Elizabeth Paulet = Sir Francis Dowse

13. Anne Dowse = Sir Philip de Carteret

14. Francis de Carteret, atty. gen. of Jersey = Anne Seale

15. Frances de Carteret = Elias Dumaresq

16. **Philip Dumaresq** of Mass. = Susan Ferry.

Sources: *NEHGR* 156 (2002): 131-39 (full Goddard line, by Paul C. Reed and Dorothy E. Hopkins) and sources cited therein; *RA* 3: 90-92 (Goddard, Gifford), 4: 325-27 (Paulet, Poynings), 5: 331-32 (Welles), 4: 187-88 (Mowbray), 4: 256-66 (Norfolk); Mss. autobiography of Edward Goddard (1675-1754) at the American Antiquarian Society in Worcester, Mass. (notably pp. 2-3); *MGH*, 5th ser., 9 (1935-37): 88-90, 142-46 (Paulet), 44-48 (Welles), 162-68 (Plantagenet, Segrave, Mowbray); *NEHGR* 17 (1863): 317-18 (reprinted in *EO* 2: 1: 693-96) (Dumaresq), W.B.H. Dowse, *Lawrence Dowse of Legbourne, England, His Ancestors, Descendants, and Connections in England, Massachusetts and Ireland* (1926), pp. 71-73; *BLG* 1952, p. 1686 (Carteret), *Collins*, vol. 2, pp. 369-70 (Paulet), and *Parliament, 1558-1603*, vol. 3, pp. 188-89 (Sir Hamden Paulet).

The Royal Descents of 900 Immigrants

1. Edward I, King of England, d. 1307 = Eleanor of Castile
2. Joan Plantagenet = Gilbert de Clare, 3rd Earl of Gloucester, 7th Earl of Hertford
3. Elizabeth de Clare = Sir Theobald de Verdun
4. Isabel de Verdun = Henry Ferrers, 2nd Baron Ferrers of Groby
5. Elizabeth Ferrers = David Strathbogie, 2nd Earl of Atholl
6. Elizabeth Strathbogie = Sir John Scrope
7. Elizabeth Scrope = Thomas Clarell
8. Elizabeth Clarell = Sir Richard FitzWilliam
9. Margaret FitzWilliam = Ralph Reresby
10. Isabel Reresby = Robert Eure
11. Jane Eure (Evers) = Richard Bellingham
12. John Bellingham = Alice Luddington
13. William Bellingham = Frances Amcotts (daughter of Alexander Amcotts and Susan Disney, daughter of Richard Disney and his first wife, Nele Hussey, not his second wife, Jane Ayscough). Their younger son, another William Bellingham, also immigrated to Mass. but died without issue.
14. **Richard Bellingham** (c. 1592-1672), colonial governor of Mass. = (1) Elizabeth Backhouse of Mass., ARD, SETH; (2) Penelope Pelham of Mass., ARD, SETH.

10. Elizabeth Reresby (sister of Isabel) = Edward Eyre
11. Anne Eyre = Thomas Revell
12. (very probably) Mary Revell = John Woolley
13. Adam Woolley = Grace Heywood
14. Edward Woolley = Mary Fritchley
15. **Emmanuel Woolley** of R.I. = Elizabeth ⸺.

The Royal Descents of 900 Immigrants

Sources: *DVY*, vol. 1, p. 327 (Reresby) and *Lincolnshire Pedigrees*, pp. 3 (Eure or Evers), 118 (Bellingham); *Parliament, 1509-1558*, vol. 2, p. 49 (Richard, Disney), *Proceedings of the Society of Antiquaries of London*, 2nd ser., 4 (1867-70), 322-27 (chart showing the FitzWilliam descent of Jane [Evers] Bellingham) and the 1527 will of Ralph Reresby in *Testamenta Eboracensia*, vol. 5, pp. 245-46 (Ralph Reresby probably had two daughters named Elizabeth/Isabel, sometimes interchangeable); forthcoming article by Jack T. Hutchinson of Dunwoody, Ga., esp. for arguments identifying the immigrant and Mary Revell; L. W. Welch, "The Wolley Family and Pedigrees" (1936), pp. 21-22 (and accompanying pedigree of Wolley of Allen Hill) (in R.A. Stokely, *The Derbyshire Connections of the Stokely Families of Iowa*, n.d., at the Derbyshire Record Office) and *BLG*, 18th ed., vol. 3 (1972), p. 259; *TG*, new ser., 8 (1891-92): 70 and *Derbyshire Archaeological Journal* 91 (1973): 143, 161 (and accompanying pedigree) (Revell); *FMG*, vol. 2, pp. 555-57 (Eyre); Rev. Joseph Hunter, *The History and Topography of the Deanery of Doncaster*, vol. 2 (1831), p. 39 (Reresby); *PCF Yorkshire*, vol. 1 (1874), FitzWilliam and Clarell pedigrees; J.W. Clay, *The Extinct and Dormant Peerages of the Northern Counties of England* (1913), p. 203 (Scrope); *CP* 1: 308-9 (Scrope, Strathbogie, Ferrers); *RA* 3: 323 (Fitzwilliam), 2: 210-11 (Clarell), 1: 193-96 (Strathbogie), 3: 153-54 (Ferrers), 5: 245-48 (Verdun), 2: 195-206 (Clare). The corrected Bellingham descent was developed and brought to my attention by John C. Brandon of Columbia, S.C.

The Royal Descents of 900 Immigrants

1. Edward I, King of England, d. 1307 = Eleanor of Castile
2. Elizabeth Plantagenet = Humphrey de Bohun, 4th Earl of Hereford and Essex
3. Eleanor de Bohun = James Butler, 1st Earl of Ormonde
4. Petronilla Butler = Gilbert Talbot, 3rd Baron Talbot
5. Richard Talbot, 4th Baron Talbot = Ankaret le Strange
6. Alice Talbot = Sir Thomas Barre
7. Elizabeth Barre = Sir Edmund Cornwall
8. Eleanor Cornwall = Sir Richard Croft
9. Anne Croft = Sir Thomas Blount. Their son, Sir John Blount, married Katherine Peshall and was the father of Elizabeth Blount, mistress of Henry VIII, King of England, and wife of Gilbert Talboys, 1st Baron Talboys of Kyme, and Edmund Clinton, 1st Earl of Lincoln, admiral.
10. Walter Blount = Isabel Acton
11. Robert Blount = Anne Fisher
12. Thomas Blount = Frances ———
13. James Blount = ———
14. **James Blount** (d. 1686) of (Va. and) N.C., colonial official, leader in Culpeper's Rebellion = (1) ———; (2) Mrs. Anna Willix Riscoe, who = (3) Seth Southill, governor of N.C., ARD, SETH.

10. Robert Blount (brother of Walter) = Elizabeth Columbell
11. George Blount = (1) Rosamond Freschville; (2) Elizabeth ———
12. (maternity uncertain, possibly illegitimate) Frances Blount = Ralph Clarke
13. Ursula Clarke = Stephen Offley
14. Robert Offley = Mary Burton

15. Stephen Offley = Anne Shute, daughter of Benjamin Shute and Patience (or Anne) Caryl, SETH and sister of Samuel Shute, colonial governor of Mass.
16. **Amelia Offley** of Mass. = Sir Francis **Bernard**, 1st Bt. (1712-1779), barrister, colonial governor of N.J. and Mass., ARD, SETH.

Sources: Virginia W. Westergard and Kyle Samuel Vanlandingham, *Parker and Blount of Florida* (1983), esp. pp. 211-12, 219, and earlier sources mentioned therein, including a 1902 chart by Helen M. Prescott, plus further research in Astley, Worcestershire by Mr. Vanlandingham, Brom Nichol and Gillian Palmer as reported on *soc.genealogy.medieval* and brought to my attention by Nathaniel L. Taylor; 1622 will of Thomas Blount and 1636/7 will of Bridget Broome Blount Stanley, both of Astley, both found at the Worcester County Record Office and both showing that the immigrant's father, an elder James Blount, was the son of Thomas by a first wife, Frances, not by Bridget Broome; William S. Powell, ed., *Dictionary of North Carolina Biography*, vol. 1, *A-C* (1979), pp. 178-79 (James Blount, no origin given) and *The Augustan* 10, #7 (Oct.-Nov. 1967), p. 380 (where the immigrant is mistakenly given as a brother of Thomas Blount of Va., almost certainly the immigrant's son instead); George Grazebrook and J.P. Rylands, eds., *Visitation of Shropshire, 1623, Part I* (*HSPVS*, vol. 28, 1889), pp. 53-54 (Blount) and William Page and J.W. Willis-Bund, eds., *The Victoria History of the County of Worcester*, vol. 4 (1924, repr. 1971), pp. 232, 236 (generations 10-12); *MGH*, 2nd ser., 5 (1894): 77 (Cornwall); *RA* 2: 310-11 (Croft, Cornwall), 5: 118-22 (Barre, Talbot), 2: 47-48 (Butler), 1: 420-24 (Bohun); *Salt*, vol. 4 (1883), p. 81 (Sir Thomas, Robert, and George Blount), Sir Alexander Croke, *The Genealogical History of the Croke Family, Originally Named le Blount* (1823, known to contain errors), esp. pp. 383-84 (George and Frances Blount) and *FMG*, vol. 1, pp. 315-17 (Clarke, Offley to Lady Bernard). Clinching confirmation that James Blount of N.C. is the James "one of the sons of my late brother James Blount Esquire, deceased" now "beyond the seas" mentioned in the 19 Dec. 1655 PCC will of Charles Blount, gent., of Astley, would be welcome. To that end note the James Blunt, planter, in Virginia by 13 Sept. 1655, in P.W. Coldham, *The Complete Book of Emigrants, 1607-1660* (1988), p. 295. The Blount-Clarke-Offley descent of Lady Bernard was brought to my attention by John C. Brandon of Columbia, S.C.

The Royal Descents of 900 Immigrants

1. Edward I, King of England, d. 1307 = Eleanor of Castile
2. Elizabeth Plantagenet = Humphrey de Bohun, 4th Earl of Hereford and Essex
3. William de Bohun, 1st Earl of Northampton = Elizabeth Badlesmere
4. Elizabeth de Bohun = Richard FitzAlan, 10th Earl of Arundel
5. Elizabeth FitzAlan = Sir Robert Goushill
6. Joan Goushill = Thomas Stanley, 1st Baron Stanley
7. Catherine Stanley = Sir John Savage
8. Sir Christopher Savage = Anne Stanley
9. Christopher Savage = Anne Lygon, sister of the William Lygon who married Eleanor Dennis, and of the Henry Lygon who married Elizabeth Berkeley, SETH, and daughter of Sir Richard Lygon (and Margaret Greville), SETH, son of Richard Lygon and Anne Beauchamp, SETH, daughter of Richard Beauchamp, 2nd Baron Beauchamp of Powyck, and Elizabeth Stafford, SETH, daughter of Sir Humphrey Stafford and Eleanor Aylesbury, SETH
10. Francis Savage = Anne Sheldon
11. Walter Savage = Elizabeth Hall
12. Ralph Savage = ——
13. **Anthony Savage**, probably the husband of Sarah Constable and immigrant to Va.
14. Alice Savage = Francis Thornton
15. Elizabeth Thornton = Edwin Conway, Jr.
16. Francis Conway = Rebecca Catlett
17. Eleanor Rose Conway = James Madison
18. James Madison, Jr. (1750/1-1836), 4th U.S. President = Mrs. Dorothea "Dolly" Payne Todd

15. Margaret Thornton (sister of Elizabeth) = William Strother, Jr.

16. Francis Strother = Susannah Dabney
17. William Strother = Sarah Bayly
18. Sarah Dabney Strother = Richard Taylor
19. Zachary Taylor (1784-1850), 12th U.S. President = Margaret Mackall Smith. A daughter, Sarah Knox Taylor, was the first wife of Jefferson Davis, later President of the Confederacy (Confederate States of America).

10. Bridget Savage (sister of Francis) = Anthony Bonner
11. Mary Bonner = William Yonge
12. Bridget Yonge (died in England) = George Wyllys, colonial governor of Conn.
13. **Amy Wyllys** of Mass. = John **Pynchon** (c. 1626-1702/3), colonial industrialist and public official, son of William Pynchon, founder of Springfield, Mass., and Anne Andrew.

Sources: *PA*, pp. 638-41 (Savage, to Anthony), *RA* 4: 557-59 (Bonner, Savage), 5: 431-32 (Wyllys, Yonge), 5: 27-28 (Stanley), 2: 610-18 (Goushill, FitzAlan), 1: 420-24 (Bohun), 3: 575-76 (Lygon), 4: 419-21 (Beauchamp of Powyck), 2: 570-75 (Ferrers); Savage research by Brice M. Clagett and Neil D. Thompson, plus *Ligon*, vol. 1, pp. 38-41 and *GVFT* 3: 474-79; *AR8*, lines 57, 20, 15, 6 and *TAG* 39 (1963): 86-89 (Mrs. Pynchon). See also *AAP* (2009, 2012), pp. 15-17, 228, 315 (Madison AT, bibliography and chart).

The Royal Descents of 900 Immigrants

1. Edward I, King of England, d. 1307 = Margaret of France
2. Thomas of Brotherton, Earl of Norfolk = Alice de Hales
3. Margaret Plantagenet, Duchess of Norfolk = John de Segrave, 4th Baron Segrave
4. Elizabeth de Segrave = John Mowbray, 4th Baron Mowbray
5. Margaret Mowbray = Sir Reginald Lucy
6. Sir Walter Lucy = Eleanor l'Archdekne
7. Eleanor Lucy = Sir Thomas Hopton
8. Elizabeth Hopton = Sir Roger Corbet, son of Robert Corbet and Margaret ——, SETH
9. Sir Richard Corbet = Elizabeth Devereux, daughter of Walter Devereux, 1st Baron Ferrers of Chartley and Anne Ferrers, SETH
10. Catherine Corbet = Robert Onslow
11. Edward Onslow = Anne Houghton
12. Roger Onslow = Margaret Poyner
14. Richard Onslow = Catherine Harding
14. Cecily Onslow = Sir Humphrey Winch
15. Onslow Winch = Judith Burgoyne
16. Sir Humphrey Winch, 1st Bt. = Rebecca Browne
17. Mary Winch = Sir Francis Bickley, 3rd Bt.
18. **Joseph Bickley** of Va. = Mrs. Sarah Shelton Gissage.

10. Mary Corbet (sister of Catherine) = Sir Thomas Lacon
11. Jane Lacon = George Bromley
12. Sir Thomas Bromley, lord chancellor = Elizabeth Fortescue
13. Elizabeth Bromley = Sir Oliver Cromwell, uncle of the lord protector
14. Elizabeth Cromwell = Sir Richard Ingoldsby
15. Sir George Ingoldsby = Mary Gould

16. Barbara Ingoldsby = William Smythe

17. Ralph Smythe = Anne Clarke

18. William Smythe = Catherine Meade Ogle

19. Anne Smythe = Thomas Wade

20. Arthur Robert Willoughby-Wade = Lucy Maria Harvey

21. **Evelyn Ada Maud Rice Willoughby-Wade** of Mass. = Alfred North **Whitehead** (1861-1947), mathematician, logician and philosopher.

Sources: *TVG* 27 (1983): 32-49 (Bickley), *TG* 10 (1989, published 1994): 55 (outline of generations 10-19 by Paul C. Reed), F.A. Blaydes, ed., *Visitations of Bedfordshire, 1566, 1582, and 1634* (*HSPVS*, vol. 19, 1884), p. 199 (Winch), Sir John MacLean, *Parochial and Family History of the Deanery of Trigg Minor*, vol. 3 (1879), pp. 398-99 (Onslow), A.E.B. Corbet, *The Family of Corbet,* vol. 2 (1920), p. 253 and chart at end esp.; *RA* 2: 292-95 (Corbet), 3: 658-61 (Hopton, Lucy), 4: 187-88 (Mowbray), 4: 256-66 (Norfolk), 2: 570-77 (Ferrers), *AR8*, lines 56B, 61, 9, 74, 70, 8 and *CP* (Lucy, Mowbray, Segrave, Norfolk, Ferrers of Chertley) (for Bickley); *ANB* and *Oxford DNB* (A.N. Whitehead), *BIFR*, pp. 1172-73 (Wade), *BLGI* 1912, p. 652 (Smythe), *Notes and Queries*, 11th ser., 8 (1913): 55 (Ingoldsby), Mark Noble, *Memoirs of the Protectoral House of Cromwell*, 3rd ed. (1787), 1: 37-58 (Cromwell, plus Ingoldsby and Bromley chapters in vol. 2) and George Grazebrook and J.P. Rylands, eds., *Visitations of Shropshire, 1623* (*HSPVS*, vols. 28-29, 1889), pp. 78 (Bromley), 306-7 (Lacon).

The Royal Descents of 900 Immigrants

1. Edward I, King of England, d. 1307 = Eleanor of Castile
2. Joan Plantagenet = Gilbert de Clare, 3rd Earl of Gloucester, 7th Earl of Hertford
3. Elizabeth de Clare = Roger Damory, 1st Baron Damory
4. Elizabeth Damory = John Bardolf, 3rd Baron Bardolf
5. William Bardolf, 4th Baron Bardolf = Agnes Poynings
6. Cecily Bardolf = Sir Brian Stapleton
7. Sir Miles Stapleton = Catherine de la Pole
8. Elizabeth Stapleton = Sir William Calthorpe
9. Anne Calthorpe = Sir Robert Drury, Speaker of the House of Commons
10. Elizabeth Drury = Sir Philip Boteler
11. Sir John Boteler = Grizel Roche
12. Sir Henry Boteler = Catharine Waller
13. John Boteler, 1st Baron Boteler of Bramfield = Elizabeth Villiers, half-sister of George Villiers, 1st Duke of Buckingham, favorite of James I, King of England
14. Helen Boteler = Sir John Drake
15. Elizabeth Drake = Sir Winston Churchill
16. Charles Churchill, English soldier (brother of John Churchill, 1st Duke of Marlborough, English commander during the War of the Spanish Succession and hero of the Battle of Blenheim, and of Arabella Churchill, wife of Charles Godfrey and mistress of James II, King of England) = Mary Gould
17. (illegitimate by ——) Charles Churchill, d. unm.
18. (illegitimate by ——) **Harriet Churchill** = (1) Sir Everard **Fawkener**; (2) Thomas **Pownall** (1722-1805), colonial governor of Mass.

12. Mary Boteler (sister of Sir Henry) = Thomas Shotbolt

13. John Shotbolt = Jane Tony
14. Mary Shotbolt = Thomas Taylor
15. William Taylor = Barbara Hanbury, his stepsister
16. **Elizabeth Taylor** of N.H. = Robert **Tufton [alias] Mason**, councillor of the Province of N.H., and of New England under Dudley and Andros, son of Joseph Tufton and Anne Mason, daughter of John Mason, grantee of N.H. as the manor of Masonhall.

Sources: *Oxford DNB* (Thomas Pownall, Sir Everard Fawkener, and Charles Churchill); *TAG* 77 (2002): 193-94 and *Parliament, 1715-1754*, vol. 1, pp. 551-52 (Charles Churchill the younger); *Chester of Chicheley*, vol. 1, pp. 139-46 (Boteler and generations 1-13 of the descent for Mrs. Pownall on pp. 140-41); *SMF* 1: 354 (Drury); *RA* 2: 472-73 (Drury), 5: 35-38 (Calthorpe, Stapleton), 1: 253-60 (Bardolf), 2: 19-22 (Damory), 2: 195-206 (Clare).

The descent of Mrs. Mason is from research by John C. Brandon of Columbia, S.C., who cites, among other published sources, *GDMNH*, pp. 464-66, J.B. Whitmore and A.W. Hughes Clarke, eds., *London Visitation Pedigrees, 1664* (*HSPVS*, vol. 92, 1940), p. 139 (Tufton alias Mason); J.L. Chester and G.J. Armitage, *Allegations for Marriage Licences Issued from the Faculty Office of the Archbishop of Canterbury at London, 1543 to 1819* (*HSPVS*, vol. 24, 1886), p. 26, W.A. Coppinger, *The Manors of Suffolk*, vol. 1 (1905), p. 300 and A. Audrey Locke, *The Hanbury Family*, vol. 2 (1916), p. 316-18 (Taylor, Hanbury and Mary [Shorbolt/Shotbolt] Taylor); Sir Henry Chauncy, *The Historical Antiquities of Hertfordshire* (1826), vol. 1, p. 123 (Taylor, Shotbolt), vol. 2, p. 57 (Boteler, with daughters of Sir Philip and Sir John), plus the 1697 PCC will of Rev. Thomas Shotbolt, nephew of Mary (Shotbolt) Taylor, which mentions Rev. Thomas's father, Philip Shotbolt, and the latter's brother-in-law, Thomas Taylor and the move from Ardeley, Hertfordshire, to Bradley, Hampshire. This descent was first posted on soc.genealogy.medieval.

Note: Sir Robert Drury (II), son of Sir Robert Drury and Anne Calthorpe above, married Elizabeth Brudenell and left a daughter, Anne Drury, who married Robert Woodliffe. Drew Woodliffe, a son of these last, married Katherine Duncombe and himself left a son, John Woodliffe of Va., who married —— and left a son and daughter but no NDTPS. The daughter, Anne Woodliffe, for whom no marriage is known, lived with her alleged "relatives" Thomas and Adria/Audrey (Hoare) Harris (Audrey was the daughter of Thomas Hoare and Julian Tripplett) at age 7 in 1624/5. Mary Harris, daughter of Thomas and Adria/Audrey, married Col. Thomas Ligon (Lygon) of Va., ARD, SETH. See *TAG* 76 (2001): 191-92, 195-200, 300-14 and *AP&P*, 4th ed., vol. 2 (2005), pp. 264-66.

The Royal Descents of 900 Immigrants

1. Edward I, King of England, d. 1307 = Margaret of France
2. Thomas of Brotherton, Earl of Norfolk = Alice de Hales
3. Margaret Plantagenet, Duchess of Norfolk = John de Segrave, 4th Baron Segrave
4. Elizabeth de Segrave = John Mowbray, 4th Baron Mowbray
5. Eleanor Mowbray = John de Welles, 5th Baron Welles
6. Eudo de Welles = Maud de Greystock
7. Lionel de Welles, 6th Baron Welles = Joan Waterton
8. Katherine de Welles = Robert Tempest
9. John Tempest = —— ——
10. Anne Tempest = Sir Edward Boleyn (uncle of Anne Boleyn, second Queen of Henry VIII, and great uncle of Elizabeth I, Queen of England), son of Sir William Boleyn and Margaret Butler, SETH
11. Elizabeth Boleyn = Thomas Payne
12. Mary Payne = William Reymes
13. William Reymes = Anne Evans
14. John Reymes = Frances ——
15. —— Reymes = Rev. Nathaniel Brewster of Brookhaven, L.I. (his first wife; he married second Sarah, almost certainly the daughter, by Mary Cogan, of Roger Ludlow of Mass. and Conn., ARD, SETH, Dep. Gov. of Mass., author of the *Fundamental Orders* of Connecticut). Rev. Nathaniel and —— (Reymes) left a son, John Brewster, whose later history is unknown, and possibly a younger daughter, Sarah, wife of Jonathan Smith of Smithtown.
16. **Abigail Brewster** of Conn. = Daniel **Burr**.

13. Anne Reymes (sister of the younger William) = Thomas Hobart
14. Mary Hobart = Thomas Colby
15. John Colby = Anne Archer
16. Mary Colby = Thomas Carthew

539

17. Thomas Carthew = Elizabeth Mitchell
18. Thomas Carthew = Anne Denny
19. Laura Carthew = Searles Wade. A son was Thomas Wade, English poet, playwright, and journalist.
20. Laura Wade = William James Linton (1812-1897), wood engraver, illustrator, poet and polemicist, in Conn. *post* 1866; his only children were by Laura's sister, Emily Wade (a common-law union begun after Laura's death)
21. **Margaret Wade Linton** of Conn. = Thomas William **Mather**. A daughter, Margaret Mather, married Thaddeus Merriman (1876-1939), civil engineer, and their daughter, Margaret Mather Merriman, married Wilbur George Parks (1904-1975), chemist and educator.

Sources: *Connecticut Ancestry* 47 (2004-5): 103-6 (Henry Bainbridge Hoff), based largely on D.L. Jacobus, *History and Genealogy of the Families of Old Fairfield*, vol. 1 (1930, rep. 1976), pp. 123-24 (Burr) and *Suffolk County Historical Society Register* 18 (1992-93): 2-5 (Smith); *TAG* 13 (1936-37): 113-16, 154-57 and H.F. Seversmith, *Colonial Families of Long Island, New York, and Connecticut,* vol. 1 (1939), pp. 359-64, 377-89 (Brewster), 96 (Colby), 84 (Hobart); *Norfolk Archaeology* 30 (1952): 34-38 and Rev. G.H. Dashwood, ed., *Visitation of Norfolk, 1563,* vol. 1 (1878), pp. 292-95 (Reymes); Walter Rye, ed., *Visitations of Norfolk, 1563, 1589 and 1613* (*HSPVS*, vol. 32, 1891), pp. 217-18, 52-53 (Payne, Boleyn); *Lincolnshire Pedigrees*, vol. 3 (*HSPVS*, vol. 52, 1904), p. 954 (Tempest), *CP* 12, part 2: 441-44 and 449-50, note j (Welles); *AR8*, lines 202, 16, 120, 15 and *RA* 2: 50-56 (Boleyn [to Sir Edward], Butler), 5: 331-36 (to Sir Edward Boleyn and Anne Tempest, but not their marriage) (Tempest, Welles), 4: 187-88 (Mowbray), 4: 256-66 (Norfolk); *WWWA*, vol. 1, *1897-1942* (1943), p. 833 (Thaddeus Merriman), vol. 6, *1974-1976* (1976), p. 316 (W.G. Parks), *Obituary Record of Graduates of Yale University Deceased During the Year Ending July 1, 1918* (1919), pp. 739-40 (T.W. Mather), *Oxford DNB* and *ANB* for W.J. Linton and F.B. Smith, *Radical Artisan: William James Linton, 1812-97* (1973), *passim*, naming the parents of Laura and Emily Wade; *BLG* 1853, vol. 2, *Supplement*, pp. 344-45 and *VC*, pp. 574-75 (Carthew); Rev. G.H. Dashwood, *Visitation of Norfolk, 1563*, vol. 1 (1878), p. 96 (Colby), 84 (Hobart). The Linton descent was developed and brought to my attention by John C. Brandon of Columbia, S.C.

The Royal Descents of 900 Immigrants

1. Edward I, King of England, d. 1307 = Margaret of France
2. Thomas of Brotherton, Earl of Norfolk = Alice de Hales
3. Margaret Plantagenet, Duchess of Norfolk = John de Segrave, 4th Baron Segrave
4. Elizabeth de Segrave = John Mowbray, 4th Baron Mowbray
5. Thomas Mowbray, 1st Duke of Norfolk = Elizabeth FitzAlan
6. Isabel Mowbray = James Berkeley, 6th Baron Berkeley, son of Sir James Berkeley (and Elizabeth Bluet), son of Maurice Berkeley, 4th Baron Berkeley (and Elizabeth le Despencer), son of Thomas Berkeley, 3rd Baron Berkeley (= [2] Katherine de Clivedon, SETH) and (1) Margaret Mortimer
7. Thomas Berkeley = Margaret Guy
8. Richard Berkeley = Margaret Dyer
9. William Berkeley = Elizabeth Burghill
10. Rowland Berkeley = Catherine Heywood
11. William Berkeley = Margaret Chettle
12. Jane Berkeley = William Jeffreys
13. **Sir Herbert Jeffreys**, colonial governor of Va. = Susanna ———.

11. Dorothy Berkeley (sister of William) = Thomas Wylde
12. Robert Wylde = Anne Rowland alias Steyner
13. Sarah Wylde = John Vernon
14. Susanna Vernon = Thomas Bund
15. William Bund = Mary Parsons
16. Thomas Bund = Susanna Johnson
17. Thomas Henry Bund = Anne Wilmot
18. Anne Susanna Kent Bund = John Walpole Willis
19. John William Willis-Bund = Harriette Penelope Temple

20. Mary Susanna Willis-Bund = John Leader MacCarthy
21. Francis Leader MacCarthy-Willis-Bund = Joan Mildred Elton Carey
22. **Alison E. MacCarthy-Willis-Bund** of Calif. and R.I. = Lewis Perry **Curtis**, Jr., b. 1932, historian, author of *Apes and Angels: The Irishman in Victorian Caricature* (1979) and *Jack the Ripper and the London Press* (2002), a U.C. Berkeley Graduate School instructor of the author, and son of Lewis Perry Curtis, historian and educator, co-leader of the History, the Arts and Letters honors program at Yale (in which the author graduated), and Jeanet Ellinwood Sullivan.

Sources: E.M. Jefferys, *Jefferys of Worcestershire, Nevis, [and] Philadelphia* (1939), pp. 6, 14-15, *BLG* 1863, pp. 89-90 (Berkeley) and *Lives of the Berkeleys*, vol. 1, pp. 86-89, vol. 2, pp. 82-83, 86-88 esp.; *MCS5*, lines 66, 63, *AR8*, line 16, and *RA* 1: 337-40 (Berkeley), 4: 187-92 (Mowbray), 4: 256-66 (Segrave, Norfolk); Wikipedia entry for L. Perry Curtis, Curtis-MacCarthy-Willis-Bund engagement announcement in *The New York Times* of 27 April 1959, a listing for F.L. MacCarthy-Willis-Bund (naming his parents) and his two wives on http://thepeerage.com/p44991.htm, various England vital and census records online, Edward Ralph Serocold Skeels (a.k.a. J.R.S. G[askell]), *A Portfolio of Royal Descents* (1902), pedigree XXXIX (entire line to Alexander Joseph Willis-Bund, brother of Mrs. J.L. MacCarthy), A.T. Butler, ed., *Visitation of Worcestershire, 1634* (*HSPVS*, vol. 90, 1938), pp. 11-12 (Berkeley), 105 (Wyld[e]), W.C. Metcalfe, ed., *Visitation of Worcestershire, 1682-83* (1883), pp. 102 (Wylde), 97 (Vernon), and *BLG*, 1925, p. 238 (Willis-Bund, to Mrs. MacCarthy).

The Royal Descents of 900 Immigrants

1. Edward I, King of England, d. 1307 = Eleanor of Castile
2. Elizabeth Plantagenet = Humphrey de Bohun, 4th Earl of Hereford and Essex
3. Margaret de Bohun = Hugh Courtenay, 2nd Earl of Devon
4. Margaret Courtenay = John Cobham, 3rd Baron Cobham
5. Joan Cobham = Sir John de la Pole
6. Joan de la Pole, Baroness Cobham = Sir Reginald Braybrooke
7. Joan Braybrooke = Sir Thomas Brooke
8. Reginald Brooke = Anne Everton
9. Edward Brooke = Florence Ashfield
10. George Brooke = Anne Carew
11. George Brooke = Alice Tyrrell, daughter of Sir John Tyrrell (and Elizabeth Munday), son of Sir Thomas Tyrrell and Margaret Willoughby, SETH
12. Anne Brooke = Sir Nicholas Salter
13. Anne Salter = Sir Henry Bowyer
14. Sir William Bowyer, 1st Bt. = Margaret Weld. They are ancestors #2928-29 of the late Diana, Princess of Wales.
15. Alice Bowyer = Sir John Clayton
16. **John Clayton** (d. 1737), Attorney-General of Va. = Lucy ⎯⎯ (parents of the botanist John Clayton, author of *Flora Virginia*, who married Elizabeth Whiting).
16. **Charlotte Clayton** of N.Y. = John Lovelace, 4th Baron **Lovelace** (d. 1709), colonial governor of N.Y., ARD, SETH.

Sources: *AP&P4*: 3: 114-17 (Salter, Bowyer, Clayton), *CB* 3: 58 (Bowyer) and *Diana 12G*, pp. 203, 310, 410, 451 (but the baronet was the grandfather, not uncle, of the Clayton immigrants); G.W.J. Gyll, *History of the Parish of Wraysbury, Ankerwycke Priory and Magna Charta Island* (1862), p. 43 (Salter); *BLG* 1853, pp. 145-46 (Brooke of Ufford Place) and the 1600 PCC will of George Brooke of Belstead,

Suffolk, naming "my son Salter"; *CP* (Cobham, Devon) and RA 5: 404-9 (Cobham to Reginald Brooke), 1: 326-31 (Courtenay), 1: 420-24 (Bohun); O.F. Brown, *The Tyrells of England* (1982), pp. 126-29, and Joan Corder, ed., *Visitations of Suffolk, 1561, Part I* (*HSPVS*, new ser., vol. 2, 1981), pp. 107-8 (Tyrrell, which lists Alice, at generation 11 above, but not her husband). This line was developed and brought to my attention by John C. Brandon of Columbia, S.C.

The Royal Descents of 900 Immigrants

1. Edward I, King of England, d. 1307 = Margaret of France
2. Thomas of Brotherton, Earl of Norfolk = Alice de Hales
3. Margaret Plantagenet, Duchess of Norfolk = John de Segrave, 4th Baron Segrave
4. Elizabeth de Segrave = John Mowbray, 4th Baron Mowbray
5. Eleanor Mowbray = John de Welles, 5th Baron Welles
6. Eudo de Welles = Maud de Greystock
7. Sir William de Welles, Lord Deputy of Ireland = Anne Barnewall
8. Ismay de Welles = Thomas Nangle
9. John Nangle = Eleanor Dowdall
10. Amy Nangle = Thomas Fagan
11. Richard Fagan = Cecily Holmes
12. John Fagan = Alice Segrave
13. John Fagan = Beale Knowles
14. Christopher Fagan = Mary Nagle
15. Patrick Fagan = Christiana FitzMaurice. Their eldest son, Christopher Alexander Fagan, was the father illegitimately, by Hyacinthe-Gabrielle Varis, wife of Pierre Roland, of Hyacinthe-Gabrielle Roland, wife of Richard Wellesley, 1st Marquess Wellesley, British foreign secretary, governor-general of India and colonial statesman (brother of Arthur Wellesley, 1st Duke of Wellington, field marshal and victor at Waterloo) and an ancestress of the late Queen Elizabeth the Queen Mother of Great Britain.
16. **Nicholas FitzMaurice Fagan** of Pa. = Mary Seton Walsh. Their son, John Francis Fagan, by second wife Emily Rogers Estell, was the father of Louis Estell Fagan, father by Mary Dorothea Colahan of Mary Dorothea Fagan, wife of H(ugh) Gilbert Cassidy and mother of Lewis Cochran Cassidy, noted lawyer, who married Clara L. McGrew and Mrs. Juanita Newton Harris.

16. Stephen Fagan (brother of Nicholas) = Helena Trant

17. Eliza Fagan = Alexander MacCarthy

18. Helen MacCarthy = James Morrogh

19. James MacCarthy-Morrogh = Anne Stubbman

20. Donal Florence MacCarthy-Morrogh = Vera Hutchinson

21. **Kathleen Helen MacCarthy-Morrogh,** known as **Kay Summersby**, 1908-1975, of N.Y., aide and confidante of General Dwight David Eisenhower during World War II, = (1) Gordon Thomas **Summersby**; (2) Reginald Heber **Morgan**.

Sources: *BIFR* 399-400, 404-5 (Fagan, to Mrs. Cassidy), 872 (Nangle), 865-66 (MacCarthy-Morrough, Morrogh and MacCarthy), *Prominent Families in America with British Ancestry* (1983, reprint of the American section of *BLG* 1939), p. 70 (Cassidy) and *WWWA*, vol. 2, *1943-1950* (1950), p. 107 (L.C. Cassidy); *ANB,* vol. 23, pp. 136-37 (Kay Summersby); *Oxford DNB* (Sir William de Welles under Lionel, Leo or Lyon de Welles, 6th Baron Welles) and *CP12*, part 1, p. 9 (forename of Anne Barnewall). See also *Prince Charles*, pp. 481 (note under F60), 1-4, *RA* 5: 331-32 (Welles), 4: 183-88 (Mowbray), 4: 256-66 (Segrave, Norfolk).

The Royal Descents of 900 Immigrants

1. Edward I, King of England, d. 1307 = Eleanor of Castile
2. Joan Plantagenet = Gilbert de Clare, 3rd Earl of Gloucester, 7th Earl of Hertford
3. Eleanor de Clare = Hugh le Despencer, 1st Baron Despencer
4. Isabel le Despencer = Richard FitzAlan, 9th Earl of Arundel
5. Sir Edmund FitzAlan = Sybil Montagu
6. Elizabeth FitzAlan = Sir Leonard Carew
7. Sir Thomas Carew = Elizabeth Bonville
8. Sir Nicholas Carew = Joan Courtenay, daughter of Sir Hugh Courtenay (and Philippa l'Archdekne), son of Sir Edward Courtenay (and Emeline Daunay), son of Hugh Courtenay, 2nd Earl of Devon, and Margaret de Bohun, SETH
9. Thomas Carew = Joan Carminow
10. Sir Nicholas Carew = Margaret Dinham
11. Sir Edmund Carew = Katherine Huddersfield
12. Katherine Carew = Sir Philip Champernowne, son of Sir John Champernowne and Margaret Courtenay, daughter of Sir Philip Courtenay and Elizabeth ——, SETH
13. Jane Champernowne = Robert Gamage, son of Sir Thomas Gamage and Margaret St. John, daughter of Sir John St. John (and Sibyl ferch Morgan ap Jenkin), son of Sir John St. John (and Alice Bradshaw), son of Sir Oliver St. John and Margaret Beauchamp (who married secondly John Beaufort, 1st Duke of Somerset [son of John Beaufort, Marquess of Somerset and Dorset, and Margaret Holand, SETH], by whom she left a daughter, Margaret Beaufort, wife firstly of Edmund Tudor, 1st Earl of Richmond and mother of Henry VII, King of England, d. 1509), daughter of Sir John Beauchamp (and Edith Stourton), son of Sir Roger Beauchamp (and Mary ——), son of Sir Roger de Beauchamp (and ——, not Joan Clopton), son of Roger de Beauchamp, 1st Baron Beauchamp of Bletsoe (and Sybil Patshull), son of Roger de Beauchamp (and ——), son of Sir Walter de Beauchamp and Alice de Toeni, daughter of Roger V de Toeni and Alice de Bohun, SETH

The Royal Descents of 900 Immigrants

14. Eleanor (or Margaret) Gamage = William Lewis
15. Joan Lewis = Edward Kemeys
16. Edward Kemeys = Alice Thomas
17. Edward Kemeys = Margaret Morgan
18. Lewis Kemeys = Mary ——
19. Nicholas Kemeys = Mary Witty
20. Edward Kemeys = Hannah Fowler
21. **William Kemeys** of N.Y. = Elizabeth Thornton. Their son, Edward Kemeys, married Gertrude Bleecker and was the father of (1) William Kemeys, who married Abby Greene and was the father of Edward Kemeys, sculptor, who married Laura Sparkes Swing; and (2) Elizabeth Thornton Kemeys, wife of Samuel Irenaeus Prime, Presbyterian clergyman, editor and author.

13. Joan Champernowne (sister of Jane) = Sir Anthony Denny
14. Mary Denny = Thomas Astley
15. Frances Astley = Sir William Harris, son of Christopher Harris (and Mary Gedge), son (by third wife Anne Ruther) of William Harris, father by second wife Joan Cooke of Arthur Harris, husband of Dorothy Waldegrave, SETH
16. Frances Harris = Oliver Raymond
17. St. Clere Raymond = Anne Warkham
18. Samuel Raymond = ——
19. William Raymond = ——
20. Samuel Raymond = Isabella Child
21. Samuel Raymond = Margaretta Bridges
22. Isabella Raymond = Henry Yeats Smythies
23. Emily Smythies = Edward Greene
24. Emily Smythies Greene = Frederic Machell Smith
25. Kathleen Machell Smith = Francis Edward Bradshaw-Isherwood

The Royal Descents of 900 Immigrants

26. Christopher William Bradshaw-Isherwood, known as Christopher Isherwood (1904-1986), of Calif., man of letters, d. unm.

23. Margaretta Smythies (sister of Emily) = John Greene, brother of Edward

24. Carleton Greene = Jane Whytt Elizabeth Ann Wilson, daughter of John Alexander Wilson (and Marion Balfour, daughter of Lewis Balfour and Henrietta Scott Smith, SETH), son of James Wilson and Martha Whytt, daughter of Robert Whytt (Whyte) of Bennochie, professor of medicine, University of Edinburgh, and Louisa Balfour, SETH

25. Marion Raymond Greene = Charles Henry Greene, a cousin

26. (Henry) Graham Greene (1904-1991), novelist = Vivien Muriel Dayrell-Browning

Sources: *BLG* 18th ed., vol. 2 (1969), pp. 363-67 (Kemeys) and *DAB* (Edward Kemeys and S.I. Prime); *M&G*, pp. 407-8 (Kemeys), 330 (Lewis), 390 (Gamage); F.A. Blaydes, ed., *Visitations of Bedfordshire, 1566, 1582 and 1634* (*HSPVS*, vol. 19, 1884), pp. 52-53 (St. John); *Charles II*, pp. 69, 118, 192, 298 (Beauchamp); *MP*, pp. 122, 125-27 (Harris to Isherwood; disregard the chronologically impossible Percy descent on pp. 1-4, a line whose failure was brought to my attention by the late David Faris); *BLG*, 1952, pp. 1362-63 (Bradshaw-Isherwood), 18th ed., vol. 1, pp. 336-37 (Greene), vol. 3, pp. 752-53 (Raymond); Walter C. Metcalfe, ed., *Visitations of Essex, 1552, 1558, 1570, 1612, 1634, Part I* (*HSPVS*, vol. 13, 1878), pp. 696-97, 59-60, 415 (Harris), 139 (Astley) and *Part II* (*HSPVS*, vol. 14, 1879), pp. 696-97 (Raymond); *RA* 2: 436-38 (Astley, Denny, Champernowne), 2: 97-102 (Carew), 1: 119-20 (FitzAlan), 2: 606-610 (FitzAlan), 2: 443-48 (le Despencer), 2: 195-206 (Clare), 2: 403-4 (Courtenay), 2: 326-34 (Courtenay), 1: 420-24 (Bohun), 3: 56-58 (Gamage), 4: 523-34 (St. John, Beauchamp), 4: 410-13 (Beauchamp), 5: 174-75 (Toeni), 5: 200-11 (Tudor) and *AR8*, lines 6, 8, 28, 84, 85, 98, 97, 96, 170; and Barbara Balfour-Melville, *The Balfours of Pilrig* (1907), *passim*, esp. pp. 237-42.

The Royal Descents of 900 Immigrants

Note: At generation 8 above, Sir Hugh Courtenay, husband firstly of Philippa l'Archdekne, married secondly Maud Beaumont and left another Sir Hugh Courtenay, who married Margaret Carminow and was the father of Elizabeth Courtenay, wife of John Tretherff. Thomas Tretherff, a son of these last, married Maud Trevisa and was the father of Margaret Tretherff, mother by a third husband, Richard Buller, of Francis Buller, husband of Thomasine Williams. Sir Richard Buller, a son of these last, married Alice Hayward and left a daughter, Catherine Buller, wife of James Parker and mother of Richard and George Parker, both of Va. Richard, sometimes confused with other Richard Parkers of Va., married a Mrs. Mary ―― Perkins and left issue but no NDTPR. George Parker's history after immigration is apparently unknown. See *RA* 2: 326-40 (Courtenay to Parker) and sources cited therein.

The Royal Descents of 900 Immigrants

1. Edward I, King of England, d. 1307 = Eleanor of Castile
2. Elizabeth Plantagenet = Humphrey de Bohun, 4th Earl of Hereford and Essex
3. William de Bohun, 1st Earl of Northampton = Elizabeth Badlesmere
4. Elizabeth de Bohun = Richard FitzAlan, 10th Earl of Arundel
5. Joan FitzAlan = William Beauchamp, Baron Abergavenny
6. Joan Beauchamp = James Butler, 4th Earl of Ormonde
7. Thomas Butler, 7th Earl of Ormonde = Anne Hankford
8. Margaret Butler = Sir William Boleyn
9. Margaret Boleyn (aunt of Anne Boleyn, second Queen of Henry VIII, and great-aunt of Elizabeth I, Queen of England) = John Sackville
10. Mary Sackville = John Lunsford
11. Sir John Lunsford = Barbara Lewknor
12. Thomas Lunsford = Katherine Fludd
13. **Sir Thomas Lunsford** (c. 1610-c. 1653) of Va., royalist army officer = (1) Anne Hudson; (2) Katherine Neville of Va., ARD, SETH, matrilineal ancestor of George John Spencer, 2nd Earl Spencer; (3) Elizabeth Wormeley, widow of Richard Kempe, secretary and act. gov. of Va., ARD, SETH, and niece of Ralph Wormeley, second husband of (Lady) Agatha Eltonhead (Kellaway) Wormeley (Chichele) of Va., ARD, SETH.

10. Christopher Sackville (brother of Mary) = Constance Colepepper [Culpeper], daughter of Thomas Colepepper [Culpeper] (and Elizabeth Hawte, sister of the Jane Hawte who married Sir Thomas Wyatt, the conspirator, SETH), son of Alexander Colepepper [Culpeper] (and Constance Chamberlaine), son of Sir John Colepepper [Culpeper] and Agnes Gainsford, SETH
11. John Sackville = Joan Downton

The Royal Descents of 900 Immigrants

12. Mary Sackville = William White

13. Joan White = Nicholas Towneley, son of Francis Towneley and Catherine Forster, SETH

14. **Richard Towneley** of N.J. = Mrs. Elizabeth Smith Lawrence de Carteret, widow of William Lawrence of L.I. and Philip de Carteret, first colonial governor of N.J., both ARD, SETH.

Sources: *RA* 3: 675-77 (Lunsford), 2: 50-57 (Sackville, Boleyn, Butler), 1: 317-19 (Beauchamp), 2: 610-16 (FitzAlan), 1: 420-26 (Bohun); *MCS5*, lines 88A, 17A, 17, 19, 18 (and *AR8*, lines 120, 15, 6) and sources cited therein, esp. *Collectanea Topographica et Genealogica* 4 (1837): 141-42, and *VM* 17 (1909): 26-33; E.L. Lomax, *Genealogy of the Virginia Family of Lomax* (1913), pp. 57-63 (Lunsford) (Sir Thomas Lunsford and Katherine Neville were ancestors #s 1054-55 of the late Diana, Princess of Wales; see *Diana 12G*, pp. 100, 156, 232, 371, 390-91, 422 [generations 11-13]); F.A. Hill, *The Mystery Solved: Facts Relating to the "Lawrence-Towneley," "Chase-Towneley" Marriages and Estate Question* (1888), chart in packet esp.; Berry's *Sussex*, p. 181 and W. Bruce Bannerman, ed., *Visitations of Sussex, 1530 and 1633-34* (*HSPVS*, vol. 53, 1905), pp. 130 (where, however, the line from William White to his daughters is carelessly omitted) (White), 183 (Sackville), *Parliament, 1509-1558*, vol. 3, p. 244 (Christopher Sackville), and *Parliament, 1558-1603*, vol. 3, pp. 313-14 (John Sackville). See also Robert Hovenden, ed., *The Visitations of Kent, 1619-1621* (*HSPVS*, vol. 42, 1898), pp. 62-63 and *Sussex Archaeological Collections*, vol. 47 (1904), chart opposite p. 56 and pp. 57-60 (Colepepper) and *Mary Isaac*, pp. 185-92. This descent was developed and brought to my attention by John C. Brandon of Columbia, S.C. The above Hawte sisters were daughters (by Mary Guilford) of Sir William Hawte, brother of Jane Hawte, wife of Thomas Goodere and Robert Wroth, SETH, and son (by Isabel Frowick, sister of the Alice Frowick who married John Goodere, SETH) of Sir Thomas Hawte, brother of Alice Hawte, who married Sir William Cromer, SETH. Mary (Guilford) Hawte was a sister of both the George Guilford who married Elizabeth Mortimer, SETH, and the Frideswide Guilford who married Sir Matthew Browne, SETH. See *Mary Isaac*, pp. 85-96 (Guil[d]ford), 175-92 (Hawte). The above Barbara Lewknor, daughter of John of Buckingham, Sussex (*RA* 3: 675) is undoubtedly somehow a kinswoman of the Lewknors treated elsewhere in this work.

The Royal Descents of 900 Immigrants

1. Edward I, King of England, d. 1307 = Eleanor of Castile
2. Elizabeth Plantagenet = Humphrey de Bohun, 4th Earl of Hereford and Essex
3. Eleanor de Bohun = James Butler, 1st Earl of Ormonde
4. Petronilla Butler = Gilbert Talbot, 3rd Baron Talbot
5. Richard Talbot, 4th Baron Talbot = Ankaret le Strange
6. Alice Talbot = Sir Thomas Barre
7. Elizabeth Barre = Sir Edmund Cornwall
8. Eleanor Cornwall = Sir Richard Croft
9. Anne Croft = Sir Thomas Blount
10. Joyce Blount = Francis Gower
11. Richard Gower = Margaret Hunt
12. Eleanor Gower = John Yarnould/Yarnall
13. Francis Yarnould/Yarnall = Alice ——
14. John Yarnall = Sarah ——
15. **Francis Yarnall** of Pa. = Hannah Baker.
15. **Philip Yarnall** of Pa. = Dorothy Baker, niece of Hannah above.

Sources: *TAG* 87 (2014): 5-24, 136-52 (Paul C. Reed and Gary E. Young), 50 (1980): 46-48 (Richard E. Brenneman), and Harry H. Yarnell and Ruth Brookman Yarnell, *A Partial History of the Name Yarnall-Yarnell, 1683-1970* (1970), esp. pp. 1-4, 361-62. See also George Grazebrook and John Paul Rylands, eds., *Visitation of Shropshire* (*HSPVS*, vol. 28, 1889), p. 53 (Blount), and *RA* 2: 310-12 (Croft), 5: 118-22 (Barre, Talbot), 2: 47-48 (Butler), 1: 420-24 (Bohun).

The Royal Descents of 900 Immigrants

1. Edward I, King of England, d. 1307 = Eleanor of Castile
2. Elizabeth Plantagenet = Humphrey de Bohun, 4th Earl of Hereford and Essex
3. William de Bohun, 1st Earl of Northampton = Elizabeth Badlesmere
4. Elizabeth de Bohun = Richard FitzAlan, 10th Earl of Arundel
5. Elizabeth FitzAlan = Sir Robert Goushill
6. Elizabeth Goushill = Sir Robert Wingfield
7. Sir Henry Wingfield = Elizabeth Rookes
8. Robert Wingfield = Margery Quarles
9. Robert Wingfield = Elizabeth Cecil, sister of William Cecil, 1st Baron Burghley, minister of Elizabeth I
10. Dorothy Wingfield = Adam Claypoole
11. John Claypoole = Mary Angell. Their eldest son, John Claypoole, married firstly Elizabeth Cromwell, daughter of Oliver Cromwell, the Lord Protector. Another son, Edward Claypoole, was sometime of Pa. but later of Barbados; by wife Abigail ―― he left two daughters but no NDTPS.
12. **James Claypoole** of Pa. = Helen Mercer.
12. **Norton Claypoole** of Del. = Rachel ――.

Sources: *RA* 5: 381-85 (Claypoole, Wingfield), 2: 610-18 (Goushill, FitzAlan), 1: 420-26 (Bohun); *TAG* 73 (1998): 131-45, 47, 67 (1992): 97-107, 47 (1971): 204-5, 18 (1941-42): 201-6 and sources cited therein, esp. J.M. Wingfield, *Some Records of the Wingfield Family* (1925), pp. 7-17, 23-26 and chart opp. p. 252 and R.I. Graff, *Genealogy of the Claypoole Family* (1893), pp. 11-52; *AR8*, lines 15, 6. See also *BLG* 1952, pp. 2762-63 (Parry-Wingfield of Tichencote).

The Royal Descents of 900 Immigrants

1. Edward I, King of England, d. 1307 = Eleanor of Castile
2. Elizabeth Plantagenet = Humphrey de Bohun, 4th Earl of Hereford and Essex
3. Eleanor de Bohun = James Butler, 1st Earl of Ormonde
4. Petronilla Butler = Gilbert Talbot, 3rd Baron Talbot
5. Richard Talbot, 4th Baron Talbot = Ankaret le Strange
6. Alice Talbot = Sir Thomas Barre
7. Elizabeth Barre = Sir Edmund Cornwall
8. Eleanor Cornwall = Sir Richard Croft
9. Edward Croft = Joyce Skull
10. Margaret Croft = Ieuan Gwyn ap James ap Rhys
11. James ab Ieuan Gwyn (or James ap Rhys) = Elizabeth Clement
12. Margaret ferch James ab Ieuan Gwyn (or Margred ferch James ap Rhys) = Owen Phillips, for whose descent from patrilineal Tudor forebears see *RD600*, pp. 495-96
13. Elen Philips = Edward Gwyn ap Hywel
14. Morgan ab Edward = ——
15. Lewis Morgan = ——
16. Evan Lewis = ——
17. **John Evans** of Radnor, Pa. = Delilah —— (children bore the name Jones). His brother Edward Evans also immigrated to Pa., but left no NDTPS.

16. Morgan Lewis (brother of Evan Lewis) = ——
17. James Morgan = Jane ——
18. **John Morgan** of Pa. = Sarah Jones, daughter of John Evans of Radnor, Pa., ARD, see above, and Delilah ——.

The Royal Descents of 900 Immigrants

Sources: *WFP1*, pedigree XIX, pp. 130-33, 165-66 esp. (generations 12-18), Sir Samuel Rush Meyrick and Lewis Dwyn, *Heraldic Visitations of Wales and Part of the Marches between the Years 1586 and 1613*, vol. 1 (1846), pp. 260 (generations 12-13), 252 (and esp. note 5) (generations 9-12), and *Bartrum 2*, pp. 1018 (generations 10-11), 53 (Barry/Barre); *RA* 2: 310-12 (Croft), 5: 118-22 (Barre, Talbot), 2: 47-48 (Butler), 1: 420-24 (Bohun). Note also *Parliament, 1386-1421*, vol. 2, pp. 132-34 (Sir Thomas de la Barre, ca. 1349-1419, father of the Sir Thomas at generation 6). This improved descent was developed and brought to my attention by Christopher Challender Child of NEHGS. The John Evans of Radnor line was first noticed by Christos Christou, Jr., who also corrected my earlier identification of the wife of John Morgan above.

The Royal Descents of 900 Immigrants

1. Edward I, King of England, d. 1307 = Margaret of France
2. Thomas of Brotherton, Earl of Norfolk = Alice de Hales
3. Margaret Plantagenet, Duchess of Norfolk = John de Segrave, 4th Baron Segrave
4. Elizabeth de Segrave = John Mowbray, 4th Baron Mowbray
5. Thomas Mowbray, 1st Duke of Norfolk = Elizabeth FitzAlan
6. Isabel Mowbray = James Berkeley, 6th Baron Berkeley
7. Alice Berkeley = Richard Arthur
8. John Arthur = Margaret Butler
9. Margaret Arthur = Roger Porter
10. Arthur Porter = Alice Arnold
11. Isabel Porter = Giles Codrington
12. Richard Codrington = Joyce Borlase, daughter of Sir John Borlase and Anne Lytton, SETH
13. Robert Codrington = Henningham Drury
14. (very probably) Robert Codrington of Barbados = Elizabeth —
15. Henningham Codrington = Paul Carrington
16. **George Carrington** of Va. = Anne Mayo.
16. Paul Carrington = Jane (Mellowes)?
17. **Elizabeth Hannah Carrington** of Pa. = Charles **Willing**, Jr., son of Charles Willing of Pa., ARD, SETH, and Anne Shippen.

Sources: *NGSQ* 70 (1982): 248-70 (252-53 esp., an article which errs, however, in the parentage of Robert Codrington, husband of Henningham Drury); V.L. Oliver, *History of the Island of Antigua*, vol. 1 (1894), pp. 143-75 (147-48 esp.), *Bristol and Gloucestershire Archaeological Society Transactions* 21 (1898): 301-45, esp. pp. 340-42 (Codrington plus Porter, Arthur and Berkeley, p. 340, from *Lives of the Berkeleys*); *RA* 1: 337-40 (Berkeley), 4: 187-92 (Mowbray), 4: 256-66 (Segrave, Norfolk). Clinching proof of the parentage of Robert Codrington of Barbados would be welcome.

The Royal Descents of 900 Immigrants

1. Edward I, King of England, d. 1307 = Eleanor of Castile
2. Elizabeth Plantagenet = Humphrey de Bohun, 4th Earl of Hereford and Essex
3. William de Bohun, 1st Earl of Northampton = Elizabeth Badlesmere
4. Elizabeth de Bohun = Richard FitzAlan, 10th Earl of Arundel
5. Elizabeth FitzAlan = Sir Robert Goushill
6. Joan Goushill = Thomas Stanley, 1st Baron Stanley
7. Sir John Stanley = Elizabeth Weever   7. Catherine Stanley = Sir John Savage
8. Margery Stanley = Sir William Torbock   8. Margaret Savage = Sir Edmund Trafford   8. Ellen Savage = Sir Peter Legh
9. Thomas Torbock = Elizabeth Moore   9. Margery Trafford = Sir Thomas Gerard   9. Peter Legh = Margaret Tyldesley

10. Sir Thomas Gerard = 10. Jane Legh

10. William Torbock = 11. Catherine Gerard

11,12. Margaret Torbock = Oliver Mainwaring

12,13. **Mary Mainwaring**, prob. of Md. = Benjamin **Gill** of Md. Whether Mary died in England or immigrated to Md. is uncertain.

13,14. Anna Maria Gill = James Neale of Md., ARD, SETH.

  10. William Gerard (brother of Sir Thomas) = Constance Rowson

  11. (illegitimate by ——) Thomas Gerard = Grace ——

  12. John Gerard = Isabel ——. Their son, Marmaduke Gerard, married —— and left two daughters, Winifred and Bridget, who seem also to have immigrated to Md. but whose later history is unknown to me.

  13. **Thomas Gerard** of Md. = (1) Susannah Snow; (2) Mrs. Rose Tucker.

The Royal Descents of 900 Immigrants

Sources: *RA* 4: 25-28 (Gill, Mainwaring, Torbock, Stanley), 5: 27-28 (Stanley), 2: 610-18 (Goushill, FitzAlan), 1: 420-26 (Bohun), 3: 556-57 (Gerard, Legh, Savage), 3: 83-86 (Gerard, to Thomas of Md.), 5: 182-83 (Trafford, Honford), 4: 557-58 (Savage); *NEHGR* 141 (1987): 104-5 and sources cited therein, including *NEHGR* 79 (1925): 110-11 (reprinted in *EO* 2:2:677), *Devon and Cornwall Notes and Queries* 5 (1908-9): 50-62, 9 (1916-17): 3-4, *Transactions of the Historic Society of Lancashire and Cheshire (for the Year 1915)* 67 (new ser., 31) (1916): 212 (Mainwaring articles by Howard M. Buck), Matthew Gregson, *Portfolio of Fragments Relative to the History and Antiquities, Topography and Genealogies of the County Palatine and Duchy of Lancaster* (1869), p. 242 and *The Reliquary* 11 (1870-1), chart opp. p. 97 (Torbock), *PCF Lancashire* (Stanley, Gerard, Trafford and Legh pedigrees), *Ormerod*, vol. 1, p. 713 (Savage), William Farrer and John Brownbill, eds., *The Victoria History of the County of Lancaster*, vol. 3 (1907, rep. 1966), p. 180 (Stanley) and *AR8*, lines 20, 15, 6 (for Oliver Mainwaring, materials assembled and brought to my attention by Robert Behra of Salt Lake City; see also an unpublished monograph by Glenn H. Goodman, "The Ancestry of Oliver Mainwaring of New London, Ct., compiled from Published Sources," n.d.); unpublished Gill research by Brice McAdoo Clagett, assembled for *Seven Centuries: Ancestors for Twenty Generations of John Brice de Treville Clagett and Ann Calvert Brooke Clagett* (mss. sent to various scholars during Brice's lifetime; Brice also believed, based on contemporary references to Benjamin Gill's wife as both Mary and Anne, that, like her daughter, she was named Anna Maria); *AR8*, line 233A and primary sources cited therein esp., and *MG1*: 478-503 (for Thomas Gerard).

The Royal Descents of 900 Immigrants

1. Edward I, King of England, d. 1307 = Eleanor of Castile
2. Elizabeth Plantagenet = Humphrey de Bohun, 4th Earl of Hereford and Essex
3. William de Bohun, 1st Earl of Northampton = Elizabeth Badlesmere
4. Elizabeth de Bohun = Richard FitzAlan, 10th Earl of Arundel
5. Elizabeth FitzAlan = Sir Robert Goushill
6. Joan Goushill = Thomas Stanley, 1st Baron Stanley
7. Sir William Stanley = (1) Joan Beaumont, (2) Elizabeth Hopton
8. (probably by 2, or an unknown wife between Joan and Elizabeth) Joan Stanley = Sir John Warburton
9. Sir Piers Warburton = Elizabeth Winnington
10. Sir John Warburton = Mary Brereton
11. Elizabeth Warburton = 11. Sir William Booth, see below.
12. Sir George Booth, 1st Bt. = Katherine Anderson
13. Sir John Booth = Dorothy St. John
14. St. John Booth = 15. Anne Owen, see below.

15,16. **Thomas Booth** of Va. = Mary Cooke.

9. Ellen Warburton (sister of Sir Piers) = Sir John Carrington
10. Margaret Carrington = Peter Domville
11. Gilbert Domville = Margaret Sneyde
12. Edward Domville = Eleanor Leycester
13. **Margaret Domville** of Md. = (1) Richard **Hatton**; (2) Richard **Banks**.

7. Catherine Stanley (sister of Sir William) = Sir John Savage
8. Margaret Savage = Sir Edmund Trafford

The Royal Descents of 900 Immigrants

9. Edmund Trafford = Elizabeth Longford
10. Elizabeth Trafford = Sir George Booth, son of Sir George Booth and Elizabeth Boteler, daughter of Sir Thomas Boteler (also of Plantagenet-Bohun-FitzAlan-Goushill-Stanley descent) and Margaret Delves, SETH
11. Sir William Booth = 11. Elizabeth Warburton, above.
12. Alice Booth = John Panton
13. Elinor Panton = Sir Edward Duke, 1st Bt.
14. **Elizabeth Duke** of Va. = (1) Nathaniel **Bacon**, colonial gov. of Virginia, leader of Bacon's Rebellion, ARD, SETH; (2) Thomas **Jarvis**; (3) Edward **Mole**.

8. Catherine Savage (sister of Margaret) = Thomas Legh
9. Eleanor Legh = Sir Piers Dutton
10. Hugh Dutton = Jane Booth (sister of the elder Sir George Booth above), who = (2) Sir Thomas Holford, SETH
11. John Dutton = Eleanor Calveley
12. Thomas Dutton = Thomasine Anderton
13. Eleanor Dutton = Gilbert Gerard, 2nd Baron Gerard of Gerard's Bromley
14. Alice Gerard = Roger Owen, son of Sir William Owen and Eleanor Needham, daughter of Robert Needham, 1st Viscount Kilmorey (and Joan Lacy), son of Sir Robert Needham and Frances Aston, SETH
15. Anne Owen = 14. St. John Booth, above.

Sources: *RA* 1: 439-40 (Booth, Boteler), 1: 446-48 (Boteler), 5: 27-28 (Stanley), 5: 182-83 (Trafford), 4: 557-58 (Savage), 2: 292-93 (Stanley to Warburton), 2: 610-18 (Goushill, FitzAlan), 1: 420-26 (Bohun), 4: 208 (Needham) and sources cited therein, esp. *Kimber,* vol. 1, pp. 26-30; Dr. and Mrs. W.C. Stubbs, *Descendants of Mordecai Cooke of "Mordecai's Mount," Gloucester Co., Va., 1650, and Thomas Booth of Ware Neck, Gloucester Co., Va., 1685* (1923), pp. 186-90; *Ormerod* 1: 524-25 (Booth),

The Royal Descents of 900 Immigrants

574 (Warburton), William Beamont, *Annals of The Lords of Warrington, Part II* (*Publications of the Chetham Society*, vol. 87, 1873), pp. 263-302, 333-421, esp. 414-15 (Boteler) and *PCF Lancashire* (Trafford and Gerard pedigrees); *TAG* 87 (2014-15): 226-35, 285-98, and sources cited therein (Nathan W. Murphy, who cites the Hatton and Domville research of William Good, noted below); *Ormerod* 1: 713 (Savage), 3: 662 (Legh), 1: 650-51 (Dutton, Gerard) and *BLG* 1952, p. 435 (Owen); George Grazebrook and J.P. Rylands, eds., *Visitations of Shropshire, 1623* (*HSPVS*, vol. 29, 1889), p. 372 (Needham) and *CP* (Kilmorey). Many documents supporting the Domville-Hatton line were first assembled and posted online by William Good of Sydney, Australia, and brought to my attention by Douglas Richardson of Salt Lake City. Mary Brereton at generation 20 above was a daughter of Sir William Brereton and Eleanor Brereton, daughter of Sir Randall Brereton and Eleanor Dutton, SETH. See Sir Robert Maitland Brereton, *The Breretons of Cheshire, 1100 to 1904 A.D.* (1904), pp. 72, 98.

When the index to this volume was nearly complete, the query of an NEHGS member brought to my attention the parentage of Mrs. Elizabeth Duke Bacon (Jarvis Mole) of Va., wife of the leader of Bacon's Rebellion, as noted in the *DAB*, *ANB*, and *Oxford DNB* articles on her husband, *EB*, p. 176, and *GVFWM*, 1: 192. From *CB*, vol. 3, p. 221, and the above-cited Booth sources, the above descent is clear. Mrs. Bacon is included on this chart because she was a second cousin once removed, not a more distant relative, of Thomas Booth of Va. In its correct order, this chart would follow that for Lady Jane (Lowe) (Sewall) Calvert, Baroness Baltimore, and Nicholas and Henry Lowe, her brothers, all of Md.

The Royal Descents of 900 Immigrants

1. Edward I, King of England, d. 1307 = Eleanor of Castile
2. Elizabeth Plantagenet = Humphrey de Bohun, 4th Earl of Hereford and Essex
3. William de Bohun, 1st Earl of Northampton = Elizabeth Badlesmere
4. Elizabeth de Bohun = Richard FitzAlan, 10th Earl of Arundel
5. Elizabeth FitzAlan = Sir Robert Goushill
6. Joan Goushill = Thomas Stanley, 1st Baron Stanley
7. Margaret Stanley = (1) Sir William Troutbeck; (2) Sir John Boteler
8. (by 1) Joan Troutbeck = Sir William Griffith
9. Sir William Griffith (whose first wife was Jane Stradling, SETH) = Jane Puleston
10. Mary Griffith = Sir Randall Brereton
11. Jane Brereton = Nicholas Robinson, Bishop of Bangor
12. Piers Robinson alias Norris = Margaret Fowke, daughter of John Fowke and Dorothy Cupper, SETH
13. Eleanor Robinson alias Norris = John Maudit
14. Isaac Maudit = Elizabeth Berryman
15. **William Mauduit** of Md. = Mercy ——.

15. Jasper Maudit (brother of William) = Elizabeth King, daughter of Thomas King (and Anne Roberts), son of Richard King and Martha Goddard, sister of William Goddard of Mass., SETH
16. Elizabeth Maudit = Thomas Wright
17. Anne Wright = Samuel Lawford
18. Samuel Lawford = Margaret Sarah Acland
19. Thomas Acland Lawford = Janet Turing Bruce
20. Sir Sydney Turing Barlow Lawford = Mrs. May Somerville Bunny Cooper Aylen

The Royal Descents of 900 Immigrants

21. **Peter (Sydney Ernest [Aylen, later]) Lawford**, known as Peter Lawford (1923-1984) of Calif., actor = (1) Patricia Helen Kennedy, daughter of Joseph Patrick Kennedy, the financier and diplomat, and sister of John Fitzgerald Kennedy, 35th U.S. President, SETH, of Robert Francis Kennedy, U.S. Senator and Attorney-General, of Edward Moore Kennedy, U.S. Senator, of Mrs. Jean Ann Kennedy Smith, diplomat, and of Mrs. (Robert) Sargent Shriver, Jr. (Eunice Mary Kennedy), wife of the Democratic vice-presidential candidate in 1972; aunt of congressmen Joseph Patrick Kennedy (III) and Patrick Joseph Kennedy and of Maria (Owings) Shriver, television newscaster and wife of Arnold (Alois) Schwarzenegger, bodybuilder, actor and governor of California; and great-aunt of Congressman Joseph Patrick Kennedy (IV); (2) Mary Anne Rowan; (3) Deborah Gould; (4) Patricia Seaton.

Sources: Will of Sir Sydney T.B. Lawford of Los Angeles, dated 4 Aug. 1932, with a codicil of 8 Sept. 1950, probated in London 7 Sept. 1953, at Somerset House, London, birth record (17 Sept. 1923) of Peter Sydney Ernest Aylen, later Lawford, and *The [London] Times* of Thurs., 21 Feb. 1924, p. 5, col. 4 (report of the Lawford and Aylen divorce cases of Lawford's parents); *BP* (Sir S.T.B. Lawford in the "Knightage" section *post* 1918); *TG*, new ser., 8 (1891-92): chart between pp. 184 and 185 (Lawford); *TG* 1 (1877): 135, 4 (1880): 87-88 (Maudit, Wright, Lawford); Reginald Ames, *Genealogical Memoranda of the Family of Ames* (1889), chart entitled "Seize Quartier [*sic*] of Elizabeth, Sister of Eleanor Maudit, Drawn upon her Marriage with a German Nobleman," pp. 12-13, 16 (Maudit, King, Goddard, Robinson, Brereton, Griffith, Fowke); *PACF,* pp. 23, 185 (Robinson, Griffith), *RA* 2: 345-46 (Griffith), 5: 190-92 (Troutbeck), 5: 27-28 (Stanley), 2: 610-18 (FitzAlan), 1: 522-23 (Brereton), 1: 448 (Boteler). See also *BRMF* 1: 308-11 (Mauduit). Via Martha (Goddard) King, Peter Lawford had a "better" royal descent from King Edward I via Thomas of Brotherton, Earl of Norfolk, Segrave, Mowbray, Welles, Poynings, Paulet, Gifford and Goddard.

Sir Randall Brereton at generation 10 above was a son of Sir Randall Brereton and Isabel Boteler (daughter of Sir Thomas Boteler [also a Stanley-Goushill descendant] and Margaret Delves, SETH), son of Sir Randall Brereton and Eleanor Dutton, SETH.

The Royal Descents of 900 Immigrants

1. Edward I, King of England, d. 1307 = Eleanor of Castile
2. Elizabeth Plantagenet = Humphrey de Bohun, 4th Earl of Hereford and Essex
3. William de Bohun, 1st Earl of Northampton = Elizabeth Badlesmere
4. Elizabeth de Bohun = Richard FitzAlan, 10th Earl of Arundel
5. Elizabeth FitzAlan = Sir Robert Goushill
6. Elizabeth Goushill = Sir Robert Wingfield
7. Sir John Wingfield = 7. Elizabeth FitzLewis, see below
8. Sir Richard Wingfield = Bridget Wiltshire
9. Thomas Maria Wingfield = —— Kerry
10. **Edward Maria Wingfield** (c. 1570-post 1613), adventurer, first president of the Virginia Colony, d. unm.

8. Sir John Wingfield (brother of Sir Richard) = Anne Touchet
9. Sir Anthony Wingfield = Elizabeth Vere, daughter of Sir George Vere (and Margaret Stafford), son of John Vere, 12th Earl of Oxford, and Elizabeth Howard, SETH
10. Richard Wingfield = Mary Hardwick, daughter of John Hardwick and Elizabeth Leke, SETH
11. Henry Wingfield = Elizabeth Risby
12. Mary Wingfield = William Dade
13. **Francis Dade** of Va. = Behethland Bernard.

2. Joan Plantagenet = Ralph de Monthermer, 1st Baron Monthermer
3. Thomas de Monthermer, 2nd Baron Monthermer = Margaret ——
4. Margaret de Monthermer = John Montagu, 3rd Baron Montagu
5. John Montagu, 1st Earl of Salisbury = Maud Francis
6. Anne Montagu = Sir Lewis (ap) John

The Royal Descents of 900 Immigrants

7. Elizabeth FitzLewis = 7. Sir John Wingfield, above.

Sources: *DAB, MCS5,* line 20 and *RA* 5: 20 and 3: 517 (Sir Richard and T.M. Wingfield), 3: 198-202 (Wingfield, FitzLewis), 5: 381-82 (Wingfield), 2: 610-18 (Goushill, FitzAlan), 1: 420-26 (Bohun), 4: 118-21 (Montagu), 2: 195-206 (Monthermer, Clare), 5: 264-68 (Vere); *GVFVM* 5:822-25 (Wingfield), 2:657-63 (Dade); Sir Henry Ellis, *Visitation of Huntingdon, 1613* (Camden Society Publications, vol. 43, 1849), pp. 125-28 (Wingfield); *AR8*, lines 15, 8A.

The Royal Descents of 900 Immigrants

1. Edward I, King of England, d. 1307 = Eleanor of Castile
2. Joan Plantagenet = Gilbert de Clare, 3rd Earl of Gloucester, 7th Earl of Hertford
3. Elizabeth de Clare = Sir Theobald de Verdun
4. Isabel de Verdun = Henry Ferrers, 2nd Baron Ferrers of Groby
5. William Ferrers, 3rd Baron Ferrers of Groby = Margaret Ufford
6. Henry Ferrers, 4th Baron Ferrers of Groby = Joan Poynings
7. William Ferrers, 5th Baron Ferrers of Groby = Philippa Clifford
8. Sir Thomas Ferrers = Elizabeth Freville, SETH
9. Sir Henry Ferrers = Margaret Heckstall, SETH
10. Sir Edward Ferrers = Constance Brome, SETH
11. Anne Ferrers = Sir Valentine Knightley, son of Sir Richard Knightley and Joan Skenard, SETH
12. Sir Richard Knightley = Mary Fermor
13. Mary Knightley = Thomas Barnardiston
14. Thomas Barnardiston = Anne Polstead
15. Samuel Barnardiston = Jane Adams
16. John Barnardiston = Miriam Saunders
17. Joseph Barnardiston = Frances Harris
18. Mary Barnardiston = Samuel Howes
19. Elizabeth Howes = John Joseph Marshall
20. Mary Anne Marshall = Charles William Meakins
21. Eliza Howes Meakins = John Harte
22. **Charles Edward Harte** of Ohio = Ruth Elizabeth Weisenstein. A son was John Joseph Meakins Harte, Episcopal bishop of Arizona (= Alice Eleanor Taylor).
22. **Ada Elinor Harte** of Ill.= Francis Frederick **Miles**. Their daughter, Ella Frances Miles, married Edwin George Schafer, agronomist.

567

The Royal Descents of 900 Immigrants

Sources: *WWWA*, vol. 15, *2002-2004* (2004), p. 105 (J.J. Harte) and vol. 7, *1977-1981* (1981), pp. 504-5 (E.G. Schafer); research by Janet (Paulette Chevalley) Wolfe of Ann Arbor, Mich. (generations 15-22); F.A. Crisp, *Visitation of England and Wales: Notes*, vol. 7 (1907), pp. 170, 173, 188 (Barnardiston, to Samuel); *Baker*, vol. 1, pp. 381-82 (Knightley) and Rev. Henry Norris, *Baddesley Clinton...* (1897), esp. pp. 113-19 (Ferrers); *RA* 2: 212-13 (Ferrers), 3: 153-58 (Ferrers), 5: 245-48 (Verdun), 2: 195-206 (Clare), 3: 39 (Freville).

The Royal Descents of 900 Immigrants

1. Edward I, King of England, d. 1307 = Eleanor of Castile
2. Elizabeth Plantagenet = Humphrey de Bohun, 4th Earl of Hereford and Essex
3. Margaret de Bohun = Hugh Courtenay, 2nd Earl of Devon
4. Sir Philip Courtenay = Anne Wake
4. Elizabeth Courtenay = Sir Andrew Luttrell
5. Sir John Courtenay = Joan Champernowne, see below
5. Sir Hugh Luttrell = Catherine Beaumont
6. Sir Philip Courtenay = Elizabeth Hungerford, see below
6. Sir John Luttrell = Margaret Touchet
7. Elizabeth Courtenay, see below = (1)
7. Sir James Luttrell
 (= [2] Sir Humphrey Audley, SETH
8. Sir Hugh Luttrell = Margaret Hill
9. Eleanor Luttrell = Roger Yorke
10. Elizabeth Yorke = Edmund Percival
11. Christian Percival = Richard Lowle
12. **Percival Lowell** of Mass. = Rebecca ———. Percival Lowell was the patrilineal ancestor of the famed Boston Lowells, who include at least three poets, a president of Harvard, an astronomer, and various other notables.

Sources: *RA* 3: 644-48 (Lowell, Percival, Yorke, Luttrell), 2: 400-3 (Courtenay), 2: 326-31 (Courtenay), 1: 420-24 (Bohun); *NEHGR* 157 (2003): 309-19 (Brandon Fradd and Douglas Richardson), based in part on *Davis* 2: 510-15; Burton W. Spear, *Search for the Passengers of the Mary and John, 1630*, vol. 25 (1996), pp. 46-47 (Somerset records extracted by Robin Bush, including an estate administration to Christiana, relict of Richard Lowle); James Anderson, *A Genealogical History of the House of Yvery, in its Different Branches of Yvery, Luvel, Percevel, and Gournay*, vol. 1 (1742), pp. 425-31 and chart between pp. 324 and 325 (with errors); a 1544-47 chancery suit (*Lists of Early Chancery Proceedings*, vol. 9 [Lists and Indexes, #54], p. 139) that identifies the wife of Edmund Percival as Elizabeth, daughter of Roger Yorke,

The Royal Descents of 900 Immigrants

serjeant-at-law; *Dunster*, vol. 1, pp. 76-133 (Luttrell); *VD*, pp. 244, 246 (Courtenay); *AR8*, lines 51, 6. For over 60 English families in Percival Lowell's ancestry see Carl Boyer, 3rd, *Ancestral Lines from Maine to North Carolina: 182 Families in England, Ireland, France, The Netherlands, Germany, Scotland, the Eastern Seaboard, Ohio, Missouri, and California, with Medieval and Royal Descents of Percival[1] Lowell of Mass. and Neill Dubh[1] and Grizel[1] (Campbell) McNeill of N.C.* (2015), *passim*. Also note Scott C. Steward and Christopher C. Child, *The Descendants of Judge John Lowell of Newburyport, Massachusetts* (2011), pp. 3-4.

The above Joan Champernowne and Elizabeth Hungerford at generations 5 and 6 above are daughters respectively of Sir Richard Champernowne and Alice Astley, SETH, and Walter Hungerford, 1st Baron Hungerford, and Catherine Peverell, SETH.

The Royal Descents of 900 Immigrants

1. Edward I, King of England, d. 1307 = Eleanor of Castile
2. Elizabeth Plantagenet = Humphrey de Bohun, 4th Earl of Hereford and Essex
3. William de Bohun, 1st Earl of Northampton = Elizabeth Badlesmere
4. Elizabeth de Bohun = Richard FitzAlan, 10th Earl of Arundel
5. Elizabeth FitzAlan = Sir Robert Goushill
6. Elizabeth Goushill = Sir Robert Wingfield
7. Elizabeth Wingfield = Sir William Brandon
8. Eleanor Brandon = John Glemham
9. Anne Glemham = Henry Pagrave
10. Thomas Pagrave = Alice Gunton
11. Edward Palgrave = ――
12. **Dr. Richard Palgrave** of Mass. = Anna ――.
13. Sarah Palgrave = John Alcock
14. Joanna Alcock = Ephraim Hunt, Jr.
15. Elizabeth Hunt = Lemuel Pope
16. Mercy Pope = Caleb Church
17. Joseph Church = Deborah Perry
18. Deborah Church = Warren Delano
19. Warren Delano, Jr. = Catherine Robbins Lyman
20. Sara Delano = James Roosevelt
21. Franklin Delano Roosevelt (1882-1945), 32nd U.S. President = (Anna) Eleanor Roosevelt

13. Mary Palgrave (sister of Sarah) = Roger Wellington
14. Benjamin Wellington = Elizabeth Sweetman
15. Elizabeth Wellington = John Fay, Jr.

The Royal Descents of 900 Immigrants

16. John Fay (III) = Hannah Child
17. Jonathan Fay = Joanna Phillips
18. Jonathan Fay, Jr. = Lucy Prescott
19. Samuel Prescott Phillips Fay = Harriet Howard
20. Samuel Howard Fay = Susan Shellman
21. Harriet Eleanor Fay = James Smith Bush
22. Samuel Prescott Bush = Flora Sheldon
23. Prescott Sheldon Bush, U.S. Senator = Dorothy Walker
24. George Herbert Walker Bush (b. 1924), 41st U.S. President = Barbara Pierce, SETH
25. George Walker Bush (b. 1946), 43rd U.S. President = Laura Lane Welch, SETH

Sources: *RA* 1: 506-13 (Palgrave, Glemham, Brandon), 5: 381-82 (Wingfield), 2: 610-18 (FitzAlan), 1: 420-26 (Bohun); *AR8*, line 15 and sources cited therein, esp. *NEHGR* 102 (1948): 87-98, 312-13, 103 (1949): 102-7, 287-95, 116 (1962): 79, all reprinted in *EO* 1: 3: 60-72, 82-96; *Moriarty*.

The Royal Descents of 900 Immigrants

1. Edward I, King of England, d. 1307 = Eleanor of Castile
2. Elizabeth Plantagenet = Humphrey de Bohun, 4th Earl of Hereford and Essex
3. Margaret de Bohun = Hugh Courtenay, 2nd Earl of Devon
4. Sir Philip Courtenay = Anne Wake
5. Sir John Courtenay = Joan Champernowne, SETH
6. Sir Philip Courtenay = Elizabeth Hungerford, SETH
7. Sir Philip Courtenay = Elizabeth ——
8. Philip Courtenay = Jane Fowell
9. Elizabeth Courtenay = William Strode
10. Elizabeth Strode = Walter Hele
11. Frances Hele = John Snelling, son of Thomas Snelling and Joan Elford, SETH
12. **John Snelling** of Mass. = Sarah ——.

Sources: *NEHGR* 52 (1898): 342-46 (reprinted in *EO* 2: 3: 274-78), 108 (1954): 179; *VD*, pp. 694 (Snelling), 462 (Hele), 718 (Strode), 244, 246, 251 (Courtenay); *RA* 2: 400-4 (Strode, Courtenay), 2: 326-31 (Courtenay), 1: 420-24 (Bohun); *AR8*, lines 51, 6. Further proof of the immigrant's identification as John Snelling, baptized 17 Jan. 1624/5 at Plympton St. Mary, Devon, son of John Snelling and Frances Hele, and nephew of William Snelling of Mass., SETH, would be desirable.

The Royal Descents of 900 Immigrants

1. Edward I, King of England, d. 1307 = Eleanor of Castile
2. Elizabeth Plantagenet = Humphrey de Bohun, 4th Earl of Hereford and Essex
3. William de Bohun, 1st Earl of Northampton = Elizabeth Badlesmere
4. Elizabeth de Bohun = Richard FitzAlan, 10th Earl of Arundel
5. Elizabeth FitzAlan = Sir Robert Goushill
6. Joan Goushill = Thomas Stanley, 1st Baron Stanley
7. Margaret Stanley = (1) Sir William Troutbeck; (2) Sir John Boteler
8. (by 1) Adam Troutbeck = Margaret Boteler, his stepsister
9. Margaret Troutbeck = 9. Sir John Talbot, see below
10. Anne Talbot = Thomas Needham
11. Robert Needham = Frances Aston
12. Dorothy Needham = Sir Richard Chetwode
13. **Grace Chetwode** of Mass. = Rev. Peter **Bulkeley** (1582/3-1658/9) of Mass., a founder and first minister of Concord, Mass., ARD, SETH.

5. Joan FitzAlan (sister of Elizabeth) = William Beauchamp, Baron Abergavenny
6. Joan Beauchamp = James Butler, 4th Earl of Ormonde
7. Elizabeth Butler = John Talbot, 2nd Earl of Shrewsbury
8. Sir Gilbert Talbot = Audrey Cotton
9. Sir John Talbot = 9. Margaret Troutbeck, see above.

Sources: *RA* 2: 10 (Bulkeley), 2: 159-60 (Chetwode), 4: 207-8 (Needham), 5: 125-28 (Talbot), 2: 50-52 (Butler), 1: 317-19 (Beauchamp), 2: 610-18 (FitzAlan, Goushill), 1: 420-26 (Bohun), 5: 190-92 (Troutbeck), 5: 27-28 (Stanley); *AR8*, lines 7, 120, 20, 15, 6; *Bulkeley*, pp. 54-89.

The Royal Descents of 900 Immigrants

1. Edward I, King of England, d. 1307 = Eleanor of Castile
2. Joan Plantagenet = Gilbert de Clare, 3rd Earl of Gloucester, 7th Earl of Hertford
3. Margaret de Clare = Hugh de Audley, 1st Earl of Gloucester
3. Eleanor de Clare = Hugh le Despencer, 1st Baron Despencer
4. Margaret de Audley = Ralph Stafford, 1st Earl of Stafford
4. Sir Edward Despencer = Anne Ferrers
5. Elizabeth Stafford = John de Ferrers, 4th Baron Ferrers of Chartley
5. Edward Despencer, 3rd Baron Despencer = Elizabeth Burghersh
6. Robert de Ferrers, 5th Baron Ferrers of Chartley = 6. Margaret Despencer
7. Sir Edmund Ferrers = Ellen Roche
8. Margaret Ferrers = John Beauchamp, 1st Baron Beauchamp of Powyck
9. Richard Beauchamp, 2nd Baron Beauchamp of Powyck = Elizabeth Stafford, daughter of Sir Humphrey Stafford and Eleanor Aylesbury, SETH
10. Anne Beauchamp = Richard Lygon
11. Elizabeth Lygon = Thomas Curzon
12. Agnes Curzon = Nicholas Backhouse
13. Samuel Backhouse = Elizabeth Borlase, daughter of Sir John Borlase and Anne Lytton, SETH
14. **Elizabeth Backhouse** of Mass. = Richard **Bellingham** (c. 1592-1672), colonial governor of Mass., ARD, SETH.

Sources: *Lincolnshire Pedigrees*, p. 118 (Bellingham); W. Harry Rylands, ed., *Visitations of Berkshire, 1532, 1566, 1623, 1665-66*, vol. 1

The Royal Descents of 900 Immigrants

(*HSPVS*, vol. 56, 1907), p. 160 (Backhouse); *Glover*, vol. 2, p. 333 and *TG*, new ser. 7 (1891): 73-74, from the 1569 visitation of Derbyshire (Curzon); *Ligon*, vol. 1, pp. 33-34, where Richard Lygon and Anne Beauchamp are given eight sons (including George, a priest, for whom his nephew George Curzon was undoubtedly named), but no daughters. Elizabeth Lygon's parentage (Richard "Liggin," but not Sir Richard, in Glover, Richard Lygon in *TG*) is confirmed by chronology and naming patterns. Note that Gov. Bellingham married firstly a cousin of the Lygon cluster and secondly a member of the Delaware-West-Pelham cluster, the largest groups of nearly kin immigrants in the colonies. See also *GM* 1, pp. 243-50 (Richard Bellingham). I first noticed the Lygon-Curzon connection in reviewing charts by Richard K. Evans on thirteenth- through eighteenth-generation ancestors of the late Diana, Princess of Wales.

The Royal Descents of 900 Immigrants

1. Edward I, King of England, d. 1307 = Eleanor of Castile
2. Joan Plantagenet = Gilbert de Clare, 3rd Earl of Gloucester, 7th Earl of Hertford
3. Margaret de Clare = Hugh de Audley, 1st Earl of Gloucester
4. Margaret de Audley = Ralph Stafford, 1st Earl of Stafford
5. Hugh Stafford, 2nd Earl of Stafford = Philippa Beauchamp
6. Katherine Stafford = Michael de la Pole, 2nd Earl of Suffolk
7. Isabel de la Pole = Thomas Morley, 5th Baron Morley
8. Anne Morley = John Hastings, *de jure* Baron Hastings
9. Sir Edmund Hastings = Mary Wodehouse
10. Anne Hastings = Richard Calthorpe
11. Edmund Calthorpe = Mary Leveson
12. Dionysia Calthorpe = Robert Woodroffe/Woodrove
13. Elizabeth Woodroffe/Woodrove = Sampson Sheffield
14. **Deliverance Sheffield**, possibly, perhaps likely of Mass., second wife of Hugh **Peter(s)** (1598-1660) of Mass., Puritan clergyman and Cromwellian politician, ARD, SETH.

Sources: G.J. Armytage, ed., *Visitation of Rutland, 1618-19* (*HSPVS*, vol. 3, 1870), p. 19 (Sheffield), *MGH*, 1st ser., 2 (1876): 379-80 (Woodroffe/Woodrove), Brig. Gen. Bulmer, ed., *Visitation of Norfolk, 1563*, vol. 2 (1895), pp. 441-42 (Calthorpe), *Norfolk Archaeology* 6 (1864): 87, 90, 94-95 (Hastings) and *RA* 2: 499 (Hastings), 4: 156-57 (Morley), 2: 416-20 (de la Pole), 5: 9-13 (Stafford), 5: 79-81 (Audley), 2: 195-206 (Clare). John C. Brandon of Columbia, S.C., first noted the possibility, perhaps likelihood, that Deliverance Sheffield of Boston and Salem, Mass., second wife of Puritan clergyman and Cromwellian politician Hugh Peter(s), was not a widow, as sometimes said, but the Deliverance Sheffield baptized at Seaton, Rutlandshire, 4 July 1613 (*Leicestershire and Rutland Notes and Queries* 3 [1893-95]: 283 and *Collectanea Topographica et Genealogica* 1 [1834]: 172), daughter of Sampson Sheffield and Elizabeth Woodroffe/Woodrove. Deliverance's only brother, a younger Sampson Sheffield, was a Parliamentary colonel, graduate of Emmanuel College, Cambridge, and of Navestock, Essex, so perhaps well known to Peters. See *Collectanea Topographica et Genealogica* 4 (1837): 259, and John and J.A. Venn, eds., *Alumni Cantabrigienses, Part I* [to 1751], vol. 4 (1927), p. 56.

Deliverance (Sheffield) Peters may have descendants in England. According to the *Oxford DNB*, her daughter, Elizabeth Peters, b. 1640, married Robert (called Thomas in the *DAB*) Barker in 1665 and had eight children. The 1711 PCC will (PROB 11/520/317, Young Quire) of Elizabeth Barker, of Deptford, near London, mentions son George and daughters Theodosia Barker (who was left Elizabeth's property in New England) and Deliverance (doubtless named for her maternal grandmother), wife of Justinian Hanchett.

The Royal Descents of 900 Immigrants

1. Edward I, King of England, d. 1307 = Margaret of France
2. Thomas of Brotherton, Earl of Norfolk = Alice de Hales
3. Margaret Plantagenet, Duchess of Norfolk = John de Segrave, 4th Baron Segrave
4. Elizabeth de Segrave = John Mowbray, 4th Baron Mowbray
5. Eleanor Mowbray = John de Welles, 5th Baron Welles
6. Eudo de Welles = Maud de Greystock
7. Lionel de Welles, 6th Baron Welles = Joan Waterton
8. Margaret de Welles = Sir Thomas Dymoke
9. Jane Dymoke = John Fulnetby
10. (probably) Katherine Fulnetby = William Dyn(e)well
11. Anne Dyn(e)well = Henry Whitgift (parents of John Whitgift, Archbishop of Canterbury)
12. William Whitgift = ——
13. Elizabeth Whitgift = Wymond Bradbury, son of William Bradbury and Anne Eden, daughter of Henry Eden and Elizabeth Heigham, daughter of Clement Heigham (and Anne Munnings), son of Clement Heigham (and Matilda Cooke), son of Thomas Heigham and Catherine Cotton, daughter of William Cotton and Alice Abbot, SETH
14. **Thomas Bradbury** of Mass. = Mary Perkins.

Sources: *NEHGR* 161 (2007): 27-36 (the late Marshall K. Kirk, edited by Martin Edward Hollick), based partly on John Brooks Threlfall, *The Ancestry of Thomas Bradbury (1611-1695) and His Wife Mary (Perkins) Bradbury (1615-1700) of Salisbury, Massachusetts*, 3rd ed. (2006), passim, esp. pp. 1-7, 13-16, 31-36 (Bradbury, Whitgift) and *Lincolnshire Pedigrees*, p. 378 (Fulnetby), 1204-5 (Dymoke); *RA* 4: 464-65 (Fulnetby, Dymoke), 5: 331-38 (Welles), 4: 187-88 (Mowbray), 4: 256-66 (Segrave, Norfolk) and *AR8*, lines 202, 16, 246A, 149, 148. For a long-rejected (because partly "faked" by Horatio Gates Somerby) but still possible kinship to Puritan leader and controversialist Rev. John Cotton (1584-1652), of Mass. (grandfather of Cotton Mather), see *New Hampshire Genealogical Record* 16 (1999): 145-70 (also by M.K. Kirk, with John Anderson Brayton).

The Royal Descents of 900 Immigrants

1. Edward I, King of England, d. 1307 = Margaret of France

2. Thomas of Brotherton, Earl of Norfolk = Alice de Hales

3. Margaret Plantagenet, Duchess of Norfolk = John de Segrave, 4th Baron Segrave

4. Elizabeth de Segrave = John Mowbray, 4th Baron Mowbray

5. Eleanor Mowbray = John de Welles, 5th Baron Welles

6. Eudo de Welles = Maud de Greystock

7. Lionel de Welles, 6th Baron Welles = Joan Waterton

8. Eleanor de Welles = Thomas Hoo, 1st Baron Hoo

9. Anne Hoo = Sir Roger Copley

10. Margaret Copley = Edward Lewknor, son of Edward Lewknor, SETH (and [1] Margaret ——), who later married [3] Anne Everard

11. Edward Lewknor = Dorothy Wroth

12. Mary Lewknor = Matthew Machell

13. Mary Machell = Ralph Cudworth. Another son, a younger Ralph Cudworth, and his daughter (by Damaris [Cradock?]), Lady Damaris (Cudworth) Masham, were both noted philosophical and theological writers treated in the *Oxford DNB*. Lady Masham was the second wife of Sir Francis Masham, 3rd Bt., and the friend, especially in his later years, of the philosopher John Locke.

14. **James Cudworth** of Mass. = Mary Parker.

Sources: *RA* 2: 363-67 (Cudworth, Machell, Lewknor), 3: 308-12 (Copley, Hoo), 5: 331-38 (Welles), 4: 187-88 (Mowbray), 4: 256-66 (Norfolk); *GM* 2: 249-58; research by Debrett Ancestry Research commissioned by Miss June E. Grunwell, proving James Cudworth's parentage but disproving that his mother was a daughter of John Machell and Jane Woodruff; W.J. Calder and A.G. Cudworth, Jr., *Records of the Cudworth Family: A History of the Ancestors and Descendants of James Cudworth of Scituate, Mass.* (1974), pp. 4-7, 22 esp.; Machell pedigree (an oversize tabular chart at NEHGS, described in *NEHGR* 30 [1876]: 464, reprinted in *EO* 2: 1: 633), a partial fraud compiled by Mrs. Harriet Bainbridge de Salis,

The Royal Descents of 900 Immigrants

corrected by the Debrett reports as indicated above; *Lewes*, pp. 159-61 (Lewknor) and *Horsham*, pp. 70-71 (Copley); *CP* (Hoo, Welles) and *AR8*, lines 202, 16. Paul C. Reed of Salt Lake City has also undertaken much research on this line; a forthcoming article may amplify the above descent. John Machell, Mary's brother, left a bequest in his 1647 PCC will to his "cousin" [niece] Jane Cudworth, a sister of the immigrant.

The Royal Descents of 900 Immigrants

1. Edward I, King of England, d. 1307 = Eleanor of Castile
2. Elizabeth Plantagenet = Humphrey de Bohun, 4th Earl of Hereford and Essex
3. Eleanor de Bohun = James Butler, 1st Earl of Ormonde
4. James Butler, 2nd Earl of Ormonde = Elizabeth Darcy
5. James Butler, 3rd Earl of Ormonde = Anne de Welles, daughter of John de Welles, 4th Baron Welles, and Maud de Ros, SETH
6. Anne Butler = John Wogan
7. Catherine Wogan = Owain Dwnn, son of Maredudd ap Henry Dwnn and Mallt ferch Gruffudd, below
8. Harry Dwnn = Margaret Wogan, a cousin
9. Janet or Sioned Dwnn = Trahaearn ap Morgan
10. Catrin ferch Trahaearn ap Morgan = Henry Barrett, son of William Barrett (and Agnes Philip ap Maredudd), son of William Barrett and Elen, daughter of Owain ap Gruffudd (and Alison Malefaunt), son of Gruffudd ap Nicholas and Mabli, daughter of Maredudd ap Henry Dwnn and Mallt, daughter of Gruffudd ap Cadwgon and Isabel, daughter of Rhys Llwyd and Goleuddydd ferch Dafydd, SETH
11. Margaret Barrett = William Dawkin
12. Jenkin Dawkin = Elizabeth Jenkin
13. Alice Dawkin = Henry Fleming
14. **Margaret Fleming** of Mass. = Griffith **Bowen** of Mass., ARD, SETH.
15. Henry Bowen = Elizabeth Johnson
16. John Bowen = Hannah Brewer
17. Abigail Bowen = Caleb Kendrick
18. Benjamin Kendrick = Sarah Harris
19. Anna Kendrick = Benjamin Pierce, Jr.
20. Franklin Pierce (1804-1869), 14th U.S. President = Jane Means Appleton

The Royal Descents of 900 Immigrants

Sources: *NGSQ* 67 (1979): 163-66 (General Herman Nickerson, Jr.), AT of Griffith Bowen and Margaret Fleming compiled by the late William Addams Reitwiesner, based partly on *M&G*, pp. 386 (Fleming, at generation 11), 483 (Dawkins, at generation 10), 476 (Barrett, at generation 9) and *Bartrum 1*, pp. 209, 210, 248, 107, 108, 618, 616 (Dwnn), 330, *Bartrum 2*, pp. 450 (Dawkin), 51 (Barrett), 396 (Trahaearn ap Morgan), 86 (Wogan). This improved line was developed and brought to my attention by Douglas Richardson of Salt Lake City after publication of *RA*, which on 2: 49 does not include Anne, wife of John Wogan, among the children of James Butler, 3rd Earl of Ormonde, and Anne de Welles.

The Royal Descents of 900 Immigrants

1. Edward I, King of England, d. 1307 = Eleanor of Castile
2. Joan Plantagenet = Gilbert de Clare, 3rd Earl of Gloucester, 7th Earl of Hertford
3. Eleanor de Clare = Hugh le Despencer, 1st Baron Despencer
4. Isabel le Despencer = Richard FitzAlan, 9th Earl of Arundel
5. Sir Edmund FitzAlan = Sybil Montagu
6. Philippa FitzAlan = Sir Richard Sergeaux
7. Alice Sergeaux = Richard de Vere, 11th Earl of Oxford
8. John de Vere, 12th Earl of Oxford = Elizabeth Howard, daughter of Sir John Howard
9. Joan de Vere = Sir William Norris/Norreys
10. Margaret Norris/Norreys = Gilbert Bullock
11. Thomas Bullock = Alice Kingsmill, sister of the Sir John Kingsmill who married Constance Goring, SETH
12. Richard Bullock = Alice Berrington
13. William Bullock = Mary Bacon. Their son, Edward Bullock, also immigrated to Mass. and married Mrs. —— Johnson, but apparently d.s.p.
14. **Elizabeth Bullock** of Mass. = Augustine **Clement(s)**.
15. Elizabeth Clement(s) = William Sumner, Jr.
16. William Sumner (III) = Hannah Henchman
17. Sarah Sumner = Nathaniel Stowe
18. Eliakim Stowe = Lydia Miller
19. Thankful Stowe = Lebbeus Ball
20. Elizabeth Ball = Aaron Jerome
21. Isaac Jerome = Aurora Murray
22. Leonard Walter Jerome, Wall Street financier = Clarissa Hall
23. Jennie Jerome, social leader = (1) Lord Randolph (Henry Spencer-) Churchill, British Chancellor of the Exchequer;

The Royal Descents of 900 Immigrants

(2) George Frederick Myddleton Cornwallis-West [who m. (2) Beatrice Stella Tanner, the actress Mrs. Patrick Campbell]; (3) Montague Phippen Porch. Her younger son, John Strange Spencer-Churchill, married Lady Gwendoline Theresa Mary Bertie and was the father of Anne Clarissa Spencer-Churchill, second wife of (Robert) Anthony Eden, 1st Earl of Avon (1897-1977), British Foreign Secretary, 1935-38, 1942-45, 1951-55, and Prime Minister, 1955-57.

24. Sir Winston (Leonard Spencer-) Churchill (1874-1965), British Prime Minister, 1940-45, 1951-55, Chancellor of the Exchequer, historian and recipient of the Nobel Prize for Literature in 1953 = Clementine Ogilvy Hozier. See *NEHGS NEXUS* 13 (1996): 166-72, 209, 211, 14 (1997): 67, Raeola Ford Cooke, "Sumner-Henchman Genealogy" (bound mss. at NEHGS, 1988), pp. 1-2, 16-17, and W.S. Appleton, *Record of the Descendants of William Sumner of Dorchester, Mass., 1636* (1879), p. 2.

16. Hannah Sumner (sister of William III) = John Goffe
17. William Goffe = Abigail Richardson
18. Martha Goffe = Ebenezer Howard
19. Samuel Howard = Anna Lillie
20. Harriet Howard = Samuel Prescott Phillips Fay
21. Samuel Howard Fay = Susan Shellman
22. Harriet Eleanor Fay = James Smith Bush
23. Samuel Prescott Bush = Flora Sheldon
24. Prescott Sheldon Bush, U.S. Senator = Dorothy Walker
25. George Herbert Walker Bush (b. 1924), 41st U.S. President = Barbara Pierce, SETH
26. George Walker Bush (b. 1946), 43rd U.S. President = Laura Lane Welch, SETH

Sources: *GM* 1, pp. 476-77 (Edward Bullock), 2, pp. 101-6, esp. 105 (Augustine Clement); W. Harry Rylands, ed., *Four Visitations of Berkshire,*

The Royal Descents of 900 Immigrants

1532, 1566, 1623, 1665-66, vol. 1 (*HSPVS*, vol. 56, 1907), pp. 19-20 (Bullock), vol. 2 (*HSPVS*, vol. 57, 1908), pp. 185-86 (Norris/Norreys) and W. Harry Rylands, ed., *Visitation of Hampshire 1530, 1575, 1622, 1634* (HSPVS, vol. 64, 1913), pp. 2-3 (Kingsmill); *NEHGR* 141 (1987): 106-7 (Bullock to Vere); *RA* 4: 269-71 (Bullock [to Thomas], Norreys), 5: 262-66 (Vere), 1: 119-22 (Sergeaux, FitzAlan), 2: 606-10 (FitzAlan), 2: 443-48 (Despencer), 2: 195-206 (Clare). This line was brought to my attention by Leslie Mahler of San Jose, California, and the name of William Bullock's wife was added by Douglas Richardson of Salt Lake City. Clinching proof (or disproof) that Mrs. Elizabeth Clement(s) was a sister of Edward Bullock of Dorchester, Mass., would be welcome. Unseen as yet is Llewellyn C.W. Bullock, *Memoirs of the Family of Bullock of Berkshire, etc.* (1905), apparently not in any American OCLC library.

The Royal Descents of 900 Immigrants

1. Edward I, King of England, d. 1307 = Eleanor of Castile
2. Joan Plantagenet = Gilbert de Clare, 3rd Earl of Gloucester, 7th Earl of Hertford
3. Elizabeth de Clare = Roger Damory, 1st Baron Damory
4. Elizabeth Damory = John Bardolf, 3rd Baron Bardolf
5. William Bardolf, 4th Baron Bardolf = Agnes Poynings
6. Cecily Bardolf = Sir Brian Stapleton
7. Brian Stapleton = Isabel (or Elizabeth) ──
8. Elizabeth Stapleton = John Richers
9. John Richers = Elizabeth Batchcroft
10. Henry Richers = Cecily Tillys
11. Frances Richers = Edmund Cushin
12. Elizabeth Cushin = William Thornton
13. Robert Thornton = Anne Smith
14. Mary Thornton = John Haynes (ca. 1594-1653/54), colonial governor of Mass. and Conn. He = (2) Mabel Harlakenden, ARD, SETH; she = (2) Samuel Eaton
15. **Elizabeth Haynes** of Mass. = Joseph **Cooke**.

Sources: *RA* 3: 273-76 (Cooke, Haynes, Thornton, Cushin), 4: 478-80 (Richers, Stapleton), 5: 35-36 (Stapleton), 1: 253-60 (Bardolf), 2: 19-22 (Damory), 2: 195-206 (Clare); *NEHGR* 148 (1994): 240-58 (Douglas Richardson), and sources cited therein, plus *AR8*, lines 257, 11, 8.

The Royal Descents of 900 Immigrants

1. Edward I, King of England, d. 1307 = Eleanor of Castile

2. Elizabeth Plantagenet = Humphrey de Bohun, 4th Earl of Hereford and Essex

3. William de Bohun, 1st Earl of Northampton = Elizabeth Badlesmere

4. Elizabeth de Bohun = Richard FitzAlan, 10th Earl of Arundel

5. Joan FitzAlan = William Beauchamp, Baron Abergavenny

6. Joan Beauchamp = James Butler, 4th Earl of Ormonde

7. Thomas Butler, 7th Earl of Ormonde = Anne Hankford

8. Margaret Butler = Sir William Boleyn (as noted SETH, parents of Thomas Boleyn, 1st Earl of Wiltshire, father by Elizabeth Howard, SETH, of Queen Anne Boleyn, mother of Queen Elizabeth I)

9. Alice Boleyn = Sir Robert Clere

10. Sir John Clere = Anne Tyrell, daughter of Sir Thomas Tyrrell (and Margaret Willoughby), son of Sir James Tyrrell and Anne Arundell, daughter of Sir John Arundell and Elizabeth Morley, daughter of Thomas Morley, 5th Baron Morley, and Isabel de la Pole, SETH. Margaret Willoughby was a daughter of Sir Christopher Willoughby, *de jure* 10th Baron Willoughby de Eresby (and Margaret Jenney), son of Sir Robert Willoughby and Cecily de Welles, daughter of Lionel de Welles, 6th Baron Welles, and Joan Waterton, SETH.

11. Sir Edward Clere = Frances Fulmerston

12. Anne Clere = William Gilbert

13. Temperance Gilbert = (1) John Alsop; (2) William Hopkins (a Temperance, wife of William Hopkins, died "overseas" before 6 Nov. 1648). Timothy and George Alsop, sons of John and Temperance and husbands of Elizabeth Heires and Dorothy Bentley respectively, also immigrated to Connecticut but apparently left no American descendants. The administrator of George Alsop's 1679 estate in Milford, Conn., was Sylvanus Baldwin, son of Richard and Elizabeth below.

14. **Elizabeth Alsop** of Conn. = (1) Richard **Baldwin**; (2) William **Fowler**.

15. Sarah Baldwin (by first husband) = Samuel Riggs

16. Ebenezer Riggs = Lois Hawkins

17. John Riggs = Hannah Johnson

18. John Riggs, Jr. = Abigail Peet

19. James Riggs = Sarah Clark

20. George Riggs = Phebe Caniff

21. Maria Riggs = Eli Doud

22. Royal Houghton Doud = Mary Cornelia Sheldon

23. John Sheldon Doud = Elivera Mathilda Carlson

24. Mamie Geneva Doud = Dwight David Eisenhower (1890-1969), 34th U.S. President

Sources: *RA* 1: 115-18 (Alsop, Gilbert, Clare), 2: 50-56 (Boleyn, Butler), 1: 317-19 (Beauchamp), 2: 610-16 (FitzAlan), 1: 420-26 (Bohun), 4: 156-60 (Tyrrell, Arundell, Morley), 5: 366-67 (Willoughby), 5: 331-36 (Welles); research of Albert H. Muth (who developed the royal descents above) and John L. Scherer, based largely on *NEHGR* 46 (1892): 366-69 (reprinted in *EO* 2:1:15-18), *TG*, new ser., 7 (1890-91): 1, and G.D. Squibb, ed., *Visitations of Derbyshire, 1662-1664, Made by William Dugdale* (*HSPVS,* new ser., vol. 8, 1989), pp. 126-27 (Alsop, and note "Cleere" Alsope among Elizabeth's siblings); L.L. Simpson, ed., *The Registers of Mickleover (1607-1812) and of Littleover (1680-1812), co. Derby* (Publications of the Parish Register Society, vol. 65, 1909), pp. 28-29, 34 (marriages of sisters Cleer and Temperance Gilbert to Robert Newton and John "Awsopp" and burial of William Gilbert, their father), plus *BLG,* 18th ed., vol. 3, p. 228 (which identifies the parents and maternal grandfather of Cleere [Gilbert] Newton); Brig. Gen. Bulmer, ed., *Visitations of Norfolk, 1563,* vol. 2 (1895), pp. 266-69 esp. (Clere), *Clutterbuck,* vol. 3, pp. 94-95 (Boleyn), and *AR8,* lines 120, 15, 6; O.F. Brown, *The Tyrells of England* (1982), pp. 125-27, 144, J.J. Howard and H.S. Hughes, *Genealogical Collections Illustrating the History of Roman Catholic Families of England, Based on the Lawson Manuscript, Part III: Arundell* (1887?), p. 224, plus *CP* (Morley, Willoughby de Eresby).

The Royal Descents of 900 Immigrants

1. Edward I, King of England, d. 1307 = Eleanor of Castile
2. Joan Plantagenet = Gilbert de Clare, 3rd Earl of Gloucester, 7th Earl of Hertford
3. Margaret de Clare = Hugh de Audley, 1st Earl of Gloucester
4. Margaret de Audley = Ralph Stafford, 1st Earl of Stafford
5. Hugh Stafford, 2nd Earl of Stafford = Philippa Beauchamp
6. Margaret Stafford = Ralph Neville, 1st Earl of Westmoreland
7. Margaret Neville = Richard Scrope, 3rd Baron Scrope of Bolton
8. Henry Scrope, 4th Baron Scrope of Bolton = Elizabeth Scrope, a cousin
9. Elizabeth Scrope = Oliver St. John, son of Sir Oliver St. John and Margaret Beauchamp, SETH
10. Sir John St. John = Jane Iwardby
11. John St. John = Elizabeth Whetehill
12. William St. John = Barbara Gore
13. Elizabeth St. John = Sir Francis Castillion
14. Barbara Castillion = Anthony Spier
15. Margaret Spier = William Sellon
16. William Sellon = Mary Hunt
17. John Sellon = Sarah Harman (parents of John and Samuel Sellon of Mass., husbands of Mrs. Elizabeth Fraiswell Reddaway and Sarah Butler, respectively, who both left issue but NDTPS).
18. William Sellon = Sarah Littlehales
19. Lydia Sellon (died in England) = Benjamin Henry Latrobe (1764-1820) of Pa. (also Va., Washington, D.C., Md. and La.), the architect and civil engineer
20. **Lydia M. Latrobe** of N.Y. = Nicholas J. **Roosevelt** (1767-1854), engineer and steamboat builder.

The Royal Descents of 900 Immigrants

Sources: Henry Bainbridge Hoff, "The Anglo-Italian Ancestry of Some Roosevelts," unpublished typescript, and sources cited therein, esp. T.F. Beard and H.B. Hoff, "The Roosevelt Family in America: A Genealogy, Part I" in *Theodore Roosevelt Association Journal,* 16: 1 (Winter, 1990), pp. 21-22; Edward C. Carter II, ed., *The Journals of Benjamin Henry Latrobe,* 3 vols. (1977-80), 1: lxviii, lxx; *Gentleman's Magazine,* July 1790, p. 673 and Aug. 1801, p. 767 (obituaries of Rev. William and Sarah [Littlehales] Sellon) and Donald McDonald, "The Family of Sellon of Clerkenwell" (1947, typescript at the Society of Genealogists in London), pp. 2-5; Charles F.H. Evans, "The Sellon Family" in *Root and Branch,* winter, 1976, pp. 103-6, published by the West Surrey Borders Family History Society, plus further Sellon research by Arthur W. Ruffell and Peter Wilson Coldham; W.H. Rylands, ed., *Visitations of Berkshire, 1532, 1566, 1623, 1665-66,* vol. 1 (*HSPVS,* vol. 56, 1907), pp. 286-87 (Spier); *TG,* new ser. 17 (1901): 76-77 (Castillion); *Friends of Lydiard Tregoz* 4 (1971): 48-50 and accompanying chart, *Berry's Hants,* pp. 148, 230-31 and G.D. Squibb, ed., *Wiltshire Visitation Pedigrees, 1623* (*HSPVS,* vol. 105-6, 1954), pp. 167-68 (St. John); *RA* 4: 523-33 (St. John, Beauchamp), 5: 167-68 (le Scrope), 4: 233-37 (Neville), 5: 9-13 (Stafford), 5: 79-81 (Audley), 2: 195-206 (Clare) and *CP* (Scrope, Westmoreland, Stafford, Gloucester).

The Royal Descents of 900 Immigrants

1. Edward I, King of England, d. 1307 = Eleanor of Castile
2. Joan Plantagenet = Gilbert de Clare, 3rd Earl of Gloucester, 7th Earl of Hertford
3. Elizabeth de Clare = Sir Theobald de Verdun
4. Isabel de Verdun = Henry Ferrers, 2nd Baron Ferrers of Groby
5. William Ferrers, 3rd Baron Ferrers of Groby = Margaret Ufford
6. Henry Ferrers, 4th Baron Ferrers of Groby = Joan Poynings
7. William Ferrers, 5th Baron Ferrers of Groby = Philippa Clifford
8. Sir Thomas Ferrers = Elizabeth Freville, daughter of Sir Baldwin Freville and Maude le Scrope, SETH
9. Sir Thomas Ferrers = Anne Hastings
10. Sir John Ferrers = Maud Stanley
11. Elizabeth Ferrers = Sir William Chetwynd
12. Thomas Chetwynd = Jane Salter
13. Mary Chetwynd = Ralph Sneyd
14. Ralph Sneyd = Felicia Archbold
15. William Sneyd = Elizabeth Audeley
16. William Sneyd = Sarah Wettenhall
17. Ralph Sneyd = Elizabeth Bowyer
18. William Sneyd = Susanna Edmonds
19. Elizabeth Sneyd = William Lloyd
20. John Robert Lloyd = Martha Shakespear, sister of the John Shakespear who married Mary Davenport, SETH
21. Louise Charlotte Lloyd = Thomas Kenyon
22. John Robert Kenyon = Mary Eliza Hawkins
23. Edward Ranulph Kenyon = Katherine Mary McCrea DeButts
24. Frances Margaret Kenyon = Geoffrey Fausitt Taylor

25. **Humphrey [John Fausitt] Taylor**, b. 1934, of N.Y., Harris Poll executive = Penelope Helen Spathis.

Sources: *WWA*, *BP*, 107th ed. (2003), pp. 2140-41 (Taylor, Kenyon), *BLG* 1952, p. 1538 (Lloyd), *BLG*, 18th ed., vol. 2 (1969), pp. 567, 569-70 (Sneyd), *BP* (Chetwynd), H.E. Chetwynd-Stapylton, *The Chetwynds of Ingestre* (1892), pp. 131-43, *SALT*, vol. 5, pt. 2 (1884), pp. 56, 79, 81 (Chetwynd, Ferrers), John Fetherston, ed., *Visitation of Warwick, 1619* (*HSPVS*, vol. 12, 1877), p. 7 (Ferrers of Tamworth Castle); *RA* 2: 212-13 (Ferrers), 3: 153-58 (Ferrers), 5: 245-48 (Verdun), 2: 195-206 (Clare), 3: 39 (Freville). See also John Shakespear, *John Shakespear of Shadwell and His Descendants, 1619-1931* (1931), pp. 21, 66, 70 and chart at end.

The Royal Descents of 900 Immigrants

1. Edward I, King of England, d. 1307 = Eleanor of Castile
2. Joan Plantagenet = Gilbert de Clare, 3rd Earl of Gloucester, 7th Earl of Hertford
3. Eleanor de Clare = Hugh le Despencer, 1st Baron Despencer
4. Isabel le Despencer = Richard FitzAlan, 9th Earl of Arundel
5. Sir Edmund FitzAlan = Sybil Montagu
6. Elizabeth FitzAlan = Sir Leonard Carew
7. Sir Thomas Carew = Elizabeth Bonville
8. Elizabeth Carew = Thomas Tremayne
9. Joan Tremayne = Sir Richard Edgcombe
10. Sir Piers Edgcombe = Joan Dernford
11. Joan Edgcomb = Sir Thomas Pomeroy
12. Thomas Pomeroy = Honor Rolle
13. Edward Pomeroy = Wilmot Periman (Peryam)
14. Samuel Pomeroy = Martha Smith
15. Martha Pomeroy = William Holmes
16. Thomas Holmes Pomeroy = Andriah Towgood
17. **George (Holmes) Pomeroy** of Pa. = Margaret ——.

Sources: William McL. and J. Nevin Pomeroy, publishers, *History and Genealogy of the Pomeroy Family and Collateral Lines, England-Ireland-America, Comprising the Ancestors and Descendants of George Pomeroy of Pennsylvania* (1958), pp. xxviii-xxix, 29-81, 147-48 (English and Irish research by Margaret Dickson Falley); *VD*, pp. 607, 609 (Pomeroy, to Edward), 730 (Tremayne), *VC*, pp. 141-42, (Edgcombe); *RA* 2: 97-98 (Carew), 1: 119-20 (FitzAlan), 2: 606-10 (FitzAlan), 2: 443-48 (le Despencer), 2: 195-206 (Clare) and *AR8*, lines 28, 8.

The Royal Descents of 900 Immigrants

1. Edward I, King of England, d. 1307 = Eleanor of Castile
2. Elizabeth Plantagenet = Humphrey de Bohun, 4th Earl of Hereford and Essex
3. Margaret de Bohun = Hugh Courtenay, 2nd Earl of Devon
4. Margaret Courtenay = John Cobham, 3rd Baron Cobham
5. Joan Cobham = Sir John de la Pole
6. Joan de la Pole, Baroness Cobham = Sir Reginald Braybrooke
7. Joan Braybrooke = Sir Thomas Brooke
8. Elizabeth Brooke = John St. Maure
9. Joan St. Maure = Walter Blewett
10. Nicholas Blewett = Joan Fitzjames
11. Edith Blewett = John Bonville
12. Humphrey Bonville = Joanna Wynslade
13. Edmund Bonville = Jane Tregion
14. Richard Bonville = ——
15. Agnes Bonville = Hugh Croker
16. Francis Croker = —— Pascoe
17. George Croker = Anstice Tripp
18. Tabitha Croker = Francis Fox
19. **Mary Fox** of Pa. = Andrew **Ellicott**.

Sources: *MG*1: 273-94; *VD*, pp. 254 (Croker), 103 (Bonville), 92 (Blewett, St. Mawr); *EP* and *CP* (Cobham, Devon), *RA* 5: 404-8 (Brooke, Braybrooke, de la Pole), 2: 326-31 (Courtenay), 1: 420-24 (Bohun), and *AR8*, line 6. A thorough monograph on the above Blewett and Bonville families would be welcome.

The Royal Descents of 900 Immigrants

1. Edward I, King of England = Eleanor of Castile
2. Elizabeth Plantagenet = Humphrey de Bohun, 4th Earl of Hereford and Essex
3. William de Bohun, 1st Earl of Northampton = Elizabeth Badlesmere
4. Elizabeth de Bohun = Richard FitzAlan, 10th Earl of Arundel
5. Joan FitzAlan = William Beauchamp, Baron Abergavenny
6. Joan Beauchamp = James Butler, 4th Earl of Ormonde
7. Thomas Butler, 7th Earl of Ormonde = Anne Hankford
8. Margaret Butler = Sir William Boleyn
9. Jane Boleyn (aunt of Anne Boleyn, second Queen of Henry VIII and great-aunt of Elizabeth I, Queen of England) = Sir Philip Calthorpe, son of Sir Philip Calthorpe (and Mary Say), son of John Calthorpe and Elizabeth Wentworth, daughter of Sir Roger Wentworth and Margery Despencer, SETH
10. Elizabeth Calthorpe = Sir Henry Parker, son of Henry Parker, 1st Baron Morley (and Alice St. John, daughter of Sir John St. John and Sybil ferch Morgan ap Jenkin, SETH), son of William Parker and Alice Lovell, daughter of William Lovell and Eleanor Morley, daughter of Robert Morley, 6th Baron Morley (and Elizabeth de Ros), son of Thomas Morley, 5th Baron Morley and Isabel de la Pole, SETH
11. Sir Philip Parker = Catherine Goodwin, daughter of Sir John Goodwin and Anne Spencer, daughter of Sir William Spencer and Susan Knightley, SETH
12. Elizabeth Parker = Sir William Cornwallis, son of Sir Charles Cornwallis (and Anne Fincham), son of Sir Thomas Cornwallis (and Anne Jernegan, daughter of Sir John Jernegan and Bridget Drury, SETH), son of Sir John Cornwallis and Mary Sulyard, SETH
13. **Thomas Cornwallis** (Cornwaleys), colonial official of Md. = (1) ——; (2) Penelope Wiseman.

The Royal Descents of 900 Immigrants

Sources: J.G. Wilson and John Fiske, eds., *Appleton's Cyclopedia of American Biography*, vol. 1 (1887), p. 743 (as Thomas Cornwalleys or Cornwallis, before the British commander alphabetically), where his father and paternal grandfather are correctly identified; G.B. Stratemeier, *Thomas Cornwallis, Commissioner and Councilor of Maryland* (vol. 2 in *Studies in American Church History*, 1922), pp. 3-4; G.E. and D.V. Russell, *The Ark and The Dove Adventurers* (2005), pp. 58-59 (and sources cited therein), A.W. Hughes Clarke and Arthur Campling, *Visitations of Norfolk, 1664* (*HSPVS*, vol. 85, 1933), p. 56 (Cornwaleys, including the immigrant, his second wife, and children), and G.W. Marshall, ed., *Visitations of Nottingham, 1569 and 1614* (*HSPVS*, vol. 4, 1871), pp. 161-62 (Cornwallis, to the immigrant as a child); Joan Corder, ed., *Visitation of Suffolk, 1561, Part 1* (*HSPVS*, new ser., vol. 2, 1981), pp. 149-53 (and *Oxford DNB* for Sir Thomas, Sir Charles and Sir William Cornwallis), *Part 2*, new ser., vol. 3 (1984), p. 335 (Jernegan); *EB*, p. 399 (Parker), W. Harry Rylands, ed., *Visitation of Buckingham, 1634* (*HSPVS*, vol. 58, 1909), p. 64 (Goodwin), and *Baker*, vol. 1, p. 109 (Spencer); *CP* (Morley) (and *RA* 4: 156-57); Walter Rye, ed., *Visitations of Norfolk, 1563, 1613* (*HSPVS*, vol. 32, 1891), p. 64 (Calthorp) and *RA* 4: 216-18 (Wentworth), 2: 50-56 (Boleyn, Butler), 1: 317-19 (Beauchamp), 2: 610-16 (FitzAlan), 1: 420-26 (Bohun), 4: 534 (St. John). This immigrant, the alternate spelling of his surname, and his Maryland offices, were brought to my attention by Christopher Carter Lee.

The Royal Descents of 900 Immigrants

1. Edward I, King of England, d. 1307 = Margaret of France
2. Thomas of Brotherton, Earl of Norfolk = Alice de Hales
3. Margaret Plantagenet, Duchess of Norfolk = John de Segrave, 4th Baron Segrave
4. Elizabeth de Segrave = John Mowbray, 4th Baron Mowbray
5. Thomas Mowbray, 1st Duke of Norfolk = Elizabeth FitzAlan
6. Isabel Mowbray = James Berkeley, 6th Baron Berkeley
7. Maurice Berkeley = Isabel Mead
8. Thomas Berkeley, 8th Baron Berkeley = Eleanor Constable
9. Joan Berkeley = Sir Nicholas Poyntz
10. Jane Poyntz = John Seymour
11. Sir Thomas Seymour = Elizabeth Webb
12. Sir John Seymour = Anne Paulet
13. Thomas Seymour = Elizabeth Lyte. Their daughter, Anne Seymour, wife of Richard Powell and Philip Lynes, also immigrated to Md. but apparently left no issue.
14. **John Seymour** (1649-1709), colonial governor of Md. = (1) Margaret Bowles, (2) Hester Newton of Md., ARD, SETH.

Sources: *BRMF* 1: 393 and Rev. Henry Thomas Ellacombe, *The History of the Parish of Bitton in the County of Gloucester* (1881), p. 89 (Seymour), plus Edward C. Papenfuse et al., eds., *A Biographical Dictionary of the Maryland Legislature, 1635-1789*, vol. 2 (1985), pp. 726 (Seymour), 558 (Lynes); John MacLean, *Historical and Genealogical Memoir of the Family of Poyntz* (1886), pp. 95-96 esp.; *Lives of the Berkeleys*, vol. 2, pp. 235-36 esp.; *RA* 4: 428 (Poyntz), 1: 337-41 (Berkeley), 4: 187-92 (Mowbray), 4: 256-66 (Segrave, Norfolk), *MCS5*, lines 66, 63 and *AR8*, line 16. The line of Gov. John Seymour was developed and brought to my attention by Henry Sutliff [III] of Pebble Beach, Calif. See also Ronny O. Bodine and Thomas W. Spalding, Jr., *The Ancestry of Dorothea Poyntz, Wife of Reverend John Owsley, Generations 1-14*, 3rd ed. (1999), *passim*.

The Royal Descents of 900 Immigrants

1. Edward I, King of England, d. 1307 = Margaret of France
2. Thomas of Brotherton, Earl of Norfolk = Alice de Hales
3. Margaret Plantagenet, Duchess of Norfolk = John de Segrave, 4th Baron Segrave
4. Elizabeth de Segrave = John Mowbray, 4th Baron Mowbray
5. Joan Mowbray = Sir Thomas Grey
6. Maud Grey = Sir Robert Ogle
7. Margaret Ogle = Sir Robert Harbottle
8. Bertram Harbottle = Joan Lumley
9. Agnes Harbottle = Sir Roger Fenwick
10. Ralph Fenwick = Margery Mitford
11. Anthony Fenwick = Isabel Selby
12. Stephen Fenwick = Elizabeth Haggerston
13. George Fenwick = Barbara Mitford
14. **Cuthbert Fenwick**, probably the Cuthbert Fenwick of Md. = (1) ——; (2) Mrs. Jane Eltonhead Moryson of Md., ARD, SETH.

Sources: *Catholic Historical Review* 5 (1919): 156-74 (Cuthbert Fenwick); John Hodgson, *A History of Northumberland*, pt. 2, vol. 2 (1832), p. 75 (Fenwick of Langshaw[e]s and Nunriding, to Cuthbert), Joseph Foster, *Visitation Pedigrees of Northumberland* (1891), pp. 50-51 (Fenwick of Langshawes and Stanton, with Cuthbert on p. 50); *NHN*, vol. 12, chart opp. p. 352 (Fenwick of Hartington), vol. 9, pp. 266-67 (Harbottle); *RA* 2: 557-58 (Fenwick, to Anthony), 3: 203-4 (Harbottle), 3: 281-82 (Ogle), 3: 106-9 (Gray/Grey), 4: 187-88 (Mowbray), 4: 256-66 (Norfolk).

The Royal Descents of 900 Immigrants

1. Edward I, King of England, d. 1307 = Margaret of France
2. Edmund of Woodstock, 1st Earl of Kent = Margaret Wake
3. Joan Plantagenet, "The Fair Maid of Kent" = Thomas Holand, 1st Earl of Kent (she later = Edward, "The Black Prince" of Wales and was the mother of Richard II, King of England)
4. Thomas Holand, 2nd Earl of Kent = Alice FitzAlan
5. Eleanor Holand = Edward Cherleton, 5th Baron Cherleton of Powis, brother of John Cherleton, 4th Baron Cherleton of Powis, who married Alice FitzAlan (niece of the above Alice), SETH
6. Joyce Cherleton = John Tiptoft (Tibetot), 1st Baron Tiptoft
7. Philippa Tiptoft = Thomas de Ros, Baron Ros
8. Eleanor de Ros = Sir Robert Manners
9. Elizabeth Manners = Sir William Fairfax
10. Sir William Fairfax = Isabel Thwaites
11. Anne Fairfax = Sir Henry Everingham
12. Eleanor Everingham = Gervase Cressy
13. Anne Cressy = William Copley
14. Lionel Copley = Frisalina Warde
15. **Lionel Copley** (d. 1693), colonial governor of Md. = Anne Boteler of Md., ARD, SETH.

Sources: *DAB* (Lionel Copley); *DVY*, vol. 2, pp. 53-54 (Copley), vol. 3, p. 118 (Cressy); *Foster's V of Yorkshire*, p. 38 (Everingham); *PCF Yorkshire* (Fairfax pedigree); *NF* 2:247 (Manners); *BP*, *EP* or *CP* (Rutland, Ros, Tiptoft, Cherleton of Powis, Kent), *AR8*, lines 155, 236, 47 and *MCS5*, lines 30, 94. See also *RA* 1: 377-78 (Fairfax), 4: 23-24 (Manners), 4: 502-4 (Ros), 3: 390-93 (Tiptoft), 2: 141-43 (Cherleton), 3: 419-36 (Holand, Kent), 2: 606-8 (FitzAlan).

The Royal Descents of 900 Immigrants

1. Edward I, King of England, d. 1307 = Eleanor of Castile
2. Elizabeth Plantagenet = Humphrey de Bohun, 4th Earl of Hereford and Essex
3. Eleanor de Bohun = James Butler, 1st Earl of Ormonde
4. James Butler, 2nd Earl of Ormonde = Elizabeth Darcy

5. James Butler, 3rd Earl of Ormonde = Anne de Welles
5. Joan Butler = Teige O'Carroll
5. Eleanor Butler = Gerald FitzGerald, 3rd Earl of Desmond

6. Sir Richard Butler = Catherine O'Reilly
6. Mulrony O'Carroll = Bibiana O'Dempsey
6. James FitzGerald 6th Earl of Desmond = Mary Burke

7. Sir Edmund Butler
7. Shile O'Carroll
7. Joan FitzGerald = Thomas FitzGerald, 7th Earl of Kildare

8. Sir James Butler = Sabina MacMorough Kavanagh
8. Gerald FitzGerald, 8th Earl of Kildare = Alison Eustace

9. Piers Butler, 8th Earl of Ormonde = 9. Margaret FitzGerald

10. Ellen Butler = Donough O'Brien, 2nd Earl of Thomond
11. Margaret O'Brien = Richard Burke, 2nd Earl of Clanricarde
12. Mary Burke = John Moore
13. Jane Moore = Sir Lucas Dillon
14. Mary Dillon = 13. John O'Carroll, son of 12. Mulrony O'Carroll (and Margaret O'Doyne), son of 11. Teige O'Carroll (and ——), son of 10. Sir William O'Carroll (and Sadhbh ní Giolla Phadraig (MacGillapatrick or Fitzpatrick), son of 9. Ferganainm O'Carroll (and ——), son of 8. Mulrony O'Carroll (and —— MacMorough Kavanagh), son of 7. John O'Carroll (and —— O'Kennedy Finn), son of 6. Mulrony O'Carroll and Bibiana O'Dempsey, see above

The Royal Descents of 900 Immigrants

14, 15. Charles O'Carroll = Clare Dunne (O'Doyne)

15, 16. **Dr. Charles Carroll** of Annapolis, Md. = (1) Dorothy Blake; (2) Anne Plater.

Sources: *Journal of the Butler Society,* vol. 3, #3 (1991): 352-62 (including an ancestor table, complete for #s 1-16 and with only two omissions through #31, of Dr. Charles Carroll's Butler descents), plus sources cited therein, including *Seven Centuries: Ancestors for Twenty Generations of John Brice de Treville Clagett and Ann Calvert Brooke Clagett* (mss. sent to various scholars during the author's lifetime), by Brice McAdoo Clagett (author also of the Carroll-Butler article). The above chart outlines only a selection of the descents of Dr. Charles Carroll from James Butler, 2nd Earl of Ormonde — the three lines through Ellen (Butler) O'Brien, Countess of Thomond, plus the patrilineal descent from Teige O'Carroll and Lady Joan Butler. The remaining Ormonde to Carroll lines are all treated in the cited article. *CP* (Clanricarde, Thomond, and Ormonde) and *BP* (Ormonde) cover the first eleven generations of this line. *RA* 2: 47-50 (Butler), 1: 420-24 (Bohun) covers only the first five generations, with a mention of Sir Richard Butler of the sixth generation.

The Royal Descents of 900 Immigrants

1. Edward I, King of England, d. 1307 = Eleanor of Castile
2. Elizabeth Plantagenet = Humphrey de Bohun, 4th Earl of Hereford and Essex
3. Eleanor de Bohun = James Butler, 1st Earl of Ormonde
4. Petronilla Butler = Gilbert Talbot, 3rd Baron Talbot
5. Richard Talbot, 4th Baron Talbot = Ankaret le Strange
6. Alice Talbot = Sir Thomas Barre
7. Elizabeth Barre = Sir Edmund Cornwall
8. Eleanor Cornwall = (1) Sir Hugh Mortimer; (2) Sir Richard Croft
9. (by 1) Elizabeth Mortimer = Thomas West, 8th Baron Delaware, who married (3) Eleanor Copley, SETH
10. Dorothy West = Sir Henry Owen, son of Sir David Owen (and Mary Bohun), illegitimate son (by ——) of Owen Tudor, founder of the Tudor dynasty and husband of Katherine of France, widow of Henry V, King of England
11. Elizabeth Owen = Nicholas Dering
12. Thomas Dering = Winifred Cotton, for whom see *AAP 2009, 2012*, pp. 660-61, 665 and *RA* 1: 106-7, 4: 1, 5: 102-4.
13. Mary Dering = Solomon Cole
14. Thomas Cole = Mary Waller
15. Margery Cole = William Fielder
16. **Anne Fielder** of Md. = (1) Thomas **Gantt**; (2) Dr. John **Wight**.

Sources: Harrison Dwight Cavanagh, *Colonial Chesapeake Families: British Origins and Descendants*, vol. 1 (2014), chapters 2-5, esp. pp. 124-36 (Fielder), 182-83, 185-89, 199 (Cole), 170-79 (Dering), vol. 2 (2014), chapter 12, esp. 412-31 (Owen-Tudor), 572-73, 599 (West), 400-1 (Mortimer), 328-29 (Cotton) and *RA* 3: 513-16, 523-27 (Dering, Owen, Tudor), 5: 348-50 (West), 2: 310-12 (Mortimer, Barre), 5: 118-22 (Barre, Talbot), 2: 47-48 (Butler), 1: 420-24 (Bohun), 1: 106 (Cotton). In addition, extensive Fielder/Feidler research of Nathan W. Murphy and others was exchanged online at soc.genealogy.medieval.

The Royal Descents of 900 Immigrants

1. Edward I, King of England, d. 1307 = Margaret of France
2. Thomas of Brotherton, Earl of Norfolk = Alice de Hales
3. Margaret Plantagenet, Duchess of Norfolk = John de Segrave, 4th Baron Segrave
4. Elizabeth de Segrave = John Mowbray, 4th Baron Mowbray
5. Eleanor Mowbray = John de Welles, 5th Baron Welles
6. Eudo de Welles = Maud de Greystock
7. Lionel de Welles, 6th Baron Welles = Joan Waterton
8. Margaret de Welles = Sir Thomas Dymoke
9. Jane Dymoke = John Fulnetby
10. Godfrey Fulnetby = Elizabeth Goodrick
11. John Fulnetby = Margaret Grantham
12. Sir Vincent Fulnetby = Jane Herenden
13. Jane Fulnetby = Sir Richard Amcotts
14. Martha Amcotts = Robert Cracroft
15. John Cracroft (of Hackthorn, Lincolnshire) = ⸺
16. (very probably) **John Cra(y)croft** of ("Hackthorn Heath"), Md. = Anne ⸺.

Sources: Research by Brice McAdoo Clagett, discussed in the Cra(y)croft bibliographical note in *Seven Centuries: Ancestors for Twenty Generations of John Brice de Treville Clagett and Ann Calvert Brooke Clagett* (mss. sent to various scholars during Brice's lifetime); *Lincolnshire Pedigrees*, pp. 279-80 (Cracroft), 16 (Amcotts), 378-79 (Fulnetby), 1204-5 (Dymoke); *AR8*, lines 202, 16 and *RA* 4: 464-65 (Fulnetby to Godfrey, Dymoke), 5: 331-38 (Welles), 4: 187-88 (Mowbray), 4: 256-66 (Segrave, Norfolk).

The Royal Descents of 900 Immigrants

1. Edward I, King of England, d. 1307 = Margaret of France
2. Thomas of Brotherton, Earl of Norfolk = Alice de Hales
3. Margaret Plantagenet, Duchess of Norfolk = John de Segrave, 4th Baron Segrave
4. Elizabeth de Segrave = John Mowbray, 4th Baron Mowbray
5. Thomas Mowbray, 1st Duke of Norfolk = Elizabeth FitzAlan
6. Margaret Mowbray = Sir Robert Howard
7. John Howard, 1st Duke of Norfolk = Katherine Moleyns
8. Thomas Howard, 2nd Duke of Norfolk = Agnes Tilney
9. William Howard, 1st Baron Howard of Effingham = Margaret Gamage. Their eldest son was Charles Howard, 1st Earl of Nottingham, commander-in-chief of the English fleet against the Spanish Armada.
10. Sir William Howard = Frances Gouldwell
11. Sir Francis Howard = Jane Monson
12. Sir Charles Howard = Frances Courthope
13. **Francis Howard, 5th Baron Howard of Effingham** (1643-1695), colonial governor of Va. = (1) Philadelphia Pelham, ARD, SETH; (2) Susan Felton, ARD, SETH.

Sources: *BP* and *CP* (Effingham or Howard of Effingham, Norfolk); *AR8*, line 16. See also *RA* 3: 333-40 (Howard, to Sir William), 4: 187-92 (Mowbray), 4: 256-66 (Segrave, Norfolk). Among younger sons of the 2nd Duke of Norfolk and Elizabeth Tilney, his first wife and a cousin of the above Agnes, Lord Edmund Howard married firstly Joyce Colepepper (Culpeper), SETH, widow of Ralph Leigh, and was the father of both Katherine Howard, the fifth wife of King Henry VIII, and Margaret Howard, SETH, who married Sir Thomas Arundell and became an ancestor of the barons (lords) Baltimore of Maryland.

The Royal Descents of 900 Immigrants

1. Edward I, King of England, d. 1307 = Eleanor of Castile
2. Joan Plantagenet = Gilbert de Clare, 3rd Earl of Gloucester, 7th Earl of Hertford
3. Elizabeth de Clare = Roger Damory, 1st Baron Damory
4. Elizabeth Damory = John Bardolf, 3rd Baron Bardolf
5. William Bardolf, 4th Baron Bardolf = Agnes Poynings
6. Cecily Bardolf = Sir Brian Stapleton
7. Sir Miles Stapleton = Catherine de la Pole
8. Elizabeth Stapleton = Sir William Calthorpe
9. Edward Calthorpe = Anne Cromer
10. Edward Calthorpe = Thomasine Gavell
11. Prudence Calthorpe = Ralph Shelton
12. Grace Shelton = John Thurton
13. Maud Thurton = Christopher Calthorpe, a cousin
14. **Christopher Calthorpe** of Va. (d. ante 1662, probably in N.C.) = Anne ——.

Sources: *RA* 2: 62 (Calthorpe, Thurton, Shelton), 5: 36-39 (Calthorpe, Stapleton), 1: 253-60 (Bardolf), 2: 19-22 (Damory), 2: 195-206 (Clare); *TVG* 40 (1996): 67-70 (John Anderson Brayton) and sources cited therein, plus *AR8*, lines 257, 11, 8.

The Royal Descents of 900 Immigrants

1. Edward I, King of England, d. 1307 = Eleanor of Castile
2. Joan Plantagenet = Gilbert de Clare, 3rd Earl of Gloucester, 7th Earl of Hertford
3. Eleanor de Clare = Hugh le Despencer, 1st Baron Despencer
4. Isabel le Despencer = Richard FitzAlan, 9th Earl of Arundel
5. Sir Edmund FitzAlan = Sybil Montagu
6. Philippa FitzAlan = Sir Richard Sergeaux
7. Elizabeth Sergeaux = Sir William Marney
8. Emma Marney = Sir Thomas Tyrrell

9. Humphrey Tyrrell = Isabel Helion	9. Sir Robert Tyrrell = Christian Hartshorn
10. Anne Tyrrell = Sir Roger Wentworth, son of Henry Wentworth and Elizabeth Howard, SETH	10. Joyce Tyrrell = Thomas Appleton
11. Margery Wentworth = John Berney	11. Roger Appleton = 9. Anne Sulyard, see below
12. John Berney = Margaret Read	10,12. Henry Appleton = Margaret Roper
	11,13. Roger Appleton = Agnes Clarke
13. Henry Berney =	12,14. Alice Appleton

13,14,15. Sir Thomas Berney = Juliana Gawdy

14,15,16. Frances Berney = Sir Edward Barkham, 1st Bt.

15,16,17. Margaret Barkham = Sir Edmund Jennings.

16,17,18. **Edmund Jennings**, acting colonial governor of Va., president of its council = Frances Corbin, daughter of Henry Corbin of Va., ARD, SETH and Mrs. Alice Eltonhead Burnham Corbin (Creek) of Va., ARD, SETH.

The Royal Descents of 900 Immigrants

1. Edward I, King of England, d. 1307 = Eleanor of Castile
2. Elizabeth Plantagenet = Humphrey de Bohun, 4th Earl of Hereford and Essex
3. Margaret de Bohun = Hugh Courtenay, 2nd Earl of Devon
4. Elizabeth Courtenay = Sir Andrew Luttrell
5. Sir Hugh Luttrell = Catherine Beaumont
6. Elizabeth Luttrell = John Stratton
7. Elizabeth Stratton = John Andrews
8. Anne Andrews = Sir John Sulyard
9. Anne Sulyard = 11. Roger Appleton, above

Sources: *RA* 3: 404-8 (Beckwith, Jennings, Barkham, Berney, Wentworth), 1: 119-26 (Appleton, Tyrrell, Markey, Sergeaux, FitzAlan), 2: 606-9 (FitzAlan), 2: 443-48 (le Despencer), 2: 195-206 (Clare), 3: 662-63 (Sulyard, Andrews, Stratton), 3: 644-45 (Luttrell), 2: 326-31 (Courtenay), 1: 420-24 (Bohun); *HSF* 4:129-30 and *VGE*, pp. 93-97, 365-66; *CB* (Barkham); Walter Rye, ed., *Visitations of Norfolk, 1563, 1589, and 1613* (*HSPVS*, vol. 32, 1891), pp. 16-17 (Berney); *Wentworth*, vol. 1, pp. 34-36; Walter C. Metcalfe, ed., *Visitations of Essex, 1552, 1558, 1570, 1612 and 1634*, vol. 1 (*HSPVS*, vol. 13, 1878), pp. 134-35 (Appleton), 300-1 (Tyrrell); Frederic Chancellor, *The Ancient Sepulchral Monuments of Essex* (1890), pp. 173-74 (Tyrrell), 20 (Marney); Sir John MacLean, *The Parochial and Family History of the Deanery of Trigg Minor in the County of Cornwall*, vol. 2 (1876), p. 507 (Marney, Sergeaux) and *MCS5*, lines 134, 34; Walter Metcalfe, ed., *Visitations of Suffolk, 1561, 1577, and 1612* (1882), p. 69 (Sulyard); *Roger Ludlow*, pp. 2322-24 (Andrews) and *AR8*, lines 12, 6.

The Royal Descents of 900 Immigrants

1. Edward I, King of England, d. 1307 = Margaret of France
2. Thomas of Brotherton, Earl of Norfolk = Alice de Hales
3. Margaret Plantagenet, Duchess of Norfolk = John de Segrave, 4th Baron Segrave
4. Elizabeth de Segrave = John Mowbray, 4th Baron Mowbray
5. Eleanor Mowbray = John de Welles, 5th Baron Welles
6. Eleanor de Welles = Sir Hugh Poynings
7. Constance Poynings = Sir John Paulet
8. William Paulet = Isabel Rodney
9. John Paulet = —— (Rawlings?)
10. William Paulet = Elizabeth Waller
11. Edward Paulet = Alice Galvington
12. Elizabeth Paulet = Sir George Paulet, a cousin
13. Edward Paulet = Dorothy Worth
14. Mary Paulet = John Buncombe
15. Edward Buncombe = Anne ——
16. Thomas Buncombe = Hester ——
17. **Edward Buncombe** (1742-1778) of N.C., planter and Revolutionary patriot = Elizabeth Dawson Taylor. Buncombe County, N.C., was named for him in 1791 and from a long-winded, rambling, irrelevant speech by Congressman (and Buncombe Co. representative, 1817-23) Felix Walker, the word (and the epithet) "bunkum" and its variant "bunk" are derived.

Sources: W.S. Powell, ed., *Dictionary of North Carolina Biography*, vol. 1 (1979), pp. 268-69 (Edward Buncombe) and *Caribbeana* 2 (1912): 275, 3 (1914): 3, 5 (1919): 314-15 (Buncombe); PRs of Goathurst, Somerset (FHL #1,526,676, items 9-10), esp. 1588 and 1661 baptisms of Edward Poulett (son of [Sir] George and Elizabeth) and Edward Buncombe (son of John and Mary) respectively, and 1706/7 burial of Mrs. Mary [Paulet Buncombe] Glassbrook, widow; F.T. Colby, ed., *Visitation of Somerset,*

The Royal Descents of 900 Immigrants

1623 (*HSPVS*, vol. 11, 1876), p. 88 ([Sir] George and Edward Poulett, before the birth of Mary) and C.G. Winn, *The Pouletts of Hinton St. George* (1976), chart opposite p. 120 (generations 7-11 esp.); *RA* 4: 325-26 (Paulet), 5: 331-32 (Welles), 4: 187-88 (Mowbray), 4: 256-66 (Norfolk). This line was developed and contributed by John Anderson Brayton of Memphis, Tenn.

The Royal Descents of 900 Immigrants

1. Edward I, King of England, d. 1307 = Eleanor of Castile
2. Elizabeth Plantagenet = Humphrey de Bohun, 4th Earl of Hereford and Essex
3. William de Bohun, 1st Earl of Northampton = Elizabeth de Badlesmere
4. Elizabeth de Bohun = Richard FitzAlan, 10th Earl of Arundel
5. Elizabeth FitzAlan = Sir Robert Goushill
6. Joan Goushill = Thomas Stanley, 1st Baron Stanley
7. Elizabeth Stanley = Sir Richard Molyneux
8. Sir Thomas Molyneux = Anne Dutton
9. Sir William Molyneux = Jane Rugge
10. Anne Molyneux = Alexander Standish
11. Alice Standish = Hugh Anderton
12. Dorothy Anderton = Edward Rigby. They are ancestors of John Venn and John Archibald Venn, editors of *Alumni Cantabrigienses*; Sir Leslie Stephen, editor of the *Dictionary of National Biography*; and the latter's daughter, the novelist (Adeline) Virginia (Stephen) Woolf. See *NEHGS NEXUS* 15 (1998): 205-6.
13. Jane Rigby = Roger Kirkby
14. Alice Kirkby = William Fleming
15. Sir Daniel Fleming, antiquary = Barbara Fletcher
16. Barbara Fleming = John Tatham
17. William Tatham = Mildred Sandford
18. Sandford Tatham = Elizabeth Marsden. Their son, Charles Tatham, also immigrated to the American colonies, and was a lieut. col. under Washington, but d.s.p.
19. **William Tatham** (1752-1819) of Va., N.C., Tenn., and Washington, D.C., civil engineer and geographer, d. unm.

The Royal Descents of 900 Immigrants

Sources: *DAB*, *Oxford DNB* and William S. Powell, ed., *Dictionary of North Carolina Biography*, vol. 6 (1996), pp. 4-5 (William Tatham); Col. W.H. Chippindall, *History of the Township of Ireby*, pp. 43-44 in *Chetham Society Publications*, new ser., vol. 95 (1935) (Tatham); Joseph Nicolson and Richard Burn, *The History and Antiquities of the Counties of Westmorland and Cumberland*, vol. 1 (1777), pp. 163-72 (Fleming), *TCWAAS*, new ser. 6 (1906), chart opp. p. 97 (Rigby, Kirkby, and Fleming) and John Venn, *Annals of a Clerical Family, Being an Account of the Family and Descendants of William Venn, Vicar of Otterton, Devon, 1600-1621* (1904), esp. p. 253 (Rigby); *PCF Lancashire* (Anderton, Standish, Molyneux, and Stanley pedigrees). Note also the *Oxford DNB* and *History of Parliament, 1660-1690*, vol. 2, pp. 331-33 (Sir Daniel Fleming) and *RA* 5: 27-28 (Stanley), 2: 610-18 (Goushill, FitzAlan), 1: 420-24 (Bohun). William Tatham was first brought to my attention, and his Tatham-Fleming-Kirkby-Rigby descent developed, by John C. Brandon of Columbia, S.C.

The Royal Descents of 900 Immigrants

1. Edward I, King of England, d. 1307 = Eleanor of Castile
2. Elizabeth Plantagenet = Humphrey de Bohun, 4th Earl of Hereford and Essex
3. William de Bohun, 1st Earl of Northampton = Elizabeth Badlesmere
4. Elizabeth de Bohun = Richard FitzAlan, 10th Earl of Arundel
5. Elizabeth FitzAlan = Sir Robert Goushill
6. Elizabeth Goushill = Sir Robert Wingfield
7. Sir John Wingfield = Elizabeth FitzLewis
8. Elizabeth Wingfield = Francis Hall
9. Alice Hall = Sir Henry Sutton
10. William Sutton = Anne Rodney
11. Sir William Sutton = Susan Cony
12. Susan Sutton = William Oglethorpe
13. Sutton Oglethorpe = Frances Mathews
14. Sir Theophilus Oglethorpe = Eleanor Wall
15. **James Edward Oglethorpe** (1696-1785), soldier, the founder of Georgia = Elizabeth Wright.
15. Eleanor Oglethorpe = Eugène-Marie de Béthisy, Marquis de Mézières
16. Catherine-Eléonore-Eugénie de Béthisy = Charles de Rohan, Prince of Rohan-Montauban
17. Louise-Julie-Constance de Rohan = Charles-Louis of Lorraine, Prince of Lambesc, Count of Brionne
18. Marie-Thérèse-Josèphe of Lorraine-Brionne = Victor Amadeus II of Savoy, Prince of Carignan
19. Charles-Emanuel of Savoy, Prince of Carignan = Marie of Saxony

20. Charles Albert, King of Sardinia = Maria Teresa of Tuscany, Archduchess of Austria

20. Elizabeth of Savoy = Rainier, Archduke of Austria, son of Leopold II, Holy Roman Emperor

21. Victor Emanuel II, = (1) King of Sardinia, 1st King of United Italy (1820-1878) = (2) Rosa Teresa Vercellana, Countess di Mirafiori and Fontanafredda (among his grandsons or great-grandsons were kings of Italy, of the Bulgarians, and of Portugal).

21. Adelaide, Archduchess of Austria

Sources: *NEHGS NEXUS* 9 (1992): 62-65, *NK* 1: 60-67, and sources cited therein; *Oxford DNB* (James Edward and Sir Theophilus Oglethorpe); *DVY*, vol. 2, pp. 299-300 (Oglethorpe); G.W. Marshall, ed., *Visitations of the County of Nottingham, 1569 and 1614* (*HSPVS*, vol. 4, 1871), p. 143 (Sutton); *Lincolnshire Pedigrees*, pp. 441-42 (Hall); J.M. Wingfield, *Some Records of the Wingfield Family* (1925), pp. 7-22 and chart at end; *MCS5*, lines 18-20 and *AR8*, lines 15, 6. For the Oglethorpe descent of the kings of Italy, see *Courcelles*, vol. 1, pp. 8-12 (Béthisy), *Anselme* (and Potier de Courcy), vol. 4, p. 63, vol. 9, part 2, pp. 204 (Rohan-Montauban), 182-83 (Lorraine-Brionne); *ES*, charts for Rohan, Lorraine-Brionne, Savoy-Carignan and Italy; and *BRFW* 1: 360, 364-68 (Italy), 59 (Bulgaria), 449 (Portugal). See also *RA* 3: 192-93 (Hall), 3: 198-200 (Wingfield), 5: 381-82 (Wingfield), 2: 610-18 (Goushill, FitzAlan), 1: 420-26 (Bohun).

As noted in the 1992 article cited above, Sir Henry Sutton at generation 9 above was a son of Sir Thomas Sutton and Catherine Bassett, sister of Mary Bassett, wife of William Beaumont, SETH, and Anne Rodney at generation 10 was a daughter of John Rodney (and Anne Mordaunt), son of Walter Rodney (and Elizabeth Compton), son of Sir John Rodney and Anne Croft, SETH.

The Royal Descents of 900 Immigrants

1. Edward I, King of England, d. 1307 = Eleanor of Castile
2. Joan Plantagenet = Gilbert de Clare, 3rd Earl of Gloucester, 7th Earl of Hertford
3. Margaret de Clare = Hugh de Audley, 1st Earl of Gloucester
4. Margaret de Audley = Ralph Stafford, 1st Earl of Stafford
5. Hugh Stafford, 2nd Earl of Stafford = Philippa Beauchamp
6. Katherine Stafford = Michael de la Pole, 2nd Earl of Suffolk
7. Elizabeth de la Pole = Sir Thomas Kerdeston
8. Margaret Kerdeston = John de Foix, 1st Earl of Kendal. Their son, Gaston II de Foix, Count of Benauges, married firstly Catherine de Foix, his cousin, niece of the half blood of Ferdinand I, first King of united Spain, and was the father of Anne de Foix, wife of Ladislaus V, King of Bohemia and Hungary and mother of Anne of Bohemia, wife of Ferdinand I (Habsburg), Holy Roman Emperor, SETH. Descendants of Anne and Ferdinand include all later Holy Roman or Austrian emperors; all kings of France after Henry IV; all kings of Spain after Philip II; Charles II, James II, Mary II, William III, and Anne of England/Great Britain, plus George III and all later (post-George III) British sovereigns; Ivan VI, Peter III, Catherine II and all later (post-Catherine) czars of Russia; all kings of Prussia and German emperors; all kings of Portugal after Peter II; all kings of the Netherlands, Belgium, Sardinia, the two Sicilies and Italy; all kings of Denmark after Christian V; Swedish sovereigns from Christina through Charles XIII and after Oscar II; all modern kings of Norway and Greece; etc.
9. Jean de Foix, Vicomte de Meille = Anne de Villeneuve
10. Marthe de Foix = Claude de Grasse, Seigneur du Bar
11. Claude de Grasse, Count du Bar = Jeanne de Brancas
12. Annibal de Grasse, Count du Bar = Claire d'Alagonia
13. Honoré de Grasse, Seigneur de Valette = Marguerite de Flotte-d'Agoult

14. Jean-Pierre-Charles de Grasse, Seigneur de Valette = Angélique de Rouxel

15. François de Grasse-Rouville, Seigneur de Valette = Véronique de Villeneuve-Trans

16. **François-Joseph-Paul de Grasse, Count de Grasse, Marquis de Tilly** (1722-1788), French admiral, commander of the French fleet in Chesapeake Bay that helped force Cornwallis's surrender at Yorktown = (1) Antoinette-Rosalie Accaron; (2) Catherine de Pien; (3) Christine de Cibon. Sylvie de Grasse, a daughter by (1), married François de Pau and left descendants in America, including a daughter, Caroline de Grasse de Pau, who married Henry Walter Livingston, Jr., nephew of Harriet Livingston, wife of steamboat inventor Robert Fulton.

Sources: Le Marquis de Grasse and M. Emile Isnard, *Histoire de la Maison de Grasse,* 2 vols. (1933), *passim,* and *D de la N* (de Grasse, de Foix); *Anselme*, vol. 3, pp. 382-83, 387-88 (Foix); *Charles II*, pp. 1-3, 5-6, 10, 18-19, 34, 58-63, 106-107, 170, 273, 397-98 (Stuart, Bourbon, de' Medici, Habsburg, Bohemia and Hungary, de Foix, Kerdeston, de la Pole, Stafford), based largely on *TG6* (1985): 160-65 (Margaret Kerdeston, by Col. Charles M. Hansen); *CP* (Suffolk, Stafford, Gloucester, Hertford) *AR8*, lines 8-10, and *RA* 2: 416-20 (Kerdeston, de la Pole), 5: 9-13 (Stafford), 5: 79-81 (Audley), 2: 195-206 (Clare). The line to de Grasse was brought to my attention by Henry Bainbridge Hoff. Another Kerdeston-Foix monograph, Donald A. Bailey, "Les Mystères de la Maison des Grailly-Foix-Candale," in *Revue de Pau et du Béarn* 33 (2006): 29-41, was brought to my attention by John Blythe Dobson of Winnipeg, Manitoba, Canada.

The Royal Descents of 900 Immigrants

1. Adolf I of Nassau-Wiesbaden, Holy Roman Emperor, d. 1298 = Imogina of Isenburg-Limburg

2. Gerlach I, Count of Nassau-Wiesbaden = Agnes of Hesse, daughter of Henry (junior), Landgrave of Hesse, and Agnes of Bavaria (sister of Louis IV, Holy Roman Emperor, d. 1337), daughter of Louis II, Duke of Bavaria and Matilda of Habsburg, daughter of Rudolf I (von Habsburg), Holy Roman Emperor, d. 1291, and Gertrude of Hohenberg

3. Elisabeth of Nassau-Wiesbaden = Louis, Herr von Hohenlohe-Uffenheim

4. Godfrey, Herr von Hohenlohe-Speckfeld = Anna of Henneberg-Schleussingen

5. Elizabeth of Hohenlohe-Speckfeld = Frederick III Schenk von Limpurg

6. Frederick IV Schenk von Limpurg = Susanna of Thierstein

7. Conrad IV Schenk von Limpurg-Gaildorf = Clara of Montfort-Tettnang

8. Albert II Schenk von Limpurg-Gaildorf = Elisabeth of Oettingen

9. Ottilia Schenk[in] von Limpurg-Gaildorf = John III, Herr zu Heideck

10. Anna zu Heideck = Georg von Polenz zu Schönberg

11. Theophil von Polenz zu Schönberg = Barbara von Eulenburg

12. Albert von Polenz zu Schönberg = Elisabeth von Zehmen

13. Christoph von Polenz zu Schönberg = Gottliebe von Bredow

14. Maria Elisabeth von Polenz zu Schönberg = Carl von der Osten-Sacken

15. Benigna von der Osten-Sacken = Christoph von Fircks

16. Maria Elisabeth von Fircks = Fromhold von der Osten-Sacken, a cousin

17. Christoph Friedrich von der Osten-Sacken = Katharina von Korff

The Royal Descents of 900 Immigrants

18. Eleanore Margarethe von der Osten-Sacken = Wilhelm Carl, Baron von Korff, a cousin

19. Nicolas, Baron von Korff = Antoinette Theodora Graun

20. Ferdinand Nicholas Victor, Baron Korff, of Russia = Nina Shishkov

21. Maria, Baroness Korff = Dimitri Nabokov, minister of justice in Russia, 1878-1885

22. Vladimir Nabokov = Elena Roukavishnikov

23. **Vladimir Nabokov** (1899-1977), the novelist (*Lolita, Pale Fire*), translator, and entomologist, sometime of N.Y. = Vera Slonin.

Sources: *WWWA*, vol. 7, *1977-1981* (1981), p. 423; Vladimir Nabokov, *Speak, Memory* [autobiography] (1966), pp. 51-61 (Nabokov, Korff, Osten-Sacken, with some genealogical errors); notes from an anonymous AT of Nicolas, Baron von Korff, #19 above (given to the novelist on his 70th birthday by his German publisher, Heinrich Maria Ledig-Rowohlt), carefully compiled but with errors and with notes added by the novelist, now in the Henry W. and Albert A. Berg Collection of English and American Literature, at the New York Public Library (the viewing of which was a courtesy to J.B. Dobson by Dr. Isaac Gerwitz, curator of the collection, with permission from Dimitri Nabokov, the novelist's son); R. von Flanβ, "Die von Zehmen (Czema) in Westpreußen (1884)," *Zeitschrift des Historischen Vereins für den Regierungsbezirk Marienwerder* 10 (1884): 33-62, which includes an abstract (naming their parents) of the marriage contract of Albert von Polenz zu Schonberg and Elisabeth von Zehmen, *ES* 2: 20: 157, 159 (Polenz), 2: 16: 116 (Heydeck), 2: 16: 137, 139 (Schenken von Limpurg), 2: 17: 2 (Hohenlohe-Uffenheim and Hohenlohe-Speckheim) and charts for Nassau-Wiesbaden, Bavaria, and Austria (Habsburg). Albert von Polenz zu Schönberg and Elisabeth von Zehmen at generation 12 are ancestors L 103-4 in *Prince Charles* but the Polenz ancestry therein contains errors. A major unseen source, not available in the U.S., is *Geschichte des Kurländischen Geschlechts von der Osten-Sacken, 1381-1991* (1992). Generations 8-23, plus other royal descents, were developed and brought to my attention by John Blythe Dobson of Winnipeg, Manitoba, Canada.

The Royal Descents of 900 Immigrants

1. Alphonso III, King of Portugal, d. 1279 = (1) Matilda of Dammartin; (2) Beatrix of Castile
2. (illegitimate by María Peres de Enxara) Afonso Dinis = María Pais Ribeira, 15th Senhora da Casa de Sousa
3. Diogo Afonso de Sousa, Senhor de Mafra e Ericeira = Violante Lopes Pacheco
4. Álvaro Dias de Sousa, Senhor de Mafra e Ericeira = María Teles de Menezes
5. Lope Dias de Sousa, Senhor de Mafra e Ericeira = Leonor Ribero
6. Isabel de Sousa = Diogo Lopes Lobo, Senhor de Alvito e Oriola
7. Branca de Sousa = Luíz Cabeza de Vaca y Guevara
8. Álvaro de Sousa y Cabeza de Vaca = Ana de Tovar y Castilla
9. Luís de Tovar, later Ludwig von Tobar, Baron von Enzesfeld, advisor to Ferdinand I, Holy Roman Emperor = Susanna Ottwein
10. Elisabeth, Baroness de Tovar = Georg Ehrenreich von Rogendorf, Baron auf Mollenburg
11. Wilhelm von Rogendorf, Baron zu Mollenburg = Agnes Streun zu Schwarzenau
12. Elisabeth, Baroness von Rogendorf = Carl, Baron Zahradecky von Zahradek und Wischenau
13. Heinrich, Baron Zahradecky von Zahradek = Eva von Schweinichen
14. Sophie Elisabeth, Baroness Zahradecky von Zahradek = Nicholas Heinrich von Haugwitz
15. Juliane Elisabeth von Haugwitz = Hans Friedrich, Baron Sandreczky von Sandraschütz
16. Hans Ferdinand, Count Sandreczky von Sandraschütz = Eleanor Charlotte von Heugel und Pollogwitz
17. Friederike Konstantine Henriette, Countess Sandreczky von Sandraschütz = Philipp Christian von Bohlen

The Royal Descents of 900 Immigrants

18. Carl Christian Ferdinand von Bohlen = Charlotte Wilhelmine Beati Jacobi

19. Wilhelmine Philippine Luise von Bohlen = Wilhelm Ernst von Finck

20. **Victor Ernst Hermann von Finck** of St. Louis, Mo. = Catharina Beck. Their daughter Clara Fink (reduced from Finck) married Henry Godfrey Gede; their daughter, Dorothy Eleanor Gede, married Franz Newell Devereux Kurie (1907-72), atomic (neutron) physicist, author of the Fermi-Kurie Plot used in the study of beta decay. Henry Frederick Gede, son of Henry Godfrey and Clara, married Faye Valeta Elder and was the father of Robert Henry Gede, who married Jacqueline Frances Strange Weske and was the father of California Republican Party official Thomas Frederick Gede, genealogist and trustee of NEHGS.

Sources: *ES* 2: 3: 3: 462-63, 467 (Sousa, together generations 1-6), Antonio Caetano de Sousa, *Historia Genealógica da Casa Real Portuguesa*, 2nd ed., vol. 12-P (1946), pp. 162, 170 and Rita Costa Gomes, *A Corte dos Reis de Portugal no Final da Idada Média* (1995), pp. 65-67, 72-73 (generations 1-9); Erhard G. Tabery, *Chronik der Geschlecht TOBAR-TOVAR* (1969), pp. S. 5-14, 16-18, 41 (generations 7-10); R.G., Graf (Count) Meraviglia, *Böhmischer Adel*, S. 161 (Rogendorf); Benjamin Schmolcke, *Sinnreiche Trost- und Trauerschriften, nebst Jacob Staalkopffs, Pastoris in St. Georgii in Wismar und des Königl. Consistorii Assessoris, Vorrede von denen Eigenschaften und Kennzeichnen eines gutes Buches*, vol. II (1725), pp. 119-124, 301-309, 317-323 (Zahradecky von Zahradek, Haugwitz); Eberhard, Graf von Haugwitz, *Die Geschichte der Familie von Haugwitz*, vol. 1 (1910), pp. 109-10, Stammtafel 9; *Gothaisches Genealogisches Taschenbuch der Gräfliche Häuser, 1855*, pp. 845-46 (Sandrezky von Sandraschütz); *Gothaisches Adelig. Taschenbuch der Uradel, 1905*, p. 102 (Bohlen); Heinrich Karl Wilhelm Berghaus, *Landbuch des Herzogthums Pommern und des Fürstenthums Rügen*, vol. 2, p. 1113 (Finck) and Finck/Fink and Gede family papers; obituary of Franz N.D. Kurie, *Physics Today* 25 (9): 76-77 and Kurie's Wikipedia entry. This line was meticulously developed by Thomas Frederick Gede of Davis, Calif.

The Royal Descents of 900 Immigrants

1. Przemysl Ottokar II, King of Bohemia, d. 1278 = (1) Margaret of Austria; (2) Kunigunde of Halicz

2. (illegitimate by ——) Nicholas I, Duke of Troppau = Adelaide ——

3. Nicholas II, Duke of Troppau = Anna of Silesia-Ratibor

4. Euphemia of Troppau = Ziemowit III, Duke of Mazovia, son of Trojden, Duke of Mazovia, and Maria of Galicia, daughter of Youri I, called King of Galicia (as were his father and paternal grandfather), d. 1308, and Euphemia of Mazovia. Youri I was the son of Leo (Lew), King of Galicia, d. 1308, and Constance of Hungary, daughter of Bela IV, King of Hungary, d. 1270, and Maria Lascaris of Byzantium.

5. John I, Duke of Mazovia = Anna of Lithuania

6. Boleslaw III, Duke of Mazovia = Anne of Holsganski

7. Boleslaw IV, Duke of Mazovia = Barbara ——

8. Conrad III, Duke of Mazovia = Anna, Princess Radziwill

9. Anna of Mazovia = Stanislaus Odrowaz

10. Sophia Odrowazowna = Jan Kostka

11. Anna Kostczanka = Alexander, Prince Ostrogski, son of Constantine Basil, Prince Ostrogski (and Sophia, Countess Tarnowska), son of Constantine, Prince Ostrogski, and Alexandra, Princess Sluka, daughter of Siemion, Prince Olelkowicz-Slucky (and Anastasia, Princess Mscislawska), son of Michael, Prince Olelkowicz-Slucky (and Anna ——), son of Alexander Olelko, Prince of Kiev, and Anastasia of Moscow, daughter of Basil II, Grand Prince of Moscow (and Sophie of Lithuania), SETH, son of Dimitri IV, Grand Prince of Moscow, and Eudoxia of Suzdal, both SETH

12. Sophia, Princess Ostrogska = Stanislaus, Prince Lubomirski

13. George (Jerzy) Sebastian, Prince Lubomirski = Konstance z Bobrku Ligezianka

14. Alexander Michael, Prince Lubomirski = Katherine Anne, Princess Sapieha

The Royal Descents of 900 Immigrants

15. George Alexander, Prince Lubomirski = (1) Joanna von Starzhausen; (2) Aniela Teresa Michowska

16. (maternity uncertain) Stanislaus, Prince Lubomirski = Louisa Honorata Pociejowna

17. Josef, Prince Lubomirski = Louisa Sosnowska

18. Frederick, Prince Lubomirski = Françoise, Countess Zaluska

19. Casimir, Prince Lubomirski = Zenaïde Holynska

20. Stanislaus Michael Heinrich, Prince Lubomirski = Wanda Marie Helena, Princess Lubomirska, a cousin

21. Adam Johann Kasimir Stanislaus, Prince Lubomirski = Marie Jelowicka

22. Martin Stanislaus, Prince Lubomirski = Jeanne-Marie de Villiers-Terrage

23. Ladislaus Jean Adam, Prince Lubomirski = Eileen Pamela Beardsell

24. **Alexi(s Jean), Prince Lubomirski**, b. 1975, of N.Y., fashion and celebrity photographer = Giada Torri.

Sources: *Almanach de Gotha*, vol. 2 (2013), pp. 542-43, which treats the photographer and his father (plus research by A.G. Hoskins below; various press items on Prince Alexi[s] mention his wife); *GH des A, Fürstliche Häuser*, vol. 14 (1991), pp. 514-15 (to the photographer's father) and among older editions of the *Almanach de Gotha*, those of 1855, pp. 182-83, and 1873, p. 165 (Lubomirski) esp.; Wlodzimierz Dworzaczek, *Genealogia* (1959), charts for Lubomirski, Ostrogski, Kostkowie, Odrowazowie, and Olelkowicz (vol. 2, #s 143, 165, 127, 109 and 161); *ES*, charts for Mazovia (Masowien), Moscow, Troppau, Bohemia, Galicia (Halicz) (2: 2: 136), and Hungary. This line was brought to my attention by Anthony Glenn Hoskins of Santa Rosa, California.

The Royal Descents of 900 Immigrants

1. Henry III, King of England, d. 1272 = Eleanor of Provence
2. Edmund Plantagenet, 1st Earl of Lancaster = Blanche of Artois
3. Henry Plantagenet, 3rd Earl of Lancaster = Maud Chaworth
4. Joan Plantagenet = John Mowbray, 3rd Baron Mowbray
5. Eleanor Mowbray = Roger La Warre, 3rd Baron La Warre
6. Joan La Warre = Sir Thomas West
7. Reynold West, 6th Baron La Warre = Margaret Thorley
8. Mary West = Sir Roger Lewknor, who had = (1) Eleanor Camoys, SETH
9. Roger Lewknor = Anne ——
10. Edmund Lewknor = Jane Tirrell
11. Elizabeth Lewknor = Thomas Stoughton
12. Sir Lawrence Stoughton = Rose Ive
13. Anthony Stoughton = Agnes Pierce
14. **Rose Stoughton** of N.H. = Richard **Otis**.
15. **Rose**, later **Françoise Otis** of Quebec = Jean **Poitevin**.

15. Richard Otis (brother of Rose) = Susanna Hussey
16. **John**, later **Jean Baptiste Otis/Hotesse** of Quebec = (1) Cecile Poulin; (2) Marie-Françoise Gagné.

15. Stephen Otis (brother of Rose and Richard) = Mary Pitman
16. **Stephen Otis, Jr.**, later **Joseph-Marie Otis/Hotesse** of Quebec = Louise Arel (Wabert, Ouabard)/Louise Hubbard, sister of Marie-Élisabeth.
16. **Nathaniel Otis**, later **Paul Hotesse** of Quebec = Marie-Élisabeth (Wabert, Ouabard)/Elizabeth Hubbard, sister of Louise; (2) Marie-Madeleine Toupin; (3) Mrs. Marie-Anne Perthius Caron.

The Royal Descents of 900 Immigrants

Sources: *RA* 5: 49-51 (Stoughton, Lewknor), 3: 572-74 (Lewknor), 5: 344-47 (West), 3: 461-62 (La Warr), 4: 183-87 (Mowbray), 4: 256-66 (Segrave, Norfolk), and sources cited therein, esp. *NEHGR* 4 (1850): 161-62 and *GDMNH*: 520-21 (Otis, which contains the best treatment also of the immigrant captives to French Canada); *EO2*: 3: 369, *Manning and Bray*, vol. 1, chart opposite p. 171 and *Parliament, 1558-1603*, vol. 3, p. 454 (Stoughton, esp. Sir Lawrence and Thomas); *Journal of the British Archaeological Association* 30 (1874) 59-61 and W. Bruce Bannerman, ed., *Visitations of Sussex, 1530 and 1633-34* (*HSPVS*, vol. 53, 1905), pp. 26-27 (with some mistakes) (Lewknor) and *CP* (West, barons, later earls, de La Warr/Delaware), plus the 1544/5 will of Edmund Lewknor of Tangmere, Sussex (d. 1545/6, on LDS film #0918267), which mentions his daughter Elizabeth, the 1509 will of Roger Lewknor, and the 1478 will of Sir Roger Lewknor. This line was developed and brought to my attention by Martin Edward Hollick of Boston, who found the will of Edmund Lewknor and examined Lewknor and Stoughton entries in the Tangmere parish register. Douglas Richardson also thanks James L. and Loretta-Marie Dimond.

For the Otis/Hotesse captive immigrants to Quebec, in addition to *GDMNH* above, René Jetté, *Dictionnaire Généalogique des Familles du Québec des origines à 1730* (1983), pp. 571, 850, contains errors but treats the French-Canadian children of the captive immigrants and William A. Otis, *A Genealogical and Historical Memoir of the Otis Family in America* (1924), p. 47-56, 59-66, 77-80 (etc., for progeny) also contains errors, but treats the captives more extensively and covers many descendants.

The Royal Descents of 900 Immigrants

1. Henry III, King of England, d. 1272 = Eleanor of Provence
2. Edmund Plantagenet, 1st Earl of Lancaster = Blanche of Artois
3. Henry Plantagenet, 3rd Earl of Lancaster = Maud Chaworth
4. Eleanor Plantagenet = John Beaumont, 2nd Baron Beaumont
5. Henry Beaumont, 3rd Baron Beaumont = Margaret de Vere
6. John Beaumont, 4th Baron Beaumont = Katherine Everingham
7. Elizabeth Beaumont = William Botreaux, 3rd Baron Botreaux
8. Margaret Botreaux = Robert Hungerford, 2nd Baron Hungerford
9. Eleanor Hungerford = John White
10. Robert White = Margaret Gainsford
11. Margaret White = John Kirton
12. Stephen Kirton = Margaret Offley
13. Thomas Kirton = Mary Sadler
14. Mary Kirton = Robert Raynsford
15. **Edward Raynsford** of Mass. = (1) ——; (2) Elizabeth ——.

11. Anne White (sister of Margaret) = Nicholas Tichborne
12. Nicholas Tichborne = Elizabeth Rythe
13. Jane Tichborne = Francis Yate
14. Thomas Yate = Dorothy Stephens
15. John Yate = Mary Tattershall
16. **George Yate** of Md. = Mrs. Mary Wells Stockett.

13. Sir Benjamin Tichborne, 1st Bt. (brother of Jane) = Amphillis Weston
14. Sir Richard Tichborne, 2nd Bt. = Ellen White, daughter of Robert White (and Mary Forster), son of Sir John White and Sybil White, daughter of Robert White (and Elizabeth Englefield), son of Robert White and Margaret Gainsford above

625

15. Amphillis Tichborne = Laurence Hyde, a first cousin of statesman and historian Edward Hyde, 1st Earl of Clarendon, who married Frances Aylesbury, SETH

16. Amphillis Hyde = Thomas Chafin

17. Amphillis Chafin = Thomas Chiffinch, son of Thomas Chiffinch, Keeper of the King's Closet and Pictures, and Dorothy Tannet

18. Elizabeth Chiffinch = George St. Lo

19. Elizabeth St. Lo = William Man

20. George St. Lo Man = Elizabeth Wiseman

21. Jane Sophia Man = Elias Walker Durnford

22. Caroline Birch Durnford = John William Dunscomb

23. **Caroline Durnford Dunscomb** of N.Y. = George **Mosle** of N.Y., ARD, SETH. Their daughter, Marie Caroline Mosle, married Keyes Winter, President Justice of the New York Municipal Court, and was the mother of (1) Henry Mosle (H.M.) West Winter (1915-2000, who married Elizabeth Tatham Dick), Pepsi-Cola executive, economic consultant, and author of *The Descendants of Charlemagne (800-1400)*, 10 vols. (1987-91), covering sixteen generations; and (2) Susan Winter, who married Murray Salisbury Stedman, Jr. (1917-2006), political scientist and educator.

Sources: *RA* 4: 463 (Raynsford), 3: 445-48 (Kirton, White), 3: 360-62 (Hungerford), 4: 97-98 (Botreaux), 1: 309-14 (Beaumont), 3: 476-86 (Lancaster), 5: 440-42 (Yate, Tichborne); *NEHGR* 139 (1985): 236-38, 296-301, 154 (2000): 219-26 (Raynsford), Sir G.J. Armytage, Bt., *Middlesex Pedigrees as Collected by Richard Mundy* (*HSPVS*, vol. 65, 1914), pp. 106-7 (Kirton), W.H. Rylands, ed., *Visitations of Hampshire, 1520, 1575, and 1622-34* (*HSPVS*, vol. 64, 1913), pp. 81-82, 12-13 (White), 125-26 (plus *BP*, Tichborne); *CP* (Hungerford, Botreaux, Beaumont, Lancaster) and *AR8*, lines 51A, 17; *NGSQ* 64 (1976): 176-80, esp. note 26, p. 180 (Yate); H.M. West Winter, "Magill and Dunscomb of Middletown, Conn., Chicago and New York" (1980, typescript at NEHGS), pp. 38-44, "Durnford Family Records" (1981, also a typescript at NEHGS), pp. 29-34, "Genealogy of the Family of St. Lo, of Somerset, Wiltshire and Dorset (1159-1873)" (1983, a third typescript at NEHGS), pp. 143-53, and "The Family of Thomas and William Chiffinch, Keepers of the King's Closet and Pictures for Charles II and James II" (1980, a fourth typescript at NEHGS), pp. 18-31, G.D. Squibb, *Wiltshire Visitation Pedigrees, 1923* (*HSPVS*, vols. 105-6, 1954), pp. 98-100 (Hyde).

The Royal Descents of 900 Immigrants

1. Henry III, King of England, d. 1272 = Eleanor of Provence
2. Edmund Plantagenet, 1st Earl of Lancaster = Blanche of Artois
3. Henry Plantagenet, 3rd Earl of Lancaster = Maud Chaworth
4. Eleanor Plantagenet = John Beaumont, 2nd Baron Beaumont
5. Henry Beaumont, 3rd Baron Beaumont = Margaret de Vere
6. John Beaumont, 4th Baron Beaumont = Katherine Everingham
7. Henry Beaumont, 5th Baron Beaumont = Elizabeth Willoughby
8. Sir Henry Beaumont = Joan Heronville
9. Sir Henry Beaumont = Eleanor Sutton, SETH
10. Sir John Beaumont = Elizabeth Mitton
11. Eleanor Beaumont = Humphrey Babington
12. Thomas Babington = Eleanor Humphrey
13. Humphrey Babington = Margaret Cave
14. Adrian Babington = Margaret Cave, a cousin
15. Catherine Babington = Edward Storer
16. **Arthur Storer** (1645-c.1687) of Md., merchant and astronomer, correspondent of Sir Isaac Newton, d. unm.
16. **Anne Storer** of Md. = (1) James **Truman**; (2) Robert **Skinner.**

14. Thomas Babington (brother of Adrian) = Catherine Kendall. Their son, another Thomas Babington, married Catherine Vermuyden and left a daughter, Elizabeth Babington, who married Sir Andrew Cooke (a Maryland immigrant of 1661) and left three sons with Md. connections – immigrants Thomas (= Anne Brooke) and Edward (= ──), and Andrew Cooke (= Anne Bowyer), this last the father of Ebenezer and Anne Cooke, both also sometime of Md. These Cooke immigrants left no NDTPS.

15. Elizabeth Babington = William Danvers
16. Henry Danvers = Anne Coke

17. William Danvers = Ellen Lacy

18. Richard Danvers = Elizabeth Cave

19. John Danvers = Mary Moore

20. John Danvers = Anne Manser

21. Richard Danvers = Mary Carline

22. **Thomas Danvers** of Pa. = Elizabeth Truxton. Their daughter, Mary Emma Danvers, married Jacob Williams Simpson and left a son, Captain Isaac Simpson, husband of Lillie Boyce Chambers and father, in turn, of NEHGS trustee (Sarah) Jayne Simpson, wife of Park William Huntington, Jr. (1923-1997), pathologist.

Sources: *TAG* 79 (2004): 13-21 (James Duvall Trabue), *ANB* 20: 882-83 (Arthur Storer), *BRMF1,* pp. 412 (Storer), 431 (Truman), 31-33 (Babington), 132-33 (Cooke), *BLG* 1906, pp. 53-54 (Babington), *TG* 5 (1984): 139-41, 156 (Beaumont, Sutton), *RA* 1: 309-17 (Beaumont), 3: 476-86 (Lancaster) and *AR8,* line 17; Danvers research of Jayne Simpson Huntington and Maryan Egan-Baker, based in part on Sculcoates and Holy Trinity parishes, Hull, Yorkshire, Yaxley, Huntingdonshire and Shepshed, Narborough, Swithland and Rothley, Leicestershire parish registers and *Nichols*, vol. 4, p. 189. See also *Journal for the History of Astronomy* 19 (1988): 77-96 (Storer) and Rev. W.G.D. Fletcher, *Leicestershire Pedigrees and Royal Descents* (1887), pp. 135 ff. (generations 9-14).

The Royal Descents of 900 Immigrants

1. Henry III, King of England, d. 1272 = Eleanor of Provence
2. Edmund Plantagenet, 1st Earl of Lancaster = Blanche of Artois
3. Henry Plantagenet, 3rd Earl of Lancaster = Maud Chaworth
4. Eleanor Plantagenet = John Beaumont, 2nd Baron Beaumont
5. Henry Beaumont, 3rd Baron Beaumont = Margaret de Vere
6. John Beaumont, 4th Baron Beaumont = Katherine Everingham
7. Henry Beaumont, 5th Baron Beaumont = Elizabeth Willoughby
8. Sir Henry Beaumont = Joan Heronville
9. Sir Henry Beaumont = Eleanor Sutton, SETH
10. Constance Beaumont = John Mitton
11. Joyce Mitton = John Harpesfield
12. Edward Harpesfield alias Mitton = Anna Skrimshire
13. Katherine Mitton = Roger Marshall
14. **Elizabeth Marshall** of Maine = Thomas **Lewis** of Maine, ARD, SETH.
15. Judith Lewis = James Gibbins
16. Hannah Gibbins = —— Hibbert
17. Mary Hibbert = Joseph Jewett
18. Nathan Jewett = Deborah Lord
19. David Jewett = Sarah Selden
20. Elizabeth Jewett = Anselm Comstock
21. Betsey Comstock = Daniel Butler
22. George Selden Butler = Elizabeth Ely Gridley
23. Amy Gridley Butler = George Manney Ayer
24. Adele Augusta Ayer = Levi Addison Gardner
25. Dorothy Ayer Gardner = (1) Leslie Lynch King; (2) Gerald Rudolf Ford

The Royal Descents of 900 Immigrants

26. Leslie Lynch King, Jr., whose name was changed to Gerald Rudolph Ford, Jr. (1913-2006), 38th U.S. President = Mrs. Elizabeth Ann (Betty) Bloomer Warren, known as Betty Ford (1918-2011), promoter of alcohol and drug rehabilitation, founder of the Betty Ford Center in Rancho Mirage, Calif., author, SETH

Sources: *RA* 4: 88-91 (Marshall, Harpersfield, Mitton), 1: 309-17 (Beaumont), 3: 476-86 (Lancaster); *AR8*, line 17; *Davis* 2: 458-65 (Lewis), 579-81 (Marshall), 618-25 (Mitton), 1:141-68 (Beaumont); *TG* 5 (1984): 131-41, 150-51, 154-56.

The Royal Descents of 900 Immigrants

1. Henry III, King of England, d. 1272 = Eleanor of Provence
2. Edmund Plantagenet, 1st Earl of Lancaster = Blanche of Artois
3. Henry Plantagenet, 3rd Earl of Lancaster = Maud Chaworth
4. Eleanor Plantagenet = Richard FitzAlan, 9th Earl of Arundel
5. John FitzAlan, 1st Baron Arundel = Eleanor Maltravers
6. Joan FitzAlan = Sir William Echyngham
7. Joan Echyngham, said to = Sir John Baynton
8. Henry Baynton = ─────
9. Joan Baynton = Thomas Prowse
10. Mary Prowse = John Gye
11. Robert Gye = Grace Dowrish, daughter of Thomas Dowrish and Anne Farringdon, daughter of Charles Farringdon and Margery Stukeley, daughter of Sir Thomas Stukeley (and Anne Wood), son of Nicholas Stukeley and Thomasine Cockworthy, SETH.
12. **Mary Gye** of Mass. = Rev. John **Maverick**. *AAP 2009, 2012*, pp. 290-91, 387, and *NEA* 10 (2009), 1: 33 (Christopher Challender Child) outlines a very likely descent from Mrs. Maverick to President George Walker Bush, as follows: 13. Elias Maverick = Anna Harris; 14. Abigail Maverick = Matthew Clarke; 15. Mary Clarke = John Stacy; 16. Nymphas Stacy = Hannah Littlehale; 17. Philemon Stacy = Mary Rand; 18. Mary Stacy, very probably = James Pierce; 19. James Pierce, Jr. = Chloe Holbrook; 20. Jonas James Pierce = Kate Pritzel; 21. Scott Pierce = Mabel Marvin; 22. Marvin Pierce = Pauline Robinson; 23. Barbara Pierce = George Herbert Walker Bush (b. 1924), 41st U.S. President, SETH; 24. George Walker Bush (b. 1946), 43rd U.S. President; = Laura Lane Welch, SETH

Sources: *RA* 3: 183-84 (Gye, Prowse, Baynton), 1: 272-73 (Baynton), 2: 482-83 (Echyngham), 1: 149-51 (FitzAlan, Arundel), 2: 606-10 (FitzAlan), 3: 476-86 (Lancaster), 5: 82-84 (Dowrish, Farringdon, Stukeley); *NEHGR* 115 (1961): 248-53, 122 (1968): 282-83 (reprinted in *EO* 1: 3: 359-66); *Davis 1*: 109-11; *AR8*, line 261, 30-32. Further proof of the identity of Joan (said to be Echyngham) Baynton is needed; a full study of generations 7-9 would be welcome.

The Royal Descents of 900 Immigrants

1. Henry III, King of England, d. 1272 = Eleanor of Provence
2. Beatrix Plantagenet = John II, Duke of Brittany
3. Marie of Brittany = Guy III de Châtillon, Count of St. Pol
4. Isabel de Châtillon = Guillaumeturinn de Coucy, Seigneur de Coucy
5. Aubert de Coucy, Seigneur de Dronai = Jeanne de Ville-Savoir
6. Marie de Coucy = Gilles VI de Mailly, Baron de Mailly
7. Colart (Nicholas) de Mailly, Baron de Mailly = Marie de Mailly, Dame de Lorsignol, a cousin
8. Jean II de Mailly, Baron de Mailly = Catherine de Mamez
9. Antoinette de Mailly = Philippe de Noyelles, Vicomte de Langle
10. Nicole de Noyelles = Jean de Villers
11. Isabella de Villers = Jan de Carpentier
12. Roelant de Carpentier = Josina van Hecke
13. Jan de Carpentier = Sophia van Culenburg (or Culemburg)
14. **Maria de Carpentier** of Del. = Jean (Jan) Paul **Jaquet**.

Sources: Edwin Jacquett Sellers, *De Carpentier Allied Ancestry: Ancestry of Maria de Carpentier, Wife of Jean Paul Jaquet* (1928); *ES*, charts for Coucy, Châtillon-St. Pol, and Brittany.

The Royal Descents of 900 Immigrants

1. (St.) Louis IX, King of France, d. 1270 = Margaret of Provence
2. Robert of France, Count of Clermont = Beatrix of Burgundy and Bourbon
3. Louis I, Duke of Bourbon = Marie of Hainault
4. Margaret of Bourbon = Jean II, Sire de Sully
5. Louis, Sire de Sully = Isabel de Craon
6. Marie de Sully = Guy V, Sire de La Trémouille
7. George, Seigneur de La Trémouille, Count of Guînes = Catherine d'Isle-Bouchard
8. Louis I de La Trémouille, Vicomte de Thouars = Marguerite d'Amboise
9. Antoinette de La Trémouille = Charles de Husson, Count de Tonnerre
10. Madeleine de Husson = Jean d'Estampes, Seigneur de La Ferté-Nabert
11. Marguerite d'Estampes = Nectaire de Senneterre, Seigneur de Saint-Nectaire
12. Marguerite de Senneterre = François de Morlhon, Seigneur d'Asprières
13. Marguerite de Morlhon = Jean III de Lupé, Seigneur de Maravat
14. Percide de Lupé = Pierre II de Rapin, Baron de Maivers
15. Jacob de Rapin, Seigneur de Thoyras = Jeanne de Pelisson
16. Paul de Rapin, Seigneur de Thoyras, historian = Marie-Anne Testard
17. Susanne-Esther de Rapin = Jean de Coninck
18. Frédéric de Coninck = Marie de Joncourt. A daughter, Louise-Philippine de Coninck, married Jean Monod. Their son, Adolphe-Louis-Frédéric-Théodore Monod, married Hannah Honyman and was the father of William Monod, who married Marie Vallette. Julien Monod, a son of these last, married Cécile Naville and was the father of Odile Monod, wife of Paul Godard and mother

of Jean-Luc Godard, the film director, who married (1) Anna Karina (born Hanne Karin Blarke Bayer/Beyer) and (2) Anne-Françoise-Sophie, Princess Wiazemsky, SETH.

19. Marie-Henriette de Coninck = Christian Wilhelm Duntzfelt
20. Cecile Olivia Duntzfelt = Jacques Louis Garrigue
21. **Rudolph Pierre Garrigue** of N.Y. (born in Copenhagen, died in Vienna) = Charlotte Lydia Whiting. Their daughter, Charlotte Garrigue, married Tomas Jan (later Tomas Garrigue) Masaryk (1850-1937), president of Czechoslovakia, 1918-35. Their son, Jan Garrigue Masaryk (1886-1948), who married Mrs. Frances Anita Crane Leatherbee of Chicago, was Czech foreign minister, 1940-48 (of the provisional government in London during World War II).

17. Marie de Rapin (sister of Susanne-Esther) = Théophile Cazenove
18. **Théophile Cazenove** (the younger) (1740-1811), sometime of Pa., agent for the Holland Land Company, financier, land speculator, and diarist, for whom Cazenovia, N.Y., is named = Margareta Helena van Jever.

18. Marie Cazenove (sister of the younger Théophile) = Antoine Liquier
19. Pauline-Victoire Liquier = François d'Albis
20. (Adrien-Henri-François-) Hippolyte d'Albis = Clarisse Bontoux
21. (Auguste-) Pauline d'Albis = Gustave Auberjonois
22. (Victor-) René Auberjonois, painter – (Madeleine-) Augusta Grenier
23. **Fernand Auberjonois** of N.Y. (a naturalized U.S. citizen) (1910-2004), journalist, foreign correspondent and writer = Princess Laure-Louise-Napoléone-Eugénie-Caroline Murat of N.Y., SETH. Their son is actor René (Murat) Auberjonois, who married Judith Helen Mahalyi.

The Royal Descents of 900 Immigrants

Sources: *NEXUS* 5 (1988): 94-98, Ruth Crawford Mitchell, *Alice Garrigue Masaryk, 1879-1966* (1980), pp. 3-16, C.H.N. Garrigues, *Silhouetten Garrigues'scher und Einiger Anderer Profile* (1930) and Patricia Wright Strati, *Our Garrigues Ancestors: French Huguenots with Connections to Charlemagne & European Royalty* (1992), pp. 116-21, 141-42 esp., confirmed by *ES* (charts for France and Bourbon), *Anselme* (vol. 2, pp. 858-59 for Sully; vol. 4, 4th ed., pp. 135-39 for de La Trémouille, pp. 842-43 for Saint-Nectaire), *Courcelles* (vol. 4, pp. 44-46 for Lupé), *Oxford DNB* (Paul de Rapin) and both *Der Deutsche Herold* 55 (1924): 20-22 and *Deutsches Familienarchiv* 77 (1981): 43-45 (generations 1-16). Generations 1-18 of this descent are also outlined in *Généalogie Magazine* #76 (Oct. 1989), p. 37, which cites *Les de Coninck* (Mulhouse, 1978). I first noticed the line to Jean-Luc Godard in Leo van de Pas, *Plantagenet Cousins* (2007), pp. 101-8 (pages that also include the Garrigue Masaryk descent). For the line to Auberjonois (and Cazenove) see the Wikipedia articles for René, Fernand and (Victor) René Auberjonois, *De Navorscher* 53 (1903), pp. 485, 567 (generations 20-23), Hippolyte de Barrau, *Documens Historiques et Généalogiques sur les Familles et les Hommes Remarquables du Rouergue dans les Temps Anciens et Modernes* (1860), pp. 166-67 and Maurice, Vicomte de Bonald, *Documens Généalogiques sur des Familles du Rouergue* (1902), p. 371 (d'Albis), Otto Schutte, *Repertorium der Nederlandse Vertegenwoordigers, Residerende in het Buitenland 1584-1810* (1976), p. 453 (the elder Antoine Liquier), Dr. and Prof. J.-B.-G. Galiffe, *Notices Généalogiques sur les Familles Genevoises*, 1st ed., vol. 4 (1857-1866), pp. 460-62 (Cazenove), *DAB* and *ANB* (Théophile Cazenove the younger), and Raoul de Cazenove, *Généalogie de la Maison de Rapin de la Chaudane en Maurienne, en France* [et] *en Prusse, 1250-1864* (1865), pp. lv-lxxvj, esp. lxxv (generations 12-18 for all three immigrants).

Note the following additional connections:

9. Louis II de La Trémouille, Vicomte de Thouars (brother of Antoinette) = Gabrielle of Bourbon-Montpensier

10. Charles de La Trémouille, Count de Taillebourg = Louise de Coëtivy

11. François de La Trémouille, Vicomte de Thouars = Anne de Laval

The Royal Descents of 900 Immigrants

12. Louis III de La Trémouille, Duc de Thouars = Jeanne de Montmorency, daughter of Anne, Duc de Montmorency, Marshal and Constable of France, and Madeleine of Savoy

13. Claude de La Trémouille, Duc de Thouars = Charlotte of Nassau-Dillenburg, SETH (their daughter, Charlotte de La Trémouille, married James Stanley, 7th Earl of Derby).

8. Louise de La Trémouille (sister of Louis I) = Bertrand VI de la Tour, Count of Auvergne and Boulogne

9. Jean I de la Tour, Count of Auvergne and Boulogne = Jeanne of Bourbon-Vendôme

10. Madeleine de la Tour d'Auvergne = Lorenzo II de' Medici, Duke of Urbino and virtual ruler of Florence

11. Catherine de' Medici, Queen of France, wife of Henry II, King of France and mother of Kings Francis II, Charles IX, and Henry III of France (all d.s.p.) and of Elizabeth, Claudia (Claude) and Margaret of France, wives respectively of Philip II, King of Spain, Charles II, Duke of Lorraine, and Henry IV, King of France.

Thus de La Trémouille figures in the ancestry of many Continental kings, French nobles, and British peers, plus at least 15 eighteenth-, nineteenth-, or twentieth-century immigrants to the U.S. (or American colonial governors). See *ES* 2: 10: 1-2 (La Trémouille), 95 (de la Tour), 1: 2: 120 (de' Medici) and *GM* 11 (1951-54): 403-9 (AT of Lady Amelia Ann Sophia Stanley, daughter of the 7th Earl of Derby and Charlotte above, and wife of John Murray, 1st Marquess of Atholl, SETH).

The Royal Descents of 900 Immigrants

1. (St.) Louis IX, King of France, d. 1270 = Margaret of Provence
2. Robert of France, Count of Clermont = Beatrix of Burgundy and Bourbon
3. Louis I, Duke of Bourbon = Marie of Hainault
4. James I of Bourbon, Count of la Marche = Jeanne de Châtillon of St. Pol
5. John I of Bourbon, Count of la Marche and Vendôme = Catherine of Vendôme. They were patrilineal forebears of Henry IV, King of France (see *ES* 2: 3: 1: 74, 2: 2: 28-29).
6. Jean I de Bourbon, Seigneur de Carency = Jeanne de Vendômois
7. Pierre de Bourbon, Seigneur de Carency = Philippote de Plaines
8. (illegitimate by ——) Jeanne-Catherine de Bourbon = Bertrand de Sallmard, Seigneur de Ressiz and de la Fay
9. Claude I de Sallmard, Seigneur de Ressiz and de la Fay = Charlotte de Sarron
10. Claude II de Sallmard, Seigneur de Ressiz and de la Fay = Marguerite de Tenay
11. Geoffrey I de Sallmard, Seigneur de Ressiz, de la Fay, and Montfort = Madeleine de Foudras
12. Geoffrey II de Sallmard, Seigneur de Ressiz and de la Fay = Éléonore de Guillens
13. Jean de Sallmard, Seigneur de Montfort = (1) Claude de Virieux; (2) Just-Madeleine de Grammont
14. (probably by 2) Louis de Sallmard, Seigneur de Montfort = Isabeau de Vangelet
15. Philippe-Guillaume de Sallmard, Seigneur de Ressiz, Montfort and Roche-Pingolet = Françoise de Guillet
16. Raymond I de Sallmard, Seigneur de Ressiz, Montfort, and Roche-Pingolet = Marie-Jeanne-Françoise de Ponchon
17. Raymond II de Sallmard, Vicomte de Ressiz = Marie-Anne de Chabrières

18. Pauline de Sallmard = Jean-Baptiste-Joseph, Count de Sibour

19. **Jean-Antonin-Gabriel, Vicomte de Sibour**, of Washington, D.C., French consular officer = Mary Louisa Johnson. Their younger son was noted architect Jules-Gabriel-Henri de Sibour, also of Washington, D.C., who married Margaret Marie Clagett.

Sources: Alfred Johnson, *History and Genealogy of One Line of Descent From Captain Edward Johnson* (1914), pp. 111-12, 125-27 (de Sibour); *Saint-Allais*, vols. 2, pp. 155-57 (de Sallmard), 8, pp. 279-80 (de Sibour); *ES*, tables for France, Bourbon, Bourbon-Vendome, Bourbon-Carency and illegitimate children of the Bourbon house (2: 2: 12, 2: 3: 1, 72, 74, 76, 2: 3: 2: 331). This line was suggested to me by the late Brice McAdoo Clagett of Washington, D.C.

The Royal Descents of 900 Immigrants

1. Wenceslaus I, King of Bohemia, d. 1253 = Cunigunde of Germany, daughter of Philip of Swabia, King of the Romans, d. 1208 (son of Frederick I Barbarossa, Holy Roman Emperor, SETH, and Beatrix of Burgundy) and Irene of Byzantium, daughter of Isaac II Angelos, Emperor of Byzantium, d. 1204, and (almost certainly) —— Taronites

2. Beatrix of Bohemia = Otto III, Margrave of Brandenburg

3. Otto V, Margrave of Brandenburg = Jutta of Henneberg

4. Beatrix of Brandenburg = (1) Bolko I of Schlesien-Liegnitz, Duke of Schweidnitz; (2) Wratislaw, Duke of Schlesien-Beuthen and Kosul

5. (by 1) Bolko II of Schlesien-Liegnitz, Duke of Fürstenberg and Münsterberg = Bonne of Savoy-Vaud

6. Nicholas IV of Schlesien-Münsterberg, Duke of Münsterberg = Agnes of Leuchtenberg

7. Bolko III of Schlesien-Münsterberg = 6. Euphemia of Kosul, daughter of 5. Boleslaw, Duke of Kosul (and Margaret von Sternberg), son of Wratislaw, Duke of Schlesien-Beuthen and Kosul and 4. Beatrix of Brandenburg above

7, 8. Euphemia of Schlesien-Münsterberg = Frederick III, Count of Oettingen-Wallerstein

8, 9. William I, Count of Oettingen-Flochberg = Beatrice della Scala of Verona

9, 10. Anna of Oettingen = John I Truchsess von Waldburg

10, 11. Frederick I Truchsess von Waldburg = Anna von Falkenberg

11, 12. Euphrosine Truchsess von Waldburg = Albert Frederick von Schlieben

12, 13. Hedwig von Schlieben = Sigmund auf Egloffstein

13, 14. Hieronymus von and zu Egloffstein = Anna Maria Schertel von Burtenbach

14, 15. Albrecht Christoph von and zu Egloffstein = Maria Dorothea von Wildenstein

The Royal Descents of 900 Immigrants

15, 16. Conrad Wilhelm Siegmund von and zu Egloffstein = Louise Magdalena, Baroness von Lassberg

16, 17. Ludwig Friedrich Heinrich von and zu Egloffstein = Hedwig Florentine Louisa Friederike von Reltzenstein

17, 18. Ernst Friedrich von and zu Egloffstein = Clara von Ebner

18, 19. Wilhelm Georg Friedrich Christian Heinrich von and zu Egloffstein = Amalie, Marquise de Montperny

19, 20. **Friedrich Ernst Sigismund Kamill von Egloffstein**, known as **Frederick W. von Egloffstein**, 1824-1885, explorer, mapmaker and engraver (esp. of the Gunnison or "Grand" River, now in Colorado, engravings long thought, erroneously, to be of the Grand Canyon), of various U.S. cities, lastly, New York, 1846-78 = Irmgard von Kiesenwetter, also of N.Y., SETH. A son was sometime of Davenport, Iowa, where his own two sons were born.

Sources: *WWWA, Historical Volume, 1607-1896* (1963), p. 553 and Wikipedia article for F.W. von Egloffstein; *GH des A*, vol. 30, *Freiherrliche Häuser A*, vol. 5 (1963), pp. 48, 50-51, 59-63 (von Egloffstein); *ES* 2: 5: 149, 151 (Truchsess von Waldburg), *ES* 2: 16: 99 (Oettingen) and charts for Schlesien-Liegnitz (Dukes of Schweidnitz and Münsterberg), Schleisen-Beuthen and Kosul, Brandenburg (*ES* 2: 1: 2: 183-84), Bohemia, and Hohenstaufen of Germany, plus *Foundations* 3 (2009-11): 349-90 (Taronites). Generation 8, 9 is O 523-24 in *Prince Charles*; generations 6 and 7 are under Q 2091-92.

The Royal Descents of 900 Immigrants

1. Amadeus IV, Count of Savoy (ruler of Milan), d. 1253 = (1) Margaret of Burgundy, daughter of Hugh III, Duke of Burgundy (and Beatrix of Albon), son of Eudes II, Duke of Burgundy, and Marie of Champagne, daughter of Theobald IV, Count of Champagne (and Maud of Carinthia), brother of Stephen, King of England, d. 1154, and son of Stephen II, Count of Blois, and Adela of England, SETH, daughter of William I the Conqueror, King of England, d. 1087, and Matilda of Flanders; (2) Cecilia de Baux

2. (by 1) Beatrix of Savoy = (1) Manfred III, Marquess of Saluzzo; (2) Manfred, King of Sicily, d. 1266. Constance of Sicily, the only child by (2), married Peter III, King of Aragón, d. 1285.

3. Thomas, Marquess of Saluzzo = Luisa di Ceva

4. Alasia of Saluzzo = Richard FitzAlan, 7th Earl of Arundel

5. Edmund FitzAlan, 8th Earl of Arundel = Alice de Warren

6. Richard FitzAlan, 9th Earl of Arundel = (1) Isabel (le) Despencer, SETH; (2) Eleanor Plantagenet, SETH

7. (prob.) (illegitimate by ———) Ralph de Arundel = Juliane (Grenville?)

8. Alice Arundel = Bartholomew Collingridge

9. William Collingridge = Sarah ———

10. Alice Collingridge = Geoffrey Dormer

11. Alice Dormer = Thomas Crocker (Croker)

12. John Crocker = Isabel Skinner

13. Margery Crocker (first of that name) = Rowland Baugh. A son, John Baugh, married Eleanor Copley and was the father of Thomas Baugh, who also immigrated to Virginia but seems to have left no descendants.

14. William Baugh = Mary Wakeman. Another son, John Baugh, immigrated to Virginia and belonged to the Virginia House of Burgesses in 1650, but also seems to have left no descendants.

15. **William Baugh** of Va. = (1) ———; (2) Mrs. Elizabeth ——— Sharp Parker (or Packer); (3) ———.

The Royal Descents of 900 Immigrants

13. Margery Crocker (second of that name) = Edward Hawten

14. Margaret Hawten = Henry Howell

15. **Edward Howell** of L.I., N.Y. = (1) Frances Paxton; (2) Eleanor ———.

16. (by 1) Richard Howell = Elizabeth Halsey

17. Josiah Howell = Mary Johnes

18. Phebe Howell = Nathaniel Smith

19. Mary Smith = Abraham Gardiner

20. Abraham Gardiner, Jr. = Phebe Dayton

21. David Gardiner = Juliana MacLachlan

22. Julia Gardiner = John Tyler (IV) (1790-1862), 10th U.S. President

Sources: Various seventeenth-century documents that link William Baugh and Richard Kemble in Gloucestershire, London, and Virginia, collected by Elizabeth Mitchell of Cambridge, Mass., plus Sir John MacLean and W.C. Heane, eds., *Visitation of Gloucestershire, 1623* (*HSPVS*, vol. 21, 1885), p. 11, which charts the kinship of the three Baugh immigrants, *Virginia Tidewater Genealogy* 12 (1981): 144-53 (which assembles Baugh material in Va.) and, although it contains errors, Mrs. J.B. Boddie, *Historical Southern Families*, vol. 11 (1967), pp. 229-30; W.H. Turner, ed., *Visitations of Oxfordshire 1566, 1574, 1634* (*HSPVS*, vol. 5, 1871), p. 185 (Croker, including the two sisters Margery), *RA* 3: 341-48 (Ralph de Arundel to Edward Howell), 2: 599-610 (FitzAlan), 4: 552-53 (Saluzzo, Savoy), 2: 28-29 (Burgundy), 1: 389-92 (Blois); Emma Howell Ross and David Faris, *Descendants of Edward Howell (1584-1655)*, 2nd ed. (1985), pp. 5-9, 11-12, 14-17, 38, 47-48, 75-76, 116 (Collingridge to Mrs. Gardiner) and *Executive Papers* 4 (2007): 15-19 (AT of Mrs. Tyler, to Edward Howell). See also Conte Pompeo Litta, *Famiglie Celebri Italiane*, vol. 10 (1874), Saluzzo section, Tables III-IV and *ES* for Savoy, Burgundy, Aragón and Sicily (the last under Hohenstaufen).

The Royal Descents of 900 Immigrants

1. Waldemar II, King of Denmark, d. 1241 = (1) Dagmar of Bohemia; (2) Berengaria of Portugal

2. (illegitimate by Helene Guttormsdatter) Knud Skarsholmslægten, Duke of Estonia = ―――― (of Pomerelia or Pomerania?)

3. Erik Skarsholmslægten, Duke of Sønder-Halland = Elisabeth ――――

4. Barnim Skarsholmslægten = Elisabeth ――――

5. Erik Skarsholmslægten, knight = Gjertrud Grubbe

6. Christine Skarsholmslægten = Torbern Galen, knight

7. Inger Galen = Bent Bille

8. Torbern Bille, knight = Sidsel Lunge

9. Regitze Bille = Peder Gyldenstierne

10. Knud Gyldenstierne = Sidsel Ulfstand, daughter of Jens Ulfstand, knight, (and Margrethe Trolle, also a descendant of 2.), son of Holger Ulfstand and Brigitte Rosensparre, daughter of Jens Rosensparre and Maeritslef Bille, daughter of Jakob Bille, knight, and Gyde Galen, daughter of 6. above

11. Margrethe Gyldenstierne = Folmer Rosenkrantz

12. Regitze Rosenkrantz = Gjord Galt, son of Peder Galt and Ingeborg Drefeld, daughter of Gjord Drefeld and Kirsten Banner, daughter of Erik Banner and Karen Gøye, daughter of Steen Gøye and Anne Bille, daughter of Peder Bille (and Margrethe Brahe), son of Jakob Bille and Gyde Galen above

13. Axel Galt = Mette Rantzau

11. Lisbeth Gyldenstierne = Jens Ulfstand, son of Holger Ulfstand, knight (and Helle Hak), son of Gregers Ulfstand and Else Bille, daughter of 8. above

12. Holger Ulfstand = Anne Skovgaard

13. Ingeborg Ulfstand = Admiral Jørgen Vind

644

The Royal Descents of 900 Immigrants

14. Birgette Galt =
Niels Harbou

14. Holger Vind, knight =
Margrethe Giedde

15. Christian Harbou =
Else Thermo

15. Anne Elisabeth Vind
= Didrik Grubbe

16. Niels Harbou =
Anna Elisabeth Buchner

17. Paul Mathias Harbou   =   16. Christiane Charlotte Grubbe

17,18. Maj. Gen. Andreas Harbou = Friderica Walter

18,19. Fredrik Hans Walter Harbou, chamberlain to Frederick VI, King of Denmark = Ane Marie Praetorius

19, 20. **Fritz Harbou** of N.Y. = Judith Fritcher.

19, 20. Andreas Paul Adolph von Harbou (brother of Fritz) = Matilde Hensen

20, 21. Theodor Carl Nicolaus von Harbou = Clotilde Constance d'Alinge

21, 22. Thea von Harbou, German novelist and screenwriter with her second husband (*Metropolis, M*), who remarried in Germany and joined the Nazi Party = (1) Rudolf Klein-Rogge, actor; (2) **Fritz Lang**, the German and American film director, longtime in Calif.

19, 20. Marie Elisabeth Wilhelmine "Mimi" Harbou (sister of Fritz and Andreas) = Nicolas Peter Diderik Toxwerdt

20, 21. Marie Gabrielle Toxwerdt = Emil Faye von Bülow

21, 22. Frits Toxwerdt von Bülow, Danish Minister of Justice = Fanny Frederikke Augusta Poulson

22, 23. Jonna von Bülow = Svend Borberg, playwright (who = [2] Eleanora Ibsen, granddaughter of dramatist Henrik Ibsen)

23, 24. **Claus** [Cecil Borberg, later] **von Bülow** of R.I., b. 1926, oil company consultant, associate of J. Paul Getty, accused but twice found innocent of the attempted murder of his comatose

The Royal Descents of 900 Immigrants

wife, Martha Sharp "Sunny" Crawford, former wife of Prince Alfred Eduard Friedrich Vincenz Martin Maria von Auersperg.

Sources: *NYGBR* 135 (2004): 163-68, 174-76 (Fritz Harbou); *Danmarks Adels Aarbog* (*DAA*) (1897), pp. 167-68, 174-76, 178-79 (Harbou), (1893), pp. 175-76 (Galt), (1985-87), pp. 693, 696 (Rosenkrantz), (1926), pp. 14-15, 17, 22 (Gyldenstierne), (1985-87), pp. 497-501, 503-5 (Bille), (1893), pp. 157-58 (Galen), (1916), pp. 422-24 (Skarsholmslægten), (1891), p. 121 (Drefeld), (1949), pp. 10-11 (Banner), (1896), p. 143 (Gøye), (1896), pp. 429-30, 432-35, 437-39 (Ulfstand), (1899), pp. 371-72 (Rosensparre), (1941), pp. 74-75, 77-78, 81 (Vind) and *Personalhistorisk Tidsskrift* (1964-65), pp. 154-55, 158 (Didrik Grubbe family), (1964): 104, 115, 103 (von Bülow). For Skarsholmslægten, Galen, and Bille (generations 1-8 above) see also W. Mollerup and Fr. Meidell, *Bille-Ættens Historie* (1893), pp. 109-28, esp. the chart on p. 113. For von Bülow see also Alan M. Dershowitz, *Reversal of Fortune: Inside the Von Bülow Case* (1985), *passim*, esp. p. xix; *GH des A*, vol. 133, *Fürstliche Häuser*, vol. 17 (2004), pp. 118-19. This descent was developed and contributed by R. Bruce Diebold of Waukegan, Ill. Patronymics, often used and preferred, have been omitted.

Torbern Bille, knight, and Sidsel Lunge, generation 8 above, were parents also of Steen Basse Bille, who married Margrethe Rønnow. Claus Bille, a son of the latter, married Lisbet Ulfstand, daughter of Jens Ulfstand, knight, and Margrethe Trolle, above at generation 9, and was the father of Beate Bille, wife of Otto Brahe. A son of these last was famed astronomer Tyge (Tycho) Brahe (1546-1601, who married Kirsten Barbara Jørgensdatter). See also *DAA* (1985-87), pp. 499-500, 502-4, 507-8, 541-43 (Bille) and (1888), p. 104-5 (Brahe).

The Royal Descents of 900 Immigrants

1. Alphonso IX, King of León, d. 1230 = Berengaria, Queen of Castile, d. 1246, daughter of Alphonso VIII, King of Castile, and Eleanor Plantagenet, daughter of Henry II, King of England, d. 1189, and Eleanor of Aquitaine
2. Berengaria of León and Castile = John de Brienne, King of Jerusalem and Emperor of Constantinople, d. 1237
3. Jean de Brienne = Jeanne de Châteaudun
4. Blanche de Brienne = Sir William de Fienes
5. Margaret de Fienes = Edmund Mortimer, 1st Baron Mortimer
6. Maud Mortimer = Theobald de Verdun, 2nd Baron Verdun
7. Margery de Verdun = Sir John Crophill (Crophull)
8. Thomas Crophill (Crophull) = Sybil Delabere
9. Agnes Crophill (Crophull) = Sir Walter Devereux
10. Walter Devereux = Elizabeth Bromwich
11. Elizabeth Devereux = John Milborne
12. Simon Milborne = Jane Baskerville
13. Anne Milborne = William Rudhall
14. John Rudhall = Isabella Whittington
15. John Rudhall = Mary Fettiplace
16. Frances Rudhall = Richard Woodward
17. Ezekias (Hezekiah) Woodward, nonconformist divine = Frances ——
18. **Frances Woodward** = Rev. John **Oxenbridge** (1608/9-1674) of Mass., Puritan clergyman, ARD, SETH.
18. **Sarah Woodward** of Mass. = Daniel **Henchman**, who later married Mary Poole, daughter of William and Jane (Greene) Poole of Mass., both ARD, SETH.
19. Hannah Henchman = William Sumner (III), SETH
20. Sarah Sumner = Nathaniel Stowe
21. Eliakim Stowe = Lydia Miller
22. Thankful Stowe = Lebbeus Ball
23. Elizabeth Ball = Aaron Jerome

The Royal Descents of 900 Immigrants

24. Isaac Jerome = Aurora Murray
25. Leonard Walter Jerome, Wall Street financier = Clarissa Hall
26. Jennie Jerome, social leader = (1) Lord Randolph (Henry Spencer-) Churchill, British chancellor of the exchequer; (2) George Frederick Myddleton Cornwallis-West [who m. (2) Beatrice Stella Tanner, the actress Mrs. Patrick Campbell]; (3) Montagu Phippen Porch. Her younger son, John Strange Spencer-Churchill, married Lady Gwendoline Theresa Mary Bertie and was the father of Anne Clarissa Spencer-Churchill, second wife of (Robert) Anthony Eden, 1st Earl of Avon (1897-1977), British foreign secretary, 1935-38, 1942-45, 1951-55, and Prime Minister, 1955-57.
27. Sir Winston (Leonard Spencer-) Churchill (1874-1965), British Prime Minister, 1940-45, 1951-55, chancellor of the exchequer, historian and recipient of the Nobel Prize for Literature in 1953 = Clementine Ogilvy Hozier. See *NEXUS* 13 (1996): 166-72, 204-7, 209-11, and Raeola Ford Cooke, "Sumner-Henchman Genealogy" (bound tss. at NEHGS, 1988), pp. 1-2, 16-17 esp.

14. Elizabeth Rudhall (sister of John) = William Hugford
15. John Hugford = Elizabeth Fettiplace
16. Margaret Hugford = John Hugford, a cousin
17. Margaret Hugford = William Laurence
18. Elizabeth Laurence = George Gwinnett
19. George Gwinnett = Elizabeth Randle
20. George Gwinnett = Elizabeth Coxe
21. Samuel Gwinnett = Anne Emes
22. **Button Gwinnett** (c. 1735-1777), president (governor) of Ga., merchant, planter, signer of the Declaration of Independence = Anne Bourne.

Sources: *RA* 5: 393-96 (Woodward, Rudhall), 4: 86-87 (Milborne), 5: 245-50 (Devereux, Crophill/hull, Verdun), 4: 168-70 (Mortimer), 1: 473-75 (Fien[n]es), 1: 536-40 (Brienne); *Oxford DNB* (Hezekiah or Ezekias Woodward) and *GGE*, pp. 1029-30 (1674 will of Hezekiah Woodward), Batsford, Gloucestershire parish register (2 Nov. 1589 baptism of Ezechias, son of "Richardi" Woodward) and research of Lothrop Withington (noted in a letter to me from Richard C. Hathaway, husband of Gertrude Bradbury Withington, Lothrop's great-niece), plus short Frances Woodward notes in *NEHGR* 53 (1899): 118 (reprinted in *EO* 2: 2: 826) and *Notes and Queries,* 3rd ser., vol. 6 (July-Dec. 1864), p. 348; W.H. Cooke, *Collections Towards the History and Antiquities of the County of Hereford,* vol. 3 (1882), p. 165 (Rudhall); F.W. Weaver, *Visitation of Herefordshire, 1569* (1886), pp. 90-91, *MGH*, 5th ser., vol. 3 (1918-19), pp. 198-99 and *Whitney*, appendix XI (Milborne); *BP* (Devereux, viscounts Hereford); George F. Farnham, *Leicestershire Medieval Pedigrees* (1925), p. 31 (Crophill/Crophull); *CP* (Verdun, Mortimer) and *AR8*, lines 114, 120; John Fetherston, ed., *Visitation of Warwickshire, 1619* (*HSPVS*, vol. 12, 1877), p. 337 and Sir John Maclean and W.C. Heane, eds., *Visitation of Gloucestershire, 1623* (*HSPVS*, vol. 21, 1885), p. 86 (Hugford); T.F. Fenwick and W.C. Metcalfe, eds., *Visitation of Gloucester, 1682-83* (1884), pp. 84-86 (Gwinnett), 110 (Laurence); Charles Francis Jenkins, *Button Gwinnett, Signer of the Declaration of Independence* (1926), pp. 7-16. Mrs. Sarah Woodward Henchman was brought to my attention by Leslie Mahler of San Jose, Calif. For proof of Sarah's immigration see W.L. Holman, *Ancestry of Colonel John Harrington Stevens and His Wife Frances Helen Miller,* vol. 2 (1952), p. 60.

The Royal Descents of 900 Immigrants

1. John "Lackland," King of England, d. 1216 = (2) Isabel of Angoulême
2. (illegitimate by Clemence ——, possibly Clemence le Botiller, wife of Nicholas de Verdun) Joan Plantagenet = Llywelyn Fawr ab Iorwerth, Prince of North Wales
3. David, Prince of North Wales (Dafydd ap Llywelyn Fawr) = Isabel de Braose
4. (illegitimate by ——) Llywelyn ap Dafydd, constable of Rhuddlau = ——
5. Cynwrig ap Llywelyn = Angharad ferch Thomas ap Gwion
6. Dafydd Llwyd ap Cynwrig = Annes ferch Gwyn ap Madog
7. Mawd ferch Dafydd Llwyd = Dafydd Goch ap Trahaearn Goch ap Madog
8. Ieuan Goch ap Dafydd Goch = Efa ferch Einion ap Celynin
9. Madog Goch ab Ieuan Goch = (perhaps) Ales ferch Ieuan ap Madog Gwenwys
10. Deicws Ddu ap Madog Goch = Gwen ferch Ieuan Dew ap Meurig
11. Einion ap Deicws Ddu = Morfudd ferch Mathew ap Llywarch
12. Hywel ab Einion = Mali Llwyd ferch Llywelyn ab Ieuan
13. Gruffudd ap Hywel = Gwenllian ferch Einion ab Ieuan Llwyd
14. Lewys ap Gruffudd = Ellyw ferch Edward ab Ieuan
15. Robert Lewis = Gwerful ferch Llywelyn ap Dafydd
16. Hugh Roberts = ——
17. Robert Pugh = Elizabeth Williams of Pa., ARD, SETH

16. Evan Robert Lewis = Jane, daughter of Cadwaladr ap Maredudd (and ——), son of Maredudd ab Ieuan and Elen, daughter of Cadwaladr ap Robert and Jane ferch Maredudd ab Ieuan, SETH

17. John ab Evan (son of Evan Robert Lewis and Jane ferch Cadwaladr ap Maredudd) = ——

18. **Jane John** of Pa. = Robert **Cadwalader**, ARD, SETH, of Pa. (their children and descendants took the surname Roberts)

18. Margaret John = David Evans

19. **Gwen Evans** of Pa. = Thomas **Foulke**, son of Edward Foulke of Pa., ARD, SETH, and Mrs. Ellen Hughes Foulke, ARD, SETH.

17. Owen ab Evan (brother of John ab Evan) = Gainor John

18. **Robert Owen** of Pa. = Rebecca Owen (sometimes called Rebecca Humphrey[s]) of Pa., ARD, SETH.

18. **Jane Owen** of Pa. = Hugh **Roberts** of Pa., ARD, SETH, son of Robert Pugh (see above) and Mrs. Elizabeth Williams Pugh of Pa., ARD, SETH.

18. Ellen Owen = Cadwalader Thomas

19. **John Cadwalader** of Pa. = Martha Jones.

17. Griffith ab Evan (brother of John and Owen ab Evan) = ——

18. Edward Griffith = ——

19. **Jane Edward** of Pa. = John **Jones**, son of Rees Jones and Mrs. Hannah Price Jones David Evans of Pa., ARD, SETH.

17. Evan Lloyd Evan (brother of John, Owen, and Griffith ab Evan) = ——

18. **Thomas Evans** of Pa. = (1) Anne ——; (2) Mrs. Hannah Price Jones David of Pa. (Thomas and Hannah left no NDTPS).

18. **Cadwalader Evans** of Pa. = Ellen Morris of Pa., ARD, SETH.

Immigrant members of this family who left no NDTPS include the following:

The Royal Descents of 900 Immigrants

1-5. Robert and Griffith John or Jones, brothers of Mrs. Jane John Cadwalader; Gwen Jones, their sister, wife of John —— and John Humphrey; Margaret Evans, their niece (and a sister of Mrs. Gwen Evans Foulke), who married Robert Humphrey; and William John, their half-brother (son of John ab Evan and Margaret John), who married Jane Pugh or Hughes, sister of Mrs. Ellen Hughes Foulke

6-10. Hugh Griffith (= Mary ——) and Catherine Griffith, wife of —— Morris, Alexander Edwards, and John Williams (this last SETH) (Catherine seems to have left issue by her first husband only), an uncle and aunt of Mrs. Jane Edward Jones; Griffith Edward (= Lowry Evans) and Margaret Edward, wife of David George, a brother and sister of Mrs. Jane Edward Jones; and Elizabeth Robert, wife of William Morgan and daughter (by ——) of Robert Griffith, a brother of Hugh and Mrs. Williams and an uncle of Mrs. Jones, Griffith Edward, and Mrs. George

11-14. Robert Evans and Sarah Evans, wife of Evan Pugh, a brother and sister of Thomas and Cadwalader Evans; and Robert Jones (= Gainor Lloyd) and Cadwalader Jones, brothers, sons of John —— and Ellen Evans, sister of the half-blood of Thomas and Cadwalader Evans (both wives of Evan Lloyd Evan are unknown).

Sources: *WFP* 2, "Owen, Evans and Allied Families," esp. pp. 75-100, 108 (generations 7-19, Mawd ferch Dafydd Llwyd to the progeny of Evan Robert Lewis); *WFP* 1, pedigree XXIV, p. 220 (Robert Pugh and family) and pedigree I, pp. 15-21 and chart facing (John Cadwalader); *Bartrum* 1, pp. 446-47, 867-68, *Bartrum* 2, p. 1657 (generations 1-14); *Curia Regis Roll,* vol. 17, pp. 281-82, on Clemence le Botiller. This identification is repeated on several subsequent charts. For some data in 6-10 above I am indebted to Stewart Baldwin; for the first five generations see *RA* 1: 43-58 (King John and the daughter above), 5: 298-304 (to the [therein said to be "alleged"] illegitimate son and daughter of David, Prince of North Wales).

Note on the following charts that all descendants of Kings John, Henry II and Henry I of England, William I "the Lion" of Scotland, and Richard Plantagenet, King of the Romans (John's son), who are not also descendants of later kings, are via illegitimate children.

The Royal Descents of 900 Immigrants

1. John "Lackland," King of England, d. 1216 = (2) Isabel of Angoulême
2. Richard Plantagenet, King of the Romans = (1) Isabel Marshall; (2) Sancha of Provence; (3) Beatrix de Falkenburg
3. (illegitimate by ——, possibly Joan de Vautort or Valletort) Sir Richard de Cornwall = Joan ——
4. Joan de Cornwall = Sir John Howard
5. Sir John Howard = Alice de Boys
6. Joan Howard = Sir Peter de Braose (Brewes), son of Sir Peter de Braose (and Agnes de Clifford), son of Sir William de Braose (Brewes) and Mary de Ros, daughter of Sir Robert de Ros and Isabel d'Aubigny, SETH
7. Beatrix de Braose = Sir Hugh Shirley
8. Sir Ralph Shirley = Joan Basset
9. Ralph Shirley = Margaret Staunton
10. John Shirley = Eleanor Willoughby, a daughter of Sir Hugh Willoughby and Margaret Freville, SETH
11. Robert Shirley = ——
12. Ralph Shirley = Amee Lolle
13. Eleanor Shirley = Nicholas Browne
14. Sir William Browne = Mary Savage
15. Percy Browne = Anne Rich
16. **Nathaniel Browne** of Conn. = Eleanor Watts.

11. Hugh Shirley (brother of Robert) = Anne Hevyn
12. John Shirley = Margaret Wroth, daughter of John Wroth and Joan (Newdigate?), SETH
13. Joyce Shirley = Richard Abington (or Habington)
14. Mary Abington (or Habington) = Richard Barnaby
15. Winifred Barnaby = Henry Davenport

The Royal Descents of 900 Immigrants

16. **Rev. John Davenport** (1597-1669/70) of Conn., non-conformist clergyman, author, founder of the New Haven Colony = Elizabeth ——.

9. Beatrix Shirley (sister of Ralph) = John Brome
10. Nicholas Brome = Katherine Lampeck
11. Elizabeth Brome = Thomas Hawes
12. William Hawes = Ursula Colles
13. Edmond Hawes = Jane Porter
14. **Edmond Hawes** of Mass. = ——. His only child, John Hawes, married Desire Gorham, daughter of John Gorham and Desire Howland, daughter of John and Elizabeth (Tilley) Howland of the *Mayflower*.

10. Isabel Brome (sister of Nicholas) = John Denton
11. Thomas Denton = Jane Webb
12. Isabel Denton = William ap Walter Thomas
13. Thomasine Walter = William Lukyn (Lucken)
14. Judith Lukyn = (almost certainly) Edward Ward
15. **Mary Ward** of Mass. = (1) John **Cutting**; (2) John **Miller**.
16. (by 1) Mary Cutting = Nicholas Noyes
17. John Noyes = Mary Poor
18. John Noyes, Jr. = Mary Thurlo
19. Elizabeth Noyes = William Adams
20. Sarah Adams = Daniel Ayer
21. Samuel Ayer = Polly Chase
22. John Varnum Ayer = Elida Vanderburgh Manney
23. George Manney Ayer = Amy Gridley Butler
24. Adele Augusta Ayer = Levi Addison Gardner

The Royal Descents of 900 Immigrants

25. Dorothy Ayer Gardner = (1) Leslie Lynch King; (2) Gerald Rudolf Ford

26. Leslie Lynch King, Jr. (whose name was changed to Gerald Rudolph Ford, Jr.) (1913-2006), 38th U.S. President = Mrs. Elizabeth Ann "Betty" Bloomer Warren, known as Betty Ford (1918-2011), promoter of drug and alcohol rehabilitation, founder of the Betty Ford Center in Rancho Mirage, Calif., author, SETH

15. **Rebecca Ward** of Mass. (sister of Mary) = Walter **Allen**.

16. Joseph Allen = Anne Brazier

17. Nathaniel Allen = Lydia Brewer

18. Mary Allen = Elisha Jones. Their daughter, Mary Jones, married Asa Dunbar and was the mother of Cynthia Dunbar, wife of John Thoreau and mother of Henry David Thoreau, the civil libertarian and essayist, author of *Walden*, who died unmarried.

19. Ephraim Jones, Loyalist soldier, Upper Canadian judge, politician, and businessman = Charlotte Coursolles

20. Sophia Jones = John Stuart, Jr.

21. Mary Stuart = Sir Allan Napier MacNab, 1st Bt., premier of the Canadas, 1854-56, legislative leader, railroad promoter

22. Sophia Mary MacNab = William Coutts Keppel, 7th Earl of Albemarle, British M.P., Superintendent of Indian Affairs for Canada, British Undersecretary for War

23. Hon. George Keppel = Alice Frederica Edmonstone, known as Mrs. Alice Keppel, social leader, confidante of King Edward VII

24. Sonia Rosemary Keppel = Roland Calvert Cubitt, 3rd Baron Ashcombe

25. Hon. Rosalind Maud Cubitt = Bruce Middleton Hope Shand

26. Camilla Rosemary Shand, b. 1947, now H.R.H. The Duchess of Cornwall = (1) Andrew Henry Parker Bowles; (2) H.R.H. Prince Charles Philip Arthur George of Great Britain, Prince of Wales, SETH

The Royal Descents of 900 Immigrants

15. Lydia Ward (sister of Mary and Rebecca) = William Markham
16. **William Markham** of Mass. = (1) Priscilla Graves; (2) Elizabeth Webster.
17. (by 1) Priscilla Markham = Thomas Hale, Jr.
18. John Hale = Abigail Gleason
19. Abigail Hale = Isaac Chandler
20. Abigail Chandler = Israel Smith
21. Chloe Smith = Rutherford Hayes
22. Rutherford Hayes, Jr. = Sophia Birchard
23. Rutherford Birchard Hayes (1822-1893), 19th U.S. President = Lucy Ware Webb

Sources: *RA* 4: 627-32 (Browne, Shirley), 5: 126-48, 1: 532-34 (Braose/Brewes), 3: 329-30 (Howard), 2: 298-308 (Cornwall), 3: 270-73 (Hawes, Brome), *MCS5*, lines 122-122D, 116-117, *AR8*, lines 230A-230B, *NEHGR* 150 (1996): 315-24 (de Braose), *TAG* 22 (1945-46): 158-63, 23 (1946-47): 109, 60 (1984): 91 (Nathaniel Browne), 52 (1976): 216-17 (Rev. John Davenport) and *TG* 7-8 (1986-1987): 132-36 (Edmond Hawes); *Shirleiana*, pp. 2-44; *Edmond Hawes*, pp. 19-65 (Hawes), 69-91 (Brome), 93-97 (Shirley); Henry James Young, *George Eldridge, Hydrographer, and Eliza Jane, His Wife: Their Ancestors and Their Descendants* (1982, which includes an ancestor table of Edmond Hawes for 33 generations, with a full bibliography) and *Hawes, Freeman and James*; *TG* 28 (2014): 137-54 (Matthew Hovious) and *TAG* 83 (2008-9): 13-18 (Leslie Mahler) (Ward, Lukyn), Walter C. Metcalfe, ed., *Visitations of Essex, 1552, 1558, 1570, 1612, 1634* (*HSPVS*, vol. 13, 1878), p. 310 (Walter) and W.H. Turner, ed., *Visitations of Oxfordshire, 1566, 1574, 1634* (*HSPVS*, vol. 5, 1871), pp. 228-29 (Denton). The parentage of Margaret Wroth, daughter of "John Wroth of Enfield" (*Shirleiana*, p. 39), is based on chronology and almost certain, and through William ap Walter the Ward sisters and their nephew may also have Welsh royal descents. The Cornwall/Howard descent of the Shirleys was developed by Douglas Richardson. For H.R.H. The Duchess of Cornwall, see *NK1*: 87-88 and Harriet Augusta Robinson, *Brewer Genealogy* (1903), p. 11.

The Royal Descents of 900 Immigrants

1. John "Lackland," King of England, d. 1216 = (2) Isabel of Angoulême
2. (illegitimate by Clemence ——, possibly Clemence le Botiller, wife of Nicholas de Verdun) Joan Plantagenet = Llywelyn Fawr ab Iorwerth, Prince of North Wales
3. David, Prince of North Wales (Dafydd ap Llywelyn Fawr) = Isabel de Braose
4. (illegitimate by ——) Annes ferch Dafydd = Elise ab Iorwerth ab Owain Brogyntyn
5. Madog ab Elise = (1) ——; (2) —— ferch Llywelyn
6. (maternity uncertain) Efa ferch Madog = Gruffudd ap Llywelyn ap Cynwrig
7. Einion ap Gruffudd = Tangwystl ferch Rhydderch ab Ieuan Llwyd
8. Gruffudd ab Einion = Lowri, daughter of Tudur ap Gruffudd Fychan (and Mawd ferch Ienaf ab Abba), brother of Welsh hero Owen Glendower and son of Gruffudd Fychan ap Gruffudd o'r Rhuddallt, SETH, and Elen ferch Thomas
9. Elise ap Gruffudd = Margred ferch Jenkin ab Ieuan
10. Dafydd Llwyd ab Elise = Gwenhwyfar ferch Richard Llwyd
11. John Wyn = Elsbeth Mostyn
12. (illegitimate by Agnes Lloyd) David Yale = Frances Lloyd, daughter of John Lloyd (and Elizabeth Pigott), son of David Lloyd ap John Griffith (and Margred ferch John ap Robert), son of John Griffith and Annes ferch John ap Maredudd, daughter of John ap Marcdudd, SETH and Gwenhwyfar ferch Gronwy ab Ieuan.
13. Thomas Yale = Anne Lloyd, later of Conn., ARD, SETH
14. **David Yale** of Conn. = Ursula Knight (parents of Elihu Yale, 1649-1721, official of the East India Company and benefactor of Yale College, for whom it was named).
14. **Thomas Yale** of Conn. = Mary Turner.

The Royal Descents of 900 Immigrants

14. **Anne Yale** of Conn. = Edward **Hopkins** (c. 1600-1657), colonial governor of Conn.

10. Lowri ferch Elise (sister of David Llwyd ab Elise) = Rheinallt ap Gruffudd ap Rhys

11. Mary ferch Rheinallt = Robert ap Dafydd Llwyd

12. Thomas ap Robert = Catrin ferch Robert ap Gruffudd

13. Ieuan ap Thomas = Dorothea Evans

14. Thomas ab Ieuan = Catrin ferch William Dafydd

15. Foulke ap Thomas = Lowri ferch Edward ap Dafydd

16. **Edward Foulke** of Pa. = Ellen Hughes of Pa., ARD, SETH.

13. Mary ferch Thomas ap Robert (sister of Ieuan ap Thomas) = Richard of Tyddin Tyfod

14. Rhys ap Richard = ——

15. Gruffudd ap Rhys = ——

16. Richard Price = ——

17. **Hannah Price** of Pa. = (1) Rees **Jones**; (2) Ellis **David**; (3) Thomas **Evans** of Pa., ARD, SETH. Edward Price (= Mably Owen) and Jane Price, wife of Cadwalader Morgan, a brother and sister of Hannah, also immigrated to Pa., but left no NDTPS.

Sources: *AR8*, line 251, *TAG* 32 (1956): 71-80, 56 (1980): 101-5 and *Journal of Royal and Noble Genealogy* 1 (1995, sponsored by The Augustan Society): 14-26 (Yales); *CVR*, pp. 69-82 (with some errors) (Foulke); *Merion*, pp. 80-81 (also with some errors), 94-95 (Foulke and Mrs. Evans); *Bartrum 1*, pp. 446-47, 51, 727, *Bartrum 2*, pp. 1415, 1416, 116, 1486 (generations 1-11 and 1-12). For English baronial ancestors of the Yales, Longespee to Henry II and Gloucester to Henry I, see *RA* 5: 434-39 (Yale, Lloyd, Pigott, Iwardby, Missenden), 4: 272-79 (Gay, Oddingseles), 2: 650-51 (FitzWalter), 3: 599-610 (Longespee), 3: 43-44 (Frome, Braose/Brewes), 1: 527-34 (Braose/Brewes), 2: 171-84 (Clare), 3: 86-90 (Gloucester), lines first explored in *TAG* 56 (1980): 1-11, 101-5 (Robert Joseph Curfman).

The Royal Descents of 900 Immigrants

1. John "Lackland," King of England, d. 1216 = (2) Isabel of Angoulême
2. (illegitimate by Clemence ——, possibly Clemence le Botiller, wife of Nicholas de Verdun) Joan Plantagenet = Llywelyn Fawr ab Iorwerth, Prince of North Wales
3. David, Prince of North Wales (Dafydd ap Llywelyn Fawr) = Isabel de Braose
4. (illegitimate by ——) Llywelyn ap Dafydd, constable of Rhuddlau = ——
5. Cynwrig ap Llywelyn = Angharad ferch Thomas ap Gwion
6. Dafydd Llwyd ap Cynwrig = Annes ferch Gwyn ap Madog
7. Mawd ferch Dafydd Llwyd = Dafydd Goch ap Trahaearn Goch ap Madog
8. Ieuan Goch ap Dafydd Goch = Efa ferch Einion ap Celynin
9. Morfudd ferch Ieuan Goch = Maredudd ap Hywel ap Tudur
10. Ieuan ap Maredudd = Lleucu ferch Hywel ap Meurig Fychan
11. Maredudd ab Ieuan = Margred ferch Einion ab Ithel
12. John ap Maredudd = Gwenhwyfar ferch Gronwy ab Ieuan
13. Elen ferch John = Hywel Fychan ap Hywel ap Gruffudd
14. Mallt ferch Hywel Fychan ap Hywel = Hywel Llwyd ap Dafydd o'r Bala, son (by Lowri ferch Dafydd ab Ieuan or Gwenllian ferch William ap Gruffudd) of Dafydd o'r Bala ap Maredudd, SETH
15. Thomas Gethin ap Hywel Llwyd = Catrin ferch Dafydd ap Gethin
16. Margred ferch Thomas Gethin = Huw ap Thomas
17. William ap Huw = ——
18. Ellis Williams (Ellis William ap Huw) = Margaret John
19. Gwen Williams = Hugh ap Cadwaladr ap Rhys
20. **John Hughes** (Hugh or Pugh) of Pa. = Martha Caimot.

20. **Ellen Hughes** (Hugh or Pugh) of Pa. = Edward **Foulke** of Pa., ARD, SETH. Ellis Pugh (= Sina ———) and Jane Pugh or Hughes, wife of William John, a brother and sister of John Hughes and of Mrs. Ellen Hughes Foulke, also immigrated to Pa., but left no NDTPS.

19. Eleanor Williams (sister of Gwen) = John Morris

20. **Ellen Morris** of Pa. = Cadwalader **Evans** of Pa., ARD, SETH.

15. Lowri ferch Hywel Llwyd (sister of Thomas Gethin) = Edward ap John Wyn, whose mother was not, according to Bartrum, Catrin, daughter of Hywel ap Jenkin and Mary Kynaston, as claimed in *WFP* 1, pedigree XVIII, p. 116 and chart following

16. Watkyn ab Edward = Grace, daughter of Cadwaladr ap Robert and Jane ferch Maredudd ab Ieuan, SETH

17. Edward ap Watkyn = ——— ferch Thomas ap Robert ap Gruffudd

18. Agnes Edwards = William Owen

19. Elizabeth Williams of Pa. = Robert Pugh, ARD, SETH

20. **Hugh Roberts** of Pa. = Jane Owen of Pa., a cousin, ARD, SETH.

20. **Gainor Roberts** of Pa. (sister of Hugh) = John **Roberts** of (Pencoyd, Lower Merion) Pa., ARD, SETH.

Sources: *WFP* 1, pedigree XXII, pp. 141-42, plus correspondence with Miriam Elliott Bertelson of Fremont, Calif. (progeny of Ellis Williams), pedigree XVIII, pp. 117-22, p. 149 and pedigree XXIV, p. 220 (plus *Merion*, pp. 98-105) (Roberts) and chart between pp. 116-17 (generations 9-17, Edward ap Watkyn); *Bartrum 1*, p. 446-47, 867, 457, *Bartrum 2*, pp. 845-46, 23, 1481, 1479 (generations 1-15).

For disproofs by Stewart Baldwin of the royal descent and placement in the above lineage of Hugh Jones, William Edwards (ab Edward or Bedward), John Edwards (ab Edward) and John Evans (the Merion and Radnor, Pa., settler), previously claimed as immigrant kinsmen of John Hughes, Ellen (Hughes) Foulke, Ellen (Morris) Evans, Hugh Roberts and Gainor (Roberts) Roberts above, see *TAG* 80 (2005): 117-20, 82 (2007): 17-31.

The Royal Descents of 900 Immigrants

1. John "Lackland," King of England, d. 1216 = (2) Isabel of Angoulême

2. Richard Plantagenet, King of the Romans = (1) Isabel Marshall; (2) Sancha of Provence; (3) Beatrix de Falkenburg

3. (illegitimate by ——, possibly Joan de Vautort or Valletort) Sir Richard de Cornwall = Joan ——

4. Joan de Cornwall = Sir John Howard

5. Sir John Howard = Alice de Boys

6. Sir Robert Howard = Margery Scales

7. Sir John Howard = (1) Joan Walton; (2) Alice Tendring

8. (by 2) Henry Howard (full brother of Sir Robert Howard, husband of Margaret Mowbray, SETH, and uncle of John Howard, 1st Duke of Norfolk) = Mary Hussey

9. Elizabeth Howard = Henry Wentworth, son of Sir Roger Wentworth and Margery Despencer, ARD, SETH

10. Margery Wentworth = Sir William Waldegrave

11. Anthony Waldegrave = Elizabeth Gray

12. Thomas Waldegrave = Elizabeth Gurdon, aunt of Brampton Gurdon, husband of Muriel Sedley, SETH, and half-sister of Thomas Appleton, husband of Mary Isaac, SETH

13. Thomas Waldegrave = Margaret Holmstead

14. **Jemima Waldegrave** = Herbert **Pelham** of Mass., 1st treasurer of Harvard College, ARD, SETH.

11. Dorothy Waldegrave (sister of Anthony) = Sir John Spring

12. Frances Spring = Edmund Wright

13. Mary Wright = William Derehaugh

14. **Anne Derehaugh** of Mass. = John **Stratton**, ARD, SETH (parents of John Stratton of Mass., Mrs. Elizabeth Stratton Thorndike of Mass., and Dorothy Stratton of Mass., SETH).

The Royal Descents of 900 Immigrants

11. Margaret Waldegrave (sister of Anthony and Dorothy) = Sir John St. John

12. Alice St. John = Edmund Elmes

13. Elizabeth Elmes = Sir Edward Apsley

14. **Alice Apsley** = (1) Sir John **Boteler**; (2) George **Fenwick** (1603-1656/7), colonist, a founder of Saybrook, Conn., ARD, SETH.

12. Oliver St. John, 1st Baron St. John of Bletso (brother of Alice) = Agnes Fisher

13. Margaret St. John = Sir Nicholas Luke

14. Anne Luke = Sir Miles Fleetwood. Martha Fleetwood, their daughter, married Robert Duckenfield and was the mother of both William Duckenfield of N.C., who married Mrs. Susanna Garraway Hartley but left no issue, and Mary Duckenfield, wife of William Barber and mother of Charles Barber of N.C., who married and left progeny but probably no NDTPS.

15. George Fleetwood, Swedish general and baron = Brita Gyllenstierna, see below

16. Gustaf Miles, Baron Fleetwood = Märta Stake

17. Gustaf Adolf, Baron Fleetwood = Anna Uggla

18. Eleonora Margareta, Baroness Fleetwood = Ulrik Gustaf Hård af Torestorp

19. Anna Hård af Torestorp = Leonard Gyllenhaal

20. Fredrik Leonard Gyllenhaal = Christina Lovisa Westling

21. **Anders Leonard Gyllenhaal** of Chicago, Ill. = Selma Amanda Nelson. Their son, Leonard Efraim Gyllenhaal, married Virginia Philo Pendleton and left a son, Hugh Anders Gyllenhaal, who married Virginia Lowrie Childs. Film director Stephen Roark Gyllenhaal, b. 1949, a son of these last, married screenwriter

The Royal Descents of 900 Immigrants

Naomi Achs Foner and is the father of actress Maggie (Ruth) Gyllenhaal, b. 1977, wife of actor (John) Peter Sarsgaard, b. 1971, and actor Jacob Benjamin (Jake) Gyllenhaal, b. 1980, unm.

1. Charles VIII (Bonde), (elected, non-hereditary) King of Sweden, d. 1470 = Brigitta Bielke
2. Christina Bonde = Erik Gyllenstierna
3. Erik Gyllenstierna = Anna Vistorp
4. Carl Gyllenstierna = Marina Grip
5. Erik Gyllenstierna = Carin Bielke
6. Carl Gyllenstierna = Anna Ribbing
7. Brita Gyllenstierna = George Fleetwood, Swedish general and baron, above

Sources: *RA* 2: 11-12 (Waldegrave), 5: 295 (Waldegrave), 3: 404-5 (Wentworth), 3: 329-33 (Howard), 2: 298-308 (Cornwall); *MCS5*, line 75A, *AR8*, lines 200, 258, *TAG* 18 (1941-42): 139-44 and *NEHGR* 154 (2000): 89-90 (for Mrs. Pelham); *BP* (Norfolk), *Cornewall*, p. 157, and *NEHGR* 119 (1965): 98, 101-2; *NEHGR* 155 (2001): 367-70, 156 (2002): 39-46, 50-55 (Mrs. Stratton, by Robert Battle of Tacoma, Wash., and sources cited therein); D.G.C. Elwes, *A History of the Castles, Mansions, and Manors of Western Sussex* (1876), chart opp. p. 250 (Apsley), Walter C. Metcalfe, ed., *Visitations of Northamptonshire, 1564 and 1618-19* (1887), p. 18 (Elmes), *CP* and F.A. Blaydes, ed., *Visitations of Bedfordshire 1566, 1582 and 1634* (*HSPVS*, vol. 19, 1884), pp. 53-54 (St. John) (and pp. 179-80 for Luke), Walter C. Metcalfe, ed., *Visitations of Essex, 1552, 1558, 1570, 1612 and 1634*, vol. 1 (*HSPVS*, vol. 13, 1878), pp. 120, 122, 309-10, 515 (Waldegrave), and *Wentworth*, vol. 1, pp. 27-28. For the English ancestry of the Gyllenhaals see *Elgenstierna*, vol. 3, pp. 275-76 (Gyllenhaal), 756 (Hård af Torestorp), vol. 2, pp. 716-18, 721 (Fleetwood); *Oxford DNB* (George Fleetwood), *Parliament, 1558-1603*, vol. 2, pp. 498-99 (Sir Nicholas Luke). For the descent from Anders Leonard Gyllenhaal to the actors, see recent volumes of *Sveriges Ridderskap och Adels Kalender* (for 2004, p. 290). This line was developed and brought to my attention by the late William Addams Reitwiesner. See also

The Royal Descents of 900 Immigrants

http://freepages.genealogy.rootsweb.com/~corpusnobiliorum/ghaal.html. The Duckenfield-Barber N.C. connections were developed by John Anderson Brayton; see *Ormerod*, vol. 3, p. 818 (Duckenfield) and J. Bryan Grimes, *North Carolina Wills and Inventories* (1912), pp. 161-66. The descent via Gyllenstierna from Charles VIII Bonde, (elected) King of Sweden, d. 1470, taken from the Internet, was developed by (Charles) Edward Gyllenhaal, grandson of Leonard Efraim and Virginia Philo (Pendleton) Gyllenhaal, confirmed by *Elgenstierna*, vol. 3, pp. 355-58, and reported to me by Stephen Robeson-Miller. Lines from earlier Scandinavian kings have been proposed but seem not to be generally accepted; see *Foundations* 2 (2006-9): 253-60.

The Royal Descents of 900 Immigrants

1. John "Lackland," King of England, d. 1216 = (2) Isabel of Angoulême
2. (illegitimate by ——) Isabel FitzRoy = Sir Richard FitzIves
3. Isabel FitzIves = Sir Belyn Heligan
4. Richard Heligan = Margaret Prideaux
5. Isabel Heligan = John Petit
6. Sir John Petit = Joanna Carminow
7. Michael Petit = Amicia Bloyou
8. John Petit = Margaret Roscarrock
9. John Petit = Margaret Trenowith
10. John Petit = Jane Anthorne
11. Jane Petit = (1) Thomas Trevanion; (2) John Killigrew
12. (by 2) Elizabeth Killigrew = Thomas Treffry
13. John Treffry = Emilyn Tresithny
14. Martha Treffry = Thomas Dyckwood, alias Peters
15. **Thomas Peter(s)** (1597-1654/5), Anglican clergyman and Connecticut colonist = Anne Rawe.
15. **Hugh Peter(s)** (1598-1660) of Mass., Puritan clergyman and Cromwellian politician = (1) Mrs. Elizabeth Cooke Reade; (2) Deliverance Sheffield, ARD, SETH.

12. (by 1) John Trevanion (half-brother of Elizabeth Killigrew) = Janet Treffry, aunt of Thomas Treffry above
13. Sir William Trevanion = Anne Edgcombe
14. Sir Hugh Trevanion = Elizabeth Pollard
15. Richard Trevanion = Margaret Chamond
16. Richard Trevanion = Mary Rolle
17. Nathaniel Trevanion = Elizabeth Sawle
18. Richard Trevanion = —— Maunder

19. Sir Nicholas Trevanion = Elizabeth Westlake
20. Arabella Trevanion = William Barlow
21. Arabella Barlow = George Smith
22. **Arabella Maria Smith** of Pa. = Alexander James **Dallas** (1759-1817), lawyer, secretary of the treasury. A son was George Mifflin Dallas, diplomat and U.S. Vice-President under Polk, for whom Dallas, Texas, is named.

Sources: *DAB* (Rev. Hugh Peter[s]), *Oxford DNB* (Revs. Thomas and Hugh) and *NEHGR* 54 (1900): 339-40 (Rev. Thomas Peter[s]), *VC*, pp. 459-60 (misnumbered 559-60) (Treffry), 267-68, 494-95, 30 (Killigrew, Petit, Heligan), 501, 504-6 (Trevanion); *Herald and Genealogist* 7 (1873): 229-31 (Heligan, FitzIves); *RA* 2: 634 (FitzIves), 1: 43-58 (King John); Raymond Walters, Jr., *Alexander James Dallas, Lawyer, Politician, Financier, 1759-1817* (1943), pp. 9-11 (and Mrs. Dallas's *Autobiographical Memoir for Her Children,* mentioned on p. 240 of that biography), plus a chart by Stanwood E. Flitner of the ancestry known in 1940 of Mrs. Trevania Barlow Dallas Blair-Smith, great-granddaughter of Mrs. A. M. Smith Dallas (this chart is now in the possession of my former NEHGS colleague, Mrs. Victoria Anne Meeks Blair-Smith, Trevania's granddaughter-in-law). For Elizabeth Westlake see A.J. Jewers, *Heraldic Church Notes from Cornwall* (1887), p. 78, a source brought to my attention by John C. Brandon of Columbia, S.C.

The Royal Descents of 900 Immigrants

1. John "Lackland," King of England, d. 1216 = (2) Isabel of Angoulême
2. (illegitimate by —— de Warenne) Richard FitzRoy = Rohese of Dover
3. Lorette de Dover = Sir William Marmion
4. John Marmion, 1st Baron Marmion = Isabel ——
5. John Marmion, 2nd Baron Marmion = Maud Furnival
6. Avice Marmion = John Grey, 1st Baron Grey of Rotherfield
7. Sir Robert Grey, later Marmion = Lora St. Quintin
8. Elizabeth Marmion = Henry FitzHugh, 3rd Baron FitzHugh
9. William FitzHugh, 4th Baron FitzHugh = Margery Willoughby
10. Lora FitzHugh = Sir John Constable
11. Margery (or Mariora) Constable = Robert Holme
12. John Holme = —— Elland
13. Anne Holme = William Cheney, son of Sir John Cheney (and Elizabeth Rempston), son of Laurence Cheney and Elizabeth Cokayne, SETH
14. William Cheney = Frances Cheney (a cousin)
15. John Cheney = Elizabeth ——
16. **Anne Cheney**, sometime of Mass. = Hanserd **Knollys** (1598-1691), Particular Baptist minister, sometime of Mass.

11. Isabel Constable (sister of Margery) = Stephen Thorpe
12. Margaret Thorpe = John Newton
13. John Newton = Margaret Grimston
14. John Newton = Mary ——
15. Lancelot Newton = Mary Lee
16. **Ellen Newton** of Mass. = Edward **Carleton** of Mass., ARD, SETH.

The Royal Descents of 900 Immigrants

11. Joan Constable (sister of Margery and Isabel) = Sir William Mallory

12. Sir John Mallory = Margaret Thwaites

13. Sir William Mallory = Jane Norton

14. Sir William Mallory = Ursula Gale

15. Thomas Mallory, Dean of Chester = Elizabeth Vaughan

16. Thomas Mallory = (1) Jane ——; (2) Mary Oldfield; (3) Frances ——

17. (prob. by Jane) **Roger Mallory** of Va. = ——. His brother, Thomas Mallory of Charles City Co., Va., left no NDTPS. Rev. Philip Mallory of York Co., Va., son of 15 above and uncle of Roger and Thomas, returned to England and also left no NDTPS. A second uncle, Richard Mallory, married Lucy Holland and left a daughter, Elizabeth Mallory, wife of Richard Halford (Holford) and mother of Thomas Halford (Holford), another immigrant to Virginia who left no NDTPS.

Sources: *Oxford DNB* article on Hanserd Knollys, Thomas Caldwall, *A Select Collection of Ancient and Modern Epitaphs and Inscriptions, to Which are Added Some on the Decease of Eminent Personages* (1796), p. 42 (monumental inscription of Anne [Cheney] Knollys at Bunhill Fields, London, which names her father), *Lincolnshire Notes and Queries* 7 (1902-3): 150-55 (which includes the 1635/6 will of Jane [Cheney] Field, widow, who mentions "my nephew Hansard Knolles, clk., of Fulletby and my niece Anne his wife"), *Lincolnshire Pedigrees*, vol. 1 (*HSPVS*, vol. 50, 1902), pp. 242-43 and George Poulson, *The History and Antiquities of the Seigniory of Holderness*, vol. 2 (1841), pp. 489-90 (Holme); *RA* 4: 247-49 (Newton, Thorpe), 4: 19-23 (Mallory [to Roger], Constable), 2: 631-33 (FitzHugh), 4: 274-76 (Grey), 4: 31-33 (Marmion), 1: 184-85 (Dover); *AR8*, lines 121D, 219, 218, 26 and *MCS5*, line 109; Walter Lee Sheppard, Jr., "The Ancestry of Edward Carleton and Ellen Newton, His Wife" (microfilm, 1978), see under Edward Carleton; *TVG* 46 (2002): 83-90 (Dean Thomas Mallory and his children), *VHG*, pp. 103-16, *GVFVM* 4: 250-70 and *VGE*, pp. 100-4 (Mallory). See also S.V. Mallory

The Royal Descents of 900 Immigrants

Smith, *A History of the Mallory Family* (1985), esp. pp. 142-43, 151, 153-54. The Cheney/Knollys descent was brought to my attention by Leslie Mahler and later John C. Brandon; the Welsh ancestry of Elizabeth Vaughan was charted, from *Bartrum 1* and *Bartrum 2*, for many generations, by the late William Addams Reitwiesner of Washington, D.C.

The Royal Descents of 900 Immigrants

1. John "Lackland," King of England, d. 1216 = (2) Isabel of Angoulême
2. (illegitimate by —— de Warenne) Richard FitzRoy = Rohese of Dover
3. Lorette de Dover = Sir William Marmion
4. John Marmion, 1st Baron Marmion = Isabel ——
5. John Marmion, 2nd Baron Marmion = Maud Furnival
6. Avice Marmion = John Grey, 1st Baron Grey of Rotherfield
7. Maud Grey = Sir Thomas Harcourt
8. Sir Thomas Harcourt = Jane Franceys
9. Sir Robert Harcourt = Margaret Byron
10. John Harcourt = Anne Norris
11. Lettice Harcourt = Humphrey Peshall
12. Eleanor Peshall = Humphrey Wolrich
13. Elizabeth Wolrich = Edward Hopton
14. Katherine Hopton = Thomas Anderson
15. Lucretia Anderson = Edmund Bressie
16. Edmund Bressie = Constance Shepherd, daughter of Thomas Shepherd (and Amphyllis Chamberlain alias Spicer), son of Thomas Shepherd and Constance Hawes, daughter of Thomas Hawes and Elizabeth Brome, SETH
17. **Thomas Bressie** of Conn. = (1) Hannah Hart; (2) Phebe Bisby. John Bressie, a brother of Thomas, was also in New Haven in the 1640s, but returned to England by 1649 and left no NDTPS.

15. Elizabeth Anderson (sister of Lucretia) = Sir William Garway
16. Elizabeth Garway = Thomas Foxall
17. Mary Foxall = Christopher Taylor
18. **James Taylor** of Mass. = (1) Elizabeth (Fuller?); (2) Rebecca Clark.

The Royal Descents of 900 Immigrants

Sources: *RA* 1: 524-27 (Bressie/ey, Anderson, Hopton, Wolrich, Peshall), 3: 209-13 (Harcourt), 4: 274-76, 4: 31-35 (Marmion), 1: 184-85 (Dover), 4: 623-24 (Shepherd), 3: 270-72 (Hawes), 5: 131-33 (Taylor, Foxall, Garway); *NEHGR* 112 (1958): 27-44, 118 (1964): 251-62 (reprinted in *EO* 2: 1: 286-304 and *EO* 1: 3: 398-409) (Bressey and Shepherd articles by W.G. Davis); Walter C. Metcalfe, ed., *Visitations of Hertfordshire, 1572, 1634* (*HSPVS*, vol. 22, 1886), 109 (Anderson); George Grazebrook and J.P. Rylands, *Visitation of Shropshire, 1623* (*HSPVS*, vols. 28-29, 1889), pp. 258-59 (Hopton), 509 (Wolrich); *Calendar of Inquisitions Post Mortem, Henry VII*, vol. 2 (1915), pp. 369-70 (IPM of "Humphrey Persall," which identifies his wife Lettice as a *sister* of Sir Robert Harcourt) and the Wolrich quarterings of Peshall and Harcourt (*HSPVS* 29: 508); *Salt*, new ser., 35 (1914), pp. 196-204 and chart opposite p. 187 (Harcourt); *AR8*, lines 50, 30, 219, 218; Taylor research by David Curtis Dearborn, late of NEHGS, based in part on manuscript GEN 1-T-199 at NEHGS ("Copy of genealogical data found in an indenture of James Taylor of Lynn, son of Christopher Taylor of London"), a 19 Oct. 1678 letter of James Taylor at the Massachusetts Historical Society, L.L. Duncan and A.O. Barron, eds., *The Register of All the Marriages, Christenings and Burials in the Church of S. Margaret, Lee, in the County of Kent, from 1579 to 1754* (1888), p. 72, item 91 Pembroke (will of Elizabeth Foxall, 16 above, which mentions her grandson James Taylor), entries for Christopher Taylor, Thomas Foxall, (Sir) William Garway, Thomas Anderson and Edward Hopton in Percival Boyd, "Pedigrees of London Citizens" (original at Society of Genealogists, London, FHL Film 94561), J.J. Howard and J.C. Chester, eds., *Visitation of London, 1633, 1634, 1635, Volume I* (*HSPVS*, vol. 15, 1880), p. 289 (Foxall, but omitting Mary, bp. 1612, wife of Christopher Taylor) and W.B. Bannerman, ed., *Visitations of Surrey, 1530, 1572, 1623* (*HSPVS*, vol. 43, 1899), p. 202 (Garway/Garraway).

The Royal Descents of 900 Immigrants

1. John "Lackland," King of England, d. 1216 = (2) Isabel of Angoulême
2. Richard Plantagenet, King of the Romans = (1) Isabel Marshall; (2) Sancha of Provence; (3) Beatrix de Falkenburg
3. (illegitimate by ——, possibly Joan de Vautort or Valletort) Joan of Cornwall = Richard de Champernowne
4. Sir Richard Champernowne = Elizabeth Valletort, daughter of Hugh de Valletort (and Lucia le Bret), son of Sir John de Valletort and —— de Columbers, daughter of Philip de Columbers and Egeline Courtenay, daughter of Sir Robert Courtenay and Mary de Vernon, SETH, but see note below
5. Sir Thomas Champernowne = Eleanor de Rohant
6. Sir Richard Champernowne = (1) Alice Astley, (2) Katherine Daubeny
7. (by 2) John Champernowne = Margaret Hamley
8. Richard Champernowne = Elizabeth Reynell
9. Elizabeth Champernowne = William Fortescue, son of John Fortescue and Joan Prutteston, SETH
10. Jane Fortescue = John Cobleigh
11. Margaret Cobleigh = Sir Roger Giffard
12. Jane Giffard = Amyas Chichester
13. Frances Chichester = John Wyatt
14. **Margaret Wyatt** of Conn. = Matthew **Allyn**.
15. Thomas Allyn = Abigail Warham
16. Abigail Allyn = John Williams
17. Elijah Williams = Lydia Dwight
18. Abigail Williams = Thomas Williams, a cousin
19. Abigail Williams = Alexander Bliss
20. Margaret Bliss = Nathan Hoyt
21. Margaret Jane Hoyt = Samuel Edward Axson

The Royal Descents of 900 Immigrants

22. Ellen Louise Axson = (Thomas) Woodrow Wilson (1856-1924), 28th U.S. President

15. Mary Allyn (sister of Thomas) = Benjamin Newberry
16. Mary Newberry = John Moseley
17. Joseph Moseley = Abigail Root
18. Abigail Moseley = John Lyman (III)
19. Mindwell Lyman = Ebenezer Pomeroy (III)
20. Eunice Pomeroy = Ebenezer Clark (III)
21. Jerusha Clark = Samuel Gates, Jr.
22. George Williams Gates (Vt. to Mo.) = Sarah D. Todd
23. George Porterfield Gates = Elizabeth Emery
24. Margaret (Madge) Gates = David Willick Wallace
25. Elizabeth Virginia "Bess" Wallace = Harry S Truman (1884-1972), 33rd U.S. President, SETH

17. Mary Moseley (sister of Joseph) = Eleazer Weller, Jr.
18. Mary Weller = Daniel Sackett
19. Daniel Sackett, Jr. = Mehitable Cadwell
20. Mehitable Sackett = Luke Francis
21. Manning Francis = Elizabeth Robbins Root
22. Frederick Augustus Francis = Jessie Anne Stevens
23. Anne Ayers Francis = John Newell Robbins
24. Kenneth Seymour Robbins = Edith Luckett, who = (2) Dr. Loyal Edward Davis, who adopted his step daughter
25. Anne Francis Robbins, whose name was changed to Nancy Davis = Ronald Wilson Reagan (1911-2004), 40th U.S. President

The Royal Descents of 900 Immigrants

7. (by 1) Joan Champernowne = Sir James Chudleigh, son of John Chudleigh and Jane (or Joan) Beauchamp, daughter of Sir John Beauchamp and Joan de Nonant, SETH, but see note below
8. James Chudleigh = (1) ——; (2) Radigond FitzWalter
9. (by 1) John Chudleigh = Margaret ——
10. Sir James Chudleigh = (1) Margaret (or Mary) Stourton; (2) Margaret Tremayne
11. (probably by 1) Petronell Chudleigh = Anthony Pollard
12. Mary Pollard = John Ayre (Eyre)
13. Margery Ayre (Eyre) = George Damerie (Amory)
14. John Damerie (Amory) = Emmot Thomas
15. Joan Damerie (Amory) = Samuel Butler
16. Almeric (Amory) Butler = ——
17. **Mary Butler** of Va. = William **Underwood**, Jr. Rev. Amory Butler, Rev. William Butler, and John Butler, brothers of Mary, also immigrated to Va., but I can find no evidence of issue.

Sources: *RA* 1: 112-15 (Wyatt, Chichester, Giffard, Cobley, Fortescue, generations 9-14), 4: 91-93 (Champernowne, generations 5-9), 2: 401 (Chudleigh), 4: 511-12 (Beauchamp), *AR8*, lines 52, 25, 246E-F, plus *CP* (Columbers) and *VD*, pp. 160, 162 and research of Todd A. Farmerie, sent via the Internet and derived in part from *Devon and Cornwall Notes and Queries* 18 (1934-5): 108-12, 19 (1936-37): 26-29 (Champernowne), 12 (1922-23): 340-42, 24 (1950-51): 229-30 (Chudleigh), and Sir John MacLean, *Parochial and Family History of the Deanery of Trigg Minor*, vol. 3 (1879), p. 427 (addendum on Chudleigh to vol. 1, p. 531, line 14), Ronny O. Bodine and Brother Thomas W. Spalding, Jr., *The Ancestry of Dorothea Poyntz, Wife of Reverend John Owsley, Generations 1-14*, 3rd ed. (1999), #s 666, 1332-33, 2664-65, 5328-31, 10658-61, 21322-23, 21136 (pp. 45, 62, 85, 116, 156-57, 206, 199), and sources cited therein (from Sir Richard Champernowne, husband of Alice and Katherine, to King John and to Egeline Courtenay) (for Mrs. Allyn); *PSECD* 2:73 (for Mrs. Underwood, undocumented), *AR8*, lines 217, 246B, F.L. Weis, *The Colonial Clergy of Virginia, North Carolina, and South Carolina* (1955), p. 9 (Amory and William Butler), John and J.A. Venn, *Alumni Cantabrigienses*, part 1, vol. 1 (1922), pp. 271, 274 (Almeric [Amory] and William Butler), and *VD*, pp. 15,

The Royal Descents of 900 Immigrants

31, 597, 189 (Amory [Damerie], Ayre [Eyre], Pollard, Chudleigh) (sources that confirm *PSECD* for generations 11-17 above). For the three Joans, wives of Sir James Chudleigh (the third Joan is 7 above), see *The Plantagenet Connection* 8 (2000): 229-30. In *TAG* 76 (2001): 46, however, Mr. Farmerie suggests that the placement of Petronell, wife of Anthony Pollard, among the Chudleighs may be indefinite. *RA* 2: 298-306 covers the first four generations but does not connect generation 4 and 5. Douglas Richardson also reports that despite the sources cited above, the Valletort descent from Courtenay and the Chudleigh descent from Beauchamp have been disproved. Definitive coverage of these three problems is eagerly awaited.

The Royal Descents of 900 Immigrants

1. John "Lackland," King of England, d. 1216 = (2) Isabel of Angoulême

2. (illegitimate by —— de Warenne) Richard Fitzroy = Rohese of Dover

3. Isabel de Dover (or de Chilham) = Sir Maurice Berkeley

4. Thomas Berkeley, 1st Baron Berkeley = Joan Ferrers

5. Maurice Berkeley, 2nd Baron Berkeley = Eve la Zouche, daughter of Eudo la Zouche and Milicent de Cantilupe, SETH

6. Thomas Berkeley, 3rd Baron Berkeley = Katherine de Clivedon

7. Sir John Berkeley = Elizabeth Betteshorne

8. Elizabeth Berkeley = John Sutton, 1st Baron Dudley, son of Sir John Sutton and Constance Blount, daughter of Sir Walter Blount and Sancha de Ayala, for whom see *AAP* (2009, 2012), pp. 660-64.

9. Eleanor Sutton = (1) Sir Henry Beaumont, SETH; (2) George Stanley

10. (by 2) Anne Stanley = John Wolseley

11. Anthony Wolseley = Margaret Blythe

12. Erasmus Wolseley = Cassandra Giffard

13. Sir Thomas Wolseley = Ellen Broughton, daughter of Edward Broughton and Anne Dixwell, SETH

14. **Anne Wolseley** of Md. = Hon. Philip **Calvert**, colonial governor of Md., half-brother of Cecil Calvert, 2nd Baron Baltimore, proprietor of Md. and of Hon. Leonard Calvert, also a colonial governor of Md., both ARD, SETH. Winifred Wolseley of Md., a sister of Anne, married Rev. William Mullet but left no issue.

14. Walter Wolseley = Mary Beauchamp

15. **Mary Wolseley** of Md. = Roger **Brooke** (who = [1] Dorothy Neale, daughter of James Neale of Md., ARD, SETH and Anna Maria Gill).

The Royal Descents of 900 Immigrants

Sources: *RA* 5: 389-92 (Wolseley, Stanley), 5: 101-4 (Sutton), 2: 589-91 (Berkeley), 1: 326-34 (Berkeley), 1: 184-85 (Dover), 1: 108-9 (Abney) and *TG* 5 (1984): 131-48, 150-52, 154-57. See also *MD* 1: 138 (Calvert), 96-97 (Brooke) and *AR8*, line 81-81C, 39, 26, *MCS5*, lines 149B, 80A, 80, 88. Ellen Wolseley, daughter of John and Anne (Stanley), married George Abney and left a son, Edmund Abney, who married Katherine Ludlam. Paul Abney, a son of these last, married Mary Brooksby and left a son, George Abney, father by Bathshua —— of the brothers Paul and Dannett Abney of Va. These last both married Mary Lee (wife firstly of Paul) and apparently left children, but I can find no NDTPS; see *TG* 5: 145-46, 150-51, 157. Sir John Sutton above, husband of Constance Blount, was the son of Sir John Sutton (and Joan ——), son of Sir John Sutton, not by Katherine Stafford, his first wife, but by Joan Clinton, his second.

The Royal Descents of 900 Immigrants

1. John "Lackland," King of England, d. 1216 = (2) Isabel of Angoulême
2. (illegitimate by —— de Warenne) Richard FitzRoy = Rohese of Dover
3. Lorette de Dover = Sir William Marmion
4. John Marmion, 1st Baron Marmion = Isabel ——
5. John Marmion, 2nd Baron Marmion = Maud Furnival
6. Avice Marmion = John Grey, 1st Baron Grey of Rotherfield
7. Maud Grey = Sir Thomas Harcourt
8. Sir Thomas Harcourt = Jane Franceys
9. Jane Harcourt = Thomas St. Barbe
10. John St. Barbe = Joan Sydenham
11. Richard St. Barbe = Margery Grey, daughter of Humphrey Grey and Anne Fielding, SETH
12. Thomas St. Barbe = Joan ——
13. Alice St. Barbe = Christopher Batt
14. Thomas Batt = Joan Byley
15. **Christopher Batt** of Mass. = Anne Bainton of Mass., ARD, SETH. Dorothy Batt, a sister of Christopher, also immigrated to Mass., and probably married there, but her later history is unknown.

Sources: *RA* 1: 266-68 (Batt, St. Barbe), 3: 209-11 (Harcourt), 4: 274-76 (Grey), 4: 31-33 (Marmion), 1: 184-85 (Dover); *Davis* 1: 77-86 (Batt), 3: 372-76 (St. Barbe), *TAG* 79 (2004): 85-99 (Brandon Fradd) and generation 9; *AR8*, lines 50, 30, 219, 218. See also *TG* 17 (2003): 92-95 (generations 11-15, also by Mr. Fradd). As brought to my attention by John C. Brandon of Columbia, S.C., Mary St. Barbe, daughter of Thomas St. Barbe and Joan ——, generation 12 above, married Edward Langford and was the mother of Mary Langford, wife of Henry Hyde and mother of statesman Edward Hyde, 1st Earl of Clarendon. This last, by second wife Frances Aylesbury, was the father of Anne Hyde, Duchess of York, first wife of James II, King of England, and mother of Mary II and Anne, Queens of England. Thus Christopher Batt of Mass. was a second cousin of the 1st Earl of Clarendon and a second cousin twice removed—and nearest immigrant kinsman with American progeny—of Queens Mary II and Anne, and of Edward Hyde, 3rd Earl of Clarendon, colonial governor of N.Y. and N.J., ARD, SETH. See *Notes and Queries* 189 (1945): 246-48, 220 (1975): 28 (the latter by Charles Frederick Holt Evans, reprinted in Steven Edwards, ed., *Complete Works of Charles Evans: Genealogy and Related Topics* [2003], p. 291) plus *TG*, new ser., 8 (1892): 44 (*seize-quartiers* of Anne Hyde, Duchess of York, by G.E. Cokayne).

The Royal Descents of 900 Immigrants

1. John "Lackland," King of England, d. 1216 = (2) Isabel of Angoulême

2. (illegitimate by Clemence ——, possibly Clemence le Botiller, wife of Nicholas de Verdun) Joan Plantagenet = Llywelyn Fawr ab Iorwerth, Prince of North Wales

3. Gwladys Ddu of Wales = Ralph de Mortimer

4. Sir Roger de Mortimer = Maud de Braose, daughter of Sir William de Braose and Eve Marshall, SETH

5. Margaret de Mortimer = Robert de Vere, 6th Earl of Oxford, son of Robert de Vere, 5th Earl of Oxford (and Alice de Sanford), son of Hugh de Vere, 4th Earl of Oxford (and Hawise de Quincy, daughter of Saire de Quincy, 1st Earl of Winchester, Magna Carta surety, and Margaret de Beaumont, SETH), son of Robert de Vere, 3rd Earl of Oxford, Magna Carta surety (and Isabel de Bolebec), son of Aubrey de Vere, 1st Earl of Oxford (and Agnes de Essex), son of Aubrey de Vere and Alice de Clare, SETH

6. Eleanor de Vere = Hugh de Naunton

7. Hugh de Naunton = Eleanor Boville

8. Peter de Naunton = Margaret Barney

9. Peter de Naunton = Margaret d'Oyley

10. Robert de Naunton = —— Tymberley

11. Thomas de Naunton = Margery Brusyard

12. Bridget Naunton = Thomas Almott

13. Catherine Almott = John Clench

14. Robert Clench = Joan Webbe

15. **Thomasine Clench** of Mass. = Edmund **Frost**.

Sources: *NEHGR* 153 (1999): 280-82, 287-99 (Clench, Almott) (Neil D. Thompson), Lord Francis Hervey, ed., *Suffolk in the XVIIth Century: The Breviary of Suffolk by Robert Reyce, 1618...From the Ms. in the British Museum* (1902), pp. 226-27 (Naunton), *RA* 5: 251-56 (Vere), 4: 164-68 (Mortimer), 5: 298-301 (Wales) and *AR8*, lines 176B (Wales, Mortimer),

The Royal Descents of 900 Immigrants

66 (Braose), 246 (Vere). This descent was first suggested by John C. Brandon on soc.genealogy.medieval. Richardson gives only a son, Sir Thomas de Vere, for the 6th Earl of Oxford, but we have no reason to disbelieve *The Breviary* and the chronology certainly fits. If Eleanor de Vere was only an *illegitimate* child of Robert de Vere, 6th Earl of Oxford (1257-1331) or Robert de Vere, 5th Earl of Oxford (ca. 1240-*ante* 1296), the best royal descent for Mrs. Frost would be to Henry I, King of France, d. 1060, via the above Margaret de Beaumont.

The Royal Descents of 900 Immigrants

1. John "Lackland," King of England, d. 1216 = Isabel of Angoulême

2. (illegitimate by Clemence ——, possibly Clemence le Botiller, wife of Nicholas de Verdun) Joan Plantagenet = Llywelyn Fawr ab Iorwerth, Prince of North Wales

3. Ellen of Wales = Sir Robert de Quincy, son of Saire de Quincy, 1st Earl of Winchester, Magna Carta surety, and Margaret de Beaumont, SETH

4. Hawise de Quincy = Sir Baldwin Wake

5. Sir Hugh Wake = Joan de Belauney

6. Mirabel Wake = Sir Thomas de Aspall/Aspale

7. Sir John de Aspall/Aspale = Katherine Pecche, SETH, who later married Sir Thomas Notbeam

8. Mirabel Aspall/Aspale = William Gedding

9. Thomas Gedding = Anne Astley

10. William Gedding = Margery Watkins

11. Constance Gedding = Henry Poley

12. Edmund Poley = Mirabel Garneys

13. Margaret Poley = Robert Knapp

14. John Knapp = Martha Bloys/Blosse

15. **Judith Knapp** of Mass. = William **Hubbard** (Hubert). A son was William Hubbard (Jr.), c. 1621-1704, noted Congregational clergyman and historian of New England, husband of Mary Rogers (?) and Mrs. Mary Giddings Pearce, widow of Samuel Pearce and daughter of George Giddings and Jane Lawrence of Mass., ARD, SETH.

Sources: *RA* 3: 349-53 (Knapp, Poley, Gedding, Aspale/Aspall), 4: 320-22 (Aspale/Aspall), 5: 287-89 (Wake), 5: 298-304 (Quincy, Wake), *GM* 3, pp. 437-43, *GGE*: 228, *NEHGR* 17 (1863): 46-47 (reprinted in *EO2*: 3: 23-24), and E.W. Day, *1000 Years of Hubbard History* (1895), pp. 167-69, 181-83 (with some mistakes or omissions); Walter C. Metcalfe, ed.,

The Royal Descents of 900 Immigrants

Visitations of Suffolk, 1561, 1577, 1612 (1882), pp. 148-49 (Knapp); Joan Corder, ed., *Visitations of Suffolk, 1561*, Part 1 (*HSPVS*, new ser., vol. 2, 1981), pp. 48, 121-24 (Poley); John Gage, *History and Antiquities of Suffolk, Thingoe Hundred* (1838), p. 47, and (Proceedings of the) *Suffolk Institute of Archaeology and Natural History* 20 (1929): 43-44 and chart opposite p. 46 (Poley, Gedding, Aspall/Aspale, Wake, Pecche), plus *TG* 10 (1989, published 1994): 3-6, 23-25, and *Calendar of the Charter Rolls 1234-1237* (1908), pp. 538-39, wherein Ellen of Wales is called niece ("nepte") by Henry III, King of England. This descent was first brought to my attention by Leslie Mahler and "improved" by Douglas Richardson.

The Royal Descents of 900 Immigrants

1. John "Lackland," King of England, d. 1216 = (2) Isabel of Angoulême
2. (illegitimate by —— de Warenne) Richard FitzRoy = Rohese of Dover
3. Lorette de Dover = Sir William Marmion
4. John Marmion, 1st Baron Marmion = Isabel ——
5. John Marmion, 2nd Baron Marmion = Maud Furnival
6. Joan Marmion = Sir John Bernacke
7. Maud Bernacke = Ralph Cromwell, 2nd Baron Cromwell
8. Maud Cromwell = Sir William FitzWilliam
9. Sir John FitzWilliam = Eleanor Greene
10. John FitzWilliam = Helen Villiers
11. Sir William FitzWilliam = Anne Hawes
12. Anne FitzWilliam = Sir Anthony Cooke (their daughters Mildred and Jane Cooke married respectively William Cecil, 1st Baron Burghley, the statesman and minister of Elizabeth I, and Sir Nicholas Bacon, the Lord Keeper and Lord Chancellor; a grandson was Francis Bacon, 1st Viscount St. Albans, the philosopher, scientist, and politician)
13. Sir Richard Cooke = Anna Caunton
14. Philippa Cooke = Hercules Meautys
15. Frances Meautys = Francis Shute, son of Robert Shute and Thomasine Burgoyne, SETH
16. Francis Shute = ——
17. Benjamin Shute = Patience (or Anne) Caryl
18. **Samuel Shute** (1662-1742), colonial governor of Mass., d. unm. His sister, Anne Shute, married Stephen Offley, SETH, and was the mother of Amelia Offley of Mass., wife of Sir Francis Bernard, 1st Bt. (1712-1779), barrister, colonial governor of N.J. and Mass., ARD, SETH.

The Royal Descents of 900 Immigrants

Sources: *Oxford DNB* (Shute and Bernard), *MCS5*, line 128A and sources cited therein, esp. *Lodge*, vol. 5, pp. 200-1; Walter C. Metcalfe, ed., *Visitations of Essex, 1552, 1558, 1570, 1612 and 1634*, vol. 1 (*HSPVS*, vol. 13, 1878), pp. 77, 247 (Meautys), 39 (Cooke), 198-99 (FitzWilliam); *PCF Yorkshire* (FitzWilliam pedigree); *RA* 5: 94 (Sir Anthony Cooke), 2: 676-79 (FitzWilliam), 2: 355-58 (Cromwell, Bernacke), 1: 343 (Bernacke), 4: 31-33 (Marmion), 1: 184-85 (Dover), and *AR8*, lines 210, 218, 26.

The Royal Descents of 900 Immigrants

1. John "Lackland," King of England, d. 1216 = (2) Isabel of Angoulême
2. (illegitimate by Clemence ——, possibly Clemence le Botiller, wife of Nicholas de Verdun) Joan Plantagenet = Llywelyn Fawr ab Iorwerth, Prince of North Wales
3. David, Prince of North Wales (Dafydd ap Llywelyn Fawr) = Isabel de Braose
4. (illegitimate by ——) Llywelyn ap Dafydd, constable of Rhuddlau = ——
5. Cynwrig ap Llywelyn = Angharad ferch Thomas ap Gwion
6. Dafydd Llwyd ap Cynwrig = Annes ferch Gwyn ap Madog
7. Mawd ferch Dafydd Llwyd = Dafydd Goch ap Trahaearn Goch ap Madog
8. Ieuan Goch ap Dafydd Goch = Efa ferch Einion ap Celynin
9. Maredudd ab Ieuan Goch = Morfudd ferch Gruffudd ap Llywelyn Fychan
10. Lleucu ferch Maredudd = Gruffudd ap Cynwrig ap Bleddyn Llwyd
11. Dafydd Llwyd ap Gruffudd = Gwen ferch Gruffudd Goch ab Ieuan
12. Dyddgu ferch Dafydd Llwyd = Llywelyn ap Gruffudd Llwyd ap Robin
13. Maredudd Llwyd ap Llywelyn = Jonet ferch Gwilym ap Llywelyn Llwyd
14. John ap Maredudd Llwyd = Margred ferch Morus Gethin ap Rhys
15. Maredudd Llwyd ap John = Jonet Conwy
16. George Lloyd, Bishop of Chester = Anne Wilkinson
17. **Anne Lloyd** of Conn. = (1) Thomas **Yale**, ARD, SETH (their three children came to Conn. with their mother and stepfather); (2) Theophilus **Eaton** (c. 1590-1657/8), colonial statesman and merchant, governor of the New Haven Colony.

Sources: *TAG* 52 (1976): 142-44; *Bartrum 1*, pp. 446-47, 867, 869, 512; *Bartrum 2*, pp. 975, 1288-89 (generations 1-15).

The Royal Descents of 900 Immigrants

1. John "Lackland," King of England, d. 1216 = (2) Isabel of Angoulême
2. (illegitimate by ——) Isabel FitzRoy = Sir Richard FitzIves
3. Sir William FitzRichard = Rose Bevyle
4. Isabel FitzWilliam = Sir Stephen de Beaupré
5. Sir Ralph de Beaupré = Margaret de Furneaux
6. Isabel de Beaupré = John de Longland
7. Margaret Longland = John Deviock
8. Margaret Deviock = John Stapleton
9. Margaret Stapleton = —— (John Stapleton?)
10. Mary Stapleton = Robert Montfort, son of Sir Baldwin Montfort (and Joan Vernon, daughter of Sir Richard Vernon and Jane ferch Rhys ap Gruffudd, SETH), son of Sir William Montfort (and Margaret Pecche), son of Sir Baldwin Montfort and Margaret de Clinton, daughter of John de Clinton, 3rd Baron Clinton (and Idonea de Say), son of John de Clinton, 2nd Baron Clinton (and Margery Corbet), son of John de Clinton, 1st Baron Clinton and Ida de Odingselles, SETH, daughter of Sir William de Odingselles and Ela FitzRobert, daughter of Sir Walter FitzRobert and Ida Longespee, daughter of William Longespee, Earl of Salisbury, and Ela, Countess of Salisbury, SETH.
11. Katherine Montfort = Sir George Booth, son of Sir William Booth and Maud Dutton, daughter of Sir John Dutton and Margaret Savage, daughter of Sir John Savage and Maud Swinnerton, SETH.
12. Sir William Booth = Ellen Montgomery
13. Jane Booth = Sir Thomas Holford, son of Sir John Holford and Margery Brereton, daughter of Ralph Brereton (and Joan ——), son of Randall Brereton and Emma Carrington, SETH.
14. Dorothy Holford = John Bruen

The Royal Descents of 900 Immigrants

15. John Bruen = Anne Fox
16. **Obadiah Bruen** of Conn. = Sarah Seeley.
17. John Bruen = Esther Lawrence
18. Sarah Bruen = Abraham Kitchell
19. Joseph Kitchell = Rachel Bates
20. Grace Kitchell = Samuel Ford, Jr.
21. Phebe Ford = Robert Marvin
22. Samuel Ross Marvin = Julia Anne Place
23. Jerome Place Marvin = Martha Anne Stokes
24. Mabel Marvin = Scott Pierce
25. Marvin Pierce = Pauline Robinson
26. Barbara Pierce = George Herbert Walker Bush (b. 1924), 41st U.S. President, SETH
27. George Walker Bush (b. 1946), 43rd U.S. President = Laura Lane Welch, SETH

Sources: *RA* 1: 585-88 (Bruen, Holford, Brereton), 1: 521-22 (Brereton), 1: 437-38 (Booth, Montfort), 4: 554-56 (Dutton, Savage), 3: 292-96 (Holand), 5: 474-77 (la Zouche), 3: 599-610 (Longespee), 4: 141-43 (Montfort), 2: 634-41 (Stapleton, Deviock, Longland, de Beaupré, FitzWilliam, FitzRichard, FitzIves, FitzRoy, and sources cited therein esp.), 2: 259-65 (Clinton), 4: 272-73 (Odingselles), 5: 280-82 (Vernon), *AR8*, lines 30-33, 86, 122, *TAG* 26 (1950): 12-25; *CP* 10:344, note b (for Margaret Pecche) and John Fetherston, ed., *Visitation of Warwick, 1619* (*HSPVS*, vol. 12, 1877), p. 56 (for Mary Stapleton). The last two items were first brought to my attention by Clyde A. Bridger.

The Royal Descents of 900 Immigrants

1. John "Lackland," King of England, d. 1216 = (2) Isabel of Angoulême
2. (illegitimate by Clemence ——, possibly Clemence le Botiller, wife of Nicholas de Verdun) Joan Plantagenet = Llywelyn Fawr ab Iorwerth, Prince of North Wales
3. David, Prince of North Wales (Dafydd ap Llywelyn Fawr) = Isabel de Braose
4. (illegitimate by ——) Annes ferch Dafydd = Elise ab Iorwerth ab Owain Brogyntyn

5. Madog ab Elise = (1) ——; (2) —— ferch Llywelyn
6. (maternity uncertain) Margred ferch Madog = Ithel ap Gwrgeneu Fychan
7. Einion ab Ithel = Mallt ferch Maredudd Ddu
8. Margred ferch Einion = Maredudd ab Ieuan
9. John ap Maredudd = Gwenhwyfar ferch Gronwy ab Ieuan
10. Elen ferch John = Howel Vaughan
11. Mary Vaughan = Maurice Owen
12. Richard Maurice (Owen) = Elen Llwyd
13. Maurice (Morris) Owen = Lucy Blaeney

5. Dafydd ab Elise = Myfanwy ferch Hwfa ab Iorwerth
6. Gruffudd ap Dafydd = ——
7. Myfanwy ferch Gruffudd = Robin ap Robert
8. Gwenhwyfar ferch Robin = Ieuan ap Hywel
9. Maud ferch Ieuan = Tudur ap Gruffudd Fychan
10. Lowri ferch Tudur = Gruffudd ab Einion
11. Tudur ap Gruffudd = Gwenhwyfar Stanley
12. Margred ferch Tudur = Hywel ap Rhys
13. Janet ferch Hywel = Owain ap John
14. Elsbeth ferch Owain = Thomas ap Humphrey
15. Humphrey Wynne = Elizabeth Herbert

The Royal Descents of 900 Immigrants

14. Rondle/Randle Owen = 16. Elen Wen/Wynn

15,17. Elizabeth Owen = Thomas ap John (ap Morgan ap Gwilym)

16,18. John Jones = Elizabeth ferch Humphrey ap Thomas

17,19. Thomas Jones = Eleanor Evans

18,20. Ellen/Ellinor Jones = Titus Evans of N.Y. Their younger daughters, Mary and Ellinor Evans, also immigrated to N.Y., married Samuel Williams (and William Locke) and James Ward Higgins respectively and left issue but no NDTPS.

19,21. **Jane Evans** of N.Y. = John **Dodge**. Their descendants include genealogist Carl Boyer, 3rd, and Organic Online founder and partners Jonathan Banks Nelson and Matthew Sherwood Nelson.

Sources: *AL 3, passim*, esp. pp. 237 (and 126-69), 244-47, 340-42, 415-43, 702-11, *AL 4, passim*, and Carl Boyer 3rd, *Medieval Welsh Ancestors of Certain Americans* (2004), *passim*, esp. pp. 162-64, 273-75, 206-9, 7, 58-59, 279-80, 24, 27-28, 30, 59-60, 174, 266, 36, 364-65, 253, 300-2, 306-7, with many references to *Bartrum 1* and *2*. This example of a "modern" Welsh immigrant (Mrs. Jane Evans Dodge was born in 1781 and died in 1860) linked to *Bartrum* will, I hope, inspire much similar research.

The Royal Descents of 900 Immigrants

1. John "Lackland," King of England, d. 1216 = Isabel of Angoulême
2. (illegitimate by —— de Warenne) Richard Fitzroy = Rohese of Dover
3. Isabel de Dover (or de Chilham) = Sir Maurice Berkeley
4. Thomas Berkeley, 1st Baron Berkeley = Joan Ferrers
5. Maurice Berkeley, 2nd Baron Berkeley = Eve la Zouche, daughter of Eudo la Zouche and Milicent de Cantilupe, SETH
6. Thomas Berkeley, 3rd Baron Berkeley = Katherine de Clivedon
7. Sir John Berkeley = Elizabeth Betteshorne
8. Elizabeth Berkeley = John Sutton, 1st Baron Dudley, SETH
9. John Dudley = Elizabeth Bramshot
10. Elizabeth Dudley (sister of Edmund Dudley, minister of Henry VII) = Thomas Ashburnham
11. Helen Ashburnham = Sir Walter Hendley
12. Anne Hendley = Richard Covert
13. John Covert = Charity Bowes
14. Anne Covert = Sir Walter Covert, a cousin
15. **Elizabeth Covert** (died in England) = John **Fenwick** (1618-1683), colonist, founder of Salem, N.J., ARD, SETH.

Sources: *Ardingly*, pp. 183-86 (Covert); W.B. Bannerman, ed., *Visitations of Kent, 1530-1, 1574, and 1592*, vol. 2 (*HSPVS*, vol. 75, 1924), p. 104 (Henley), and *Visitations of Sussex, 1530 and 1633-4* (*HSPVS*, vol. 53, 1905), p. 18 (Ashburnham); Dean Dudley, *The History of the Dudley Family* (1886-98), esp. p. 60 (Elizabeth Dudley); *AR8*, lines 81, 39, 26, *MCS5*, lines 149B, 80A, 80, 88, *TG* 5 (1984): 131-39, 154-56, and *RA* 2: 340-44 (Covert, Hendley, Ashburnham, Dudley), 5: 101-4 (Sutton), 2: 589-91 (Berkeley), 1: 326-34 (Berkeley), 1: 184-85 (Dover).

The Royal Descents of 900 Immigrants

1. John "Lackland," King of England, d. 1216 = (2) Isabel of Angoulême

2. (illegitimate by Clemence ——, possibly Clemence le Botiller, wife of Nicholas de Verdun) Joan Plantagenet = Llywelyn Fawr ab Iorwerth, Prince of North Wales

3. David, Prince of North Wales (Dafydd ap Llywelyn Fawr) = Isabel de Braose

4. (illegitimate by ——) Annes ferch Dafydd = Elise ab Iorwerth ab Owain Brogyntyn

5. Madog ab Elise = (1) ——; (2) —— ferch Llywelyn

6. (maternity uncertain) Efa ferch Madog = Gruffudd ap Llywelyn ap Cynwrig

7. Einion ap Gruffudd = Tangwystl ferch Rhydderch ab Ieuan Llwyd

8. Ieuan ab Einion = Angharad ferch Dafydd

9. Mali ferch Ieuan = Dafydd ap Rhys ab Ieuan

10. Lowri ferch Dafydd = Gruffudd ap Hywel ap Madog

11. Margred ferch Gruffudd = Morus ap Gruffudd ab Ieuan

12. Thomas ap Morus = —— (Bartrum gives him only a daughter, Jonet Anwyl, by Catrin ferch Edward ap Gruffudd)

13. Robert Thomas Morris = ——

14. Richard Roberts = Margaret Evans

15. **John Roberts** of (Pencoyd, lower Merion) Pa. = Gainor Roberts of Pa., ARD, SETH.

Sources: *Merion*, pp. 100-5 (generations 11-15); *CRFP*, vol. 1, pp. 451-54 (generations 5-15); *Bartrum 1*, pp. 446-47, 51, 727-28, *Bartrum 2*, pp. 117, 807, 803 (generations 1-12). Further research should be undertaken to confirm the parentage of Robert Thomas Morris.

The Royal Descents of 900 Immigrants

1. John "Lackland," King of England, d. 1216 = (2) Isabel of Angoulême
2. (illegitimate by Clemence ——, possibly Clemence le Botiller, wife of Nicholas de Verdun) Joan Plantagenet = Llywelyn Fawr ab Iorwerth, Prince of North Wales
3. David, Prince of North Wales (Dafydd ap Llywelyn Fawr) = Isabel de Braose
4. (illegitimate by ——) Annes ferch Dafydd = Elise ab Iorwerth ab Owain Brogyntyn
5. Madog ab Elise = (1) ——; (2) —— ferch Llywelyn
6. (maternity uncertain) Lleucu ferch Madog = Gronwy Llwyd ab Y Penwyn
7. Margred ferch Gronwy Llwyd = Hywel y Gadair ap Gruffudd ap Madog
8. Gronwy ap Hywel y Gadair = (1) Gwen ferch Gruffudd; (2) —— ferch Gronwy
9. (maternity uncertain) Tudur ap Gronwy = Gwerful ferch Ieuan ab Einion
10. (not by Gwerful) Mali ferch Tudur = Madog ab Ieuan
11. Dafydd ap Madog = Mali ferch Gruffudd (Dafydd and Mali left two daughters and a son, Thomas, according to Bartrum, but no Dafydd Fychan)
12. Dafydd Fychan ap Dafydd = ——
13. Huw ap Dafydd Fychan = ——
14. Ellis ap Huw = ——
15. William Ellis = ——
16. William ap William = ——
17. **John Williams** of Pa. = (1) Mary Evans; (2) Mrs. Catherine Griffith Morris Edwards, SETH (no children by 2).

Sources: *CVR*, pp. 301-5 (generations 10-17); *Bartrum 1*, pp. 446-47, 51, 694, 751-52, *Bartrum 2*, p. 155 (generations 1-11). Further research should be undertaken to confirm the last seven generations of this descent (the immigrant's patrilineal descent from Dafydd ap Madog).

The Royal Descents of 900 Immigrants

1. John "Lackland," King of England, d. 1216 = (2) Isabel of Angoulême

2. (illegitimate by Clemence ——, possibly Clemence le Botiller, wife of Nicholas de Verdun) Joan Plantagenet = Llywelyn Fawr ab Iorwerth, Prince of North Wales

3. David, Prince of North Wales (Dafydd ap Llywelyn Fawr) = Isabel de Braose

4. (illegitimate by ——) Llywelyn ap Dafydd, constable of Rhuddlau = ——

5. Cynwrig ap Llywelyn = Angharad ferch Thomas ap Gwion

6. Dafydd Llwyd ap Cynwrig = Annes ferch Gwyn ap Madog

7. Mawd ferch Dafydd Llwyd = Dafydd Goch ap Trahaearn Goch ap Madog

8. Ieuan Goch ap Dafydd Goch = Efa ferch Einion ap Celynin

9. Morfudd ferch Ieuan Goch = Maredudd ap Hywel ap Tudur

10. Ieuan ap Maredudd = Lleucu ferch Hywel ap Meurig Fychan

11. Maredudd ab Ieuan = Margred ferch Einion ab Ithel

12. John ap Maredudd = Gwenhwyfar ferch Gronwy ab Ieuan

13. Morus ap John = Angharad ferch Elise ap Gruffudd

14. Margred ferch Morus = Maredudd ab Ieuan ap Robert

15. Jane ferch Maredudd = Cadwaladr ap Robert

16. Hywel ap Cadwaladr (Hywel Fychan) = ——

17. Robert ap Hywel = ——

18. Cadwaladr ap Robert = ——

19. **Robert Cadwalader** of Pa. = Jane John of Pa., ARD, SETH (their children and descendants took the surname Roberts).

Sources: *WFP* 2, "Roberts of Gwynedd," esp. pp. 24-26, 43-46 (generations 15-19); *Bartrum 1*, pp. 446-47, 867, 457, *Bartrum 2*, pp. 845-47, 851 (generations 1-15).

The Royal Descents of 900 Immigrants

1. John "Lackland," King of England, d. 1216 = (2) Isabel of Angoulême
2. (illegitimate by ——) Isabel FitzRoy = Sir Richard FitzIves
3. Sir William FitzRichard = Rose Bevyle
4. Isabel FitzWilliam = Sir Stephen de Beaupré
5. Sir Ralph de Beaupré = Margaret de Furneaux
6. Isabel de Beaupré = John Longland
7. Joan Longland = John Roynon
8. Joan Roynon = Hugh Malet, son of Baldwin Malet and Amice Lyffe, daughter of Richard Lyffe and Margery Stawell, daughter of Matthew Stawell (and Eleanor Merton), son of Geoffrey Stawell (and Juliana Gastelin), son of Geoffrey Stawell and Joan de Columbers, daughter of John de Columbers (and Alice Peneshurst), son of Philip de Columbers and Egeline Courtenay, daughter of Sir Robert Courtenay and Mary de Vernon, SETH
9. Thomas Malet = Joan Wadham
10. William Malet = Alice Young
11. Hugh Malet = Isabel Michell
12. Elizabeth Malet = Thomas Ivye
13. Judith Ivye = Anthony Prater/Prather
14. Thomas Prater/Prather = Margaret Quintyne
15. **Thomas Prather** of Va. = Mary (Powell?)
16. Jonathan Prather = Jane (MacKay?)
17. Jonathan Prather, Jr. = Elizabeth Bigger
18. Anne Prather = Henry Odell
19. Thomas Odell = Keziah Offutt
20. Eleanor Odell = Benjamin Jacob
21. Martha Eleanor Jacob = Nathaniel Thomas Halley
22. Martha Ellen Halley = James Fulford

The Royal Descents of 900 Immigrants

23. Mary Eleanor Fulford = William Henry Bell

24. Sarah Eleanor Bell = Wilburn Juriston Smith

25. Wilburn Edgar Smith = Frances Allethea Murray

26. (Eleanor) Rosalyn Smith = James Earl Carter, Jr., b. 1924, 39th U.S. President, gov. of Georgia, SETH

Sources: Thomas Benjamin Hertzel, *The Royal Descents of Judith Ivye, Wife of Anthony Prater* (2015), esp. pp. v, vii, 1, 3-6, 170-71 and among sources cited therein John W. Prather, *Praters in Wiltshire, 1480-1670*, vol. 1 (1987), esp. pp. 22, 43-44, 51-56, 156-57, and *Prater, Prather, Prator, Praytor in America, 1620-1800, 1-5 Generations*, vol. 2 (1994), pp. 5-9, 11-12, 18-19, 42, 118 (generations 11-21), *HSF* 6: 21-23, and Arthur Malet, *Notices of an English Branch of the Malet Family* (1885), esp. pp. 35-36, 38-44, *RA* 2: 634-38 (generations 2-9), 1: 43-58 (King John and Isabel FitzRoy). For the line to Mrs. Carter, not widely known, see Jeff(rey) Carter, *Ancestors of Jimmy and Rosalyn Carter* (2012), pp. 142-43, 145, 147, 149-52, 162, 198-200, and sources cited therein, esp. a manuscript family history by Mrs. Sarah Eleanor Bell Smith, Mrs. Carter's grandmother, and Sharon J. Doliante, *Maryland and Virginia Colonials* (1991), pp. 651-54, 714, 595-99 (Prather, Odell, Jacob to Mrs. Halley). In *TAG* 87 (2014-15): 320, Nathaniel Lane Taylor urges caution in accepting the patrilineal Prater/Prather descent at generations 13-16.

The Royal Descents of 900 Immigrants

1. John "Lackland," King of England, d. 1216 = (2) Isabel of Angoulême
2. (illegitimate by —— de Warenne) Richard FitzRoy = Rohese of Dover
3. Richard de Dover = Maud of Angus
4. Isabel de Dover = David Strathbogie, 8th Earl of Atholl
5. John Strathbogie, 9th Earl of Atholl = Marjory of Mar
6. David Strathbogie, 10th Earl of Atholl = Joan Comyn
7. Sir Aymer de Atholl = Mary ——
8. Isabel de Atholl = Sir Ralph Eure
9. Margaret Eure = Sir John Pudsey
10. Sir Ralph Pudsey = Margaret Tunstall
11. Sir John Pudsey = Grace Hamerton
12. Henry Pudsey = Margaret Conyers
13. Rowland Pudsey = Edith Hore
14. William Pudsey = Eleanor Montfort, daughter of Thomas Montfort and Elizabeth Gresley, daughter of Sir John Gresley and Anne Stanley, SETH
15. Robert Pudsey = Eleanor Harman
16. George Pudsey = Maud Cotton
17. Dorothy Pudsey = Gawen Grosvenor, son of Walter Grosvenor and Joyce Fowke, daughter of Roger Fowke and Margery Morton, daughter of Richard Morton and Cecily Charlton, daughter of William Charlton (and Alicia Horde), son of Richard Charlton and Anne Mainwaring, SETH
18. Winifred Grosvenor = Thomas Corbin, a descendant of Amy de Gaveston via Faunt, Vincent, Grimsby, Moton, Malory and Driby
19. **Henry Corbin** of Va. = Mrs. Alice Eltonhead Burnham of Va., ARD, SETH.

The Royal Descents of 900 Immigrants

13. Margaret Pudsey (sister of Rowland) = Thomas Wandesford

14. Christopher Wandesford = Anne Norton, daughter of Sir John Norton and Margaret Warde, daughter of Sir Roger Warde and Joan Tunstall, daughter of Sir Thomas Tunstall and Eleanor FitzHugh, daughter of Henry FitzHugh, 3rd Baron FitzHugh, and Elizabeth Marmion, SETH

15. Susan Wandesford = Francis Lascelles, possibly, but the chronology is very tight, the Francis, fifth son (per his brother, Sir Thomas Lascelles, and nephew, William Lascelles, in visitations) of Francis Lascelles and Anne Thwaites, daughter (a second Anne, almost certainly the younger) of William Thwaites and Elizabeth Redman (or Redmayne), daughter of Thomas Redman (or Redmayne) and Anne Scrope, daughter of Hon. Robert Scrope (and Katherine Zouche), son of Henry Scrope, 4th Baron Scrope of Bolton, and Elizabeth Scrope, SETH

16. Anne Lascelles = Edward Hutton

17. Margaret Hutton = Robert Joplin(g)

18. Arthur Joplin(g) = Mary Featherstonehalgh

19. **Ralph Joplin**(g) of Va., patrilineal immigrant ancestor of singer and rock star Janis Lyn Joplin, = ——.

Sources: *RA* 2: 296-97 (Corbin, Faunt), 4: 432-36 (Grosvenor, Pudsey), 2: 525-26 (Eure), 1: 184-92 (Atholl, Strathbogie, Dover), 4: 144 (Montfort), 4: 451-56 (to Piers de Gaveston via Faunt, Vincent, Grimsby, Moton, Mallory, and Driby); *Ligon*, vol. 1, pp. 160-63, 806-11 (Corbin); *GVFVM* 2: 313 esp. (Grosvenor), plus *Shaw*, vol. 2, part I, p. 60 (Fowke), and George Grazebrook and J.P. Rylands, eds. *Visitation of Shropshire, 1623* (*HSPVS*, vols. 28-29, 1889), pp. 368 (Morton), 101 (Charlton); John Fetherston, ed., *Visitation of Warwick, 1619* (*HSPVS*, vol. 12, 1887), pp. 250-51, W.H. Turner, ed., *Visitations of Oxfordshire, 1566, 1574, 1634* (*HSPVS*, vol. 5, 1871), pp. 248-49, Sir William Dugdale, *The Antiquities of Warwickshire*, 2nd ed., vol. 2 (1730), p. 923 (link between 12 and 13 above), *Foster's V of Yorkshire,* pp. 254, 564 (all Pudsey); *NHN* 12: 495, 497 (Eure), *SP* and *CP* (Atholl, Angus) and *TG*, new ser., 22 (1906): 105-10 (Richard Fitz Roy and his heirs); *RA* 5: 218-20 (Wandesford, Norton, Warde, Tunstall, FitzHugh), Hardy Bartram McCall, *Story of the*

The Royal Descents of 900 Immigrants

Family of Wandesforde of Kirklington and Castlecomer (1904), pp. 28-32, Joseph Foster, ed., *Visitations of Durham, 1575, 1615, 1666* (1887), p. 181 (Hutton, which includes Margaret, daughter of Edward and Anne), plus Lascelles, Hutton and Joplin(g) research of Neil D. Thompson of Salt Lake City for James R. Bedwell of Vancouver, Washington. Neil found or confirmed the 10 Feb. 1673/4 birth of Ralph Jopling in Wolsingham, Durham, the 19 April 1653 marriage of Arthur Joplin and Mary Fetherstonhalgh in Brancepeth, Durham, the 26 April 1618 marriage of Robert Joplin and Margaret Hutton at Durham St. Mary le Bow, the 30 Sept. 1593 baptism of Margaret Hutton at St. Mary in the South Bailey, Durham, and the 30 Nov. 1585 marriage of Edward Hutton and Anne Lascelles in Kirklington, Yorkshire, and deduced Lascelles kinships from location and chronology. For the possible Scrope descent, which Mr. Thompson accepted, but I think just barely possible, see Foster's *V of Yorkshire*, p. 61 (Lascelles), J.W. Walker, ed., *Yorkshire Pedigrees, T-Z* (*HSPVS*, vol. 96, 1944), pp. 367-68 (Thwaites), W[illiam] Greenwood, *The Redmans of Levens and Harewood* (1905), pp. 117-19 and *RA* 5: 167-68 (Scrope).

Ralph Joplin(g), a late addition to this work, is charted here, rather than in a section near this book's end, among "Immigrants Whose Royal Descents Were Received or Developed After Much of This Volume Had Been Indexed" since he shared twelve generations of the descent from King John to Henry Corbin. In its correct order, this chart would follow that for Mrs. Anne Wolseley Calvert and her niece, Mrs. Mary Wolseley Brooke, both of Md.

The Royal Descents of 900 Immigrants

1. William I the Lion, King of Scotland, d. 1214 = Ermengarde de Beaumont
2. (illegitimate by a daughter of Richard Avenal) Isabel of Scotland = Robert de Ros, Magna Carta surety
3. Sir William de Ros = Lucy FitzPiers
4. Sir William de Ros = Eustache FitzHugh
5. Lucy de Ros = Sir Robert Plumpton
6. Sir William Plumpton = Christiana Mowbray
7. Alice Plumpton = (1) Sir Richard Sherburne; (2) Sir John Boteler
8. (by 1) Margaret Sherburne = Richard Bayley
9. Richard Bayley alias Sherburne = Agnes Harington, daughter of Sir Nicholas Harington and Isabel English, SETH
10. Richard Sherburne = Matilda Hamerton
11. Isabel Sherburne = John Towneley
12. Lawrence Towneley = ──
13. Henry Towneley = ──
14. Lawrence Towneley = Helen Hesketh
15. Lawrence Towneley = Margaret Hartley
16. Lawrence Towneley = Jennet Halstead
17. **Mary Towneley** of Va. = Augustine **Warner**.
18. Augustine Warner, Jr. = Mildred Reade
19. Mildred Warner = Lawrence Washington
20. Augustine Washington = Mary Ball
21. George Washington (1731/2-1799), 1st U.S. President = Mrs. Martha Dandridge Custis

17. Lawrence Towneley (brother of Mrs. Warner) = Alice Calvert

The Royal Descents of 900 Immigrants

18. **Lawrence Towneley** of Va. = Sarah Warner, his first cousin, daughter of Augustine Warner and Mary Towneley of Va., see above.

17. Elizabeth Towneley (sister of Mrs. Warner) = Christopher Smith
18. **Lawrence Smith**, almost certainly the immigrant to Va. = Mary Debnam. Mary Towneley, a second sister of Mrs. Warner, married Samuel Hoyle and left a son, Edward Hoyle, who also immigrated to Va. and married Ann Debnam but left no NDTPS.

12. Grace Towneley (sister of Lawrence) = Roger Nowell
13. John Nowell = Elizabeth Kay
14. Laurence Nowell, Dean of Lichfield = Mary ——
15. Alexander Nowell = Sarah Smyth
16. **Increase Nowell** (1593-1655), secretary of Mass. = Mrs. Parnell Gray Parker, daughter of Thomas Gray and Katherine Myles, who later married Rowland Coytmore, SETH.

14. Elizabeth Nowell (sister of Laurence) = Thomas Whitaker
15. William Whitaker, master of St. John's College, Cambridge = —— Culverwell
16. **Alexander Whitaker** (c. 1585-1616/7) of Va., Anglican clergyman, d. unm.
16. **Jabez Whitaker** of Va. = Mary Bourchier of Va., ARD, SETH.

11. Agnes Sherburne (sister of Isabel) = Henry Rushton (Rishton)
12. Nicholas Rushton = Margaret Radcliffe
13. Agnes Rushton = Richard Worthington
14. Peter Worthington = Isabel Anderton
15. Isabel Worthington = Robert Worden (Werden)

The Royal Descents of 900 Immigrants

16. **Peter Worden** of Mass. = Mrs. Margaret Grice Wall.
17. Peter Worden, Jr. = Mary ——
18. Mary Worden = John Burgess
19. Martha Burgess = Samuel Storrs, Jr.
20. Mary Storrs = Joseph Jacob, Jr.
21. Sarah Jacob = Elias Birchard
22. (illegitimate by Sarah and —— Cornwall) Roger Cornwall alias Birchard = Drusilla Austin
23. Sophia Birchard = Rutherford Hayes, Jr.
24. Rutherford Birchard Hayes (1822-1893), 19th U.S. president = Lucy Ware Webb

8. (by 2) Alice Boteler (full sister of Sir William) = John Gerard
9. Constance Gerard = Sir Alexander Standish
10. Oliver Standish = ——
11. Grace Standish = Ralph Faircloth
12. Lawrence Faircloth = Elizabeth ——
13. Thomas Faircloth = Millicent Barr
14. Mary Faircloth = Thomas Allen
15. **Jane Allen**, who died in England = Rev. Peter **Bulkeley** of Mass.
16. Edward Bulkeley = Lucian ——
17. Peter Bulkeley = Rebecca Wheeler
18. Rebecca Bulkeley = Jonathan Prescott, Jr.
19. Abel Prescott = Abigail Brigham
20. Lucy Prescott, sister of Dr. Samuel Prescott, who completed Paul Revere's "Midnight Ride" of 19 April 1775 = Jonathan Fay, Jr.
21. Samuel Prescott Phillips Fay = Harriet Howard

The Royal Descents of 900 Immigrants

22. Samuel Howard Fay = Susan Shellman
23. Harriet Eleanor Fay = James Smith Bush
24. Samuel Prescott Bush = Flora Sheldon
25. Prescott Sheldon Bush, U.S. senator = Dorothy Walker
26. George Herbert Walker Bush (b. 1924), 41st U.S. President = Barbara Pierce, SETH
27. George Walker Bush (b. 1946), 43rd U.S. President = Laura Lane Welch, SETH

Sources: *RA* 5: 178-81 (Towneley, Sherburne), 1: 444-45 (Alice Plumpton), 4: 386-89 (Plumpton), 4: 489-90 (de Ros), 4: 583-90 (William I, the Lion), 5: 359-60 (Whitaker, Nowell), 5: 396-97 (Worden, Worthington, Rushton), 1: 109-11 (Allen, Faircloth, Standish), 3: 82 (Gerard), 1: 444-45 (Boteler); *GVFVM* 5: 538-90; *Baines 1,* vol. 3, chart between pp. 572 and 573 (Sherburne) plus 2004 and 2005 website articles by Douglas Hickling of Piedmont, Calif., "Who Were the Parents of Richard Sherburne's wife Agnes, and of Isabel (Sherburne) Towneley and Agnes (Sherburne) Rushton?" and "Which John de Mowbray was the Brother of Christiana de Plumpton?," which for Haringtons cite esp. T.D. Whitaker, *A(n) History of Richmondshire in the North Riding of the County of York*, vol. 2 (1823), p. 250; *AR8*, line 170; David A. Avant, Jr., *Some Southern Colonial Families*, vol. 1 (1983), pp. 316-25 and *TVG* 40 (1996): 5-6 (Lawrence Smith); *Stephen Bull*, pp. 91-92 (corrected by *GMB*, pp. 1342-46) and *Oxford DNB* notices for Alexander (Dean of St. Paul's, brother of Laurence), Increase and Laurence Nowell; Sarah C.W. Allen, *Our Children's Ancestry* [Whitaker family] (1935), pp. 31-65 (Whitaker, Nowell, Towneley) and *DAB* (Alexander Whitaker); George L. Bolton, *Worden Origins: A Study of the Origins of the Immigrant Peter Worden of Lancashire, England* (1997), pp. 15, 23-29, 55-65, 77-83, 85-100, 107-16, 119-24, 131-34, P.M. Worthington, *The Worthington Families in Medieval England* (1985), pp. 118-19, 131-39, 171-75, and T.D. Whitaker, J.G. Nichols, and Rev. P.A. Lyons, *An* [sic] *History of the Original Parish of Whalley and Honor of Clitheroe*, 4th ed., vol. 2 (1876), p. 298 (Rushton); *PCF Lancashire* (Whitaker, Nowell, and Towneley pedigrees); William Beamont, *Annals of the Lords of Warrington, Part 1* (Publications of the Chetham Society, vol. 86, 1872), pp. 199-262 (Boteler); *MCS5*, lines 116,

The Royal Descents of 900 Immigrants

116A, *Bulkeley*, pp. 38-51, *TAG* 42 (1966): 129-35, and F.L. Weis, *The Families of Standish, Lancashire, England* (1959), pp. 14-15 (Mrs. Bulkeley). In addition, Jerome E. Anderson has assembled many English Nowell documents that add considerably to data in print and support the above descent for Increase Nowell. The Peter Worden descent was developed and brought to my attention by Sara B. Doherty. For Sherburne, Towneley, Nowell and Whitaker (pedigrees and/or biographical notices), see *History of the Original Parish of Whalley,* as above, 4th ed., vol. 2, esp. pp. 475-76, 255-56, chart between 40 and 41, 204, 535-40, 558-64.

The Royal Descents of 900 Immigrants

1. William I the Lion, King of Scotland, d. 1214 = Ermengarde de Beaumont

2. (illegitimate by a daughter of Richard Avenal) Isabel of Scotland = Robert de Ros, Magna Carta surety

3. Sir William de Ros = Lucy FitzPiers

4. Sir Robert de Ros = Isabel d'Aubigny

5. Isabel de Ros = Walter de Fauconberge, 2nd Baron Fauconberge

6. Anice de Fauconberge = Sir Nicholas Engaine

7. John Engaine, 2nd Baron Engaine = Joan Peveral

8. Elizabeth Engaine = Sir Laurence Pabenham

9. Katherine Pabenham = (1) Sir William Cheyne/Cheney; (2) Sir Thomas Aylesbury

10. (by 1) Laurence Cheney = Elizabeth Cokayne, daughter of John Cokayne and Ida Grey, daughter of Reginald de Grey, 2nd Baron Grey of Ruthyn, and Eleanor le Strange, SETH

11. Elizabeth Cheney = (1) Sir Frederick Tilney (parents of Elizabeth Tilney, wife of Sir Humphrey Bourchier and Thomas Howard, 2nd Duke of Norfolk, all SETH, and matrilineal great-grandmother of Elizabeth I, Queen of England); (2) Sir John Saye

12. (by 2) Elizabeth Saye = Thomas Sampson

13. Margery Sampson = Robert Felton

14. Thomas Felton = Cecily Seckford

15. Cecily Felton = John Stratton. Cecily was thus a third cousin of the half blood of Elizabeth I, Queen of England. Cecily was also a full third cousin of Edward VI, King of England, since Ann Saye, a sister of Elizabeth, married Sir Henry Wentworth, SETH, and was the mother of Margery Wentworth, wife of Sir John Seymour and mother of Queen Jane Seymour.

16. Thomas Stratton = Dorothy Nicolls (their son, Joseph Stratton, mariner, settled in James City, Va., married Joan――, and may have left descendants through his possible son, Edward Stratton of Henrico Co.).

The Royal Descents of 900 Immigrants

17. John Stratton = Anne Derehaugh of Mass., ARD, SETH

18. **John Stratton** of Mass. = —— (a daughter, Anne Stratton, married William Lake and William Stevens).

18. **Elizabeth Stratton** of Mass. = **John Thorndike** (Dorothy Stratton, a sister of John and Elizabeth, also came to Mass.; her later history is uncertain, but she perhaps married William Pester).

10. (by 2) Isabel Aylesbury = Sir Thomas Chaworth

11. Catherine Chaworth = William Leke

12. Thomas Leke = Margaret Fox

13. Elizabeth Leke (SETH, wife firstly of John Hardwick and mother of "Bess of Hardwick," Countess of Shrewsbury, and Mary Hardwick, SETH, wife of Richard Wingfield) = (2) Ralph Leech

14. Margaret Leech = Richard Slater

15. Elizabeth Slater = John Digby

16. Elizabeth Digby = Gregory/George Walker

17. John Walker = Ursula Royston

18. **Dorothy Walker** of Va. = Roger **Jones**.

Sources: *RA* 5: 71-75 (Stratton, Felton, Sampson, Say, Tilney), 2: 160-62 (Cheney/Cheyne, Cokayne), 2: 505-8 (Pabenham, Engaine), 2: 549 (Fauconberg), 4: 487-91 (de Ros), 3: 125-26 (Grey), 3: 336-40 (Howard), 2: 56-57 (Boleyn), 4: 219-20 (Wentworth), 4: 618-20 (Seymour), 4: 377 (Leech/Leche), 3: 554-55 (Leeke, Chaworth), 1: 265-66 (Aylesbury); *NEHGR* 135 (1981): 287-90, reprinted in *EO* 2: 3: 378-81 (Stratton), 160 (2006): 101-8 (Harold Wheeler [Hal] Bradley), Harriet Russell Stratton, *A Book of Strattons*, vol. 1 (1908), pp. 43-60, 75-83 and chart opposite p. 42, M.H. Stafford, Scott C. Steward and J. Bradley Arthaud, *A Thorndike Family History* (2000), pp. 17-28. See also Walter C. Metcalfe, ed., *Visitations of Suffolk, 1561, 1577 and 1612* (1882), p. 190 (Felton), and *Proceedings of the Suffolk Institute of Archaeology and Natural History* 4

The Royal Descents of 900 Immigrants

(1874): 14-41 (Felton, Sampson); Judge L.H. Jones, *Captain Roger Jones of London and Virginia, Some of His Antecedents and Descendants* (1891), pp. 4-34 (esp. 31-34), 196-200 (Jones, Walker), *FMG*, pp. 1006-7 (Walker) and *Paver's Marriage Licences* (*Yorkshire Archaeological Society, Record Series*, vol. 40, 1909), p. 152 (1639 marriage of John Walker of Mansfield, age 28, and Ursula Royston, spinster, age 21, of Tadcaster), G.D. Squibb, ed., *Visitations of Nottinghamshire, 1662-64* (*HSPVS*, new ser., vol. 5, 1986), pp. 70-71 (Digby); M.P. Siddons, ed., *Visitation of Herefordshire, 1634* (*HSPVS*, new ser., vol. 15, 2002), pp. 119-20 (Slater/Slaughter) and 1575 will (Archdeaconry of Lincoln Wills, vol. 1575, pt. 1, 139 [FHL #198834]) of Richard Slater/Slaughter; *The Topographer* 3 (1790-91): 317-18 (Leech of Chatsworth) and 1549/50 IPM of Ralph Leech/Leche. The Stratton/Felton/Sampson/Say descent was developed and brought to my attention by Dr. David A. Sandmire of Madison, Wisconsin, and the Walker/Digby/Slater/Leech/Leke/Chaworth/Aylesbury descent (generations 9-18) was developed and brought to my attention by John Anderson Brayton of Memphis, Tenn.

The Royal Descents of 900 Immigrants

1. William I the Lion, King of Scotland, d. 1214 = Ermengarde de Beaumont
2. (illegitimate by a daughter of Richard Avenal) Isabel of Scotland = Robert de Ros, Magna Carta surety
3. Sir Robert de Ros of Wark = ——
4. Robert de Ros of Wark = Margaret de Brus
5. Robert de Ros of Wark = Laura ——
6. Margaret de Ros = John Salvayn
7. Sir Gerard Salvayn = Agnes Mauleverer
8. John Salvayn = ——
9. Sir Gerard Salvayn = Alice ——
10. Muriel Salvayn = Sir Gerard Sotehill
11. Sir Gerard Sotehill = —— Percehay/Pereshay
12. Richard Sotehill = Agnes ——
13. Isabel Sotehill = Oliver Wentworth
14. William Wentworth = Ellen Gilby
15. Christopher Wentworth = Katherine Marbury, sister of Francis Marbury, husband of Bridget Dryden, SETH.
16. William Wentworth = Susanna Carter
17. **William Wentworth** of N.H. = (1) ——; (2) Elizabeth Knight.

16. Anne Wentworth (sister of William) = John Lawson
17. **Christopher Lawson** of Mass. = Elizabeth James.

Sources: Paul C. Reed, commissioned by Shirley Goodwin Bennett, undertook extensive research on this descent and an article or monograph is eagerly awaited. This line was also developed in a 15 Oct. 2001 posting on soc.genealogy.medieval by Michael Anne Guido, referring to (1) Chancery suits C1/593/45, C1/596/7 and C1/186/88, for proof that the wife of Oliver Wentworth was Isabel, daughter of Richard Sotehill

The Royal Descents of 900 Immigrants

(an item brought to my attention by Nathaniel Lane Taylor); (2) *Lincolnshire Pedigrees*, p. 915 and J.W. Walker, ed., *Yorkshire Pedigrees, G-S* (*HSPVS*, vol. 95, 1943), p. 342 (Sotehill); (3) *Surtees*, vol. 4, pt. 2, p. 118 (Salvayn); and (4) *NF1*, pp. 225-26, 228-29 (de Ros). Nat Taylor has also outlined and shown me lesser Wentworth-Lawson RDs, and note especially the possible descent from Alphonso IX, King of León, d. 1230, and Berengaria, Queen of Castile, d. 1246, pp. 647, 909, 948, 964 herein, via Sancha de Ayala, d. 1418, wife of Sir Walter Blount. See *AAP*, pp. 365-66, and *NEHGR* 152 (1998): 36, 39-44.

Note: The Sotehill-FitzWilliam-Cromwell descent suggested by p. 342 of Yorkshire Pedigrees G-S (and for the Cromwell descent from King John see p. 684 herein) was disproved by John P. Ravilious in a post of 15 Oct. 2001 ("Sothill Genealogy" on soc.genealogy.medieval). Parliament 1386-1421, vol. 4, p. 408, does not positively identify the parents of Sir Gerard Sotehill. Pages 342-45 of the cited Sotehill pedigree makes Henry Sotehill, Sir Gerard's alleged brother, the grandfather of the John Sotehill who married Elizabeth Plumpton, SETH.

The Royal Descents of 900 Immigrants

1. William I the Lion, King of Scotland, d. 1214 = Ermengarde de Beaumont
2. (illegitimate by a daughter of Richard Avenal) Isabel of Scotland = Robert de Ros, Magna Carta surety
3. Sir William de Ros = Lucy FitzPiers
4. Sir Robert de Ros = Isabel d'Aubigny
5. William de Ros, 1st Baron Ros of Helmsley = Maud Vaux
6. Agnes de Ros = Pain de Tibetot, 1st Baron Tibetot
7. John de Tibetot, 2nd Baron Tibetot = (1) Margaret Badlesmere
8. Robert de Tibetot, 3rd Baron Tibetot = Margaret Deincourt
9. Elizabeth de Tibetot = Sir Philip Despencer
10. Margery Despencer = Sir Roger Wentworth. Their son, Henry Wentworth, married Jane FitzSimon (a second wife; his first was Elizabeth Howard, SETH) and left a son, Sir Nicholas Wentworth, who married Jane Josselyn and was the father of Elizabethan Parliamentary leaders Paul and Peter Wentworth, the former of whom married Helen Agmondesham and left a daughter Helen Wentworth, wife of William Day. Wentworth Day, a son of these last, was probably the immigrant to Mass. who married Elizabeth Story, left children but no NDTPS, and probably returned to England.
11. Margaret Wentworth = Sir William Hopton
12. Margaret Hopton = Sir Philip Booth
13. Audrey Booth = Sir William Lytton
14. Sir Robert Lytton = Frances Calverley
15. Anne Lytton = Sir John Borlase
16. Anne Borlase = Sir Euseby Isham
17. William Isham = Mary Brett
18. **Henry Isham** of Va. = Mrs. Katherine Banks Royall.
19. Mary Isham = **William Randolph** (c. 1651-1711) of Va., planter, merchant, and colonial official, ARD, SETH.

The Royal Descents of 900 Immigrants

20. Isham Randolph = Jane Rogers
21. Jane Randolph = Peter Jefferson
22. Thomas Jefferson (1743-1826), 3rd U.S. President = 22. Mrs. Martha Wayles Skelton, his third cousin, see below

22. Mary Jefferson (sister of Thomas) = John Bolling (III), a great-great-great-grandson of Pocahontas and John Rolfe
23. Archibald Bolling = Catherine Payne
24. Archibald Bolling, Jr. = Anne E. Wigginton
25. William Holcombe Bolling = Sallie Spiers White
26. Edith Bolling = (1) Norman Galt; (2) (Thomas) Woodrow Wilson (1856-1924), 28th U.S. President

19. Anne Isham (sister of Mary) = Francis Epes (III)
20. Francis Epes (IV) = Sarah ——
21. Martha Epes = John Wayles
22. Martha Wayles = (1) Bathurst Skelton; (2) 22. Thomas Jefferson (1743-1826), 3rd U.S. President, her third cousin, see above. For Martha's Isham line see *AP&P*, pp. 263-64 and J.F. Dorman, *Ancestors and Descendants of Francis Epes I of Virginia (Epes-Eppes-Epps)*, vol. 1 (1992), pp. 150-53.

15. Elizabeth Lytton (sister of Anne) = Edward Barrett
16. Anne Barrett = Thomas Corbett
17. Catherine Corbett = Sir John Mede
18. Jane Mede = Thomas Talbot
19. **John Talbot** (c. 1645-1727) of N.J., Anglican missionary clergyman = (1) Isabel Jenney, ARD, SETH; (2) Mrs. Anne Herbert.

Sources: *RA* 3: 402-4 (Isham, Borlase, Lytton), 3: 684-85 (Lytton, Booth), 3: 314-15 (Hopton), 4: 216-18 (Wentworth, le Despencer), 5: 163-

The Royal Descents of 900 Immigrants

66 (Tibetot), 4: 487-93 (Ros), 1: 216-23 (Badlesmere, Clare), 3: 404-5 (Henry Wentworth); *TG* 9 (1988): 194-96, 223-25; *AR8*, lines 200, 65A, 89, 54, and *MCS5*, lines 2, 1, 117, 116, 74 (Isham — see also *Isham*, pp. 32-35, 44-45, 50-55; *TG*, new ser., 2 [1885]: 228-30 [Borlase]; and *Clutterbuck*, vol. 2, p. 377 [Lytton]). For John Talbot see *Oxford DNB*; A.W.H. Clarke and Arthur Campling, eds., *Visitation of Norfolk, 1664*, vol. 2 (*HSPVS*, vol. 86, 1934), p. 214 (Talbot); Walter C. Metcalfe, ed., *Visitations of Essex, 1552, 1558, 1570, 1612 and 1634*, vol. 1 (*HSPVS*, vol. 13, 1878), pp. 448 (Me[a]de), 146 (Barrett); Walter Rye, ed., *Visitations of Norfolk, 1563, 1589, and 1613* (*HSPVS*, vol. 32, 1891), pp. 84-85 (Corbett). For Wentworth Day of Mass., brought to my attention by Thomas S. Erwin, see *Wentworth* 1:26-29, W.H. Rylands, ed., *The Four Visitations of Berkshire, 1532, 1623, 1665-66*, vol. 1 (*HSPVS*, vol. 56, 1907), p. 83 (Day) and James Savage, *A Genealogical Dictionary of the First Settlers of New England*, 4 vols. (1860-62), 2: 28.

The Royal Descents of 900 Immigrants

1. William I the Lion, King of Scotland, d. 1214 = Ermengarde de Beaumont

2. (illegitimate by a daughter of Richard Avenal) Isabel of Scotland = Robert de Ros, Magna Carta surety

3. Sir William de Ros = Lucy FitzPiers

4. Sir Robert de Ros = Isabel d'Aubigny

5. William de Ros, 1st Baron Ros of Helmsley = Maud Vaux

6. William de Ros, 2nd Baron Ros of Helmsley = Margery de Badlesmere

7. Elizabeth de Ros = William la Zouche, 2nd Baron Zouche of Haryngworth

8. William la Zouche, 3rd Baron Zouche of Haryngworth = Agnes Greene

9. (probably) Katherine la Zouche = John Tyndal

10. Sir William Tyndal = Alana de Felbrigg, daughter of Sir Simon de Felbrigg (and Margaret of Teschen, alleged daughter of Przemysl I Nosak, Duke of Teschen and Glogau, and Eliska of Beuthen-Kosel), son of Sir Roger Bigod alias Felbrigg and Elizabeth Scales, daughter of Robert, 3rd Baron Scales (and Katherine de Ufford), son of Robert, 2nd Baron Scales and Egeline de Courtenay, daughter of Sir Hugh Courtenay and Eleanor le Despencer, SETH

11. Sir Thomas Tyndal = Margaret Yelverton

12. Sir William Tyndal = Mary Mondeford

13. Sir John Tyndal = Amphyllis Coningsby

14. Sir Thomas Tyndal = Anne Fermor

15. Sir John Tyndal = Anna Egerton. Their son, Arthur Tyndal, also immigrated to Mass., but returned to England and died unmarried.

16. **Margaret Tyndal (Tindal)** of Mass. = John **Winthrop** (1587/8-1649), the colonial statesman, founder and governor of

The Royal Descents of 900 Immigrants

the Massachusetts Bay Colony (his third wife; Winthrop married secondly Thomasine Clopton, ARD, SETH)

17. Samuel Winthrop of Antigua = Elizabeth ——
18. Joseph Winthrop = Catherine Slicer
19. Sarah Winthrop = George Thomas
20. **Sir George Thomas, 1ˢᵗ Bt.** (c. 1695-1774), colonial governor of Pa. and Del. = Elizabeth King.

Sources: *RA* 5: 221-24 (Winthrop, Tyndal), 2: 552-55 (Felbrigg), 4: 573-74 (Scales), 2: 317-23 (Courtenay), 2: 91-95 (la Zouche, but not including Katherine), 4: 487-96 Ros); *DAB* (Sir George Thomas, 1ˢᵗ Bt. and John Winthrop); Ellery Kirke Taylor, *The Lion and the Hare* [Winthrop family] (1939), chart Q, *BIFR,* pp. 643, 648-9 and Robert Charles Winthrop, *Evidences of the Winthrops of Groton* (1894-96, later vol. 1 of *SMF*), pp. 26, 28, 153 esp. (Winthrop, Tyndal, Felbrigg, Bigod); *Parliament, 1386-1421*, vol. 4, pp. 679-81 (John Tyndale, husband of Katherine Zouche), plus *CP* (Zouche, Ros of Helmsley) and *AR8*, line 232. See also *Chester of Chicheley,* vol. 1, pp. 252-59, 263-83 (Tindal) and *Blackmansbury* 2 (1965-66): 3-7 and *TAG* 79 (2004): 283-91 (Charles F.H. Evans and Charles M. Hansen on Margaret of Teschen). Col. Hansen thinks that the wife of Sir Simon de Felbrigg was simply a noblewoman in the train of Anne of Bohemia, Queen of Richard II, King of England. Douglas Richardson, who questions the la Zouche descent, thinks, however, that the Teschen descent is correct (see the *RA* references above).

The Royal Descents of 900 Immigrants

1. William I the Lion, King of Scotland, d. 1214 = Ermengarde de Beaumont
2. (illegitimate by a daughter of Richard Avenal) Isabel of Scotland = Robert de Ros, Magna Carta surety
3. Sir William de Ros = Lucy FitzPiers
4. Sir Robert de Ros = Isabel d'Aubigny
5. William de Ros, 1st Baron Ros of Helmsley = Maud Vaux
6. William de Ros, 2nd Baron Ros of Helmsley = Margery de Badlesmere
7. Maud de Ros = John de Welles, 4th Baron Welles
8. Margery de Welles = Stephen le Scrope, 2nd Baron Scrope of Masham
9. Maud le Scrope = Sir Baldwin Freville, son of Sir Baldwin Freville and Joyce de Botetourte, daughter of John de Botetourte, 2nd Baron Botetourte (and Joyce la Zouche de Mortimer), son of Thomas de Botetourte (and Joan de Somery), son of John de Botetourte, 1st Baron Botetourte, and Maud (or Matilda) FitzThomas, SETH
10. Margaret Freville = Sir Hugh Willoughby
11. Margery Willoughby = Godfrey Hilton, Baron Luttrell
12. Elizabeth Hilton = Richard Thimbleby
13. Anne Thimbleby = John Booth
14. Elizabeth Booth = Edward Hamby
15. William Hamby = Margaret Blewett
16. Robert Hamby – Elizabeth Arnold
17. **Catherine Hamby** of Mass. = Edward **Hutchinson**.
18. Elisha Hutchinson = (1) Hannah Hawkins; (2) Elizabeth Clarke
19. (by 2) Edward Hutchinson = Lydia Foster
20. Elizabeth Hutchinson = Nathaniel Robbins
21. Edward Hutchinson Robbins = Elizabeth Murray

The Royal Descents of 900 Immigrants

22. Anne Jean Robbins = Joseph Lyman (III)
23. Catherine Robbins Lyman = Warren Delano, Jr.
24. Sara Delano = James Roosevelt
25. Franklin Delano Roosevelt (1882-1945), 32nd U.S. President = (Anna) Eleanor Roosevelt

19. (by 1) Hannah Hutchinson = John Ruck
20. Hannah Ruck = Theophilus Lillie
21. John Lillie = Abigail Breck
22. Anna Lillie = Samuel Howard
23. Harriet Howard = Samuel Prescott Phillips Fay
24. Samuel Howard Fay = Susan Shellman
25. Harriet Eleanor Fay = James Smith Bush
26. Samuel Prescott Bush = Flora Sheldon
27. Prescott Sheldon Bush, U.S. Senator = Dorothy Walker
28. George Herbert Walker Bush (b. 1924), 41st U.S. President = Barbara Pierce, SETH
29. George Walker Bush (b. 1946), 43rd U.S. President = Laura Lane Welch, SETH

11. Isabel Willoughby (sister of Margery) = Philip Boteler, son of Sir Philip Boteler and Elizabeth Cokayne, daughter of John Cokayne and Ida Grey, SETH
12. John Boteler = Constance Vane
13. Elizabeth Boteler = Thomas Lovett
14. Thomas Lovett = Anna Danvers, daughter of Sir John Danvers and Anna Stradling, daughter of John Stradling and Alice Langford (who later married Sir Richard Pole, who later married Margaret Plantagenet, Countess of Salisbury, SETH), daughter of Edward Langford and Senche (Sancha) Blount, daughter of Sir Thomas Blount and Margaret Gresley, for whom

see the Sancha de Ayala-Ferdinand I, King of Spain-Habsburg chart in *AAP 2009, 2012*, pp. 660-64, where the Sancha de Ayala descent of RD immigrant ancestors (all SETH) of U.S. presidents are charted.

15. Elizabeth Lovett = Anthony Cave, brother of (1) Bridget Cave, wife of Francis Tanfield, SETH, and (2) Sir Thomas Cave, who married Elizabeth Danvers (a cousin but not a Stradling descendant) and was the father of Roger Cave, SETH, who married Margaret Cecil. Mary and Anne Cave, daughters of Elizabeth and Anthony, married Sir Jerome Weston and Griffith Hampden, both SETH.

16. Martha Cave = John Newdigate, son of John Newdigate (and Mary Cheyney), son of John Newdigate (and Mary Hylton), son of John Newdigate and Amphyllis Neville, daughter of John Neville (and Anne Maplethorpe), son of Thomas Neville and Elizabeth Babington, SETH

17. Grizel Newdigate = Edward Shillingford alias Isode/Izard

18. William Shillingford alias Isode/Izard = Marian [Mary-Ann] Greenglass

19. Ralph Izard = Elizabeth Prior/Pryor. Their sons George and Benjamin Izard also immigrated to S.C. but George probably returned to England, not leaving American descendants, and Benjamin married Elizabeth —— and apparently left a son Benjamin, who probably died s.p.

20. **Ralph Izard** of S.C. = (1) Mrs. Mary —— Smith Middleton; (2) Mrs. Dorothy —— Smith.

Sources: *RA* 3: 194-95 (Hamby, Booth), 5: 328-29 (Thimbleby, Hilton), 3: 39-40 (Freville), 4: 604-6 (le Scrope), 5: 331 (Welles), 4: 487-96 (de Ros), 3: 635-38 (Cave, Lovett, Boteler), 2: 160-62 (Boteler, Cokayne, Grey), 2: 399-400 (Danvers, Stradling, Langford), 4: 243-44 (Newdigate, Neville), 3: 615-17 (Neville, Langford, le Boteler), 5: 130-31 (Cave, Tanfield); *AR8*, lines 224A, 74A, 216, 122A, 30, *NEHGR* 145 (1991): 99-121, 258-68 (Wayne H.M. Wilcox) and sources cited therein, esp. those listed in *NEHGR* 141 (1987): 96-97; G.W. Marshall, ed.,

The Royal Descents of 900 Immigrants

Visitations of Nottingham, 1569 and 1614 (*HSPVS,* vol. 4, 1871), pp. 146-47 (Willoughby); *GM* 21 (1983-85): 185-90 (Freville); *CP* (Scrope of Masham, Welles, Ros of Helmsley); W. Harry Rylands, ed., *Visitation of Warwick, 1682-83* (*HSPVS,* vol. 62, 1911), pp. 33-34 (Newdigate) and Vivienne Larminie, *Wealth, Kinship and Culture: The Seventeenth-Century Newdigates of Arbury and Their World* (1995), *passim,* esp. the chart on pp. 208-9, and John Dunkin, *The History and Antiquities of the Hundreds of Bullington and Ploughley* (1835), vol. 1, p. 100 (Shillingford alias Isode/Izard). Other Izard, plus Blount and Cave sources, include *SGC2*, pp. 417-18 (Izard), *Survey of London,* vol. 17, pt. 1, *The Parish of St. Pancras* [including] *the Village of Highgate* (1936), p. 17 (Pryor, Izard), *Gresleys of Drakelowe,* p. 240 (Blount) and *Chester of Chicheley,* vol. 1, pp. 89-99 and J.W. Walker, ed., *Yorkshire Pedigrees* (*HSPVS,* vol. 94, 1942), pp. 96-97 (Cave).

The Royal Descents of 900 Immigrants

1. William I the Lion, King of Scotland, d. 1214 = Ermengarde de Beaumont
2. (illegitimate by a daughter of Richard Avenal) Isabel of Scotland = Robert de Ros, Magna Carta surety
3. Sir William de Ros = Lucy FitzPiers
4. Sir Robert de Ros = Isabel d'Aubigny
5. William de Ros, 1st Baron Ros of Helmsley = Maud Vaux
6. Agnes de Ros = Pain de Tibetot, 1st Baron Tibetot
7. John de Tibetot, 2nd Baron Tibetot = (1) Margaret Badlesmere
8. Robert de Tibetot, 3rd Baron Tibetot = Margaret Deincourt
9. Elizabeth de Tibetot = Sir Philip Despencer
10. Margery Despencer = Sir Roger Wentworth
11. Agnes Wentworth = Sir Robert Constable
12. Sir William Constable = Joan Fulthorpe
13. Robert Constable = —— Arden
14. Francis Constable = Margaret Brigham
15. —— Constable (daughter) = Walter Fenwick
16. George Fenwick = Margaret ——
17. Walter Fenwick = Magdalen Hunt
18. **Thomas Fenwick** of Del. = (1) Mrs. Mary Savill Porter Lawson; (2) Mary ——.

12. Anne Constable (sister of Sir William) – Sir William Tyrwhit
13. Sir Robert Tyrwhit = Maud Talboys, SETH
14. (alleged, poss. illegitimate) Anna Tyrwhit = Edward Kaye
15. Lucy Kaye = John Pickering
16. Elizabeth Pickering = Robert Throckmorton, son of Gabriel Throckmorton (and Emma Lawrence), son of Richard Throckmorton and Jane Beaufoe, SETH

The Royal Descents of 900 Immigrants

17. Gabriel Throckmorton = Alice Bedell

18. **Robert Throckmorton** of Va. = (1) Anne Chare/Chaire; (2) Judith Hetley.

Sources: Edwin Jaquett Sellers, *Fenwick Allied Ancestry: Ancestry of Thomas Fenwick of Sussex County, Delaware* (1916) and *Supplement to Genealogies* (1922), pp. 40-49; *RA* 5: 224-26 (Tyrwhit, but no wife of Edward Kaye), 2: 284-85 (Constable, to Sir William), 4: 216-18 (Wentworth, le Despencer), 5: 163-66 (Tibetot), 4: 487-93 (Ros), 1: 216-23 (Badlesmere, Clare); *AR8*, lines 200, 65A, 89, 54 and *MCS5*, lines 2, 1, 117, 116, 74, 76, 8B (generations 1-11 and 13-18 for Throckmorton); *BP* (Throckmorton of Ellington and Virginia, under the baronets of Coughton, in editions since 1928), *Throckmorton*, pp. 256-68, 273-76, 287-91, 295-303, *NGSQ* 60 (1974): 22-24 (Pickering, Kaye, Tyrwhit); *Lincolnshire Pedigrees*, p. 1019 (Tyrwhit); *DVY* 2:289, 3:47-48 (Constable). *RA* 5: 225-26 states that Agnes or Anne Tyrwhit, daughter of Sir Robert and Maud, married —— Bolle, but the Harleian Manuscript 890 cited by John G. Hunt in *NGSQ* 60: 24, note 8, is stated to show that Lucy Kaye's maternal grandfather was Sir Robert Tyrwhit of Ketelby, Lincolnshire. Possibly Anne Tyrwhit was illegitimate, but Paul C. Reed tells me that he has disproved the Tyrwhit-Kaye-Pickering descent altogether. Publication of this disproof is eagerly awaited. Minus Tyrwhit ancestry, the "best" royal descent for Robert Throckmorton of Va. may be the cross-referenced line from Louis IV, King of France.

The Royal Descents of 900 Immigrants

1. William I the Lion, King of Scotland, d. 1214 = Ermengarde de Beaumont
2. (illegitimate by a daughter of Richard Avenal) Isabel of Scotland = Robert de Ros, Magna Carta surety
3. Sir William de Ros = Lucy FitzPiers
4. Alice de Ros = Sir John Comyn
5. Sir John Comyn = Maud ——
6. Isabel Comyn = Sir Thomas Clarell
7. William Clarell = Elizabeth Reygate
8. Thomas Clarell = Maud Montgomery, daughter of Sir Nicholas Montgomery and Joan Delves, SETH
9. Elizabeth Clarell = Sir John Gresley
10. Sir John Gresley = Anne Stanley
11. Thomasine Gresley = Thomas Darrell
12. Henry Darrell = Elizabeth Cheney/Cheyne
13. Thomas Darrell = Elizabeth Horne
14. Thomas Darrell = Mary Roydon, daughter of Thomas Roydon and Margaret Whetenhall, daughter of William Whetenhall and Anne Cromer, SETH
15. Frances Darrell = Robert Greene
16. Sir Thomas Greene = Margaret (Webb?). Their son, Robert Greene, also immigrated to Md. but left no NDTPS.
17. **Thomas Greene** (1609-ca. 1651), colonial governor of Md. = (1) Anne Cox; (2) Mrs. Winifred Seyborne Harvey.

10. Katherine Gresley (sister of Sir John) = William Peyto
11. John Peyto = Eleanor Manfield
12. Edward Peyto = Goditha Throckmorton, daughter of Sir Thomas Throckmorton and Margaret Olney, SETH
13. John Peyto = Margaret Baynham

The Royal Descents of 900 Immigrants

14. Audrey Peyto = John Cupper

15. Dorothy Cupper = John Fowke

16. Roger Fowke = Mary Bayley. Their son, Thomas Fowke, also immigrated to Va. and married Susanna ——, but d.s.p.

17. **Col. Gerard Fowke** of Va. = Anne Thoroughgood.

18. Elizabeth Fowke = William Dent

19. Peter Dent = Mary Brooke

20. Peter Dent, Jr. = Mary Eleanor ——

21. George Dent = Susannah Dawson

22. Frederick Fayette Dent = Ellen Bray Wrenshall

23. Julia Boggs Dent = Ulysses Simpson Grant (1822-1885), 18th U.S. President

Sources: *RA* 3: 114-19 (Greene, Darrell, Gresley), 2: 206-10 (Clarell, Comyn), 4: 487-90 (de Ros), 4: 362-65 (Peyto), 3: 13-14 (Fowke); *MCS5*, line 16E and *BRMF1*, pp. 218-19, 152-53 (Greene, Darell), H.W. Newman, *The Flowering of the Maryland Palatinate* (1961, repr. 1984), pp. 213-18 and Edward Hasted, *The History and Topographical Survey of the County of Kent*, vol. 2 (1782), p. 639 (Greene), W.B. Bannerman, ed., *Visitations of Kent, 1530-1, 1574, and 1592*, vol. 2 (*HSPVS*, vol. 75, 1924), pp. 94 (Darell), 116 (Whetenhall), *Gresleys of Drakelow*, pp. 225-26 (Gresley), 245 (Clarell), 248 (Darrell), *PCF Yorkshire* (Clarell pedigree) and C.H. Dudley Ward, *The Family of Twysden and Twisden* (1939), Roydon charts at end; *Shaw*, vol. 2, part 1, p. 60, *VGE*, pp. 583-85, *HVG*, pp. 154-56, 743-44 and E.W. Schieffelin, *In Search of a Magna Carta Signer, A Tale of Adventure* (1990) (Fowke), Rev. Herbert Barnett, *Glympton: The History of an Oxfordshire Manor* (*Publications of the Oxfordshire Record Society*, vol. 5, 1923), p. 23 (Cupper), Sir William Dugdale, *The Antiquities of Warwickshire*, 2nd ed., vol. 1 (1730), p. 472 (Peto), and *Throckmorton,* pp. 82-85. This "improved" Peyto-Darrell-Gresley-Clarell descent, developed by Douglas Richardson, was brought to my attention by Christopher Carter Lee.

The Royal Descents of 900 Immigrants

1. William the Lion, King of Scotland, d. 1214 = Ermengarde de Beaumont
2. (illegitimate by a daughter of Richard Avenal) Isabel of Scotland = Robert de Ros, Magna Carta surety
3. Sir Robert de Ros of Wark = ――
4. Isabel de Ros = Sir Roger Merlay
5. Isabel de Merlay = Sir Robert de Somerville
6. Sir Philip de Somerville = Margaret de Pipe
7. Joan de Somerville = Sir Rhys ap Griffith
8. Rhys (ap Rhys) ap Griffith = Isabel de Stackpole
9. Joan ferch Rhys ap Gruffudd = Sir Richard Vernon
10. Sir Richard Vernon = Benedicta Ludlow
11. Isabella Vernon = Nicholas Montgomery
12. Sir Nicholas Montgomery = Joan Delves
13. Margaret Montgomery = John Kniveton
14. John Kniveton = Anne Dethick
15. Barbara Kniveton (daughter certainly of 13 or 14, probably 14) = Richard Weston
16. Ralph Weston = Anna Smyth
17. **Thomas Weston** (c. 1576, bp. 1584-1647) of Mass., ironmonger, merchant adventurer, agent of the London syndicate that underwrote the sailing of the Pilgrims to Plymouth in 1620, a New England resident for an unknown period post 1622 = Elizabeth Weaver.

Sources: *DAB, Oxford DNB, NGSQ* 62 (1974): 163-72 and Sampson Erdeswick, *A Survey of Staffordshire* (1844), chart opposite p. 164 (Weston); *TG*, new ser. 7 (1890-91): 226-27 (Kniveton); Montgomery notes by Rosie Bevan sent to me by Brice McAdoo Clagett, which cite *Calendar of Papal Letters, 1471-1484*, vol. 13, pt. 1 (1955), p. 404, for the identification of Isabella, #11 above, wife of Nicholas Montgomery,

The Royal Descents of 900 Immigrants

as a Vernon, I.H. Jeayes, *Descriptive Catalogue of Derbyshire Charters* (1906), p. 2394, for Vernon-Montgomery associations, and Susan M. Wright, *Derbyshire Gentry in the Fifteenth Century* (*Derbyshire Record Society* [*Publications*], vol. 8, 1983), pp. 39, 161, 216, 226 esp., for generations 15-17; *BP* (Vernon); *CP* (Canville/Camville) and *RA* 5: 281-82 (Vernon, including Isabel, wife of Nicholas Montgomery), 4: 665-69 (Griffith, Somerville, de Merlay), 4: 301-2 (de Ros of Wark), 4: 487-89 (de Ros), *AR8*, lines 56A, 63A, 63, 124 (first 14 generations). See *NEHGR* 141 (1987): 99-100 for the chronological reasons (and suggestive naming patterns) leading to my conclusion that Barbara Kniveton, wife of Richard (not Ralph) Weston, was almost certainly a daughter of John Kniveton the younger and Anne Dethick. A definitive Kniveton monograph would be welcome.

The Royal Descents of 900 Immigrants

1. William I the Lion, King of Scotland, d. 1214 = Ermengarde de Beaumont
2. (illegitimate by a daughter of Richard Avenal) Isabel of Scotland = Robert de Ros, Magna Carta surety
3. Sir William de Ros = Lucy FitzPiers
4. Sir William de Ros = Eustache FitzHugh
5. Alice de Ros = Sir Geoffrey St. Quintin
6. Geoffrey St. Quintin = Margery Constable
7. Sir William St. Quintin = Joan (or Elizabeth) de Thwenge
8. Sir John St. Quintin = Agnes Herbert
9. Anthony St. Quintin = Elizabeth Gascoigne
10. (probably illegitimate by Margaret Swynho) Margaret St. Quintin = Sir John Conyers
11. Sir Christopher Conyers = Ellen Rolleston
12. Joan Conyers = John FitzRandolph, a descendant of Hugh Capet, King of France, via FitzRandall/Ranulph/Ralph, and Bigod, de Vere, de Clare, Clermont, Montdidier, Roucy, and Hainault; see *RD500*, pp. 446-47, *MCS5*, lines 164, 155, 154, and *AR8*, lines 246, 151, 106
13. John FitzRandolph = ——
14. Christopher FitzRandolph = Jane Langton
15. Christopher FitzRandolph = ——
16. Edward FitzRandolph = Frances Howis
17. **Edward FitzRandolph** of Mass. and N.J. = Elizabeth Blossom.
18. Nathaniel FitzRandolph = Mary Holley
19. Samuel FitzRandolph = Mary Jones
20. Prudence FitzRandolph = Shubael Smith
21. Mary Smith = Jonathan Dunham
22. Samuel Dunham = Hannah Chenoweth

The Royal Descents of 900 Immigrants

23. Jacob Dunham = Catherine Goodnight

24. Jacob Mackey Dunham = Louise Eliza Stroup

25. Jacob William Dunham = Mary Ann Kearney

26. Ralph Waldo Emerson Dunham = Ruth Lucille Armour

27. Stanley Armour Dunham = Madelyn Lee Payne

28. Stanley Ann Dunham = Barack Hussein Obama

29. Barack Hussein Obama, Jr., b. 1961, 44th U.S. President = Michelle LaVaughn Robinson

18. Benjamin FitzRandolph (brother of Nathaniel) = Sarah Dennis

19. Isaac FitzRandolph = Rebecca Seabrook

20. James FitzRandolph = Deliverance Coward

21. Isaac FitzRandolph = Eleanor Hunter

22. Rebecca Longstreet FitzRandolph = Isaac Stockton Keith Axson

23. Samuel Edward Axson = Margaret Jane Hoyt

24. Ellen Louise Axson = (Thomas) Woodrow Wilson (1856-1924), 28th U.S. President

Sources: *MCA* 1: 342-43 (FitzRandolph), *MCS5*, lines 164 (and notes and sources therein, by John Insley Coddington), and 116; *AR8*, line 170, and Oris H.F. Randolph, *Edward FitzRandolph Branch Lines: Allied Families and English and Norman Ancestry*, 2nd ed. (1980), pp. 585-89; C.B. Norcliffe, ed., *Visitation of Yorkshire, 1563-64* (*HSPVS*, vol. 16, 1881), p. 74 (Conyers); V.J. Watney, *The Wallop Family and Their Ancestry*, vols. 2 and 3 (1928), pp. 225 (#265), 683 (#869) (Conyers, St. Quintin), plus William Page, ed., *Victoria History of the County of York: North Riding*, vol. 1 (1914, repr. 1968), p. 315 (generations 7-11) and *PCF Yorkshire* (St. Quintin pedigree). See also *Parliament, 1386-1421*, vol. 4, pp. 284-86 (Sir John St. Quintin). This "improved" FitzRandolph line was brought to my attention by Jay A. Cary of Lyme, N.H., and several years ago by Sam and Marcia Henderson of Denton, Texas. The chronology of generations 8-12 is tight but seems possible; a confirming or corrective St. Quintin article is eagerly awaited.

The Royal Descents of 900 Immigrants

1. William I the Lion, King of Scotland, d. 1214 = Ermengarde de Beaumont
2. (illegitimate by a daughter of Richard Avenal) Isabel of Scotland = Robert de Ros, Magna Carta surety
3. Sir William de Ros = Lucy FitzPiers
4. Sir Robert de Ros = Isabel d'Aubigny
5. William de Ros, 1st Baron Ros of Helmsley = Maud Vaux
6. William de Ros, 2nd Baron Ros of Helmsley = Margery de Badlesmere
7. Elizabeth de Ros = William la Zouche, 2nd Baron Zouche of Haryngworth
8. Elizabeth la Zouche = Sir John Basynges (Basing)
9. Alice Basynges (Basing) = Thomas Mackworth
10. Henry Mackworth = ——
11. John Mackworth = Beatrix ——
12. George Mackworth = Anne Sherard
13. Francis Mackworth = Ellen Hercy, daughter of Humphrey Hercy and Elizabeth Digby, SETH
14. Catherine Mackworth = John Baldwin
15. Francis or John (= Mrs. Joan —— Spendly) or Oliver (probably not James or Henry) Baldwin
16. **Frances Baldwin** of Va. = (1) Richard **Townshend**; (2) Richard **Jones**; (3) Robert **Williams**. Her brother, William Baldwin, also came to Va., married ——, and left at least three daughters but no NDTPS. William's daughters and Frances's three sons (Francis Townshend, d.s.p., Robert Townshend and Cadwalader Jones) were fourth cousins of Anne Hyde, Duchess of York, first wife of James II, King of England.

Sources: *TVG* 48 (2004): 170-84 (John Anderson Brayton), 50 (2006): 121-29 (Jeffery A. Duvall) and sources cited therein, esp. *Blore*, pp. 127-30 (Mackworth); *RA* 2: 91-94 (Basynges/Basing, la Zouche), 4: 487-96 (Ros).

The Royal Descents of 900 Immigrants

1. William I the Lion, King of Scotland, d. 1214 = Ermengarde de Beaumont
2. (illegitimate by a daughter of Richard Avenal) Isabel of Scotland = Robert de Ros, Magna Carta surety
3. Sir William de Ros = Lucy FitzPiers
4. Sir Robert de Ros = Isabel d'Aubigny
5. William de Ros, 1st Baron Ros of Helmsley = Maud Vaux
6. William de Ros, 2nd Baron Ros of Helmsley = Margery de Badlesmere
7. Maud de Ros = John de Welles, 4th Baron Welles
8. Margery de Welles = Stephen le Scrope, 2nd Baron Scrope of Masham
9. Maud le Scrope = Sir Baldwin Freville, son of Sir Baldwin Freville and Joyce de Botetourte, daughter of John de Botetourte, 2nd Baron Botetourte (and Joyce la Zouche de Mortimer), son of Thomas de Botetourte (and Joan de Somery), son of John de Botetourte, 1st Baron Botetourte, and Maud (or Matilda) Fitz Thomas, SETH
10. Joyce Freville = Sir Roger Aston
11. Sir Robert Aston = Isabella Brereton
12. John Aston = Elizabeth Delves
13. Sir John Aston = Joan Lyttleton
14. Sir Edward Aston = Joan Bowles
15. Leonard Aston = Elizabeth Barton
16. Walter Aston = Joyce Nason
17. **Col. Walter Aston** of Va. = Hannah Jordan.
18. Mary Aston = Richard Cocke
19. Richard Cocke the younger (of two brothers both named Richard) = Elizabeth (Littleberry?)
20. Anne Cocke = Robert Bolling, Jr.

The Royal Descents of 900 Immigrants

21. Elizabeth Bolling = James Munford
22. Robert Munford/Montfort = Anne Brodnax
23. Clarissa Montfort = John Shellman, Jr.
24. Susan Shellman = Samuel Howard Fay
25. Harriet Eleanor Fay = James Smith Bush
26. Samuel Prescott Bush = Flora Sheldon
27. Prescott Sheldon Bush, U. S. Senator = Dorothy Walker
28. George Herbert Walker Bush (b. 1924), 41st U.S. President = Barbara Pierce, SETH
29. George Walker Bush (b. 1946), 43rd U.S. President = Laura Lane Welch, SETH

Sources: *TAG* 89 (2017): 1-20 (Paul C. Reed and Nathan W. Murphy), which corrects *TAG* 76 (2001): 234-36; *RA* 1: 175-82 (Aston, to the immigrant), 3: 39 (Freville), 4: 604-6 (Scrope), 5: 331 (Welles), 4: 487-96 (Ros); and among other sources, *MCS5*, lines 101, 101A and *VHG*, pp. 272-78 (but note the Burley correction in *MCS4/5*), *VGE*, pp. 390-92, *Tixall*, pp. 146-49 (Aston), and *GM* 21 (1983-85): 185-90 (Freville).

The Royal Descents of 900 Immigrants

1. William the Lion, King of Scotland, d. 1214 = Ermengarde de Beaumont
2. (illegitimate by a daughter of Richard Avenal) Isabel of Scotland = Robert de Ros, Magna Carta surety
3. Sir William de Ros = Lucy Fitzpiers
4. Lucy de Ros = Sir William de Kyme
5. Philip de Kyme, 1st Baron Kyme = Joan Bigod, daughter of Sir Hugh Bigod and Joan de Stuteville, SETH
6. Lucy de Kyme = Robert de Umfreville, 2nd Earl of Angus
7. Elizabeth de Umfreville = Sir Gilbert de Burradon or Boroughdon
8. Eleanor de Burradon or Boroughdon = Sir Henry Talboys
9. Sir Walter Talboys = Margaret (Deincourt?)
10. Sir Walter Talboys = (1) ——
11. Margaret Talboys = Richard Pinchbeck
12. John Pinchbeck = ——
13. Grace Pinchbeck = Christopher Browne
14. Francis Browne = Margaret Mathew. Their son, Anthony Browne, married Dorothy Boteler, daughter of Sir Philip Boteler and Elizabeth Drury, SETH, and was the father of Robert Browne, the Separatist, who married Alice —— and Elizabeth Warrener.
15. Joyce Browne = William Hone
16. Thomas Hone = Jane Allen
17. William Hone = Elizabeth Parsons
18. Thomas Hone = Judith Aylmer
19. **Theophilus Hone** of Va. = (1) ——; (2) Mrs. Sarah —— Edwards Richardson.
20. (by 1) Judith Hone = John Armistead
21. Elizabeth Armistead = William Churchill
22. Elizabeth Churchill = William Bassett (IV)
23. Elizabeth Bassett = Benjamin Harrison (V), Signer of the Declaration of Independence

24. William Henry Harrison (1773-1841), 9th U.S. President = Anna Tuthill Symmes
25. John Scott Harrison = Elizabeth Ramsey Irwin
26. Benjamin Harrison (1833-1901), 23rd U.S. President = (1) Caroline Lavinia Scott; (2) Mrs. Mary Scott Lord Dimmick

Sources: Hone and Browne research of John Anderson Brayton, author of an unpublished monograph, "Major Theophilus Hone and Judith Aylmer of James City Co., Va."; *RA* 4: 376 (Pinchbeck), 5: 109-13 (Talboys, Burradon/Boroughdon), 4: 14-17 (Umfreville), 3: 452-55 (Kyme). Much material was also assembled independently by Patricia Law Hatcher and published in *American Ancestors Journal, Fourth Annual Supplement to NEHGR* 166 (2012): 352-64. Note as well the 1541, proved 1542, PCC 6 Spert will of Francis Browne, which mentions "son Hone and dau. Joane" [not Joyce therein]; the 1590 PCC 85 Drury will of Anthony Browne, Joyce's brother, which mentions "Thomas Hone and Dorothy Hone, my nephew and niece," *Parliament, 1509-1558*, vol. 1, pp. 521-22 (Francis Browne), W. Harry Rylands and W. Bruce Bannerman, eds., *Visitation of Rutland, 1681-82* (*HSPVS*, vol. 73, 1922), pp. 8-10 (Browne) and the *Oxford DNB* for Robert Browne. The placement of John Pinchbeck is based largely on chronology and place, and his nephew of the same name, son of Sir Thomas Pinchbeck and Anne Greene, was a knight. In the Rutland visitation Grace Pinchbeck is said to be one of three daughters of John Pinchbeck of Pinchbeck, Lincolnshire, about whom a separate monograph would be welcome.

The Royal Descents of 900 Immigrants

1. William I the Lion, King of Scotland, d. 1214 = Ermengarde de Beaumont
2. (illegitimate by ——) Ada of Scotland = Patrick Dunbar, 4th Earl of Dunbar
3. Patrick Dunbar, 5th Earl of Dunbar = Eupheme Bruce
4. Patrick Dunbar, 6th Earl of Dunbar = Cecily FitzJohn
5. Patrick Dunbar, 7th Earl of Dunbar = Marjory Comyn
5. Sir Alexander Dunbar = ——
6. Sir Patrick Dunbar = Isabel Randolph
7. Sir David Dunbar of Cumnock and Blantyre (brother of George Dunbar, 9th Earl of Dunbar) = ——
8. Sir Patrick Dunbar of Cumnock and Mochrum = ——
9. Cuthbert Dunbar of Blantyre and Enterkine = ——
10. John Dunbar of Blantyre and Enterkine = ——
11. John Dunbar of Blantyre and Enterkine = Agnes Mure
12. Alexander Dunbar of Machermore = ——
13. Antonie Dunbar of Machermore = (1) Mary Montgomery; (2) —— Stewart
14. (maternity uncertain) John Dunbar of Machermore = Jean Murdoch
15. Jean Dunbar = Andrew Heron of Kirrouchtrie
16. Andrew Heron of Bargaly = Mary Graham
17. Patrick Heron = Ann Vining
18. **Benjamin Heron** of N.C. = Mary Howe.

Sources: *LDBR*1, pp. 755, 757-58 and *TG* 4 (1983): 238-39, 241, 245, 255, 258, 262 (generations 14-17); P.H. McKerlie, *History of the Lands and Owners in Galloway*, vol. 4 (1878), pp. 423-24, 448-50 (Heron), 435-39 (Dunbar); *The Herald and Genealogist* 6 (1871): 309-11, *Drummond*, vol. 2, *SP, CP,* and *BP* (Dunbar). For Cecily FitzJohn, daughter of John FitzRobert and Ada Baliol, see *The Genealogist* 9 (1988): 229-241 (Andrew B. W. MacEwen). A thorough monograph on generations 7-15 would be welcome.

The Royal Descents of 900 Immigrants

1. Philip of Swabia, King of the Romans, d. 1208 (son of Frederick I Barbarossa, Holy Roman Emperor, SETH, and Beatrix of Burgundy) = Irene of Byzantium, daughter of Isaac II Angelos, Emperor of Byzantium, d. 1204, and (almost certainly) —— Taronites
2. Marie of Swabia = Henry II, Duke of Brabant
3. Matilda of Brabant = (2) Guy II de Châtillon, Count of St. Pol
4. Jacques de Châtillon, Seigneur de Leuze = Catherine de Carency
5. Hugh de Châtillon, Seigneur de Leuze, etc. = Jeanne d'Argies
6. Catherine de Châtillon = Jean de Picquigny, Seigneur d'Ailly
7. Marguerite de Picquigny = Hugh I de Melun, Seigneur d'Antoing and d'Épinoy
8. Isabel de Melun = Bertrand de La Bouverie
9. Catherine de La Bouverie, dit de Viane = Jean de Haynin
10. Jacques de Haynin, Seigneur de Haynin, etc., author of *Les Mémoires de Messire Jean, Seigneur de Haynin et de Louvegnies, Chevalier 1465-1477*, 2 vols., continued by his son François, below = Marie de Roison
11. François, Seigneur de Haynin, etc. = Antoinette de Tenremonde
12. François, Seigneur de Haynin, etc. = Marie d'Estaples
13. Marguerite de Haynin = Johan van Alendorp
14. Louise van Alendorp = Philippe de Gonnes
15. Adolf de Gonnes, Heer van Vuylcoop = Paschina Ruysch
16. Maria de Gonnes = Johan van Weede, Heer van Groot Weede
17. Cornelia Henriette van Weede = Daniel de Leeuw
18. Antonia Louise de Leeuw = Maximilian van Hangest d'Ivoy
19. Catharina Frederica Cornelia van Hangest d'Ivoy = Johan Frederic Hoffman
20. Johan Frederic Hoffman = Anna Josina van der Pot
21. Willem Johan Hoffman = Johanna Maria Catharina Havelaar

The Royal Descents of 900 Immigrants

22. Jan Jacob Hoffman = Mathilda Petronella Hermanna Schadee
23. **Willem Johan Hoffman**, known as **William J. Hoffman**, 1882-1955, of N.Y., genealogist, author of *An Armory of American Families of Dutch Descent* (Francis S. Sypher, ed., NYGBS, 2010, a consolidation of many articles in *NYGBR*) = Kathryn Teresa Marguerite Cary.

Sources: *NYGBR* 87 (1956): 78 (obituary), 146 (2015): 23-30 (J.B. Dobson) and sources cited in the latter (esp. in notes 4, 9, 18); several rare Hoffman works by W.J. Hoffman mentioned or cited by Dobson, notably *Geschiedenis van de Familie Hoffman uit Hachenburg*, 2 vols. (1925-28), esp. vol. 2, pp. 240, 258-71 (generations 13-23, but omitting generation 14); *Nederland's Adelsboek*, vol. 7 (1909), p. 184 (Hangest d'Ivoy, generations 17-19); *Taxandria* 10, pt. 2 (1903): 266, 305 (tombstone heraldic quartiers of Philippe and Adolf de Gonnes), plus *Genealogische en Heraldische Bladen* 8 (1913), p. 378 (Gonnes, Heers von Vuylcoop); Abraham Ferwerde and Jacobus Kok, *Nederlandsch Geslacht-Stam-en Wapen-Boek*, vol. 1 (1785), Alendorp article; the *Haynin Mémoires* mentioned at generation 10, plus *De Wapenheraut* 22 (1918): 447, *Compte-Rendu des Séances de la Commission Royale d'Histoire* [*de Belgique*] 12 (1846): 80 (where de la Bouverie dit de Viane at generation 9 is mistakenly given as Clesonne), Jean Le Carpentier, *Histoire Généalogique des Païs-Bas, ou Histoire de Cambray et du Cambresis*, 4 parts in 2 vols. (1664), pt. 3, pp. 676-79 and ____ Dumont, *Recueil Généalogique de Familles Originaires des Pays-Bas ou y Établies*, 2 vols. (1775-78), 2: 30-79 (Haynin, Bouverie); *Anselme*, vol. 5, pp. 228-29 (Melun), vol. 6, pp. 106-8 (Châtillon) and *ES* 2, charts for Brabant and Hohenstaufen of Swabia and Germany.

CPSIA information can be obtained
at www.ICGtesting.com
Printed in the USA
LVHW020150100920
665474LV00010B/221

9 780806 320755